Warman's® American Records

CHUCK MILLER

Published by

700 E. State Street • Iola, WI 54990-0001
Telephone: 715/445-2214

Please, call or write us for our free catalog of publications. Our toll-free number to place an order or obtain a free catalog is 800-258-0929 or please use our regular business telephone 715-445-2214 for editorial comment and further information.

Library of Congress Catalog Number: 2001088587

ISBN: 0-87349-259-5

Printed in the United States of America

ACKNOWLEDGMENTS

Even though my name is on the spine of this book, that doesn't mean I wrote this book myself. There were dozens of people who, both personally and professionally, helped me get this book off the ground, allowed me to photograph their collections and archives, and guided me in the completion of a dream I thought might never come to fruition.

Finding rare records to add to this book was difficult, but not impossible. A special thanks goes out the Last Vestige Music Store in Albany, New York, whose staff helped me find everything from Sub Pop 45s to vintage Hendrix pressings.

The staff of *Collectors Universe and Good Rockin' Tonight*, one of the Internet's most successful and reputable collectible auction houses, also helped in providing rare images for this book. Thanks to Dave Gioia, Kelly Lawler and the rest of the staff at Good Rockin' Tonight for all their help and advice.

Val Shively and his staff at his House of Oldies in Philadelphia were very supportive and helped find many of the rare photos that you see in this book. Besides the photos, Val and his team were able to answer many of my questions and showed me some of the rarest records in their store. Thanks to all.

This book could not be written without the guidance and support of Krause Publications and *Goldmine magazine*, with whom I have been associated for the past five years. A hearty thanks to the staff of *Goldmine magazine*, including editor Greg Loescher, assistant editor Cathy Bernardy, former editor Michael Metzger and former assistant editor Irwin Soonachan. Each of these people, as well as those behind the scenes at *Goldmine*, have guided me throughout my continued association with the magazine. And thanks also to Paul Kennedy, Kris Manty, Rick Jones, and the Krause Publications Book Department, who took a chance with an unknown writer. Hopefully I haven't let you down.

Two big thank-yous to Tim Neely, a fellow record collector and book editor for Krause Publications, and to writer-journalist Catherine Saunders-Watson. Both have dozens of published collectible books to their credit, and I consider both of them my personal mentors in completing this project.

Many of the record shows I attended while working on this project contained dealers and experts who were more than willing to help answer, explain and demonstrate concepts and collecting tips that could be passed to you. Much thanks also go to those who sent rare images from their own personal collection, who took the time to take a snapshot or forward a photocopy (or even the original records) to me. Special thanks go to Kenneth Schwartz and the members of the Keystone Record Collector Club, Ross Bacon of Shyney Records, George Russo "The Wanderer," Pete Battistini, Lothar Fohrn, Mark and Elaine Klein, Stephen Caraco and the Madonna Collectors Club, Jon "Bermuda" Schwartz, DCC Compact Classics, Garry Bryan, Mark Anderson, R. Michael Murray, Val Shively, Bob Szuszzewicz, Bruce Spizer, and Mark Pisani. Much appreciation also goes to my "Board of Advisors," whose valuable expertise in musical collecting genres made this book happen.

There have been three generations of Millers who helped to make this project a success. Both my grandmother, Betty Miller, and my aunt Elaine Miller, have scoured the New England yard sales and flea markets and collector's shops for 30 years, and have found some significant treasures for my collection. Thanks to my mother-in-law, Doris Robinson, who used the power of inter-library loan to help me find dozens of books and research materials for this project. And a special thanks to my wife Vicki, without whose support this book could never have been finished, and who never lost faith in me.

And a special thanks to you, the person holding this book now. I want to hear from you about Warman's American Records. I want your ideas, your opinions, your stories about your collection. There may be a monetary value placed on a record because of its age, its rarity, or the rare performance by a soon-to-be superstar. But with records, there is also an emotional bond. These are songs you heard at your senior prom. Or when you were cruising down the highway in your '65 GTO. Or in your '73 Pinto. Or in your '97 Mazda 626.

I'm also looking forward to hearing from you—let me know what you liked or didn't like about this book and its contents, and let me know what records and genres should be considered for future volumes of this book.

Chuck Miller
c/o O&A
100 State Street
Albany NY 12207-1885
email: boardwalk7@aol.com
http://members.aol.com/boardwalk7

CONTENTS

INTRODUCTION

Welcome to *Warman's American Records.* If you've purchased this book, or even if you're in a bookstore thumbing through this introduction, it's a good assumption that you either have a record collection, or are considering starting one.

And why not? These records may have been in your attic for years. Or your brother went to college and said you could have them. You've seen them at flea markets, yard sales, estate sales, and specialized weekend sales. Some of them have sold at auctions for thousands of dollars. Others sit forlornly in old boxes and crates, unsold for even the "50 cents" price on the crate cover.

Perhaps you heard a song on the radio, and wanted a copy of that song for your own listening pleasure. Or you enjoy a particular singer's music so much, you'll purchase their recordings on reputation alone.

You might be a musicologist, looking for that elusive 45 that proves Artist "A" was influenced by Artist "B," and in turn influenced Artist "C." Or you may be a fan not only of classic music, but of the tools and equipment used to produce and replicate sound from those 45s and LPs.

If you want to become a true collector, it helps if you are a music lover. Music is an extensive and integral part of our lives; it has infiltrated our culture and our language; its very existence has brought together cultures and nationalities, and has provided a mnemonic roadsign to our consciousness.

For the past 100 years, this music has been stored on records. Whether these records are cylindrical or circular; whether they were pressed on shellac, vinyl, styrene or paraffin; whether those records contain the operatic acrobatics of Enrico Caruso or the axe-playing dexterity of Eddie Van Halen, records have been a part of our culture. Before motion pictures and radio, cylinder records have captured the earliest sounds. They have survived wars, economic depressions, oil embargoes, and the changing tastes of music aficionados. And against all odds, records have even survived the digital technology of compact discs—the very equipment that was to send vinyl records into obsolescence.

A record is a work of art, not just in sound, but in appearance as well. An album cover can double as fine art, whether it's 25 Elvis Presleys in gold lamé, or the half-silhouette photographs of the Beatles on their first album, or the artwork of an Egyptian sphinx with a futuristic superstructure in an Earth Wind & Fire cover. Holding a record in your hand, you can see the grooves and know that the song starts when the grooves wind tight on the disc—when the grooves space apart, there is silence until they tighten up again. On a 12" disco disc, you can almost see where the drums mark the beat, as you watch the spiral groove pinwheel over the vinyl.

It's a feeling one has trouble receiving from any other musical format. Every cassette looks the same; the back of every CD is a mirrored surface. A record is unique—what looks like a simple black circle with a pretty picture in the center can contain melodies and lyrics as complex as an All-Star midnight jam.

These records are also the collected works and evolutions of thousands of musicians, singers, writers, producers, and arrangers. It's akin to a Van Gogh collector admiring the painter's first furtive works, then seeing how the artist evolved his craft into *Starry Night* and *Self-Portrait with Bandaged Ear.* How fascinating it is to hear four shaggy-haired Liverpudlians recreating the American pop and soul they heard in 1963—and a few short years later, creating *Sgt. Pepper's Lonely Hearts Club Band*, an album cited by legions of artists as an influence to their own work. With your collection, you can trace where the Beatles' creativity bloomed—the moments they went from "yeah, yeah, yeah" to "all my troubles seemed so far away," and eventually to "imagine there's no heaven" and "give me love, give me peace on earth."

Like you, I am also a record collector. Since 1975, when my grandmother bought me a box of 45s from a flea market, I've been hooked. Over the next 25 years, I've visited record stores, used record shops, flea markets, conventions, record shows, estate sales, the Internet, my grandmother's basement, almost anywhere records could be found. My search for 45s and albums has outlasted many of the music stores I once patronized. There's been treasure and trash in all my searches, and sometimes when I think I've seen too many copies of "Have You Never Been Mellow" or "Weekend in New England," I would find a rare record, almost forgotten by its original owners, looking for a collector to take it home.

Record collecting is a hobby that I've enjoyed for more than 25 years. And whether you're a first-time collector or someone looking to organize or streamline your own record collection, *Warman's American Records* is the book for you. By using this book, you can tell which of two visually equal records is the rarer recording. You will discover the wonders of colored vinyl and picture discs—how they're made and the special appeal collectors have for them. You'll learn about ring wear, edge warps, scratches, mispressings, cue burn, bootlegs, stickers, counterfeits, and reproductions.

And you'll also discover a new appreciation for your vinyl collection. You might clean off an album, put it on your turntable, and suddenly discover a forgotten masterpiece. Once again, an artist's work brings a smile and a tear to a new heart and new ears.

Terminology

There are dozens of nicknames for records: discs; platters; 7-inchers; 12-inchers; LPs; 45s; golden oldies; stacks of wax; Frisbees.

Whatever term we use for them, not all records are the same—and that's not just because different records contain different songs. Think about the physical characteristics of the record itself: What is it made of? Why are some center labels rendered in full color, while others barely have the artist's name and the song title on a monochromatic background? And why would two records vary in price, despite the fact that they contain the same song in their grooves?

To understand these questions, one must first understand how a record is made. All records start with a master tape of an artist's performance. A mastering agent plays the tape, and feeds the sound from that tape to a cutting lathe, electronically transcribing the song into the grooves of a circular black lacquer disc. This disc, also known as an "acetate," can be played on a normal phonograph—but because an acetate disc is very pliable, it can be damaged if played more than a few times. Mastering agents sometimes test-play acetates to confirm the sonic quality of the recording, to make sure there are no spacing or timing errors on the disc, and that the songs on an album are in the proper running order.

The finished acetate is then sprayed with a metal film. Once the film dries, the acetate is peeled away (which, because of its pliable surface, is destroyed in the process). This new metal disc, with its raised groove pattern, is called a "master." Because of its raised groove pattern, a "master" cannot be played on a phonograph.

Another metallic compound will be sprayed on the master, and once this compound is carefully removed from the master, you now have a "mother" disc. The mother disc has lowered grooves, but still cannot be played on a phonograph (playing a mother would wear away the stylus from the friction of metal upon needletip).

The mother disc is sprayed with yet another metallic compound. When that compound is peeled away from the mother, you now have a new disc called a "stamper." This stamper may have additional information printed on the runout grooves, information pertaining to which plant the record was pressed at, the date of pressing, or the number of records made before this stamper was used.

What we call a "vinyl" 45 or LP is actually a disc made of polyvinyl chloride (PVC). After the stampers are made, hot PVC is pressed between the A-side and B-side of the stampers by compression molding, squeezing the vinyl compound into playable records. The stampers are heated by steam at the start of the pressing cycle, and then cooled to solidify the record. Excess PVC that squirts from the sides of the stamping process is usually recycled to make new records. Since recycled vinyl does not reheat and re-cool to a smooth, glossy surface, sometimes even near-mint 45s can have hissy surface noises if the record was cut with recycled vinyl. The mixture of new and old vinyl can also make the record look grainy or pockmarked, especially in the runout groove area. And because stampers eventually wore down from the changing temperatures and pressures used to make records, the plates were usually replaced after 1,000 pressings (although some companies pressed pop records until the stampers fell apart, then made new stampers from the mothers and continued on).

Both 45s and LPs were originally pressed from vinyl. And although vinyl is still used for LPs, record companies have switched from vinyl 45s to ones made of cheaper polystyrene. Instead of being stamped in a press, polystyrene is heated to a liquid, and then squirted or injected into closed stampers, similar to the methods used for making the parts for plastic model kits. The labels are then glued or painted on after the record leaves the press. Unlike vinyl records, where the label is stamped into the cooling vinyl and stays there forever, paper labels sometimes lose their adherence to the record, and can cause labels to pucker or rip—or in some extreme cases, fall off completely.

Some record companies in the 1960s, most notably Amy, Mala, Bell, Sphere Sound, and Page One, didn't even bother with paper labels. In many cases, these companies simply inked a label directly onto the styrene. While other paper labels may show "ring wear" over time, the information on these "spray-painted styrene" discs can actually wear right off the disc—sometimes down to a black center. Today, these pressings are much harder to find in near-mint condition than their paper-labeled brethren.

This is an example of a painted-on label on a styrene record. Notice that the lines run right to the edge of the center hole. Notice also the huge print on the label; it was not feasible to paint small text on a styrene record.

Most record companies use styrene for 45s because the master stampers actually last longer, as they are not "heated" for styrene pressings. Styrene can also be recycled without a noticeable change to its moulding properties. Thus, a near-mint styrene record will have virtually no surface noise. But after only a few plays, especially with an imbalanced tonearm or a worn needle, styrene records will develop surface noise quickly. Club DJs who backcue styrene 45s also notice those discs acquiring "cue burn" (a slight hiss before the beginning of the song).

Styrene records are also extremely light, so light in fact that they don't work very well in the drop-changer phonographs of the 1960s and 1970s. Here's a physics lesson—if you place a stack of three styrene 45s on your dropchanger, by the time the tonearm rests upon the third disc, that top record will spin slower than the two below it—the tonearm actually exerts more pressure on the disc than do the records spinning underneath. Stack enough styrene discs high enough on a dropchanger, and eventually the tonearm could actually stop the record cold while the turntable (and discs between) continue to spin.

There are many ways to tell the difference between styrene and vinyl records. Vinyl records are thicker and heavier than styrene records; 7" vinyl 45s don't bend, and the record's circumference is not flared to the edge (flared edges are styrene pressings). If you hold a vinyl record and flick its edge with your finger, you'll hear a deep thunk. Do the same with a styrene record, and you'll hear a tinny clink. If the center label is one color with the information seemingly engraved or spraypainted into the center, the 45 is polystyrene.

Grading

The best and most accepted method of grading a record is by using the *Goldmine* grading system. This system is used by dealers and collectors alike, and offers a universal standard for collectors.

There are many different factors involved in grading a record—the physical condition of the album jacket or picture sleeve; the visual condition of the record; and if possible, how the record sounds when played on a turntable with a properly calibrated stylus and balanced tonearm. For visual quality, look at the record under a strong light. Take into consideration how the label looks, if there are any scratches, scuffs, cracks or discolorations on the grooved portion of the record.

After you've examined the disc, give it a grade based on the following requirements.

Mint (M): The record is perfect. No flaws, scratches, or scuffs on the grooves. A clean, crisp cardboard jacket or picture sleeve, with no disfigurations whatsoever. There is an argument that even a record coming straight out of the factory to your hands cannot be completely "mint" like a coin or a stamp, and therefore the "mint" grade should be used rarely, if at all.

Near Mint (NM) or **Mint-Minus** (M-): The record is as close to perfect as possible. No marks whatsoever on the grooves. The label is clean, unmarked, and unscuffed. There is no ring wear on the album cover or the picture sleeve. There is no background surface noise on the disc. Some dealers will not give a record a grade higher than "near-mint," as it may be their belief that no record can ever be truly "perfect." For purposes of this book, "near-mint" will be the standard for which all other conditions will be based. This figure is approximately the highest a dealer will sell a record in such condition.

A near-mint example of Heart's "Magic Man." Notice the crisp label and clean grooves.

Very Good Plus (VG+). The record has been played, but by someone who took extremely good care of his or her record collection. There might be some slight "scuffs" or "warps" on the grooves; which on a VG+ record should not affect the sound quality when played. You may see a faint outline of ring discoloration on the album jacket or picture sleeve (ring discoloration occurs when albums are stored together on a shelf, and time causes some of the album artwork to rub off, causing a circular "ring" on the album jacket). There might be a tiny dent in the corner of the album cover, or a small split in one of the jacket's seams. If a record has one or two of these flaws, it is considered "VG+"—just missing the final cut for Near Mint. Records in VG+ condition should sell for approximately 50% of the same record in NM condition.

Very Good (VG): Records in this condition have more pronounced defects. You'll hear a small hiss when you play the record, but you'll still be able to hear the music without difficulty. There may be scratches on the record, but they won't affect the record's playability.

The album cover may have more pronounced ringwear or a bigger split in one of the seams. There might be the residue of a mailing label or sticker on the album cover or on the label. Part of the label may have scratches or may have lost some adherence to the vinyl.

Some 45s may contain plastic or metal center hole adapters, to allow the large-holed 45 to be played on a phonograph's small spindle. If the adapter can be removed without causing nicks to the record's inner hole, do so. If not, it's okay to leave the adapter in the record.

In this "very good" pressing, you can see some ring wear, but the grooves still look crisp.

A "very good" record may have one or two of these defects or aberrations, but not all of them. Records in VG condition should sell for approximately 25% of the same record in NM condition. If your record is in NM condition and you wish to sell it to a dealer, he may only pay you the VG price so that he can make a profit with the disc in a future transaction. Most music collectible books will not list values for less than VG condition, and this book is one of them.

Good or Good Plus (G, G+): You can play a "good" or "good plus" record on your turntable and listen to the music. You might not mind that the record was formerly owned by Barbara Rinaldo of Ypsilanti, Michigan (you know that because she affixed a mailing sticker on the record label, covering up the label trademark). You will need some tape to repair the splits in two of the album jacket seams. The jacket or picture sleeve will have severe ring wear, rips, folds, pockmarks, or damage from water or some other stain.

There may be cracks in the record, which will cause a pop when the needle passes over it. The record might have a moderate warp, which might affect the tonearm's operation. The record may have been pressed off-center, causing the tonearm to sway back and forth like a hypnotist's pendant. Or the label itself may have been pressed off-center, so much so that the paper itself actually touches the runout grooves. The scratches on the record give a "recorded near a bonfire" quality to the song. If the disc is made of styrene, the grooves of the record may have turned white from constant play.

Not only is there ringwear on the label, but you can see where the label is slightly worn. This record may have been previously owned by someone with a drop-changer phonograph.

A rule of thumb is that if you have been looking for this record for most of your life, and you find it in this condition, you should buy it only with the mindset that you will keep looking for a better copy, and eventually use the record now in your collection as a backup copy. If the record was once certified multi-platinum, that means there are millions of copies of this record somewhere, and you can pass up this "well-loved" copy someday. Records in G or G+ condition should sell for approximately 10% of the same record in NM condition.

Poor or Fair (P, F): These records are virtually worthless. The record label has magic marker or crayon all over it, or decorated with stamps and stickers and other defacings. The record is cracked to the point where pieces of the groove are missing. The edge warps look like mountain peaks, and playing the record will cause your tonearm to fly out of the grooves.

This label is starting to peel, and there is more worn sections on this disc than is normally acceptable.

If the album jacket hasn't fallen apart, it's holding on by a couple of unsplit corners. There's graffiti on the front cover—if not the previous owner's name, some artwork defacing the singer or least favorite band member. Or a young lady has decided Mick Jagger is her favorite Rolling Stone, and the lipstick prints near his picture on the album cover is clear proof of this. The 45s picture sleeve is wrinkled and splitting, or its center may have been cut out.

Another example of a "poor" record—as can be seen in the upper portion of this disc, somebody carved the words, "To my 1961 future husband Jan."

Unless this record is an extremely rare piece that would normally sell for four figures in NM condition, one should pay no more than a few pennies—if at all—for records in this condition.

Some people try to embellish the worth of their record collection by suggesting their discs are **Mint Plus** (M+), which would erroneously assume that the record is better than perfect. Watch out for listings for **Near Mint Plus** (NM+), which also blurs the line between near-mint and mint. Some records are also listed as **Good Plus Plus** (G++), which borders on Orwellian doublespeak.

It is not the case that the condition of the record is caused by the care—or lack thereof—of the purchaser or owner. Sometimes a record company's quality control division misses a mispressed or off-center 45. The glue on a 45 label may have lost its adherence due to age, and the label may have simply fallen off the record.

Other Definitions in this Book

Mono: The record was produced in monaural sound, one audio channel of music. Virtually all records made before the 1950s, and many records up until the late 1960s, were produced in mono.

Stereo: The record was produced in stereophonic sound, offering two distinct audio channels of music. Widespread use of stereo record production began in the mid-1950s. Until the late 1960s, you could purchase your choice of records in either mono or stereo (not all monaural phonographs could play stereo records).

No, this is not an optical illusion. The label is about an inch off-center, to the point where the edge of the label is actually in the runout grooves.

Electrically Channeled Stereo: Sometimes used by producers to turn a mono track into a stereo track—the left channel might include all the bass notes, while the right channel might incorporate all the higher-frequency instruments and vocals.

Quadraphonic: In the early 1970s, some record companies experimented with quadraphonic sound, allowing specially-designed phonographs to play sounds into four different speakers.

Picture Disc: An album or 45 that has a photograph or artwork pressed into the vinyl. Usually a picture disc has a representation of the album's original front cover on the vinyl; other times the record contains photographs of the band members or representative artwork. Depending on the artwork, a picture disc can also exist in non-circular formats (the grooves will remain circular, but the perimeter of the record may be uniquely shaped).

Picture Sleeve: A special paper holder for 45s. It often contains specialized artwork and a photo of the artist or group. In near-mint condition, some picture sleeves can attain a value worth more than the records they once contained. You may also see a 45 stored in a **company sleeve**, which often contains an artistic representation of the record company's trademark logo. A 45 may also appear in a generic **white sleeve**, or in a generic cardboard sleeve (mostly sold by record supply companies), or in no sleeve at all.

When the last song on a record is played, the needle will ride the **runout groove** to an infinite loop bordering the label. A record's **dead wax** is the black, grooveless area surrounding the label, and often contains engraved mastering numbers and the mastering agent's initials or company name. Sometimes the dead wax contains cryptic messages from the band, phrases or messages designed to entertain, confuse, titillate or mystify.

A vinyl album is usually stored in an **inner sleeve.** This is usually made of paper, plastic or some other protective compound, and protects the album when it is stored in its **outer sleeve** or **cover.** Inner sleeves can contain liner notes, song lyrics, fan club information, and/or photographs of other records in a record company's catalog.

How Can There Only Be One Copy of This Record in Existence?

It seems illogical that a record company would go through all the effort of signing a group, putting them in the studio to record a blockbuster album, commission their art department to design a knockout cover—and then press only a few records.

That sometimes happens, but only in rare instances where a successful artist may press only a handful of copies of a certain title, which he or she will give to friends, family, or fan club members.

Actually, there has been at least one instance where an artist pressed ONE copy of an album. In 1983, avant-garde composer Jean-Michel Jarre recorded an album called *Music For Supermarkets.* Only one copy of this album was pressed, and it was auctioned at an art exhibition for more than 69,000 francs ($10,000.00). After the auction, Jarre broadcast one airing of *Music For Supermarkets* on Radio Luxembourg, then he ceremoniously smashed the only existing master to pieces. Now that's a rare record.

The reality of the situation is that record companies did press thousands of copies of an album or 45. When the record stayed on the store shelves for too long, the records were shipped back from the stores to the record company, which then proceeded to melt down the unsold records to make new vinyl releases.

This process continued until the 1970s. By then, instead of destroying the records and making new copies, record companies simply notched the album covers and drilled tiny holes in the 45 labels. These "cutouts" were then sent to discount stores and bargain shops, which could sell the vinyl at a fraction of its original price. These albums can still be found in those bargain shops today, especially during the Christmas season, when the boxes of cutout Christmas albums are brought out in the hopes someone will purchase them for the holidays.

Another instance where only a few records would be pressed can occur when, at the last minute, a producer or artist doesn't like the final product. Normally the materials would be destroyed and the artist would start over, but often a few "orphan pressings" escape the pressing plants. These discs either end up in the record company archives, or in the collections of pressing plant employees.

Frank Wilson's "Do I Love You (Indeed I Do)," one of the most popular "Northern Soul" songs of all time, is one of these "destroy the pressings" records. Wilson, who produced dozens of Motown hits, was encouraged to record an uptempo track in an effort to see if he could have a hit. At the last minute, even after some promo copies were pressed, Motown president Berry Gordy convinced Wilson that although he was a decent singer, he should concentrate on his duties as a producer. Gordy destroyed the remaining copies, leaving a scarce few for the Motown archive (he even had Wilson's voice wiped off the master tape, replacing it with another singer, Chris Clark).

Eventually that archive copy ended up in the hands of a British club DJ, who filled the dance floor of his club every time he played "Do I Love You (Indeed I Do)." A second copy of "Do I Love You" eventually sold at auction for more than £15,000 in 1999, and the song's legendary status has made Frank Wilson a musical legend in northern England.

If Two Records Look the Same, Why isOne Worth $500 and the Other Worth Only $2?

This is a very good question. These two records may look the same, but there is something about disc A that disc B doesn't have. Maybe it's a song that was originally part of the album, but was removed from later pressings. The artwork on the label in the center of the record could have changed due to a subsequent pressing or reissue. Something on the album jacket may have been mispelled, or a song title may be listed for a song that's not on the record.

Yes, albums like *Sgt. Pepper's Lonely Hearts Club Band, Exile on Main Street, 461 Ocean Boulevard and Songs in the Key of Life* are considered masterpieces of rock music, each one a million-seller. Now think about this. Being a "million-seller" means that there are at least one million copies of each record out there.

Let's put this in perspective: The 1970s supergroup Boston sold 17 million copies of their debut album, one copy for every 15 people living in the United States today. That alone means that a standard copy of *Boston* has little resale value, even in near-mint condition. But if that record were a half-speed mastered audiophile pressing by the Mobile Fidelity Sound Lab or if the record was a "picture disc," with the album art pressed directly into the vinyl, those copies would have more worth to both Boston collectors and arena rock fans.

Sometimes an artist or band will release an album, only to have it yanked from shelves when somebody discovers something offensive or unsettling on the cover or the obverse. In coin collecting, this is the equivalent of a 1916 dollar coin with a bare-breasted Liberty. In baseball cards, it's the same as a Fleer Billy Ripken card that was photographed with an obscenity scrawled on the bat knob. Whether it involves a bare-breasted woman holding a model airplane (Blind Faith's *Blind Faith*), clearly visible canine genitals (David Bowie's *Diamond Dogs*), or even some ground beef and doll heads (The Beatles' *Yesterday and Today*), many of these covers can go for hundreds, even thousands, of dollars in near-mint condition—much more, in fact, than the replacement covers plastered over them.

Since small record companies may have their discs made at various independent pressing plants, it is possible for a record to have a variation in its label text or artwork. The label's font—the width, height and style of the lettering—may vary from company to company, and sometimes collectors have taken rulers and protractors with them to record shows, in an effort to confirm the proper angle or width of the rarest pressing. As an example, while many bootleg copies of the Beatles' *Introducing the Beatles* (Vee Jay 1062) exist today, some pressings have been misidentified as bootlegs, and are really albums from a legitimate California pressing plant.

Look at the size of the record. Does it seem smaller in diameter than an album should be? In the 1950s, many record companies pressed 10-inch long-playing albums, containing at least six to eight songs by the featured artist or band. Some years later, these same record companies would re-release the album in a 12-inch format, and add four or six more songs to the record and sell it as a new release. While the 12-inch LPs from the 1950s do command a decent price, some of those 10-inch records have crossed the four-figure threshold. This 10-inch album concept continued into the 1980s, as some companies released selected albums in a 10-inch budget format (the Clash's "Black Market Clash" and Rickie Lee Jones' "Girl At Her Volcano" were originally released as 10-inch albums).

This first release by parodist Tom Lehrer was as a 10-inch album. This record is even rarer—it was custom-pressed for Lehrer Records.

Most Jimmy Clanton 45s have a white label, including this title.

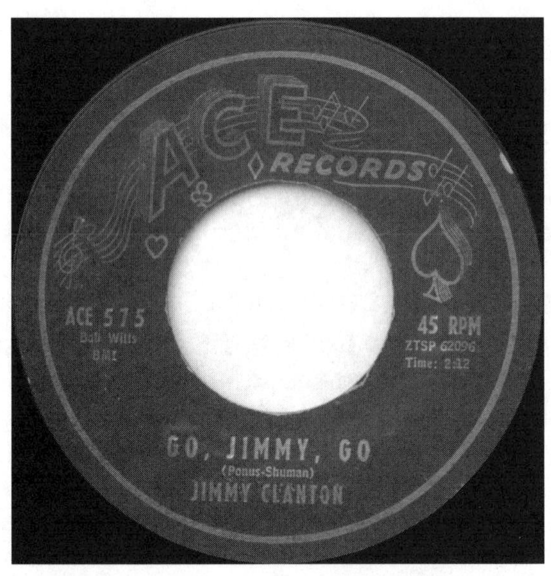

But this pressing of "Go Jimmy Go" has a purple label, and is worth more because of that variation.

Sometimes the rarity comes from a record being re-titled, or songwriting credits being added or deleted. Roy Orbison's big hit "Oh, Pretty Woman" (Monument 851) was originally titled "Pretty Woman," until the publishing group that represented Cole Porter's catalog (which had a song called "Pretty Woman") ordered Orbison to change the lyric. The original record is worth $25 in near-mint condition; if the "Oh" is on the title, it is more common and worth only $15 in near-mint condition.

Here's another example: the Doors once released one of their songs on 45 as "Hello! I Love You, Won't You Tell Me Your Name" (Elektra 45635) before shortening the title to the first four words. The longer-titled record can command prices as high as $20; shorten the title and the record's best price is $12.

Sometimes a record is released just as the record company itself is converting its label artwork from one style to another. Releases on the older artwork invariably command a higher price—the first release by Ricky Nelson on Verve, "I'm Walkin'" (Verve 10047) exists in two label variations—an orange-yellow label worth $50 in near-mint condition; and a more common black-and-white Verve label worth only $40 in near-mint condition.

Another rarity can occur when a song has to be re-recorded because a lyric might be too sensitive for broadcast. Artists from the Kinks to the Knack, from the Steve Miller Band to Pink Floyd, have recorded one version of a popular song, then had to change a lyric or refrain for cleaner airplay. A classic example of this is Lou Christie's "Rhapsody in the Rain" (MGM 13473). Some stations refused to play the original 45 because of its lyrics, which were, by 1960s standards, rather risqué: "We were makin' out in the rain/And in this car, our love went much too far." Christie recorded a "clean" version, with the lyrics edited thusly: "We fell in love in the rain/And in this car, love came like a falling star." Only by a close examination of the dead wax numbers in the runout grooves can a collector tell, without playing the song, which version is which (the "makin' out" version has the numbers 66-XY-308 in the grooves; the "fell in love" version adds the letters "DJ" to the runout groove). In case you're wondering, the "makin' out" version commands a higher price: $20 in near mint, as opposed to $15 for the cleaner version.

Have you ever heard of the following labels: Singular, Fee Bee, Jerden, Hib-Tone, or Magic Lamp? These were the original labels for artists like Danny and the Juniors, the Dell Vikings, the Kingsmen, R.E.M., and the Carpenters. These early recordings inspired major labels to sign the bands and propel them to rock music immortality. And for collectors of these artists, finding those rare, short-printed songs on those labels can be the crown jewels for their collection.

Another variation can occur when a band records its first song, then changes its name. Sometimes the name change will be very subtle, such as a respelling of the group name (what was once "Huang Chung" became "Wang Chung"). Other times, the name change will be as different as night and day.

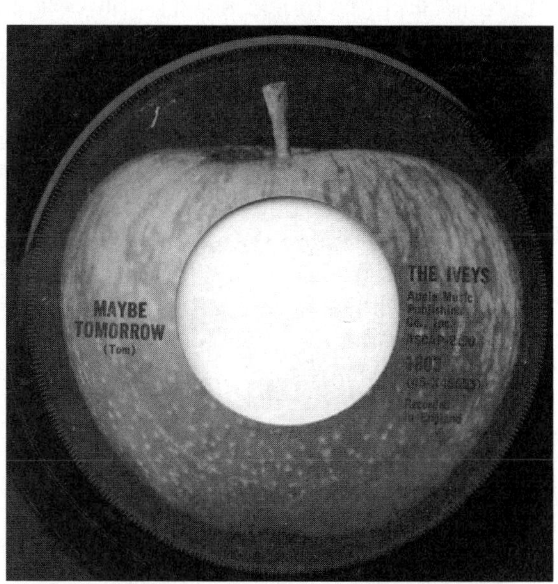

The Iveys had a minor hit with "Maybe Tomorrow." You might know the group by its later name—Badfinger.

One of the biggest myths about record collecting is that an artist's most significant work will be the most desirable and collectible. I would never argue that the Beach Boys' greatest songs, "Good Vibrations," "I Get Around," "Wouldn't It Be Nice" and "Surfer Girl," are classics. But even a near-mint copy of "Good Vibrations" is only worth $15. Meanwhile, a song they recorded in 1971, "Cool, Cool Water" (Reprise 0998) can command a near-mint price tag of $80. Why? It was a minor hit on the Beach Boys' custom label Brother, and it was poorly distributed. So for Beach Boys' collectors, this song is hard to find. And their earliest recording of "Surfin" can command $200-$300 on the Candix label, and four figures on "X," both the names of a record company the group was associated with before its major-label signing with Capitol.

Another myth about records is that because of the popularity of compact discs, nobody makes vinyl records any more. Actually, more titles are available on vinyl today than were in the past ten years. Even though record production decreased in the 1990s, some artists have always released their singles and albums on vinyl, as well as on compact disc and on cassette (Pearl Jam, R.E.M., and Madonna, to name a few). And some musical genres—country music, for example—never stopped making 45s. For most of his career, Garth Brooks did not release cassette singles or CD singles (notwithstanding his "Chris Gaines" period), but he did release all his hits on hard-to-find 7" 45s. Some 45s are being pressed to serve two markets, the United States and the United Kingdom—both countries have millions of vinyl-playing jukeboxes that, without a steady stream of 45s to play, would eventually enter obsolescence.

And still another myth about collecting is that in order to keep a record in near-mint condition, it should never be played or even touched. If you've spent $100 on a rare non-sealed record, wouldn't you like to know what's on it, to hear what lies in the grooves that makes this record worth choosing over new furniture? Well, if you have a good turntable with a well-adjusted tonearm and proper stylus—and if you properly clean the record after each playing—and you're making a personal copy to your cassette player so that you can listen to this album in a non-eroding format, then that's fine. If you properly store your vinyl with care and attention, your records can maintain their near-mint or VG+ grade for years, even decades.

Yet another myth about record collecting is that these prices are hard and fast—no dickering, no bargaining, and that's that. Since records are considered collectibles the same way trading cards and rare coins are considered collectible, prices can fluctuate. And like trading cards, some records can increase in value depending on where, or to whom, they are sold. A doo-wop collector in New York may not want to buy a rare short-printed Guns 'n Roses LP, but he may be more willing to spend an extra dollar to secure a near-mint Criterions 45.

Are 78s and cylinder recordings still collectible?

Although the focus of this book is on recordings made after 1950, it would be ludicrous to suggest that those albums and 45s are the only collectible recordings. There are many collectors who specialize in both cylinder recordings and in 78s, and whose collections are indeed impressive.

Before Thomas Edison and Emile Berliner invented their separate versions of a phonograph, the only way to reproduce popular songs was through the use of sheet music, or with metal discs for music boxes, or with perforated player piano rolls. Edison's cylinder machine was able to reproduce not only the melody, as did player pianos and music boxes, but it was also able to reproduce the instrument or orchestra that played the melody. The Edison label's early successes include recordings by John Philip Sousa's band, as well as built-in studio orchestras such as the Edison Conservatory Band.

Berliner's phonograph played records that were not cylinders, but were instead flat discs. The discs themselves could carry three minutes of music per side, as opposed to the two-minute-maximum cylinders. And although many of the popular artists and singers of the day, including Ada Jones, Billy Murray, Al Collins, and Cal Stewart, recorded both for Edison's cylinder label and for the Columbia and Victor flat-disc companies, the flat disc eventually surpassed cylinders as the phonograph medium of choice. Because thousands of Edison cylinder machines were still available throughout the South, the Edison company continued to make cylinder recordings into the late 1920s.

But today, although many of these cylinders may look similar, they are not all playable on the same equipment. Because there are differences in cylinder size, composition and rotation speed, some cylinder phonographs are actually incapable of playing certain cylinders. Today, unless the title is extremely recognizable ("Take Me Out To The Ball Game," "Liberty Bell March," or "The Preacher and the Bear"), many of these early cylinders have been forgotten and ignored, except by a small legion of dedicated musicologists and archivists. There was a slight resurgence in cylinder recordings, thanks to the motion picture *Titanic*, which mentioned such titles as "Come Take A Trip In My Air-Ship," and "Nearer My God To Thee."

Another problem is that many cylinders simply have not survived the elements. Those cylinders that have been stored in hot attics or damp basements have either expanded or shrunk over the years, causing devastating cracks or mold spores on the cylinders. But of the cylinders that have survived, the music captured from their grooves is both striking and breathtaking. For more information on cylinder recordings, one should visit *http://www.tinfoil.com* on the Internet. And if you do have some cylinders and are looking for a machine that will play them today, Nauck's Vintage Antiques offers a modern multi-cylinder machine called the Archeophone, a device that can be hooked up to your modern stereo system. For more information, visit Nauck's at *http://www.78rpm.com.*

As for 78s, from 1900 to the mid-1950s, the most popular music format was 10-inch flat discs rotating at 78.26 RPM (pre-World War I discs had varying sizes and speeds before the 10-inch 78 was standardized). Every type of music, from big-band music to vocal harmonies, from jazz to blues, from opera to doo-wop, was pressed on 78s.

Does this mean that all these 78s have high collectible value?

Well, not all of them.

First, let's talk about what's NOT collectible in the 78 format. CD re-issues have lowered the price for popular big band and swing 78s. The 78s of popular vocalists, such as Dinah Shore, Rosemary Clooney, and Perry Como, also have a minimal collector value outside of fans of those artists' repertoire. While Frank Sinatra's music is still highly collectible, only his earliest 78s on RCA and Columbia have risen on the collector's market.

Those 78s that ARE collectible have to be rare—extremely rare. The most collectible 78s are blues and jazz records that weren't initially sold in "white" record shops to "white" patrons. These include original recordings by Muddy Waters, Robert Johnson, Charlie Patton, Blind Lemon Jefferson, and Louis Armstrong. The first recordings by country-western artists are collectible as well–Gene Autry on Supertone, Hank Williams on the Sterling label.

An early Louis Armstrong 78 of a song the Mills Brothers would make famous, "Lazy River."

During the Second World War, most musical bands and singers recorded "V-Discs," one-of-a-kind recordings as entertainment for soldiers and sailors in the theaters of war. Many of these V-Discs contained performances by artists collaborating together for the first time. And because of a 1942 musician's strike against the major record companies, V-Discs (the label was exempt from the strike) are the only surviving examples of mid-1940s blues and jazz. Since V-Discs had to travel across the ocean to the soldiers and sailors–and then back to America—any V-Discs existing today are worth at least $20 in near-mint condition, with the price rising for a Sinatra or rare jazz V-Disc.

"Picture disc" 78s, with the grooves spinning over a full-color artwork, also have a high collector value. A great example of this is the Vogue Picture Disc. From 1946 to 1948, more than 75 different picture disc titles were pressed for the Vogue Picture Disc company, and some Vogue collectors will pay anywhere from $50 to $3,000 for discs in this genre.

When the 45 RPM record was born in 1948, it signaled the slow demise of the 78. Within the next ten years, record companies gradually switched their record production from 78s to 45s, which were more durable and less expensive to produce. Between 1950 and 1955, more 78s were pressed than 45s, and for collectors today, the 45 copy of a song is twice to five times as valuable as its 78 counterpart.

But as record companies eventually phased out 78s in favor of the 45, any 78s made after 1956 are rarer and have a higher collectible value than the same song on a 45. And some 78s pressed in 1959, including Elvis Presley titles like "Wear My Ring Around Your Neck," can be worth five to ten times the concurrent 45s value.

Weren't CDs Supposed to Take the Place of Vinyl Albums?

In theory, digital compact discs were designed as the next wave for future music collectors and artists—recordings so pure you can hear an artist inhale before singing a verse; sound and melodies so sharp and clear, you can make out every instrument in an orchestra.

And although there has been major improvements in sound quality with compact discs, many audiophiles, collectors, and record owners aren't ready to toss their vinyl just yet. Even though the compact disc is now the most popular music platform today, there are still people who claim its sonic reproductions may be inferior to a well-pressed vinyl album.

Ostensibly, CDs can be released with different mixes of popular songs, but in this age of .mp3 and Napster, even those rarities can circulate around the Internet for years, easily downloadable to anyone with a moderately speedy computer.

With CDs, one must also consider the source from which the CD was originally mastered. When David Bowie's RCA albums were initially released on CD, the sound quality was actually *inferior* to the same albums that were pressed on vinyl. Quality did not improve until Bowie acquired the rights to his back catalog, and released the albums on Rykodisc, overseeing the data transfer and every step of the mastering process.

CDs that are collectible include radio-only concerts and interviews, promotional CDs with different remixes of popular songs, and pre-1985 titles that were taken out of circulation due to initial poor sales (such titles include Dennis DeYoung's *Desert Moon* and Big Country's self-titled debut album).

Proper Care and Maintenance of Your Record Collection

Records need attention. They need to be cleaned. They need to be properly stored—and when you want to play them, they must be played on proper equipment. Some common sense tips can also ensure that your near-mint records stay in near-mint condition.

Albums and 45s must be stored vertically, never laid flat. Laying albums flat on a pile can cause ringwear on the album cover, and create problems if you want to play a certain LP on the bottom of the pile. For small collections, most standard bookshelves will suffice. Make sure there is a 13" spacing between each shelf, so that you can easily extract albums. Never overpack your shelves—while it may look impressive to have your entire collection filling a bookshelf, you don't want the records packed so tightly that you can't pull an album out without taking six or seven other albums with it.

For larger collections, think about building your own bookshelf or purchasing a rack system. Stay away from metal shelving units; besides their lack of supporting walls, which could cause the first or last album on the shelf to get scraped or notched against the shelving unit screws, poorly assembled metal shelving units can become top-heavy and will eventually fall down or collapse. Many record collecting magazines have advertisers who offer stackable shelving units (such as ICE for CDs, and the Rackit series for LPs and tapes); make sure that whatever cabinets you choose will allow you unbarriered access to your records. Outfitting a large record collection in Rackit or ICE shelves might be an expensive proposition, so make sure you budget wisely.

You can also build your own customized shelving units. Your local home improvement store will have modular closet shelves that can hold your albums and 45s with ease. Depending on your collection, you may outgrow that unit fast and have to buy a second (or third) one. Be aware that these closet shelves are made out of pressed wood (as opposed to the Rackit system, made out of whole oak), and a shelf with two feet of albums on it may start to sag.

Overexposure to sunlight and humidity, in time, can damage your record collection. Make sure that wherever you store your records, they are located away from direct sunlight or radiators. If you want to store your collection in a basement, make sure you invest in a dehumidifier and pour out its excess water every day.

If you want to keep your picture sleeves and rare company sleeves in mint condition, it's a good idea to store the records and sleeves separately; 45 sleeves are more prone to ringwear, seam splits, and tearing. Some 1970s Capitol 45s can also produce gear-like ridges around the center of your picture sleeve. The best way to store your 45s is in plain white paper sleeves. Place your picture sleeves in separate plastic or mylar cover sleeves and store them elsewhere.

Some people purchase white generic cardboard sleeves to store their 45s. If you do store your records this way, make sure you clean out any slivers of loose cardboard inside the sleeve (usually blowing inside will force the cardboard fragments to float away). If you don't clean out the sleeves, the loose scraps of cardboard will eventually stick to the 45s static charge.

Yes, vinyl albums and 45s can actually become magnetized—not to the point where they can pick up a nail, but...remember that old science experiment where you rubbed an inflated balloon on your hair, then watched in amazement as it magically stuck to your woolen sweater? Well, that same static electric charge is generated every time you play a record. Notice that after you play an album and remove it from your turntable, airborne dust, dirt, and pollen seem to leap to the vinyl. After playing a record, you should use a zerostat gun, a plastic appliance that sprays harmless neutral ions on your record and removes the record's static charge. Or spray a non-alcohol-based static spray into a dry cloth and wipe the record with the cloth.

White paper sleeves are also acceptable for albums, but if you can find a dealer that still sells rice-paper sleeves, buy as many as you can. Rice-paper sleeves envelop your album in a thin, pillowy material that both protects the vinyl from everyday use, and keeps it scratch-free inside. Placing your records on polypropylene protective sleeves is also a good idea, and you can purchase them at companies like Bags Unlimited for a very reasonable price (approximately $24.50 for a package of 100 sleeves, available at *http://www.bagsunlimited.com).* If you choose to use standard poly-lined sleeves (Radio Shack sells them at 10 to the bag), don't use them for your most expensive or rarest albums—standard poly-lined sleeves have a tendency to break down in heat and stick to albums, as opposed to polypropylene sleeves, which do not break down over time.

There has been considerable discussion about whether to leave shrink-wrap on an album cover or to remove it. If you haven't opened the disc up, you can leave the shrinkwrap alone. If you've already opened the disc, unless the shrinkwrap has some identifying sticker on it (i.e., "contains the new #1 hit 'Mrs. Robinson'"), you should remove it before it gets too tattered and dusty. There are 12-inch clear polypropylene or mylar sleeves available if you want to protect your album art, and some companies like Bags Unlimited sell shrink-wrap machines so you can hermetically re-seal your discs.

If there are some identifying stickers you want to save, or a price tag that you want to take off without tearing the plastic, you can use either lighter fluid, or a household adhesive dissolver called UN-du. A few drops of UN-du on the price tag or sticker will temporarily loosen the glue backing, allowing you to peel the sticker off and re-apply it on an index card.

Some people actually believe that if shrink-wrap remains on a record, it will be protected from water damage. This is wrong. In reality, records that sustain water damage (floods, rain storms, leaky pipes dripping on collections) can be *more* damaged if the shrink-wrap is left on. Often the water will seep through a hole in the shrink-wrap, or at the opening of the jacket. Once the water gets inside the shrink-wrap to the jacket, the shrink-wrap actually keeps the moisture inside the record, causing it to stain and mold quickly.

If your records and album jackets have been damaged from floods or rain, there are ways to make them playable and storable again. Take the water-damaged records out of the sleeves, wash them with a mixture of distilled lukewarm water and very mild detergent. Dab off the excess water with a soft sponge and store the records in a dish rack until dry. Place your album covers between dry white paper towels (insert paper towels in the jackets themselves through the album opening if necessary). Stack them for about 24 hours in a dry warm room, then replace the paper towels with clean ones. The sleeves may show signs of water damage, but they can be re-used in a few days.

Everybody has an opinion on what to use to clean your vinyl—rubbing alcohol, distilled water, hydrogen peroxide, de-ionized water, etc. A serious collector should invest in a cleaning machine with a built-in vacuum, like a Nitty Gritty or a VPI machine. Cleaning fluids like Discwasher D4 and Vinyl-Zyme Gold will clean your grooves when used in conjunction with a carbon fiber brush (also available through Discwasher, although Radio Shack does sell a nice one). You can also make your own record-cleaning "home brew" out of the following recipe: three parts of distilled water to one part isopropyl alcohol, and adding a little Woolite. You may also want to add a few drops of Kodak Photoflow so that your mixture flows evenly over the grooves and doesn't bead up. After cleaning out the grooves, rinse your records thoroughly with distilled water—not spring water, mineral water, or tap water, all of which have impurities that can settle in the grooves. Use a clean cloth diaper or chamois to wipe any excess water off, then place your disc in a rack to dry. If you use a home brew, test it out on some old 45s to make sure you have mixed the right formula for your purposes.

Never use any "home brew" originally concocted for 45s and LPs on 78s—an alcohol-based cleaner will eat shellac like candy. You can, however, use a non-alcoholic, non-ammonia window cleaner to clean 78s. Spray the window cleaner onto a clean white cloth or woolen towel. Wiping carefully, gently, and firmly, following the path of the grooves, you should be able to remove dirt and grime from 78s. Depending on the age of the 78, you may even find yourself removing minuscule iron filings from the grooves, the residue of steel needles from generations past.

If you've invested all this money in your record collection, you should also think about adding an insurance policy. Talk with an insurance agent to make sure you receive the right insurance policy for your needs, and remember that the agent who sells insurance is not the same person who will settle the damage claim. Insurance is only for the physical property, not for the equivalent of the music.

In conjunction with your insurance policy, you should maintain an itemized list of your collection. If you have a computer, you should invest in inventory software—nobody can remember every single album or 45 they own at the snap of a finger. There are music-specific databases like "Organize Your Collection" or Mr. Lister, which have specific fields (artist, title, label, condition) all ready for your data. Or you can invest in a standard spreadsheet database program like Quattro Pro, Excel or dBASE, and tailor the information to your specific needs (variations in label design, RCA master number, beats per minute, etc.). Be sure that the company you purchase your data software from will be able to provide upgrades. I know one person who's forced to still use his Apple IIe because the software he stored his 10,000 classical albums on is incompatible with modern computers.

Once you've entered all the information into your database, you should print out an inventory list at least once every two months and store it in a binder with your record collection. Not only will this tell you at a glance what records you have and their condition, you can take this binder to any record show and avoid spending $25 for a $15 record you forgot you owned.

Naturally you want to listen to your music whenever it suits your fancy. This means we come to the most important part of your record collection outside of the vinyl itself—your record player. No matter how cool it looks to play your priceless 50s records on a 1950s-era turntable, don't play them on those players unless they have been upgraded and updated with new needles. There are many phonograph repair and upgrade services on the Internet that specialize in modifying your RCA 45-Y-3 or Silvertone or GE Wildcat so that it can play today's music without sacrificing its original looks and charm, and are worth contacting if you so choose.

Although multi-record drop-changing turntables are great examples of 1970s kitsch, don't use them without serious upgrades to their needles and tonearm tracking. Even then, although the myth of record grooves scraping against each other on dropchanger phonographs is apocryphal at best (since the album edge and label are raised, stacked grooves seldom touch), the labels do rub against each other, causing scrapes and wear in the labels.

Among electronic companies that still make turntables, Technics still makes its SL-1200, a direct-drive turntable with pitch adjustment, for $200-$300. Another company, KAB of New Jersey, still makes top-of-the-line triple-speed players (33-45-78) for $300, as well as a transcriber turntable that will play 17" AFRS military discs for $375.

If you want to play large-holed 45s in your collection and can't find the 45 adapter that came with your turntable, it never hurts to pick up some single-use 45 adapters. Plastic three-armed adapters are cheap enough, and 10-20 inserts for a dollar is a fair price. Zinc Pfanstiehl "Push-Up" adapters are more expensive—about 6 inserts for a dollar, and if you place it in a record, it should not be removed (zinc Pfanstiehls won't damage your discs, unlike Webster Chicago steel adapters that were made in the 1950s, which can cause damage to 45s if they're removed improperly).

By following these simple guidelines for record care, your discs should last a lifetime; your investment will not depreciate over time; and your friends and family will be amazed at the fantastic record collection you've maintained over the years.

Record Collecting and the Internet

There is no doubt that the Internet has changed the way most record collectors acquire those rare and hard-to-find titles. Those same collectors who five years ago went from collecting show to collecting show, now purchase rare records with a click of the mouse and a mailed money order.

The Internet has also spawned a new type of collecting speculator—one who purchases rare records at shows, then turns around and sells them on eBay or Amazon.com to the highest bidder. In many cases, people are unloading the record collection they've amassed for 20 years onto Internet auction sites, while new collectors find those rare pieces are easier to acquire on the Internet than ever before. Instead of visiting record shows or the neighborhood record shop, people are now using the computer for instant purchase gratification.

Speaking from personal experience, I know the highs and lows of Internet record purchasing and selling. By typing in a simple request for a group name or song title, a plethora of selectable choices pop up on my computer screen faster than Rimsky-Korsakov's bumblebee flight. I have met and befriended fantastic record collectors from all over the world, and have built entire collections from genres that were unknown to me a scant few years ago.

But there are as many downsides with online selling and auctioning as there are upsides. Sometimes prices are set enormously high, with the claim that a "rare Michael Jackson *Thriller*" record is worth an opening bid of $3,000 (for this dealer, "rare" must mean "less than 25 million copies"). Or the ubiquitous "grab bag 'o records," where a sealed package of 50 discs can be yours for only a $25 opening bid (and upon receiving your prize through the mail, you marvel at how many different Shaun Cassidy records are in the "grab bag").

Sometimes the descriptions of items for Internet auction take "poetic license" to new lows. I've purchased records advertised as having "minor scuffs" and receiving records that look as if they were cleaned with Brillo. Covers with "slight wear" that barely have a photo attached. How about "tiny splits" on the jacket that are as wide as the record slot?

Another problem with using the Internet for record collecting is that buyers can not physically see the record (unless the seller took a digital photo of the album and posted it with his advertisements), nor can a buyer ensure that the record will arrive intact to the seller. One seller informed me he had completed a transaction with a purchaser and sent an album to him. A few days later, the purchaser contacted the seller, admonishing the seller for advertising a record in near-mint condition, but sending a record with a deep gouge in the vinyl. The seller asked the purchaser to send the record back. Upon careful examination, the seller discovered a deep gouge not only in the vinyl, but in the album's jacket as well. After some thought, the seller figured out that when the buyer received his mail-order package, he took a box cutter and sliced the box open—and applied enough pressure when he cut the box to cut both the record jacket and the vinyl.

And believe it or not, some Internet auction sites will not allow the sale or auctioning of white label promos. Since selling bootleg or counterfeit records is taboo on many auction sites, some web auction houses lump white label promos into that group, because the promos are often listed as "for promotional use only," or "not for sale," which some Internet sites have interpreted to mean "not for sale under any circumstances."

What about Napster and all the Internet file-swapping sites?

In less than a year, many computer file-swapping programs, including Napster, Gnutella, and Freenet, have brought a new dimension to record collecting. Now you can send, trade, or swap music files, which are encoded in .mp3 format, to anyone in the world who owns a computer and a link to the Internet.

The first thing to understand is that there is no such thing as a "rare .mp3 file." Only a few years ago, there were .mp3 sites online that allowed visitors to download files, as long as they uploaded an .mp3 file of their own up to the site, or signed up for a monthly subscription service at the .mp3 site. Today, that technology has evolved into Napster, which allows computer users to swap files quickly, effortlessly, and anonymously.

For collectors, Napster allows them to search out recordings they may never have heard before, and actually listen to music before they hunt for the original recordings. Ostensibly, in a perfect world, Napster would actually encourage people to purchase more music at record stores or at collector's shows.

But if you have a choice between purchasing a $500 doo-wop classic and acquiring the same song for free through Napster, that $500 record may stay on the shelf for a long time. But what you are getting from Napster is a sound file. A copy of a sound from a record. It has about as much face value as a laser photocopy of a Honus Wagner T-206 baseball card, or of a photograph of Van Gogh's *Starry Night* painting. If I made a cassette tape of *Y Kant Tori Read* and gave you the tape, would that have the same value as my original CD copy? Do I even have to answer this question?

Even though Napster has entered into "strategic alliances" with music industry giant A.G. Bertlesmann, someone is still getting hurt in this battle—and it's not the artists, and it's not the record companies, and it's not Napster. It's mom-and-pop record stores, especially the ones near college campuses. These are the family owned businesses, the ones who live and die on the sale of used records and tapes, stores that have been operating for as long as phonographs have existed. It's used record stores who get dumped-off copies of records and CDs that some computer user "ripped" into .mp3s, placed them on his Napster download directory, and took the disc back to the store, made some comment about it being "the wrong purchase," and getting his money back.

The long-range effects of Napster and .mp3s on the record collecting world are still too early to fathom, but it definitely is a subject worth more study and consideration.

Why Isn't My Favorite Album or Artist Listed in This Price Guide?

I have no bad feelings for any musical artist or group, and I would love to list every single album ever made, every 45 ever pressed, every picture sleeve ever printed. Such a book would be the size of the New York City phone directory, would cost at least $500 apiece, and would kill more trees than a California wildfire.

Warman's American Records was written for beginning and intermediate record collectors. It's for people who want to start their own record collection. It's for collectors who want to visit a record collecting show, and make educated purchases without fear of overspending.

For more information on specific types of record collecting, and to find out more about the artists, singers, and genres, each subdivision of this book contains a bibliography, specific magazines, and Internet webpages loaded with discographies, discussions and downloadable data.

Most of all, this book was written to explain why certain records are collectible, while others are not. Ten years ago, 1950s instrumental albums by Esquivel and Enoch Light took up space in thrift store bargain bins. Today, with the rediscovery and appreciation of "space age pop," these records are quickly increasing in value. On the other end of the spectrum, despite their elaborate packaging and promise of high quality, many Longines Symphonette box sets have actually dropped in value over the years, to the point where only a few titles can attain a higher resale value than the product's original price.

Despite the ornate packaging and the heavy vinyl used to create this Herb Alpert/Baja Marimba Band boxed set, this Longines Symphonette album has not risen above its initial sale price.

How were the prices arrived at for this book?

Darts. Plain and simple.

Actually, the prices for the records in this book were arrived at from various sources from within the Krause Publications family of books, including *The Standard Catalog of American Records* (2nd Edition), *The Goldmine Price Guide to 45 RPM Records* (2nd Edition), *The Goldmine Record Album Price Guide, The Goldmine Promo Record and CD Price Guide, The Goldmine 45 RPM Picture Sleeve Price Guide, The Goldmine Country West-*

ern Record and CD Price Guide, The Goldmine Price Guide to Alternative Records, The Goldmine Heavy Metal Price Guide and The Goldmine Jazz Album Price Guide.

Within these books, the authors were in contact with thousands of used record shops, sifted through millions of advertisements and auction results, and listened to legions of record collectors. While these prices may constitute an educated listing of millions of titles, they should only be considered a reference guide and in no way a listing of iron-clad prices. Krause Publications does not set prices for records; it only reflects the trends shown in the marketplace for collectible and desirable vinyl. The publisher of *Warman's American Records* does not buy and sell records. So therefore, none of the items in this book are "offers to buy" or "offers to sell" from either Krause Publications, *Warman's American Records,* or this author.

BOARD OF ADVISORS

Mark Anderson
email: manderso@theriver.com
Specialty: Quad Recordings

Thomas R. Grosh
P.O. Box 7061
Lancaster PA 17604-7061
email: vears@lancnews.infi.net
Specialty: British Invasion, Rolling Stones

Bruce Spizer
925 Common St.
New Orleans LA 70112
email: bruce@beatle.net
Specialty: Beatles

Norm Katuna
P.O. Box 80154
San Diego CA 92138
email: normk@operamail.com

Tim Neely
c/o Krause Publications
700 East State St.
Iola WI 54990-0001
email: neelyt@krause.com

Jim Parker
2002 West Main St., Lot 33
Ephrata PA 17522
Specialty: Movie Soundtracks

Ken Jarrell
4314 16th Street, #5
Lubbock, TX 79416-5834
email: vinylville@door.net
http://members.tripod.com/~Vinylville

Leslie Gerber
Parnassus Records
51 Goat Hill Road
Saugerties NY 12477-3008
(845) 246-3332
Specialty: Classical Music

Boo's Blasts From The Past
3875 Alberta Place
Philadelphia PA 19154
Specialty: Oldies, Motown

Val Shively
Box B
Havertown PA 19083
Specialties: Doo-wop, 1950s music

Stephen M. Caraco
email: steve@madonnacatalog.com
Specialty: Madonna

Pete Battistini
6576 Lake Forest Drive
Avon, IN 46123-7405
email: at40@aol.com
Specialty: American Top 40

Rocky Kruegel
6814 West Highland Road 128N
Mequon WI 53092
(262) 236-4391

APPLE RECORDS

History: Apple Corps Ltd. was born in early 1968, as an attempt by the Beatles to create their own corporate empire. Ostensibly, Apple was a record company, a clothing boutique, a book publishing company, and an electronics firm. While the non-musical projects folded after only a few months, Apple Records survived for almost eight years. It was still around when the Beatles broke up in 1970, and was the home of all four Beatles' solo projects until 1975.

Badfinger's first chart hit, when they were originally known as the Iveys.

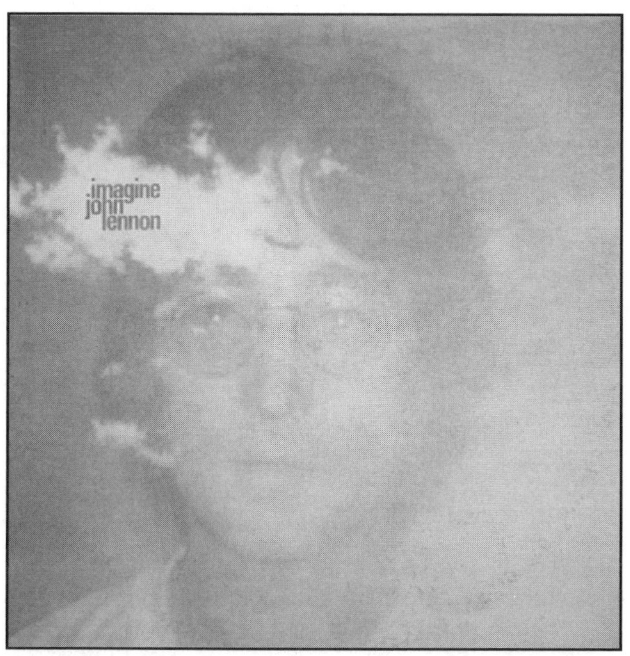

John Lennon's *Imagine*. His post-Beatles solo work appeared on Apple, the label he and the other Beatles formed in 1968.

Apple was also the home for other groups, some of whom received songwriting and/or instrumental assistance by the Beatles, eventually achieving Top 10 hits of their own. The biggest of these "non-Beatles" groups on Apple was the band Badfinger. The British group, led by lead singer/songwriter Peter Ham, was originally signed to the Apple label as the Iveys (and charting with the song "Maybe Tomorrow"). Badfinger had five U.S. chart hits, including the Paul McCartney composition "Come and Get It," as well as "Baby Blue," "No Matter What," and "Day After Day," all written within the group. They also recorded four albums for Apple, including *Magic Christian Music* and *Ass*.

Badfinger's *No Dice* album contained "Without You," which became a smash hit for both Harry Nilsson and Mariah Carey. Courtesy Last Vestige Music Store, Albany, N.Y.

Another Apple success story is Welsh singer Mary Hopkin. In 1968, she took the old Russian folk song "Dear For Me" and, with new lyrics written by Paul McCartney, had a Top 5 hit with "Those Were The Days." Hopkin also hit the Top 40 with songs like "Goodbye" and "Temma Harbour."

Mary Hopkin's "Those Were The Days."

Other artists who recorded singles or albums for Apple include Ronnie Spector, who recorded a George Harrison composition called "Try Some, Buy Some"; Billy Preston, whose Apple singles included a version of Harrison's "My Sweet Lord"; and James Taylor, who had a minor chart hit with an early version of "Carolina In My Mind."

Written by George Harrison, *Try Some Buy Some* became Ronnie Spector's first hit since her days as lead singer of the Ronettes.

Between 1968 and 1970, Apple 45s contained a tiny Capitol logo on the label's B-side. This is a key point in identifying the age of an Apple 45. In 1971, the Beatles' entire singles catalog, going back to "Love Me Do" and "Please Please Me," was re-released on Apple, and the Capitol logo disappeared from the B-side label. If these 1971 releases have a star on the A-side, they are worth $7.50 in VG condition, $30 in near-mint. Without the star, their value drops to one-third of those pressings with a star. In 1975, when the Beatles' entire Apple-Capitol singles catalog was once again re-released, those pressings have the words "All Rights Reserved" on the label, and are worth $3.75 to $15, depending on condition.

After 1976, Apple Records remained silent for almost 20 years. In 1996, however, the label was resurrected as the imprint for the Beatles' *Live at the BBC* album and three double-disc *Anthology* releases, as well as for the 45s "Baby, It's You," "Free As A Bird," and "Real Love."

While most Apple artists received a generic Apple company sleeve, the Beatles were provided their own company sleeve. If you look at the perimeter of the label for this Beatles 45, the B-side of "Let It Be," you can see a tiny Capitol logo, denoting this record as an original first pressing and not a reissue.

Trivia

While recording solo material on Apple, each of Ringo Starr's former bandmates either produced, wrote, or performed on the drummer's solo hits. George Harrison produced "It Don't Come Easy" and sang harmony vocals on "Photograph," John Lennon wrote and played piano on "It's All Down To Goodnight Vienna," and Paul McCartney played kazoo on Starr's remake of "You're Sixteen."

The Beatles' "Free As A Bird," which resurrected the Fab Four's Apple label.

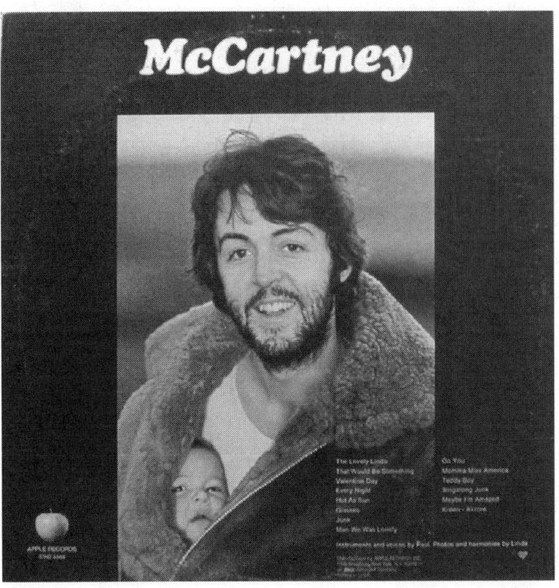

Paul McCartney's first solo album on Apple.

What To Look For: The Beatles' material will always be collectible, no matter what label they appear on. Apple's single releases were first pressed with a black star on the "A" side, and these first pressings command higher prices than non-starred material.

Beatles picture sleeves are always collectible, and picture sleeves from their Apple labelmates are also desirable. Since Apple was distributed by Capitol, and Capitol releases had a grooved gear-like ridge along the label, many of these picture sleeves will have a circular groove or wear pattern in their center. This wear pattern automatically brings the sleeve down one grade—a near-mint sleeve containing this wear pattern is downgraded to VG+.

Trivia

Because of a defective stamper when pressing John Lennon's "Cold Turkey" 45 (Apple 1813), the song has a skip during the third chorus, causing Lennon to sing about "Cold Tea" rather than "Cold Turkey." Pressings that play the complete song can be identified by larger, bolder print on the label.

Until 1976, all four Beatles released their solo works on Apple. When a Beatle moved on to another record company, that later record company often re-released the original Apple albums with a new record company imprint. For example, Paul McCartney's *McCartney* album exists with an Apple label, as well as on Columbia and Capitol labels.

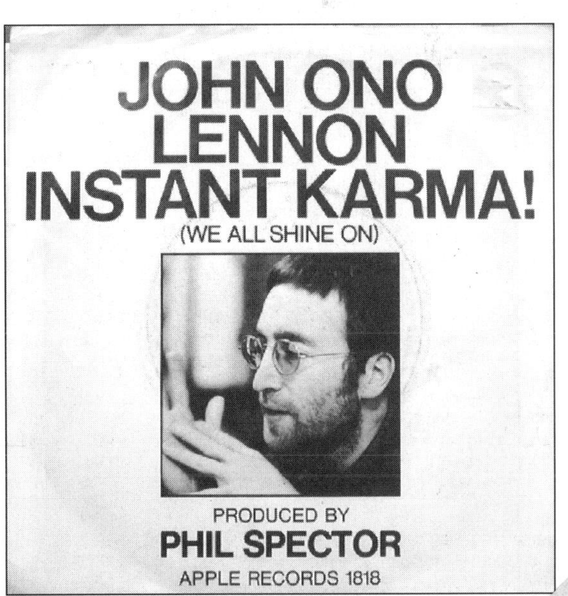

You can see the geared edge on John Lennon's *Instant Karma*; finding copies without this geared edge is difficult. Courtesy Last Vestige Music Store, Albany, N.Y.

References: Wiener, Allen I., *The Beatles: The Ultimate Recording Guide* (3rd Rev. Ed.), Bob Adams, Inc., Holbrook, Mass., 1994.

Trivia

Because George Harrison's "My Sweet Lord"/"Isn't It A Pity" 45 was considered a "Double-A"-sided record—that is, both sides were considered worthy of airplay—this record was one of the few Apple 45s that had an unsliced apple on both sides of the record.

George Harrison's biggest solo hit, "My Sweet Lord" was a #1 worldwide smash.

Web pages: Mitch McGeary's Beatles Web site, which contains label scans of many Apple artists: *http://www.rarebeatles.com.*

45s	Year	VG	VG+	NM
Badfinger, "Come And Get It" / "Rock Of All Ages" (Apple 1803)				
(with Capitol logo on bottom of B-side of label)	1969	$2.00	$4.00	$8.00
(without logo)	1969		$3.00	$6.00
Badfinger, "Day After Day" / "Money" (Apple 1841)				
(with star on A-side label)	1971	$5.00	$10.00	$20.00
(without star)	1971		$3.00	$6.00
(white label promo DJ pressing)	1971	$30.00	$60.00	$120.00
Badfinger, "Baby Blue" / "Flying" (Apple 1844)	1972		$3.00	$6.00
(white label promo)	1972	$30.00	$60.00	$120.00
The Beatles, "Hey Jude" / "Revolution" (Apple 2276)				
(small Capitol logo on the B-side)	1968	$3.75	$7.50	$15.00
(if "Mfd. by Apple")	1968	$2.50	$5.00	$10.00
The Beatles, "The Ballad of John and Yoko" / "Old Brown Shoe" (Apple 2531)	1969	$2.50	$5.00	$10.00
(with picture sleeve, add:)	1969	$25.00	$50.00	$100.00
The Beatles, "Something" / "Come Together" (Apple 2654)				
(small Capitol logo on the B-side)	1969	$25.00	$50.00	$100.00
(if "Mfd. by Apple")	1969	$2.50	$5.00	$10.00
The Beatles, "Let It Be" / "You Know My Name (Look Up My Number")" (Apple 2764)	1970	$2.50	$5.00	$10.00
(with picture sleeve, add:)	1970	$25.00	$50.00	$100.00
The Beatles, "Free As A Bird" / "Christmas Time (Is Here Again)" (Apple 58497)	1995		$2.00	$4.00
(with picture sleeve, add:)	1995		$2.00	$4.00
Elephant's Memory, "Liberation Special" (Apple 1854)				
(if B-side is "Power Boogie")	1972	$100.00	$200.00	$400.00
(if B-side is "Madness", second and subsequent pressings)	1972	$2.00	$4.00	$8.00
(if picture sleeve for "Liberation Special" / "Madness", add:)	1972	$2.50	$5.00	$10.00
George Harrison, "My Sweet Lord" / "Isn't It A Pity" (Apple 2995)				
(if black star on label)	1970	$10.00	$20.00	$40.00
(if label says "Mfd. by Apple")	1970	$2.00	$4.00	$8.00
(with picture sleeve, add:)	1970	$10.00	$20.00	$40.00
(with "All Rights Reserved" disclaimer, 1975 reissue)	1975	$6.25	$12.50	$25.00
George Harrison, "What Is Life" / "Apple Scruffs" (Apple 1828)				
(if black star on label)	1971	$3.75	$7.50	$15.00
(without star on label)	1971	$2.00	$4.00	$8.00
(with picture sleeve, add:)	1971	$10.00	$20.00	$40.00
Mary Hopkin, "Those Were The Days" / "Turn, Turn, Turn" (Apple 1801)	1968	$2.50	$5.00	$10.00
Mary Hopkin, "Goodbye" / "Sparrow" (Apple 1806)	1969	$2.00	$4.00	$8.00
(with picture sleeve, add:)	1969	$3.00	$6.00	$12.00
The Iveys, "Maybe Tomorrow" / "And Her Daddy's A Millionaire" (Apple 1803)				
(if black star on label)	1969	$7.50	$15.00	$30.00
(without star on label)	1969	$5.00	$10.00	$20.00
John Lennon / Plastic Ono Band, "Cold Turkey" / "Don't Worry Kyoko" (Apple 1813)	1969	$2.50	$5.00	$10.00
(some copies skip on the third lyric because of a pressing defect; if this happens, deduct 50% from price of an unskipping copy)				
John Ono Lennon, "Instant Karma (We All Shine On)" / "Who Has Seen The Wind" (Apple 1818)				
(if single-sided DJ copy)	1970	$50.00	$100.00	$200.00
(if stock copy with B-side)	1970		$2.00	$4.00
John Lennon and Yoko Ono, "Happy Xmas (War Is Over)" / "Listen, The Snow Is Falling" (Apple 1842)				
(if catalog number S45X-47663/4, white label on styrene pressing)	1971	$187.50	$375.00	$750.00
(if on Apple 1842, green vinyl, faces label)	1971	$3.75	$7.50	$15.00
(if on Apple 1842, green vinyl, Apple label)	1971	$2.50	$5.00	$10.00
Jackie Lomax, "Sour Milk Sea" / "The Eagle Laughs At You" (Apple 1802)	1968	$5.00	$10.00	$20.00
Paul McCartney, "Another Day" / "Oh Woman, Oh Why" (Apple 1829)				
(with star on A-side)	1971	$3.00	$6.00	$12.00
(without star)	1971	$2.00	$4.00	$8.00
(promo copy, Apple PRO-6193/4)	1971	$20.00	$40.00	$80.00
Paul McCartney and Wings, "Jet" (Apple 1871)				
(if B-side is "Mamunia", running time on A-side incorrectly listed at 2:49)	1974	$25.00	$50.00	$100.00
(if B-side is "Mamunia", running time on A-side is correct, at 4:51)	1974	$2.50	$5.00	$10.00
(if B-side is "Let Me Roll It")	1974	$2.00	$4.00	$8.00
(if "Jet" is on both sides, promo copy, edited mono / stereo)	1974	$12.50	$25.00	$50.00
Paul McCartney and Wings, "Band on the Run" (Apple 1873)				
(stock copy, has "Nineteen Hundred and Eighty-Five" on B-side)	1974	$2.00	$4.00	$8.00
(promotional copy; has edited mono on A-side, full-length stereo of "Band on the Run" on B-side)	1974	$10.00	$20.00	$40.00
(promotional copy, has edited mono on A-side, edited stereo of "Band on the Run" on B-side)	1974	$25.00	$50.00	$100.00
Ronnie Spector, "Try Some Buy Some" / "Tandoori Chicken" (Apple 1832)				
(with star on A-side)	1971	$2.00	$4.00	$8.00
(without star on A-side)	1971		$3.50	$7.00
(with picture sleeve, add:)	1971	$2.50	$5.00	$10.00
Ringo Starr, "Back Off Boogaloo" / "Birdman" (Apple 1849)				
(if label has blue background)	1972	$18.75	$37.50	$75.00
(if label has green background)	1972	$2.00	$4.00	$8.00
(white label promo)	1972	$37.50	$75.00	$150.00
(with flat finish, black paper sleeve, add:)	1972	$3.75	$7.50	$15.00
(with glossy finish on one or both sides of paper sleeve, add:)	1972	$10.00	$20.00	$40.00
Ringo Starr, "You're Sixteen" / "Devil Woman" (Apple 1870)				
(if standard Apple label)	1973	$6.25	$12.50	$25.00
(if label features Ringo in a star-shaped bedsheet)	1973		$3.00	$6.00
(white label promo, mono-stereo "You're Sixteen" on both sides)	1973	$12.50	$25.00	$50.00
James Taylor, "Carolina In My Mind" (Apple 1805)				
(first pressing, if B-side is "Taking It In")	1969	$75.00	$150.00	$300.00
(second pressing, if B-side is "Something's Wrong," with Star on "Carolina" side)	1970	$2.50	$5.00	$10.00
(if B-side is "Something's Wrong," no star on "Carolina" side)	1970	$2.00	$4.00	$8.00
(DJ pressing, song is listed as "Carolina On My Mind")	1970	$7.50	$15.00	$30.00

Apple-Americom four-inch flexi-discs	Year	VG	VG+	NM
The Beatles, "Yellow Submarine" / "Eleanor Rigby" (Apple/Americom 5715)	1969	$1,000	$1,500	$2,000
The Beatles, "Hey Jude" / "Revolution" (Apple/Americom 2276/M-221)	1969	$75.00	$150.00	$300.00
The Beatles, "Get Back" / "Don't Let Me Down" (Apple/Americom 2490/M-335)	1969	$250.00	$500.00	$1,000.00
The Beatles, "The Ballad of John and Yoko" / "Old Brown Shoe" (Apple/Americom 2531/M-382)	1969	$200.00	$400.00	$800.00

Apple-Americom four-inch flexi-discs	Year	VG	VG+	NM
Mary Hopkin, "Those Were The Days" / "Turn, Turn, Turn" (Apple/Americom 1801P/M-238)	1969	$150.00	$300.00	$600.00
The Iveys, "Maybe Tomorrow" / "And Her Daddy's A Millionaire" (Apple/Americom 1803P/ M-300)	1969	$150.00	$300.00	$600.00

Albums	Year	VG	VG+	NM
Badfinger, Magic Christian Music (Apple ST 3364)				
(with Capitol logo on Side 2 bottom)	1970	$7.50	$15.00	$30.00
(without Capitol logo)	1970	$5.00	$10.00	$20.00
Badfinger, No Dice (Apple SKAO 3367)	1970	$7.50	$15.00	$30.00
Badfinger, Straight Up (Apple SW 3387)	1971	$15.00	$30.00	$60.00
Badfinger, Ass (Apple SW 3411)	1973	$5.00	$10.00	$20.00
The Beatles, The Beatles (Apple SBO-101) (2 LP's)				
(numbered copy, contains four pictures and a large poster; mint copies extremely hard to find)	1968	$37.50	$75.00	$200.00
(unnumbered copy, contains four pictures and a large poster)	197?	$15.00	$30.00	$60.00
(with "All Rights Reserved" on labels, title in black on cover, posters and pictures on thinner paper stock)	1975	$17.50	$35.00	$70.00
The Beatles, Abbey Road (Apple SO-383)				
(with Capitol logo on Side 2 bottom, contains words "Her Majesty" on jacket and label)	1969	$10.00	$20.00	$40.00
(with Capitol logo on Side 2 bottom, no reference to "Her Majesty")	1969	$18.75	$37.50	$75.00
(with "Mfd. by Apple" on label)	1969	$5.00	$10.00	$20.00
(with "All Rights Reserved" on labels)	1975	$6.25	$12.50	$25.00
The Beatles, Anthology I (Apple CI-8-34445) (3 LP's)	1995	$10.00	$20.00	$40.00
The Beatles, Anthology II (Apple CI-8-34448) (3 LP's)	1996	$12.50	$25.00	$50.00
The Beatles, Anthology III (Apple CI-8-34451) (3 LP's)	1996	$10.00	$20.00	$40.00
Elephant's Memory, Elephant's Memory (Apple SMAS-3389)	1972	$6.25	$12.50	$25.00
George Harrison, All Things Must Pass (Apple STCH-639) (3 LP's)	1970	$10.00	$20.00	$40.00
(1988 reissue, has Apple labels and Capitol cover, and large sticker on back cover)	1988	$20.00	$40.00	$80.00
George Harrison and Friends, The Concert for Bangla-Desh (Apple STCX-3385) (3 LP's)				
(1971 release, contains 64-page booklet and special record sleeves)	1971	$10.00	$20.00	$40.00

Albums	Year	VG	VG+	NM
(1975 reissue, has "All Rights Reserved" on labels)	1975	$12.50	$25.00	$50.00
Mary Hopkin, Those Were The Days (Apple SW-3395)	1972	$10.00	$20.00	$40.00
John Lennon and Yoko Ono, Wedding Album (Apple SMAX-3361)	1969	$37.50	$75.00	$150.00
(to be considered near mint, this record must contain, in addition to a clean cover and pristine vinyl, all the following inserts: a photo strip, postcard, poster of wedding photos, poster of lithographs, "Bagism" bag, booklet, photo of slice of wedding cake)				
John Lennon and Yoko Ono, Two Virgins - Unfinished Music No. 1 (Apple T-5001)				
(price with brown bag)	1968	$37.50	$75.00	$150.00
(price without brown bag)	1968	$12.50	$25.00	$50.00
(price with die-cut bag)	1968	$37.50	$75.00	$150.00
John Lennon, Imagine (Apple SW-3379)	1971	$5.00	$10.00	$20.00
Paul and Linda McCartney, Ram				
(if Apple MAS-3375, mono record in stereo cover, for radio station use only)	1971	$1,000	$2,000	$4,000
(if Apple SMAS-3375, Apple label with small Capitol logo on B-side)	1971	$12.50	$25.00	$50.00
(if Apple SMAS-3375, unsliced apple logo on both labels)	1971	$7.50	$15.00	$30.00
(if Apple SMAS-3375, "All Rights Reserved" on label)	1975	$25.00	$50.00	$100.00
Paul McCartney and Wings, Band on the Run (Apple SO-3415) (with photo innersleeve and poster)	1973	$5.00	$10.00	$20.00
Ringo Starr, Sentimental Journey (Apple SW-3365)	1970	$5.00	$10.00	$20.00
Ringo Starr, Ringo (Apple SWAL-3413)				
(with a 5:26 version of "Six O'Clock." On later copies, the song is shortened to 4:05, although the label still says "5.26". All known copies have a promo punch-hole in top corner of jacket; on side 2 of the record, "Six O'Clock" will be the widest track)	1973	$100.00	$200.00	$400.00
(standard issue with booklet; Side 1, Song 2 listed on cover as "Hold On")	1973	$5.00	$10.00	$20.00
(later pressing with booklet; Side 1, Song 2 listed on cover as "Have You Seen My Baby")	1974	$6.25	$12.50	$25.00
James Taylor, James Taylor (Apple SKAQ 3352)				
(first pressing, with name in black print)	1969	$6.25	$12.50	$25.00
(subsequent pressing, with name in orange print)	1970	$5.00	$10.00	$20.00

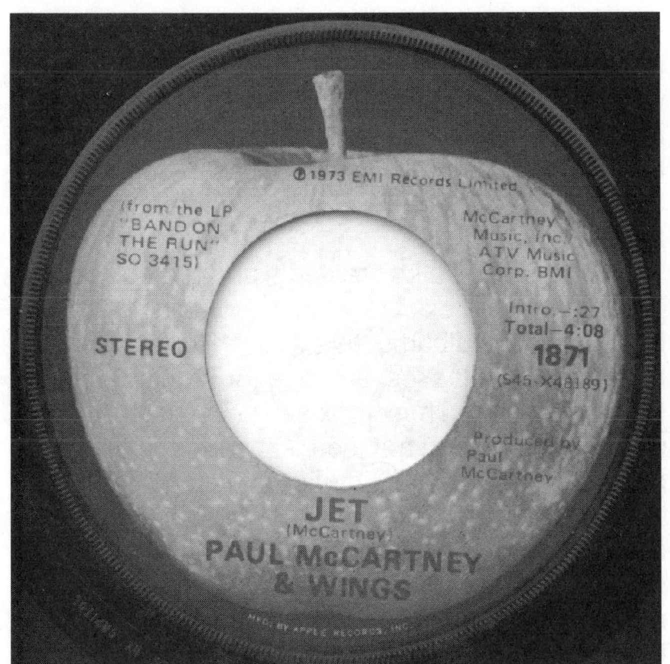

The B-side of "Jet" was originally "Let Me Roll It," another verbal volley in the songwriting war of words between John Lennon and Paul McCartney—but the B-side was later replaced with the song "Mammunia."

Despite George Harrison producing and performing on this track, Jackie Lomax' "Sour Milk Sea" did not crack the American pop charts. It is today, however, a rare Apple collectible.

AUDIOPHILE RELEASES

History: In the 1970s, a new type of music collector appeared—the "audiophile," a Latin word that literally means "lover of sound." As advances in electronics produced better-operating turntables and amplifiers, audiophiles willingly spent thousands of dollars on top-of-the-line stereo equipment. No longer content with phonographs from their local S.S. Kresge's or W.T. Grants, audiophiles based their musical collection not on the all-in-one dropchanger phonograph, but toward individual electronic components—a turntable here, an amplifier there, another unit for cassettes, still another unit for 8-tracks (this is the 1970s, after all).

But while music equipment evolved, the music product itself remained constant—for better or worse. Records were pressed in such huge quantities, but the quality of the vinyl itself had not improved since the start of the rock era. And when audiophiles placed these albums on their expensive turntables, and played the sound through their top-of-the-line speakers, they heard everything—thin sound from records that were pressed with worn stampers; crackly sound from recycled vinyl; wow and flutter from records with off-center spindle holes.

It was for this type of consumer that a new recording format was born: the audiophile record. Companies like Nautilus, DCC Compact Classic, and Mobile Fidelity Sound Lab created the highest quality vinyl, cassette, and CD re-releases from major labels, all for consumers willing to pay an extra couple of dollars for better quality sound and packaging.

Mobile Fidelity Sound Lab: The label most associated with the "audiophile" sound is Mobile Fidelity Sound Lab, which released more than 300 different albums between 1977 and 1999. In 1977, the people who created Mobile Fidelity Sound Lab had an idea—reissue popular albums, press them on 200-gram virgin vinyl, use only the album's original mater tapes for the best sound quality, then master the record at one-half its normal mastering speed, so that twice as much sound and ambiance could reach the final product. Today, Mobile Fidelity pressings are hot collectibles, where Steely Dan's *Katy Lied* can sell for $100, as opposed to its original ABC pressing, which goes for $12 in near-mint condition.

Every part of a Mobile Fidelity disc was produced for perfection: reinforced cardboard jackets' rice paper inner sleeves; virgin vinyl that was so pure you could hold it up in the air and see the sun through its black grooves. And the consumer response was tremendous. One of its first reissue projects, Pink Floyd's *The Dark Side of the Moon* (MFSL-1-017) became the hit of the 1979 Consumer Electronics Show, and near-mint copies today sell for approximately $50 apiece.

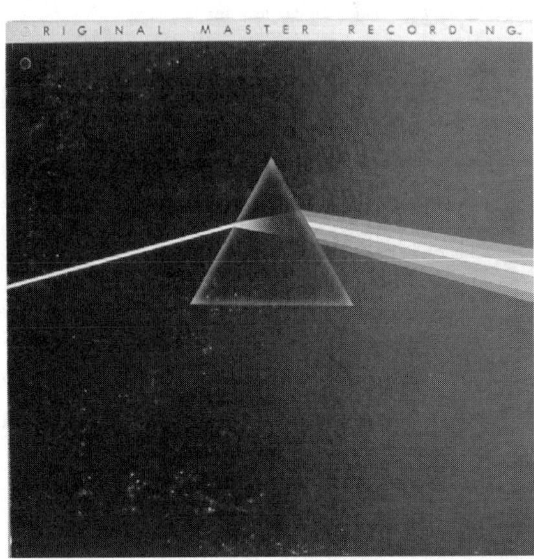

Pink Floyd, *The Dark Side of the Moon,* an early Mobile Fidelity classic. Courtesy Last Vestige Music Shop, Albany, N.Y.

Some Mobile Fidelity discs include extra added material—the master tapes for the Who's *Tommy* were lost years ago, but MoFi was able to acquire Pete Townshend's personal master tapes. Townshend's tapes included different mixes of songs such as "Eyesight for the Blind," an added treat for Who fans.

Mobile Fidelity also created elaborate box sets. Three such sets exist today: one containing the Beatles' 1960s albums, one for the Rolling Stones' London label releases; and one for Frank Sinatra's Reprise albums. These box sets, containing elaborate liner notes and a "Geo-disc" cartridge alignment tool, sell for $400 in near-mint condition.

In the 1980s, Mobile Fidelity entered the compact disc market, although it continued to make vinyl records sporadically until 1996. While subjecting the new aluminum-sputtered CDs to humidity and aging tests in its labs, essentially to stimulate years of use in a couple of weeks, the company found these discs developed pinholes or oxidation, a sign of poor aluminum bonding. Mobile Fidelity was able to later produce a series of gold-spattered CDs, once again with better sound quality and improved durability.

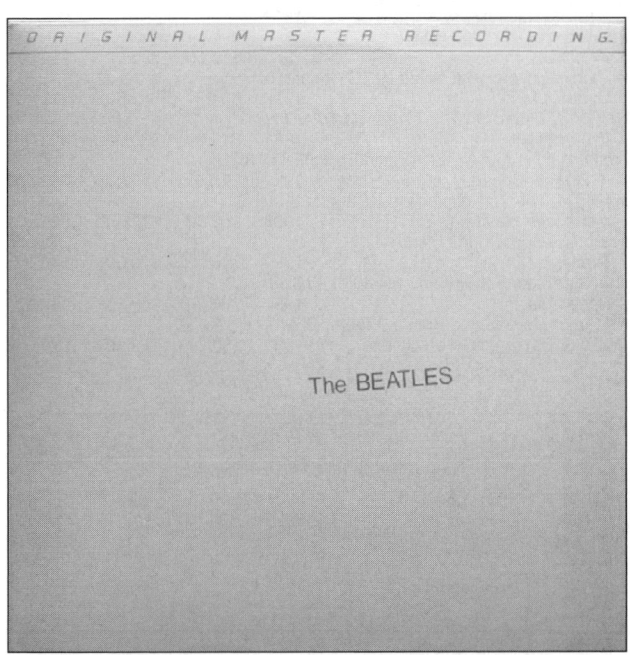

The Beatles' *White Album,* on Mobile Fidelity. Courtesy Last Vestige Music Shop, Albany, N.Y.

In the late 1980s, Mobile Fidelity worked with Soviet record label Melodiya to restore hundreds of Soviet classical and jazz albums, restoring aging master tapes and preserving both state-sanctioned and "underground" Soviet music.

Mobile Fidelity continued making gold CDs and virgin vinyl albums throughout the 1990s. When the company finally closed its doors in 1999, the audiophile world lost one of its great record labels.

Nautilus, DCC Compact Classics and "Quiex II": Not to be outdone by Mobile Fidelity, the audiophile label Nautilus released a series of "SuperDiscs," reissuing such titles as the Cars' debut album, Heart's *Dreamboat Annie* and Styx' *Pieces of Eight.*

Between 1979 and 1983, major record companies released their own high-quality vinyl, oftentimes with mixed results. The Warner/Elektra/Atlantic record conglomerate pressed some of its albums on "Quiex II" vinyl, a lighter compound designed to reduce surface noise. These were often radio-only pressings, and contain a black sticker on the album jacket announcing that the record was pressed on such vinyl. CBS also released some of its catalog titles in a "half-speed mastered" version, but the sound quality did not match the heights Mobile Fidelity and Nautilus set for their vinyl releases.

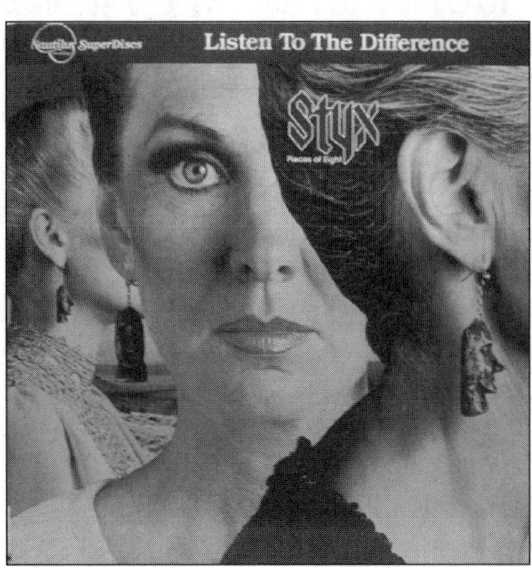

An example of a Nautilus SuperDisc pressing, Styx' *Pieces of Eight.*

In 1997, a new audiophile record company, DCC Compact Classics, released some 1970s LPs on 180-gram virgin vinyl. Some of the DCC titles include Cream's *Fresh Cream*, The Beach Boys' *Pet Sounds*, and Jefferson Starship's *Red Octopus*. Although the front covers of these albums are indistinguishable from their original label releases, DCC audiophile records add a gold sticker on the accompanying polybag, a DCC trademark label on the back cover, and a DCC catalog number on the spine. The record itself contains a custom DCC label.

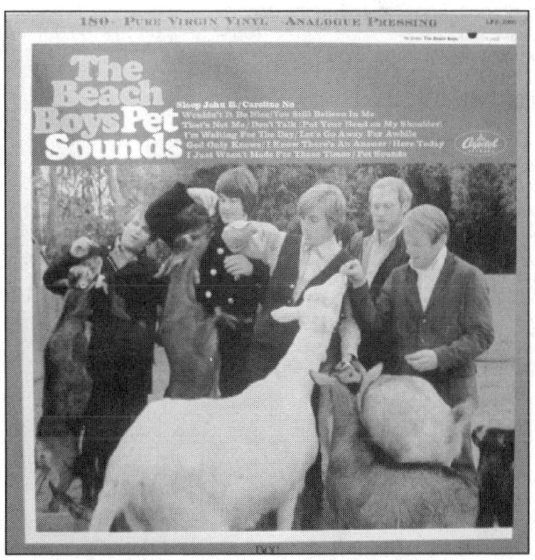

The Beach Boys' *Pet Sounds,* on 180-gram virgin vinyl. Courtesy DCC Compact Classics.

Another new company, Classic Records, has also reissued albums on virgin vinyl. Its catalog includes many rare recordings from the RCA Victor Red Seal and Mercury Living Presence classical labels, as well as contemporary works from pop and rock artists.

What To Look For: Audiophiles took care of their audiophile records, so many of them remain in good to near mint condition. Because of their low print run and high-quality output, many audiophile discs have retained their collectible value—and if the reissue was a major artist like the Beatles, the Rolling Stones, Nirvana, or Frank Sinatra, the record has increased in value.

Web pages: The Mobile Fidelity Sound Lab discography on Mike Callahan's Both Sides Now webpage: *http://www.bsnpubs.com/mofi.html*; DCC Compact Classics' homepage: *http://www.dcccompactclassics.com*; Classic Records' homepage: *http://www.classicrecs.com.*

Mobile Fidelity Sound Lab vinyl LPs	**Year**	**VG**	**VG+**	**NM**
The Beach Boys, Surfer Girl (Mobile Fidelity 1-116)	1984	$7.50	$15.00	$30.00
The Beatles, The Beatles Collection (Mobile Fidelity BC-1, 13 LP's)	1982	$125.00	$250.00	$500.00
Creedence Clearwater Revival, Cosmo's Factory (Mobile Fidelity 1-037)	1979	$17.50	$35.00	$70.00
Neil Diamond, The Jazz Singer (Mobile Fidelity 1-071)	1981	$7.50	$15.00	$30.00
The Grateful Dead, American Beauty (Mobile Fidelity 1-014)	1980	$12.50	$25.00	$50.00
Elton John, Goodbye Yellow Brick Road (Mobile Fidelity 2-160) (2 LP's)	1984	$10.00	$20.00	$40.00
Barry Manilow, Manilow I (Mobile Fidelity 1-097)	1981	$5.00	$10.00	$20.00
The Manhattan Transfer, Manhattan Transfer Live (Mobile Fidelity 1-022)	1979	$10.00	$20.00	$40.00
The Moody Blues, Days of Future Passed (Mobile Fidelity 1-042)	1980	$15.00	$30.00	$60.00
The Alan Parsons Project, I Robot (Mobile Fidelity 1-084)	1982	$10.00	$20.00	$40.00
(if above title is a "UHQR" pressing, Mobile Fidelity MFQR-084)	1982	$20.00	$40.00	$80.00
Pink Floyd, The Dark Side of the Moon (Mobile Fidelity 1-017)	1980	$12.50	$25.00	$50.00
(if above title is a "UHQR" pressing, Mobile Fidelity MFQR-017)	1982	$75.00	$150.00	$300.00
The Rolling Stones, The Rolling Stones (Mobile Fidelity RC-1, 11 LP's)	1984	$75.00	$150.00	$300.00
Simon and Garfunkel, Bridge Over Troubled Water (Mobile Fidelity 1-173)	198??	$10.00	$20.00	$40.00
Frank Sinatra, Sinatra (Mobile Fidelity SC-1, 16 LP's)	1983	$100.00	$200.00	$400.00
Steely Dan, Katy Lied (Mobile Fidelity 1-007)	1979	$20.00	$40.00	$80.00
Woodstock (original motion picture soundtrack) (Mobile Fidelity 5-200, 5 LP's)	1985	$50.00	$100.00	$200.00

Nautilus, DCC, CBS Half-Speed Master, Quiex II and others	**Year**	**VG**	**VG+**	**NM**
The Beach Boys, Pet Sounds (DCC Compact Classics LPZ-2006)	1995	$6.25	$12.50	$25.00
The Cars, The Cars (Nautilus NR-14)	1981	$7.50	$15.00	$30.00
Creedence Clearwater Revival, Willie and the Poor Boys (DCC Compact Classics LPZ-2019)	1996	$5.00	$10.00	$20.00
Dire Straits, Love Over Gold (Warner Bros. 23728-DJ) (pressed on Quiex II vinyl)	1982	$12.50	$25.00	$50.00
Dire Straits, Brothers In Arms (Warner Bros. 25264-DJ) (pressed on Quiex II vinyl)	1985	$12.50	$25.00	$50.00
The Grateful Dead, Terrapin Station (Direct Disk SD-16619)	1980	$25.00	$50.00	$100.00
Heart, Dreamboat Annie (Nautilus NR-3)	1980	$10.00	$20.00	$40.00
Jefferson Starship, Red Octopus (DCC Compact Classics LPZ-2036)	1997	$6.25	$12.50	$25.00
Elton John, Madman Across The Water (DCC Compact Classics LPZ-2004)	1994	$5.00	$10.00	$20.00
Elton John, Elton John's Greatest Hits (Nautilus NR-42)	198??	$25.00	$50.00	$100.00
Billy Joel, The Stranger (Columbia HC-34987) (CBS half-speed master)	1981	$7.50	$15.00	$30.00
(if on Columbia HC-44987, a reissue)	1982	$6.25	$12.50	$25.00
John Lennon and Yoko Ono, Double Fantasy (Nautilus NR-47) (if black and white front cover)	1982	$20.00	$40.00	$80.00
(if yellow and red colors added to black and white front cover, alternate cover pressing)	1982	$500.00	$1,000.00	$2,000.00
GHSP 2023) (pressed on Quiex II vinyl)	1982	$12.50	$25.00	$50.00
Joni Mitchell, Court and Spark (Nautilus NR-11)	1980	$12.50	$25.00	$50.00
Joni Mitchell, Court and Spark (DCC Compact Classics LPZ-2044)	1997	$6.25	$12.50	$25.00
The Moody Blues, On The Threshold Of A Dream (Nautilus NR-21)	1981	$15.00	$30.00	$60.00
Mike Oldfield, Tubular Bells (Virgin/Epic HE 44116) (CBS Half-Speed Master)	1982	$7.50	$15.00	$30.00
Pink Floyd, The Wall (Columbia HC2 46183) (CBS half-speed master) (2 LP's)	1983	$62.50	$125.00	$250.00
The Police, Ghost in the Machine (Nautilus NR-40)	1982	$10.00	$20.00	$40.00
Santana, Abraxas (Columbia HC 40130) (CBS Half-Speed Master)	1981	$20.00	$40.00	$80.00
Paul Simon, Hearts and Bones (Warner Bros. 23942-DJ) (pressed on Quiex II vinyl)	1983	$5.00	$10.00	$20.00

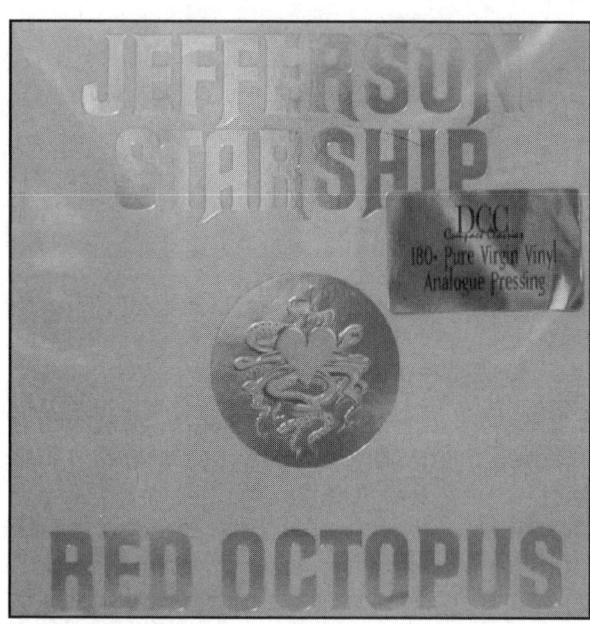

Jefferson Starship's *Red Octopus,* with DCC sticker on the polybag. Courtesy DCC Compact Classics.

Mike Oldfield's *Tubular Bells,* a CBS half-speed mastered disc. Courtesy Last Vestige Music Shop, Albany, N.Y.

THE BEATLES

History: John Lennon. Paul McCartney. George Harrison. Ringo Starr. These four men, along with their producer George Martin, revolutionized popular music forever. From their early days performing in the Liverpool Cavern Club, to their last public performance on the roof of their Apple Corps, Ltd. building, the Beatles were the heralds for a generation of music fans and collectors.

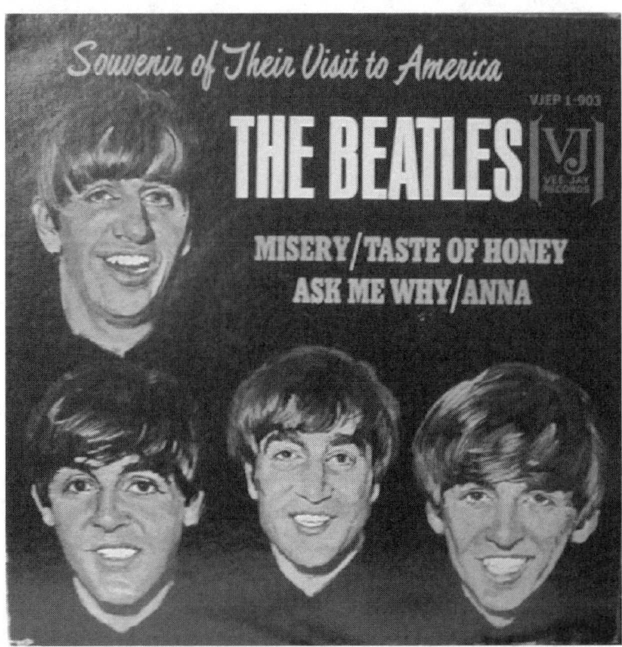

This four-song EP was issued by Vee Jay as part of the Beatles' first American tour. From the Collection of Val Shively.

It seems hard to believe, even today, that this group was actually passed over for a Decca recording contract, or that Capitol Records of America initially allowed other labels, such as Swan and Vee Jay, to release Beatles 45s.

The Beatles evolved in Liverpool, England, where John Lennon and Paul McCartney were members of the Quarry Men, one of many skiffle groups throughout England. The Quarry Men later became the Silver Beatles, and then "The Beatles"—with a lineup of Lennon, McCartney, George Harrison, Stuart Sutcliffe, and Peter Best. The Beatles honed their skills in live concerts at the Star Club in Hamburg, Germany; they eventually became headliners at the Cavern Club in Liverpool.

Stuart Sutcliffe eventually left the band, and Pete Best was replaced as drummer by Ringo Starr. With this lineup, the Beatles auditioned for London's record labels. An audition at Decca Records proved fruitless, as the label signed a local band, Brian Poole and the Tremoloes, instead. EMI Records eventually signed the Beatles, assigning them to their low-budget Parlophone label.

Working at Parlophone was a young producer, George Martin, who had previously produced the comedy albums that were Parlophone's stock in trade. But with the Beatles, Martin found a group capable of writing their own songs and working hard to make those rough songs polished gems.

Vee Jay Records released some early Beatles records in America; their early commitment to the band, however, was not as thorough as one would expect—notice the misspelling of the band's name as "Beattles" on the record. From the Collection of Bruce Spizer.

By 1963, the Beatles had conquered England. Conquering America, on the other hand, was more difficult. EMI's sister label in America, Capitol, had turned down various Beatles singles, allowing small companies like Vee Jay and Swan to pick up the rights. Unfortunately, those songs invariably did not chart, initially confirming Capitol's decision as a correct one.

But when the Beatles made their first concert appearances in America, their record sales soared. Where a generation once remarked about where they were when Franklin Delano Roosevelt died, this generation now asked, "Where were you when the Beatles played on 'The *Ed Sullivan Show*'?"

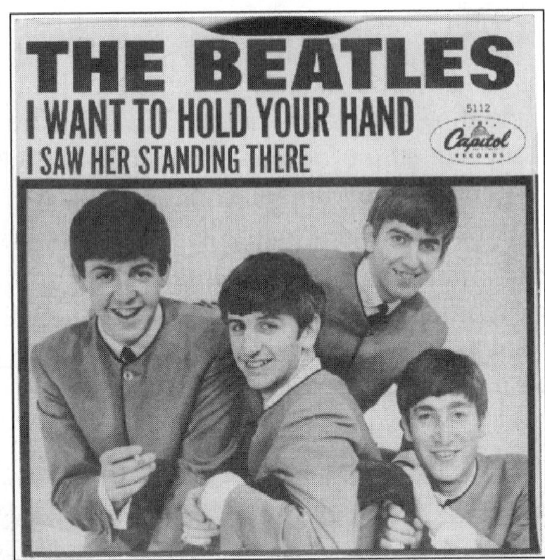

After the Beatles appeared on the "Ed Sullivan Show," millions of their new fans snapped up copies of their first Capitol single, "I Want To Hold Your Hand." From the collection of Bruce Spizer.

Beatlemania was at such a fever pitch in America, that in April 1964, the top five songs on the *Billboard* singles chart were Beatles songs. Of those five songs, two were official Capitol releases ("Can't Buy Me Love" and "I Wanna Hold Your Hand"), while the other three were from Vee Jay and Swan Records, which both had previously been offered the license to certain early Beatles recordings. And as other labels like Atco and MGM were able to find Beatles recordings to release (even in releasing "My Bonnie," when the Fab Four were backup musicians for Tony Sheridan), it eventually gave the Beatles 14 songs in a single week on *Billboard's* Hot 100 charts, a feat never duplicated. Demand for Beatles music was so great that "Roll Over Beethoven," a Capitol of Canada pressing, was able to cross the border and chart in America. There were even two Beatles tribute songs on the charts that week: the Carefrees' "We Love You Beatles," and the Four Preps' tongue-in-cheek "A Letter To The Beatles."

Even if the Beatles continued with the same Merseybeat rock that propelled them to stardom, their fans would have been satisfied. But one of the major strengths within the band was the ability to experiment within the studio, to challenge each other to write stronger songs, to raise the bar for every future album and single, to make each recording better than the last. Within that framework, the talents and assistance of producer George Martin should not be forgotten. John Lennon and Paul McCartney would bounce ideas off Martin, who in turn would show the group what could and could not be done in a four-track studio. It was Martin, for example, who took two distinctly different recordings of "Strawberry Fields Forever" and, by using variable speed tape recorders, merged both versions into a seamless pop smash.

The Beatles' "She Loves You" was released on Swan; the "Don't Drop Out" was added by the record company president as a plea for kids to stay in school.

Many classic Beatles 45s and LPs are hard to find in any decent condition; fans often bought the records, took them home, then added special identification stickers to the label, as can be seen by the actions of this "Lennon nut."

The Beatles were also pioneers in creating the "concept album," an LP where all or most of the tracks revolved around a certain theme. For the Beatles, that album was *Sgt. Pepper's Lonely Hearts Club Band*, with the Beatles dressed as orchestral military troubadours, their songs filled with the melodies and lyrics of their concert tours and of their trips to India and the Far East. Many have hailed *Sgt. Pepper* as the greatest Beatles album of all time; others have gone so far as to acclaim it as the greatest *album* of all time.

The group released three more albums after *Sgt. Pepper:* an eponymous double album (often called *The White Album* because of its stark white cover), the soundtrack to the film *Let It Be*, and their final studio album together, *Abbey Road*.

Although the Beatles officially disbanded in 1970, fans worldwide hoped for a reunion, a tour, possibly one more album. Those fans would have to be content with themed reissue LPs (*Rock and Roll Music, Love Songs, Reel Music*) and previously unreleased live concerts and demo tracks (*The Beatles at the Hollywood Bowl, Rarities*). All hopes of a live reunion show were dashed on December 8, 1980, when an assassin's bullet took John Lennon's life.

But in the late 1990s, the surviving Beatles recorded two new tracks for a documentary series, *The Beatles Anthology*. John Lennon was part of the sessions, as his voice was digitally enhanced from unreleased cassette tapes to create the songs "Free As A Bird" and "Real Love."

Interest in the Beatles has not wavered, even to this day. The release of *The Beatles 1*, a compilation of all their #1 hits, became a multi-platinum smash in the winter of 2000.

Trivia

Since Vee Jay did not have its own pressing plant, it used independent facilities to manufacture its Beatles 45s and LPs. At one point during the pressing of "Please Please Me"/"From Me To You," when the pressing plants ran out of Vee Jay preprinted labels, they simply made labels with the words "VEE JAY" or "VJ" in block printing—creating more than fifteen different label variations of that title.

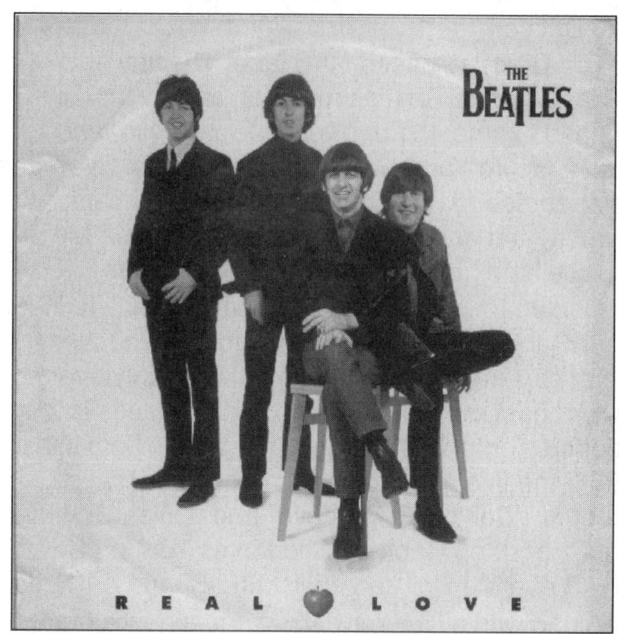

Adding their voices to an unreleased John Lennon demo tape, the Beatles reunited for their song "Real Love."

What To Look For: Without a doubt, the Beatles are the most highly collected music group of the rock era. Their early LPs can command thousands of dollars in near-mint condition. Because of this, bootlegs and counterfeits abound, and more than one collector has been fooled by a Beatles album with a price tag "too good to be true."

By the mid-1980s, the surviving Beatles requested that all subsequent Beatles album and CD releases from around the world, including America, feature the original album artwork and track listings of the British Parlophone albums. This meant American titles like *Beatles '65, Something New and Yesterday and Today* were deleted from the Capitol (U.S.) catalogs, to be replaced by *Beatles for Sale, With the Beatles, and Please Please Me.* The value of near-mint copies of the original 1960s Capitol LPs has steadily risen because of this.

The two most highly sought Beatles albums are 1963's *Introducing the Beatles* (Vee Jay 1062) and 1966's *Yesterday and Today* (Capitol 2553). The factors making these albums more collectible than other titles in the Beatles catalog are deep and varied, but will be explained in an abridged format below.

In 1963, the Beatles were dominating the UK pop scene, as their albums and 45s on Parlophone Records were rising up the charts. Parlophone's sister label in the USA, Capitol, was offered the opportunity to release Beatles records in America. Capitol initially refused, and Beatles songs appeared on other US labels—among them Swan, Tollie, Atco, and Decca.

The Chicago-based R&B label Vee Jay also released some Beatles material, and eventually released some 45s of "Please Please Me" and "From Me To You," two early Beatles hits. Even Vee Jay seemed to have the Beatles on their back burner—the early copies of "Please Please Me" misspell the group's name as the "Beattles."

One year later, Capitol released "I Want To Hold Your Hand," which shot to #1 and ushered the American wave of Beatlemania. Suddenly every record company that ever owned a Beatles track flooded it onto the market, to the point where in April 1965, the five biggest-selling 45s were Beatles records: "Can't Buy Me Love" and "I Want To Hold Your Hand" on Capitol, "She Loves You" on Swan, and "Love Me Do" and "Twist and Shout" on Tollie.

Along with all the new 45s came a new album, as Vee Jay had leased enough Beatles songs to issue a twelve-song LP. The album, *Introducing the Beatles*, was sold in both mono and stereo copies—then its running tracks were rearranged, with some songs added and others deleted—then the disc was issued as part of a double-LP with Vee Jay's other pop hitmakers at the time, the Four Seasons.

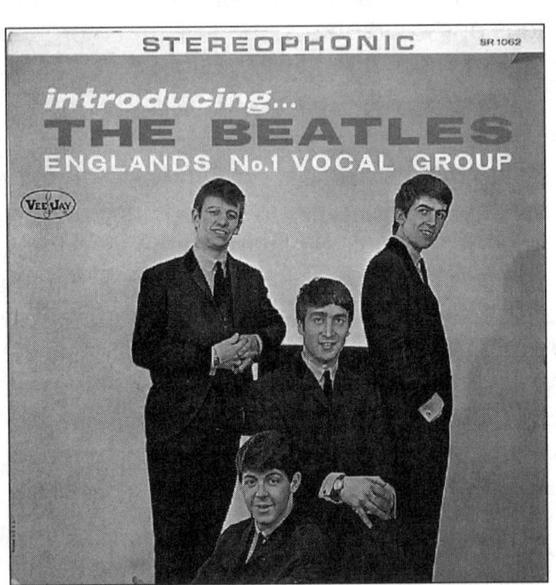

Because of the high value of legitimate stereo copies of Introducing the Beatles, there are literally more counterfeit copies than original pressings existing of this title. Courtesy Good Rockin' Tonight/Collectors Universe.

The mono copies of *Introducing the Beatles* are rare enough, but legitimate stereo copies of this title are extremely hard to find. Notice that word "legitimate." Because stereo copies of this album can command up to $12,000 in near-mint condition, *Introducing the Beatles* is one of the most bootlegged and counterfeited albums of the rock era. An explanation of how to determine a true copy from a counterfeit is listed as part of the price guide below.

Believe it or not, *Introducing the Beatles* isn't even the rarest Beatles disc on the Vee Jay label! Since Vee Jay tried to milk its Beatles cash cow for all it was worth, it released discs of the Beatles being interviewed (*Hear The Beatles Tell All*), it released albums containing early Beatles history (*Songs, Pictures and Stories of the Fabulous Beatles*), and it even released albums that were half-Beatles, half-other artist (*Jolly What! The Beatles and Frank Ifield On Stage*). Some copies of these records are worth as much as $18,000 in near-mint condition to a Beatles collector.

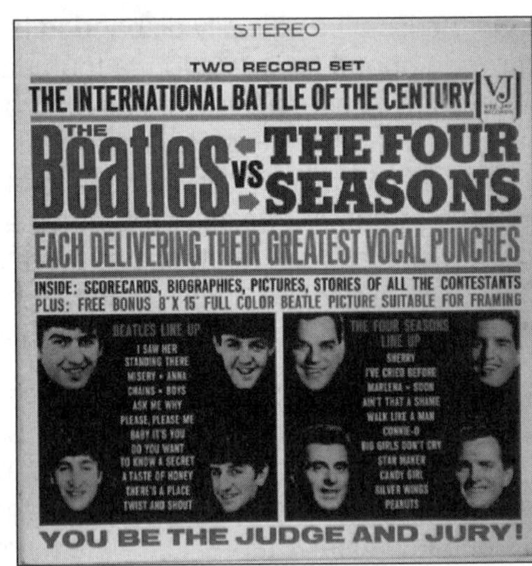

At one time, Vee Jay's two biggest-selling artists were the Beatles and the Four Seasons. This two-record set featured both groups' biggest hits, allowing fans to decide who won the "tale of the tape." Courtesy Good Rockin' Tonight/Collectors Universe.

Another highly collectible Beatles album is *Yesterday and Today* (Capitol 2553). During the Beatles' early hitmaking years, Capitol Records would trim two tracks from a British EMI/Parlophone album, and release the album with a new title (*Beatles '65* or *Something New*). By 1966, it was able to create an album featuring the Beatles' new hit single "Yesterday," along with tracks that had been culled from previous albums. Instead of the standard Beatles photographs that were used for Capitol album releases, the foursome posed for their new American album cover wearing butcher's smocks, their bodies covered with raw meat and baby-doll parts. Capitol printed thousands of these covers before somebody realized the Beatles album cover looked like the Fab Four had just committed infanticide in a butcher shop.

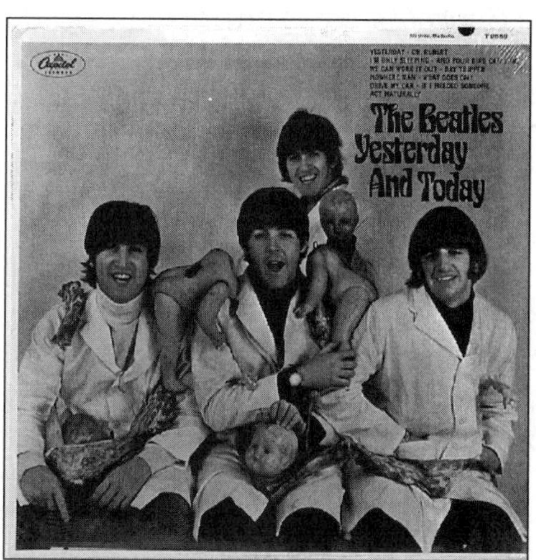

A "first state" copy of the Beatles' *Yesterday and Today*, featuring the Fab Four with their original album cover art. Courtesy Good Rockin' Tonight/Collectors Universe.

The albums were recalled to the factories, and a new album jacket was printed, an innocuous photo of the Beatles sitting around a steamer trunk. Besides printing new album art, some of the Capitol factories were able to recycle the old albums by applying the new "trunk" photo over the original "butcher" album art. Because of the major difference in cover art, *Yesterday and Today* has become an extremely collectible album, if not the most collectible album cover in rock history. A "first state" cover features the Beatles in their butcher smocks. A "second state" cover will have the Beatles sitting around the steamer trunk, but with the "trunk" artwork covering up a "butcher" cover. If you see a black triangle on the right side of the "trunk" cover, that's Ringo Starr's black sweater in the "butcher" photo underneath. Without that triangle, it's a standard "trunk" cover.

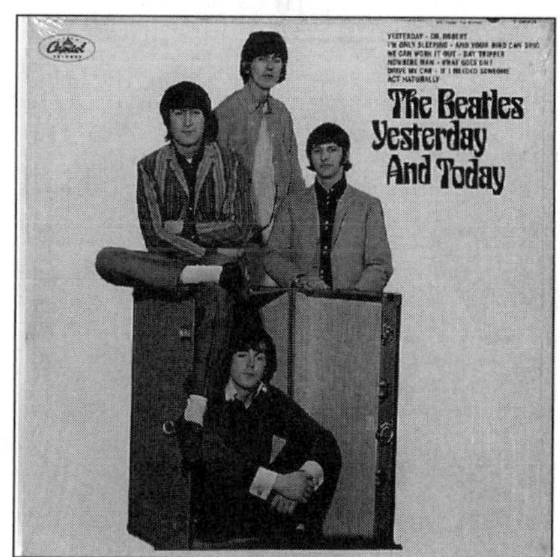

Capitol Records recalled as many copies of *Yesterday and Today* as it could find. Many of the records were placed in new "trunk" covers, while others simply had a trunk cover pasted over the original jacket. Courtesy Good Rockin' Tonight/Collectors Universe.

Many of these "second state" covers have been steamed or peeled away to find the "butcher" artwork. A peeled cover is known as "third state." The value of a "third state" *Yesterday and Today* Beatles album is proportional to the success of the peel.

Some art-restoring companies will peel your "second state" Beatles album to reveal the "third state" butcher cover underneath. Don't try to do it yourself unless you know what you're doing—as can be seen in this photo, where the jacket is torn down to the cover, it is easy to render a collectible cover worthless. From the Collection of Bruce Spizer.

The Apple Issues and Reissues: In 1968, beginning with the "Hey Jude"/"Revolution" 45 and *The Beatles* (the "White Album"), the Beatles switched their American label from Capitol to their own custom label, Apple (which Capitol distributed). One year later, however, every American Beatles release was reissued on Apple. On albums, these 1969 reissues can be identified by a Capitol logo on side two of the record label. The Beatles catalog was reissued again in 1971 and these discs have the words "Mfd. by Apple" on the label. Another reissue, this time in 1975, will have the words "All Rights Reserved" on the label. Surprisingly, while the label on the record changed, albums that were originally released before 1968 still sported a prominent Capitol logo on their jackets!

Apple 45s also have a prominent dating pattern. Beginning with "Hey Jude"/"Revolution" (Apple 2276), first pressings of new Beatles recordings would have a small Capitol logo on the record's B-side (the "split" Apple side). By 1971, the Beatles' 45 reissue singles no longer had a Capitol logo, and instead had the words "Mfd. by Apple" on the label. The A-side of the record (the "unsplit" Apple side) may contain a printed star on the label; non-starred labels from 1971 are worth only one-third of the value of starred labels. Apple reissued the Beatles' singles catalog one more time, in 1975, and those copies have the words "All Rights Reserved" on the label.

The Post-1975 Beatles Releases: In 1976, the Beatles' back catalog was reissued on Capitol. A two-LP collection of uptempo Beatles songs, *Rock and Roll Music*, was released, and both it and a single version of "Got To Get You Into My Life" hit the Top 10 on the charts. Capitol 45 reissues in 1976 were orange with a serifless "Capitol" printed on the bottom of the label. In 1978, Capitol went to an all-purple label with a grooved perimeter, and the Beatles 45s appear in that format as well. Beatles reissues also appeared in Capitol's 1983 color scheme (black label with colorband on the perimeter), and its 1988 label pattern (light purple label, smooth label perimeter).

In 1994, the Beatles' greatest hits were reissued on 45, this time in colored vinyl. Most of these titles only sell for about $4 in near-mint condition, with the exception of "Birthday"/"Taxman" (Capitol S7-17488), which was "accidentally" pressed on black vinyl, and can sell for $50 in near-mint condition.

The Beatles' album titles and content have also changed in the post-Apple period. In 1978, three of the Beatles' two-LP sets were pressed, in a limited edition, on colored vinyl. They were *The Beatles: 1962-1966* (red vinyl), *The Beatles: 1967-1970* (blue vinyl) and *The Beatles* (on white vinyl). All feature the Capitol logo.

In 1987, while the Beatles' first albums were released on CD for the first time, their vinyl albums were re-released. Both the vinyl and CD versions of these albums followed the original EMI/Parlophone album art and track listings. These were released on the Capitol label. One year later, the American albums were re-released for the last time. These copies have UPC codes on the back covers. In 1995, the British album versions were re-released one more time on vinyl, with an Apple logo on the album and on the jacket.

References: *The Beatles Anthology*, Chronicle Books LLC, San Francisco, 2000; Cox, Perry, *The Official Price Guide to the Beatles Records and Memorabilia*, House of Collectibles/Ballantine Publishing, New York, 1999; Neely, Tim; Thompson, Dave, *Goldmine British Invasion Record Price Guide*, Krause Publications, Iola, Wisconsin, 1997; Riley, Tim, *Tell Me Why: A Beatles Commentary*, Alfred A. Knopf, N.Y., 1988; Spizer, Bruce, *Songs, Pictures and Stories of the Fabulous Beatles Records on Vee Jay*, 498 Productions, New Orleans, La., 1998; Spizer, Bruce, *The Beatles' Story on Capitol Records* (two volumes), 498 Productions, New Orleans, La., 2000; *The Goldmine Beatles Digest*, Krause Publications, Iola, Wisconsin, 2000.

Trivia

Most of the Beatles' Capitol singles were pressed in two separate printing plants. The East Coast Capitol pressings, with labels made in Scranton, Pa., feature fatter font letters and larger catalog numbers. The West Coast Capitol pressings, made in its Hollywood pressing plant, have thinner letters and smaller catalog numbers.

An East Coast pressing of the Beatles' "Help." From the Collection of Bruce Spizer.

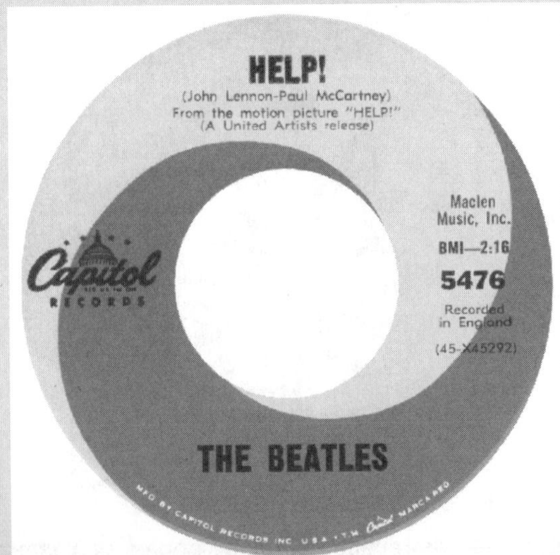

The West Coast pressings have thinner letters and smaller catalog numbers. From the Collection of Brice Spizer.

Web pages: The Beatles' homepage, *http://www.beatles.com*; Bruce Spizer's Beatles page: *http://www.beatle.ne*; Mitch McGeary's Beatles online museum: *http://www.rarebeatles.com*

Magazines: *Beatlefan*, Box 33515, Decatur GA 30033; *The Beatletter,* P.O. Box 13, St. Clair Shores MI 48080; *Beatlemania Magazine*, PSF 565, Erfurt, 99011, Germany; *Beatles Fans Unite*, P.O. Box 50123, Cicero IL 60650; *Beatles Monthly*, 45 St. Mary's Road, Ealing, London W5 5RQ, England; *BU Magazine (Beatles Unlimited)*, P.O. Box 602, 3430 AP Nieuwegein, The Netherlands; *Reseau Quebecois des Ami(e)s des Beatles*, 6-20-69, Chadelaine, Ste-Foy, Quebec, PQ G1V 1M5, Canada; *Good Day Sunshine*, P.O. Box 1008, Mar Vista, CA 90066-1008.

45s	Year	VG	VG+	NM
The Beatles, "Please Please Me" / "Ask Me Why" (Vee Jay 498)				
(if group is "The Beattles," number is #498)	1963	$800.00	$1,200.00	$1,600.00
(if group is "The Beattles," number is "VJ 498")	1963	$750.00	$1,125.00	$1,500.00
(if group is "The Beatles," number is "VJ 498", thick print)	1963	$300.00	$600.00	$900.00
(if group is "The Beatles," number is #498)	1963	$800.00	$1,200.00	$1,600.00
(if group is "The Beatles," number is "VJ 498", "VJ" in brackets)	1963	$1,000	$1,500	$2,000
The Beatles, "Please Please Me" / "From Me To You" (Vee Jay 581)				
(if label has rainbow perimeter on black background, oval "Vee Jay" logo)	1964	$12.50	$25.00	$50.00
(if on plain black label with no horizontal lines)	1964	$18.75	$37.50	$75.00
(if on yellow label)	1964	$18.75	$37.50	$75.00
(if on white label)	1964	$40.00	$80.00	$160.00
(if on purple label)	1964	$62.50	$125.00	$250.00
(if on plain black label, block letters "VEE JAY" standing alone)	1964	$15.00	$30.00	$60.00
(if on plain black label, block letters 'VJ' standing alone)	1964	$16.25	$32.50	$65.00
(if label has rainbow perimeter on black ground, brackets logo)	1964	$15.00	$30.00	$60.00
(if on plain black label, with oval logo)	1964	$15.00	$30.00	$60.00
(if on white label, blue print, "Promotional Copy" on label)	1964	$200.00	$400.00	$800.00
(if on white label, blue print, no mention of promotional copy)	1964	$300.00	$600.00	$900.00
(with "The Record That Started Beatlemania" promo-only sleeve, add:)	1964	$1,250	$1,875	$2,500
The Beatles, "Love Me Do" / "P.S. I Love You"				
(if on Tollie 9008, yellow label, black print)	1964	$12.50	$25.00	$50.00
(if on Tollie 9008, yellow label, blue-green print)	1964	$12.50	$25.00	$50.00
(if on Tollie 9008, black label, silver print)	1964	$15.00	$30.00	$60.00
(if on Tollie 9008, white label promo)	1964	$100.00	$200.00	$400.00
(with picture sleeve, add:)	1964	$37.50	$75.00	$150.00
(if on Capitol S7-56785, red vinyl)	1992	$7.50	$15.00	$30.00
(if on Capitol S7-56785, black vinyl)	1992		$2.00	$4.00
The Beatles, "I Wanna Hold Your Hand" / "I Saw Her Standing There" (Capitol 5112)				
(if Walter Hofer is credited with publishing "I Saw Her Standing There")	1964	$10.00	$20.00	$40.00
(if George Pincus and Sons are credited with publishing "I Saw Her Standing There")	1964	$8.75	$17.50	$35.00
(if Gil Music is credited with publishing "I Saw Her Standing There")	1964	$7.50	$15.00	$30.00
(with picture sleeve, die-cut at top, George Harrison's head is cropped in photo, add:)	1964	$25.00	$50.00	$100.00
(with picture sleeve, straight cut at top, George Harrison's head is uncropped, add:)	1964	$25.00	$50.00	$100.00
(with picture sleeve, giveaway from WMCA radio, photo of WMCA DJ's on B-side)	1964	$500.00	$1,000.00	$2,000.00

45s	Year	VG	VG+	NM
(if 20th anniversary reissue, black print on label perimeter [1964 pressings have white print on perimeter])	1984		$2.50	$5.00
(if 30th anniversary reissue, "NR-58123" engraved in dead wax of runout groove)	1994		$2.50	$5.00
The Beatles, "She Loves You" / "I'll Get You" (Swan 4152)				
(if semi-glossy white label with red print, no reference to "Don't Drop Out")	1963	$150.00	$300.00	$600.00
(if semi-glossy white label with red print, "Don't Drop Out")	1963	$162.50	$325.00	$650.00
(if flat, white label with red print, no reference to "Don't Drop Out")	1963	$162.50	$325.00	$650.00
(if semi-glossy white label with blue printing)	1963	$150.00	$300.00	$600.00
(if black label, silver print, no reference to "Don't Drop Out")	1964	$10.00	$20.00	$40.00
(if black label, silver print, "Don't Drop Out")	1964	$7.50	$15.00	$30.00
(if black label, silver print, "Produced by George Martin" on both sides)	1964	$12.50	$25.00	$50.00
(if black label, silver print, only one side says "Produced by George Martin")	196??	$12.50	$25.00	$50.00
(if black label, silver print, no reference to "Don't Drop Out," smaller numbers in dead wax)	196??	$5.00	$10.00	$20.00
(if on white label, with red or maroon print, same as above)	196??	$12.50	$25.00	$50.00
(if promo copy, thick print, no reference to "Don't Drop Out")	1963	$125.00	$250.00	$500.00
(if promo copy, thin print, "Don't Drop Out")	1963	$112.50	$225.00	$450.00
(if promo copy, flat white label, no reference to "Don't Drop Out")	1963	$125.00	$250.00	$50.00
(with picture sleeve, add:)	1964	$30.00	$60.00	$120.00
The Beatles, "Sweet Georgia Brown" / "Take Out Some Insurance On Me" (Atco 6302)	1964	$50.00	$100.00	$200.00
The Beatles, "Ain't She Sweet" / "Nobody's Child" (Atco 6308)				
(with "Vocal by John Lennon" on left side of label)	1964	$12.50	$25.00	$50.00
(with "Vocal by John Lennon" under "The Beatles")	1964	$15.00	$30.00	$60.00
(with picture sleeve - sleeves with black and green print are reproductions - add:	1964	$125.00	$250.00	$500.00
The Beatles, "Can't Buy Me Love" / "You Can't Do That" (Capitol 5150)				
(if first pressing, orange-yellow swirl label, no reference to "A Subsidiary of..." in perimeter of label)	1964	$7.50	$15.00	$30.00
(if on yellow vinyl, unauthorized "after hours" pressing)	1964	$2,000	$3,000	$4,000
(if on yellow-black vinyl, unauthorized "after hours" pressing)	1964	$1,000	$1,500	$2,000
(with picture sleeve (which has been counterfeited, see an expert if unsure), add:)	1964	$200.00	$400.00	$800.00
The Beatles, "And I Love Her" / "If I Fell" (Capitol 5235)				
(if orange-yellow swirl label, no reference to "A Subsidiary of..." in perimeter of label)	1964	$7.50	$15.00	$30.00
(if "A Subsidiary of Capitol" in white along perimeter)	1968	$12.50	$25.00	$50.00
(if "A Subsidiary of Capitol" in black along perimeter)	1968	$18.75	$37.50	$75.00
(with picture sleeve, add:)	1964	$30.00	$60.00	$120.00
The Beatles, "Help!" / "I'm Down" (Capitol 5476)				
(if orange-yellow swirl label, no reference to "A Subsidiary of..." in perimeter of label)	1965	$7.50	$15.00	$30.00
(if "A Subsidiary of Capitol" in white along perimeter)	1968	$25.00	$50.00	$100.00
(if "A Subsidiary of Capitol" in black along perimeter)	1968	$15.00	$30.00	$60.00
(with picture sleeve, add:)	1965	$18.75	$37.50	$75.00
The Beatles, "Nowhere Man" / "What Goes On" (Capitol 5587)				
(if orange-yellow swirl label, no reference to "A Subsidiary of..." in perimeter of label, B-side credited to "John Lennon-Paul McCartney")	1966	$6.25	$12.50	$25.00
(if same as above, except B-side credited to "Lennon-McCartney-Starkey")	1966	$12.50	$25.00	$50.00
(with picture sleeve, add:)	1966	$10.00	$20.00	$40.00
The Beatles, "Hello Goodbye" / "I Am The Walrus" (Capitol 2056)				
(if orange-yellow swirl label, no reference to "A Subsidiary of..." in perimeter of label)	1967	$7.50	$15.00	$30.00
(with picture sleeve, add:)	1967	$25.00	$50.00	$100.00
The Beatles, "Hey Jude" / "Revolution" (Apple 2276)				
(small Capitol logo on the B-side)	1968	$3.75	$7.50	$15.00
(if "Mfd. by Apple")	1968	$2.50	$5.00	$10.00
The Beatles, "The Ballad of John and Yoko" / "Old Brown Shoe" (Apple 2531)	1969	$2.50	$5.00	$10.00

45s	Year	VG	VG+	NM
(with picture sleeve, add:)	1969	$25.00	$50.00	$100.00
The Beatles, "Something" / "Come Together" (Apple 2654)				
(small Capitol logo on the B-side)	1969	$25.00	$50.00	$100.00
(if "Mfd. by Apple")	1969	$2.50	$5.00	$10.00
The Beatles, "Let It Be" / "You Know My Name (Look Up My Number") (Apple 2764)	1970	$2.50	$5.00	$10.00
(with picture sleeve, add:)	1970	$25.00	$50.00	$100.00
The Beatles, "Got To Get You Into My Life" / "Helter Skelter" (Capitol 4274)				
(if orange label with "Capitol" on bottom, no reference to George Martin on label)	1976		$3.00	$6.00
(if orange label with "Capitol" on bottom, George Martin's name is listed)	1976	$2.50	$5.00	$10.00
(with picture sleeve, add:)	1976		$2.50	$5.00
The Beatles, "Sgt. Pepper's Lonely Hearts Club Band - With A Little Help From My Friends" / "A Day In The Life" (Capitol 4612)				
(if purple label with geared edge surrounding label)	1978	$2.00	$4.00	$8.00
(with picture sleeve, add:)	1978	$5.00	$10.00	$20.00
The Beatles, "Free As A Bird" / "Christmas Time (Is Here Again)" (Apple 58497)	1995		$2.00	$4.00
(with picture sleeve, add:)	1995		$2.00	$4.00

Beatles reissue 45s	Year	VG	VG+	NM
1965 reissue: on Oldies 45, titles previously issued on Vee-Jay and its subsidiary labels, cat #'s 149-152)	1965	$3.75	$7.50	$15.00
1968 reissue: on Capitol, "A Subsidiary of Capitol" around the perimeter of the label	1968	$15.00	$30.00	$60.00
1969 reissue: on Capitol, if red-orange "target" label, round logo, "Capitol" in serifless font	1969	$6.25	$12.50	$25.00
1971 reissue: on Apple, with star on label	1971	$7.50	$15.00	$30.00
1971 reissue: on Apple, without star on label	1971	$2.50	$5.00	$10.00
1975 reissue: on Apple, with "All Rights Reserved" disclaimer on label	1975	$5.00	$10.00	$20.00
1976 reissue: on Capitol, if red-orange "target" label, dome logo	1976	$2.50	$5.00	$10.00
1978 reissue: on Capitol, if on purple label with geared perimeter	1978	$3.75	$7.50	$15.00
1982 reissue: on Collectables, Catalog nos. 1501-1515)	1982		$3.00	
1983 reissue: on Capitol, black label with rainbow perimeter	1983		$3.00	$6.00
1988 reissue: on Capitol, purple label with smooth perimeter	1988		$2.50	$5.00
1994 reissue: on Capitol, catalog number begins with S7-17 plus other numbers, colored vinyl)	1994		$2.00	$4.00
(exception: "Birthday" / "Taxman", on Capitol S7-17488, pressed on black vinyl)	1994	$12.50	$25.00	$50.00
1996 reissue: on Capitol, catalog number begins with S7-18, plus other numbers, colored vinyl)	1996		$2.00	$4.00

LPs	Year	VG	VG+	NM
The Beatles, Introducing the Beatles (Vee Jay 1062)				
(if mono, "Ad Back" cover, with "Love Me Do" and "P.S. I Love You," oval Vee-Jay logo with rainbow)	1964	$1,500.00	$2,750.00	$4,000.00
(if mono, blank back cover, with "Love Me Do" and "P.S. I Love You," oval Vee-Jay logo with rainbow)	1964	$400.00	$800.00	$1,200.00
(if mono, blank back cover, with "Please Please Me" and "Ask Me Why," oval Vee-Jay logo with rainbow)	1964	$250.00	$500.00	$1,000.00
(if mono, song titles cover, with "Love Me Do" and "P.S. I Love You," oval Vee-Jay logo with rainbow)	1964	$200.00	$400.00	$800.00
(if mono, song titles cover, with "Please Please Me" and "Ask Me Why," oval Vee-Jay logo with rainbow)	1964	$75.00	$150.00	$300.00
(if mono, song titles cover, with "Please Please Me" and "Ask Me Why," brackets VJ logo with rainbow)	1964	$62.50	$125.00	$250.00
(if mono, song titles cover, with "Please Please Me" and "Ask Me Why," plain Vee-Jay logo, black label)	1964	$62.50	$125.00	$250.00
(if mono, song titles cover, with "Please Please Me" and "Ask Me Why," oval Vee-Jay logo, black label)	1964	$75.00	$150.00	$300.00
(if mono, song titles cover, with "Please Please Me" and "Ask Me Why," brackets VJ logo, black label)	1964	$250.00	$500.00	$1,000.00
(if stereo, "Ad Back" cover, with "Love Me Do" and "P.S. I Love You," oval Vee-Jay logo with rainbow)	1964	$4,000	$8,000	$12,000
(if stereo, blank back cover, with "Love Me Do" and "P.S. I Love You," oval Vee-Jay logo with rainbow)	1964	$625.00	$1,250.00	$2,500.00

LPs	Year	VG	VG+	NM
(if stereo, song titles cover, with "Love Me Do" and "P.S. I Love You," oval Vee-Jay logo with rainbow)	1964	$3,000	$5,500	$8,000
(if stereo, song titles cover, with "Please Please Me" and "Ask Me Why," oval Vee-Jay logo with rainbow)	1964	$400.00	$800.00	$1,600.00
(if stereo, song titles cover, with "Please Please Me" and "Ask Me Why," brackets VJ logo with rainbow)	1964	$375.00	$750.00	$1,500.00
(if stereo, song titles cover, with "Please Please Me" and "Ask Me Why," plain Vee-Jay logo, black label)	1964	$400.00	$800.00	$1,600.00
The Beatles, Meet the Beatles! (Capitol T 2047) (mono)				
(if black label with rainbow, "Beatles" on front cover in tannish brown print)	1964	$50.00	$100.00	$200.00
(if black label with rainbow, "Beatles" on front cover in green print)	1964	$25.00	$50.00	$100.00
(if on Capitol ST-2047, all true stereo except "I Want To Hold Your Hand" and "This Boy," which are rechanneled; "Beatles" on cover in tannish brown print)	1964	$37.50	$75.00	$150.00
(if on Capitol ST-2047, stereo, "Beatles" on front cover in green print)	1964	$18.75	$37.50	$75.00
(if on Capitol ST-8-2047, Capitol Record Club edition, black label with rainbow)	1964	$125.00	$250.00	$500.00
(if on Capitol ST-2047, stereo, lime green label)	1969	$10.00	$20.00	$40.00
(if on Capitol ST-8-2047, Capitol Record Club edition, green label)	1969	$50.00	$100.00	$200.00
The Beatles, Beatles 65 (Capitol T 2228) (mono)	1964	$30.00	$60.00	$120.00
(if on Capitol ST-2228, all tracks stereo except "She's A Woman" and "I Feel Fine," both are rechanneled)	1964	$20.00	$40.00	$80.00
The Beatles, Yesterday and Today (Capitol 2553)				
Mono, first state ("Butcher")	1966	$2,000	$3,000	$4.000
Mono, second state ("trunk" photo over butcher cover)	1966	$250.00	$500.00	$1,000.00
Mono, third state ("peeled" cover, trunk cover removed to reveal butcher cover underneath)	1966	$400.00	$800.00	$1,200.00
Mono, trunk cover	1966	$37.50	$75.00	$150.00
Partial stereo, first state	1966	$4,000	$6,000	$8,000
Partial stereo, second state	1966	$500.00	$750.00	$1,000.00
Partial stereo, third state	1966	$375.00	$750.00	$1,500.00
Partial stereo, trunk cover	1966	$20.00	$40.00	$80.00
(if on Capitol ST-8-2553, Capitol Record Club edition, trunk cover)	1966	$75.00	$150.00	$300.00
(if on Capitol ST-8-2553, Capitol Record Club edition, green label, all tracks in full stereo)	1969	$37.50	$75.00	$150.00
The Beatles, Sgt. Pepper's Lonely Hearts Club Band (Capitol MAS 2653) (mono)	1967	$75.00	$150.00	$300.00
(if on Capitol SMAS 2653, stereo, black label with rainbow)	1967	$25.00	$50.00	$100.00
The Beatles, The Beatles (Apple SBO-101) (2 LPs)				
(numbered copy, contains four pictures and a large poster; mint copies extremely hard to find)	1968	$37.50	$75.00	$200.00
(unnumbered copy, contains four pictures and a large poster)	197?	$15.00	$30.00	$60.00
(with "All Rights Reserved" on labels, title in black on cover, posters and pictures on thinner paper stock)	1975	$17.50	$35.00	$70.00
The Beatles, Abbey Road (Apple SO-383)				
(with Capitol logo on Side 2 bottom, contains words "Her Majesty" on jacket and label)	1969	$10.00	$20.00	$40.00
(with Capitol logo on Side 2 bottom, no reference to "Her Majesty")	1969	$18.75	$37.50	$75.00
(with "Mfd. by Apple" on label)	1969	$5.00	$10.00	$20.00
(with "All Rights Reserved" on labels)	1975	$6.25	$12.50	$25.00
The Beatles, Greatest Hits 1962-1966 (Apple SKBO-3403) (2 LPs)	1973	$7.50	$15.00	$30.00
(if red Apple labels say "All Rights Reserved")	1975	$12.50	$25.00	$50.00
The Beatles, Greatest Hits 1967-1970 (Apple SKBO-3404) (2 LPs)	1973	$7.50	$15.00	$30.00
(if blue Apple labels say "All Rights Reserved")	1975	$12.50	$25.00	$50.00
The Beatles, The Beatles Live at the Hollywood Bowl (Capitol SMAS-1638)				
(if first pressing, embossed cover)	1977	$5.00	$10.00	$20.00
(if second pressing, flat cover)	1980	$3.75	$7.50	$15.00
(if third pressing, with UPC code)	1989	$10.00	$20.00	$40.00
The Beatles, Anthology I (Apple CI-8-34445) (3 LPs)	1995	$10.00	$20.00	$40.00
The Beatles, Anthology II (Apple CI-8-34448) (3 LPs)	1996	$10.00	$20.00	$40.00
The Beatles, Anthology III (Apple CI-8-34451) (3 LPs)	1996	$7.50	$15.00	$30.00

BLUES

History: The sound of blues music can be traced back over 150 years, from the songs of the slaves and the sharecroppers, to the road houses on the Mississippi delta, and the clubs in the heart of Chicago. The blues not only was the forefather of rock and roll, its music has inspired the titles of rock groups and of magazines. Over the years, rock's biggest stars have brought blues music back to public consciousness.

The blues legend of Houston, Texas, Lightnin' Hopkins. This is one of his hard-to-find LPs. Courtesy Good Rockin' Tonight/Collectors Universe.

Although one might think of the blues as songs involving "my woman she done left me, all I've got are the strings on my guitar," the music of the blues is actually an emotive statement by the artist about his life, about the world in general, as told through his guitar, a harmonica, a piano, some drums, a bass—and his voice of a thousand emotions.

Describing the blues, however, is similar to asking someone to describe sport. There are different types of blues, depending on the region where the artist recorded, the instruments used, the era the recording was made, and whether the instruments used were electric or acoustic.

Some of the different genres of blues include the uptempo jump blues, featuring Louis Jordan and Wynonie Harris; *piano blues*, featuring the work of Professor Longhair and Otis Spann; *country blues*, such as Leadbelly and Mississippi John Hurt; and regional styles from places like Chicago (Big Bill Broonzy, Tampa Red and Howlin' Wolf), Texas (Lightnin' Hopkins and Blind Lemon Jefferson), and Memphis (B.B. King and Gus Cannon).

A former Memphis disc jockey, B.B. King truly became the king of the blues. From the Collection of Val Shively.

Some of the earliest recorded blues artists, such as Robert Johnson, Blind Lemon Jefferson, and Charlie Patton, recorded their 78s on small subsidiary labels of the major record companies. Instead of recording on RCA Victor or Columbia or Decca, these artists made 78s for Okeh, Vocalion, and Paramount. Even worn-out, cracked copies of Johnson's Vocalion 78s and Patton's Paramount recordings are worth thousands of dollars today, if for no other reason than these were the recordings that planted the seeds for rock 'n' roll music.

The post-World War II blues explosion occurred when southern black musicians, many of whose families toiled as sharecroppers, migrated north in search of jobs and new opportunities. Many of these musicians performed in Chicago clubs with such legends as Big Bill Broonzy, Washboard Sam, Earl Hooker, and the first Sonny Boy Williamson. The best record label for Chicago blues at the time was the Chess family of labels: Chess, Checker, Aristocrat, Cadet, and Argo, all of which chronicled the birth of Chicago blues, rock 'n' roll and jazz.

Trivia

The earliest recorded blues artists were women. Mamie Smith, Ma Rainey, and Bessie Smith recorded in the 1920s and 1930s, and the first national blues hit, "Crazy Blues," was recorded by Mamie Smith and her Jazz Hounds.

During his stay on Vee-Jay Records in the 1950s and 1960s, John Lee Hooker recorded two of his biggest hits, "Dimples" and "Boom Boom," both of which are part of this greatest hits package. Courtesy Last Vestige Music Store, Albany, N.Y.

In the late 1940s, brothers Leonard and Phil Chess owned a series of nightclubs and bar rooms, and many of these clubs played live blues music from artists who left sharecropping towns in Mississippi, Tennessee, and Alabama, moving north to Chicago for a new life. Since the Chess brothers felt that none of these musicians were being properly recorded, they formed their own label, Aristocrat, in 1947, and signed many of these artists to record for them.

Among the first—and most successful—of these blues artists on Aristocrat was McKinley Morganfield, known to millions of blues afficionados as Muddy Waters. Waters' classics, including "I'm Your Hoochie Coochie Man," "Rollin' Stone," "I Just Wanna Make Love To You," and "I Can't Be Satisfied," are blues masterpieces that influenced generations of musicians. "Rollin' Stone," for example, inspired Bob Dylan to write "Like A Rolling Stone," inspired Mick Jagger and Keith Richards to name their band the Rolling Stones; and inspired a magazine for which Dr. Hook and the Medicine Show aspired to appear on its cover.

Muddy Waters was arguably the most influential blues musician of all time. Courtesy Last Vestige Music Store, Albany, N.Y.

In 1951, Aristocrat was renamed Chess Records, and Muddy Waters' labelmates now included Howlin' Wolf, Little Walter, Sonny Boy Williamson, John Lee Hooker, and Al Hibbler. Chess also released a jump boogie track, "Rocket 88" by Jackie Brenston and his Delta Cats (Chess 1458), which some musicologists feel is the first true "rock 'n' roll" record (actually, it was Ike Turner and his Kings of Rhythm on the track; the credited Brenston was one of Turner's saxophone players).

By the 1960s, British bands such as the Rolling Stones, the Yardbirds, John Mayall's Bluesbreakers, Cream, and Led Zeppelin all embraced and incorporated the blues music of Muddy Waters, Willie Dixon, Howlin' Wolf, and Robert Johnson into classic rock songs. Many of these same British bands and artists invited surviving blues musicians to tour with them, introducing these legends to a new appreciative audience.

Today's blues legends and masters include Robert Cray, Kenny Wayne Shepherd, Bonnie Raitt, Taj Mahal, Rory Block, the late Stevie Ray Vaughan, and the bands Roomful of Blues and the Fabulous Thunderbirds.

Trivia

Little Walter's harmonica classic "Juke" was recorded as the last song of a Muddy Waters session. The song stayed at #1 on the R&B charts for two months, and established Little Walter as a premier blues harpist.

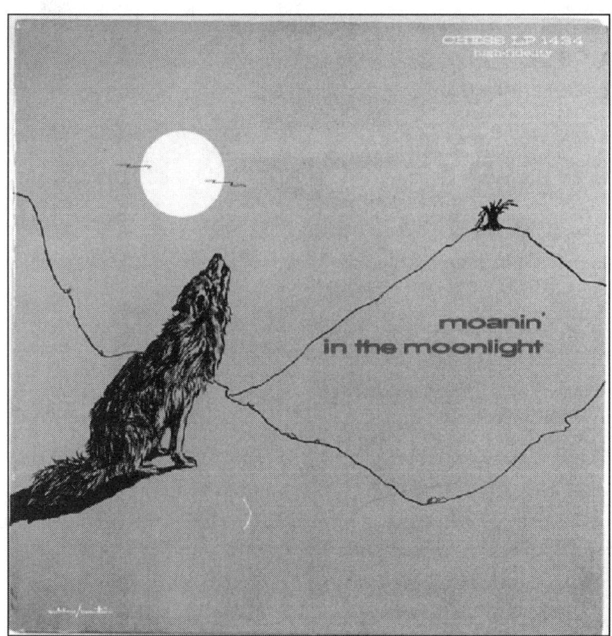

Howlin' Wolf's music influenced generations of blues and rock musicians. This copy of *Moanin' in the Moonlight* is one of his rarest albums. Courtesy Good Rockin' Tonight / Collectors Universe.

What To Look For: If you want to start your own blues music collection, your first decision should be whether you want to base your collection on vinyl releases or CDs. While compact disc reissues are less expensive than original vinyl releases, and though a respectable blues collection can exist with reissue CDs, many blues collectors search out the old vinyl recordings—the 78s, the 10-inch LPs, and the albums pressed by small independent labels.

But if you plan to start your collection in vinyl, make sure you have lots of money and are not afraid to spend it. In many cases, there may be fewer copies of a specific blues 78 than there are fingers on your hands; 78s of the earliest blues legends—Charlie Patton, Blind Lemon Jefferson and Robert Johnson—can command high prices, even if the vinyl is in less-than-fair condition. Even original 45s and 78s of some 1950's blues artists, including Muddy Waters, Howlin' Wolf, John Lee Hooker, Lightnin' Hopkins, etc. are difficult to find, especially in good condition.

When the Chess studios in Chicago finally shut down in 1975, the new owners of the building threw out all the 78s and 45s that were left in the Chess storerooms. This means that thousands of Muddy Waters and Howlin' Wolf records are now in a Chicago landfill. While this may make a blues fan sing the blues, it also increases the rarity of the 45s and LPs that made it to the record stores and to private collections.

One logical fallacy among blues collectors is to equate a blues record's collectible price with its musical value. The rarity of some blues 78s, including some classic and seminal recordings, does warrant a higher value than today's LPs, but this does not mean the musical performance on these early discs are greater or lesser than today's current musical output.

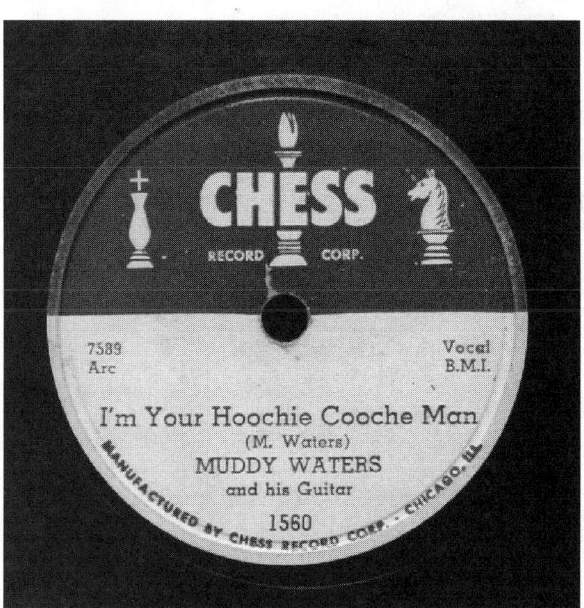

Muddy Waters' Chess 78s are very collectible; "I'm Your Hoochie Coochie Man" was one of his big hits.

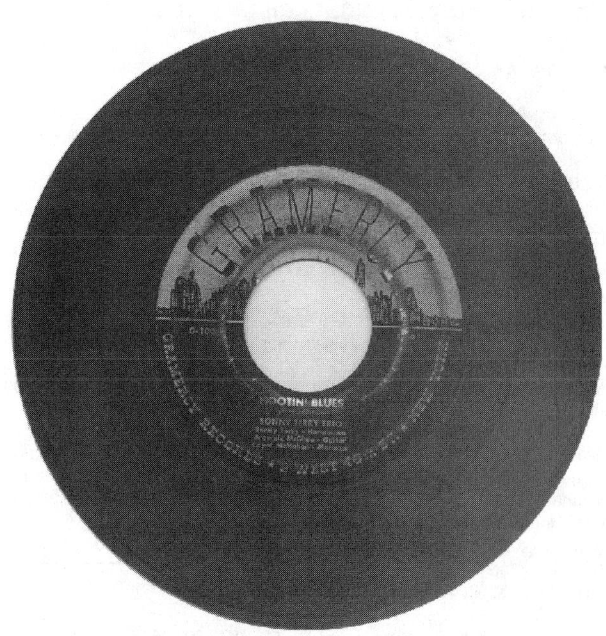

Harpist Sonny Terry's greatest performances came when he collaborated with guitarist Brownie McGhee. This copy of "Hootin' Blues" was available both on black and red vinyl.

Trivia

One would not know it from their Top 40 hits, but the 1960s band The Lovin' Spoonful took their name from a Mississippi John Hurt blues song "Coffee Blues," with its lyric, "I wanna see my baby 'bout a lovin' spoonful."

References: Brooks, Lonnie; Koda, Cub; Brooks, Wayne Baker, *Blues for Dummies*, IDG Books Worldwide, Foster City, CA, 1998; Collis, John, *The Story of Chess Records*, Bloomsbury Publishing, New York, N.Y., 1998; Hansen, Barry, *Rhino's Cruise Through the Blues*, Miller Freeman Books, Los Angeles, Calif., 2000; Leigh, Keri, *Stevie Ray: Soul To Soul*, Taylor Publishing Company, Dallas, Tex., 1993; Patoski, Joe Nick and Crawford, Bill, *Stevie Ray Vaughan: Caught in the Crossfire*, Little, Brown, Boston 1993.

Organizations: The Blues Foundation, 49 Union Avenue, Memphis TN 38103.

Web pages: The Blues Foundation, *http://www.blues.org*; A history of Muddy Waters: *http://www.muddywaters.com*; Both Sides Now: The Chess Story, *http://www.bsnpubs.com/chess-check.html;* The Blue Flame Café, an interactive biographical encyclopedia of the great blues singers and singers of the blues, *http://www.blueflame-cafe.com*; Usenet newsgroups: alt.music.blues, alt.fan.stevie-ray-vaughan, alt.fan.robert-cray.

45s	Year	VG	VG+	NM
Jackie Brenston and his Delta Cats, "Rocket 88" / "Come Back Where You Belong" (Chess 1458)	1951	$5,000	$7,500	$10,000
(the original 78 was pressed in 1949, even so, these 45's are unbelievably rare)				
Jackie Brenston, "What Can It Be" / "Gonna Wait For My Chance" (Federal 12283)	1956	$12.50	$25.00	$50.00
Big Bill Broonzy, "Little City Woman" / "Lonesome" (Chess 1546)	1953	$100.00	$200.00	$400.00
Albert Collins, "Albert's Alley" / "Defrost"				
(if on Great Scott 007)	1963	$7.50	$15.00	$30.00
(if on Hallway 1913)	1963	$3.00	$6.00	$12.00
Wynonie Harris, "Lovin' Machine" / "Luscious Woman" (King 4485)				
(if on red vinyl)	1951	$100.00	$200.00	$400.00
(if on black vinyl)	1951	$30.00	$60.00	$120.00
John Lee Hooker, "High Priced Woman" / "Union Station Blues" (Chess 1505)	1952	$250.00	$500.00	$1,000.00
John Lee Hooker, "Boom Boom" / "Drug Store Woman" (Vee Jay 438)	1962	$5.00	$10.00	$20.00
Lightnin' Hopkins, "Contrary Mary" / "I'm Begging You"				
(if on Jax 321)	1953	$75.00	$150.00	$300.00
(If on Harlem 2321)	1954	$50.00	$100.00	$200.00
Lightnin' Hopkins, "Coffee Blues" / "New Short Haired Woman"				
(if on Sittin' In With 635)	1952	$75.00	$150.00	$300.00
(if on Jax 635)	1954	$62.50	$125.00	$250.00
Lightnin' Hopkins, "Sinner's Prayer"/				
(if on Bluesville 822, backed with "Angel Child")	1962	$5.00	$10.00	$20.00
(if on Prestige 391, backed with "Got To Move Your Baby")	1965	$2.50	$5.00	$10.00

45s	Year	VG	VG+	NM
Hot Shot Love, "Wolf Call Boogie" / "Harmonica Jam" (Sun 196)	1954	$1,000	$2,000	$4,000
Howlin' Wolf, "Passing By Blues" / "Crying at Daybreak" (RPM 340)	1952	$1,000	$2,000	$3,000
Howlin' Wolf, "Oh! Red" / "My Last Affair" (Chess 1528)	1952	$175.00	$350.00	$700.00
Howlin' Wolf, "Smoke Stack Lightning" / "You Can't Be Beat" (Chess 1618)	1956	$10.00	$20.00	$40.00
Howlin' Wolf, "Wang Dang Doodle" / "Back Door Man" (Chess 1777)	1961	$7.50	$15.00	$30.00
B.B. King, "3 O'Clock Blues" / "Ain't That The Way To Do It" (RPM 339)	1951	$225.00	$450.00	$900.00
B.B. King, "Whole Lot of Loving" / "Down Now" (Kent 388)	1963	$3.00	$6.00	$12.00
B.B. King, "The Thrill Is Gone" / "You're Mean" (Bluesway 61032)	1969	$3.00	$6.00	$12.00
(with picture sleeve, add:)	1969	$5.00	$10.00	$20.00
Little Walter, "Juke" / "Can't Hold On Much Longer" (Checker 758)	1952	$50.00	$100.00	$200.00
Little Walter, "Boom, Boom – Out Goes the Light" / "Temperature" (Checker 867)	1957	$10.00	$20.00	$40.00
Tampa Red, "If You Ever Change Your Ways" / "Chicago Breakdown" (RCA Victor 50-0002) (on orange "cerise" vinyl)	1950	$30.00	$60.00	$120.00
Sonny Terry Trio, "Hootin' Blues" / (B-side unknown) (Gramercy 1004)				
(if on black vinyl)	1952	$12.50	$25.00	$50.00
(if on red vinyl)	1952	$25.00	$50.00	$100.00
Stevie Ray Vaughan, "Pride and Joy" / "Rude Mood" (Epic 04031)	1983		$2.50	$5.00
Stevie Ray Vaughan and Dick Dale, "Pipeline" / "Love Struck Baby" (Epic 07340)	1987		$2.00	$4.00
(with picture sleeve, add:)	1987		$2.50	$5.00
Muddy Waters, "I'm Your Hoochie Coochie Man" / "You're So Pretty" (Chess 1560)	1954	$25.00	$50.00	$100.00
Muddy Waters, "Manish Boy" / "Young Fashion Ways" (Chess 1602)	1955	$17.50	$35.00	$70.00
Muddy Waters, "Muddy Waters Twist" / "You Shook Me" (Chess 1827)	1962	$6.25	$12.50	$25.00

LPs	Year	VG	VG+	NM
Big Bill Broonzy, Blues Concert (Dial LP-306) (10-inch LP)	1952	$125.00	$250.00	$500.00
Big Bill Broonzy, Folk Blues (Emarcy MG-26034) (10-inch LP)	1954	$50.00	$100.00	$200.00
Albert Collins, Showdown! (Alligator AL-4743) (also feat. Robert Cray and Johnny Copeland)	1985	$2.50	$5.00	$10.00
Cream, Wheels of Fire (Atco 2-700) (2 LPs)				
(if on white label promo, mono - all stock copies are stereo)	1968	$50.00	$100.00	$200.00
(if stereo, foil-like cover, purple-brown Atco label)	1968	$12.50	$25.00	$50.00
(if stereo, dull gray cover, yellow Atco label)	1969	$5.00	$10.00	$20.00
Billie Holiday, An Evening With Billie Holiday (Clef MGC-144) (10-inch LP)	1953	$45.00	$90.00	$180.00
Billie Holiday, Lady Sings The Blues				
(if on Clef MGC-721)	1956	$30.00	$60.00	$120.00
(if on American Recording Society G-431, reissue)	1957	$15.00	$30.00	$60.00
(if on Verve MGV-8099, reissue)	1957	$10.00	$20.00	$40.00
(if on Verve V-8257, reissue)	1957	$5.00	$10.00	$20.00
Billie Holiday, Lover Man (Decca DL-5345) (10-inch LP)	1951	$50.00	$100.00	$200.00
Wynonie Harris, Good Rockin' Blues (King 1086)	1970	$6.25	$12.50	$25.00
Son House and J.D. Short, Blues from the Mississippi Delta				
(If on Verve Folkways FV-9035, mono)	1966	$10.00	$20.00	$40.00
(if on Verve Folkwahs FVS-9035, rechanneled stereo)	1966	$5.00	$10.00	$20.00
John Lee Hooker, I'm John Lee Hooker (Vee Jay 1007)				
(if record has a maroon label, first pressing)	1959	$50.00	$100.00	$200.00
(if record has a rainbow perimeter, second pressing)	1960	$20.00	$40.00	$80.00
(if record is VJLP-1007, on thin flimsy vinyl)	1986	$2.00	$4.00	$8.00
John Lee Hooker, John Lee Hooker Plays and Sings the Blues (Chess LP-1454)				
(if black label)	1961	$75.00	$150.00	$300.00
(if blue-white label)	1966	$12.50	$25.00	$50.00
(if on Chess CH-9199, 1980s reissue)	1986	$2.00	$4.00	$8.00
John Lee Hooker, The Healer (Chameleon D1-74808)	1989	$2.50	$5.00	$10.00
Lightnin' Hopkins, Lightnin' and the Blues (Herald LP-1012)				
(if label is black, first pressing)	1959	$750.00	$1,125.00	$1,500.00
(if label is yellow, second pressing)	1959	$200.00	$400.00	$800.00
(if label is multicolored)	196??	$125.00	$250.00	$500.00

LPs	Year	VG	VG+	NM
Lightnin' Hopkins, Lightnin' Strikes (Vee Jay LP-1044) (mono)	1962	$12.50	$25.00	$50.00
Lightnin' Hopkins, Lightnin' Hopkins Sings the Blues (Crown CLP-5224) (mono)				
(if black label, silver "CROWN")	1962	$25.00	$50.00	$100.00
(if gray label)	1962	$12.50	$25.00	$50.00
(if black label, multi-colored logo)	196??	$6.25	$12.50	$25.00
Howlin' Wolf, Moanin' In The Moonlight				
(if Chess LP-1434)	1958	$150.00	$300.00	$600.00
(if Chess CH-9195, reissue)	1986	$2.00	$4.00	$8.00
Howlin' Wolf, Howlin' Wolf a/k/a Chester Burnett (Chess CH-60016) (2 LPs)	1972	$6.25	$12.50	$25.00
Mississippi John Hurt, Folk Songs and Blues (Piedmont PLP-13157) (mono)	1963	$20.00	$40.00	$80.00
Mississippi John Hurt, The Best of Mississippi John Hurt (Vanguard VSD-19/20) (2 LPs)	197??	$6.25	$12.50	$25.00
Blind Lemon Jefferson, The Folk Blues of Blind Lemon Jefferson (Riverside 1014) (10-inch LP)	1953	$62.50	$125.00	$250.00
Blind Lemon Jefferson, Black Snake Moan (Milestone MLP-2013)	1970	$6.25	$12.50	$25.00
Robert Johnson, King of the Delta Blues Singers (Columbia CL 1654)				
(if red and black label, with six Columbia "eye" logos)	1961	$125.00	$250.00	$500.00
(if label says "High Fidelity")	1963	$12.50	$25.00	$50.00
(if label says "360 Sound Mono")	1965	$6.25	$12.50	$25.00
(if orange label, has the word "Columbia" around the perimeter)	1970	$3.00	$6.00	$12.00
Robert Johnson, The Complete Recordings (Columbia C3 46222) (3 LPs)	1990	$12.50	$25.00	$50.00
B.B. King, B.B. King Wails (Crown CLP-8115)				
(if on black label, mono, "Crown" is silver)	1959	$25.00	$50.00	$100.00
(if on gray label, mono, "Crown" is black)	1963	$5.00	$10.00	$20.00
(if on black label, mono, "Crown" is multicolored)	1960's	$3.00	$6.00	$12.00
(if on CST-147, rechanneled stereo, black vinyl)	1960	$3.00	$6.00	$12.00
(if on CST-147, rechanneled stereo, red vinyl)	1960	$25.00	$50.00	$100.00
Taj Mahal, Recycling the Blues & Other Related Stuff (Columbia KC 31605)	1972	$3.00	$6.00	$12.00
(if on Columbia PC-31605, 1980's reissue)	198??	$2.00	$4.00	$8.00
Taj Mahal, Live and Direct (Crystal Clear 5011) (direct-to-disc recording)	1980	$6.25	$12.50	$25.00
John Mayall, Blues Breakers with Eric Clapton				
(if on London PS 492) (stereo)	1966	$7.50	$15.00	$30.00
(if on London LL 4392) (mono)	1966	$6.25	$12.50	$25.00
(if on London LC-50009, reissue)	1977	$2.50	$5.00	$10.00
(if on London 800 086-1, reissue)	1983	$2.00	$4.00	$8.00
Tampa Red, Don't Tampa With The Blues (Bluesville BVLP-1030)				
(if first pressing, blue label, silver print)	1961	$30.00	$60.00	$120.00
(if reissue, with trident logo at right)	1963	$7.50	$15.00	$30.00
Muddy Waters, The Best of Muddy Waters (Chess LP-1427)				
(if DJ white label promo)	1957	$500.00	$1,000.00	$1,500.00
(if stock copy)	1957	$125.00	$250.00	$500.00
(if reissue, catalog number CH-9255)	1987	$2.50	$5.00	$10.00
Muddy Waters, Muddy Waters Sings Big Bill (Chess LP-1444)				
(if DJ white label promo)	1960	$250.00	$500.00	$1,000.00
(if stock copy)	1960	$100.00	$200.00	$400.00
(if reissue, catalog number CH-9197)	1986	$2.50	$5.00	$10.00

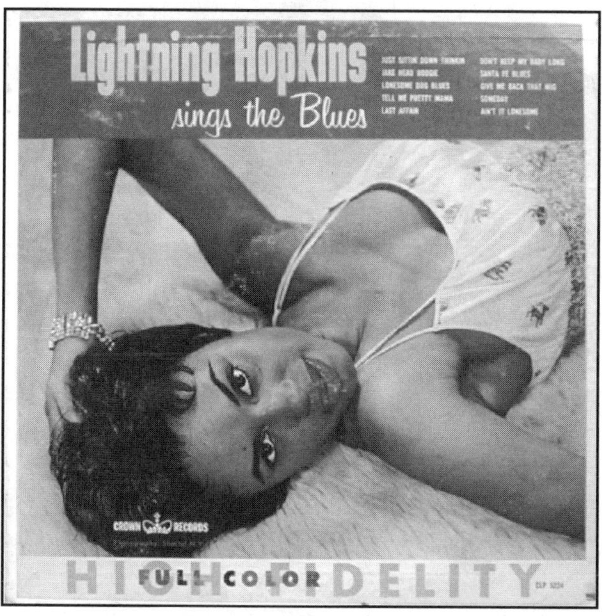

The inside label for this album can determine its value. A gray label is worth $50 in near-mint condition. If the label is black and has a silver "CROWN" on it, you have a $100 near-mint record. A multi-colored logo, on the other hand, can only bring you $25 in near-mint condition. Courtesy Last Vestige Music Store, Albany, N.Y.

Robert Cray's first Top 40 hit, "Smoking Gun," appears on the *Strong Persuader* album. Before this album, Cray spent 14 years on the road, backing up Albert Collins. You might have spotted him in National Lampoon's Animal House; he's the bass player for Otis Day and the Knights. Courtesy Last Vestige Music Store, Albany, N.Y.

BREAK-IN RECORDS

History: "Break-in" or "splice" records follow a common theme. A reporter or interviewer asks someone a question, with the interviewee being a political figure, an athlete, or a movie star. But instead of that person answering the question, the response actually comes from the lyric of a popular Top 40 song—a lyric taken totally out of context, with the ultimate goal to poke fun at the interviewee or the contrived situation. These discs are called "break-in" records because most times the record begins with standard music, until the reporter "breaks in" with a spurious news story.

The first "break-in" record appeared in 1955, when down-on-their-luck New York songwriters Bill Buchanan and Dickie Goodman stitched together a record satirizing UFO sightings and how people would respond to the extraterrestrials. The song, "The Flying Saucer (Parts 1 and 2)," was an instant success, selling nearly a million copies and inspiring various copycat "break-in" records (some even using "The Flying Saucer" as part of their snippets).

The record that started it all; "The Flying Saucer" is available as a 45 and as a 78.

Although "The Flying Saucer" became a Top 5 smash, it also drew the ire of music publishers, record companies, and musicians, who felt the hit song "borrowed" material without permission or remuneration. A judge later ruled that Buchanan and Goodman had created a burlesque—in effect, a new record from the old ones—and that no copyright infringement had occurred. Buchanan and Goodman's response to all this? They made another snippet record, "Buchanan and Goodman on Trial," which was a minor hit.

The pair split in 1957. Dickie Goodman continued to create "break-in" records for the next 30 years, including the 1975 hit "Mr. Jaws" and the political satire record "Watergrate." Bill Buchanan worked with a number of partners for more break-in discs, including a partnership with Neil Sedaka's songwriting partner Howard Greenfield on a Beatles break-in record.

The first compilation of Dickie Goodman's work, with liner notes by Shelly Berman.

While Buchanan and Goodman were the first and most notable break-in artists, they were not the only ones. The success of "The Flying Saucer" prompted DJs and other musicians to create their own snippet compilations—even Alan Freed recorded a break-in disc. WMCA disc jockey Jack Spector recorded the Top 40 break-in disc "Moonflight" under the pseudonym Vik Venus. In 1972, two record producers called themselves "The Delegates" and had a Top 10 break-in hit with "Convention '72." Even Dickie Goodman spread his talent around: he created a series of R&B break-in discs like "Superfly Meets Shaft" and "Soul President Number One" with friends John Free and Ernest Smith.

Trivia

Dickie Goodman's "Mr. Jaws" was the biggest-selling novelty record of 1975, and topped the *Record World and Cashbox* singles charts. The recording sold more copies than the 45 release of John Williams' "Theme From Jaws."

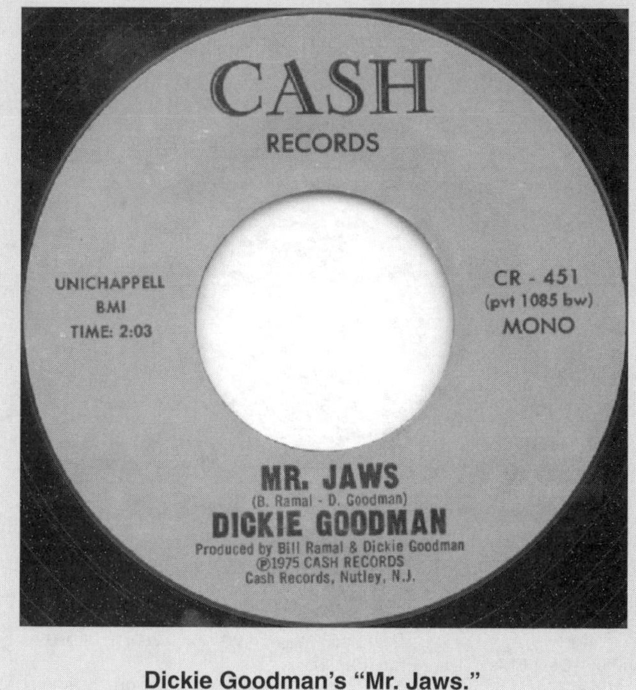

Dickie Goodman's "Mr. Jaws."

What To Look For: Because of the simplicity in creating these break-in records—in most cases such an artist only needs a microphone, a cassette player, and lots of 45s—there are dozens of "break-in" discs out there, based on everything from Presidential campaigns to blockbuster movies. Many collectors who specialize in "break-in" records acknowledge that these recordings are the first use of "sampling" in popular music, and consider Dickie Goodman and Bill Buchanan legendary pioneers in this field. Even Goodman's son Jon has created some break-in singles of his own, as a tribute to his father's work.

Most break-in records were recorded on tiny independent labels, and print runs were very low. This factor may increase a break-in record's collectibility, or may keep the record from discovery.

Collectors interested in Dickie Goodman's singles history have another problem to overcome. Many break-in artists operated under nicknames or pseudonyms, partially to avoid paying royalties for the songs they sampled. Dickie Goodman also recorded some break-in discs under phony names or studio-created groups: "The Casual Three" and "Spencer and Spencer" are two such confirmed sobriquets. He also produced break-in records for other artists, including John and Ernest's "Super Fly Meets Shaft." But because information on lesser-known break-in discs is extremely sketchy, some break-in releases have been attributed to Goodman, whether or not he had any involvement on that record.

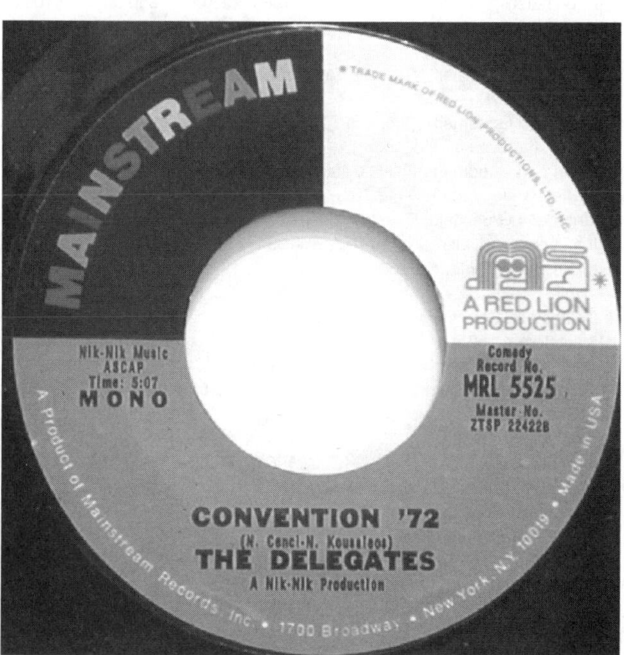

"Convention '72," by the Delegates.

Dickie Goodman co-wrote and produced this Top 40 break-in hit, "Super Fly Meets Shaft."

One such example of an "is it Dickie Goodman or not" recording is "The Chariot Race," by Ben Blur. The song was released on Mark-X Records, one of the labels associated with Goodman. But no writing credit exists on the record, and none of the voices on the record are distinctly Goodman's. No recording information exists today from Mark-X to confirm or deny Goodman's participation.

Is "Ben Blur" Dickie Goodman in disguise?

The first pressings of "The Flying Saucer" are extremely rare and highly coveted by break-in collectors. The original discs were pressed on Universe Records, but when it was discovered that *another* Universe Records existed, Bill Buchanan and Dickie Goodman changed their label's name to Luniverse Records—and marked a handwritten "L" on 2,000 pressed copies of their first single.

Many collectors of political memorabilia also search out these break-in discs, as do fans of such movies as *Star Wars* (Dickie Goodman recorded at least four different "Star Wars"-themed break-ins).

Known Bootlegs / Reproductions: At the height of its popularity in 1956, copies of "The Flying Saucer" were pressed by numerous independent record pressing plants. Any 45s of "The Flying Saucer" pressed on "Radioactive Records" are bootlegs. A version of "The Flying Saucer" titled "Back To Earth" is a legitimate release; it was renamed due to an error at one of the company pressing plants.

By the mid-1970s, some of the samples used on tracks of Dickie Goodman albums were either re-recorded or deleted entirely. This process continued through Goodman's CD re-releases, as both bootleg and legitimate greatest-hits CDs contained poorly recorded soundalike samples of Little Richard, the Everly Brothers, and the O'Jays.

Reference Books: Goodman, Jon, *The King of Novelty*, Xlibris Corporation, *www.xlibris.com*, 2000.

Web pages: The Dickie Goodman homepage, as maintained by his son Jon: *http://www.dickiegoodman.com*

A collection of Dickie Goodman's greatest hits, released by Rhino in 1983.

45s	Year	VG	VG+	NM
Audrey, "Dear Elvis" / "Dear Elvis (Part 2)" (Plus 104)	1956	$20.00	$40.00	$80.00
Buchanan and Goodman, "The Flying Saucer" (Pt. 1) / (Pt. 2) (Universe 101) (handwritten "L" on label)	1956	$25.00	$50.00	$100.00
Buchanan and Goodman, "The Flying Saucer" (Pt. 1) / (Pt. 2) (Luniverse 101)	1956	$12.50	$25.00	$50.00
Buchanan and Goodman, "Back To Earth" (Pt. 1) / (Pt. 2) (Luniverse 101x)	1956	$50.00	$100.00	$200.00
Buchanan and Goodman, "Buchanan and Goodman on Trial" / "Crazy" (Luniverse 102)	1956	$10.00	$20.00	$40.00
Buchanan and Goodman, "Flying Saucer the Second" / "Martian Melody" (Luniverse 107)	1957	$10.00	$20.00	$40.00
Buchanan and Greenfield, "The Invasion" / "What A Lovely Party" (Novel 711)				
(If first pressing, all red label)	1964	$7.50	$15.00	$30.00
(If reissue pressing, red and white label)	1972	$2.00	$4.00	$8.00
The Delegates, "Convention '72" / "Funky Butt" (Mainstream 5525)	1972		$3.00	$6.00
The Delegates, "Richard M. Nixon Faces The Issues" / "Touzie's Blues" (Mainstream 5530)	1972	$2.50	$5.00	$10.00
Dickie Goodman, "The Touchables" (Mark-X 8009)				
(If on yellow label)	1961	$7.50	$15.00	$30.00
(If on black label)	1961	$5.00	$10.00	$20.00
Dickie Goodman, "Presidential Interview (Flying Saucer '64)" / "Paul Revere" (Audio Spectrum 75)	1964	$10.00	$20.00	$40.00
Dickie Goodman, "Batman And His Grandmother" / "Surprise" (Red Bird 10-058)	1966	$5.00	$10.00	$20.00
Dickie Goodman, "White House Happening" / "President Johnson" (Davy Jones 663)	1967	$6.25	$12.50	$25.00
(with picture sleeve, add:)	1967	$10.00	$20.00	$40.00
Dickie Goodman, "Mr. Jaws" / "Irv's Theme" (Cash 451)	1975		$2.50	$5.00

45s	Year	VG	VG+	NM
John and Ernest, "Super Fly Meets Shaft" / "Problems" (Rainy Wednesday 201)	1973		$2.50	$5.00
John and Ernest, "Soul President Number One" / "Crossover" (Rainy Wednesday 203)	1973		$2.50	$5.00
Spencer and Spencer, "Russian Bandstand" / "Brass Wail" (Argo 5331)	1959	$6.25	$12.50	$25.00
Spencer and Spencer, "Stagger Lawrence" / "Stroganoff Cha Cha" (Gone 5053)	1959	$6.25	$12.50	$25.00
Vik Venus, "Moonflight" / "Everybody's On Strike " (Buddah 118)	1969	$2.50	$5.00	$10.00

LPs	Year	VG	VG+	NM
Dickie Goodman, The Many Heads of Dickie Goodman (Rori 3301)	1962	$20.00	$40.00	$80.00
Dickie Goodman, The Original Flying Saucers (IX Chains 9000) (contains the Delegates' "Election '72", a break-in record with no Dickie Goodman involvement)	1973	$10.00	$20.00	$40.00
Dickie Goodman, Mr. Jaws and Other Fables (Cash 6000)	1975	$6.25	$12.50	$25.00
Dickie Goodman, Dickie Goodman's Greatest Hits (Rhino RNLP-811)	1983	$3.75	$7.50	$15.00

Trivia

The first pressings of Buchanan and Goodman's "Buchanan and Goodman on Trial" feature their signatures in the dead wax. A second version of "Buchanan and Goodman on Trial" replaced one of the samples of Fats Domino with a sample of Jim Lowe's "The Green Door," after Fats Domino threatened a lawsuit against Buchanan and Goodman. Those replacement copies of "Buchanan and Goodman on Trial" do not have the duo's signatures in the dead wax.

Buchanan and Goodman's second break-in release; available on both 45 and 78.

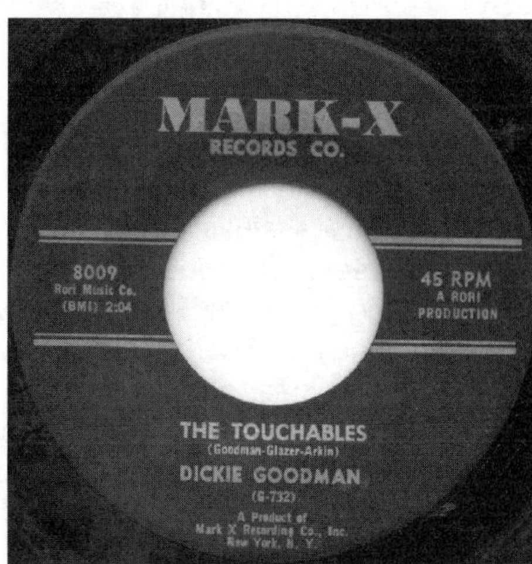

Goodman made three break-in records based on the 1950s TV show; this was the first.

Mickey Shorr worked with Dickie Goodman as "Spencer and Spencer"; this was his solo break-in record.

Dozens of break-in records were made over the years, and not all of them involved Dickie Goodman; this one, by Ed Solomon, dealt with the arrival of the Beatles in America.

THE BRITISH INVASION

History: The "British Invasion" is not so much a musical genre as it is a reaction to the success of the Beatles and of the Rolling Stones. After those two bands proved successful in America, American record company executives signed nearly every rock band and pop group from England, hoping for the same Beatle-like success from these new artists. It was a risky gamble: before 1964, very few British bands ever achieved success outside of the United Kingdom. Even the biggest selling singer at the time, Cliff Richard, couldn't break through to American audiences.

British music, however, was influenced greatly by American bands, whether it was the blues of Muddy Waters and Howlin' Wolf; the Motown soul of the Marvelettes and the Temptations; or the rockabilly recordings from Charlie Feathers and Carl Perkins. When the British groups finally broke through and achieved their own success, they were actually bringing American music back to the States.

What the British Invasion did do was effectively derail the recording careers of dozens of rock and pop artists from the early 1960s. The Drifters, the Tokens, the Chiffons, and the Coasters never had another hit after 1964. Teen idols such as Bobby Rydell, Frankie Avalon, Fabian, and Connie Francis were surpassed by new teen idols from across the Atlantic Ocean.

At one point, Gerry and the Pacemakers actually outsold the Beatles in England. In America, they had some chart successes, including this song.

As far as record buyers were concerned, this new wave of British performers were all part of London or Liverpool, no matter if the group was actually from Manchester, Leeds, or Stratford-on-Avon.

Many of the British-Invasion groups continued the Merseybeat sound of early Beatles records; it can be heard in the songs of the Dave Clark Five, of Gerry and the Pacemakers, and of Billy J. Kramer and the Dakotas.

The "British Invasion" also included chanteuses like Petula Clark and Shirley Bassey, whose musical careers predated the Beatles, yet were able to ride the British Invasion into the American pop radio charts. The early strains of progressive rock appeared with the Moody Blues; while Freddie and the Dreamers and Herman's Hermits established their own teen-pop music. Hard-rocking British bands like the Who and the Kinks actually outlasted the initial British invasion; both groups had hits well into the 1980s, during a second new-wave-themed British invasion.

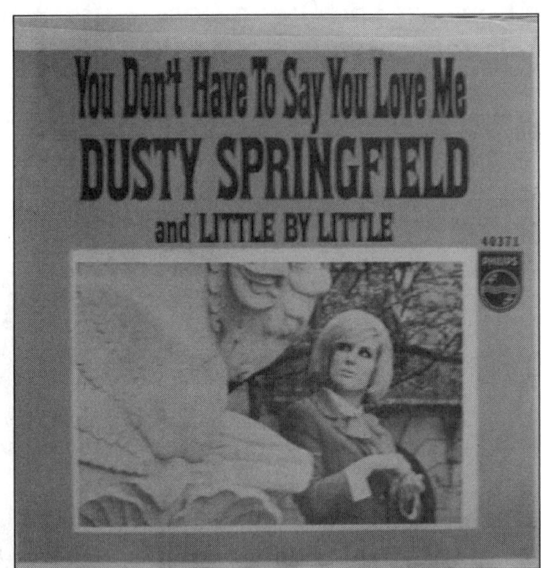

Dusty Springfield's British Invasion hit singles included this song; she later recorded such hits as "Son-of-a-Preacher Man" and "What Have I Done To Deserve This," the latter with the Pet Shop Boys. From the Collection of Val Shively.

One of the drawbacks of signing British-Invasion acts in America was that sometimes two labels would claim to own the rights to portions of a British group's catalog. The bulk of Freddie and the Dreamers' catalog was on Mercury, but their biggest hit, "I'm Telling You Now," was released on Tower. And the Troggs' #1 hit, "Wild Thing," was pressed by both the Atco and Fontana labels.

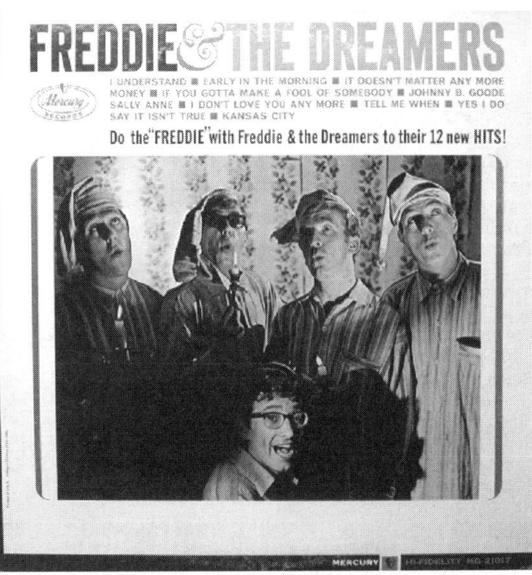

This Freddie and the Dreamers album had 12 of the group's biggest US and UK hits—except for "I'm Telling You Now," which was not part of Mercury's catalog. Courtesy Boo's Blasts From the Past.

What To Look For: During the British Invasion, American record companies still pressed two types of albums per release; a monaural copy and a stereo copy. Unfortunately, trying to find true stereo copies of 1960s hits can be a difficult endeavor. Many of the 1960s stereo albums are either rechanneled or fake stereo—low notes in one channel, high notes in the other; or music in one channel, vocalists in the other. True stereo copies of songs by the Dave Clark Five, for example, were not released in America until the early 1970s.

True stereo copies of the Dave Clark Five's greatest hits did not appear in America until the early 1970s. Courtesy Boo's Blast from the Past.

Trivia

Four of Peter and Gordon's Top 40 hits, including their #1 song, "A World Without Love," were written by John Lennon and Paul McCartney. Another one of their hits, "I Go To Pieces," was written for them by Del Shannon.

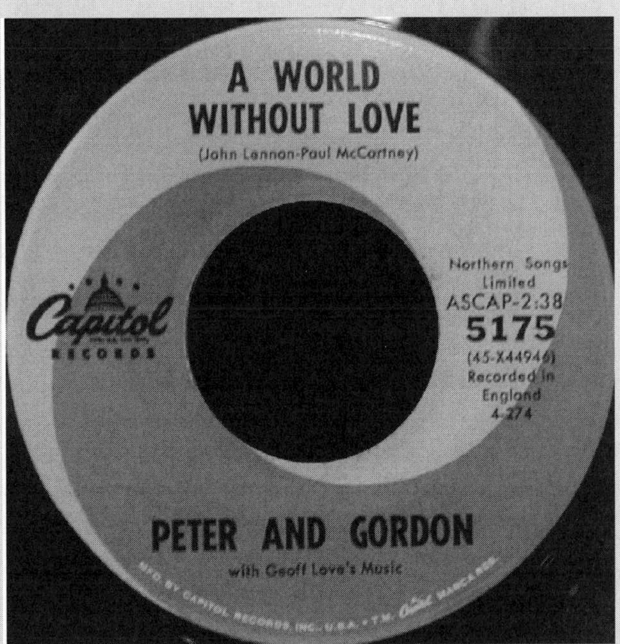

Peter and Gordon's "A World Without Love" was the first non-Beatles #1 song during the British Invasion. From the Collection of Val Shively.

The most collectible releases by British Invasion artists are those records that actually predate the British Invasion—American releases from 1963 and earlier. Many of these records sold poorly upon their initial release, but when such artists became popular through the British Invasion, many fans avidly searched out those early American pressings.

Some British acts did not have solid Top 40 hits until after the first British Invasion wave ended, in 1969. David Bowie's early work with the Lower Third is part of the selected price guide below; his later work can be found in the Seventies Rock chapter.

References: Neely, Tim; Thompson, Dave, *Goldmine British Invasion Record Price Guide*, Krause Publications, Iola, Wisconsin, 1997.

Web pages: Peter and Gordon's official homepage: *http://www.peterandgordon.com*; a fan-based homepage for Freddie and the Dreamers: *http://users.aol.com/bocad/freddie.htm*; a fan-based homepage for the Tremeloes: *http://www.tremeloes.oldiemusic.de/english.html;* Rod Argent and

Colin Blunstone of the Zombies have built their own Web sites: *http://www.rodargent.com, and http://www.colinblunstone.com*; usenet newsgroups: *alt.fan.kinks, alt.rock-n-roll.classic, rec.music.rock-pop-r+b.1960s*

45s	Year	VG	VG+	NM
The Animals, "The House of the Rising Sun" / "Talkin' About You" (MGM 13264)	1964	$3.00	$6.00	$12.00
(with picture sleeve, add:)	1964	$6.25	$12.50	$25.00
The Animals, "We Gotta Get Out Of This Place" / "I Can't Believe It" (MGM 13382)	1965	$3.00	$6.00	$12.00
Shirley Bassey, "Goldfinger" / "Strange How Love Can Be" (United Artists 790)	1964	$2.50	$5.00	$10.00
Peter Best, "Boys" / "Kansas City" (Cameo 391)	1965	$20.00	$40.00	$80.00
(with picture sleeve, add:)	1965	$25.00	$50.00	$100.00
Peter Best, Peter Best, "Casting My Spell" / "I'm Blue" (Mr. Maestro 712)	1965	$37.50	$75.00	$150.00
(if on blue vinyl)	1965	$50.00	$100.00	$200.00
Cilla Black, "You're My World" / "Suffer Now I Must" (Capitol 5196)	1964	$3.75	$7.50	$15.00
David Bowie and the Lower Third, "Can't Help Thinking About Me" / "And I Say To Myself" (Warner Bros. 5815)	1966	$125.00	$250.00	$500.00
David Bowie, "Love You Till Tuesday" / "Did You Ever Have A Dream" (Deram 85016)	1967	$12.50	$25.00	$50.00
Eric Burdon and the Animals, "San Franciscan Nights" / "Good Times" (MGM 13769)	1967	$2.50	$5.00	$10.00
(with picture sleeve, add:)	1967	$6.25	$12.50	$25.00
Chad and Jeremy, "Willow Weep For Me" / "If She Was Mine" (World Artists 1034)	1964	$2.50	$5.00	$10.00
(with picture sleeve, add:)	1964	$5.00	$10.00	$20.00
Chad and Jeremy, "Before and After" / "Fare The Well" (Columbia 43277)	1965	$2.50	$5.00	$10.00
(if on red vinyl)	1965	$10.00	$20.00	$40.00
The Dave Clark Five, "Glad All Over" / "I Know You" (Epic 9656)	1964	$3.75	$7.50	$15.00
(with picture sleeve, add:)	1964	$5.00	$10.00	$20.00
The Dave Clark Five, "Over and Over" / "I'll Be Yours (My Love)" (Epic 9863)	1965	$3.00	$6.00	$12.00
(with picture sleeve, add:)	1965	$5.00	$10.00	$20.00
(if "Over and Over" on both sides, red vinyl, DJ promo)	1965	$10.00	$20.00	$40.00
Petula Clark, "I Will Follow Him" / "Darling Cheri" (Laurie 3156)	1963	$3.75	$7.50	$15.00
Petula Clark, "Downtown" / "You'd Better Love Me" (Warner Bros. 5494)				
(if first pressing, with red label and arrows)	1964	$3.75	$7.50	$15.00
(if second pressing, with orange label and triangles)	1964	$2.50	$5.00	$10.00
Petula Clark, "This Is My Song" / "High" (Warner Bros. 7002)	1967	$2.50	$5.00	$10.00
Spencer Davis Group, "I'm A Man" / "Can't Get Enough of It" (United Artists 50144)	1967	$3.00	$6.00	$12.00
Spencer Davis Group, "Time Seller" / "Don't Want You No More" (United Artists 50202)	1967	$2.50	$5.00	$10.00
(with picture sleeve, add:)	1967	$5.00	$10.00	$20.00
Dave Dee, Dozy, Beaky, Mick & Tich, "Bend It" / "She's So Good" (Fontana 1559)	1966	$3.00	$6.00	$12.00
Donovan, "Catch the Wind" / "Why Do You Treat Me Like You Do" (Hickory 1492)	1965	$3.75	$7.50	$15.00
Donovan, "Sunshine Superman" / "The Trip" (Epic 10045)	1966	$2.50	$5.00	$10.00
(with picture sleeve, add:)	1966	$3.75	$7.50	$15.00
(if pressed on red vinyl)	1966	$10.00	$20.00	$40.00
Marianne Faithfull, "As Tears Go By" / "Greensleeves" (London 9697)	1964	$3.00	$6.00	$12.00
Marianne Faithfull, "Sister Morphine" / "Something Better" (London 1022)	1969	$25.00	$50.00	$100.00
(with picture sleeve, add:)	1969	$12.50	$25.00	$50.00
Wayne Fontana and the Mindbenders, "Game of Love" / "Since You've Been Gone" (Fontana 1503)	1965	$3.75	$7.50	$15.00
Wayne Fontana and the Mindbenders, "Game of Love" / "One More Time" (Fontana 1509)	1965	$3.00	$6.00	$12.00
Freddie and the Dreamers, "I'm Telling You Now" / "What Have I Done To You" (Capitol 5053)	1963	$5.00	$10.00	$20.00
(if on Tower 125)	1964	$3.75	$7.50	$15.00
Gerry and the Pacemakers, "Ferry Cross the Mersey" / "Pretend" (Laurie 3284)	1965	$3.00	$6.00	$12.00

45s	Year	VG	VG+	NM
Herman's Hermits, "Mrs. Brown You've Got a Lovely Daughter" / "I Gotta Dream On" (MGM 13341)	1965	$2.50	$5.00	$10.00
(with picture sleeve, add:)	1965	$3.75	$7.50	$15.00
The Hollies, "Just One Look" / "Keep Off That Fence of Mine" (Imperial 66026)	1964	$5.00	$10.00	$20.00
The Hollies, "Bus Stop" / "Don't Run and Hide" (Imperial 66186)	1966	$3.00	$6.00	$12.00
The Hollies, "Carrie-Anne" / "Signs That Will Never Change" (Epic 10180)	1967	$2.00	$4.00	$8.00
(with picture sleeve, add:)	1967	$3.75	$7.50	$15.00
Tom Jones, "What's New Pussycat" / "Once Upon A Time" (Parrot 9765)	1965	$2.50	$5.00	$10.00
(with picture sleeve, add:)	1965	$3.75	$7.50	$15.00
Tom Jones, "Thunderball" / "Key To My Heart" (Parrot 9801)	1965	$2.00	$4.00	$8.00
(with picture sleeve featuring a dead woman and a spear gun, add:)	1965	$5.00	$10.00	$20.00
(with picture sleeve, reissued to remove dead woman and spear gun, add:)	1965	$3.00	$6.00	$12.00
Jonathan King, "Everyone's Gone to the Moon" / "Summer's Coming" (Parrot 9774)	1965	$2.50	$5.00	$10.00
The Kinks, "You Really Got Me" / "It's All Right" (Reprise 0306)				
(if first pressing, with peach-colored label)	1964	$6.25	$12.50	$25.00
(if second pressing, orange-brown label)	1964	$3.75	$7.50	$15.00
The Kinks, "Waterloo Sunset" / "Two Sisters" (Reprise 0612)	1967	$10.00	$20.00	$40.00
Lulu, "Shout" / "Forget Me Baby" (Parrot 9678)	1964	$5.00	$10.00	$20.00
(if on Parrot 40021, B-side is "When He Touches Me")	1967	$2.50	$5.00	$10.00
Lulu, "To Sir With Love" / "The Boat That I Row" (Epic 10187)	1967	$2.50	$5.00	$10.00
Manfred Mann, "Do Wah Diddy Diddy" / "What You Gonna Do?" (Ascot 2157)	1964	$3.00	$6.00	$12.00
The Mindbenders, "A Groovy Kind of Love" / "Love is Good" (Fontana 1541)	1966	$3.00	$6.00	$12.00
The Moody Blues, "Go Now!" / "Lose Your Money" (London 9726)				
(if first pressing, white-purple-blue label)	1965	$6.25	$12.50	$25.00
(if second pressing, blue swirl label, "London" in white)	1965	$3.00	$6.00	$12.00
(if blue swirl label, "London" in black)	1965	$2.00	$4.00	$8.00
The Moody Blues, "Nights In White Satin" / "Cities" (Deram 85023)				
(if "Nights in White Satin" is credited to "Redwave")	1968	$2.50	$5.00	$10.00
(if "Nights in White Satin" is credited to "Justin Hayward")	1968	$2.00	$4.00	$8.00
(if "Nights in White Satin" is credited to "Redwave-Hayward")	1968	$2.00	$4.00	$8.00
The New Vaudeville Band, "Winchester Cathedral" / "Wait For Me Baby" (Fontana 1562)	1966	$2.00	$4.00	$8.00
Peter and Gordon, "A World Without Love" / "If I Were You" (Capitol 5175)	1964	$3.00	$6.00	$12.00
Peter and Gordon, "I Go To Pieces" / "Love Me, Baby" (Capitol 5335)	1965	$3.00	$6.00	$12.00
(with picture sleeve, add:)	1965	$4.00	$8.00	$16.00
The Searchers, "Needles and Pins" / "Ain't That Just Like Me" (Kapp 577)	1964	$3.00	$6.00	$12.00
(with picture sleeve for this A-side/B-side combination only, add:)	1964	$7.50	$15.00	$30.00
(if B-side is "Saturday Night Out")	1964	$2.50	$5.00	$10.00
(with picture sleeve on promo copies only, add:)	1964	$12.50	$25.00	$50.00
The Searchers, "Love Potion Number Nine" / "Hi-Heel Sneakers" (Kapp Winner's Circle KCS-27)	1964	$2.50	$5.00	$10.00
The Seekers, "Georgy Girl" / "When The Stars Begin To Fall" (Capitol 5756)	1966	$3.00	$6.00	$12.00
Sandie Shaw, "(There's) Always Something There To Remind Me" / "Don't You Know" (Reprise 0320)	1964	$3.00	$6.00	$12.00
The Small Faces, "Tin Soldier" / "I Feel Much Better" (Immediate 5003)	1968	$2.50	$5.00	$10.00
(with picture sleeve, add:)	1968	$6.25	$12.50	$25.00
Dusty Springfield, "You Don't Have To Say You Love Me" / "Little by Little" (Philips 40371)	1966	$2.50	$5.00	$10.00
(with picture sleeve, add:)	1966	$5.00	$10.00	$20.00
Dusty Springfield, "Son-of-a-Preacher Man" / "Just A Little Lovin' (Early In the Morning)" (Atlantic 2580)	1968	$2.50	$5.00	$10.00
(with picture sleeve, add:)	1968	$3.75	$7.50	$15.00
Them, "Gloria" / "Baby, Please Don't Go" (Parrot 9727)	1965	$4.00	$8.00	$16.00
(if Gloria is on Parrot 365, with "Bring 'em On In" as the B-side)	1971	$2.50	$5.00	$10.00

45s	Year	VG	VG+	NM
The Tornadoes, "Telstar" / "Jungle Fever" (London 9561)	1962	$6.25	$12.50	$25.00
The Troggs, "Wild Thing" / "With A Girl Like You" (Atco 6415)				
(if "Wild Thing" is incorrectly credited to "Presley")	1966	$5.00	$10.00	$20.00
(if "Wild Thing" is credited to "Taylor")	1966	$4.00	$8.00	$16.00
(if B-side is "I Want You")	1966	$4.00	$8.00	$16.00
The Troggs, "Wild Thing" / "From Home" (Fontana 1548)	1966	$2.50	$5.00	$10.00
The Who, "I Can't Explain" / "Bald Headed Woman" (Decca 31725)	1965	$7.50	$15.00	$30.00
The Who, "Anyway, Anyhow, Anywhere" / "Anytime You Want Me" (Decca 31801)	1965	$15.00	$30.00	$60.00
The Who, "Happy Jack" / "Whiskey Man" (Decca 32114)	1967	$3.00	$6.00	$12.00
(with picture sleeve, add:)	1967	$7.50	$15.00	$30.00
The Yardbirds, "Heart Full of Soul" / "Steeled Blues" (Epic 9823)	1965	$3.75	$7.50	$15.00
(with picture sleeve, add:)	1965	$12.50	$25.00	$50.00
The Yardbirds, "Happenings Ten Years Time Ago" / "The Nazz Are Blue" (Epic 10094)	1966	$3.75	$7.50	$15.00
(with picture sleeve, add:)	1966	$10.00	$20.00	$40.00
The Zombies, "Tell Her No" / "Leave Me Be" (Parrot 9723)	1965	$3.00	$6.00	$12.00
(with picture sleeve, add:)	1965	$6.25	$12.50	$25.00
The Zombies, "Time of the Season" / "I'll Call You Mine" (Date 1604)	1968	$5.00	$10.00	$20.00
(if on Date 1628, B-side is "Friends of Mine")	1968	$3.00	$6.00	$12.00

LPs	Year	VG	VG+	NM
The Animals, The Animals (MGM E-4264, mono) (with short version of "House of the Rising Sun")	1964	$10.00	$20.00	$40.00
(if on MGM E-4264, mono, yellow label promo)	1964	$25.00	$50.00	$100.00
(if on MGM SE-4264, rechanneled stereo)	1964	$7.50	$15.00	$30.00
The Animals, The Best of the Animals (MGM E-4324) (mono) (full-length "House of the Rising Sun")	1966	$5.00	$10.00	$20.00
(if on MGM E-4324, mono, yellow label promo)	1966	$20.00	$40.00	$60.00
(if on MGM SE-4324, rechanneled stereo)	1966	$6.25	$12.50	$25.00
Peter Best, Best of the Beatles (Savage BM-71) (legit copies have a white circle around the word "Savage" and around Peter Best's head)	1966	$50.00	$100.00	$200.00
Cilla Black, Is It Love? (Capitol T 2308) (mono)	1965	$6.25	$12.50	$25.00
(if on Capitol ST 2308, stereo)	1965	$10.00	$20.00	$40.00
David Bowie, David Bowie (Deram DE 16003) (mono)	1967	$25.00	$50.00	$100.00
(if on Deram DES 18003, stereo)	1967	$37.50	$75.00	$150.00
Chad and Jeremy, Of Cabbages and Kings (Columbia CL 2671) (mono)	1967	$5.00	$10.00	$20.00
(if on Columbia CS 9471, stereo)	1967	$6.25	$12.50	$25.00
The Dave Clark Five, Glad All Over				
(if on Epic LN 24093, mono, group photo, no instruments)	1964	$20.00	$40.00	$80.00
(if on Epic LN 24093, mono, group photo, with instruments)	1964	$10.00	$20.00	$40.00
(if on Epic BN 26093, rechanneled stereo, group photo, no instruments)	1964	$15.00	$30.00	$60.00
(if on Epic BN 26093, rechanneled stereo, group photo, with instruments)	1964	$7.50	$15.00	$30.00
The Dave Clark Five, The Dave Clark Five Interview (Epic XEM 77238/9) (white label promo)	1964	$150.00	$300.00	$600.00
Petula Clark, Pet Clark (Imperial LP-9079) (mono)	1959	$12.50	$25.00	$50.00
(if on Imperial LP-9281, mono, reissue)	1965	$5.00	$10.00	$20.00
(if on Imperial LP-12079, stereo)	1959	$20.00	$40.00	$80.00
(if on Imperial LP-12281, stereo, reissue)	1965	$6.25	$12.50	$25.00
Petula Clark, Downtown (Warner Bros. W 1590) (mono, gray labels)	1965	$3.00	$6.00	$12.00
(if on Warner Bros. W 1590, mono, gold labels, reissue)	1966	$3.00	$6.00	$12.00
(if on Warner Bros. WS 1590, stereo, gold labels)	1965	$5.00	$10.00	$20.00
The Spencer Davis Group, Gimme Some Lovin' (United Artists UAL 3578) (mono)	1967	$12.50	$25.00	$50.00
(if on United Artists UAS 6578, rechanelled stereo)	1967	$10.00	$20.00	$40.00
Dave Dee, Dozy, Beaky, Mick & Tich, Time To Take Off (Imperial LP-12402) ("Zabadak" is rechanneled)	1968	$10.00	$20.00	$40.00

LPs	Year	VG	VG+	NM
Donovan, Catch the Wind (Hickory LPM-123) (mono)	1965	$6.25	$12.50	$25.00
(if on Hickory LPS-123, rechanneled stereo)	1965	$5.00	$10.00	$20.00
Donovan, Mellow Yellow (Epic LN 24239) (mono)	1967	$7.50	$15.00	$30.00
(if on Epic BN 26239, rechanneled stereo)	1967	$3.75	$7.50	$15.00
Marianne Faithfull, Go Away From My World (London LL 3452) (mono)	1965	$3.75	$7.50	$15.00
(if on London PS 452, stereo)	1965	$5.00	$10.00	$20.00
Wayne Fontana and the Mindbenders, The Game of Love (Fontana MGF-27542) (mono)	1965	$7.50	$15.00	$30.00
(if on Fontana SRF-67542, rechanneled stereo)	1965	$6.25	$12.50	$25.00
Freddie and the Dreamers, Do The Freddie (Mercury MG-21026) (mono)	1965	$5.00	$10.00	$20.00
(if on Mercury SR-61026, stereo)	1965	$6.25	$12.50	$25.00
Gerry and the Pacemakers, Don't Let The Sun Catch You Crying (Laurie LLP-2024) (mono)	1964	$7.50	$15.00	$30.00
(if on Laurie SLP-2024, rechanneled stereo)	1964	$6.25	$12.50	$25.00
(if on Laurie T-90555, Capitol Record Club issue, mono)	1964	$10.00	$20.00	$40.00
(if on Laurie DT-90555, Capitol Record Club issue, rechanneled stereo)	1964	$7.50	$15.00	$30.00
Herman's Hermits, Introducing Herman's Hermits (MGM E-4282) (mono)				
(if first pressing, cover promotes hit single "I'm Into Something Good")	1965	$6.25	$12.50	$25.00
(if second pressing, contains sticker announcing hit single "Mrs. Brown You've Got a Lovely Daughter")	1965	$5.00	$10.00	$20.00
(if third pressing, cover now promotes "Mrs. Brown You've Got a Lovely Daughter")	1965	$3.75	$7.50	$15.00
Herman's Hermits, Introducing Herman's Hermits (MGM SE-4282) (rechanneled stereo)				
(if first pressing, cover promotes hit single "I'm Into Something Good")	1965	$5.00	$10.00	$20.00
(if second pressing, contains sticker announcing hit single "Mrs. Brown You've Got a Lovely Daughter")	1965	$3.75	$7.50	$15.00
(if third pressing, cover now promotes "Mrs. Brown You've Got a Lovely Daughter")	1965	$2.50	$5.00	$10.00
The Hollies, Here I Go Again (Imperial LP-9265) (mono)				
(if label is black with stars)	1964	$25.00	$50.00	$100.00
(if label is black and pink)	1964	$12.50	$25.00	$50.00
(if on Imperial LP-12265, rechanneled stereo, black label with silver print)	1964	$18.75	$37.50	$75.00
(if on Imperial LP-12265, rechanneled stereo, black and pink label)	1964	$7.50	$15.00	$30.00
Tom Jones, It's Not Unusual (Parrot PA 61004) (mono)	1965	$3.75	$7.50	$15.00
(if on Parrot PAS 71004, stereo)	1965	$3.75	$7.50	$15.00
Jonathan King, Jonathan King or Then Again... (Parrot PA 61013) (mono)	1967	$10.00	$20.00	$40.00
(if on Parrot PAS 71013, all tracks except "Where The Sun Has Never Shown," in true stereo)	1967	$12.50	$25.00	$50.00
The Kinks, You Really Got Me (Reprise R-6143) (mono)	1965	$10.00	$20.00	$40.00
(if white label promo)	1965	$100.00	$200.00	$400.00
(if on Reprise RS-6143, pink-gold-green label, some songs in stereo)	1965	$12.50	$25.00	$50.00
(if on Reprise RS-6143, orange label with "r:" and steamboat, some songs in stereo)	1971	$2.50	$5.00	$10.00
The Kinks, God Save the Kinks (Reprise PRO 328) (mail-order box with decal, postcard, bag of grass, two pins, letter, Kinks consumer guide and "Then Now and In Between" LP. Price is for complete package)	1969	$125.00	$250.00	$500.00
(if only "Then Now and In Between" album exists, with no extra goodies)	1969	$12.50	$25.00	$50.00
Lulu, To Sir With Love (Epic LN 24339) (mono)	1967	$6.25	$12.50	$25.00
(if on Epic BN 26339, some songs in stereo)	1967	$7.50	$15.00	$30.00
Manfred Mann, The Mighty Quinn (Mercury SR-61168)	1968	$6.25	$12.50	$25.00
The Mindbenders, A Groovy Kind of Love (Fontana MGF-27554) (mono)				
(if above has the song "Don't Cry No More")	1966	$7.50	$15.00	$30.00
(if above has the song "Ashes to Ashes")	1966	$6.25	$12.50	$25.00
(if on Fontana SRF-67554, rechanneled stereo, has the song "Don't Cry No More")	1966	$6.25	$12.50	$25.00
(if above has the song "Ashes to Ashes")	1966	$5.00	$10.00	$20.00

LPs	Year	VG	VG+	NM
The Moody Blues, Days of Future Passed (Dearm DE 16012) (mono)	1968	$62.50	$125.00	$250.00
(if on Deram DES 18012, stereo)	1968	$5.00	$10.00	$20.00
(if on Mobile Fidelity 042, stereo, audiophile pressing)	1980	$15.00	$30.00	$60.00
(if on Deram 820 006-1, stereo, reissue)	1985	$2.00	$4.00	$8.00
Peter and Gordon, A World Without Love (Capitol T 2115) (mono)	1964	$5.00	$10.00	$20.00
(if on Capitol ST 2115, stereo)	1964	$6.25	$12.50	$25.00
Sandie Shaw, Sandie Shaw (Reprise R-6166) (mono)	1965	$10.00	$20.00	$40.00
(if on Reprise R-6191, stereo)	1965	$12.50	$25.00	$50.00
Dusty Springfield, Stay Awhile (Philips PHM-200-133 M) (mono)	1964	$7.50	$15.00	$30.00
(if on Philips PHS-600-133 P, some songs in stereo)	1964	$10.00	$20.00	$40.00
Dusty Springfield, Dusty in Memphis (Atlantic SD 8214)				
(if first pressing, with purple-brown label)	1969	$7.50	$15.00	$30.00
(if second pressing, with green-red label)	1969	$3.75	$7.50	$15.00
Them, Them Again (Parrot PA 61008)	1966	$20.00	$40.00	$80.00
(if on Parrot PAS 71008, rechanneled stereo)	1966	$12.50	$25.00	$50.00
Them, Time Out! Time In For Them (Tower ST 5116)	1968	$25.00	$50.00	$100.00
The Tornadoes, Telstar (London LL 3279) (mono)	1963	$37.50	$75.00	$150.00
The Tornadoes, The Sounds of the Tornadoes (London LL 3293) (same as above album, except new cover, new track order and one song swapped for another)	1963	$50.00	$100.00	$200.00

LPs	Year	VG	VG+	NM
The Who, The Who Sell Out (Decca DL 4950) (mono)	1967	$25.00	$50.00	$100.00
(if white label promo, side 1 banded for airplay, all the commercials on one side)	1967	$75.00	$150.00	$300.00
(if white label promo, songs in the same order as on stock copy)	1967	$50.00	$100.00	$200.00
The Who, The Who Sell Out (Decca DL 74950) (stereo)	1967	$12.50	$25.00	$50.00
(if white label promo, side 1 banded for airplay, all the commercials on one side)	1967	$100.00	$200.00	$400.00
(if white label promo, songs in the same order as on stock copy)	1967	$62.50	$125.00	$250.00
The Who, Magic Bus - The Who On Tour (Decca DL 75064) (rechanneled except for "Magic Bus," "Tattoo" and "I Can't Reach You," in true stereo)	1968	$12.50	$25.00	$50.00
(if on white label promo, rechanneled stereo except as above noted)	1968	$37.50	$75.00	$150.00
(if on Decca DL 5064, white label promo, mono pressing - no stock mono copies are known to exist)	1968	$50.00	$100.00	$200.00
The Yardbirds, For Your Love (Epic LN 24167) (mono)	1965	$25.00	$50.00	$100.00
(if white label promo)	1965	$100.00	$200.00	$400.00
(if on Epic BN 26167, all songs in true stereo except for "Sweet Music")	1965	$20.00	$40.00	$80.00
The Zombies, The Zombies (Parrot PA-61001) (mono)	1965	$15.00	$30.00	$60.00
(if on Parrot PAS 71001, rechanneled stereo)	1965	$10.00	$20.00	$40.00
The Zombies, Odyssey and Oracle (Date TES-4103)				
(if "Time of the Season" is not mentioned on front cover)	1968	$7.50	$15.00	$30.00
(if "Time of the Season" is mentioned, second pressing)	1969	$5.00	$10.00	$20.00

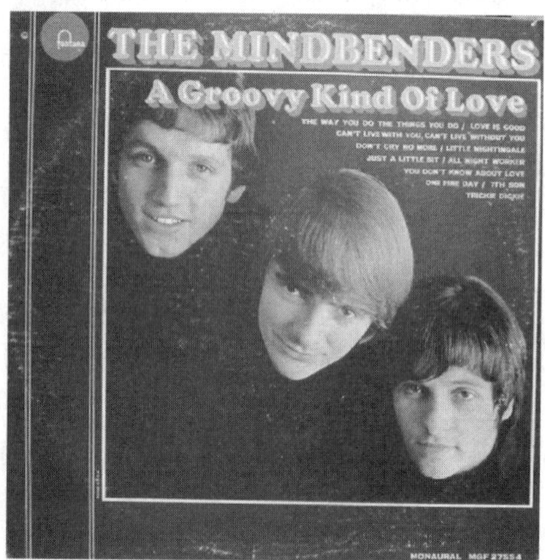

The Mindbenders' #1 hit "Groovy Kind of Love" was later covered by Phil Collins; the Mindbenders' lineup included future members of 10cc.

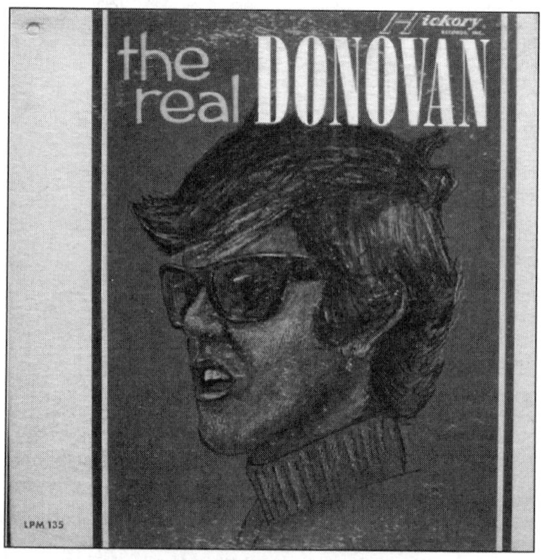

Although the bulk of Donovan's hits were on Epic, his first American releases were on the tiny Hickory label. From the Collection of Mark and Elaine Klein.

Singing background vocals on Donovan's "Mellow Yellow" is none other than Paul McCartney.

BUBBLEGUM MUSIC

History: On the surface, "bubblegum music" may have seemed as innocuous as novelty music. But many bubblegum songs had lyrics with hints of double entendre, a creamy center of sexual overtones coated in a rich chocolate shell. While radio stations in the late 1960s were filled with folk-rock, protest songs, and psychedelic excursions, some disaffected teens wanted simpler songs with more "fun" to them. For them, bubblegum music was the cure. Many bubblegum songs were built around children's nursery rhymes and recess games, with the lyrics using those childhood themes as metaphors for love (or maybe sex, if you were a little older and knew about such things).

Many of the original bubblegum groups were garage and psychedelia bands looking for their first big break. Those groups found their breaks on small independent labels such as Laurie (The Balloon Farm and the Music Explosion) and Kama Sutra (whose roster included the Lovin' Spoonful and the Sopwith "Camel").

It was Buddah Records that brought bubblegum music to the national stage. Buddah was run by record producer/executive Neil Bogart, a former head man at MGM and at Cameo-Parkway. His top songwriters/producers were Jerry Kasenetz and Jeff Katz, who had produced successful hits for a group called the Music Explosion ("Little Bit O' Soul").

The Ohio Express became the first bubblegum success story for Buddah. Originally known as the Rare Breed, the Ohio Express' first hit was a Kasenetz-Katz production on the Cameo-Parkway label ("Beg, Borrow and Steal"). While on Buddah, the Ohio Express, now augmented by lead singer Joey Levine, had monster hits like "Yummy, Yummy, Yummy" and "Chewy, Chewy."

> ### Trivia
> **Tommy James and the Shondells' pre-bubblegum hit, "Hanky Panky," was a flop in 1963. Three years later, a Pittsburgh radio DJ gave the record a spin, and the response was so positive that James formed a new set of Shondells and had a successful recording career.**

One of the earliest proponents of bubblegum music, the Ohio Express.

Kasenetz-Katz didn't stop with the Ohio Express—Buddah Records added a New Jersey bubblegum group, the 1910 Fruitgum Company, to the label roster, and Kasenetz-Katz gave them nursery rhyme hits with "Simon Says," "1, 2, 3, Red Light," and "Indian Giver." At one point, the Buddah songwriting-producing duo created a 40-piece all-star band from the Buddah roster, called themselves the Kasenetz-Katz Singing Orchestral Circus, and earned a moderate top 40 bubblegum hit with "Quick Joey Small (Run Joey Run)."

Another producer who created bubblegum smashes in the 1960s was Don Kirshner. Rather than use a single songwriting team, Kirshner had contacts with the entire Brill Building songwriting enclave, guaranteeing him a plethora of hit songs, as long as he could find someone to record them.

At this time, Kirshner provided music for the first season of the TV series *"The Monkees,"* and was responsible for the group's early hits "Last Train to Clarksville" and "I'm A Believer." But after the Monkees and Kirshner parted ways over creative differences, Kirshner eventually worked with the Archies, a group that literally couldn't fire him—after all, pen-and-ink cartoon characters won't disagree with a musical director, now will they?

At the time, the Archies had a successful comic strip, a Saturday Morning TV show, and a decent bubblegum music career. This picture sleeve for "Bang Shang-A-Lang" shows the group performing for their upcoming tour through Toontown.

Originally recorded as a studio B-side for up-and-coming singer Gary DeCarlo, Steam's bubblegum hit became a #1 smash and a worldwide sports anthem.

Based on the Bob Montana comic strip, *"The Archies"* was a successful CBS Saturday morning cartoon series. The animated teenagers on the show also sang and played music, and sold tons of records based on many of the same pop songs the Monkees previously rejected. The Archies' biggest hit, "Sugar Sugar," became both a bubblegum classic and a popular dance hit (and a soul smash when Wilson Pickett covered the song).

The Archies were not the only "studio band" wrapped up in the bubblegum sound. Other bubblegum bands that existed only on vinyl were the Banana Splits (another Saturday morning musical cartoon show), the Cuff Links (whose lead singer, Ron Dante, was also the mystery lead singer of the Archies), and Steam (a studio group created for a knockoff B-side that eventually became the worldwide hit "Na Na Hey Hey Kiss Him Goodbye").

Trivia

The title of John Fred and his Playboy Band's bubblegum chart-topper "Judy In Disguise (With Glasses)" came when Fred misheard the lyrics to the Beatles' "Lucy in the Sky with Diamonds" as "Lucy in Disguise with Diamonds." Once he understood what the real lyrics were, Fred decided to write a song based on the misheard lyrics.

Not every band who recorded bubblegum music was a bubblegum band; in fact, many groups who were more based in garage music, psychedelia or folk music have been pigeonholed as "bubblegum bands" because their biggest single was... well... Such groups in this "one-bubblegum song" phalanx include the Lemon Pipers, a psychedelic group from New Jersey who recorded the song "Green Tambourine" because it allowed them to keep their recording contract; John Fred, and his Playboy Band, whose garage classics were overshadowed by "Judy In Disguise (With Glasses"), and Melanie (five albums of folk-pop classics, but her most notable song involved a pair of roller-skates and a "Brand New Key").

Bubblegum bands may have had noteworthy names (come on, you never heard of the Rock and Roll Dubble Bubble Trading Card Co. of Philadelphia 1941?), but their members were interchangeable. In many cases, groups were supplemented (or replaced) by studio musicians during their career. Ron Dante and Joey Levine sang as lead on more than one hitmaking group (Levine, the lead singer of the Ohio Express, also sang lead for Crazy Elephant's "Gimme Gimme Good Lovin'," and was also involved in the group Reunion, who had the bubblegum hit "Life Is A Rock [But The Radio Rolled Me]").

Other groups that were on the bubblegum fringe—that is, their music may have been predominantly rock, garage, or psychedelic, but a bubblegum song snuck in now and again—include Paul Revere and the Raiders, Tommy James and the Shondells, and the Royal Guardsmen. While songs like "Hanky Panky," "Hungry," and "Snoopy vs. the Red Baron" may fall within the bubblegum music mold, these groups were closer to rock and garage bands than they were to the Kasenetz-Katz factory sound.

The Royal Guardsmen, a Florida-based band, made a bubblegum/garage band career out of Charlie Brown's dog Snoopy's imaginary World War I battles with the Red Baron.

The residue of bubblegum music lasted into the 1970s, as groups like Bo Donaldson and the Heywoods ("Billy, Don't Be a Hero") and Paper Lace ("The Night Chicago Died") recorded story-songs with thumping rhythms reminiscent of the classic Kasenetz-Katz Buddah hits.

Bubblegum music finally popped in the early 1970s, but its influence can be heard on power pop bands, new wave artists and disco/dance groups today. Neil Bogart, who supervised the Buddah bubblegum sound, later formed Casablanca Records, the home for Donna Summer and Kiss. Andy Kim, who wrote bubblegum hits for the Archies, had his own #1 bubblegum-disco song, "Rock Me Gently." The Ramones have covered various Kasenetz-Katz songs on their early albums, and R.E.M.'s early soundchecks sometimes included the Banana Splits nugget "I Enjoy Being A Boy (In Love With You)."

Trivia

Tony Burrows was the lead singer for the bubblegum group Edison Lighthouse ("Love Grows Where My Rosemary Goes"), as well as for White Plains ("My Baby Loves Lovin'") and the Pipkins ("Gimme Dat Ding"). In fact, if you count his work on the Brotherhood of Man's schmaltz chorale, "United We Stand," Burrows headlined four different groups with four different hits—all in a four-month period. And for completists, Burrows also sang lead on the surf-knockoff group First Class' song "Beach Baby."

What To Look For: Most of the great bubblegum hits have already been reissued as "greatest hits" packages on CD, although some bubblegum fans hope the newly resurrected Buddha Records (apparently the label's name was misspelled in the 1960s and 70s) will create a full-fledged retrospective on the works of the Ohio Express and the 1910 Fruitgum Company.

Finding 45s of bubblegum classics is easy—finding clean copies is tough. And finding picture sleeves and albums of these bubblegum artists is more difficult. Since most bubblegum groups barely had three or four hit singles in their career, their albums did not sell as well as their 45s, which makes any surviving albums today very collectable.

Web pages: Yummy, yummy, chewy, chewy, it's the Classic Bubblegum Music Page: *http://home.att.net/~bubblegumusic;* Both Sides Now: The Kama Sutra and Buddah Story, along with album discographies: *http://www.bsnpubs.com/buddah/buddahstory.html;* a site devoted to the bubblegum work of Kasenetz-Katz: *http://www.unclebuzz.com/bubblegum.html.*

45s	Year	VG	VG+	NM
The Archies, "Bang Shang-A-Lang" / "Truck Driver" (Calendar 63-1006)	1968	$2.00	$4.00	$8.00
(with picture sleeve, add:)	1968	$4.00	$8.00	$16.00
The Archies, "Sugar Sugar" / "Melody Hill" (Calendar 63-1008) (also on Kirshner 63-1008)	1969	$2.50	$5.00	$10.00
The Archies, "A Summer Praye For Peace" / "Maybe I'm Wrong" (Kirshner 63-5014)	1971	$2.00	$4.00	$8.00
(with picture sleeve, add:)	1971	$4.00	$8.00	$16.00
The Balloon Farm, "A Question of Tempature" / "Hurtin' For Your Lovin'" (Laurie 3405) (A-side misspells "Temperature")	1967	$5.00	$10.00	$20.00
The Balloon Farm, "A Question of Temperature" / "Hurtin' For Your Lovin'" (Laurie 3405) (A-side spelled correctly)	1967	$2.50	$5.00	$10.00
The Banana Splits, "The Tra-La-La Song (One Banana, Two Banana)" / "Toy Piano Medley" (Decca 32429)	1968	$3.00	$6.00	$12.00
(with picture sleeve, add:)	1968	$6.25	$12.50	$25.00
The Banana Splits, "Doin' The Banana Split" / "I Enjoy Being A Boy (In Love With You)" / "The Beautiful Calliopa" / "Let Me Remember You Smiling"				

LPs	Year	VG	VG+	NM
(four-song EP, available through Kellogg's breakfast cereals as a promotional product)	1969	$3.00	$6.00	$12.00
(with picture sleeve, add:)	1969	$5.00	$10.00	$20.00
Crazy Elephant, "Gimme Gimme Good Lovin'" / "Dark Part Of My Mind" (1969)	1969	$2.00	$4.00	$8.00
Bo Donaldson and the Heywoods, "Billy Don't Be A Hero" / "Don't Ever Look Back" (ABC 11435) (also on ABC 12011)	1974		$2.00	$4.00
Bo Donaldson and the Heywoods, "Who Do You Think You Are" / "Fool's Way of Lovin'" (ABC 12006)	1974		$2.00	$4.00
Edison Lighthouse, "Love Grows (Where My Rosemary Goes)" / "Every Lonely Day" (Bell 858)	1970		$3.00	$6.00
John Fred and his Playboy Band, "Judy In Disguise (With Glasses)" / "When The Lights Go Out" (Paula 282)				
(if label is yellow)	1967	$3.00	$6.00	$12.00
(if label is white)	1967	$2.50	$5.00	$10.00
(if label is pink)	1967	$2.00	$4.00	$8.00
Gunhill Road, "Back When My Hair Was Short" / "We Can't Ride The Roller Coaster Anymore" (Kama Sutra 569)	1973		$3.00	$6.00
Tommy James and the Shondells, "Hanky Panky" / "Thunderbolt"				
(if on Snap 102, group listed as "The Shondells," no mention of Red Fox Records on label)	1963	$20.00	$40.00	$80.00
(if on Snap 102, group listed as "The Shondells," "Dist. by Red Fox Records, Pgh, Pa." on label)	1966	$7.50	$15.00	$30.00
(if on Red Fox 110, group listed as "The Shondells")	1966	$10.00	$20.00	$40.00
(if on Roulette 4686)	1966	$2.00	$5.00	$10.00
The Kasenetz-Katz Singing Orchestral Circus, "Quick Joey Small (Run Joey Run)" / "Mr. Jensen" (Buddah 64)	1968	$2.00	$4.00	$8.00
The Lemon Pipers, "Green Tambourine" / "No Help From Me" (Buddah 23)	1967	$3.00	$6.00	$12.00
The Lemon Pipers, "Rice Is Nice" / "Blueberry Blue" (Buddah 31)	1968	$2.50	$5.00	$10.00
(with picture sleeve, add:)	1968	$3.75	$7.50	$15.00
The Music Explosion, "Little Bit O' Soul" / "I See The Light" (Laurie 3380)	1967	$3.00	$6.00	$12.00
1910 Fruitgum Company, "Simon Says" / "Reflections from the Looking Glass" (Buddah 24)	1968	$2.50	$5.00	$10.00
1910 Fruitgum Company, "Goody Goody Gumdrops" / "Candy Kisses" (Buddah 71)	1968	$2.00	$4.00	$8.00
The Ohio Express, "Yummy Yummy Yummy" / "Zig Zag (Buddah 38)	1968	$2.50	$5.00	$10.00
The Ohio Express, "Chewy Chewy" / "Firebird" (Buddah 70)	1968	$2.50	$5.00	$10.00
Paper Lace, "The Night Chicago Died" / "Can You Get It When You Want It" (Mercury 73492)				
(if on red label)	1974		$3.00	$6.00
(if on Chicago skyline label)	1974		$2.00	$4.00
The Royal Guardsmen, "Snoopy vs. the Red Baron" / "I Needed You" (Laurie 3366)	1966	$3.00	$6.00	$12.00
The Royal Guardsmen, "Snoopy's Christmas" / "It Kinda Looks Like Christmas" (Laurie 3416)	1967	$2.50	$5.00	$10.00
(with picture sleeve, add:)	1967	$5.00	$10.00	$20.00
Steam, "Na Na Hey Hey Kiss Him Goodbye" / "It's The Magic In You Girl" (Fontana 1667)	1960	$2.00	$4.00	$8.00
(if on Mercury 30160, reissue from 1976 backed with "Don't Stop Lovin' Me")	1976		$2.00	$4.00
(with 1976 picture sleeve, celebrating the Chicago White Sox, originally only available in Chicago)	1976	$5.00	$10.00	$20.00
White Plains, "My Baby Loves Lovin'" / "Show Me Your Hand" (Deram 85058)	1970	$2.00	$4.00	$8.00

LPs	Year	VG	VG+	NM
The Archies, The Archies (Calendar KES-101)	1968	$6.25	$12.50	$25.00
The Archies, Everything's Archie (Calendar KES-103)	1969	$6.25	$12.50	$25.00
The Archies, Everything's Archie Box (Kirshner KES-103) (promo box with LP, photos, press kit, and buttons)	1969	$25.00	$50.00	$100.00
The Banana Splits, We're The Banana Splits (Decca DL 75075)	1969	$50.00	$100.00	$200.00
Crazy Elephant, Crazy Elephant Bell 6034)	1969	$5.00	$10.00	$20.00
Bo Donaldson and the Heywoods, Bo Donaldson and the Heywoods (ABC D-824)	1974	$2.50	$5.00	$10.00
The Lemon Pipers, Green Tambourine (Buddah BD-5009 mono, BDS-5009 stereo)	1968	$6.25	$12.50	$25.00
The Lemon Pipers, Jungle Marmalade (Buddah BDS-5016)	1968	$6.25	$12.50	$25.00
The Music Explosion, Little Bit O' Soul (Laurie LLP-2040) (mono)	1967	$5.00	$10.00	$20.00
(if on Laurie SLLP-2040, stereo)	1967	$6.25	$12.50	$25.00

LPs	Year	VG	VG+	NM
1910 Fruitgum Company, Simon Says (Buddah BDS-5010)	1968	$6.25	$12.50	$25.00
1910 Fruitgum Company, Juiciest Fruitgum (Buddah BDS-5057)	1970	$6.25	$12.50	$25.00
The Ohio Express, Beg, Borrow and Steal (Cameo C 20,000) (mono)	1967	$7.50	$15.00	$30.00
(if on Cameo CS 20,000, stereo)	1967	$10.00	$20.00	$40.00
The Ohio Express, Chewy Chewy (Buddah BDS 5018)	1968	$5.00	$10.00	$20.00
The Ohio Express, The Very Best of the Ohio Express (BDS 5058)	1970	$5.00	$10.00	$20.00
Paper Lace, Paper Lace (Mercury SRM-1-1008)	1974	$3.00	$6.00	$12.00
Steam, Steam (Mercury SR 61254)	1969	$5.00	$10.00	$20.00
Various Artists, Bubble Gum Music Is The Naked Truth, Volume 1 (Buddah BDA 5032)	1969	$6.25	$12.50	$25.00
Various Artists, Buddah's 360 Degree Dial-A-Hit (Buddah BDA 5039)	1969	$7.50	$15.00	$30.00

The Jaggerz only had one bubblegum hit, "The Rapper," but their lead singer, Donnie Iris, had a respectable solo career in the early 1980s.

Although Joey Levine sang lead on many bubblegum hits for the Ohio Express and such, he did not sing lead on hits for the 1910 Fruitgum Company—those duties were handled by the band's lead singer, Mark Gutkowski.

CAMEO-PARKWAY

History: Cameo Records, a Philadelphia-based record label, was formed in 1957 by musician-songwriter Bernie Lowe. Lowe, along with the songwriting team of Kal Mann and Dave Appell, created dance records and teen idols that were an integral part of early 1960s Top 40 radio and dance rock.

The success of Cameo-Parkway Records, along with other Philadelphia-based record companies such as Swan and Chancellor, can be directly linked to the television show "American Bandstand." When the series was broadcast from Philadelphia in the 1950s and early 1960s, stars of the local record companies could quickly appear on "Bandstand" and perform their songs for a nationwide audience. And if host Dick Clark noticed a new dance style on his dance floor, the Cameo-Parkway songwriting team of Mann and Appell could have a dance song written, recorded, and pressed for their label in less than a week.

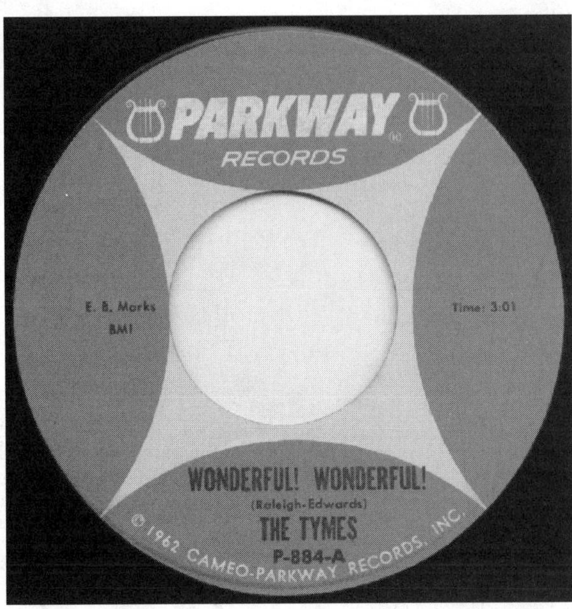

The Tymes had a hit with the Johnny Mathis ballad "Wonderful! Wonderful!"

Dee Dee Sharp's biggest hit on Cameo, "Mashed Potato Time."

Successful recordings for Cameo and its sister label Parkway included Charlie Gracie's "Butterfly," Bobby Rydell's "Wild One" and "Kissin' Time," Dee Dee Sharp's "Mashed Potato Time," the Orlons' "Wah-Watusi" and "Don't Hang Up," the Dovells' "Bristol Stomp" and "You Can't Sit Down," and the Tymes' "So Much In Love" and "Wonderful! Wonderful!" In fact, by 1963 the Cameo-Parkway family of labels was the third most prolific record company in America, in terms of 45 RPM sales.

One song that was not originally written by Mann and Appell, but still made the top of the charts for the label, was "The Twist." Originally written and recorded by Hank Ballard and the Midnighters, "The Twist" initially was only the B-side of Ballard's ballad "Teardrops On Your Letter." But when dancers on "American Bandstand" began a new hip-shifting dance called "The Twist," based on Ballard's B-side underground hit, Dick Clark wanted someone in the Philadelphia music community to record a cover version.

At the time, Cameo-Parkway had a new singer on their roster, Chubby Checker (born Ernest Evans, he changed his name to "Chubby Checker" as a sly twist on Fats Domino's name). Checker had a minor hit with "The Class," a song where he mimicked the singing styles of the pop singers of the day. "The Class" was originally recorded as a special Christmas card for Dick Clark's family and friends, but eventually was released nationally and received some radio airplay.

Trivia

Actor Clint Eastwood recorded for Cameo-Parkway. At the time, Eastwood starred on the TV series "Rawhide," which explains the subject material of his Cameo album Clint Eastwood Sings Cowboy Favorites.

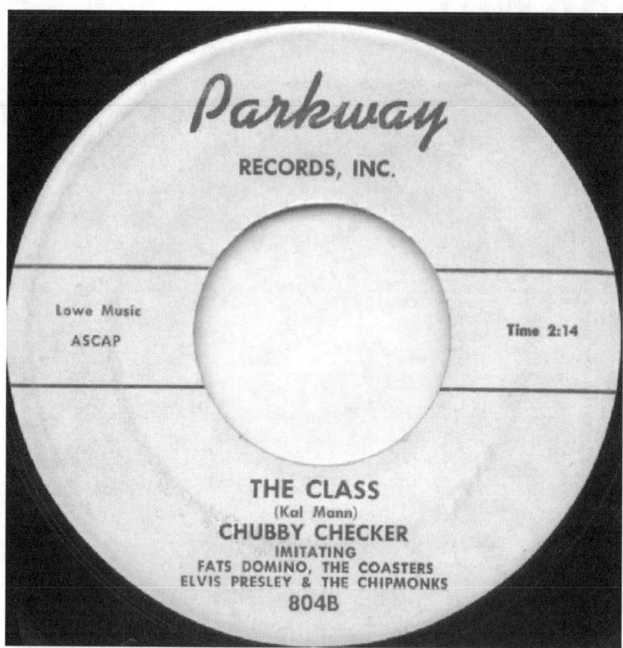

Chubby Checker's first hit, "The Class."

After Freddy "Boom Boom" Cannon passed over the song, Cameo-Parkway recorded "The Twist" with Chubby Checker. Checker's version of "The Twist" hit #1 in 1960, and as the dance became a nationwide craze, "The Twist" was re-released two years later—and returned to the top of the charts. Chubby Checker, now known as the "King of the Twist," recorded dozens of successful party and dance recordings for Cameo-Parkway, including "The Hucklebuck," "Pony Time," and "Popeye The Hitchhiker."

Chubby Checker, King of the Twist. Courtesy Last Vestige Music Store, Albany, N.Y.

In 1964, Dick Clark moved his "American Bandstand" show to Los Angeles, and the Philadelphia record companies lost the local show that turned their local artists into national stars. The British Invasion also began in 1964, which also squeezed those same companies off the pop charts. Cameo-Parkway continued to have hits for a few more years, including recordings by ? and the Mysterians ("96 Tears"), Sounds Orchestral! ("Cast Your Fate To the Wind"), as well as early recordings by the Kinks ("Long Tall Sally") and the Ohio Express ("Beg, Borrow and Steal").

A classic garage hit, ? and the Mysterians with "96 Tears."

What To Look For: One reason Cameo/Parkway releases are so collectible is that very few of the recordings have ever been released on compact disc, forcing music lovers of "The Twist," "Mashed Potato Time," "96 Tears," and "Bristol Stomp" to save their original 45s for those songs. Cameo-Parkway was purchased by Allen Klein in 1967, and was eventually renamed ABKCO Records (which still exists today). Although Klein and ABKCO did release some of the original Cameo-Parkway recordings on some reissue 45s in 1972, and a series of mono LPs in the 1980s, almost none of the old recordings have made their way to CD. Some of the Cameo-Parkway artists, most notably Chubby Checker, eventually re-recorded their classic songs on small independent labels so that at least the music could be heard on compact disc. Some bootleg unauthorized Cameo-Parkway "best of" CDs, using albums or 45s for source material, have appeared on the market.

A 1972 ABKCO reissue of Chubby Checker's "Let's Twist Again."

Because most of their recordings were dance songs, and were played often at dances or parties, Cameo-Parkway 45s are usually found only in fair condition. They tend to suffer from scratches and heavy ring wear.

Cameo-Parkway albums are very collectible, including the recordings by Chubby Checker, Bobby Rydell, and Dee Dee Sharp. As part of a promotional tool, many of these albums also contained bonus 45s, or peelable stickers. Since the 45s eventually were separated from the albums, and since the stickers often appeared on bathroom mirrors, book covers, diaries and the like, finding albums with all the peripheral material still intact can be difficult.

Trivia

The Dreamlovers were the vocal group that backed up Chubby Checker on "The Twist." They also did session work for other Cameo-Parkway artists, including Dee Dee Sharp and Bobby Rydell. They eventually recorded their own Top 10 hit, "When We Get Married," but it was for another Philadelphia-based record label, Heritage Records.

A Chubby Checker album, containing "Pull-Off-Pix" and a removable poster.

Reference Books: Jackson, John A., American Bandstand: Dick Clark and the Making of a Rock 'n' Roll Empire, Oxford University Press, New York, N.Y., 1997.

Web pages: Cameo Records Album Discography, from Both Sides Now: *http://www.bsnpubs.com/cameo.html*; Parkway Records Album Discography, from Both Sides Now: *http://www.bsnpubs.com/parkway.html*; Chubby Checker's home page: *http://chubbychecker.com.*

Trivia

The Cameo-Parkway studios at 309 South Broad Street in Philadelphia is now home to another record company, Kenny Gamble and Leon Huff's Philadelphia International Records. Coincidentally, Gamble co-wrote and Huff played on a minor hit, "The '81," for Cameo recording artists Candy and the Kisses.

Candy and the Kisses' "The 81," a regional dance hit.

45s	Year	VG	VG+	NM
The Cameos, "Merry Christmas" / "New Year's Eve" (Cameo 123)	1957	$37.50	$75.00	$150.00
(if 1970s reissue, with original 1957 label artwork)	197??	$2.50	$5.00	$10.00
Candy and the Kisses, "The 81" / "Two Happy People" (Cameo 336)	1964	$5.00	$10.00	$20.00
Chubby Checker, "The Class" / "Schooldays, Oh Schooldays" (Parkway 804)	1959	$7.50	$15.00	$30.00
Chubby Checker, "The Twist" / "Toot" (Parkway 811)				
(if on white label with blue print, first pressing)	1960	$7.50	$15.00	$30.00
(if on orange label with black print, second pressing)	1960	$5.00	$10.00	$20.00
Chubby Checker, "Pony Time" / "Oh Susannah" (Parkway 818)	1960	$3.75	$7.50	$15.00
Chubby Checker, "The Twist" / "Twistin' U.S.A." (Parkway 811)				
(if standard stock copy on black vinyl)	1961	$3.75	$7.50	$15.00
(if promotional copy on yellow vinyl)	1961	$37.50	$75.00	$150.00
(if promotional copy on red vinyl)	1961	$50.00	$100.00	$200.00
(with picture sleeve, add:)	1961	$6.25	$12.50	$25.00
Chubby Checker, "Limbo Rock" / "Popeye the Hitch-Hiker" (Parkway 849)	1962	$3.75	$7.50	$15.00
(with picture sleeve, add:)	1962	$6.25	$12.50	$25.00
The Dovells, "Bristol Stomp" / "Out In the Cold Again" (Parkway 827)	1961	$7.50	$15.00	$30.00
The Dovells, "Bristol Stomp" / "Letters of Love" (Parkway 827)	1961	$3.75	$7.50	$15.00
The Dovells, "You Can't Sit Down" / "Stompin' Everywhere" (Parkway 867)	1963	$3.00	$6.00	$12.00
(with picture sleeve, add:)	1963	$10.00	$20.00	$40.00
The Dovells, "You Can't Sit Down" / "Wildwood Days" (Parkway 867)	1963	$3.75	$7.50	$15.00
(with picture sleeve, add:)	1963	$10.00	$20.00	$40.00
Charlie Gracie, "Butterfly" / "Ninety-Nine Ways" (Cameo 105)	1957	$6.25	$12.50	$25.00
Charlie Gracie, "I Love You So Much It Hurts" / "Wandering Eyes" (Cameo 111)	1957	$5.00	$10.00	$20.00
The Kinks, "Long Tall Sally" / "I Took My Baby Home" (Cameo 308)	1964	$150.00	$300.00	$600.00
(if on Cameo 345, re-release)	1965	$75.00	$150.00	$300.00
The Ohio Express, "Beg Borrow and Steal" / "Maybe" (Cameo 483)	1967	$3.00	$6.00	$12.00
The Orlons, "The Wah-Watusi" / "Holiday Hill" (Cameo 218)	1962	$5.00	$10.00	$20.00
The Orlons, "South Street" / "Those Terrible Boots" (Cameo 243)	1963	$5.00	$10.00	$20.00
(with picture sleeve, add:)	1963	$10.00	$20.00	$40.00
? and the Mysterians, "96 Tears" / "Midnight Hour" (Cameo 428)	1966	$5.00	$10.00	$20.00
? and the Mysterians, "Can't Get Enough Of You Baby" / "Smokes" (Cameo 467)	1967	$3.75	$7.50	$15.00
The Rays, "Silhouettes" / "Daddy Cool" (Cameo 117)	1957	$6.25	$12.50	$25.00
Bobby Rydell, "Please Don't Be Mad" / "Makin' Time" (Cameo 160)	1959	$12.50	$25.00	$50.00
Bobby Rydell, "Wild One" / "I'd Do It Again" (Cameo 171)	1960	$3.75	$7.50	$15.00
(with picture sleeve, add:)	1960	$6.25	$12.50	$25.00
Bobby Rydell, "Wildwood Days" / "Will You Be My Baby" (Cameo 252)	1963	$3.00	$6.00	$12.00
(with picture sleeve, add:)	1963	$5.00	$10.00	$20.00
Bobby Rydell and Chubby Checker, "Teach Me To Twist" / "Swingin' Together" (Cameo 214)	1962	$3.75	$7.50	$15.00
(with picture sleeve, add:)	1962	$6.25	$12.50	$25.00
Senator Bobby, "Wild Thing" / Senator McKinley, "Wild Thing" (Parkway 127)	1966	$3.00	$6.00	$12.00
Dee Dee Sharp, "Mashed Potato Time" / "Set My Heart At Ease" (Cameo 212)	1962	$5.00	$10.00	$20.00
Dee Dee Sharp, "Gravy (For My Mashed Potatoes)" / "Baby Cakes" (Cameo 219)	1962	$3.75	$7.50	$15.00
(with picture sleeve, add:)	1962	$6.25	$12.50	$25.00
Dee Dee Sharp and Chubby Checker, "Do You Love Me?" / "One More Time" (Cameo 103) (DJ pressing)	1962	$10.00	$20.00	$40.00
Sounds Orchestral!, "Cast Your Fate To The Wind" / "To Wendy With Love" (Parkway 942)	1965	$2.50	$5.00	$10.00
Sounds Orchestral!, "Thunderball" / "Mr. Kiss Kiss Bang Bang" (Parkway 973)	1966	$2.00	$4.00	$8.00
The Tymes, "So In Love" / "Roscoe James McClain" (Parkway 871)	1963	$6.25	$12.50	$25.00
The Tymes, "So Much In Love" / "Roscoe James McClain" (Parkway 871)	1963	$3.75	$7.50	$15.00
(with picture sleeve, add:)	1963	$7.50	$15.00	$30.00
The Tymes, "Wonderful! Wonderful!" / "Come With Me To The Sea" (Parkway 884)	1963	$3.75	$7.50	$15.00
(with picture sleeve, add:)	1963	$6.25	$12.50	$25.00
John Zacherle, "Igor" / "Dinner with Drac" (Cameo 130)	1958	$10.00	$20.00	$40.00
John Zacherle, "Dinner With Drac" (Pt. 1) / (Pt. 2) (Cameo 130)				
(if orange label)	1958	$7.50	$15.00	$30.00
(if red-black label)	1960	$5.00	$10.00	$20.00

LPs	Year	VG	VG+	NM
Jo Ann Campbell, All The Hits of Jo Ann Campbell (Cameo C-1026) (mono)	1962	$12.50	$25.00	$50.00
(if stereo, Cameo SC-1026)	1962	$25.00	$50.00	$100.00
Chubby Checker, Twist With Chubby Checker (Parkway P-7001) (mono)				
(if all-orange label)	1960	$10.00	$20.00	$40.00
(if orange-yellow label)	1960	$7.50	$15.00	$30.00
Chubby Checker, It's Pony Time (Parkway P-7003) (mono)				
(if all-orange label)	1961	$10.00	$20.00	$40.00
(if orange-yellow label)	1961	$7.50	$15.00	$30.00
Chubby Checker, Discotheque (Parkway P-7045) (mono)	1965	$7.50	$15.00	$30.00
(if stereo pressing SP-7045)	1965	$10.00	$20.00	$40.00
The Dovells, The Bristol Stomp (Parkway P-7006) (mono)				
(if orange label)	1961	$20.00	$40.00	$80.00
(if orange-yellow label)	1962	$12.50	$25.00	$50.00
The Dovells, You Can't Sit Down (Parkway P-7025) (mono)	1963	$12.50	$25.00	$50.00
The Dovells, Len Barry Sings With the Dovells (Cameo C-1082) (mono)	1965	$7.50	$15.00	$30.00
(if stereo, Cameo SC-1082)	1965	$12.50	$25.00	$50.00
Clint Eastwood, Clint Eastwood Sings Cowboy Favorites (Cameo C-1056) (mono)	1963	$25.00	$50.00	$100.00
(if stereo, Cameo SC-1056)	1963	$37.50	$75.00	$150.00
The Ivy League, Tossin' and Turnin' (Cameo-Parkway C-2000, mono; Cameo-Parkway CS-2000, rechanneled stereo))	1965	$7.50	$15.00	$30.00
Terry Knight and the Pack, Reflections (Cameo-Parkway C-2007) (mono)	1967	$5.00	$10.00	$20.00
(if stereo, Cameo-Parkway C-2007)	1967	$6.25	$12.50	$25.00
The Ohio Express, Beg, Borrow and Steal (Cameo C-20,000) (mono)	1967	$7.50	$15.00	$30.00
(if on Cameo SC-20,000, stereo)	1967	$10.00	$20.00	$40.00
The Orlons, The Wah-Watusi (Cameo C-1020) (mono)	1962	$15.00	$30.00	$60.00
The Orlons, South Street (Cameo C-1041) (mono)	1963	$15.00	$30.00	$60.00
? and the Mysterians, 96 Tears (Cameo-Parkway C-2004) (mono)	1966	$25.00	$50.00	$100.00
(if on Cameo-Parkway CS-2004, stereo)	1966	$17.50	$35.00	$70.00
? and the Mysterians, Action (Cameo-Parkway C-2006) (mono)	1967	$37.50	$75.00	$150.00
(if on Cameo-Parkway CS-2006, stereo)	1967	$25.00	$50.00	$100.00
Bobby Rydell, We Got Love (Cameo C-1006) (mono)	1959	$15.00	$30.00	$60.00
Bobby Rydell, Bobby's Biggest Hits (Cameo C-1009)				
(if first pressing, has die-cut cover and textured inner sleeve)	1961	$20.00	$40.00	$80.00
(if second pressing, standard cover and sleeve)	1961	$6.25	$12.50	$25.00
Bobby Rydell, All The Hits (Cameo C-1019)				
(if on red vinyl)	1962	$37.50	$75.00	$150.00
(if on black vinyl)	1962	$6.25	$12.50	$25.00
Dee Dee Sharp, It's Mashed Potato Time (Cameo C-1018) (mono)	1962	$15.00	$30.00	$60.00
Dee Dee Sharp, Songs of Faith (Cameo C-1022)				
(if on Cameo C-1022, mono)	1962	$10.00	$20.00	$40.00
(if on Cameo SC-1022, stereo)	1962	$12.50	$25.00	$50.00
Dee Dee Sharp and Chubby Checker, Down To Earth (Cameo C-1029)				
(if on Cameo C-1029, mono)	1962	$10.00	$20.00	$40.00
(if on Cameo SC-1029, stereo)	1962	$12.50	$25.00	$50.00
Bunny Sigler, Let The Good Times Roll (Parkway P-50,000, mono; SP-50,000, stereo)	1967	$10.00	$20.00	$40.00
Sounds Orchestral!, Cast Your Fate To The Wind (Parkway SP 7046) (stereo)	1965	$5.00	$10.00	$20.00
The Swagmen, Meet The Swagmen (Parkway P-7015) (mono)	1962	$12.50	$25.00	$50.00
The Tymes, So Much In Love (Parkway 7032) (mono)				
(if front cover shows group standing)	1963	$10.00	$20.00	$40.00
(if front cover has only head and shoulders of group)	1963	$50.00	$100.00	$200.00
The Tymes, 18 Greatest Hits (Parkway P 7049) (mono)	1964	$10.00	$20.00	$40.00
John Zacherle, Monster Mash (Parkway P-7018) (mono)	1962	$15.00	$30.00	$60.00

CHRISTMAS/SEASONAL

History: Christmas music has brought music lovers thousands of December memories. Sleigh rides and carolers; mistletoe and holly; chestnuts roasting on an open fire; the humble yet world-fulfilling birth of the Son of God in a Bethlehem manger; Santa Claus and his nine reindeer—including the frontrunner with the high-beam nose. Old Rudolph may not have been paying attention; reports are he had a hit-and-run with Grandma.

Christmas music has evolved from hymns dedicated to the birth of Christ ("Hark The Herald Angels Sing," "Silent Night"), into carols about Christmas miracles ("Good King Wenceslas," "We Three Kings of Orient Are"). Christmas music can appeal to the young (the Chipmunks' "The Christmas Song [Christmas Don't Be Late]," Gene Autry's "Rudolph the Red-Nosed Reindeer"). It can appeal to the young-at-heart (Bing Crosby's "White Christmas," Nat King Cole's "The Christmas Song [Chestnuts Roasting on an Open Fire]").

Producer Phil Spector went one step further in creating a Christmas album: he had his entire Philles singing roster—the Ronettes, the Crystals, Bob B. Soxx and the Blue Jeans, Darlene Love—record rock versions of Christmas music, and released it as a special sampler for the holidays.

Other songs use the Christmas holidays as a spotlight on social issues. When Boomtown Rats lead singer Bob Geldof saw famine-scorched African tribes on the evening news, he rounded up as many recording stars as he could, and recorded "Do They Know It's Christmas?" under the name Band Aid. Proceeds from the sale of the song were funneled to African famine relief charities, and the song itself spurred a series of collaborative musical fundraisers around the world. A few years later, A&M Records had contemporary artists perform classic and original Christmas songs for "A Very Special Christmas," with proceeds benefiting the Special Olympics.

Gene Autry's classic "Rudolph The Red-Nosed Reindeer," on a Columbia Microgroove 7-inch 33 RPM record.

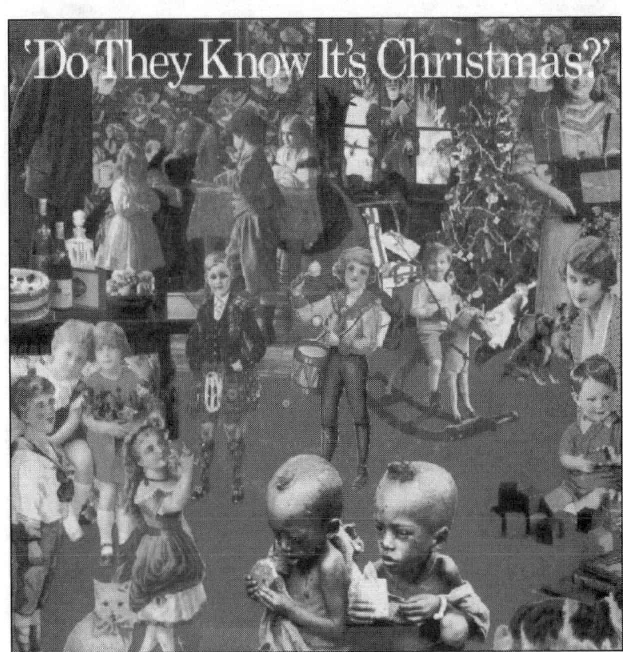

Band Aid's "Do They Know It's Christmas?"

Nearly every musician has recorded a Christmas song or album at one time in their career. Elvis Presley recorded full-length albums of Christmas standards. Phil Spector utilized his entire Philles roster for a rock 'n roll Christmas album. R.E.M., the Manhattan Transfer, and the Beatles have sent special Christmas recordings to the members of their fan clubs.

Some artists' biggest hits have been their Christmas releases—Bobby Helms may have sung "My Special Angel," but try to imagine Christmas music without his "Jingle Bell Rock." Likewise, the Waitresses may have had the classic New Wave track "I Know What Boys Like," but their seasonal song "Christmas Wrapping" has endured throughout the years. Other artists are known only by their Christmas releases—The Harry Simeone Chorale's "The

Little Drummer Boy" is a perfect example. Other groups, such as Mannheim Steamroller and the Trans-Siberian Orchestra, have found their successful Christmas recordings have caused a demand for their music even after the snow has melted and the ornaments are boxed away.

Christmas novelty and satirical songs have perennial staying power, and first pressings of these witty songs are highly collectible. Elmo 'n Patsy's "Grandma Got Run Over By A Reindeer" was a regional hit in the late 1970s, but eventually gathered enough momentum that it was picked up by a major label. Stan Freberg's "Green Chritma," where the holiday spirit is threatened by overcommercialism, is popular with both holiday and Freberg music collectors.

The B-side of Freberg's "Green Chritma" is called "The Meaning of Christmas," and includes four carols performed absolutely straight.

A Christmas music collectible that has been growing in popularity is the non-music store record releases. Companies such as True Value, Firestone, Hallmark, and Tupperware have produced albums and CD's as holiday items for customers to purchase. Most of these releases are compilations of various Christmas songs by contemporary artists, and the value of these records is a combination of available product and track lineup.

Firestone Tire's Christmas sampler.

The soundtracks to many Christmas television specials have found their way to the record bins. Whether it's the Rankin-Bass retelling of "Rudolph The Red-Nosed Reindeer," the Vince Guaraldi stylings for "A Charlie Brown Christmas," the mawkish duet between Fred Gwynne and Johnnie Whittaker from "The Littlest Angel," or the spectacular made-for-TV operetta "Amahl and the Night Visitors," Christmas soundtrack albums allowed viewers to relive their favorite moments from those classic TV specials.

What To Look For: Since Christmas records were pressed in very small quantities, when compared to the year-round pressings of non-Christmas records, these albums and 45s already have a built-in rarity.

Some Christmas 45s were reissued every year, and although the song itself did not change, the center label did. When collecting Christmas 45s, the earliest pressings are the most desirable.

Colored vinyl and picture disc releases are very prevalent in this genre, with many discs pressed in red or green vinyl, the colors of Christmas.

Trivia

Bing Crosby's "White Christmas" (first pressing on Decca 18429, a 78 RPM disc) hit the top of the charts in 1942. It also hit #1 in 1945 and in 1946, and is arguably the biggest-selling song of the 20th century.

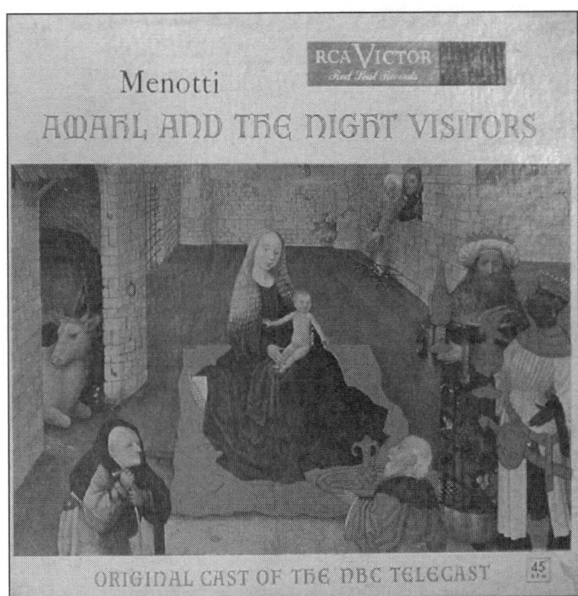

The 1951 NBC opera "Amahl and the Night Visitors" was so successful, a 4-record, 7-inch 45 box set was produced for the 1952 telecast.

Christmas ornament collectors desire to own an entire year-by-year run of a particular ornament, and "store-brand" Christmas album collectors do the same. The "Volume 1" pressings are naturally the most desirable, but clean copies of "store-brand" albums are getting harder to find, and their collectible value reflects this. The True Value Hardware Christmas series, for example, has released more than 30 volumes of Christmas music, with no sign of stopping.

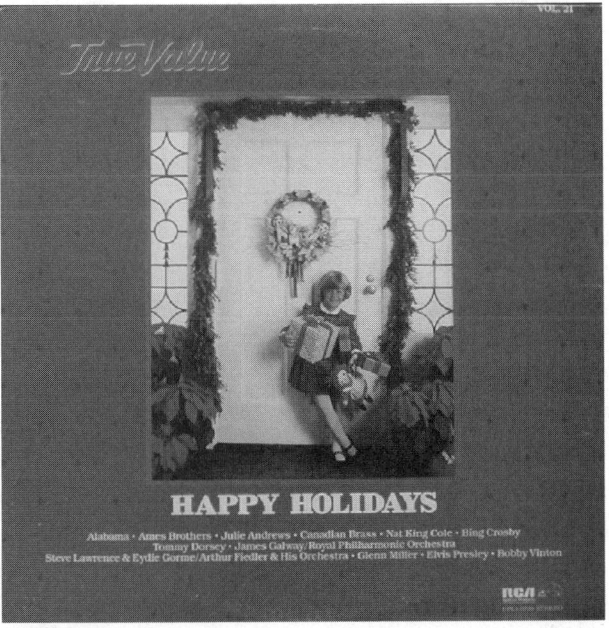

One of the many albums in the True Value Christmas series.

Trivia

"The Chipmunk Song (Christmas Don't Be Late)" by the Chipmunks sold more than four million records in its first five weeks of release. Its creator, David Seville (the pseudonym of Ross Bagdasarian), once created a national novelty hit with "Witch Doctor," by recording his voice at half-speed, switching the tape to full speed, and creating a high-pitched duetting partner. Some time later, he repeated this success, creating three high-pitched rodent crooners—Alvin, Simon and Theodore—for a Christmas single. Not only was the song a complete success, it spawned two television series ("The Alvin Show" and "Alvin and the Chipmunks"), and a series of popular albums that continue to this day (Bagdasarian's son Ross Jr. continues and oversees the family business).

The fastest selling single in the history of Liberty Records, The Chipmunks' "The Chipmunk Song."

Known Counterfeits / Bootlegs: Christmas compilations containing Elvis Presley or the Beatles have been prime candidates for counterfeiting. Because the Beatles released rare Christmas records to members of the Beatles Fan Club, counterfeit compilation albums containing those tracks have appeared. And a promo-only collection called Christmas Programming from RCA Victor (RCA Victor SP-33-66), containing the Elvis Presley track, "I'll Be Home For Christmas," has been counterfeited. Original copies have color covers; counterfeits are in black and white.

References: Neely, Tim, *Goldmine Christmas Record Price Guide*, Krause Publications, Iola, Wisconsin, 1997.

Web pages: Tony Paris' review of the best and worst **Christmas records:** *http://web.cln.com/archives/atlanta/newsstand/121397/amusic.htm.*

45s	Year	VG	VG+	NM
Original soundtrack, Amahl and the Night Visitors (four 7" 45s in box set, RCA Red Seal WDM-1701)	1952	$10.00	$20.00	$40.00
Louis Armstrong, "White Christmas" / "Winter Wonderland" (Decca 28443)	1952	$3.75	$7.50	$15.00
Gene Autry, "Rudolph The Red Nosed Reindeer"				
(if on Columbia 1-375, microgroove 33 1/3 rpm 7" single, "If It Doesn't Snow on Christmas" on B-side)	1949	$10.00	$20.00	$40.00
(if on Columbia 6-375, 45 reissue of Columbia 1-375, "If It Doesn't Snow on Christmas" on B-side)	1950	$6.25	$12.50	$25.00
(if on Columbia 4-56 (90049), on yellow label, "If It Doesn't Snow on Christmas" on B-side)	1951	$5.00	$10.00	$20.00
(with picture sleeve, add:)	1951	$6.25	$12.50	$25.00
(if on Columbia 38610, "If It Doesn't Snow on Christmas" on B-side)	1951	$3.75	$7.50	$15.00
(if on Columbia 39463, "Here Comes Santa Claus [Down Santa Claus Lane]" on B-side)	1951	$3.00	$6.00	$12.00
(if on Challenge 1010, re-recordings, with "Here Comes Santa Claus" on B-side)	1957	$3.00	$6.00	$12.00
(if on Challenge 59030, re-recordings, with "Here Comes Santa Claus" on B-side)	1958	$3.00	$6.00	$12.00
(with picture sleeve, add:)	1958	$5.00	$10.00	$20.00
(if on Cricket CX-6, with "Tinker Town Santa Claus" on the B-side)	196?	$3.00	$6.00	$12.00
(if on Mistletoe 801, "Up on the House Top" on B-side)	196?	$2.00	$4.00	$8.00
(if on Republic 1405, "Here Comes Santa Claus" on B-side)	1969	$2.00	$4.00	$8.00
(if on Columbia Hall of Fame 33165, red-black label, "Here Comes Santa Claus" on B-side)	1970		$2.50	$5.00
(if on Republic 326, "Here Comes Santa Claus" on B-side)	1976		$2.00	$4.00
(if on Columbia Hall of Fame 33165, gray label, "Here Comes Santa Claus" on B-side)	198?			$3.00
Band Aid, "Do They Know It's Christmas" / "Feed The World" (Columbia 04749)	1984		$2.50	$5.00
(with picture sleeve, add:)	1984		$2.50	$5.00
The Beatles, "Season's Greetings from the Beatles" (Beatles Fan Club 1964) (soundsheet)	1964	$75.00	$150.00	$300.00
The Beatles, "Beatles Third Christmas Record" (Beatles Fan Club 1965, Lyntone 948e) (soundsheet)	1965	$20.00	$40.00	$80.00
(with picture sleeve, add)	1965	$25.00	$50.00	$100.00
Cheech and Chong, "Santa Claus and His Old Lady" / "Dave" (Ode 66021)	1971	$2.00	$4.00	$8.00
(with picture sleeve, add)	1971	$3.00	$6.00	$12.00
The Chipmunks, "The Chipmunk Song" / "Almost Good" (Liberty 55168)				
(if on blue-green label)	1958	$6.25	$12.50	$25.00
(if on black label)	1958	$7.50	$15.00	$30.00
The Chipmunks, "The Chipmunk Song" / "Alvin's Harmonica" (Liberty 55250)				
(if on blue-green label, no horizontal lines)	1959	$3.75	$7.50	$15.00
(with picture sleeve, artwork looks like real chipmunks, add:)	1959	$10.00	$20.00	$40.00
(if on blue-green label, horizontal lines on label)	1961	$3.00	$6.00	$12.00
(with picture sleeve depicting Chipmunks as the cartoon characters we've come to know and love)	1961	$7.50	$15.00	$30.00
Bing Crosby, "White Christmas" / "God Rest Ye Merry Gentlemen"				
(if on Decca 23778, lines label, Sides 5 and 6 of "Album No. 9-65")	1950	$3.00	$6.00	$12.00
(if on Decca 23778, star on label	1955	$2.50	$5.00	$10.00
(if on Decca 23778, rainbow bars on label)	1960	$2.00	$4.00	$8.00
(with picture sleeve on 1960 release, add:)	1960	$3.75	$7.50	$15.00

45s	Year	VG	VG+	NM
(if on MCA 65022, black label with rainbow)	1973		$2.00	$4.00
(if on MCA 40830, B-side is "When the Blue of the Night Meets the Gold of the Day")	1977		$2.50	$5.00
(with picture sleeve on 1977 release, add:)	1977		$2.50	$5.00
(if on MCA 65022, blue label with rainbow)	1980			$3.00
The Drifters, "White Christmas" / "The Bells of St. Mary's" (Atlantic 1048)				
(first pressing, yellow label, no pinwheel below the "A" in Atlantic)	1954	$10.00	$20.00	$40.00
(second pressing, red label, no pinwheel below the "A" in Atlantic)	1956	$6.25	$12.50	$25.00
(white label promo)	1956	$6.25	$12.50	$25.00
(third pressing, red label, pinwheel below the "A" in Atlantic)	1962	$2.00	$4.00	$8.00
(glossy yellow label, with pinwheel)	197?		$2.50	$5.00
Elmo 'n Patsy, "Grandma Got Run Over By A Reindeer" / "Christmas"				
(if on "Elmo 'n Patsy" records, first pressings)	1979	$5.00	$10.00	$20.00
(if on Oink 2984, second pressings)	1979	$2.00	$4.00	$8.00
(if on Soundwaves 4658, third pressings)	1979		$3.00	$6.00
(if on Epic 04703, new recording, "Percy, the Puny Poinsettia" on the B-side)	1984		$2.00	$4.00
(with picture sleeve, add:)	1984		$2.00	$4.00
(if on Epic 05479, gray label reissue of Epic 04703)	1985			$3.00
The Five Keys, "It's Christmas Time" / "Old Mac Donald" (Aladdin 3113)	1951	$200.00	$400.00	$800.00
The Four Seasons, "Santa Claus is Coming to Town" / "Christmas Tears" (Vee Jay 478)	1962	$6.25	$12.50	$25.00
Dickie Goodman and the Polar Bears, "Santa and the Touchables" / "North Pole Rock"	1961	$6.25	$12.50	$25.00
Vince Guaraldi, "Christmas Time Is Here" / "What Child Is This" (Fantasy 608)	1966	$5.00	$10.00	$20.00
Jimi Hendrix, "Medley: The Little Drummer Boy - Silent Night" / "Auld Lang Syne" (Reprise PRO 595, white label promo)	1974	$45.00	$90.00	$180.00
John Lennon and Yoko Ono, "Happy Xmas (War Is Over)" / "Listen, The Snow Is Falling" (Apple 1842)				
(if catalog number S45X-47663/4, white label on styrene pressing)	1971	$187.50	$375.00	$750.00
(if on Apple 1842, green vinyl, faces label)	1971	$3.75	$7.50	$15.00
(if on Apple 1842, green vinyl, Apple label)	1971	$2.50	$5.00	$10.00
Darlene Love, "Christmas (Baby Please Come Home)"				
(if on Philles 119, B-side is "Harry and Milt Meet Hal B.")	1963	$10.00	$20.00	$40.00
(if on Philles 125, B-side is "X-Mas Blues")	1964	$100.00	$200.00	$400.00
(if on Philles 125X, B-side was replaced by "Winter Wonderland")	1965	$6.25	$12.50	$25.00
(if on Warner-Spector 0401, B-side is "Winter Wonderland")	1974	$2.50	$5.00	$10.00
(if on Passport 7926, B-side is "Playing For Keeps")	1983	$3.00	$6.00	$12.00
The Manhattan Transfer, "The Christmas Song" (same on both sides) (no label) (issued to fan club and friends)	1984	$7.50	$15.00	$30.00
(with picture sleeve, add:)	1984	$7.50	$15.00	$30.00
R.E.M., "Parade of the Wooden Soldiers" / "See No Evil" (Fan Club U-23518M) (issued to fan club, exists in both white and green vinyl, value is equal)	1988	$12.50	$25.00	$50.00
Frank Sinatra, "White Christmas" / "The Christmas Waltz"				
(if on Capitol F2954)	1954	$5.00	$10.00	$20.00
(if on Capitol 2954, red-yellow swirl label)	1962	$2.50	$5.00	$10.00
The Soul Stirrers, "Christmas Joy" / "I Know I'll Be Free" (Checker 5007)	195?	$3.00	$6.00	$12.00
The Supremes, "Children's Christmas Song" / "Twinkle Twinkle Little Me" (Motown 1085)				
(if on red vinyl)	1965	$6.25	$12.50	$25.00
(if on black vinyl)	1965	$3.75	$7.50	$15.00
"Weird Al" Yankovic, "Christmas At Ground Zero" / "One Of These Days" (Rock 'n Roll 06588)	1986		$2.50	$5.00
(with picture sleeve, add:)	1986		$2.50	$5.00

LPs	Year	VG	VG+	NM
Original Soundtrack, Amahl and the Night Visitors (RCA Red Seal LM-1701, 1951 NBC soundtrack)				
(if on 10" LP)	1952	$12.50	$25.00	$50.00

LPs	Year	VG	VG+	NM
(if on 12" record in hinged box with booklet)	1952	$10.00	$20.00	$40.00
Original Soundtrack, Amahl and the Night Visitors (1963 NBC soundtrack)				
(if mono, RCA Red Seal LM-2762)	1964	$3.75	$7.50	$15.00
(if stereo, RCA Red Seal LSC-2762, large "RCA Victor" and dog at top of label)	1964	$3.75	$7.50	$15.00
(if stereo, RCA Red Seal LSC-2762, red label, no dog)	1969	$3.00	$6.00	$12.00
(if stereo, RCA Red Seal LSC-2762, red label, no dog, UPC bar code on back cover)	198?	$2.50	$5.00	$10.00
Original Soundtrack, Rudolph The Red-Nosed Reindeer				
(if on Decca DL-4815, mono pressing)	1964	$15.00	$30.00	$60.00
(if on Decca DL-74815, stereo pressing)	1964	$20.00	$40.00	$80.00
(if on Decca DL-34327, custom pressing)	1965	$10.00	$20.00	$40.00
(if on MCA 15003, reissue)	1973	$5.00	$10.00	$20.00
The Boston Pops Orchestra, Arthur Fiedler, Cond., Pops Christmas Party				
(if RCA Red Seal LSC-2329, "shaded dog," small "RCA" logo)	1959	$20.00	$40.00	$80.00
(if RCA Red Seal LSC-2329, "white dog" with large "RCA" logo)	1964	$7.50	$15.00	$30.00
(if RCA Gold Seal AGL1-3436)	1979	$2.50	$5.00	$10.00
James Brown, Christmas Songs (King 1010)				
(if cover has wreath on gray wall, no song titles on back, mono LP)	1966	$25.00	$80.00	$160.00
(if cover has wreath on gray wall, no song titles on back, stereo LP)	1966	$37.50	$75.00	$150.00
(if cover has wreath on white wall, song titles on back, mono LP)	1967	$20.00	$40.00	$80.00
(if cover has wreath on white wall, song titles on back, stereo LP)	1967	$25.00	$50.00	$100.00
Bing Crosby, Merry Christmas (Decca DL 5019) (10-inch LP)	1949	$15.00	$30.00	$60.00
The Vince Guaraldi Trio, A Charlie Brown Christmas (Fantasy 8431)				
(if dark blue label)	1971	$6.25	$12.50	$25.00
(if light blue label, "1988" stamped on back cover)	1988	$3.75	$7.50	$15.00
Original Motion Picture Soundtrack, The Littlest Angel (Mercury 1-603)	1969	$4.00	$8.00	$16.00
Mannheim Steamroller, Mannheim Steamroller Christmas (American Gramophone AG-1984)	1984	$3.75	$7.50	$15.00
Elvis Presley, Elvis' Christmas Album				
(if on RCA Victor LOC-1035, mono, gatefold cover, gold print on LP spine)	1957	$150.00	$300.00	$600.00
(if on RCA Victor LOC-1035, mono, gatefold cover, silver print on LP spine)	1957	$175.00	$350.00	$700.00
(with golden sticker, "To ________ From _______", add:)	1957	$37.50	$75.00	$150.00
(red vinyl, may have been custom-pressed by factory employee after hours)	1957	$7,500.00	$11,250.00	$15,000.00
(if on RCA Victor LPM-1951, standard non-gatefold cover, "Long Play" on bottom of label)	1958	$25.00	$50.00	$100.00
(if on RCA Victor LPM-1951, "mono" on bottom of label, "RE" on lower left front cover)	1963	$12.50	$25.00	$50.00
(if on RCA Victor LPM-1951, "monaural" on bottom of label, "RE" on lower left front cover)	1964	$10.00	$20.00	$40.00
(if on RCA Victor LSP-1951(e), dog and gramophone on top of label, rechanneled stereo)	1964	$12.50	$25.00	$50.00
(if on RCA Victor LSP-1951(e), orange label, stiff vinyl)	1968	$7.50	$15.00	$30.00
(if on RCA Camden CAL-2428, blue label, mono, stiff vinyl)	1970	$6.25	$12.50	$25.00
(if on RCA Camden CAL-2428, blue label, mono, flexible vinyl)	1971	$3.00	$6.00	$12.00
(if on Pickwick CAL-2428, mono, no Christmas trim on jacket border)	1975	$3.00	$6.00	$12.00
(if on Pickwick CAL-2428, mono, Christmas trim is on jacket border)	1976	$2.50	$5.00	$10.00
(if on RCA Victor AFM1-5486, green vinyl with booklet)	1985	$3.00	$6.00	$12.00
(if on RCA Victor AFM1-5486, black vinyl with booklet)	1985	$3.75	$7.50	$15.00
(if on RCA Special Products CAL-2428, mono, reissue for The Special Music Company)	1986	$3.75	$7.50	$15.00
Various Artists, Christmas Through The Years (Reader's Digest RDA-143) (5 LPs)	1984	$5.00	$10.00	$20.00
Various Artists, A Christmas Gift For You From Phil Spector				
(if on Philles PHLP-4005, mono, first pressings have blue-black labels)	1963	$37.50	$75.00	$150.00
(if on Philles PHLP-4005, mono, second pressings have red-yellow labels)	1964	$20.00	$40.00	$80.00
(if on Apple SW 3400, mono, retitled "Phil Spector's Christmas Album")	1972	$7.50	$15.00	$30.00
(if on Warner/Spector SP 9103, mono, retitled "Phil Spector's Christmas Album")	1974	$5.00	$10.00	$20.00
(if on Pavillion PZ 37686, true stereo, retitled "Phil Spector's Christmas Album")	1981	$3.75	$7.50	$15.00
(if on Passport PB 3604, true stereo, retitled "Phil Spector's Christmas Album")	1984	$3.00	$6.00	$12.00
(if on Phil Spector/Rhino RNLP 70235, mono)	1987	$3.00	$6.00	$12.00
(if on Phil Spector/Abkco D1-4005, mono)	1989	$5.00	$10.00	$20.00
(if part of 5-LP set "Phil Spector: Back to Mono 1958-1969", value is for entire set)	1991	$25.00	$50.00	$100.00
Various Artists, Favorite Christmas Carols from the Voice of Firestone (Firestone MLP 7005)	1962	$3.75	$7.50	$15.00
Various Artists, Goodyear Presents The Great Songs of Christmas (RCA Special DLP1-0285)	1977	$2.50	$5.00	$10.00
Various Artists, Happy Holidays, Volume III (RCA Victor PRS-255) (sold only at True Value stores)	1967	$3.75	$7.50	$15.00

A Calypso Christmas album with Harry Belafonte.

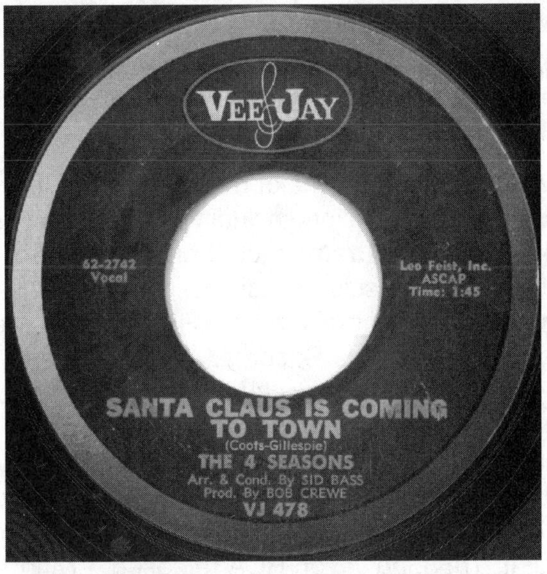

The Four Seasons doo-wop version of "Santa Claus is Coming to Town."

CLASSICAL

History: Classical music encompasses the greatest composers in history, whose last names alone delineate their accomplishments. Bach. Beethoven. Brahms. Haydn. Handel. Verdi. Mozart. Rimsky-Korsakov. Gershwin. Vivaldi. Chopin. Debussy.

Their music has been interpreted by symphony orchestras from Boston to Paris, from London to Minneapolis, orchestras guided by conductors such as Sergei Ozawa, Michael Tilson-Thomas, Arthur Fiedler, Fritz Reiner, and Leopold Stokowski. And collectors of their music avidly search out the most vibrant, breathtaking and sonically superior performances, searching for the greatest compositions of all time—by the greatest orchestras of all time.

While nearly every major record label had its own classical music division, including Columbia Masterworks, Deutsche Gramophon, London, and Angel, the two labels classical music collectors search for today are RCA Victor Red Seal Records and Mercury Living Presence Records.

The "Red Seal" division of RCA Records, dedicated to classical and opera music, had been around since the first Victor 78s at the turn of the century. Up until 1958, RCA had a respectable classical album line, although all its releases were monaural. In 1958, however, RCA released "Living Stereo" albums, allowing audiophiles and music lovers the opportunity to hear works by the great masters in thrilling stereo sound.

The front cover of an RCA Victor Red Seal "Living Stereo" album will have a 1-1/2-inch black strip along its top, with the words "Living Stereo" inside. Later issues will only have a 1-inch black strip, but the word "Living Stereo" will still be visible.

RCA's inside labels during that time period were also breathtaking. The "His Master's Voice" trademark (a gramophone and Nipper the fox terrier) were in full color on a red background. A deep shade of gray exists behind Nipper and his gramophone, so much so that these pressings are referred to as "Shaded Dogs," and generally are the most collectible of all RCA Red Seal issues.

Known for his PBS concert shows in the 1970s, Arthur Fiedler is one of the most well-recognized symphony conductors of the 20th century.

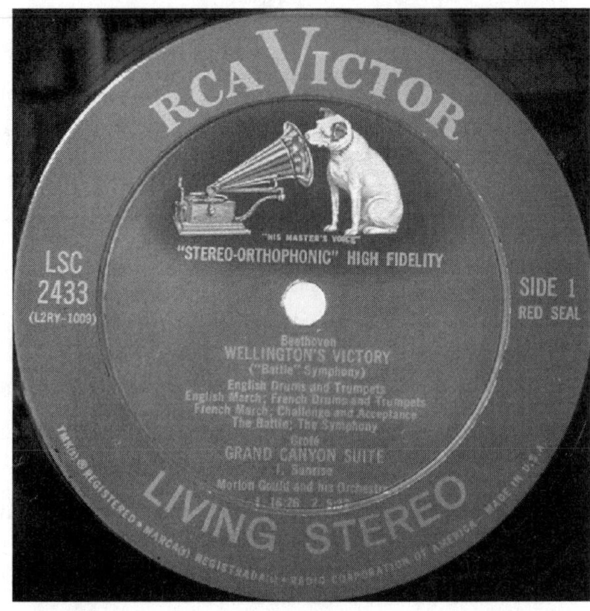

An example of an RCA Victor Red Seal "Shaded Dog" release. Notice the dark gray background behind Nipper and the gramophone. Courtesy Last Vestige Music Store, Albany, N.Y.

By the early 1960s, however, RCA had reissued many of its titles with a new label scheme. This time the labels were bright red, without any shading. These pressings are known as "White Dogs" because of the striking contrast of Nipper's body against the red label.

The end of RCA's "Golden Era" of classical music came in 1964, when the company invented a new recording technology called "Dynagroove." Dynagroove was an equalization recording process that made records sound better on low-end equipment—you could get the same sound from your GE Wildcat portable phonograph as did your neighbor with his $3,000 hi-fi system. But for audiophiles and wide range equipment owners, the records on Dynagroove-pressed albums were too brassy and boomy. The records were pressed on flimsy, flexible "dynaflex" vinyl. And to top it all off, many of the classical albums continued to use the "Living Stereo" imprint on their album jackets. In these instances, always check the record inside to make sure that you're purchasing a "Shaded Dog" RCA Victor Red Seal album, and not a poor-quality "Dynagroove" version.

The other collectible classical albums are from the Mercury Living Presence label. Although the company pressed monaural and stereo albums, the stereo recordings are the most collectible in the series. Look for the word "STEREO" on top of the album jacket, on a 1-1/2-inch wide strip. The words "Hi-Fi" will be above the "T" in "STEREO." The words "Mercury Living Presence" can be found on the right side of the cover, in a small banner.

The first Mercury Living Presence releases have deep maroon labels. There should be no reference on the label to "Vendor: Mercury Record Corporation"; if you see those words, you have a later pressing. Other late pressings have light maroon labels; some have orange labels.

This label artwork, without any reference to "Vendor: Mercury Record Corporation," is much more collectible than a variation with those four words on the label. Courtesy Last Vestige Music Store, Albany, N.Y.

Another collectible classical label are London "blue backs." They will have a red "ffss" on the label, and the earliest pressings of these records are collectible. What is more collectible in this line are the equivalent titles pressed from Decca Records in England, American London's British parent label.

This does not mean that these labels were the only ones that produced classical music albums. They are, however, the companies which took the greatest care with their recordings. The orchestras were miked for proper stereo separation. The best and heaviest vinyl available was used for pressings. Surface noise was reduced to infinitesimal levels. In other words, during the 1950s and early 1960s, these records were as close to a living performance as one could achieve.

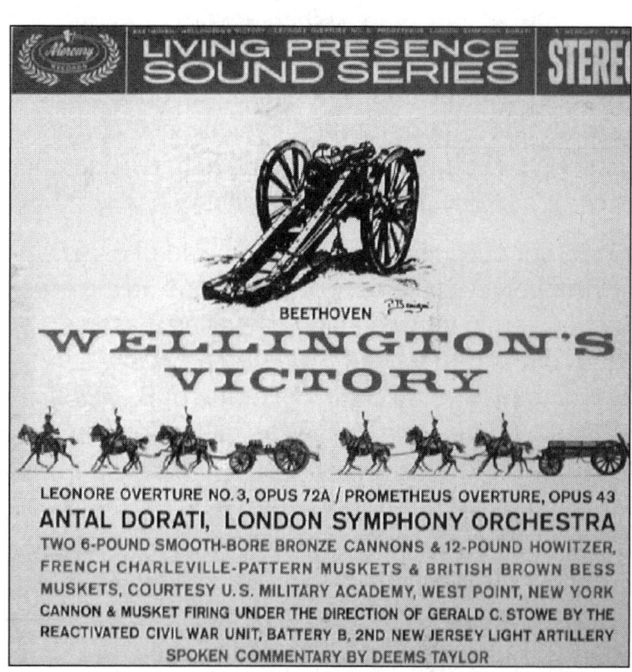

Mercury Living Presence albums had some of the thickest cover jackets of the era. This jacket even had a laminated cellophane cover. Courtesy Last Vestige Music Store, Albany, N.Y.

What To Look For: With the birth of compact discs in the 1980s, many audiophiles left their record collections for the promise of superior sonic performance from a 5-inch mirrored aluminum disc. But while many audiophiles stuck with the compact disc as a viable listening alternative, others felt the digitally-created output from CDs did not match the analog recording output of a phonograph record, and those collectors continued to search for classical vinyl.

In 1997, the audiophile label Classic Records started reissuing many rare classical albums, including titles from the RCA Victor Red Seal and Mercury Living Presence labels. Although these reissues have limited collectible value in comparison to the original releases, they are produced with the same care and quality control that both classical music lovers and audiophiles expect from their albums.

Some classical record collectors specialize in 78 RPM releases. Although the works of Enrico Caruso are considered musical masterpieces of their day, his Victor releases are very common and languish in flea market bins; 78 RPM classical collectors will search for Caruso's earliest recordings on Zon-O-Phone and Pathé, as these discs are extremely rare and few have survived to this day.

Among classical music genres, the most desirous recordings are violin solos. Soloists from the 1940s to the 1960s, including Jascha Heifitz, Mischa Elman and Josef Szigeti, are highly prized by collectors today. For example, the three-LP boxed set of Bach sonatas, as performed by violinist George Enescu, is extremely rare and, despite its existence on compact disc, is highly collectible on vinyl.

Another collectible genre in the field of classical music involves classical interpretations on the Moog synthesizer. In fact, the biggest selling classical album of the 1960s was *Switched-on Bach*, a recording by Wendy Carlos of some of Bach's greatest sonatas and concertos, all performed on the earliest Moog synthesizers. The *Switched-on Bach* album eventually spawned a whole series of imitators, with performers playing everything from Beethoven to the Beatles on their electric keyboards.

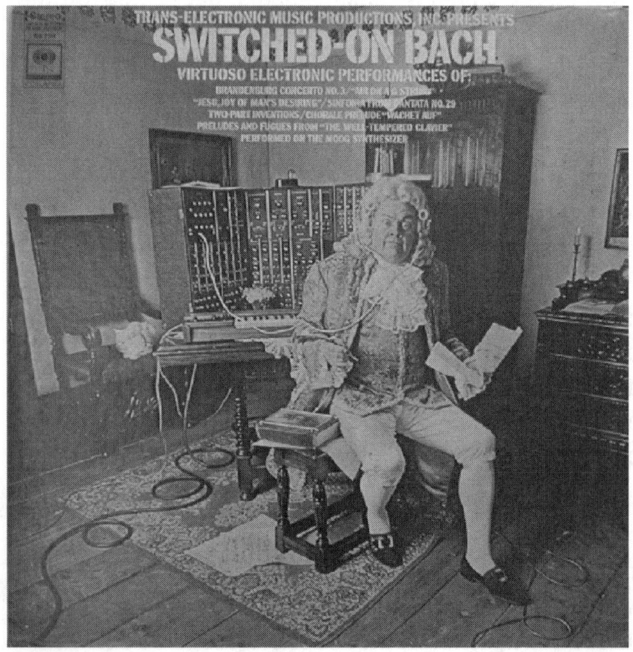

The first pressings of *Switched-On Bach* featured Bach sitting in front of the synthesizer. Notice his headphones are plugged into an input jack.

In later pressings, Bach is seen standing in front of the synthesizer, as if to proudly present the future of classical music.

References: Canfield, David, *The Canfield Guide to Classical Recordings* (5th Edition), 2000. Available at 812-876-6553, or at *http://www.arsantiqua.com*; Mitchell, James A., *The Golden Era of RCA Records*, 16th Ed., Irvington Music, Portland, Ore., 1990, *http://www.irvmusic.com*; Pogue, David, and Speck, Scott, *Classical Music for Dummies*, IDG Books Worldwide, Foster City, CA, 1997.

Museums: The American Classical Music Hall of Fame and Museum, The Herschede Building, 4 West Fourth St., Cincinnati, Ohio 45202, 1-800-499-3263, h*ttp://www.classicalhall.org*

Web pages: Parnassus Records, a seller and buyer of classical albums: *http://www.parnassusrecords.com*; A discography of all Mercury Living Presence classical LPs: *http://www.4music.net/hifiheaven/mercury*; Wendy Carlos' personal home page: *http://www.wendycarlos.com.*

LPs	Year	VG	VG+	NM
Gina Bachauer, Chopin: Piano Concerto No. 2 in F; Fantasy in F (Mercury Living Presence SR 90432) (stereo) (with maroon label, and no reference to "Vendor: Mercury Record Corporation")	1965	$10.00	$20.00	$40.00
The Boston Pops Orchestra, Arthur Fiedler, Conductor, Pops Stoppers (RCA Victor Red Seal LSC-2270) (stereo) (if original with "shaded dog" label)	1959	$5.00	$10.00	$20.00
The Boston Pops Orchestra, Arthur Fiedler, Conductor, Pops Christmas Party (RCA Victor Red Seal LSC-2329) (stereo) (if original with "shaded dog" label, large "Living Stereo" on cover)	1959	$20.00	$40.00	$80.00
(if reissue, with "white dog" on label, small "Living Stereo" on cover)	1964	$7.50	$15.00	$30.00
The Boston Pops Orchestra, Arthur Fiedler, Conductor, Gershwin: Rhapsody in Blue; An American In Paris (RCA Victor Red Seal LSC-2367) (stereo) (Earl Wild on piano, originals have "shaded dog" label)	1960	$5.00	$10.00	$20.00

LPs	Year	VG	VG+	NM
The Boston Pops Orchestra, Arthur Fiedler, Conductor, Everything But The Beer (RCA Victor Red Seal LSC-6082) (2 LPs) (stereo)				
(if original with "shaded dog" label)	1959	$30.00	$60.00	$120.00
Boston Symphony Orchestra, Pierre Monteux, Conductor, Tchaikovsky: Symphony No. 6 "Pathetique" (RCA Victor Red Seal LSC-1901) (stereo)				
(if original with "shaded dog" label)	1958	$12.50	$25.00	$50.00
(if Classic Records reissue, same catalog number)	199??	$6.25	$12.50	$25.00
Boston Symphony Orchestra, Charles Munch, Conductor, Ravel: Daphne and Chloe (RCA Victor Red Seal LSC-1893) (stereo)				
(if original with "shaded dog" label)	1958	$75.00	$150.00	$300.00
(if Classic Records reissue, same catalog number)	199??	$6.25	$12.50	$25.00
Boston Symphony Orchestra, Charles Munch, Conductor, Debussy: Images (RCA Victor Red Seal LSC-2282) (stereo)				
(if original with "shaded dog" label)	1959	$37.50	$75.00	$150.00
(if on RCA Victor Red Seal LM-2282, mono)	1959	$5.00	$10.00	$20.00
Boston Symphony Orchestra, Charles Munch, Conductor, Milhaude: La Creation du Monde; Suite Provencale (RCA Victor Red Seal LSC-2625) (stereo)				
(if original with "shaded dog" label)	1962	$50.00	$100.00	$200.00
(if later pressing, with "white dog" label)	1962	$37.50	$75.00	$150.00
(if Classic Records reissue, same catalog number)	199??	$6.25	$12.50	$25.00
Walter Carlos / Wendy Carlos, Switched-on Bach (Columbia MS 7194)				
(no performer credit on cover, gray label, "360 Sound Stereo")	1968	$3.75	$7.50	$15.00
("Walter Carlos" on cover, orange Columbia logos, "360 Sound Stereo")	1970	$3.00	$6.00	$12.00
Chicago Symphony Orchestra, Fritz Reiner, Conductor, Strauss: Also Sprach Zarathustra (RCA Victor Red Seal LSC-1806) (stereo)				
(if original with "shaded dog" label)	1958	$37.50	$75.00	$150.00
(if Classic Records reissue, same catalog number)	199??	$6.25	$12.50	$25.00
Chicago Symphony Orchestra, Fritz Reiner, Conductor, Mussorgsky-Ravel: Pictures at an Exhibition (RCA Victor Red Seal LSC-2201) (stereo)				
(if original with "shaded dog" label)	1959	$20.00	$40.00	$80.00
(if second pressing with "white dog" label)	1964	$7.50	$15.00	$30.00
Chicago Symphony Orchestra, Fritz Reiner, Conductor, Strauss, Richard: Don Quixote (RCA Victor Red Seal LDS-2384) (stereo)				
(if original with "shaded dog" label)	1960	$12.50	$25.00	$50.00
(if on RCA Victor Red Seal LSS-2384, limited edition of 200 in box with booklet)	1960	$30.00	$60.00	$120.00
Chicago Symphony Orchestra, Fritz Reiner, Conductor, The Heart of the Symphony (RCA Victor Red Seal LSC-2496) (stereo)				
(if original with "shaded dog" label)	1961	$10.00	$20.00	$40.00
Van Cliburn, Tchaikovsky: Piano Concerto No. 1 (RCA Victor Red Seal LSC-2252)				
(if original with "shaded dog" label)	1958	$7.50	$15.00	$30.00
(if later pressing with "white dog" label)	1965	$5.00	$10.00	$20.00
(if on RCA Victor Red Seal LM-2252, mono)	1958	$6.25	$12.50	$25.00
Van Cliburn, Prokofiev: Piano Concerto No. 3; MacDowell: Piano Concerto No. 2 (RCA Victor Red Seal LSC-2507)				
(if original with "shaded dog" label)	1961	$12.50	$25.00	$50.00
(if later pressing with "white dog" label)	1965	$5.00	$10.00	$20.00
Detroit Symphony Orchestra, Paul Paray, Conductor, Debussy: La Mer; Iberia (Mercury Living Presence SR 90010) (stereo)				
(if maroon label, no reference to "Vendor: Mercury Record Corporation")	1959	$50.00	$100.00	$200.00
Detroit Symphony Orchestra, Paul Paray, Conductor, Schumann: Symphony No. 3, "Rhenish" (Mercury Living Presence SR 90133) (stereo)				
(if maroon label, no reference to "Vendor: Mercury Record Corporation")	1960	$7.50	$15.00	$30.00
Detroit Symphony Orchestra, Paul Paray, Conductor, Franck: Symphony in D (Mercury Living Presence SR 90285) (stereo)				
(if maroon label, no reference to "Vendor: Mercury Record Corporation")	196??	$17.50	$35.00	$70.00
(if maroon label, "Vendor: Mercury Record Corporation" is on label)	196??	$7.50	$15.00	$30.00
Marcel Dupré, Dupre at Saint-Sulpice, Vol. 1 (Mercury Living Presence SR 90227) (stereo)				
(if maroon label, no reference to "Vendor: Mercury Record Corporation")	196??	$15.00	$30.00	$60.00
Marcel Dupré, Organ Recital (Mercury Living Presence SR 90169) (stereo)				
(if maroon label, no reference to "Vendor: Mercury Record Corporation")	196??	$30.00	$60.00	$120.00
(if maroon label, "Vendor: Mercury Record Corporation" is on label)	196??	$60.00	$120.00	$240.00
Eastman-Rochester Orchestra, Frederick Fennell, Conductor, Hi-Fi A La Espanola (Mercury Living Presence SR 90144) (stereo)				
(if maroon label, no reference to "Vendor: Mercury Record Corporation")	196??	$250.00	$500.00	$1,000.00
(if Classic Records reissue, with same catalog number)	199??	$6.25	$12.50	$25.00
Eastman-Rochester Orchestra, Howard Hanson, Conductor, The Composer and His Orchestra (Mercury Living Presence SR 90175) (stereo)				
(if maroon label, no reference to "Vendor: Mercury Record Corporation")	196??	$17.50	$35.00	$70.00
(if maroon label, "Vendor: Mercury Record Corporation" on label)	196??	$6.25	$12.50	$25.00
Eastman-Rochester Wind Ensemble, Frederick Fennell, Conductor, British Band Classics, Vol. 2 (Mercury Living Presence SR 90197) (stereo)				
(if maroon label, no reference to "Vendor: Mercury Record Corporation")	196??	$18.75	$37.50	$75.00
(if maroon label, "Vendor: Mercury Record Corporation" is on label)	196??	$15.00	$30.00	$60.00
(if dark red - not maroon - label)	196??	$7.50	$15.00	$30.00
Mischa Elman, Grieg: Violin Sonatas 1 and 3 (London LL 1253)	1955	$62.50	$125.00	$250.00
George Enescu, Bach: Six Sonatas and Partitas (Continental CLP 104) (3 LP's)				
(in original box)	1948??	$2,500	$5,000	$10,000
Festival Quartet, Schubert: Trout Quintet (RCA Victor Red Seal LSC-2147) (stereo)				
(if original with "shaded dog" label)	1958	$37.50	$75.00	$150.00
(if later pressing with "white dog" label)	1964	$30.00	$60.00	$120.00
Morton Gould, Tchaikovsky: 1812 Overture; Ravel: Bolero (RCA Victor Red Seal LSC-2345) (stereo)				
(if original with "shaded dog" label)	1960	$5.00	$10.00	$20.00
Halle Orchestra, John Barbirolli, Conductor, Williams, Vaughan: Symphony No. 8; Bax: Garden of Fand; Butterworth: Shropshire Lad (Mercury Living Presence SR 90115) (stereo)				
(if maroon label, no reference to "Vendor: Mercury Record Corporation")	1960	$12.50	$25.00	$50.00
Jascha Heifitz, Tchaikovsky: Violin Concerto (RCA Victor Red Seal LSC-2129) (stereo)				
(with Fritz Reiner/Chicago Symphony Orchestra; if original with "shaded dog" label)	1958	$7.50	$15.00	$30.00
(if Classic Records reissue, with same catalog number)	1999	$6.25	$12.50	$25.00
Jascha Heifitz, Glazunov: Violin Concerto; Mozart: Sinfonia Concertante (RCA Victor Red Seal LSC-2734) (stereo)				
(if original with "shaded dog" label)	1963	$25.00	$50.00	$100.00
Julliard String Quartet, Schubert: String Quartet No. 14, "Death and the Maiden" (RCA Victor Red Seal LSC-2378) (stereo)				
(if original with "shaded dog" label)	1960	$37.50	$75.00	$150.00
Julliard String Quartet, Beethoven: String Quartet in C# Minor (RCA Victor Red Seal LSC-2616) (stereo)				
(if original with "shaded dog" label)	1962	$10.00	$20.00	$40.00
London Proms Symphony Orchestra, Charles Mackerras, Conductor, Sibelius: Finlandia (RCA Victor Red Seal LSC-2336) (stereo)				
(if original with "shaded dog" label)	1960	$17.50	$35.00	$70.00
(if Classic Records reissue, with same catalog number)	199??	$6.25	$12.50	$25.00
London Symphony Orchestra, Antal Dorati, Conductor, Respighi: The Birds; Brazilian Impressions (Mercury Living Presence SR 90153) (stereo)				
(if maroon label, no reference to "Vendor: Mercury Record Corporation")	196??	$45.00	$90.00	$180.00
(if maroon label, "Vendor: Mercury Record Corporation" is on label)	196??	$20.00	$40.00	$80.00
London Symphony Orchestra, Antal Dorati, Conductor, Liszt: Hungarian Rhapsodies Nos. 1, 4, 5 and 6 (Mercury Living Presence SR 90371) (stereo)				
(if maroon label, no reference to "Vendor: Mercury Record Corporation")	196??	$100.00	$200.00	$400.00
(if maroon label, "Vendor: Mercury Record Corporation" is on label)	196??	$15.00	$30.00	$60.00
(if dark red - not maroon - label)	196??	$7.50	$15.00	$30.00
London Symphony Orchestra, Alexander Gibson, Conductor, Sibelius: Symphony No. 5 (RCA Victor Red Seal LSC-2405) (stereo)				
(if original with "shaded dog" label)	1960	$37.50	$75.00	$150.00
(if Classic Records reissue, with same catalog number)	199??	$6.25	$12.50	$25.00
Minneapolis Symphony Orchestra, Antal Dorati, Conductor, Mussorgsky: Pictures at an Exhibition (Mercury Living Presence SR 90217) (stereo)				
(if maroon label, no reference to "Vendor: Mercury Record Corporation")	196??	$30.00	$60.00	$120.00
(if maroon label, "Vendor: Mercury Record Corporation" is on label)	196??	$5.00	$10.00	$20.00
Minneapolis Symphony Orchestra, Stanislaw Skrowaczewski, Conductor, Khachatourian: Gayne Ballet; Shostakovich: Symphony No. 5 (Mercury Living Presence SR 90060) (stereo)				

LPs	Year	VG	VG+	NM
(if maroon label, no reference to "Vendor: Mercury Record Corporation")	1960	$50.00	$100.00	$200.00
Minneapolis Symphony Orchestra, Stanislaw Skrowaczewski, Conductor, Schubert: Symphony No. 7 (9) in C (Mercury Living Presence SR 90272) (stereo)				
(if maroon label, no reference to "Vendor: Mercury Record Corporation")	196??	$10.00	$20.00	$40.00
NBC Symphony Orchestra, Leopold Stokowski, Conductor, The Sound of Stokowski and Wagner (RCA Victor Red Seal LSC-2555) (stereo)				
(if original with "shaded dog" label)	1961	$7.50	$15.00	$30.00
New York Philharmonic Orchestra, Bruno Walter, Conductor, Mendelssohn: Violin Concerto (Columbia Masterworks ML 4001) (mono)				
(Violinist Nathan Milstein performs on this, the very first Microgroove LP)	1948	$10.00	$20.00	$40.00
(if Classic Records reissue, with same catalog number)	1999	$6.25	$12.50	$25.00
Paris Conservatoire Orchestre, Jean Martinon, Conductor, Prokofiev: Symphony No. 7 (RCA Victor Red Seal LSC-2288) (stereo)				
(if original with "shaded dog" label)	1959	$37.50	$75.00	$150.00
(if Classic Records reissue, with same catalog number)	199??	$6.25	$12.50	$25.00
Paris Conservatoire Orchestre, Albert Wolff, Conductor, Adam: Giselle (RCA Victor Red Seal LSC-2301) (stereo)				
(if original with "shaded dog" label)	1959	$17.50	$35.00	$70.00
RCA Victor Symphony Orchestra, Kiril Kondrashin, Conductor, Khachaturian: Masquerade Suite; Kabalevsky: The Comedians (RCA Victor Red Seal LSC-2398) (stereo)				
(if original with "shaded dog" label)	1960	$62.50	$125.00	$250.00
(if second edition with "white dog" label)	1964	$25.00	$50.00	$100.00
(if third edition with no dog on label)	1969	$6.25	$12.50	$25.00
(if Classic Records reissue, with same catalog number)	199??	$6.25	$12.50	$25.00
RCA Victor Symphony Orchestra, Leopold Stokowski, Conductor, Handel: Royal Fireworks Music, Water Music (RCA Victor Red Seal LSC-2612) (stereo)				
(if original with "shaded dog" label)	1962	$7.50	$15.00	$30.00
(if second edition with "white dog" label)	1964	$5.00	$10.00	$20.00
Arthur Rubenstein, Chopin: Scherzos 1-4 (RCA Victor Red Seal LSC-2368) (stereo)				
(if original with "shaded dog" label)	1960	$5.00	$10.00	$20.00
Josef Szigeti, Prokofiev: Violin Sonatas No. 1 and 2 (Mercury Living Presence SR 90319) (stereo)				
(if maroon label, no reference to "Vendor: Mercury Record Corporation")	196??	$37.50	$75.00	$150.00
Josef Szigeti, Mieczyslaw Horszowski, John Barrows, Brahms: Horn Trio; Violin Sonata No. 2 (Mercury Living Presence SR 90210) (stereo)				
(if maroon label, no reference to "Vendor: Mercury Record Corporation")	196??	$30.00	$60.00	$120.00

LPs	Year	VG	VG+	NM
(if maroon label, "Vendor: Mercury Record Corporation" on label)	196??	$12.50	$25.00	$50.00
Vienna Philharmonic Orchestra, Wilhelm Furtwangler, Conductor, Beethoven: Symphony No. 3 (Urania URLP-7095) (mono)				
(may have been withdrawn from the market when it was discovered the record was mastered too fast)	195??	$125.00	$250.00	$500.00
Vienna Philharmonic Orchestra, Fritz Reiner, Conductor, Strauss: Till Eulenspiegel (RCA Victor Red Seal LSC-2077) (stereo)				
(if original with "shaded dog" label)	1959	$20.00	$40.00	$80.00
(if Classic Records reissue, with same catalog number)	199??	$6.25	$12.50	$25.00

Classical albums can often be found with breathtaking vistas, exquisite artwork—or in the case of this album, a pretty face.

COLORED VINYL

History: Literally, every record ever made is pressed on colored vinyl. That's assuming, of course, that you're counting black as a color.

But for more than 100 years, record companies have pressed non-black records as special prizes for consumers, as collectible one-of-a-kind pressings, or to delineate the musical style on the record. Colored vinyl records are one of the hottest music collectibles today, as records are designed both to be played and to be shown off.

Colored vinyl records are not a new or recent phenomenon. Vinyl pressings go as far back as the dawn of the 20th century, when various companies mixed pigment into their shellac pressings, producing shades of red and blue and yellow in the finished product. But it wasn't until the 1950s, when record companies used polyvinyl chloride (PVC) for records, that colored vinyl pressings became more predominant and collectible.

The band Grand Funk went through a "colored vinyl" period—both this single and the album of the same name were pressed on clear yellow vinyl.

Before records are pressed, PVC pellets arrive at the record plant. The pellets are melted down and poured between the record stampers. A few seconds later, a black vinyl record is made. But black is not the only color of PVC available for pressing. PVC is also available in shades of red, green, blue, white, gold and clear. The careful mixture of each of these colors can create, when the PVC is melted, any color in the visual rainbow. Once the mixture is heated, it can come out looking like a frosty snow cone, it can come out in a pancake form and shaped like a hockey puck, or it can come out in noodle-like strips. The pressing agents keep records of every possible color formula, and can create enough of a color mixture so that the 50,000th pressing is as close to the same exact color as the first pressing.

A single color in a record is one thing, but some artists may want two or more colors in their pressings. A starburst pressing, for example, might require two melting machines, one for each separate color needed. Instead of the vinyl being processed as a flat disc, it is processed in noodle form, and the PVC noodles are placed on top of the stampers. Depending on how creative the stamping operators are, one can create starbursts, two-tone discs, or various other patterns.

In 1948, in an attempt to promote the new 45 RPM product that RCA Victor had designed, the company pressed its records with different colored vinyl—red vinyl for classical music, dark blue for "light classics," green for country, reddish orange, or "cerise" for blues or soul music, yellow for children's records, sky blue for international—and black vinyl for popular songs. Many of the red and blue records can still be found today, but the "cerise" recordings of Tampa Red, the Four Tunes, and the Five Trumpets are extremely difficult to find and are highly collectible.

Some colored vinyl records are truly one of a kind—and that's often because only one copy was pressed. During the 1960s, some pressing plant employees made "after-hours" pressings—in effect, a single record made from whatever colored vinyl is left in the office, the pressing made after hours at an employee's whim. "After hours" vinyl pressings exist of Elvis Presley recordings, Rolling Stones albums, and Ronettes 45s. Most of these pressings were made at independent record plants by late-night employees. When these records do come to light, they sell for large sums of money at auctions. Because there is no way of knowing how many "after hours" pressings were made, or where they were pressed, there is no way of actually knowing how many of these surreptitious albums exist today.

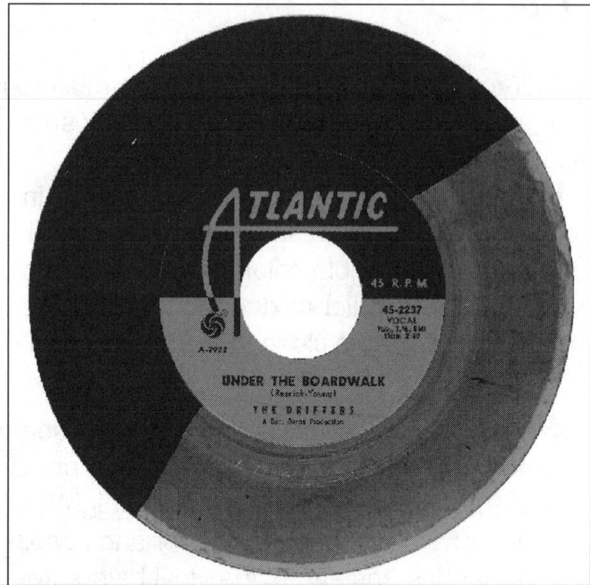

A rare example of an after-hours two-tone pressing, where sheets of both black and purple PVC were used in a pressing of a Drifters classic. Courtesy Good Rockin' Tonight/Collectors Universe.

Many colored vinyl releases were made concomitant to the standard black vinyl release. While the black vinyl records were sold in stores, colored vinyl pressings were often sent to disc jockeys in the hopes that a bright orange 45 might get played sooner than the 30th black vinyl 45 that appeared in the studio.

With few exceptions, virtually every colored vinyl 45 and LP is worth more than its black vinyl counterpart. One of the reasons this is so is because colored vinyl records are pressed in smaller runs; it is harder to maintain the same color consistently throughout a print run, while black vinyl records will always remain black from first pressing to last.

However, there are some instances where a black vinyl record is worth more than its colored vinyl counterpart. An example is Elvis Presley's album Moody Blue. Originally, the plan was to press blue vinyl copies for the first two months, then switch to black vinyl for the rest of the copies. Just as the record company changed over to black vinyl, Elvis Presley passed away. Immediately the company switched back to pressing blue-vinyl copies, ostensibly to provide Elvis Presley fans with a collectible souvenir. If it had only known that 20 years later, people would search out the rare black vinyl pressings (and some green, red, and white test pressings that were even rarer).

Colored vinyl records also tend to appear around Christmastime. Many holiday songs are pressed in red and green vinyl, the colors of Christmas. These pressings tend to be of translucent, or see-through vinyl, rather than of the opaque, or non-see-through, variety.

This promotional pink vinyl pressing may have impressed disc jockeys when they received it, but someone at the Big Top Records proofreading department mistitled Del Shannon's song "Two Kinds of Teardrops." Courtesy Good Rockin' Tonight/Collectors Universe.

John Lennon's peaceful Christmas song is very common—but desirable—in green Christmas vinyl.

During the 1960s, Columbia Records, along with its sister label Epic, pressed many of their biggest 45s in clear red vinyl, as special promotional records for radio stations. This means that red vinyl 45s exist for such artists as Bob Dylan, the Dave Clark Five, Simon and Garfunkel, the Cyrkle, Paul Revere and the Raiders, and Donovan.

A red vinyl "radio station copy" of a Simon and Garfunkel hit.

Record companies continued to produce promo-only colored vinyl 45s and LPs throughout the 1970s and 1980s, oftentimes with the color matching up with a particular artist's song. Madonna's "True Blue," for example, would appear on blue vinyl, while her album Like a Virgin would be pressed on virgin white vinyl.

Today, in an effort to bring back collectibility to current 45s, many reissue pressings are now on colored vinyl. Entire runs of Beatles singles, of Elvis Presley 45s and of Phil Spector's Philles recordings have been pressed on colored vinyl, and although these records do not contain the same collectibility as the original pressings did, they do have fans who can hold a record up to a light, see the colored light stream through the vinyl grooves, and say, "Cool, man."

What To Look For: Colored vinyl collecting is an easy collecting niche to get involved with; some people only collect red vinyl pressings (red is the most popular colored vinyl release), while others search for every possible hue in the spectrum.

Be aware that in the 1990s, many reissue companies have pressed colored vinyl pressings of 1950s and 1960s popular songs. Some of these companies even issue their colored vinyl product in boxed sets.

If you are unsure of whether a colored vinyl record exists as an original pressing or as a reproduction, examine the label carefully. For original pressings, the label artwork should be crisp and sharp; the letters should have sharp points, the lines should be straight. A reproduction may have rounded corners on the letters, or the lines might have small bulges in them, as if they were photocopied labels.

References: Neely, Tim, *Goldmine Price Guide to 45 RPM Records*, Krause Publications, Iola, Wisconsin, 1999; Neely, Tim, *Goldmine Price Guide to Alternative Records*, Krause Publications, Iola, Wisconsin, 1996.

Web pages: Erika Records is the leading producer of colored vinyl and picture disc records. Its Web site is as follows: *http://www.erikarecords.com*

Trivia

Sometimes the best way to see a colored vinyl 45 is through a bread-bag sleeve. Some record companies will bag their records in these clear plastic sleeves, which are very flimsy and wear down very quickly. Some examples of bread-bagging a colored vinyl record include Prince's "Purple Rain" and Kraftwerk's "Pocket Calculator" 45s.

The techno-rock pioneers Kraftwerk, with a song from their Computer World album. The B-side, "Dentaku," is actually the "Pocket Calculator" song in Japanese.

45s	Year	VG	VG+	NM
Faye Adams, "Shake a Hand" / "I've Got To Leave You" (Herald 416) (red vinyl)	1953	$25.00	$50.00	$100.00
Duane and Gregg Allman, "Morning Dew" (same on both sides) (Bold 200) (promo) (red vinyl)	1973	$5.00	$10.00	$20.00
Eddy Arnold, "The Lily Of the Valley" / "Evil, Tempt Me Not" (RCA Victor 48-0165) (green vinyl)	1950	$12.50	$25.00	$50.00
Chet Atkins, "Main Street Breakdown" / "Under the Hickory Nut Tree" (RCA Victor 48-0329) (green vinyl)	1950	$12.50	$25.00	$50.00
Donnie Baker and the Demensionals, "Drinkin' Pop Sodee-Odee (Pop Pop)" / "Sleepy Time Gal" (Rainbow 219) (red vinyl)	1953	$37.50	$75.00	$150.00
The Beatles, "Can't Buy Me Love" / "You Can't Do That" (Capitol 5150) (yellow vinyl) (after-hours pressing, unauthorized, value is conjecture)	1964	$2,000	$3,000	$4,000
The Beatles, "Norwegian Wood" / "If I Needed Someone" (Capitol S7-18888) (green vinyl, 1,000 copies pressed, given by Collector's Choice Music to buyers of Beatles reissue LPs)	1995	$12.50	$25.00	$50.00
Peter Best, "Casting My Spell" / "I'm Blue" (Mr. Maestro 712) (blue vinyl)	1965	$50.00	$100.00	$200.00
Pat Boone, "Blue Jean" / "Dancing with the Big Boys" (EMI America 8231) (blue vinyl)	1984	$2.00	$4.00	$8.00
Roy Brown, "Bar Room Blues" / "Good Rockin' Man" (Deluxe 3319) (blue vinyl)	1951	$100.00	$200.00	$400.00
The Byrds, "Mr. Tamourine Man" (same on both sides) (Columbia 43271) (red vinyl)	1965	$37.50	$75.00	$150.00
Al Casey, "Surfin' Hootenany" / "Easy Pickin'" (Stacy 962) (red vinyl)	1963	$10.00	$20.00	$40.00
The Champs, "Tequila" / "Train to Nowhere" (Challenge 1016) (blue vinyl; one copy is known to exist)	1958	$150.00	$300.00	$600.00
Chubby Checker, "The Twist" / "Twistin' U.S.A." (Parkway 811) (red vinyl)	1961	$50.00	$100.00	$200.00
(if on yellow vinyl)	1961	$37.50	$75.00	$150.00
Dave Clark Five, "Over and Over" (same on both sides) (Epic 9863) (red vinyl)	1965	$10.00	$20.00	$40.00
Ray Coniff, "Blue Moon" / "Honeycomb" (Columbia 42967) (blue vinyl)	1964	$3.00	$6.00	$12.00
The Coronets, "It Would Be Heavenly" / "Baby's Coming Home" (Chess 1453) (red vinyl)	1953	$200.00	$400.00	$800.00
The Crests, "No One To Love" / "Wish She Was Mine" (Times Square 2) (red vinyl)	1962	$5.00	$10.00	$20.00
The Crows, "Gee" / "I Love You So" (Rama 5) (red vinyl)	1953	$100.00	$200.00	$400.00
The Cyrkle, "Red Rubber Ball" (same on both sides) (Columbia 43589) (red vinyl)	1966	$10.00	$20.00	$40.00
Fats Domino, "Blueberry Hill" / "Honey Chile" (Imperial 5407) (red vinyl)	1956	$37.50	$75.00	$150.00
Donovan, "Sunshine Superman" / "The Trip" (Epic 10045) (red vinyl)	1966	$10.00	$20.00	$40.00
The Du Droppers, "Can't Do Sixty No More" / "Chain Me Baby (Blues of Desire)" (Red Robin 108) (red vinyl)	1952	$125.00	$250.00	$500.00
The Elegants, "It's Just A Matter of Time" / "Lonesome Weekends" (Bim Bam Boom 121) (colored vinyl)	1974		$3.00	$6.00
The Everly Brothers, "Ebony Eyes" / "Walk Right Back" (Warner Bros. 5199) (promo) (gold vinyl)	1961	$25.00	$50.00	$100.00
The Fascinators, "The Bells of My Heart" / "Sweet Baby" (Your Copy 1135) (red vinyl)	1954	$500.00	$1,000.00	$2,000.00
The Five Trumpets, "When The Saints Go Marching In" / "Preach My Word" (RCA Victor 50-0034) (cerise vinyl)	1950	$17.50	$35.00	$70.00
The Flamingos, "If I Can't Have You" / "Someday, Somehow" (Chance 1133) (red vinyl)	1953	$1,000	$1,500	$2,000
The Four Tunes, "May That Day Never Come" / "Carry Me Back to the Lone Prairie" (RCA Victor 50-0131) (cerise vinyl)	1951	$37.50	$75.00	$150.00
Aretha Franklin, "Jumpin' Jack Flash" / "Integrity" (Arista 9028) (clear vinyl)	1986		$2.50	$5.00
Lowell Fulson, "Night and Day" / "Stormin' and Rainin'" (Aladdin 3104) (green vinyl)	1951	$50.00	$100.00	$200.00
Grand Funk, "We're An American Band" / "Creepin'" (Capitol 3660) (gold vinyl)	1973		$3.00	$6.00
Bill Haley and the Comets, "Rock the Joint" / "Icy Heart" (Essex 303) (red vinyl)	1952	$900.00	$1,350.00	$1,800.00
Daryl Hall and John Oates, "Jingle Bell Rock from Daryl" / "Jingle Bell Rock from John" (RCA JR-14259) (available in red and green vinyl, value is equal for both)	1985	$2.50	$5.00	$10.00
The Iridescents, "Three Coins in the Fountain" / "Strong Love" (Hudson 8102)	1963	$25.00	$50.00	$100.00
Jethro Tull, "Christmas Song" / "Skating Away on the Thin Ice of a New Day" (Chrysalis S7-18211) (green vinyl)	1994		$2.50	$5.00
Lonnie Johnson, "My Woman is Gone" / "Don't Make Me Cry Baby" (Rama 9) (red vinyl)	1953	$37.50	$75.00	$150.00
Kraftwerk, "Pocket Calculator" / "Dentaku" (Warner Bros. 49723) (opaque yellow vinyl)	1981		$2.50	$5.00
Smiley Lewis, "Play Girl" / "Big Mamou" (Imperial 5234) (red vinyl)	1953	$62.50	$125.00	$250.00
Little Walter, "Off The Wall" / "Tell Me Mama" (Checker 770) (red vinyl)	1953	$750.00	$1,500.00	$3,000.00
Shorty Long, "A Bottle and a Blonde" / "Waltz of Colorado" (RCA Victor 48-0347) (green vinyl)	1950	$10.00	$20.00	$40.00
Barbara Mandrell, ""Fast Lanes and Country Roads" (same on both side) (MCA 52737) (yellow vinyl)	1985	$2.50	$5.00	$10.00
Al Martino, "Here In My Heart" / "I Cried Myself To Sleep" (BBS 101)	1952	$15.00	$30.00	$60.00
Lucky Millinder, "D Natural Blues" / "Little Girl, Don't Cry" (RCA Victor 50-0054) (gray label, cerise vinyl)	1949	$15.00	$30.00	$60.00
The Moody Blues, "The Other Side of Life" / "The Spirit" (Polydor 885201-7) (blue vinyl)	1986		$2.50	$5.00
(with specially designed picture sleeve, add:)	1986		$2.50	$5.00
Rick Nelson, "Lonesome Town" / "I Got A Feeling" (Imperial 5545) (red vinyl)	1958	$150.00	$300.00	$600.00
Rick Nelson, "Travelin' Man" / "Hellow Mary Lou" (Imperial 5741) (red vinyl)	1961	$200.00	$400.00	$800.00
Willie Nelson, "Pretty Paper" / "Rudolph the Red Nosed Reindeer" (Columbia AE7 1183) (red vinyl)	1979	$6.25	$12.50	$25.00
The Oak Ridge Boys, "When You Give It Away" / "The Voices of Rejoicing Love" (MCA S45-17233) (promo) (green vinyl)	1986	$3.75	$7.50	$15.00
The Orioles, "Teardrops On My Pillow" / "Hold Me, Thrill Me, Kiss Me" (Jubilee 5108) (red vinyl)	1953	$375.00	$750.00	$1,500.00
Patti Page, "Mister and Mississippi" / "These Things I Offer You" (Mercury 5645) (red vinyl)	1951	$10.00	$20.00	$40.00
The Penetrations, "Bring 'Em In" / "Fackin' Out" (Icon 1002) (blue vinyl)	196??	$15.00	$30.00	$60.00
Elvis Presley, "King of the Whole Wide World" / "King Creole" (RCA DME1-1803) (test pressings on green, blue, white and clear vinyl. Value is equal for all pressings)	1997	$100.00	$200.00	$400.00
(with picture sleeve, add:)	1997	$2.00	$4.00	$8.00
Charley Pride, "Stagger Lee" (same on both sides) (RCA JK-13754) (red vinyl)	1984	$2.50	$5.00	$10.00
Eddie Rabbitt, "Song of Ireland" (same on both sides) (Elektra 378) (small center hole, green vinyl)	1978	$3.75	$7.50	$15.00
Rare Earth, "What'd I Say" (stereo/mono) (Rare Earth 960/961) (blue vinyl)	1972	$6.25	$12.50	$25.00
Jim Reeves, "Bimbo" / "Gypsy Heart" (Abbott 148) (red vinyl)	1953	$15.00	$30.00	$60.00
Paul Revere and the Raiders, "Kicks" (same on both sides) (Columbia 43556) (red vinyl)	1966	$12.50	$25.00	$50.00
The Rip Chords, "Hey Little Cobra" (same on both sides) (Columbia 42921) (yellow vinyl)	1963	$12.50	$25.00	$50.00
Billy Joe Royal, "Down in the Boondocks" (same on both sides) (Columbia 43305) (red vinyl)	1965	$10.00	$20.00	$40.00
Bob Seger, "We've Got Tonight" (mono/stereo) (Capitol 4653) (promo) (silver vinyl)	1978	$2.50	$5.00	$10.00
Simon and Garfunkel, "The Sounds of Silence" (same on both sides) (Columbia 43396) (red vinyl)	1965	$12.50	$25.00	$50.00
The Surfaris, "Wipe Out" / "Wipe Out" (Dot 144) (promo) (red vinyl)	1966	$25.00	$50.00	$100.00
Sonny Terry, "I Don't Worry (Sittin' on Top of the World)" / "Man Ain't Nothin' But A Fool" (Jax 305) (colored vinyl)	195??	$100.00	$200.00	$400.00
Slim Whitman, "Indian Love Call" / "China Doll" (Imperial 8156) (opaque red vinyl)	1952	$12.50	$25.00	$50.00
Yes, "Roundabout" (mono/stereo) (Atlantic 2854) (yellow vinyl)	1972	$25.00	$50.00	$100.00

LPs	Year	VG	VG+	NM
Adrian and the Sunsets, Breakthrough (Sunset 63-601) (mono) (multi-colored vinyl)	1963	$37.50	$75.00	$150.00

LPs	Year	VG	VG+	NM
(if on Sunset SD 63-601, stereo, multi-colored vinyl)	1963	$75.00	$150.00	$300.00
The Beatles, The Beatles (Capitol SEBX-11841) (2 LPs) (white vinyl)	1978	$12.50	$25.00	$50.00
The Beatles, The Beatles 1962-1966 (Capitol SEBX-11842) (2 LPs) (red vinyl)	1978	$10.00	$20.00	$40.00
The Beatles, The Beatles 1967-1970 (Capitol SEBX-11843) (2 LPs) (blue vinyl)	1978	$10.00	$20.00	$40.00
Pat Boone, Moonglow (Dot DLP-25270) (blue vinyl)	1960	$12.50	$25.00	$50.00
Lenny Bruce, Interviews of Our Times (Fantasy 7001) (opaque, non-flexible red vinyl)	1959	$25.00	$50.00	$100.00
(if translucent flexible red vinyl)	1962	$10.00	$20.00	$40.00
Johnny Burnette, Tear It Up (Solid Smoke SS-8001)	1978	$3.75	$7.50	$15.00
The Challengers, (Lloyd Thaxton Goes) Surfin' with the Challengers (Vault VS-101) available in orange, red, yellow or blue vinyl; title might not mention Lloyd Thaxton; value is equal)	1963	$62.50	$125.00	$250.00
Dion, Runaround Sue (Laurie LLP 2009) (mono) (exists in gold, green and blue vinyl pressings, value is equal)	1961	$200.00	$400.00	$800.00
Allen Ginsburg, Howl and Other Poems (Fantasy F-7006) (mono) (red vinyl)	1959	$100.00	$200.00	$400.00
Grand Funk, We're An American Band (Capitol SMAS-11207) (gold vinyl)	1973	$5.00	$10.00	$20.00
Vince Guaraldi, Jazz Impressions of Black Orpheus (Cast Your Fate To The Wind) (Fantasy 3337) (mono) (red vinyl)	1962	$10.00	$20.00	$40.00
(if on Fantasy 8089, stereo, blue vinyl)	1962	$10.00	$20.00	$40.00
Jan and Dean, Jan and Dean (The Dore Album) (Sundazed LP-5022) (2 LP's) (colored vinyl)	1996	$2.50	$5.00	$10.00
The Jazz Crusaders, Lookin' Ahead (Pacific Jazz ST-43) (stereo) (yellow vinyl)	1962	$15.00	$30.00	$60.00
Paul Kantner and Jefferson Starship, Blows Against the Empire, RCA Victor LSP-4448) (clear vinyl promo)	1970	$37.50	$75.00	$150.00
Kiss, Alive III (Mercury 522 647-1) (2 LP's) (pressed on red, white, blue or black vinyl, value is equal)	1994	$6.25	$12.50	$25.00

LPs	Year	VG	VG+	NM
Smiley Lewis, I Hear You Knocking (Imperial LP-9141) (green vinyl; only one copy known to exist)	1961	$1,500	$3,000	$6,000
Les McCann, On Time (Pacific Jazz PJ-56) (mono) (yellow vinyl)	1962	$10.00	$20.00	$40.00
(if on Pacific Jazz ST-56, stereo, yellow vinyl)	1962	$12.50	$25.00	$50.00
Madonna, Like A Virgin (Sire 25157) (white vinyl, silver spine)	1984	$15.00	$30.00	$60.00
(if white vinyl, cream spine)	1984	$12.50	$25.00	$50.00
The Monkees, More of the Monkees (Sundazed LP 5046) (colored vinyl)	1996	$2.50	$5.00	$10.00
Nirvana, Bleach (Sub Pop 34) (if on white vinyl, first 1,000 copies pressed)	1989	$12.50	$25.00	$50.00
(if on red vinyl)	1989	$5.00	$10.00	$20.00
Korla Pandit, Latin Holiday (Fantasy 3284) (mono) (red vinyl)	1959	$10.00	$20.00	$40.00
(if on Fantasy 8027, stereo, blue vinyl)	1960	$12.50	$25.00	$50.00
Pink Floyd, The Division Bell (Columbia C 64200) (blue vinyl)	1994	$5.00	$10.00	$20.00
Planet Patrol, Planet Patrol (Tommy Boy TBLP 1002) (yellow-purple marbled vinyl)	1986	$3.00	$6.00	$12.00
Elvis Presley, A Valentine Gift For You (RCA AFL1-5353) (red vinyl)	1985	$5.00	$10.00	$20.00
? and the Mysterians, Featuring 96 Tears (Collectibles COL 2004) (orange vinyl) (tracks are re-recorded)	1997	$3.00	$6.00	$12.00
The Remains, The Remains (Spoonfed SFD-3205) (red vinyl)	1978	$3.75	$7.50	$15.00
Bobby Rydell, All The Hits (Cameo C-1019) (red vinyl)	1962	$37.50	$75.00	$150.00
Simple Minds, New Gold Dream (81-82-83-84) (A&M SP-6-4928) (wine-stained starburst vinyl)	1982	$3.00	$6.00	$12.00
Jimmy Witherspoon, Jimmy Witherspoon Sings the Blues (Crown CST-215) (red vinyl, true stereo)	1961	$37.50	$75.00	$150.00
Brenton Wood, Baby You Got It (Double Shot 5003) (multi-colored vinyl)	1967	$50.00	$100.00	$200.00

COMEDY/NOVELTY RECORDS

History: Comedy and novelty music has been part of recorded media ever since Thomas Edison enlisted Mark Twain to record some humorous narratives on a new cylinder phonograph. One could successfully argue that the genre of comedy and novelty music has been the longest-sustained musical genre in recorded history, rivaling the longevity of classical and opera music.

Those who search out comedy and novelty records today currently search for various subgenres in the comedy music field: stand-up comedy monologues, song parodies, humorous sketches, topical/controversial humorists, and the like.

Bill Cosby's first comedy album, which was produced by comedy legend Allan Sherman.

The earliest recorded comedy and novelty material can be heard on Edison cylinder recordings of the 1900s and 1910s, with Cal Stewart's "Uncle Josh" monologues, and the various renditions of the novelty classic "The Preacher and the Bear." By the 1920s, comedy duos such as William Jones and Earnest Hare (The Happiness Boys) and Moran and Mack (Two Black Crows) recorded their routines on flat, double-sided shellac 78s.

By the 1930s and 1940s, as more Americans received their music via radio, comedy monologues were on the wane—who wanted to purchase a comedy routine on record, when they could hear one on the radio for free? Musical comedy, however, still held strong. The most successful musical comedy band of the 1940s, Spike Jones and his City Slickers, sold millions of cacophonous copies of "Cocktails for Two," "Der Fuhrer's Face," and "All I Want For Christmas Is My Two Front Teeth."

By the 1950s, a new type of comedy record, the nightclub monologue, began to achieve popularity. Many of these comedians built their fame in small nightclubs and hotel ballrooms; and since radio stations were playing this new rock and roll music, and only the larger cities had more than two television channels, records became a new avenue for promoting nightclub comedians.

Trivia

When Allan Sherman recorded his classic album *My Son, The Folk Singer*, he had just been fired from the "Steve Allen" show, and was living on unemployment. The album became an overnight sensation, spawning dozens of copycats, including break-in legend Dickie Goodman, whose album *My Son, The Joke* was his only album to not have a single snippet-based song.

Dickie Goodman's parody of Allan Sherman's LP even featured him mimicking Sherman's album cover.

Lack of available airtime was not the only reason these performers were not played on the radio or shown on television. Many of these comedy records discussed taboo subjects for 1950s America: sex, religion, sex, politics, sex, drinking, and sex. Many of the songs were filled with racy double—and sometimes triple—entendre. Performers such as Ruth Wallis and Benny Bell would sing songs that sounded like something naughty was about to happen, but instead, they added a few extra words to "swerve" the listener. Such songs included Benny Bell's "Shaving Cream," with its lyric seeking a rhyme of "bit," or "split," or "kit," followed by word sounding like "sh - - shaving cream, be nice and clean..." A song by Ruth Wallis, "The Dinghy Song," talks about how a sailor has the "cutest little dinghy in the navy..." (wink wink).

An early Ruth Wallis album. Wallis' double-entrende humor earned her the nickname "Queen of the Wicked Ditties."

These records were seldom on display in record stores; you could find them, however, sold "under the counter" for an extra dollar or two. In 1961, singer/cabaret artist Rusty Warren turned her nightclub act into a series of successful albums, including Songs for Sinners, Sin-sational, and her only Top 10 album, Knockers Up! (in the 1960s, "knockers" were round-knobbed wooden mallets that people used to bang on tables in lieu of clapping—that's the other definition).

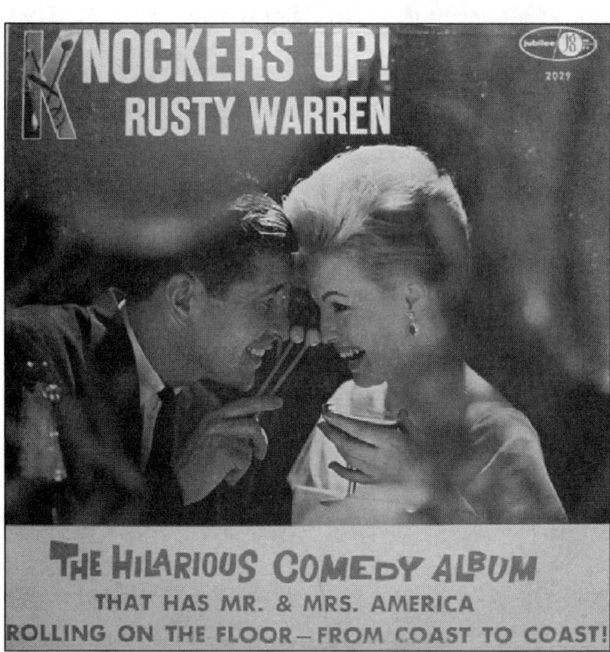

Rusty and a friend sharing a pair of knockers together.

Stand-up comedy records in the 1950s and 1960s were quick and easy to make: simply start the tape recorder rolling when the comedian or monologuist takes the stage, turn the tape off when the show is over, and master it into an album. Labels such as Dooto and Laff built their fortunes on quickie recordings by Redd Foxx and Richard Pryor.

There were other records that were kept off radio stations, not for their salacious content, but for their mature, macabre themes. Among stand-up comedians on vinyl, Lenny Bruce's records are extremely collectible. His barrier-breaking comedy and censorship battles with the law have elevated his recordings to legendary status. Some of his rarest records include two self-produced albums, a release on Phil Spector's Philles label, and some red vinyl recordings for Fantasy Records.

Tom Lehrer, a Harvard mathematics professor, released a series of collectible albums with sick and twisted lyrical humor, with song titles like "Poisoning Pigeons in the Park," "The Masochism Tango," and "The Old Dope Peddler." His early self-produced recordings are very collectible, as are the first pressings of his Reprise albums.

But other parody artists became million-selling singer-composers, especially in the 1960s. Among the most successful in this genre was former television scriptwriter Allan Sherman. Sherman's parodies of old public domain songs, mixed with his own Borscht Belt humor, sold millions of albums in the 1960s, and influenced such artists as "Weird Al" Yankovic to try their hand at musical parody and satire. Besides recording such successful albums as *My Son, The Folk Singer* and songs like "Hello Mudduh, Hello Fadduh! (A Letter From Camp)," Sherman also produced Bill Cosby's first comedy albums.

Allan Sherman's debut album, containing parodies of popular songs. It also spawned a popular catchprase, "My Son, the ..."

Sometimes comedy records are more than just an audio recording of a nightclub act. In fact, thematic comedy records have taken their cue from early radio comedies, where the humor was heard, but only seen in the imagination. Thanks to new innovations in recording techniques, comedy artists could record different voices on multi-tracked recording tapes, adding carefully selected sound effects and music, a patchwork quilt of sound and humor. Such proponents of this 1950s aural comedy include Stan Freberg, Mike Nichols & Elaine May, and Bob Elliot & Ray Goulding. These comedy artists paved the way for similar concept albums by the Firesign Theatre, Monty Python and the National Lampoon Radio Show.

Reinventing many of their television skits for albums, the Monty Python comedy troupe released a series of collectible albums in the 1970s.

Trivia

Kermit Schaefer created a cottage industry with a series of "Blooper" albums. Schaefer collected "Bloopers," which were gaffes, mistakes, malaprops, and spoonerisms accidentally broadcast over live radio and television, compiled them, and successfully sold them as comedy albums. Be aware, however, that the early "Blooper" albums contain recreations of classic bloopers, whose voices sound like the same five broadcasters covering every local radio station in America.

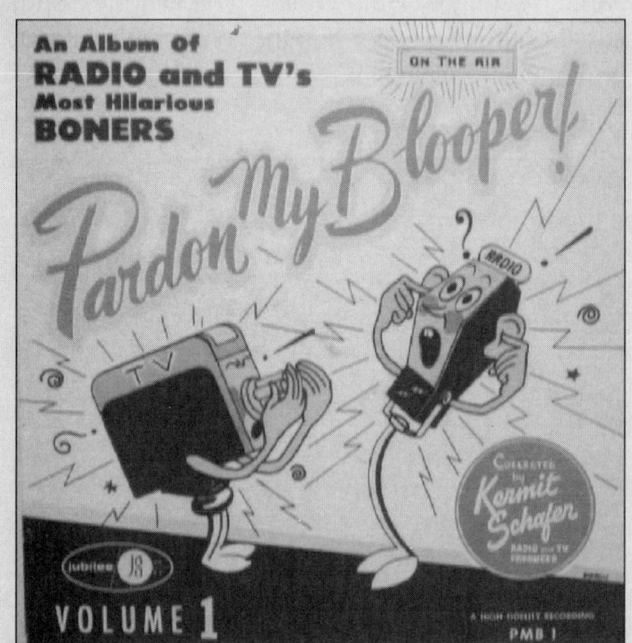

Schaefer's *"bloopers"* have remained in print for years; the original pressings can be found on the Jubilee label.

Another successful comedy record format involved concept albums, with entire troupes of comedians creating LPs of political and pop culture satire. One of the most famous and best-selling of these sketch comedy records is Vaughn Meader's 1962 recording *The First Family* (Cadence CLP 3060). This album, a tongue-in-cheek satire of President Kennedy, his family and his staff, was at one time listed in the *Guinness Book of World Records* as the fastest selling record in history. The success of *The First Family* spawned imitation records, as well as a sequel LP from Meader himself. After the assassination of John F. Kennedy, record collectors tossed their copies of *The First Family* away, and the remaining copies languished in cutout bins for years.

Even John F. Kennedy bought a copy of *The First Family,* although he said in news reports that Vaughn Meader sounded more like Ted Kennedy than the President.

Even after that release, other presidential satire records have made their way to the store shelves, and for a while it seemed as if every President was due for a comedy record satirizing their years in office: *LBJ in the Catskills, The Washington Hillbillies* (for Jimmy Carter) and *The First Family Rides Again* (for Ronald Reagan).

This 1980s version of *The First Family* starred impressionist Rich Little and "Seinfeld's" Kramer, Michael Richards—that's him on the lower right, wearing a tutu.

By the 1970s, the most popular comedy records often involved more taboo subjects: either drugs (Cheech and Chong), sexual prowess (Blowfly) or seven words you cannot say on television (George Carlin). Actors from television sketch-comedy shows like "Saturday Night Live" and "SCTV" also recorded albums (or the soundtracks from their shows were simply transferred to vinyl).

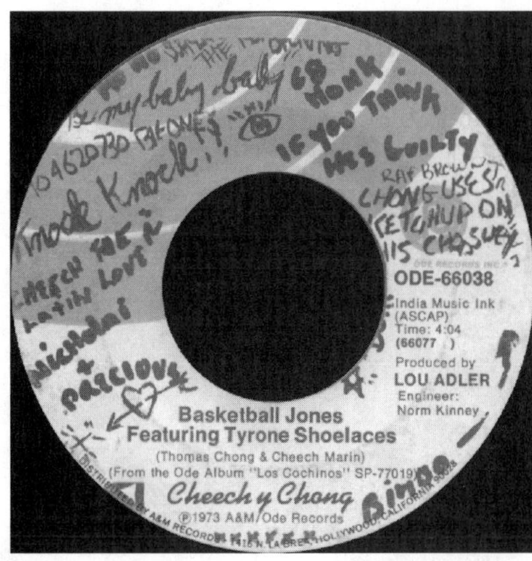

This record "intentionally" has graffiti all over it. "Basketball Jones," Cheech and Chong's first hit.

The 1970s also produced a new avenue for comedy and novelty records—the Doctor Demento radio show. For two hours every weekend, Doctor Demento (born Barry Hansen) played classic comedic and off-the-wall recordings, and still broadcasts the program to this very day. Rhino Records has even released some "Doctor Demento" humor compilation albums, containing such classics in dementia as Barnes and Barnes' "Fish Heads," the Frantics' "Ti Kwan Leep/Boot to the Head," and Fred Blassie's "Pencil Neck Geek."

"Weird Al" Yankovic's parody of Queen's "Another One Rides The Bus" was recorded live on the Dr. Demento radio show. Courtesy Jon "Bermuda" Schwartz.

What To Look For: Comedy records either sold millions of copies or they sold very few,—there seems to be no middle ground. Albums like *The First Family* and Allan Sherman's *My Son, the Folk Singer* are readily available and at reasonable prices. For some comedy recordings, especially those with limited press runs, the value increases dramatically.

Allan Sherman's ode to summer camp may be funny as anything, but to collectors it is a very easily obtainable recording.

Other comedy albums are highly prized—not just by comedy collectors, but by other genre collectors. One such album, *Musically Mad*, is a "must-have" for comedy collectors, as well as for RCA "Living Stereo" collectors (the album was released on this label), and for *Mad* magazine collectors (including a classic front cover shot of Mad poster boy Alfred E. Newman). And although some comedy collectors still look for Moran and Mack's "Two Black Crows" series of Columbia 78s, these records are more desired by collectors of racially insensitive and politically incorrect historical artifacts.

References: *Incredibly Strange Music*, Vols. I and II, Re/Search Publications, San Francisco, 1993, 1994; Nash, Bruce; Zullo, Allan; *The Wacky Top 40*, Bob Abrams, Inc., Holbrook, Mass., 1993; Smith, Ronald L., *Goldmine Comedy Record Price Guide*, Krause Publications, 700 East State St., Iola, Wisconsin, 1996.

Web pages: "Weird Al" Yankovic's home page: *http://www.weirdal.com*; Dr. Demento's home page: *http://www.drdemento.com;* "The Blue Pages," a great site for the history of blue comedy records of the 1940s, 1950s and 1960s, *http://www.hensteeth.com*; Usenet newsgroups: rec.music.dementia, alt.fan.weird-al

Trivia

Woody Woodbury was a popular Florida nightclub performer, playing piano and spinning some humorous anecdotes. He even had his own fan club and fraternal organization, with a motto patterned after Woodbury's own catchphrase—"Booze is the only answer."

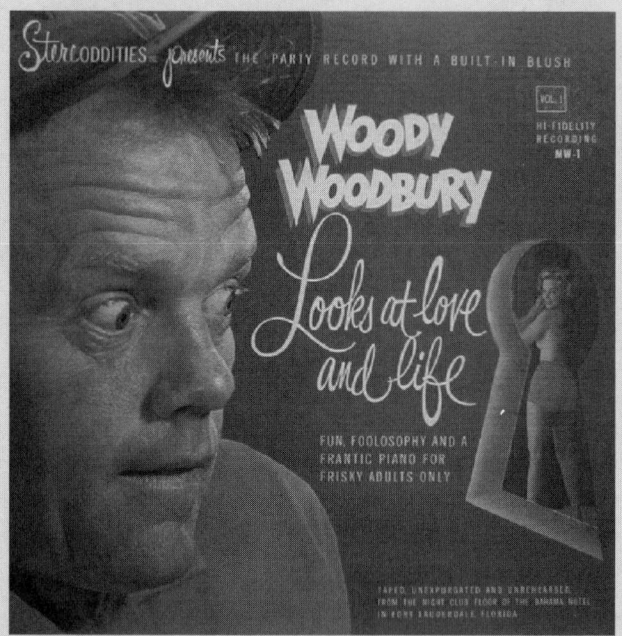

One of Woody Woodbury's many releases on the Stereoddities label.

45s	Year	VG	VG+	NM
George Carlin, "Wonderful WINQ" / "Al Sleet, Your Hippy Dippy Weatherman" (RCA Victor 47-9110)	1967	$2.50	$5.00	$10.00
Cheech and Chong, "Earache My Eye Featuring Alice Bowie" / "Turn That Thing Down" (Ode 66102)	1974		$2.00	$4.00
(with picture sleeve, add:)	1974		$3.00	$6.00
Bill Cosby, "Little Ole Man (Uptight - Everything's Alright)" / "Don'cha Know" (Warner Bros. 7072)	1967	$2.00	$4.00	$8.00
The Firesign Theatre, "Forward Into The Past" / "Station Break" (Columbia 45052)	1969	$2.50	$5.00	$10.00
(with picture sleeve, add:)	1969	$10.00	$20.00	$40.00
Stan Freberg, "St. George and the Dragonet" / "Little Blue Riding Hood" (Capitol F2596)	1953	$7.50	$15.00	$30.00
(if on Capitol F1697, reissue)	1954	$5.00	$10.00	$20.00
Stan Freberg, "The Old Payola Roll Blues" (Pt. 1) / (Pt. 2) (Capitol F4329)	1960	$5.00	$10.00	$20.00
(with picture sleeve, add:)	1960	$7.50	$15.00	$30.00
Hudson and Landry, "Ajax Liquor Store" / "The Hippie and the Redneck" (Dore 855)	1971	$2.50	$5.00	$10.00
Spike Jones and his City Slickers, The Nutcracker Suite (RCA Victor WP 143) (3 7-inch singles, aqua labels, gold print)	1949	$20.00	$40.00	$80.00
(if on black labels, white print, Nipper on left of label)	1951	$15.00	$30.00	$60.00
Tom Lehrer, "Pollution" / "Who's Next" (Reprise 0862)	1969	$2.00	$4.00	$8.00
Vaughn Meader, "St. Nick Visits the White House" / "Twas The Night Before Christmas" (Verve 1009)	1963	$5.00	$10.00	$20.00

45s	Year	VG	VG+	NM
Monty Python, "They Won't Play This Song On the Radio" / "Sit On My Face - Farewell To John Denver" (Arista 0578)	1980	$2.00	$4.00	$8.00
Napoleon XIV, "They're Coming To Take Me Away, Ha-Haaa!" / "!aaaH-aH, yawA mE ekaT oT gnimoC er'yehT"				
(if on Warner Bros. 5831)	1966	$3.00	$6.00	$12.00
(if on Warner Bros. 7726, reissue)	1973	$2.00	$4.00	$8.00
National Lampoon, "Deteriorata" / "Those Fabulous Sixties" (Blue Thumb 218)	1972	$2.00	$4.00	$8.00
Mort Sahl, "Nixon's Odyssey" / "Watergate" (GNP Crescendo 467)	1973		$2.50	$5.00
Allan Sherman, "Hello Muddah! Hello Fadduh! (A Letter From Camp)" / "Here's To The Crabgrass" (Warner Bros. 5378)	1963	$3.75	$7.50	$15.00
Allan Sherman, "Hello Muddah! Hello Fadduh! (A Letter From Camp)" / "Rat Fink" (Warner Bros. 5378)	1963	$3.00	$6.00	$12.00
(with picture sleeve, add:)	1963	$5.00	$10.00	$20.00
Ray Stevens, "Jeremiah Peabody's Poly Unsaturated Quick Dissolving Fast Acting Pleasant Tasting Green and Purple Pills" / "Teen Years" (Mercury 71843)	1961	$3.75	$7.50	$15.00
(with picture sleeve, add:)	1961	$6.25	$12.50	$25.00
Ray Stevens, "The Streak" / "You've Got The Music Inside" (Barnaby 600)				
(if on white label, not a promo)	1974		$2.50	$5.00
(if on Salvador Dali-esque label)	1974		$2.00	$4.00
"Weird Al" Yankovic, "My Bologna" / "School Cafeteria" (Capitol 4816)	1980	$5.00	$10.00	$20.00
"Weird Al" Yankovic, "Another One Rides The Bus" / "Gotta Boogie" (TK 1043)	1981	$5.00	$10.00	$20.00
(if above songs, with "Happy Birthday" and "Mr. Frump in the Iron Lung" on 7" EP, Placebo 3626)	1981	$2.50	$5.00	$10.00
(with Placebo picture sleeve, add:)	1981	$2.50	$5.00	$10.00

LPs	Year	VG	VG+	NM
Woody Allen, Woody Allen (Colpix CP 518)	1964	$7.50	$15.00	$30.00
Lenny Bruce, Interviews of Our Times (Fantasy 7001)				
(if opaque, non-flexible red vinyl, Bruce's name blacked out on back cover)	1959	$25.00	$50.00	$100.00
(if non-flexible black vinyl, blue-tinted cover)	1959	$10.00	$20.00	$40.00
(if flexible red vinyl)	1962	$10.00	$20.00	$40.00
(if flexible black vinyl)	1962	$5.00	$10.00	$20.00
Lenny Bruce, Lenny Bruce Is Out Again				
(if on Lenny Bruce LB-3001/2, privately pressed version, white labels, Bruce's address on cover)	196??	$75.00	$150.00	$300.00
(if on Philles PHLP-4010, reissue)	1966	$25.00	$50.00	$100.00
George Carlin, FM & AM (Little David LD 7214)	1972	$2.50	$5.00	$10.00
Cheech and Chong, Big Bambu (Ode SP 77014)	1972	$3.00	$6.00	$12.00
(with souvenir rolling paper, add:)	1972	$1.50	$3.00	$6.00
(if on Warner Bros. BSK 3251, reissue)	1978	$2.00	$4.00	$8.00
Cheech and Chong, Cheech and Chong's Wedding Album (Ode SP-77025)	1974	$3.00	$6.00	$12.00
(if on Ode PE 34954, reissue)	1977	$2.50	$5.00	$10.00
(if on Warner Bros. BSK 3253, reissue)	1978	$2.00	$4.00	$8.00
Bill Cosby, Bill Cosby Is A Very Funny Fellow Right! (Warner Bros. W-1518)	1964	$3.75	$7.50	$15.00
The Firesign Theatre, How Can You Be In Two Places At Once When You're Not Anywhere At All (Columbia CS 9884)				
(with "360 Sound" on the label)	1969	$3.75	$7.50	$15.00
The Firesign Theatre, I Think We're All Bozos On This Bus (Columbia C 30737)	1971	$3.75	$7.50	$15.00
(if on Columbia CQ 30737, quadraphonic)	1972	$5.00	$10.00	$20.00
Stan Freberg, Stan Freberg Presents the United States of America (Capitol W1573) (mono)	1961	$7.50	$15.00	$30.00
(if on Capitol SW1573, stereo)	1961	$6.25	$12.50	$25.00
Dickie Goodman, My Son The Joke (Comet 69) (see the "Break-in" section for more on Dickie Goodman's work)	1963	$10.00	$20.00	$40.00
Spike Jones, Spike Jones Murders Carmen and Kids the Classics (RCA Victor LPM-3128) (10-inch LP)	1953	$50.00	$100.00	$200.00

LPs	Year	VG	VG+	NM
Tom Lehrer, Songs By Tom Lehrer (Lehrer 101) (10-inch LP)	1952	$20.00	$40.00	$80.00
Tom Lehrer, An Evening Wasted with Tom Lehrer				
(if on Lehrer TL-202, mono)	1959	$6.25	$12.50	$25.00
(if on Lehrer TL-202S, stereo)	1959	$10.00	$20.00	$40.00
(if on Reprise R 6199, mono)	1966	$5.00	$10.00	$20.00
(if on Reprise RS 6199, stereo)	1966	$6.25	$12.50	$25.00
Tom Lehrer, That Was The Week That Was (Reprise 6179)				
(if on Reprise R 6179, mono)	1965	$5.00	$10.00	$20.00
(if on Reprise RS-6179, stereo, pink-yellow-green label)	1965	$6.25	$12.50	$25.00
(if on Reprise RS-6179, stereo, two-tone orange label, with "W7" and "r:" logos)	1968	$3.75	$7.50	$15.00
(if on Reprise RS-6179, stereo, tan label with "r:" logo)	1970	$2.50	$5.00	$10.00
Original Cast Recording, The Mad Show (Columbia Masterworks OL 6530) (mono)	1965	$12.50	$25.00	$50.00
(if on Columbia Masterworks OS 2930, stereo)	1965	$25.00	$50.00	$100.00
Vaughn Meader, The First Family (Cadence CLP 3060)	1962	$3.75	$7.50	$15.00
Vaughn Meader, The First Family, Volume 2 (Cadence CLP 3065)	1963	$5.00	$10.00	$20.00
(if on Cadence CPL 25065, stereo)	1963	$7.50	$15.00	$30.00
Monty Python, Matching Tie and Handkerchief (Arista AL 4039)				
(original pressings have two grooves on side 2; the comedy routine is different depending on the groove)	1975	$5.00	$10.00	$20.00
(if on Arista 8357, reissue, may only have one groove on side 2)	198??	$2.00	$4.00	$8.00
Napoleon XIV, They're Coming To Take Me Away, Ha-Haaa! (Warner Bros. W 1661) (mono)	1966	$15.00	$30.00	$60.00
(if on Warner Bros. WS 1661, stereo)	1966	$25.00	$50.00	$100.00
(if on Rhino RNLP 816, reissue)	1985	$3.00	$6.00	$12.00
National Lampoon, Radio Dinner (Banana BTS 38)	1972	$3.75	$7.50	$15.00
(if on MCA 27024, reissue)	198??	$2.00	$4.00	$8.00
Richard Pryor, Craps: After Hours (Laff 146)	1971	$3.00	$6.00	$12.00
Richard Pryor, Is It Something I Said? (Reprise MS 2227)	1975	$3.00	$6.00	$12.00
(if on Reprise MSK 2285, reissue)	1977	$2.50	$5.00	$10.00
Mort Sahl, 1960: Look Forward In Anger (Verve MGV-15004) (mono)	1959	$5.00	$10.00	$20.00
Mort Sahl, Mort Sahl on Relationships (Reprise R-5003) (mono) (Joan Collins on cover)	1961	$10.00	$20.00	$40.00
(if on Reprise R9-5003, stereo, Joan Collins on cover)	1961	$12.50	$25.00	$50.00
Allan Sherman, My Son The Folk Singer (Warner Bros. 1475) (mono)	1962	$3.75	$7.50	$15.00
(if on Warner Bros. WS 1475, stereo)	1962	$5.00	$10.00	$20.00
Ray Stevens, 1,837 Seconds of Humor (Mercury MG-20732) (mono)	1962	$10.00	$20.00	$40.00
(if on Mercury SR-60732, stereo)	1962	$12.50	$25.00	$50.00
Ray Stevens, He Thinks He's Ray Stevens (MCA 5517)	1984	$2.50	$5.00	$10.00
Ruth Wallis, Rhumba Party (King 265-6) (10-inch LP)	1952	$30.00	$60.00	$120.00
Ruth Wallis, Ruth Wallis (Wallis Original 2) (mono)	1957	$10.00	$20.00	$40.00
Ruth Wallis, Here's Looking Up Your Hatch (King 986) (mono)	1966	$7.50	$15.00	$30.00
Rusty Warren, Songs for Sinners (Jubilee JLP 2024)	1960	$6.25	$12.50	$25.00
Rusty Warren, Knockers Up! (Jubilee JLP 2029)	1960	$6.25	$12.50	$25.00
(if both above albums reissued as a 2 LP set on GNP Crescendo 2079)	1975	$3.75	$7.50	$15.00
"Weird Al" Yankovic, "Weird Al" Yankovic (Rock 'n Roll BFZ 38679)	1983	$2.50	$5.00	$10.00
(if on Rock n' Roll PZ 38679, budget reissue)	1985	$2.00	$4.00	$8.00

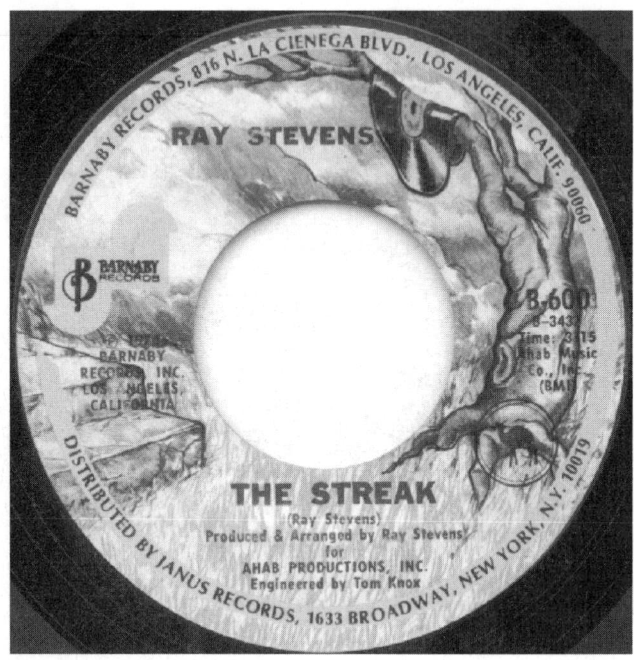

Topical events often spawn theme-based comedy records. The "streaking" fad of the 1970s gave birth to some "streaking"-based records; Ray Stevens' "The Streak" hit #1.

"Weird Al" Yankovic has had a long and successful recording career; here's his first 45, a parody of the Knack's "My Sharona."

A Top 10 hit for Cheech and Chong, satirizing the power-chord glam rockers of the early 1970s.

Rusty Warren's albums are easy to find—this EP of her bawdy songs, with a picture sleeve, is not.

COUNTRY/WESTERN

History: Country music grew from the small towns and southern farmlands, a mixture of violin or "fiddle songs," and Irish ballads. Today, it is one of the most popular and profitable forms of music, as artists from Garth Brooks to the Dixie Chicks have sold millions of 45s, albums, and CDs.

One of the most collectible country albums, Jim Reeves' debut LP on the Abbott label is a country collector's dream. Courtesy Good Rockin' Tonight/Collectors Universe.

The earliest recorded country music were "fiddle songs" from the 1920s. An A&R man from Victor Records, Ralph Peer, set up a portable recording studio in Bristol, Tennessee, and searched the town for new talent for his label. On August 1, 1927, Peer recorded two legends of country music—Jimmie Rodgers and the Carter Family—in a makeshift recording studio in a Bristol barn. From these recordings came the earliest sounds of country music.

With the birth of radio, country music was transported to millions of homes outside of country's rural base. The most popular radio show to feature country music, WSM's "Grand Ole Opry," is still on the air today, and features every form of country music, from bluegrass to western bop, from contemporary country to old-time country gospel.

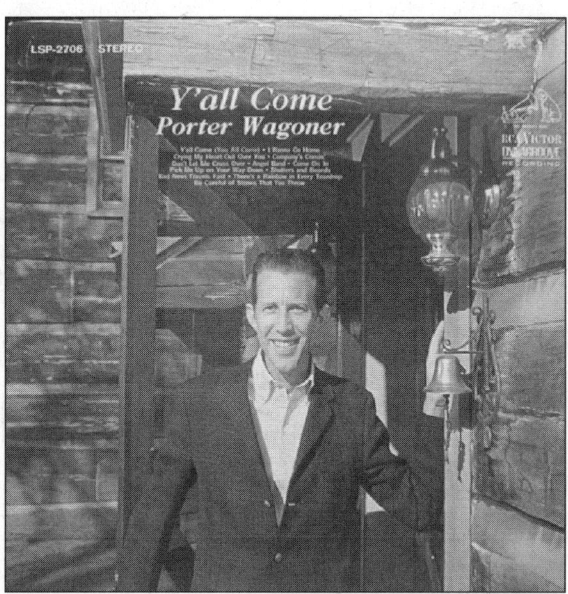

Besides joining the Grand Ole Opry in 1957, Porter Wagoner hosted his own syndicated television show for 20 years, and helped Dolly Parton on the road to stardom. Courtesy Last Vestige Music Store, Albany, N.Y.

WSM's first major star was Roy Acuff and his Tennessee Crackerjacks. Acuff, who was as popular among country music fans as Frank Sinatra was among pop music fans of the time, performed with the Opry for more than 50 years. Acuff's biggest hits included "The Great Speckle Bird," "The Precious Jewel," and "The Wabash Cannonball."

But in the 1940s, the country music that most people heard came not from the south, but from the west—Hollywood, to be more precise. "Singing Cowboys" like Gene Autry and Roy Rogers starred in successful motion pictures and serials, and always stopped the bandits, kissed the girl, strummed on their guitar and sang "Back in the Saddle Again," "Don't Fence Me In," or "Happy Trails" into the sunset.

Roy Rogers was once a member of a harmony group called the Pioneer Trio. That group eventually evolved into the Sons of the Pioneers, whose western songs included "Tumbling Tumbleweeds" and "Cool Water." The Sons of the Pioneers also appeared in many of Roy Rogers' movies, starred in their own radio show, and were one of the first country/western groups to incorporate vocal harmonies into their songs.

Originally known as the Pioneer Trio, the Sons of the Pioneers changed their name to honor the Native American heritage of some of their members. Courtesy Last Vestige Music Store, Albany, N.Y.

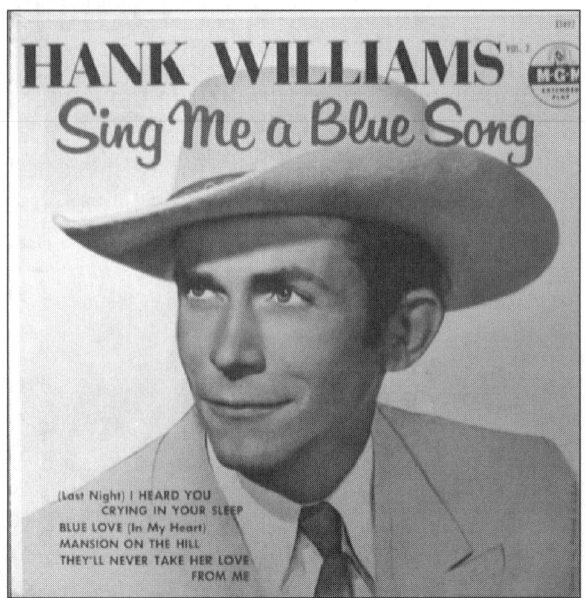

After Williams' death, MGM re-released many of his songs on albums, EPs and 45s for years. Some recordings even have new orchestrations; while the original versions were not re-released until the compact disc era.

In the 1960s, a new type of country singer appeared—the "country crooner." With lush orchestrations and soothing background singers, artists such as Eddy Arnold, Bill Anderson, and Jim Reeves were able to "cross over" from their traditional country fan base to the pop charts.

During the 1940s, a new form of country music appeared—western swing. This type of music, which mixed traditional country sounds with swing and jazz music, had its biggest proponent in Bob Wills and His Texas Playboys. Between 1935 and the early 1950s, Wills and his orchestra, which featured vocalist Tommy Duncan and steel guitarist Leon McAuliffe, had major country and pop hits with "San Antonio Rose," "We Might As Well Forget It," and "Stars and Stripes on Iwo Jima."

After World War II, the most popular country singer—in fact, one of the forefathers of rock 'n' roll—was Hank Williams. Between 1949 until the time of his death in 1953, Hank Williams dominated the country charts, with such #1 songs as "Lovesick Blues," "Cold Cold Heart," "Hey Good Lookin'," "Jambalaya (on the Bayou)," and "Your Cheating Heart." His songs were as tortured as his life; his emotive voice wrenched in doubt and sadness over the loves he lost and the ones he never had. At the height of his popularity, Williams made $1,000 a night in front of capacity crowds. But drugs and drink wrecked his marriages and ruined his career, eventually causing his death in 1953.

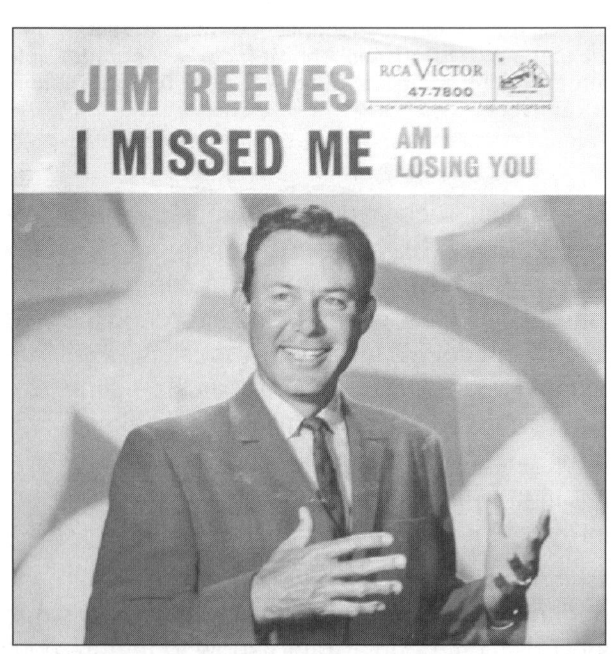

Even after his death in 1964, Reeves's voice appeared on new albums and 45s for the next twenty years—thanks to thousands of hours of previously unknown home recordings. Photo Credit: From the Collection of Val Shively.

Trivia

Mt. Airy, North Carolina was Andy Griffith's hometown, and early in his performing career Griffith had country hits with "What it Was, Was Football." Mt. Airy was also the hometown of Donna Fargo, who had a #1 hit with her self-penned, "The Happiest Girl in the Whole U.S.A."

The title track from this song was voted "Song of the Year" by the Country Music Association in 1973. Courtesy Last Vestige Music Store, Albany, N.Y.

During this period, country music singers also recorded "answer" records and "Part 2" records. "Answer" records were usually a female singer's response to a male singer's popular song. After Claude King's song "Wolverton Mountain" hit the top of the charts, Jo Ann Campbell recorded an answer record, "(I'm the Girl On) Wolverton Mountain." Jim Reeves' "He'll Have To Go" was answered by Jeanne Black, who sang "He'll Have To Stay."

"Part 2" records were parody and comedy songs, mostly satirizing the top hits of the day. The comedy duo Homer and Jethro had hits by poking fun at Red Foley's "Tennessee Border" (Homer and Jethro's version was "Tennessee Border—No. 2"), or Johnnie Horton's "Battle of New Orleans" (which, to Homer and Jethro, was the "Battle of Kookamonga").

Female country singers have always been revered by their fans; whether it was the bigger-than-life personae of Dolly Parton, the heartfelt, emotive voice of Patsy Cline, or the down-to-earth success stories of Tammy Wynette and Loretta Lynn, these singers have captured the hearts of generations.

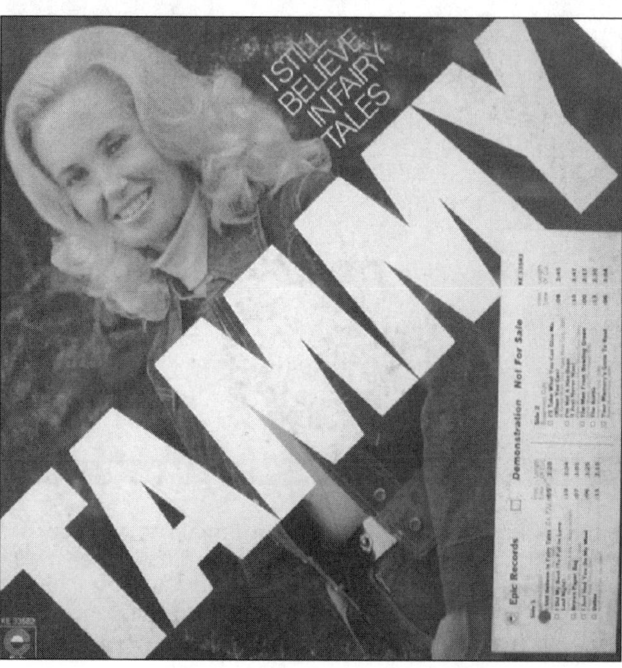

"The First Lady of Country Music," Tammy Wynette's most famous recordings included "Stand By Your Man," and "We're Gonna Hold On," one of her many duets with George Jones. Courtesy Last Vestige Music Store, Albany, N.Y.

While radio shows like the "Grand Ole Opry" helped spread country music throughout the 1920s and 1930s, television shows like "Hee Haw" promoted country music's biggest stars in the 1960s and 1970s. Hosted by country music singers Roy Clark and Buck Owens, "Hee Haw" brought together all facets of country music; every show had at least four musical numbers, featuring a special "guest artist." And even though the humor was as corny as the Kornfield Kounty location of the show, the program did provide viewers with a reverent and honored approach to popular country music. "Hee Haw" also provided new exposure for established country singers Minnie Pearl, Grandpa Jones, and Archie Campbell.

In the 1970s, some artists broke away from traditional country music and created "outlaw country," or progressive country songs. They embraced new musical genres, and wrote songs incorporating more mature themes of love and loss. Legends of outlaw country included Willie Nelson, Waylon Jennings, Jessi Colter, Merle Haggard, and Johnny Cash.

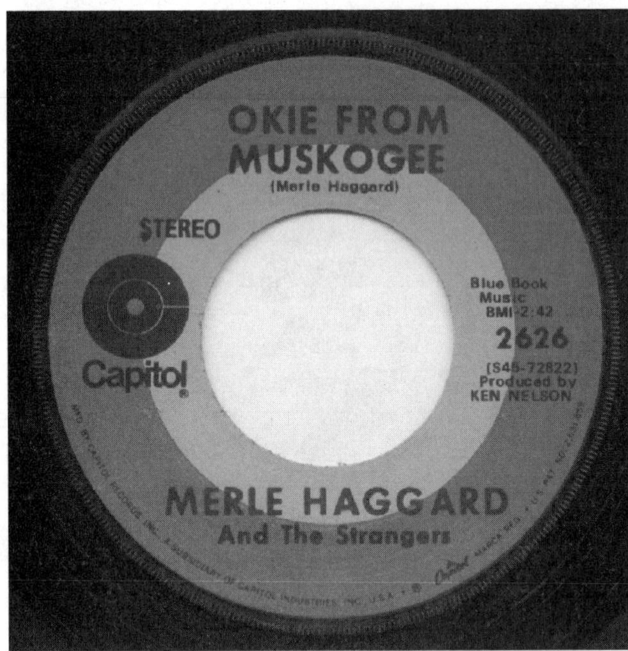

Merle Haggard went from prison inmate to the top of the charts, as his song "Oakie from Muskogee" was voted the Single of the Year by the Country Music Association in 1969.

By the 1990s, as more country artists added music videos to their musical repertoire, the old country establishment was shaken up once more. Garth Brooks marketed his music to both country and rock 'n' roll fans; Shania Twain combined her vocal abilities with her glamorous music videos. And new stars such as LeAnn Rimes, the Dixie Chicks, and Tim McGraw perform on that same Grand Ole Opry stage as did Roy Acuff and Eddy Arnold.

What To Look For: Major label country music 45s from the 1970s and 1980s are very easy to find, as are the albums from that same period. Vinyl items that are more difficult to locate are mono LPs from the 1960s, stereo LPs from the 1950s, and 10-inch albums from the 1950s.

Many country artists originally had success on the pop charts; country singers Conway Twitty and Sonny James had pop hits in the early days of rock 'n' roll. Because of this, some artists who had their biggest hits in the 1960s may have released a 45 or two in the 1950s. If these records are on small independent labels and received poor distribution upon their initial release, those records have a very high collectible value today.

Trivia

Country music has often been criticized for its elaborate song titles. But upon listening to these tracks, many people discover that the lyrics deftly combine symbolism and metaphors to describe love and loss. Playing cards, for example, have often been used as the starting point for many country songs, including Tex Ritter's "Deck of Cards," Juice Newton's "Queen of Hearts," George Strait's "Ace in the Hole," and Ned Miller's "From a Jack To a King."

Ned Miller's Top 10 song describes how to play cards and win a girl at the same time.

While record companies abandoned vinyl 45s and LPs in the early 1990s, there have always been 45s for country music artists. Garth Brooks, in fact, has released all his singles on 7" vinyl, as have Trisha Yearwood, the Dixie Chicks, Shania Twain, and Alan Jackson. And vinyl LPs for many of these stars also exist—many record and tape clubs continued to make albums long after the major record companies stopped doing so.

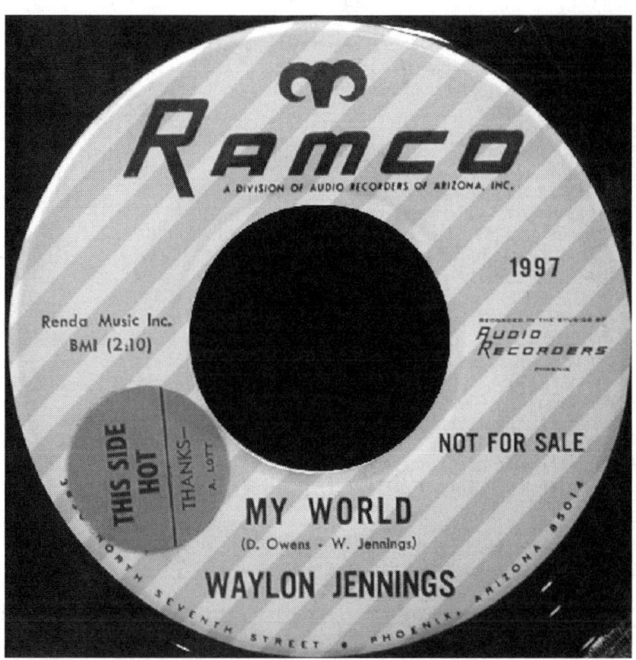

In the 1960s, Waylon Jennings recorded this song on the tiny Ramco label. This record today is one of the hardest to find for Waylon Jennings fans and collectors. Notice the promotional sticker on the label that says "THIS SIDE HOT—Thanks, A. Lott." From the Collection of Val Shively.

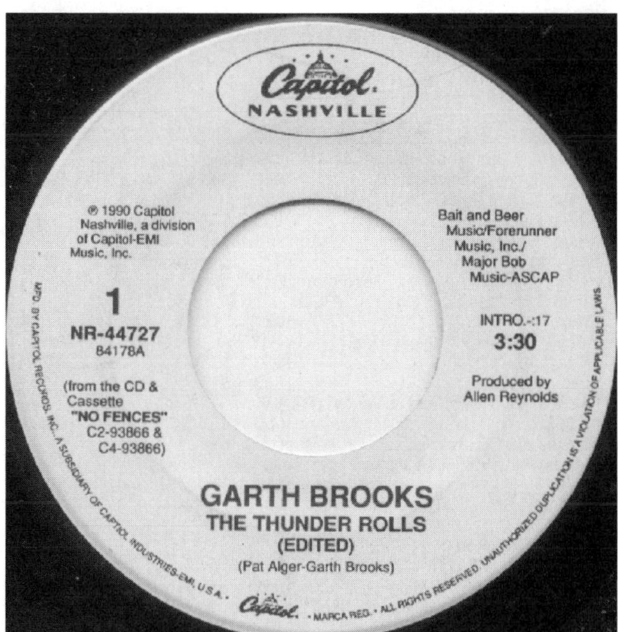

One of Garth Brooks' many hits, all of which are currently available as 7-inch 45s.

References: Heggeness, Fred, *Goldmine Country Western Record and CD Price Guide*, Krause Publications, Iola, Wisconsin, 1996; Mason, Michael, Ed., *The Country Music Book*, Charles Scribner's Sons, New York, N.Y. 1985; Osborne, Jerry, *The Official Price Guide to Country Music Records*, House of Collectibles/Ballantine Publishing, New York, 1996; Whitburn, Joel, *Billboard Top Country Singles 1944-1997*, Record Research, Inc., Menomonee Falls, Wisconsin, 1998.

Web pages: Roughstock's Country Music history page: *http://www.roughstock.com/country*; The Country Music Association: *http://www.cma-world.com*; Hank Williams Jr.'s homepage: *http://www.hankjr.com;* a history of the Grand Ole Opry, as well as other information, can be found at this site: *http://www.grandoleopry.com*; Usenet newsgroups: rec.music.country.old-time, rec.music.country.western, alt.music.country-classic.

Museums: The Grand Ole Opry Museum, at 2802 Opryland Drive, Nashville, Tennessee 37214; (615) 889-3060; the Alabama Music Hall of Fame, whose honorees include Jimmie Rodgers and Tammy Wynette, U.S. Highway 72 West, Tuscumbia, Alabama, (800) 239-2643.

Trivia

In the 1980s, some country music stars teamed up with techno-dance producers in a series of unique collaborations. Kon Kan's "I Beg Your Pardon" features several sound-alike lyrics from Lynn Anderson's "Rose Garden"; and Tammy Wynette added her voice to the KLF's "Justified and Ancient," giving the First Lady of Country Music her highest-charting pop record ever.

Lynn Anderson was a regular on the Lawrence Welk TV show when "Rose Garden" hit the top of the country charts.

45s	Year	VG	VG+	NM
Alabama, "My Home's in Alabama" / "I Wanna Come Over" (RCA PB-12008)	1980		$2.00	$4.00
(with picture sleeve, add:)	1980		$3.00	$6.00
Eddy Arnold, "Make the World Go Away" / "The Easy Way" (RCA Victor 47-8679)	1965	$2.00	$4.00	$8.00
(with picture sleeve, add:)	1965	$3.75	$7.50	$15.00
Garth Brooks, "The Dance" / "Two of a Kind, Workin' on a Full House" (Capitol Nashville NR-44701)	1991		$3.00	$6.00
Garth Brooks, "The Thunder Rolls" / "Victim of the Game" (Capitol Nashville NR-44727)	1991		$3.00	$6.00
Johnny Cash, "I Walk The Line" / "Get Rhythm" (Sun 241)	1956	$10.00	$20.00	$40.00
Johnny Cash, "Ballad of a Teenage Queen" / "Big River" (Sun 283)	1958	$6.25	$12.50	$25.00
Johnny Cash, "Ring of Fire" / "I'd Still Be There" (Columbia 42788)	1963	$2.50	$5.00	$10.00
(if "Ring of Fire" is on both sides, red vinyl promo)	1963	$10.00	$20.00	$40.00
Roy Clark, "Yesterday, When I Was Young" / "Just Another Man" (Dot 17246)	1969		$2.50	$5.00
Patsy Cline, Walkin' After Midnight" / "A Poor Man's Roses (Or a Rich Man's Gold)" (Decca 30221)	1957	$5.00	$10.00	$20.00
Patsy Cline, "Crazy" / "Who Can I Count On" (Decca 31317)	1961	$3.00	$6.00	$12.00
Billy "Crash" Craddock," "Broken Down in Tiny Pieces" / "Shake It Easy" (ABC Dot 17659)	1976		$2.00	$4.00
The Charlie Daniels Band, "The Devil Went Down To Georgia" / "Rainbow Ride" (Epic 50700)	1979		$2.00	$4.00
The Dixie Chicks, "Goodbye Earl" / "Cowboy Take Me Away" (Monument 79352)	2000		$2.00	$4.00
Dave Dudley, "Six Days On The Road" / "I Feel A Cry Coming On" (Golden Wing 3020)	1963	$3.00	$6.00	$12.00
Everly Brothers, "Bye Bye Love" / "I Wonder If I Care As Much" (Cadence 1315)	1957	$6.25	$12.50	$25.00
Everly Brothers, "Wake Up Little Susie" / "Maybe Tomorrow" (Cadence 1337)	1957	$7.50	$15.00	$30.00
(with picture sleeve, add:)	1957	$62.50	$125.00	$250.00
Narvel Felts, "Reconsider Me" / "Foggy Misty Morning" (ABC Dot 17549	1975		$2.50	$5.00
Lester Flatt and Earl Scruggs, "Foggy Mountain Breakdown" / "You're Not a Drop in the Bucket" (Columbia 21295)	1954	$5.00	$10.00	$20.00
Lefty Frizzell, "If You've Got The Money I've Got The Time" / "I Love You 1000 Ways" (Columbia 20739)	1950	$10.00	$20.00	$40.00
Merle Haggard, "Okie from Muskogee" / "If I Had Left It Up To You" (Capitol 2626)	1969	$2.00	$4.00	$8.00
(with picture sleeve, add:)	1969	$2.00	$4.00	$6.00
Emmylou Harris, "I'll Be Your Baby Tonight" / "I'll Never Fall In Love Again" (Jubilee 5679)	1969	$5.00	$10.00	$20.00
Hawkshaw Hawkins, "Lonesome 7-7203" / "Everything Has Changed" (King 5712)	1963	$3.75	$7.50	$15.00
Highway 101, "Just Say Yes" / "I'll Be Missing You" (Warner Bros. 27867)	1988			$3.00
(with picture sleeve, add:)	1988		$2.00	$4.00
Ferlin Husky, "Wings of a Dove" / "Next to Jimmy" (Capitol 4406)	1960	$3.00	$6.00	$12.00
Waylon Jennings, "My World" / "Another Blue Day" (Ramco 1997)	1968	$3.00	$6.00	$12.00
Waylon Jennings, "Luckenbach, Texas (Back to the Basics of Love)" / "Belle of the Ball" (RCA PB-10924)	1977		$2.50	$5.00
Corky Jones, "Hot Dog" / "Rhythm and Booze" (Dixie 505) (later became Buck Owens)	1956	$100.00	$200.00	$400.00
George Jones, "Why Baby Why" / "Season Of My Heart" (Starday 202)	1955	$12.50	$25.00	$50.00
George Jones, "White Lightning" / "Long Time To Forget" (Mercury 71406)	1959	$3.75	$7.50	$15.00
George Jones, "Still Doin' Time" / "Good Ones and Bad Ones" (Epic 02526)	1981			$3.00
Grandpa Jones, "The All-American Boy" / "Pickin' Time" (Decca 30823)	1959	$5.00	$10.00	$20.00
The Kendalls, "Heaven's Just A Sin Away" / "Live and Let Live" (Ovation 1103)	1977		$3.00	$6.00
Brenda Lee, "Fool #1" / "Anybody But Me" (Decca 31309)	1961	$3.75	$7.50	$15.00
Jerry Lee Lewis, "What's Made Milwaukee Famous (Has Made A Loser Out Of Me)" / "All the Good Is Gone" (Smash 2186)	1968	$2.50	$5.00	$10.00
Loretta Lynn, "I'm A Honky Tonk Girl" / "Whispering Sea" (Zero 107)	1960	$125.00	$250.00	$500.00

45s	Year	VG	VG+	NM
Loretta Lynn, "Don't Come Home A-Drinkin' (With Lovin' On Your Mind)" / "A Saint To A Sinner" (Decca 32045)	1966	$2.50	$5.00	$10.00
Loretta Lynn, "Lyin', Cheatin', Woman Chasin', Honky Tonkin', Whiskey Drinkin' You" / "Star Light, Star Bright" (MCA 52219)	1983		$2.00	$4.00
Barbara Mandrell, "(If Loving You Is Wrong) I Don't Want To Be Right" / "I Feel The Hurt Coming On" (MCA 12451)	1979		$2.00	$4.00
C.W. McCall, "Old Home Filler-Up An' Keep On-a-Truckin' Café" / "Old 30" (American Gramophone 351)	1974	$3.75	$7.50	$15.00
(if on MGM 14738)	1974		$2.00	$4.00
C.W. McCall, "Convoy" / "Long Lonesome Road" (MGM 14839)	1975		$2.50	$5.00
Roger Miller, "Poor Little John" / "My Fellow" (Mercury 71212)	1957	$6.25	$12.50	$25.00
Roger Miller, "King of the Road" / "Atta Boy Girl" (Smash 1965)	1965	$3.00	$6.00	$12.00
Ronnie Milsap, "A Thousand Miles From Nowhere" / "When It Comes To My Baby" (Scepter 12127)	1966	$3.00	$6.00	$12.00
Ronnie Milsap, "It Was Almost Like A Song" / "It Don't Hurt To Dream" (RCA Victor PB-10976)	1977		$2.00	$4.00
Ronnie Milsap, "Time, Love and Money" / "Livin' on Love" (Virgin 58853)	2000			$3.00
Willie Nelson, "Night Life" / "Rainy Day Blues" (Belaire 107)	1963	$7.50	$15.00	$30.00
(if pressed on colored vinyl)	1963	$15.00	$30.00	$60.00
Willie Nelson, "A Storm Has Just Begun" / "When I Sing My Last Hillbilly Song" (Sarg 260)	196??	$12.50	$25.00	$50.00
Willie Nelson, "Blue Eyes Cryin' in the Rain" / "Bandera" (Columbia 10176)	1975		$2.50	$5.00
The Oak Ridge Boys, "This Ole House" / "Early in the Morning" (Warner Bros. 5359)	1963	$5.00	$10.00	$20.00
The Oak Ridge Boys, "Elvira" / "A Woman Like You" (MCA 51084)	1981		$2.00	$4.00
Buck Owens, "I've Got A Tiger by the Tail" / "Cryin' Time" (Capitol 5336)	1965	$2.50	$5.00	$10.00
(with picture sleeve, add:)	1965	$3.75	$7.50	$15.00
Buck Owens and Ringo Starr, "Act Naturally" / "The Key's in the Mailbox" (Capitol B-44409)	1989	$2.50	$5.00	$10.00
Dolly Parton, "Puppy Love" / "Girl Left Alone" (Gold Band 1086)	1959	$150.00	$300.00	$600.00
Dolly Parton, "Dumb Blonde" / "The Giving and the Taking" (Monument 982)	1967	$2.50	$5.00	$10.00
Dolly Parton, "Jolene" / "You're So Beautiful Tonight" (RCA Victor APBO-0145)	1973		$2.50	$5.00
Johnny Paycheck, "Take This Job And Shove It" / "Colorado Kool-Aid" (Epic 8-50469)	1977	$2.00	$4.00	$8.00
Webb Pierce, "That Heart Belongs To Me" / "So Used To Loving You" (Decca 9-28091)	1952	$6.25	$12.50	$25.00
Ray Price, "Crazy Arms" / "You Done Me Wrong" (Columbia 21510)	1956	$3.75	$7.50	$15.00
Ray Price, "For The Good Times" / "Grazin' in Greener Pastures" (Columbia 45178)	1970		$3.00	$6.00
Charley Pride, "Kiss An Angel Good Mornin' / "No One Could Ever Take Me From You" (RCA Victor 74-0550)	1971		$3.00	$6.00
Jim Reeves, "Bimbo" / "Gypsy Heart" (Abbott 148)	1953	$6.25	$12.50	$25.00
(if on red vinyl)	1953	$15.00	$30.00	$60.00
Jim Reeves, "Bimbo" / "Penny Candy" (RCA Victor 47-6625)	1956	$5.00	$10.00	$20.00
Jim Reeves, "He'll Have To Go" / "In A Mansion Stands My Love" (RCA Victor 47-7643)	1959	$3.00	$6.00	$12.00
LeAnn Rimes, "Blue" / "The Light In Your Eyes" (Curb 76959)	1996		$2.00	$4.00
Tex Ritter, "I Dreamed of a Hill-Billy Heaven" / "The Wind and the Tree" (Capitol 4567)	1961	$3.00	$6.00	$12.00
Roy Rogers, "Don't Fence Me In" / "Roll On Texas Moon" (RCA Victor 0008) (green vinyl)	1949	$10.00	$20.00	$40.00
Hank Snow, "Lady's Man" / "Married by the Bible, Divorced by the Law" (RCA Victor 47-4733)	1952	$6.25	$12.50	$25.00
The Sons of the Pioneers, "Ballad of Davy Crockett" / "The Graveyard Filler of the West" (RCA Victor WBY-25)	1955	$7.50	$15.00	$30.00
(with picture sleeve, add:)	1955	$12.50	$25.00	$50.00
Red Sovine, "Teddy Bear" / "Daddy" (Starday 142)	1976		$2.50	$5.00
Shania Twain, "Whose Bed Have Your Boots Been Under?" / "Any Man of Mine" (Mercury 856 488-7)	1995	$2.50	$5.00	$10.00

45s	Year	VG	VG+	NM
Tanya Tucker, "Would You Lay With Me (In A Field Of Stone)" / "No Man's Land" (Columbia 45991)	1974		$2.50	$5.00
Conway Twitty, "Hello Darlin'" / "Girl at the Bar" (Decca 32661)	1970		$3.50	$7.00
Porter Wagoner, "Takin' Chances" / "I Can't Live With You" (RCA Victor 47-5086)	1952	$7.50	$15.00	$30.00
Porter Wagoner and Dolly Parton, "We'll Get Ahead Someday" / "Jeannie's Afraid of the Dark" (RCA Victor 47-9577)	1968	$2.00	$4.00	$8.00
Kitty Wells, "Guilty Street" / "Shape Up or Get Out" (Decca 32455)	1969	$2.00	$4.00	$8.00
(with picture sleeve, add:)	1969	$5.00	$10.00	$20.00
Hank Williams, "Lonesome Blues" / "Never Again" (MGM 8010)	1949	$15.00	$30.00	$60.00
(if on MGM 10352, reissue)	1950	$10.00	$20.00	$40.00
Hank Williams, "Hey, Good Lookin'" / "My HeartWold Know" (MGM 11000)	1951	$7.50	$15.00	$30.00
Hank Williams, "Kaw-Liga" / "Your Cheatin' Heart" (MGM 11416)	1953	$7.50	$15.00	$30.00
Hank Williams, Jr., "All My Rowdy Friends (Have Settled Down)" / "Everytime I Hear That Song" (Elektra 47191)	1981		$2.50	$5.00
Hank Williams, Jr., "All My Rowdy Friends Are Coming Over Tonight" / "Video Blues" (Warner Bros. 29184)	1984		$2.00	$4.00
Hank Williams and Hank Williams, Jr., "There's A Tear In My Beer" / "You Brought Me Down To Earth" (Warner Bros. 27584)	1989		$2.00	$4.00
Tammy Wynette, "Stand By Your Man" / "I Stayed Long Enough" (Epic 10398)	1968	$2.50	$5.00	$10.00
Trisha Yearwood, "She's In Love With The Boy" / "Victim of the Game" (MCA 54076)	1991	$2.00	$4.00	$8.00
Faron Young, "Hello Walls" / "Congratulations" (Capitol 4533)	1961	$3.75	$7.50	$15.00

LPs	Year	VG	VG+	NM
Alabama, The Alabama Band (Alabama ALA-78-9-01)	1978	$100.00	$200.00	$400.00
Alabama, 40 Hour Week (RCA Victor AHL1-5339)	1985	$2.00	$4.00	$8.00
Eddy Arnold, Lonely Again (RCA Victor LPM-3753) (mono)	1967	$5.00	$10.00	$20.00
(if on RCA Victor LSP-3753, stereo)	1967	$3.75	$7.50	$15.00
Garth Brooks, Ropin' the Wind (Capitol Nashville C1-596330) (vinyl available only through Columbia House)	1991	$12.50	$25.00	$50.00
Archie Campbell, Bedtime Stories for Adults (Starday 167)	1962	$7.50	$15.00	$30.00
The Carter Family, In Memory of A.P. Carter (Acme LP-2)	1960	$50.00	$100.00	$200.00
Johnny Cash, Johnny Cash With His Hot And Blue Guitar (Sun SLP-1220) (mono)	1956	$25.00	$50.00	$100.00
Johnny Cash, Johnny Cash at San Quentin (Columbia CS 9827)	1969	$3.00	$6.00	$12.00
(if on Columbia CQ 30961, quadraphonic)	1971	$5.00	$10.00	$20.00
Roy Clark, The Lightning Fingers of Roy Clark (Capitol T 1780) (mono)	1962	$5.00	$10.00	$20.00
(if on Capitol ST 1780, stereo)	1962	$6.25	$12.50	$25.00
Patsy Cline, Patsy Cline (Decca DL 8611) (mono)				
(if first pressing, black label with silver print)	1957	$25.00	$50.00	$100.00
(if second pressing, black label with color bars)	1960	$12.50	$25.00	$50.00
Patsy Cline, Sweet Dreams – The Life and Times of Patsy Cline (MCA 6149)	1985	$2.50	$5.00	$10.00
The Charlie Daniels Band, Million Mile Reflections (Epic JE 35751)	1979	$2.50	$5.00	$10.00
(if on Epic PE 35751, budget reissue)	198??	$2.00	$4.00	$8.00
(if on Mobile Fidelity 1-176, audiophile vinyl)	1984	$7.50	$15.00	$30.00
Dave Dudley, Six Days on the Road (Golden Ring 110)	1963	$12.50	$25.00	$50.00
Lester Flatt and Earl Scruggs, Songs of the Famous Carter Family (Columbia CL 1664) (mono)	1961	$5.00	$10.00	$20.00
(if on Columbia CS 8464, stereo)	1961	$6.25	$12.50	$25.00
Merle Haggard, A Tribute to the Best Damn Fiddle Player in the World (Or, My Salute to Bob Wills) (Capitol ST-638)	1970	$6.25	$12.50	$25.00
(if on Capitol SN-16279, budget reissue)	1982	$2.00	$4.00	$8.00
Homer and Jethro, The Worst of Homer and Jethro (RCA Victor LPM-1560)	1958	$12.50	$25.00	$50.00
Ferlin Husky, Ferlin's Favorites (Capitol T 1280) (mono)				
(if black label with rainbow perimeter, Capitol logo at left)	1960	$10.00	$20.00	$40.00
(if black label with rainbow perimeter, Capitol logo at top)	1962	$6.25	$12.50	$25.00
Waylon Jennings, Willie Nelson, Jessi Colter, Tompall Glaser, Wanted! The Outlaws (RCA Victor APL1-1321)				
(if tan label, first pressing)	1976	$3.00	$6.00	$12.00

LPs	Year	VG	VG+	NM
(if black label, dog near top)	1976	$2.50	$5.00	$10.00
(if on RCA AAL1-1321, reissue)	198??	$2.00	$4.00	$8.00
George Jones, The Grand Ole Opry's New Star (Starday SLP 101) (mono)	1958	$300.00	$600.00	$1,200.00
George Jones, George Jones Sings White Lightning And Other Favorites (Mercury MG-20477) (mono)	1959	$37.50	$75.00	$150.00
Grandpa Jones, Grandpa Jones Sings His Biggest Hits (King 554)	1958	$25.00	$50.00	$100.00
Jerry Lee Lewis, Who's Gonna Play This Old Piano ... (Think About It Darlin') (Mercury SR-61366)	1972	$3.75	$7.50	$15.00
Loretta Lynn, Your Squaw Is On The Warpath (Decca DL 75084)				
(if first pressing, includes song "Barney")	1969	$10.00	$20.00	$40.00
(if second pressing, "Barney" is deleted)	1969	$6.25	$12.50	$25.00
Barbara Mandrell, Midnight Angel (ABC Dot DOSD-2067)	1976	$3.00	$6.00	$12.00
C.W. McCall, Wolf Creek Pass (MGM M3G-4989)	1975	$2.50	$5.00	$10.00
Roger Miller, Roger and Out (Smash MGS-27049) (mono)	1964	$3.75	$7.50	$15.00
(if retitled "Dang Me/Chug-a-Lug," with the same catalog number)	196??	$3.00	$6.00	$12.00
Roger Miller, Roger and Out (Smash SRS-67049) (stereo)	1964	$5.00	$10.00	$20.00
(if retitled "Dang Me/Chug-a-Lug," with the same catalog number)	196??	$3.75	$7.50	$15.00
Ronnie Milsap, A Legend In My Time (RCA Victor APL1-0846)	1975	$3.75	$7.50	$15.00
(if on RCA Victor APD1-0846, quadraphonic)	1975	$5.00	$10.00	$20.00
Willie Nelson, Red Headed Stranger (Columbia PC 34482)	1975	$3.75	$7.50	$15.00
(if back cover has UPC bar code, reissue)	1979	$2.00	$4.00	$8.00
(if on Columbia HC 43482, half-speed mastered pressing)	1982	$10.00	$20.00	$40.00
Buck Owens, Buck Owens (Labrea 1017) (mono)	1961	$25.00	$50.00	$100.00
(if on Labrea 8017, stereo)	1961	$37.50	$75.00	$150.00
Dolly Parton, Just Because I'm A Woman (RCA Victor LPM-3949) (mono)	1968	$25.00	$50.00	$100.00
(if on RCA Victor LSP-3949, stereo, black label)	1968	$7.50	$15.00	$30.00
(if on RCA Victor LSP-3949, stereo, orange label)	1968	$5.00	$10.00	$20.00
Ray Price, For The Good Times (Columbia C 30106)	1970	$3.00	$6.00	$12.00
(if on Columbia CQ 30106, quadraphonic)	1972	$5.00	$10.00	$20.00
Jim Reeves, Jim Reeves Sings (Abbott LP-5001) (mono)	1956	$1,000.00	$1,500.00	$2,000.00
Jim Reeves, Bimbo (RCA Victor LPM-1410) (reissue of Abbott LP)	1957	$50.00	$100.00	$200.00
Jim Reeves, The Best of Jim Reeves (RCA Victor LPM-2890) (mono)	1964	$5.00	$10.00	$20.00
(if on RCA Victor LSP-2890, stereo)	1964	$6.25	$12.50	$25.00
Hank Snow, Heartbreak Trail (RCA Victor LPM-3471) (mono)	1966	$6.25	$12.50	$25.00
(if on RCA Victor LSP-3471, stereo)	1966	$7.50	$15.00	$30.00
The Sons of the Pioneers, Cool Water (RCA Victor LPM-2118)	1960	$6.25	$12.50	$25.00
(if on RCA Victor LSP-2118, stereo)	1960	$7.50	$15.00	$30.00
Tanya Tucker, Delta Dawn (Columbia KC 31742)	1972	$3.75	$7.50	$15.00
(if on Columbia PC 31742, budget reissue)	198??	$2.00	$4.00	$8.00
Porter Wagoner, Y'all Come (RCA Victor LPM-2706)	1963	$6.25	$12.50	$25.00
(if on RCA Victor LSP-2650, stereo)	1963	$7.50	$15.00	$30.00
Wild Country, Deuces Wild (LSI 0177) (group later became Alabama)	1977	$300.00	$600.00	$1,200.00
Hank Williams, Moanin' the Blues (MGM E-168) (10-inch LP)	1952	$100.00	$200.00	$400.00
(if on MGM E-3330, 12-inch LP, yellow label)	1956	$25.00	$50.00	$100.00
(if on MGM E-3330, 12-inch LP, black label)	1960	$10.00	$20.00	$40.00
Hank Williams, Reflections of Those Who Loved Him (MGM PRO-912) (3 LPs) (promo-only box set)	1975	$62.50	$125.00	$250.00
Hank Williams, Jr., Bocephus (MGM M3G-4988)	1974	$3.00	$6.00	$12.00
Bob Wills, For the Last Time (United Artists UA-LA216-J) (2 LPs)	1974	$10.00	$20.00	$40.00
Tammy Wynette, Your Good Girl's Gonna Go Bad (Epic LN 24305) (mono)	1967	$7.50	$15.00	$30.00
(if on Epic BN 26305, stereo)	1967	$5.00	$10.00	$20.00

DISCO

History: The 1970s were the years of disco. It was the most successful dance music since the "Twist" records of the early 1960s—a studio orchestra draped over a syncopated 4/4 beat, with lyrical topics ranging from steamy sex to goofy double entendre.

This new music originally came from dance clubs, or "discotheques," in the early 1970s. Club DJs would play a mixture of funk music, salsa, and popular dance songs, keeping the beat hot and the dance floor packed. The patrons boogied to James Brown's "Sex Machine," Eddie Kendricks' "Girl, You Need a Change of Mind," and Manu DiBango's "Soul Makossa," dancing to music at a time when AM stations were playing bubblegum music, and FM stations were hooked on album-oriented rock.

Blondie's "Heart of Glass," featuring Deborah Harry on the 12-inch label graphic.

Disco music broke into the mainstream in 1974, as groups like Harold Melvin and the Blue Notes, MFSB, and the O'Jays brought a new sound to the clubs—a pulsing beat, combined with a full orchestra and soulful lyrics, and extended mixes that lasted as long as there was recording tape in the studio. Whether it was slow jams like Silver Convention's "Fly, Robin, Fly," hot Florida salsa rhythms like K.C. and the Sunshine Band's "Get Down Tonight," tease-me disco songs like Donna Summer's "Love To Love You Baby," or even funk-based disco like Parliament's "Tear the Roof Off the Sucker," disco was now a dominant force in 1970s' music.

Disco also popularized a new recording format: the 12-inch disc. Also known as a "maxi-single" or "disco disc," 12-inch discs allowed club DJs to play extended versions of popular dance songs of the day. While Santa Esmerelda's version of the Animals' "Don't Let Me Be Misunderstood" only clocked in at 3:48 on radio, the 12-inch version was extended to more than 20 minutes. Club DJs would memorize such minutiae as a song's beats per minute and musical key, then by using two turntables and an electronic cross-fader, they would synchronize the end of one disco song to the beginning of another, matching the beats and tempo in a seamless segue.

A 12-inch "disco disc," featuring Gino Soccio. The "0770" in the upper left corner was probably a disc jockey's inventory indexing code.

By 1978, the biggest-selling album of the year was the soundtrack to a film about disco life, *Saturday Night Fever.* Among the many artists featured on this album were the Bee Gees, who had changed their image from syrupy balladeers to disco legends. And if the Bee Gees could do it, well so could—and did—the Rolling Stones ("Miss You"), the Kinks ("Wish I Could Fly Like Superman"), and Rod Stewart ("Da Ya Think I'm Sexy").

Trivia

The group A Taste of Honey came up with their signature bass riff for "Boogie Oogie Oogie" when guitarist/bass player Janice Marie Johnson was tuning her bass during rehearsals. The group liked the staccato riffs so much, they added it to the song.

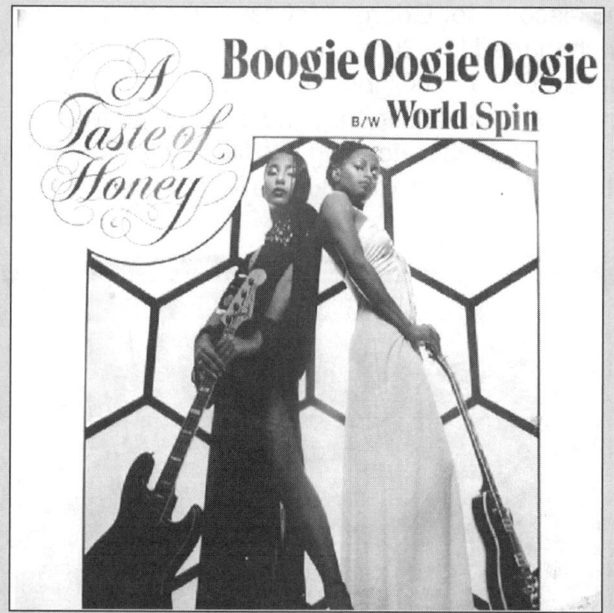

The 1978 Grammy Award winner for Best New Artist, A Taste of Honey. Courtesy Last Vestige Music Store, Albany, N.Y.

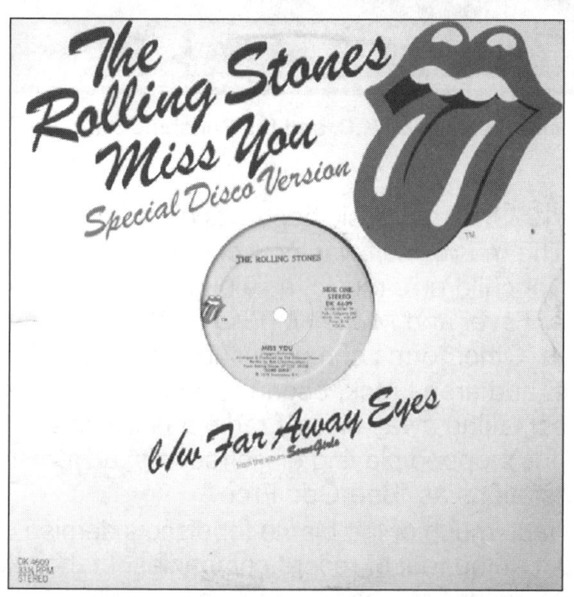

Even the Rolling Stones did a disco song, "Miss You." Courtesy Last Vestige Music Store, Albany, N.Y.

Late '70s disco music also featured thumping bass beats, and is probably one of the few musical styles (surf instrumental being another) where the bass guitarist has as much of a prominent role as a guitarist or pianist. Two perfect examples of bass-heavy disco include A Taste of Honey's "Boogie Oogie Oogie," and a million-selling disco groove called "Le Freak."

Chic, the group behind "Le Freak," parlayed the success of that song into a string of dance club disco classics, including "Good Times" and "I Want Your Love." Two of the members of Chic, Nile Rodgers and Bernard Edwards, expanded upon their disco beginnings, becoming successful producers and songwriters for other artists. And one of Chic's classic tracks, "Good Times," became the soundtrack for early rap records such as the Sugarhill Gang's "Rapper's Delight."

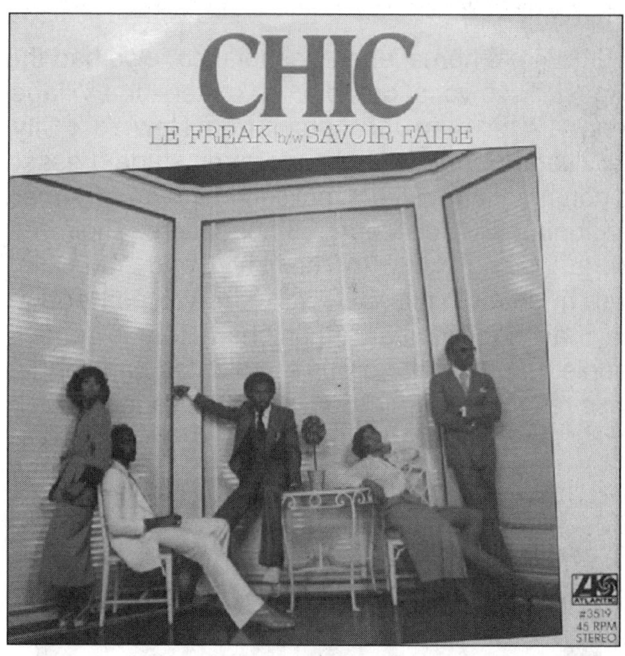

Chic's "Le Freak" single was one of the top-selling songs, disco or otherwise, of 1978. Courtesy Last Vestige Music Store, Albany, N.Y.

The most popular female disco singer, the "Queen of Disco," was Donna Summer. From her first song, where she purred "Love To Love You Baby" to a sultry beat, and throughout the disco music era, Summer was a multi-platinum performer whose every dance track was a "must-hear" in discos. Songs like "Hot Stuff," "Bad Girls," "On the Radio," and "I Feel Love" were not only disco smashes, they were also early successful forays into techno-pop and social commentary.

The long version of Donna Summer's "Love To Love You Baby" takes up the whole first side of this LP.

Summer's home label, Casablanca, also had the biggest disco vocal group on its roster—the Village People. A six-man vocal group from New York City, the Village People would perform on stage dressed as construction workers, policemen, even an American Indian with full feathered headdress. Their songs "Macho Man," "In The Navy," and "Y.M.C.A." were huge radio hits, and while the Village People may have looked like cartoon characters to some people, to others the group's costumes and song lyrics reflected homosexual stereotypes in New York's Greenwich "Village."

The Village People, "In The Navy."

Eventually every group that recorded a song which made people dance were grouped into the Disco mode, even if their sound came from another genre. One such group was K.C. and the Sunshine Band, who even though their music reflected the salsa and Latin rhythms around their Hialeah, Florida studios, are grouped into the disco category simply because their music made people get up and shake their booties. The band's two main songwriters, Harry Wayne Casey and Richard Finch, produced other artists for TK Records, including "Rock Your Baby," a #1 pop and disco hit for George McCrae. When Casey and Finch formed the Sunshine Band, their earliest funk songs, "Queen of Clubs" and "Sound Your Funky Horn," became hits in England, and paved the way for American chart-topping hits like "That's The Way (I Like It)" and "I'm Your Boogie Man."

An early release by K.C. and the Sunshine Band.

In 1979, disco music began its descent into oblivion. The music itself was now considered a suitable beat for children's music, as albums like *Sesame Street Fever* and *Mickey Mouse Disco* appeared in stores. Other forms of music, such as punk, new wave, and arena rock, began to dominate the airwaves, taking away disco's radio base. Some radio stations stopped playing disco records, advertising their stations as "Bee-Gee Free."

In fact, much of the blame for disco's demise can be laid at the feet of record companies. In the late 1970s, record companies could press millions of copies of an artist's debut single, send them to stores, and if the stores didn't sell all the records, they could be returned for credit. In one case, when Cher was about to receive a gold record for sales of 500,000 copies of her 12-inch disco single "Take Me Home," her record label noticed she had only sold 380,000 copies. So the day before Cher was to receive the award, the record label printed 120,000 copies of "Take Me Home" and sent them to stores—even if they were returned, the total made Cher's gold record a legitimate award.

But what happened to all those 12-inch discs? Many of them clogged cutout bins for years. If record collectors in 1979 didn't like disco, they would show their contempt to anybody who would listen. During a baseball doubleheader in Chicago, fans were asked to bring their disco records to the stadium for use in "Disco Demolition Night." After the first game of the doubleheader, thousands of disco records were strewn all over Comiskey Park—and blown up. (The second game of the doubleheader had to be forfeited because the field was now as unplayable as the chunks of vinyl littering the grass and basepaths.)

Trivia

Bryan Adams' first hit was a disco song—not by his choosing, though. Remix expert John Luongo took Adams' track "Let Me Take You Dancing," sped up his vocals and added a disco beat. It became a Top 5 dance track, but has never resurfaced on any Adams' greatest hits or reissue package.

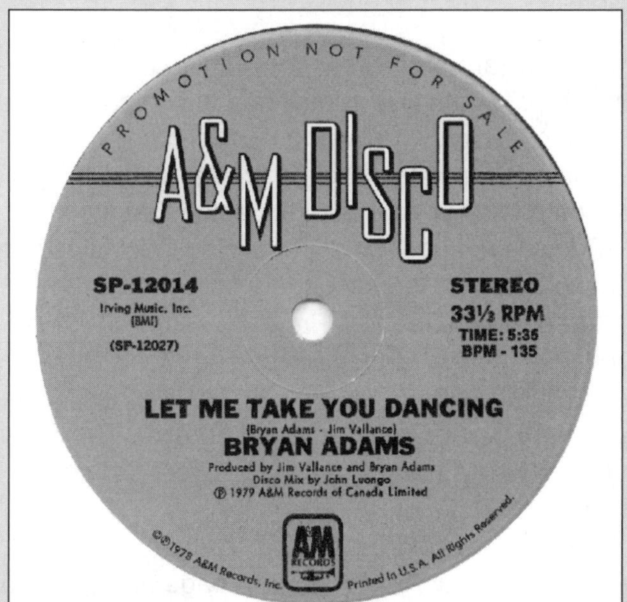

Bryan Adams' first hit was a disco song, "Let Me Take You Dancing."

The last remaining profitable disco labels were small independent companies like Prelude Records in New York City. Prelude's biggest disco group, "D" Train, may have been just the duo of Hubert Eaves III and James "D Train" Williams, but their keyboard-influenced disco-funk sound replicated what originally took a full orchestra to produce.

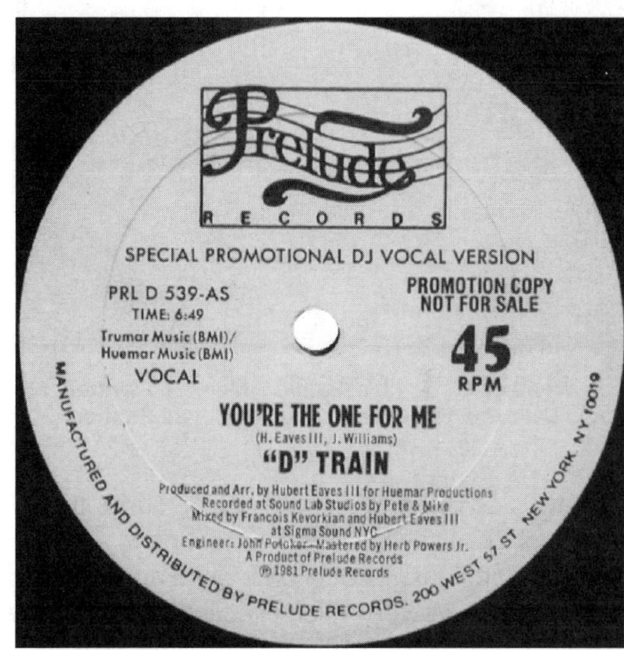

"D" Train's biggest hit, this promo copy specifically informed DJ's to play this record at 45 RPM—a unique request, because most American disco 12-inch discs played at 33-1/3 RPM.

Even though disco was considered a "four-letter" word by musical elitists, disco-themed songs still continued to fill dance floors and cross over to the pop charts. Many of these early 1980s disco songs were classified as "Hi-NRG" ("high-energy") songs, and contained female vocalists cooing about the availability of male suitors. The biggest disco/dance songs of this era included Miquel Brown's "So Many Men, So Little Time" and the Weather Girls' "It's Raining Men."

The "disco sound" would sporadically appear over the next few years, but people were quick to call the new discs "dance records," trying to avoid the five-letter word as much as possible. Even when the band U2 recorded a song called "Discotheque," employed 1970s dance rhythms, and even dressed up in the music video as the Village People, the record itself was considered a poor seller for the band.

The Weather Girls' "It's Raining Men," co-written by David Letterman's keyboard sidekick, Paul Shaffer.

What To Look For: With the 1970s currently experiencing a kitschy revival period, people are hunting for original disco records once again. Disco 45s and LPs have very little collectible value (many titles are barely worth $10 with both vinyl and picture sleeve in near-mint condition), but 12-inch disco discs are especially prized; 12-inch discs often contained extended mixes that were not available on LP, and are currently not available on any CD reissue. Be aware that many 12-inch discs may contain "cue burn," caused when a disc jockey backspins a record to its beginning notes and holds it with his fingers, while the turntable spins underneath. Once the DJ releases his fingers on the vinyl, the record spins almost exactly to the beat (called "slip-cueing"). But since records weren't designed for a needle to travel anti-clockwise on the groove, you may hear a slight hissing before the song's intro. That's cue burn.

Many of the original disco labels, such as TK, RSO, and Casablanca, no longer exist. Records may still be pressed with those company names on the label; in these cases, the trademark may have been licensed by another company, so double-check the fine print around the label's perimeter to see if the record is a first pressing or a reissue. Because disco music was only around for a few years, the colorful 12-inch company sleeves often remained consistent throughout disco's reign, with only an advertising sticker marking the difference between two artists using the same label. Company sleeves should be crisp and even; 12-inch covers are often subjected to seam splitting, heavy ringwear, and even magic marker graffiti (usually from a DJ scribbling beats-per-minute or personal information on the jacket).

A "special package for disco DJs," as noted in the lower left-hand corner of this France Joli release—two copies of the record, allowing the DJ to remix the song while at the dance club. Since two records were jammed into a single disc sleeve, ringwear is very common on these jackets.

Another rare and lesser known disco item is the remix disc. Some DJs subscribed to companies like Rockpool, which would send them records filled with unique remixes of hot dance tracks. Although the companies specifically requested that their remix discs not be resold, some Rockpool titles still surface today on the secondary collectors' market.

References: Dannon, Frederic, *Hit Men: Power Brokers and Fast Money Inside The Music Business*, Vintage Books, New York, 1991; Jones, Alan; Kantonen, Jussi, *Saturday Night Forever: The Story of Disco*, Mainstream Publishing, Great Britain, 1999.

Web pages: Andrea Izzotti's '70s dance/disco page: *http://www.70disco.com;* a page dedicated to the most famous disco of them all, New York's Studio 54: *http://www.geocities.com/westhollywood/heights/5939.*

Trivia

Evelyn "Champagne" King's father once sang for the Orioles and for the Harptones. While working as a cleaning lady at the Sigma Sound Studios in Philadelphia, a producer overheard her singing as she worked. That producer helped her get a contract with RCA, where, as Evelyn "Champagne" King, she had a string of disco hits. Even when disco died, she continued to have hits like "Love Come Down" and "I'm In Love," but by then she had dropped the word "Champagne" from her name.

Evelyn "Champagne" King's big disco hit, "Shame."

45s	Year	VG	VG+	NM
The Bee Gees, "Jive Talkin'" / "Wind of Change" (RSO 510)	1975		$2.00	$4.00
The Bee Gees, "You Should Be Dancing" / "Subway" (RSO 853)	1976		$2.00	$4.00
The Bee Gees, "Night Fever" / "Down The Road" (RSO 889)	1978		$2.00	$4.00
Blondie, "Heart of Glass" / "11:59" (Chrysalis 2295)	1979		$2.00	$4.00
(with picture sleeve, add:)	1979		$2.00	$4.00
Rick Dees and his Cast of Idiots, "Disco Duck" (Pt. 1) / (Pt. 2) (RSO 857)	1976		$2.00	$4.00
Marvin Gaye, "Got To Give It Up" (Pt. 1) / (Pt. 2) (Tamla 54280)	1977		$2.00	$4.00
(with picture sleeve, add:)	1977	$2.50	$5.00	$10.00
Gloria Gaynor, "Never Can Say Goodbye" / "We Can Just Make It" (Columbia 14748)	1974		$2.00	$4.00
Gloria Gaynor, "I Will Survive" / "Substitute" (Polydor 14508)	1978		$2.00	$4.00
Thelma Houston, "Don't Leave Me This Way" / "Today Will Soon Be Yesterday" (Tamla 54278)	1977		$2.00	$4.00
(if white label promo, contains long and short versions of "Don't Leave Me This Way")	1977		$3.00	$6.00

45s	Year	VG	VG+	NM
KC and the Sunshine Band, "That's The Way (I Like It)" / "What Makes You Happy" (TK 1015)	1975		$2.00	$4.00
KC and the Sunshine Band, "Keep It Comin' Love" / "Baby I Love You" (TK 1023)	1977		$2.00	$4.00
(with picture sleeve, add:)	1977		$2.50	$5.00
Eddie Kendricks, "Girl, You Need A Change of Mind" (Pt. 1) / (Pt. 2) (Tamla 54230)	1973		$2.50	$5.00
Ben E. King, "Supernatural Thing" (Pt. 1) / (Pt. 2) (Atlantic 3241)	1975		$2.50	$5.00
Van McCoy and the Soul City Symphony, "The Hustle" / "Hey Girl, Come and Get It" (Avco 4653)	1975		$2.00	$4.00
George McCrae, "Rock Your Baby (parts 1 and 2) (TK 1004)	1974		$2.50	$5.00
Gwen McCrae, "Rockin' Chair" / "It Keeps On Raining" (Cat 1996)	1975		$2.50	$5.00
MFSB, "TSOP (The Sound of Philadelphia)" / "Something For Nothing" (Philadelphia International 3540)	1974		$2.50	$5.00
Vicki Sue Robinson, "Turn The Beat Around" / "Lack of Respect" (RCA PB-10435)	1975		$2.50	$5.00
Silver Convention, "Fly Robin Fly" / "Chains of Love" (Midland International MB-10339)				
(if "Fly Robin Fly" is over 4 minutes long, matrix number 10339-A)	1975		$3.00	$6.00
(if "Fly Robin Fly" is 3:05 minutes long, matrix number 10339-Z)	1975		$2.00	$4.00
Rod Stewart, "Da Ya Think I'm Sexy?" / "Scarred and Scared" (Warner Bros. 8724)	1978		$2.00	$4.00
(with picture sleeve, add:)	1978		$2.50	$5.00
Donna Summer, "Love To Love You Baby" / "Need-A-Man Blues" (Oasis 401) (original first mix of song)	1975	$3.00	$6.00	$12.00
Donna Summer, "Love To Love You Baby" (4:55 time) / "Love To Love You Baby" (3:24 time) (Oasis 401 AA)	1975		$3.00	$6.00
Donna Summer, "I Feel Love" / "Can't We Just Sit Down (And Talk It Over)" (Casablanca 884)				
(if "I Feel Love" is listed as B-side, first pressings)	1977		$3.00	$6.00
(if "I Feel Love" is listed as A-side, second pressings)	1977		$2.50	$5.00
Donna Summer, "Hot Stuff" / "Journey To The Center Of Your Heart" (Casablanca 978)	1979		$2.00	$4.00
A Taste of Honey, "Boogie Oogie Oogie" / "World Spin" (Capitol 4565)	1978		$2.00	$4.00
(with picture sleeve, add:)	1978		$2.50	$5.00
The Trammps, "Disco Inferno" / "You Touch My Hot Line" (Atlantic 3389)	1977		$3.00	$6.00
(with picture sleeve, add:)	1977	$2.00	$4.00	$8.00
(if B-side is "That's Where The Happy People Go")	1978		$2.50	$5.00
The Village People, "Y.M.C.A." / "The Women" (Casablanca 973)	1978		$2.50	$5.00
The Village People, "In The Navy" / "Manhattan Woman" (Casablanca 973)	1979		$2.50	$5.00
(with promo-only picture sleeve, add:)	1979	$5.00	$10.00	$20.00

12-inch	Year	VG	VG+	NM
Marvin Gaye, "A Funky Space Reincarnation" / (instrumental) (Motown 00014)	1978	$3.00	$6.00	$12.00
K.C. and the Sunshine Band, "Do You Wanna Go Party" (2 versions) (Sunshine Sound 207)	1979	$2.00	$4.00	$8.00
Van McCoy and the Soul City Symphony, "Rhythms of the World" / "Soul Cha Cha" / "That's The Joint" (H&L 2002)	1976	$5.00	$10.00	$20.00
Vicki Sue Robinson, "Turn The Beat Around" / "Hold Tight" (RCA PC-11507)	1979	$3.00	$6.00	$12.00
The Rolling Stones, "Miss You" / "Far Away Eyes" (Rolling Stones DK 4609)				
(with standard Atlantic-Atco sleeve)	1978	$2.50	$5.00	$10.00
(with custom Rolling Stones sleeve)	1978	$3.00	$6.00	$12.00
Donna Summer, "Love To Love You Baby" / "Try Me, I Know We Can Make It" (Casablanca NBLP 7041)	1976	$3.75	$7.50	$15.00
(if B-side is Parliament's "Flash Light," Casablanca PRO 1148, promo-only reissue)	1994	$5.00	$10.00	$20.00
Donna Summer, "Hot Stuff" / "Bad Girls" (Casablanca NBD 20167) (one-sided 12", both songs are on Side A)	1979	$3.75	$7.50	$15.00
The Trammps, "The Night The Lights Went Out" / "Hooked For Life" (Atlantic DSKO 173)	1977	$3.75	$7.50	$15.00
The Whispers, "And The Beat Goes On" / "Can You Do The Boogie" (Solar 11895)	1979	$3.75	$7.50	$15.00
Barry White, "I Love To Sing The Songs I Sing" / (b-side unknown)	1979	$3.00	$6.00	$12.00

LPs	Year	VG	VG+	NM
B.T. Express, Non-Stop (Roadshow 41001)	1975	$3.00	$6.00	$12.00
Gloria Gaynor, "Substitute" / "Substitute" (Polydor PD-D-504) (white label promo)	1978	$2.00	$4.00	$8.00
The Hues Corporation, Freedom for the Stallion (RCA Victor APL1-0323)	1973	$2.50	$5.00	$10.00
KC and the Sunshine Band, Do It Good (TK 500)	1974	$3.00	$6.00	$12.00
KC and the Sunshine Band, Greatest Hits (TK 612)	1980	$2.50	$5.00	$10.00
George McCrae, Rock Your Baby (TK 501)	1974	$2.50	$5.00	$10.00
Gwen McCrae, Rockin' Chair (Cat 2605)	1974	$2.50	$5.00	$10.00
MFSB, Love Is The Message (Philadelphia International KZ 32707)	1974	$2.50	$5.00	$10.00
Silver Convention, Silver Convention (Midland International BKL1-1369)	1976	$2.50	$5.00	$10.00
(if on Midsong International BXL1-1369, reissue)	1978	$2.00	$4.00	$8.00

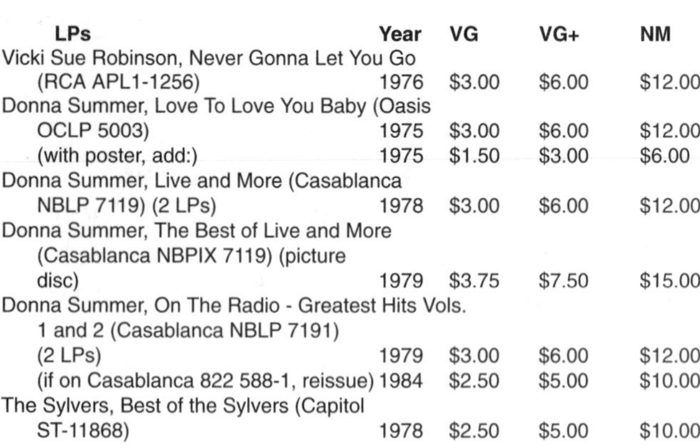

LPs	Year	VG	VG+	NM
Vicki Sue Robinson, Never Gonna Let You Go (RCA APL1-1256)	1976	$3.00	$6.00	$12.00
Donna Summer, Love To Love You Baby (Oasis OCLP 5003)	1975	$3.00	$6.00	$12.00
(with poster, add:)	1975	$1.50	$3.00	$6.00
Donna Summer, Live and More (Casablanca NBLP 7119) (2 LPs)	1978	$3.00	$6.00	$12.00
Donna Summer, The Best of Live and More (Casablanca NBPIX 7119) (picture disc)	1979	$3.75	$7.50	$15.00
Donna Summer, On The Radio - Greatest Hits Vols. 1 and 2 (Casablanca NBLP 7191) (2 LPs)	1979	$3.00	$6.00	$12.00
(if on Casablanca 822 588-1, reissue)	1984	$2.50	$5.00	$10.00
The Sylvers, Best of the Sylvers (Capitol ST-11868)	1978	$2.50	$5.00	$10.00

Not every 12" disco hit became a subsequent radio hit. A rare Barry White 12" of "I Love To Sing The Songs I Sing."

Vicki Sue Robinson's "Turn The Beat Around," a prime example of disco with a full orchestra.

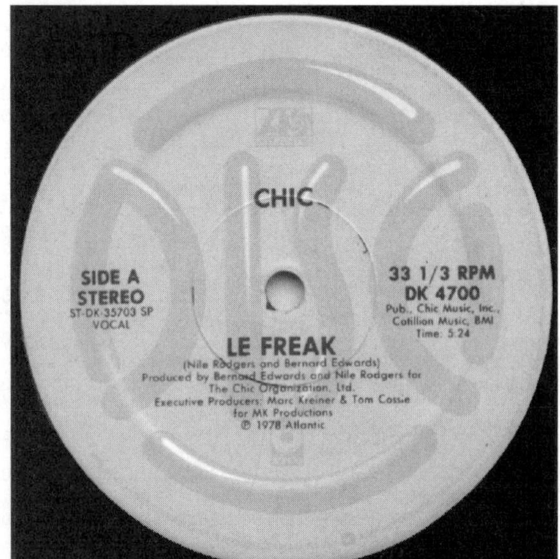

And as more consumers purchased 12" singles, many labels reissued classic dance tracks in that format. Here's Chic's "Le Freak," not just available for DJ's any more.

First pressings of Donna Summer's "Love To Love You Baby" contain a different mix and a different B-side, "Need-A-Man Blues." As can be seen from this B-side, this pressing is normal.

DOO-WOP

History: Doo-wop groups and music achieved their greatest popularity during the early years of rock 'n' roll, from 1954 to 1963, and the doo-wop sound can still be heard in some of today's hits. Early doo-wop began in the 1950s, when high school friends would sing in assemblies and glee clubs by day, but at night, under the iridescent warmth of a street lamp, singers would blend their voices together, snapping their fingers for a drum beat.

The earliest doo-wop groups were R&B acts from the 1950s, many of whom were influenced by the intricate harmonies of gospel choirs. Groups like the Ravens, the Orioles, the Dominoes, and the Crows had hits on the R&B charts, and made some inroads into the pop music field before their songs were "covered" by white vocal groups and artists. But by the mid-1950s, both white and black vocal harmony groups co-existed on the pop charts, all unified in doo-wop music.

An early doo-wop classic, a 78 pressing of the Crows song "Gee."

The characteristics of doo-wop records include vocal harmony of three to seven singers, with vocal parts ranging from falsetto to bass. The lyrics are easy to hear and to understand—except maybe the nonsense syllables scatted throughout the verses, refrains, and bridges.

Hundreds of doo-wop groups in major cities were offered record contracts and promises of fame and fortune. Many of these groups performed on rock 'n' roll package tours, and groups like Dion and the Belmonts, Frankie Lymon and the Teenagers, the Moonglows, and the Del-Vikings found stardom. Other groups, such as the Platters, the Coasters, the Drifters, and the Four Seasons, rose from doo-wop backgrounds to offer their full vocal harmonies to the tapestry of rock 'n' roll.

While the Del Vikings' "Come Go With Me" is extremely common on the Dot label, this first version on Fee Bee is highly collectible. Photo Credit: Courtesy Good Rockin' Tonight/Collectors Universe.

Doo-wop in the 1950s was an urban sound—its greatest popularity came from the groups in New York, Los Angeles, Philadelphia, Boston, and Pittsburgh, from the men who sang on street corners, the women who sang at assemblies and social functions. In these major cities, the music of the Jive Five, the Harptones, Lee Andrews and the Hearts, the Marcels, and the Chords, survived and thrived.

Legend has it that if two doo-wop groups ever met each other on the street corner, the groups might challenge each other to a musical duel, endeavoring to discover who could attach better harmonies to "Sunday Kind of Love" or "Somewhere Over the Rainbow," each group fiercely guarding their vocal territories as if they were streets of gold.

While other groups used "Over the Rainbow" to prove their vocalistic prowess, the Dimensions actually turned their doo-wop version into a Top 40 hit.

This beat-up copy of the Four Lovers' "You're The Apple Of My Eye" might stay in a junk box for years—unless one knew this was one of the first recordings for a group that would later become Frankie Valli and the Four Seasons.

Interest in doo-wop groups and the music they sang has been augmented by the release of successful nostalgia films like *"American Graffiti," "The Five Heartbeats," "Why do Fools Fall In Love" and "American Hot Wax,"* as well as the Broadway show *"Forever Plaid."* Today, thanks to successful CD box sets of classic and rare doo-wop music from labels like Rhino and Collectibles, fans are discovering—many for the first time—some of the most intricate vocal harmonies of the rock era.

Since the most popular doo-wop hits were pressed on millions of 45s and 78s, their value has not significantly risen. As a point of reference, the most common doo-wop records are the ones most often heard on oldies stations today. But for some doo-wop songs, especially those tracks that were not hits upon their original release, or those containing performances by bands which would later change their name and achieve superstardom, collectors may spend thousands of dollars searching for near-mint copies of these extremely rare recordings. Some of these high-priced doo-wop records either contain a legendary doo-wop recording rarely heard today, or if an album exists for a doo-wop group known only for its hit singles.

Many doo-wop groups of the 1950s only recorded a couple of songs, not enough tracks for an album. But for those who did have enough material and time to record an album, these 12-inch LPs, with their low print runs, are very hard to find and are extremely collectible today. In the 1950s, the single release—either on 45 or on 78—was the most popular musical format; an album was recorded only so that a record company could cash in on the single's success.

Trivia

Arthur Lee Maye sang lead vocal for his doo-wop group the Crowns, but he also played professional baseball for the Milwaukee Braves. His musical hits included "Gloria" and "Set My Heart Free"; his baseball hits included a .274 lifetime batting average and, in 1964, Maye led the major leagues with 44 doubles.

This version of the Chantels' LP is very rare, as the cover shows the vocal quintet on the cover. Later pressings show two teenagers hunched over a jukebox. Courtesy Good Rockin' Tonight / Collectors Universe.

Have you seen a 45 RPM copy of this record? Only three 78 pressings have survived to this day; a legitimate 45 copy of the Five Sharps' "Stormy Weather" is the Holy Grail of all doo-wop records. Photo Credit: From the Collection of George Russo, "The Wanderer."

The Story of "Stormy Weather"

One of the rarest doo-wop records in history is the Five Sharps' 1952 doo-wop song "Stormy Weather." The song begins with thunderstorm sound effects and a mournful piano intro, an aural concept that preceded Phil Spector's "wall of sound" work by a decade. The Sharps sang "Stormy Weather" in a slow, emotional yet impassioned manner, a classic doo-wop rendition of its time. Unfortunately, very few people have ever heard the song. The master tape for this song was lost years ago, and only three copies of this song exist in 78 RPM format—and of those three, one known copy is cracked. Desire for this record has been so great, however, that 20-year-old reproductions of "Stormy Weather" have appeared, mastered on red vinyl from a transcription of that cracked 78. Jubilee Records, where the Five Sharps originally recorded "Stormy Weather," eventually released a new version by a new group of "Five Sharps"—but because these new singers are "Five Sharps" in name only, the value of this version is slight at best. The 1960s re-recording eliminates the introductory piano solo and has more thunderstorm effects throughout the song. Although theoretically a 45 should exist of the original "Stormy Weather"—Jubilee Records was pressing 45s at that time—no 45s of that title have surfaced in nearly 50 years. If a legitimate 45 of "Stormy Weather" ever appeared, the selling price could rival any rare Elvis Presley or Beatles record ever made.

Just be aware—this 45 of "Stormy Weather" is not a legitimate pressing of the original Five Sharps song. It is, however, a re-recording of the song, as done by a new group of Five Sharps. From the Collection of Val Shively.

What To Look For: For doo-wop collectors, the most desirable recordings are songs that were pressed on small independent labels with poor distribution. Many doo-wop groups had their first release on a regional label, then were later picked up by a major label. Because of the low print runs by most independent labels, doo-wop pressings on these labels are much more desirable to collectors, even though both the minor and major labels may contain the exact same song.

Even the format of an album can make a huge difference to doo-wop collectors. The 12-inch album *Billy Ward and His Dominoes* (Federal 548), released in 1958, can command up to $3,000 in near-mint condition. But if you have the 10-inch version released three years earlier, and kept it in near-mint condition, it's worth more than $25,000 to a doo-wop collector.

Since the popularity of doo-wop music coincided with the rise of 45s and decline of 78s as a popular format, most collectors will look for a doo-wop group on 45 rather than 78, but will purchase a 78 if the song was never pressed on a 45.

Doo-wop music existed during the last years of 78 RPM discs, and their value varies proportionately. Although doo-wop 78s garner a lesser price than the same song on a 45, things change after 1958, when the major labels stopped offering 78s for sale. Some smaller labels continued pressing 78s, and in fact those late 50s 10-inch artifacts are actually worth more than the simultaneous 45 recordings.

The Flamingos hit from 1959, "I Only Have Eyes For You," is very common on 45.

But on 78 RPM, this record is extremely rare, as 1959 was one of the last years for pressing 78's in America. Courtesy Good Rockin' Tonight/Collectors Universe.

Trivia

The Capris' "There's A Moon Out Tonight" was recorded in 1958 on Planet Records, a tiny label. Three years and one label change later, the song became a Top 10 hit on the Old Town label.

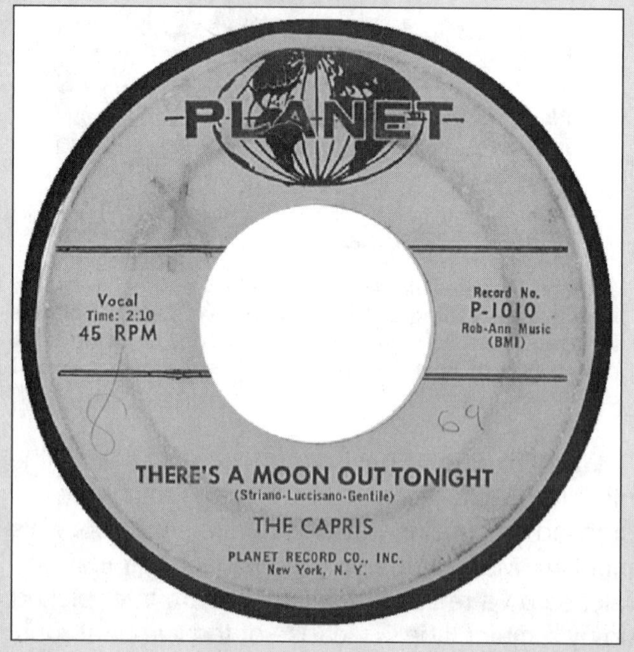

The first pressings of "There's A Moon Out Tonight" on Planet Records. Courtesy Good Rockin' Tonight / Collectors Universe.

If you want to collect doo-wop 78s, make sure the 78 label is from the same company as the 45. Frankie Lymon and the Teenagers' "Why Do Fools Fall In Love" was pressed on Gee Records, and exists in both 45 and 78 formats. It also exists in Canadian pressings on the Apex label, and in New Zealand pressings as a Columbia release. Some countries continued to press 78s long after American record companies ceased using the format; for example, in the 1960s, some Beatles records were pressed on 78s in India.

On the 78 of "Why Do Fools Fall In Love," the "GEE" logo touches the small center hole. Courtesy Last Vestige Music Store, Albany, N.Y.

The Skyliners' debut LP is hard enough to find—but in their hometown of Pittsburgh, the album can fetch premium prices—if you can find it. Courtesy Last Vestige Music Store, Albany, N.Y.

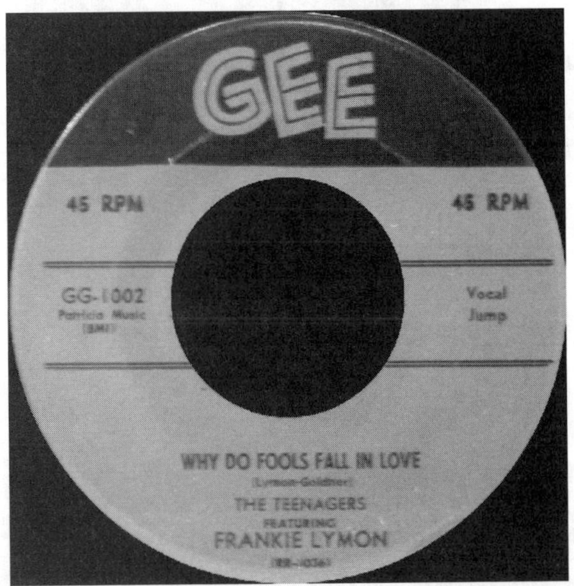

The label artwork is much smaller on the 7" pressing, but was released at the same time as the 78. From the Collection of Val Shively.

Although there are doo-wop collectors across North America, there are more doo-wop collectors in major metropolitan cities like New York, Boston, Los Angeles, Philadelphia, Baltimore and Pittsburgh, partially because doo-wop was born on the street corners of these cities. In fact, more than any other musical genre, the collectible value of doo-wop records can vary from city to city, and many doo-wop groups can command a higher price in their hometown.

Because of their high collectible value, some of the rarest doo-wop 45s have been bootlegged. Copies of the Five Keys' "Red Sails in the Sunset," the Royals' "Starting From Tonight" and the Clovers' "Yes Sir That's My Baby" exist both as legitimate pressings and as cheap bootlegs. Make sure you are working with a reputable dealer who is willing to offer a money-back guarantee if you are not satisfied with the record's authenticity.

By the same token, some record companies have re-issued classic 45s, many of whom have been "enhanced" (electronic stereo, additional instruments, even re-recorded vocals). The Penguins' "Earth Angel" exists in two versions: the first version with the Penguins' harmonies against a subdued musical background (on Dootone 348, B-side is "Hey Senorita"); the second version with the music almost drowning out the Penguins (on Mercury 70943, B-side is "Ice"). Doo-wop collectors often want the first version of any doo-wop record, and may acquire the second version only to complete a collection.

The doo-wop era may have coincided with the last pressings of 78 RPM records, but it also coincided with the earliest uses of stereo recordings for the rock era. While many of these stereo 45 pressings had terrible stereo separation—singer in one speaker, music in the other—some doo-wop singers actually re-recorded their classic hits with true stereo separation.

This pressing of the Fleetwoods' *"Come Softly To Me"* on Liberty Records has the monaural version of the trio's doo-wop hit.

The stereo version, on the other hand, is a re-recording—the percussion heard on this stereo record is actually lead singer Gary Troxel shaking car keys in his hand.

Reference Books: Gribin, Dr. Anthony J., and Schiff, Dr. Matthew M., *Doo Wop: The Forgotten Third of Rock and Roll*, Krause Publications, Iola, Wisconsin, 1992; Gribin, Dr. Anthony J.; Schiff, Dr. Matthew M., *The Complete Book of Doo-Wop*, Krause Publications, Iola, Wisconsin, 2000; Groia, Phil, *They All Sang On The Corner*, Phillie Dee Enterprises, New Rochelle, New York, 1983; Propes, Steve, *Those Oldies But Goodies: A Guide To 50s Record Collecting*, The MacMillan Company, New York, 1973; Shannon, Bob; Javna, John, *Behind the Hits: Inside Stories of Classic Pop and Rock and Roll*, Warner Books, New York, N.Y. 1986.

Trivia

"Little Darlin'" was originally recorded by Maurice Williams and the Gladiolas. But just as the song began to generate some airplay, a white cover version of "Little Darlin'" by the Diamonds became a runaway hit. A few years later, Williams, with his new group the Zodiacs, recorded the song "Stay," and watched that song rise all the way to #1.

The Diamonds' cover version. From the Collection of Val Shively.

The Gladiolas' original "Little Darlin'".

Maurice Williams and the Zodiacs' "Stay" has been covered by both the Four Seasons and by Jackson Browne.

Web pages: The Vocal Group Harmony Web site: *http://www.vocal-harmony.com*; The Platters' Web site: *http://www.theplatters.com*; Primarily A Cappella, a site dedicated to instrument-less vocalists and groups: *http://www.singers.com*; The Wanderer, the "First Oldies Site on the Net," has sections devoted to rare doo-wop and to other 1950s and 1960s music: *http://www.wanderers.com/wanderers.*

Museums: The Vocal Group Hall of Fame and Museum, 98 East State St., Sharon, Pennsylvania 16146; 1-800-753-1648; *http://www.vocalhalloffame.com.*

45s	Year	VG	VG+	NM
The Aquatones, "You" / "She's The One For Me" (Fargo 1001)	1958	$6.25	$12.50	$25.00
The Blue Belles, "The Story of a Fool" / "Cancel the Call" (Atlantic 987) (Patti LaBelle's first group)	1953	$37.50	$75.00	$150.00
The Bobbettes, "Mr. Lee" / "Look at the Stars" (Atlantic 1144)	1957	$6.25	$12.50	$25.00
The Bobbettes, "I Shot Mr. Lee" / "Untrue Love" (Atlantic 2069)	1960	$7.50	$15.00	$30.00
The Cadillacs, "Speedoo" / "Let Me Explain" (Josie 778)	1955	$12.50	$25.00	$50.00
The Capris, "There's A Moon Out Tonight" / "Indian Girl"				
(if on Planet 1010, first pressings)	1958	$400.00	$800.00	$1,200.00
(if on Old Town 1094, light blue label)	1961	$7.50	$15.00	$30.00
(if on Old Town 1094, black label, second pressing)	1962	$5.00	$10.00	$20.00
(if on Trommers 101, either red or white label)	1961	$6.25	$12.50	$25.00
(if on Lost Nite 101, first pressings on pink label)	1961	$12.50	$25.00	$50.00
(if on Lost Nite 101, later pressings on yellow label)	196?	$2.00	$4.00	$8.00
The Chantels, "Maybe" / "Come, My Little Baby" (End 1005)				
(if on black label, first pressing)	1957	$20.00	$40.00	$80.00
(if on gray-white label, second pressing)	1958	$10.00	$20.00	$40.00
(if on multi-colored label, subsequent pressing)	1959	$5.00	$10.00	$20.00
The Chiffons, "Tonight's The Night" / "Do You Know?" (Big Deal 6003)	1960	$12.50	$25.00	$50.00
The Chiffons, "He's So Fine" / "Oh My Lover" (Laurie 3152)	1963	$5.00	$10.00	$20.00
The Chords, "Sh-Boom" (Cat 104)				
(if B-side is "Cross Over The Bridge")	1954	$30.00	$60.00	$120.00
(if B-side is "Little Maiden")	1954	$15.00	$30.00	$60.00
(if on Atco 6213, group listed as "The Sh-Booms")	1961	$3.75	$7.50	$15.00
The Cleftones, "Heart and Soul" / "How Do You Feel" (Gee 1064)	1961	$6.25	$12.50	$25.00
The Coasters, "Searchin'" / "Young Blood" (Atco 6087)				
(if maroon label, first pressing)	1957	$17.50	$35.00	$70.00
(if yellow-white label, second and subsequent pressings)	1957	$6.25	$12.50	$25.00
The Coasters, "Yakety Yak" / "Zing Went The Strings Of My Heart" (Atco 6116)	1958	$6.25	$12.50	$25.00
The Crescendos, "Oh Julie" / "My Little Girl"				
(if on Nasco 6005)	1957	$6.25	$12.50	$25.00
(if on Tap 7027)	1962	$3.75	$7.50	$15.00
(with picture sleeve, add:)	1962	$6.25	$12.50	$25.00
The Crowns, "Kiss And Make Up" / "I'll Forget About You" (R&B 6901) (group became the second Drifters)	1958	$12.50	$25.00	$50.00
The Crows, "Gee" / "Love You So" (Rama 5)				
(with blue label, red vinyl)	1953	$62.50	$125.00	$250.00
(with blue label, black vinyl)	1953	$17.50	$35.00	$70.00
(with red label, black vinyl)	1953	$7.50	$15.00	$30.00
Danny and the Juniors, "At the Hop" / "Sometimes When I'm All Alone"				
(if on Singular 711, blue label, machine-stamped numbers in dead wax, "Orchestra directed by Artie Singer" on label, song begins with a "count-in")	1957	$300.00	$600.00	$1,200.00
(if on Singular 711, same as above except no mention of Artie Singer on label)	1957	$250.00	$500.00	$1,000.00
(any Singular copies without the "count-in" are probably reproductions)				
(if on ABC-Paramount 9871, label picked the song up for national release)	1957	$7.50	$15.00	$30.00
The Del Vikings, "Come Go With Me" / "How Can I Find True Love"				

45s	Year	VG	VG+	NM
(if on Fee Bee 205, orange label, bee on top)	1957	$125.00	$250.00	$500.00
(if on Fee Bee 205, orange label, only one side has a bee drawing)	1957	$62.50	$125.00	$250.00
(if on Fee Bee 205, orange label, no bees)	1957	$7.50	$15.00	$30.00
(if on Dot 15538)	1957	$7.50	$15.00	$30.00
(if on Dot 16092)	1960	$5.00	$10.00	$20.00
(if on Dot 16236, B-side is "Whispering Bells")	1961	$5.00	$10.00	$20.00
(if on Fee Bee 205, B-side is "Whispering Bells")	1964	$5.00	$10.00	$20.00
The Del Vikings, "Somewhere Over The Rainbow" / "Hey, Seniorita" (Luniverse 106)	1957	$25.00	$50.00	$100.00
The Demensions, "Over The Rainbow" / "Nursery Rhyme Rock" (Mohawk 116)				
(if label is maroon)	1960	$12.50	$25.00	$50.00
(if label is brown)	1960	$7.50	$15.00	$30.00
(if label is red)	1960	$6.25	$12.50	$25.00
Dion and the Belmonts, "I Wonder Why" / "Teen Angel" (Laurie 3013)				
(if on gray label, first pressing)	1958	$15.00	$30.00	$60.00
(if on light blue label)	1958	$7.50	$15.00	$30.00
(if on black-red-white label)	1958	$5.00	$10.00	$20.00
Dion and the Belmonts, "A Teenager in Love" / "I've Cried Before" (Laurie 3027)				
(if mono, Laurie 3027)	1959	$6.25	$12.50	$25.00
(if stereo, Laurie S-3027)	1959	$12.50	$25.00	$50.00
The Dreamlovers, "When We Get Married" / "Just Because" (Heritage 102)	1961	$5.00	$10.00	$20.00
The Dreamlovers, "Amazons and Coyotes" / "Together" (Swan 4167)				
(if white label)	1963	$5.00	$10.00	$20.00
(if black label)	1963	$3.00	$6.00	$12.00
The Drifters, "Such A Night" / "Lucille" (Atlantic 1019)	1954	$17.50	$35.00	$70.00
The Drifters, "There Goes My Baby" / "Oh My Love" (Atlantic 2025)	1959	$6.25	$12.50	$25.00
The Drifters, "This Magic Moment" / "Baltimore" (Atlantic 2050)	1960	$5.00	$10.00	$20.00
The Duprees, "You Belong To Me" / "Take Me As I Am" (Coed 569)	1962	$5.00	$10.00	$20.00
The Edsels, "Rama Lama Ding Dong" / "Bells"				
(if on Dub 2843, A-side is "Lama Rama Ding Dong")	1958	$17.50	$35.00	$70.00
(if on Dub 2843, correctly spelled A-side)	1958	$12.50	$25.00	$50.00
(if on Twin 700, both the Twin and the above Dub versions are the same recording)	1961	$6.25	$12.50	$25.00
(if on Musictone 1144)	1961	$3.00	$6.00	$12.00
(if on Dub 2843, 1970s reproduction of label with alternate take on A-side)	197?		$2.50	$5.00
The Elegants, "Little Star" / "Getting Dizzy" (Apt 25005)				
(if on all-black Apt label)	1958	$12.50	$25.00	$50.00
(if on Apt black label with rainbow)	1958	$10.00	$20.00	$40.00
The Falcons, "You're So Fine" / "Goddess of Angels"				
(if on Flick 001)	1959	$100.00	$200.00	$400.00
(if on Unart 2013, mono)	1959	$7.50	$15.00	$30.00
(if on Unart 2013-S, rechanneled stereo)	1959	$20.00	$40.00	$80.00
The Five Satins, "I'll Remember (In The Still of The Nite)" / "The Jones Girl"				
(if on Standord 200, original title listed as "In the Still of the Nite")	1956	$300.00	$600.00	$900.00
(if on Standord 200, same as above, but with "Produced by Martin Kuegell" credit)	1956	$1,000	$1,500	$2,000
(if on Ember 1005, red label, has "6016A" in the trail-off vinyl)	1956	$50.00	$100.00	$200.00
(if on Ember 1005, red label, has "E-2015-45" in the trail-off vinyl)	1956	$12.50	$25.00	$30.00
(if on Ember 1005, red label, has "E-1005" in the trail-off vinyl)	1956	$7.50	$15.00	$30.00
(if on Ember 1005, red label, now retitled "I'll Remember (In The Still Of The Nite)")	1956	$12.50	$25.00	$50.00
(if on Ember 1005, multi-colored "logs" label, marked "Special Demand Release")	1959	$7.50	$15.00	$30.00
(if on Ember 1005, multi-colored "logs" label, no reference to a special demand release)	1961	$7.50	$15.00	$30.00
The Five Sharps, "Stormy Weather" / "Sleepy Cowboy"				
(A legitimate 45 copy on Jubilee 5104 has not been found yet; three copies exist on 78, one of those is cracked - if a legitimate 45 pressing ever turned up, the owner could name his or her own price)				
(if on Jubilee 5478, B-side is "Mammy Jammy," a different group with the same name)	1964	$3.00	$6.00	$12.00
(if on Bim Bam Boom 103, mastered from the "cracked" 78)	1972	$2.00	$4.00	$8.00
The Fleetwoods, "Come Softly To Me" / "I Care So Much"				
(if on Dolphin 1)	1959	$6.25	$12.50	$25.00
(if on Liberty 55188, mono)	1959	$6.25	$12.50	$25.00

45s	**Year**	**VG**	**VG+**	**NM**
(if on Liberty 77188, stereo mix)	1959	$12.50	$25.00	$50.00
(if on Dolton 307, B-side is "I'm Not Jimmy," new re-recording of hit)	1965	$2.50	$5.00	$10.00
The Four Lovers, "You're The Apple Of My Eye" / "The Girl Of My Dreams" (RCA Victor 6518)	1956	$10.00	$20.00	$40.00
The Four Seasons, "Sherry" / "I've Cried Before" (Vee Jay 456)	1962	$6.25	$12.50	$25.00
The Four Seasons, "Walk Like A Man" / "Lucky Ladybug" (Vee Jay 485)	1963	$3.75	$7.50	$15.00
The Harptones, "Sunday Kind of Love" / "I'll Never Tell" (Bruce 101)				
(if "Bruce" is in script lettering)	1953	$1,000	$2,000	$3,000
(if "Bruce" is in block lettering)	1953	$20.00	$40.00	$80.00
The Jive Five, "My True Story" / "When I Was Single" (Beltone 1006)	1961	$7.50	$15.00	$30.00
Gladys Knight and the Pips, "Every Beat of My Heart" / "Room In Your Heart"				
(if on Huntom 2510, original recording, credited to "The Pips")	1961	$125.00	$250.00	$500.00
(if on Vee Jay 386, credited to "Pips")	1961	$5.00	$10.00	$20.00
(if on Vee Jay 386, B-side is the same song, retitled "Ain'tcha Got Some Room (In Your Heart For Me)")	1961	$5.00	$10.00	$20.00
(if on Fury 1050, credited to "Gladys Knight and the Pips," different than Huntom and Vee Jay copies)	1961	$6.25	$12.50	$25.00
Little Anthony and the Imperials, "Tears On My Pillow" / "Two People in the World) (End 1027)				
(first pressing, group simply listed as "The Imperials")	1958	$10.00	$20.00	$40.00
(second pressing, Little Anthony's name is added)	1958	$6.25	$12.50	$25.00
Frankie Lymon and the Teenagers, "Why Do Fools Fall In Love" / "Please Be Mine" (Gee 1002)				
(if red and gold label)	1956	$20.00	$40.00	$80.00
(if red-black label, B-side is a vocal duet)	1956	$12.50	$25.00	$50.00
(if red-black label, B-side is a solo vocal)	1956	$7.50	$15.00	$30.00
The Marcels, "Blue Moon" / "Goodbye To Love" (Colpix 186)	1961	$7.50	$15.00	$30.00
(with picture sleeve, add:)	1961	$15.00	$30.00	$60.00
Arthur Lee Maye and the Crowns, "Set My Heart Free" / "I Wanna Love" (Modern 944)	1954	$150.00	$300.00	$600.00
Arthur Lee Maye and the Crowns, "Gloria" / "Oo-Rooba-Lee" (Specialty 573)	1956	$15.00	$30.00	$60.00
The Midnighters, "Work With Me Annie" / "Until I Die" (Federal 12169)				
(if label has a silver top, credited to "The Midnighters (Formerly Known as the Royals)")	1954	$25.00	$50.00	$100.00
(if label is all green, credited to "The Midnighters (Formerly Known as the Royals)")	1954	$10.00	$20.00	$40.00
Hank Ballard and the Midnighters, "The Twist" / "Teardrops On Your Letter" (King 5171)	1959	$7.50	$15.00	$30.00
Harvey and the Moonglows, "The Ten Commandments of Love" / "Mean Old Blues" (Chess 1705)	1958	$7.50	$15.00	$30.00
The Orioles, "I Miss You So" / "You Are My First Love" (Jubilee 5051)				
(if on red vinyl)	1951	$1,000.00	$1,500.00	$2,000.00
(if on black vinyl)	1951	$200.00	$400.00	$800.00
Shirley Gunter and the Queens, "Oop Shoop" / "It's You" (Flair 1050)				
The Rays, "Silhouettes" / "Daddy Cool"				
(if on XYZ 102, gray label)	1957	$42.50	$85.00	$170.00
(if on XYZ 102, blue label)	1957	$15.00	$30.00	$60.00
(if on Cameo 117)	1957	$6.25	$12.50	$25.00
The Rivingtons, "Papa-Oom-Mow-Mow" / "Deep Water"				
(if on Liberty 55427)	1962	$6.25	$12.50	$25.00
(if on Wand 11253, B-side is "I Don't Want A New Baby")	1973		$2.50	$5.00
The Skyliners, "Since I Don't Have You" / "One Night, One Night"				
(if on Calico 103 or 104)	1959	$12.50	$25.00	$50.00
(if on Original Sound 35)	1963	$3.75	$7.50	$15.00
(if on Motown 1046, B-side is "I'd Die," only two promo copies are known to exist)	1963	$1,000.00	$1,500.00	$2,000.00
The Spaniels, "Goodnight, Sweetheart, Goodnight" / "You Don't Move Me" (Vee Jay 107)				
(if on black vinyl, group erroneously listed as "Spanials")	1953	$75.00	$150.00	$300.00
(if on black vinyl, group's name spelled correctly)	1953	$50.00	$100.00	$200.00
(if on red vinyl, no "Trade Mark Reg" on label)	1953	$200.00	$400.00	$800.00
(if on red vinyl, "Trade Mark Reg" is on label, bonus 7" inserted in CD box set)	1993	$2.00	$4.00	$8.00
Tico and the Triumphs, "Motorcycle" / "I Don't Believe Them" (Paul Simon was a member of this doo-wop group)				
(if on Madison 169)	1961	$50.00	$100.00	$200.00
(if on Amy 835)	1961	$25.00	$50.00	$100.00
The Tokens, "The Lion Sleeps Tonight" / "Tina" (RCA Victor 7954)	1961	$6.25	$12.50	$25.00
(if on RCA 47-7954, "Compact Single 33")	1961	$12.50	$25.00	$50.00
The Tymes, "So Much In Love" / "Roscoe James McClain" (Parkway 871)				
(if on Parkway 871A, A-side says "So In Love")	1963	$6.25	$12.50	$25.00
(if on Parkway 871C, A-side title is correct)	1963	$3.75	$7.50	$15.00
(with picture sleeve, add:)	1963	$7.50	$15.00	$30.00
Maurice Williams and the Zodiacs, "Stay" / "Do You Believe" (Herald 552)	1960	$5.00	$10.00	$20.00

78s	**Year**	**VG**	**VG+**	**NM**
The Chantels, "Maybe" / "Come, My Little Baby" (End 1005)	1958	$30.00	$60.00	$120.00
The Coasters, "Yakety Yak" / "Zing Went The Strings Of My Heart" (Atco 6116)	1958	$25.00	$50.00	$100.00
The Crescendos, "Oh Julie" / "My Little Girl" (Nasco 6005)	1957	$20.00	$40.00	$80.00
The Crows, "Gee" / "Love You So" (Rama 5)	1953	$10.00	$20.00	$40.00
Danny and the Juniors, "At the Hop" / "Sometimes When I'm All Alone" (ABC-Paramount 9871)	1957	$30.00	$60.00	$120.00
Danny and the Juniors, "Rock and Roll Is Here To Stay" / "School Boy Romance" (ABC-Paramount 9888)	1958	$50.00	$100.00	$200.00
The Del Vikings, "Come Go With Me" / "How Can I Find True Love"				
(if on Fee Bee 205)	1957	$37.50	$75.00	$150.00
(if on Dot 15538)	1957	$12.50	$25.00	$50.00
The Drifters, "There Goes My Baby" / "Oh My Love" (Atlantic 2025)	1959	$125.00	$250.00	$500.00
The Five Keys, "The Glory of Love" / "Hucklebuck With Jimmy" (Aladdin 3099)	1951	$50.00	$100.00	$200.00
The Five Sharps, "Stormy Weather" / "Sleepy Cowboy" (Jubilee 5104)	1953	$12,500	$18,750	$25,000
The Harptones, "Sunday Kind of Love" / "I'll Never Tell" (Bruce 101)	1953	$30.00	$60.00	$120.00
Harvey and the Moonglows, "The Ten Commandments of Love" / "Mean Old Blues" (Chess 1705)	1958	$12.50	$25.00	$50.00
Sonny Til and the Orioles, "Maybe You'll Be There" / "Drowning Every Hope I Ever Had" (Jubilee 5143)	1954	$10.00	$20.00	$40.00
The Spaniels, "Goodnight, Sweetheart, Goodnight" / "You Don't Move Me" (Vee Jay 107)	1954	$20.00	$40.00	$80.00
Frankie Lymon and the Teenagers, "Why Do Fools Fall In Love" / "Please Be Mine" (Gee 1002)	1955	$12.50	$25.00	$50.00

LPs	**Year**	**VG**	**VG+**	**NM**
The Aquatones, The Aquatones Sing (Fargo 3001) (mono)	1964	$50.00	$100.00	$200.00
The Belmonts, The Belmonts' Carnival of Hits (Sabina SALP-5001) (mono)	1962	$37.50	$75.00	$150.00
The Belmonts, Cigars, Acapella, Candy (Buddah BDS-5123)	1972	$12.50	$25.00	$50.00
The Cadillacs, The Fabulous Cadillacs (Jubilee JGM-1045)				
(if blue label)	1957	$125.00	$250.00	$500.00
(if flat black label)	1959	$62.50	$125.00	$250.00
(if glossy black label)	1960	$25.00	$50.00	$100.00
The Chantels, We're The Chantels (End LP-301) (mono)				
(if group photo on front cover)	1958	$500.00	$1,000.00	$1,500.00
(jukebox on front cover, trail off wax does not contain the number "1962")	1959	$100.00	$200.00	$400.00
(jukebox on front cover, "1962" in trail off wax)	1962	$50.00	$100.00	$200.00
The Chiffons, He's So Fine (Laurie LLP-2018) (mono)	1963	$50.00	$100.00	$200.00
(if on Laurie ST-90775, Capitol Record Club, r echanneled stereo)	1965	$75.00	$150.00	$300.00
The Cleftones, Heart and Soul (Gee GLP-705) (mono)	1961	$50.00	$100.00	$200.00
(if on Gee SGLP-705, stereo)	1961	$125.00	$250.00	$500.00
The Coasters, The Coasters (Atco 33-101) (mono)				
(if label has a harp on it, first pressing)	1958	$75.00	$150.00	$300.00
(if label is gold and dark blue, second pressing)	196??	$15.00	$30.00	$60.00
The Crescendos, Oh Julie (Guest Star G-1453) (mono)	1962	$12.50	$25.00	$50.00
(if on Guest Star GS-1453, rechanelled stereo)	1962	$5.00	$10.00	$20.00
The Del Vikings, Come Go With The Del Vikings (Luniverse LP-1000) (mono)	1957	$125.00	$250.00	$500.00
(this album has been counterfeited; originals have eight tracks and a cover made from slicks; bootlegs and counterfeits have more tracks and a pre-printed cover)				
The Drifters, Clyde McPhatter and the Drifters (Atlantic 8003) (mono)				
(if black label)	1956	$125.00	$250.00	$500.00

LPs	Year	VG	VG+	NM
(if reddish label)	1959	$15.00	$30.00	$60.00
The Drifters, Save The Last Dance For Me (Atlantic 8059)				
(mono) (red label, white pinwheel logo)	1962	$30.00	$60.00	$120.00
(if on Atlantic SD 8059, stereo, red label, white pinwheel logo)	1962	$50.00	$100.00	$200.00
The Duprees, You Belong To Me (Coed LPC-905)				
(mono)	1962	$75.00	$150.00	$300.00
The Five Satins, The Five Satins Sing (Ember ELP-100) (mono)				
(if on red Ember label, group pictured on front cover, blue vinyl)	1957	$1,000	$1,500	$2,000
(if on red Ember label, group pictured on front cover, black vinyl)	1957	$150.00	$300.00	$600.00
(if on white Ember "logs" label, group pictured on front cover)	1959	$75.00	$150.00	$300.00
(if on white Ember "logs" label, no picture on front cover)	1959	$50.00	$100.00	$200.00
(if on black label, no picture on cover)	1961	$25.00	$50.00	$100.00
The Four Seasons, Golden Hits of the Four Seasons				
(Vee Jay LP-1065) (mono)	1963	$7.50	$15.00	$30.00
(if on Vee Jay SR-1065, stereo)	1963	$10.00	$20.00	$40.00
Frankie Lymon and the Teenagers, The Teenagers Featuring Frankie Lymon (Gee GLP-701)				
(if on red label, first pressing)	1956	$125.00	$250.00	$500.00
(if on gray label, second pressing)	1961	$37.50	$75.00	$150.00
(if on white label, thin vinyl)	197??	$3.00	$6.00	$12.00
The Marcels, Blue Moon (Colpix CP-??) (mono)				
(if on gold label, first pressing)	1961	$87.50	$175.00	$350.00

LPs	Year	VG	VG+	NM
(if on blue label, second pressing)	1963	$30.00	$60.00	$120.00
The Midnighters, Their Greatest Hits (Federal 295-90)				
(10-inch record)	1954	$4,000	$6,000	$8,000
The Midnighters, Their Greatest Hits (Federal 541) (mono)				
(if red album cover)	1955	$375.00	$750.00	$1,500.00
(if yellow album cover)	1955	$250.00	$500.00	$1,000.00
The Penguins, The Cool, Cool Penguins (Dooto DTL-242) (mono)				
(if red-yellow label or blue-yellow label, value is equal)	1959	$175.00	$350.00	$700.00
(if black label with gold-orange-blue ring, a legitimate pressing)	196??	$50.00	$100.00	$200.00
The Rivingtons, Doin' The Bird (Liberty LRP-3282)				
(mono)	1963	$25.00	$50.00	$100.00
(if on Liberty LST-7282, stereo)	1963	$50.00	$100.00	$200.00
The Skyliners, The Skyliners (Calico LP-3000) (mono)				
(if yellow-blue label)	1959	$200.00	$400.00	$600.00
(if on blue label)	196??	$50.00	$100.00	$200.00
The Spaniels, Goodnight, It's Time To Go (Vee Jay LP-1002)				
(if maroon label, group on cover)	1958	$150.00	$300.00	$600.00
(if black label, dogs on cover)	1961	$50.00	$100.00	$200.00
(if on VJLP-1002, 1980s reissue on flimsy vinyl)	198??	$3.00	$6.00	$12.00
The Tokens, The Lion Sleeps Tonight (RCA Victor LPM-2514) (mono)	1961	$20.00	$40.00	$80.00
(if on RCA Victor LSP-2514, stereo)	1961	$37.50	$75.00	$150.00

The first pressings of "Why Do Fools Fall in Love" have a red label with black printing, the word "GEE" is in capital letters at the top of the label. The copy here is a reissue pressing; this label design was used in the early 1960s.

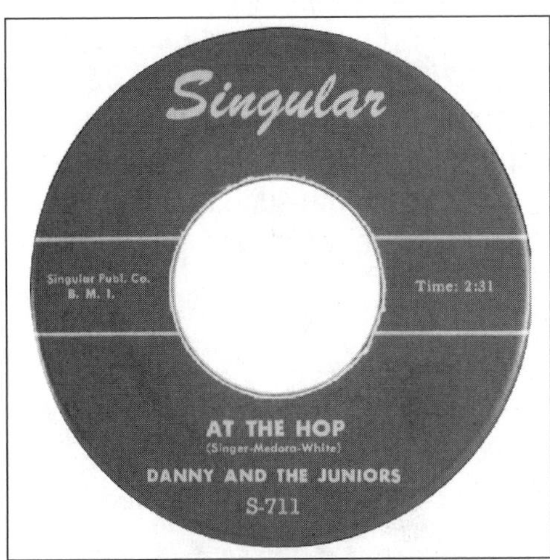

This pressing of "At the Hop" by Danny and the Juniors contains a countoff at the beginning of the song, which their major-label pressing on ABC-Paramount did not. Because of its rarity, this record has been counterfeited—copies without the "count-in" are reproductions.

If you listen very closely to this doo-wop classic by Harvey and the Moonglows, you might notice they only list nine commandments in the lyrics.

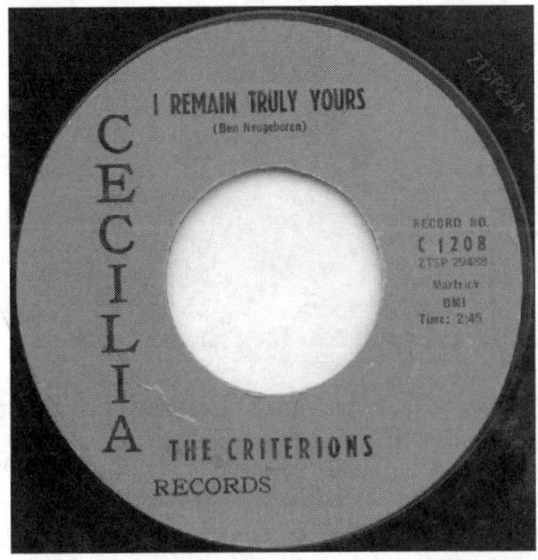

This doo-wop record may never have hit the big time, but one of its members did—vocalist Tim Hauser, who later formed the Manhattan Transfer.

EASY LISTENING/ADULT CONTEMPORARY

History: The most important part of "easy listening" or "adult contemporary" music was in its name—the music should be easy to listen to. No screeching guitars, no jarring raps, just continuous "soft" music, as many adult contemporary radio stations advertised.

Adult-contemporary music evolved from the soft instrumental music of the 1950s, and the "traditional pop" of the 1960s. "Soft instrumental" orchestras and chorales created a niche by recording string-laden remakes of popular songs, allowing the listener to enjoy the hits of the day without jarring guitars or thumping drums. Such orchestral groups included the Hollyridge Singers, the 101 Strings, and the Ray Conniff Singers.

"Traditional pop," a mixture of ballads, Broadway standards, and light uptempo songs, were the core of easy listening music in the 1960s. Artists such as Glen Campbell, Jim Nabors, and Ed Ames sold millions of albums filled with such standards as "By The Time I Get To Phoenix" and "My Cup Runneth Over."

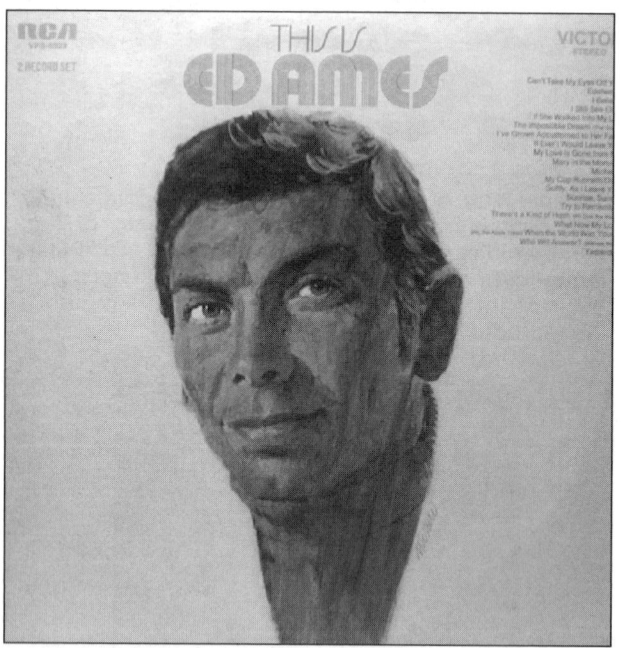

This collection of Ed Ames' greatest hits is a prime example of 1960s "traditional pop."

Another branch of traditional pop, the "country crooner," achieved its own success with lushly orchestrated ballads and smooth vocals. Many of these "country crooner" songs featured ballads of lost love or unrequited love. Bill Anderson, Jim Reeves, Floyd Cramer, and Eddy Arnold were part of this musical genre.

Jim Reeves crossed over from country balladeer to country/pop crooner with his soft baritone voice and lush orchestrations.

By the 1970s, popular music had fragmented into different musical genres, and radio stations changed their formats to fit one musical style or another. Whether a listener liked hard rock, heavy metal, Top 40, country-western, or R&B, there was a station for them that played ONLY those songs.

Some stations were programmed for "easy listening," which featured the traditional pop of the 1950s and '60s, as well as ballads and soft pop contemporary hits. On these stations, artists like the Carpenters, Helen Reddy, Tony Orlando and Dawn, Bread, Barry Manilow, the Captain and Tennille, and Leo Sayer were heard. "Easy listening" was also applied to artists such as John Denver, whose blend of country, folk, and pop spanned multiple genres. Teen idols of the 1950s, including Paul Anka and Neil Sedaka, were able to resurrect their careers with middle-of-the-road pop ballads.

This pressing is the second of three attempts for Barry Manilow to have a hit with this song (the first was a dance-pop version when he was a member of the group Featherbed). His third version, on Arista Records, eventually hit #1.

Richard Harris' "MacArthur Park" appears in different label variations; the solitary "Dunhill" was the first, while other pressings have an "ABC" on them.

By the 1980s, adult-contemporary stations had new musical styles to work with: the "power ballad," the "theatrical pop song," and the "lite dance track." Power ballads were soft love songs recorded by hard rock bands, and such recordings often outsold the bands' harder songs. Such songs included REO Speedwagon's "Keep On Loving You" and "Can't Fight This Feeling," Styx's "Babe" and "Lady," Journey's "Open Arms" and "Don't Stop Believin'," Night Ranger's "Sister Christian," and Survivor's "The Search Is Over."

"Theatrical pop" mostly encompassed the works of producer-songwriter Jim Steinman. Steinman, who had previously collaborated with Meat Loaf on the groundbreaking *Bat Out Of Hell* album, created six-minute over-the-top recordings with elaborate lyrics and dramatic volume changes—in other words, from glissando to pianoforte in a matter of seconds. His adult-contemporary productions include Barry Manilow's "Read 'Em And Weep," Air Supply's "Making Love Out of Nothing At All," Celine Dion's "It's All Coming Back To Me Now," Bonnie Tyler's "Total Eclipse of the Heart," and his reunion with Meat Loaf on "I'd Do Anything For Love (But I Won't Do That)" and "Objects In The Rearview Mirror May Appear Closer Than They Are." Other theatrical pop songs in the adult contemporary mode include Richard Harris' "MacArthur Park" and Don McLean's "American Pie," both for their lyrical content and for their length, as both songs clocked in at more than seven minutes apiece.

Trivia

One of Daryl Hall and John Oates' early singles was a track called "She's Gone." It stiffed in its first release (even though the soul group Tavares had a Top 10 R&B hit with it). But after Hall and Oates signed with another label, and had a Top 10 hit with "Sara Smile," their old label re-released "She's Gone"—and the song followed "Sara Smile" into the Top 10.

This is the first pressing of "She's Gone," later pressings were on Atlantic 3332.

"Lite dance" uptempo songs were the purview of artists such as Melissa Manchester, Daryl Hall and John Oates, and the Pointer Sisters. The typical ballads were still available for those who desired them, as Air Supply and Michael Bolton had a steady stream of hit love songs throughout the 1980s. There was even an adult-contemporary musical genre called "Quiet Storm," featuring R&B ballads and soft soul from Dionne Warwick, Luther Vandross, Lionel Richie, and Phyllis Hyman.

What To Look For: Many easy listening artists already have dedicated fan bases, and those fans have snapped up the lion's share of these recordings. The difficult records to find are the first releases, songs that some artists have recorded *before* their biggest hits. The rarest of these adult contemporary songs include the Captain and Tennille's "The Way I Want To Touch You" on their self-pressed Butterscotch Castle label; Barry Manilow's version of "Could It Be Magic" when he recorded under the band name Featherbed; and the Carpenters' "I'll Be Yours," which was recorded under the Magic Lamp label and credited only to Karen Carpenter.

One of Karen Carpenter's first recordings, it also features her brother Richard on background vocals. Courtesy Good Rockin' Tonight / Collectors Universe.

Other rare pressings by easy listening/adult contemporary artists are those on quadraphonic records. These four-channel albums were highly touted as the next successful recording format, but the inability to agree on a standard recording and playback system eventually doomed the concept. However, many adult contemporary artists, including the Carpenters, Bread, and Seals & Crofts, had nearly their entire catalog pressed on quadraphonic records. With the proper playback equipment, these recordings offer new mixes and unique interpretations on an artist's 1970s output.

Other than an artist's earliest releases, many adult contemporary albums and 45s are very common, and even in near-mint condition will not sell for more than a couple of dollars.

Trivia

James Taylor's first recording contract was with Apple Records—in fact, he was the first American solo singer signed to the Beatles' custom label. He recorded one album for Apple, and the song "Carolina In My Mind" was released twice by the label, and each time it flopped. Taylor would later move to Warner Bros. Records, and a re-recorded version of "Carolina In My Mind" would eventually become a hit.

James Taylor's first single; if the B-side is "Taking It In," the record can be worth as much as $300 in near-mint condition.

Seals and Crofts' Diamond Girl LP, available in one of the many quadraphonic formats of the 1970s. From the Collection of Mark Anderson.

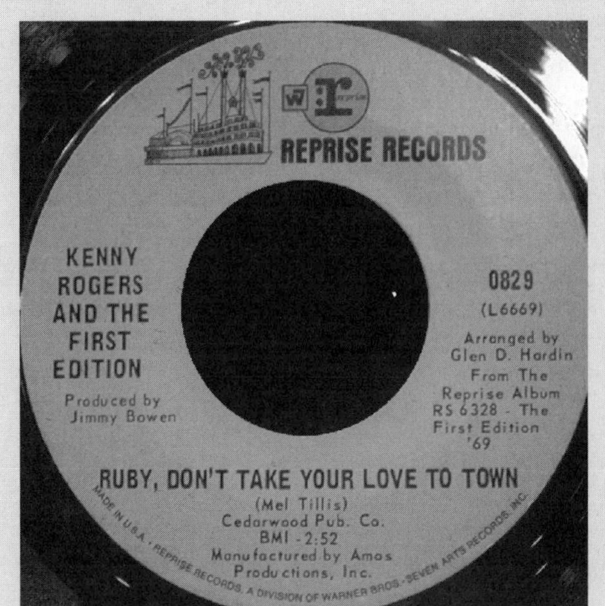

The original recording of Kenny Rogers and the First Edition's "Ruby, Don't Take Your Love To Town." From the Collection of Val Shively.

A United Artists "Silver Spotlight Series" reissue, featuring a new recording of this song. Five former First Edition songs were re-recorded for the new label. From the Collection of Val Shively.

Reference Books: Hyatt, Wesley, *The Billboard Book of Number One Adult Contemporary Hits*, Billboard Books, Watson-Guptill Publications, BPI Communications, New York, N.Y., 1999.

Web pages: From About.com, a list of radio stations that broadcast adult contemporary music over the Internet: *http://radio.about.com/cs/adultcontemporary/index.htm?terms=adult+contemporary.*

Trivia

Five songs Kenny Rogers recorded for his previous band, The First Edition, were re-recorded and reissued as B-sides for his reissued solo hits. His 45s on United Artists' "Silver Spotlight Series" (catalog numbers XW1151 to XW1155) have re-recordings of "Ruby, Don't Take Your Love To Town," "Something's Burning," "But You Know I Love You," "Just Dropped In (To See What Condition My Condition Was In)," and "Reuben James," all of which were previously issued on the Reprise label. The United Artists re-recordings also note that the songs were "originally released 12/77."

45s	Year	VG	VG+	NM
Ed Ames, "Try To Remember" / "Love Is Here To Stay" (RCA Victor 47-8483)	1964	$2.00	$4.00	$8.00
Ed Ames, "My Cup Runneth Over" / "It Seems A Long, Long Time" (RCA Victor 47-9002)	1966	$2.00	$4.00	$8.00
Bill Anderson, "Still" / "You Make It Easy" (Decca 31458)	1963	$2.50	$5.00	$10.00
Paul Anka, "Times of Your Life" / "Water Runs Deep" (United Artists XW-737)	1975		$2.00	$4.00
(with picture sleeve, add:)	1975		$2.00	$4.00
Paul Anka, "Hold Me 'Til the Mornin' Comes" / "This Is The First Time" (Columbia 03897)	1983			$3.00
(with picture sleeve, add:)	1983		$2.00	$4.00

45s	Year	VG	VG+	NM
Eddy Arnold, "Make The World Go Away" / "The Easy Way" (RCA Victor 47-8679)	1965	$2.00	$4.00	$8.00
(with picture sleeve, add:)	1965	$3.75	$7.50	$15.00
Michael Bolotin, "You Make Me Feel Like Lovin' You" / "If I Had Your Lovin'" (RCA PB-10650)	1976	$2.50	$5.00	$10.00
Michael Bolton, "How Am I Supposed To Live Without You" / "Forever Eyes" (Columbia 73017)	1989			$3.00
Pat Boone, "Love Letters In The sand" / "Bernardine" (Dot 15570)	1957	$3.75	$7.50	$15.00
(with picture sleeve, add:)	1957	$7.50	$15.00	$30.00
Pat Boone, "Don't Forbid Me" / "April Love" (Dot 16034)	1960	$2.50	$5.00	$10.00
Bread, "Make It With You" / "Why Do You Keep Me Waiting" (Elektra 45686) (first pressing on red-black-white label, second pressing on yellow-black label, value is equal)	1970		$2.00	$4.00
Bread, "If" / "Take Comfort" (Elektra 45720)	1971		$2.00	$4.00
(with picture sleeve, add:)	1971	$2.00	$4.00	$8.00
Glen Campbell, "Death Valley" / "Nothin' Better Than A Pretty Woman" (Capehart 5008)	1961	$6.25	$12.50	$25.00
Glen Campbell, "Guess I'm Dumb" / "That's All Right" (Capitol 5441)	1965	$25.00	$50.00	$100.00
Glen Campbell, "Wichita Lineman" / "Fate of Man" (Capitol 2302)	1968		$2.50	$5.00
The Captain and Tennille, "The Way I Want To Touch You" / "Disney Girls"				
(if on Butterscotch Castle 001, independent first pressing)	1974	$20.00	$40.00	$80.00
(if on Joyce 101, second pressing)	1974	$10.00	$20.00	$40.00
(if on A&M 1624, first major label pressing)	1974		$3.00	$6.00
(if on A&M 1725, pressed after hit "Love Will Keep Us Together," B-side is "Broddy Bounce")	1975		$2.00	$4.00
(with picture sleeve for A&M 1725, add:)	1975		$2.00	$4.00
Eric Carmen, "All By Myself" / "Everything" (Arista 0165)	1975		$2.00	$4.00
Karen Carpenter, "I'll Be Yours" / "Looking For Love" (Magic Lamp 704)	1967	$500.00	$1,000.00	$2,000.00
The Carpenters, "(They Long To Be) Close To You" / "I Kept On Loving You" (A&M 1183)	1970		$2.50	$5.00
The Carpenters, "Yesterday Once More" / "(They Long To Be) Close To You - We've Only Just Begun" (A&M 2735)	1985	$5.00	$10.00	$20.00
(with picture sleeve, add:)	1985	$5.00	$10.00	$20.00
Charlene, "I've Never Been To Me" / "It's Really Nice To Be In Love Again" (Prodigal 0636)	1977	$5.00	$10.00	$20.00
(if on Motown 1611, B-side is "Somewhere In My Life")	1982			$3.00
Chicago, "Does Anybody Really Know What Time It Is?" / "Listen" (Columbia 45264)	1970		$2.50	$5.00
(with picture sleeve, add:)	1970	$2.00	$4.00	$8.00
Chicago, "Hard To Say I'm Sorry" / "Sonny Think Twice" (Full Moon 29979)	1982		$2.00	$4.00
Perry Como, "Catch A Falling Star" / "Magic Moments" (RCA Victor 47-7128)	1957	$3.00	$6.00	$12.00
Rita Coolidge, "We're All Alone" / "Southern Lady" (A&M 1965)	1977		$2.00	$4.00
(with picture sleeve, add:)	1977		$2.00	$4.00
Alice Cooper, "I Never Cry" / "Go To Hell" (Warner Bros. 8228) (only the A-side is "easy listening")	1976		$2.00	$4.00
Floyd Cramer, "Last Date" / "Sweetie Baby" (RCA Victor 47-7775)	1960	$3.00	$6.00	$12.00
John Denver with Fat City, "Take Me Home, Country Roads" / "Poems, Prayers and Promises" (RCA Victor 74-0445)	1971	$2.00	$4.00	$8.00
John Denver, "Rocky Mountain High" / "Spring" (RCA Victor 74-0829)	1972		$2.50	$5.00
(if on RCA's "Gold Standard Series," GB-10477)	1975			$3.00
Barry DeVorzon and Perry Botkin, Jr., "Nadia's Theme (The Young and the Restless)" / "Down the Line" (A&M 1856)				
(if label only lists Perry Botkin, Jr.'s name)	1976	$2.50	$5.00	$10.00
(with picture sleeve listing only Perry Botkin, Jr., add:)	1976	$2.50	$5.00	$10.00
(if Barry DeVorzon's name is added to label)	1976		$2.00	$4.00
(with green picture sleeve, both names on sleeve, add:)	1976		$2.00	$4.00
(with blue picture sleeve, both names on sleeve, add:)	1976		$3.00	$6.00
(with black picture sleeve, both names on sleeve, add:)	1976		$3.00	$6.00
Neil Diamond, "Clown Town" / "At Night" (Columbia 52809)	1963	$125.00	$250.00	$500.00
(if white label promo)	1963	$62.50	$125.00	$250.00
Neil Diamond, "I Thank The Lord For The Night Time" / "The Long Way Home" (Bang 547)	1967	$3.75	$7.50	$15.00
(if second pressing, title corrected to "Thank The Lord For The Night Time")	1967	$2.50	$5.00	$10.00
Neil Diamond, "Sweet Caroline" (Good Times Never Seemed So Good)" / "Dig In" (Uni 55136)	1969		$3.00	$6.00
Neil Diamond, "We Wrote A Song Together" / "Beautiful Noise" (Continuum II 001) (private pressing done for the grade school class of Neil's son Jesse Diamond. All were autographed by Neil Diamond. The version of "Beautiful Noise" is an alternate take. There may be as few as 30 copies that were pressed.)	1976	$500.00	$1,000.00	$2,000.00
Neil Diamond, "Heartlight" (one-sided pressing) (Columbia CNR-03345)	1982		$2.50	$5.00
Dr. Hook, "Sharing The Night Together" / "You Make My Pants Want To Get Up And Dance" (Capitol 4621)	1978		$2.00	$4.00
England Dan and John Ford Coley, "I'd Really Love To See You Tonight" / "Not The Same" (Big Tree 16069)	1976		$2.00	$4.00
The Fifth Dimension, "I'll Be Loving You Forever" / "Train, Keep On Moving" (Soul City 752)	1966	$15.00	$30.00	$60.00
The Fifth Dimension, "Up-Up and Away" / "Which Way To Nowhere" (Soul City 756)	1967	$2.00	$4.00	$8.00
Dan Fogelberg, "Longer" / "Along the Road" (Full Moon/Epic 50824)	1980		$2.00	$4.00
Dan Fogelberg, "Same Old Lang Syne" / "Hearts and Crafts" (Full Moon/Epic 50961)	1980		$2.00	$4.00
(with picture sleeve, add:)	1980		$3.00	$6.00
Art Garfunkel, "I Only Have Eyes For You" / "Looking For The Right One" (Columbia 10190)	1975		$2.50	$5.00
David Gates, "Goodbye Girl" /"Sunday Rider" (Elektra 45450)	1977		$2.00	$4.00
(with picture sleeve, add:)	1977		$2.50	$5.00
Daryl Hall and John Oates, "She's Gone" / I'm Just A Kid (Don't Make Me Feel Like A Man)"				
(if on Atlantic 2993, first pressing)	1973	$2.00	$4.00	$8.00
(if on Atlantic 3332, pressed after "Sara Smile" became a hit)	1976		$2.00	$4.00
Daryl Hall and John Oates, "Rich Girl" / "London Luck & Love" (RCA PB-10860)	1976		$2.00	$4.00
(with picture sleeve, add:)	1976	$2.00	$4.00	$8.00
Hamilton, Joe Frank and Reynolds, "Don't Pull Your Love" / "Funk-in-Wagnall" (ABC Dunhill 4276)	1971		$3.00	$6.00
Richard Harris, "MacArthur Park" / "Didn't We"				
(if on Dunhill 4134, first pressing)	1968	$2.00	$4.00	$8.00
(with special promotional issue sleeve, add:)	1968	$3.75	$7.50	$15.00
(if on ABC/Dunhill 4134, second pressing)	1968		$3.00	$6.00
Rupert Holmes, "Escape (The Pina Colada Song)" / "Drop It" (Infinity 50035)	1979		$2.50	$5.00
(if on MCA 50035)	1979		$2.00	$4.00
Journey, "Open Arms" / "Little Girl" (Columbia 02687)	1982			$3.00
(with picture sleeve, add:)	1982		$2.00	$4.00
The Lettermen, "When I Fall In Love" / "Smile" (Capitol 4658)	1961	$3.00	$6.00	$12.00
(with picture sleeve, add:)	1961	$5.00	$10.00	$20.00
The Lettermen, "I Only Have Eyes For You" / "Love Letters" (Capitol 5649)	1966	$2.00	$4.00	$8.00
(with picture sleeve, add:)	1966	$3.00	$6.00	$12.00
The Lettermen, "Goin' Out of My Head - Can't Take My Eyes Off You" / "I Believe" (Capitol 2054)	1967	$2.00	$4.00	$8.00
Barry Manilow, "Mandy" / "Something's Comin' Up" (Bell 45613)	1974		$2.50	$5.00
Barry Manilow, "Even Now" / "I Was A Fool (To Let You Go)" (Arista 0330)	1978		$2.00	$4.00
(with picture sleeve, add:)	1978		$2.00	$4.00
Sergio Mendes and Brasil '66, "The Look of Love" / "Like a Lover" (A&M 924)	1968		$2.50	$5.00
(with picture sleeve, add:)	1968	$2.00	$4.00	$8.00
Sergio Mendes, "Never Gonna Let You Go" / "Carnival" (A&M 2623)	1983			$3.00
Michael Murphey, "Wildfire" / "Night Thunder" (Epic 50084)	1975		$2.50	$5.00
Anne Murray, "Snowbird" / "Just Bidin' My Time" (Capitol 2738)	1970		$3.00	$6.00
Anne Murray, "You Needed Me" / "I Still Wish The Very Best For You" (Capitol 4574)	1978		$2.00	$4.00
Gilbert O'Sullivan, "Alone Again (Naturally)" / "Save It" (MAM 3619)	1972		$3.00	$6.00
Pablo Cruise, "Love Will Find A Way" / "Always Be Together" (A&M 2048)	1978		$2.00	$4.00

45s	Year	VG	VG+	NM
(with picture sleeve, add:)	1978		$2.50	$5.00
The Poppy Family, "Which Way You Goin', Billy?" / "Endless Sleep" (London 129)	1970		$3.00	$6.00
Helen Reddy, "I Am Woman" / "More Than You Could Take" (Capitol 3350)				
(if on red-orange "target" label)	1972		$2.50	$5.00
(if on orange label with "Capitol" on bottom)	1972		$2.00	$4.00
Helen Reddy, "You And Me Against The World" / "Love Song for Jeffrey" (Capitol 3897)	1974		$2.00	$4.00
Jim Reeves, "He'll Have To Go" / "In A Mansion Stands My Love" (RCA Victor 47-7643)	1959	$3.00	$6.00	$12.00
Jim Reeves, "Welcome To My World" / "Good Morning Self" (RCA Victor 47-8289)	1963	$2.50	$5.00	$10.00
Cliff Richard, "Living Doll" / "Apron Strings" (ABC-Paramount 10042)	1959	$6.25	$12.50	$25.00
Cliff Richard, "Devil Woman" / "Love On (Shine On)" (Rocket 40574)	1976		$2.50	$5.00
Kenny Rogers, "Lucille" / "Till I Get It Right" (United Artists XW929)	1976		$2.00	$4.00
Kenny Rogers, "Lucille" / "Something's Burning" (United Artists XS 1154) ("Something's Burning" is a re-recording of a previous hit by Kenny Rogers and the First Edition)	1978		$2.00	$4.00
Seals and Crofts, "In Tune" / "Seldom's Sister" (T-A 188)	1969	$2.00	$4.00	$8.00
Seals and Crofts, "Summer Breeze" / "East of Ginger Tree" (Warner Bros. 7606)	1972		$2.50	$5.00
Neil Sedaka, "Laughter in the Rain" / "Endlessly" (Rocket 40313)	1974		$2.00	$4.00
Neil Sedaka, "The Immigrant" / "Hey Mister Sunshine" (Rocket 40370)				
(if the words "Dedicated to John Lennon" are printed on the label)	1975	$2.50	$5.00	$10.00
(if John Lennon is not mentioned on the record)	1975		$2.00	$4.00
Phoebe Snow, "Poetry Man" / "Either or Both" (Shelter 40353)	1974		$3.00	$6.00
Cat Stevens, "Moon Shadow" / "I Think I See The Light" (A&M 1265)	1971		$2.00	$4.00
(with picture sleeve, add:)	1971		$2.00	$4.00
Cat Stevens, "Father and Son" / "Father and Son" (A&M 2711) (white label promo only)	1985	$2.50	$5.00	$10.00
Ray Stevens, "Everything Is Beautiful" / "A Brighter Day" (Barnaby 2011)	1970		$3.00	$6.00
James Taylor, "Carolina In My Mind" / "Taking It In" (Apple 1805)	1969	$75.00	$150.00	$300.00
James Taylor, "Carolina In My Mind" / "Something's Wrong" (Apple 1805)				
(if label has a star on A-side)	1970	$2.50	$5.00	$10.00
(if label has no star)	1970	$2.00	$4.00	$8.00
(if A-side is misprinted as "Carolina on My Mind")	1970	$7.50	$15.00	$30.00
James Taylor, "How Sweet It Is (To Be Loved By You)" / "Sarah Maria" (Warner Bros. 8109)	1975		$2.50	$5.00
Three Dog Night, "Joy To The World" / "I Can Hear You Calling" (ABC Dunhill 4272)	1971		$2.50	$5.00
The Vogues, "You're The One" / "Some Words"				
(if on Blue Star 229, original pressing)	1965	$6.25	$12.50	$25.00
(if on Co and Ce 229, major label debut)	1965	$3.00	$6.00	$12.00
The Vogues, "Turn Around, Look At Me" / "Then" (Reprise 0686)	1968	$2.00	$4.00	$8.00
Roger Whittaker, "The Last Farewell" / "Paradise" (RCA PB-50030) (Canadian serial number, but pressed in US)	1975		$2.00	$4.00
Glenn Yarborough, "Baby The Rain Must Fall" / "I've Been To Town" (RCA Victor 47-8498)	1965	$2.00	$5.00	$10.00
(with picture sleeve, add:)	1965	$3.75	$7.50	$15.00

LPs	Year	VG	VG+	NM
Ed Ames, My Cup Runneth Over (RCA LPM-3774) (mono)	1967	$2.50	$5.00	$10.00
(if on RCA LSP-3774, stereo)	1967	$3.00	$6.00	$12.00
Ed Ames, Apologize (RCA LPM-4028) (his last mono recording)	1968	$5.00	$10.00	$20.00
(if on RCA LSP-4028, stereo)	1968	$2.50	$5.00	$10.00
Bill Anderson, I Love You Drops (Decca DL 4771) (mono)	1966	$3.75	$7.50	$15.00
(if on Decca DL 74711, stereo)	1966	$5.00	$10.00	$20.00
Eddy Arnold, The Romantic World of Eddy Arnold (RCA Victor LSP-4009)	1968	$3.75	$7.50	$15.00
Michael Bolotin, Every Day Of My Life (RCA Victor APL1-1551)	1976	$5.00	$10.00	$20.00
Michael Bolton, Time, Love and Tenderness (Columbia C 46771)	1991	$3.75	$7.50	$15.00
Bread, Bread (Elektra EKS-7044)				
(if label is red, with large stylized "E")	1969	$3.75	$7.50	$15.00

LPs	Year	VG	VG+	NM
(if label has a butterfly, later pressing)	1971	$2.50	$5.00	$10.00
Bread, Baby I'm-A-Want You (Elektra EKS-75015)				
(if album cover is a gatefold, with raised photo on front)	1971	$3.75	$7.50	$15.00
(if second pressing, front cover photo is not raised)	197??	$2.50	$5.00	$10.00
Glen Campbell, By The Time I Get To Phoenix (Capitol T 2851) (mono) (also on Capitol ST 2851, stereo, value is equal)	1967	$3.75	$7.50	$15.00
Glen Campbell, Rhinestone Cowboy (Capitol SW-11430)	1975	$2.50	$5.00	$10.00
The Captain and Tennille, Love Will Keep Us Together (A&M SP 3045)	1975	$3.00	$6.00	$12.00
(if on A&M SP-4552, reissue)	1975	$2.50	$5.00	$10.00
(if on A&M QU-54552, quadraphonic)	1975	$3.75	$7.50	$15.00
Eric Carmen, Eric Carmen (Arista AL 4057)				
(if cover has a simulated gold shine)	1975	$3.00	$6.00	$12.00
(if cover has a flat color composition, no shine)	1975	$2.00	$4.00	$8.00
(if on AQ 4057, quadraphonic)	1975	$4.50	$9.00	$18.00
The Carpenters, Offering (A&M SP-4205)	1969	$20.00	$40.00	$80.00
The Carpenters, Ticket To Ride (A&M SP-4205) (new cover and title for album "Offering")	1970	$3.00	$6.00	$12.00
The Carpenters, The Singles 1969-1973 (A&M SP-3601)	1973	$3.00	$6.00	$12.00
(if on A&M QU-53601, quadraphonic)	1974	$5.00	$10.00	$20.00
Chicago, Chicago (Columbia, no number) (17 LP's) (promo-only, first 10 Chicago albums, gold stamps on covers, box, side panel and wraparound)	1976	$62.50	$125.00	$250.00
Chicago, Chicago at Carnegie Hall (Columbia C4X 30865) (4 LP's, with posters, box and program)	1971	$10.00	$20.00	$40.00
(if on C4Q 30865, quadraphonic)	1971	$10.00	$20.00	$40.00
Perry Como, A Sentimental Date with Perry Como (RCA Victor LPM-1177) (mono)	1956	$7.50	$15.00	$30.00
Floyd Cramer, Last Date (RCA Victor LPM-2350) (mono)	1961	$5.00	$10.00	$20.00
(if on RCA Victor LSP-2350, stereo)	1961	$6.25	$12.50	$25.00
John Denver, John Denver Sings (HJD 66) (300 copies pressed by Denver as Christmas gifts to friends, contains original version of "Leaving On A Jet Plane")	1966	$125.00	$250.00	$500.00
John Denver, Rocky Mountain High (RCA LSP-4731) (orange label)	1972	$3.00	$6.00	$12.00
(if on RCA LSP-4731, black label, dog near top)	1975	$2.50	$5.00	$10.00
(if on RCA AFL1-4731 or RCA AqL1-4731, reissues)	197??	$2.00	$4.00	$8.00
Neil Diamond, Brother Love's Traveling Salvation Show				
(if on Uni 73047, does not include "Sweet Caroline")	1969	$7.50	$15.00	$30.00
(if on Uni 73047, second pressing, includes "Sweet Caroline")	1969	$5.00	$10.00	$20.00
(if on MCA 2011, now known as Sweet Caroline (Brother Love's Traveling Salvation Show))	1973	$2.50	$5.00	$10.00
(if on MCA 37057, now known as Sweet Caroline / Brother Love's Traveling Salvation Show)	1980	$2.00	$4.00	$8.00
Neil Diamond, Hot August Night (MCA 2-8000) (2 LP's)	1972	$5.00	$10.00	$20.00
(if on MCA 6896, reissue)	1980	$3.00	$6.00	$12.00
(if on Mobile Fidelity 2-024, audiophile reissue)	1979	$10.00	$20.00	$40.00
Dr. Hook, A Little Bit More (Capitol ST-11522)	1976	$2.50	$5.00	$10.00
England Dan and John Ford Coley, Nights Are Forever (Big Tree 89517)	1976	$2.50	$5.00	$10.00
The Fifth Dimension, The Age of Aquarius (Soul City SCS-92005)	1969	$3.75	$7.50	$15.00
Dan Fogelberg, Phoenix (Columbia FE 35634)	1979	$2.50	$5.00	$10.00
(if on HE 45634, half-speed mastered edition)	1981	$7.50	$15.00	$30.00
(if on PE 35364, budget reissue)	198??	$2.00	$4.00	$8.00
David Gates, Goodbye Girl (Elektra 6E-148)	1978	$3.00	$6.00	$12.00
Daryl Hall and John Oates, Abandoned Luncheonette (Atlantic SD 7269)	1973	$3.00	$6.00	$12.00
Daryl Hall and John Oates, Private Eyes (RCA Victor AFL1-4028)	1981	$2.50	$5.00	$10.00
Hamilton, Joe Frank and Reynolds, Fallin" In Love (Playboy PB-407)	1975	$2.50	$5.00	$10.00
(if on Playboy PZ 34741, reissue)	1977	$2.00	$4.00	$8.00
The Lettermen, The Lettermen In Concert (Capitol ST 1936) (stereo)	1963	$5.00	$10.00	$20.00

LPs	Year	VG	VG+	NM
(if on Capitol T 1936, mono)	1963	$3.75	$7.50	$15.00
The Lettermen, The Lettermen (Capitol STCL-577) (3 LP's)	1970	$6.25	$12.50	$25.00
Barry Manilow, Barry Manilow (Bell 1129)	1973	$6.25	$12.50	$25.00
(if on Arista AL 4007, with a remixed version of "Could It Be Magic")	1975	$2.50	$5.00	$10.00
Sergio Mendes and Brasil '66, The Beat of Brazil (A&M 1480) (mono)	1967	$5.00	$10.00	$20.00
(if on A&M SD 1480, stereo)	1967	$3.75	$7.50	$15.00
Anne Murray, Snowbird (Capitol ST-579)	1970	$3.00	$6.00	$12.00
Jim Nabors, Jim Nabors Sings Love Me With All Your Heart (Columbia CL 2558) (mono)	1966	$3.00	$6.00	$12.00
(if on Columbia CS 9358, stereo)	1966	$3.75	$7.50	$15.00
Gilbert O'Sullivan, Gilbert O'Sullivan - Himself (MAM 4)	1972	$3.75	$7.50	$15.00
Pablo Cruise, A Place In The Sun				
(if on A&M SP-4625)	1977	$2.50	$5.00	$10.00
(if on Mobile Fidelity 1-029, audiophile vinyl)	1979	$5.00	$10.00	$20.00
(if on A&M SP-3236, budget reissue)	198??	$2.00	$4.00	$8.00
Helen Reddy, I Am Woman (Capitol ST-11068)	1972	$2.50	$5.00	$10.00
(if on Capitol SN-16099, budget-line reissue)	1980	$2.00	$4.00	$8.00
Jim Reeves, The Best of Jim Reeves (RCA Victor LPM-2890) (mono)	1964	$5.00	$10.00	$20.00
(if on RCA Victor LSP-2890, stereo)	1964	$6.25	$12.50	$25.00
Cliff Richard, Cliff Sings (ABC-Paramount 321) (mono)	1960	$20.00	$40.00	$80.00
(if on ABC-Paramount S-321, stereo)	1960	$25.00	$50.00	$100.00
Cliff Richard, I'm Nearly Famous (Rocket PIG-2210)	1976	$3.00	$6.00	$12.00
(if on EMI-America SN-16221)	1981	$2.00	$4.00	$8.00
Kenny Rogers, The Gambler (United Artists UA-LA934-H)	1978	$2.50	$5.00	$10.00
(if on Mobile Fidelity 1-044, audiophile pressing)	1981	$5.00	$10.00	$20.00
(if on Liberty LO-934, budget reissue)	1981	$2.00	$4.00	$8.00
(if on Liberty LN-10247, budget reissue)	1984	$3.00	$6.00	
Seals and Crofts, Diamond Girl (Warner Bros. BS 2699)				
(if label has palm trees and references to Burbank, first pressings)	1973	$3.00	$6.00	$12.00
(if label is white or tan, reissue)	1979	$2.00	$4.00	$8.00
(if on Warner Bros. BS4 2699, quadraphonic)	1974	$5.00	$10.00	$20.00
Neil Sedaka, Sedaka's Back (Rocket MCA-463)	1974	$3.00	$6.00	$12.00
(if on MCA 2357, reissue)	1978	$2.50	$5.00	$10.00
Cat Stevens, Tea for the Tillerman				
(if on A&M SP-4280, brown label)	1971	$3.00	$6.00	$12.00
(if on A&M SP-4280, silver label with half-faded A&M)	1974	$2.50	$5.00	$10.00
(if on A&M QU-54313, quadraphonic)	1974	$5.00	$10.0	$20.00
(if on Mobile Fidelity 1-035, audiophile pressing)	1979	$10.00	$20.00	$40.00
(if on Mobile Fidelity MFQR-035, Ultra High Quality recording)	1984	$30.00	$60.00	$120.00
Ray Stevens, Everything Is Beautiful (Barnaby Z12-35005)	1970	$3.75	$7.50	$15.00
James Taylor, James Taylor (Apple SKAO 3352)				
(if title is in black print, first pressing)	1969	$6.25	$12.50	$25.00
(if title is in orange print)	1970	$5.00	$10.00	$20.00
James Taylor, Sweet Baby James (Warner Bros. WS 1843)				
(if first pressing, with "W7" logo)	1970	$6.25	$12.50	$25.00
(with green "WB" label, no reference to other songs on front cover)	1970	$3.75	$7.50	$15.00
(with green "WB" label, "Contains Fire and Rain and Country Road" listed on front cover)	1970	$2.50	$5.00	$10.00
(if on "Burbank" palm trees or cream-colored label)	1973	$2.00	$4.00	$8.00
(if on Warner Bros. ST-93138, Capitol Record Club edition)	1970	$5.00	$10.00	$20.00
Three Dog Night, It Ain't Easy (ABC Dunhill DS-50078)				
(if first pressing, band is in the nude on front cover)	1970	$25.00	$50.00	$100.00
(second pressing, regular front cover with gatefold)	1970	$3.00	$6.00	$12.00
The Vogues, Five O'Clock World (Co and Ce LP-1230) (mono) (no known stereo copies of this LP exist)	1966	$12.50	$25.00	$50.00
Glenn Yarborough, Each Of Us Alone (The Words and Music of Rod McKuen (Warner Bros. WS 1736)	1968	$3.00	$6.00	$12.00

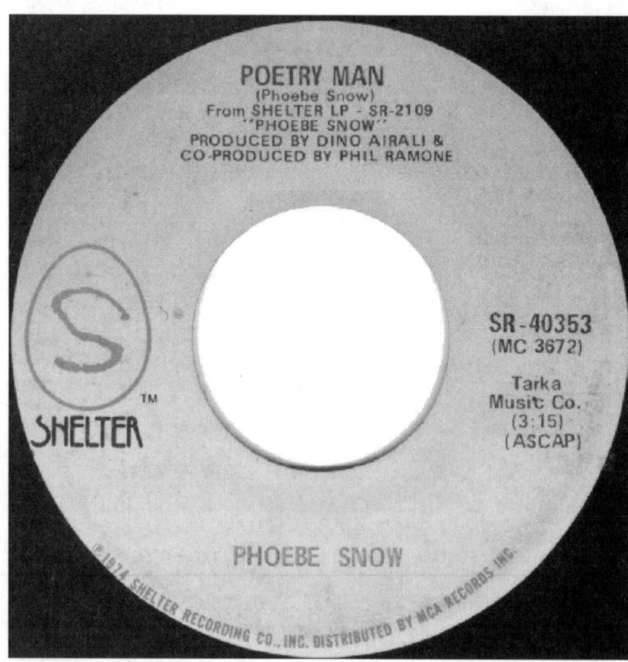

Phoebe Snow's first hit was her biggest; "Poetry Man" hit the top of the Adult Contemporary charts in 1975.

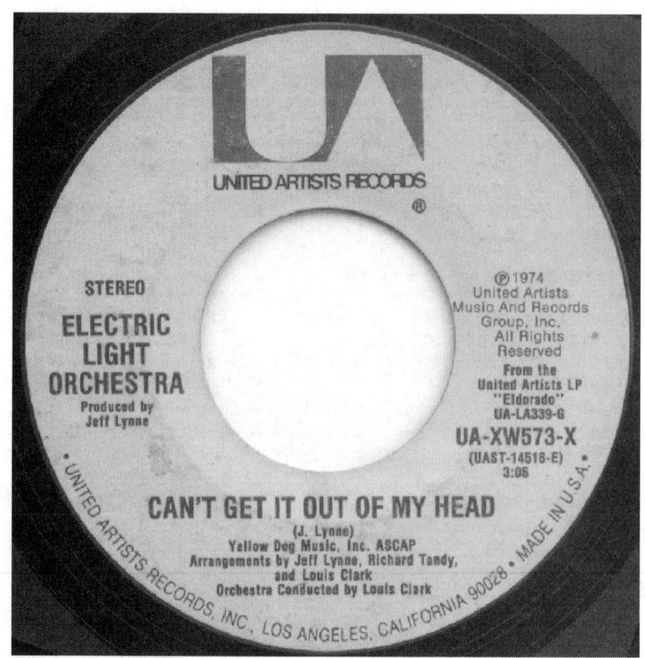

Although the Electric Light Orchestra ran the gamut from art-rock to rock and roll, "Can't Get It Out Of My Head" became a hit both on the pop and adult contemporary charts.

FOLK

History: Songs of childhood, songs of freedom, songs of the open road, and songs of the common man; The ballads of English troubadours, the chants and cadences of American work songs, the trials and triumphs of stories from around the world, all these musical styles have been grouped into folk music. Folk music was passed from generation to generation, telling lyrical stories of heroes, of loves lost and found, of songs to make the workday go faster to protest deplorable working or living conditions.

Many of the historical folk songs would have been lost today, without the foresightedness of musicologists like John Lomax and Francis Child. John Lomax, along with his son Alan, traveled with a portable tape recorder through the highways and byways of 1930s America. Along with the blues and jazz recordings they made for the Smithsonian library, they also recorded hundreds of American folk songs. In 19th century England, Francis Child collected hundreds of oral ballads and their variations— and transcribed them on paper before Child's efforts. Between the "Child Ballads" and the Smithsonian recordings from the Lomaxes, folk music was transferred from private music to a format that could be shared by music lovers around the world.

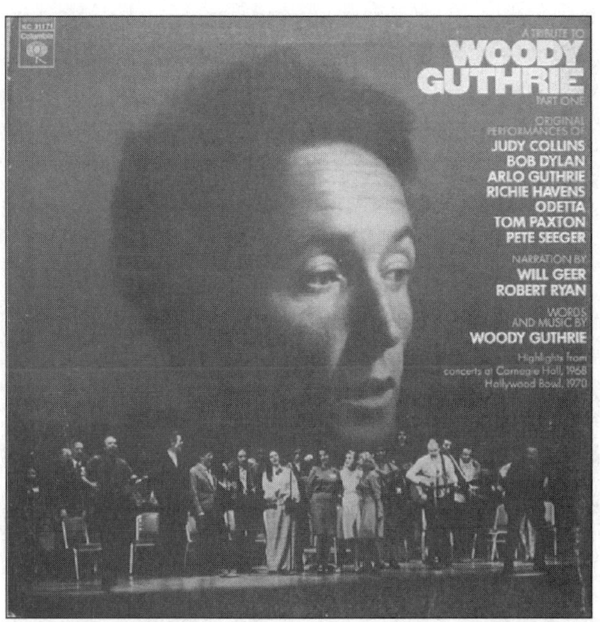

In 1968 and 1970, the most popular folk musicians of that time paid tribute to folk singer Woody Guthrie with a series of concerts honoring the legend.

By the early 1950s, folk performers like Pete Seeger, Woody Guthrie, and the Weavers were playing to appreciative crowds across America. But because many popular folk songs of that time, including "This Land Is Your Land" and "We Shall Not Be Moved," had a heavy pro-labor, pro-union content, some senators in Washington thought the lyrics might also have a pro-Communist slant.

And in the 1950s, with everybody looking for "the dreaded Communist influence," many popular folk singers and groups of the 1950s were accused, at one time or another, of either being Communists, knowing Communists, or not denouncing Communism fervently enough. Woody Guthrie and Pete Seeger were called to testify before the House Un-American Activities Committee; while the Weavers were under investigation on charges of sedition.

A rare 10-inch LP from The Weavers, one of the most popular folk acts of the 1950s.

Because of these investigations, many folk musicians were blacklisted from television and radio—"forced underground" by the Red Scare. But some sympathetic producers and record labels were able to give blacklisted performers a home for a time.

Other labels ignored the blacklist, signing folk artists and releasing new and stirring folk music. One such label was Vanguard Records. Although its first releases were a series of Bach cantatas, Vanguard was one of the first labels to break the "blacklist" barrier, releasing albums by Paul Robeson and the

Weavers. They also recorded performances at the Newport Folk Festival, such recordings being a historical overview of a changing period in folk music.

Another strong folk label was Elektra Records. Created by Jaq Holzman in 1950, Elektra's first releases were by world-renowned folk artists, performing the songs, ballads and compositions of their homelands. Holzman produced many of these early records, including discs by Jean Ritchie, Theodore Bikel and Cynthia Gooding. He also produced recordings by blacklisted folk performer Josh White, at a time when White was unable to get a recording contract because of his alleged ties to the Communist Party.

The Kingston Trio, with songs like "Tom Dooley" and "M.T.A.," were the most popular folk act of the late 1950s and early 1960s.

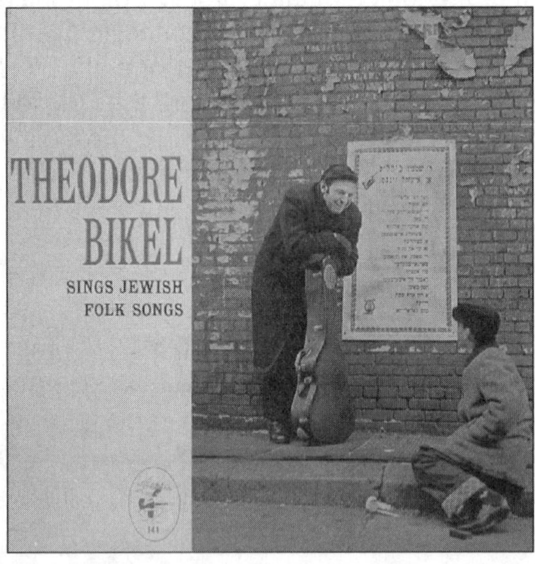

An early release on Elektra, starring folk singer Theodore Bikel.

By 1955, the Weavers outwardly defied the Communist blacklist and gave a triumphant performance at New York's Carnegie Hall, effectively jump-starting the career of a second wave of folk musicians. These new performers now found their audiences in cafés and coffee houses throughout New York's Greenwich Village, like the Café Wha? and the Commons, and in Los Angeles clubs like the Troubadour and the Hungry i. The new performers of folk included the Kingston Trio, Peter Paul and Mary, and The New Christy Minstrels.

Trivia

The Weavers' 1955 Carnegie Hall concert was not only a triumphant return of folk musicians from the blacklist, it also inspired the musical lives of Arlo Guthrie and Don McLean, who were in the audience on that fateful night.

Two other members of the folk revival, vocalists who would take folk music to new and exciting directions, were Joan Baez and Bob Dylan. Baez' first performing successes came in the Boston-area coffeehouses. By 1959, her spectacular performance at the Newport Folk Festival allowed her to sign with Vanguard Records, and release the first of many folk albums that would inspire generations.

Legendary singer-songwriter Joan Baez, on an early Vanguard release. Photo Credit: From the Collection of Mark and Elaine Klein.

Bob Dylan's influence can be heard on not only folk music, but on almost every musical genre today. His early albums, *Bob Dylan and The Freewheelin' Bob Dylan*, inspired a new generation of folk and folk-rock musicians. His later recordings electrified folk music; while it may have offended some purists, it eventually paved the way for such diverse musicians and acts as Simon & Garfunkel, the Band, the Byrds, and the Eagles. Eventually Dylan transcended folk music, recording folk-rock albums with The Band, country albums, gospel albums—in fact, recording music in whatever genre or style fitted his mood at the time.

One of the greatest and most prolific singer-songwriters in history, Bob Dylan. Courtesy Last Vestige Music Store, Albany, N.Y.

Among British folk musicians, the most popular folk group was Fairport Convention. The group, featuring singer/songwriters Richard Thompson, Sandy Denny, Ian Matthews, and Martin Lamble, took original British folk songs and reinterpreted them with contemporary harmony vocals. They also recorded popular versions of songs by Joni Mitchell, Bob Dylan, and Emitt Rhodes. While the original lineup evaporated from Fairport Convention by the mid-1970s (Richard Thompson, Ian Matthews, and Sandy Denny had successful solo careers, Fairport member Trevor Lucas became a successful producer, and Ashley Hutchings worked with Steeleye Span), the band itself, with new members, continues to tour and carry on the tradition of British folk music.

The influence of many British folk musicians, Fairport Convention. Courtesy Last Vestige Music Store, Albany, N.Y.

The 1970s folk singers were also known as "singer-songwriters," and composed their ballads and story-songs with minimal orchestrations. Some of these legendary singer-songwriters included Harry Chapin, Don McLean, Tom Rush, and Nick Drake. A new branch of the folk music tree, "women's music," also appeared in the 1970s, with the release of successful albums on the Olivia and Redwood record labels by Cris Williamson, Holly Near, and Meg Christian. Williamson's debut album, *The Changer and the Changed*, is the biggest-selling women's music album in history, with more than 500,000 copies sold since 1974—and all of them sold without a single second of commercial airplay; sold on the strength of "word-of-mouth" alone.

Trivia

The Kingston Trio's "M.T.A. ," one of their most popular songs, was actually a campaign song for a 1948 Boston mayoral candidate. The song protested higher subway tolls by having an unsuspecting rider put ten cents in, but not have another nickel for the increased fare. The song won a Grammy for Best Folk Performance in 1959.

Cris Williamson's groundbreaking independent LP *The Changer and the Changed,* one of the biggest-selling independent records of the 1970s. Courtesy Last Vestige Music Store, Albany, N.Y.

What To Look For: Many folk titles have remained in print over the years, so the first pressings are the most collectible. For these reasons, double check the label to make sure you are not purchasing a budget-line reissue (with the exception of audiophile pressings from Mobile Fidelity, Nautilus and Analogue Productions, whose reissues may be worth more than the original record).

Since folk music had a successful run through the 1950s, be aware that many artists had their material released on 10-inch LPs, which are highly collectible today. Especially collectible in this format are recordings by Woody Guthrie and Pete Seeger, whose material was in conflict with the Communist-hunting senators.

Folk songs have made inroads into the Top 40, so 7-inch singles do exist and are collectible, especially with picture sleeves intact. Be aware that some 7-inch singles do contain truncated or edited lyrics, especially if the song does feature some sort of expletive in the album version or if the song is just too long for 7-inch release.

Among folk music artists, Bob Dylan's records are the most collectable, especially his early Columbia recordings. Be aware that some of his albums, especially *The Freewheelin' Bob Dylan and Highway 61 Revisited*, may contain alternate takes or different songs from one pressing to the next. This is extremely important—a stereo copy of *The Freewheelin' Bob Dylan*, containing such songs as "Let Me Die In My Footsteps" and "Rocks and Gravel," can sell for as much as $30,000 in near-mint condition, while a "corrected version," one that does not contain those songs, will only sell for about $50 in near-mint condition.

Although Pete Seeger sang folk songs of various origins and genres—including children's folk songs, as shown on this album—he was under investigation in the 1950s on charges of supporting Communism. From the collection of Mark and Elaine Klein.

There are variations in pressings on *The Freewheelin' Bob Dylan*, some of which contain additional songs. Does your album copy have more songs than are listed here? Courtesy Last Vestige Music Store, Albany, N.Y.

Trivia

Bob Dylan's "Subterranean Homesick Blues," with its stream-of-consciousness lyrics, was enhanced by an early music video in which Dylan tossed cue cards featuring the song's lyrics.

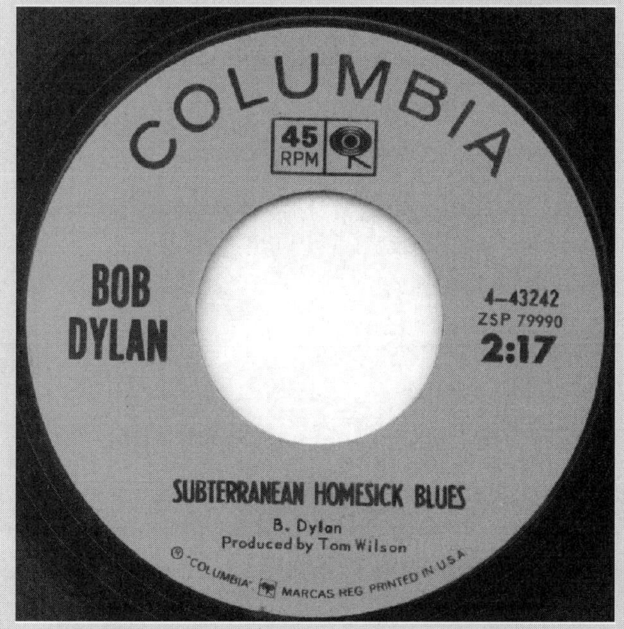

Bob Dylan's first song to crack the Billboard Top 40, "Subterranean Homesick Blues."

Reference Books: Holzman, Jac; Daws, Gavan, *Follow The Music: The Life and Hard Times of Elektra Records in the Great Years of American Pop Culture*, FirstMedia Books, Santa Monica, Calif. 1998.

Web pages: Go to the *about.com* Web site *(http://www.about.com)*, and type in the keywords "Folk Music 101." Hugh Blumenfeld's folk music sites are very educational, descriptive, and informative; Christine A. Spivey has an excellent dissertation on the effects of the "Red Scare" on 1950s folk musicians: *http://www.loyno.edu/~history/journal/1996-7/Spivey.html*; a fansite devoted to the history and lineage of Fairport Convention: *http://www.musikfolk.com/expletive-delighted/welcome.htm*; the Vanguard Records homepage: *http://www.vanguardrecords.com.*

45s	Year	VG	VG+	NM
Joan Baez, "We Shall Overcome" / "What Have They Done To the Rain" (Vanguard 35023)	1963	$2.00	$4.00	$8.00
Joan Baez, "There But For Fortune" / "Daddy You Been On My Mind" (Vanguard 35031)	1965	$2.00	$4.00	$8.00
(with picture sleeve, add:)	1965	$7.50	$15.00	$30.00

45s	Year	VG	VG+	NM
Harry Chapin, "Taxi" / "Empty" (Elektra 45770)	1972		$2.50	$5.00
Harry Chapin, "Cat's In The Cradle" / "Vacancy" (Elektra 45203)	1974		$2.00	$4.00
Leonard Cohen, "Suzanne" / "That's No Way To Say Goodbye" (Columbia 44439)	1968		$3.00	$6.00
Judy Collins, "Both Sides Now" / "Who Knows Where The Time Goes) (Elektra 45639)				
(if label is red, white and black, first pressing)	1968	$2.00	$4.00	$8.00
(if label is yellow and black, second pressing)	1968		$3.00	$6.00
Judy Collins, "Send In The Clowns" / "Houses" (Elektra 45253)				
(if titles are in large print, first pressing)	1975		$2.50	$5.00
(if titles are in smaller print, reissue)	1977		$2.00	$4.00
Bob Dylan, "Mixed-Up Confusion" / "Corrine, Corrina" (Columbia 42656)	1962	$500.00	$750.00	$1,000.00
Bob Dylan, "Blowin' In The Wind" / "Don't Think Twice, It's All Right" (Columbia 42856)	1963	$125.00	$250.00	$500.00
(if on white label promo)	1963	$100.00	$200.00	$400.00
(if on Columbia JZSP 75606/7, "Special Album Excerpt" promo)	1963	$75.00	$150.00	$300.00
(with "Rebel With A Cause" promotional flyer picture sleeve, add:)	1963	$200.00	$400.00	$800.00
Bob Dylan, "Subterranean Homesick Blues" / "She Belongs To Me" (Columbia 43242)	1965	$3.00	$6.00	$12.00
(if promo copy with "Subterranean Homesick Blues" on both sides, pressed on red vinyl)	1965	$50.00	$100.00	$200.00
(with picture sleeve, available only on some promos, add:)	1965	$500.00	$750.00	$1,000.00
(if stock copy on gray label, 1972 reissue)	1972	$7.50	$15.00	$30.00
Bob Dylan, "All Along The Watchtower" / "It Ain't Me Babe" (Asylum 45212)	1974	$3.00	$6.00	$12.00
Bob Dylan, "Hurricane" (Pt. 1) / (Pt. 2) Columbia 10245)	1975	$3.00	$6.00	
(with picture sleeve, add:)	1975	$3.00	$6.00	$12.00
(if radio station reissue, plays at 33 1/3 RPM, does not contain "Special Rush Reservice" on label)	1975	$5.00	$10.00	$20.00
(if radio station reissue, plays at 33 1/3 RPM, contains "Special Rush Reservice" on label)	1975	$3.75	$7.50	$15.00
(with picture sleeve for "Special Rush Reservice" pressing, add:)	1975	$3.75	$7.50	$15.00
Fairport Convention, "Fotheringay" / "I'll Keep It With Mine" (A&M 1108)	1969	$3.00	$6.00	$12.00
Fairport Convention, "Journeyman's Grace" / "The World Has Surely Lost Its Head" (A&M 1333)	1972	$2.00	$4.00	$8.00
Kinky Friedman, "Wiled Man From Borneo" / "Popeye The Sailor Man" (ABC 12107)	1975		$2.50	$5.00
Arlo Guthrie, "Alice's Rock & Roll Restaurant" / "Coming Into Los Angeles" (Reprise 0877)	1969	$3.00	$6.00	$12.00
The Highwaymen, "Michael" / "Santiano" (United Artists 258)	1960	$3.75	$7.50	$15.00
Janis Ian, "Society's Child" (Baby I've Been Thinking" / "Letter to Jon" (Verve Folkways 5027)	1966	$3.00	$6.00	$12.00
(if on Verve 5027, second pressing)	1967	$2.50	$5.00	$10.00
(if on Verve Forecast 5027, third pressing)	1967	$2.00	$4.00	$8.00
It's A Beautiful Day, "White Bird" / "Wasted Union Blues" (Columbia 44928)	1969	$2.00	$4.00	$8.00
The Limeliters, "A Dollar Down" / "When Twice The Moon Has Come And Gone" (RCA Victor 47-7859)	1961	$2.00	$4.00	$8.00
(with picture sleeve, add:)	1961	$3.00	$6.00	$12.00
The Chad Mitchell Trio, "Lizzie Borden" / "Super Skier" (Kapp 439)	1961	$3.00	$6.00	$12.00
(with picture sleeve, add:)	1961	$5.00	$10.00	$20.00
The Chad Mitchell Trio, "The Marvelous Toy" / "Bonny Streets of Fyve-10" (Mercury 72197)	1963	$2.50	$5.00	$10.00
(with picture sleeve, add:)	1963	$3.75	$7.50	$15.00
Joni Mitchell, "Big Yellow Taxi" / "Woodstock" (Reprise 0906)	1970	$2.00	$4.00	$8.00
The New Christy Minstrels, "This Land Is Your Land" / "Don't Cry, Suzanne" (Columbia 42592)	1962	$2.50	$5.00	$10.00
(with picture sleeve, add:)	1962	$3.75	$7.50	$15.00
Phil Ochs, "The War Is Over" / "The Harder They Fall" (A&M 932)	1968	$2.00	$4.00	$8.00
Phil Ochs, "Here's To The State Of Richard Nixon" / "Power and Glory" (A&M 1509)	1974	$2.00	$4.00	$8.00

45s	Year	VG	VG+	NM
Peter Paul and Mary, "Puff" / "Pretty Mary" (Warner Bros. 5348)	1963	$3.00	$6.00	$12.00
Peter Paul and Mary, "Puff (The Magic Dragon)" / "Pretty Mary" (Warner Bros. 5348)	1963	$2.50	$5.00	$10.00
The Rooftop Singers, "Tom Cat" / "Shoes" (Vanguard 35019)	1963	$2.00	$4.00	$8.00
(with picture sleeve, add:)	1963	$3.00	$6.00	$12.00
Tom Rush, "Diamond Joe" / "Every Day in the Week" (Prestige 289)	1964	$3.00	$6.00	$12.00
Buffy Sainte-Marie, "Until It's Time For You To Go" / "The Flower and the Apple Tree" (Vanguard 35028)	1963	$2.50	$5.00	$10.00
(if on Vanguard 35050, B-side is "Jusqu'au Jour Ou Tu Partiras")	1967	$2.00	$4.00	$8.00
Pete Seeger, "Waist Deep in the Big Muddy" / "Down By The Riverside" (Columbia 44273)	1967	$2.00	$4.00	$8.00
Simon and Garfunkel, "The Sounds of Silence" / "We've Got A Groovey Thing Goin'" (Columbia 43396)	1965	$2.50	$5.00	$10.00
(if both sides are "The Sounds of Silence," red vinyl pressing)	1965	$12.50	$25.00	$50.00
Simon and Garfunkel, "Bridge Over Troubled Water" / "Keep The Customer Satisfied" (Columbia 45079)	1970		$3.00	$6.00
(with picture sleeve, add:)	1970	$2.00	$4.00	$8.00
Steeleye Span, "Gaudete" / "Royal Forester" (Chrysalis 2008)	1972		$3.00	$6.00
(if on Chrysalis 2102, reissue)	1974	$2.50	$5.00	
The Weavers, "Goodnight Irene" / "Tzena, Tzena, Tzena" (Decca 27077)	1950	$3.75	$7.50	$15.00
The Weavers, "Wimoweh" / "Old Paint" (Decca 27928)	1952	$3.75	$7.50	$15.00

10-inch LPs	Year	VG	VG+	NM
Pete Seeger, A Pete Seeger Sampler (Folkways FA-2043)	1954	$20.00	$40.00	$80.00
Woody Guthrie, Dust Bowl Ballads (Folkways FP-11)	1950	$150.00	$300.00	$600.00
(if on Folkways FA-2011, reissue)	195??	$125.00	$250.00	$500.00
The Weavers, We Wish You A Merry Christmas (Decca DL-5373)	1952	$25.00	$50.00	$100.00

LPs	Year	VG	VG+	NM
Joan Baez, Joan Baez (Vanguard VRS-9078) (mono)	1960	$5.00	$10.00	$20.00
(if on Vanguard VSD-2077, stereo)	1960	$6.25	$12.50	$25.00
Joan Baez, Farewell, Angelina (Vanguard VRS-9200) (mono)	1965	$3.75	$7.50	$15.00
(if on Vanguard VSD-79200, stereo)	1965	$5.00	$10.00	$20.00
Joan Baez, Diamonds and Rust (A&M SP-4527)	1975	$2.50	$5.00	$10.00
(if on A&M SP-3233, budget line reissue)	198??	$2.00	$4.00	$8.00
(if on Nautilus NR-12, audiophile vinyl)	1980	$10.00	$20.00	$40.00
(if on Mobile Fidelity 1-238, audiophile vinyl)	1996	$6.25	$12.50	$25.00
Harry Chapin, Heads and Tales (Elektra EKS-75023)	1972	$2.50	$5.00	$10.00
Leonard Cohen, Leonard Cohen (Columbia CL 2733) (mono)	1967	$6.25	$12.50	$25.00
(if on Columbia CS 9533, stereo, "360 Sound" on red label)	1967	$3.00	$6.00	$12.00
(if on Columbia CS 9533, stereo, orange label)	1970	$2.50	$5.00	$10.00
(if on Columbia PC 9533, stereo, reissue)	198??	$2.00	$4.00	$8.00
Judy Collins, Maid of Constant Sorrow				
(if on Elektra EKL-209, guitar player on label, mono)	1961	$10.00	$20.00	$40.00
(if on Elektra EKL-209, gold-tan label, mono)	1966	$5.00	$10.00	$20.00
(if on Elektra EKS-7209, rechannelled stereo, gold-tan or red label with large stylized "E" logo)	196??	$3.00	$6.00	$12.00
(if on Elektra EKS-7209, rechannelled stereo, butterfly logo, no reference to Warner Communications)	1971	$2.50	$5.00	$10.00
(if on Elektra EKS-7209, rechannelled stereo, contains logo for Warner Communications)	1975	$2.00	$4.00	$8.00
Nick Drake, Pink Moon (Island SMAS-9318)	1971	$6.25	$12.50	$25.00
Bob Dylan, The Freewheelin' Bob Dylan				
(if on Columbia CL 1986, mono, "Guaranteed High Fidelity" on label, plays "Let Me Die In My Footsteps," "Rocks and Gravel," "Uncle John Birch Blues," "Gamblin' Willie's Dead Man's Hand," Label does NOT list these songs. Stamper number in dead wax ends in "-1," followed by a letter)	1963	$5,000	$10,000	$15,000
(if on Columbia CL 1986, mono, white label promo, label and timing strip lists the deleted tracks, but record plays the "correct" tracks)	1963	$2,000	$3,000	$4,000
(if on Columbia CL 1986, mono, white label promo, label lists deleted tracks, but timing strip lists, and record plays, the "correct" tracks)	1963	$250.00	$500.00	$1,000.00
(if on Columbia CL 1986, mono, white label promo, timing strip lists deleted tracks, but label lists, and record plays, the "correct" tracks)	1963	$200.00	$400.00	$800.00
(if on Columbia CL 1986, mono, white label promo, label AND timing strip list, and record plays, "correct" tracks)	1963	$125.00	$250.00	$500.00
(if on Columbia CL 1986, mono, "Guaranteed High Fidelity" on label, corrected version (record plays what label says)	1963	$10.00	$20.00	$40.00
(if on Columbia CS 8786, stereo, "360 Sound Stereo" in black on label, no arrows, record plays, and label lists, "Let Me Die In My Footsteps," "Rocks and Gravel," "Talkin' John Birch Blues," and "Gamblin' Willie's Dead Man's Hand." No known stereo copies play these songs without listing them on the label)	1963	$15,000	$22,500	$30,000
(if on Columbia CS 8786, stereo, "360 Sound Stereo" in black on label, no arrows)	1963	$12.50	$25.00	$50.00
(if on Columbia CS 8786, stereo, "360 Sound Stereo" in black on label, with arrows)	1964	$10.00	$20.00	$40.00
(if on Columbia CS 8786, stereo, "360 Sound Stereo" in white on label)	1965	$6.25	$12.50	$25.00
(if on Columbia CS 8786, stereo, orange label)	1970	$3.00	$6.00	$12.00
(if on Columbia CS 8786, stereo, orange label, red vinyl (unauthorized pressing))	197??	$250.00	$500.00	$1,000.00
(if on Columbia KCS 8786)	197??	$2.50	$5.00	$10.00
(if on Columbia PC 8786, budget line reissue)	198??	$2.00	$4.00	$8.00
Bob Dylan, Highway 61 Revisited				
(if on Columbia CL 2389, mono, white label promo)	1965	$100.00	$200.00	$400.00
(if on Columbia CL 2389, mono, stock copy)	1965	$15.00	$30.00	$60.00
(if on Columbia CS 9189, stereo, with alternate take of "From A Buick 6," the matrix number on side 1 will end in "-1," plus a letter)	1965	$50.00	$100.00	$200.00
(if on Columbia CS 9189, stereo, with regular take of "From A Buick 6," the matrix number on side 1 will end in "-2" or higher, plus a letter)	1965	$7.50	$15.00	$30.00
(if on Columbia CS 9189, stereo, orange label)	197??	$30.00	$6.00	$12.00
(if on Columbia KCS 9643, stereo)	197??	$2.50	$5.00	$10.00
(if on Columbia PC 9189, stereo, budget reissue)	198??	$2.00	$4.00	$8.00
Bob Dylan, Dylan and the Dead (Columbia OC 45056)	1989	$3.00	$6.00	$12.00
Fairport Convention, Fairport Convention (Cotillion SD 9024)	1968	$7.50	$15.00	$30.00
Fairport Convention, Fairport Convention (A&M SP 4185) (actually US copy of UK LP "What We Did On Our Holidays")	1969	$3.75	$7.50	$15.00
(if on Carthage CGLP-4430, reissue with UK title restored)	198??	$2.50	$5.00	$10.00
Kinky Friedman, Lasso from El Paso (Epic PE 34304)	1976	$2.50	$5.00	$10.00
Arlo Guthrie, Alice's Restaurant (Reprise 6267)				
(if on Reprise R 6267, mono)	1967	$5.00	$10.00	$20.00
(if on Reprise RS 6267, stereo, pink-green-gold label)	1967	$3.75	$7.50	$15.00
(if on Reprise RS 6267, stereo, with "W7" and "r:" logos on two-tone orange color)	1968	$3.00	$6.00	$12.00
(if on Reprise RS 6267, stereo, with only "r:" logo, all-orange or tan label)	1970	$2.50	$5.00	$10.00
Woody Guthrie, Bound for Glory: Songs and Stories of Woody Guthrie (Folkways FA-2481) (mono)	1956	$37.50	$75.00	$100.00
Woody Guthrie, Bonneville Dam and Other Columbia River Songs (Verve Folkways FV-9036) (mono)	1965	$7.50	$15.00	$30.00
(if on Verve Folkways FVS-9036, rechannelled stereo)	1965	$5.00	$10.00	$20.00
The Highwaymen, Standing Room Only! (United Artists UAL 3168) (mono)	1962	$3.75	$7.50	$15.00
(if on United Artists UAS 6168, stereo)	1962	$5.00	$10.00	$20.00
Janis Ian, For All The Seasons Of Your Mind (Verve Forecast FT-3024) (mono)	1967	$5.00	$10.00	$20.00

LPs	Year	VG	VG+	NM
(if on Verve Forecast FTS-3024, stereo)	1967	$3.75	$7.50	$15.00
The Limeliters, The Limeliters (Elektra EKM-180) (mono)	1960	$5.00	$10.00	$20.00
(if on Elektra EKS-7180, stereo)	1960	$6.25	$12.50	$25.00
The Chad Mitchell Trio, The Best of the Chad Mitchell Trio (Kapp KL-1334) (mono)	1963	$5.00	$10.00	$20.00
(if on Kapp KS-3334, stereo)	1963	$6.25	$12.50	$25.00
Joni Mitchell, Court and Spark (Asylum 7E-1001)	1974	$2.50	$5.00	$10.00
(if on Asylum EQ-1001, quadraphonic)	1974	$5.00	$10.00	$20.00
(if on Nautilus NR-11, audiophile vinyl)	1980	$12.50	$25.00	$50.00
(if on DCC Compact Classics LPZ-2004)	1997	$6.25	$12.50	$25.00
The New Christy Minstrels, The New Christy Minstrels (Columbia CL 1872) (mono)	1962	$5.00	$10.00	$20.00
(if on Columbia CS 8672, stereo)	1962	$6.25	$12.50	$25.00
Phil Ochs, All The News That's Fit To Sing				
(if on Elektra EKL-269, mono, gold label with guitar player logo)	1964	$7.50	$15.00	$30.00
(if on Elektra EKS-7269, stereo, gold label with guitar player logo)	1964	$10.00	$20.00	$40.00
(if on Elektra EKL-269, mono, gold label with stylized "E" logo)	1966	$5.00	$10.00	$20.00
(if on Elektra EKS-7269, stereo, gold label with stylized "E" logo)	1966	$6.25	$12.50	$25.00
(if on Carthage CGLP-4427, reissue)	198??	$2.50	$5.00	$10.00
Peter Paul and Mary, Peter Paul and Mary in Concert (Warner Bros. 2W 1555) (mono) (2 LPs)	1964	$6.25	$12.50	$25.00
(if on Warner Bros. 2WS 1555, stereo, gold label)	1964	$7.50	$15.00	$30.00
(if on Warner Bros. 2WS 1555, stereo, any other Warner Bros. label except gold color)	1968	$3.00	$6.00	$12.00
The Rooftop Singers, Walk Right In (Vanguard VRS-9123) (mono)	1963	$3.75	$7.50	$15.00
(if on Vanguard VSD-2136, stereo)	1963	$5.00	$10.00	$20.00

LPs	Year	VG	VG+	NM
Tom Rush, Got a Mind to Ramble (Folklore FRLP-14003) (mono)	1964	$5.00	$10.00	$20.00
(if on Folklore FRST-14003, stereo)	1964	$6.25	$12.50	$25.00
Tom Rush, Tom Rush (Columbia CS 9972)				
(if on red "360 Sound" label)	1970	$3.75	$7.50	$15.00
(if on orange label)	1970	$3.00	$6.00	$12.00
Buffy Sainte-Marie, The Best of Buffy Sainte-Marie (Vanguard VSD 3/4) (2 LPs)	1970	$5.00	$10.00	$20.00
Simon and Garfunkel, Wednesday Morning 3 A.M.				
(if on Columbia CL 2249, mono, "Guaranteed High Fidelity" on label)	1964	$6.25	$12.50	$25.00
(if on Columbia CL 2249, mono, "Mono" on label)	1965	$3.75	$7.50	$15.00
(if on Columbia CS 9049, stereo, "360 Sound Stereo" in black on label)	1964	$6.25	$12.50	$25.00
(if on Columbia CS 9049, stereo, "360 Sound Stereo" in white on label)	1965	$3.75	$7.50	$15.00
(if on Columbia CS 9049, stereo, orange label)	1970	$2.50	$5.00	$10.00
(if on Columbia PC 9049, stereo, budget-line reissue)	197??	$2.00	$4.00	$8.00
Steeleye Span, All Around My Hat (Chrysalis CHR 1091)				
(if on green label, address listed as "3300 Warner Blvd.")	1975	$3.75	$7.50	$15.00
(if on blue label, with New York address)	1977	$3.00	$6.00	$12.00
(if on Mobile Fidelity 1-027, audiophile pressing)	1980	$6.25	$12.50	$25.00
(if on Shanachie 79059, reissue)	1989	$3.00	$6.00	$12.00
Richard and Linda Thompson, Shoot Out The Lights (Hannibal HNBL 1303)	1982	$2.50	$5.00	$10.00
The Weavers, Reunion at Carnegie Hall, 1963 (Vanguard VRS 9130) (mono)	1963	$5.00	$10.00	$20.00
(if on Vanguard VSD 2150, stereo)	1963	$7.50	$15.00	$30.00
(if on Analogue Productions 005, audiophile release)	199??	$7.50	$15.00	$30.00

The Chad Mitchell Trio, while not as popular as the Kingston Trio, did have some folk hits of their own—including "Lizzie Borden," a satirical song about the trial of the century—the 19th century, that is.

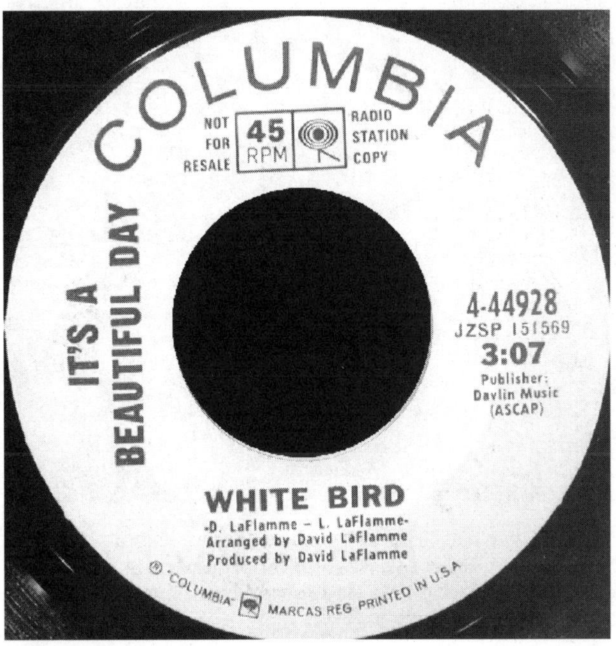

Written and produced by David LaFlamme, It's a Beautiful Day's "White Bird" became a staple on FM radio stations in the late 1960s.

FUNK

History: Funk music is hard-edged dance music designed to get your rump off the couch and boogie. With its thick, jumpy baselines, rhythmic drums, trumpet blasts and call-and-response vocals, funk has become a harder-edged version of soul music, or a danceable version of rock—take your pick.

James Brown may be the "Godfather of Soul," but he was also one of the popularists of funk. While his ballads "Try Me" and "Please, Please, Please" were pure soul, he added a bass-heavy melody to his recordings, punctuating certain breaks in the song with drum solos and horn riffs. While with King Records, he recorded tracks like "Papa's Got A Brand New Bag," "I Got You (I Feel Good)," "Cold Sweat," and "Mother Popcorn"—songs which catapulted Brown across all radio and racial barriers. He brought funk music to black and white fans alike, and Brown's Famous Flames backup band laid down such a funky beat that concert theaters they performed in became dance clubs that night.

James Brown's "Please Please Please" was a hit when he recorded it on the Federal label; when he moved to King Records, the title was re-released, eventually selling a million copies.

By 1971, James Brown disbanded the Famous Flames, and formed the JBs with former Famous Flame Jimmy Nolen, and new additions Maceo Parker, St. Clair Pinckney, and Fred Wesley. He also left King Records, the label for which he had recorded his greatest hits, and signed a long-term deal with Polydor. He also created a new record label, People Records, so that Polydor could distribute recordings by Lyn Collins and Donald Byrd.

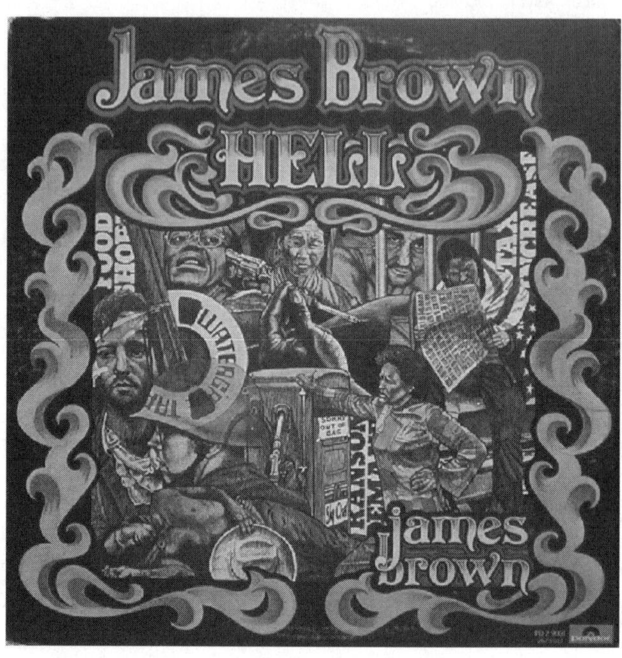

James Brown's music was just as hot in the 1970s, which would create the multiple meaning of the album title Hell.

Many of the ex-Famous Flames joined up with George Clinton's Parliament/Funkadelic operation. Clinton's funk band evolved from the Parliaments, a doo-wop group which had a Top 20 hit in 1967 on Revilot, "(I Wanna) Testify." In 1969, when a contract dispute took Clinton's right to call his group the "Parliaments" away from him, he renamed the band Funkadelic and signed with Westbound Records (and eventually to Warner Bros. in the mid-1970s). A year later, when he regained the rights to the name "Parliaments," he rechristened his band Parliament and signed them to a competing record company, Invictus (that version of Clinton's band moved to Casablanca in 1976).

As more members of James Brown's band joined up with Clinton, including Bootsy Collins and Gary Shider, the Parliament/Funkadelic combination became a musical entity in itself. Besides Parliament and Funkadelic, George Clinton oversaw spinoff groups such as Bootsy's Rubber Band, Parlet, and the Brides of Funkenstein, all backed up by the Horny Horns. While Parliament had massive hits with "Flash Light" and "Tear the Roof Off the Sucker," Funkadelic matched it with "One Nation Under A Groove," "(Not Just) Knee Deep," and "Up For The Down Stroke."

With a mixture of funk and science fiction, George Clinton launched his Mothership Connection with Parliament. Notice the record was produced and "conceived" by Clinton.

George Clinton's other band Funkadelic, featuring many of the musicians in his band Parliament.

The Clinton funk bands continued until 1980, when another legal wrangling took the names Parliament and Funkadelic away from him. Undaunted, he signed with Capitol Records as a solo artist, and released the funk hits "Atomic Dog" and "Loopzilla," backing himself with the "P-Funk All-Stars."

The third person who brought funk into the mainstream was Sylvester Stewart, the "Sly Stone" of Sly and the Family Stone. A former disc jockey and songwriter, Sly mixed funk with psychedelia, and created a series of funk and dance anthems like "Dance to the Music," "Thank You (Falletinme Be Mice Elf Agin)," and "Everyday People."

Sly and the Family Stone, who brought psychedelia and "flower power" to funk music.

More than any other musical genre, funk music brought the electric bass guitar to the forefront of the band. Bass guitarists, who formerly plucked their instruments in virtual anonymity, now slapped and thumped and pounded those strings with reckless abandon and fervor. By the 1970s, the next generation of funk-based artists would now layer their musical compositions around their bass player's thick, bouncing instrumental riffs.

Some of these groups mixed funk with a Latin beat (War), while others expanded on the call-and-response vocals of James Brown and Parliament-Funkadelic (such as the Ohio Players, Con Funk Shun). Bands like Tower of Power and Charles Wright and the Watts 103rd Street Rhythm Band brought West Coast urban funk to radio; groups such as the Brothers Johnson, the Gap Band and Cameo incorporated funk into slick, polished productions that captured millions of fans.

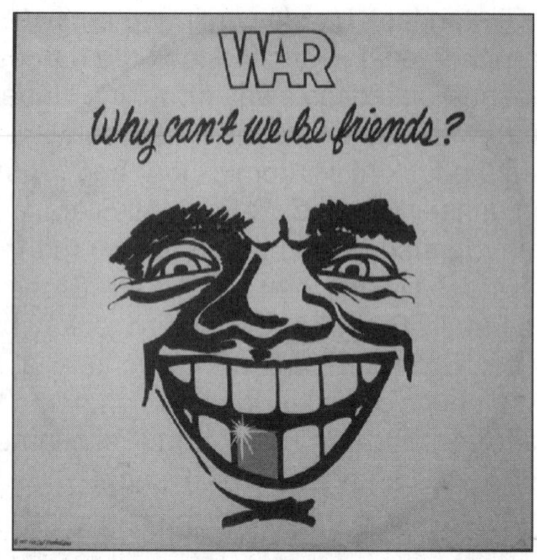

The former backup band for Eric Burdon, War evolved into a funk-salsa superband of the 1970s. Courtesy of Last Vestige Music Store, Albany, N.Y.

By the 1980s, the two biggest names in funk were Rick James and Prince. Both artists mixed their funk beats with salacious, double-entendre lyrics; both artists could lay down a killer beat that would keep people dancing all night.

Rick James and the Stone City Band had funk hits in the 1970s, but it wasn't until the success of his breakthrough album Street Songs, with its hits "Super Freak" and "Give It To Me Baby," that James was able to achieve musical superstardom. He would later build that success into a stable of funk and soul artists at Motown, producing and writing songs for Teena Marie, the Mary Jane Girls and the Stone City Band. And when M.C. Hammer needed a funky rhythm track for his song "U Can't Touch This," Rick James' "Super Freak" was the perfect choice.

Rick James' biggest hit, "Super Freak," features Daniel Lemelle's extended funky saxophone riff on this 12-inch dance disc.

Not to be outdone, Prince Rogers Nelson mixed funky bass lines with synthesizer riffs and off-the-wall lyrical subject matter. His early songs "I Wanna Be Your Lover," "Dirty Mind," and "Controversy" paved the way for the success of his albums *1999 and Purple Rain.* During his career, Prince found time to produce another funk band, The Time; an all-girl trio, Vanity 6 (later renamed Apollonia 6 when the group switched lead singers), and an all-instrumental crew, Madhouse. He also wrote music for the movies *"Under the Cherry Moon"* and *"Graffiti Bridge"* (he also starred in both), and recorded songs to promote the movie *"Batman."*

The double-album *1999* established Prince as a performer on Top 40 radio; R&B stations had known about his electric funk for years.

What To Look For: James Brown's earliest 45s on the Federal label are the hardest to find. His King and Smash releases, while plentiful, are hard to find in near-mint condition, and their value reflects their rarity. His 1970s recordings on Polydor are very common, and their collectible value is very low. Brown's 1980s comeback on Scotti Bros., while a shot in the arm to his career and legacy, are also not as collectible as his earlier work.

Prince's rarer records were his early, pre-*Purple Rain issues.* Although his albums after *Diamonds and Pearls* were released on CD only, he has allowed some of his songs to be released on 7-inch vinyl. Prince's picture sleeves are getting harder to find, especially in good condition. Although most of his picture sleeves were the standard glossy artwork most artists used for their 45s, some picture sleeves exist in bread-bag plastic (*Purple Rain*), foldout (*Delirious*), and plastic (*Alphabet St. and Glam Slam*). Other sleeves were pulled from the marketplace when the songs they promoted were either not released as A-sided singles or were just pulled for reasons known only to the Artist.

Trivia

The Ohio Players' funk hit "Love Rollercoaster" features an urban legend. Approximately 90 seconds into the song, one can hear a bloodcurdling scream over an instrumental track. Some conspiracy theorists have argued that the "scream" came from a woman who was stabbed in the next studio, or that the sound came from a woman who was thrown off a moving rollercoaster to her death. Although common sense dictates that the scream is nothing more than a party yell by a backup singer, the Ohio Players have played up the "controversy" by not stating exactly how they got that scream on tape.

This rare picture sleeve of Prince's hit "Delirious" folds out to become a poster/calendar—albeit released in 1983, the calendar is for the year 1999.

George Clinton's earliest recordings, both with the Parliaments and with Parliament/Funkadelic, have increased in value over the years, as have Rick James' earliest albums. One of the reasons is that many musicians today are using song samples for their own projects. Songs such as Rick James' "Super Freak," Funkadelic's "(not just) Knee Deep," and James Brown's "Funky Drummer" have become the frame to which a whole nation of samplers have draped their musical tapestries.

Both of these songs have been sampled by other artists—the last ten seconds of "Funky Drummer" became the West Side Mob's "Break Dance—Electric Boogaloo," and Funkadelic's "(not just) Knee Deep" eventually was used by De La Soul for their song "Me Myself and I."

Reference Books: Ward, Ed; Stokes, Geoffrey; Tucker, Ken, *Rock of Ages: The Rolling Stone History of Rock and Roll*, Rolling Stone Press, Summit Books, Simon & Schuster, New York, 1986; Whitburn, Joel, *Top R&B Singles 1942-1995*, Record Research Inc., Menomonee Falls, Wisconsin, 1996; Whitburn, Joel, *Top R&B Albums 1965-1998*, Record Research Inc., Menomonee Falls, Wisconsin, 1999.

Web pages: NPG Online Ltd., Prince's official site: *http://www.npgonlineltd.com;* a fan page devoted to James Brown: *http://www.funky-stuff.com*; a homepage with plenty of funk biographies: *http://www.soul-patrol.com/funk.*

Trivia

A 1987 funk album Prince recorded, *The Black Album*, was yanked from shelves days before its release; stock and promo copies do exist and are worth thousands of dollars in near-mint condition (songs from *The Black Album* eventually ended up on future Prince releases). Bootlegs of *The Black Album* exist; as well as legitimate promo copies pressed on either orange, black or white vinyl. Warner Bros. eventually released *The Black Album* in 1994, but only promotional copies are available on vinyl. Check with an expert in Prince memorabilia before you purchase any copies of this LP.

45s	Year	VG	VG+	NM
James Brown, "Please, Please, Please" / "Why Do You Do Me?" (Federal 12258)	1956	$10.00	$20.00	$40.00
James Brown, "Try Me" / "Tell Me What I Did Wrong" (Federal 12337)	1958	$7.50	$15.00	$30.00
James Brown, "Please, Please, Please" / "In The Wee Wee Hours" (King 5853)	1964	$3.75	$7.50	$15.00
James Brown, "Out of Sight" / "Maybe The Last Time" (Smash 1919)	1964	$3.00	$6.00	$12.00
James Brown, "Papa's Got A Brand New Bag (Pt. 1)" / "Papa's Got A Brand New Bag (Pt. 2)" (King 5999)	1965	$3.75	$7.50	$15.00
James Brown, "I Got You (I Feel Good)" / "I Can't Help It (I Just Do, Do, Do)" (King 6015)	1965	$3.75	$7.50	$15.00
James Brown, "I Loves You Porgy" / "Yours and Mine" (Bethlehem 3089)	1969	$3.75	$7.50	$15.00
James Brown, "Funky Drummer (Pt. 1)" / "Funky Drummer (Pt. 2)" (King 6290)	1970	$2.00	$4.00	$8.00
James Brown, "Sex Machine Part 1" / "Sex M achine Part 2" (Polydor 14270)	1975		$2.50	$5.00
James Brown, "Get Up Offa That Thing" / "Release The Pressure" (Polydor 14326)	1976		$2.50	$5.00
James Brown, "Rapp Payback (Where Iz Moses) (Pt. 1)" / "Rapp Payback (Pt. 2)" (TK 1039)	1980		$2.00	$4.00
James Brown, "Living In America" / "Farewell" (Scotti Bros. 05682)	1985			$3.00
Cameo, "Find My Way" / "Good Company" (Chocolate City 001)	1975		$2.00	$4.00
Cameo, "Word Up" / "Urban Warrior" (Atlanta Artists 884993-7)	1986			$3.00
(with picture sleeve, add:)	1986			$3.00
George Clinton, "Loopzilla" / "Pot Sharing Tots" (Capitol B-5160)	1982		$2.00	$4.00
George Clinton, "Atomic Dog" / (instrumental)	1982		$2.00	$4.00
(with picture sleeve, add:)	1982		$2.00	$4.00
Lyn Collins, "Rock Me Again & Again & Again & Again & Again & Again" / "Wide Awake In A Dream" (People 641)	1974		$3.00	$6.00
Funkadelic, "Music For My Mother" / (instrumental) (Westbound 148)	1969	$2.50	$5.00	$10.00
Funkadelic, "I Wanna Know If It's Good To You?" (Pt. 1) / (Pt. 2) (Westbound 167)	1970	$2.50	$5.00	$10.00
Funkadelic, "Standing on the Verge of Getting It On" / "Jimmy's Got A Little Bit of Bitch In Him" (Westbound 224)	1974	$2.50	$5.00	$10.00
Funkadelic, "One Nation Under A Groove" (Pt. 1) / (Pt. 2) (Warner Bros. 8618)	1978		$2.50	$5.00
(with picture sleeve, add:)	1978		$2.50	$5.00
Funkadelic, "(Not Just) Knee Deep - Part 1" / "(Not Just) Knee Deep - Part 2" (Warner Bros. 49040)	1979		$2.50	$5.00
Isaac Hayes, "Precious Precious" / "Going to Chicago Blues" (Enterprise 002)	1969	$2.00	$4.00	$8.00
Isaac Hayes, "Theme From Shaft" / "Café Regio's" (Enterprise 9038)	1971		$2.50	$5.00
Rick James, "Funkin' Around" / "My Mama" (A&M 1615)	1974	$6.25	$12.50	$25.00
Rick James, "Give It To Me Baby" / "Don't Give Up On Love" (Gordy 1981)	1981		$2.00	$4.00
Rick James, "Super Freak" (Pt. 1) / (Pt. 2) (Gordy 7205)	1981		$2.00	$4.00
The Ohio Players, "Funky Worm" / "Paint Me" (Westbound 214)	1973		$3.00	$6.00
The Ohio Players, "Love Rollercoaster" / "It's All Over" (Mercury 73734)	1975		$2.50	$5.00
The Parliaments, "(I Wanna) Testify" / "I Can Feel The Ice Melting" (Revilot 207)	1967	$3.75	$7.50	$15.00
The Parliaments, "A New Day Begins" / "I'll Wait" (Revilot 228)	1968	$7.50	$15.00	$30.00
Parliament, "I Call My Baby Pussy Cat" / "Little Ole Country Boy" (Invictus 9077)	1970	$2.50	$5.00	$10.00
Parliament, "Tear The Roof Off The Sucker (Give Up The Funk)" / "P Funk" (Casablanca 856)				
(if on blue "Bogart" label)	1976		$2.50	$5.00
(if on tan "Camels" label)	1976		$2.00	$4.00
Parliament, "Flashlight" / "Swing Down, Sweet Chariot" (Casablanca 909)	1978		$2.00	$5.00
Parliament, "Aqua Boogie (A Psychoalphadi scobetabioaquadoloop)" / "(You're a Fish and I'm a) Water Sign" (Casablanca 950)	1978		$2.00	$5.00
Prince, "Soft and Wet" / "So Blue" (Warner Bros. 8619)	1978	$10.00	$20.00	$40.00
Prince, "Dirty Mind" / "When We're Dancing Close And Slow" (Warner Bros. 49638)	1980	$3.75	$7.50	$15.00
Prince, "1999" / "How Come U Don't Call Me Anymore" (Warner Bros. 29826)	1982		$2.50	$5.00
(with picture sleeve, add:)	1982	$2.50	$5.00	$10.00
Prince, "Batdance" / "200 Balloons" (Warner Bros. 22924)	1989			$3.00
(with picture sleeve, add:)	1989			$3.00
Sly and the Family Stone, "I Ain't Got Nobody" / "I Can't Turn You Loose" (Loadstone 3951)	1967	$5.00	$10.00	$20.00
Sly and the Family Stone, "Dance To The Music" / "Let Me Hear It From You" (Epic 10256)	1969	$2.50	$5.00	$10.00
Sly and the Family Stone, "Thank You (Falettinme Be Mice Elf Agin" / "Everybody Is A Star" (Epic 10555)	1969		$3.00	$6.00
(with picture sleeve, add:)	1969	$2.50	$5.00	$10.00
Tower of Power, "What Is Hip?" / "Clever Girl" (Warner Bros. 7748)	1973		$3.00	$6.00
War, "The Cisco Kid" / Beetles in the Bog" (United Artists XW163)	1973		$2.50	$5.00
War, "Low Rider" / "So" (United Artists XW706)	1975		$2.50	$5.00
(with picture sleeve, add:)	1975		$2.00	$4.00
Charles Wright and the Watts 103rd Street Rhythm Band, "Express Yourself" / "Living on Borrowed Time" (Warner Bros. 7417)	1970		$3.00	$6.00

LPs	Year	VG	VG+	NM
James Brown, Please Please Please (King 619)				
(if mono, "woman's and man's legs" cover, "King" on label is two inches wide)	1958	$300.00	$600.00	$1,200.00
(if mono, "woman's and man's legs" cover, "King" on label is three inches wide)	1961	$250.00	$500.00	$1,000.00
(if on King 909, mono, reissue of King 619) ("crownless King" label)	1964	$25.00	$50.00	$100.00
(if on King 909, mono, reissue of King 619) ("crowned King" label)	1966	$12.50	$25.00	$50.00
James Brown, Think! (King 683)				
(if mono, "Baby" cover, "King" on label is three inches wide)	1961	$150.00	$300.00	$600.00
(if mono, James Brown on cover, "crownless King" label)	1963	$25.00	$50.00	$100.00
(if mono, James Brown on cover, "crowned King" label)	1966	$12.50	$25.00	$50.00
James Brown, Live at the Apollo (King 826)				
(if mono, custom back cover, "crownless King" label)	1963	$50.00	$100.00	$200.00

LPs	Year	VG	VG+	NM
(if stereo, custom back cover, "crownless King" label)	1963	$75.00	$150.00	$300.00
(if mono, other King albums on back cover, "crownless King" label)	1963	$37.50	$75.00	$150.00
(if stereo, other King albums on back cover, "crownless King" label)	1963	$50.00	$100.00	$200.00
(if mono, "crowned King" label)	1966	$12.50	$25.00	$50.00
(if stereo, "crowned King" label)	1966	$17.50	$35.00	$70.00
James Brown, Out of Sight (Smash MGS-27058) (mono)	1965	$25.00	$50.00	$100.00
(if on SRS-67058, stereo)	1965	$37.50	$75.00	$150.00
James Brown, Get On The Good Foot (Polydor PD2-3004) (2 LPs)	1972	$15.00	$30.00	$60.00
James Brown, The Payback (Polydor PD2-3007) (2 LPs)	1973	$12.50	$25.00	$50.00
James Brown, Get Up Offa That Thing (Polydor PD-1-6089)	1976	$10.00	$20.00	$40.00
James Brown, Love Overdue (Scotti Bros. 75225)	1991	$5.00	$10.00	$20.00
Cameo, Word Up! (Atlanta Artists 830265-1)	1986	$2.50	$5.00	$10.00
George Clinton, Black Vampire (Invictus ST-9815)	1973	$5.00	$10.00	$20.00
George Clinton, The George Clinton Band Arrives (ABC D-831)	1974	$3.75	$7.50	$15.00
George Clinton, Computer Games (Capitol ST-12246)	1982	$2.50	$5.00	$10.00
George Clinton, The Cinderella Theory (Paisley Park 25994)	1989	$3.00	$6.00	$10.00
Funkadelic, Free Your Mind... And Your Ass Will Follow (Westbound 2001)	1970	$12.50	$25.00	$50.00
(if on Westbound 217, reissue)	1975	$6.25	$12.50	$25.00
(if on Westbound 2001, bar code on cover, reissue)	1990	$3.75	$7.50	$15.00
Funkadelic, Standing on the Verge of Getting It On (Westbound 1001)	1974	$12.50	$25.00	$50.00
(if on Westbound 208, reissue)	1975	$6.25	$12.50	$25.00
(if on Westbound 1001, with bar code on cover, reissue)	1991	$3.75	$7.50	$15.00
Funkadelic, One Nation Under A Groove (Warner Bros. BS 3209) (with bonus 7" single, reduce by 20% if missing))	1978	$6.25	$12.50	$25.00
(if on Scarface/Priority 53872, reissue)	1993	$3.75	$7.50	$15.00
Isaac Hayes, Presenting Isaac Hayes (Enterprise E-100) (mono)	1968	$10.00	$20.00	$40.00
(if on Enterprise ES-100, stereo)	1968	$7.50	$15.00	$30.00
Rick James, Bustin' Out of L. Seven (Gordy G7-984)	1979	$2.50	$5.00	$10.00
Rick James, Street Songs (Gordy G8-1002)	1981	$2.00	$4.00	$8.00
Rick James, Greatest Hits (Motown 5382 ML)	1986	$2.00	$4.00	$8.00
The Ohio Players, Observations in Time (Capitol ST-192)	1969	$12.50	$25.00	$50.00
The Ohio Players, Honey (Mercury SRM-1-1038)	1975	$2.50	$5.00	$10.00
Parliament, Osmium (Invictus ST-7302)	1970	$25.00	$50.00	$100.00
Parliament, Up For The Down Stroke				
(if on Casablanca NBLP 9003, distributed by Warner Bros.)	1974	$12.50	$25.00	$50.00
(if on Casablanca NBLP 7002, distributed by Polydor)	1974	$10.00	$20.00	$40.00
Parliament, Chocolate City (Casablanca NBLP 7014)	1975	$10.00	$20.00	$40.00
Parliament, Parliament Live / P. Funk Earth Tour (Casablanca NBLP 7053) (2 LPs)	1977	$10.00	$20.00	$40.00
Parliament, Gloryhallastoopid (Or Pin The Tale On the Funky) (Casablanca NBLP 7195)	1979	$7.50	$15.00	$30.00
Prince, Prince (Warner Bros. BSK 3150) (with palm trees and "Burbank" label)	1977	$5.00	$10.00	$20.00
Prince, Controversy (Warner Bros. BSK 3601) (with poster)	1980	$3.00	$6.00	$15.00
Prince and the Revolution, Purple Rain (Warner Bros. 25110) (purple vinyl, with poster)	1984	$12.50	$25.00	$50.00

LPs	Year	VG	VG+	NM
(if on black vinyl, with poster)	1984	$2.50	$5.00	$10.00
Prince, The Black Album (Paisley Park 25677)	1987	$500.00	$1,000.00	$2,000.00
Prince, The Black Album (Paisley Park 25677DJ) (two 12" 45 RPM records)	1987	$750.00	$1,500.00	$3,000.00
Prince, The Black Album (Warner Bros. PRO-A-7330) (white label promo-only vinyl release)	1994	$12.50	$25.00	$50.00
Sly and the Family Stone, Sly and the Family Stone's Greatest Hits (Epic KE 30325) (with gatefold cover)	1970	$3.00	$6.00	$12.00
(if on Epic EQ 30325, quadraphonic, featuring true stereo mixes of "Hot Fun in the Summertime," "Thank You (Falettinme Be Mice Elf Agin)" and "Everybody Is A Star," while the original release of this album only had rechanneled stereo versions of these three songs)	1971	$25.00	$50.00	$100.00
(if on Epic PE 30325, budget line reissue, no gatefold cover)	1989	$2.00	$4.00	$8.00
Sly and the Family Stone, There's A Riot Goin' On (Epic KE 30986) (with gatefold cover)	1981	$3.00	$6.00	$12.00
Sly and the Family Stone, Everything You Always Wanted To Hear By Sly and the Family Stone But Were Afraid To Ask For (Epic AS 234, white label promo)	1976	$6.25	$12.50	$25.00
Tower of Power, Tower of Power (Warner Bros. BS 2681)				
(if first pressing, green "WB" label)	1973	$3.75	$7.50	$15.00
(if second pressing, "Burbank" palm trees label)	1973	$3.00	$6.00	$12.00
(if on white or tan label)	1979	$2.00	$4.00	$8.00
War, Radio Free War (United Artists SP-103) (white label promo, on blue vinyl)	1974	$6.25	$12.50	$25.00
War, Why Can't We Be Friends? (United Artists UA-LA441-G)	1975	$2.50	$5.00	$10.00
(if on Lax PW37113, reissue)	1981	$2.50	$5.00	$10.00
Charles Wright and the Watts 103rd Street Rhythm Band, Together (Warner Bros. WS 1761)				
(if green label with "W7" logo)	1969	$5.00	$10.00	$20.00
(if green label with "WB" logo)	1970	$3.75	$7.50	$15.00
Charles Wright and the Watts 103rd Street Rhythm Band, Doin' What Comes Naturally (ABC Dunhill DS-50162) (2 LP's)	1973	$3.75	$7.50	$15.00

If you played the B-side of this Parliament 12-inch disco disc, you would literally be playing a black hole—this was a one-sided record, the B-side was left blank.

GARAGE BAND

History: Garage music, or more literally, a sound so raw and unpolished that it had to have originated not in a studio, but in the guitarist's family garage, got its start in the early 1960s. The Kingsmen's "Louie Louie," with its vocals buried so low in the mix that parents thought there might be vulgar vocals in the song, epitomized what would follow in garage band music—a do-it-yourself attitude and work ethic, a raw attempt to replicate the pop and rock songs of the day and perform them in a raucous rendition.

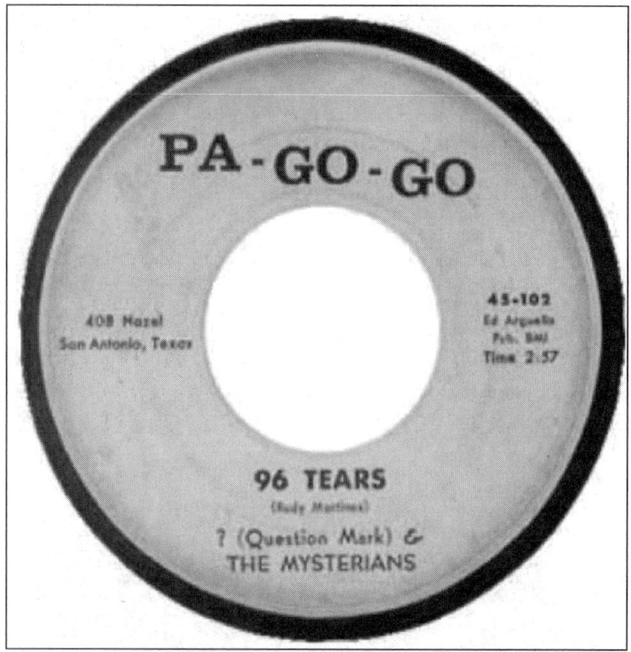

? and the Mysterians' success began with their garage-rock classic "96 Tears," originally released on the tiny Pa-Go-Go label. Photo Credit: Courtesy Good Rockin' Tonight / Collectors Universe.

The 1960s British Invasion gave garage bands a new infusion of energy. Suddenly groups and combos appeared in every American neighborhood, groups blasting out three-chord songs and howling lyrics. The guitarist might have learned his craft from listening to Duane Eddy or Surfaris records and practicing along. The drummer and bass player followed along, learning their instruments in literally on-the-job training.

Garage music influences include the smoking surf instrumentals of the early 1960s, by artists like Dick Dale and the Del-Tones, Duane Eddy, Link Wray, the Ventures, and the Surfaris—and adding the brash raucousness of British Invasion groups like the Rolling Stones and the Yardbirds. But garage bands also had an aura about them—a sense of do-it-yourself that could propel them to the top of the charts.

The Standells' "Dirty Water," a garage band classic. From the Collection of Val Shively.

And for some garage bands, that did happen—? and the Mysterians, the Syndicate of Sound, the Shadows of Knight, and the Seeds all had their moment in the sun. Other groups, such as the Chocolate Watchband, the Thirteenth Floor Elevators, and Thee Midnighters, had regional hits and a rabid cult following.

The music of many of the early garage bands might have faded into history, had it not been for *Nuggets.* This multi-volume anthology series compiled garage and do-it-yourself music, and became a successful reissue package, while bringing garage music to a new generation of aspiring musicians. Today, such musical styles as power pop and grunge can be traced back to those early days in the garage.

What To Look For: Every musical genre has its legendary performers, and garage music is no exception to this rule. Hardcore garage music collectors want vinyl singles and LPs from such bands as the Chocolate Watchband, the Thirteenth Floor Elevators, and the Monks.

Trivia

The Thirteenth Floor Elevators' garage band hit "You're Gonna Miss Me" exists on both the Hanna-Barbera and Contact labels. The International Artists label picked the group up, giving them the closest thing they ever had to a major hit record.

An early pressing of "You're Gonna Miss Me" by the Thirteenth Floor Elevators. Courtesy Good Rockin' Tonight/Collectors Universe.

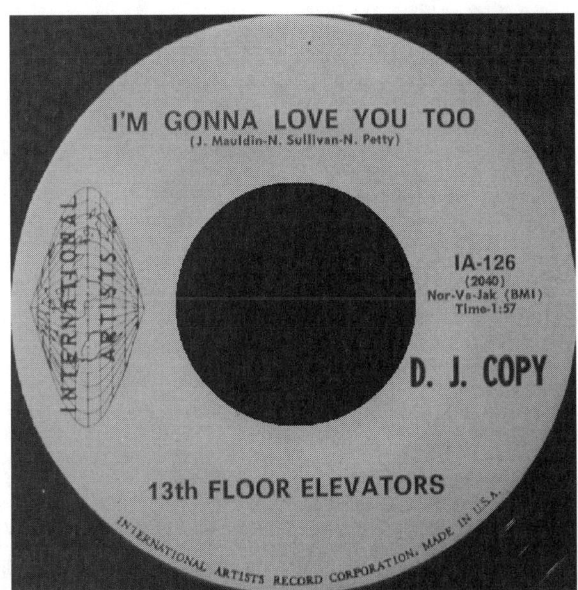

A promo pressing of the Thirteenth Floor Elevators' cover of a Buddy Holly classic. From the Collection of Val Shively.

Trivia

The Sir Douglas Quintet was a Texas band that was actually promoted as being from England. Doug Sahm, the Quintet's lead singer, would go on to have his own solo career.

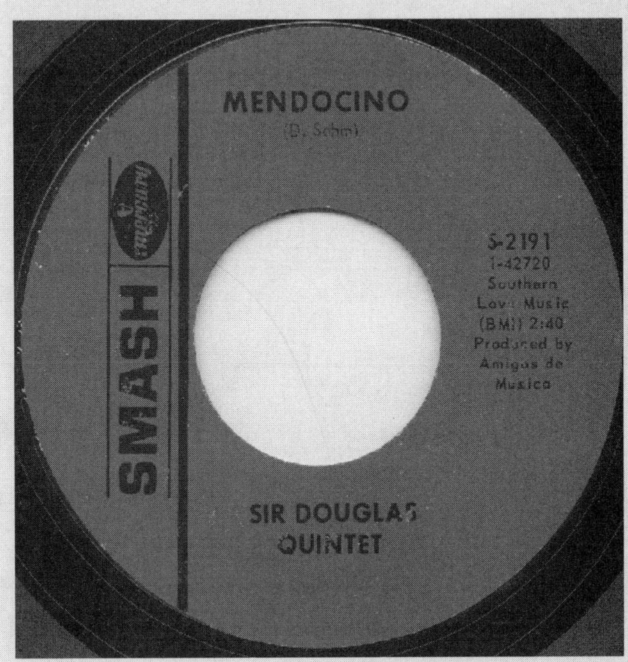

The Sir Douglas Quintet's big hit, "Mendocino."

Those bands' vinyl output was low in comparison to groups like the Seeds or the Shadows of Knight, who had Top 40 hits. But even those bands recorded songs on small independent labels before they hit the big time, and finding pressings on Hush or Zero (or even Hanna-Barbera) are more collectible than their major label counterparts.

Garage vinyl may be collectible, but picture sleeves are even more so. Some picture sleeves, especially for songs that weren't hits, can command as much as ten times the price of the vinyl alone.

Reference: Joynson, Vernon, *Fuzz, Acid and Flowers: A Comprehensive Guide To American Garage, Psychedelic and Hippie Rock (1964-1975)* (4th Ed.), Borderline, Glasgow, Scotland, 1997.

Web pages: Dennis A. Blackledge's tribute page to the Mojo Hands, as well as a place where you can purchase his book *We Gotta Go Now, at http://www.wegottagonow.com;* the Chocolate Watchband's Web site: *http://www.chocolatewatchband.com;* the former drummer for the Thirteenth Floor Elevators, Danny Thomas, maintains this Web site for the history of the group: *http://www.geocities.com/ucdnlo/.*

Trivia

The Count Five may have had only one hit, "Psychotic Reaction," but the title of that song became the title of a collection of essays and reviews by author Lester Bangs.

The Count Five's only hit, "Psychotic Reaction."

Trivia

45s	Year	VG	VG+	NM
The Barbarians, "Hey Little Bird" / "You've Got To Understand" (Joy 290)	1964	$12.50	$25.00	$50.00
The Barbarians, "Are You A Boy or Are You A Girl" / "Take It Or Leave It" (Laurie 3308)	1965	$5.00	$10.00	$20.00
The Chocolate Watchband, "Are You Gonna Be There (At the Love-In)" / "No Way Out" (Tower 373)	1967	$12.50	$25.00	$50.00
The Chocolate Watchband, "Baby Blue" / "Sweet Young Thing" (Uptown 740)	1967	$75.00	$150.00	$300.00
The Count Five, "Psychotic Reaction" / "They're Gonna Get You" (Double Shot 104)				
(if first pressing, label logo on top)	1966	$3.75	$7.50	$15.00
(if second pressing, label logo on side)	1966	$3.00	$6.00	$12.00
The Daybreakers, "Psychedelic Siren" / "Afterthoughts"	1967	$7.50	$15.00	$30.00
The Five Americans, "Western Union" / "Now That It's Over" (Abnak 118)	1967	$3.00	$6.00	$12.00
(if on yellow vinyl, promo only)	1967	$6.25	$12.50	$25.00
The Gants, "Road Runner" / "My Baby Don't Care"				
(if on Statue 608)	1965	$12.50	$25.00	$50.00
(if on Liberty 55829)	1965	$3.75	$7.50	$15.00
The Golliwogs, "Don't Tell Me No Lies" / "Little Girl, Does Your Mama Know" (Fantasy 590)	1964	$15.00	$30.00	$60.00
Gonn, "Blackout of Gretley" / "Pain In My Heart"				
(if on Emir 9217)	1966	$100.00	$200.00	$400.00
(if on Emir-MCCM 88-9217, black vinyl)	1988		$2.50	$5.00
(if on Emir-MCCM 88-9217, colored vinyl)	1988	$3.75	$7.50	$15.00
The Hogs, "Loose Lip Sync Ships" / "Blues Theme" (Hanna-Barbera 511) (A-side produced by Frank Zappa)	1967	$37.50	$75.00	$150.00

45s	Year	VG	VG+	NM
Faine Jade, "Introspection" / (B-side unknown) (RSVP 1130)	1968	$6.23	$12.50	$25.00
Kenny and the Kasuals, "I'm Gonna Make It" / "Journey To Tyme" (Mark IV 1006)	1966	$10.00	$20.00	$40.00
(if on United Artists 50085)	1966	$5.00	$10.00	$20.00
The Kingsmen, "Louie Louie" / "Haunted Castle"				
(if on Jerden 712)	1963	$15.00	$30.00	$60.00
(if on Wand 143)	1963	$5.00	$10.00	$20.00
The Lost, "Back Door Blues" / "Maybe More Than You Do" (Capitol 5519)	1965	$3.75	$7.50	$15.00
The Mojo Men, "Surfin' Fat Man" / "Paula" (Tide 2000)	1964	$10.00	$20.00	$40.00
The Mojo Men, "Sit Down, I Think I Love You" / "Don't Leave Me Crying Like Before" (Reprise 0539)	1966	$2.50	$5.00	$10.00
Mouse and the Traps, "Sometimes You Just Can't Win" / "Cryin' Inside" (Fraternity 1005)	1968	$3.75	$7.50	$15.00
(with picture sleeve, add:)	1968	$20.00	$40.00	$80.00
Mouse and the Traps, "Streets of a Dusty Town" / "Mouse" (Capitol 2460)	1969	$2.50	$5.00	$10.00
The Music Machine, "Talk Talk" / "Come On In" (Original Sound 61)	1966	$3.00	$6.00	$12.00
The Music Machine, "Mother Nature - Father Earth" / "Advise and Consent" (Bell 764)	1969	$2.00	$4.00	$8.00
The Outsiders, "Time Won't Let Me" / "Was It Really Bad" (Capitol 5573)	1966	$3.00	$6.00	$12.00
? and the Mysterians, "96 Tears" / "Midnight Hour"				
(if on Pa-Go-Go 102, first release)	1965	$175.00	$350.00	$700.00
(if on Cameo 428, national release)	1966	$5.00	$10.00	$20.00
Sam the Sham and the Pharaohs, "Wooly Bully" / "Ain't Gonna Move"				
(if on XL 906, first release)	1965	$75.00	$150.00	$300.00
(if on MGM 13322, national release)	1965	$3.75	$7.50	$15.00
The Seeds, "Pushin' Too Hard" / "Try To Understand" (GNP Crescendo 372)				
(if "GNP Crescendo" is unboxed at top of label)	1966	$3.75	$7.50	$15.00
(if "GNP Crescendo" is boxed at top of label)	1966	$2.00	$4.00	$8.00
The Seeds, "Mr. Farmer" / "Up In Her Room" (GNP Crescendo 383)	1967	$2.00	$4.00	$8.00
(with picture sleeve, add:)	1967	$12.50	$25.00	$50.00
The Shadows of Knight, "Gloria" / "Dark Side" (Dunwich 116)				
(if on gold label, no mention of Atco Records)	1966	$6.25	$12.50	$25.00
(if on yellow label, label has "Distributed by Atco Record Sales Co.")	1966	$5.00	$10.00	$20.00
(if on dark pink-yellow label)	1966	$3.75	$7.50	$15.00
The Shadows of Knight, "Bad Little Woman" / "Gospel Zone" (Dunwich 128)	1966	$3.75	$7.50	$15.00
(with picture sleeve, add:)	1966	$12.50	$25.00	$50.00
The Smoke, "Choose It" (Pt. 1) / (Pt. 2) (Uni 55154)	1969	$2.50	$5.00	$10.00
The Sonics, "The Witch" / "Like No Other" (Jerden 810)	1966	$3.75	$7.50	$15.00
The Sonics, "Anyway The Wind Blows" / "Lost Love"				
(if on Piccadilly 244)	1967	$5.00	$10.00	$20.00
(if on Uni 55039, national release)	1967	$3.75	$7.50	$15.00
The Spades, "You're Gonna Miss Me" / "We Sell Soul" (Zero 10002) (later became the 13th Floor Elevators)	1966	$100.00	$200.00	$400.00
The Squires, "Going All The Way" / "Go Ahead" (Atco 6442)	1966	$10.00	$20.00	$40.00
The Standells, "The Boy Next Door" / "B.J. Quetzal" (Vee Jay 643)	1965	$5.00	$10.00	$20.00
(with picture sleeve, add:)	1965	$50.00	$100.00	$200.00
The Standells, "Dirty Water" / "Rari" (Tower 185)	1966	$5.00	$10.00	$20.00
Syndicate of Sound, "Little Girl" / You"				
(if on Hush 228)	1966	$12.50	$25.00	$50.00
(if on Bell 640)	1966	$5.00	$10.00	$20.00
Thee Midnighters, "Land of a Thousand Dances" (Pt. 1) / "Ball O'Twine" (Chattahoochie 666-2)	1965	$3.75	$7.50	$15.00
Thee Midnighters, "You're Gonna Make Me Cry" / "Make Ends Meet" (Whittier 511)	1968	$50.00	$100.00	$200.00
Things To Come, "I'm Not Talkin'" / "Til The End" (Dunwich 124)	1966	$12.50	$25.00	$50.00
The Thirteenth Floor Elevators, "You're Gonna Miss Me" / "Tried To Hide"				
(if on Hanna-Barbera 492)	1966	$50.00	$100.00	$200.00

45s	Year	VG	VG+	NM
(if on Contact 5269)	1966	$25.00	$50.00	$100.00
(if on International Artists 107, blue label)	1967	$7.50	$15.00	$30.00
(if on International Artists 107, yellow label)	1967	$5.00	$10.00	$20.00
The Trashmen, "Surfin' Bird" / "King of the Surf" (Garrett 4002)	1963	$7.50	$15.00	$30.00
The Trashmen, "Whoa Dad" / "Walkin' My Baby" (Garrett 4012)	1964	$5.00	$10.00	$20.00
(with picture sleeve, add:)	1964	$62.50	$125.00	$250.00
The Vejtables, "Feel The Music" / "Shadows" (Uptown 741)	1967	$2.50	$5.00	$10.00

LPs	Year	VG	VG+	NM
The Barbarians, Are You A Boy Or Are You A Girl? (Laurie LLP-2033) (mono)	1966	$37.50	$75.00	$150.00
(if on Laurie SLP-2033, stereo)	1966	$50.00	$100.00	$200.00
The Chocolate Watchband, No Way Out (Tower T-5096) (mono)	1968	$75.00	$150.00	$300.00
(if on Tower ST-5096, stereo)	1968	$100.00	$200.00	$400.00
The Chocolate Watchband, The Inner Mystique (Tower T-5106) (mono)	1968	$100.00	$200.00	$400.00
(if on Tower ST-5106, stereo)	1968	$75.00	$150.00	$300.00
The Count Five, Psychotic Reaction (Double Shot DSM-1001) (mono)	1966	$10.00	$20.00	$40.00
(if on Double Shot DSS-5001, rechanelled stereo)	1966	$6.25	$12.50	$25.00
The Fantastic Dee Jays, The Fantastic Dee Jays (Stone SLP-4003)	1966	$250.00	$500.00	$1,000.00
The Five Americans, Western Union / Sound of Love (Abnak AB-1967) (mono)	1967	$5.00	$10.00	$20.00
(if on Abnak ABST-2067, stereo)	1967	$7.50	$15.00	$30.00
Faine Jade, Introspection: A Faine Jade Recital (RSVP 8002)	1968	$100.00	$200.00	$400.00
Kenny and the Kasuals, The Impact Sound of Kenny and the Kasuals Live at the Studio Club (Mark 5000) (mono)	1966	$250.00	$500.00	$1,000.00
(if 1977 re-release, "reissue, 1977" appears on cover)	1977	$6.25	$12.50	$25.00
The Kingsmen, The Kingsmen In Person (Wand WD-657) (mono)	1964	$7.50	$15.00	$30.00
(if on Wand WDS-657, some tracks in stereo)	1965	$10.00	$20.00	$40.00
The Mojo Men, Mojo Magic (GRT 10003)	1969	$6.25	$12.50	$25.00
The Music Machine, (Turn On) The Music Machine (Original Sound 5015) (mono)	1966	$10.00	$20.00	$40.00
(if on Original Sound 8875, stereo)	1966	$12.50	$25.00	$50.00
The Outsiders, Time Won't Let Me (Capitol T-2501) (mono)	1966	$7.50	$15.00	$30.00
? and the Mysterians, 96 Tears (Cameo C-2004) (mono)	1966	$25.00	$50.00	$100.00
(if on Cameo CS-2004, some songs in stereo)	1966	$20.00	$40.00	$80.00
The Rising Storm, Calm Before the Rising Storm (Remnant BBA-3571)	1968	$600.00	$900.00	$1,200.00
(if on Stanton Park 001, reissue)	1991	$5.00	$10.00	$20.00
Sam the Sham and the Pharaohs, Wooly Bully				
(if on MGM E-4297, mono)	1965	$7.50	$15.00	$30.00
(if on MGM SE-4297, stereo)	1965	$10.00	$20.00	$40.00
(if on MGM T-90422, mono, Capitol Record Club edition)	1965	$10.00	$20.00	$40.00
(if on MGM ST-90422, stereo, Capitol Record Club edition)	1965	$12.50	$25.00	$50.00
The Seeds, The Seeds (GNP Crescendo GNP-2023) (mono)	1966	$15.00	$30.00	$60.00
(if on GNP Crescendo GNPS-2023, stereo)	1966	$10.00	$20.00	$40.00
The Shadows of Knight, Gloria (Dunwich 666) (mono)	1966	$12.50	$25.00	$50.00
(if on Dunwich S-666, stereo)	1966	$20.00	$40.00	$80.00
(if on Sundazed LP 5034, 180-gram vinyl reissue)	1999	$3.00	$6.00	$12.00
The Smoke, The Smoke (Sidewalk ST 5912)	1968	$10.00	$20.00	$40.00
(if on Uni 73052, national release)	1969	$6.25	$12.50	$25.00
The Sonics, Here Are The Sonics!				
(if on Etiquette ETALB-024, mono, red label)	1965	$62.50	$125.00	$250.00
(if on Etiquette ETALB-024, mono, purple label)	1965	$50.00	$100.00	$200.00
(if on Etiquette ETLPS-024, stereo, red label)	1965	$100.00	$200.00	$400.00
(if on Etiquette ETLPS-024, stereo, purple label)	1965	$75.00	$150.00	$300.00
(if on Etiquette ETLPS, purple label, flimsy vinyl, 1984 date on back cover)	1984	$2.50	$5.00	$10.00
The Standells, The Standells In Person at P.J.'s (Liberty LRP-3384) (mono)	1964	$20.00	$40.00	$80.00
(if on Liberty LST-7384, stereo)	1964	$25.00	$50.00	$100.00
The Syndicate of Sound, Little Girl (Bell 6001) (mono)	1966	$12.50	$25.00	$50.00
(if on Bell S-6001, stereo)	1966	$20.00	$40.00	$80.00
T.C. Atlantic, T.C. Atlantic (Dove LP-4459)	1966	$25.00	$50.00	$100.00
Thee Midnighters, Thee Midnighters (Chattahoochie C-1001) (mono)	1965	$15.00	$30.00	$60.00
(if on Chattahoochie CS-1001, stereo)	1965	$20.00	$40.00	$80.00
The Thirteenth Floor Elevators, Psychedelic Sounds (International Artists 1)				
(if on green-yellow label, mono)	1967	$62.50	$125.00	$250.00
(if on all-yellow label, mono or stereo)	1968	$37.50	$75.00	$150.00
(if on aqua-blue label, stereo)	1968	$50.00	$100.00	$200.00
(if 1979 reissue, "Masterfonics" in dead wax)	1979	$7.50	$15.00	$30.00
The Trashmen, Surfin' Bird (Garrett GA-200) (mono)	1964	$55.00	$110.00	$220.00
(if on Garrett GAS-200, rechannelled stereo)	1964	$87.50	$175.00	$350.00
(if on Beat Rocket BR-107, 180-gram vinyl reissue)	1999	$3.00	$6.00	$12.00
Various Artists, Nuggets (Elektra 7E-2006) (2 LPs)	1972	$10.00	$20.00	$40.00

Although most garage bands were American, their names tended to promote an English connection, such as this band calling itself "Thee" Prophets.

Many garage bands had one major hit. The Five Americans were one such group, as their hit "Western Union" was a Top 10 smash.

GOSPEL AND MUSIC OF FAITH

History: In the Bible, a gospel is the word of the Lord. In music, the word "Gospel" means the music that praises the Lord and all His work. Gospel music collectors search high and low for rare LPs and 78s, whether the music contains a choir, a solo vocalist—or both.

Trivia

An offshoot of gospel-music collecting involves searching for transcriptions of famous sermons and speeches. The most collectible of these speeches involves the works of Dr. Martin Luther King, Jr. Because King's speeches were considered part of the "public domain," his "I Have A Dream" sermon from the 1963 March on Washington was pressed for more than a few different labels. Many of these labels re-issued that speech in 1968, when the civil rights leader and man of faith was murdered.

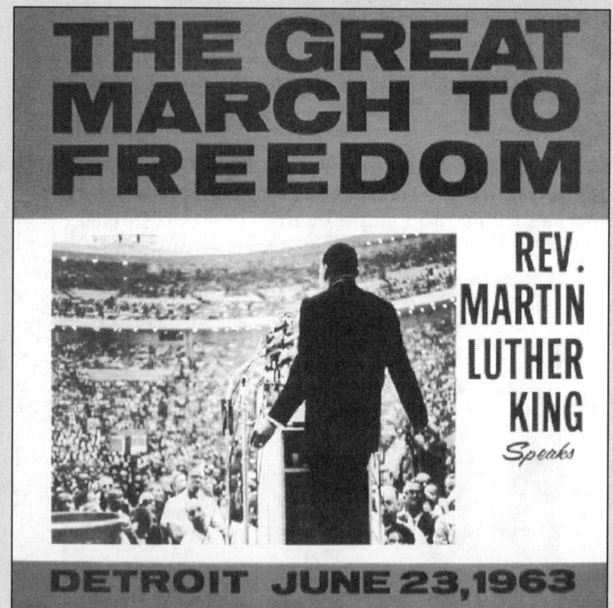

Unlike most albums that contain Dr. Martin Luther King's "I Have A Dream" speech, this album does not contain the version heard in the August 1963 March on Washington; this track was recorded in June 1963, at a Freedom Rally in Detroit's Cobo Hall. This album has stayed in print for years, and contains the old-style "Gordy" logo, even though the record itself contains the contemporary triangle "Gordy" label.

"Black Gospel" evolved from traditional 19th-century Negro spirituals, and is often based around a choir or quintet. Some of the great vocal groups in this field include the Wings Over Jordan Choir, the Five Blind Boys of Mississippi, The Mighty Clouds of Joy, the Dixie Hummingbirds, and the Five Blind Boys of Alabama. Solo vocalists in this field include Kirk Franklin, BeBe and CeCe Winans, and Mahalia Jackson. Among the compositions sung by such performers are the works of Thomas A. Dorsey, the grandfather of gospel music, whose compositions include "Take My Hand, Precious Lord," "Peace in the Valley," and "Alone."

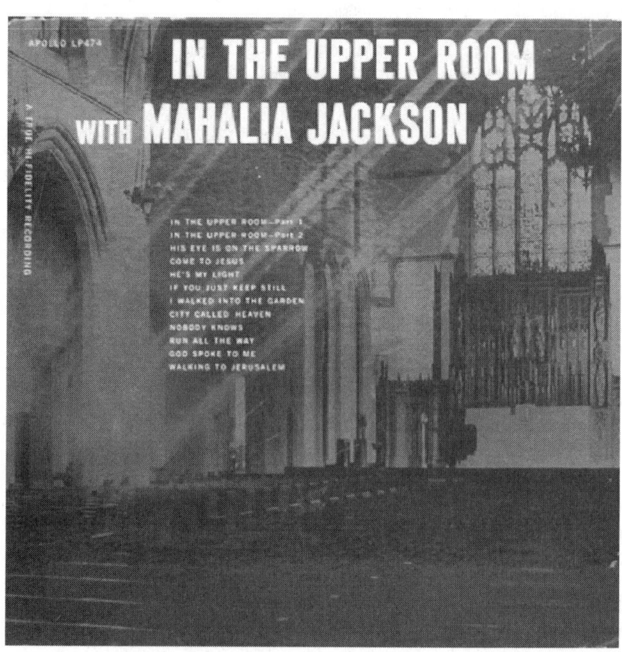

Mahalia Jackson's name is still spoken with reverence among gospel music afficionados.

One of the most famous gospel groups, at least in terms of its contributions to rock and roll, were the Soul Stirrers. Formed in 1926 in Trinity, Texas by Senior Roy Crain, the Soul Stirrers were the first gospel group to break away from traditional gospel music, adding more emotion and passion to their performances (after one early performance, an audience member told Crain the music had "stirred his soul," and Crain used that reference to name his group). By the 1950s, the Soul Stirrers were one of the most popular gospel groups in the Midwest, and recorded many sides for the Specialty label. In 1950, the Soul Stirrers added a new member, Sam Cooke, to their lineup, and their first song with

Cooke, "Jesus Gave Me Water," was a major hit. Cooke left the Soul Stirrers a few years later for a successful solo career in the secular music field; his replacement, Johnnie Taylor, would also enjoy a solo career of his own. Cooke never forgot the choir that gave him his first major break; when Cooke formed his own label, Sar, in 1961, he signed the Soul Stirrers to it.

Sam Cooke and the Soul Stirrers with their first recording together, "Jesus Gave Me Water," backed with the gospel standard "Peace in the Valley."

Other forms of early gospel music include country gospel and blues gospel—essentially the same musical genres as country and blues, but with lyrics praising the Lord and His work. Country gospel, also known as "southern gospel," contains four-part and five-part harmonies. Such groups include the Happy Goodman Family, the Speers, and the Chuck Wagon Gang.

Many contemporary artists recorded songs in the gospel music field, some under their own names, some by using aliases. Tennessee Ernie Ford, for example, recorded dozens of gospel and spoken-word albums and spirituals. Hank Williams, for example, recorded some spirituals under the name "Luke the Drifter." His son, Hank Williams Jr., also recorded some gospel music as "Luke the Drifter, Jr."

Some gospel records include entire sermons by such legendary clergymen as the Rev. C.L. Franklin and the Rev. James Cleveland. Chess/Checker Records often recorded gospel music by Franklin's New Bethel Baptist Church of Detroit choir, which included a teen-aged Aretha Franklin.

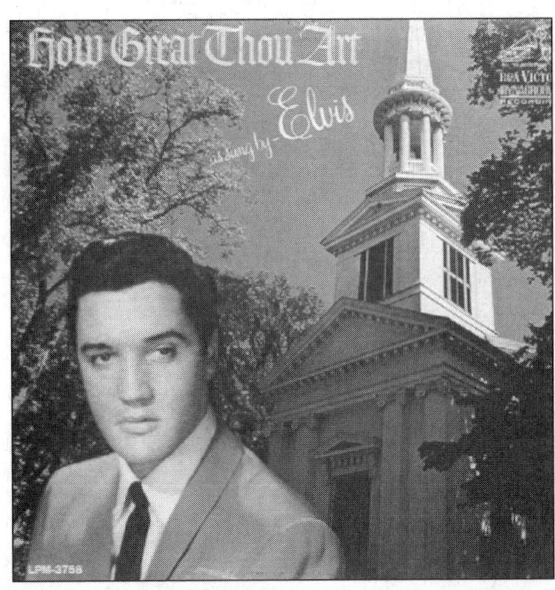

Elvis Presley may have sold billions of records worldwide, but the only Grammy awards he ever received were related to his gospel recordings.

Trivia

Elvis Presley's backup singers, the Jordanaires, were famous on the country gospel circuit. Besides backing up Presley, they also recorded gospel singles and albums for their own release. They even backed up artists like Ernest Tubb on his gospel recordings.

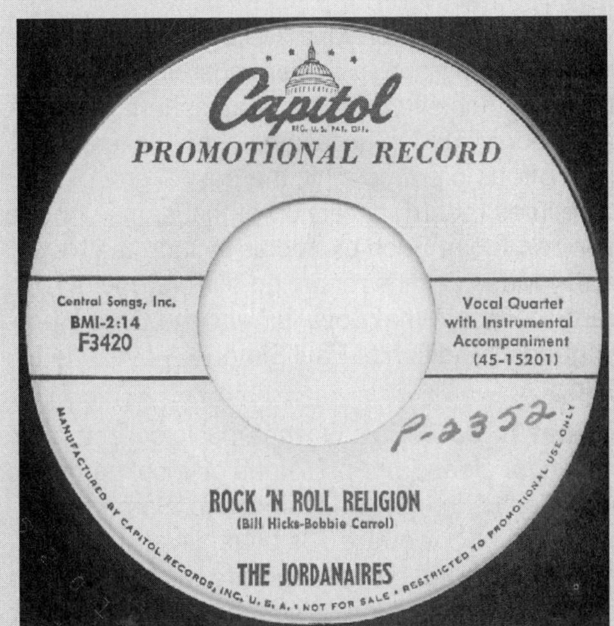

A white label promo pressing of a Jordanaires gospel classic.

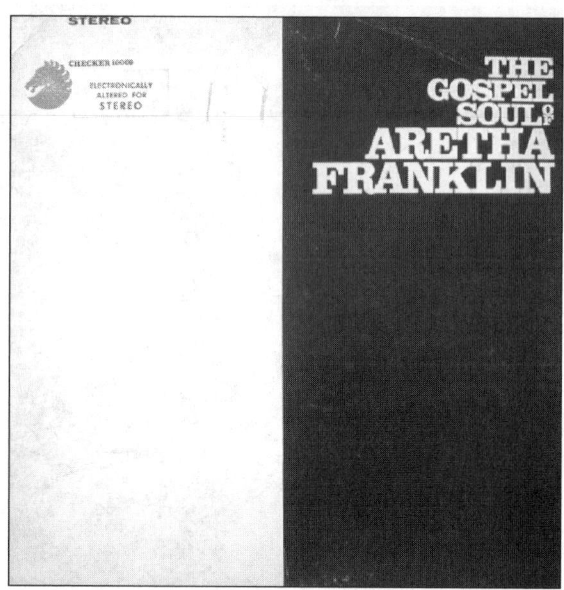

The Gospel Soul of Aretha Franklin is actually a rechanneled, retitled version of an earlier Checker album, Songs of Faith. That album cover features Aretha Franklin sitting at a piano, and is very collectible by both gospel collectors and fans of the Queen of Soul. Photo Credit: Courtesy Last Vestige Music Store, Albany, N.Y.

The Dixie Hummingbirds backed Paul Simon on his version of "Loves Me Like A Rock"; the version the gospel group recorded was a minor hit on the R&B charts. Photo Credit: From the Collection of Val Shively.

In the 1970s, another form of gospel music "Inspirational" or "Contemporary Christian Music," appeared. While these recordings also praise the Lord, their music is more influenced by country and adult contemporary musical styles. Artists in this field include Amy Grant, Michael W. Smith, and Jaci Velasquez.

It is not uncommon for a secular artist to team up with a gospel group or singer, most often in an attempt to achieve a "holier" atmosphere in the finished recording. On occasion, when these combined efforts produce a hit, the gospel group sometimes records a version of that same song for their own label. Such examples include the New Jersey Mass Choir's recording of Foreigner's "I Want To Know What Love Is," and the Dixie Hummingbirds' rendition of Paul Simon's "Loves Me Like A Rock."

What To Look For: Gospel-music collectors are looking for clean, rare pressings of vocal harmonies and religious integrity in their music. Some collectors will hunt down rare 78s by relatively unknown choirs and choral groups, and are willing to pay top dollar for these rare pressings. Among such collectors, black gospel is more collectible than white gospel, because fewer runs of black gospel recordings were pressed.

Many collectors will treat these records as if the Lord Himself had recorded the tracks. This is why it is easier to find gospel records in better condition than a rock or R&B record from the same era. Rock and pop artists have recorded gospel or contemporary Christian albums, however, and it is intriguing to hear the interpretations on such standards as "Take My Hand, Precious Lord," "Swing Low Sweet Chariot" and "Amen."

A collaboration by Jackie Wilson and new singer Linda Hopkins on a minor hit, "Shake A Hand," produced this album of gospel and spiritual music. Photo Credit: Courtesy Last Vestige Music Store, Albany, N.Y.

Web pages: A site for buying and selling rare gospel albums: *http://www.gospelgallery.com*; another site for rare gospel recordings: *http://www.island.net/~blues/gospel.htm.*

Trivia

In 1985, a 21-piece youth evangelical choir called Powersource recorded an album, *Shelter From the Storm.* Other than some sales in religious bookstores, the album was not a major seller. Two years later, a young girl named Lisa Steinberg was beaten to death by her adoptive father. To honor Steinberg's memory, some disc jockeys in New York played a song from *Shelter From the Storm* in her memory, an anti-child abuse track from the album, "Dear Mr. Jesus," as sung by 6-year-old Powersource member Sharon Batts. As Christmas 1987 approached, "Dear Mr. Jesus" became a left-field hit across the country, and stayed on some radio stations' playlists as a Christmas perennial.

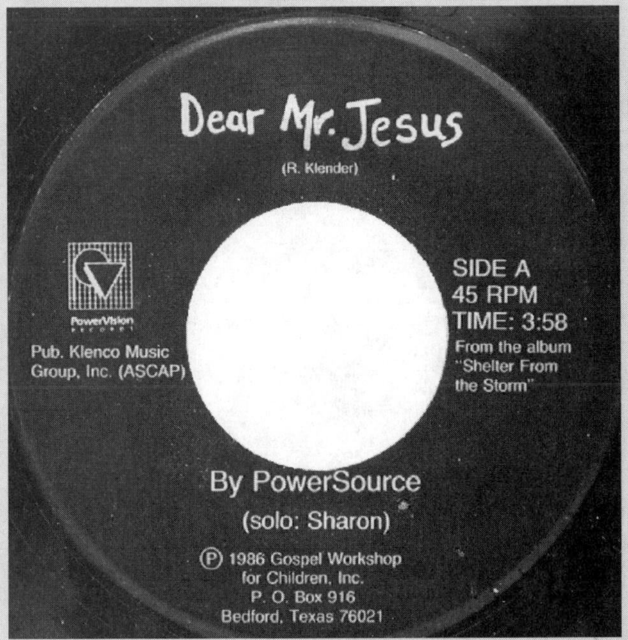

Powersource's "Dear Mr. Jesus," featuring the voice of 6-year-old Sharon Batts.

45s	Year	VG	VG+	NM
The Chuck Wagon Gang, "When the Saints Go Marching In" / "I'm Telling The World About His Love" (Columbia 4-20966)	1952	$5.00	$10.00	$20.00
The Chuck Wagon Gang, "That We Might Know" / "Open Up Them Pearly Gates" (Columbia 4-43048)	1964	$2.50	$5.00	$10.00
Perry Como, "Ave Maria" / "The Lord's Prayer" (RCA Victor 52-0071)				
(if pressed on blue vinyl)	1949	$6.25	$12.50	$25.00
(if pressed on black vinyl)	1949	$3.00	$6.00	$12.00
Dixie Hummingbirds, "Loves Me Like A Rock" / "I've Been Born Again" (Peacock 3198)	1973		$3.00	$6.00
The Five Blind Boys, "Waiting at the River" / "Where There's A Will" (Vee-Jay 872)	1959	$6.25	$12.50	$25.00
Tennessee Ernie Ford, "I Am A Pilgrim" / "His Hands" (Capitol F3135)	1955	$3.75	$7.50	$15.00
Tennessee Ernie Ford, "Joshua Fit De Battle" / "Oh Mary, Don't You Weep" (Capitol 4416)	1960	$2.00	$4.00	$8.00
Aretha Franklin, "Precious Lord, Part 1" / "Precious Lord, Part 2" (Checker 941)	1960	$3.75	$7.50	$15.00
The Gospel Stars, "He Lifted Me" / "Behold the Saints of God" (Tamla 54037)				
(if label has horizontal lines)	1961	$37.50	$75.00	$150.00
(if label has globes)	1961	$15.00	$30.00	$60.00
The Edwin Hawkins Singers, "Oh Happy Day" / Jesus, Lover of My Soul" (Pavilion 20001)	1969		$3.00	$6.00
Mahalia Jackson, "Bless This House" / "The Lord's Prayer" (Apollo 245)	1951	$5.00	$10.00	$20.00
Mahalia Jackson, "I Walked Into The Garden" / "I'm Going To Tell God" (Apollo 291)	1955	$5.00	$10.00	$20.00
Mahalia Jackson, "A Rusty Old Halo" / "The Treasure of Love" (Columbia 40411)	1955	$3.75	$7.50	$15.00
Mahalia Jackson, "Take My Hand, Precious Lord" / "We Shall Overcome" (Columbia 44529)	1968		$2.50	$5.00
Mahalia Jackson, "Abraham, Martin and John" / "Day Is Done" (Columbia 45068)	1970		$2.50	$5.00
Wanda Jackson, "Jesus Put A Yodel In My Soul" (mono/stereo) (Myrrh 143)	1974		$2.50	$5.00
The Jordanaires, "Rock and Roll Religion" / "Do Unto Others" (Capitol 3420)	1957	$2.50	$5.00	$10.00
Mighty Clouds of Joy, "Jesus Lead Us Safely" / "Ain't Got Long Here" (Peacock 1823)	1961	$3.00	$6.00	$12.00
Mighty Clouds of Joy, "A Friend in Jesus" / "Two Wings" (Peacock 3050)	1965	$2.50	$5.00	$10.00
Mighty Clouds of Joy, "Mighty High" / "Touch My Soul" (ABC 12164)	1976		$2.00	$4.00
The Oak Ridge Boys, "Where the Soul Never Dies" / "No Earthly Good" (Columbia 10320)	1976		$2.50	$5.00
Powersource featuring Sharon Batts, "Dear Mr. Jesus" / "Love, Sharon" (Powervision 8603)	1987	$3.00	$6.00	$12.00
Jim Reeves, "Take My Hand, Precious Lord" / "Snowflake" (RCA Victor 47-8719)	1965	$2.00	$4.00	$8.00
The Stamps Quartet, "This Ole House" / "Promise You'll Meet Me" (Columbia 4-21323)	1954	$6.25	$12.50	$25.00
The Staple Singers, "God's Wonderful Love" / "If I Could Hear My Mother" (Vee Jay 169)	1956	$5.00	$10.00	$20.00
The Staple Singers, "Swing Low, Sweet Chariot" / "I'm So Glad" (Vee Jay 930)	1963	$3.00	$6.00	$12.00
The Statler Brothers, "How Great Thou Art" / "Noah Found Grace in the Eyes of the Lord" (Mercury 73732)	1975		$2.50	$5.00
Bebe and Cece Winans, "Heaven" / "Silent Night, Holy Night" (Capitol B-44261)	1988		$2.00	$4.00

LPs	Year	VG	VG+	NM
Shirley Caesar, Christmasing (Rejoice WR 8347)	1986	$2.50	$5.00	$10.00
Ray Charles, A Message from the People (ABC X-755)	1972	$3.00	$6.00	$12.00
Floyd Cramer, Sounds of Sunday (RCA Victor LSP-4500)	1971	$3.75	$7.50	$15.00
Jimmy Dean, Most Richly Blessed (RCA Victor LPM-3824) (mono)	1967	$5.00	$10.00	$20.00

45s	Year	VG	VG+	NM
(if on RCA Victor LSP-3727, stereo)	1967	$3.75	$7.50	$15.00
Aretha Franklin, Songs of Faith (Checker 10009) (mono) (cover shows Aretha Franklin sitting at a piano)	1965	$125.00	$250.00	$500.00
(if album is titled "Gospel Soul", reissue of above title with new name and cover)	1967	$5.00	$10.00	$20.00
Bill Gaither Trio, Christmas ... Back Home in Indiana (Heart Warming R 3197)	1972	$5.00	$10.00	$20.00
(if on Word 8825, reissue)	198??	$3.00	$6.00	$12.00
Edwin Hawkins, Let Us Go Into the House of the Lord (Pavilion 10001)	1969	$3.75	$7.50	$15.00
(if reissued on Buddah BDS-5070, retitled "Oh Happy Day")	1970	$3.00	$6.00	$12.00
Mahalia Jackson, Spirituals (Apollo 201/202) (mono)	1954	$7.50	$15.00	$30.00
Mahalia Jackson, Newport 1958 (Columbia Cl 1244)	1959	$5.00	$10.00	$20.00
(if on CS 8071, stereo)	1959	$7.50	$15.00	$30.00
Mahalia Jackson, The Best-Loved Hymns of Dr. Martin Luther King Jr. (Columbia CS 9686)	1968	$3.75	$7.50	$15.00
(if on Columbia PC 9686, budget reissue)	198??	$2.00	$4.00	$8.00
Wanda Jackson, Country Gospel (Word WST-8614)	197??	$3.00	$6.00	$12.00
Pope John XXIII, Pope John XXIII (Mercury 200) (mono)	1963	$3.75	$7.50	$15.00
The Jordanaires, Beautiful City (RCA Victor LPM-3081) (10-inch disc)	1953	$25.00	$50.00	$100.00
The Jordanaires, Peace in the Valley (Decca DL 8681) (mono)	1957	$12.50	$25.00	$50.00
The Jordanaires, Land of Jordan (Capitol T 1311) (mono)	1960	$7.50	$15.00	$30.00
(if on Capitol ST 1311, stereo)	1960	$10.00	$20.00	$40.00
Rev. Dr. Martin Luther King, Jr., Martin Luther King at Zion Hill (Dooto DTL-831) (mono)	1962	$7.50	$15.00	$30.00

45s	Year	VG	VG+	NM
Rev. Dr. Martin Luther King, Jr., Freedom March on Washington (20th Century TCF-3110)	1963	$7.50	$15.00	$30.00
Rev. Dr. Martin Luther King, Jr., Free At Last (Gordy G-929) (with gatefold cover)	1968	$7.50	$15.00	$30.00
The Louvin Brothers, Nearer My God To Thee (Capitol 825)	1957	$25.00	$50.00	$100.00
Mighty Clouds of Joy, The Best of Mighty Clouds of Joy (Peacock 136)	196??	$5.00	$10.00	$20.00
(if on MCA 2809, reissue)	198??	$2.00	$4.00	$8.00
Mighty Clouds of Joy, It's Time (ABC-Dunhill DSX-50177)	1974	$2.50	$5.00	$10.00
The Mighty Faith Increasers, The Mighty Faith Increasers With Willa Dorsey (King 806) (mono)	1962	$37.50	$75.00	$150.00
The Mighty Faith Increasers, A Festival of Spiritual Songs (King 814) (mono)	1962	$37.50	$75.00	$150.00
Elvis Presley, He Touched Me (RCA LSP-4690) (if first pressing, on orange label)	1972	$10.00	$20.00	$40.00
(if promo copy, orange label, timing sticker on front cover)	1972	$25.00	$50.00	$100.00
(if second pressing, on tan label)	1975	$5.00	$10.00	$20.00
(if later pressing, RCA dog near top of black label)	1976	$3.75	$7.50	$15.00
(if on RCA AFL1-4690, black label, dog near top, some copies have stickers with new catalog number)	1977	$3.00	$6.00	$12.00
Jim Reeves, My Cathedral (RCA Victor LPM-3903) (mono)	1967	$7.50	$15.00	$30.00
(if on RCA Victor LSP-3903, stereo)	1967	$6.25	$12.50	$25.00
The Staple Singers, Best of the Staple Singers (Vee Jay LP-5019) (mono)	1962	$7.50	$15.00	$30.00
The Staple Singers, The Staple Singers, Vol. 2 (Archive of Gospel Music 72)	1969	$3.00	$6.00	$12.00
Jackie Wilson and Linda Hopkins, Shake a Hand (Brunswick BL 54113) (mono)	1964	$6.25	$12.50	$25.00
(if on Brunswick BL 754113, stereo)	1964	$7.50	$15.00	$30.00
Various Artists, Gospel Stars in Concert (Specialty SPS-2153)	1971	$5.00	$10.00	$20.00

This recording is a souvenir 7-inch picture disc, containing a performance of the carillon at St. Peter's Basilica in Vatican City, along with some benediction from the Pope.

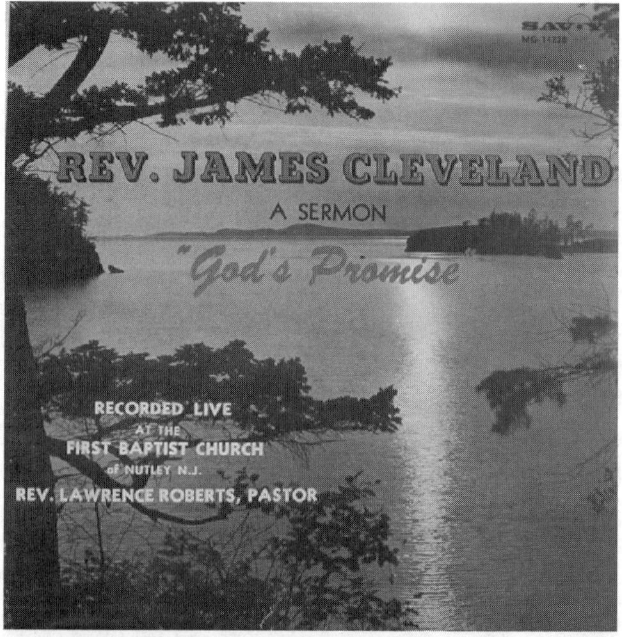

Recordings by popular ministers such as the Rev. James Cleveland are not only collectible for gospel music lovers, but also for spoken word enthusiasts. Photo Credit: Courtesy Last Vestige Music Store, Albany, N.Y.

THE GRATEFUL DEAD

History: They fused blues, folk, and bluegrass into a free-flowing mind-opening experience, enjoyable both with drugs and without them. They inspired generations to follow them, like mice to the Pied Piper, from city to city. Truly, it was a long, strange trip for the Grateful Dead.

The roots of the Grateful Dead began in the early 1960s, when bluegrass enthusiast Jerry Garcia joined various folk and bluegrass bands around Palo Alto, California. Garcia would later, along with keyboardist Ron "Pigpen" McKernan and rhythm guitarist Robert Weir, form Mother McCree's Uptown Jug Champions, and garner some success around the San Francisco clubs. Eventually the band renamed themselves the Warlocks, and added bassist Phil Lesh and drummer Bill Kreutzmann.

The Dead's first single on the tiny Scorpio label, "Stealin'." From the Collection of Eric Schwartz.

By 1966, the Warlocks were the band of choice for Ken Kesey's Acid Tests, a series of then-legal experimentations with LSD in San Francisco. After the band changed its name to the Grateful Dead, it developed a loyal and dedicated following throughout the Bay Area.

Although the band recorded some demo tracks for MGM, the Grateful Dead released its debut album in 1967 through Warner Brothers. With the addition of a second drummer, Mickey Hart, the Dead played the Monterey Pop Festival (they performed after the Who, and just before the Jimi Hendrix Experience).

A rare picture sleeve for the Grateful Dead single "Dark Star." From the Collection of Eric Schwartz.

Albums such as *Anthem of the Sun* and *Aoxomoxoa* were balances between short songs that could be released as singles (which the record company wanted), and longer, in-studio experiments and jams (which the Dead's fans wanted). The band bowed to the wishes of the fans, and included more jams on their 1969 album *Live/Dead*—such as a 24-minute jam on "Dark Star," and a 15-minute run on the soul hit "Turn On Your Love Light."

Between 1970 and 1971, the Grateful Dead's studio albums *American Beauty* and *Workingman's Dead* contained the songs most associated with the group—songs like "Uncle John's Band," "Truckin'," "Friend of the Devil," and "Casey Jones," and it was these albums that would form the core catalog of every Dead fan's record collection. Many of the songs in this fertile recording period showed the strength of Garcia's songwriting partnership with Robert Hunter, who provided the lyrics to Garcia's melodies. The Grateful Dead ended their association with Warner Brothers with two more live albums, including the three-disc *Europe '72*. This album was the last to feature Pigpen McKernan, who died of liver failure on March 8, 1973.

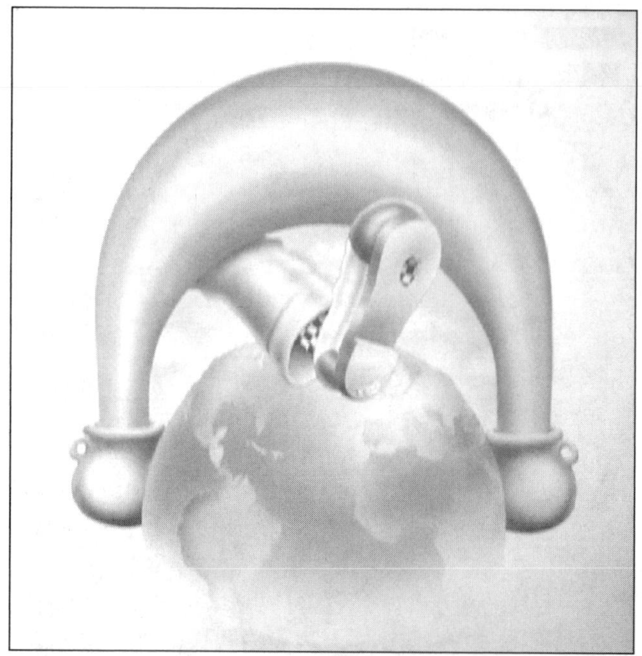

The last album to feature Ron "Pigpen" McKernan, the three-LP set Europe '72. Photo Credit: Courtesy Last Vestige Music Store, Albany, N.Y.

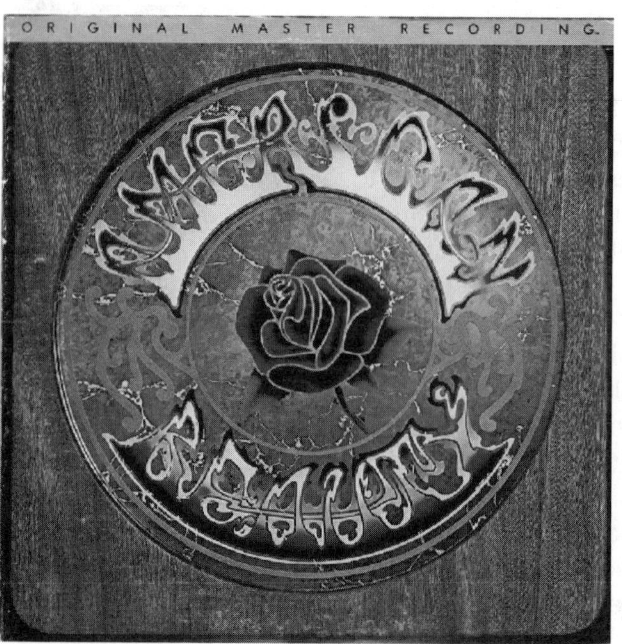

The Grateful Dead's American Beauty album, later released in an audiophile format for Mobile Fidelity Sound Lab. From the Collection of Gerry Bryan.

During the mid-1970s, the Grateful Dead recorded four albums for their own custom label, Grateful Dead Records. With their new keyboardist Keith Godchaux (and his wife Donna on background vocals), the Dead's music evolved into unchartered folk-rock and country-rock territories. But by 1974, the band took a sabbatical so their members could record solo projects.

The Dead reformed in 1976, and signed with Arista Records. While their albums *Terrapin Station* and *Shakedown Street* had their fans, the group found more pleasure in touring than in their studio work.

Along with the Grateful Dead concerts came hundreds of tie-dyed fans, who would pitch camp in the concert city, sell souvenirs, and spread their own concepts of peace, love, and harmony. "Deadheads" created a their own city near a stadium or arena, creating their own Shakedown Alley of vendors, performance artists, and life-affirming citizens. Not only were Deadheads the Grateful Dead's most loyal fans, Deadheads were arguably the most recently evolved indigenous cultural tribe in America.

The Godchauxes left the Grateful Dead in 1979, to be replaced by a new keyboardist, Brent Mydland. Undaunted, the band continued to tour throughout the 1980s, even though it had not recorded any new material since the decade began.

But in 1986, a hospitalized Jerry Garcia slipped into a five-day near-fatal coma. When he awoke from the coma, he had to undergo therapy to relearn how to play the guitar. By 1987, Garcia had returned to the band, and the Grateful Dead geared up for another tour, this time supporting a new studio album, *In the Dark*.

This tour, however, had one thing previous Dead shows didn't—a major hit single. A song from In the Dark, "Touch of Grey," broke through Top 40 radio, propelling the Dead onto the Top 10 pop charts for the first time in their career. They even had a music video for the song, which received heavy rotation on MTV—a rarity for a band whose members were old enough to remember monaural LPs.

Trivia

The Grateful Dead album *Wake of the Flood* was pressed on green vinyl for their fan club. Ironically, many of those copies were damaged when a warehouse was flooded.

The Grateful Dead's first Top 10 hit, "Touch of Gray," was pressed on gray vinyl and enclosed in a foldout poster sleeve.

The last lineup changes for the Dead occurred in 1990, after the drug-induced death of keyboardist Brent Mydland. Former Tubes keyboardist Vince Welnick took Mydland's place, and singer-pianist Bruce Hornsby added his talents on piano from 1990 to 1992.

The year 1995 was not a good one for the Dead. Jerry Garcia had fought both heroin addiction and diabetes, and throughout the 1990s had checked in and out of rehab centers and hospitals. On the morning of August 9, 1995, while enrolled at a health clinic in Forest Knolls, California, Garcia suffered a heart attack and died in his sleep.

In that moment, the long strange trip had finally ended for the Grateful Dead and their fans. Three generations of Deadheads held worldwide candlelight vigils. In San Francisco, the birthplace of the Grateful Dead, the music and art communities were in mourning.

But the Grateful Dead's music continues to this day. Volumes of classic "Dick's Picks" concerts have been released on CD. Dead souvenirs, from bean bag bears to neckties to ice cream, still raise millions for charities. The surviving members of the Grateful Dead still tour and perform today, under such group names as Ratdog, the Other Ones, and Mystery Box. And thirty-five years of music—from the days as Ken Kesey's house band to the worldwide concerts—still make a difference in millions of lives.

What To Look For: Even though the Grateful Dead are the undisputed kings of unreleased concert tapes, as their fans have recorded the band's live performances since the Ken Kesey Acid Test days, this book focuses on their vinyl releases on Warner Bros. and Arista, as well as the material released on their own Grateful Dead label. Bootleg recordings are not included in this book, nor are the thousands of concert tapes Dead fans have treasured over the years. More appropriate and scholarly books that cover Dead concert tapes are listed in the bibliography below.

Although the band's albums have always remained in print, especially the Warner Bros. recordings, be aware that although the front cover artwork has remained the same, the record inside may have a center label from the late 1970s or 1980s, with the Warner Bros. "Burbank" or "white stock label" artwork. Warner Bros. albums with a UPC bar code on the back cover are definitely reissues.

Because the Dead released very few singles in comparison to other artists of similar recording longevity, those 45s that have survived are very collectible. And since very few of those singles ever hit the pop charts, finding stock copies of the 45s, with their colorful picture sleeve intact, is difficult.

Artwork for the Grateful Dead single "U.S. Blues." From the Collection of Eric Schwartz.

References: Dodd, David G.; Spaulding, Diana, Eds., *The Grateful Dead Reader*, Oxford University Press, New York, N.Y., 2000; Dodd, David G.; Weiner, Robert G.; *The Grateful Dead and the Deadheads: An Annotated Bibliography*, Greenwood Press. Westport, Conn. 1997; Getz, Michael M.; Dwork, John R., *The Deadhead's Taping Companion*, Owl Books/Henry Holt & Co., New York 2000 (three volumes); Shenk, David; Silberman, Steve; *Skeleton Key: A Dictionary of Deadheads,* Doubleday, New York, 1994; Trager, Oliver, *The American Book of the Dead: The Definitive Grateful Dead Encyclopedia*, Fireside/Simon and Schuster Inc., New York, N.Y., 1997; a Grateful Dead FAQ (Frequently Asked Questions) is also available through the University of California at Berkeley, through FTP:

Part 1: *ftp://gdead.berkeley.edu/pub/gdead/miscellaneous/faq1.2*

Part 2: *ftp://gdead.berkeley.edu/pub/gdead/miscellaneous/faq2.2*

Web pages: The Grateful Dead's official Web page: *http://www.dead.net*; the Grateful Dead Family Discography, a complete discography of Grateful Dead and solo material: *http://www.deaddisc.com*; Eric Schwartz hosts a Grateful Dead radio show on Dallas public radio. His Dead homepage: *http://www.conservatory.com/eric/45s.htm;* Grateful Dead Usenet newsgroups: rec.music.gdead

Magazines: Relix Magazine covers not only the Grateful Dead, but the entire San Francisco music scene. Ordering information available through *http://www.relix.com.*

45s	Year	VG	VG+	NM
The Grateful Dead, "Stealin'" / "Don't Ease Me In" (Scorpio 201)	1966	$150.00	$300.00	$600.00
(counterfeits exist; originals have "Commercial Records" in the dead wax)				
The Grateful Dead, "The Golden Road (To Unlimited Devotion)" / "Cream Puff War" (Warner Bros. 7016)	1967	$6.25	$12.50	$25.00
The Grateful Dead, "Dark Star" / "Born Cross-Eyed" (Warner Bros. 7186)	1968	$6.25	$12.50	$25.00
(with picture sleeve, add:)	1968	$125.00	$250.00	$500.00
The Grateful Dead, "Dupree's Diamond Blues" / "Cosmic Charlie" (Warner Bros. 7324)	1969	$6.25	$12.50	$25.00
The Grateful Dead, "Truckin'" / "Ripple" (Warner Bros. 7464)	1971	$3.00	$6.00	$12.00
The Grateful Dead, "Sugar Magnolia" / "Mr. Charlie" (Warner Bros. 7667)	1972	$3.00	$6.00	$12.00
Jerry Garcia, "Deep Hour" / "Sugaree" (Warner Bros. 7551)	1972		$3.00	$6.00
Mickey Hart, "Blind John" / "Pump Man" (Warner Bros. 7644)	1972	$2.50	$5.00	$10.00
Robert Weir, "One More Saturday Night" / "Casidy" (Warner Bros. 7611)	1972	$3.00	$6.00	$12.00
The Grateful Dead, "Here Comes Sunshine" / "Let Me Sing Your Blues Away" (Grateful Dead 01)	1973	$2.50	$5.00	$10.00
The Grateful Dead, "U.S. Blues" / "Loose Lucy" (Grateful Dead 03)	1974	$2.50	$5.00	$10.00
(with picture sleeve, add:)	1974	$5.00	$10.00	$20.00
The Grateful Dead, "Franklin's Tower" / "Help On The Way" (Grateful Dead XW 762)	1976	$5.00	$10.00	$20.00

45s	Year	VG	VG+	NM
Jerry Garcia, "Let It Rock" / "Midnight Town" (Round 4504)	1974		$3.00	$6.00
Robert Weir, "I'll Be Doggone" / "Shade of Grey" (Arista 0336)	1978	$3.00	$6.00	$12.00
The Grateful Dead, "Dancin' In The Streets" / "Terrapin Station" (Arista 0276)	1977		$3.00	$6.00
The Grateful Dead, "Good Lovin'" / "Stagger Lee" (Arista 0383)	1978		$3.00	$6.00
The Grateful Dead, "Alabama Getaway" / "Far From Me" (Arista 0519)	1980		$2.50	$5.00
(with picture sleeve, add:)	1980		$2.50	$5.00
The Grateful Dead, "Touch of Grey" / "My Brother Esau" (Arista 9606)				
(if on gray vinyl)	1987		$2.50	$5.00
(with foldout picture sleeve, add $2 if sticker is still attached to shrink-wrap)	1987		$2.50	$5.00
(if on black vinyl, no foldout sleeve issued in this configuration)	1987			$3.00
The Grateful Dead, "Foolish Heart" / "We Can Run" (Arista 9899)	1989		$2.00	$4.00
(with picture sleeve, add:)	1989		$2.00	$4.00

LPs	Year	VG	VG+	NM
The Grateful Dead, The Grateful Dead (Warner Bros. 1689)				
(if on Warner Bros. W 1689, mono)	1967	$20.00	$40.00	$80.00
(if on Warner Bros. WS 1689, stereo, gold label)	1967	$15.00	$30.00	$60.00
(if on Warner Bros. WS 1689, stereo, green label, "W7" logo)	1968	$6.25	$12.50	$25.00
(if on Warner Bros. WS 1689, stereo, green label, "WB" logo)	1970	$3.75	$7.50	$15.00
(if on Warner Bros. WS 1689, stereo, "Burbank" label with palm trees)	1973	$3.00	$6.00	$12.00
(if on Warner Bros. WS 1689, stereo, white or tan stock label)	1979	$2.00	$4.00	$8.00
The Grateful Dead, Anthem of the Sun (Warner Bros. WS 1749)				
(if on green label, "W7" logo)	1968	$7.50	$15.00	$30.00
(if on green label, "WB" logo, purple cover)	1970	$3.75	$7.50	$15.00
(if on green label, "WB" logo, white background on cover, album has been remixed)	197??	$12.50	$25.00	$50.00
(if on "Burbank" label with palm trees)	1973	$3.00	$6.00	$12.00
(if on white or tan stock label)	1979	$2.00	$4.00	$8.00
The Grateful Dead, Aoxomoxoa (Warner Bros. WS 1790)				
(if on green label, "W7" logo)	1969	$7.50	$15.00	$30.00
(if on green label, "WB" logo)	1970	$3.75	$7.50	$15.00
(if on "Burbank" label with palm trees)	1973	$3.00	$6.00	$12.00
(if on white or tan stock label)	1979	$2.00	$4.00	$8.00
The Grateful Dead, Workingman's Dead (Warner Bros. WS 1869)				
(if on green label, "WB" logo, textured cover with back cover slick upside down)	1970	$6.25	$12.50	$25.00
(if on "Burbank" label with palm trees, standard cover, back cover right side up)	1973	$3.00	$6.00	$12.00
(if on white or tan stock label)	1979	$2.00	$4.00	$8.00
The Grateful Dead, Vintage Dead (Sunflower SUN-5001) (counterfeit covers are 1/4" shorter than normal LP covers)	1970	$10.00	$20.00	$40.00
The Grateful Dead, Historic Dead (Sunflower SNF-5004)	1971	$10.00	$20.00	$40.00
The Grateful Dead, Europe '72 (Warner Bros. 2WS 1935) (2 LPs)				
(if on green label, "WB" logo)	1972	$10.00	$20.00	$40.00
(if on "Burbank" label with palm trees)	1973	$5.00	$10.00	$20.00
(if on white or tan stock label)	1979	$3.00	$6.00	$12.00
Jerry Garcia, Garcia (Warner Bros. BS 2582)				
(green label with "WB" logo)	1972	$10.00	$20.00	$40.00
(if on Round RX-102)	1974	$6.25	$12.50	$25.00
Mickey Hart, Rolling Thunder (Warner Bros. BS 2635)	1972	$7.50	$15.00	$30.00
(if on Relix 2026)	1987	$3.00	$6.00	$12.00
Robert Weir, Ace (Warner Bros. BS 2627)				
(if color photo on back cover)	1972	$10.00	$20.00	$40.00
(if black and white photo on back cover)	1972	$7.50	$15.00	$30.00
The Grateful Dead, Wake of the Flood (Grateful Dead GD-01)				
(if no contributing artists on back cover)	1973	$5.00	$10.00	$20.00
(if on green vinyl for fan club members)	1973	$100.00	$200.00	$400.00
(if contributing artists are listed, United Artists distribution is mentioned)	1975	$3.75	$7.50	$15.00

LPs	Year	VG	VG+	NM
The Grateful Dead, From the Mars Hotel (Grateful Dead GD-102)				
(if no mention of United Artists distribution)	1974	$5.00	$10.00	$20.00
(with mention of United Artists distribution)	1975	$3.75	$7.50	$15.00
Keith and Donna, Keith and Donna (Round RX-104)	1975	$7.50	$15.00	$30.00
The Grateful Dead, Blues for Allah (Grateful Dead GD-LA494-G)	1975	$5.00	$10.00	$20.00
The Grateful Dead, Steal Your Face (Grateful Dead GD-LA620-J2) (2 LPs)	1976	$6.25	$12.50	$25.00
The Grateful Dead, Terrapin Station (Arista AL 7001)	1977	$3.75	$7.50	$15.00
(if white label promo copy, tracks are banded for radio airplay)	1977	$12.50	$25.00	$50.00
(if on Direct Disc SD-16619, audiophile vinyl)	1980	$50.00	$100.00	$200.00
(if on Arista AL 8329, budget line reissue)	198??	$2.00	$4.00	$8.00
Jerry Garcia, Cats Under the Stars (Arista AB 4160)	1978	$3.00	$6.00	$12.00
Robert Weir, Heaven Help the Fool (Arista AL 4155)	1978	$2.50	$5.00	$10.00
The Grateful Dead, Go To Heaven (Arista AL 9508)	1980	$3.00	$6.00	$12.00
(if on Arista AL 3332, budget line reissue)	198??	$2.00	$4.00	$8.00
The Grateful Dead, In The Dark (Arista AL 8452)	1987	$2.50	$5.00	$10.00
The Grateful Dead, Without A Net (Arista AL3 8634) (3 LPs)	1990	$6.25	$12.50	$25.00

The Grateful Dead skeleton, wearing a jester's costume, appears here on this copy of "Franklin's Tower." This 45 also mentions that Grateful Dead Records are now being distributed through United Artists. From the Collection of Eric Schwartz.

A Grateful Dead improvisation on the Young Rascals classic "Good Lovin'." From the Collection of Eric Schwartz.

Although the writer's credit on "The Golden Road" is given to "McGannahan Skjellyfetti," the track was actually co-written by Jerry Garcia, Bill Kreutzmann, Phil Lesh, Pigpen McKernan and Bob Weir. From the Collection of Eric Schwartz.

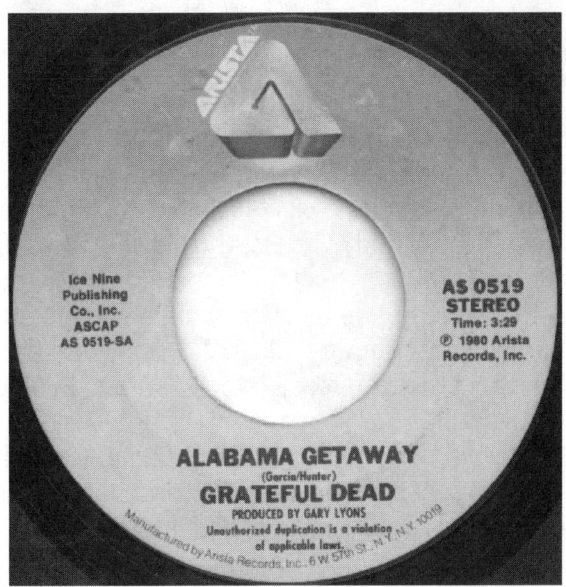

"Alabama Getaway" and the album it came from, Go To Heaven, are extremely common and easily findable records today.

HEAVY METAL

History: What we know today as "heavy metal" music began in the mid-1960s. Rock bands used their electric guitars to re-interpret blues and soul songs, increasing the volume and feedback on their guitars in an effort to make their records sound thicker and heavier. Some of these early excursions include Iron Butterfly's "In A Gadda-Da-Vida," Vanilla Fudge's "You Keep Me Hanging On," Blue Cheer's "Summertime Blues," and Steppenwolf's "Born To Be Wild" (which contains the lyrics "heavy metal thunder").

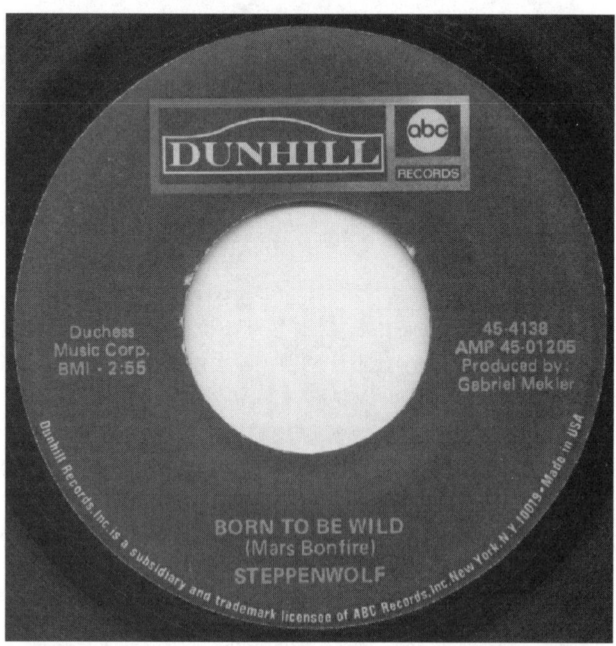

From this humble Steppenwolf 45 came the term "heavy metal."

In England, the hard chords and thumping bass led to bands like Led Zeppelin and Black Sabbath. Many of these bands took classic blues songs from such artists as Muddy Waters and Howlin' Wolf, and played them with as much volume as humanly possible. Before long, the musical sonic boom included the bands Deep Purple and Uriah Heep, who had evolved from the progressive rock genre to this new powerful sound.

Meanwhile, American "hard rock" acts Aerosmith and Ted Nugent added more R&B and boogie to their sonic palate. Over-the-top theatrics were added by Kiss and Alice Cooper (and by an Australian band named AC/DC), who wanted their fans to both see and hear a heavy-metal experience.

But in the 1980s, American groups would begin to dominate not only heavy metal sales, but pop and rock sales as well. Groups such as Motley Crue, Guns 'n' Roses, Quiet Riot, Twisted Sister, and Bon Jovi became multi-platinum superstars, as they mixed punk and pop with heavy metal sounds of the 1970s. Not to be outdone, European groups like Def Leppard, Europe, and the Scorpions also became worldwide metal sensations.

Motley Crue burst from the Los Angeles punk-metal scene and became one of the top heavy metal bands of the 1980s.

Eventually copycat metal groups appeared, groups who tried to emulate the 1980s metal bands for their own successes. Some of these groups included Poison, Ratt, Warrant, Cinderella, Winger and L.A. Guns. Many of these groups were also called "hair bands" because of their teased hairstyles and androgynous wardrobes.

The popularity of hair-metal bands waned in the early 1990s with the arrival of grunge music. Bands like Nirvana, Alice in Chains, Soundgarden, and Rage Against the Machine, with their raw musical style and stripped-down appearances, broke new ground in hard-rock music. Other groups embraced a type of heavy-metal music called "speed metal," which involved songs with a faster tempo and darker lyrics. The first "speed metal" groups were Judas Priest and Motorhead, who would later be followed by Metallica and Slayer.

Trivia

Jon Bongiovi swept floors in a recording studio by day, and cut his own rock songs at that same studio at night. Eventually one of those tracks, "Runaway," became a Top 40 radio hit and started Bongiovi—now known as Jon Bon Jovi—on the road to success.

Jon Bon Jovi's first hard rock hit, "Runaway."

A picture sleeve for Metallica's single "One."

One of the main perceptions by people who don't like heavy-metal music is that the artists and their songs are either satanic or have a devil-worshipping agenda. Allegedly some records can be played backwards to reveal a satanic message, while others artists use pentagrams or demonic artwork on their covers. Because of this, some people have claimed that heavy metal music is the work of the devil, and is the tool used by the devil to command teenagers to kill their parents or themselves. Of course, if backward messages actually worked, if some heavy metal band recorded "get a job, pay your bills, respect animals" into a backward message on their songs...

Today's hardcore/metal/punk/hip-hop melange bands owe a tremendous debt to their heavy-metal forefathers. Alice Cooper, for example, shocked audiences long before Marilyn Manson was born. The Insane Clown Posse's face paint was pioneered by Kiss a generation ago. And the sonic noise of Korn and Limp Bizkit have their lineage in Black Sabbath, Motorhead, and Slayer.

What To Look For: If a heavy-metal music collector has a choice between an American pressing and a European or Japanese pressing, they will often choose the import rather than the domestic product. Imported metal albums often are pressed on cleaner vinyl, and may contain bonus tracks or alternate mixes more often than do the American pressings. Also, some metal albums exist on vinyl only as imports, as the American record company may have stopped making albums for its entire roster in favor of CD's.

That being said, the rarer American copies of heavy-metal records often come from tiny independent labels, or from shortprinted albums that may have been taken off the market for a controversial lyric or album cover.

Although 45s are listed in the following price guide, most values for heavy-metal 45s are very low. Heavy metal music is a genre specifically geared towards albums, with only a few rare 45s garnering a collectible value of more than a few dollars.

References: Eddy, Chuck, *Stairway To Hell: The 500 Best Heavy Metal Albums In The Universe*, Da Capo Press, New York, 1998; Popoff, Martin, *The Collector's Guide to Heavy Metal*, CG Publishing, Inc., Burlington, Ontario, 1997; Popoff, Marvin, *Goldmine Heavy Metal Record Price Guide*, Krause Publications, Iola, Wisconsin, 1999; Strong, Martin C., *The Great Metal Discography*, Canongate Books, Edinburgh, Great Britain, 1998.

Trivia

Taking their name from the biblical passage "by his stripes we are healed," the Christian heavy-metal band Stryper achieved some success in the mid-1980s with songs like "Honestly" and "Calling On You."

Instead of singing for the Devil, Stryper's albums contained songs like *"To Hell With the Devil."* This 12-inch single of "Calling On You" was released to radio while their video was in heavy rotation on MTV.

Web pages: Addicted to Metal, a homepage devoted to heavy metal music: *http://www.atmetal.com*; the Ring of Zeppelin, a list of fan-based pages devoted to Led Zeppelin: *http://www.crickrock.com/cgi-bin/webring/list.pl?ringid=zepring*; Pantera's homepage: *http://www.pantera.com;* the official Iron Maiden Web site: *http://www.ironmaiden.com;* Usenet newsgroups: alt.music.judas-priest, alt.music.led-zeppelin.

45s	Year	VG	VG+	NM
AC/DC, "High Voltage" / "It's A Long Way To The Top" (Atco 7068)	1976	$2.00	$4.00	$8.00
AC/DC, "Back in Black" / "What Do You Do For Money Honey" (Atlantic 3787)	1980		$2.50	$4.00
Black Sabbath, "Paranoid" / "Wizard" (Warner Bros. 7437)	1970	$2.50	$5.00	$10.00
Blue Cheer, "Summertime Blues" / "Out of Focus" (Philips 40516)	1968	$3.00	$6.00	$12.00
(with picture sleeve, add:)	1968	$6.25	$12.50	$25.00
Blue Öyster Cult, (Don't Fear) The Reaper" / "Tattoo Vampire" (Columbia 10384)	1976		$3.00	$6.00
Alice Cooper, "Reflected" / "Living" (Straight 101)	1959	$75.00	$150.00	$300.00
Alice Cooper, "Welcome To My Nightmare" / "Cold Ethyl" (Atlantic 3298)	1975		$2.50	$5.00
Deep Purple, "Hush" / "One More Rainy Day" (Tetragrammaton 1503)	1968	$3.00	$6.00	$12.00
(with picture sleeve, add:)	1968	$7.50	$15.00	$30.00
Def Leppard, "Photograph" / "Action, Not Words" (Mercury 811 215-7)				
(if on Chicago skyline label)	1983		$2.50	$5.00
(if on black label)	1983	$2.00	$4.00	
(with picture sleeve, add:)	1983	$2.50	$5.00	$10.00
Guns 'n' Roses, "Welcome To The Jungle" / "Mr. Brownstone" (Geffen 27759)	1988		$2.00	$4.00
(with picture sleeve, add:)	1988		$2.00	$4.00
Iron Butterfly, "In-A-Gadda-Da-Vida" / "Iron Butterfly Theme" (Atco 6606)	1968	$2.50	$5.00	$10.00
Iron Maiden, "Flight of Icarus" / "I've The Fire" (Capitol B-5248)	1983	$2.50	$5.00	$10.00
Led Zeppelin, "Stairway To Heaven" (mono/stereo) (Atlantic PR 175) (promo only)	1972	$25.00	$50.00	$100.00
(with promo picture sleeve, add:)	1972	$62.50	$125.00	$250.00
(if on Atlantic PR 269, both sides in stereo)	1973	$12.50	$25.00	$50.00
Metallica, "One" / "The Prince" (Elektra 69329)	1988		$2.50	$5.00
(with picture sleeve, add:)	1988		$2.50	$5.00
Mötley Crüe, "Stick To Your Guns" / "Toast of the Town" (Leathur 001)	1981	$20.00	$40.00	$80.00
(with picture sleeve, add:)	1981	$37.50	$75.00	$150.00
Mötley Crüe, "Girls, Girls, Girls" / "Sumthin' for Nothin'" (Elektra 69465)	1987			$3.00
(with picture sleeve, add:)	1987			$3.00
Ted Nugent, "Cat Scratch Fever" / "Wang Dang Sweet Poontang" (Epic 50425)	1977		$2.50	$5.00
Ozzy Osbourne, "Crazy Train" / "Steal Away (The Night)" (Jet 02079)	1981		$2.50	$5.00
(if on CBS Associated 07168, studio and live versions of "Crazy Train")	1987			$3.00
Poison, "Talk Dirty To Me" / "Want Some, Need Some" (Capitol B-5686)	1987			$3.00
(with picture sleeve, add:)	1987		$2.00	$4.00
Rage Against the Machine, "Bullet in the Head" / "Darkness" (Epic 74927)	1993		$2.50	$5.00
(with picture sleeve, add:)	1993		$2.50	$5.00
Blackmore's Rainbow, "Snake Charmer" / "Man on the Silver Mountain" (Polydor 14290)	1975		$3.00	$6.00
Rainbow, "Stone Cold" / "Rock Fever" (Mercury 76146)	1982		$2.00	$4.00
(with picture sleeve, add:)	1982		$2.50	$5.00
Soundgarden, "Black Hole Sun" / "Spoonman" (A&M 31458 0766 7)	1994			$3.00
Starz, "Cherry Baby" / "Rock Six Times" (Capitol 4399)	1977		$2.00	$4.00
(if on yellow vinyl)	1977	$3.00	$6.00	$12.00
(with picture sleeve, add:)	1977		$3.00	$6.00
Steppenwolf, "Born To Be Wild" / "Everybody's Next One" (ABC Dunhill 4138)	1968	$2.00	$4.00	$8.00
UFO, "Too Hot To Handle" / "Electric Phase" (Chrysalis 2157)	1977		$2.50	$5.00

LPs	Year	VG	VG+	NM
AC/DC, Live at the Atlantic Studios (Atlantic LAAS-001)	1977	$15.00	$30.00	$60.00
AC/DC, Back in Black (Atlantic SD-16018)	1980		$2.50	$5.00
Aerosmith, Aerosmith (Columbia KC 32005)				
(if orange cover, back cover lists song as "Walking the Dig")	1973	$5.00	$10.00	$20.00
(if orange cover, corrected title as "Walking the Dog")	1973	$3.75	$7.50	$15.00
(if light blue cover, often says "featuring Dream On" on front)	1973	$3.00	$6.00	$12.00
(if on Columbia PC 32005, no bar code)	1976	$2.50	$5.00	$10.00
(if on Columbia JC 32005)	1977	$2.00	$4.00	$8.00
(if on Columbia PC 32005, with bar code)	1984	$2.00	$4.00	$8.00
Aerosmith, Pure Gold From Rock 'n' Roll's Golden Boys (Columbia A3S 187)				
(white label promo, compilation from "Aerosmith," "Get Your Wings" and "Toys in the Attic")	1976	$12.50	$25.00	$50.00
Alice in Chains, Sap / Jar of Flies (Sony C257804) (2 LPs)	1994	$5.00	$10.00	$20.00
Black Sabbath, Black Sabbath (Warner Bros. WS 1871)				
(if first pressing, on green label)	1970	$3.75	$7.50	$15.00

LPs	Year	VG	VG+	NM
(if on "Burbank" label with palm trees)	1973	$2.50	$5.00	$10.00
(if on white or tan label)	1979	$2.00	$4.00	$8.00
Blue Cheer, Vincebus Eruptum (Philips PHM200264) (mono)	1968	$20.00	$40.00	$80.00
(if on Philips PHS 600264, stereo)	1968	$10.00	$20.00	$40.00
Blue Öyster Cult, Agents of Fortune (Columbia PC-34164)				
(if original gatefold, no bar code on cover)	1976	$2.50	$5.00	$10.00
(if on Columbia PC 36164, budget reissue with bar code)	198??	$2.00	$4.00	$8.00
Bon Jovi, Slippery When Wet (Mercury 830264)	1986			$3.50
(if on Mercury PD 830822, picture disc)	1986	$4.00	$8.00	$16.00
The Cherry Bombz, 100 Degrees in the Shade (PVC 5913)	1986	$3.25	$6.50	$13.00
Alice Cooper, Pretties For You (Straight ST51501) (yellow label)	1969	$37.50	$75.00	$150.00
(if on Straight ST51501, white label promo)	1969	$50.00	$100.00	$200.00
(if on Straight ST51501, pink label)	1970	$15.00	$30.00	$60.00
Deep Purple, Concerto for Group and Orchestra (Tetragrammon T131)	1970	$75.00	$150.00	$300.00
(if on Warner Bros. WS 1860)	1970	$3.00	$6.00	$12.00
Deep Purple, Machine Head (Warner Bros. BS 2607)				
(if green label)	1972	$3.00	$6.00	$12.00
(if "Burbank" labels with palm trees)	1973	$2.50	$5.00	$10.00
(if on Warner Bros. BS4 2607, quadraphonic)	1974	$6.25	$12.50	$25.00
Def Leppard, Pyromania (Mercury 810308)	1983		$2.00	$4.00
Dokken, Breakin' The Chains (Elektra 60290)	1981		$2.00	$4.00
Girlschool, Screaming Blue Murder (Mercury SRM 14066)	1982	$2.00	$4.25	$8.50
Guns 'n Roses, Appetite for Destruction				
(if on Geffen XXXG24148, "rape" cover)	1988	$12.50	$25.00	$50.00
(if on Geffen G24148, "cross" cover)	1988	$2.50	$4.00	$8.00
Hanoi Rocks, Two Steps from the Move (Columbia 39614)	1984		$2.50	$5.00
Iron Butterfly, In-A-Gadda-Da-Vida (Atco 33-250) (mono)	1968	$12.50	$25.00	$50.00
(if on Atco SD-33-250, stereo, brown-purple label)	1968	$6.25	$12.50	$25.00
(if on Atco SD-33-250, stereo, yellow label)	1969	$3.75	$7.50	$15.00
(if on Atco SD-33-250, any other later Atco label)	197??	$2.50	$5.00	$10.00
Iron Maiden, The Number of the Beast (EMI ST 12141)	1981		$2.75	$5.50
(if on EMI SEAX 12219, picture disc)	1982	$12.50	$25.00	$50.00
Iron Maiden, Best of the Beast (Capitol 53185) (4 LPs)	1996	$20.00	$40.00	$80.00
Judas Priest, Screaming for Venegance (Columbia AS99 1543) (picture disc)				
(if disc plays correct album on both sides)	1982	$5.00	$10.00	$20.00
(if disc actually plays Neil Diamond's "Heartlight" but has Judas Priest picture disc artwork)	1982	$7.50	$15.00	$30.00
Led Zeppelin, Led Zeppelin (Atlantic 7208)				
(album also known as Led Zeppelin IV, Runes or Zoso)				
(if on Atlantic 7208, mono, white label promo only)	1971	$75.00	$150.00	$300.00
(if on Atlantic SD 7208, stereo, white label promo)	1971	$37.50	$75.00	$150.00
(if on Atlantic SD 7208, stereo, "1841 Broadway" address on label)	1971	$3.00	$6.00	$12.00
(if on Atlantic SMAS-94019, Capitol Record Club)	1972	$10.00	$20.00	$40.00
(if on Atlantic SD 7208, stereo, "75 Rockefeller Plaza" address on label)	1974	$2.50	$5.00	$10.00
(if on Atlantic SD 19129, reissue)	1977	$2.00	$4.00	$8.00
(if on Atlantic SD 7208, Classic Records reissue on audiophile vinyl)	2000	$6.25	$12.50	$25.00
Loudness, Thunder in the East (Atlantic 90246)	1985		$2.75	$5.50
Mahogany Rush, Child of the Novelty (20th Century T-451)	1974	$6.25	$12.50	$25.00
Mahogany Rush, Mahogany Rush IV (Columbia PC 34190) (no bar code on back)	1976	$3.75	$7.50	$15.00
(with bar code on back cover)	198??	$2.00	$4.00	$8.00
Yngwie Malmsteen, Yngwie Malmsteen's Rising Force (Polydor 825324)	1985		$2.50	$5.00
Megadeth, So Far, So Good... So What! (Capitol 48148)	1988		$2.75	$5.50
(if on picture disc)	1988	$6.25	$12.50	$25.00

LPs	Year	VG	VG+	NM
Metallica, Kill 'Em All (Megaforce MRI 069)	1983	$7.50	$15.00	$30.00
(if on picture disc, numbered limited edition version, same catalog number)	1983	$20.00	$40.00	$80.00
(if on picture disc, un-numbered version, same catalog number)	1983	$10.00	$20.00	$40.00
Metallica, Ride the Lightning (Megaforce MRI 769)	1984	$7.50	$15.00	$30.00
Metallica, Garage Inc. (Elektra 62299) (3 LP's)	1998	$5.00	$10.00	$20.00
Montrose, Jump On It (Warner Bros. BS 2963)	1976	$3.00	$6.00	$12.00
Mötley Crüe, Too Fast For Love (Leathur LR 123)				
(if first pressing, white lettering on cover)	1981	$75.00	$150.00	$300.00
(if second pressing, red lettering on cover)	1981	$37.50	$75.00	$150.00
(if on Elektra 60174, deletes the song "Stick To Your Guns")	1981		$2.25	$4.50
Motörhead, Ace of Spades (Mercury SRM 14011)	1980		$4.25	$8.50
Mountain, Nantucket Sleighride (Windfall 5500)	1971	$3.00	$6.00	$12.00
(with inserts, add:)	1971	$1.00	$2.00	$3.00
Nine Inch Nails, The Downward Spiral (Nothing/TVT/Interscope PR 5509) (2 LP's, promo copies on vinyl only)	1994	$6.25	$12.50	$25.00
Ted Nugent, State of Shock (Epic FE 36000)	1979	$2.50	$5.00	$10.00
(if on Epic AS99-607, promo-only picture disc)	1979	$10.00	$20.00	$40.00
(if on Epic PE 36000, budget reissue)	198??	$2.00	$4.00	$8.00
Ozzy Osbourne, Diary of a Madman (Jet FZ 37492)	1981		$2.50	$5.00
(if on Epic AS99 1372, picture disc, promo only)	1981	$7.00	$14.00	$28.00
Pantera, Projects in the Jungle (Metal Magic MMR 1984)				
(with fan club insert)	1984	$18.75	$37.50	$75.00
(if on yellow vinyl)	1984	$18.75	$37.50	$75.00
Poison, Look What The Cat Dragged In (Capitol ST512523)	1986		$2.25	$4.50
Queensryche, Operation: Mindcrime (EMI 48640)	1988		$2.25	$4.50
(if on EMI SPRO1436, picture disc)	1988	$11.25	$22.50	$45.00
Rage Against the Machine, Evil Empire (Epic E 57523)	1996	$2.50	$5.00	$10.00
Rainbow, Rainbow Rising (Oyster OY-1-1601)	1976	$3.00	$6.00	$12.00
(if on Polydor 823655-1, reissue)	1985	$2.00	$4.00	$8.00
Ratt, Invasion of Your Privacy (Atlantic 81257)	1985		$2.25	$4.50
Saxon, Strong Arm of the Law (Carrere 37679)	1980		$3.50	$7.00
Scorpions, Lonesome Crow (Billingsgate 1004)	1974	$7.50	$15.00	$30.00
Scorpions, Love at First Sting (Mercury 814981-1)				
(if first pressing, with man and woman on cover)	1984	$2.50	$5.00	$10.00
(if second pressing, with band on cover)	1984	$3.00	$6.00	$12.00
Slayer, Show No Mercy (Metal Blade 71034)	1983		$4.25	$8.50
(if on Metal Blad 72214, picture disc)	1987	$6.25	$12.50	$25.00
Soundgarden, Superunknown (A&M 31454 0198 1) (2 LPs) (available on gold, blue or clear vinyl, value is equal)	1994	$3.75	$7.50	$15.00
Starz, Violation (Capitol ST 11617)	1977	$2.50	$5.00	$10.00
(if on (yellow vinyl, promo only)	1977	$5.00	$10.00	$20.00
Stryper, The Yellow and Black Attack (Enigma E1064)	1986		$3.50	$7.00
(if on Enigma ST73207, blue or yellow vinyl, round cover)	1986	$5.00	$10.00	$20.00
Twisted Sister, You Can't Stop Rock 'n' Roll (Atlantic 80074)	1983		$2.50	$5.00
UFO, UFO 1 (Rare Earth RS 624)	1971	$6.25	$12.50	$25.00
UFO, The Wild, The Willing and the Innocent (Chrysalis PV 41307)	1983	$2.00	$4.00	$8.00
Van Halen, 1984 (Warner Bros. 23985)	1984		$2.25	$4.50
(if promo copy, pressed on Quiex II vinyl)	1984	$6.25	$12.50	$25.00
Van Halen, For Unlawful Carnal Knowledge (Warner Bros. 1W-26594) (vinyl only available through Columbia House)	1991	$5.00	$10.00	$20.00
W.A.S.P., W.A.S.P. (Capitol ST512343)	1985		$2.50	$5.00
Wargasm, Why Play Around? (Profile PRO 1254)	1988		$3.75	$7.50
White Zombie, Astro Creep 2000 (Geffen 24802) (purple vinyl)	1995	$5.75	$11.50	$23.00
Winger, Winger (Atlantic 81867)	1988		$2.25	$4.50
Y&T, In Rock We Trust (A&M SP5007)	1984		$2.50	$5.00

JIMI HENDRIX

History: It seemed all too short. A superstar career that spanned less than half a decade, with a drug overdose taking the life of one of the greatest guitarists of all time. But if truth be told, Jimi Hendrix spent years working as a session guitarist, honing his skills by performing as a backup musician for everybody from the Isley Brothers to Little Richard, from Curtis Knight to Joey Dee and the Starliters.

But when the Jimi Hendrix Experience, a trio with bassist Noel Redding and drummer Mitch Mitchell, released their first singles and albums, they became instant superstars in England. And although Hendrix was originally from Seattle, Washington, his group was able to ride the wave of the British Invasion, becoming a popular and successful live act in America.

This picture sleeve for "Gloria" was part of a 7-inch bonus disc for a Jimi Hendrix greatest hits package. Courtesy Last Vestige Music Store, Albany, N.Y.

What set Jimi Hendrix apart from other guitarists of his era was his ability to use every part of his equipment—his guitar, his amplifier, and a wah-wah pedal—to create new and unique sounds. He was able to use controlled feedback from his amplifiers to generate new chords and complex orchestrations. He could make his guitar scream in pain, or moan in ecstasy.

Chas Chandler, the bass player for the Animals, discovered Hendrix performing at Café Wha?, a New York City nightclub. Chandler immediately brought Hendrix to England, where he teamed the guitarist with Redding and Mitchell, and christened the trio as the Jimi Hendrix Experience.

The Experience's first singles, "Hey Joe" and "Purple Haze," rocketed to the top of the UK charts. By the time the Experience returned to America, they had a full-length album, *Are You Experienced?*, which reached the *Billboard* Top 10 in 1967.

One of the early singles from the Jimi Hendrix Experience. From the Collection of Val Shively.

In June 1967, at the Monterey International Pop Festival, the Jimi Hendrix Experience stole the show. During a performance of "Wild Thing," Hendrix played his guitar with his teeth, played it behind his back, then at he end of the performance, lit the guitar on fire. Movie footage from this concert showed millions of music lovers a new type of theatrical musician, someone who could perform both musically and sonically.

The Experience would produce two more albums, *Axis: Bold as Love and Electric Ladyland*. Both albums showed Hendrix maturing as a musician and as a producer; the guitarist's legendary perfection in the studio required dozens of takes until the sound was just right. *Electric Ladyland* reached #1 on the *Billboard* album charts, and spawned Hendrix's first Top 40 hit in America, "All Along The Watchtower."

From the psychedelic cover to the sonic experimentation on the grooves, Axis: Bold as Love proved that Jimi Hendrix was a musical force to be reckoned with.

One of the many Hendrix recordings that were released without his consent or control. Courtesy Last Vestige Music Store, Albany, N.Y.

A common misconception is that unauthorized Hendrix albums were released only after the guitar legend died. In fact, Hendrix's legitimate releases were often competing with recordings he made years before. In his early years, Hendrix would record for anybody and everybody, and signed recording contracts as often as baseball players sign autographs. Thus, once he achieved stardom, his early recordings with Curtis Knight and with Little Richard were ripe for reissue.

By 1969, in fact, because of the rapacious contracts Hendrix signed, he found he was obligated to Capitol Records for an album, even though the Experience was bound to Reprise Records. By this time, he had already broken up the Experience, and began work with other musicians. After a spectacular appearance at the Woodstock Festival, in which Hendrix woke the crowd with a feedback-influenced version of "The Star Spangled Banner," Hendrix recorded the album *Band of Gypsys* on New Year's Eve, 1969, at the Fillmore East.

On September 18, 1970, Jimi Hendrix, one of the greatest guitarists in music history, died of a drug overdose. His last studio album, *The Cry of Love*, was released posthumously.

But after Hendrix died, anybody who had as little as a Hendrix guitar riff on tape suddenly had Hendrix "previously unreleased" material on their hands, and could release it on LP for an avid legion of Hendrix devotees.

A series of Hendrix legitimate releases were attempted by producer Alan Douglas. Douglas took some unfinished Hendrix recordings, fleshed them out with studio musicians, and released *Crash Landing and Midnight Lightning*, both with reasonable success.

In 1995, the rights to all of Jimi Hendrix's previous recordings reverted to Hendrix's father. Today, Experience Hendrix LLC is the umbrella company that maintains licensing, reissue, and repackaging of various classic and posthumous Hendrix songs.

Trivia

Jimi Hendrix did session work for many artists throughout his career. His guitar can be heard on the Isley Brothers' "Testify," and on albums by the Last Poets.

This pressing of "The Star Spangled Banner," with die-cut stars around the record's blue vinyl perimeter, was a gift for Capitol Records' promotions staff in 1999. Courtesy Erika Records, Downey, California.

What To Look For: Hendrix's classic albums came when record companies were finally phasing out separate-but-equal stereo and mono releases. A few mono pressings were made of Hendrix's first two albums (and a radio-only mono run for the third LP), making these discs extremely rare.

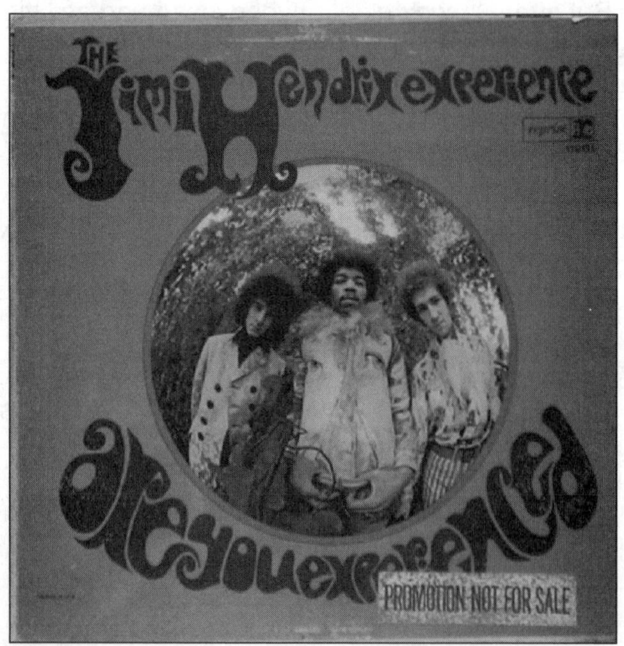

The Jimi Hendrix Experience's first album, *Are You Experienced*, is difficult to find in a mono pressing. Here's what one looks like; the top of the record jacket has a black "MONO" box on the fold. Courtesy Good Rockin' Tonight/Collectors Universe.

Jimi Hendrix's work was best suited for albums. Although he had Top 40 hits in England, he only hit the U.S. Top 40 once in his entire career, with "All Along The Watchtower." Therefore, his other American singles are highly collectible, and their accompanying picture sleeves even more so.

The most valuable prices are for recordings made during Hendrix's lifetime. After he died in 1970, major and minor record companies continued to raid old tape vaults for unreleased works by the guitar virtuoso. These recordings sold well in their original release, some of them even cracking the Top 10 on the LP charts, but today do not have the same collectibility as Hendrix's early albums.

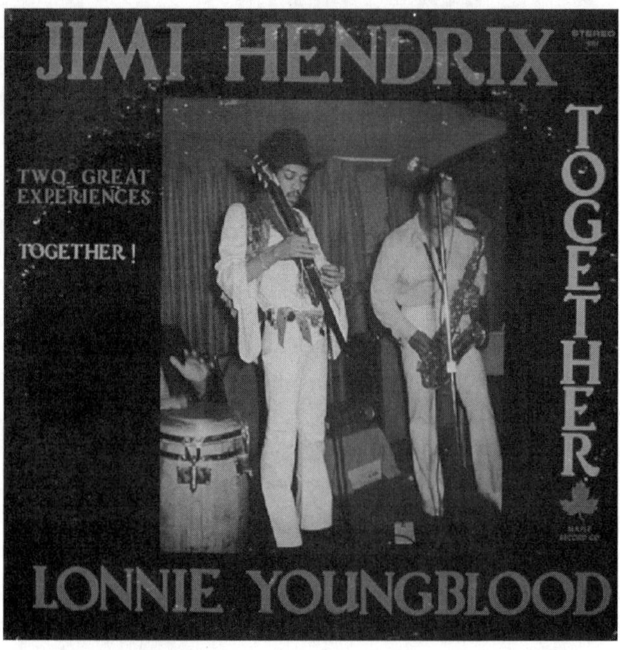

This album contains songs Jimi Hendrix recorded with Lonnie Youngblood in 1963. The album was released in 1971, a year after Hendrix died. Courtesy Last Vestige Music Store, Albany, N.Y.

References: Brown, Tony, *Jimi Hendrix: The Final Days*, Omnibus Press, 1997; Hopkins, Jerry, *Hit and Run: The Jimi Hendrix Story*, Putnam Publishing, New York, 1983; Murray, Charles S., *Crosstown Traffic: Jimi Hendrix and the Post-War Rock 'n' Roll Revolution*, Saint Martin's Press, New York, 1991; Redding, Noel; Appleby, Carol, *Are You Experienced?: The Inside Story of Jimi Hendrix*, Fourth Estate, London, 1990; Shapiro, Harry; Glebbeek, Caesar, *Jimi Hendrix: Electric Gypsy*, Mandarin, London, 1995; Welch, Chris, *Hendrix: A Biography*, Omnibus Press, 1972.

Web pages: The official Jimi Hendrix homepage: *http://www.jimi-hendrix.com*; the Jimi Hendrix Family Foundation, dedicated to developing resources and funds for charities: *http://www.jimihendrix.org*; Usenet newsgroups: *alt.fan.jimi-hendrix*, alt.music.jimi.hendrix.

Museums: The Experience Music Project, near the Seattle Space Needle, is home to the largest collection of Jimi Hendrix memorabilia and equipment. For more information, contact the museum at (206) EMP-LIVE (367-5483), or on its Web page at *http://www.experience.org*.

45s	Year	VG	VG+	NM
The Jimi Hendrix Experience, "Hey Joe" / "51st Anniversary" (Reprise 0572)	1967	$25.00	$50.00	$100.00
(with picture sleeve, add:)	1967	$250.00	$500.00	$1,000.00
The Jimi Hendrix Experience, "Purple Haze" / "The Wind Cries Mary" (Reprise 0597)	1967	$6.25	$12.50	$25.00
The Jimi Hendrix Experience, "Foxey Lady" / "Hey Joe" (Reprise 0641)	1967	$6.25	$12.50	$25.00
The Jimi Hendrix Experience, "Up From The Skies" / "One Rainy Wash" (Reprise 0665)	1968	$7.50	$15.00	$30.00
The Jimi Hendrix Experience, "Purple Haze" /"Foxey Lady" (Reprise 0728) ("Back to Back Hits", has both "r:" and "W7" logos)	1968	$3.75	$7.50	$15.00
The Jimi Hendrix Experience, "All Along The Watchtower" / "Burning of the Midnight Lamp" (Reprise 0767)	1968	$7.50	$15.00	$30.00
The Jimi Hendrix Experience, "Crosstown Traffic" / "Gypsy Eyes" (Reprise 0792)	1968	$7.50	$15.00	$30.00
The Jimi Hendrix Experience, "If 6 Were 9" / "Stone Free" (Reprise 0853)	1970	$10.00	$20.00	$40.00
Jimi Hendrix and Band of Gypsys, "Stepping Stone" / "Izabella" (Reprise 0905)	1970	$25.00	$50.00	$100.00
Jimi Hendrix, "No Such Animal" (Pt. 1) / (Pt. 2) (Audio Fidelity 167)	1970	$3.75	$7.50	$15.00
(with picture sleeve, add:)	1970	$10.00	$20.00	$40.00
Jimi Hendrix, "Freedom" / "Angel" (Reprise 1000)	1971	$3.75	$7.50	$15.00
Jimi Hendrix, "Dolly Dagger" / "Star Spangled Banner" (Reprise 1044)	1971	$3.75	$7.50	$15.00
Jimi Hendrix, 'All Along the Watchtower" / "Crosstown Traffic" (Reprise 0742, "Back to Back Hits")	1971		$3.00	$6.00
Jimi Hendrix, "Hot Trigger" / "Suspicious" (Trip 3002)	1972		$2.50	$5.00
Jimi Hendrix and Little Richard, "Goodnight Irene" / "Why Don't You Love Me" (Ala 1175)	1972	$2.00	$4.00	$8.00
Jimi Hendrix, "Medley: The Little Drummer Boy - Silent Night" / "Auld Lang Syne" (Reprise PRO 595) (white label promo)	1974	$37.50	$75.00	$150.00
(with picture sleeve, "... and a happy new year," add:)	1974	$20.00	$40.00	$80.00
Jimi Hendrix, "Gloria" (Reprise EP 2239) (one-sided single, included in "The Essential Jimi Hendrix, Vol. II")	1979		$2.50	$5.00
(with picture sleeve, add:)	1979		$2.50	$5.00
Jimi Hendrix, "Can You Please Crawl Out Your Window?" / "Burning of the Midnight Lamp" (MCA 55454) (promo, orange vinyl)	1988		$2.00	$4.00
(with cardboard picture sleeve, add:)	1988		$2.00	$4.00
The Jimi Hendrix Classic Singles Collection (Experience Hendrix/Classic RTH-1007) (boxed set of 10 45s, price is for full set)	1998	$15.00	$30.00	$60.00
Jimi Hendrix, "Little Drummer Boy - Auld Lang Syne" / "Three Little Pigs" (Experience Hendrix/Classic 5851-7) (red vinyl, small hole)	1999	$3.00	$6.00	$12.00
(with picture sleeve, add:)	1999	$3.00	$6.00	$12.00
Jimi Hendrix, "The Star Spangled Banner" (same on both sides) (Capitol SPRO-11284) (blue vinyl, stars die-cut along the vinyl perimeter, pressed as a gift for Capitol record promoters)	1999	$12.50	$25.00	$50.00

LPs	Year	VG	VG+	NM
The Jimi Hendrix Experience, Are You Experienced? (Reprise 6261)				
(if on Reprise R-6261, mono)	1967	$50.00	$100.00	$200.00
(if on Reprise RS-6261, stereo, with pink-green-gold label)	1967	$12.50	$25.00	$50.00
(If on Reprise RS-6261, stereo, with "W7" and "r:" logos on orange label)	1968	$6.25	$12.50	$25.00
(if on Experience Hendrix/MCA 11602, 2 LPs, heavy vinyl, booklet)	1997	$12.50	$25.00	$50.00
Jimi Hendrix, Get That Feeling (Capitol T 2856) (mono)	1967	$20.00	$40.00	$80.00
(if on Capitol ST 2856, stereo)	1967	$10.00	$20.00	$40.00
The Jimi Hendrix Experience, Axis: Bold as Love (Reprise 6281)				
(if on Reprise R-6281, mono)	1968	$625.00	$1,250.00	$2,500.00
(if on Reprise RS-6281, stereo, with pink-green-gold label)	1968	$20.00	$40.00	$80.00
(if on Reprise RS-6281, stereo, with "W7" and "r:" logos on orange label)	1968	$6.25	$12.50	$25.00
(if on Experience Hendrix/MCA 11601, heavy vinyl, booklet)	1997	$12.50	$25.00	$50.00
The Jimi Hendrix Experience, Electric Ladyland (Reprise 6307) (2 LPs)				
(if on Reprise 2R 6307, mono, promo only)	1968	$2,000	$3,000	$4,000
(if on Reprise 2RS 6307, stereo, with "W7" and "r:" logos on orange label)	1968	$25.00	$50.00	$100.00
(if on Experience Hendrix/MCA 11600, 2 LPs, heavy vinyl, booklet)	1997	$10.00	$20.00	$40.00
Jimi Hendrix, Flashing Capitol T 2894) (mono)	1968	$25.00	$50.00	$100.00
(if on Capitol ST 2894, stereo)	1968	$10.00	$20.00	$40.00
The Jimi Hendrix Experience, Smash Hits (Reprise MS 2025) (with "W7" and "r:" logos on orange label)	1969	$10.00	$20.00	$40.00
(with bonus poster, add:)	1969	$10.00	$20.00	$40.00
(if on Reprise MSK 2276, reissue)	1977	$2.50	$15.00	$30.00
Jimi Hendrix, Band of Gypsys (Capitol STAO-472)	1970	$5.00	$10.00	$20.00
(if on Capitol SN-16319, budget reissue)	1985	$2.50	$5.00	$10.00
(if on Capitol C1-96414, numbered reissue)	1995	$3.75	$7.50	$15.00
Jimi Hendrix, Get That Feeling/Flashing (Capitol SWBB-659) (2 LPs)	1971	$6.25	$12.50	$25.00
(if on Experience Hendrix/Capitol 11607, heavy vinyl, booklet)	1997	$6.25	$12.50	$25.00
Jimi Hendrix, The Cry of Love (Reprise MS 2034) (with "W7" and "r:" logos on orange label)	1971	$125.00	$250.00	$500.00
Jimi Hendrix, Superpak (Trip 3509) (2 LPs)	197??	$3.75	$7.50	$15.00
Jimi Hendrix, Rainbow Bridge (Reprise MS 2040)	1971	$5.00	$10.00	$20.00
Jimi Hendrix and Lonnie Youngblood, Two Great Experiences Together (Maple 6004)	1971	$12.50	$25.00	$50.00
Jimi Hendrix, Rare Hendrix (Trip TLP-9500)	1972	$3.75	$7.50	$15.00
Jimi Hendrix, Roots of Hendrix (Trip TLP-9501)	1972	$3.00	$6.00	$12.00
Jimi Hendrix, Hendrix in the West (Reprise MS 2049)	1972	$5.00	$10.00	$20.00
Jimi Hendrix, War Heroes (Reprise MS 2103)	1972	$5.00	$10.00	$20.00
Jimi Hendrix, Moods (Trip TLP-9512)	1973	$3.00	$6.00	$12.00
Jimi Hendrix, The Genius of Jimi Hendrix (Trip TLP-9523)	1973	$3.00	$6.00	$12.00
Jimi Hendrix and Little Richard, Jimi Hendrix and Little Richard Together (Pickwick SPC-3347)	1973	$3.00	$6.00	$12.00
Original Motion Picture Soundtrack, Soundtrack Recordings from the Film Jimi Hendrix (Reprise 2RS 6481) (2 LPs)	1973	$6.25	$12.50	$25.00
Jimi Hendrix, Crash Landing (Reprise MS 2204)	1975	$3.75	$7.50	$15.00
Jimi Hendrix, Midnight Lightning (Reprise MS 2229)	1975	$3.75	$7.50	$15.00
Jimi Hendrix, The Very Best of Jimi Hendrix (United Artists UA-LA505-E)	1975	$3.00	$6.00	$12.00
Jimi Hendrix, The Essential Jimi Hendrix (Reprise 2RS 2245) (2 LPs)	1978	$5.00	$10.00	$20.00

LPs	Year	VG	VG+	NM
Jimi Hendrix, The Essential Jimi Hendrix, Volume II (Reprise HS 2293) (2 LPs) (double value if "Gloria" with picture sleeve included)	1979	$3.75	$7.50	$15.00
Jimi Hendrix, Kaleidoscope (Accord SN-7101)	1981	$2.50	$5.00	$10.00
Jimi Hendrix, Before London (Accord SN-7112)	1981	$2.50	$5.00	$10.00
Jimi Hendrix, Cosmic Feeling (Accord SN-7139)	1981	$2.50	$5.00	$10.00
Jimi Hendrix, The Jimi Hendrix Concerts (Reprise 22306) (2 LP's)	1982	$3.00	$6.00	$12.00
Jimi Hendrix, Band of Gypsys 2 (Capitol SJ-12416) (side two lists three songs, actually plays four other songs - vinyl has four tracks)	1986	$37.50	$75.00	$150.00
Jimi Hendrix, Live at Winterland (Ryko Analogue RALP-0038) (2 LPs)	1988	$3.75	$7.50	$15.00
Jimi Hendrix, Radio One (Ryko Analogue RALP-0078) (2 LPs, clear vinyl)	1988	$3.75	$7.50	$15.00
Jimi Hendrix, Axis: Bold as Love (Track 612003) (reissue by Classic Records of original UK mono mix, reproduction of UK label)	2000	$6.25	$12.50	$25.00

Hendrix' only Top 40 hit in America, "All Along The Watchtower," was written by Bob Dylan. From the Collection of Val Shively.

This collection of Jimi Hendrix' recordings for England's Radio One was issued with an "obi," a paper sash commonly found on Japanese albums. From the Collection of Mark Pisani.

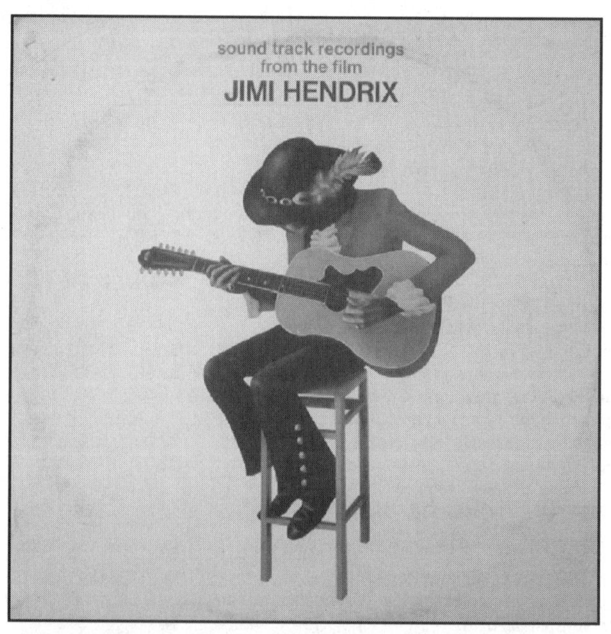

The soundtrack to the motion picture Jimi Hendrix was released as one of many posthumous Jimi Hendrix albums. Courtesy Last Vestige Music Store, Albany, N.Y.

JAZZ

History: Describing "jazz" is akin to describing "sport." The term "jazz music" is an all-encompassing definition, covering such musical styles as bebop, hard bop, fusion, free form, New Orleans jazz, Midwestern jazz—even traditional Dixieland, swing and big band sounds have been grouped into the jazz definition, whether or not they actually are part of that sound.

Jazz is also one of the few musical genres where collectors search for not only a particular musical style, but also how a particular musical instrument is used in that style. There are jazz saxophone fans who search for recordings by Coleman Hawkins, John Coltrane, Charlie "Yardbird" Parker, and Cannonball Adderly. Jazz trumpet collectors will gravitate toward the works of Louis Armstrong, Bix Beiderbecke, Miles Davis, and Dizzy Gillespie. Keyboard enthusiasts will search out the early recordings of Earl "Fatha" Hines, Fats Waller, Thelonious Monk, Dave Brubeck, and Vince Guaraldi.

The legendary saxophone player John Coltrane, an influence on thousands of musicians worldwide. From the Collection of Val Shively.

Even the voice itself has become a powerful jazz instrument, as collectors of music by Bessie Smith, Ethel Waters, Connee Boswell, or Billie Holiday will attest. Among vocal jazz fans, there are also popular "vocalese" performers, artists who use their vocal skills to replace a trumpet solo, adding lyrics that match perfectly with the music and theme. Proponents of "vocalese" jazz include Lambert Hendricks and Ross, Eddie Jefferson, King Pleasure, and the Manhattan Transfer.

King Pleasure, a master of the art of "vocalese."

The first jazz sounds came from New Orleans, a multicultural melting pot where blues, spirituals, Dixieland, and ragtime could be heard from Storyville to the French Quarter. Such New Orleans jazz proponents include Jelly Roll Morton, Kid Ory, Sidney Bechet, and the legendary Buddy Bolden. In 1917, the Original Dixieland Jazz Band recorded "Livery Stable Blues" for Victor Records, the first jazz recording ever preserved on a record.

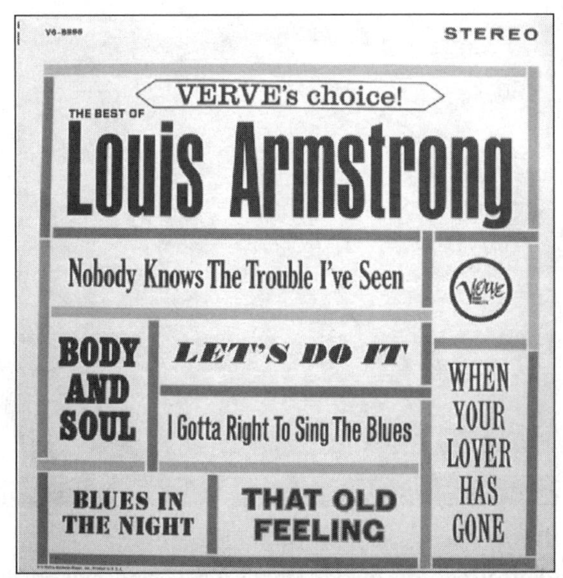

One of the many "Greatest Hits" albums of Louis Armstrong's music; this one was released on the Verve label.

By the 1920s, thousands of African-Americans migrated north to industrial cities like Chicago, Detroit, and Pittsburgh, where factory jobs were plentiful. Chicago became a hotbed for jazz music in the 1920s, as Louis Armstrong, Joe "King" Oliver and Bix Beiderbecke helped jazz to evolve.

Jazz music survived the Depression-era 1930's, evolving into "big band" music. Orchestras and combos crisscrossed America, performing in clubs, halls and arenas, spreading jazz as a new musical message. Fletcher Henderson's big band included, at various times, Coleman Hawkins and Louis Armstrong. Paul Whiteman's big band included Jack Teagarden and Bix Biederbecke. Cab Calloway brought excitement to the stage with every "hi-de-ho"; while Lionel Hampton held double duty as vibraphonist and conductor in his own orchestra.

Some of the greatest big band conductors in the 1930's and 1940's include Duke Ellington, Count Basie, Glenn Miller, Benny Goodman, Tommy Dorsey and James Dorsey. Their orchestras brought swing to jazz music, while their musical orchestrations allowed their musicians the freedom to experiment within the jazz/big band framework.

Roulette Records owner Morris Levy also owned the legendary New York City jazz club Birdland; this cross-promotional Count Basie package has some tremendous recordings.

By 1945, saxophonist Charlie Parker and trumpeter Dizzy Gillespie created new jazz sounds from New York. With its high-spirited melodies and daring orchestrations, this new form of jazz music, known as "bebop," found new popularity in New York's smoky jazz clubs. Besides Parker and Gillespie, other bebop legends include Coleman Hawkins, Buddy Rich, Thelonious Monk, and Sonny Stitt.

Bebop itself eventually split into two different musical styles—Cool Jazz and Hard Bop. West Coast cool jazz was sweeter and mellower, its sound a mixture of bebop and swing, along with classical music from Claude Debussy and George Gershwin. Among the proponents of cool jazz were Miles Davis, whose early 78s were collected into the seminal album *Birth of the Cool*; Dave Brubeck, whose experiments with time signatures created the masterpiece Take Five; and Shorty Rogers, whose albums *Portrait of Shorty and The Shorty Rogers Quintet* are staples of cool jazz libraries.

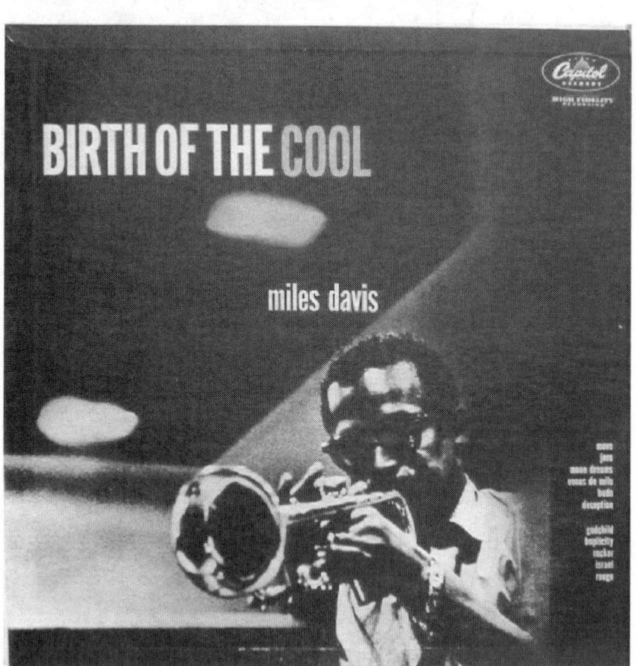

Miles Davis' early 78s were gathered into this LP masterpiece, Birth of the Cool.

Hard bop was not as mellow as cool jazz, but it did have more emotion and passion, its musicians turning their New York City life experiences into powerful musical excursions. Legends of hard bop include Art Blakey and his Jazz Messengers, Dexter Gordon, Clifford Brown, and Sonny Rollins.

Dexter Gordon, one of the proponents of "Hard Bop," with a rare Dootone album release. Courtesy of Good Rockin' Tonight / Collectors Universe.

By the 1960s, jazz evolved into "free jazz," with the soaring sax solos of John Coltrane, the intricate "harmolodics" of Ornette Coleman, and the intergalactic adventures of Sun Ra and his various Arkestras. The 1970s brought a mixture of jazz to rock and roll, creating "fusion." Proponents of this style of jazz music include Chick Corea and Return to Forever; Pat Metheny, Keith Jarrett, Weather Report, and Herbie Hancock.

Many labels had their own jazz division, with special artwork and labels. For this Herbie Mann 45, Atlantic used a blue-and-silver color pattern to their classic label design.

An offshoot of free jazz became "new age" music. This form of jazz music involves lighter, calmer musical excursions, relaxing the mind and freeing the soul. The label most associated with new age music is Windham Hill Records. Windham Hill has featured electic jazz and new age releases by such artists as William Ackerman, Michael Hedges, Alex DeGrassi and Shadowfax. Windham Hill's most successful artist has been pianist George Winston, whose album *December* has become a holiday perennial since its release in 1982.

Windham Hill's biggest selling record, George Winston's December.

Almost every record label had its own jazz division, and re-releases and box sets were not uncommon. In fact, these box sets may have actually increased the popularity of jazz music, by making these recordings more available to consumers today who could not afford rare 1940s and 1950s pressings.

What To Look For: More than any other musical style, the price of collectible jazz has fluctuated greatly. One collector I spoke with even suggested that to get the most accurate prices for rare jazz, you should go to Tokyo for a week, visit the collectible jazz shops, write down the prices in yen, then convert those figures to U.S. dollars.

That being said, the works of many of the original masters are still highly collectible—including first pressings of albums by Charlie Parker, John Coltrane, and Sun Ra. Because of the prolific output of many jazz artists, many of their albums appear as budget-line reissues. These reissues are great to listen to and enjoy while your early pressings of the same title stay safe on the shelves.

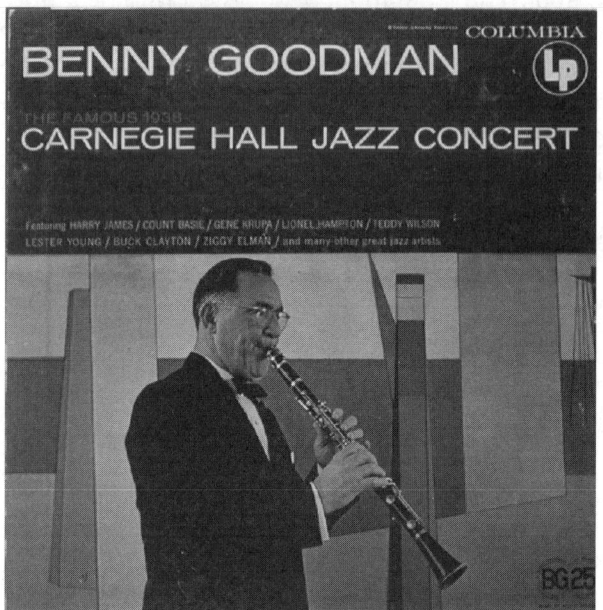

Jazz records as both music and history; this Benny Goodman reissue, timed with the 25th anniversary of Goodman's performing career, chronicles a classic concert with an all-star lineup at Carnegie Hall.

Trivia

The Blue Note record label is one of the most desirous jazz labels, with a rich history of recorded sound. However, many jazz collectors will want the first pressings of a Blue Note album, and to properly determine that the Blue Note disc you own is either an original or a reissue, one needs to examine the record's paper label.

1950s up to 1956: Blue Note albums are pressed with a deep groove that actually penetrates the paper label to the vinyl below.

1956: The label cites Blue Note's address as Lexington Avenue.

1957: The label cites Blue Note's address as West 63rd Street.

1963: The label now says Blue Note's address is New York, USA.

1960s: The label acknowledges Blue Note's affiliation with Liberty Records.

1984: Blue Note labels now say that Blue Note is "The Finest in Jazz Since 1939."

Trivia

Jazz music constantly evolves, as the performers of the present adapt the sound of the past and infuse it with their own stylings and musicianship. For example, in the late 1930s, Coleman Hawkins interpreted the classic song "Body and Soul" into a jazz standard. Twenty years later, Eddie Jefferson used his voice to replicate, with new lyrics and vocals, Coleman Hawkins' version of "Body and Soul." And in 1980, the Manhattan Transfer used Jefferson's techniques to record a version of "Body and Soul" that paid tribute to both jazz legends.

From Coleman Hawkins...

... to Eddie Jefferson...

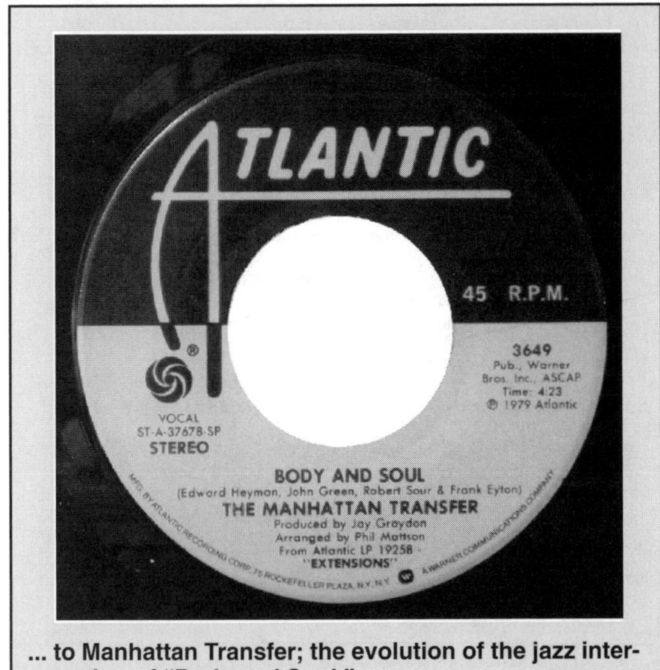

... to Manhattan Transfer; the evolution of the jazz interpretation of "Body and Soul."

Between 1948 and 1955, many record companies pressed 10-inch albums as a standard format. Eventually the 12-inch album became the dominant format for multi-song recordings, but the original 10-inch discs have leaped in value, commanding anywhere from $60 to $500 for near-mint examples of legendary jazz performances.

References: Kofsky, Frank, *Black Nationalism and the Revolution in Music*, Pathfinder Press, New York, N.Y., 1970. Contains insightful interviews and essays on the life of John Coltrane and the jazz culture of the 1940s and 50s. Neely, Tim, *Goldmine Jazz Album Price Guide*, Krause Publications, Iola, Wisconsin, 2000; Sutro, Dirk, *Jazz for Dummies*, IDG Books Worldwide, Foster City, Calif., 1998; Ward, Geoffrey C.; Burns, Ken, *Jazz: A History of America's Music*, Knopf, New York 2000.

Museums: American Jazz Museum, 18th and Vine Streets, Kansas City, Missouri, (816) 474-8463. *http://www.americanjazzmuseum.com*; Graystone International Jazz Museum and Hall of Fame, 249 Washington Boulevard, Suite 201, Detroit, Michigan 48226, (313) 963-3813, *http://hometown.aol.com/gjazzmuseu/front.html.*

Web pages: Blue Note Records, the legendary jazz label: *http://www.bluenote.com.* For the history of jazz before 1930, visit this page: *http://www.redhotjazz.com.* The year 2000 is the 100th anniversary of the birth of Louis Armstrong; this Web page has a history of the man and the legend: *http://www.satchmo.com.* A Web page devoted to the music and careers of John Coltrane and McCoy Tyner: *http://www.jazz.route66.net.* A complete discography of the music of Sun Ra, available at this site: *http://www.dpo.uab.edu/~moudry/discintr.htm.* Usenet newsgroups: *rec.music.bluenote, rec.music.makers.jazz, tw.bbs.music.jazz*

45s	Year	VG	VG+	NM
Cannonball Adderly, "Autumn Leaves" (Pt. 1) / (Pt. 2) (Blue Note 1737)	1959	$2.50	$5.00	$10.00
Cannonball Adderly, "Mercy, Mercy, Mercy" / "Games" (Capitol 5798)	1966		$3.50	$7.00
Louis Armstrong, "Basin Street Blues" (Pt. 1) / (Pt. 2) (Decca 29102)	1954	$3.75	$7.50	$15.00
Louis Armstrong, "Hello Dolly!" / "A Lot Of Lovin' To Do" (Kapp 573)	1964	$3.00	$6.00	
(with picture sleeve, add:)	1964	$2.50	$5.00	$10.00
Count Basie, "Jumpin' At The Woodside" / "Rusty Dusty Blues" (Roulette 4124)	1958	$2.50	$5.00	$10.00
Dave Brubeck, "Take Five" / "Blue Rondo A La Turk" (Columbia 41479)	1960	$3.00	$6.00	$12.00
Chick Corea and Return to Forever, "Spain" / "Captain Marvel" (Polydor 15067)	1973		$3.00	$6.00
Duke Ellington, "The Sidewalks Of New York" / "Don't Get Around Much Anymore" (RCA Victor 47-2955)	1949	$5.00	$10.00	$20.00
Duke Ellington, "Satin Doll" / "Without A Song" (Capitol F2458)	1953	$3.00	$6.00	$12.00
Erroll Garner, "Misty" / "Exactly Like You" (Mercury 70442)	1954	$3.75	$7.50	$15.00
Stan Getz and Astrud Gilberto, "The Girl From Ipanema" / "Corcovado" (Verve 10322)	1964	$2.50	$5.00	$10.00
(if B-side is "Blowin' In The Wind," on Verve 10323)	1964	$2.00	$4.00	$8.00
Herbie Hancock, "Watermelon Man "/ "Three Bags Full" (Blue Note 1862)	1962	$2.00	$4.00	$8.00
Woody Herman, "Prelude To A Kiss" / "Cuban Holiday" (MGM 11661)	1954	$3.75	$7.50	$15.00
Billie Holiday, "Stormy Weather" / "Tenderly" (Mercury 89064)	1953	$5.00	$10.00	$20.00
Manhattan Transfer, "Four Brothers" / "It's Not The Spotlight" (Atlantic 3491)	1978		$2.50	$5.00
Thelonious Monk, "'Round Midnight" / "In Walked Bud" (Blue Note 1664)	195??	$3.75	$7.50	$15.00
Thelonious Monk, "Bye-Ya" / "Hackensack" (Columbia 42825)	1963	$2.50	$5.00	$10.00
Wes Montgomery, Celebrity Scene: Wes Montgomery (Verve CS?-5) (5 7" singles)				
(near-mint condition must include all five singles, jukebox strips, bio and box)	1966	$15.00	$30.00	$60.00
(individual singles, catalog #10440-10444)	1966	$2.50	$5.00	$10.00
George Shearing, "When Your Lover Has Gone" / "Carnegie Horizons" (MGM 10763)	1950	$5.00	$10.00	$20.00
Sonny Stitt, "Thirty-Three Ninety-Six" (Pt. 1) / (Pt. 2) (Prestige 282)	1963	$2.50	$5.00	$10.00
McCoy Tyner, "Duke's Place" / "Searchin'" (Impulse! 240)	1965	$2.00	$4.00	$8.00
Sarah Vaughan, "Tenderly" / "I'll Wait And Pray" (MGM 10705)	1950	$7.50	$15.00	$30.00
Sarah Vaughan, "C'est La Vie" / "Never" (Mercury 70727)	1955	$3.75	$7.50	$15.00
Weather Report, "Birdland" / "Palladium" (Columbia 10532)	1977		$2.50	$5.00

10-inch LPs	Year	VG	VG+	NM
Louis Armstrong, Armstrong Classics (Brunswick BL 58004)	1950	$25.00	$50.00	$100.00
Louis Armstrong and the Mills Brothers, Louis Armstrong and the Mills Brothers (Decca DL 5509)	1954	$15.00	$30.00	$60.00
Count Basie, Count Basie and his Orchestra Collates (Clef MCG-120)	1953	$50.00	$100.00	$200.00
Count Basie, Dance Parade (Columbia CL 6079)	1949	$25.00	$50.00	$100.00
Count Basie, Jazz Royalty (Emarcy MG-26023)	1954	$17.50	$35.00	$70.00
Sidney Bechet, Sidney Bechet's Blue Note Jazz Men (Blue Note BLP-7001)	1950	$100.00	$200.00	$400.00
Art Blakey and his Jazz Messengers, A Night At Birdland, Volume 1 (Blue Note BLP-5037)	1954	$75.00	$150.00	$300.00
Bob Brookmeyer, Bob Brookmeyer with Jimmy (Prestige PRLP-214)	1954	$37.50	$75.00	$150.00
Clifford Brown, New Star on the Horizon (Blue Note BLP-5032)	1953	$125.00	$250.00	$500.00
Cab Calloway, Cab Calloway (Brunswick BL 58101)	1954	$25.00	$50.00	$100.00

10-inch LPs	Year	VG	VG+	NM
Kenny Drew, Introducing the Kenny Drew Trio (Blue Note BLP-5023)	1953	$100.00	$200.00	$400.00
Duke Ellington, Ellingtonia, Volume 1 (Brunswick BL 58002)	1950	$25.00	$50.00	$100.00
Maynard Ferguson, Dimensions (Emarcy MG-26024)	1954	$25.00	$50.00	$100.00
Ella Fitzgerald, Ella Fitzgerald Sings Gershwin Songs (Decca DL 5300)	1951	$30.00	$60.00	$120.00
Erroll Garner, Overture To Dawn, Volume 1 (Blue Note BLP-5007)	1952	$50.00	$100.00	$200.00
(there are five 10-inch LP volumes to "Overture To Dawn," all have equal value as the first volume)				
Stan Getz, The Artistry of Stan Getz (Clef MGC-143)	1953	$50.00	$100.00	$200.00
Dizzy Gillespie, Horn of Plenty (Blue Note BLP-5017)	1953	$75.00	$150.00	$300.00
Lionel Hampton, Rockin' and Groovin' (Blue Note BLP-5046)	1954	$75.00	$150.00	$300.00
Coleman Hawkins, Classics In Jazz (Capitol H 327)	1952	$62.50	$125.00	$250.00
Billie Holiday, Billie Holiday at Jazz at the Philharmonic (Clef MGC-169)	1955	$45.00	$90.00	$180.00
Gene Krupa, Drummin' Man (Columbia CL 2515)	1955	$12.50	$25.00	$50.00
Thelonious Monk, Genius of Modern Music, Vol. 1 (Blue Note BLP-5002)	1952	$100.00	$200.00	$400.00
James Moody, James Moody and His Modernists (Blue Note BLP-5006)	1952	$75.00	$150.00	$300.00
Charlie Parker, Charlie Parker (Dial LP-203)	1949	$200.00	$400.00	$800.00
Charlie Parker, Charlie Parker With Strings				
(if on Mercury MG-35010)	1950	$150.00	$300.00	$600.00
(if on Mercury MGC-101)	1950	$125.00	$250.00	$500.00
(if on Mercury MGC-501)	1951	$125.00	$250.00	$500.00
(if on Clef MGC-501)	1954	$100.00	$200.00	$400.00
Charlie Parker, A Night at Carnegie Hall (Birdland 425)	1956	$75.00	$150.00	$300.00
Ma Rainey, Ma Rainey, Vol. 1 (Riverside RLP-1003)	1953	$62.50	$125.00	$250.00
Max Roach, Max Roach Quartet Featuring Hank Mobley (Debut DLP-13)	1954	$75.00	$150.00	$300.00
Sonny Stitt, Jazz at the Hi-Hat (Roost LP-418)	1954	$75.00	$150.00	$300.00
Art Tatum, Art Tatum (Asch ALP-356)	1950	$37.50	$75.00	$150.00
Sarah Vaughan, The Divine Sarah (Mercury MG-25188)	1955	$25.00	$50.00	$100.00
Fats Waller, Fats Waller Favorites (RCA Victor LPT-14)	1951	$37.50	$75.00	$150.00

12-inch LPs	Year	VG	VG+	NM
Cannonball Adderly, Presenting Cannonball (Savoy MG-12018) (mono)				
(if album cover features the group)	1955	$20.00	$40.00	$80.00
(if album cover features cannonballs, reissue)	196??	$10.00	$20.00	$40.00
(if album is on Savoy Jazz SJC-401, reissue)	1985	$2.50	$5.00	$10.00
Cannonball Adderly, Somethin' Else				
(if on Blue Note BLP-1595, mono, deep groove pressed into label)	1958	$37.50	$75.00	$150.00
(if on Blue Note BST-1595, stereo, deep groove pressed into label)	1959	$25.00	$50.00	$100.00
(if on Blue Note BLP-1595, mono, West 63rd Street address on label)	1958	$25.00	$50.00	$100.00
(if on Blue Note BST-1595, stereo, West 63rd Street address on label)	1959	$18.75	$37.50	$75.00
(if on Blue Note BLP-1595, mono, New York USA address on label)	1963	$6.25	$12.50	$25.00
(if on Blue Note BST-81595, stereo, New York USA address on label)	1963	$5.00	$10.00	$20.00
(if on Blue Note BST-81595, stereo, "A Division of Liberty Records" on label)	1966	$3.75	$7.50	$15.00
(if on Blue Note BM-LA169-F, reissue)	1973	$2.50	$5.00	$10.00
(if on Blue Note LT-169, reissue)	1981	$2.50	$5.00	$10.00
(if on Blue Note BST-81595, stereo, "The Finest in Jazz Since 1939" on label)	1984	$2.50	$5.00	$10.00
(if on Blue Note B1-46338, audiophile reissue)	1997	$5.00	$10.00	$20.00
(if on Blue Note BST-81595, Classic Records reissue)	199??	$6.25	$12.50	$25.00
Louis Armstrong, A Rare Batch of Satch (RCA Victor LPM-2322)	1961	$6.25	$12.50	$25.00
Louis Armstrong, The Louis Armstrong Story, Vol. 1 (Columbia Masterworks ML 4383) (mono)	1951	$12.50	$25.00	$50.00

12-inch LPs	Year	VG	VG+	NM
(if on Columbia CL 851, reissue)	1956	$7.50	$15.00	$30.00
Louis Armstrong, The Complete Decca Recordings of Louis Armstrong And The All-Stars (Mosaic MQ8-146) (8 LP's)	199??	$37.50	$75.00	$150.00
Count Basie, Basie (Roulette R-52003) (mono)	1958	$7.50	$15.00	$30.00
(if on Roulette SR-52003) (stereo) (black vinyl)	1958	$7.50	$15.00	$30.00
(if on Roulette SR-52003) (stereo) (red vinyl)	1958	$25.00	$50.00	$100.00
Sidney Bechet, Jazz Classics, Volume 1 (Blue Note)				
(if on Blue Note BLP-1201, mono, deep groove pressed into label)	1955	$37.50	$75.00	$150.00
(if on Blue Note BLP-1201, mono, Lexington Avenue address on label)	1955	$25.00	$50.00	$100.00
(if on Blue Note BST-81201, rechanelled stereo, label says "A Division of Liberty Records")	1968	$3.00	$6.00	$12.00
Art Blakey and the Jazz Messengers, A Night at Birdland, Volume 1 (Blue Note BLP-1521) (mono)				
(if deep groove pressed into label)	1956	$50.00	$100.00	$200.00
(if Lexington Avenue address on label)	1956	$25.00	$50.00	$100.00
(if West 63rd Street address on label)	1957	$12.50	$25.00	$50.00
(if New York, USA address on label)	1963	$6.25	$12.50	$25.00
Connee Boswell, Connee Boswell and the Original Memphis Five (RCA Victor LPM-1426) (mono)	1957	$10.00	$20.00	$40.00
Clifford Brown, Clifford Brown Memorial Album (Blue Note BNLP-1526) (mono)				
(if deep groove pressed into label)	1956	$50.00	$100.00	$200.00
(if Lexington Avenue address on label)	1956	$37.50	$75.00	$150.00
(if West 63rd Street address on label)	196??	$12.50	$25.00	$50.00
(if New York, USA address on label)	196??	$6.25	$12.50	$25.00
(if on Blue Note BST-81526, rechanelled stereo, "A Division of Liberty Records" on label)	1967	$3.00	$6.00	$12.00
(if on Blue Note BST-81526, "The Finest in Jazz Since 1939" on label)	1985	$2.50	$5.00	$10.00
Dave Brubeck, Time Out Featuring "Take Five"				
(if on Columbia CL 1397, mono, album title is "Time Out")	1960	$6.25	$12.50	$25.00
(if on Columbia CL 1397, mono, "Guaranteed High Fidelity" on red label)	1962	$3.75	$7.50	$15.00
(if on Columbia CL 1397, mono, "360 Sound" on red label)	1966	$3.00	$6.00	$12.00
(if on Columbia CS 8192, stereo, album title is "Time Out")	1960	$7.50	$15.00	$30.00
(if on Columbia CS 8192, stereo, "360 Sound" in black letters on red label)	1962	$5.00	$10.00	$20.00
(if on Columbia CS 8192, stereo, "360 Sound" in white letters on red label)	1966	$3.75	$7.50	$15.00
(if on Columbia CS 8192, orange label)	1971	$3.00	$6.00	$12.00
(if on Columbia PC 8192, album title is "Time Out")	1981	$2.00	$4.00	$8.00
(if on Columbia Jazz Masterpieces CJ 40585, album title is "Time Out")	1987	$2.50	$5.00	$10.00
(if on Columbia/Classic CS 8192, audiophile vinyl)	1995	$6.25	$12.50	$25.00
John Coltrane, Giant Steps				
(if on Atlantic 1311, mono, black label)	1959	$12.50	$25.00	$50.00
(if on Atlantic 1311, mono, orange-purple label with white pinwheel)	1960	$6.25	$12.50	$25.00
(if on Atlantic 1311, mono, orange-purple label with black pinwheel)	1962	$3.75	$7.50	$15.00
(if on Atlantic SD 1311, stereo, green label)	1959	$15.00	$30.00	$60.00
(if on Atlantic SD 1311, stereo, green-blue label with white pinwheel)	1960	$6.25	$12.50	$25.00
(if on Atlantic SD 1311, stereo, green-blue label with black pinwheel)	1962	$3.75	$7.50	$15.00
(if on Atlantic SD 1311, stereo, red-green label)	1969	$3.00	$6.00	$12.00
John Coltrane, The Heavyweight Champion: The Complete Atlantic Recordings (Atlantic-Rhino R1-71984) (12 LPs)	1995	$50.00	$100.00	$200.00
John Coltrane, Blue Train				
(if on Blue Note BLP-1577, mono, deep groove pressed into label)	1957	$37.50	$75.00	$150.00
(if on Blue Note BLP-1577, mono, West 63rd Street address on label)	1957	$25.00	$50.00	$100.00
(if on Blue Note BLP-1577, mono, New York USA address on label)	196??	$7.50	$15.00	$30.00
(if on Blue Note BST-1577, stereo, deep groove pressed into label)	1959	$30.00	$60.00	$120.00
(if on Blue Note BST-1577, stereo, West 63rd Street address on label)	1959	$20.00	$40.00	$80.00
(if on Blue Note BST-1577, stereo, New York USA address on label)	196??	$6.25	$12.50	$25.00

45s	Year	VG	VG+	NM
(if on Blue Note BST-81577, stereo, "A Division of Liberty Records" on label)	1967	$3.75	$7.50	$15.00
(if on Blue Note BST-81577, "The Finest in Jazz Since 1939" on label)	198??	$2.50	$5.00	$10.00
(if on Blue Note B1-81577)	1988	$2.50	$5.00	$10.00
(if on Blue Note B1-46095)	1997	$3.75	$7.50	$15.00
Chick Corea, Now He Sings, Now He Sobs (Solid State SS-18039)	1969	$5.00	$10.00	$20.00
(if on Pacific Jazz LN-10057)	1981	$2.50	$5.00	$10.00
(if on Blue Note B1-90055)	1988	$3.00	$6.00	$12.00
Miles Davis, Birth of the Cool (Capitol T-762) (mono)	1956	$37.50	$75.00	$150.00
(if on Capitol T-1974)	1963	$7.50	$15.00	$30.00
(if on Capitol DT-1974, rechanelled stereo)	196??	$3.00	$6.00	$12.00
(if on Capitol N-16168)	198??	$2.00	$4.00	$8.00
Miles Davis, Bitches Brew (Columbia GP 26) (2 LPs)				
(if "360 Sound Stereo" on red label)	1970	$10.00	$20.00	$40.00
(if orange Columbia label)	1970	$3.75	$7.50	$15.00
(if on Columbia GQ 30997, quadraphonic)	1972	$10.00	$20.00	$40.00
(if on Columbia PG 26, orange label)	1977	$3.00	$6.00	$12.00
(if on Columbia Jazz Masterpieces CJ2 40577)	1987	$3.00	$6.00	$12.00
Kenny Drew, The Modernity of Kenny Drew (Norgran MGN-1066) (mono)	1956	$37.50	$75.00	$150.00
Duke Ellington, The Complete Capitol Recordings of Duke Ellington (Mosaic MQ8-160) (8 LPs)	1997	$37.50	$75.00	$150.00
Duke Ellington, Ellington at Newport '56 (Columbia CL-934)				
(if on red-black label with six "eye" logos) (mono)	1957	$10.00	$20.00	$40.00
(if on red label, "Guaranteed High Fidelity" or "360 Sound" on label) (mono)	1963	$3.75	$7.50	$15.00
(if on Columbia CS 8648, rechanelled stereo)	1963	$3.00	$6.00	$12.00
(if on Columbia PC 8648, budget reissue)	198??	$2.00	$4.00	$8.00
(if on Columbia Jazz Masterpieces, CJ 40587)	1987	$2.50	$5.00	$10.00
Maynard Ferguson, Maynard Ferguson Plays Jazz For Dancing (Roulete R-52038 mono, SR 52038 stereo)	1959	$6.25	$12.50	$25.00
Ella Fitzgerald, Ella Fitzgerald Sings the George and Ira Gershwin Song Book (Verve MGV-4029-5) (5 LPs) (mono)				
(5-album set, must also contain bonus 1 0-inch LP)	1959	$62.50	$125.00	$250.00
(if albums are in walnut box with leather pockets)	1959	$125.00	$250.00	$500.00
Erroll Garner, The Greatest Garner (Atlantic 1227)				
(if on black label)	1956	$10.00	$20.00	$40.00
(if on multi-colored label with white pinwheel)	1961	$3.75	$7.50	$15.00
(if on multi-colored label with black pinwheel)	196??	$3.00	$6.00	$12.00
Stan Getz and Charlie Byrd, Jazz Samba				
(if on Verve V-8432, mono)	1962	$5.00	$10.00	$20.00
(if on Verve V6-8432, stereo)	1962	$6.25	$12.50	$25.00
(if on Verve UMJ-3158, reissue)	198??	$2.50	$5.00	$10.00
(if on Verve 810 061-1, reissue)	198??	$2.50	$5.00	$10.00
(if on DCC Compact Classics LPZ-2011, audiophile vinyl)	1995	$6.25	$12.50	$25.00
Dizzy Gillespie, The Greatest of Dizzy Gillespie (RCAVictor LPM-2398) ("Long Play" on label)	1961	$12.50	$25.00	$50.00
Dizzy Gillespie and Charlie Parker, The Beginning: Diz and Bird (Roost SK-106) (2 LP's) (mono)	1960	$25.00	$50.00	$100.00
Vince Guaraldi, Jazz Impressions of Black Orpheus (Cast Your Fate To The Wind)				
(if on Fantasy 3337, mono, red vinyl)	1962	$10.00	$20.00	$40.00
(if on Fantasy 3337, mono, black vinyl, red label, vinyl is flexible)	1962	$3.75	$7.50	$15.00
(if on Fantasy 3337, mono, black vinyl, red label, vinyl does not flex)	1962	$6.25	$12.50	$25.00
(if on Fantasy 8089, stereo, blue vinyl)	1962	$10.00	$20.00	$40.00
(if on Fantasy 8089, stereo, black vinyl, blue label, vinyl is flexible)	1962	$3.75	$7.50	$15.00
(if on Fantasy 8089, stereo, black vinyl, blue label, vinyl does not flex)	1962	$6.25	$12.50	$25.00
(if on Mobile Fidelity 1-102, audiophile vinyl)	1983	$12.50	$25.00	$50.00
(if on Fantasy OJC-437, reissue)	198??	$2.50	$5.00	$10.00
Lionel Hampton, All American Award Concert at Carnegie Hall (Decca DL 8088) (mono)				
(if label is black with silver print)	1955	$12.50	$25.00	$50.00
(if label has color bars, reissue)	196??	$5.00	$10.00	$20.00
Herbie Hancock, Head Hunters				
(if on Columbia KC 32371)	1973	$3.00	$6.00	$12.00

45s	Year	VG	VG+	NM
(if on Columbia CQ 32371, quadraphonic)	1973	$6.25	$12.50	$25.00
(if on Columbia PC 32371, budget issue)	197??	$2.00	$4.00	$8.00
Coleman Hawkins, At Ease With Coleman Hawkins				
(if on Moodsville MVLP-7, green label)	1960	$12.50	$25.00	$50.00
(if on Moodsville MVLP-7, blue label with trident logo)	1965	$6.25	$12.50	$25.00
(if on Fantasy OJC-181, reissue)	1985	$2.50	$5.00	$10.00
Billie Holiday, Lady Day				
(if on Columbia CL 637, mono, maroon label with gold print)	1954	$17.50	$35.00	$70.00
(if on Columbia CL 637, mono, red-black label with six "eye" logos)	1956	$10.00	$20.00	$40.00
(if on Columbia CL 637, red "Guaranteed High Fidelity" or "360 Sound" on label)	1962	$3.75	$7.50	$15.00
Gene Krupa, Drummin' Man (Columbia C2L 29) (2 LPs) (mono)				
(if red-black labels, six "eye" logos, box set with booklet)	1962	$12.50	$25.00	$50.00
(if booklet is missing from above)	1962	$10.00	$20.00	$40.00
(if red labels, "Guaranteed High Fidelity" or "360 Sound Mono" on label)	1963	$5.00	$10.00	$20.00
Lambert, Hendricks and Ross, Sing A Song of Basie				
(if on ABC-Paramount ABC-223, mono)	1958	$12.50	$25.00	$50.00
(if on ABC-Paramount ABCS-223, stereo)	1958	$12.50	$25.00	$50.00
(if on Impulse! A-83, mono)	1965	$6.25	$12.50	$25.00
(if on Impulse! AS-83, stereo)	1965	$7.50	$15.00	$30.00
(if on ABC Impulse! AS-83, stereo)	1968	$3.75	$7.50	$15.00
Manhattan Transfer, Vocalese (Atlantic 81266)	1985	$2.50	$5.00	$10.00
Pat Metheny, Offramp (ECM 1216)	1983	$3.00	$6.00	$12.00
Charles Mingus, The Jazz Experiment of Charlie Mingus (Bethlehem BCP-65)	1956	$25.00	$50.00	$100.00
Charles Mingus, Mingus at Monterrey (Charles Mingus Records JWS-001/2) (2 LPs)				
(if single-pocket jacket, with sepia-tone photo on front)	1966	$175.00	$350.00	$700.00
(if gatefold jacket, color photo on front, reference to album's availability only by mail order on back cover)	1966	$75.00	$150.00	$300.00
(if gatefold jacket, color photo on front, reference to distribution by Fantasy)	1968	$15.00	$30.00	$60.00
(if on Fantasy JWS/001/2, reissue)	1969	$5.00	$10.00	$20.00
(if on Prestige 24100, reissue)	198??	$3.75	$7.50	$15.00
Thelonious Monk, Genius of Modern Music, Vol. 1 (Blue Note BLP-1510)				
(if on Blue Note BLP-1510, mono, deep groove pressed into label)	1956	$50.00	$100.00	$200.00
(if on Blue Note BLP-1510, mono, Lexington Avenue address on label)	1956	$37.50	$75.00	$150.00
(if on Blue Note BLP-1510, mono, "New York, USA" address on label)	1963	$6.25	$12.50	$25.00
(if on Blue Note BLP-81510, rechanelled stereo)	1968	$2.50	$5.00	$10.00
(if on Blue Note BST-81510, "The Finest in Jazz Since 1939" on label, reissue)	1985	$2.50	$5.00	$10.00
Thelonious Monk and John Coltrane, Thelonious Monk with John Coltrane				
(if on Jazzland JLP-46, mono)	1961	$10.00	$20.00	$40.00
(if on Jazzland JLP-946, stereo)	1961	$12.50	$25.00	$50.00
(if on Riverside RLP-490, mono reissue)	1965	$6.25	$12.50	$25.00
(if on Riverside RS-94090, stereo reissue)	1965	$7.50	$15.00	$30.00
(if on Fantasy OJC-039, reissue)	198??	$2.00	$5.00	$10.00
James Moody, Moody's Mood For Love				
(if on Argo LP-613, mono, first pressings)	1957	$10.00	$20.00	$40.00
(if on Cadet LP-613, mono, reissue)	1966	$3.75	$7.50	$15.00
Oliver Nelson, The Blues and the Abstract Truth				
(if on Impulse! A-5, mono, art cover)	1961	$12.50	$25.00	$50.00
(if on Impulse! A-5, mono, photo cover)	196??	$5.00	$10.00	$20.00
(if on Impulse! AS-5, stereo, art cover)	1961	$25.00	$50.00	$100.00
(if on Impulse! AS-5, stereo photo cover)	196??	$7.50	$15.00	$30.00
(if on ABC Impulse! AS-5)	1968	$3.75	$7.50	$15.00
(if on MCA 29063)	1980	$2.50	$5.00	$10.00
(if on MCA Impulse! MCA-5659)	1985	$3.00	$6.00	$12.00
(if on GRP Impulse! IMP-154, on audiophile vinyl)	1995	$3.75	$7.50	$15.00
Ken Nordine, Word Jazz (Dot DLP-3075) (mono)	1958	$10.00	$20.00	$40.00
(if on Dot DLP-25075, stereo)	1959	$12.50	$25.00	$50.00
Charlie Parker, The Bird Blows the Blues				
(if on Dial LP-1, available through mail-order only)	1949	$1,000.00	$2,000.00	$4,000.00

45s	Year	VG	VG+	NM
(if on Dial LP-901, mono)	1950	$150.00	$300.00	$600.00
Charlie Parker, The Complete Dean Benedetti Recordings of Charlie Parker (Mosaic 129) (10 LPs)	199??	$25.00	$50.00	$100.00
Ma Rainey, Ma Rainey (Riverside RLP 12-108)	1955	$50.00	$100.00	$200.00
Return To Forever, The Best of Return To Forever (Columbia JC 36359)	1980	$2.50	$5.00	$10.00
(if on Columbia PC 36359, budget reissue)	198??	$2.00	$4.00	$8.00
Max Roach, Jazz in 3/4 Time				
(if on Emarcy MG-36108, mono)	1957	$25.00	$50.00	$100.00
(If on Emarcy SR-80002, stereo)	1959	$20.00	$40.00	$80.00
(if on Trip 5559, reissue)	197??	$2.50	$5.00	$10.00
(if on Mercury 826 456-1, reissue)	1986	$2.50	$5.00	$10.00
Sonny Rollins, A Night at the Village Vanguard				
(if on Blue Note BLP-1581, mono, deep groove pressed into label)	1958	$30.00	$60.00	$120.00
(if on Blue Note BLP-1581, mono, W. 63rd St. address on label)	1958	$20.00	$40.00	$80.00
(if on Blue Note BLP-1581, mono, "New York, USA" address on label)	1963	$6.25	$12.50	$25.00
(if on Blue Note BST-81581, rechanelled stereo, "A Division of Liberty Records" on label)	1967	$3.00	$6.00	$12.00
(if on Blue Note BST-81581, mono, "The Finest in Jazz Since 1939" on label, now listed as Volume 1)	1987	$2.50	$5.00	$10.00
George Shearing, The Complete Capitol Live Recordings of George Shearing (Mosaic MQ7-157) (7 LPs)	199??	$30.00	$60.00	$120.00
Spiro Gyra, Morning Dance				
(if on Infinity INF-9004)	1979	$3.00	$6.00	$12.00
(if on Nautilus NR-9, audiophile vinyl)	1979	$10.00	$20.00	$40.00
(if on MCA 37148, reissue)	198??	$2.00	$4.00	$8.00
Sonny Stitt, Stitt Plays Bird (Atlantic 1418) (mono)	1964	$7.50	$15.00	$30.00
(if on Atlantic SD 1418, stereo)	1964	$10.00	$20.00	$40.00
Sun Ra, Super-Sonic Jazz (Saturn SRLP-0216)				
(if blank cover)	1957	$37.50	$75.00	$150.00
(if silkscreened cover)	1957	$75.00	$150.00	$300.00
(if purple "keyboard" cover)	1958	$37.50	$75.00	$150.00
(if blue or green cover, reissue)	1965	$12.50	$25.00	$50.00
Sun Ra, A Black Mass (Jihad 1968)				
(if colored cover)	1968	$25.00	$50.00	$100.00

45s	Year	VG	VG+	NM
(if black-white cover)	1968	$37.50	$75.00	$150.00
Art Tatum, Here's Art Tatum (Brunswick BL 54004) (mono)	1955	$30.00	$60.00	$120.00
Art Tatum, The Tatum Solo Masterpieces (Pablo 2625 703) (13 LPs)	197??	$25.00	$50.00	$100.00
Toots Thielmans, Man Bites Harmonica (Riverside RLP 12-257) (mono)	1958	$25.00	$50.00	$100.00
(if on Fantasy OJC-1738, reissue)	198??	$2.50	$5.00	$10.00
Stanley Turrentine, Look Out!				
(if on Blue Note BLP-4039, mono, deep groove pressed into label)	1960	$30.00	$60.00	$120.00
(if on Blue Note BLP-4039, mono, W. 63rd St. address on label)	1960	$20.00	$40.00	$80.00
(if on Blue Note BLP-4039, mono, "New York, USA" address on label)	1963	$6.25	$12.50	$25.00
(if on Blue Note BST-84039, stereo, W. 63rd St. address on label)	1960	$15.00	$30.00	$60.00
(if on Blue Note BST-84039, stereo, "New York, USA" address on label)	1963	$5.00	$10.00	$20.00
(if on Blue Note BST-94039, stereo, "A Division of Liberty Records" on label)	1967	$3.75	$7.50	$15.00
McCoy Tyner, Inception				
(if on Impulse! A-18, mono)	1962	$6.25	$12.50	$25.00
(if on Impulse! AS-18, stereo)	1962	$6.25	$12.50	$25.00
(if on ABC Impulse! AS-18)	1968	$3.00	$6.00	$12.00
(if on GRP Impulse! 220, on audiophile vinyl)	1997	$5.00	$10.00	$20.00
Weather Report, Heavy Weather (Columbia PC 34418) (without UPC bar code on back cover)	1977	$3.00	$6.00	$12.00
(if on Columbia PC 34418, with bar code, budget reissue)	198??	$2.00	$4.00	$8.00
(if on Columbia HC 44418, half-speed mastered audiophile release)	198??	$10.00	$20.00	$40.00
Paul Whiteman Orchestra, The Night I Played At 666 Fifth (Grand Award GA-241 SD) (stereo)	1960	$7.50	$15.00	$30.00
(if on GA-33-409, mono)	1960	$5.00	$10.00	$20.00
George Winston, December				
(if on Windham Hill C-1025, "December" in black letters)	1982	$3.75	$7.50	$15.00
(if on Windham Hill WD-1025, distributed by A&M, "December" in raised white letters)	1982	$3.00	$6.00	$12.00

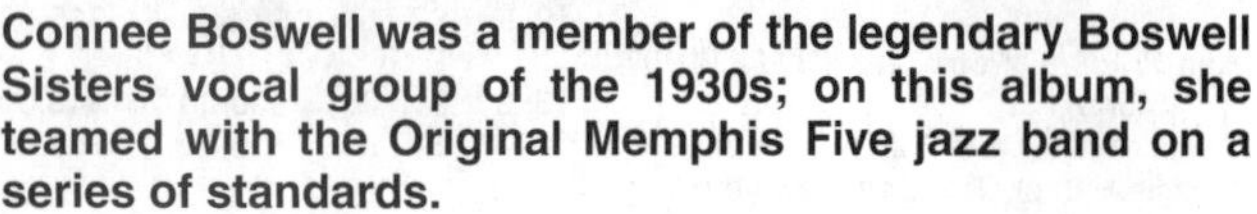
Connee Boswell was a member of the legendary Boswell Sisters vocal group of the 1930s; on this album, she teamed with the Original Memphis Five jazz band on a series of standards.

While today's pop music fans might appreciate the Johnny Mathis version (or the Ray Stevens "banjo and fiddle" version), pianist Erroll Garner wrote the classic song "Misty."

JUKEBOX RECORDS AND TITLE STRIPS

History: Jukeboxes have been an essential staple in bars, soda shops, and diners, almost as much a part of Americana diner chic as white-suited soda jerks and chrome-edged Formica tables. Customers dropped their pocket change into the jukebox coin slot, selected a series of titles by pushing an alphanumeric combination of buttons, then they watched (or danced) as the jukebox's inner mechanism extracted their favorite song from a rack of 45s, and played that very record.

The first coin-operated jukebox was created in San Francisco in 1889. A saloon owner offered four acoustic listening tubes to his Edison phonograph, and for a few coins in hand, listeners could enjoy two minutes of a cylinder disc. By 1927, a jukebox that could electronically reproduce sound, as opposed to the previous acoustic models, was successfully released to the market. The price of a song—five cents per play—was economically feasible to millions of listeners, who poured millions of nickels into jukeboxes throughout the Great Depression and World War II.

The major manufacturers of the day—Seeburg, Wurlitzer, Rock-ola—not only built functional music machines, but some jukeboxes, including the legendary Wurlitzer 1015, have become works of art, both in the industrial and pop culture fields. The jukebox has also made its way into Top 40 music, with references in such songs as Olivia Newton-John's "Please Mr. Please," the Stray Cats' "Rock This Town," Jim Reeves' "He'll Have To Go," and the Flirts' "Jukebox (Don't Put Another Dime In the Jukebox)."

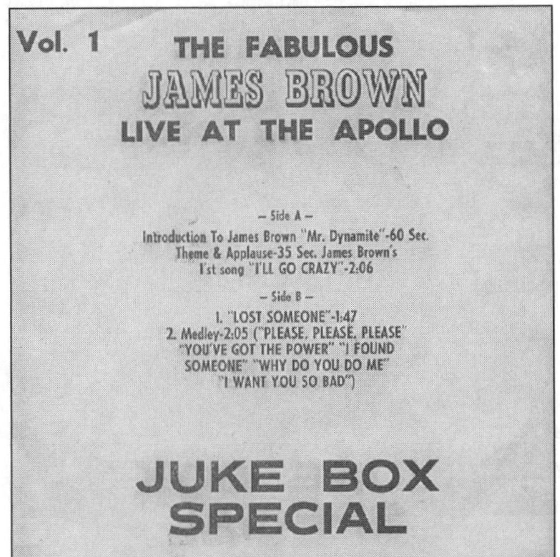

King Records released this 4-song 45 RPM EP so James Brown fans can get a taste of the Godfather of Soul's performance at the Apollo Theatre. Courtesy Good Rockin' Tonight/Collectors Universe.

Independent contractors, the same people who maintained the pinball machine at the diner, would insert new records into the jukebox every month, and remove the less profitable or out-of-date singles. The contractor and the diner owner might split the profits from the jukebox's coin slots, with other portions from the proceeds going to the record companies, the publishing houses, and the artists. Truly this was a "pay-for-play" operation.

While record companies supplied jukebox operators with plenty of the top hits, the jukebox companies had to produce their own specialized title strips—little sheets of paper that were inserted into the jukebox's front grid.

Ronnie Dove's classic ballad, "One Kiss For Old Time's Sake," along with five title strips (on page 157).

But by the late 1950s, some jukeboxes were specially modified to allow a new recording format—the "Little LP," a 7-inch, 33 rpm miniaturized replica of the most popular record albums of the day (albeit with only four to six tracks listed). These records were placed in special 33 RPM jukebox slots, so that when a customer selected this "little LP," the mechanism would automatically play the record at a slower speed. Naturally, the most collectible "Little LPs" from the 1960s are by popular artists like the Beatles, the Monkees, James Brown and the Rolling Stones; since these recordings were pressed in such small quantities, their collectible value is very high.

Trivia

Even jazz labels put out their own "Little LPs" for jukeboxes. As can be seen below, Donald Byrd's A New Perspective comes complete with title strips, 2 x 2 miniature album images, and—most of all—some hot jazz.

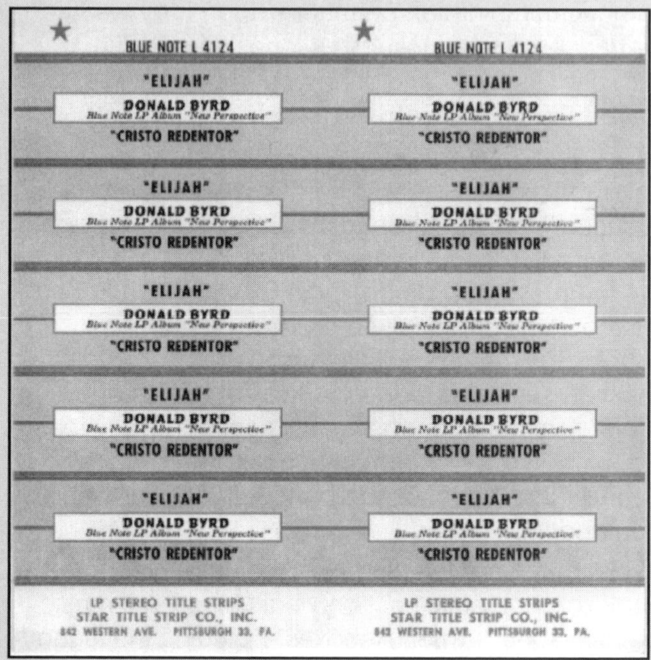

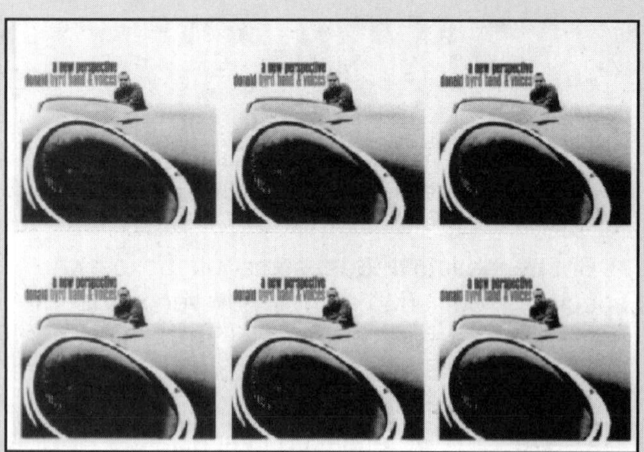

A full package for a jukebox LP; Blue Note Records artist Donald Byrd is part of a complete package. Courtesy Ross Bacon of Shyney Records

These "Little LPs" came with at least ten title strips and six 2" x 2" replications of the original album artwork. This allowed the jukebox owner or operator to put a title strip and the cover into the main jukebox at a diner or club, and put strips and miniature graphics into the "wallboxes" adorning the dining tables. Some record companies even produced an "Operator Pack," which incorporated the title strips and miniature graphics into the picture sleeve artwork itself.

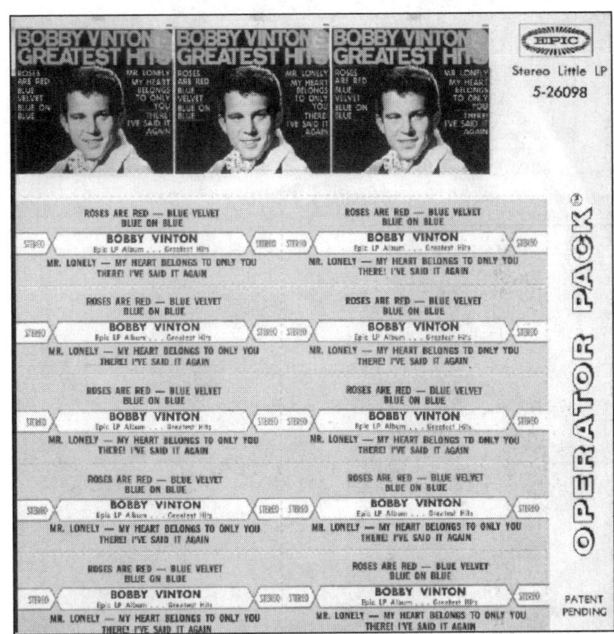

An example of an "Operator Pack," with the title strips attached as part of the record cover.

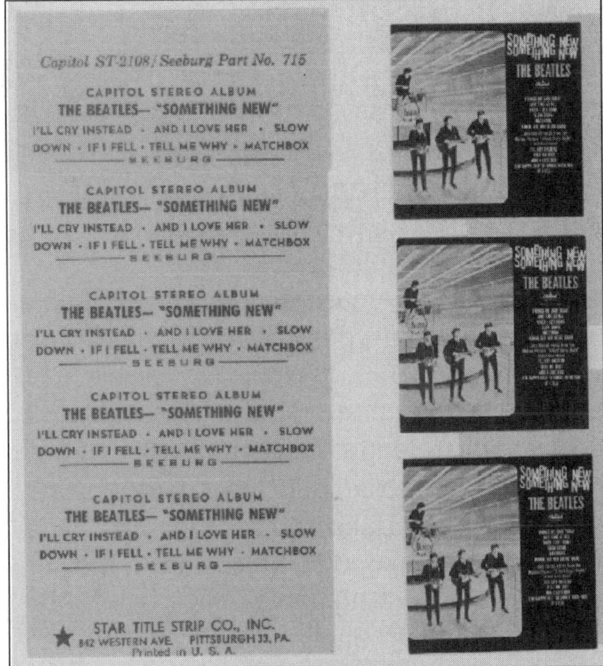

Selections from the Beatles' first three Capitol LPs were also released as jukebox-only mini-albums. These title strips came from the Beatles mini-album Something New. From the Collection of Bruce Spizer.

In the 1970s, a new company made "Little LPs" for jukeboxes. The "Little LPs Unlimited" company of Danbury, Connecticut received a license to press 7-inch, 33 1/3 RPM small-holed records, and made some collectible pressings by Steely Dan, the Grateful Dead, Alice Cooper, and Three Dog Night. Unlike the previous jukebox albums, Little LPs had monochromatic artwork, almost as if the original album jacket was photocopied onto colored paper. The paper label on the vinyl releases, however, were full color and replicated the major label releases of the day. Once again, the recordings came with ten detachable title strips, suitable for insertion into a jukebox title rack. The Danbury company also pressed some quadraphonic 45s for four-speaker jukeboxes; these records are extremely hard to find today.

A "Little LP" version of the Grateful Dead's album *American Beauty*, including the title strips.

Eventually, of course, the title strips would disappear or tear, forcing the jukebox owner to insert generic strips of handwritten or typed paper into the title slots. As you can imagine, even if those slips say "Elvis," "Beatles," or "Springsteen," if they're handwritten, they're worthless. Unless that's Bruce Springsteen's autograph on that title strip...

Although today's jukeboxes are designed to play CDs instead of 45s, there are still thousands of working 45 RPM jukeboxes in America; and many record companies still make a few 7-inch titles for the jukebox market. These 45s will often say "For Jukeboxes Only!" on the label, but may contain colored vinyl or a different mix of the song.

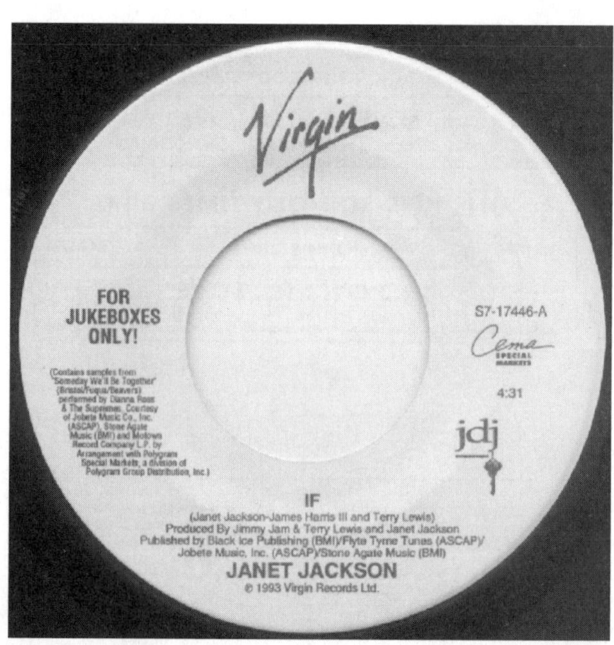

A #1 hit for Janet Jackson, but the 7-inch vinyl copies of *"If"* were stamped "For Jukeboxes Only!"

Since 1989, the Amusement and Music Operators Association have posted a list of the 40 most played jukebox hits. Of these, Patsy Cline's "Crazy" is at the top of this chart, followed by Bob Seger and the Silver Bullet Band's "Old Time Rock and Roll," Elvis Presley's double-sided "Hound Dog"/"Don't Be Cruel", and Bobby Darin's "Mack the Knife." And depending on the mood of the customer, the jukebox can play everything from tender ballads (the Righteous Brothers "Unchained Melody"), a singalong (Garth Brooks' "Friends in Low Places") or a happy birthday wish (it seemed every jukebox had a copy of "Happy Birthday" as one of the last selections available).

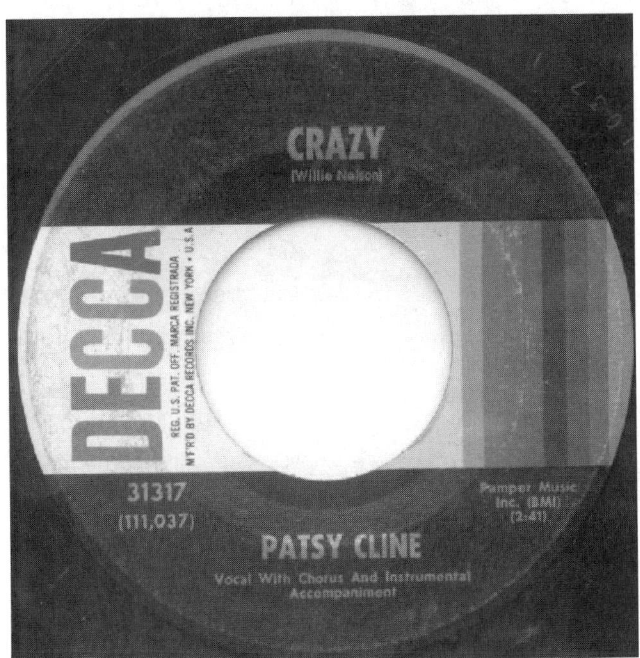

The most popular jukebox song of all time, Patsy Cline's "Crazy."

What To Look For: Thanks to new computer programs that can allow you to make your own custom title strips that look as authentic as the original strips, title strip counterfeiting is rampant. But here are some clues to alert you to real strips and to reproductions.

Original title strips were machine-printed on very thin cardstock, and are pre-perforated. The colored lines were already pre-printed on the paper. The backgrounds will have a checkerboard pattern of tiny colored dots against a white background, that give the illusion of a lighter shade. And titles often are misspelled or edited, in an effort to squeeze a long name onto a short piece of paper.

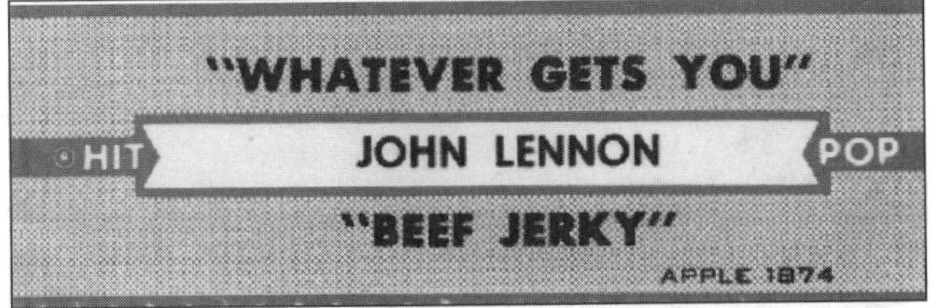

John Lennon's "Whatever Gets You Though The Night" title strip, with a few words missing.

Since blank title strips are often too small to fit through ink printers or laser printers, most computer programs will print both the frame and the titles simultaneously. Reproductions have been printed on everything from photographic paper to white bond. The edges may show signs of scissors cutting, and will have no perforation points. In other words, the reproductions look much better than the originals.

For a jukebox LP to be considered "near mint," not only must the vinyl and jacket conform to the near-mint standards listed in this book's introduction, but the title strips and 2 x 2 squares must be in an uncut, untorn, unperforated state. If the paper inserts are missing, the value of the record drops by at least one-third. If the inserts are still with the package, but are decollated, or if some strips are torn or missing, deduct anywhere from 10-20% of the record's grade.

Trivia

Although jukebox LPs often contained the one or two hit singles from an artist's concurrent 12-inch album, it also contained three or four duds or filler songs. And often the two hits were on either side of the jukebox LP, which was perfect for maximizing profits. You could put the two 45s in and play each one for 10 cents a song—or spend 50 cents for two plays of a jukebox LP.

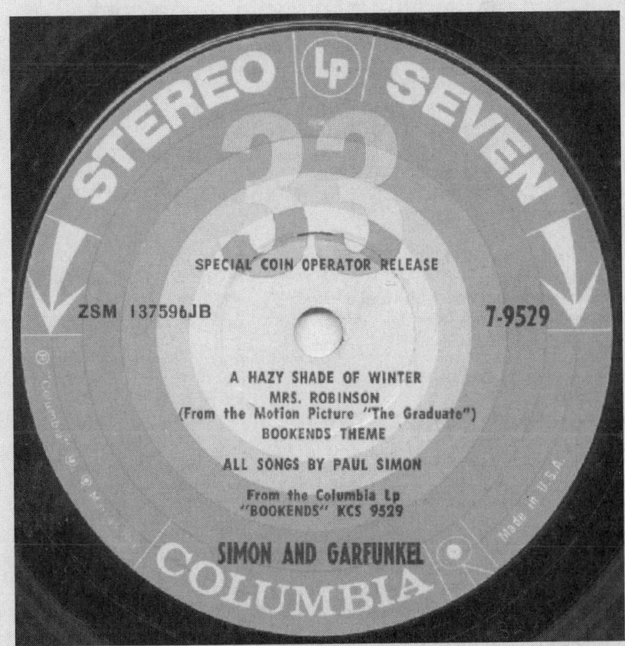

Simon and Garfunkel's *Bookends* jukebox LP, which featured "Mrs. Robinson" sandwiched between two lesser-known tracks.

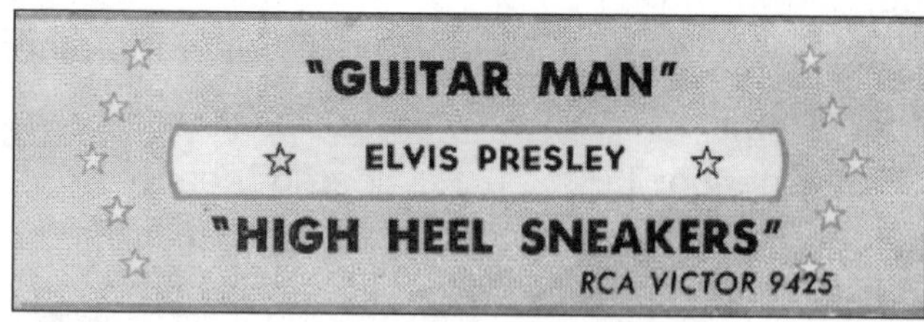

Among title strip collectors, Elvis Presley's "Guitar Man" is about as common as the 45 it represents. The difficulty in finding Presley's original jukebox title strips have caused a boom in counterfeit and "fantasy" title strips, most made on a home computer.

Jukebox records that are in the best possible condition are the ones that never were put in the machine. Because of a jukebox's heavy tracking tonearm, records extracted from jukeboxes are usually worn and hissy. The label will often have scuff or wear marks on one side, depending on the jukebox's disc selection mechanism.

Web pages: For more information on jukeboxes and their contents, visit this site: *http://tomszone.com.* Jay Hardwig wrote an excellent article for the *Austin Chronicle* on the jukebox and its effect on country music and Texas bars, "Hot Line to Jesus." It is accessible at this Web page: *http://www.auchron.com/issues/vol17/issue51/music.jukebox.htm.* The Amusement and Music Operators Association, a trade association dedicated to jukeboxes and the like, has its their own homepage: *http://www.amoa.com.*

Little LPs (6-song, 33 1/3 rpm, 7")	Year	VG	VG+	NM
(must include all paper material, including title strips, to qualify as near-mint)				
The Beach Boys, Surfer Girl (Capitol SXA-1981)	1963	$75.00	$150.00	$300.00
The Beatles, Meet the Beatles (Capitol SXA-2047)	1964	$187.50	$375.00	$750.00
The Beatles, The Beatles' Second Album (Capitol SXA-2080)	1964	$187.50	$375.00	$750.00
The Beatles, Something New (Capitol SXA-2108)	1964	$312.50	$625.00	$1,250.00
Bill Black's Combo, Bill Black's Combo Goes Big Band (Hi SBG 26)	196??	$5.00	$10.00	$20.00
Blood Sweat & Tears, Blood Sweat & Tears 4 (Columbia 7-30590)	1971	$6.25	$12.50	$25.00
James Brown, Live at the Apollo (King 826)	1963	$50.00	$100.00	$200.00
Chicago, Colour My World (Columbia 7-KGP 24)	1971	$8.75	$17.50	$35.00
The Dave Clark Five, The Dave Clark Five's Greatest Hits (Epic E 26185)	1966	$35.00	$70.00	$150.00
Alice Cooper, Muscle of Love (Little LP's 235)	1973	$10.00	$20.00	$40.00
Deep Purple, Burn (Warner Bros. S 2766)	1974	$6.25	$12.50	$25.00
The Doobie Brothers, What Were Once Vices Are Now Habits (Warner Bros. S 2750)	1974	$5.00	$10.00	$20.00
The Four Seasons, Genuine Imitation Life Gazette (Philips 2704)	1968	$10.00	$20.00	$40.00
Freddie and the Dreamers, Fun Lovin' Freddie (Mercury SRC 661-C)	1965	$10.00	$20.00	$40.00
Marvin Gaye, Marvin Gaye Greatest Hits (Tamla 5708)	1967	$12.50	$25.00	$50.00
Robert Goulet, My Love, Forgive Me (Columbia 7-9096)	1964	$5.00	$10.00	$20.00
The Grateful Dead, American Beauty (Warner Bros. S 1893)	1973	$12.50	$25.00	$50.00

Little LPs (6-song, 33 1/3 rpm, 7")	Year	VG	VG+	NM
The Ink Spots, Best of the Ink Spots (Decca 7182)	1972	$2.50	$5.00	$10.00
Elton John, Tumbleweed Connection (Uni 1903)	1971	$8.75	$17.50	$35.00
Elton John, Don't Shoot Me, I'm Only The Piano Player (MCA 349671)	1973	$7.50	$15.00	$30.00
Led Zeppelin, Led Zeppelin IV (Atlantic 7208)	1971	$50.00	$100.00	$200.00
Led Zeppelin, Houses of the Holy (Atlantic 7255)	1973	$37.50	$75.00	$150.00
Lulu, Lulu Sings To Sir With Love (Epic 5-26339)	1967	$7.50	$15.00	$30.00
The Monkees, The Monkees (Colgems CGLP-101)	1967	$75.00	$150.00	$300.00
The Monkees, More of the Monkees (Colgems CGLP-102)	1967	$75.00	$150.00	$300.00
Ricky Nelson, Best Always (Decca 34319)	1966	$18.75	$37.50	$75.00
Roy Orbison, Roy Orbison's Greatest Hits (Monument 506-1)	1967	$12.50	$25.00	$50.00
Peter Paul and Mary, Late Again (Warner Bros. 1751)	1968	$6.25	$12.50	$25.00
Elvis Presley, Aloha From Hawaii Via Satellite (RCA Victor 2006)	1973	$25.00	$50.00	$100.00
The Rascals, Once Upon A Dream (Atlantic 8169)	1968	$6.25	$12.50	$25.00
Jim Reeves, The Best of Jim Reeves, Vol. II (RCA Victor 3482)	1966	$6.25	$12.50	$25.00
The Rolling Stones, 12 x 5 (London 23)	1968	$100.00	$200.00	$400.00
The Rolling Stones, Their Satanic Majesties Request (London 54) (flat image, no 3-D cover)	1968	$112.50	$225.00	$450.00
The Rolling Stones, Exile on Main Street (Atlantic 22900)	1973	$50.00	$100.00	$200.00
Todd Rundgren, Something/Anything (Bearsville 2066)	1972	$10.00	$20.00	$40.00
Seals and Crofts, Unborn Child (Warner Bros. S 2761)	1974	$3.00	$6.00	$12.00
The Supremes, I Hear A Symphony (Motown 643)	1965	$6.25	$12.50	$25.00
The Supremes and the Four Tops, The Magnificent Seven (Motown 60717)	1970	$4.50	$9.00	$18.00
Conway Twitty, Look Into My Teardrops (Decca 34437)	1966	$6.25	$12.50	$25.00
Bobby Vinton, Sealed With A Kiss (Epic 31642)	1970	$3.00	$6.00	$12.00
Neil Young, Harvest (Reprise LLP 183)	1972	$10.00	$20.00	$40.00

This label for songs from Elton John's album *Don't Shoot Me, I'm Only The Piano Player* features the last images of the rainbow Decca label, even though the stock album and 45 of "Crocodile Rock" were released on the "black rainbow" MCA label.

KISS

History: Kiss took theatrical rock to a new level. With their kabuki face paint, studded leather costumes, and a pyrotechnic stage show, Kiss brought the theatrical style of Alice Cooper and David Bowie to a new level. Their thunder-crunching, fist-pounding rock songs captured the ears of millions of fans, and the band's self-marketing schemes brought promotional tactics to a whole new level.

Kiss was formed in 1974 by New Yorkers Gene Simmons and Paul Stanley. Peter Criss and Ace Frehley joined the group after answering newspaper ads. While their early albums sold respectably, Kiss made their mark as a touring band, winning thousands of fans over with their theatrical live shows.

Their unique face paint, which transformed the four musicians into the Star Child (Stanley), the Demon (Simmons), the Cat (Criss), and the Space Ace (Frehley), changed the group from mild-mannered musicians to full-fledged superhero rockers. The makeup also allowed fans in the back rows to clearly see the musicians on stage—and when the makeup was wiped off, the band could leave an arena unrecognized.

By 1975, Kiss started to win over radio stations. Their first Top 40 hit was a live recording of one of their early songs, "Rock and Roll All Nite." Other rock anthems followed, including "Shout It Out Loud," "Detroit Rock City" and "Calling Dr. Love."

This promotional greatest hits package of Kiss' *First Kiss Last Licks* has a very unique cover: The band members are shown both with and without makeup. No other album shows the group in both formats.

But surprisingly, it was their non-rock songs that made the most impact on radio. The power ballad "Beth" was originally the B-side of "Detroit Rock City," but was flipped over to the A-side when radio stations couldn't stop playing the tender song.

During the late 1970s, the Kiss image was marketed for almost every souvenir product available: there were Kiss dolls, you could play a Kiss pinball machine (which played "Rock and Roll All Nite" when you gave it a quarter), you could eat your lunch out of a Kiss lunchbox, and you could even read Kiss comic books (as part of a publicity stunt, each Kiss member donated a vial of his own blood, which was poured into the comic book publisher's ink presses).

Their promotional excursion continued into 1978, when all four members released simultaneous solo albums and singles. Of the four LPs, Gene Simmons' album sold the most copies, while Ace Frehley's "New York Groove" was the biggest solo single.

Ace Frehley's solo hit during his years with Kiss; he would later form a band called Frehley's Comet.

The 1980s saw a change in lineup; while Stanley and Simmons remained with the band, Frehley and Criss quit for solo careers. A rotating series of guitarists and drummers came and went, while Kiss recorded songs in new genres—power ballads ("World Without Heroes"), disco ("I Was Made For Lovin' You"), and speed metal ("Creatures of the Night").

By 1984, Kiss did something their fans would not think possible—they appeared at a press conference without their traditional facepaint. The publicity stunt worked, and their albums and singles returned to the charts. Stanley and Simmons remained constants with the band, but the drumming and guitar positions continued to be filled by other musicians.

In 1996, the old wounds between the four original Kiss members finally healed. Proving that one can go home again, Kiss put the makeup and facepaint back on, and toured to sold-out crowds all over North America.

Trivia

Kiss' first national TV appearance was on a Paul Lynde holiday special. They performed "Detroit Rock City" and "Beth," and had to endure Lynde's one-liner about how as kids, the bandmembers fought with each other, until their parents told them to "kiss and make up."

Peter Criss wrote and sang lead on "Beth," Kiss' biggest radio hit.

What To Look For: Almost from their first releases, Kiss knew the importance of collectibility in terms of their vinyl releases. Almost every record was packed with fan club applications, souvenir catalogs, and special prizes like temporary tattoos, posters, and cardboard cutouts. For near-mint condition, all these "prizes" must remain in the record jacket, uncut, untrimmed, and un-tattooed.

During the 1970s, Kiss' 45s were packaged in simple Casablanca sleeves. A couple of their singles, however, were packaged with picture sleeves. One of the rarest sleeves is for "Flaming Youth"/"God of Thunder," and in near-mint condition can fetch $60 for a Kiss collector.

Be aware that thousands of Kiss albums from the late 1970s, including the band's four simultaneous solo albums, may have a notched cover. Kiss may have sold millions of records, but sometimes their record company over-estimated sales and printed more albums that were sold. These discs eventually made their way to the "cutout bin" of the record store, where they were sold for less than cost.

Kiss' early records were on the Casablanca label, and the label artwork changed styles over the years. In 1974, their records were on blue "Bogart" labels, with a stylized rendering of Humphrey Bogart at the 8:00 position of the label. The first singles were distributed by Warner Bros. Records, and says so on the lower perimeter of the label.

This early Kiss single was released during the time when Casablanca Records was distributed by Warner Bros. From the Collection of Val Shively.

Between 1974 and 1976, the "Bogart" artwork remained on the label, but the Warner Bros. references were deleted from the perimeter. At this time, Kiss' albums were selling extremely well, but their singles had not yet cracked the charts. It was not until a live version of "Rock and Roll All Nite" hit the charts, that Kiss' singles began to find radio airplay.

In 1976, Casablanca changed its labels again, this time to a tan label with an oasis-and-camels motif. Kiss' first single on this label was the double-sided "Detroit Rock City" and "Beth." "Detroit Rock City" was initially the planned "A" side of the single, but "Beth" received more airplay and later became Kiss' first Top 10 hit.

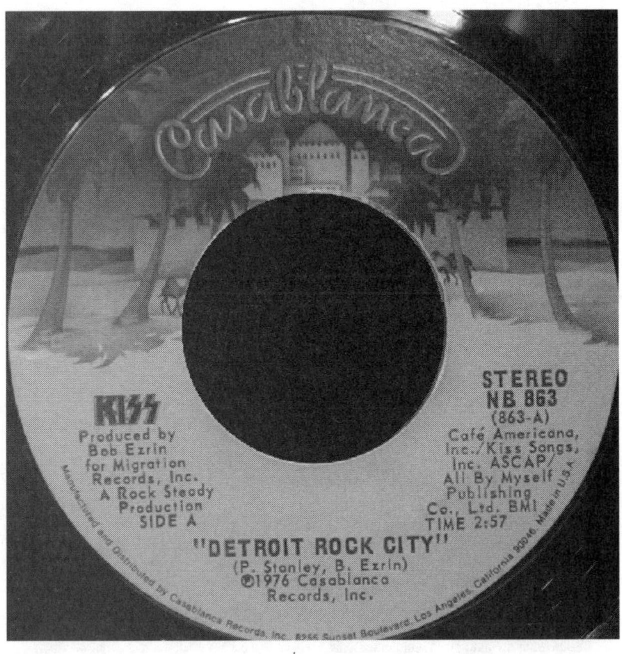

Pressings that list "Detroit Rock City" as the "A" side are hard to find today. From the Collection of Val Shively.

By 1977, Casablanca Records acquired a film studio, and the label was changed again, this time adding cameras and lights to the oasis. The company sleeves also were changed—1976 sleeves were covered with camel silhouettes; 1977 sleeves showed camels morphing into cameras.

Collecting Kiss albums and 45s is one thing, but Kiss is one of the most merchandised bands in rock music. What's available on the market? Besides the products one could buy in the 1970s, today you can purchase Kiss action figures, Kiss wine and beer, Kiss golf balls, Kiss mousepads, Kiss lava lamps. If you can name it, it's probably available with a Kiss logo (or in packs of four, one for each band member). And you can even purchase it with your own Kiss credit card!

Kiss' power ballad "A World Without Heroes" was their last hit for Casablanca; the label was absorbed by Polygram and Kiss' contract was transferred to Mercury Records. From the Collection of Val Shively.

References: Lendt, C.K., *Kiss and Sell: The Making of a Supergroup*, Billboard Books, Watson-Guptill Publications, BPI Communications, New York, N.Y., 1997; Shannon, Tom, *Goldmine Kiss Collectibles Price Guide*, Krause Publications, Iola, Wisconsin, 2000; Sherman, Dale., *Black Diamond II: The Illustrated Collector's Guide To Kiss*, CB Publishing, Toronto 1997.

Web pages: Kiss' homepage: *http://www.kissonline.com.*

Kiss 45s	Year	VG	VG+	NM
Kiss, "Love Theme From Kiss" / "Nothin' To Lose" (Casablanca 0004)	1974	$3.00	$6.00	$12.00
Kiss, "Strutter" / "100,000 Years" (Casablanca 0011)	1974	$3.00	$6.00	$12.00
Kiss, "Rock and Roll All Nite (live)" / "Rock and Roll All Nite (studio)" (Casablanca 850)	1975	$2.50	$5.00	$10.00
Kiss, "Shout It Out Loud" / "Sweet Pain" (Casablanca 854)	1976	$2.50	$5.00	$10.00
Kiss, "Flaming Youth" / "God of Thunder" (Casablanca 858)	1976	$2.50	$5.00	$10.00
(with picture sleeve, add:)	1976	$15.00	$30.00	$60.00
Kiss, "Detroit Rock City" / "Beth" (Casablanca 863) ("Detroit Rock City" is listed as A-side)	1976	$2.50	$5.00	$10.00
Kiss, "Beth" / "Detroit Rock City" (Casablanca 863) ("Beth" is listed as A-side)	1976		$2.50	$5.00
Kiss, "Christine Sixteen" / "Shock Me" (Casablanca 889)	1977		$3.00	$6.00
Kiss, "I Was Made For Lovin' You" / "Hard Times" (Casablanca 983)	1979		$2.50	$5.00
Kiss, "A World Without Heroes" / "Dark Light" (Casablanca 2343)	1981		$2.50	$5.00
Kiss, "I Love It Loud" / "Danger" (Casablanca 2365)	1982		$2.50	$5.00
(with picture sleeve, add:)	1982	$5.00	$10.00	$20.00
Kiss, "Lick It Up" / "Dance All Over Your Face" (Mercury 814 671-7)	1983		$2.00	$4.00

Kiss 45s	Year	VG	VG+	NM
Kiss, "Heaven's On Fire" / "Lonely Is The Hunter" (Mercury 880 205-7)	1984		$2.00	$4.00
Kiss, "Tears Are Falling" / "Any Way You Slice It" (Mercury 884 141-7)	1985		$2.00	$4.00
(with picture sleeve, add:)	1985		$2.50	$5.00
Kiss, "Forever" / "The Street Giveth And The Street Taketh Away" (Mercury 876 716-7)	1990		$2.50	$5.00
Kiss, "Detroit Rock City" / The Mighty Mighty Bosstones, "Detroit Rock City" (Mercury 818 216-7)				
(on green vinyl, small hole)	1994		$2.00	$4.00
(with picture sleeve, add:)	1994		$2.00	$4.00

Solo 45s	Year	VG	VG+	NM
Peter Criss, "Don't You Let Me Down" / "Hooked On Rock and Roll" (Casablanca 952)	1978		$3.00	$6.00
Peter Criss, "You Still Matter To Me" / "Hooked On Rock and Roll" (Casablanca 961)	1979		$3.00	$6.00
Peter Criss, "I Found Love" / "By Myself" (Casablanca 2311)	1980		$2.50	$5.00
Ace Frehley, "New York Groove" / "Snowblind" (Casablanca 941)	1978		$2.50	$5.00
Ace Frehley, "Into the Night" / "Fractured Too" (Atlantic 89255)	1987		$3.00	
Frehley's Comet, "Insane" / "The Acorn Is Spinning" (Atlantic 89072)	1988		$3.00	
Gene Simmons, "Radioactive" / "See You In Your Dreams" (Casablanca 951)	1978		$3.00	$6.00
Paul Stanley, "Goodbye" / "Hold Me, Touch Me" (Casablanca 940)	1978		$3.00	$6.00

Kiss LPs	Year	VG	VG+	NM
Kiss, Kiss (Casablanca NB 9001) (does not contain the song "Kissin' Time")	1974	$20.00	$40.00	$80.00
Kiss, Kiss (Casablanca NBLP 7001) (contains the song "Kissin' Time")	1974	$7.50	$15.00	$30.00
Kiss, Hotter than Hell (Casablanca NBLP 7006) (dark blue "Bogart" label)	1974	$7.50	$15.00	$30.00
Kiss, Dressed to Kill (Casablanca NBLP 7016) (dark blue "Bogart" label)	1975	$7.50	$15.00	$30.00
Kiss, Alive! (Casablanca NBLP 7020) (2 LPs) (dark blue "Bogart" label)	1975	$10.00	$20.00	$40.00
(if above is on tan Casablanca "camels" label, no motion picture cameras or "Filmworks" reference)	1976	$5.00	$10.00	$20.00
Kiss, The Originals (Casablanca NBLP 7032) (3 LPs)				
(if above is on tan "Casablanca" camel label, with booklet, four kiss cards and Kiss Army sticker)	1976	$37.50	$75.00	$150.00
(if above does not have the booklet, cards or sticker)	1976	$25.00	$50.00	$100.00
(if above is on tan "Casablanca Records and Filmworks" label, with extras)	1977	$18.75	$37.50	$75.00
(if above "Filmworks" copy does not have booklet, cards or sticker)	1977	$6.25	$12.50	$25.00
Kiss, Love Gun (Casablanca NBLP 7037) (mint copy must contain inserted cardboard gun)	1977	$10.00	$20.00	$40.00
Kiss, Alive II (Casablanca NBLP 7076) (2 LPs)				
(if back cover and record itself has "Take Me", "Hooligan" and "Do You Love Me")	1977	$100.00	$200.00	$400.00
(if cover lists above three songs, but they do not appear on the record; with sheet of Kiss tattoos)	1977	$25.00	$50.00	$100.00
(if cover lists above three songs, but they do not appear on the record; no Kiss tattoos)	1977	$18.75	$37.50	$75.00
(if cover does not have the three songs listed, but does have Kiss tattoos)	1977	$10.00	$20.00	$40.00
Kiss, Music From The Elder (Casablanca NBLP 7261)	1981	$7.50	$15.00	$30.00
Kiss, Creatures Of The Night (Casablanca NBLP 7270) (first pressings have band with face paint)	1982	$10.00	$20.00	$40.00
Kiss, First Kiss, Last Licks (Mercury 792-1) (white label promo sampler)	1990	$25.00	$50.00	$100.00
Kiss, Alive III (Mercury 522 647-1) (2 LPs) (pressed on red, white, blue or black vinyl, value is equal)	1994	$6.25	$12.50	$25.00

Solo LPs	Year	VG	VG+	NM
Chelsea, The Chelsea Album (Decca DL 75262) (Peter Criss played drums on this pre-Kiss album)	1972	$37.50	$75.00	$150.00
Peter Criss, Peter Criss (Casablanca NBLP-7122)	1978	$5.00	$10.00	$20.00
(if above is Casablanca NBPIX-7122, picture disc)	1978	$12.50	$25.00	$50.00
Peter Criss, Out Of Control (Casablanca NBLP-7240)	1980	$6.25	$12.50	$25.00
Ace Frehley, Ace Frehley (Casablanca NBLP-7121)	1978	$5.00	$10.00	$20.00
(if above is Casablanca NBPIX-7121, picture disc)	1978	$12.50	$25.00	$50.00
Ace Frehley, Frehley's Comet (Megaforce 81749)	1987	$2.75	$5.50	
Gene Simmons, Gene Simmons (Casablanca NBLP-7120)	1978	$6.25	$12.50	$25.00
(if above is Casablanca NBPIX-7120, picture disc)	1978	$15.00	$30.00	$60.00
Paul Stanley, Paul Stanley (Casablanca NBLP-7123)	1978	$6.25	$12.50	$25.00
(if above is Casablanca NBPIX-7120, picture disc)	1978	$15.00	$30.00	$60.00

"Shout It Out Loud" was one of the last Kiss singles to be released with the "Humphrey Bogart" Casablanca label.

In 1978, all four Kiss members released solo albums and singles. Paul Stanley's ballad "Hold Me, Touch Me" did not hit the Top 40, but is not hard to find as Casablanca Records pressed millions of Kiss solo records during the late 1970s.

MADONNA

History: Madonna changed the way female singers are perceived. Her music, her image, her publicity were all dictated—and completed—on her own terms. She broke the original perception of the winsome, wistful female pop singer, using music videos and previously taboo musical themes to create a new personae—a truly/liberated full-dimensional woman.

In 1977, a teenage Madonna Ciccone arrived in New York City from her native Bay City, Michigan, with dreams of becoming a ballet dancer. She worked with the Alvin Ailey troupe for two years, then sang backup vocals for disco singer Patrick Hernandez. She later sung and played drums for other groups, including the new-wave band The Breakfast Club (they had a hit in 1986 with "Right On Track," long after she left the band).

By 1982, Madonna recorded some dance-oriented tracks with her then-boyfriend, Steven Bray. These tracks eventually caught the ear of club DJ Mark Kamins, who helped Madonna acquire a recording contract with Sire Records. Her early singles, "Everybody" and "Physical Attraction," became smash hits in the New York City dance clubs, and received some college radio airplay throughout the East Coast.

The cover of one of Madonna's early hits, "Burning Up" b/w "Physical Attraction." From the Collection of Stephen M. Caraco.

By the time her third single, "Holiday," was released, Madonna's music had crossed over to the pop charts. During an appearance on *American Bandstand*, when asked by host Dick Clark what she hoped to accomplish with her career, Madonna prophetically yet coyly replied, "To rule the world."

She was well on her way to that goal, as her self-titled debut album generated two more radio hits, "Borderline" and "Lucky Star." Music videos for these songs gave television viewers their first look at Madonna, as an eye-winking, lace-wearing, midriff-bearing coquette who had some semblance of dance training. These early videos inspired thousands of fans to adopt "the Madonna look"—mesh blouses, short skirts, junk jewelry, and blonde locks.

Madonna's debut album has two pressing variations—one copy has a longer running time on "Burning Up" than does the other.

It also inspired controversy. Whether it involved the titles of her albums, the lyrics of her songs, or even her personal appearance, parents' groups had plenty of ammunition to protest almost anything Madonna did. An album called "Like a Virgin?" A song called "Papa Don't Preach," where she extols about how she's going to "keep her baby"—did she mean an unwed pregnancy? Or another song called "Like a Prayer," whose music video showed her cavorting with saints and idols and burning crosses?

But the more controversy Madonna received, the more albums she sold. And while she did give critics plenty of grist to chew on, she also showed her audience that she was capable of material that was not "boy toy" dance-pop. Her ballads, including "Crazy For You," "This Used To Be My Playground," "Rain," and "Live To Tell" demonstrated Madonna's considerable vocal range and her emotive lyrical interpretations.

Trivia

One of Madonna's most popular radio hits was not initially released on a 45. "Into The Groove," despite its popularity as the theme from Madonna's first mainstream movie "Desperately Seeking Susan," was only commercially available as the B-side of the 12-inch disc of another Madonna hit, "Angel." "Into The Groove" was eventually released as a reissue 45 with "Dress You Up" (Sire GSRE 0539), and fetches $3 in near-mint condition.

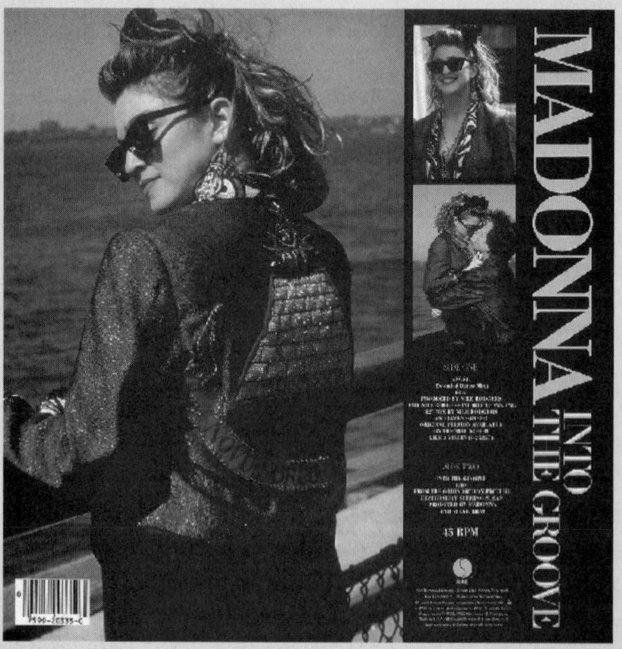

The 12-inch cover contains photos from Madonna's movie Desperately Seeking Susan, and "Into The Groove" was part of the movie. But it was not initially released as a 7-inch single. From the Collection of Stephen M. Caraco.

Madonna's "Crazy For You," from the motion picture "Vision Quest," showed critics that the Material Girl could handle a tender ballad as well as she could a dance track.

Madonna also acted in several motion pictures, the most successful of which were "Desperately Seeking Susan," "A League of Their Own," and "Evita." She married (and later divorced) actor Sean Penn, romanced (and later left) Warren Beatty, and befriended a Hollywood A-list of stars. She also continued to record, with songs like "Vogue" (a new dance based on the fashion runway poses of supermodels), "Justify My Love" (whose video, with its myriad of late-night boudoir escapades, was banned by MTV), and "Take A Bow" (her collaboration with producer Babyface; a song that stayed atop the *Billboard* Hot 100 chart for seven straight weeks).

Trivia

In the early 1980s, Madonna and remixer John "Jellybean" Benitez worked together, both professionally and personally. Benitez remixed many of Madonna's early hits, while she wrote his first Top 40 hit, "Sidewalk Talk." Although some people who hear "Sidewalk Talk" think the female lead vocalist on the song is Madonna, singer Catherine Buchanan sings lead on this track.

While Madonna's "This Used To Be My Playground" was heard in the motion picture A League of Their Own, it does not appear on the soundtrack album of the same name. From the Collection of Stephen M. Caraco.

Madonna's most recent recordings have been influenced by the techno and electronica sound of the Chemical Brothers and Prodigy. Her songs "Ray of Light" and "Frozen" are the first electronica songs by an established artist, and have successfully legitimized the musical style as more than just a dance beat and synthesizer riffs.

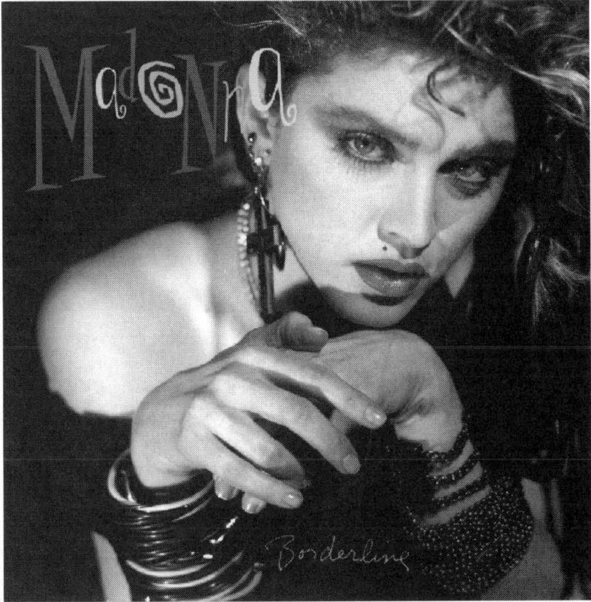

Because this picture sleeve for Madonna's "Borderline" folds out to a poster, finding the sleeve without seam splits or fold splits is very difficult. From the Collection of Stephen M. Caraco.

What To Look For: Considering Madonna's albums and singles have sold millions of copies over the years, finding her pre-1990 vinyl stock singles and albums is relatively easy. What is not so easy, however, is finding white label promo copies of her Sire and Maverick recordings. Madonna's picture sleeves may also prove difficult to locate, especially for the songs "Borderline" (in which the sleeve folds out to a poster) and "Keep It Together" (one of the few Madonna picture sleeves in the CD era).

While most of Madonna's dance tracks were commercially released on 12-inch dance discs, many Madonna collectors avidly seek the promotional copies of these same discs. Many of them have alternate remixes or colored vinyl; others may have promotional cover art not available on the stock recordings. This is also true of Madonna's 45s and LPs. The first promo copies of her *Like a Virgin* LP, for example, were pressed on "virgin white" vinyl.

Trivia

Madonna is one of the few superstar musicians today whose work is still pressed on 45s. Even recent Madonna hits like "Music" are still available as stock 7-inch vinyl singles, as well as on promotional 12-inch disco discs.

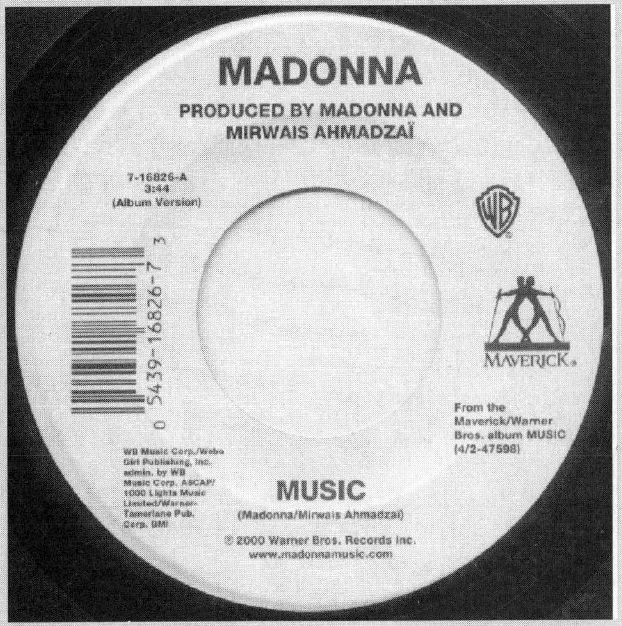

A recent Madonna 45, of "Music"—complete with bar code and a plug for Madonna's Web site.

Madonna's "Oh Father" picture sleeve, only available with promo copies of her 7-inch single of the same name. From the Collection of Stephen M. Caraco.

Even though Madonna collectors will often search for rare and unique Madonna mixes from around the world, this book focuses only on her American releases.

References: Bego, Mark, *Madonna: Blonde Ambition* (updated edition), Cooper Square Press, New York, N.Y., 2000; Dickerson, James, *Women on Top: The Quiet Revolution That's Rocking The American Music Industry*, Billboard Books, an imprint of Watson-Guptill Publications, a division of BPI Communications, New York, N.Y., 1998.

Web pages: Madonna's web page: *http://www.madonnamusic.com*; the Madonna Catalog, a collector's page for domestic and international Madonna collectibles: *http://www.madonnacatalog.com.*

45s	**Year**	**VG**	**VG+**	**NM**
Madonna, "Everybody" / (instrumental) (Sire 29841)	1982	$5.00	$10.00	$20.00
(if promotional copy, "Everybody" on both sides)	1982	$2.50	$5.00	$10.00
Madonna, "Holiday" / "I Know It" (Sire 29478)	1983		$2.00	$4.00
Madonna, "Borderline" / "Think of Me" (Sire 29534)	1984		$2.00	$4.00
(with foldout picture sleeve, add:)	1984	$20.00	$40.00	$80.00
Madonna, "Like A Virgin" / "Stay" (Sire 29210)	1984		$3.00	
(with picture sleeve, add:)	1984		$3.00	
Madonna, "Crazy For You" / Berlin, "No More Words" (Geffen 29051)	1985		$3.00	
(with picture sleeve, add:)	1985		$3.00	
Madonna, "Dress You Up" / "Shoo-Be-Doo" (Sire 28919)	1985		$3.00	
(with picture sleeve, add:)	1985	$12.50	$25.00	$50.00
Madonna, "Papa Don't Preach" / "Pretender" (Sire 28660)	1986		$3.00	
(with picture sleeve, add:)	1986		$3.00	
Madonna, "True Blue" / "Ain't No Big Deal" (Sire 28591)	1986		$3.00	

45s	**Year**	**VG**	**VG+**	**NM**
(with picture sleeve, add)	1986		$3.00	
(if on blue vinyl)	1986	$2.50	$5.00	
(with picture sleeve that says "Limited edition blue vinyl pressing", add:)	1986		$2.50	$5.00
Madonna, "Who's That Girl?" / "White Heat" (Sire 28341)	1987			$3.00
(with picture sleeve, add:)	1987			$3.00
Madonna, "Oh Father" / "Pray for Spanish Eyes" (Sire 22723)	1989			$3.00
(with picture sleeve, available only on promo copies)	1989	$37.50	$75.00	$150.00
Madonna, "Keep It Together" / (instrumental) Sire 19986)	1990		$3.00	
(with picture sleeve, add:)	1990	$20.00	$40.00	$80.00
Madonna, "Vogue" / "Vogue (Bette Davis Dub)" (Sire 19863)	1990			$3.00
Madonna, "This Used To Be My Playground" / (long version) (Sire 18822)	1992			$3.00
Madonna, "Erotica" / (instrumental) (Maverick 18782)	1992			$3.00
Madonna, "Rain" / "Waiting" (Maverick 18505)	1993			$3.00
Madonna, "Human Nature" / "Sanctuary" (Maverick 17882)	1995			$3.00
Madonna, "Frozen" / "Shanti-Ashtangi" (Maverick 17244)	1998			$3.00
Madonna, "Ray of Light" / "Has To Be" (Maverick 17206)	1998			$3.00

12-inch (all pressings with PRO-A are promo copies)	**Year**	**VG**	**VG+**	**NM**
Madonna, "Everybody" (two versions)				
(if on Sire 29899)	1982	$2.50	$5.00	$10.00
(if on Sire PRO-A-1083, promo)	1982	$15.00	$30.00	$60.00
Madonna, "Burning Up" / "Physical Attraction" (Sire 29715)	1983	$2.50	$5.00	$10.00
Madonna, "Lucky Star" / "Holiday" (Sire PRO-A-2069)	1983	$7.50	$15.00	$30.00
Madonna, "Borderline" / "Lucky Star" (Sire 20212)	1984	$2.50	$5.00	$10.00
Madonna, "Borderline" (2 versions) (Sire PRO-A-2120)	1984	$6.25	$12.50	$25.00
Madonna, "Material Girl" (both sides are the same) (Sire PRO-A-2257)	1985	$6.25	$12.50	$25.00
Madonna, "Angel" / "Into The Groove" (Sire 20335)	1985	$2.00	$4.00	$8.00
Madonna, "Dress You Up" (2 versions) / "Shoo-Be-Doo" (Sire 20369)	1985	$2.00	$4.00	$8.00
Madonna, "True Blue" (2 versions) / "Ain't No Big Deal" (2 versions) (Sire 20533)	1986	$2.00	$4.00	$8.00
Madonna, "Like A Prayer" (5 versions) / "Act of Contrition" (Sire 21170)	1989	$2.50	$5.00	$10.00
Madonna, "Justify My Love" (3 versions) / "Express Yourself" (Sire 21820)	1990	$2.00	$4.00	$8.00
Madonna, "Erotica" (6 versions) (Maverick 40585)	1992	$2.00	$4.00	$8.00
Madonna, "Erotica" (11 versions) (Maverick PRO-A-5860) (2 12" discs)	1992	$7.50	$15.00	$30.00
Madonna, "Deeper and Deeper" (6 versions) (Maverick 40722)	1992	$2.00	$4.00	$8.00
Madonna, "Deeper and Deeper" (12 versions) (Maverick PRO-A-5928) (2 12" discs)	1992	$10.00	$20.00	$40.00
Madonna, "I'll Remember" (4 versions) (Maverick 41355)	1994	$3.75	$7.50	$15.00
Madonna, "Human Nature" (6 versions) (Maverick PRO-A-7719) (clear vinyl)	1995	$5.00	$10.00	$20.00
(if "Advance Only" on label, Maverick PRO-A-7719-A)	1995	$5.00	$10.00	$20.00
Madonna, "Don't Cry For Me Argentina" (6 versions) (Maverick PRO-A-8544)	1997	$5.00	$10.00	$20.00
(if "Advance Only" on label, Maverick PRO-A-8544-A)	1997	$6.25	$12.50	$25.00
Madonna, "Frozen" (3 versions) (Maverick PRO-A-9254)	1998	$12.50	$25.00	$50.00

LPs	**Year**	**VG**	**VG+**	**NM**
Madonna, Madonna (Sire 23867)				
(if "Burning Up" is 4:48, first pressing)	1983	$5.00	$10.00	$20.00
(if "Burning Up" is 3:49, second pressing)	1983	$2.50	$5.00	$10.00
(if on Sire W1-23867, Columbia House pressing)	1984	$3.75	$7.50	$15.00
(if on Sire R 164288, RCA Music Service Edition)	1984	$3.75	$7.50	$15.00

LPs	Year	VG	VG+	NM
Madonna, Like A Virgin (Sire 25157)				
(if stock copy)	1984	$2.50	$5.00	$10.00
(if white vinyl, silver spine)	1984	$15.00	$30.00	$60.00
(if white vinyl, cream spine)	1984	$12.50	$25.00	$50.00
(if on Sire W1-25157, Columbia House pressing)	1985	$3.75	$7.50	$15.00
(if on Sire R 161153, RCA Music Service Edition)	1985	$3.75	$7.50	$15.00
Madonna, True Blue (Sire 25442)	1986	$2.00	$4.00	$8.00
(with poster, add:)	1986	$1.00	$2.00	$4.00
(if on Sire W1-25442, Columbia House Pressing, with poster)	1986	$3.75	$7.50	$15.00
(if on Sire R 143811, RCA Music Service Edition, with poster)	1986	$3.75	$7.50	$15.00
Madonna, You Can Dance (Sire 25535)	1987	$2.00	$4.00	$8.00
(if record contains gold obi strip that says "Madonna and Dancing"; price is for record and obi)	1987	$3.00	$6.00	$12.00
(if on Sire W1-25535, Columbia House pressing, no obi)	1987	$3.75	$7.50	$15.00
(if on Sire R 134536, RCA Music Service Edition, no obi)	1987	$3.75	$7.50	$15.00
(if on Sire PRO-A-2892, single edits of the 7 dance songs on the stock copy)	1987	$7.50	$15.00	$30.00
Madonna, Like A Prayer (Sire 25444)	1989	$2.50	$5.00	$10.00
(if on Sire W1-25844, Columbia House pressing)	1989	$3.75	$7.50	$15.00
(if on Sire R 101029, BMG Direct Marketing Edition)	1989	$3.75	$7.50	$15.00
Madonna, I'm Breathless (Sire 26209)	1990	$2.50	$5.00	$10.00
(if on Sire W1-26209, Columbia House pressing)	1990	$3.75	$7.50	$15.00
(if on Sire R 100572, BMG Direct Marketing Edition)	1990	$3.75	$7.50	$15.00
Madonna, The Immaculate Collection (Sire 26440) (2 LPs)	1990	$3.75	$7.50	$15.00
(if on Sire W1-26440, Columbia House pressing)	1990	$5.00	$10.00	$20.00
(if on Sire R 254164, BMG Direct Marketing Edition)	1990	$5.00	$10.00	$20.00
Madonna, Erotica (Maverick PRO-A-5904) (promo-only 2 LPs)	1992	$12.50	$25.00	$50.00
Madonna, Bedtime Stories (Maverick PRO-A-7311) (promo-only 2 LPs) (pink vinyl)	1994	$12.50	$25.00	$50.00

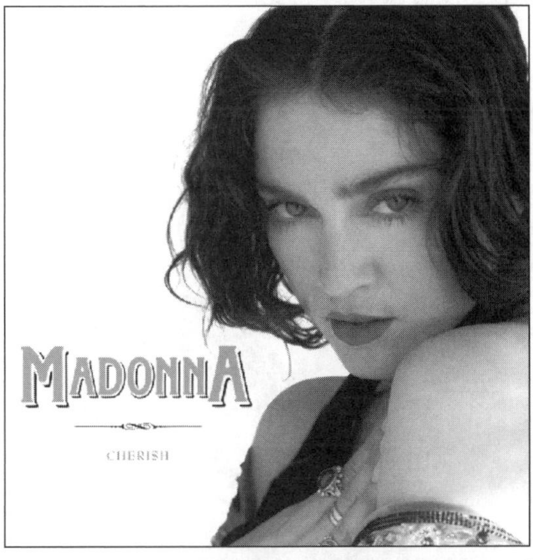

One of the many picture sleeves for Madonna's 45s. This sleeve for "Cherish" is rather common… From the Collection of Stephen M. Caraco.

Some of Madonna's promo pressings have special treats—including this 12" copy of "Human Nature," which was pressed on clear vinyl. From the Collection of Stephen M. Caraco.

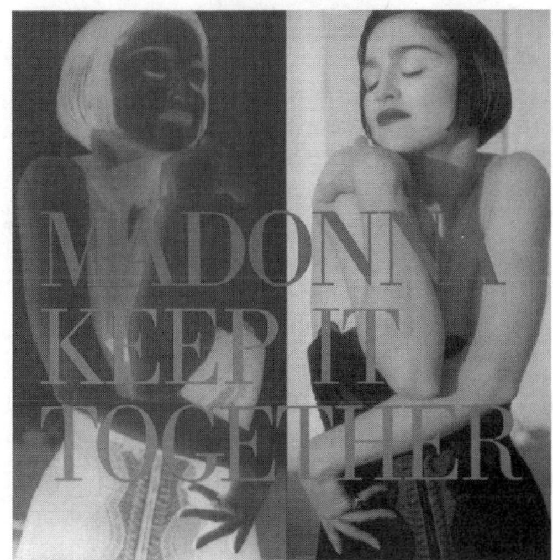

...but this one, for "Keep It Together," is quite rare—in fact, this is currently the last picture sleeve for a Madonna 7-inch single. From the Collection of Stephen M. Caraco.

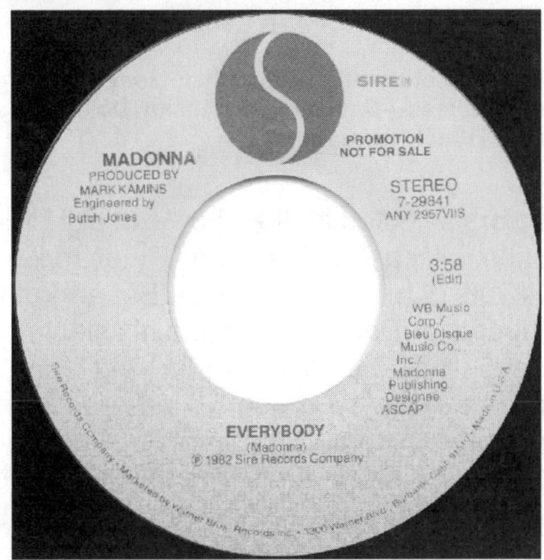

This promo copy of "Everybody" is rare enough, but a stock copy, with an instrumental version of "Everybody" on the B-side, is worth twice as much as a promo copy.

THE MONKEES

History: It was life imitating art. Four actors were hired to play knockabout musicians on a television situation comedy. Within two years, the actors were now a cohesive band of their own, headlining sold-out concerts and writing their own Top 40 songs.

Thus began the story of The Monkees—and *"The Monkees."*

"The Monkees" was an NBC-TV situation comedy that aired between 1966 and 1968. The premise of the show was the wacky adventures of four musicians living in a California beach house, and was based on the humorous antics of the Beatles in their motion pictures "A Hard Days' Night" and "Help!"

On their first picture sleeve together, from left to right, are the Monkees—Davy Jones, Micky Dolenz, Peter Tork and Michael Nesmith.

The actors selected for the show—Micky Dolenz, Davy Jones, Michael Nesmith, and Peter Tork—had varying levels of music experience. But armed with music supervisor Don Kirshner and his stable of songwriters—Neil Diamond, Carole King, John Stewart, Tommy Boyce & Bobby Hart—the Monkees were able to dominate pop radio almost from the first week the show aired. The Monkees, along with Ricky Nelson, were the first performers to use television to promote their performances, their shows essentially acting as 30-minute music videos. Their first few songs—"Last Train to Clarksville," "I'm A Believer," and "(I'm Not Your) Stepping Stone," dominated Top 40 radio. Their first two albums, *The Monkees and More of the Monkees* held the #1 spot on *Billboard's* album chart for a phenomenal 31 consecutive weeks.

Although the Monkees' songs and LPs were million-sellers, the foursome were dogged by accusations that they didn't play on their own recordings. Eager to prove they could perform as a band outside of their TV series, the group fired Don Kirshner and recorded their next album, *Headquarters*, performing and singing all the songs on every track. *Headquarters* hit #1 on the *Billboard* album charts, only to be nudged out of the top spot by the Beatles' *Sgt. Pepper's Lonely Hearts Club Band* album.

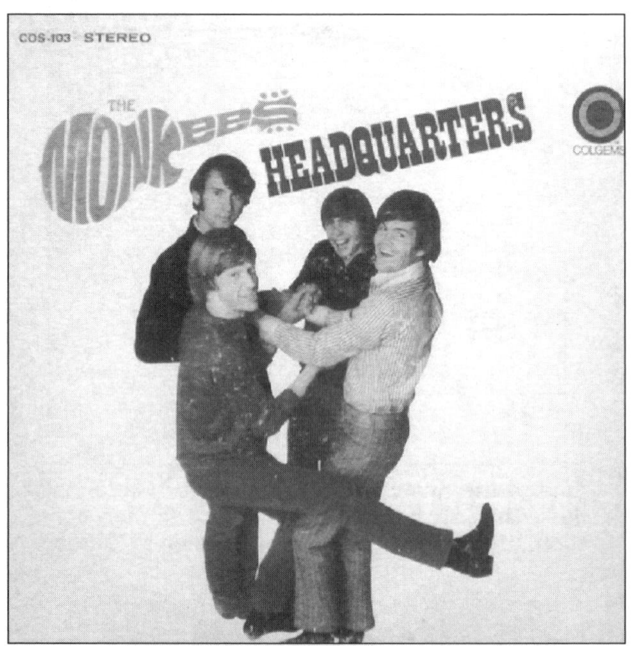

Art imitates life: The Monkees' *Headquarters* album, proof that the quartet could play their instruments as well as sing and act.

Their TV series lasted only two seasons, and although the Monkees continued to have hits with songs like "Pleasant Valley Sunday," "Words," and "Daydream Believer," they no longer had a television series to promote their latest hits. Undaunted, the Monkees continued as a live rock band (even having Jimi Hendrix open for them at a few dates). They later made the critically panned motion picture *"Head"* and the TV special "33 1/3 Revolutions per Monkee," after which Peter Tork left the group. By 1970, Michael Nesmith had left the band for a solo career, and the unsuccessful album *Changes* featured only Davy Jones and Micky Dolenz.

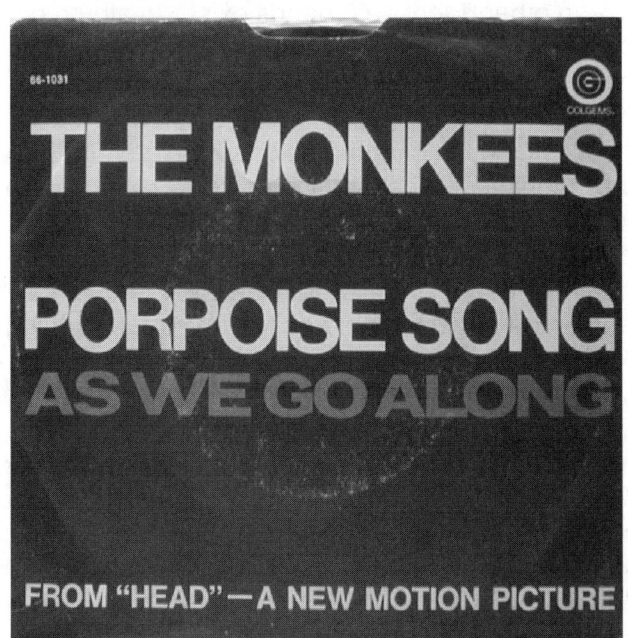

Written by Carole King, "The Porpoise Song" was featured in the Monkees' motion picture Head. The song was also the first Monkees A-side to fail to reach the Billboard Top 40 pop charts.

All four Monkees worked on solo projects throughout the 1970s. Of all the releases during that period, only Michael Nesmith was able to reach the Top 40 again, with his ballad "Joanne." A pioneer in music video production and experimental film presentation, Nesmith later won a Grammy for his long-form music video "Elephant Parts" (which later spawned a 1984 summer TV series, "Michael Nesmith in Television Parts").

"Joanne," Michael Nesmith's solo Top 40 hit.

In 1986, MTV ran a marathon of all 58 *"Monkees"* episodes. The marathon later spiked a new run of Monkee-mania, and eventually Micky Dolenz and Peter Tork recorded a Top 20 single, "That Was Then, This Is Now." Along with Davy Jones, they reunited as the Monkees and performed their classic hits in concert (Nesmith eventually joined them for a few shows).

What To Look For: Monkees 45s and LPs in NM condition are highly collectible; 45s released on the Colgems label are original pressings—anything pressed on Arista and Rhino are either reproductions or 1980s releases. Original Monkees picture sleeves in near-mint condition are also desirable.

Beginning collectors will have no problem finding the Monkees' biggest hits, as millions of 45s were pressed for each title. Finding near-mint copies will be more difficult, as these records were usually played to death. Monkees 45s with a serial number of 5000 or higher are harder to find, as these were pressed after the Monkees' TV show had been canceled. These include songs like "Tear Drop City," "Good Clean Fun," and "Listen to the Band."

Original Monkees albums are on the Colgems label. They have been re-released on vinyl by both the Rhino and Sundazed labels, both of which command lesser collectible prices than the original. Photo Credit: Courtesy Last Vestige Music Store, Albany, N.Y.

There are two versions of the Monkees' 45 "A Little Bit Me, A Little Bit You." The first unreleased pressings list the B-side as "She Hangs Out." After Don Kirshner and the Monkees parted company, the B-side was replaced with the song "The Girl I Knew Somewhere," and became the first Top 40 hit that was actually written by a Monkee (Michael Nesmith).

Trivia

As the Monkees' popularity resurged in the 1980s, Arista re-released one of the Monkees' earlier hits, "Daydream Believer." It also issued a picture sleeve replicating the original Colgems sleeve.

The original 1967 picture sleeve. The Peter Tork autograph was added for a fan in 1986.

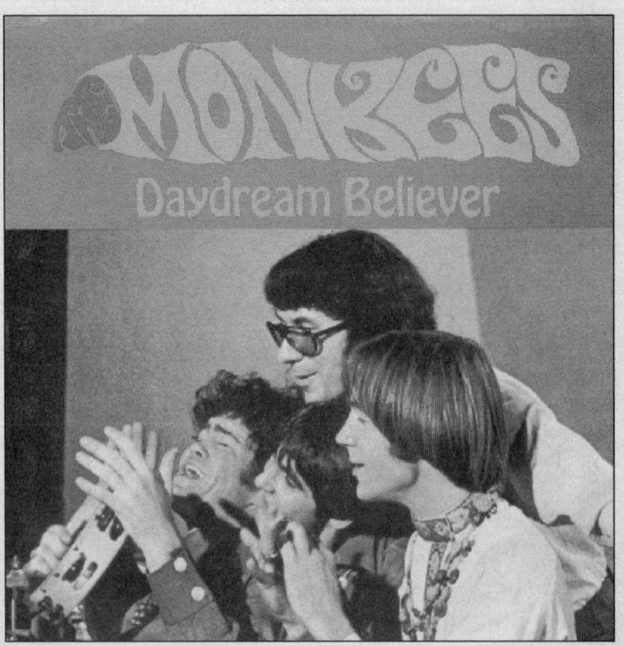

The 1986 Arista reissue.

Two other "Monkees" bands exist. An album on the Wyncote label, "Monkey Business," are an unrelated barrel of Monkees. In 1987, after the reissued success of the original Monkees show, a new quartet of singing knockabout actors premiered in "The New Monkees." The syndicated show lasted 13 episodes, with many stations dropping the program long before that. This "New Monkees" did release an album and a single, and are only desirable for fans of the original Monkees to prove that lightning does not always strike twice in the same place.

References: Baker, Glenn A., *Monkeemania: The Story of the Monkees*, Plexus Publishing Ltd., London (3rd Ed.), 2000; Dolenz, Micky; Bego, Mark, *I'm A Believer: My Life of Monkees, Music and Madness*, Hyperion, New York, 1993; Eck, Marty, *The Monkees Collectibles Price Guide*, Antique Trader Books, Dubuque, Iowa, 1998; Jones, Davy; Green, Alan W., *Mutant Monkees Meet the Masters of the Multimedia Manipulation Machine*, Click! Publishing, Selinsgrove, Pa., 1992; Lefcowitz, Eric, *The Monkees Tale*, Last Gasp, Berkeley, Calif., 1989; Massingill, Randi L., *Total Control: The Michael Nesmith Story*, FLEXquarters, Mesa, Ariz., 1997.

Web pages: The Monkees' home page: *http://www.monkees.net*; Micky Dolenz' home page: *http://www.mickydolenz.com*; Davy Jones' home page: *http://www.davyjones.net*; Michael Nesmith's home page: *http://www.videoranch.com*; Peter Tork's home page: *http://www.petertork*.com.

Monkees 45s	Year	VG	VG+	NM
The Monkees, "Last Train to Clarksville" / "Take A Giant Step" (Colgems 66-1001)	1966	$3.75	$7.50	$15.00
(with picture sleeve, no mention of Monkees fan club, add:)	1966	$7.50	$15.00	$30.00
(with picture sleeve, "Write the Monkees")	1966	$5.00	$10.00	$20.00
The Monkees, "I'm A Believer" / "(I'm Not Your) Stepping Stone" (Colgems 66-1002)	1966	$3.75	$7.50	$15.00
(with picture sleeve, add:)	1966	$7.50	$15.00	$30.00
The Monkees, "A Little Bit Me, A Little Bit You" / "The Girl I Knew Somewhere" (Colgems 66-1004)	1967	$3.75	$7.50	$15.00
The Monkees, "Daydream Believer" / "Goin' Down" (Colgems 66-1012)	1967	$3.75	$7.50	$15.00
(with picture sleeve, add:)	1967	$7.50	$15.00	$30.00
The Monkees, "Tear Drop City" / "A Man Without A Dream" (Colgems 66-5000)	1969	$2.50	$5.00	$10.00
(with picture sleeve, add:)	1969	$6.25	$12.50	$25.00
The Monkees, "Listen To The Band" / "Someday Man" (Colgems 66-5004)	1969	$2.50	$5.00	$10.00
(with picture sleeve, "Listen to the Band" listed first)	1969	$6.25	$12.50	$25.00
(with picture sleeve, "Someday Man" listed first)	1969	$5.00	$10.00	$20.00
The Monkees, "Daydream Believer" / "Monkee's Theme" (Arista 0201)	1976	$2.50	$5.00	$10.00
The Monkees, "That Was Then, This is Now" / "(Theme From) The Monkees" (Arista 9505)				
(if group is listed as "The Monkees")	1986	$2.50	$5.00	$10.00
(if group is listed as "Mickey Dolenz and Peter Tork [Of The Monkees]")	1986			$3.00
(with "Monkees" picture sleeve, add:)	1986	$2.50	$5.00	$10.00
(with "Mickey Dolenz and Peter Tork [Of The Monkees]" picture sleeve, add:)	1986			$3.00
The Monkees, "Daydream Believer" / "Randy Scouse Git" (Arista 9532)	1986		$2.00	$4.00

Monkees 45s	Year	VG	VG+	NM
(with "20th anniversary" picture sleeve, add:)	1986		$2.00	$4.00
Monkees solo 45s	**Year**	**VG**	**VG+**	**NM**
Mickey Dolenz, "Don't Do It" / "Plastic Symphony III" (Challenge 59353)	1967	$5.00	$10.00	$20.00
(with picture sleeve, add:)	1967	$15.00	$30.00	$60.00
Mickey Dolenz, "Buddy Holly Tribute" / "She's So Young" (Romar 715)	1974	$5.00	$10.00	$20.00
Mickey Dolenz and Davy Jones, "Do It In The Name Of Love " / "Lady Jane" (Bell 986)	1971	$12.50	$25.00	$50.00
Dolenz, Jones, Boyce and Hart, "You and I" / "Remember The Feeling" (Capitol 4180)	1975	$2.50	$5.00	$10.00
Dolenz, Jones and Tork, "Christmas Is My Time Of Year" / "White Christmas" (Christmas 700)	1976	$5.00	$10.00	$20.00
Davy Jones, "Dream Girl" / "Take Me To Paradise" (Colpix 764)	1965	$5.00	$10.00	$20.00
(with picture sleeve, add:)	1965	$7.50	$15.00	$30.00
Davy Jones, "The Girl From Chelsea" / "Theme For A New Love" (Colpix 789)	1965	$5.00	$10.00	$20.00
(with picture sleeve, add:)	1965	$10.00	$20.00	$40.00
Davy Jones, "Girl" / "Take My Love" (Bell 45,159)	1971	$12.50	$25.00	$50.00
Michael Blessing, "The New Recruit" / "A Journey" (Colpix 787)	1965	$37.50	$75.00	$150.00
Michael Nesmith, "Just A Little Love" / "Curson Terrace" (Edan 1001)	1965	$30.00	$60.00	$120.00
Michael Nesmith and the First National Band, "Joanne" / "One Rose" (RCA Victor 74-0368)	1977	$3.00	$6.00	$12.00
Michael Nesmith, "Casablanca Moonlight" / "Rio" (Pacific Arts 104)	1977	$2.00	$4.00	$8.00
(with picture sleeve, add:)	1977	$3.00	$6.00	$12.00
Monkees LPs	**Year**	**VG**	**VG+**	**NM**
The Monkees, The Monkees (Colgems COM-101 in mono, COS-101 in stereo)				
(if fifth song on side one is spelled "Papa Jean's Blues")	1966	$6.25	$12.50	$25.00

Monkees LPs	Year	VG	VG+	NM
(second pressing, song is spelled "Papa Gene's Blues," upper right back cover has "RE")	1966	$5.00	$10.00	$20.00
The Monkees, More of the Monkees (Colgems COM-102 in mono, COS-102 in stereo)	1966	$5.00	$10.00	$20.00
The Monkees, Headquarters (Colgems COM-103 in mono, Colgems COS-103 in stereo)				
(if back cover, bottom picture has pictures of Monkees with beards)	1967	$7.50	$15.00	$30.00
(if back cover, bottom picture is of producers)	1967	$5.00	$10.00	$20.00
The Monkees, Pisces, Aquarius, Capricorn and Jones, Ltd.				
(if on Colgems COM-104, mono)	1967	$10.00	$20.00	$40.00
(if on Colgems COS-104, stereo)	1967	$5.00	$10.00	$20.00
The Monkees, The Birds, The Bees and the Monkees				
(if on Colgems COM-109, mono)	1968	$25.00	$50.00	$100.00
(if on Colgems COS-109, stereo)	1968	$5.00	$10.00	$20.00
(if any of the above titles are 1980's reissues on Rhino)	1987	$3.00	$6.00	$12.00
(if any of the above titles are Sundazed reissues, pressed on colored vinyl)	1996	$2.50	$5.00	$10.00
The Monkees, Changes (Colgems COS-119)	1970	$18.75	$37.50	$75.00
The Monkees, Pool It! (Rhino RNIN-70706)	1987	$2.50	$5.00	$10.00
Solo Monkees LPs	**Year**	**VG**	**VG+**	**NM**
Dolenz, Jones, Boyce and Hart, Dolenz, Jones, Boyce and Hart (Capitol ST-11513)	1976	$3.75	$7.50	$15.00
David Jones, David Jones (Colpix CP-493) (mono)	1965	$6.25	$12.50	$25.00
(if on Colpix CPS-493, stereo)	1965	$10.00	$20.00	$40.00
Davy Jones, Davy Jones (Bell 6067)	1971	$5.00	$10.00	$20.00
Michael Nesmith, Magnetic South (RCA Victor LSP-4371)	1970	$7.50	$15.00	$30.00
Michael Nesmith, The Prison				
(if on Pacific Arts 7-101, standard cover)	197??	$5.00	$10.00	$20.00
(if on Pacific Arts 11-101A, box cover with booklet)	1975	$17.50	$25.00	$50.00
Michael Nesmith, The Newer Stuff (Rhino R1-70168)	1989	$3.00	$6.00	$12.00

Colgems 45s with serial numbers of 5000 and higher are hard to find, as they were released after the Monkees TV show was canceled. And if you heard this song on the radio, you might not know it as "Good Clean Fun"—because those words are never mentioned in the lyrics of this song.

Two versions of this 20th anniversary picture sleeve exist; the first pressings credit the recording to "The Monkees," while second pressings credit only Micky Dolenz and Peter Tork (of the Monkees).

MOTOWN

History: From its inception, Motown was a success in both business and in music. Its fusion of black soul and white pop was as dominant during the 1960s as the music of the Beatles or the Rolling Stones. The singing groups that formed Motown's musical core—Diana Ross and the Supremes, the Temptations, the Four Tops, Smokey Robinson and the Miracles, Stevie Wonder, Marvin Gaye, the Jackson Five—were part of a sound that, for lack of any other descriptive term, came to be known as the "Motown Sound."

This early album by the Supremes features three of their #1 hits—as well as some songs recorded before they hit it big.

The brains behind Motown Records was its founder, Berry Gordy, Jr. Gordy left his 9-to-5 job at the local Lincoln-Mercury factory in Detroit, after the songs he wrote, "Reet Petite" and "Lonely Teardrops," became hits for Jackie Wilson. Gordy wrote more songs for Wilson, and eventually created his own record company, Tamla.

Tamla's earliest recordings were eventually licensed to other national labels. These included Marv Johnson's "Come To Me" on United Artists, the Miracles' "Bad Girl" on Chess, and Barrett Strong's "Money (That's What I Want)" on Anna. But by 1960, Gordy stopped licensing tracks to other labels, instead concentrating on making Tamla a national label.

The Miracles were Tamla's first successful group. Led by lead singer William "Smokey" Robinson, the Miracles evolved from a successful doo-wop group to a pop-soul band that brought Gordy his own label's hits. Songs like "Shop Around," "Mickey's Monkey," "You Really Got A Hold On Me," and "What's So Good About Good-By" established the Miracles as Gordy's first superstars.

Motown's first big hits was the Miracles' "Shop Around," on the Tamla label. Notice the horizontal stripes on the label of this early pressing.

Eventually Gordy moved his record company into a house at 2648 West Grand Boulevard. For the next decade, the greatest singers and musicians in the Detroit area converged on this small house, recording the most dominant hits of an era.

Tamla's first #1 record, "Please Mr. Postman," was recorded by the Marvelettes, a four-member girl group from Detroit's Inkster High School. The song was so successful, the Beatles recorded it on one of their early albums; ten years later, the Carpenters recorded a version of "Please Mr. Postman" that also topped the pop charts. Led by Gladys Horton, the Marvelettes would have a string of Top 40 hits, including "Don't Mess With Bill" and "Beechwood 4-5789."

By 1962, Tamla Records had more singers and hits. Martha Reeves, a former secretary within the Motown complex, became the lead singer of the Vandellas, and had hits with "Heat Wave," "Jimmy Mack," and "Dancing In The Streets." Her vocal group also backed up a new singer, Marvin Gaye, on songs like "Stubborn Kind of Fellow" and "Pride and Joy."

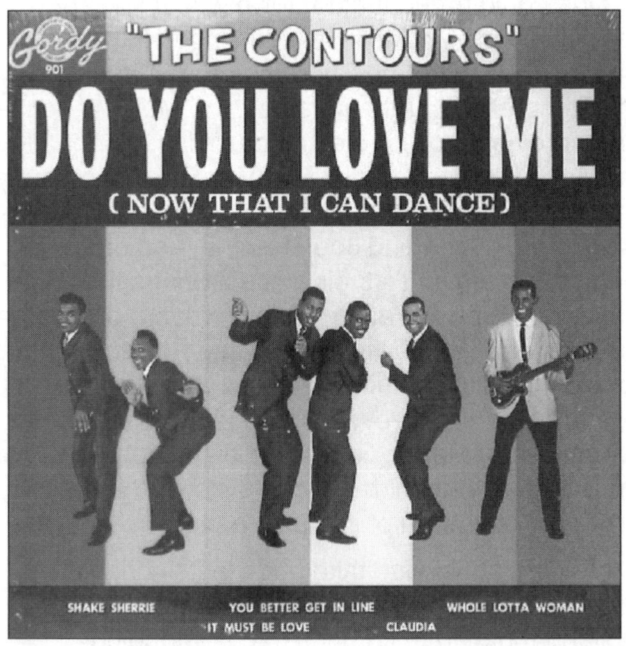

While the single for the Contours' "Do You Love Me" is relatively easy to find, the Contours' debut album is not. Courtesy Good Rockin' Tonight / Collectors Universe.

Gordy Records, a sister label to Tamla, made its initial splash with the Contours' raucous "Do You Love Me." The song, with its party atmosphere and false ending, eventually reached the Top 10. Meanwhile, another sister label, Motown Records, provided Mary Wells and the Four Tops with their first Top 40 hits.

From 1962 to 1964, Mary Wells was Motown's most consistent recording artist. This early Motown label artwork existed before the "Map of Detroit" label that would grace Motown 45s and LPs for the next 35 years. Courtesy Good Rockin' Tonight/Collectors Universe.

In 1963, a blind piano/harmonica player named Stevie Wonder joined the Motown lineup. His recording of "Fingertips" became the first concert recording to top the pop charts, beginning a 40-year-long association with Berry Gordy's record company. Wonder would eventually grow from a child prodigy to a musical *wunderkind,* embracing soul, pop, funk and rock into albums filled with new grooves and beats. Some of Stevie Wonder's biggest hits in the 1960's included "Uptight—Everything's Alright," "For Once In My Life," "A Place In The Sun," and "Signed, Sealed, Delivered, I'm Yours."

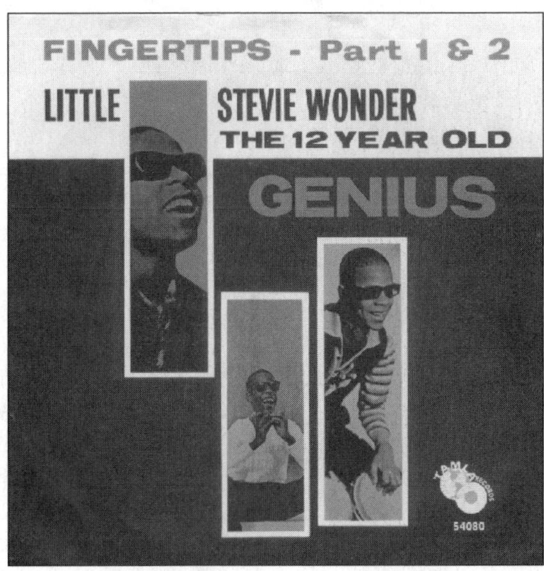

A picture sleeve of Stevie Wonder's breakthrough hit, "Fingertips Part 2." Motown's earliest picture sleeves are very difficult to find today.

But Motown's biggest artists made their claim to fame in 1964. That's when the Supremes, after recording a dozen singles that failed to chart, finally broke through with their #1 hit "Baby Love." The Supremes would have five straight #1 songs in a row, and twelve #1 songs overall. What began as three girls from Detroit's Brewster housing projects developed into a trio of international singing superstars, playing Las Vegas and the *"Ed Sullivan"* show on a regular basis.

Trivia

Except for its regional issues before it became a national label, the Tamla 45 numbering system actually begins in the 54000s. This is because Berry Gordy wanted to pay tribute to Jackie Wilson, who sang Gordy's song "Reet Petite" and made it a pop hit. "Reet Petite" is on Brunswick 55024.

Diana Ross, Mary Wilson and Florence Ballard were the singing trio behind some of Motown's greatest hit songs. Photo Credit: Courtesy Last Vestige Music Store, Albany, N.Y.

The year 1964 was also when the Temptations established themselves as hitmakers extraordinaire. The group was formed in 1960, as the merger of two vocal groups, the Primes and the Elgins. With the dueling lead vocal skills of David Ruffin and Eddie Kendricks, the Temptations had major hits with songs like "The Way You Do The Things You Do," "Beauty Is Only Skin Deep," and their #1 smash, "My Girl."

One of the Temptations' classic hits, "Ain't Too Proud to Beg."

One could argue that Motown was a solitary recording act with multiple lead singers. Whether the vocalists were the Supremes or the Vandellas, the Temptations or the Miracles, the Motown house band provided top-of-the-line musicianship for all of them. Led by keyboardist Earl Van Dyke, the house band consisted of bassist James Jamerson, guitarists Robert White and Joe Messina, and drummer Benny Benjamin. It's their orchestrations that can be heard on nearly every Motown record during the 1960s. And their ability to tailor their musical style for each artist, whether it was the party-dance sound of Martha Reeves and the Vandellas, the icy roughness of Marvin Gaye, or the emotional cries of the Four Tops, provided their artists with a flexibility previously unheard of in studio bands.

Motown could also take pride in its songwriting teams. The Brian Holland-Lamont Dozier-Eddie Holland triumvirate composed chart-topping smashes for Diana Ross and the Supremes, while Norman Whitfield and Barrett Strong gave the Temptations some of their greatest hits. Another songwriting duo, Nickolas Ashford and Valerie Simpson, wrote their first big hits for the duo of Marvin Gaye and Tammi Terrell.

According to legend, after the success of the Four Tops' "I Can't Help Myself," Columbia Records was about to reissue an old Four Tops song from their vaults. The Holland-Dozier-Holland songwriting team immediately wrote a new song for the Four Tops, and Motown rush-released it, eventually killing off the Columbia reissue. The song they wrote, "It's The Same Old Song," eventually hit the Top 10.

Not only was one expected to be a top-notch singer in the Motown stable, one also had to be able to perform on stage. Everything, from the Supremes' hand-signals during "Stop! In the Name of Love," to the Temptations' dance steps during "My Girl," were choreographed by Motown's Cholly Atkins. Artists were groomed on everything from stage appearance to diction, as Gordy wanted his stars to appeal both to black and white audiences.

By the late 1960s, Motown was a dominant force on the pop and soul charts. Songs like Marvin Gaye's "I Heard It Through The Grapevine," Smokey Robinson and the Miracles' "The Tears of a Clown," the Temptations' "Just My Imagination (Running Away With Me)," and Diana Ross and the Supremes' "Love Child" were part of every radio station's playlists.

Diana Ross and the Supremes, dressing down for the cover of their new album *Love Child.* Courtesy Boo's Blast from the Past, Philadelphia, Pa.

The 1970s were a time of sweeping change in the Motown studios. Albums full of three-minute pop songs, a formula that had sustained Motown's album division for over a decade, changed as Marvin Gaye's social awareness album *What's Goin' On* and Stevie Wonder's innovative double-LP *Songs in the Key of Life* both topped the album charts. Motown itself moved in a different direction, as Berry Gordy moved his musical hit factory to Los Angeles in 1972, in an effort to help Motown enter the motion picture industry and to establish Diana Ross as an actress.

While Diana Ross did have major hits in the 1970s, including "Ain't No Mountain High Enough," "Love Hangover," and "Theme From 'Mahogany' (Do You Know Where You're Going To)," the group she left, the Supremes, continued to have major hits, including "Up The Ladder To The Roof," "Nathan Jones," and "Stoned Love."

In fact, during the 1970s, many of Motown's greatest acts splintered apart, yet still were able to garner Top 10 hits. Such successes included former Temptations Eddie Kendricks ("Keep On Truckin'") and David Ruffin ("Walk Away From Love"); both Smokey Robinson ("Cruisin'") and the Miracles ("Love Machine"); and the Jackson 5's Jermaine Jackson ("Let's Get Serious") and Michael Jackson ("Ben," and "Rockin' Robin").

Trivia

Many of Motown's early album covers have generic artwork on the front cover. This was because many record store owners in the South would not sell an album by a black artist, especially if said artist was on the front cover. The worst example of this was when the Isley Brothers' album *This Old Heart of Mine* featured two WHITE people on the front cover.

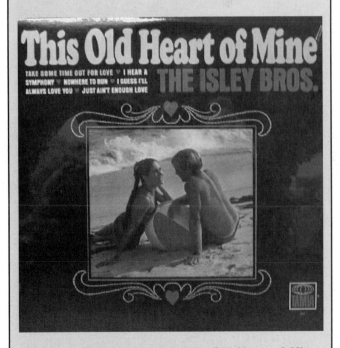

The Isley Brothers' album *This Old Heart of Mine.* Note—neither of the two people on the front cover are Isley Brothers. Courtesy Boo's Blasts from the Past.

In the 1980s, Motown's most successful stars were Stevie Wonder, Lionel Richie, and Rick James. Wonder continued to dominate the pop, soul, and adult contemporary charts with "I Just Called To Say I Love You," "That Girl," and "Part-Time Lover." Lionel Richie, the former lead singer of the Commodores, strung together a series of #1 ballads like "Truly," "You Are," "My Love," and "All Night Long (All Night)."

Today, Motown is a subsidiary of Universal Music Group, and Berry Gordy has long since sold his stock in the company. The label still continues on, however, as artists such as Boyz II Men, Erykah Badu, and Brian McKnight continue the tradition that began with Berry Gordy and the house-turned studio on 2648 West Grand Boulevard.

What To Look For: The most collectible Motown/Tamla/Gordy recordings are the earliest ones. The pre-1964 recordings by artists such as Marv Johnson, Mary Wells, the Miracles, Eddie Holland, the Elgins, and "Little" Stevie Wonder are difficult to find. Early albums by these groups are also collectible; be aware that Motown has reissued their back catalog many times, and will often place a "originally recorded" box on the back of the album jacket.

Brenda Holloway had a million-selling record with the title track from this album. Both that single and this album are very hard to find today. Courtesy Good Rockin' Tonight / Collectors Universe.

The earliest Tamla and Motown record labels have vertical lines. From 1962 to 1964, Tamla used a tan label with two circles at the top; one circle was a globe, the other was the name "TAMLA." From 1964 until the label was shut down in the mid-1980s, the word "TAMLA" appeared in a box at the top of the 45 label.

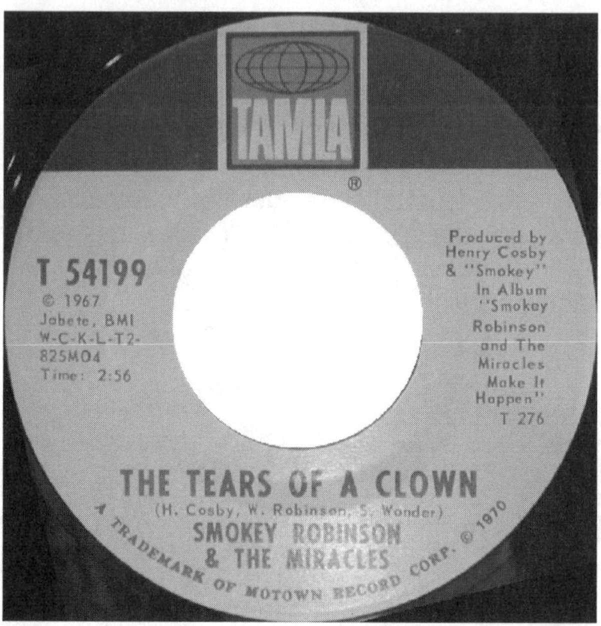

"Tears of a Clown" actually appeared on a 1967 *Miracles* album. It wasn't until 1970, when the song became a hit in England, that Motown released it as a single in America. From the Collection of Val Shively.

Motown went from their vertical lines label to a map of Detroit in 1962, with the word "MOTOWN," in red-gold-green letters, superimposed over the map. The bottom of the label was a dark blue, with the recording information stamped in white or silver.

Gordy Records, the home of the Temptations and Rick James, originally had the name "Gordy" in script at the 12:00 of the label, with the words "It's what's in the grooves that count" surrounding the "Gordy." By 1965, that was replaced with a magenta label and a yellow triangle running from the label's 9:00 edge to the 3:00 edge. The word "GORDY" appeared inside the triangle, with a large "G" as part of the artwork.

The 1960s Motown classics were recorded to be heard on AM car radios. Because of this, many of Motown's greatest songs sound better in mono than in stereo. Some of the stereo recordings were rechanneled, putting the drums in one speaker and the rest of the instruments in the other. On Marvin Gaye's "I Heard It Through The Grapevine," Gaye's voice is in both speakers, but the drums are in the left channel and the strings are in the right.

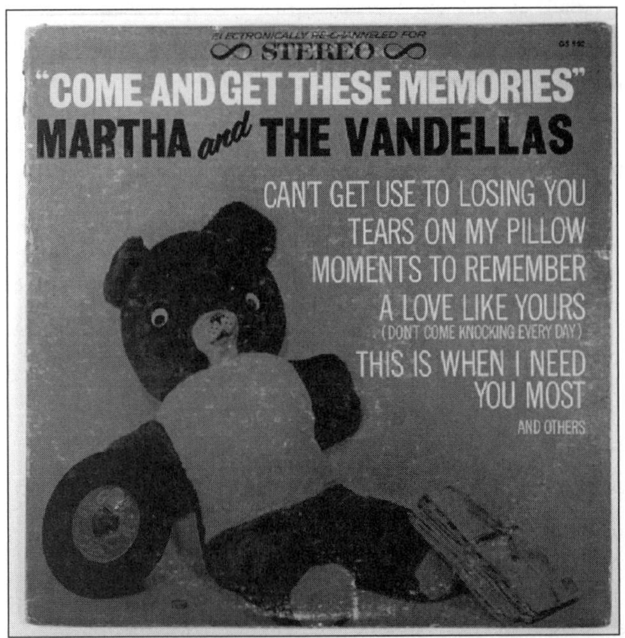

Notice the top of the album jacket for Martha and the Vandellas' *Come and Get These Memories.* This means the album was recorded in mono, but the tracks were separated to give an illusion of stereo. Courtesy Good Rockin' Tonight / Collectors Universe.

Some records are surprisingly expensive on the collectible market. One of the reasons is that many Motown records that did not become hits upon their first release, eventually became hits overseas, in the "Northern Soul" British dance clubs. This makes the few copies that were pressed extremely rare today. Other times, a song will be pulled from production at the last minute, many times for reasons known only to Berry Gordy. The few copies that were pressed became instant collectibles.

References: Smith, Suzanne E., *Dancing In The Street: Motown and the Cultural Politics of Detroit*, Harvard University Press, Cambridge, Mass., 1999; Walker, Don, *The Motown Story*, Charles Scribner's Sons, New York, N.Y., 1985.

Museums: The Motown Historical Museum, 2648 West Grand Boulevard, Detroit, Michigan 48208-1237. Phone: (313) 875-2264. E-mail: *MotownMus@aol.com.*

Web pages: Motown's homepage, celebrating the company's 40th anniversary: *http://www.motown.com*; a page devoted to Mary Wilson of the Supremes: *http://www.marywilson.com*; the Unofficial Stevie Wonder Internet Archive: *http://www.insoul.com/stevie;* the Motown Alumni Association, a 10,000-member organization dedicated to maintaining a brotherhood among former musicians, singers and employees of Motown: *http://members.aol.com/maainc.*

Trivia

Motown had some rock and roll hits in the 1970s. A garage band called Rare Earth, who recorded on the custom-made Rare Earth label, had psychedelic rock hits with "(I Know) I'm Losing You" and "I Just Want to Celebrate." Motown even had a country music label, Melodyland. Their most popular singer on that label was T.G. Sheppard, who sang "Devil in the Bottle" and "Tryin' To Beat The Morning Home."

45s	Year	VG	VG+	NM
Commodores, "I'm Looking for Love" / "At the Zoo" (Mowest 5009)	1972	$2.00	$4.00	$8.00
Commodores, "Brick House" / "Captain Quickdraw" (Motown 1425)	1977		$2.00	$4.00
The Darnells, "Too Hurt to Cry, Too Much In Love To Say Goodbye" / "Come On Home" (Gordy 7024) (group is actually the Marvelettes)	1963	$20.00	$40.00	$80.00
The Downbeats, "Request of a Fool" / "Your Baby's Back" (Tamla 54056)				
(if first pressing, with "Tamla" circling globe at top of label)	1962	$75.00	$150.00	$300.00
(if second pressing, with "Tamla" in globe at top of label)	1962	$7.50	$15.00	$30.00
The Downbeats, "Darling Baby" / "Put Yourself In My Place" (V.I.P. 25029)	1965	$50.00	$100.00	$200.00
The Elgins, "Darling Baby" / "Put Yourself In My Place" (V.I.P. 25029) (the Downbeats changed their name)	1965	$5.00	$10.00	$20.00
The Four Seasons, "Walk On, Don't Look Back" / "Sun Country" (Mowest 5026)	1972	$2.50	$5.00	$10.00
The Four Tops, "It's The Same Old Song" / "Your Love is Amazing" (Motown 1081)	1965	$3.75	$7.50	$15.00
The Four Tops, "Reach Out I'll Be There" / "Until You Love Someone" (Motown 1098)	1966	$3.75	$7.50	$15.00
(with picture sleeve, add:)	1966	$20.00	$40.00	$80.00
Marvin Gaye, "Let Your Conscience Be Your Gude" / "Never Let You Go" (Tamla 54041)	1961	$100.00	$200.00	$400.00
Marvin Gaye, "Baby Don't You Do It" / "Walk On The Wild Side" (Tamla 54101)	1964	$3.75	$7.50	$15.00
(with picture sleeve, add;)	1964	$15.00	$30.00	$60.00
Marvin Gaye, "I Heard It Through The Grapevine" / "You're What's Happening (In The World Today)" (Tamla 54176)	1968	$2.50	$5.00	$10.00
Marvin Gaye and Tammi Terrell, "Your Precious Love" / "Hold Me Oh My Darling" (Tamla 54156)	1967	$2.00	$4.00	$8.00
Eddie Holland, "Merry-Go-Round" / "It Moves Me" (Tamla 102)	1959	$62.50	$125.00	$250.00
Eddie Holland, "Jamie" / "Take A Chance On Me" (Motown 1021)	1961	$6.25	$12.50	$25.00
Brenda Holloway, "Every Little Bit Hurts" / "Land of 1,000 Boys" (Tamla 54094)	1964	$3.00	$6.00	$12.00
Brenda Holloway, "When I'm Gone" / "I've Been Good To You" (Tamla 54111)	1965	$3.75	$7.50	$15.00
(with picture sleeve, add:)	1965	$25.00	$50.00	$100.00
The Jackson Five, "I Want You Back" / "Who's Lovin' You" (Motown 1157)	1969	$2.00	$4.00	$8.00
The Jackson Five, "Dancing Machine" / "It's Too Late to Change the Time" (Motown 1286)	1974		$3.00	$6.00
Jermaine Jackson, "Let's Get Serious" / "Je Vous Aime Beaucoups" (Motown 1469)	1980		$2.00	$4.00
Michael Jackson, "I Wanna Be Where You Are" / "We Got A Good Thing Going" (Motown 1202)	1972		$2.50	$5.00
(with picture sleeve, add:)	1972	$2.50	$5.00	$10.00

45s	Year	VG	VG+	NM
Marv Johnson, "Come to Me" / "Whisper" (Tamla 101)				
(with no address on label)	1959	$75.00	$150.00	$300.00
(with Gladstone St., Detroit address on label)	1959	$62.50	$125.00	$250.00
Eddie Kendricks, "Keep On Truckin'" (Part 1) / (Part 2) (Tamla 54238)	1973		$2.50	$5.00
Gladys Knight and the Pips, "I Heard It Through The Grapevine" / "It's Time To Go Now" (Soul 35039)	1967	$2.50	$5.00	$10.00
Martha and the Vandellas, "Come and Get These Memories" / "Jealous Love" (Gordy 7014)	1963	$7.50	$15.00	$30.00
Martha and the Vandellas, "Dancing in the Street" / "There He Is (At My Door)" (Gordy 7033)	1964	$3.75	$7.50	$15.00
(with picture sleeve, add:)	1964	$30.00	$60.00	$120.00
The Marvelettes, "Please Mr. Postman" / "So Long Baby" (Tamla 54046)	1961	$6.25	$12.50	$25.00
(with picture sleeve, add:)	1961	$30.00	$60.00	$120.00
The Marvelettes, "Beechwood 4-5789" / "Someday, Someway" (Tamla 54065)	1962	$5.00	$10.00	$20.00
The Miracles, "What's So Good About Good-By" / "I've Been Good To You" (Tamla 54053)	1962	$7.50	$15.00	$30.00
(with picture sleeve, add:)	1962	$30.00	$60.00	$120.00
Smokey Robinson and the Miracles, "The Tears of a Clown" / "Promise Me" (Tamla 54199)	1970		$3.00	$6.00
The Miracles, "Love Machine" (Part 1) / (Part 2) (Tamla 54262)	1975		$2.50	$5.00
The Originals, "Baby I'm For Real" / "The Moment of Truth" (Soul 35066)	1969	$2.00	$4.00	$8.00
Diana Ross, "Ain't No Mountain High Enough" / "Can't It Wait Until Tomorrow" (Motown 1169)	1970		$2.50	$5.00
(with picture sleeve, add:)	1970	$3.00	$6.00	$12.00
Diana Ross and Marvin Gaye, "My Mistake (Was To Love You)" / "Include Me In Your Life" (Motown 1269)	1973		$2.50	$5.00
Diana Ross, Marvin Gaye, Smokey Robinson, Stevie Wonder, "Pops, We Love You (Tribute to Father)" / (instrumental) (Motown 1455)	1979		$2.00	$4.00
David Ruffin, "My Whole World Ended (The Moment You Left Me)" / "I've Got To Find A Brand New Baby" (Motown 1140)	1968		$3.00	$6.00
David Ruffin, "Walk Away From Love" / "Love Can Be Hazardous To Your Health" (Motown 1376)	1975		$2.50	$5.00
The Spinners, "In My Diary" / "(She's Gonna Love Me) At Sundown" (Motown 1155)	1969	$375.00	$750.00	$1,500.00
The Spinners, "It's A Shame" / "Together We Can Make Such Sweet Music" (V.I.P. 25057)	1970	$3.00	$6.00	$12.00
The Supremes, "I Want A Guy" / "Never Again" (Motown 1008)	1961	$75.00	$150.00	$300.00
(if on Tamla 54038, "lines" label)	1961	$31.25	$62.50	$125.00
(if on Tamla 54038, "globe" label)	1961	$15.00	$30.00	$60.00
The Supremes, "A Breath Taking, First Sight Soul Shaking, One Night Love Making, Next Day Heart Breaking Guy" / "Rock and Roll Banjo Band" (Motown 1044)	1963	$25.00	$50.00	$100.00
(if later pressing, title of A-side shortened to "A Breath Taking Guy")	1963	$6.25	$12.50	$25.00
The Supremes, "Where Did Our Love Go" / "He Means The World To Me" (Motown 1060)	1964	$5.00	$10.00	$20.00
(with picture sleeve, add:)	1964	$5.00	$10.00	$20.00
The Supremes, "You Keep Me Hangin' On" / "Remove This Doubt" (Motown 1101)	1966	$3.75	$7.50	$15.00
(with picture sleeve, add:)	1966	$7.50	$15.00	$30.00
Diana Ross and the Supremes, "Love Child" / "This Will Be The Day" (Motown 1135)	1968	$2.00	$4.00	$8.00
Diana Ross and the Supremes, "Someday We'll Be Together" / "He's My Sunny Boy" (Motown 1156)	1969	$2.00	$4.00	$8.00
The Supremes, "Stoned Love" / "Shine on Me" (Motown 1172)	1970		$3.00	$6.00
Bobby Taylor and the Vancouvers, "Does Your Mama Know About Me" / "Fading Away" (Gordy 7069)	1968	$5.00	$10.00	$20.00
The Temptations, "My Girl" / "Nobody But My Baby" (Gordy 7038)	1965	$3.75	$7.50	$15.00
(with picture sleeve, add:)	1965	$30.00	$60.00	$120.00

45s	Year	VG	VG+	NM
The Temptations, "Beauty Is Only Skin Deep" / "You're Not An Ordinary Girl" (Gordy 7055)	1966	$3.75	$7.50	$15.00
(with picture sleeve, add:)	1966	$10.00	$20.00	$40.00
The Temptations, "Just My Imagination (Running Away With Me)" / "You Make Your Own Heaven And Hell Right Here On Earth" (Gordy 7105)	1971		$3.00	$6.00
The Undisputed Truth, "Smiling Faces Sometimes" / "You Got the Love I Need" (Gordy 7108)	1971		$3.00	$6.00
The Velvelettes, "A Bird in the Hand (Is Worth Two in the Bush)" / (B-side unknown) (VIP 25021)	1965	$200.00	$400.00	$800.00
(if B-side is "Since You've Been Loving Me," on VIP 25030)	1965	$5.00	$10.00	$20.00
Jr. Walker and the All Stars, "Shotgun" / "Hot Cha" (Soul 35008)	1965	$3.75	$7.50	$15.00
(with picture sleeve, add:)	1965	$6.25	$12.50	$25.00
Jr. Walker and the All Stars, "What Does It Take (To Win Your Love)" / "Brainwasher - Part 1" (Soul 35062)	1969	$2.00	$4.00	$8.00
Mary Wells, "Bye Bye Baby" / "Please Forgive Me" (Motown 1003)	1960	$12.50	$25.00	$50.00
Mary Wells, "You Beat Me To The Punch" / "Old Love (Let's Try It Again)" (Motown 1032)	1962	$5.00	$10.00	$20.00
(with picture sleeve, add:)	1962	$30.00	$60.00	$120.00
Mary Wells, "My Guy" / "Oh Little Boy (What Did You Do To Me)" (Motown 1056)	1964	$5.00	$10.00	$20.00
Kim Weston, "Helpless" / "A Love Like Yours (Don't Come Knocking Every Day)" (Gordy 7050)	1966	$5.00	$10.00	$20.00
Little Stevie Wonder, "Fingertips" (Pt. 2) / "Fingertips" (Pt. 1) (Tamla 54080)	1963	$5.00	$10.00	$20.00
(with picture sleeve, add:)	1963	$12.50	$25.00	$50.00
Stevie Wonder, "Uptight (Everything's Alright)" / "Purple Rain Drops" (Tamla 54124)	1965	$3.75	$7.50	$15.00
Stevie Wonder, "Superstition" / "You've Got It Bad Girl" (Tamla 54226)	1972		$3.00	$6.00

LPs	Year	VG	VG+	NM
The Elgins, Darling Baby (V.I.P. 400) (mono)	1966	$17.50	$35.00	$60.00
(if on V.I.P. S-400, stereo)	1966	$25.00	$50.00	$100.00
The Four Tops, Four Tops Reach Out (Motown 660) (mono)	1967	$6.25	$12.50	$25.00
(if on Motown MS-660, stereo)	1967	$6.25	$12.50	$25.00
The Four Seasons, Chameleon (Mowest MW 108L)	1972	$3.00	$6.00	$12.00
Marvin Gaye, The Soulful Moods of Marvin Gaye (Tamla T 221) (mono)	1961	$250.00	$500.00	$1,000.00
Marvin Gaye, How Sweet It Is To Be Loved By You (Tamla T 258) (mono)	1965	$10.00	$20.00	$40.00
(if on Tamla TS 258, stereo)	1965	$12.50	$25.00	$50.00
Marvin Gaye, What's Going On (Tamla TS-310)	1971	$3.75	$7.50	$15.00
Eddie Holland, Eddie Holland (Motown 604) (mono)	1963	$100.00	$200.00	$400.00
Brenda Holloway, Every Little Bit Hurts (Tamla T 257) (mono)	1964	$50.00	$100.00	$200.00
(if on Tamla TS 257, rechanneled stereo)	1964	$37.50	$75.00	$150.00
(if on Motown 5242 ML, reissue)	1982	$3.00	$6.00	$12.00
The Jackson Five, Diana Ross Presents the Jackson Five (Motown MS 700)	1969	$6.25	$12.50	$25.00
(if on Motown M5-129V1, reissue)	1981	$2.00	$4.00	$8.00
Jermaine Jackson, Come Into My Life (Motown M-775)	1973	$2.50	$5.00	$10.00
Michael Jackson, Ben (Motown M 755)				
(if Michael Jackson is on top half of cover, rats on the bottom half)	1972	$15.00	$30.00	$60.00
(if only Michael Jackson on front cover)	1972	$3.75	$7.50	$15.00
(if on Motown M5-153V1, reissue)	1981	$2.50	$5.00	$10.00
Michael Jackson, Michael Jackson and the Jackson 5 - 14 Greatest Hits (Motown 6099 ML) (picture disc with white glove)	1984	$2.50	$5.00	$10.00
Eddie Kendricks, Boogie Down! (Tamla T6-330)	1974	$2.50	$5.00	$10.00
Gladys Knight and the Pips, Everybody Needs Love (Soul S 706) (mono)	1967	$5.00	$10.00	$20.00

45s	Year	VG	VG+	NM
(if on Soul SS 706, stereo)	1967	$6.25	$12.50	$25.00
(if on Motown M5-126V1, reissue)	1981	$3.00	$6.00	$12.00
Martha and the Vandellas, Come and Get These Memories (Gordy G-902)				
(mono)	1963	$100.00	$200.00	$400.00
(if on Gordy GS-902, stereo)	1963	$200.00	$400.00	$800.00
Martha and the Vandellas, Heat Wave				
(Gordy 907) (mono)	1963	$37.50	$75.00	$150.00
(if on Gordy GS-907, rechanneled stereo, "stereo" banner pre-printed on cover)	1963	$37.50	$75.00	$150.00
(if on Gordy GS-907, stereo, mono cover with "Stereo" sticker)	1963	$100.00	$200.00	$400.00
(if on Motown M5-145V1, reissue)	1981	$2.50	$5.00	$10.00
The Marvelettes, Please Mr. Postman (Tamla T 228) (mono)				
(if white label on record)	1961	$150.00	$300.00	$600.00
(if on Tamla "globes" yellow label)	1963	$7.50	$150.00	$300.00
(if on Motown 5266 ML, reissue)	1982	$2.50	$5.00	$10.00
The Miracles, Hi We're the Miracles				
(Tamla T 220) (mono) (white label)	1961	$150.00	$300.00	$600.00
(if on Motown M5-160V1, reissue)	1981	$2.00	$4.00	$8.00
Smokey Robinson and the Miracles, Make It Happen (Tamla T 276) (mono)	1967	$6.25	$12.50	$25.00
(if on Tamla TS 276, stereo)	1967	$7.50	$15.00	$30.00
(if on Tamla TS 276, stereo, renamed "The Tears of a Clown")	1970	$3.75	$7.50	$15.00
The Originals, Baby I'm For Real (Soul SS-716)	1969	$10.00	$20.00	$40.00
The Spinners, 2nd Time Around (V.I.P. 405)	1970	$10.00	$20.00	$40.00
The Supremes, Meet the Supremes (Motown 606) (mono)				
(if group is sitting on stools)	1963	$225.00	$450.00	$900.00
(if cover is comprised of faces)	1963	$7.50	$15.00	$30.00
(if on Motown MS 606, stereo, cover is comprised of faces)	1964	$10.00	$20.00	$40.00
The Supremes, Where Did Our Love Go				
(Motown M 621) (mono)	1964	$7.50	$15.00	$30.00
(if on Motown MS 621, stereo)	1964	$10.00	$20.00	$40.00
The Supremes, I Hear A Symphony				
(Motown 643) (mono)	1966	$6.25	$12.50	$25.00
(if on Motown MS 643, stereo)	1966	$7.50	$15.00	$30.00
The Supremes, New Ways but Love Stays (Motown MS 720)	1970	$3.75	$7.50	$15.00
The Temptations, Meet the Temptations				
(Gordy G 911) (mono)	1964	$7.50	$15.00	$30.00
(if on Gordy GS 911, stereo, script "Gordy" on top of label)	1964	$10.00	$20.00	$40.00
(if on Gordy GS 911, stereo, black "GORDY" inside "G" on left of label, reissue)	1967	$5.00	$10.00	$20.00
The Temptations, Temptin' Temptations				
(Gordy 914) (mono)	1965	$6.25	$12.50	$25.00
(if on Gordy GS 914, stereo, script "Gordy" on top of label)	1965	$7.50	$15.00	$30.00
(if on Gordy GS 914, stereo, black "GORDY" inside "G" on left of label, reissue)	1967	$5.00	$10.00	$20.00
The Temptations, Live at the Copa (Gordy 938)	1968	$5.00	$10.00	$20.00
Jr. Walker and the All-Stars, Shotgun (Soul 701) (mono)				
(if white label, "SOUL" at left)	1965	$15.00	$30.00	$60.00
(if purple swirl label, "SOUL" at top)	1965	$5.00	$10.00	$20.00
(if on Soul SS-701, stereo)	1965	$7.50	$15.00	$30.00
(if on Motown M5-141V1, reissue)	1981	$2.50	$5.00	$10.00
Mary Wells, Bye Bye Baby / I Didn't Want To Take A Chance (Motown M 600) (mono)				
(if white label, stock copy)	1961	$75.00	$150.00	$300.00
(with map of Detroit, label address above center hole)	1962	$62.50	$125.00	$250.00
(if on Motown M5-161V1, reissue)	1981	$2.50	$5.00	$10.00
Little Stevie Wonder, Recorded Live / Little Stevie Wonder / The 12 Year Old Genius				
(Tamla T 240) (mono)	1963	$37.50	$75.00	$150.00
(if on Motown MS-131V1, reissue)	1981	$3.00	$6.00	$12.00
Stevie Wonder, I Was Made To Love Her				
(Tamla T 279) (mono)	1967	$5.00	$10.00	$20.00
(if on Tamla TS 279, stereo)	1967	$6.25	$12.50	$25.00
Stevie Wonder, Talking Book (Tamla T 319L)				
(if first pressing, with Braille note on cover)	1972	$3.75	$7.50	$15.00
(if second pressing, with no Braille)	1973	$2.50	$5.00	$10.00

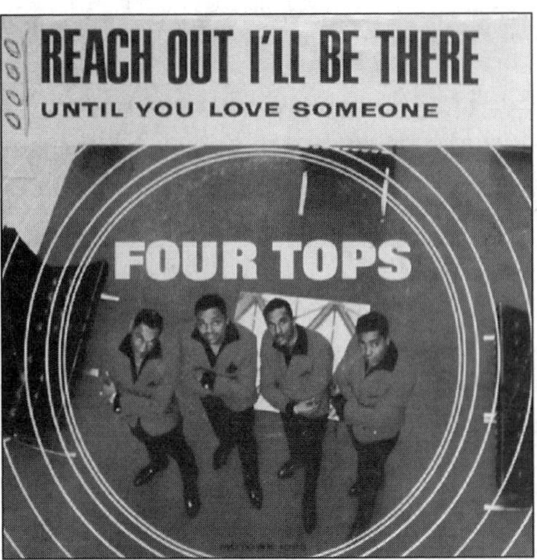

Picture sleeves didn't often survive the years as well as 45s did. Here's a picture sleeve for one of the Four Tops' biggest hits. From the Collection of Val Shively.

The original title of this song was "How Can I Forget You," but the promo copy lists the title differently. In the 1960s, most promo pressings simply had the name printed above, with little artwork or design. Courtesy Good Rockin' Tonight/Collectors Universe.

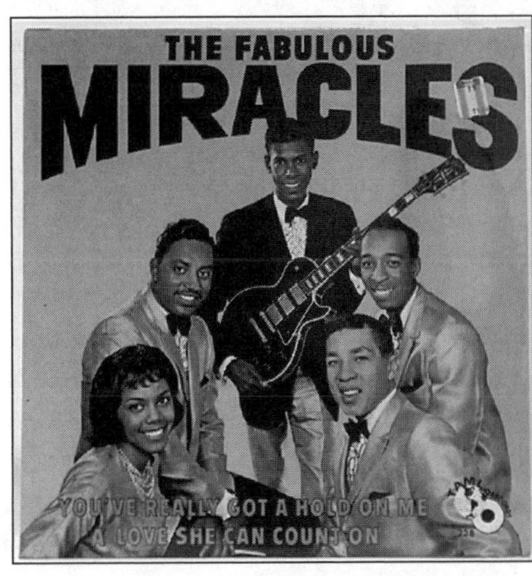

This Miracles' album was titled *The Fabulous Miracles,* but the album was later retitled to match with their biggest hit at the time, "You Really Got A Hold On Me." Courtesy Good Rockin' Tonight / Collectors Universe.

NEW WAVE AND ALTERNATIVE

History: The music was not as angry as the punk that preceded it. It was danceable, yet the lyrics were not as repetitive as the disco that preceded it. And it introduced the music world to the possibilities of a digital synthesizer as a viable component to a rock group.

This was New Wave music, a "new wave" of pop, rock, and dance songs to wash the angry punk bands and the mind-clogging disco groups away. While some American new wave bands started their careers with quirky, left-of-center recordings (the B-52s' "Rock Lobster," Devo's "Whip It," and Talking Heads' "Psycho Killer"), other groups expanded on punk's angry thrash and three-chord construction, creating a satire of punk-pop (the Ramones, Richard Hell, and the Voidoids).

The B-52's, so named for the hairdos the women wore in the group, had new wave hits with "Rock Lobster" and "Planet Claire," before breaking into the Top 40 with "Love Shack" and "Roam." This 12-inch EP remixes some of their early hits.

In England, an anti-punk "new romantic" musical movement appeared. Artists wore blazers and ties, their faces painted in David Bowie-esque androgynous makeup. Their musical heroes were part Bryan Ferry, part Henry Mancini. Their songs were a balance of dance tracks and ballads, with most bands in the new romantic genre employing synthesizers and drums. The most successful of these groups was Duran Duran, but other examples of New Romantic music include Spandau Ballet, Ultravox, and Gary Numan. Some New Romantic groups went one step further—they went for a more theatric look, whether it meant performing in gold lamé tuxedos (ABC) or in full Native American garb (Adam and the Ants).

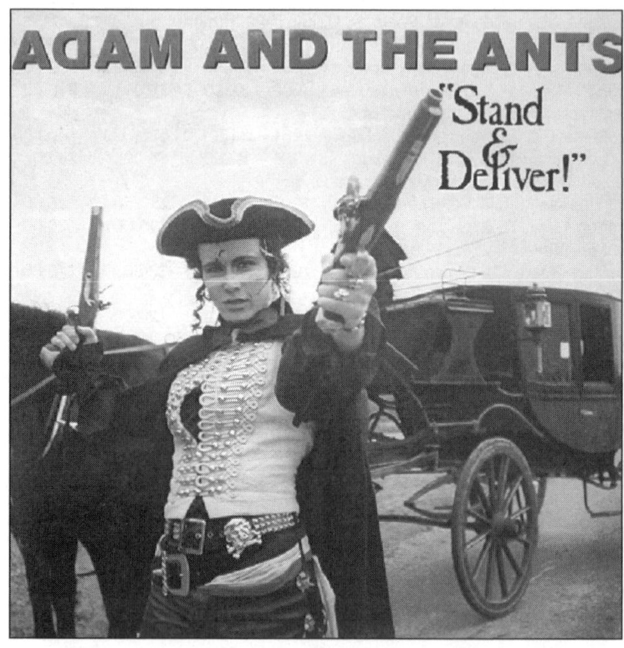

Stuart Goddard, the "Adam" of Adam and the Ants, dominated the British pop charts (and American alternative radio stations) with songs like "Stand and Deliver" and "Antmusic."

These groups found radio airplay from a previously untapped source—college radio stations. In the late 1970s, student-run college radio stations were playing Squeeze, Split Enz and Elvis Costello. These stations embraced a new wave variant simply called "new music," whether it belonged to independent California rock bands like Green on Red, the Blasters and X; or to Atlanta-based artists like the B-52s, R.E.M., and Let's Active; or to British synth-pop bands like Depeche Mode, Yaz, and Orchestral Maneuvers in the Dark. College radio helped many small and independent labels promote their recorded product, and even if these groups weren't heard on Top 40 stations, they sure were heard on the college stations on the low side of the FM dial. Eventually those college kids graduated, and the bands they listened to—R.E.M., Depeche Mode, and U2—eventually broke through to the mainstream.

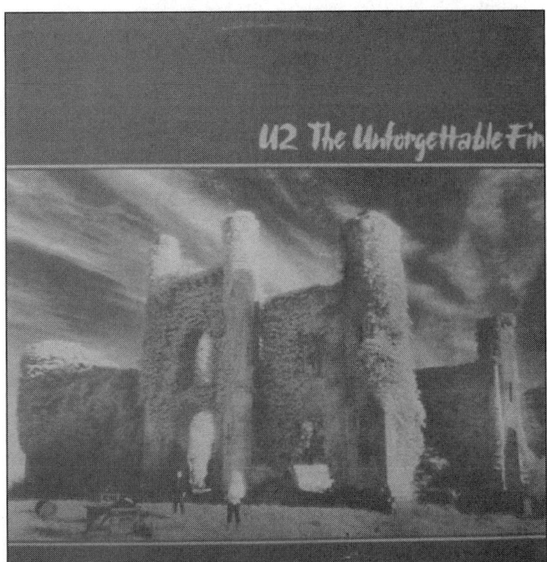

Thanks to college radio, many bands received valuable musical exposure. Many of these groups, like U2, would later achieve worldwide stardom.

New wave music also brought the digital synthesizer into mainstream music. Originally used for atmospheric or "spooky" music, the digital synthesizer could replicate the sound of any instrument—guitar, trumpet, drum—at the touch of a finger. While "techno" artists are featured in another chapter of this book, many new-wave bands incorporated synthesizers into their group, if only to create new sounds and project a futuristic image. Mainstream rock bands tended to look down on "synth-pop" bands, as electronic equipment had the appearance of "cheating," of pressing a button to create music.

Although Eurythmics started out as a do-it-yourself synth-pop alternative band, their music evolved into rock, funk and soul genres; and turned lead singer Annie Lennox (she's on the right) into a powerful pop chanteuse.

Trivia

The band R.E.M.'s earliest songs had incomprehensible lyrics, meaning people could interpret the songs any way they wished. In fact, in the music video for one of their later songs, "Fall on Me," the words were superimposed in big block letters on the front of the screen. No misinterpretation here.

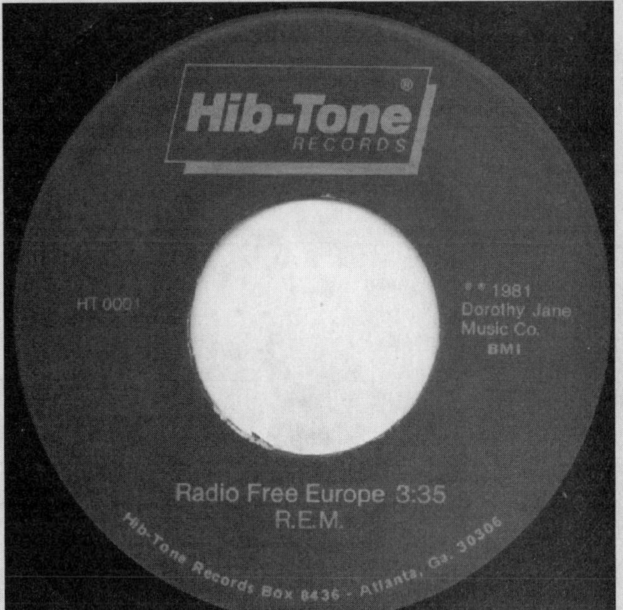

R.E.M.'s first single was released on the tiny Hib-Tone label in Georgia.

The song was later re-recorded when the band signed with IRS Records. The lyrics are almost impossible to decipher in either version.

One of the major paradoxes of "new wave" music was that it favored more artists from the United Kingdom rather than from America or any other country; one of the reasons was that these groups had actually topped the pop charts in England, and many record companies felt that if the group could hit #1 in England, it should have no trouble hitting #1 in America. Of course, this meant groups like the Minutemen, Innocence in Danger, Love Tractor, the dB's, and Blotto were left in the dust while a new wave "British Invasion" took over the airwaves.

The new wave/party band Blotto had a college radio hit with "I Wanna Be A Lifeguard." Their four-song EP has the entire history of the band, in typewritten font, as the background of the album cover.

Trivia

It took the Pet Shop Boys at least two different tries before their alternative dance hit "West End Girls" reached the top of the charts. An earlier version of this song was recorded with dance-pop wizard Bobby Orlando, and although that version did hit the dance charts, it failed to cross over to the pop world.

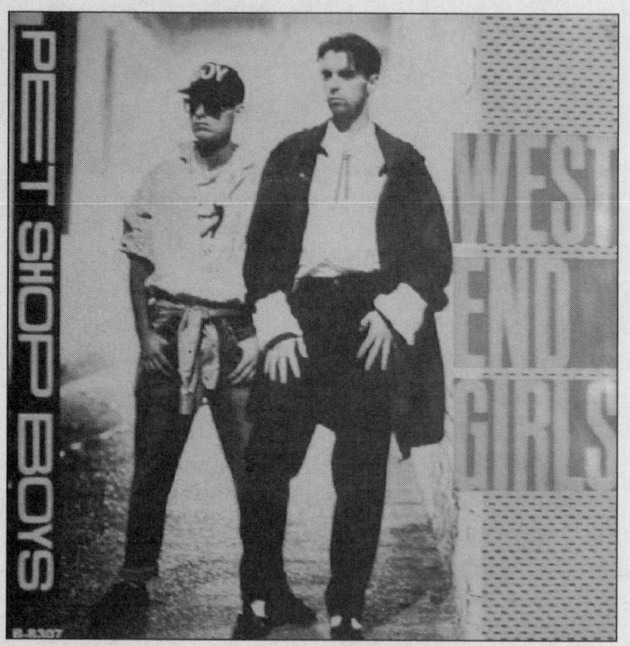

This is the picture sleeve for the Pet Shop Boys' "West End Girls," which hit #1 in 1986.

Eventually record companies looked to other countries for their pop music superstars, until the college radio and alternative broadcast stations sounded like the United Nations. In the span of an hour, you could hear German groups (Nena), Austrian singers (Falco), French groups (Telephone), Polish groups (Lady Pank), South African interracial groups (Juluka), Australian groups (InXs, Divinyls) and Japanese bands (Yellow Magic Orchestra).

What was known as "new wave" faded in the 1980s, as its musicians and artists either were reclassified as "pop" artists or as "alternative," depending on how often their music was heard on Top 40 radio.

Christina Amphlett and the Divinyls had some college radio and alternative broadcast hits in America; setting the groundwork for their biggest song, "I Touch Myself."

Early "alternative" music didn't always have a dance beat. It might encompass other musical rhythms, other world cultures, and the music itself was indeed an "alternative" to pop songs. In the 1970s, alternative tracks were musical experiments of their own, a combination of polyphonic notes and rhythms with poetry or anti-lyricism. Laurie Anderson used her alternative music as an extension of her acclaimed theatrical pieces. David Byrne experimented with new instruments and lyrics, just as Les Baxter had experimented with Polynesian instruments decades before. Synthesizers were now used by Brian Eno to create ambient sounds and dreamscapes, not just as fancy pianos.

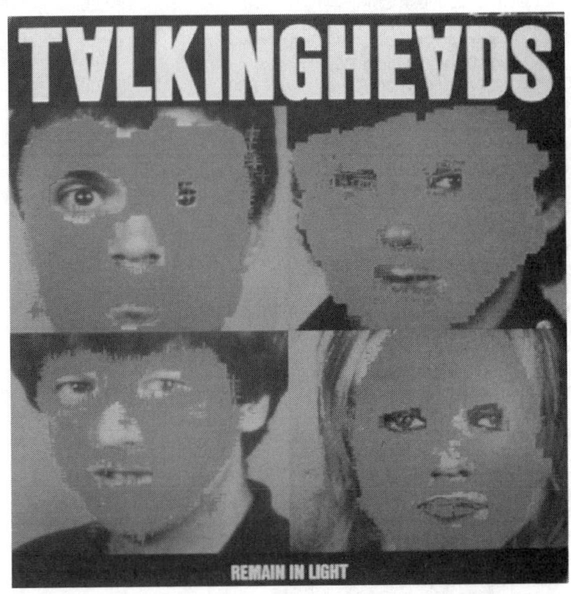

David Byrne and Talking Heads went from experimental new wavers to funk musicians (in the Tom Tom Club) and sonic excursions (David Byrne's soundtrack to The Catherine Wheel).

Today, "alternative" music is the bastion of rock bands whose songs are a mixture of punk and power pop, groups such as Green Day, the Presidents of the United States of America, Blink 182, and SR-71. Alternative music also encompasses those who create from samples and digital collages, such as Beck and Moby.

What To Look For: New wave and alternative music is readily plentiful and easy to find. Early pressings are difficult, especially those where artists have made print runs of less than 5,000 copies. Also, some artists may have had limited success with a major label, despite every college radio station in the country playing their songs. These groups may not have initially "caught on," but when their material goes to a more supportive record company and the group finally "breaks through," their early recordings suddenly become very collectible.

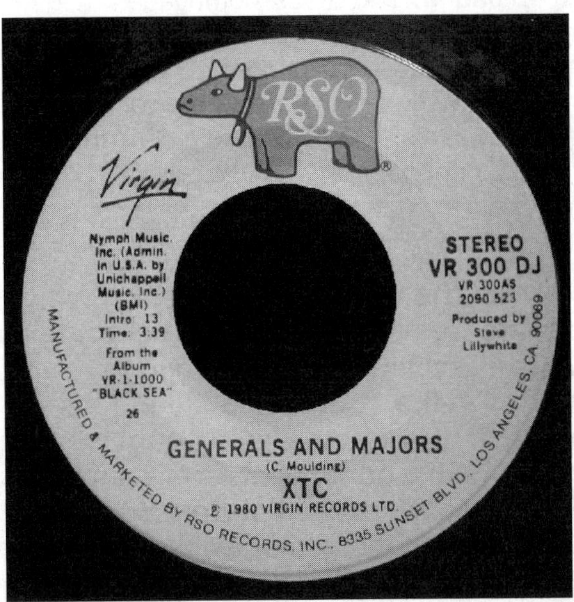

The alternative band XTC went through three different major labels in America, beginning with the disco label RSO.

Some 45s for 1970s new-wave artists may only be available as promo pressings; stock copies of lesser-known titles are more collectible than their promo-only counterparts; 12-inch promo discs are very collectible, as they often contain remixed or extended versions of classic new-wave recordings.

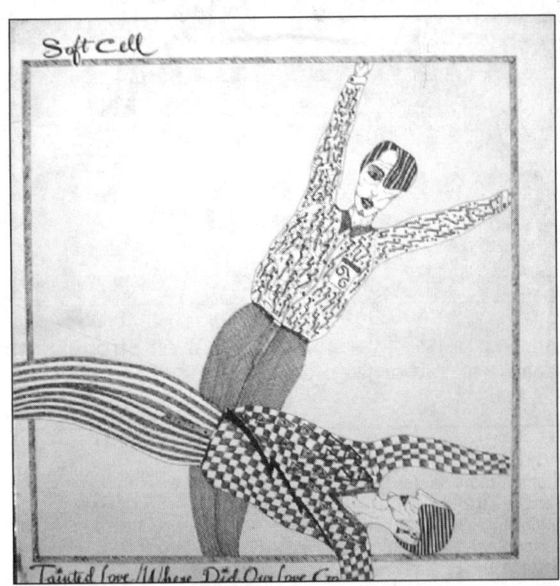

Merging Gloria Jones' "Tainted Love" with the Supremes' "Where Did Our Love Go" and soldering them to a synth-pop beat, Soft Cell had arguably the biggest international dance hit of 1982. This 12-inch version contains a dub remix on the B-side.

References: Neely, Tim, *Goldmine Price Guide to Alternative Records*, Krause Publications, Iola, Wisconsin, 1996.

Web pages: The B-52s' homepage: *http://www.theb52s.com*; the Ramones' homepage: *http://www.officialramones.com*; R.E.M.'s homepage: *http://www.remhq.com*; a page for fans of They Might Be Giants: *http://www.tmbg.com*; the homepage for Blotto: *http://www.blotto.net*.

Trivia

Many of the weird noises on the Flying Lizards' remake of "Money" occurred when the piano player wedged toys and fabrics in the stringed section of his piano. If this sounds weird, consider that in the 1960s, some performers, including Ferrante and Teicher, performed with "prepared pianos" that were altered to create new and unique tones.

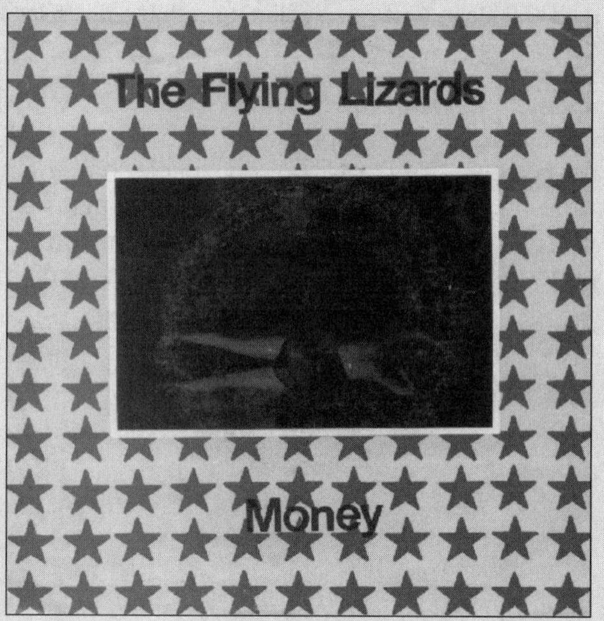

This freeze-dried version of the Barrett Strong classic became an underground hit in 1979.

45s	Year	VG	VG+	NM
ABC, "The Look of Love" (Part One) / "Theme From Mantrap" (Mercury 76168)	1982		$3.00	
(with picture sleeve, add:)	1982		$2.00	$4.00
Adam and the Ants, "Stand and Deliver" / "Beat My Guest" (Epic AE7 1236)	1981		$3.00	
(with picture sleeve, add:)	1981		$3.00	
The Alarm, "The Stand" / "Reason 41" (IRS 9922)	1983		$2.00	$4.00
(with picture sleeve, add:)	1983	$2.50	$5.00	$10.00
The Alarm, "Sixty Eight Guns" / "Pavilion Steps" (IRS 9924)	1984		$2.00	$4.00
(with picture sleeve, add:)	1984		$2.00	$4.00
Laurie Anderson, "O Superman (For Massinet)" / "Walking The Dog"				
(if on One Ten Records, catalog number unknown)	1981	$2.50	$5.00	$10.00
(with picture sleeve, add:)	1981	$2.50	$5.00	$10.00
The Art of Noise, "Close (To The Edit)" / (b-side unknown) (Island 97754)	1984		$2.00	$4.00
(with picture sleeve, add:)	1984		$2.00	$4.00

45s	Year	VG	VG+	NM
The B-52s, "Rock Lobster" / "52 Girls" (DB 52)	1978	$6.25	$12.50	$25.00
(with picture sleeve, add:)	1978	$6.25	$12.50	$25.00
The B-52s, "Rock Lobster" / "6060-842" (Warner Bros. 49173)	1980		$2.00	$4.00
(with picture sleeve, add:)	1980		$3.00	$6.00
Blondie, "In The Flesh" / "Man Overboard" (Private Stock 45141)	1977	$5.00	$10.00	$20.00
Blondie, "Heart of Glass" / "11:59" (Chrysalis 2295)	1979		$2.00	$4.00
(with picture sleeve, add:)	1979		$2.00	$4.00
The Boomtown Rats, "I Don't Like Mondays" / "It's All The Rage" (Columbia 11117)	1979	$2.50	$5.00	
Bow Wow Wow, "I Want Candy" / "Elimination Dancing" (RCA PB-13204)	1982		$3.00	
(with picture sleeve, add:)	1982		$3.00	
Kate Bush, "Wuthering Heights" / "Kite" (EMI America 8003)	1978		$2.00	$4.00
(with picture sleeve, add:)	1978	$2.00	$4.00	$8.00
Cabaret Voltaire, "Seconds Too Late" / "Control Addict" (Rough Trade RT-US-003)	1985		$2.50	$5.00
(with picture sleeve, add:)	1981		$2.50	$5.00
The Call, "Walls Come Down" / "Upperbirth" (Mercury 811 487-7)	1983		$2.00	$4.00
The Jim Carroll Band, "People Who Died" / "I Want The Angel" (Atco 7314)	1980		$3.00	
The Cars, "Just What I Needed" / "I'm In Touch With Your World" (Elektra 45491)	1978		$3.00	
(if pressed on red vinyl)	1978	$2.50	$5.00	$10.00
(with picture sleeve, add:)	1978		$2.50	$5.00
The Church, "Under the Milky Way" / "Musk" (Arista 9673)	1988		$3.00	
(with picture sleeve, add:)	1988		$3.00	
Concrete Blonde, "True" / "True II (instrumental)" (IRS 55053)	1987		$2.50	$5.00
(with picture sleeve, add:)	1987		$3.00	
Elvis Costello and the Attractions, "Alison" / "Miracle Man" (Columbia 10641)	1977	$2.50	$5.00	$10.00
Elvis Costello and the Attractions, "Alison" / "Watching The Detectives" (Columbia 10705)	1978	$2.50	$5.00	$10.00
The Cure, "Let's Go To Bed" / "Boys Don't Cry" (Elektra 69537)	1986		$3.00	
(with picture sleeve, add:)	1986		$3.00	
The Cure, "Love Song" / "2 Late" (Elektra 69280)				
(if first pressing, red-black label)	1989		$3.00	
(if second pressing, gray label)	1989		$2.00	$4.00
Depeche Mode, "Just Can't Get Enough" / "Tora, Tora, Tora" (Sire 50029)	1982		$2.50	$5.00
Depeche Mode, "Enjoy The Silence" / "Memphisto" (Sire 19885)	1990		$3.00	
Devo, "Jocko Homo" / "Mongoloid" (Booji Boy 7033-14)	1977	$2.00	$4.00	$8.00
(with picture sleeve, add:)	1977	$2.00	$4.00	$8.00
Devo, "Whip It" / "Turn Around" (Warner Bros. 49550)	1980		$3.00	
Dinosaur Jr., "Freak Scene" / "Keep The Glove" (SST 220)				
(if large hole, clear vinyl)	1988	$2.50	$5.00	$10.00
(if small hole, black vinyl)	1988		$2.50	$5.00
(with picture sleeve, add:)	1988		$2.50	$5.00
Duran Duran, "Rio" / "Hold Back The Rain"				
(if on Harvest 5175, custom label)	1982	$3.00	$6.00	$12.00
(if on Capitol 5215)	1983		$3.00	
(with Capitol picture sleeve, add:)	1983		$3.00	$6.00
Duran Duran, "Girls On Film" / "Faster Than Light" (Harvest 5070)	1981	$6.25	$12.50	$25.00
Duran Duran, "A View To A Kill" / "A View To A Kill (That Fatal Kiss)" (Capitol 5475)	1985		$3.00	
(with picture sleeve, add:)	1985		$2.00	$4.00
Ian Dury and the Blockheads, "Hit Me With Your Rhythm Stick" / "There Ain't Half Been Some Clever Bastards" (Stiff/Epic 50726)	1979		$2.00	$4.00
(with picture sleeve, add:)	1979		$2.00	$4.00
Echo and the Bunnymen, "The Cutter" / "Gods Will Be Gods" (Sire 29664)	1983		$3.00	
The Flying Lizards, "Money" / "Money B" (Virgin 67003)	1979		$2.00	$4.00
(with picture sleeve, add:)	1979		$2.00	$4.00
Frankie Goes To Hollywood, "Relax" / "One September Monday" (Island 99805)				
(if first pressing, time 3:02, dark purple label, no picture sleeve)	1983		$3.00	$6.00
(if second pressing, remixed single with 3:35 time, dark purple label, no picture sleeve)	1983		$2.00	$4.00

45s	Year	VG	VG+	NM
(later pressing, light blue label)	1983		$3.00	
(with picture sleeve, available only with later pressings, add:)	1983		$2.50	$5.00
Heaven 17, "Let Me Go" / "I'm Your Money" (Arista 1050)	1983		$3.00	
The Human League, "Don't You Want Me" / "Seconds" (A&M 2397)	1982		$3.00	
(with picture sleeve, add:)	1982		$3.00	$6.00
The Jam, "In The City" / "Takin' My Love" (Polydor 14442)	1977	$2.50	$5.00	$10.00
The Jam, "A Town Called Malice" / "Precious" (Polydor 2206)	1982		$3.00	$6.00
Joy Division, "Love Will Tear Us Apart" / "These Days" (Factory FACTUS 23)	1980	$3.00	$6.00	$12.00
(if white label promo)	1980	$25.00	$50.00	$100.00
(with picture sleeve, add:)	1980	$3.00	$6.00	$12.00
Let's Active, "Water's Part" / "Blue Line" (IRS 70983)	1984	$2.00	$4.00	$8.00
Modern English, "I Melt With You" / "After The Snow" (Sire 29775)	1983		$2.50	$5.00
New Order, "Bizarre Love Triangle" / "Every Little Bit Counts" (Qwest 28241)	1987	$2.50	$5.00	$10.00
Gary Numan, "Cars" / "Metal" (Atco 7211)	1980		$2.00	$4.00
Oingo Boingo, "Wake Up (It's 1984)" / "No Spill Blood" (A&M 2610)	1983		$2.00	$4.00
Orchestral Manœuvres in the Dark, "Telegraph" / "This Is Helena" (Virgin/Epic 03891)	1983		$2.50	$5.00
Orchestral Manœuvres in the Dark, "If You Leave" / "La Femme Accident" (A&M 2811)	1986		$3.00	
(with picture sleeve, add:)	1986		$2.00	$4.00
Pere Ubu, "30 Seconds Over Tokyo" / "Heart of Darkness" (Hearthan HR-101)				
(if first pressing, black label)	1975	$12.50	$25.00	$50.00
(if second pressing, brown on white label)	1975	$8.75	$17.50	$35.00
(with picture sleeve, add:)	1975	$25.00	$50.00	$100.00
The Pet Shop Boys, "Opportunities (Let's Make Lots of Money)" / "In The Night" (EMI America 8321)	1986	$2.50	$5.00	$10.00
(with picture sleeve, which was withdrawn shortly after release, add:)	1986	$2.50	$5.00	$10.00
The Pet Shop Boys, "Opportunities (Let's Make Lots of Money)" / "Was That What It Was" (EMI America 8330)	1986		$2.00	$4.00
(with picture sleeve, add:)	1986		$2.00	$4.00
The Psychedelic Furs, "Pretty In Pink" (2 versions) (A&M 2826)	1986		$3.00	
(with very rare picture sleeve, add:)	1986	$6.25	$12.50	$25.00
R.E.M., "Radio Free Europe" / "Standing Still" (Hib-Tone 001)				
(if label does not have address for Hib-Tone Records, first pressing)	1981	$18.75	$37.50	$75.00
(if label has address for Hib-Tone Records, second pressing)	1981	$12.50	$25.00	$50.00
(with picture sleeve, add:)	1981	$18.75	$37.50	$75.00
R.E.M., "Radio Free Europe" / "There She Goes Again" (IRS 9916)	1983	$2.50	$5.00	$10.00
(with picture sleeve, add:)	1983	$7.50	$15.00	$30.00
R.E.M., "Fall On Me" / "Rotary Ten" (IRS 52883)	1986		$2.50	$5.00
(with picture sleeve, add:)	1986		$2.50	$5.00
R.E.M., "Losing My Religion" / "Rotary Eleven" (Warner Bros. 19392)	1991		$3.00	
The Ramones, "Blitzkrieg Bop" / "Havana Affair" (Sire 725)	1976	$10.00	$20.00	$40.00
The Ramones, "I Wanna Be Sedated" / "The Return of Jackie and Judy" (RSO 1055)	1980		$2.50	$5.00
The Ramones, "I Wanna Be Sedated" / "I Wanna Be Sedated (Ramones on 45 Mega-Mix)" (Sire 27663)	1988		$2.00	$4.00
(with picture sleeve, add:)	1988		$2.00	$4.00
Sigue Sigue Sputnik, "Love Missile F-111" / "Hack Attack" (Manhattan 50035)	1986		$2.00	$4.00
Soft Cell, "Tainted Love" / "Memorabilia" (Sire 49855)	1981		$3.00	
(with rare picture sleeve, add:)	1981		$3.00	$6.00
Talking Heads, "Take Me To The River" / "Thank You For Sending Me An Angel (Version)" (Sire 1032)	1978		$2.00	$4.00
(with picture sleeve, add:)	1978		$2.00	$4.00
Talking Heads, "Burning Down The House" / "I Get Wild - Wild Gravity" (Sire 29565)	1983		$3.00	
(with picture sleeve, add:)	1983		$3.00	
They Might Be Giants, "Birdhouse In Your Soul" / "Hot Cha" (Elektra 64998)	1990		$2.50	$5.00
Tom Tom Club, "Genius of Love" / "Lorelei" (Sire 49882)	1981		$3.00	

45s	Year	VG	VG+	NM
Ultravox, "Reap The Wild Wind" / "Hosanna (In Excelsis Deo)" (Chrysalis 42682)	1983		$2.00	$4.00
U2, "I Will Follow" / "Out of Control (Live)" (Island 49716)	1980	$2.50	$5.00	$10.00
(with picture sleeve, add:)	1980	$2.50	$5.00	$10.00
(with picture sleeve and poster announcing tour dates, promo only, add:)	1980	$6.25	$12.50	$25.00
U2, "I Still Haven't Found What I'm Looking For" / "Spanish Eyes" "Deep in the Heart" (Island 99430)	1987		$3.00	
(with paper picture sleeve, add:)	1987		$3.00	
(with cardboard picture sleeve, add:)	1987		$2.00	$4.00
Veruca Salt, "Seether" / "All Hail Me" (Minty Fresh MF-6)				
(if first 100 copies, clear orange vinyl, hand-numbered)	1994	$6.25	$12.50	$25.00
(if next 2000 copies, clear orange vinyl, no numbering)	1994	$3.75	$7.50	$15.00
(if third pressing, opaque orange vinyl)	1994	$2.50	$5.00	$10.00
(with picture sleeve, add:)	1994	$2.50	$5.00	$10.00

12-inch	Year	VG	VG+	NM
Blondie, "Heart of Glass" (disco version) / (instrumental) (Chrysalis CHS-12-2275)	1979	$2.50	$5.00	$10.00
The Boomtown Rats, "Up All Night" / "Mood Mambo" / "Banana Republic" (Columbia AS 920)	1981		$3.50	$7.00
Cabaret Voltaire, "The Drain Train" (5 versions) (Caroline CAROL 2452) (2 12-inch discs)	1986	$5.00	$10.00	$20.00
The Call, "Time Of Your Life" / "All About You" (Mercury MK 242)	1983	$2.00	$4.00	$8.00
Concrete Blonde, "God Is A Bullet" / "Free" / "Little Wing" (IRS 74001)	1989	$4.50	$9.00	$18.00
Elvis Costello and the Attractions, "Everyday I Write The Book" (2 versions) / "Heathen Town" / " Night Time" (Columbia 04115)	1983	$2.00	$4.00	$8.00
Depeche Mode, "Leave In Silence" / "Photograph" / "My Secret Garden" (2 versions) (Sire PRO-A-1084)	1982	$7.50	$15.00	$30.00
Depeche Mode, "Master and Servant" / "Remotivate Me" / "Are People People?" (Sire 20283)	1984	$2.50	$5.00	$10.00
Depeche Mode, "Blasphemous Rumors" / "Something To Do" / "Remotivate Me" (Edit) (Sire PRO-A-2271)	1985	$12.50	$25.00	$50.00
Devo, "Jerkin' Back 'n' Forth" / "Going Under" / "Through Being Cool" (Warner Bros. PRO-A-993)	1981	$2.00	$4.00	$8.00
Duran Duran, "Hungry Like The Wolf" / "Lonely In Your Nightmare" / "Rio" (Harvest SPRO-9876/7)	1982	$5.00	$10.00	$20.00
Ian Dury and the Blockheads, "Hit Me With Your Rhythm Stick" / "Reasons To Be Cheerful Pt. 3" (Stiff/Epic 50779)	1979	$3.75	$7.50	$15.00
Echo and the Bunnymen, "Lips Like Sugar" (3 versions) / "Rollercoaster" (Sire 20784)	1987		$3.00	$6.00
Heaven 17, "We Live So Fast" (2 versions) / "Temptation" (Arista 9030)	1983	$2.50	$5.00	$10.00
Heaven 17, "Penthouse and Pavement" (4 versions) (Virgin 12667) (promo only)	1993	$2.00	$4.00	$8.00
The Human League, "Don't You Want Me" (Extended) / "Love Action" (A&M 12045)	1982	$3.00	$6.00	$12.00
Ministry, "Revenge" / "Effigy" / "I Wanted To Tell Her" (Arista 9062)	1983	$3.75	$7.50	$15.00
New Order, "Blue Monday" / "The Beach" (Factory FACTUS 10)	1983	$2.00	$4.00	$8.00
New Order, "Confusion" (4 versions) (Streetwise 2213)	1984	$2.00	$4.00	$8.00
Oingo Boingo, "Weird Science" (two versions) (MCA 17048)	1985	$2.50	$5.00	$10.00
Orchestral Manœuvres in the Dark, "If You Leave" (remix) / "La Femme Accident" (A&M 12176)	1986	$3.75	$7.50	$15.00
Pet Shop Boys, "West End Girls" / "One More Chance" (Bobcat 05019) (early version, produced by Bobby Orlando)	1984	$7.50	$15.00	$30.00
Pet Shop Boys, "West End Girls" (2 versions) / "A Man Could Get Arrested" (EMI America 19208)	1985	$3.75	$7.50	$15.00
R.E.M., "The One I Love" / "The One I Love (Live)" / "Maps and Legends" (IRS 23792)	1987	$3.00	$6.00	$12.00

12-inch	Year	VG	VG+	NM
Soft Cell, "Tainted Love - Where Did Our Love Go" / "Memorabilia" / "Tainted Dub" (Sire 49856)	1981	$2.00	$4.00	$8.00
Talking Heads, "Wild Wild Life" (2 versions) / "People Like Us" (Movie Version) (Sire 20593)	1986	$2.50	$5.00	$10.00
Tears for Fears, "Everybody Wants To Rule The World" (2 versions) / "Pharaohs" (Mercury 880 659-1)	1985	$2.50	$5.00	$10.00
Tom Tom Club, "Genius of Love" / "Lorelei" (Sire PRO-A-996)	1981	$2.50	$5.00	$10.00
Ultravox, "Sleepwalk" (2 versions) (Chrysalis CHS-22-PDJ)	1980	$2.50	$5.00	$10.00

LPs	Year	VG	VG+	NM
ABC, The Lexicon of Love (Mercury SRM-1-4059)	1982	$2.50	$5.00	$10.00
Adam and the Ants, Kings of the Wild Frontier (Epic NJE 37033)	1981	$3.00	$6.00	$12.00
(if on Epic PE 37033, budget line reissue)	1985	$2.00	$4.00	$8.00
The Alarm, The Alarm (IRS SP 70504) (EP)	1984	$3.50	$7.00	$14.00
The Alarm, Declaration (IRS SP 70608)	1984	$2.50	$5.00	$10.00
Laurie Anderson, The United States Live (Warner Bros. 25192) (5 LP's)	1984	$7.50	$15.00	$30.00
The Art of Noise, (Who's Afraid Of) The Art of Noise (Island 90179)	1985	$3.00	$6.00	$12.00
(if on Island 842 473-1, reissue)	1990	$2.50	$5.00	$10.00
The B-52's, Wild Planet (Warner Bros. BSK 3471) (first pressings have red labels, deduct 33% if label is another color)	1980	$3.00	$6.00	$12.00
Blondie, Parallel Lines				
(if on Chrysalis CHR 1192, first pressing, with short version of "Heart of Glass" as fourth song on side 2)	1978	$3.75	$7.50	$15.00
(if on Chrysalis CHR 1192, second pressing, longer disco "Heart of Glass" as fourth song on side 2)	1979	$2.50	$5.00	$10.00
(if on Mobile Fidelity 1-050, audiophile vinyl)	1980	$7.50	$15.00	$30.00
(if on Chrysalis FV 41192, reissue)	1983	$2.00	$4.00	$8.00
(if on Chrysalis PV 41192, reissue)	1986	$2.00	$4.00	$8.00
Blotto, Hello, My Name Is Blotto! What's Yours (Blotto 001)	1979	$3.75	$7.50	$15.00
Blotto, Combo Akimbo (Blotto BLP 004)	1982	$4.00	$8.00	$16.00
The Boomtown Rats, The Fine Art of Surfacing (Columbia JC 36248)	1979	$2.50	$5.00	$10.00
Kate Bush, Hounds of Love (EMI America ST-17171)				
(if on marbled vinyl)	1985	$7.50	$15.00	$30.00
(if on black vinyl)	1985	$2.50	$5.00	$10.00
The Call, Reconciled (Elektra 60440)	1986	$2.50	$5.00	$10.00
(if on Elektra R 141152, RCA Music Service Edition)	1986	$3.00	$6.00	$12.00
The Jim Carroll Band, Catholic Boy (Atco 38-132)	1980	$3.75	$7.50	$15.00
The Cars, Candy-O				
(if on Elektra 5E-507, title and artist information listed only on a sticker on the shrink-wrap)	1979	$2.50	$5.00	$10.00
(if on Elektra R 123334, RCA Music Service, "The Cars Candy-O" listed on front of cover)	1979	$3.00	$6.00	$12.00
(if on Nautilus NR-49, audiophile pressing)	1982	$7.50	$15.00	$30.00
The Church, Starfish (Arista AL 8521)	1988	$2.50	$5.00	$10.00
(if on Arista R 173703, BMG Direct Marketing Edition)	1988	$3.00	$6.00	$12.00
Concrete Blonde, Bloodletting (IRS X1-13037)				
(red vinyl)	1990	$5.00	$10.00	$20.00
(if on IRS 82037, promo only, sticker on generic cover, black vinyl)	1990	$6.25	$12.50	$25.00
Elvis Costello, My Aim Is True (Columbia JC 35037)				
(if yellow back cover, first pressing)	1977	$3.75	$7.50	$15.00
(if white back cover, no bar code, second pressing)	1978	$2.50	$5.00	$10.00
(if on Columbia PC 35037, reissue, bar code on back cover)	1984	$2.00	$4.00	$8.00
The Cure, Disintegration (Elektra 60855)	1989	$2.50	$5.00	$10.00
(if on Elektra R 101109, BMG Direct Marketing edition)	1989	$3.00	$6.00	$12.00
Depeche Mode, Some Great Reward (Sire 25194)	1984	$3.00	$6.00	$12.00
Devo, Q: Are We Not Men? A: We Are Devo! (Warner Bros. BSK 3329)	1978	$2.50	$5.00	$10.00
Devo, Smooth Noodle Maps				
(if on Enigma EPRO 326, promo only, no picture cover)	1990	$5.00	$10.00	$20.00
(if on Dutch East India DE-112008-1, red vinyl, 1000 copies pressed)	1991	$3.75	$7.50	$15.00
Duran Duran, Rio (Harvest ST-12211)				
(if no mention of remixes by David Kirshenbaum, first pressing)	1982	$3.75	$7.50	$15.00
(if remixes by David Kirshenbaum are mentioned, second pressing)	1982	$3.00	$6.00	$12.00
(if on Capitol ST-12211)	1983	$2.50	$5.00	$10.00
(if on Capitol R-163452, RCA Music Service Edition)	1983	$3.00	$6.00	$12.00
Duran Duran, Duran Duran (Harvest ST-12158) (without "Is There Something I Should Know?")	1981	$3.75	$7.50	$15.00
(if on Capitol ST-12158, "Is There Something I Should Know?" added)	1983	$2.50	$5.00	$10.00
Ian Dury and the Blockheads, New Boots and Panties (Stiff STF 0002)	1978	$2.50	$5.00	$10.00
(if on Stiff USE 02, reissue)	1980	$2.50	$5.00	$10.00
Brian Eno, Working Backwards: 1983-1973 (Editions EG EGBS-2) (11 LP's)	1984	$15.00	$30.00	$60.00
Frankie Goes To Hollywood, Welcome To The Pleasuredome (Island 90232) (2 LPs)	1985	$3.75	$7.50	$15.00
Fugazi, Steady Diet of Nothing (Dischord 60)	1991	$2.00	$4.00	$8.00
Nina Hagen, Nunsexmonkrock (Columbia ARC 38008)	1982	$3.00	$6.00	$12.00
(if on Columbia PC 38008, reissue)	198??	$2.50	$5.00	$10.00
Heaven 17, How Men Are (Arista AL8-8259)	1987	$2.50	$5.00	$10.00
The Human League, Travelogue (Virgin International VI 2160)	1980	$3.75	$7.50	$15.00
(if on Virgin 90881, 1988 reissue)	1988	$2.50	$5.00	$10.00
The Human League, Dare (A&M SP6-4892)	1981	$2.50	$5.00	$10.00
The Jam, In The City (Polydor PD1-6110)	1977	$6.25	$12.50	$25.00
(if on Polydor 817 124-1, reissue)	198??	$2.50	$5.00	$10.00
Joy Division, Closer (Factory Fact US 6)				
(if purple-tinted vinyl)	1980	$12.50	$25.00	$50.00
(if red-tinted vinyl)	1980	$6.25	$12.50	$25.00
(if on Warner Bros. 25841, 1989 reissue)	1989	$2.50	$5.00	$10.00
Let's Active, Cypress (IRS SP-70648)	1984	$2.50	$5.00	$10.00
The Lords of the New Church, The Lords of the New Church (IRS SP-70029)	1982	$3.75	$7.50	$15.00
Ministry, With Sympathy (Arista AL 6608)	1983	$3.50	$7.00	$14.00
(if on Arista AL6 8016, reissue)	1983	$2.50	$5.00	$10.00
Modern English, After The Snow (Sire 23821)	1982	$2.50	$5.00	$10.00
New Order, Power, Corruption and Lies (Factory FAC US 12)	1983	$5.00	$10.00	$20.00
(if on Qwest 25308, reissue)	1985	$2.50	$5.00	$10.00
New Order, Substance (Qwest 25621) (2 LPs)	1987	$3.75	$7.50	$15.00
Gary Numan, The Pleasure Principle (Atco SD 38-120)	1979	$3.00	$6.00	$12.00
Orchestral Manœvres in the Dark, Architecture and Morality (Virgin/Epic ARE 37721)	1981	$3.00	$6.00	$12.00
Pere Ubu, The Art of Walking (Rough Trade ROUGH US 4)				
(first 1,800 copies were incorrectly mastered)	1980	$8.75	$17.50	$35.00
(later pressings, vocal added on "Arabia", "Miles" is shortened)	1980	$6.25	$12.50	$25.00
Pet Shop Boys, Actually (EMI Manhattan ELJ-46972)	1987	$3.00	$6.00	$12.00
(if on EMI Manhattan R 153678, BMG Direct Marketing Edition)	1987	$3.50	$7.00	$14.00
(if on EMI Manhattan E1-90263, two LP set, the extra LP contains remixes)	1988	$5.00	$10.00	$20.00
The Plasmatics, Coup d'Etat (Capitol ST-12237)	1982	$3.75	$7.50	$15.00
R.E.M., Chronic Town (IRS SP-70502)				
(first pressings have custom label with gargoyle)	1982	$3.00	$6.00	$12.00
(if second pressing, standard IRS label)	1982	$3.00	$6.00	
R.E.M., Life's Rich Pageant (IRS 5783)	1986	$3.00	$6.00	$12.00
(if on IRS R 173669, RCA Music Service pressing)	1986	$3.50	$7.00	$14.00
The Ramones, Ramones Leave Home				
(if on Sire SASD-7528, first pressing, contains "Carbona Not Glue," distributed by ABC)	1977	$12.50	$25.00	$50.00

LPs	Year	VG	VG+	NM
(if on Sire SASD-7528, second pressing, replaces "Carbona Not Glue" with "Sheena is a Punk Rocker")	1977	$6.25	$12.50	$25.00
(if on Sire SR-6031, distributed by Warner Bros., tracks as on second issue, no UPC code)	1978	$4.50	$9.00	$18.00
The Ramones, End of the Century (Sire SRK 6077)	1980	$3.75	$7.50	$15.00
Sigue Sigue Sputnik, Flaunt It (Manhattan ST-53033) (album actually has commercials between the songs)	1986	$2.50	$5.00	$10.00
Talking Heads, More Songs About Buildings and Food (Sire SR 6058)	1978	$3.00	$6.00	$12.00
(if on Sire SRK 6058, reissue)	1979	$2.00	$4.00	$8.00
Talking Heads, Speaking In Tongues (Sire 23771) (clear vinyl, oversize cover, designed by Robert Rauschenberg)	1983	$3.75	$7.50	$15.00
(if on Sire 23883, standard black vinyl and cardboard cover issue)	1983	$2.50	$5.00	$10.00
Tears for Fears, Songs from the Big Chair (Mercury 824 300-1)	1985	$2.50	$5.00	$10.00
(if on Mercury R 143666, BMG Direct Marketing edition)	1985	$3.00	$6.00	$12.00
10,000 Maniacs, Secrets of the I Ching (Christian Burial P-3001)	1984	$31.25	$62.50	$125.00

LPs	Year	VG	VG+	NM
10,000 Maniacs, The Wishing Chair (Elektra 60428)	1985	$3.00	$6.00	$12.00
Ultravox, Vienna (Chrysalis CHR 1296)	1980	$2.50	$5.00	$10.00
U2, War (Island 90067)				
(if first pressing, dark purple label)	1983	$3.00	$6.00	$12.00
(if second pressing, light blue label)	1983	$2.50	$5.00	$10.00
(if third pressing, black label)	1983	$2.00	$4.00	$8.00
(if on Island R 114632, RCA Music Service edition)	1983	$3.00	$6.00	$12.00
(if on Island 811 148-1, actually stickered over leftover Island/Atco pressings)	1990	$2.00	$4.00	$8.00
U2, Under a Blood Red Sky (Island 90127-B)				
(first pressing contains long version of "The Electric Co.," where Bono sings "Send in the Clowns" and West Side Story's "America" during the instrumental break)	1983	$5.00	$10.00	$20.00
(second pressings have edited version of "The Electric Co.")	1983	$2.50	$5.00	$10.00
(if on Island R 153598, BMG Direct Marketing edition)	1983	$3.00	$6.00	$12.00
(if on Island 818 008-1, actually stickered over leftover Island/Atco pressings)	1990	$3.00	$6.00	
Ween, Chocolate and Cheese (Grand Royal GR 010)	1994	$3.00	$6.00	$12.00

Bananarama were once the backup singers for the ska band Fun Boy Three. They eventually made their own name with a series of neo-Motown songs, including this remake of the Velvelettes' near-hit.

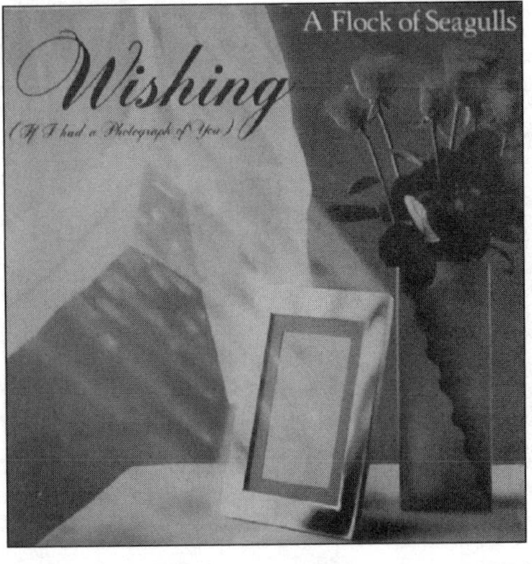

A Flock of Seagulls mixed guitars and synthesizers for a string of popular dance-pop songs. One of their songs, "D.N.A.," even won a Grammy for best instrumental recording.

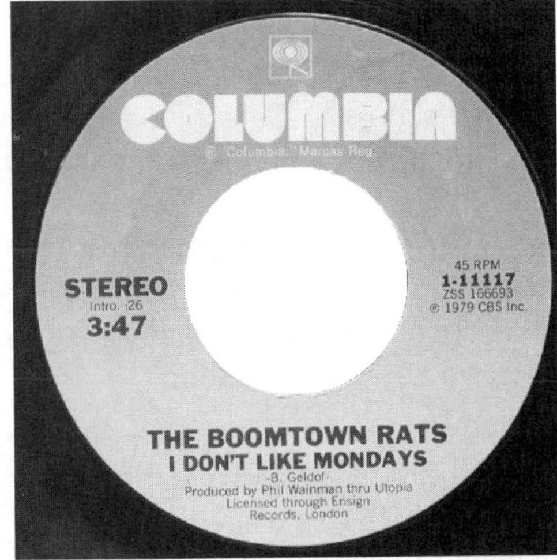

Before his work with African famine relief and charity superstar concerts, Bob Geldof was the lead singer of the Boomtown Rats. This is a stock copy of their biggest hit, "I Don't Like Mondays."

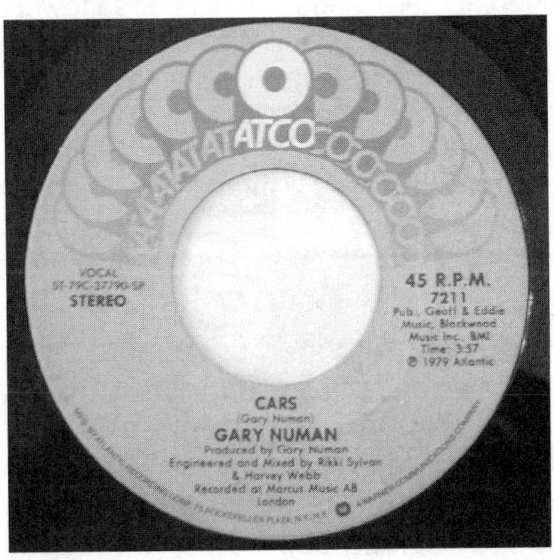

Thanks to some pre-MTV music videos, Gary Numan's "Cars" became a Top 10 hit, one of the earliest synth-rock new wave songs to cross over to popular music.

NORTHERN SOUL

History: Coined by reporter Dave Godin in a September 1971 edition of *Blues and Soul* magazine, "Northern Soul" is both a musical style—a pulsing Motown-like beat, with the horns and lyrics of a Chicago blues club or a Memphis roadhouse—as well as a musical fad, as British club DJs searched for rare, exclusive dance songs they could play in their own clubs for the "punters" on the dance floor.

Long before his #1 hit "Show and Tell," Al Wilson had a Northern Soul hit with "The Snake." From the Collection of Val Shively.

Bobby Freeman's hit song "C'mon and Swim," which became a Northern Soul classic, was written by Sylvester Stewart, who later fronted Sly and the Family Stone.

In the late 1960s, British club DJs noticed that the current crop of soul music wasn't filling the dance floors as it once did. The musical tastes of the original clubgoers, the "mods," were headed toward psychedelia and flower power. What remained was a hardcore legion of soul fans, eager to hear the classic American soul sounds. They wanted uptempo Motown music, they wanted Memphis dance records from Stax, they wanted Chicago and New York R&B classics.

> **Trivia**
>
> **Many other artists had successful Northern Soul solo careers, including Bobby Sheen of Bobb B. Soxx and the Blue Jeans, Tony Middleton of the Willows, and Tommy Hunt of the Flamingos. Earl Van Dyke, whose combo played music for hundreds of Motown classics, had successful Northern Soul stompers with "6 x 6" and "Too Many Fish In The Sea."**

The first club catering to this type of rare soul music was the Twisted Wheel Club of Manchester. It was also one of the first venues to offer R&B music as an all-night dance party (also known as "Nighters" or "All-Nighters"). The records played at the Twisted Wheel Club were moderate soul hits in the UK, but either because of poor distribution or poor sales, there were so few of these pressings in existence that the records instantly became collector's items.

When the Twisted Wheel closed down in 1970, almost every northern England city and town had their own R&B club—the Catacombs, the Junction, the Golden Torch, to name a few. And their DJs made dance hits out of "newies," records that missed hit status the first time around, but were now played alongside classic "oldies." This mixture of "flyers" (fast songs) and "stompers" (heavy beat) became known as "Northern Soul."

In the 1970s, the most famous Northern Soul clubs were the Wigan Casino and the Blackpool Mecca. The Mecca's DJs played 1960s soul, as recorded only by black artists. The Wigan Casino, led by DJ Russ Winstanley, would play black and white artists, oldies, newies, and "current" songs, all in a credo of "if it's danceable, play it."

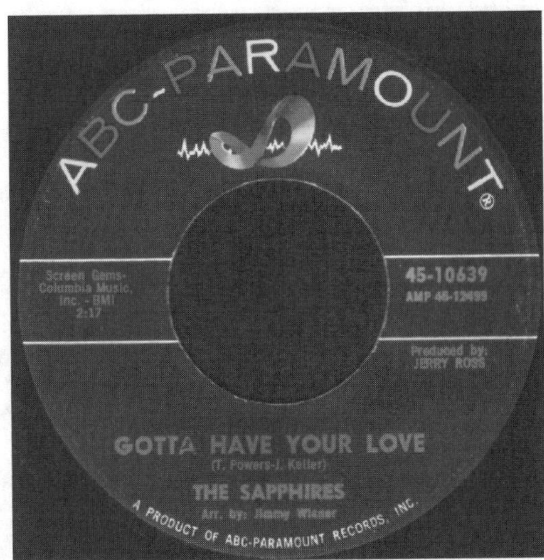

Many of Philadelphia producer Jerry Ross' artists either hit the Top 40 in America—or, like the Sapphires, became superstars in Northern Soul clubs. From the Collection of Nick Crocker.

By the mid-1970s, the current crop of British "Northern Soul" 45s had dried up, forcing DJs to search through American 45s for their top dance records. Many of these discs sold for very high prices, as the DJs kept searching for "exclusives," records that could pack the floor at their club exclusively.

Many of these songs found a new life of their own, as British pop groups remade their favorite Northern Soul songs as Top 40 hits of their own. The best example of this happening is when Gloria Jones' "Tainted Love," a Northern Soul staple, became a Top 10 worldwide hit for Soft Cell in 1982. Most recently, Fatboy Slim's hit "Rockafella Skank" borrows heavily from the Just Brothers' "Sliced Tomatoes," a Northern Soul classic.

Gloria Jones' stomper hit "Tainted Love," which would be covered two decades later by the techno-pop duo Soft Cell. From the Collection of Nick Crocker.

One of the great Northern Soul success stories is Major Lance. While he only had two Top 10 hits in America, even his smallest-selling records became Northern Soul classics, to the point where Lance's UK concerts were instant sellouts. Other artists and performers who had minimal success in America, but thundering adulation in England, were Archie Bell and the Drells, Betty Wright, Barbara Lynn, Gene Chandler, and Al Wilson.

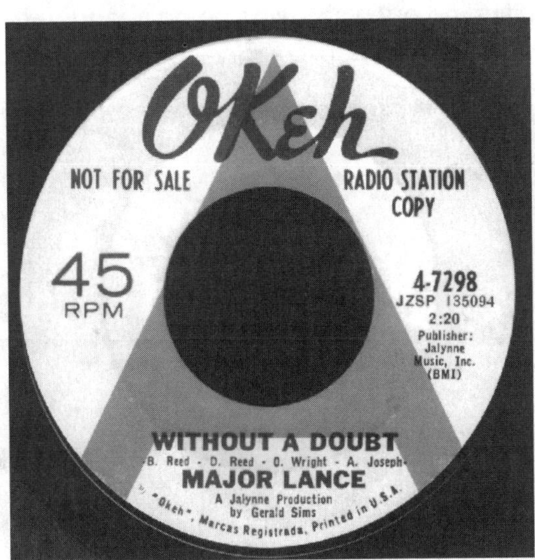

Northern Soul collectors will pay more for a promo pressing, especially if the "A" side is clearly marked, as is this pressing for a Major Lance song. From the collection of Nick Crocker.

What To Look For: There are many distinct factors that determine a Northern Soul record—a raw 1960's soul record, with an early Motownish beat and Chicago blues horn section. Most of these records were never hits in their own right, either in America or in the UK, but to club DJs looking for rare, exclusive soul they could play in their clubs, these records were just the treat.

By the early 1970s, the American pressings of some rare Northern Soul 45s changed hands for hundreds of British pounds. Other Northern Soul classics were bootlegged or reissued for general purchase.

The rarest Northern Soul record, in fact one of the rarest records of all time, is Frank Wilson's "Sweeter as the Days Go By"/"Do I Love You" (Soul 35019). This record was not officially released, and only two copies are known to exist today. In 1999, a collector from Scotland paid more than £15,000 for a copy of the rare disc, making this song one of the most expensive collectible records of all time, rivaling the most expensive Elvis Presley Sun 45s and Beatles Vee-Jay albums.

Northern Soul collectors are most desirous of white label promo copies of both American and UK 45s. Many of the British 45s will have a gigantic "A" on the front label. The British demo pressings may have a plastic removable center adapter, this must remain in the record or its collectible value is considerably diminished. Some Northern Soul records may have white mailing stickers pasted over the labels—this was a common practice among club DJs, in an attempt to keep rival DJs from seeing the record, finding out who's singing on it, and getting a copy for their own club.

The Platters on Mercury were not a dance band. But the Platters on Musicor, produced by Luther Dixon, were perfectly tailored for the Northern Soul dance floor. From the Collection of Nick Crocker.

Many of these titles have been reissued by smaller independent companies—and some, including Frank Wilson's "Do I Love You," have been bootlegged. Don't be afraid to ask questions from a dealer if they say a record is "Northern Soul" and you're unfamiliar with the title or song. Don't be fooled into purchasing a record just because someone marked it as a "Northern Soul" title.

Northern Soul music is driven by 45s. Rarely do Northern Soul collectors hunt out albums, unless it contains that rare track they have not been able to find on 45.

Trivia

A classic Northern Soul track by Richard Berry and the Pharaohs, "Have Love Will Travel," was once issued with a B-side that would achieve its own greatness—the original version of "Louie, Louie."

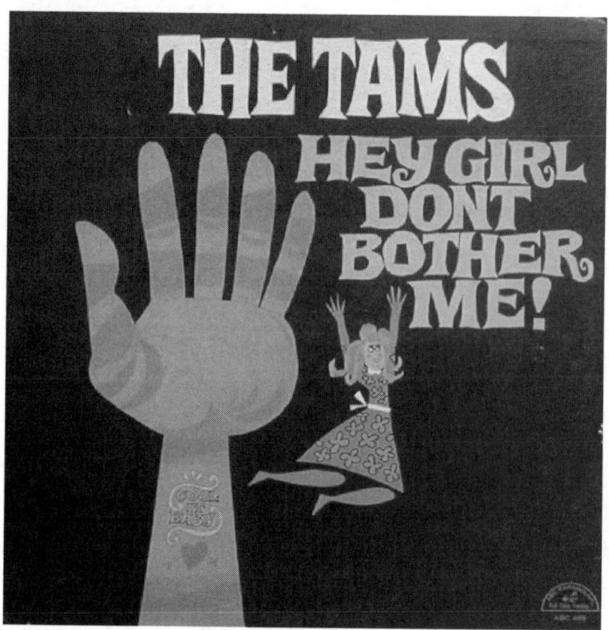

The title track to this Tams album is a great song indeed; it is much more collectible among Northern Soul fans on a 45.

References: Guralnick, Peter, Sweet Soul Music: Rhythm & Blues & the Southern Dream of Freedom, HarperTrade, New York, 1986; McKenna, Pete, *Nightshift: Personal Recollections Of Growing Up In And Around The Casino Soul Club, Empress Hall, Wigan, Sept. 1973 to Dec. 1981*, S.T. Publishing, Dunoon, U.K., 1996; Roberts, Kev, *The Northern Soul Top 500*, Goldmine/Soul Supply Ltd., Todmorden, U.K., 2000; Winstanley, Russ; Nowell, David, *Soul Survivors: The Wigan Casino Story*, Robson Books, London, 1996. ISBN: 1861050534.

Web pages: The Night Owl Club, a Web page devoted to Northern Soul music and culture, *http://www.nightowlclub.com*; the Northern Soul Webring, a listing of dozens of sites dedicated to "keeping the faith," can be accessed through this site: *http://www.soul-source.co.uk/welcome.htm*; an excellent essay by Paul Wynne comparing Northern Soul collectors with archeologists: *http://homepage.ntlworld.com/paul.wynne/NS/; Nick Crocker's* Northern Soul page, a good starting point for anyone looking for Northern Soul history and images: *http://www.soulsurfin.co.uk.*

45s	Year	VG	VG+	NM
The Ad Libs, "The Boy From New York City" / "Kicked Around" (Blue Cat 102)	1965	$3.75	$7.50	$15.00
The Ad Libs, "The Boy From New York City" / "Nothing Worse Than Being Alone" (Share 106)	1969	$2.00	$4.00	$8.00
Yvonne Baker, "You Didn't Say A Word" / "To Prove My Love Is True" (Parkway 140)	1967	$25.00	$50.00	$100.00
Jerry Butler, "Moody Woman" / "Go Away - Find Yourself" (Mercury 72929)	1969	$2.00	$4.00	$8.00
The Contours, "Do You Love Me" / "Mr. Man" (Gordy 7005)	1962	$5.00	$10.00	$20.00

45s	Year	VG	VG+	NM
The Contours, "Just A Little Misunderstanding" / "Determination" (Gordy 7052)	1966	$3.00	$6.00	$12.00
Darrell Banks, "Open the Door To Your Heart" / "Our Love Is In The Pocket" (Revilot 201)	1966	$3.75	$7.50	$15.00
Shirley Ellis, "Soul Time" / "Waitin'" (Columbia 44021)	1967	$2.00	$4.00	$8.00
Bobby Freeman, "C'mon and Swim" / "C'mon and Swim [Pt. 2]" (Autumn 2)				
(if white label, red print)	1964	$3.00	$6.00	$12.00
(if on tan label)	1964	$2.50	$5.00	$10.00
Dobie Gray, "Out On The Floor" / "No Room To Cry" (Charger 115)	1966	$2.50	$5.00	$10.00
Roy Hamilton, "Walk Hand In Hand" / "Crackin' Up Over You" (RCA Victor 47-8960)	1966	$6.25	$12.50	$25.00
Patrice Holloway, "Love and Desire" / "Ecstacy" (Capitol 5778)	1967	$15.00	$30.00	$60.00
The Impressions - "I Loved And I Lost" / "Up, Up and Away" (ABC 11103)	1968	$2.00	$4.00	$8.00
Gloria Jones, "Tainted Love" / (B-side unknown) (Champion 14003)	1964	$3.00	$6.00	$12.00
Major Lance, "The Monkey Time" / "Mama Didn't Know" (Okeh 7175)	1963	$3.75	$7.50	$15.00
Major Lance, "Um, Um, Um, Um, Um, Um" / "Sweet Music" (Okeh 7187)	1964	$3.75	$7.50	$15.00
(with picture sleeve, add:)	1964	$7.50	$15.00	$30.00
Major Lance, "Ain't No Soul (In These Shoes)" / "I" (Okeh 7266)	1966	$3.75	$7.50	$15.00
Barbara McNair, "Touch of Time" / "You're Gonna Love My Baby" (Motown 1087)	1965	$6.25	$12.50	$25.00
Tony Middleton, "Don't Ever Leave Me" / "To The Ends Of The Earth" (MGM 13493)	1966	$10.00	$20.00	$40.00
The Sapphires, "Gee I'm Sorry, Baby" / "Gotta Have Your Love" (ABC-Paramount 10639)	1965	$3.75	$7.50	$15.00
The Tams, "Hey Girl Don't Bother Me" / "Take Away" (ABC-Paramount 10573)	1964	$3.00	$6.00	$12.00
The Tams, "Hey Girl Don't Bother Me" / "Weep Little Girl"	1971		$3.00	$6.00
(with picture sleeve that says "#1 in England," add:)	1971	$2.50	$5.00	$10.00
The Three Degrees, "I Wanna Be Your Baby" / "Tales Are True" (Swan 4253)	1966	$3.00	$6.00	$12.00
Earl Van Dyke and the Soul Brothers, "All For You" / "Too Many Fish in the Sea" (Soul 35009)	1965	$200.00	$400.00	$800.00
Earl Van Dyke and the Motown Brass, "6 x 6" / "There Is No Greater Love" (Soul 35028)	1967	$5.00	$10.00	$20.00
Gino Washington, "Gino is a Coward" / "Puppet on a String"				
(if on Correc-Tone 503)	1962	$15.00	$30.00	$60.00
(if on Sonbert 3770)	1963	$6.25	$12.50	$25.00
(if on Ric-Tic 100)	1964	$5.00	$10.00	$20.00
Danny Wagner and Kindred Spirit, "I Lost A True Love" / "My Buddy" (Imperial 66305)	1967	$7.50	$15.00	$30.00
Kim Weston, "It Should Have Been Me" / "Love Me All The Way" (Tamla 54076)	1963	$12.50	$25.00	$50.00
Kim Weston, "A Little More Love" / "Go Ahead And Laugh" (Tamla 54106)	1964	$25.00	$50.00	$100.00
Kim Weston, "I'll Never See My Love Again" / "A Thrill A Moment" (Gordy 7041)	1965	$5.00	$10.00	$20.00
Kim Weston, "Helpless" / "A Love Like Yours (Doesn't Come Knockin' Every Day") (Gordy 7050)	1966	$5.00	$10.00	$20.00
Al Wilson, "The Snake" / "Getting Ready for Tomorrow" (Soul City 767)	1968	$2.00	$4.00	$8.00
Frank Wilson, "Sweeter as the Days Go By" / "Do I Love You" (Soul 35019)	1966	$10,000	$15,000	$20,000
Jackie Wilson, "Because of You" / "Go Away" (Brunswick 55495)	1973		$3.00	$6.00

Northern Soul fans and DJ's are still pouring through the Motown catalog, looking for future club smashes. Even 30-year-old records like this song by the Fantastic Four are receiving a new life in Northern England clubs.

The O'Jays would become soul superstars in the 1970s, but their 1960s dance tracks and ballads have been Northern Soul staples for years. Especially prized are their recordings on the Neptune label, years before their first hits on the Philadelphia International label.

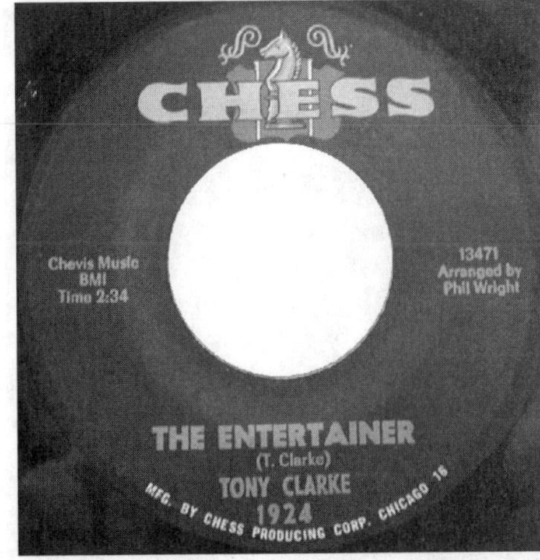

Tony Clarke's "The Entertainer" was a Top 10 soul hit in America—and a top floor-packer in Northern Soul clubs. From the Collection of Val Shively.

PHILLES RECORDS

History: Philles Records was born through the collaboration of producers Phil Spector and Lester Sill. Phil Spector, a New York City producer and performer, was first the drummer for the trio The Teddy Bears ("To Know Him Is To Love Him"). He would later mature into a producer/songwriter for such artists as Ben E. King, Curtis Lee, Gene Pitney and the Paris Sisters.

Spector partnered up with Lester Sill, whose background included production work for Duane Eddy and other artists on the Jamie/Guyden labels. The two combined their first names and formed Philles Records in 1961. One year later, Spector purchased Sill's interest in the company, and between 1962 and 1966, Spector created for his label artists a sound never before heard on pop radio—the "Phil Spector Wall of Sound."

Previously, orchestral pop was limited to classical music and a few instrumental Top 40 hits. But in Spector's hands, the "Wall of Sound" was a multi-tracked symphony of strings, guitars, drums, and piano, all modeled to accentuate both the singer and the song. What Spector called "little symphonies for the kids" were classic pop tracks from Brill Building songwriters, mixed with Spector's aural orchestrations.

Philles' biggest successes involved five major vocal acts: the Crystals, the Ronettes, the Righteous Brothers, Darlene Love, and Bob B. Soxx and the Blue Jeans. The Crystals, a Brooklyn girl group, was Philles' first success story, with hits like "There's No Other (Like My Baby)," "Da Doo Ron Ron," and "Then He Kissed Me."

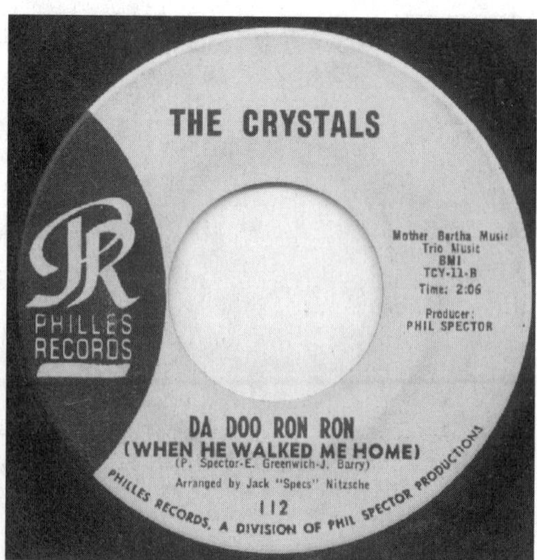

The Crystals had Philles Records' first big hits.

Whereas the Crystals were the typical "good-girl" vocal group, the Ronettes were the "bad girls of rock 'n' roll." With their beehive hairdos, tight skirts, and impassioned vocals, the Ronettes melted the hearts of millions of teenage boys with songs like "Be My Baby," "Baby I Love You," and "Walking In The Rain."

The Righteous Brothers were two unrelated singers, Bobby Hatfield and Bill Medley, who had some minor hits on the Moonglow label. On Philles, they became "blue-eyed soul" superstars, recording such rock classics as "You've Lost That Lovin' Feelin'," "Just Once In My Life," and "Unchained Melody."

A hit in both the 1960s and 1990s, thanks to its inclusion into the soundtrack of the motion picture "Ghost."

Darlene Love was a session singer who had previously recorded background vocals for Bobby Day's "Rock-In Robin," Shelly Fabares' "Johnny Angel" and Sam Cooke's "Chain Gang." With her group the Blossoms, she sang "He's A Rebel" and "He's Sure The Boy I Love" on records Spector credited to the Crystals. Love would later record with Philles under her own name, both on Top 40 singles like "Today I Met (The Boy I'm Gonna Marry,") and on Phil Spector's all-star Christmas album *A Christmas Gift For You From Phil Spector.* Love, along with Bobby Sheen and Fanita James, also recorded for Philles as Bob B. Soxx and the Blue Jeans, with hits like "Why Do Lovers Break Each Others' Hearts" and a guitar-fuzz remake of the Disney classic "Zip-A-Dee Doo Dah."

Darlene Love's Christmas song, which grew from the Phil Spector Christmas album to a life of its own.

No description of Phil Spector's "Wall of Sound" can be complete without mentioning the "Wrecking Crew," the best studio musicians in Los Angeles. With their music engineered by Larry Levine and arranged by Jack "Specs" Nitzche, the "Wrecking Crew" featured such legendary studio musicians as drummer Hal Blaine, guitarist Glen Campbell, keyboardists Leon Russell and Larry Knechtel, saxophonist Nino Tempo and percussion player Sonny Bono. And if you listen closely on some tracks, you might even hear Cher on background vocals (as "Bonnie Jo Mason," Cher recorded a novelty song, "Ringo I Love You," for the Philles subsidiary label Annette).

Even though the 1964 British Invasion forced many American singers off the charts, Philles was still able to sell records, as tracks such as "You've Lost That Lovin' Feelin'" and "The Best Part of Breakin' Up" still had chart success. But by 1966, Philles was in desperate need of a hit, and Spector thought he had a classic. Signing Ike and Tina Turner to Philles, he recorded one of the biggest "Wall of Sound" productions ever, "River Deep—Mountain High," and put Tina Turner's vocals in the center of his music. Although the record was a Top 10 hit in England, it flopped in America, eventually signaling the end of Philles Records as a viable recording label.

By the late 1960s, all of Philles' artists had signed with other labels (with the exception of Ronettes lead singer Veronica Bennett, whom Phil Spector married). The most successful of these post-Philles artists were the Righteous Brothers, who reached the top of the charts with "(You're My) Soul and Inspiration," and later charted with 1974s "Rock and Roll Heaven."

Of the other artists, Bob B. Soxx and the Blue Jeans singer Bobby Sheen had hits in England, as part of the Northern Soul movement. Veronica Bennett, now known as Ronnie Spector, eventually divorced Phil Spector and recorded critically acclaimed singles with Bruce Springsteen's E Street Band and Eddie Money. The Crystals signed with United Artists Records, but no hits came from their association with that label.

As for Phil Spector, he later produced albums for the Beatles, as well as for ex-Beatles John Lennon and George Harrison. He also worked on albums for Dion, the Ramones and Leonard Cohen, but was unable to recapture the magic of those glory years at Philles Records.

Trivia

Knowing that the Righteous Brothers' song "You've Lost That Lovin' Feelin'" was too long for standard radio airplay, Spector simply listed the running time as "3:05" instead of the correct "3:50." Although radio stations discovered the 3:05 fadeout was a false ending, the song continued to receive airplay and became a #1 worldwide smash.

The title track to this album is one of the most played songs of the rock and roll era—even if Phil Spector did fudge the running time on the label.

Trivia

Not every Crystals record was sung by "The Crystals." Depending on how fast Spector wanted a song on the market, he often hired another vocal trio, the Blossoms, and recorded them as "The Crystals" (the Blossoms' lead singer, Darlene Love, is clearly audible on "He's A Rebel" and "He's Sure The Boy I Love"). And on at least three tracks of the album The Crystals Sing Today's Hits, the Ronettes' Veronica Bennett is singing lead.

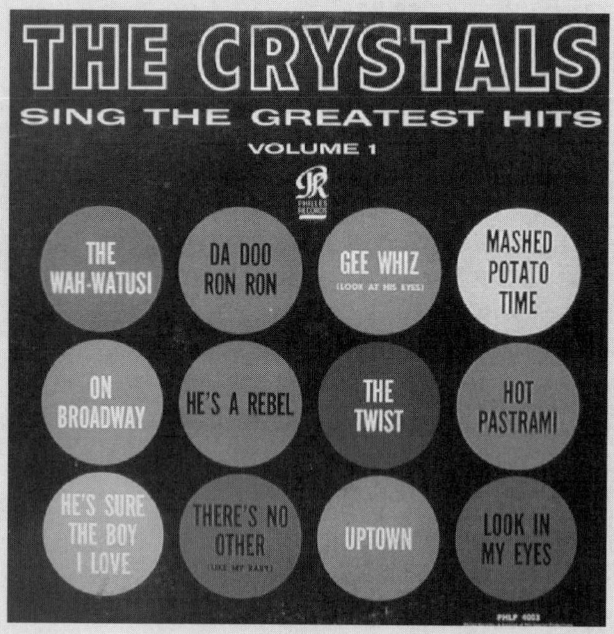

To fill out this album, the Ronettes sung three of the "Crystals" greatest hits.

What To Look For: One of the rarest records in the Philles catalog came from a lawsuit settlement. Spector was required, as part of a settlement agreement with his former partners Lester Sill and Harry Finfer, to give them a portion of the profits from the next two Crystals 45s. For the first song, Spector brought in the Blossoms, recorded the song "He's Sure The Boy I Love" under the Crystals' name, and watched as it hit the Top 20. The next song, however, was designed as a kiss-off to his former partners. Spector had the Crystals record "(Let's Dance) The Screw" (Pts. 1 and 2) (Philles 111), a five-minute raunchy, suggestive track. Some promo copies were sent to disc jockeys, who wouldn't play such a record for fear of losing their FCC licenses.

As popular as the Philles 45s are, the albums are worth more. Two holy grails in the Philles collection are the LP *Presenting the Fabulous Ronettes Featuring Veronica*, and an all-star Christmas record called *A Christmas Gift To You From Phil Spector.* An album by Ike and Tina Turner, *River Deep—Mountain High* (Philles 4011), is extremely rare; although the album was pressed, Spector removed it from sale when its title track bombed on the pop charts. The album by itself is worth $8,000 in near-mint condition; an album jacket was never created for it.

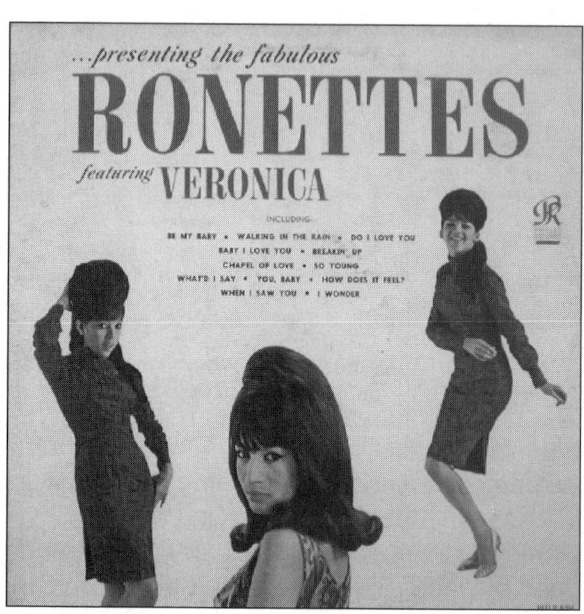

A difficult album to acquire, but lots of hits make it a worthwhile search. Courtesy Last Vestige Music Store, Albany, N.Y.

Any red vinyl or gold vinyl copies of Philles records are reproductions, made by Collectibles Records as part of a commemorative box set.

The Crystals' "(Let's Dance) The Screw" have been counterfeited. Original copies will have machine-stamped numbers in the dead wax. Counterfeit copies have hand-scratched numbers in the dead wax.

References: Ribowski, Mark, *Phil Spector: He's A Rebel*, Cooper Square Press, New York, 2000; Spector, Ronnie, with Waldron, Vince, *Be My Baby: How I Survived Mascara, Miniskirts, and Madness or My Life as a Fabulous Ronette*, Harmony Books/Crown Publishers, Inc., New York, N.Y. 1990.

Web pages: Mike Callahan's "Both Sides Now" Philles album discography: *http://www.bsnpubs.com/philles.html*; Jon Rausch's fan tribute site, "Phil Spector's Wall of Sound Page," *http://members.tripod.com/~rauschj*; a fan tribute site devoted to the Ronettes, *http://www.geocities.com/SunsetStrip/Studio/2469*; Mark Landwehr's Phil Spector Label Gallery, which contains a complete run of Philles records: *http://www.toltbbs.com/~msland/Spector/PSindex.htm.*

Trivia

***The Dirty Dancing* soundtrack featured a quasi-reunion of Philles artists. The Ronettes' "Be My Baby" was featured on the soundtrack, as was a duet with Righteous Brother Bill Medley and Jennifer Warnes, the #1 single "(I've Had) The Time Of My Life."**

45s	Year	VG	VG+	NM
The Alley Cats, "Puddin 'n Tain" / "Feel So Good" (Philles 108)	1965	$3.00	$6.00	$12.00
Bob B. Soxx and the Blue Jeans, "Zip-A-Dee-Doo-Dah" / "Flip & Nitty" (Philles 107)	1963	$5.00	$10.00	$20.00
Bob B. Soxx and the Blue Jeans, "Why Do Lovers Break Each Others' Hearts?" / "Dr. Kaplan's Office" (Philles 110)	1963	$5.00	$10.00	$20.00
Bob B. Soxx and the Blue Jeans, "Not Too Young To Get Married" / "Annette" (Philles 113)	1963	$5.00	$10.00	$20.00
The Crystals, "There's No Other (Like My Baby)" / "Oh Yeah, Maybe Baby" (Philles 100)	1961	$10.00	$20.00	$40.00
The Crystals, "Uptown" / "What a Nice Way To Turn 17" (Philles 102)	1962	$10.00	$20.00	$40.00
The Crystals, "He Hit Me (And It Felt Like A Kiss)" / "No One Ever Tells You" (Philles 105)	1962	$25.00	$50.00	$100.00
The Crystals, "He's A Rebel" / "I Love You Eddie" (Philles 106)				
(if on orange label)	1962	$15.00	$30.00	$60.00
(if on light blue label)	1962	$10.00	$20.00	$40.00
(if on yellow-red label, 1964 reissue)	1964	$6.25	$12.50	$25.00
The Crystals, "He's Sure The Boy I Love" / "Walkin' Along (La-La-La)" (Philles 109x)	1962	$7.50	$15.00	$30.00
The Crystals, "(Let's Dance) The Screw" (Pt. 1) / (Pt. 2) (Philles 111)				
(with white label)	1963	$2,000	$3,000	$4,000
(if on light blue label)	1963	$3,000	$4,500	$6,000
The Crystals, "Da Doo Ron Ron (When He Walked Me Home)" / "Git' It" (Philles 112)	1963	$7.50	$15.00	$30.00
The Crystals, "Then He Kissed Me" / "Brother Julius" (Philles 115)				
(if on light blue label)	1963	$10.00	$20.00	$40.00
(if on yellow-red label)	1963	$6.25	$12.50	$25.00
Darlene Love, "(Today I Met) The Boy I'm Gonna Marry" / "My Heart Beat A Little Bit Faster" (Philles 111)	1963	$7.50	$15.00	$30.00
Darlene Love, "(Today I Met) The Boy I'm Gonna Marry" / "Playing for Keeps" (Philles 111)	1963	$5.00	$10.00	$20.00
Darlene Love, "Wait Til My Bobby Gets Home" / "Take It From Me" (Philles 114)	1963	$5.00	$10.00	$20.00
Darlene Love, "Christmas (Baby Please Come Home)" / "Harry and Milt Meet Hal B." (Philles 119)	1963	$10.00	$20.00	$40.00
Darlene Love, "Stumble and Fall" / "(He's A) Quiet Guy" (Philles 123)				
(if on yellow-red stock copy label)	1964	$200.00	$400.00	$800.00
(if on yellow-red label, stamped "DJ Copy Not For Sale")	1964	$75.00	$150.00	$300.00
(if on white label promo)	1964	$37.50	$75.00	$150.00
The Righteous Brothers, "You've Lost That Lovin' Feelin'" / "There's A Woman" (Philles 124)	1964	$3.75	$7.50	$15.00
The Righteous Brothers, "Just Once In My Life" / "The Blues" (Philles 127)	1965	$3.75	$7.50	$15.00
(with picture sleeve, add:)	1965	$7.50	$15.00	$30.00
The Righteous Brothers, "Unchained Melody" / "Hung On You" (Philles 129)	1965	$3.75	$7.50	$15.00
The Righteous Brothers, "Ebb Tide" / "For Sentimental Reasons" (Philles 130)	1965	$3.75	$7.50	$15.00
(with picture sleeve, add:)	1965	$7.50	$15.00	$30.00
The Righteous Brothers, "White Cliffs of Dover" / "She's Mine All Mine" (Philles 132)	1966	$5.00	$10.00	$20.00
The Ronettes, "Be My Baby" / "Tedesco & Pittman" (Philles 116)	1963	$7.50	$15.00	$30.00
The Ronettes, "Baby I Love You" / "Miss Joan and Mr. Sam" (Philles 118)	1963	$7.50	$15.00	$30.00

45s	Year	VG	VG+	NM
The Ronettes, "(The Best Part Of) Breakin' Up" / "Big Red" (Philles 120)	1964	$7.50	$15.00	$30.00
The Ronettes, "Walking In The Rain" / "How Does It Feel?" (Philles 123)	1964	$10.00	$20.00	$40.00
(with picture sleeve, add:)	1964	$37.50	$75.00	$150.00
The Ronettes, "Is This What I Get For Loving You?" / "Oh I Love You" (Philles 128)	1965	$6.25	$12.50	$25.00
(with picture sleeve, add:)	1965	$37.50	$75.00	$150.00
Ike and Tina Turner, "River Deep - Mountain High" / "I'll Keep You Happy" (Philles 132)	1966	$5.00	$10.00	$20.00
Ike and Tina Turner, "A Man Is A Man Is A Man" / "Two to Tango" (Philles 134)	1966	$3.75	$7.50	$15.00

LPs	Year	VG	VG+	NM
Bob B. Soxx and the Blue Jeans, Zip A Dee Doo Dah (Philles PHLP-4002) (mono)	1963	$125.00	$250.00	$500.00
Lenny Bruce, Lenny Bruce is Out Again (Philles PHLP-4010)	1966	$25.00	$50.00	$100.00
The Crystals, Twist Uptown				
(if mono, blue label, Philles PHLP-4000)	1962	$150.00	$300.00	$600.00
(if mono, Capitol Record Club, Philles T-90722)	1965	$150.00	$300.00	$600.00
(if in electronically channeled stereo, Capitol Record Club, Philles DT-90722)	1965	$300.00	$600.00	$1,200.00
The Righteous Brothers, You've Lost That Lovin' Feelin'				
(if in mono, Philles PHLP-4007)	1964	$6.25	$12.50	$25.00
(if some songs in stereo, Philles PHLPST-4007)	1964	$10.00	$20.00	$40.00
(if in mono, Capitol Record Club, Philles T-90692)	1965	$12.50	$25.00	$50.00
(if some songs in stereo, Capitol Record Club, Philles ST-90692)	1965	$12.50	$25.00	$50.00
The Ronettes, Presenting the Fabulous Ronettes Featuring Veronica				
(if in mono, blue label, Philles PHLP-4006)	1964	$200.00	$400.00	$800.00
(if in mono, yellow-red label, Philles PHLP-4006)	1964	$100.00	$200.00	$400.00
(if in stereo, yellow-red label, Philles PHLPST-4006)	1964	$150.00	$300.00	$600.00
(if in mono, Capitol Record Club, Philles T-90721)	1965	$62.50	$125.00	$250.00
(if in stereo, Capitol Record Club, Philles ST-90721)	1965	$100.00	$200.00	$400.00
Ike and Tina Turner, River Deep - Mountain High (Philles PHLP-4011) (mono)	1966	$2,000	$4,000	$8,000
Various Artists, A Christmas Gift For You From Phil Spector				
(if on Philles PHLP-4005, mono, first pressings have blue-black labels)	1963	$37.50	$75.00	$150.00
(if on Philles PHLP-4005, mono, second pressings have red-yellow labels)	1964	$20.00	$40.00	$80.00

The piano intro to "Baby I Love You" was played by Leon Huff, who later formed a successful soul music partnership with Kenny Gamble.

PICTURE DISCS

History: Picture discs—records containing a photograph or artwork embedded inside the record—have been around since the early days of 78s. In the 1930s, RCA Victor released some special-edition picture discs of its most popular singers and bandleaders. By the late 1930s, French and German pressing plants made picture discs of "Le Hot Jazz" recordings.

By 1947, Thomas Saffady's Vogue Picture Disc company had perfected an automatic assembly-line process for constructing picture discs. Two paper color illustrations were placed on either side of an aluminum core. The illustrations and core were coated with a clear vinylite polymer, and the grooves were stamped onto the final product. Unfortunately, initial sales were very poor—pretty picture records could not compensate many subpar performances in the grooves—and the company filed for bankruptcy barely a year after opening its doors.

In the 1970s, some record companies pressed picture discs as a novelty—mostly the pictures replicated the front of the album cover—but their existence sparked a picture disc collecting craze. Most of the collectors who purchased picture discs in the late 1970s either hung them on the wall like fine art, or displayed them with plate stands to show their full-color glory. These discs were rarely played; many picture disc collectors at the time already had the black vinyl version of those albums, and played the picture disc maybe once to make sure the correct album was in the grooves.

Boston's first four studio LPs are available on picture disc. Their debut disc is the most common of the four; the discs for *Third Stage* and *Walk On* are European imports.

Today's picture discs are more durable than their 78 RPM ancestors. The paper illustrations are now affixed to a polyvinyl chloride center disc, then sheets of mylar are placed over each picture, like the bread slices of a sandwich. The mylar-artwork-vinyl collage is then stamped by the pressing machines—and 45 seconds later, a picture disc is born.

While most picture discs feature album art found on the black vinyl albums, some discs contain rare band photos or specially modified art. Other picture discs contain interviews with the band or lead singer, and these interviews exist only in the picture-disc format.

This shaped-disc pressing contains an interview Presley conducted with a Little Rock, Arkansas reporter in 1956. The 1996 shaped disc is the first such pressing authorized by the estate of Elvis Presley. Courtesy Erika Records, Downey, Calif.

The majority of picture discs are round, but some discs are irregularly shaped, in an effort to follow the picture disc's artwork. In this case, the record is pressed with the paper insert and the mylar sheets, but a 7-inch odd-shaped disc is pressed in a 12-inch format, then the record is cut with a special pre-sculpted die, similar to a cookie cutter. This gives the illusion of a bigger-than-life 7-inch record, even though the grooves still spin in a circular pattern.

Many record collectors have mixed feelings about picture discs. These records are more likely to end up on a wall or display shelf than on a turntable—and if the mylar used to press the record was from thin sheets, the record itself will have a muffled sound when played. If a record company or pressing plant uses thicker mylar, however, the record will sound as clear as its vinyl counterpart.

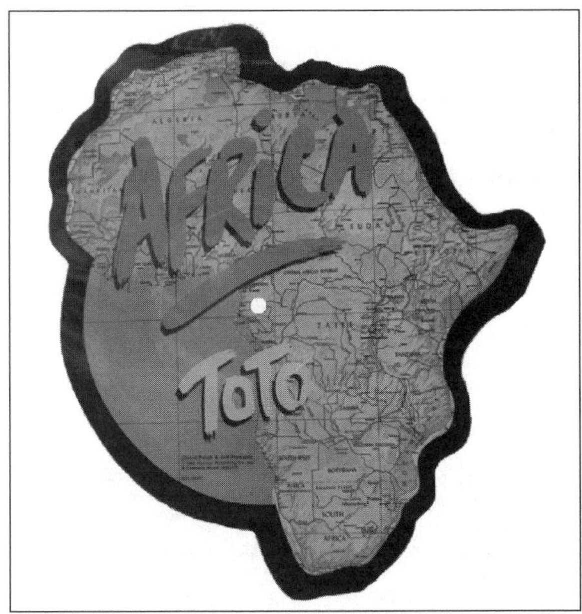

Toto's #1 hit "Africa" is available on this continent-shaped picture disc.

Another type of picture disc, the "laser-etched" album, also appeared in the late 1970s. Using special tools similar to those employed by engravers to make dollar bill pressing plates, the record lacquer is scraped or "etched" before the grooves are cut. The finished product is striking—when viewed in reflected light, the black vinyl contains rainbow-colored patterns which shimmer as the record spins on the turntable.

Split Enz' *True Colours* LP was "laser etched," which produced rainbow-shaped geometric patterns in the vinyl when held to reflected light. This album also contains their quirky hit, "I Got You."

Trivia

The Police released some odd-shaped picture discs in their career, including "Don't Stand So Close To Me" and "Message In A Bottle"—but their rarest picture disc, in fact the band's rarest collectible, was a specially designed picture disc for their Ghost in the Machine album. Once the record was placed on the turntable, a connection between the metal spindle and some electrodes around the spindle hole actually allowed the disc to light up, showing the calculator-diode motif of that album.

What To Look For: For most picture-disc collectors, a clean vinyl image is key. Picture discs are one of the few record collectibles in which the visual appearance is more important than the sound on the grooves.

Most picture discs were sold in 12-inch jackets, whose front covers were die-cut so that consumers could see the entire album in all its full-color glory. These jackets tend to wrinkle and split over time, with most of the splits occurring where the surface area between the seam and the die-cut circle is the thinnest. Those who want the jackets, as well as the picture disc, also look for jackets that have not been "notched" by the record company for discount sales. The discs themselves were stored inside clear plastic inner sleeves; if the record was improperly placed inside the jacket, the inner lining will wrinkle and tear.

Some classic recordings on the Sun label; as arranged on a Rhino Records picture disc.

Trivia

Bobby Caldwell's biggest hit, "What You Won't Do For Love," was available for a limited time both as a regular black vinyl 45, and as a red vinyl heart-shaped record. The heart-shaped version was originally pressed as a 10-inch circular record, then was die-cut to create the heart shape.

It was both a hit record and an instant Valentine gift, Bobby Caldwell's "What You Won't Do For Love."

Trivia

Picture discs are still being made today, and the sound quality has improved to the point where surface noise is virtually eliminated. These current picture discs are pressed in extremely low print runs, as compared to their 1970s' counterparts.

Not only did the punk-ska band Less Than Jake release their *Hello Rockview* album on both vinyl and CD, it also pressed some picture disc versions of their major-label album. Courtesy Erika Records, Downey, Calif.

If you plan to display your records on a wall, don't just hang them up by putting a nail in the wall and slipping the record on through its spindle hole. These are works of art; a 12 x 16 frame can be purchased at any art supply store or framing shop (if you bring the disc in, the framers can even create a customized matte to enhance your picture disc). And avoid hanging your picture disc on a wall that receives direct sunlight—the picture inside can fade in just a few years from direct sunshine.

References: Curry, Edgar L., *Vogue: The Picture Record (2nd Edition)*, self-published by the author, 1998, available through *jancur@halcyon.com.*

Web pages: Erika Records of Downey, California, is America's largest producer of colored vinyl and picture disc records. They can be reached at: *http://www.erikarecords.com.*

Picture Discs	Year	VG	VG+	NM
The Beatles, Sgt. Pepper's Lonely Hearts Club Band (Capitol SEAX-11840) (deduct 25% if cover is notched or cut)	1978	$5.00	$10.00	$20.00
Blondie, Parallel Lines (Chrysalis CHP 5001)	1979	$6.25	$12.50	$25.00
Boston, Boston (Epic E99 44188)	1978	$3.75	$7.50	$15.00
The Cars, Shake It Up (Elektra 5E-567)				
(if "KMET-FM" stamped on back)	1981	$12.50	$25.00	$50.00
(with blank back)	1981	$10.00	$20.00	$40.00
Cheap Trick, Dream Police (Epic 35773)	1979	$7.50	$15.00	$30.00
Elvis Costello, My Aim Is True / This Year's Model (Columbia, no number) (promo-only picture disc, one side is dedicated to each album)	1978	$12.50	$25.00	$50.00
Culture Club, Colour By Numbers (Virgin/Epic 9E9-39237)	1983	$6.25	$12.50	$25.00
Neil Diamond, Primitive (Columbia 9C9-39915)	1984	$5.00	$10.00	$20.00
Heart, Dreamboat Annie (Mushroom MRS-2-SP)	1978	$6.25	$12.50	$25.00
Iron Maiden, The Number of the Beast (Capitol SEAX-12219)	1982	$12.50	$25.00	$50.00
Jag Panzer, Ample Destruction (Azra Iron Works 1001) (allegedly only 250 were pressed as picture discs)	1985	$6.25	$12.50	$25.00
Elton John, A Single Man (MCA 14951)	1978	$5.00	$10.00	$20.00
(if on MCA L33-1995, promo only)	1978	$10.00	$20.00	$40.00

Picture Discs	Year	VG	VG+	NM
Judas Priest, Great Vinyl and Concert Hits (Columbia 9C9 39926)	1984	$15.00	$30.00	$60.00
Original Motion Picture Soundtrack, Jurassic Park (MCA/BMG, no number) (promo only)	1993	$300.00	$600.00	$1,200.00
Kiss, Smashes, Thrashes and Hits (Mercury 836 887-1)	1988	$6.25	$12.50	$25.00
Less Than Jake, Hello Rockview (Drive-Thru Records L-50959)	1996	$3.75	$7.50	$15.00
Barry Manilow, Greatest Hits (Arista A2L 8601) (2 LP's)	1979	$10.00	$20.00	$40.00
Paul McCartney and Wings, Band on the Run (Capitol SEAX-11901)	1978	$10.00	$20.00	$40.00
Meat Loaf, Bat Out Of Hell (Epic E99 34974)	1978	$5.00	$10.00	$20.00
Metallica, Kill 'Em All (Megaforce MRI 069)				
(if picture disc is numbered)	1983	$20.00	$40.00	$80.00
(if picture disc is not numbered)	1983	$10.00	$20.00	$40.00
Mudhoney, Every Good Boy Deserves Fudge (Sub Pop 105 PD) (2,500 copies pressed)	1991	$7.50	$15.00	$30.00
National Lampoon, That's Not Funny, That's Sick! (Label 21 PIC-2001)	1978	$5.00	$10.00	$20.00
Oingo Boingo, Dark at the End of the Tunnel (MCA L33-18137, promo only)	1990	$10.00	$20.00	$40.00
Ozzy Osbourne, Diary of a Madman (Jet AS99 1372) (promo only)	1981	$10.00	$20.00	$40.00
The Alan Parsons Project, Vulture Culture (Arista ALPD 8263) (promo only)	1985	$6.25	$12.50	$25.00
Pink Floyd, The Dark Side of the Moon (Capitol SEAX-11902)	1978	$7.50	$15.00	$30.00
The Police, Ghost in the Machine (A&M-SP-3730) (picture disc that lights up when placed on turntable)	1981	$250.00	$500.00	$1,000.00

Picture Discs	Year	VG	VG+	NM
Queensryche, Operation: Mindcrime (EMI Manhattan SPRO-04136/7) (promo only)	1988	$20.00	$40.00	$80.00
The Residents, Meet The Residents (Ralph RZ 7707) (side one is original jacket cover, side two is replacement cover)	1986	$6.25	$12.50	$25.00
The Rolling Stones, Still Life (American Concert 1981) (Rolling Stones COC 39114)	1982	$10.00	$20.00	$40.00
Rufus Featuring Chaka Khan, Street Player (ABC 1049) (promo only)	1978	$6.25	$12.50	$25.00
Bob Seger, Night Moves (Capitol, no number) (promo only)	1977	$10.00	$20.00	$40.00
The Smithereens, Especially For You (Enigma SEAX-73258)	1986	$5.00	$10.00	$20.00
Stryper, To Hell with the Devil (Enigma SEAX-73277)	1986	$6.25	$12.50	$25.00
Styx, Pieces of Eight (A&M PR-4724)	1978	$6.25	$12.50	$25.00
Supertramp, Breakfast in America (A&M 3730) (in-house disc featuring A&M staff members and the cover model)	1979	$125.00	$250.00	$500.00
Toto, Turn Back (Columbia PD-36813) (promo only)	1981	$6.25	$12.50	$25.00
Toto, "Africa" / "Rosanna" (Columbia 8C8 38685) (disc shaped like the African continent)	1983	$5.00	$10.00	$20.00
Wham!, Make It Big (Columbia 9C9 40062)	1985	$6.25	$12.50	$25.00
Neil Young, "Southern Pacific" / "Motor City" (Reprise 49895) (triangle-shaped picture disc)	1982	$75.00	$150.00	$300.00

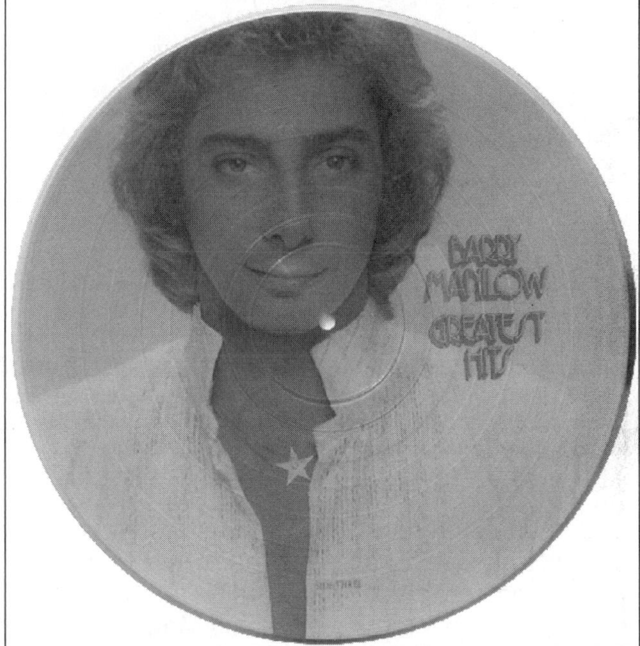

While Barry Manilow's *Greatest Hits* album has little collectible value outside of Manilow's fans, the picture disc version of that same album can garner as much as $50 in near-mint condition.

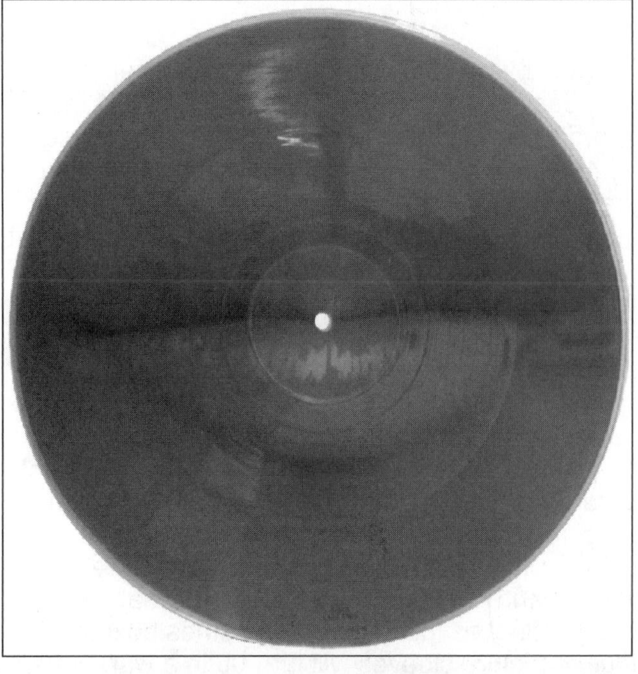

No, this is not the opening scene from the Rocky Horror Picture Show. It's a promotional picture disc by a group named *Fandango.* Although the song they recorded, "Last Kiss," was not a hit, this record is still collectible on its kitschy looks alone.

PICTURE SLEEVES

History: Picture sleeves have been part of record collecting ever since records were first pressed. Even some of the earliest 78s had special paper sleeves that advertised a label's singing roster, with crisp line drawings of such singers as Enrico Caruso, Jenny Lind and Nellie Melba.

While most 45s were sold either in white paper sleeves or in "company sleeves," a select number of records were sold with a full-color picture of the artist, the band, or a representative drawing of the song's concept. These "picture sleeves" can often be as valuable—in some cases, even more valuable—than the records contained inside.

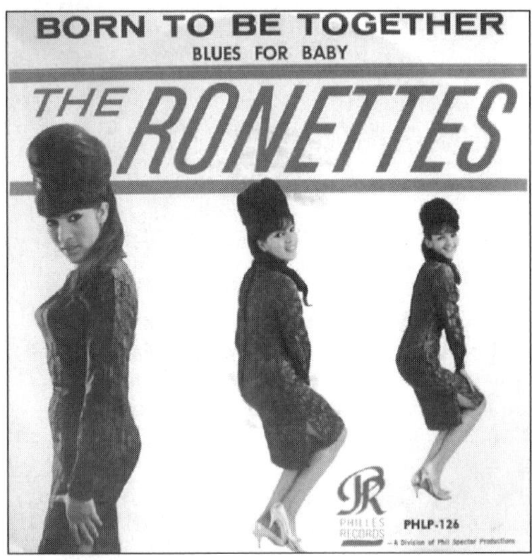

This Ronettes picture sleeve is very rare; very few Philles 45s had picture sleeves, and this song was not a big hit. From the Collection of Val Shively.

By their very nature and existence, paper sleeves were designed to catch a purchaser's eye at the record store; and act as a carrying pouch to guide the 45 safely home. Unfortunately, after that the picture sleeve would be subject to every sort of wear and tear—splits on the seams, tears and wrinkles at the sleeve's opening, ringwear around the artist's face, etc. Because many record collectors stored their 45s in the accompanying picture sleeve, not expecting the sleeve to increase in any value, finding picture sleeves in near-mint condition becomes more difficult with each year.

In many cases, a picture sleeve will be made only for radio stations and promotional use. Sometimes a record will become such a quick hit, that the record company will simply run out of picture sleeves and package the hot discs in whatever generic sleeves it can find. Sometimes boxes of unused picture sleeves will turn up in a warehouse; in fact, the picture sleeve for Bruce Springsteen's first hit, "Blinded By The Light," is so rare that many of the copies existing today were allegedly found in a CBS dumpster.

Not every picture sleeve is limited to a snazzy photo of the artist or group. Record companies have used many eye-catching tactics to make their records stand out, whether it includes foldout sleeves, label variations, or non-paper sleeves. Besides being a holder for the 45, picture sleeves often contained information on how to join an artist's fan club, what new releases were soon to be available, a concert tour schedule, or whether that artist would be appearing on a popular TV show.

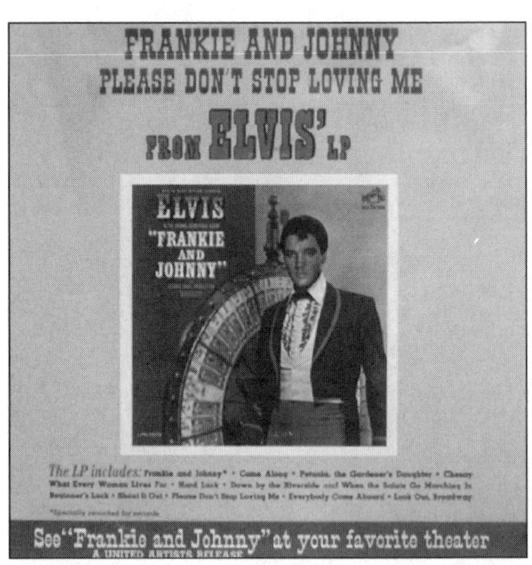

This picture sleeve for Elvis Presley's single "Frankie and Johnny" advertised not only the single, but also the album and the motion picture of the same name. From the Collection of Val Shively.

Sometimes a record would be stored in a "foldout" picture sleeve, allowing the owner to get a bonus poster for their wall. Finding intact, near-mint copies of such foldout sleeves as Madonna's "Borderline," Duran Duran's "The Reflex," or the Grateful Dead's "Touch of Grey" has become more difficult, as these foldout sleeves may have tack holes in the corners (when they were put up on a bedroom wall), or the folds themselves may have split their seams (because the record was still stored inside).

Other picture sleeves become rare collectibles because the content may have been changed—either the artwork was too salacious for initial release, or the band felt that a new cover was more appropriate for the music. The sleeve for Queen's "Body Language," for example, was yanked off the market because the cover showed a naked couple. The sleeve was replaced with a stark black sleeve, containing only the band's name and the song title.

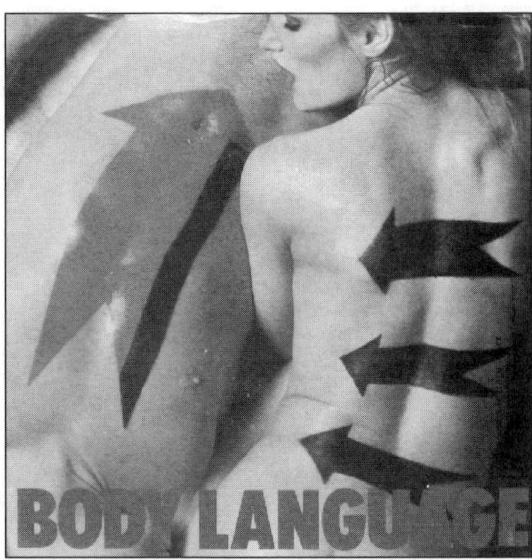

This was the original sleeve for Queen's "Body Language."

Some other picture sleeves were made of thin plastic, the same material used for bread bags. These sleeves tend to wrinkle easily, and the printed material on them can peel or scrape off quickly.

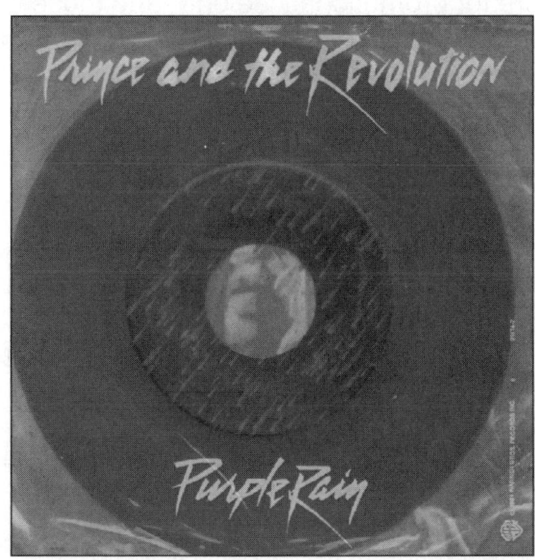

The clear bread-bag sleeve for Prince's "Purple Rain" shows off the purple vinyl and custom label contained therein.

Records that aren't sold with picture sleeves are often sold in generic "company sleeves." The sleeve, often made of thin paper stock instead of glossy paper, barely contains a mention of the record company. Some record companies, however, use "company sleeves" to promote other artists on the label, or to promote a certain artist's back catalog. Motown and Philadelphia International Records were two such labels that used their company sleeves to help sell other records within the organization.

Trivia

Some of the rarest picture sleeves were issued for 45s by artists that had not yet made the big time.

The B-52's picture sleeve for an early single, "Planet Claire."

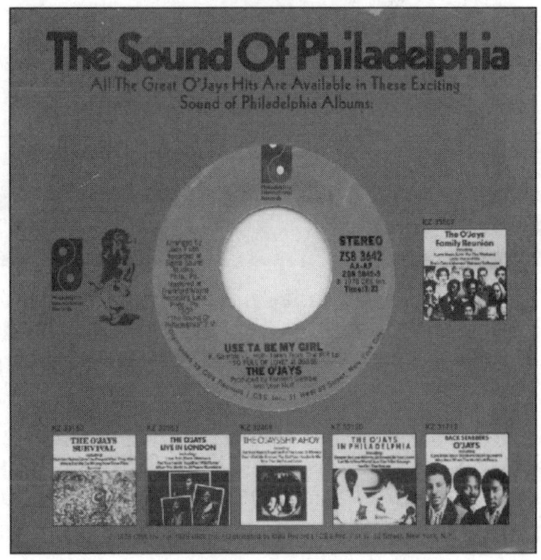

In purchasing the O'Jays' single "Use Ta Be My Girl," Philadelphia International Records hoped you would consider purchasing five other O'Jays albums, as advertised on the company sleeve.

To store your sleeves properly, first make sure they don't have records in them. This may sound odd—that the very item sleeves were designed to hold would do the most damage—but your records can be stored in inexpensive white paper sleeves.

As for the colored picture sleeves, they can be stored in clear plastic sleeves, available through most equipment supply companies. Comic books also store non-PVC jackets, in which a 45 picture sleeve will fit nicely.

What To Look For: Picture sleeve storage is almost a Catch-22 situation. Optimally, you would want to store the record and the sleeve together. But the longer a record is stored in a picture sleeve, the more likely the sleeve will develop ringwear. If you want to collect picture sleeves, you should remove the record from the picture sleeve, storing the record in a white generic sleeve.

Glossy picture sleeves are very fragile; besides ringwear, they can also suffer from split seams, ridge cuts, and wrinkling. Sometimes the sleeve's internal glue may break down, causing the sleeve to come apart at the folds. And since these sleeves were made of paper, they tended to rip over time anyway.

Even records pressed today have picture sleeves. The sleeve for Pearl Jam's hit "Given to Fly" is made of durable cardstock rather than flimsy paper.

Picture sleeves that were once owned by jukebox companies are rarely kept in good condition; sometimes the jukebox employees would cut a circular hole in the front of the sleeve, so they could reuse the sleeve for another record.

While most picture sleeves will have artwork from the original album, or a group shot of the band, some picture sleeves may contain original artwork that represents the song's lyrics. Although picture sleeves in the 1950s and 1960s contained shots of the artist, by the 1970s the sleeve was considered by many artists to be part of the whole musical experience, and care was taken with the picture sleeve artwork.

The cover artwork to Styx' "Come Sail Away" may give away the final secret of the song; but this unique artwork does not exist on any other Styx album or promotional material.

The most desirable picture sleeves are ones that are short-printed or were only available in a certain geographic area. Other rare sleeves include those that were for promotional use only, and those where something is edited out of the picture (early Beatles picture sleeves for "I Want To Hold Your Hand" show Paul McCartney with a cigarette in his fingers; when the sleeve was reissued for a 20th anniversary pressing, the cigarette was airbrushed out).

The prices listed below in this section are for the picture sleeve only, not for the 45 contained inside.

References: Neely, Tim, *Goldmine Price Guide to 45 RPM Records*, Krause Publications, Iola, Wisconsin, 1999; Szabla, Charles, *Goldmine 45 RPM Picture Sleeve Price Guide*, Krause Publications, Iola, Wisconsin, 1998.

Web pages: You can see one-of-a-kind rare and unique Beatles picture sleeves at this site: *http://www.rarebeatles.com.*

Picture Sleeves	Year	VG	VG+	NM
a-ha, "Take On Me" / "Love Is Reason" (Warner Bros. 29011-7) (comic book picture sleeve)	1985	$2.00	$4.00	$8.00
Annette, "How Will I Know My Love" / "Don't Jump To Conclusions" (Disneyland F-102)	1958	$12.50	$25.00	$50.00
Louis Armstrong, "Hello Dolly!" (Kapp 573)	1964	$2.50	$5.00	$10.00
Asia, "Heat of the Moment" / "Ride Easy" (Geffen 50040)	1982		$2.50	$5.00
The Beach Boys, "Barbara Ann" / "Girl Don't Tell Me" (Capitol 5561)				
(if on coated paper, glossy finish)	1965	$37.50	$75.00	$150.00
(if on non-coated paper, not glossy)	1965	$50.00	$100.00	$200.00
The Beatles, "Leave My Kitten Alone" / "Ob La Di Ob La Da (alternate version)" (Capitol B-5439) (no record was ever pressed for this sleeve)	1985	$12.50	$25.00	$50.00
The B-52's, "Planet Claire" / "There's A Moon In The Sky (Called The Moon)" Warner Bros. 49212)	1979		$3.00	$6.00
Boston, "Amanda" (MCA 52756)	1986		$3.00	
David Bowie, "Time" / "The Prettiest Star" (RCA APBO-0001)	1973	$200.00	$400.00	$800.00

Picture Sleeves	Year	VG	VG+	NM
David Bowie, "Tonight" / "Tumble and Twirl" (EMI America B-8246) (foldout poster sleeve)	1984		$2.50	$5.00
James Brown, "Living in America" (Scotti Bros. ZS4-05682)	1985		$3.00	
(if marked "Demonstration Only - Not For Sale")	1985		$2.00	$4.00
The Byrds, "Eight Miles High" / "Why?" (Columbia 4-43578)	1966	$15.00	$30.00	$60.00
Cheech and Chong, "Earache My Eye Featuring Alice Bowie" (Ode 66102)	1974		$3.00	$6.00
Jimmy Clanton and Mary Ann Mobley, "Down the Aisle" / "No Longer Blue" (Ace 616)	1961	$7.50	$15.00	$30.00
The Clash, "Should I Stay Or Should I Go?" / "First Night Back In London" (Epic 14-03061) (Ronald Reagan on sleeve)	1982	$3.00	$6.00	$12.00
The Clash, "Should I Stay Or Should I Go?" / "Cool Confusion" (Epic 34-03547) (entire band on sleeve)	1983		$2.50	$5.00
Bobby Darin, "Ave Maria" / "O Come All Ye Faithful" (Atco 6211)	1961	$40.00	$80.00	$160.00
Dexys Midnight Runners and the Emerald Express, "Come On Eileen" / "Let's Make This Precious" (Mercury 76189)	1982	$2.00	$4.00	$8.00
Bob Dylan, "Blowin' In The Wind" / "Don't Think Twice" (Columbia 4-42856)	1963	$200.00	$400.00	$800.00
The Everly Brothers, "Wake Up Little Susie" / "Maybe Tomorrow" (Cadence 1337)	1957	$62.50	$125.00	$250.00
The 5th Dimension, "Aquarius - Let The Sunshine In" (Soul City 772)	1969	$3.75	$7.50	$15.00
The Fixx, "One Thing Leads To Another" / "Opinions" (MCA 52264)	1983		$2.00	$4.00
Foreigner, "Waiting For A Girl Like You" / "I'm Gonna Win" (Atlantic 3868)	1981		$2.50	$5.00
Peter Gabriel, "Sledgehammer" / "Don't Break This Rhythm" (Geffen 28247-7)	1986		$3.00	
The Go-Go's, "We Got The Beat" / "Can't Stop The World" (IRS 9903)	1981		$3.00	
The Grateful Dead, "Dark Star" / "Born Cross-Eyed" (Warner Bros. 7186)	1968	$125.00	$250.00	$500.00
Bill Haley and the Comets, "(You Hit The Wrong Note) Billy Goat" / "Rockin' Rollin' Rover" (Decca 30314)	1957	$30.00	$60.00	$120.00
The Jimi Hendrix Experience, "Hey Joe" / "51st Anniversary" (Reprise 0572)	1967	$250.00	$500.00	$1,000.00
The Human League, "Don't You Want Me" / "Seconds" (A&M/Virgin 2397)	1982		$3.00	$6.00
Billy Idol, "Hot in the City" / "Hole in the Wall" (Chrysalis 2605)	1982		$2.50	$5.00
The Jackson Five, "Mama's Pearl" / "Darling Dear" (Motown 1177)	1971	$3.75	$7.50	$15.00
Joan Jett and the Blackhearts, "I Love Rock and Roll" / "You Don't Know What You've Got" (Boardwalk NB7-11-135)	1982	$2.50	$5.00	$10.00
Joy Division, "Love Will Tear Us Apart" / "These Days" (Factory FACTUS 23)	1980	$3.00	$6.00	$12.00
Katrina and the Waves, "Walking on Sunshine" / "Going Down To Liverpool" (Capitol B-5466)	1985		$3.00	
Kiss, "Flaming Youth" / "God of Thunder" (Casablanca 858)	1976	$15.00	$30.00	$60.00
Brenda Lee, "Sweet Nothin's" / "Weep No More My Baby" (Decca 30967)	1959	$30.00	$60.00	$120.00
Little Richard, "Keep A Knockin'"/ "Can't Believe You Wanna Leave" (Specialty 611)	1957	$15.00	$30.00	$60.00
The Lovin' Spoonful, "Daydream" (Kama Sutra 208)	1966	$3.75	$7.50	$15.00
Madonna, "Borderline" / "Think of Me" (Sire 29534) (foldout poster sleeve)	1984	$20.00	$40.00	$80.00
The Mamas and the Papas, "Creeque Alley" (Dunhill 4083) (promotional only)	1967	$10.00	$20.00	$40.00
Johnny Mathis, "Chances Are" / "The Twelfth of Never" (Columbia 4-40983)	1957	$5.00	$10.00	$20.00
Paul McCartney and Wings, "Girls School" / "Mull of Kintyre" (Capitol 4504)	1977	$3.00	$6.00	$12.00
Men Without Hats, "The Safety Dance" / "Living in China" (Backstreet 52232)	1984		$2.50	$5.00
Milli Vanilli, "Girl You Know It's True" / "Magic Touch" (Arista 9781)	1988		$3.00	
Mötley Crüe, "Girls Girls Girls" / "Sumthin' for Nothin'" (Elektra 7-69465)	1987		$3.00	
New Order, "Blue Monday 1988" / "Touched By The Hand of God" (Qwest 27979-7)	1988		$3.00	
Roy Orbison, "Crying" / "Candy Man" (Monument 447)	1961	$10.00	$20.00	$40.00

Picture Sleeves	Year	VG	VG+	NM
Orchestral Manœuvres in the Dark, "If You Leave" (A&M 2811)	1986		$2.00	$4.00
Robert Palmer, "Addicted To Love" (Island 7-99570) (two versions of this picture sleeve, one with Palmer solo, one with four women, value is equal)	1986		$2.00	$4.00
Carl Perkins, "Hambone" / "Sister Twister" (Columbia 4-42514)	1962	$100.00	$200.00	$400.00
Elvis Presley, "Don't Be Cruel" / "Hound Dog" (RCA Victor 47-6604)				
(if "Hound Dog!" is listed above "Don't Be Cruel")	1956	$30.00	$60.00	$120.00
(if "Don't Be Cruel" is listed above "Hound Dog!")	1956	$50.00	$100.00	$200.00
Prince and the Revolution, "Let's Go Crazy" / Prince with Sheila E., "Erotic City" (Warner Bros. 29216)	1984	$2.00	$4.00	$8.00
Queen, "We Will Rock You" / "We Are The Champions" (Elektra 45441)	1977	$2.50	$5.00	$10.00
Queen, "Body Language" (Elektra 47452)				
(if first pressing, with a naked couple on cover)	1982	$3.75	$7.50	$15.00
(if second pressing, white cover, B-side "Life is Real" listed)	1982	$2.50	$5.00	$10.00
The Ramones, "I Wanna Be Your Boyfriend" / "California Sun" / "I Don't Wanna Walk Around With You (Live)" (Sire 734)	1976	$3.50	$7.00	$14.00
R.E.M., "Radio Free Europe" / "Standing Still" (Hib-Tone 001)	1981	$18.75	$37.50	$75.00
R.E.M., "Radio Free Europe" / "There She Goes Again" (IRS 9916)	1983	$7.50	$15.00	$30.00
The Rolling Stones, "Not Fade Away" / "I Wanna Be Your Man" (London 9657)	1964	$75.00	$150.00	$300.00
The Rolling Stones,"(I Can't Get No) Satisfaction" / "The Under Assistant West Coast Production Man" (London 9766)	1965	$50.00	$100.00	$200.00
Run-D.M.C., "Walk This Way" / "King of Rock" (Profile 5112)	1986		$2.00	$4.00
Neil Sedaka, "Breaking Up Is Hard To Do" (As Long As I Live" (RCA Victor 47-8046)	1962	$6.25	$12.50	$25.00
Sheriff, "When I'm With You" (Capitol B-5199) (1982 release; the 1989 re-release did not have a picture sleeve)	1982		$2.50	$5.00
Simon and Garfunkel, "At The Zoo" (Columbia 4-44046)	1967	$10.00	$20.00	$40.00
Simon and Garfunkel, "My Little Town" / Art Garfunkel, "Rag Doll", Paul Simon, "You're Kind" (Columbia 3-10230)	1975		$2.50	$5.00
The Smashing Pumpkins, "1979" / "Bullet with Butterfly Wings" (Virgin 7243 8 38522 7 7)	1996		$2.50	$5.00
Bruce Springsteen, "Blinded By The Light" / "The Angel" (Columbia 4-45805)	1973	$100.00	$200.00	$400.00
Starz, "Cherry Baby" / "Rock Six Times" (Capitol 4399)	1976		$3.00	$6.00
Styx, "Come Sail Away" / "Put Me On" (A&M 1977)	1977		$3.00	$6.00
Talking Heads, "Psycho Killer" (Sire 1013)	1978	$2.00	$4.00	$8.00
.38 Special, "Caught Up In You" / "Firestarter" (A&M 2412)	1982		$2.00	$4.00
Times Two, "Strange But True" (Reprise 27998-7) (poster sleeve)	1988		$2.00	$4.00
The Turtles, "Happy Together" / "Like The Seasons" (White Whale 244)	1967	$5.00	$10.00	$20.00
U2, "Two Hearts Beat As One" / "Endless Sleep" (Island 7-99861)	1983	$2.00	$4.00	$8.00
The Velvet Underground, "All Tomorrow's Parties" / "I'll Be Your Mirror" (Verve 10427)	1966	$2,000	$4,000	$8,000
Wham!, "Wake Me Up Before You Go-Go" (Columbia 38-04552)	1984	$2.00	$4.00	$8.00
Whitesnake, "Here I Go Again" (Geffen 28339-7)	1984		$2.00	$4.00
XTC, "The Mayor of Simpleton" / "One of the Millions" (Geffen/Virgin 27552-7)	1989		$3.00	
Y Kant Tori Read, "Cool On Your Island" / "Heart Attack At 23" (Atlantic 7-89021) (lead singer is Tori Amos)	1988	$20.00	$40.00	$80.00
Warren Zevon, "Leave My Monkey Alone" (Virgin 99440-7)	1987		$3.00	

POWER POP

History: At the start of 1978, very few people outside of Southern California ever heard of the Knack. Six months later, the Knack, their hit album *Get the Knack*, and the hit song from that album, "My Sharona," was seemingly everywhere. Some critics erroneously considered the Knack an American punk band, but in fact they were a "power pop" band, and shared their heritage with groups like the Raspberries and Badfinger, and would share a lineage with XTC, Cheap Trick, and the Plimsouls.

Power pop evolved from two distinct musical styles of the late 1960s—the Beatles' *White Album* and *Abbey Road* recordings, and the bubblegum music from the Don Kirshner and Kasenetz-Katz music factories. Power pop songs contained intricate melodies and ear-catching hooks, and were laced over with jangly guitar solos. The lyrics to power pop songs were intricate and emotional, mixing love ballads with passionate energy, throwing a wry rhyme or a terse verse into an unrestrained refrain.

"Come And Get It" was the first of four Top 10 "power pop" hits for Badfinger.

In the early 1970s, power pop groups like Badfinger and the Raspberries had major Top 40 hits. Badfinger originally benefited from their early association with the Beatles, but songs like "Day After Day" and "Baby Blue" showed they were hitmakers on their own. The Raspberries, led by classically trained pianist Eric Carmen, had hits with short Top 40 rockers like "Go All The Way" and "I Wanna Be With You," and with longer emotional songs like "Don't Wanna Say Goodbye" and "Overnight Sensation (Hit Record)."

The Raspberries' "Go All The Way," featuring lead singer Eric Carmen.

A third power pop group from the 1970s was Big Star. Led by former Box Tops member Alex Chilton, Big Star's three 1970s albums were the favorites of critics and college radio DJs, although poor distribution by their record companies, Ardent and PVC, may have kept their records from hitting nationwide. Big Star's songs "September Gurls" and "When My Baby's Beside Me" may not have hit the Top 40, but they were covered by appreciative groups like the Bangles and the Replacements (who also recorded the song "Alex Chilton," a tribute to the Big Star leader).

Big Star's 45s are harder to find than their albums; here's a promo copy of "When My Baby's Beside Me."

Trivia

On the 45 version of the Knack's follow-up to "My Sharona," "Good Girls Don't (But I Do)," there are at least three different lyric changes, causing the Knack to essentially release a PG-rated 45 rather than the R-rated LP track.

Although their albums never cracked the charts, Big Star has developed a major worldwide appreciation, and their albums have risen in value over the years. At last report, Ardent Records, Big Star's original label, is producing a 25th anniversary Big Star tribute album, featuring many of the pop bands who were influenced by the legendary power pop group.

Besides the Knack, other popular power pop groups in the late 1970s were Cheap Trick, the Dwight Twilley Band, the Smithereens, and the Romantics. Groups like the Plimsouls, the Rubinoos, and the Shoes had regional and college radio hits, and their records have been harder to find over the years.

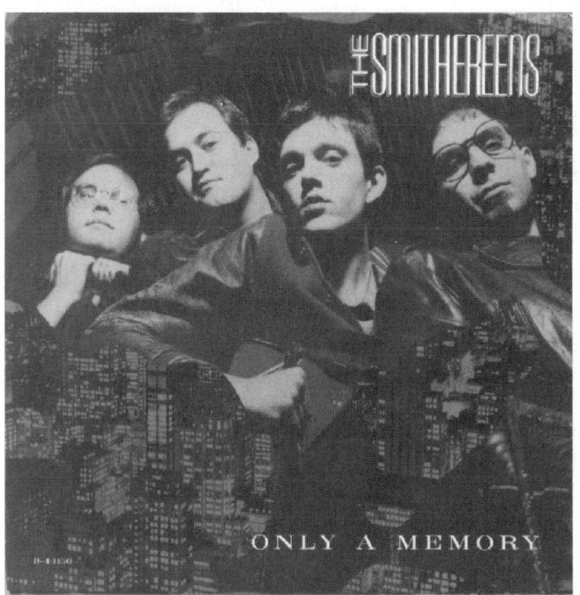

A favorite on 1980s college radio stations, the Smithereens' "Only A Memory" was their major label debut single.

Although power pop bands are predominantly American, power pop's lyrical twists and flowing melodies can also be found in British, Australian, and New Zealand groups such as Squeeze, Split Enz, and XTC; although these groups can also be classified as rock alternative, songs like "Pulling Mussels From A Shell," "The Mayor of Simpleton," and "I Got You" have power pop leanings as well.

Power pop's influence can still be heard in songs from the 1980s and 1990s, including melodic pop singles like Matthew Sweet's "Girlfriend," Enuff Z'Nuff's "New Thing," The Smithereens' "A Girl Like You," and Toad the Wet Sprocket's "All I Want."

What To Look For: The most successful "power pop" album, The Knack's *Get The Knack*, sold millions of copies and is maddeningly easy to find. The Knack's biggest hit single, "My Sharona," is also easily obtainable. Finding the picture sleeve for "My Sharona" is more difficult, especially in near-mint condition. The gear-tooth edge of the Capitol label frayed thousands of picture sleeves, and many others were pinned on the bedroom walls of lonely teenage boys.

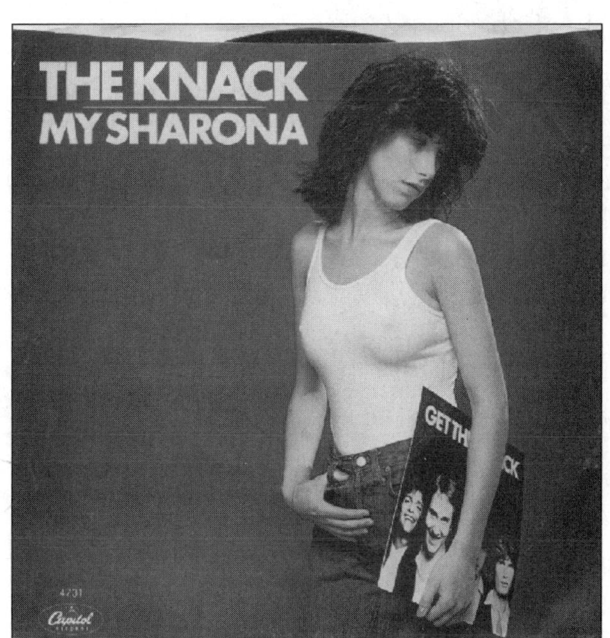

The hard-to-find picture sleeve for the Knack's "My Sharona."

When collecting power pop, look for the independent pressings and pre-major label recordings. Some power pop artists resorted to gimmick pressings; on the Raspberries' self-titled album, the cover had a "scratch and sniff" raspberry scent. Now the music fan could hear the Raspberries—and smell them, if he or she so chose.

Another example of rarity in collecting power pop involves the group Cheap Trick. While their biggest hits barely go for $4 in near-mint condition, a pressing of "I Want You To Want Me" as the B-side of an earlier release, on Epic 50265, can net $10 in near-mint condition. That recording was released in America a full year before the domestic release of their *Live at Budokan* album.

Trivia

When recording the song "Overnight Sensation (Hit Record)," the Raspberries simulated the sound of an AM station playing their song—by playing their master tape through a miked transistor radio.

During the 1990s, many of these power pop groups have released new recordings on vinyl, even though compact disc is the prevailing medium of preference. Sometimes the record company presses the albums and 45s; but other times the bands or singers will press the singles and LPs out of their own budgets.

References: Neely, Tim, *The Goldmine Price Guide to Alternative Records*, Krause Publications, Iola, Wisconsin, 1996.

Web pages: Lee Coursey's Power Pop history site, an excellent resource for power pop history and group links (how can you go wrong when the homepage splash screen has the opening riff of Badfinger's "No Matter What"): *http://www.powerpopradio.com.*

45s	Year	VG	VG+	NM
Badfinger, "No Matter What" / "Carry On Till Tomorrow" (Apple 1822)				
(with star on A-side label)	1970	$5.00	$10.00	$20.00
(without star)	1970		$3.00	$6.00
(white label promo DJ pressing)	1971	$30.00	$60.00	$120.00
Badfinger, "Baby Blue" / "Flying" (Apple 1844)	1972		$3.00	$6.00
(white label promo)	1972	$30.00	$60.00	$120.00
Badfinger, "Lost Inside Your Love" / "Come Down Hard" (Elektra 46022)	1979		$2.50	$5.00
The Beat, "Let Me Into Your Life" / "Walking Out On Love" (Columbia 11161)	1979	$2.00	$4.00	$8.00
Big Star, "When My Baby's Beside Me" / "In The Street" (Ardent 2902)	1972	$6.25	$12.50	$25.00
Big Star, "O My Soul" / "Morphatoo - I'm In Love With A Girl" (Ardent 2909)	1974	$5.00	$10.00	$20.00
Cheap Trick, "Oh, Candy" / "Daddy Should Have Stayed In High School" (Epic 50375)	1977	$2.50	$5.00	$10.00
Cheap Trick, "California Man" / "I Want You To Want Me" (Epic 50625)	1978	$2.50	$5.00	$10.00
Cheap Trick, "I Want You To Want Me" / "Clock Strikes Ten" (Epic 50680)	1979		$2.00	$4.00
(with picture sleeve, add:)	1979	$2.50	$5.00	$10.00
Joan Jett and the Blackhearts, "I Love Rock and Roll" / "You Don't Know What You've Got" (Boardwalk NB7-11-135)	1982		$3.00	
(with rare picture sleeve, add:)	1982	$2.50	$5.00	$10.00
Joan Jett, "Dirty Deeds" / "Let It Bleed" (Blackheart 73215)	1990	$2.00	$4.00	$8.00
The Knack, "My Sharona" / "Let Me Out" (Capitol 4731)	1979		$2.00	$4.00
(with picture sleeve, add:)	1979		$3.00	$6.00
The Knack, "Baby Talks Dirty" / "End of the Game" (Capitol 4822)	1980		$2.00	$4.00
(with picture sleeve, add:)	1980	$2.50	$5.00	$10.00
The Plimsouls, "Zero Hour" / "Hush Hush" / " Dizzy Miss Lizzie" (Planet 47930)	1981	$15.00	$30.00	$60.00
The Plimsouls, "A Million Miles Away" / "I'll Get Lucky" (Shaky City 134)	1982		$2.00	$4.00
(with picture sleeve, add:)	1982		$2.00	$4.00
The Plimsouls, "A Million Miles Away" / "Play The Breaks" (Geffen 29600)	1983		$2.00	$4.00
(with picture sleeve, add:)	1983	$3.00	$6.00	$12.00
The Raspberries, ""Don't Want TO Say Goodbye" / "Rock and Roll Mama" (Capitol 3280)	1972	$2.00	$4.00	$8.00
(with picture sleeve, add:)	1972	$6.25	$12.50	$25.00
The Raspberries, "Go All The Way" / "With You In My Life" (Capitol 3348)	1972		$3.00	$6.00
The Raspberries, "Overnight Sensation (Hit Record)" / "Hands On You" (Capitol 3946)	1974		$3.00	$6.00
The Replacements, "I'm In Trouble" / "If Only You Were Lonely" (Twin/Tone 8120)	1981	$3.00	$6.00	$12.00
(with picture sleeve, add:)	1981	$3.00	$6.00	$12.00
The Replacements, "I'll Be You" / "Date to Church" (Sire 22992)	1989		$3.00	
(with picture sleeve, add:)	1989		$3.00	
Jonathan Richman and the Modern Lovers, "Ne England" / "Here Comes the Martians" (Beserkley 5743)	1976	$2.50	$5.00	$10.00
(with picture sleeve, add:)	1976	$2.50	$5.00	$10.00
The Smithereens, "Behind the Wall of Sleep" / "Blood and Roses" (Enigma 75052)	1986	$2.50	$5.00	$10.00
(with picture sleeve, add:)	1986	$2.50	$5.00	
The Smithereens, "Only A Memory" / "The Seeker" (Capitol/Enigma 44150)	1988		$2.50	$5.00
(with picture sleeve, add:)	1988		$2.50	$5.00
Split Enz, "I Got You" / "Double Happy" (A&M 2252)	1980		$2.00	$4.00
(with picture sleeve, add:)	1980	$2.00	$4.00	$8.00
Squeeze, "Another Nail In My Heart" / "Going Crazy" "What The Butler Saw" (A&M 2263)	1980		$2.00	$4.00
(with picture sleeve, add:)	1980	$2.00	$4.00	$8.00
Squeeze, "If I Didn't Love You" / "Another Nail In My Heart" (A&M 1616) (5-inch record, plays at 33 1/3 rpm)	1980	$2.50	$5.00	$10.00
(with "Tiny Collector's Edition" picture sleeve, add:)	1980	$2.50	$5.00	$10.00
XTC, "Making Plans for Nigel" / "This Is Pop" / "Meccanik Dancing" (Virgin 67009)	1980		$3.50	$7.00
(with picture sleeve, add:)	1980		$3.00	
(if "Making Plans for Nigel" on both sides, mono/stereo, white label promo)	1980		$3.00	
XTC, "Generals and Majors" / "Living Through Another Cuba" (RSO/Virgin 300)	1981		$2.50	$5.00

LPs	Year	VG	VG+	NM
The Beat, The Kids Are The Same (Columbia ARC 36794)	1982	$2.50	$5.00	$10.00
Big Star, #1 Record (Ardent ADS-2803)	1972	$6.25	$12.50	$25.00
Big Star, Radio City (Ardent ADS-1501)	1974	$7.50	$15.00	$30.00
Big Star, Big Star's Third (PVC 7903)	1978	$6.25	$12.50	$25.00
Cheap Trick, From Tokyo To You (Epic AS-518) (white label promo EP)	1978	$7.50	$15.00	$30.00
Cheap Trick, Cheap Trick at Budokan (Epic 35795)	1978		$2.50	$5.00
The Knack, Get The Knack (Capitol SO-11948)	1979	$3.00	$6.00	$12.00
The Knack, ... but the little girls understand (Capitol SOO-12045)	1980	$2.50	$5.00	$10.00
The Plimsouls, Zero Hour (Beat BE-1001) (EP)	1980	$6.25	$12.50	$25.00
The Plimsouls, The Plimsouls (Planet 13)	1981	$5.00	$10.00	$20.00
The Raspberries, Fresh (Capitol ST-11123)	1972	$5.00	$10.00	$20.00
The Raspberries, Raspberries (Capitol SK-11036)				
(if record has red label, cover is "scratch and sniff," with raspberry scent)	1972	$7.50	$15.00	$30.00
(if Capitol ST-11036, orange label with "Capitol" at 6:00)	1973	$5.00	$10.00	$20.00
The Replacements, Sorry, Ma, Forgot To Take Out The Trash (Twin/Tone TTR 8123)	1981	$3.75	$7.50	$15.00
The Replacements, Don't Tell A Soul (Sire 25831)	1989	$2.50	$5.00	$10.00
(if above is on Sire R 101024, BMG Music Service edition)	1989	$3.00	$6.00	$12.00
Jonathan Richman and the Modern Lovers, Jonathan Richman and the Modern Lovers				
(if on Beserkley BZ-0048, distributed by GRT)	1976	$7.50	$15.00	$30.00
(if on Bezerkley JBZ 0048, distributed by Playboy/CBS)	1976	$6.25	$12.50	$25.00
(if on Rhino RNLP 70092, reissue)	1986	$3.00	$6.00	$12.00
The Smithereens, Beauty and Sadness (Little Ricky 103)	1983	$10.00	$20.00	$40.00
(if on Enigma 73220, remixed version of above album with one track deleted)	1988	$2.00	$4.00	$8.00
Squeeze, U.K. Squeeze (A&M SP-4687)	1978	$3.00	$6.00	
(if pressed on red vinyl, promo only)	1978	$3.75	$7.50	$15.00
(if on A&M SP-3185, budget reissue)	198??	$2.00	$4.00	$8.00
Squeeze, Six Squeeze Songs Crammed Into One Ten-Inch Record (A&M SP-3719, 10" LP)	1980	$2.50	$5.00	$10.00
Split Enz, True Colours (A&M SP-4822)				
(vinyl is laser-etched)	1980	$2.50	$5.00	$10.00
(if on A&M SP-3153, reissue, no laser etching on vinyl)	198??	$2.00	$4.00	$8.00
Matthew Sweet, Girlfriend (Zoo/Classic 11015) (Audiophile pressing of 1991 CD release)	1995	$4.50	$9.00	$18.00
XTC, Skylarking (Geffen GHS 24117)				
(if first pressing, does not have the song "Dear God")	1986	$3.75	$7.50	$15.00
(if second pressing, contains the song "Dear God")	1986	$2.50	$5.00	$10.00

Boston's first four studio LPs are available on picture disc. Their debut disc is the most common of the four; the discs for *Third Stage* and *Walk On* are European imports.

This shaped-disc pressing contains an interview Elvis conducted with a Little Rock, Arkansas reporter in 1956. The 1996 shaped disc is the first such pressing authorized by the estate of Elvis Presley. Courtesy of Erika Records, Downey, Calif.

Not only did the punk-ska band Less Than Jake release their *Hello Rockview* album on both vinyl and CD, they also pressed some picture disc versions of their major-label album. Courtesy of Erika Records, Downey, Calif.

Bobby Caldwell's "What You Won't Do For Love" was both a hit record and an instant Valentine gift.

Toto's #1 hit "Africa" is available on this continent-shaped picture disc.

Amahl and the Night Visitors.

Eddy Arnold, “I'll Hold You in My Heart.”

Perry Como, “Ave Maria.” From the Collection of Val Shively.

Four Tunes, “You're Heartless.” From the Collection of Val Shively.

The Little Red Hen.

Desi Arnaz, “Babalu.”

In 1948, when RCA Victor introduced the 45 RPM 7-inch record to the world, it experimented with different colored vinyl to represent different musical styles. Classical music was represented with red vinyl (to continue RCA's Red Seal division). Country and western 45s were pressed in green vinyl. Different shades of blue were used for light classics and international music. A reddish-orange or cerise vinyl was reserved for R&B or blues artists. For the children, RCA designated its Little Nipper series of yellow vinyl records; and for popular music, RCA pressed those singles in black vinyl; which it still does today.

Smashing Pumpkins, "Tristessa." Courtesy of the Last Vestige Music Store, Albany, N.Y.

Afghan Whigs, "Conjure Me." Courtesy of the Last Vestige Music Store, Albany, N.Y.

Bewitched, "Hey White Homey."

Fastbacks, "Impatience." Courtesy of the Last Vestige Music Store, Albany, N.Y.

Love Battery, "Foot." Courtesy of the Last Vestige Music Store, Albany, N.Y.

Tad, "Pig Iron." Courtesy of the Last Vestige Music Store, Albany, N.Y.

Forty years after RCA "color-coded" its 45s, the Sub Pop label began its mail-order singles club. Every month subscribers received a one-of-a-kind pressing, and each record in the singles club was pressed on a different colored vinyl. Because of the low print runs on these records, their value has increased dramatically—and records by some artists, such as Smashing Pumpkins, Nirvana, Soundgarden, and Fugazi, have become increasingly difficult to find.

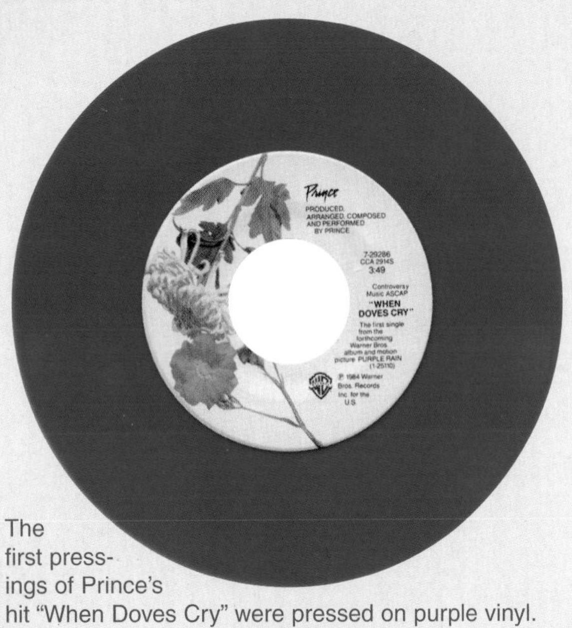

The first pressings of Prince's hit "When Doves Cry" were pressed on purple vinyl.

In the 1950s, red-vinyl records were the most common non-black color; this translucent pressing is from the singing rage, Miss Patti Page. From the Collection of Val Shively.

Madonna's "Like a Virgin" album, pressed on "virgin" white vinyl. From the Collection of Stephen M. Caraco.

Bread-bag sleeves were often used to show off a colored vinyl record. As can be seen in this picture, Kraftwerk's yellow-greenish vinyl copy of "Pocket Calculator" is clearly visible through the plastic sleeve.

The soundtrack album to the Jerry Lewis movie, "Cinderfella," was pressed with rainbow colors in the vinyl. From the Collection of R. Michael Murray.

Radio station "promo-only" colored vinyl pressings continued throughout the 1970s and 1980s. Here's a blue vinyl 45 of Todd Rundgren's hit "I Saw The Light." From the Collection of Val Shively.

Like Columbia did in the 1960s, Cameo-Parkway Records produced colored-vinyl 45s of its biggest hits for promotional purposes.

The Electric Light Orchestra released some colored vinyl pressings, many of which came with customized picture sleeves. The black vinyl counterpart pressings often did not have the picture sleeves.

Although "Touch of Grey" was the Grateful Dead's biggest hit, this gray vinyl pressing has only a slightly higher collectible value than its black vinyl counterpart.

The first 50,000 copies of Simple Minds' New Gold Dream album were pressed in a spectacular wine-stained vinyl.

While Barry Manilow's *Greatest Hits* album has little collectible value outside of Manilow's fans, the picture disc version of that same album can garner as much as $50 in near-mint condition.

Most picture discs either replicated the cover artwork, or used photos taken from the same session, as this picture disc for Blondie's *Parallel Lines* shows. Courtesy Last Vestige Music Store, Albany, N.Y.

No, this is not the opening scene from the "Rocky Horror Picture Show." It's a promotional picture disc by a group named Fandango. Although the song they recorded, "Last Kiss," was not a hit, this record is still collectible on its kitschy looks alone.

Split Enz' *True Colours* LP was "laser etched," which produced rainbow-shaped geometric patterns in the vinyl when held to reflected light. This album also contains their quirky hit, "I Got You."

Some classic recordings on the Sun label, as arranged on a Rhino Records picture disc.

Dukays, "Nite Owl." From the Collection of Val Shively.

Another version of "Nite Owl" by Dukays. From the Collection of Val Shively.]

Gene Chandler, "Duke of Earl." From the Collection of Val Shively.

Duke of Earl, "The Duke of Earl." From the Collection of Val Shively.

Yet another version of Dukays' "Nite Owl." From the Collection of Val Shively.

Pearlettes, "Duchess of Earl." From the Collection of Val Shively.

Some collectors like to acquire not only the hit, but the songs that came before that hit—and any answer records that followed. Case in point: The Dukays were a struggling doo-wop group that recorded some sides, including "Nite Owl" on the Nat label. One of the songs the Dukays recorded, "Duke of Earl," so impressed the people at Vee Jay Records that they signed the Dukays' lead singer, Eugene Dixon, to a solo contract. Dixon changed his name to "Gene Chandler," and "Duke of Earl" hit #1 on the pop and soul charts. Vee Jay eventually reissued the Dukays' "Nite Owl," and it recharted. Vee Jay also pressed copies of "Duke of Earl" as being performed by "The Duke of Earl." And to top it all off, an answer record, "Duchess of Earl," was recorded by another group, the Pearlettes.

Elvis Presley, "Milkcow Blues Boogie," on a Sun 45 label.

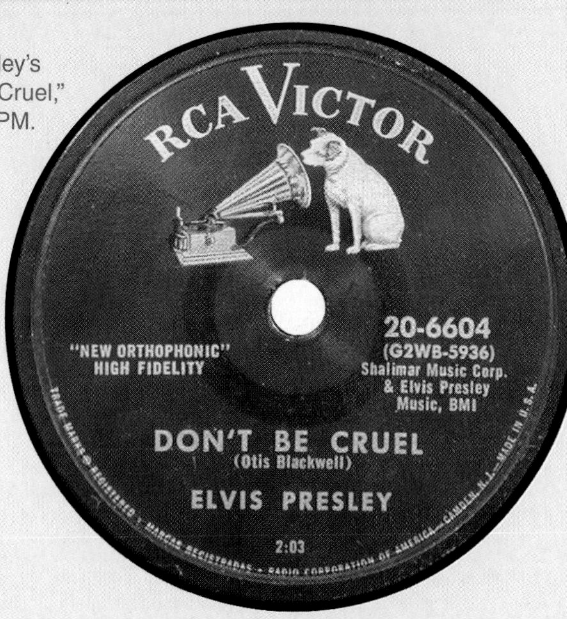

Elvis Presley's "Don't Be Cruel," on a 78 RPM.

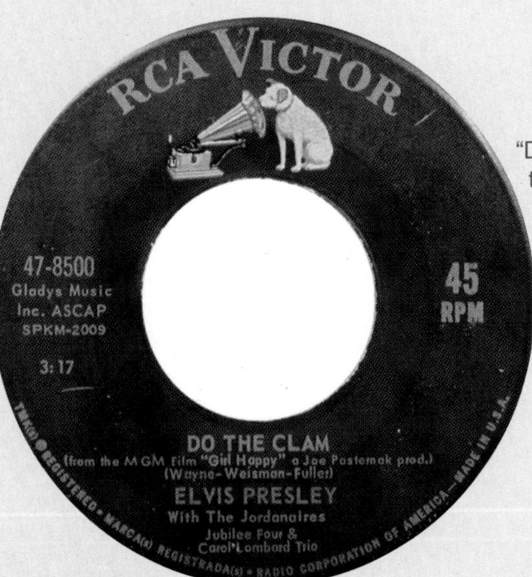

"Do the Clam" is significant in that this is the last Elvis Presley 45 with the RCA logo on top - at least until 1976, when the dog-and-gramophone logo was resurrected.

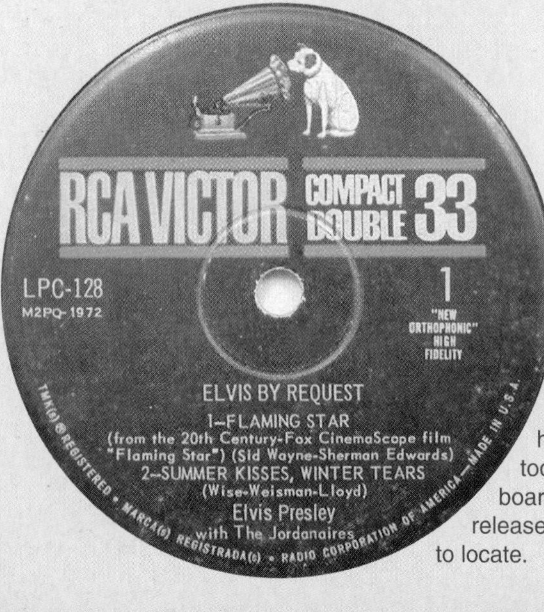

The "Compact Double 33" series contained four RCA songs - in this case, four Elvis Presley songs - and are very hard to find today. The cardboard jacket for this release is even harder to locate.

An extremely rare "gold picture disc" of Elvis Presley's "Jailhouse Rock." One such copy sold at auction for more than $7,900. Courtesy of Good Rockin' Tonight/Collectors Universe.

Swan Records had the rights to press copies of this song, "She Loves You," as well as its German-language counterpart, "Sie Liebt Dich." When Swan released "Sie Liebt Dich," the record credited the group by their German name, "Die Beatles" - which is what millions of people wanted them to do after John Lennon commented that the Beatles were more popular than Jesus. From the collection of Bruce Spizer.

The Beatles' "Real Love" picture sleeve.

Capitol Records issued some of its 1960s releases on soundsheets, which were sold from vending machines. Naturally, the Beatles' soundsheets are the most desired collectible in the line. Notice the 3:25 length on "Hey Jude." From the collection of Bruce Spizer.

Jimi Hendrix, "The Star Spangled Banner," on die-cut star 10-inch disc.

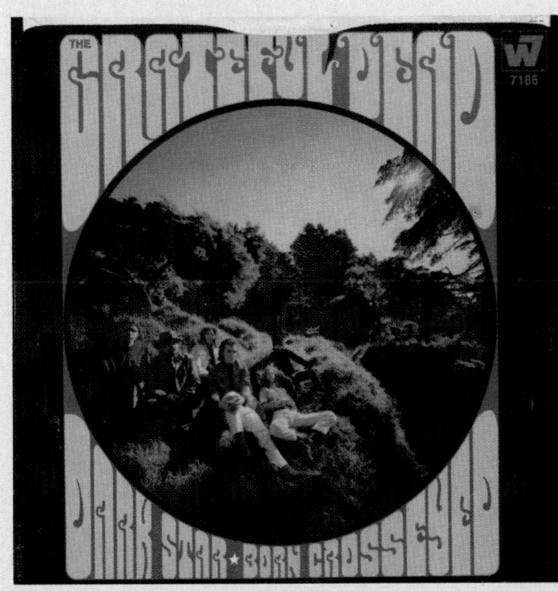

The Grateful Dead, "Dark Star" picture sleeve.

In order to entice radio stations to play their songs, sometimes a white label promo will arrive on colored vinyl, as in the case with this Jr. Walker and the All-Stars track. Courtesy of the Last Vestige Music Store, Albany, N.Y.

The Gladiolas, "Little Darlin'," on an Excello 45 label.

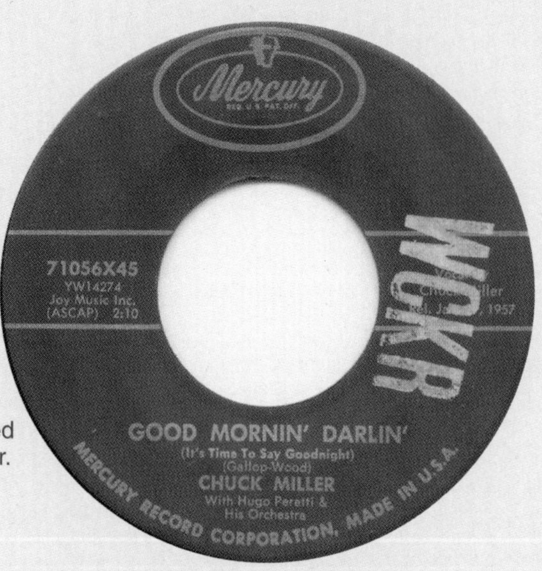

Stations will often stamp or write their call letters on a record label or album jacket to protect their inventory from theft or loss. By the way, the Chuck Miller on this record is a boogie piano player from the 1950s, and is not related in any way to the author.

Allan Sherman's *My Son the Folk Singer* LP.

The Ventures' *Golden Greats* LP.

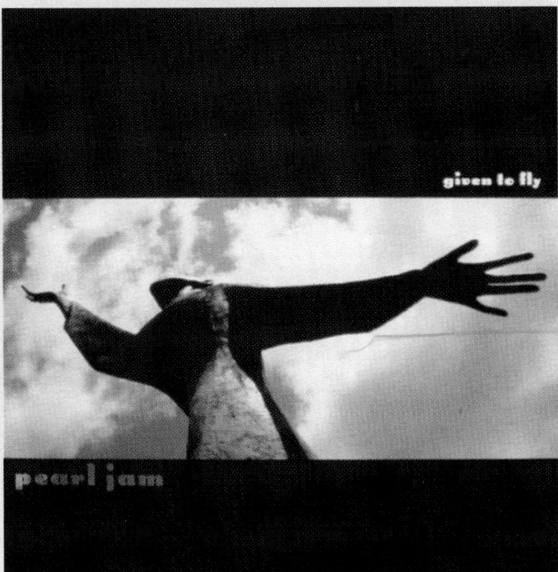

Pearl Jam's "Given to Fly" picture sleeve.

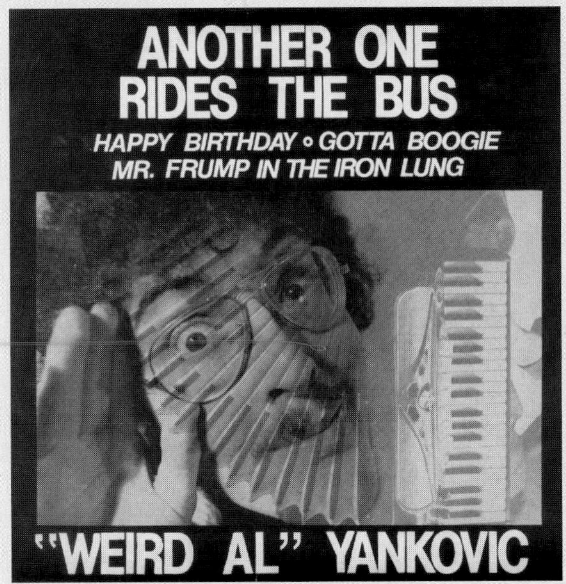

"Weird Al" Yankovic's *Placebo* EP, containing his early version of "Another One Rides the Bus."

R.E.M.'s "Radio Free Europe," on their first label, Hib Tone.

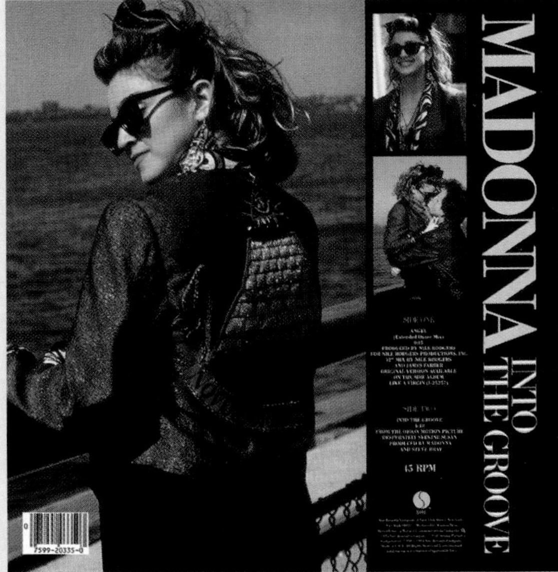

Madonna, "Into the Groove," 12-inch picture sleeve.

Gloria Jones, "Tainted Love," on Champion 45.

Frank Sinatra's "New York New York" picture sleeve.

The Original Motion Picture Soundtrack to "And God Created Woman."

Columbia Records produced this collection of jazz music classics as a tie-in with the television game show, "The $64,000 Question." The artists on this record are a representative cross-section of the Columbia jazz lineup at that time - and *that* is our final answer.

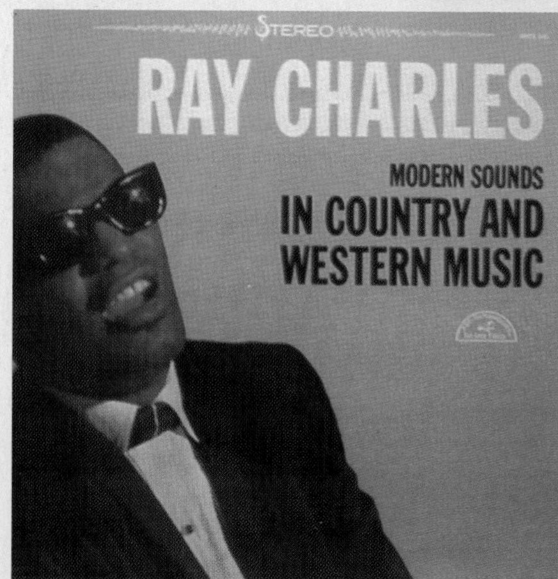

Ray Charles' *Modern Sounds in Country and Western Music* LP.

Duke Ellington transcends jazz - his work ranks among the greatest recordings of the 20th century. This album, *Ellington Uptown*, was originally released with the Columbia Masterworks numbering system, originally reserved for classical music.

Bob Marley and the Wailers, "I Shot the Sheriff," on an Island 45 label.

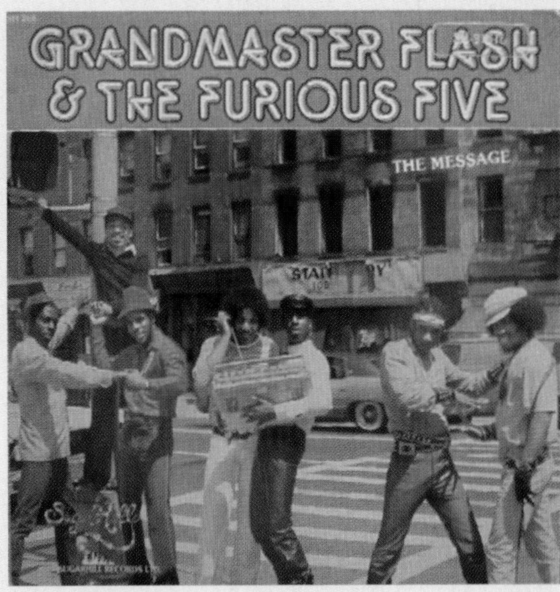

Grandmaster Flash and the Furious Five's LP *The Message*.

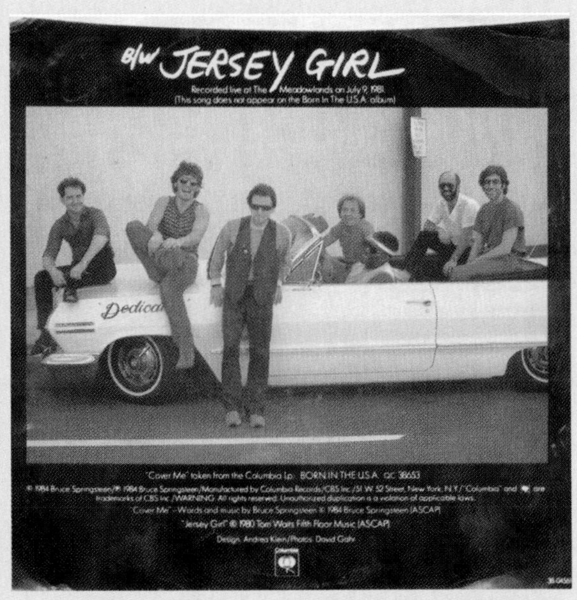

This B-side of Bruce Springsteen's "Cover Me" contains a live version of "Jersey Girl," but does it also contain a Springsteen introduction? The picture sleeve doesn't tell...

And looking at the 45 doesn't tell....

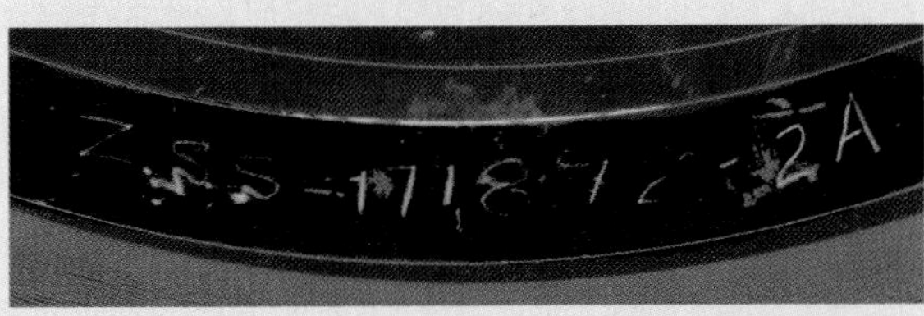

But the stamper numbers tell all: "2A" at the end of the stamper number means a second pressing, which deleted the spoken-word introduction (those copies contained a "1A" in the dead wax).

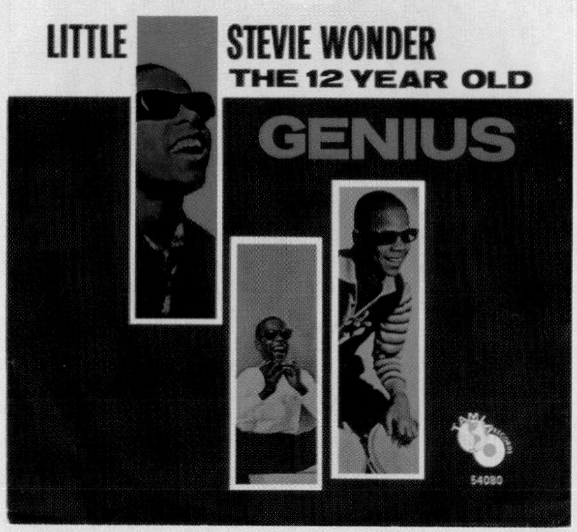

FINGERTIPS - Part 1 & 2
LITTLE
STEVIE WONDER
THE 12 YEAR OLD
GENIUS
54080

Stevie Wonder's early picture sleeve "Fingertips."

ULTRA HIGH FIDELITY
KENT
45x388B
Modern Music Publ.
BMI
HI-FI
Time: 2:40
WHOLE LOT OF LOVIN'
(King-Taub)
B. B. KING
KENT RECORDS • CULVER CITY • CALIF.

B.B. King, "Whole Lot of Lovin'," on a Kent 45 label.

Mahalia Jackson's LP *In the Upper Room.*

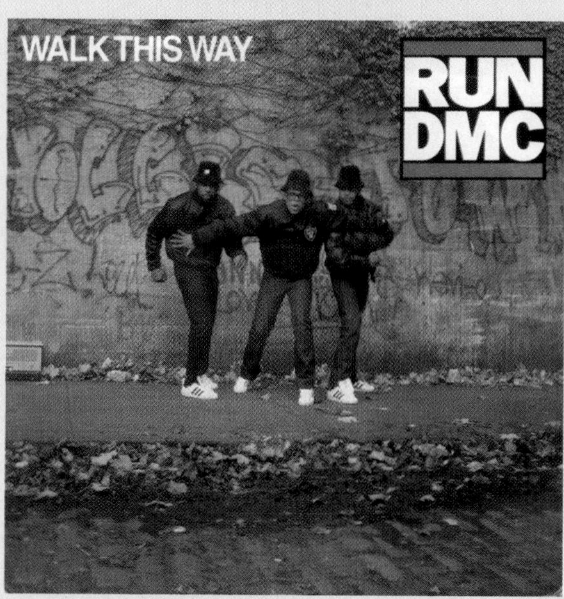

The picture sleeve for Run-D.M.C.'s "Walk This Way."

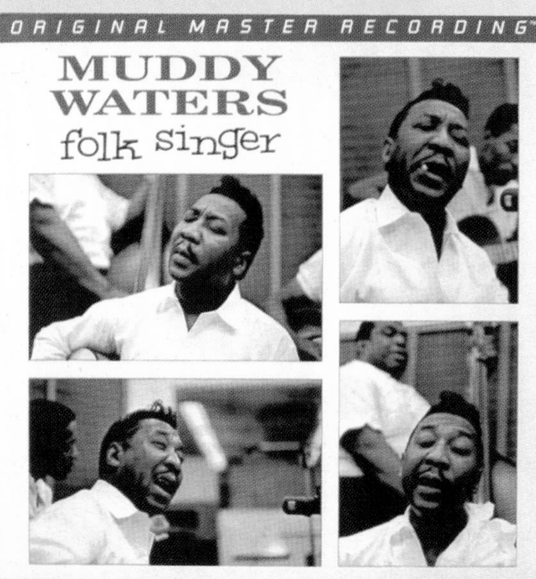

This Mobile Fidelity Sound Lab pressing captures Muddy Waters' music in clear half-speed mastered audiophile sound. From the Collection of Mark Pisani.

The first blues records were recorded by women, and women today still sing the blues as well as any man can. Koko Taylor's blues/R & B hit "Wang Dang Doodle" was written by Willie Dixon, who also sings background vocals on the song. Courtesy of the Last Vestige Music Store, Albany, N.Y.

Buddy Holly's "That'll Be the Day."

Patsy Cline's "Walking After Midnight."

Ritchie Valens' "La Bamba."

"Midnight in Heaven" by Cowboy Copas.

"Chantilly Lace," by the Big Bopper. From the Collection of Val Shively.

"Lonesome 7-7203" by Hawkshaw Hawkins.

The Day the Music Died: Some collectors reserve special places in their collections for those artists whose lives and careers were taken away at such young ages. Buddy Holly's early Decca single is listed above, and his backup band is credited to "The Three Tunes." The Ritchie Valens' "La Bamba" shown has bluish-green circles; other label variations include a sawtooth perimeter and a black background. The Big Bopper's "Chantilly Lace" was originally released on the tiny "D" label, but his Mercury release is more familiar to collectors. In almost an eerie coincidence to the 1959 Iowa plane crash that took the lives of Buddy Holly, Ritchie Valens, and the Big Bopper, a plane crash in Tennessee five years later stole the lives of Patsy Cline, Cowboy Copas, and Hawkshaw Hawkins. Cline's first big hit, "Walking After Midnight," is harder to find on a 78 than it is on a 45. Cowboy Copas put together nine Top 10 country songs between 1946 and 1961, recording for the King and Starday labels. And Hawkshaw Hawkins' "Lonesome 7-7203" became a posthumous #1 country hit for the Grand Ole Opry legend.

The Spaniels' "Goodnite Sweetheart, Goodnite" on a 78.

The Spaniels' "Goodnite Sweetheart, Goodnite" on a black 45. From the Collection of Val Shively.

The Spaniels' red 45 version of "Goodnite Sweetheart, Goodnite."

Some collectors try to acquire all known versions of a song's release. Above are three of the many different pressings of the Spaniels' doo-wop classic "Goodnite Sweetheart, Goodnite." The original 78 can cost as much as $80 in near-mint condition. The 78 label has silver print over a maroon background, and the print can wear down over time. The black vinyl 45 exists in two versions; if the group's name is spelled correctly, the record can be worth up to $200 in near-mint condition. However, if the group's name is misspelled "SPANIALS," a near-mint copy is worth $300. The red-vinyl pressing of this 45 can be worth up to $800 in near-mint condition. But the red vinyl copy you see on this page is not worth $800—in fact, it's only worth about $8 at best. In 1993, Vee Jay Records released a CD box set, which included a red vinyl pressing of "Goodnite, Sweetheart." The vinyl was the right color and the label artwork was meticulously reproduced—except that if you look under the "V" in the label name in the above picture, you can see the words "TRADE MARK REG." The original 1953 pressing does not have those words, either in the black or red vinyl editions.

ELVIS PRESLEY

History: Singer, performer, cultural icon. In simple terms, these words may describe Elvis Presley. The emotional attachment millions of his fans have to his music surpass simple adoration—to his fans, Elvis was the greatest pop singer of his generation, rivaling Frank Sinatra, Bing Crosby and Enrico Caruso as the greatest male vocalist of the 20th century.

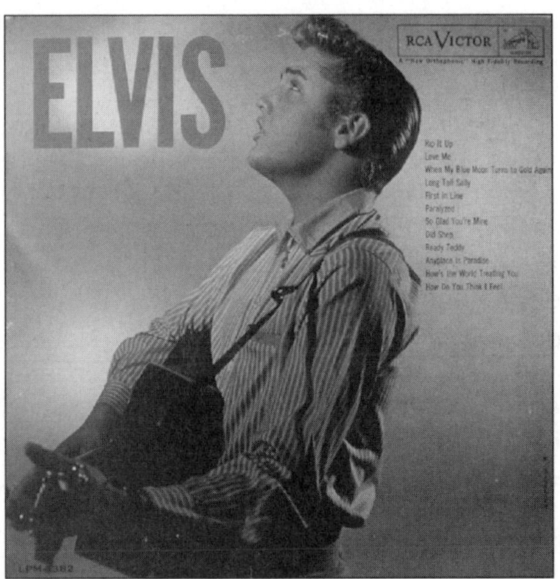

An early album by Elvis Presley. Courtesy Last Vestige Music Store, Albany, N.Y.

Elvis' first Sun recordings, a fusion of country twang with rhythm and blues, became early rockabilly classics. His early output for RCA included such rock classics as "Heartbreak Hotel," "Don't Be Cruel," "Hound Dog," and "Jailhouse Rock." His gyrating stage performances in the 1950s drove female fans into ecstasy; his late 1960s television specials proved that despite suggestions to the contrary, the King had not left the building. And upon his death in 1977, Presley's soul may have ascended into heaven, but his legend ascended into icon status.

Among Presley's most coveted and collectible recordings are the ten sides he recorded for Sam Phillips' Sun Records. These Memphis-based recordings were Elvis' first commercial tracks, but within these songs were the beginnings of a musical legend. He could sing deep haunting ballads like "Blue Moon," he could belt out the blues with "I Got A Woman" and "Milkcow Blues Boogie," and rock the room with "That's All Right" and "Blue Moon of Kentucky." Those Sun sessions, where Presley performed with bassist Bill Black and guitarist Scotty Moore, became hits—first in Memphis, then throughout the South.

"Milkcow Blues Boogie" was one of ten songs released on the Sun label, Elvis Presley's first recording label. These 45s (and the 78s of the same titles) are among the most highly prized record collectibles today. Courtesy Good Rockin' Tonight/Collectors Universe.

Eventually Presley acquired a new manager; Col. Tom Parker, who had previously worked with country legend Eddy Arnold. He also acquired a new recording label—Sam Phillips sold Presley's contract, as well as the Sun recordings, to RCA Victor for the unheard-of sum of $35,000. No record company ever paid that much for an artist, but in retrospect, RCA Victor received a bargain.

The original Sun recordings were reissued with RCA catalog numbers and labels. They were quickly followed by Presley's first RCA recording, "Heartbreak Hotel." The song stormed up the charts, hitting #1 on both the pop and country listings. There was no turning back. By 1956, Elvis Presley was the #1 recording artist in the country.

Elvis Presley's first major hit, "Heartbreak Hotel," hit #1 on Billboard's Top 40 charts for eight straight weeks.Courtesy Last Vestige Music Store, Albany, N.Y.

Not since the days when Frank Sinatra's bobbysoxed followers swooned *en masse* before the Brooklyn Paramount had there ever been such a show of adulation for any singer. Presley's impact in 1956 was nearly unstoppable—as a rock-'n'-roll singer, he influenced a new generation of musicians, vocalists, and songwriters. As an entertainer, his swiveling hips and deep vocals drove female fans into hysteria. In fact, when performing on the *"Ed Sullivan"* variety show, Sullivan ordered the cameras to show the performing Presley only from the chest up, so as not to offend the viewing public with the singer's pelvic gyrations.

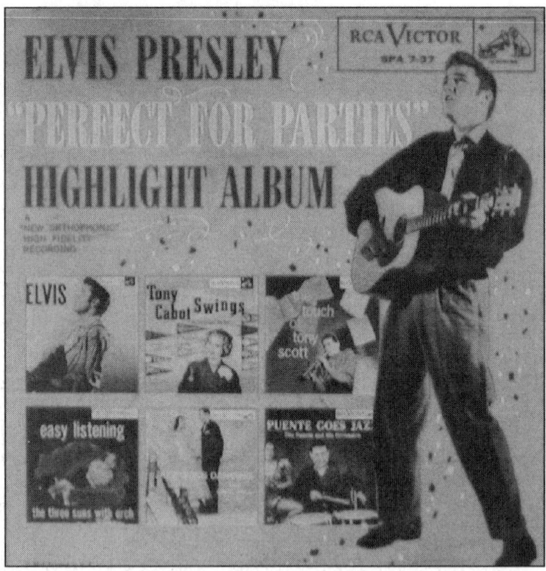

Such was the appeal of Elvis Presley that his image could sell this EP, Perfect for Parties, despite the inclusion of only ONE Elvis song, "Love Me." From the Collection of Val Shively.

For the next twenty years, Elvis Presley released a stream of albums and 45s, appeared in more than 30 motion pictures, and performed on television with Frank Sinatra (during a musical number, Sinatra sang "Love Me Tender," while Presley sang "Witchcraft"). With the Jordanaires as his backup singers, Presley now branched into different musical styles—tender ballads like "Love Me Tender" and "Are You Lonesome Tonight," uptempo rockers like "Hard Headed Woman" and "Jailhouse Rock," and poppish love songs like "(Let Me Be Your) Teddy Bear" and "Stuck On You."

Nothing could dim Presley's popularity—not a stint in the Army, not the declining quality of his movies. Even though other musicians' careers were curtailed during the British Invasion, he was able to have hits like "Crying in the Chapel," one of the few Americans to still have hits during this period. His return to prominence came during a 1968 television variety special, in which a leather-clad Elvis still showed he could rock and roll with the best of them.

In 1973, Presley gave another stellar performance—this time from Hawaii, to a television audience of more than one billion viewers. The subsequent soundtrack album from that concert, *Hello From Hawaii Via Satellite*, was a worldwide million-seller, both in stereo and the new quadraphonic (four speakers) album format.

When Presley passed away on August 16, 1977, his millions of loyal fans grieved. Then they went to the stores and bought nearly every Elvis Presley 45 and LP they could. RCA's pressing plants worked round the clock to satisfy the demand for Presley's back catalog. They also released new Presley singles, either as "in concert" performances ("My Way"), remixed versions ("Guitar Man"), or even novelty recordings ("The Elvis Medley").

Today, Elvis Presley's music is still as popular as ever, as new compilations and reissues continue to appear on store shelves. His opulent Memphis estate Graceland is now a museum and tourist attraction, attracting legions of Elvis followers every year.

Of the many Elvis Presley tribute records released after the King's death, Ronnie McDowell's "The King Is Gone" was the biggest hit of them all. In fact, McDowell later recorded Elvis songs for motion pictures and TV shows based on the King's life.

What To Look For: The toughest task for an Elvis collection is to find his five Sun 45s (they are also available on 78s). Reproductions abound on these titles, and some of the reproductions actually use original out-of-stock Sun labels.

Any Sun Elvis recording pressed on colored or swirled vinyl is a reproduction; the originals were pressed only in black. There were never any "picture sleeves" for Elvis Sun recordings, either. And Sun never made any four-song EPs of Elvis' songs, so any that you find are phonies.

Of Presley's five Sun releases, legitimate copies of his first four releases have "push marks"—three circles pressed into the label itself. Not all the originals have push marks, but because the collectible value of a Sun 45 is extremely high, and since so many counterfeit and reproduced Sun 45s exist because of this, collectors look for the "push marks" to confirm a true Memphis pressing.

Presley's fifth Sun release, "Mystery Train"/"I Forgot to Remember to Forget" (Sun 223) does not contain push marks on the label. If the record has a triangle in the dead wax, the record was pressed by Monarch Record Pressing in Los Angeles. Even before his signing with RCA Victor, Elvis was already an established country music star from these Sun recordings, with "I Forgot To Remember To Forget" hitting #1 on the *Billboard* country charts.

During Presley's RCA tenure, the record company pressed millions of copies of his 45s and LPs. It is important to know not only the variations in label design throughout Elvis' recording career, but also when RCA changed their label patterns so that a collector can determine an original from a repressing.

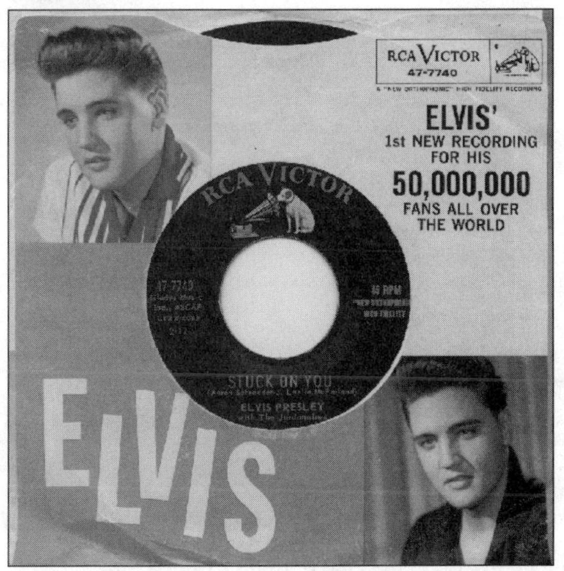

This die-cut sleeve was designed for Elvis Presley's hit "Stuck on You," and was a tie-in to his "50,000,000 Elvis Fans Can't Be Wrong" greatest hits album.

Even though the front of an Elvis Presley album may contain the traditional RCA logos and trademarks of the 1950s, oftentimes the company would continue to press an old-style jacket with old-style logos, while inserting a new recording inside. The following is a short list of label variations for RCA 45s and LPs, as well as the first and last Presley records in each format.

Elvis Presley RCA 45s: 1955-1965: "RCA VICTOR" in white or gray capital serif letters, along the 12:00 perimeter (top of label). Beneath the letters, in full color, is the RCA dog and gramophone trademark ("Nipper"). Black background. Copies exist with gray-white horizontal line through the spindle hole; copies also exist without the line. Unless specifically listed below, the value for the lined and line-less pressings are equal. Elvis' first RCA-recorded 45 in this format: "Heartbreak Hotel"/"I Was The One" (RCA Victor 47-6420). Presley's five Sun 45s were also reissued on this label prior to the release of "Heartbreak Hotel." The last Elvis 45 on this format: "Do the Clam"/"You'll Be Gone" (RCA 47-8500).

"Love Me Tender," on an RCA label design that lasted until 1965.

1965-1968: "RCA VICTOR" in thin tall white letters, at 3:00; full-color Nipper at 9:00. Black background. The first Elvis 45 on this format was actually part of the RCA "Gold Standard" reissue series: "Crying in the Chapel"/"I Believe In The Man In The Sky" (RCA Victor 447-0643). The first Elvis 45 in the standard numbering series in this format: "(Such An) Easy Question"/"It Feels So Right) (RCA Victor 47-8585). Last Elvis 45 on this format: "A Little Less Conversation"/"Almost In Love" (RCA Victor 47-9610).

1968-1976: "RCA" in futuristic print at 9:00, orange label. First Elvis 45 on this format: "If I Can Dream"/"Edge of Reality" (RCA 47-9670). Now here's where it gets tricky.

1974-1975: Same as above, except on tan or gray label. At this time, RCA had three major record pressing plants—Indianapolis, Indiana; Hollywood, California, and Rockaway, New York. Although Rockaway had ceased pressing records by 1974,

Indianapolis and Hollywood were still cranking out Elvis vinyl. Although Hollywood still used orange labels for its 45s, the last Elvis record that plant pressed with an orange label was "Bringing It Back"/"Pieces Of My Life" (RCA PB-10401).

Elvis Presley's big hit "Burning Love," on an orange RCA label.

Beginning in 1974, the Indianapolis plant pressed RCA 45s first with a gray label. Among Elvis 45s, the only single in this color was "Promised Land"/"It's Midnight" (PB-10074). By the time the next Elvis 45, "My Boy"/"Thinking About You" (RCA PB-10191) was pressed, the Indianapolis factor used a tan label. So until RCA's pressing plants were consolidated into one Indianapolis factory, some Presley records exist with both tan backgrounds and orange backgrounds.

Trivia

The first copies of Elvis Presley's album *Moody Blue* were pressed on translucent blue vinyl, and the plan was for that record to be pressed in black vinyl for the remaining pressings. And some copies were pressed on black vinyl—until Elvis Presley died. The decision was then made to resume blue vinyl pressing, making this record one of the few in history where the black vinyl pressing is rarer than its colored vinyl counterpart. Also, RCA made *Moody Blue* test pressings in other colors—red, white, green—all of which have much more value than do the blue or black pressings.

"Promised Land," on a gray RCA label from Indianapolis. Courtesy Last Vestige Music Store, Albany, N.Y.

The last Elvis Presley 45 with a tan background was "Hurt"/"For The Heart" (RCA PB-10601). Eventually Elvis would be reunited with his "hound dog," and subsequent RCA pressings would restore "His Master's Voice" to the paper label.

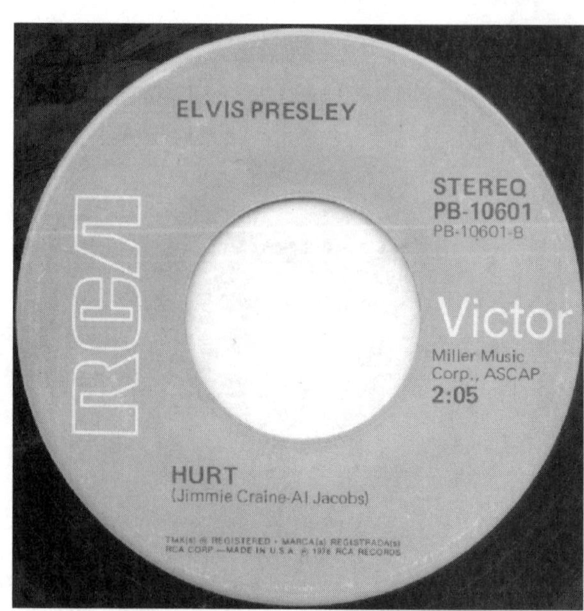

"Hurt," the last "dog-less" Elvis Presley 45.

1976-1988: Futuristic "RCA" at 12:00, Nipper returns at 1:00, black label. Many of these pressings will have a frosty dust layer on the paper label; this can be removed by gently wiping with a soft cloth. Elvis' last living recordings are on this label format. First Elvis 45 on this format was a second pressing of "Hurt"/"For The Heart" (RCA PB-10601). Last living Elvis 45 on this format: "Way Down"/"Pledging My Love" (RCA PB-10998). Presley died as that record was rising up the pop charts.

Presley's last living single, "Way Down."

Elvis Presley RCA Albums

1956-1964: "RCA VICTOR" in gray capital serif letters, along the 12:00 perimeter. Nipper underneath the letters, above the spindle hole. First Elvis album on this format: *Elvis Presley* (RCA LPM-1254). Last Elvis album on this format: *Roustabout* (RCA RCA LSP-2999).

1964-1968: "RCA VICTOR" in white serif letters, along the 12:00 perimeter. The letters are fatter and take up more of the perimeter than do previous gray-letter pressings. Nipper sits underneath the letters, above the spindle hole. This is also known as a "White Dog Pressing" among classical music fans. First Elvis album in this format: *Girl Happy* (RCA LSP-3338). The last Elvis album with this label design: *Speedway* (RCA LSP-3989).

1968-1975: "RCA" in futuristic print at 9:00, orange label. No sign of Nipper. First Elvis album on this format: *The Elvis TV Special ('68 Special)* (RCA LPM-4088). Last Elvis album on this format: *Today* (RCA APL-1039).

1975-1976: "RCA" in futuristic print at 9:00, tan label. Still no sign of Nipper. These were pressed in Indianapolis, after RCA's record pressing facilities in Hollywood and Rockaway were shut down. *The Elvis Sun Sessions* (RCA APM-1675) and *From Elvis Presley Boulevard, Memphis, Tennessee* (RCA APL-1506) have these tan labels.

Trivia

Elvis Presley's career coincided with the last pressings of 78 RPM records. His five Sun singles are available as black vinyl 10-inch 78s (colored vinyl 78s are reproductions). Even though RCA actively promoted the 45 RPM record as the musical format of choice, many of Presley's early recordings exist on RCA 78s. Some, including "Wear My Ring Around Your Neck," command higher prices than their 7-inch counterparts.

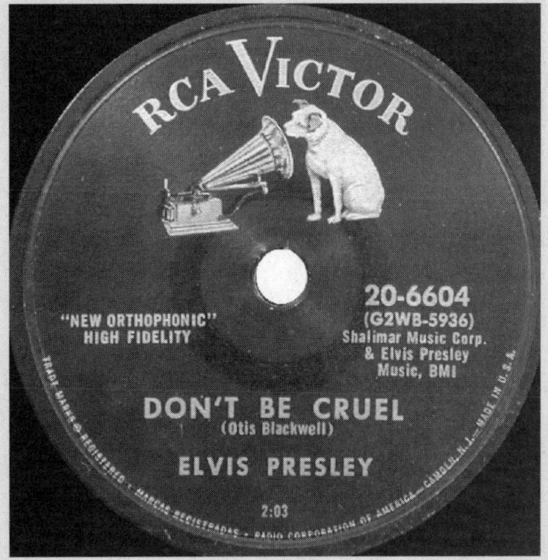

An example of an Elvis Presley 78 for "Don't Be Cruel." This is the pressing from their Indianapolis facility. Courtesy Last Vestige Music Store, Albany, N.Y.

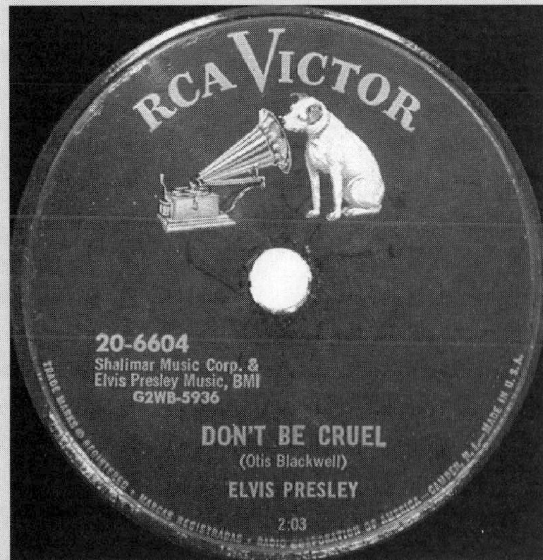

This 78 was pressed at RCA's Rockaway, N.Y. plant. Notice the absence of the words "New Orthophonic High Fidelity," and the thinner text font. Courtesy Last Vestige Music Store, Albany, N.Y.

In the early 1970s, some of Elvis Presley's albums were re-released on RCA's budget label, Camden. In 1975, some of these same albums were licensed to Pickwick Records, another budget label.

1976-1988: "RCA" at 1:00, Nipper returns at 2:00, black label. Elvis' last living recordings are on this label format. First Elvis album on this format: *Welcome To My World* (RCA APL-2274). Last living Elvis album on this format: *Moody Blue* (RCA AFL-2428).

Any RCA 45s with the words "Gold Standard Series," no matter what the format, is a reissue. These records will contain a "447" before the serial number. Although some of these "447" numbers became hits on their own ("Crying in the Chapel" is a perfect example), *Presley* is one of very few artists whose company-produced reproductions have collectible value.

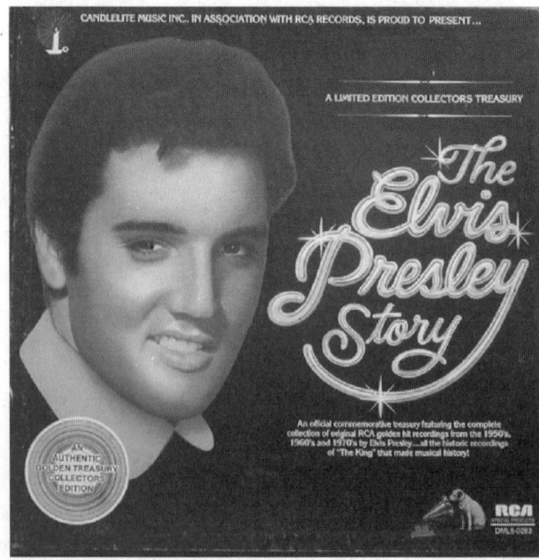

After his death, Elvis Presley's music was reissued in various box sets. This one was available only through a mail-order offer from Candelite Music.

In 1984, to honor Presley's 50th birthday, RCA released two box sets of six 45s apiece, each one pressed on golden vinyl. In 1986, Collectibles Records released a boxed set of Presley's greatest hits on black vinyl. Six years later, it re-released the set on gold vinyl. And in 1997, it released a second set, this time on marbled gray vinyl.

Many of the rarest Presley recordings are pressings that have some slight variation from the standard pressing. The name of the song might be misspelled, a songwriting or backup singer's credit might be added or deleted, the record might have been mastered at an incorrect speed, or the RCA "His Master's Voice" trademark might have disappeared from some copies. If an album or single may have an alternate track, and you don't have a phonograph available to confirm this, look at the stamper numbers in the dead wax. Certain stamper numbers may provide the clue to an alternate pressing, and those records, for which the stamper number will provide a clue to its contents, are listed below in the selected discography.

Almost all of Elvis Presley's RCA releases came with a picture sleeve. After Presley's death, RCA reissued most of Presley's releases as "Gold Standard Singles," and printed new picture sleeves for them. Picture sleeves printed for singles with serial numbers RCA 47-9610 and lower (between the years 1956 and 1968) should have the old-style serifed "RCA VICTOR" logo, along with Nipper and the gramophone. Reprinted sleeves will have the futuristic "RCA" logo, and no sign of Nipper. They may also say "COLLECTOR'S EDITION" or "GOLD STANDARD SERIES" on the sleeve.

Elvis' albums, especially the soundtracks to his movies, may contain promotional postcards or posters. For an album to qualify as near-mint, these postcards and posters must be part of the package, with no tack holes or pen marks.

References: Hawkins, Martin; Escott, Colin, *Elvis: The Illustrated Discography*, Omnibus Press, London, 1981; Jorgensen, Ernst, *Elvis Presley, A Life In Music: The Complete Recording Sessions*, St. Martin's Press, New York, N.Y., 1998; Kingsbury, Paul; Axelrod, Alan, Eds. *Country: The Music and the Musicians,* Abbeville Press, New York, N.Y. 1988; Worth, Fred L.; Tamerous, Steven, *Elvis: His Life From A-Z*, Contemporary Books, Chicago, 1988.

Museums: Graceland, Elvis' home and current museum/shrine to the King. 3734 Elvis Presley Boulevard, Memphis, Tennessee, 38186-0508. (800) 238-2000. http://www.elvis-presley.com/graceland; the Elvis-A-Rama Museum, 3401 Industrial Road, Las Vegas, Nevada. (702) 309-7200. *http://www.elvisarama.com.*

Web pages: Elvis Presley's official page: *http://www.elvis-presley.com*; Usenet newsgroups: *alt.fan.elvis-presley, alt.elvis.king.*

45s	Year	VG	VG+	NM
Elvis Presley, "That's All Right" / "Blue Moon of Kentucky" (Sun 209)	1954	$2.000.00	$4,000.00	$6,000.00
Elvis Presley, "Good Rockin' Tonight" / "I Don't Care if The Sun Don't Shine" (Sun 210)	1954	$1,000.00	$2,000.00	$3,000.00
Elvis Presley, "Milkcow Blues Boogie" / "You're A Heartbreaker" (Sun 215)	1955	$2,000.00	$3000.00	$4,000.00
Elvis Presley, "Baby Let's Play House" / "I 'm Left, You're Right, She's Gone" (Sun 217)	1955	$1,000.00	$2,000.00	$3,000.00
(if any of the above four are on RCA Victor 47-6380 to 47-6383)	1955	$15.00	$30.00	$60.00
Elvis Presley, "I Forgot To Remember To Forget" / "Mystery Train" (Sun 223)	1955	$500.00	$1,000.00	$2,000.00
(if above is on RCA Victor 47-6357)	1955	$15.00	$30.00	$60.00
Elvis Presley, "Heartbreak Hotel" / "I Was The One" (RCA Victor 47-6420)	1956	$10.00	$20.00	$40.00
Elvis Presley, "I Want You, I Need You, I Love You" / "My Baby Left Me" (RCA Victor 47-6540)	1956	$10.00	$20.00	$40.00
Elvis Presley, "Don't Be Cruel" / "Hound Dog" (RCA Victor 47-6604)	1956	$7.50	$15.00	$30.00
(with picture sleeve, if "Hound Dog!" is listed above "Don't Be Cruel", add:)	1956	$30.00	$60.00	$120.00
(with picture sleeve, if "Don't Be Cruel" is listed above "Hound Dog!", add:)	1956	$50.00	$100.00	$200.00
Elvis Presley, "I Got A Woman" / "I'm Countin' On You" (RCA Victor 47-6637)	1956	$20.00	$40.00	$80.00
Elvis Presley, "Lawdy Miss Clawdy" / "Shake, Rattle and Roll" (RCA Victor 47-6642)				
(with horizontal line, but no Nipper or gramophone)	1956	$50.00	$100.00	$200.00
(with Nipper and gramophone)	1956	$10.00	$20.00	$40.00
Elvis Presley, "Love Me Tender" / "Anyway You Want Me (That's How I Will Be)" (RCA Victor 47-6643)				
(if record refers to movie "Love Me Tender")	1956	$7.50	$15.00	$30.00
(if record has no reference to "Love Me Tender")	1956	$10.00	$20.00	$40.00
(with black/white picture sleeve, add:)	1956	$45.00	$90.00	$180.00
(with black/green picture sleeve, add:)	1956	$18.75	$37.50	$75.00
(with black/dark pink picture sleeve, add:)	1956	$10.00	$20.00	$40.00
(with black/light pink picture sleeve, add:)	1956	$7.50	$15.00	$30.00
Elvis Presley, "Too Much" / "Playing For Keeps" (RCA Victor 47-6800)				
(with horizontal line, but no Nipper or gramophone)	1957	$50.00	$100.00	$200.00
(with Nipper and gramophone)	1957	$7.50	$15.00	$30.00
Elvis Presley, "Let Me Be Your TEDDY BEAR" / "Loving You" (RCA Victor 47-7000) (no parentheses in title)	1957	$10.00	$20.00	$40.00
Elvis Presley, "(Let Me Be Your) Teddy Bear" / "Loving You" (RCA Victor 47-7000) (title has parentheses)	1957	$7.50	$15.00	$30.00
Elvis Presley, "It's Now or Never" / "A Mess of Blues" (RCA Victor 47-7777)				
(if "It's Now or Never" is missing the piano part, stamper numbers L2WW-0100-3S or L2WW-0100-4S)	1960	$250.00	$500.00	$1,000.00
(if "It's Now or Never" has the overdubbed piano)	1960	$5.00	$10.00	$20.00
(with picture sleeve, add:)	1960	$15.00	$30.00	$60.00
(if on RCA 61-7777, stereo single, 45 rpm, large hole)	1960	$100.00	$200.00	$400.00
Elvis Presley, "Surrender" / "Lonely Man" (RCA Victor 47-7850)	1961	$5.00	$10.00	$20.00
(with picture sleeve, add:)	1961	$15.00	$30.00	$60.00
(if on RCA Victor 61-7850, "Living Stereo" single, 45 rpm, large hole)	1961	$200.00	$400.00	$800.00
(if on RCA Victor 61-7850, "Compact Stereo 33", in "Living Stereo")	1961	$1,000.00	$1,500.00	$2,000.00
Elvis Presley, "Can't Help Falling In Love" / "Rock-a-Hula Baby" (RCA Victor 47-7968)	1961	$5.00	$10.00	$20.00
(with picture sleeve, add:)	1961	$15.00	$30.00	$60.00
Elvis Presley, "Viva Las Vegas" / "What'd I Say" (RCA Victor 47-8360)	1964	$3.00	$6.00	$12.00
(with "Coming Soon" on picture sleeve, add:)	1964	$6.25	$12.50	$25.00
(with "Ask For" on picture sleeve, add:)	1964	$12.50	$25.00	$50.00
Elvis Presley, "Guitar Man" / "High Heel Sneakers" (RCA Victor 47-9425)	1968	$2.50	$5.00	$10.00
(with picture sleeve ["Coming Soon" and "Ask For" variations have equal value], add:)	1968	$6.25	$12.50	$25.00
Elvis Presley, "You'll Never Walk Alone" / "We Call On Him" (RCA Victor 47-9600)	1968	$3.00	$6.00	$12.00
(with rare picture sleeve, add:)	1968	$25.00	$50.00	$100.00
Elvis Presley, "If I Can Dream" / "Edge of Reality" (RCA Victor 47-9670)	1968	$2.00	$4.00	$8.00
(with picture sleeve [some sleeves mention his NBC special, some don't, value is equal], add:)	1968	$5.00	$10.00	$20.00

45s	Year	VG	VG+	NM
Elvis Presley, "Suspicious Minds" / "You'll Think of Me" (RCA Victor 47-9764)	1969	$2.00	$4.00	$8.00
(with picture sleeve, add:)	1969	$5.00	$10.00	$20.00
Elvis Presley, "He Touched Me" / "The Bosom of Abraham" (RCA Victor 74-0651)				
(if stamper number is AWKS-1277, "He Touched Me" incorrectly mastered at 35 rpm)	1972	$37.50	$75.00	$150.00
(if stamper number is APKS-1277, both songs play correctly)	1972	$2.00	$4.00	$8.00
(with picture sleeve, add:)	1972	$30.00	$60.00	$120.00
Elvis Presley, "Burning Love" / "It's A Matter Of Time" (RCA Victor 74-0769)				
(if on orange label)	1972	$3.00	$6.00	
(with picture sleeve, add:)	1972	$3.75	$7.50	$15.00
(if on gray label, very rare reissue)	1974	$37.50	$75.00	$150.00
Elvis Presley, "If You Talk In Your Sleep" / "Help Me" (RCA Victor APBO-0280)				
(if A-side title is all on one line)	1974	$3.00	$6.00	$12.00
(if title is split to two lines)	1974	$3.00	$6.00	
(with picture sleeve, add:)	1974	$3.75	$7.50	$15.00
Elvis Presley, "T-R-O-U-B-L-E" / "Mr. Songman" (RCA Victor PB-10278)				
(if on orange label)	1975	$2.50	$5.00	
(if on tan label)	1975	$2.50	$5.00	$10.00
(if on gray label)	1975	$25.00	$50.00	$100.00
(with picture sleeve, add:)	1975	$2.50	$5.00	$10.00
Elvis Presley, "Bringing It Back" / "Pieces Of My Life" (RCA Victor PB-10401)				
(if on orange label)	1975	$50.00	$100.00	$200.00
(if on tan label)	1975	$2.50	$5.00	
(with picture sleeve, add:)	1975	$2.50	$5.00	$10.00
Elvis Presley, "Moody Blue" / "She Thinks I Still Care" (RCA PB-10587)	1976	$2.50	$5.00	
(with picture sleeve, add:)	1976	$2.50	$5.00	$10.00
Elvis Presley, "Lovin' Arms" / "You Asked Me To" (RCA JB-12205) (if promo only on green vinyl)	1981	$75.00	$150.00	$300.00
(if standard stock copy on black vinyl, not issued with picture sleeve)	1981	$3.00	$6.00	

78 RPM	Year	VG	VG+	NM
Elvis Presley, "That's All Right" / "Blue Moon of Kentucky" (Sun 209)	1954	$750.00	$1,500.00	$3,000.00
Elvis Presley, "Good Rockin' Tonight" / "I Don't Care if The Sun Don't Shine" (Sun 210)	1954	$450.00	$900.00	$1,800.00
Elvis Presley, "Milkcow Blues Boogie" / "You're A Heartbreaker" (Sun 215)	1955	$625.00	$1,250.00	$2,500.00
Elvis Presley, "Baby Let's Play House" / "I 'm Left, You're Right, She's Gone" (Sun 217)	1955	$375.00	$750.00	$1,500.00
Elvis Presley, "I Forgot To Remember To Forget" / "Mystery Train" (Sun 223)	1955	$250.00	$500.00	$1,000.00
Elvis Presley, "Heartbreak Hotel" / "I Was The One" (RCA Victor 20-6420)	1956	$25.00	$50.00	$100.00
Elvis Presley, "Don't Be Cruel" / "Hound Dog" (RCA Victor 20-6604)	1956	$25.00	$50.00	$100.00
Elvis Presley, "Love Me Tender"/ " Anyway You Want Me (That's How I Will Be)" (RCA Victor 20-6643)	1956	$25.00	$50.00	$100.00
Elvis Presley, "Wear My Ring Around Your Neck" / "Doncha' Think It's Time" (RCA Victor 20-7240)	1958	$30.00	$60.00	$120.00
Elvis Presley, "One Night" / "I Got Stung" (RCA Victor 20-7410)	1958	$125.00	$250.00	$500.00

LPs	Year	VG	VG+	NM
Elvis Presley, Elvis Presley (RCA Victor LPM-1254) (mono)				
(if "Long Play" on label, "Elvis" in pale pink, "Presley" in pale green on cover, pale green logo box in upper right front cover)	1956	$125.00	$250.00	$500.00
(if "Long Play" on label, "Elvis" in pale pink, "Presley" in neon green on cover, neon green logo box in upper right front cover)	1956	$100.00	$200.00	$400.00
(if "Long Play" on label, "Elvis" in pale pink, "Presley" in neon green on cover, black logo box in upper right front cover)	1956	$62.50	$125.00	$250.00
(if "Long Play" on label, "Elvis" in neon pink, "Presley" in neon green on cover, black logo box in upper right front cover)	1958	$50.00	$100.00	$200.00
(if "Mono" on label, cover photo is off-center but resembles 1958 release)	1963	$30.00	$60.00	$120.00
(if "Monaural" on label)	1964	$15.00	$30.00	$60.00
(if on RCA Victor LSP-1254(e), "Stereo Electronically Reproduced" and silver "RCA Victor" on label)	1962	$50.00	$100.00	$200.00
(if on RCA Victor LSP-1254(e), same as above, except white "RCA Victor" on label)	1965	$10.00	$20.00	$40.00
(if on RCA Victor LSP-1254(e), orange label, stiff non-flexible vinyl)	1968	$7.50	$15.00	$30.00
(if on RCA Victor LSP-1254(e), tan label)	1975	$3.75	$7.50	$15.00
(if on RCA Victor LSP-1254(e), black label, dog near top)	1976	$3.00	$6.00	$12.00
(if on RCA Victor AFL1-1245(e), some copies have stickers over original catalog numbers)	1977	$3.00	$6.00	$12.00
Elvis Presley, Elvis (RCA Victor LPM-1382) (mono)				
(if matrix number is 15S, 17S or 19S, containing alternate take of "Old Shep" with lyrics "he grew old AND his eyes were growing dim")	1956	$200.00	$400.00	$800.00
(if songs are listed as "Band 1" through "Band 6" on label)	1956	$100.00	$200.00	$400.00

45s	Year	VG	VG+	NM
(if back cover has ads for other albums)	1956	$75.00	$150.00	$300.00
(if back cover has no ads for other albums, "Long Play" on label)	1956	$75.00	$150.00	$300.00
(if "Mono" on label)	1963	$20.00	$40.00	$80.00
(if "Monaural" on label)	1965	$15.00	$30.00	$60.00
(if on RCA Victor LSP-1382(e), "Stereo Electronically Reprocessed" and silver "RCA Victor" on label)	1962	$50.00	$100.00	$200.00
(if on RCA Victor LSP-1382(e), same as above, except white "RCA Victor" on label)	1964	$12.50	$25.00	$50.00
(if on RCA Victor LSP-1382(e), orange label, non-flexible vinyl)	1968	$7.50	$15.00	$30.00
(if on RCA Victor LSP-1382(e), orange label, flexible vinyl)	1971	$5.00	$10.00	$20.00
(if on RCA Victor LSP-1382(e), tan label)	1975	$3.75	$7.50	$15.00
(if on RCA Victor LSP-1382(e), black label, dog near top)	1976	$3.00	$6.00	$12.00
(if on RCA Victor AFL1-1382(e), some copies have stickers over original catalog numbers)	1977	$3.00	$6.00	$12.00
Elvis Presley, Elvis' Golden Records (RCA Victor LPM-1707) (mono)				
(if title on cover in light blue letters, no song titles listed on front cover)	1958	$62.50	$125.00	$250.00
(if title on cover in light blue letters, no song titles listed on front cover, "RE" on back cover)	1958	$37.50	$75.00	$150.00
(if "MONO" on cover, title in white letters, song titles added to front cover)	1963	$15.00	$30.00	$60.00
(if "Monaural" on label, "RE2" on back cover)	1964	$10.00	$20.00	$40.00
(if on RCA Victor LSP-1707(e), "Stereo Electronically Reprocessed" and silver "RCA Victor" on label)	1962	$50.00	$100.00	$200.00
(if on RCA Victor LSP-1707(e), same as above, except white "RCA Victor" on label)	1964	$12.50	$25.00	$50.00
(if on RCA Victor LSP-1707(e), orange label, non-flexible vinyl)	1968	$7.50	$15.00	$30.00
(if on RCA Victor LSP-1707(e), orange label, flexible vinyl)	1971	$5.00	$10.00	$20.00
(if on RCA Victor LSP-1707(e), tan label)	1975	$3.75	$7.50	$15.00
(if on RCA Victor LSP-1707(e), black label, dog near top)	1976	$3.00	$6.00	$12.00
(if on RCA Victor AFL1-1707(e), some copies have stickers over original catalog numbers)	1977	$3.00	$6.00	$12.00
(if on RCA Victor AQL1-1707(e), reissue with new prefix)	1979	$2.50	$5.00	$10.00
(if on RCA 07863-67642-1, with six extra tracks, sold through Tower Records stores)	1997	$7.50	$15.00	$30.00
Elvis Presley, Elvis' Golden Records Volume 2 - 50,000,000 Elvis Fans Can't Be Wrong (RCA Victor LPM-2075) (mono)				
(if "Long Play" on label, "Magic Millions" on upper right front cover with RCA Victor logo)	1960	$50.00	$100.00	$200.00
(if "Mono" on label, "RE" on lower right front cover)	1963	$20.00	$40.00	$80.00
(if "Monaural" on label, label says "50,000,000 Elvis Presley Fans Can't Be Wrong")	1964	$12.50	$25.00	$50.00
(if "Monaural" on label, label only says "Elvis' Gold Records - Vol. 2")	1964	$12.50	$25.00	$50.00
(if on RCA Victor LSP-2075(e), "Stereo Electronically Reprocessed," label says "50,000,000 Elvis Presley Fans Can't Be Wrong")	1962	$37.50	$75.00	$150.00
(if on RCA Victor LSP-2075(e), "Stereo Electronically Reproduced," white "RCA Victor" on label)	1964	$12.50	$25.00	$50.00
(if on RCA Victor LSP-2075(e), orange label, non-flexible vinyl)	1968	$7.50	$15.00	$30.00
(if on RCA Victor LSP-2075(e), orange label, flexible vinyl)	1971	$5.00	$10.00	$20.00
(if on RCA Victor LSP-2075(e), tan label)	1975	$5.00	$10.00	$20.00
(if on RCA Victor LSP-2075(e), black label, dog near top)	1976	$3.00	$6.00	$12.00
(if on RCA Victor AFL1-2075(e), some copies have stickers over original catalog numbers)	1977	$3.00	$6.00	$12.00
(if on RCA 07863-67631-1, with ten extra tracks, sold through Tower Records stores)	1997	$7.50	$15.00	$30.00
Elvis Presley, Fun in Acapulco (RCA Victor LPM-2756) (mono)				
(if "Mono" on label)	1963	$20.00	$40.00	$80.00
(if "Monaural" on label)	1964	$12.50	$25.00	$50.00
(if on RCA Victor LSP-2756, "stereo" and silver "RCA Victor" on black label)	1963	$25.00	$50.00	$100.00
(if on RCA Victor LSP-2756, "stereo" and white "RCA Victor" on black label)	1964	$15.00	$30.00	$60.00
(if on RCA Victor LSP-2756, stereo, orange label, non-flexible vinyl)	1968	$10.00	$20.00	$40.00

45s	Year	VG	VG+	NM
(if on RCA Victor LSP-2756, stereo, tan label)	1975	$6.25	$12.50	$25.00
(if on RCA Victor LSP-2756, stereo, black label, dog near top)	1976	$3.00	$6.00	$12.00
(if on RCA Victor AFL1-2756, some copies have stickers over original catalog numbers)	1977	$3.00	$6.00	$12.00
Elvis Presley, Roustabout (RCA Victor LPM-2999) (mono)				
(if "Mono" on label)	1964	$25.00	$50.00	$100.00
(if "Monaural" on label)	1965	$15.00	$30.00	$60.00
(if on RCA Victor LSP-2999, "stereo" and silver "RCA Victor" on black label)	1963	$150.00	$300.00	$600.00
(if on RCA Victor LSP-2999, "stereo" and white "RCA Victor" on black label)	1964	$15.00	$30.00	$60.00
(if on RCA Victor LSP-2999, stereo, orange label, non-flexible vinyl)	1968	$10.00	$20.00	$40.00
(if on RCA Victor LSP-2999, stereo, orange label, flexible vinyl)	1971	$5.00	$10.00	$20.00
(if on RCA Victor LSP-2999, stereo, tan label)	1975	$5.00	$10.00	$20.00
(if on RCA Victor LSP-2999, stereo, black label, dog near top)	1976	$3.00	$6.00	$12.00
(if on RCA Victor AFL1-2999, some copies have stickers over original catalog numbers)	1977	$3.00	$6.00	$12.00
Elvis Presley, Speedway (RCA Victor LPM-3989) (mono)	1968	$500.00	$1,000.00	$2,000.00
(with bonus photo, add:)	1968	$12.50	$25.00	$50.00
(if on RCA Victor LSP-3989, "stereo" on black label)	1968	$15.00	$30.00	$60.00
(if on RCA Victor LSP-3989, stereo, orange label, non-flexible vinyl)	1968	$10.00	$20.00	$40.00
(if on RCA Victor LSP-3989, stereo, orange label, flexible vinyl)	1971	$5.00	$10.00	$20.00
(if on RCA Victor LSP-3989, stereo, tan label)	1975	$5.00	$10.00	$20.00
(if on RCA Victor LSP-3989, stereo, black label, dog near top)	1976	$3.00	$6.00	$12.00
(if on RCA Victor AFL1-3989, some copies have stickers over original catalog numbers)	1977	$3.00	$6.00	$12.00
Elvis Presley, Elvis Country (I'm 10,000 Years Old) (RCA Victor LSP-4460)				
(if on orange label, non-flexible vinyl)	1971	$10.00	$20.00	$40.00
(if on orange label, flexible vinyl)	1971	$6.25	$12.50	$25.00
(with bonus photo, add:)	1971	$3.75	$7.50	$15.00
(if on tan label)	1975	$6.25	$12.50	$25.00
(if on black label, dog near top)	1976	$3.75	$7.50	$15.00
(if on green vinyl, black label, dog near top)	197??	$500.00	$1,000.00	$2,000.00
(if on RCA Victor AFL1-4460, some copies have stickers over original catalog numbers)	1977	$3.00	$6.00	$10.00
(if on RCA Victor A&L1-3956, budget reissue)	1981	$2.00	$4.00	$8.00
Elvis Presley, Moody Blue (RCA AFL1-2428)				
(if on blue vinyl)	1977	$2.50	$5.00	$10.00
(if on black vinyl, short printed)	1977	$50.00	$100.00	$200.00
(if on any other color vinyl, promo copies only)	1977	$500.00	$1,000.00	$2,000.00
(if on RCA AQL1-2428, reissue with new prefix)	1979	$6.25	$12.50	$25.00
Elvis Presley, The Elvis Story (RCA Special Products DML5-0263) (available only through Candelite Music TV mail-in)	1977	$15.00	$30.00	$60.00
Elvis Presley, Elvis Aron Presley (RCA CPL8-3699) (8 LP's)	1980	$25.00	$50.00	$100.00
(if box says "Reviewer Series" on cover)	1980	$62.50	$125.00	$250.00
(if on RCA DJL1-3781, promo-only selections on one disc from album				
Elvis Presley, His Greatest Hits (Reader's Digest RD-10/A) (8 LP's)	1979	$25.00	$50.00	$100.00
(if on Reader's Digest 010/A, 7 LP's, yellow box)	1983	$15.00	$30.00	$60.00
(if on Reader's Digest 010/A, 7 LP's, white box)	1990	$10.00	$20.00	$40.00
Elvis Presley, Love Songs (K-Tel NU 9900)	1981	$5.00	$10.00	$20.00
Elvis Presley, The Legend Lives On (Reader's Digest RB4-191/A) (7 LP's)	1986	$15.00	$30.00	$60.00
Elvis Presley, Early Elvis (1954-1956 Live at the Louisiana Hayride (Premore PL-589)	1989	$7.50	$15.00	$30.00
Elvis Presley, The Million Dollar Quartet (RCA 2013-1-R) (featuring Johnny Cash, Jerry Lee Lewis and Carl Perkins)	1990	$3.00	$6.00	$12.00
Elvis Presley, Windows of the Soul (Erika GLCD 13047777) (Elvis-shaped picture disc, contains 1956 interview)	1996	$5.00	$10.00	$20.00

PROGRESSIVE ROCK

History: Progressive rock, also known as "prog-rock" or "art-rock," began in the late 1960s as artists started to base their music not just on their rock 'n' roll pioneers, but on those who came before—classical composers like Beethoven, Handel, and Bach. The term "progressive rock" can be interpreted as rock music evolving, or "progressing" from its present state. Songs might encompass far-reaching concepts of jealousy, passion, history, or fantasy. Non-traditional rock instruments may be added to the mix, such as violins, cellos, piccolos, harpsichords, theremins, bassoons, or early synthesizers.

A prog-rock song could be 10-15 minutes long (Mike Oldfield's prog-rock classic *"Tubular Bells"* album contains two 20+ minute songs, one for each side of the disc). Some prog-rock groups experimented with the standard 4/4 beat, as groups like Pink Floyd and Rush have released songs in different time signatures. The group Magma even created a whole new language for their songs.

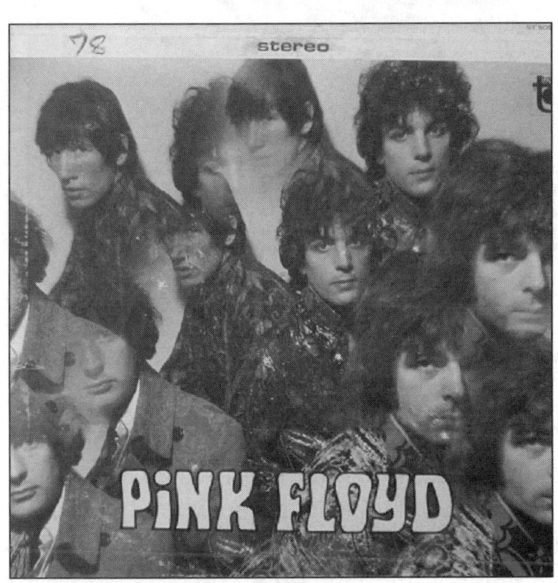

The first album by Pink Floyd, featuring the single "See Emily Play." Courtesy Last Vestige Music Store, Albany, N.Y.

Another form of progressive rock came from early experiments with synthesizers. The influences for these bands were the early tonal experiments of John Cage and Karlheinz Stockhausen, who generated electronic sound in a new sonic symphony. In 1968, Robert Moog created the Moog synthesizer, an instrument capable of creating whole new musical landscapes from an electronic piano keyboard. Some of the earliest artists and groups to incorporate synthesizers and other electronic instruments into their music include Kraftwerk, Tangerine Dream, and Jean-Michael Jarre. These groups, with their synthesizers and tone generators, create musical masterpieces like *Autobahn, Phaedra, and Oxygene.*

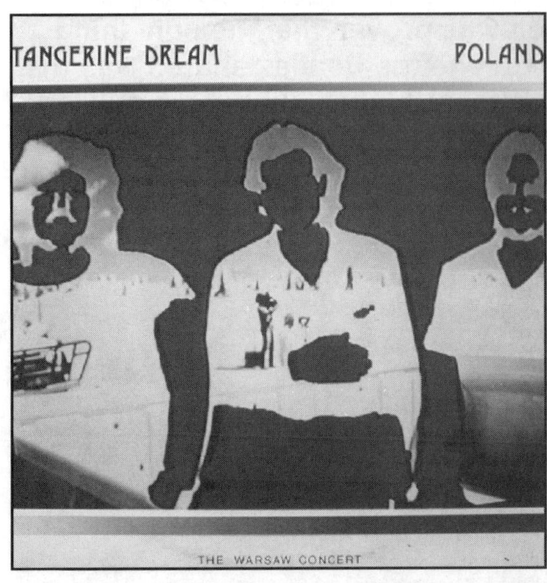

Whereas Kraftwerk experimented with dance rhythms on their albums, Tangerine Dream used their synthesizers to create spectacular aural landscapes. Courtesy Last Vestige Music Store, Albany, N.Y.

Progressive rock has also been labeled "art-rock," but while prog-rock allows for more jazz and classical improvisation, "art-rock" leans toward the gothic and mystical, incorporating demons, wizards, and dragons into their compositions.

Progressive rock bands arguably have the most loyal fan bases, almost rivaling the Grateful Dead in terms of fan devotion. Even if an act like Renaissance or Jethro Tull has not released an album in years (or if they have released some albums, yet the radio stations have ignored the new LP in favor of classic "oldies" tracks), they could still pack an arena or theater nearly on word of mouth alone.

Trivia

Someone at ABC Records must have thought the new band they signed, Genesis, was a jazz band. Which would explain why their first American album, *Trespass*, was released on ABC's Impulse! jazz label. The record was later re-released on the main ABC label, making the Impulse! pressing a hard-to-find collectible.

Trivia

The Canadian prog-rock band Klaatu released their debut album in 1976, and it sold poorly—until a rumor circulated that this band was actually the Beatles in disguise. Then the record took off. Eventually it was proven that the only thing Klaatu and the Beatles shared was the same record label, but people still look for that debut album to see how close the band really sounded to the Fab Four.

Outside of the "are these guys the Beatles?" connection, Klaatu's other claim to fame is that one of their songs, "Calling Occupants of Interplanetary Craft," was recorded by the Carpenters as a Top 40 hit. Courtesy Last Vestige Music Store, Albany, N.Y.

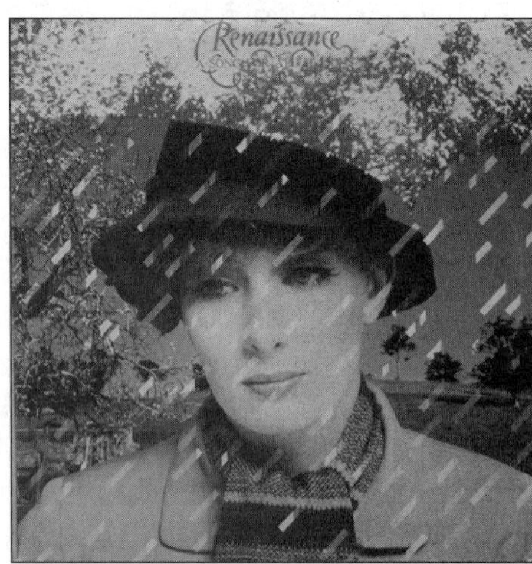

The first Renaissance group featured ex-Yardbirds member Keith Relf, and was a folk-rock band. Renaissance's second incarnation included lead singer Annie Haslam, with her three-octave vocal range. Courtesy Last Vestige Music Store, Albany, N.Y.

Trivia

Some listeners think that Kraftwerk's "Autobahn" was inspired by the Beach Boys song "Fun, Fun, Fun." This conclusion was arrived at because Kraftwerk's German lyrics, "Wir fahr'n fahr'n fahr'n auf der Autobahn," sound like "The Fun, Fun, Fun of the Autobahn" (it actually means, "We're driving, driving, driving on the autobahn").

From driving on the autobahn to racing in the world's greatest bicycle race, Kraftwerk's albums do not follow a traditional rock and roll path.

What To Look For: Some progressive rock artists did release 45s, but album tracks like "Autobahn" and "Tubular Bells" paled when heavily edited down to a 3-minute 45. In many cases, though, an artist's earliest releases on 45 do have some collectible value, but these recordings are few and far between.

The cleaner a progressive rock album sounds, the more collectible it becomes. While the standard album pressing does contain a collectible value, collectors will search for audiophile discs if they exist.

References: Jones, Cliff, *Another Brick In The Wall: The Stories Behind Every Pink Floyd Song*, Carlton Books, London, 1999; Neely, Tim, *Goldmine Record Album Price Guide*, Krause Publications, Iola, Wisconsin, 1999; Neely, Tim, *Goldmine Price Guide to Alternative Records*, Krause Publications, Iola, Wisconsin, 1996.

Web pages: A progressive rock homepage, with links to many bands: *http://www.progrock.com*; Kraftwerk home page, with Flash and Quicktime movies based on their most popular compositions: *http://www.kraftwerk.com*; the homepage of former Renaissance singer Annie Haslam: *http://www.annie-haslam.com*; Pink Floyd's homepage: *http://www.pinkfloyd-co.com*; Tangerine Dream's home page: *http://www.tangerine-dream.de;* Usenet newsgroups: alt.music.jethro-tull, alt.music.pink-floyd.

45s	Year	VG	VG+	NM
Blodwyn Pig, "Dear Jill" / "Summer Day" (A&M 1158)	1969		$3.00	$6.00
Emerson Lake and Palmer, "Lucky Man" / "Knife's Edge" (Cotillion 44106)	1971		$3.00	$6.00
Emerson Lake and Palmer, "Fanfare for the Common Man" / "Brain Salad Surgery" (Atlantic 3398)	1977		$2.50	$5.00
Genesis, "Silent Sun" / "That's Me" (Parrot 3018)				
(if stock copy, black label, green-yellow bird)	1968	$100.00	$200.00	$400.00
(if DJ copy, orange label, black bird)	1968	$25.00	$50.00	$100.00
Genesis, "Watcher of the Skies" / "Willow Farm" (Charisma 103)	1973	$12.50	$25.00	$50.00
Genesis, "The Lamb Lies Down on Broadway" / "Counting Out Time" (Atco 7013)	1975	$5.00	$10.00	$20.00
Genesis, "Abacab" / "Who Dunnit?" (Atlantic 3891)	1982		$2.00	$4.00
(with picture sleeve, add:)	1982		$2.00	$4.00
Gentle Giant, "Cogs in Cogs" / "I'm Turning Around" (Capitol 4464)	1977		$2.50	$5.00
Jethro Tull, "Hymn 43" / "Mother Goose" (Reprise 1024)	1971		$2.50	$5.00
Jethro Tull, "Bungle in the Jungle" / "Back Door Angels" (Chrysalis 2101)	1974		$2.50	$5.00
(with picture sleeve, add:)	1974	$2.50	$5.00	$10.00
King Crimson, "In The Court of the Crimson King" (Part 1) / (Part 2) (Atlantic 2702)	1970	$3.00	$6.00	$12.00
Klaatu, "Calling Occupants" / "Doctor Marvello" (Capitol 4377)	1976	$2.00	$4.00	$8.00
Klaatu, "Calling Occupants" / "Sub-Rosa Subway" (Capitol 4412)	1977		$2.50	$5.00
Kraftwerk, "Autobahn" / "Morgen Spaziergance" (Vertigo 203)	1975	$2.00	$4.00	$8.00
Kraftwerk, "Pocket Calculator" / "Dentaku" (Warner Bros. 49723) (opaque yellow vinyl)	1981		$2.50	$5.00
(with bread-bag plastic picture sleeve, add:)	1981		$2.50	$5.00
Marillion, "Kayleigh" / "Heart of Lothian" (Capitol B-5493)	1985		$2.00	$4.00
The Alan Parsons Project, "(The System of) Doctor Tarr and Professor Feather" / "Dream Within A Dream" (20th Century 2297)	1976		$2.50	$5.00
The Alan Parsons Project, "Eye in the Sky" / "Gemini" (Arista 0696)	1982		$2.00	$4.00
Pink Floyd, "See Emily Play" / "Scarecrow" (Tower 356)	1967	$50.00	$100.00	$200.00
(with promotional title sleeve, add:)	1967	$175.00	$350.00	$700.00
(with promotional photo sleeve, add:)	1967	$200.00	$400.00	$800.00
Pink Floyd, "Money" / "Any Colour You Like" (Harvest 3609)	1973	$3.75	$7.50	$15.00
Pink Floyd, "Another Brick In the Wall (Part 2)" / "One of My Turns" (Columbia 11187)				
(if customized "wall" label)	1980		$2.50	$5.00
(if standard Columbia label)	1980		$2.00	$4.00
(with picture sleeve, add:)	1980	$2.00	$4.00	$8.00
Renaissance, "Prologue" / "Spare Some Love" (Capitol 3487)	1972	$2.00	$4.00	$8.00
Rush, "Finding My Way" / "Need Some Love" (Mercury 73623)	1974	$12.50	$25.00	$50.00
Rush, "Tom Sawyer" / "Witch Hunt" (Mercury 76109)	1981	$2.50	$5.00	$10.00
(with picture sleeve, add:)	1981	$6.25	$12.50	$25.00
Tangerine Dream, "Moonlight (Part 2)" / "Coldwater Canyon (Part 2)" (Virgin 9516)	1977	$2.50	$5.00	$10.00
Uriah Heep, "Easy Livin'" / "All My Life" (Mercury 73307)	1972	$2.00	$4.00	$8.00
Yes, "Your Move" / "Clap" (Atlantic 2819)	1971		$2.50	$5.00
Yes, "Roundabout" / "Long Distance Runaround" (Atlantic 2854)	1972		$2.50	$5.00
(if "Roundabout" on both sides, promo, yellow vinyl)	1972	$25.00	$50.00	$100.00

LPs	Year	VG	VG+	NM
Blodwyn Pig, Ahead Rings Out (A&M SP-1210)	1969	$3.75	$7.50	$15.00
(if on A&M SP-3180, budget reissue)	1982	$2.00	$4.00	$8.00
Emerson Lake and Palmer, Pictures at an Exhibition (Cotillion ELP 66666)	1971	$3.00	$6.00	$12.00
(if on Atlantic SD 1912)	1977	$2.00	$4.00	$8.00
Emerson Lake and Palmer, Trilogy (Cotillion SD 9903)	1972	$3.00	$6.00	$12.00
(if on Cotillion SMAS-94773, Columbia Record Club edition)	1972	$3.75	$7.50	$15.00
(if on Atlantic SD 19123)	1977	$2.00	$4.00	$8.00
Genesis, Trespass (ABC Impulse! ASD-9205)	1971	$7.50	$15.00	$30.00
(if on ABC X-816, reissue)	1971	$3.00	$6.00	$12.00
(if on MCA 816)	1979	$2.50	$5.00	$10.00
(if on MCA 37151)	198??	$2.00	$4.00	$8.00
Genesis, Nursery Cryme (Charisma CAS-1052)	1971	$3.75	$7.50	$15.00
(if on Atlantic 80030)	1982	$2.00	$4.00	$8.00
Genesis, Abacab (Atlantic SD 19313) (four different covers, lettered "A" through "D" on spine, value is equal)	1981	$2.50	$5.00	$10.00
Gentle Giant, Acquiring the Taste (Vertigo VE-1005)	1971	$3.75	$7.50	$15.00
Gentle Giant, The Power and the Glory (Capitol ST-11337)	1974	$2.50	$5.00	$10.00
(if on Capitol SN-16044, budget reissue)	1980	$2.00	$4.00	$8.00
Jean-Michel Jarre, Oxygene				
(if on Polydor PD-1-6112)	1977	$2.50	$5.00	$10.00
(if on Dreyfus/Polydor 827 885-1)	1987	$2.00	$4.00	$8.00
(if on Mobile Fidelity 1-212)	1995	$5.00	$10.00	$20.00
Jethro Tull, Living in the Past (Reprise 2MS 2106) (2 LPs) (original pressings have sleeves attached to booklet)	1972	$6.25	$12.50	$25.00
(if on Chrysalis 2CH 1035, green labels)	1972	$5.00	$10.00	$20.00
(if on Chrysalis CHR 1035, blue labels, New York address)	1977	$2.50	$5.00	$10.00
Jethro Tull, 20 Years of Jethro Tull (Chrysalis V5X 41653) (5 LPs)	1988	$20.00	$40.00	$80.00
(if on Chrysalis V2X 41665, 2 LP's, abridged version of above)	1989	$6.25	$12.50	$25.00
King Crimson, In the Court of the Crimson King - An Observation by King Crimson (Atlantic SD 8245)	1969	$5.00	$10.00	$20.00
(if on Atlantic SD 19155, reissue)	1978	$3.00	$6.00	$12.00
(if on Mobile Fidelity 1-075, audiophile pressing)	1981	$20.00	$40.00	$80.00
(if on Editions EG EGKC-1, reissue)	1985	$2.50	$5.00	$10.00
Klaatu, Klaatu (Capitol ST-11542)	1976	$3.75	$7.50	$15.00
(if on Capitol SN-16060, budget reissue)	1980	$2.00	$4.00	$8.00
Kraftwerk, Autobahn				
(if on Vertigo VEL-2003)	1974	$5.00	$10.00	$20.00
(if on Mercury SRM-1-3704)	1977	$3.75	$7.50	$15.00
(if on Warner Bros. 25326)	1985	$3.00	$6.00	$12.00
(if on Elektra 60987)	1988	$2.00	$4.00	$8.00
Mike Oldfield, Tubular Bells				
(if on Virgin VR 13-105)	1973	$3.75	$7.50	$15.00
(if on Virgin QR 13-105, quadraphonic version)	1974	$6.25	$12.50	$25.00
(if on Virgin PZ 34116)	1976	$3.00	$6.00	$12.00
(if on Virgin SD 13135)	1979	$2.50	$5.00	$10.00
(if on Virgin/Epic PE 34116, contains bar code)	1982	$2.00	$4.00	$8.00
(if on Virgin/Epic HE 44116, half-speed mastered edition)	1982	$6.25	$12.50	$25.00
(if on Virgin 90589)	1987	$2.00	$4.00	$8.00
Pink Floyd, The Piper at the Gates of Dawn (Tower T 5093) (mono)	1967	$62.50	$125.00	$250.00
(if on Tower ST-5093, stereo, orange label)	1967	$20.00	$40.00	$80.00
(if on Tower ST-5093, stereo, multicolored label)	1967	$10.00	$20.00	$40.00
Pink Floyd, The Dark Side of the Moon				
(if on Harvest SMAS-11163, with poster and two stickers)	1973	$6.25	$12.50	$25.00
(if on Harvest SMAS-11163, no inserts)	1973	$3.00	$6.00	$12.00

LPs	Year	VG	VG+	NM
(if on Capitol SEAX-11902, picture disc)	1978	$7.50	$15.00	$30.00
(if on Mobile Fidelity 1-017, audiophile pressing)	1980	$12.50	$25.00	$50.00
(if on Mobile Fidelity MFQR-017, "Ultra High Quality Recording" in box)	1982	$75.00	$150.00	$300.00
Renaissance, Scheherazade and Other Stories (Sire SASD-7510)	1975	$3.00	$6.00	$12.00
(if on Sire SR 6107, budget reissue)	1977	$2.50	$5.00	$10.00
(if on Mobile Fidelity 1-099, audiophile pressing)	1982	$12.50	$25.00	$50.00
Renaissance, Time Line (IRS SP-70033)	1983	$2.50	$5.00	$10.00
Rush, 2112 (Mercury SRM-1-1079)	1976	$2.50	$5.00	$10.00
(if on Mercury 822545-1, reissue)	1985	$2.00	$4.00	$8.00

LPs	Year	VG	VG+	NM
Tangerine Dream, Phaedra				
(if on Virgin 13-108)	1974	$3.75	$7.50	$15.00
(if on Virgin 2010, a reissue)	1979	$2.50	$5.00	$10.00
Uriah Heep, Uriah Heep (Mercury SR-61294)	1970	$3.00	$6.00	$12.00
Uriah Heep, Abominog (Mercury SRM-1-4057)	1982	$2.00	$4.00	$8.00
Yes, Close To The Edge (Atlantic SD 7244)	1972	$3.00	$6.00	$12.00
(if white label mono copy, banded for airplay)	1972	$12.50	$25.00	$50.00
(if on Atlantic SD 19133, reissue)	1977	$2.00	$4.00	$8.00
(if on Mobile Fidelity 1-077, audiophile pressing)	1982	$15.00	$30.00	$60.0

Former Jethro Tull guitarist Mick Abrahams formed his own progressive rock group Blodwyn Pig. The group recorded some albums in the 1970s, but were not able to equal Jethro Tull's success and longevity. Courtesy Last Vestige Music Store, Albany, N.Y.

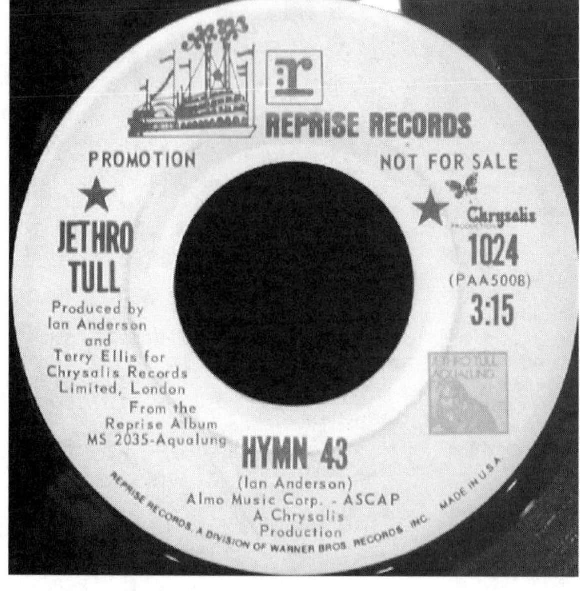

This white label promo for the Jethro Tull song *"Hymn 43"* features not only the artwork of two record companies—Reprise and Chrysalis—but also a small photo of the album "Hymn 43" came from, *Aqualung*. From the Collection of Val Shively.

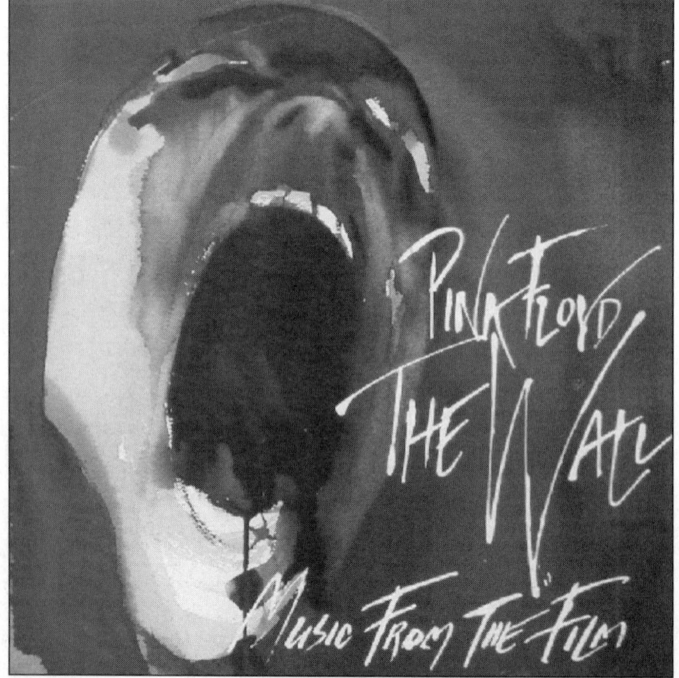

Pink Floyd's "When The Tigers Broke Free" did appear in the motion picture *Pink Floyd the Wall*, and the album jacket announced the song would appear on Pink Floyd's forthcoming album *The Final Cut*. But when *The Final Cut* was released, "When The Tigers Broke Free" was not on the album. Perhaps that song was indeed—the final cut.

PROMOTIONAL RECORDS

History: A promotional record, or "promo," is a different type of pressing than a standard record. Whereas a "stock copy" is a record sold in stores, a "promo copy" will be given away to radio stations, so they can play the record on the air and "promote" the artist.

Promo records are part of an artist's contract with the record company. A certain number of records are made for promotional use only, and the artist does not receive any royalties or remuneration from the existence of those pressings. These records often have a different label scheme than their equivalent stock copies; most of the promo pressings have a white background. Because of this, promotional records are often called "white label promos" by collectors.

Although the standard Vee Jay stock copies of the Beatles' 45s were printed on black labels with a rainbow perimeter, promotional 45s were pressed on a white label with blue printing. From the Collection of Bruce Spizer.

Promo albums that are sent to radio stations often contain a "timing strip" on their front cover. This allows radio personnel to know exactly what songs are on what side, their proper running time, and which songs the record company wants promoted first. These strips can be peeled off, but many collectors leave them on as proof that the record was originally used to promote the artist.

The "timing strip" on the front cover can often provide clues as to how the record was received at a radio station, and what the station's program director thought of the album. In this case, the PD selected three songs for airplay—but not the song "Let It Shine," which was released as the first single from the album.

Besides the white label on a promo, the label will often contain words like "Audition Copy," "Promotional Copy—Not For Sale," "Demonstration Copy," etc. Promo singles will often carry the same song on both sides—one side in stereo, the other in a mono pressing.

Liberty Records called their promotional 45s "audition records." Notice the label design and the bar-code-like horizontal stripes on the left side of the label. Courtesy Last Vestige Music Store, Albany, N.Y.

Trivia

Even though in the early 1970s, Top 40 radio songs rarely exceeded three minutes in length ("American Pie" notwithstanding), Bruce Springsteen recorded his signature hit "Born To Run" in such a way that it could not be cleanly edited or trimmed from its four-minute-plus length.

Not only is this a radio promo copy of "Born to Run," but it also contains a monaural version of the song.

The rarity and collectible value of a promo disc is proportional to the number of stock copies pressed of that title. In other words, if an artist sells two million stock copies of a 45, the white label promo copies will be harder to find and more desirable to a collector. However, if the song did not sell well, the few stock copies that exist will have more collectible value than their white label counterparts.

Another type of promotional record is the "designate promo." This is a stock copy record "designated" for promotional purposes. Designate promo albums will have a gold stamp or sticker on the cover, declaring the record for promotional use only and that the record company has the right to reclaim the record at any time. Designate promo 45s will have the stock copy label, but will also have a rubber-stamped "not for sale" on the label face.

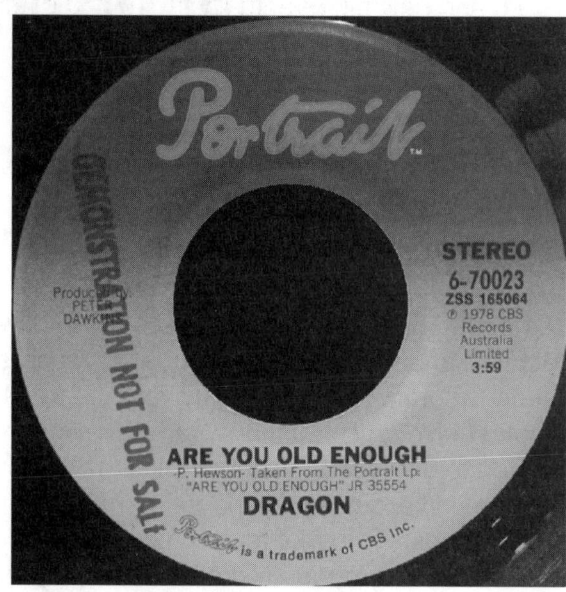

An example of a "designate" promo, as this stock copy has been stamped for promo use.

Some promotional 45s may contain red circular stickers. These stickers were often affixed to the disc by a person hired by the record company to promote the record. With the sea of white label promo 45s arriving at a radio station every week, promotion people will do anything—or say anything—in order to get a record into a radio station's heavy rotation.

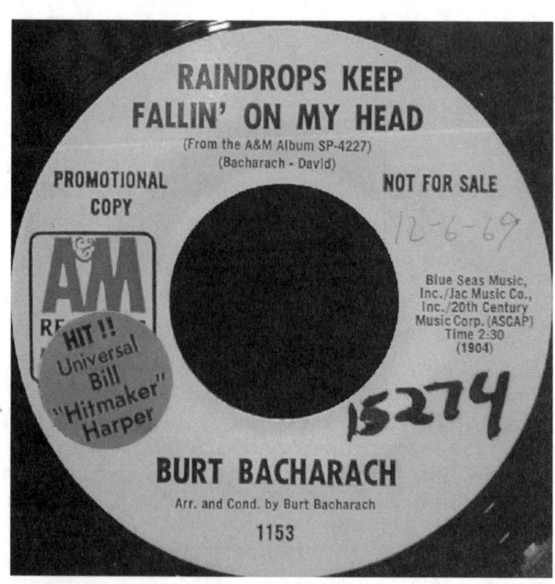

Bill "Hitmaker" Harper was right about this song becoming a hit... but it would top the charts with B.J. Thomas singing it, not Burt Bacharach. From the Collection of Val Shively.

In the 1950s and 1960s, white label promos usually contained the same A-sides and B-sides as the stock copies. Sometimes a disc jockey would accidentally play the B-side of the record, and eventually create a brand new hit. Eventually the record companies pressed promo copies with a huge "A" on the "plug side" of the record, an image that left no doubt which side the DJ was supposed to play.

An example of a "Big A" side on a promo 45. Courtesy Last Vestige Music Store, Albany, N.Y.

What To Look For: Promo albums will often be pressed on cleaner vinyl (in the late 1970s and early 1980s, Warner Bros. released its promo albums on "Quiex II" audiophile vinyl). They may also contain biographical or promotional material packed inside the album jacket.

Some promo recordings may have a drill hole through the cover; or the UPC bar code may have been blacked out to prevent it from being read at a record store's checkout scanner. At the other end of the spectrum, some elaborate promotional copies may be pressed on colored vinyl. Columbia Records, for example, pressed many of their 1960s 45s on red vinyl.

Be aware that these records were pressed in such a way that the artist does not receive a royalty or payment of any sort. Therefore, many Internet auction companies will not let you sell a promotional record on their sites. The debate on whether promotional records can be sold on the secondary market continues to this day, and there are arguments both for and against this practice.

References: Heggeness, Fred; Neely, Tim, *Goldmine Promo Record and CD Price Guide*, Krause Publications, Iola, Wisconsin, 1998.

Trivia

The Isley Brothers' "Fight the Power" contains a word that, according to George Carlin, can't be said on TV—or on radio, for that matter. The 7-inch pressing contains an "edited for radio" version with the offensive word bleeped. The B-side, however, contains the entire unexpurgated version of the song.

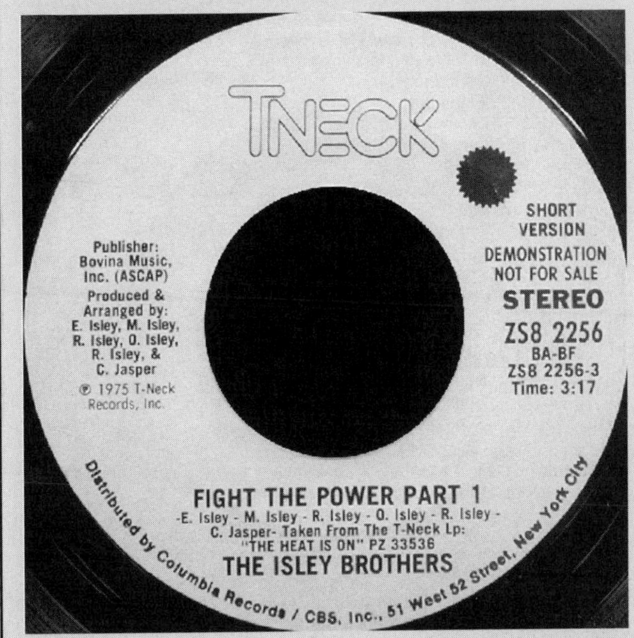

The Isley Brothers' "Fight the Power" promo 45, containing both a censored and an uncensored version of the song. Courtesy Last Vestige Music Store, Albany, N.Y.

45s	Year	VG	VG+	NM
Alabama, "Mountain Music" (RCA Victor 13019) (green vinyl, brown promo label)	1981	$3.00	$6.00	$12.00
The Animals, "The House of the Rising Sun" (MGM 13264) (yellow label)	1964	$6.25	$12.50	$25.00
The Beach Boys, "Surfin" (Candix 301) (promo label)	1963	$375.00	$750.00	$1,500.00
The Beatles, "Please Please Me" / "From Me To You" (Vee Jay 581) (if white label and blue print, "Promotional Copy" on label)	1964	$200.00	$400.00	$600.00
(if white label and blue print, no listing of "Promotional Copy" anywhere on label)	1964	$300.00	$600.00	$900.00
The Beatles, "Lady Madonna" / "The Inner Light" (Capitol P 2138) (light green label promo)	1968	$50.00	$100.00	$200.00
The Bee Gees, "New York Mining Disaster 1941" / "I Can't See Nobody" (Atco 6487) (Bee Gees not listed on label)	1967	$6.25	$12.50	$25.00
Chuck Berry, "Thirty Days" (Chess 1610) (label must also say "Promotion, Not For Sale")	1955	$43.75	$87.50	$175.00
The Cars, "Just What I Needed" (Elektra 45491) (red vinyl promo)	1978	$6.25	$12.50	$25.00
Chicago, "Questions 67 and 68" (Columbia 67E68) (in English and Japanese)	1971	$6.25	$12.50	$25.00
Phil Collins, "In The Air Tonight" (Atlantic PR 655) (white label promo)	1981	$5.00	$10.00	$20.00
The Crickets, "That'll Be The Day" (Brunswick 55009) (yellow promo)	1957	$37.50	$75.00	$150.00
Def Leppard, "Let It Go" (same on both sides) (Mercury 76120)	1981	$2.50	$5.00	$10.00

45s	Year	VG	VG+	NM
Neil Diamond, "Clown Town" / "At Night" (Columbia 42809)	1963	$150.00	$300.00	$600.00
The Doors, "Light My Fire" (Elektra 45615) (white-black promo label, 2:52 version)	1967	$12.50	$25.00	$50.00
Bob Dylan, "Blowin' in the Wind" / "Don't Think Twice, It's All Right" (Columbia 42856)	1963	$100.00	$200.00	$400.00
(if label says "Special Album Excerpt")	1963	$75.00	$150.00	$300.00
Eagles, "Lyin' Eyes" (two versions) (Asylum 45279)	1975	$2.50	$5.00	$10.00
The Five Keys, "I'll Follow You" (Groove 0031) (extremely rare promo)	195??	$1,000.00	$2,000.00	$4,000.00
Foreigner, "Blue Morning, Blue Day" (Atlantic 3543) (silver label, blue vinyl promo)	1978	$6.25	$12.50	$25.00
Peter Gabriel, "I Don't Remember" (Mercury 76086) (blue vinyl promo)	1980	$2.50	$5.00	$10.00
Sammy Hagar, "I Can't Drive 55" (Geffen 29173) (contains "traffic ticket" insert)	1984	$3.00	$6.00	$12.00
Richard Harris, "MacArthur Park" (Dunhill D-32) (stereo single, small hole, long version)	1968	$4.50	$9.00	$18.00
Heart, "Magic Man" ("AM" short version and "FM" long version) (Mushroom 7011)	1975	$2.50	$5.00	$10.00
The J. Geils Band, "Flamethrower" (two versions) (EMI SPRO 9743)	1981	$2.50	$5.00	$10.00
Michael Jackson, "Someone In The Dark" (two versions) (MCA 1786)	1982	$37.50	$75.00	$150.00
Jan and Dean, "Surf City" (Liberty 55580)	1963	$4.50	$9.00	$18.00
Joy Division, "Love Will Tear Us Apart" / "These Days" (Factory FAC US 23) (white label promo)	1980	$25.00	$50.00	$100.00
The Larks, "Honey From The Bee" (Apollo 475) (white label promo)	1955	$25.00	$50.00	$100.00
John Lennon, "Slippin' and Slidin' (mono/stereo versions) (Apple P-1883)	1975	$50.00	$100.00	$200.00
The Mamas and the Papas, "Go Where You Wanna Go" (Dunhill 4018) (white label promo)	1966	$5.00	$10.00	$20.00
Barry Manilow, "Could It Be Magic (7:17 version)" / "Cloudburst" (Bell 45,422)	1970	$5.00	$10.00	$20.00
Paul McCartney and Wings, "Silly Love Songs" (2 versions) (Capitol P-4256)	1976	$6.25	$12.50	$25.00
The Moody Blues, "Nights in White Satin" (Deram 85023) (brown-white promo label, star on "plug side")	1968	$3.75	$7.50	$15.00
Dolly Parton, "9 to 5" (RCA 12133) (pink label, blue vinyl)	1980	$5.00	$10.00	$20.00
Pink Floyd, "Arnold Layne" (Tower 333)	1967	$37.50	$75.00	$150.00
(with rare picture sleeve, add:)	1967	$187.50	$375.00	$750.00
REO Speedwagon, "Roll With The Changes" (long/short versions) (Epic 50545)	1978	$2.50	$5.00	$10.00
Linda Ronstadt, "Lago Azul" (Asylum 45464) ("Blue Bayou" in Spanish)	1977	$2.50	$5.00	$10.00
Bob Seger, "Ramblin' Gamblin' Man" (Capitol 2297) (green label promo)	1968	$2.50	$5.00	$10.00
Simon and Garfunkel, "7 O'Clock News - Silent Night" (same on both sides) (Columbia JZSP 116469)	1966	$6.25	$12.50	$25.00
Ronnie Spector and the E Street Band, "Say Goodbye To Hollywood" (same on both sides) (Epic ASF 350)	1977	$8.75	$17.50	$35.00
Bruce Springsteen, "Born To Run" (mono/stereo) (Columbia 10209)	1975	$12.50	$25.00	$50.00
10cc, "Rubber Bullets" (UK 49015) (blue promo label)	1973	$3.00	$6.00	$12.00
The Traveling Wilburys, "Handle With Care" (Wilbury 27732) (brown Warner promo label)	1988	$3.75	$7.50	$15.00
U2, "New Year's Day" (Island 99915) (blue promo label)	1983	$4.50	$9.00	$18.00
The Who, "Who Are You" (long/short versions) (MCA 40948)	1978	$3.00	$6.00	$12.00
Stevie Wonder, "A Place In The Sun" (Tamla 54139) (red vinyl, white promo)	1966	$6.25	$12.50	$25.00
Neil Young, "Everybody Knows This Is Nowhere" (Reprise 0819) (if acoustic version, first pressing)	1969	$75.00	$150.00	$300.00
(if rock version, second pressing, "RE-1" in dead wax)	1969	$5.00	$10.00	$20.00

12-inch	Year	VG	VG+	NM
The B-52s, "Give Me Back My Man" / "Strobe Light" (Warner Bros. PRO-A-927)	1980	$3.00	$6.00	$12.00
Beck, "Loser" (same on both sides) (DGC 4629)	1993	$2.50	$5.00	$10.00
David Bowie, "Space Oddity" / "Ashes to Ashes" (RCA DJL1-3795)	1980	$5.00	$10.00	$20.00
(if above contains a set of stamps, add:)	1980	$2.50	$5.00	$10.00
The Clash, "The Magnificent Seven" / Lightning Strikes" / "One More Time" / "One More Dub" (Epic AS 905)	1980	$3.75	$7.50	$15.00
Creedence Clearwater Revival, "I Heard It Through The Grapevine" (11:05) (same on both sides) (Fantasy 759-D-LP)	1976	$5.00	$10.00	$20.00
Depeche Mode, "Leave in Silence" / "Photograph" / "My Secret Garden" (2 versions) (Sire PRO-A-1084)	1982	$7.50	$15.00	$30.00
Duran Duran, "Hungry Like The Wolf" / "Lonely In Your Nightmare" / "Rio" (Harvest SPRO-9786/7)	1982	$5.00	$10.00	$20.00
The English Beat, "Tears of a Clown" / "Hands Off... She's Mine" / "Twist and Crawl" (Sire PRO-A-874)	1980	$3.75	$7.50	$15.00
Fleetwood Mac, "Tusk" / "Never Make Me Cry" (Warner Bros. PRO-A-831)	1979	$3.00	$6.00	$12.00
The Go-Go's, "Vacation" / "Beatnik Beach" (IRS 70961)	1982	$2.00	$4.00	$8.00
Michael Jackson, "Jam" (13 versions) (Epic ES 4580)	1991	$7.50	$15.00	$30.00
Howard Jones, "New Song" (2 versions) / "Conditioning" / "Change the Man" (Elektra 4944)	1983	$2.50	$5.00	$10.00
Kid Creole and the Coconuts, "Annie I'm Not Your Daddy" (two versions) (Sire PRO-A-2005)	1983		$3.00	$6.00
Living Colour, "Cult of Personality" (and four live songs) (Epic EAS 01265)	1988	$2.50	$5.00	$10.00
Madness, "One Step Beyond" / "My Girl" / "Madness" (Sire PRO-A-852)	1980	$3.75	$7.50	$15.00
Barry Manilow, "En El Copa" (same on both sides) (Arista SP-21) (Spanish-language version of "Copacabana")	1978	$6.25	$12.50	$25.00
Meat Loaf, "Paradise By The Dashboard Light" (3 versions) (Epic/Cleveland International AS 477) (one version does not have the play-by-play commentary, allowing local jocks to "make their own")	1978	$5.00	$10.00	$20.00
Olivia Newton-John with the Electric Light Orchestra, "Xanadu" (MCA 2315) (10-inch single, picture disc promo)	1980	$150.00	$300.00	$600.00
Nirvana, "Smells Like Teen Spirit" / "Even In His Youth" / "Aneurysm" (DGC 4344) (yellow vinyl)	1991	$5.00	$10.00	$20.00
Orchestral Manœuvres in the Dark, "Georgia" / "Souvenir" / "She's Leaving" / "Joan of Arc" (Virgin/Epic AE 1403)	1981	$3.75	$7.50	$15.00
Pet Shop Boys, "West End Girls" (Bobcat 05019) (rare early version)	1984	$10.00	$20.00	$40.00
The Plimsouls, "A Million Miles Away" / "The Oldest Story" /Magic Touch" (Geffen PRO-A-2068)	1983	$3.00	$6.00	$12.00
Prince, "1999" (short/long versions) (Warner Bros. PRO-A-1070)	1982	$15.00	$30.00	$60.00
The Ramones, "I Wanna Be Sedated" (Sire PRO-A-3193)	1988	$5.00	$10.00	$20.00
Scorpions, "Rock You Like A Hurricane" (same on both sides) (Mercury MK 212)	1982	$2.00	$4.00	$8.00
Simply Red, "If You Don't Know Me By Now" (same on both sides) (Elektra ED 5378)	1989	$2.00	$4.00	$8.00
Frank Sinatra, "Night and Day" / "Everybody Ought To Be In Love" (Reprise RPO-A-674)	1977	$20.00	$40.00	$80.00
Tears for Fears, "Everybody Wants To Rule The World" (same on both sides) (Mercury PRO-340-1)	1985	$2.00	$4.00	$8.00
U2, "I Will Follow" / Steve Winwood, "Night Train" (Island PRO-A2-940 RE-1)	1980	$17.50	$35.00	$70.00
X, "Breathless" / "Riding With Mary" (Elektra 4912)	1983	$2.50	$5.00	$10.00

LPs	Year	VG	VG+	NM
Frankie Avalon, The Young Frankie Avalon (Chancellor 5002) (white label promo)	1959	$15.00	$30.00	$60.00
The Beach Boys, Surf's Up (Brother/Reprise RS 6453) (white label promo)	1971	$10.00	$20.00	$40.00
The Beatles, Rarities (Capitol SN-12209) (green label, withdrawn after release, all copies have generic white sleeve)	1979	$75.00	$150.00	$300.00
James Brown, Live at the Apollo (King 826) (white label promo, timing strip on front cover)	1963	$125.00	$250.00	$500.00
Chicago, Chicago (Columbia, no number) (17 LP's)	1976	$50.00	$100.00	$200.00
Eric Clapton, Slowhand (RSO 035) (white vinyl)	1977	$6.25	$12.50	$25.00

LPs	Year	VG	VG+	NM
Concrete Blond, Bloodletting (IRS 82037) (promo-only, black vinyl, generic cover with sticker)	1990	$6.25	$12.50	$25.00
Dire Straits, Love Over Gold (Warner Bros. 23728-DJ) (pressed on Quiex II vinyl)	1982	$12.50	$25.00	$50.00
Bob Dylan, The Freewheelin' Bob Dylan				
(if on Columbia CL 1986, mono, "Guaranteed High Fidelity" on label, plays "Let Me Die In My Footsteps," "Rocks and Gravel," "Uncle John Birch Blues," "Gamblin' Willie's Dead Man's Hand," Label does NOT list these songs. Stamper number in dead wax ends in "-1," followed by a letter)	1963	$5,000.	$10,000.	$15,000.
(if on Columbia CL 1986, mono, white label promo, label and timing strip lists the deleted tracks, but record plays the "correct" tracks)	1963	$2,000.	$3,000.	$4,000.
(if on Columbia CL 1986, mono, white label promo, label lists deleted tracks, but timing strip lists, and record plays, the "correct" tracks)	1963	$250.00	$500.00	$1,000.00
(if on Columbia CL 1986, mono, white label promo, timing strip lists deleted tracks, but label lists, and record plays, the "correct" tracks)	1963	$200.00	$400.00	$800.00
(if on Columbia CL 1986, mono, white label promo, label AND timing strip list, and record plays, "correct" tracks)	1963	$125.00	$250.00	$500.00
(if on Columbia CL 1986, mono, "Guaranteed High Fidelity" on label, corrected version (record plays what label says)	1963	$10.00	$20.00	$40.00
The Electric Light Orchestra, Ole ELO (United Artists SP-123)				
(if gold vinyl promo with generic cover)	1976	$12.50	$25.00	$50.00
(if red, blue or white vinyl promo with generic cover)	1976	$20.00	$40.00	$80.00
(if gold vinyl, stock cover except for single line "Ole ELO" without "Electric Light Orchestra" underneath at top of front cover)	1976	$25.00	$50.00	$100.00
Fleetwood Mac, Rumours (Warner Bros. PRO-A-652) (embossed cover)	1977	$12.50	$25.00	$50.00
Stan Freberg, Uncle Stan Wants You (Capitol 80700) (promo only LP)	1961	$31.25	$62.50	$125.00
Green Day, Dookie (Reprise 45529)				
(if on clear green vinyl, plain white cover)	1994	$8.75	$17.50	$35.00
(if on pale green vinyl)	1994	$7.50	$15.00	$30.00
Ice-T, O.G. Original Gangster (Sire PRO-A-4959) (radio-ready version, not available otherwise on U.S. vinyl)	1991	$10.00	$20.00	$40.00
Jethro Tull, Thick as a Brick (Reprise 2072) (banded for airplay)	1972	$7.50	$15.00	$30.00
Elton John, Captain Fantastic and the Brown Dirt Cowboy (MCA 2142) (brown vinyl, autographed by Elton John and Bernie Taupin)	1975	$75.00	$150.00	$300.00
The Kinks, The Kink Kontroversy (Reprise R-6197) (white label promo)	1966	$50.00	$100.00	$200.00
Led Zeppelin, Led Zeppelin (Atlantic 7208) (album also known as Led Zeppelin IV, Runes or Zoso)				
(if on Atlantic 7208, mono, white label promo only)	1971	$75.00	$150.00	$300.00
(if on Atlantic SD 7208, stereo, white label promo)	1971	$37.50	$75.00	$150.00
Lynyrd Skynyrd, "One More From The Road" (MCA L-33-1946)				
(if on black vinyl)	1976	$6.25	$12.50	$25.00
(if on red, blue, gold or purple vinyl, value is equal for all versions)	1976	$12.50	$25.00	$50.00
Bob Marley and the Wailers, Rastaman Vibration (Island ILPS 9383) (promo package with burlap box and press kit)	1976	$25.00	$50.00	$100.00
The Steve Miller Band, Greatest Hits 1974-1978 (Capitol SOO-11872) (blue vinyl promo)	1978	$7.50	$15.00	$30.00
P.M. Dawn, The Bliss Album (Gee Street 6768) (promo-only vinyl)	1993	$5.00	$10.00	$20.00
Elvis Presley, Special Palm Sunday Programming (RCA Victor 461) (contains record and programming booklet)	1967	$375.00	$750.00	$1,500.00
Queen, Queen (Elektra 75064) (gold embossing on front cover)	1973	$12.50	$25.00	$50.00
Tommy Roe, Sheila (ABC Paramount 432)	1962	$12.50	$25.00	$50.00
Todd Rundgren, Something/Anything (Bearsville 2066) (2 LPs) (one red vinyl, the other blue vinyl)	1972	$75.00	$150.00	$300.00
Rush, Rush 'n Roulette (Mercury MK-185) ("trick-tracked" for six grooves; each groove contains a different song)	1981	$25.00	$50.00	$100.00
Santana, Santana (Columbia 9781)	1969	$3.75	$7.50	$15.00
Sonny and Cher, Baby Don't Go (Reprise 6177) (white label promo)	1965	$12.50	$25.00	$50.00

LPs	Year	VG	VG+	NM
Rod Stewart, Every Picture Tells A Story (Mercury 609) (white label promo)	1971	$6.25	$12.50	$25.00
Talking Heads, Speaking In Tongues (Warner Bros. 23771) (clear vinyl, plastic box; some stock copies were pressed this way as well)	1983	$10.00	$20.00	$40.00
Toto, Toto IV Columbia 37928) (promo-only picture disc)	1981	$4.50	$9.00	$18.00
Gene Vincent, Bluejean Bop (Capitol 764) (yellow promo label)	1957	$100.00	$200.00	$400.00
War, Radio Free War (United Artists 103) (blue vinyl, promo only)	1974	$6.25	$12.50	$25.00
Yes, Close to the Edge (Atlantic 7244) (white label mono copies, banded for airplay)	1972	$12.50	$25.00	$50.00

While the Temptations' "Since I Lost My Baby" was a big hit, most promo collectors will search out a white label pressing because it was pressed in smaller quantities than the stock copy. From the Collection of Val Shively.

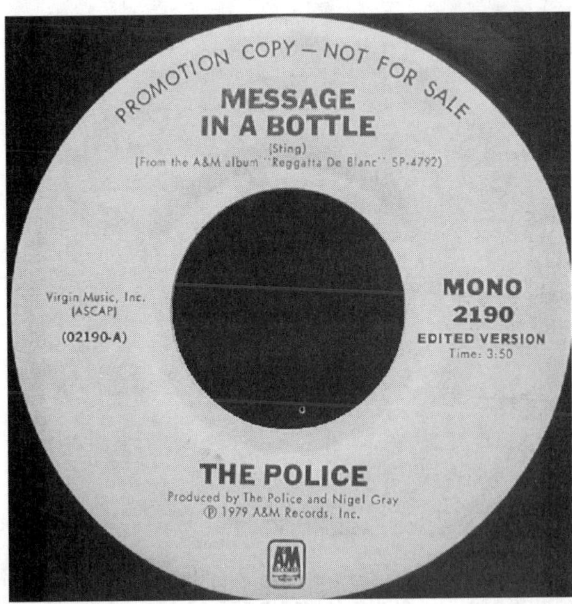

A typical A&M white label promo pressing. Usually the print is color-coded—black print for monaural pressings (like this 45 in 1979), red print on the B-side for stereo pressings.

PUNK

History: Punk music was born in London, as disaffected teens rebelled against glam music and disco, creating their own sound with angry, jarring guitars, coarse lyrics, and an attitude that nothing is sacred.

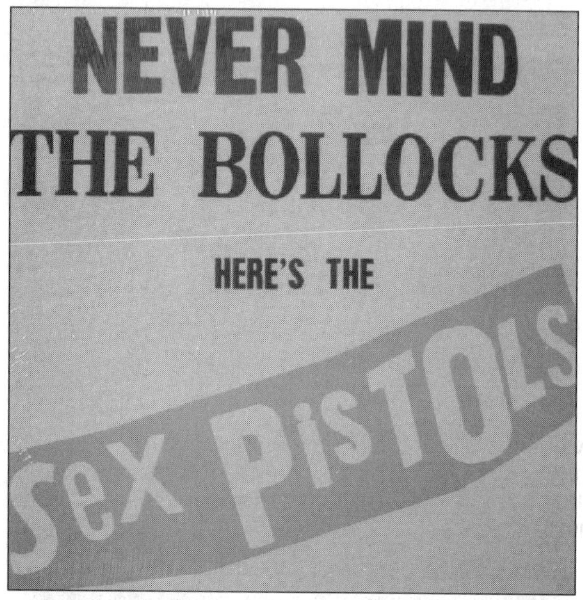

The Sex Pistols' first, last and only licensed LP, *Never Mind the Bollocks Here's the Sex Pistols.* Courtesy Last Vestige Music Store, Albany, N.Y.

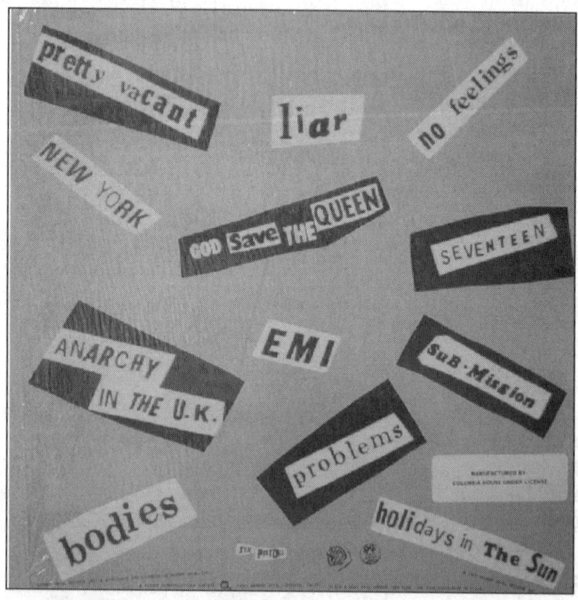

In case you're wondering what the title of the song in the white box on the lower right of the back of this album is, it's actually "Manufactured by Columbia House Under License." Amazing what one can purchase through mail order catalogs. Courtesy Last Vestige Music Store, Albany, N.Y.

The first punk group to achieve worldwide fame (or notoriety, depending on how you look at it) was the Sex Pistols. Led by sneering lead singer Johnny Rotten, the Pistols were confrontational in interviews, taunted the audiences, and played three-chord rock like it was their last breath of life. Their first UK singles, on EMI and A&M respectively, were quickly pulled from shelves because of their confrontational material; the band finally signed with Virgin UK, which released their anti-monarchy song "God Save The Queen" during Queen Elizabeth's 50th birthday celebration. The Pistols eventually toured America, then broke up after that tour ended.

The Sex Pistols may have been the first punk band to achieve fame and fortune, but they were not the last. Before long, punk groups were appearing throughout England, including groups like the Clash, Siouxie and the Banshees, X-Ray Spex, and the Buzzcocks.

Although the most famous proponents of punk music came from England, the American punk scene had its own stars, many of whom recorded collectible singles and albums. Early American punk bands included Iggy and the Stooges, the Ramones, and MC5, all of whom still have a loyal following today. Many other American punk recordings were on small labels like SST, Alternative Tentacles, or Ism, and the lyrics were more vulgar than their British counterparts. Such groups included the Dead Kennedys, Black Flag, the Minutemen, X, and the Butthole Surfers. The prices listed are for American pressings only.

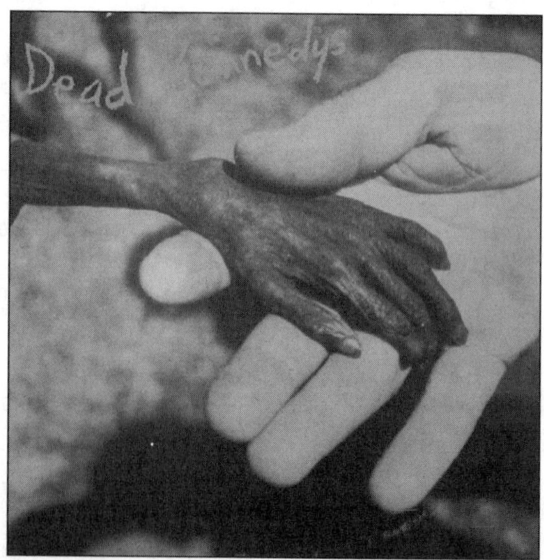

Undoubtedly the most vocal American punk band, the Dead Kennedys tested the boundaries of free speech in almost every song they ever performed. Courtesy Last Vestige Music Store, Albany, N.Y.

Trivia

Wendy O. Williams and the Plasmatics may have been the first group—punk or otherwise—to incorporate chainsaws and shaving cream as musical instruments. They lasted long enough to have one major-label release; their other recordings were on independent labels.

The Plasmatics' major-label debut, *Coup d'Etat,* was also their last album before Wendy O. Williams embarked on a solo career. Photo Credit: Courtesy Last Vestige Music Store, Albany, N.Y.

What To Look For: With British punk bands, the UK pressings are more desirable to punk collectors than the American releases, unless the American album has different tracks or a different running order (some copies of the Sex Pistols' *Never Mind the Bullocks* and the Clash's *The Clash* fall into this category). Sex Pistols collectors, for example, are more interested in finding the rare UK 7-inch pressings of "Anarchy in the U.K." on EMI (UK), and of "God Save The Queen" on A&M (UK). As for American releases, some punk labels like SST and Alternative Tentacles have actually kept their artists' records in print for years, meaning the discs and songs are as easily obtainable today as they were 20 years ago.

The rare items in this genre are radio and promotional pressings, as well as 10-inch "gimmick" releases. The records of one punk group, the Misfits, have sold for as much as $350 in near-mint condition. Many of their records were pressed on colored vinyl, in very small print runs (some as low as 16 copies!). Because of this, many Misfits records have been counterfeited, so check with a reputable dealer who is an expert in alternative/punk music.

Even though the lyrics on this record reference old 70s shows like "Fridays," "That's Incredible" and "Quincy," Black Flag's *TV Party* has remained in print well into the 1990s.

If this picture sleeve from the Misfits' single "Halloween" contains a lyric sheet, the sleeve may be worth $40 in near-mint condition. Without the lyric sheet, deduct up to $5 from a near-mint copy. Courtesy Good Rockin' Tonight / Collectors Universe.

References: McNeil, Legs and McCann, Gillian, *Please Kill Me: The Uncensored History of Punk*, Penguin, New York 1996; Neely, Tim, *Goldmine Price Guide to Alternative Records*, Krause Publications, Iola, Wisconsin, 1996; Southern, Terry, *Virgin: A History of Virgin Records*, A Publishing Company, Axminster, Devon, England, 1996.

Trivia

The song "Ça Plane Pour Moi" by Belgian punk-rocker Plastic Bertrand was a minor hit in America. The melody for the song was later appropriated by the punk group The Damned for their song "Jet Boy Jet Girl."

The actual title of "Ça Plane Pour Moi," in English, is "This Life's For Me."

Web pages: House of the Rising Punk, a directory of punk Web sites from around the world: *http://www.punkrock.org*; a page for the Misfits: *http://www.misfits.com.*

45s	Year	VG	VG+	NM
Bad Religion, "Atomic Garden" (Sympathy for the Record Industry 158)	1991		$2.00	$4.00
(with picture sleeve, add:)	1991		$2.00	$4.00
Black Flag, "Nervous Breakdown" / "Fix Me" / "I've Had It" / "Wasted" (SST 001)				
(if red SST label, first pressing)	1978	$2.50	$5.00	$10.00
(if blue SST label, subsequent pressings)	1978		$2.00	
Black Flag, "TV Party" / "I've Got To Run" / "My Rules"				
(if on SST 101)	1981		$2.00	$4.00
(if on SST/Unicorn 95006, contains "TV Party" on both sides)	1981	$4.00	$8.00	$16.00
The Butthole Surfers, "Hurdy Gurdy Man" / "Barking Dogs" (Rough Trade RUS 97-3)				
(pressed on gold vinyl)	1990		$3.00	$6.00
The Buzzcocks, "Everybody's Happy Nowadays" / "Why Can't I Touch It" (IRS 9001)	1979		$2.50	$5.00
(with picture sleeve, add:)	1979		$2.50	$5.00
The Clash, "Rock the Casbah"				
(if on Epic 03245, B-side is "Long Time Jerk")	1982			$3.00
(if on Epic 05540, B-side is "Long Time Jerk")	1984			$3.00
(if on Epic 08470, gray label, B-side is "Should I Stay or Should I Go")	1988			$3.00
The Cramps, "Surfin' Bird" / "The Way I Walk" (Vengeance 666)	1978	$7.50	$15.00	$30.00
(with picture sleeve, add:)	1978	$8.75	$17.50	$35.00
The Damned, "Dr. Jeckyl and Mr. Hyde" / "Looking At You (live)" (IRS 9022)	1981	$2.00	$4.00	$8.00
(with picture sleeve, add:)	1981	$2.00	$4.00	$8.00
The Dead Boys, "Sonic Reducer" / "Down In Flames" (Sire 1004)	1977	$3.00	$6.00	$12.00
(with picture sleeve, add:)	1977	$3.00	$6.00	$12.00
The Dead Kennedys, "California Uber Alles" / "The Man With The Dogs"				
(if on Alternative Tentacles AT-95-41)	1979	$5.00	$10.00	$20.00
(if on Optional Music OPT-2)	1979	$3.00	$6.00	$12.00
The Dickies, "Nights In White Satin" / "Manny, Moe and Jack" (A&M 2225)	1980	$2.50	$5.00	$10.00
(with picture sleeve [sleeve withdrawn because it showed Dickies in KKK robes], add:)	1980	$12.50	$25.00	$50.00
Fear, "I Love Livin' In The City" / "Now You're Dead" (Criminal Records, no number)	1978	$61.50	$125.00	$250.00
(with picture sleeve, add:)	1978	$61.50	$125.00	$250.00
Flipper, "Love Canal" / "Ha Ha Ha" (Thermidor/Suberranean T 1 / SUB 7)	1980		$3.00	$6.00
(with picture sleeve, add:)	1980		$3.00	$6.00
The Germs, "Lexicon Devil" / "Circle One" / "No God" (Slash 101)	1978	$5.00	$10.00	$20.00
(with picture sleeve, add:)	1978	$5.00	$10.00	$20.00
The Injections, "Prison Walls" / "Lies" (Radio Active 04)	1980	$50.00	$100.00	$200.00
Ism, "I Think I Love You" / "A7" (S.I.N. 003)	1983	$5.00	$10.00	$20.00
(with picture sleeve, add:)	1983	$5.00	$10.00	$20.00
The Minutemen, "Courage" / "What Is It?" / "Stories" (SST PSST E58)	1985	$2.00	$4.00	$8.00
(with rubberstamped picture sleeve, add:)	1985	$3.00	$6.00	$12.00
The Misfits, "Horror Business" / "Teenagers from Mars" / "Children in Heat" (Plan 9 PL 1009)				
(if on yellow vinyl, 5000 copies pressed)	1979	$15.00	$30.00	$60.00
(if on black vinyl, 25 copies pressed)	1979	$50.00	$100.00	$200.00
(with picture sleeve and insert, add:)	1979	$25.00	$50.00	$100.00
(with picture sleeve only, add:)	1979	$12.50	$25.00	$50.00
The Saints, "(I'm) Stranded" / "No Time" (Sire 1005)	1977	$3.75	$7.50	$15.00
(if marked "promotional copy")	1977	$3.75	$7.50	
(with picture sleeve, add:)	1977	$3.50	$7.00	
The Sex Pistols, "Pretty Vacant" / "Sub-Mission" (Warner Bros. 8516)	1978	$5.00	$10.00	$20.00
(with picture sleeve, add:)	1978	$2.50	$5.00	$10.00
Siouxie and the Banshees, "Hong Kong Garden" / "Overground" (Polydor 14561)	1979	$10.00	$20.00	$40.00
Siouxie and the Banshees, "Dear Prudence" / "Tattoo" (Geffen 29358)	1984			$3.00
(with picture sleeve, add:)	1984			$3.00
Suicidal Tendencies, "I'll Hate You Better" /"Mandatory Love Songs" / "Just Another Love Song" / "Won't Fall In Love Today" (Epic 74868)				
(heart-shaped purple vinyl pressing)	1993	$2.00	$4.00	$8.00
X, "Adult Books" / "We're Desperate" (Dangerhouse D-88)	1978	$10.00	$20.00	$40.00
(with picture sleeve, add:)	1978	$10.00	$20.00	$40.00
X, "Blue Spark" / "Dancing With Tears In My Eyes" (Elektra 69885)	1982	$3.00	$6.00	$12.00
(with picture sleeve, add:)	1982	$3.00	$6.00	$12.00

12-inch	Year	VG	VG+	NM
The Clash, "This Is Radio Clash" / "Radio Clash" / "Outside Broadcast" / "Radio 5" (Epic 02262)	1981	$2.00	$4.00	$8.00
The Clash, "Rock The Casbah" / "Mustapha Dance" (Epic 03144)	1982	$3.00	$6.00	$12.00
The Cramps, "Bikini Girls With Machine Guns" (same on both sides) (Enigma EPRO 253) (DJ)	1989	$2.50	$5.00	$10.00
The Damned, "Eloise" / "Beat Girl" / "Temptation" (MCA 23625)	1986	$2.00	$4.00	$8.00
Siouxie and the Banshees, "Peek-a-Boo" (2 versions) / "False Face" / "Catwalk" (Geffen 20977)	1988	$2.00	$4.00	$8.00

LPs	Year	VG	VG+	NM
Black Flag, Everything Went Black (SST 015) (2 LPs)	1982	$3.75	$7.50	$15.00
The Butthole Surfers, Pschic ... Powerless ... Another Man's Sac (Touch N Go 5)				
(if on clear vinyl)	1985	$5.00	$10.00	$20.00
(if on black vinyl)	1985	$2.50	$5.00	$10.00
The Buzzcocks, Singles Going Steady (IRS SP-001)	1979	$3.00	$6.00	$12.00
(if on IRS SP-75001, reissue)	198??	$2.50	$5.00	$10.00
The Clash, Sandinista! (Epic E3X 37037) (3 LP's)	1981	$5.00	$10.00	$20.00
The Clash, Combat Rock				
(if Epic AS 99-1592, picture disc)	1982	$10.00	$20.00	$40.00
(if Epic AS 99-1595, camouflage green vinyl promo)	1982	$7.50	$15.00	$30.00

LPs	Year	VG	VG+	NM
(if Epic FE 37689, a commercial appears in the middle of "Innoculated City")	1982	$3.75	$7.50	$15.00
(if Epic FE 37689, no commercial in "Innoculated City")	1982	$2.50	$5.00	$10.00
The Damned, Light at The End Of The Tunnel (MCA 2-8024) (2 LP's)	1988	$3.75	$7.50	$15.00
The Dead Boys, We Have Come For Your Children (Sire SRK-6054)	1978	$5.00	$10.00	$20.00
The Dead Kennedys, Fresh Fruit for Rotting Vegetables				
(if on IRS/Faulty Products SP-70014, original with orange cover to distinguish it from imports)	1980	$5.00	$10.00	$20.00
(if on IRS/Faulty Products SP-70014, black front cover, both reissues and imports have this cover)	1980	$3.75	$7.50	$15.00
(if on Faulty Products 70014, nursing home back cover, no mention of IRS Records)	1982	$8.75	$17.50	$35.00
(if on Alternative Tentacles VIRUS 1)	1988	$3.00	$6.00	$12.00
The Dead Kennedys, Frankenchrist (Alternative Tentacles VIRUS 45) (with H.R. Giger poster insert)	1985	$2.50	$5.00	$10.00
The Dickies, The Incredible Shrinking Dickies (A&M SP-4742)				
(if first pressing on yellow vinyl)	1979	$5.00	$10.00	$20.00
(if second pressing on black vinyl)	1979	$3.75	$7.50	$15.00
The Germs, Recorded Live at the Whiskey, June, 1977 (Mohawk SCALP-001)				
(if numbered edition with sticker, first pressing)	1981	$12.50	$25.00	$50.00
(if unnumbered edition, with sticker, second pressing)	1981	$5.00	$10.00	$20.00
The MC5, Kick Out The Jams (Elektra EKS-74042)				
(if gatefold jacket, contains John Sinclair liner notes, brownish Elektra label)	1969	$12.50	$25.00	$50.00
(all other editions)	1969	$5.00	$10.00	$20.00
The Meat Puppets, Too High to Die (London 828 484-1)				
(if bonus 10-inch record is inside and DJ sticker is on jacket, double listed price)	1994	$3.00	$6.00	$12.00

LPs	Year	VG	VG+	NM
The Meatmen, We're The Meatmen... And You Suck (Touch N Go TGLP 001)	198??	$6.25	$12.50	$25.00
The Minutemen, Double Nickels on the Dime (SST 028) (2 LPs)	1984	$3.00	$6.00	$12.00
The Misfits, Legacy of Brutality (Plan 9 PL9-06)				
(if pressed on pink vinyl, 16 copies pressed)	1986	$25.00	$50.00	$100.00
(if pressed on white vinyl, 500 copies pressed)	1986	$6.25	$12.50	$25.00
(if pressed on red vinyl, 500 copies pressed)	1986	$6.25	$12.50	$25.00
(if pressed on black vinyl)	1986	$3.00	$6.00	$12.00
The Plasmatics, Coup d'Etat (Capitol ST-12237)	1982	$3.75	$7.50	$15.00
Redd Kross, Teen Babies from Monsanto (Gasatanka E 1170)	1984	$3.00	$6.00	$12.00
The Sex Pistols, Never Mind The Bollocks Here's The Sex Pistols (Warner Bros. BSK 3147)				
(with sticker "Contains Sub-Mission")	1978	$7.50	$15.00	$30.00
(with custom label)	1978	$6.25	$12.50	$25.00
(with white Warner Bros. label)	1978	$2.50	$5.00	$10.00
Siouxie and the Banshees, The Scream				
(if on Polydor PD1-6207)	1978	$7.50	$15.00	$30.00
(if reissued on Geffen 24046)	1984	$2.50	$5.00	$10.00
Siouxie and the Banshees, The Rapture (Geffen GEF 24630)	1995	$3.00	$6.00	$12.00
The Stooges, The Stooges (Elektra EKS 74051)				
(if first pressing, red label)	1969	$12.50	$25.00	$50.00
(if second pressing, "butterfly" label)	197?	$5.00	$10.00	$20.00
Suicidal Tendencies, How Will I Laugh Tomorrow When I Can't Even Smile Today (Epic FE 44288)	1988	$3.00	$6.00	$12.00
X-Ray Spex, Germ Free Adolescents (Blue Plate CAROL-1813-1)	1992	$3.75	$7.50	$15.00
(first US issue of their 1978 UK album; that disc is worth twice the value of the US copy)				

This Meat Puppets album contains a bonus 10-inch disc. The value of the record increases if the 10-inch disc is inside, and if an identifying DJ sticker is on the front cover. Courtesy Last Vestige Music Store, Albany, N.Y.

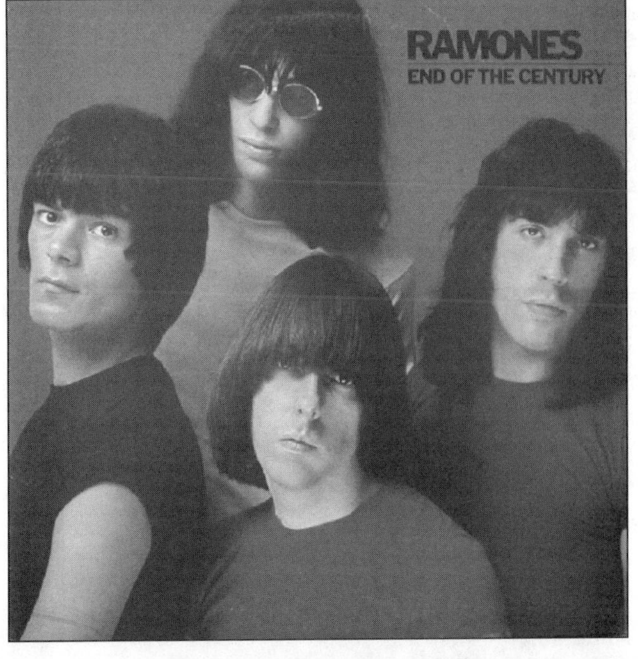

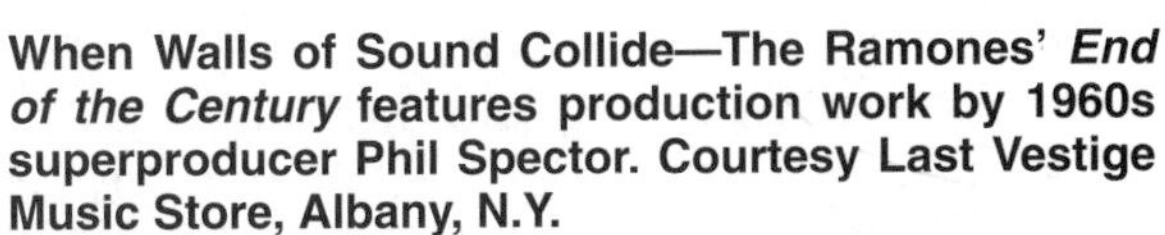

When Walls of Sound Collide—The Ramones' *End of the Century* features production work by 1960s superproducer Phil Spector. Courtesy Last Vestige Music Store, Albany, N.Y.

QUADRAPHONIC RECORDS

History: Quadraphonic recordings were the music industry's first true attempt at "surround sound" albums. Instead of left-right stereo recordings, quad records required four speakers, as well as a new pickup and stereo system. For the listening audience, the sonic benefits would be staggering. One could hear a concert performance as if they were in the center of a symphony orchestra. Or they could hear dazzling special effects, like a screaming guitar swirling from speaker to speaker, traveling around the listener in ways never before attempted.

For the records, the original plan was to provide a disc that could transfer a single signal to the tonearm stylus, which in turn would decode it into four separate signals, each signal sent to a different speaker and providing the listener with sound in front, on the sides, and in back.

Quad made its commercial debut in 1969, when Vanguard Records demonstrated a four-channel reel-to-reel tape at the AES electronics show. One year later, quadraphonic 8-track tapes were successfully introduced into the marketplace.

Also in 1970, Peter Scheiber invented a formula to encode four channels of sound into two, then have it decoded by a home audio equipment attachment. CBS purchased the rights and called this new format "SQ" (for Surround Quadraphonic). By 1970, the CBS family of labels had released enough titles to make quad a viable new format, and companies like Sony, Lafayette, Marantz, Pioneer and Fisher followed suit with new quad-compatible turntables and amplifiers.

A CBS "SQ" Santana quadraphonic record. CBS Quad records are identifiable by a huge gold border around the original cover photo. From the Collection of Mark Anderson

Trivia

When Sly and the Family Stone's Greatest Hits was originally released, the master tapes for three of the songs—"Hot Fun In The Summertime," "Everybody Is A Star," and "Thank You (Falettinme Be Mice Elf Agin)"—were not immediately available. The only mixes available were the 45 single mixes of those three songs; they were placed on Greatest Hits in rechanneled stereo. Six months later, the missing master tapes for those three songs turned up, and they were used on the quad version of Greatest Hits. For more than 20 years, the quad LP of Greatest Hits contained the only true stereo copies of Sly and the Family Stone's most popular recordings.

A rare and highly collectible quadraphonic LP, Sly and the Family Stone's "Greatest Hits." From the Collection of Mark Anderson.

But while CBS was developing a quad format, other record companies, hesitant of paying royalties to a rival record company, began work on their own quad records. RCA's Japanese subsidiary label JVC created the CD-4 quad format, which used a carrier frequency to decode the signals on the record into four distinct channels. After development of a stylus capable of decoding the information, as well as the introduction of "Super Vinyl" to handle all the information on the disc, by 1973 RCA had its own successful CD-4 quad records (which were incompatible with CBS's SQ format). Armed with their new quad format, RCA immediately released four-channel records by Elvis Presley, the Jefferson Airplane and John Denver.

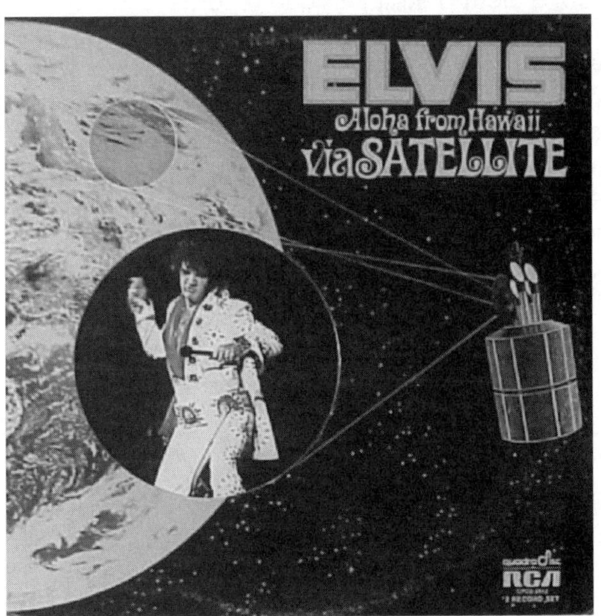

Elvis Presley's *Aloha From Hawaii Via Satellite,* one of the biggest selling quad LPs of all time. From the Collection of Mark Anderson.

While those two formats battled it out for the consumer dollar, an electronics company decided to add a third format. The electronics company Sansui developed its own Quadrasonic-Stereo (QS) home entertainment equipment, and offered the technology for free to any record company who wanted it (Sansui expected to make the profits back on the sales of its audio equipment). So all the non-CBS and non-RCA record companies snatched up Sansui's quad format.

Alice Cooper's "Billion Dollar Babies," heavy metal in the Quadrasonic-Stereo decoding format. From the Collection of Mark Anderson.

For the next few years, the record companies and electronics companies battled and jockeyed over which quad format would stand alone. And consumers who were able to purchase the various quad records found their home entertainment equipment was often not capable of properly decoding the four-channel albums. In many cases, the records sounded muddy (SQ), noisy (CD-4) or indecipherable (QS) And if a home stereo system could play a certain format, it didn't mean it could play *all formats.*

Electronics stores and stereo shops began offering quadraphonic test albums, so their patrons could experience the wonders of four-channel stereo, and would eventually purchase a quad system of their own.

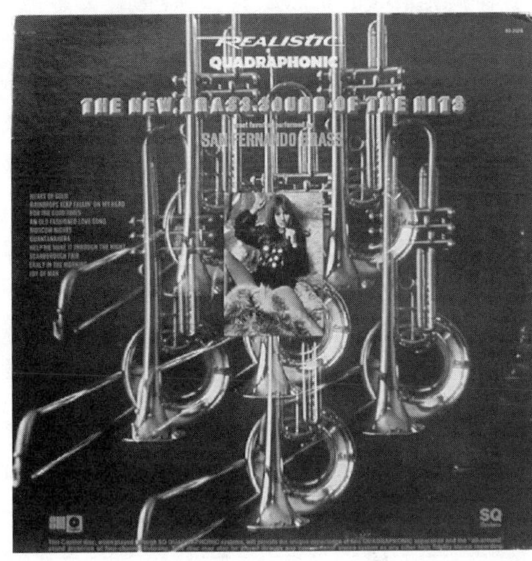

A demonstration album from Radio Shack's "Realistic" division.

Some audio companies compromised by offering multi-format equipment—by 1975, there were new amplifiers on the market capable of decoding all three formats with the flip of a toggle switch. But by then, it was too late. RCA stopped making its CD-4 quad records that year, and CBS and the Sansui formats limped along for another few years before calling it quits.

There were many reasons why the quad record format was a noble failure. Besides the non-uniform decoding system, quad records were priced an extra $1 to $2 over the price of a standard stereo record, despite the quad discs being released six months after the original stereo release. And with the Energy Crisis and oil embargoes of 1974, there was barely enough petroleum to make gasoline, let alone vinyl for records, and some companies sacrificed their quad output in favor of stereo albums and 45s.

Trivia

In the 1970s, some jukebox companies experimented with quadraphonic jukeboxes. Very few of these quad music machines exist today, and the quad 45s that were pressed to stock these four-channel coin machines are extremely rare.

A rare jukebox "Little LP," a four-song quadraphonic pressing of Three Dog Night hits.

As you can see from the "cutout" lower right corner of this Billy Joel album, quad records quickly landed in the cutout bins as the desire for four-channel surround sound ended. From the Collection of Mark Anderson.

But a clear benefit of quad records is that it allowed listeners to hear entirely new mixes of their favorite songs. While the first stereo albums were produced with the artist and the producer working together on the final audio mix, quad records were often made after hours by a technician working off the original master tapes. The guitars may be punched up in quad; the drums may be enhanced or reduced. Some background vocals are more discernable in quad than they were in the stereo mixes.

Many of Pink Floyd's 1970s albums were released in quad, including *The Dark Side of the Moon* and Wish You Were Here. From the Collection of Mark Anderson.

This doesn't mean that every quad LP is a sonic masterpiece in comparison to its stereo LP counterpart. Creedence Clearwater Revival's *Gold* quad LP has very little stereo separation, while ZZ Top's *Tres Hombres* quad LP split the entire group into four different speakers, with almost no centering.

Although quad records had some successes (Elvis Presley's *Aloha From Hawaii Via Satellite* sold a million quad copies), for a while even quad discs took a back seat to quad 8-tracks. Even though the quad 8-tracks were not compatible with standard 8-tracks, there was only one standard format of quad 8-tracks, which allowed record companies to produce more titles in that format. In fact, the only domestic versions of John Lennon's *Imagine* and Paul McCartney's *Band on the Run* are on quad 8-tracks. The quad 8-track format, however, faded away in the late 1970s, as did its standard stereo 8-track counterpart.

What To Look For: Quad albums were not pressed in large numbers, so finding them can be difficult. Quad-equipped turntables and amplifiers have dropped considerably in price; while in the 1970s a deck could sell for as much as $750, today one can find a deck on the Internet or at a yard sale for one third of its original cost.

Trivia

Mike Oldfield's *Tubular Bells* was released in America as a CD-4 record (Virgin QD13-105) and at the same time in England as a SQ record (Virgin QV-2001). Years later, a box set contained a different SQ mix of *Tubular Bells*, including the use of his "original" Sailor's Hornpipe coda.

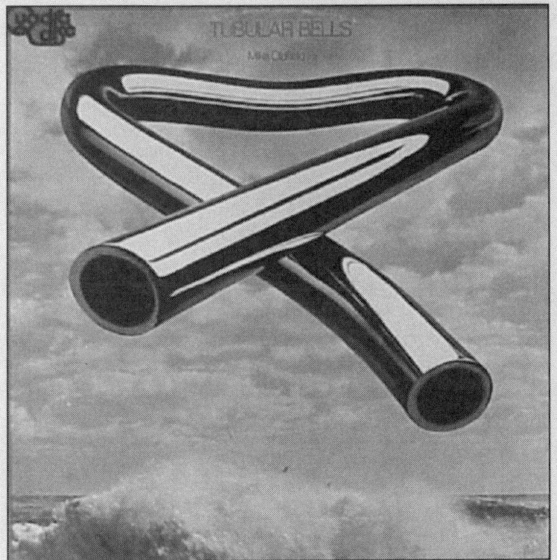

Mike Oldfield's American pressing of *Tubular Bells*. From the Collection of Mark Anderson.

If the quad disc has a considerably different mix than its stereo counterpart, that could increase the record's value. Be aware that not all quad players can play every quad record—CBS records played SQ, RCA records were in CD-4, and everything else appeared in QS format. And for records that were pressed overseas, there are even more quad vinyl and tape formats, none of which are compatible with the U.S. quad formats.

Web pages: Mark Anderson's Quadraphonics page: *http://personal.riverusers.com/~manderso.*

Quadraphonic LPs	Year	VG	VG+	NM
Joan Baez, Diamonds and Rust (A&M QU-54527)	1975	$5.00	$10.00	$20.00
Black Sabbath, Paranoid (Warner Bros. WS4 1887) (with palm trees on label)	1974	$7.50	$15.00	$30.00
The Carpenters, The Singles 1969-1973 (A&M QU-53601)	1974	$5.00	$10.00	$20.00
Johnny Cash, Johnny Cash at San Quentin (Columbia CQ 30961)	1971	$5.00	$10.00	$20.00
Chicago, Chicago at Carnegie Hall (Columbia C4Q 30865) (4 LPs)	1971	$12.50	$25.00	$50.00
Alice Cooper, Billion Dollar Babies (Warner Bros. BS4 2685)	1974	$6.25	$12.50	$25.00
Deep Purple, Stormbringer (Warner Bros. PR4 2832)	1974	$6.25	$12.50	$25.00
The Doors, Best of the Doors (Elektra EQ-5035)	1973	$5.00	$10.00	$20.00
Bob Dylan, Planet Waves (Asylum EQ-1003)	1974	$12.50	$25.00	$50.00
The Eagles, On The Border (Asylum EQ 1004)	1974	$5.00	$10.00	$20.00
The Four Tops, Keeper of the Castle (Command CQD-40011)	1974	$5.00	$10.00	$20.00
Art Garfunkel, Breakaway (Columbia PCQ 33700)	1975	$5.00	$10.00	$20.00
Herbie Hancock, Head Hunters (Columbia CQ 32371)	1973	$6.25	$12.50	$25.00
The Isley Brothers, Go For Your Guns (T-Neck PZQ 34432)	1977	$5.00	$10.00	$20.00
Jefferson Airplane, Volunteers (RCA APD1-0320)				
(if yellow-orange RCA label)	1973	$20.00	$40.00	$80.00
(if tan label reissue)	1975	$12.50	$25.00	$50.00
Billy Joel, Turnstiles (Columbia PCQ 33848)	1976	$5.00	$10.00	$20.00
Quincy Jones, Mellow Madness (A&M QU-54526)	1975	$5.00	$10.00	$20.00
Enoch Light, Big Hits of the Seventies (Project 3 PR4C-6003/4) (2 LP's)	1974	$5.00	$10.00	$20.00
Johnny Mathis, Johnny Mathis In Person (Columbia 2CQ 30979) (2 LP's)	1972	$6.25	$12.50	$25.00
Harold Melvin and the Blue Notes, Wake Up Everybody (Philadelphia International PZQ 33808)	1975	$5.00	$10.00	$20.00
The Mothers of Invention, Over-Nite Sensation (DiscReet MS4 2149)	1973	$10.00	$20.00	$40.00
Mike Oldfield, Tubular Bells (Virgin QR 13-105)	1974	$6.25	$12.50	$25.00
Dolly Parton, My Tennessee Mountain Home (RCA Victor APD1-0033)	1973	$5.00	$10.00	$20.00
Billy Paul, 360 Degrees of Billy Paul (Philadelphia International ZQ 31793)	1972	$5.00	$10.00	$20.00
Pink Floyd, Wish You Were Here (Columbia HC 43453)	1975	$50.00	$100.00	$200.00
Elvis Presley, Aloha From Hawaii Via Satellite (RCA VPSX-6089) (2 LPs)				
(if DJ pressing, with orange label on record, and white timing strip on album jacket)	1973	$500.00	$1,000.00	$2,000.00
(if "Chicken of the Sea" sticker on front cover, Stokely-Van Camp special pressing)	1973	$2,500.00	$3,750.00	$5,000.00
(if dark orange label, "QuadraDisc" on top, "RCA" on bottom)	1973	$25.00	$50.00	$100.00
(if light orange label, "RCA" on side)	1973	$10.00	$20.00	$40.00
(if tan 1975 reissue)	1975	$7.50	$15.00	$30.00
Pure Prairie League, If The Shoe Fits (RCA Victor APD1-1247)	1976	$5.00	$10.00	$20.00
Jerry Reed, Lord, Mr. Ford (RCA Victor APD1-0238)	1973	$6.25	$12.50	$25.00
Santana, Abraxas (Columbia CQ 30130)	1972	$5.00	$10.00	$20.00
Seals and Crofts, Diamond Girl (Warner Bros. BS4 2699)	1974	$5.00	$10.00	$20.00
Simon and Garfunkel, Bridge Over Troubled Water (Columbia CQ 30995)	1971	$6.25	$12.50	$25.00
Paul Simon, Still Crazy After All These Years (Columbia PCQ 33540)	1975	$5.00	$10.00	$20.00
Sly and the Family Stone, Sly and the Family Stone's Greatest Hits (Epic EQ 30325)	1971	$25.00	$50.00	$100.00
Steely Dan, Pretzel Logic (Command QD-40015)	1974	$5.00	$10.00	$20.00
Three Dog Night, Hard Labor (Command QD-40014)	1974	$5.00	$10.00	$20.00
Various Artists, Magnavox Album of Christmas Music (Columbia Special Prod. CSQ 11093)	1972	$5.00	$10.00	$20.00
Rick Wakeman, Journey to the Center of the Earth (A&M QU-53621)	1974	$6.25	$12.50	$25.00
Dionne Warwicke, Then Came You (Warner Bros. BS4 2846)	1975	$5.00	$10.00	$20.00
Frank Zappa, Apostrophe (') (DiscReet DS4 2175)	1974	$8.75	$17.50	$35.00

RAP

History: What we know as Rap today evolved from a myriad of sources. It was doo-wop music without the melody. It was a double-dutch rope-skipping chant without the rope. It was the original poetry and social commentary of the Last Poets and Gil Scott-Heron, and later evolved, with the addition of turntables, rhymes, and samples, into one of the most dominant musical styles in contemporary music.

The Last Poets were one of the first groups to mix poetry and rhetoric with a rhythmic beat.

With a sound that was born in the streets of the Bronx, Harlem, Brooklyn, and Manhattan in the 1970s, early rap records took instrumental backings from other songs while groups of poets "rapped" over the instrumental tracks. This actually evolved from Jamaican club DJs, who "toasted" or recited poetry over their instrumental dub jams. The first Bronx-based rap-turntable pioneers were Pete "DJ" Jones, Grandmaster Flowers and Reggie Wells; by the mid-1970s, the Bronx rap scene included Afrika Bambaataa and the SoulSonic Force, Cool Herc, Kurtis Blow, Grandmaster Flash and the Furious Five, and DJ Hollywood.

Some early rap recordings were actually released on major labels, and became R&B hits, such as DJ Hollywood's "Shock, Shock the House" and Kurtis Blow's "The Breaks." Rap also made early appearances in pop music, either through established artists like Blondie ("Rapture") or through novelty studio acts like the Afternoon Delights ("General Hospi-Tale," a rapping history of the soap opera *"General Hospital"*).

Trivia

Grandmaster Flash may have been the first rap DJ to ever be mentioned in a #1 pop song, as Blondie mentions his name (along with hip-hop legend Fab 5 Freddy) in the rapping section of her song "Rapture." She learned of Flash's turntable prowess when she attended an MC tournament in the Bronx, which Flash had won.

Many Sugarhill albums, including this one, have been recently reissued by Rhino. Look on the back cover for a Rhino reissue listing—it may be on the record's shrinkwrap.

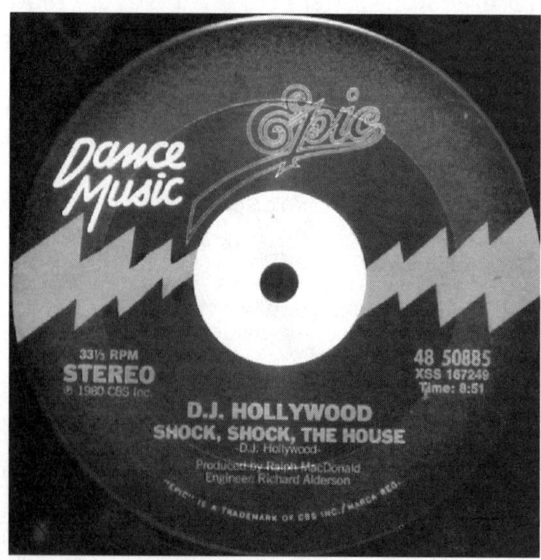

DJ Hollywood was one of the first rap artists to receive a major-label release, as "Shock Shock the House" became a club hit.

Trivia

The Sugarhill Gang's "Rapper's Delight" has lyrics about "never let an MC steal your rhyme," but in fact that's exactly what happened with this song. Rapper Big Bank Hank makes references in the song to "Casanova," which in fact was rapper Grandmaster Kaz. Kaz was supposed to receive compensation for letting Big Bank Hank use the lyrics (including a Sugar Hill contract for his rap group, the Cold Crush Brothers), but he never received compensation or a contract. Never let an MC steal your rhyme, indeed.

But it wasn't until 1979, when Sugar Hill Records released a song called "Rapper's Delight," that most of America received their first taste of rap. Recorded by a studio group called the "Sugarhill Gang," "Rapper's Delight" became the first 12-inch dance record to reach the Top 40 on *Billboard's* singles chart. It also sent record company representatives on a feeding frenzy through the Bronx, looking for rap artists and groups that could give their label that same success.

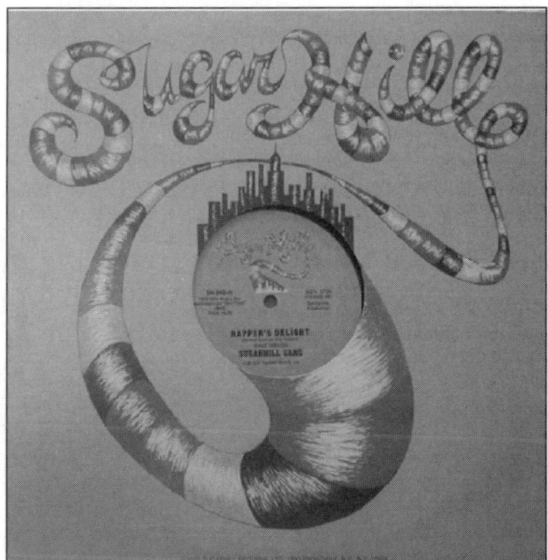

Wonder Mike, Big Bank Hank and Master G, also known as the Sugarhill Gang, with the first "crossover" rap record, "Rapper's Delight."

In the early 1980s, the predominant rap theme was the prowess—lyrically, physically, and sexually—of the rappers behind the microphone, and the party-all-night call-and-response between them and the audience. But in 1983, Grandmaster Flash and the Furious Five's "The Message" changed all that. With its lyrics of inner-city slums, poverty, urban desolation, and despair, "The Message" has been hailed as one of the most important records—rap or otherwise—in music history. It projected Grandmaster Flash and the Furious Five to the rap forefront, and proved to the music world that rap was more than just party music.

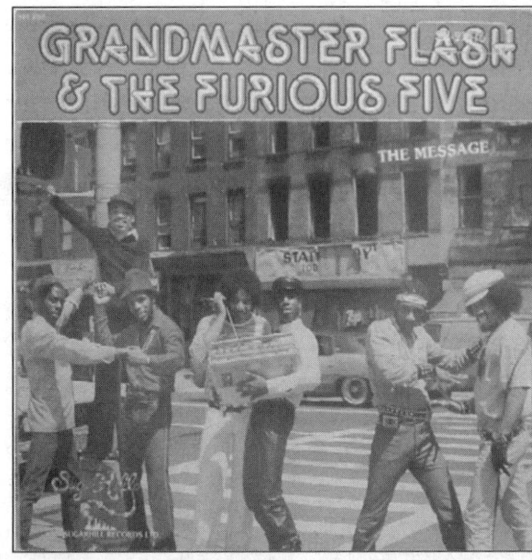

The title song on this album changed rap music forever, Grandmaster Flash and the Furious Five's *The Message.*

That hard-edged rap evolved when two other New York City-based rap troupes, Run-D.M.C. and Public Enemy, took the stage. Run-D.M.C. was one of the first rap groups to embrace rock music as part of rap. Their first single, "Rock Box," had screaming guitars throughout the song, and their hit songs "King of Rock" and "Jam-Master Jammin'" continued this trend. In 1986, Run-D.M.C. collaborated with Steven Tyler and Joe Perry of Aerosmith for a new rap-meets-rock version of the Aerosmith classic "Walk This Way," which became a Top 10 rock, pop, and soul hit.

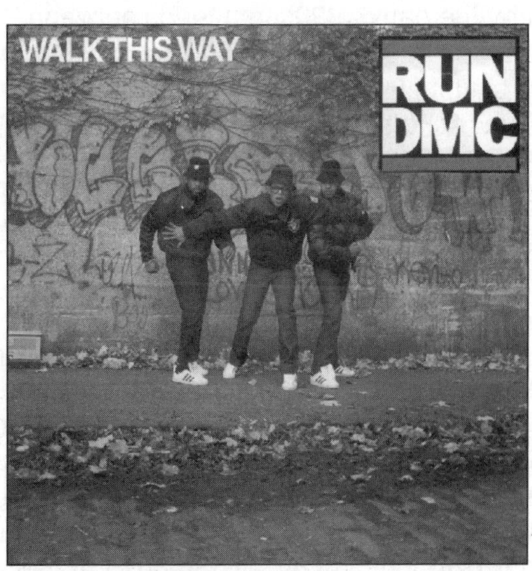

The pride of Hollis, Queens, New York, Run-D.M.C. with their biggest hit, *"Walk This Way."*

Public Enemy, on the other hand, made rap political. Their raps included the imagery of Martin Luther King and Malcolm X, layered over funk and electronic rhythms, creating a rap concept that was part funk, part hip-hop, part social commentary, and part shock. With songs like "Fight the Power," "911 is a Joke," and "Night of the Living Baseheads," Public Enemy's Chuck D issued a rallying call to all disaffected youth to stand up and fight for their rights.

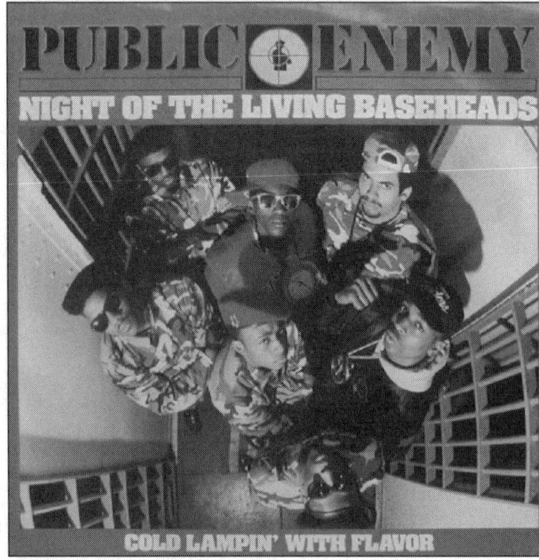

A single from Public Enemy's album *It Takes A Nation of Millions To Hold Us Back.*

By the late 1980s, rap groups such as N.W.A. and the Wu-Tang Clan gave birth to "gangsta rap," which extolled the dilemmas and pleasures of inner-city "thug life." Eventually N.W.A. splintered into separate successful rap acts and groups, including Dr. Dre, Easy-E, and Ice Cube, each influencing rap in their own way.

But by the early 1990s, rap feuds between "West Coast" rappers (which included Dr. Dre, Snoop Doggy Dogg, and Tupac Shakur) and "East Coast" rappers (the Wu-Tang Clan, Notorious B.I.G., and producer Sean "Puff Daddy" Combs) escalated from attacks on each others' albums to verbal sparring at awards shows. The feud eventually culminated with the shooting deaths of rappers Tupac Shakur and the Notorious B.I.G., both of whose assailants were never found and remain anonymous to this day.

Rap itself has continued to evolve, as rap artists experiment with blues (Arrested Development), psychedelia (De La Soul), rock and hard funk (LL Cool J), and Caribbean and Third World polyrhythms (the Fugees). Rap lyrics have even evolved, whether through their meter (the ultra-quick raps of Bone-Thugs-n-Harmony's "Tha Crossroads") or their content (Snoop Doggy Dogg's "Murder Was The Case").

Rap music has also been at the forefront of major censorship issues. When the rap group 2 Live Crew released their album *As Nasty As They Wanna Be*, the lyrical content was so full of sex and adult themes—their Top 40 single "Me So Horny" was on this album—that a Florida record store owner was arrested and served jail time for selling a copy of the album to a minor—the first time in American history that someone went to jail for selling music. 2 Live Crew eventually endured a series of obscenity trials in Florida, both for their album and their live performances, and eventually turned the entire experience into another Top 40 single, "Banned in the U.S.A."

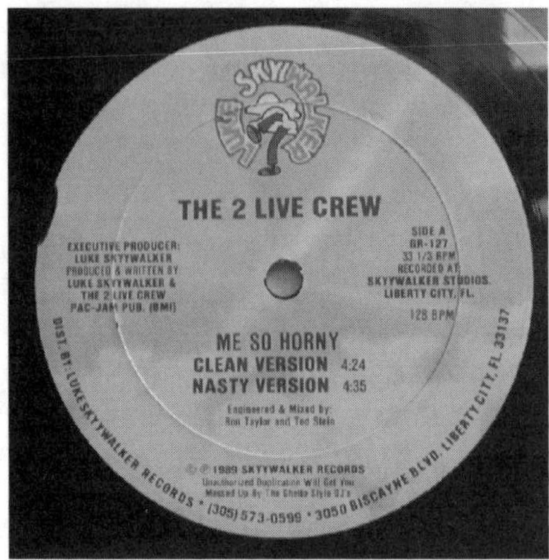

Despite releasing their songs in two versions, clean and adult, 2 Live Crew battled censorship and First Amendment rights throughout their career.

While African-American men have dominated the rap music scene, white male rappers (the Beastie Boys, Third Bass, Vanilla Ice, Eminem), and female rappers (Queen Latifah, the Sequence, Salt-n-Pepa) have broken the mold. Rap music has even re-embraced its Jamaican "toasting" heritage, as artists like Shabba Ranks, Snow, and Shaggy have had rap-reggae hits like "Boombastic," "Informer," and "It Wasn't Me."

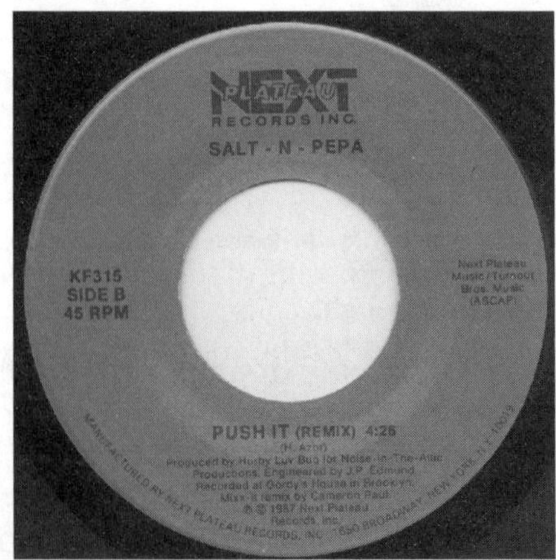

Originally the B-side of a song called "Tramp," Salt-n-Pepa's "Push It" became the first Top 40 hit by a female rap group.

Trivia

A hefty rap trio called the Disco 3 had a massive R&B hit with their first rap single, "Fat Boys." They later changed their name to the Fat Boys, and had a series of successful rap hits, including collaborations with the Beach Boys and with Chubby Checker. Their lineup included "the human beat box," one of their members who could replicate drum beats and scratches with his own voice.

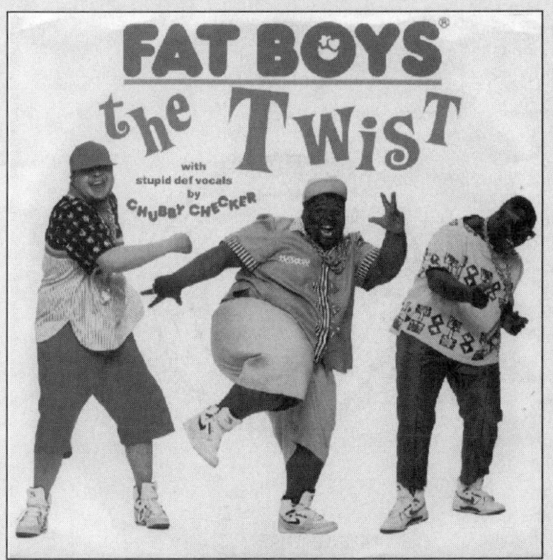

The Fat Boys' most successful hits were rap remakes of 60s hits like "Wipe Out," "Louie Louie," and "The Twist," with "stupid def vocals by Chubby Checker."

What To Look For: Early recordings by rap artists are very hard to come by, especially in good condition. Many of these records were pressed on small labels, with print runs tailored more for sales throughout New York City. Between 1976 and 1984, some of the most desirable East Coast rap labels included Sugarhill, Streetwise, Sutra, Sunnyview, Tommy Boy, Profile, Def Jam, and Prelude. Groups like the Fat Boys, the Beastie Boys, the Sugarhill Gang, Run-D.M.C., and Spoonie Gee recorded early hits on these labels.

The more common rap hits are readily available on 12-inch dance discs, although some reproductions do exist. Some of the repressings even recreate the original label art from record companies that have long since folded. In many cases, the reissue labels will have a silver or brown background; most New York City old school rap records will have multicolored labels, while their promo copies will have a white background.

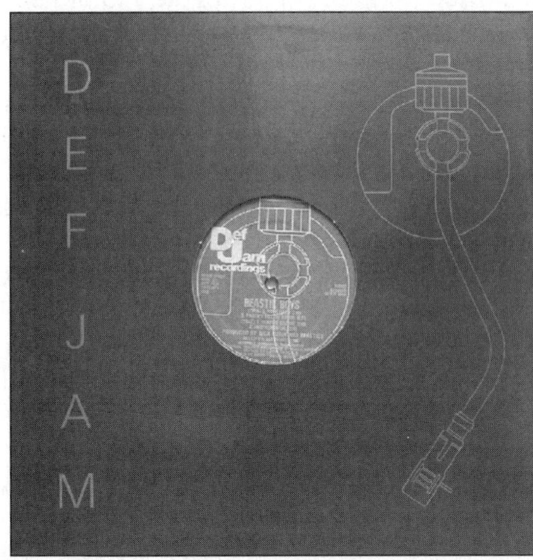

An early Beastie Boys release on Def Jam, where the group raps over the instrumental track to AC/DC's "Back in Black." Note the Def Jam disc cover, which resembles the tonearm of a modern turntable.

While many rap 45s exist, their value is very low in comparison to rap albums and 12-inch discs. Because of the space limitations of a 45, most 7- to 9-minute rap songs were trimmed down to 4 to 5 minutes on a 45, and many of the single edits were haphazard or jarring.

A 7-inch promotional copy of a Grandmaster Flash 12-inch disc.

References: Brewster, Bill, and Broughton, Frank, *Last Night a DJ Saved My Life: The History of the Disc Jockey*, Headline Book Pub., London, 1999; Gregory, Hugh, *Soul Music A-Z*, Da Capo Press, New York, N.Y., 1995; Toop, David, *Rap Attack 2: African Rap to Global Hip Hop*, Pluto Press, London, England, 1984.

Web pages: A Web page devoted to old school rap: *http://www.geocities.com/~tothebeat/*; a dissertation by Professors Steven Best and Douglas Kellner on the history of rap and its racial and social ramifications: *http://utminers.utep.edu/best/rap.htm*; Grandmaster Flash's Web page: *http://www.grandmasterflash.com*; Public Enemy's Web page: *http://www.publicenemy.com*; interviews with old school rappers like Afrika Bambaataa and Grandmixer D.S.T. can be found on the Hip-Hop.com Web site: *http://www.hip-hop.com*; Def Jam Records' homepage, home to LL Cool J, Public Enemy and the early recordings of the Beastie Boys: *http://www.defjam.com.*

45s	Year	VG	VG+	NM
Afrika Bambaataa and the SoulSonic Force, "Planet Rock" / (instrumental) (Tommy Boy 823)	1982	$2.00	$4.00	$8.00
The Beastie Boys, "She's On It" / "Slow and Low" (Def Jam 05683)	1985		$2.50	$5.00
(with picture sleeve, add:)	1985		$2.50	$5.00
Blondie, "Rapture" / "Walk Like Me" (Chrysalis 2485)	1980			$3.00
(with picture sleeve, add:)	1980			$3.00
Digital Underground, "The Humpty Dance" / "The Humpty Dance" (Tommy Boy / Collectibles 944)	1992			$3.00
The Fatback Band, "King Tim III (Personality Jock)" /"You're My Candy Sweet" (Spring 199)	1979		$3.00	$6.00
The Fat Boys, "Twist (Yo Twist)" / "The Twist (Buffapella)" (Tin Pan Apple 887 571-7)	1988			$3.00
(with picture sleeve, add:)	1988			$3.00
Grandmaster Flash and the Furious Five, "Freedom" / (instrumental) (Sugar Hill 756)	1980	$2.50	$5.00	$10.00
Grandmaster Flash, "Girls Love The Way He Spins" / "Larry's Dance Theme" (Elektra 69643)	1985			$3.00
Grandmaster Melle Mel and the Furious Five, "Beat Street Breakdown" (Pt. 1) / (Pt. 2) (Atlantic 89659)	1984			$3.00
(with picture sleeve, add:)	1984			$3.00
House of Pain, "Shamrocks and Shenanigans" (2 versions) (Sub Pop 188)				
(pressed on "lucky green vinyl")	1992	$2.50	$5.00	$10.00
(with picture sleeve, add:)	1992	$2.50	$5.00	$10.00
House of Pain, "Jump Around" (same on both sides) (Tommy Boy 526)				
(without "Collectibles" logo)	1992		$2.00	$4.00
(with "Collectibles" logo)	1993			$3.00
DJ Jazzy Jeff and the Fresh Prince, "Parents Just Don't Understand" / (instrumental) (Jive 1099-7)	1988			$3.00
(with picture sleeve, add:)	1988			$3.00
Oran "Juice" Jones, "The Rain" / "Your Song" (Def Jam 06209)	1986		$2.00	$4.00
LL Cool J, "Mama Said Knock You Out" / "Around The Way Girl" (Def Jam 73609)	1991			$3.00
Naughty By Nature, "O.P.P." / "Everything's Gonna Be Alright" (Tommy Boy 512)				
(first pressing, on green-bluish label)	1991		$2.50	$5.00
(second pressing, on white label)	1991			$3.00
Public Enemy, "Fight The Power" / "Flavor Flav Meets Spike Lee" (Motown 1972)				
Run-D.M.C., "It's Like That" / (instrumental) (Profile 5019)	1983		$2.50	$5.00
Run-D.M.C., "Walk This Way" / "King of Rock" (Profile 5112)	1986		$2.00	$4.00
(with picture sleeve, add:)	1986		$2.00	$4.00
Salt-n-Pepa, "Push It" / (instrumental) (Next Plateau KF 315)	1987		$2.50	$5.00
Gil Scott-Heron, "Johannesburg" / "Fell Together" (Arista 0152)	1975		$2.50	$5.00

12-inch	Year	VG	VG+	NM
Afrika Bambaataa and the SoulSonic Force, "Planet Rock" "Bonus Beats" / (instrumental) (Tommy Boy 823)	1983	$2.50	$5.00	$10.00
The Beastie Boys, "Cooky Puss" (Rat Cage 026) (12" EP)	1983	$8.00	$16.00	$32.00
Blondie, "Rapture" (9 versions) (Chrysalis 58277) (2 discs)	1994	$2.50	$5.00	$10.00
De La Soul, "A Roller Skating Jam Named Saturdays" (8 versions) (Tommy Boy 586)	1993	$2.00	$4.00	$8.00
Digital Underground, "The Humpty Dance" (3 versions) (Tommy Boy 944)	1989	$2.50	$5.00	$10.00
The Fatback Band, "King Tim III (Personality Jock)") / "You're My Candy Sweet" (Spring 402)	1979	$2.50	$5.00	$10.00
Grandmaster Flash and the Furious Five, "Freedom" / (instrumental) (Sugar Hill 549)	1980	$2.50	$5.00	$10.00
Grandmaster Flash and the Furious Five, "The Message" / (instrumental) (Sugar Hill 584)	1982	$2.50	$5.00	$10.00
Gil Scott-Heron, "Re-Ron" / "Re-Ron" (Special Mix) (Arista 9216)	1984	$2.50	$5.00	$10.00
Ice Cube, "You Know How We Do It" / (instrumental) (Priority 7046)	1994	$2.00	$4.00	$8.00
Ice-T, "Original Gangster" (3 versions) / "Bitches" (2 versions) (Sire 40104)	199	$2.00	$4.00	$8.00
DJ Jazzy Jeff and the Fresh Prince, "Girls Ain't Nothing But Trouble"				
(if on Word Up WD-001, four versions)	1985	$3.00	$6.00	$12.00
(if on Word Up WD-002, two versions)	1985	$3.75	$7.50	$15.00
(if on Jive 1146-1, three versions, different mixes and lyrics than the Word Up versions)	1988		$3.00	$6.00
LL Cool J, "Mama Said Knock You Out" (7 versions) (Def Jam 73703)	1991	$2.00	$4.00	$8.00
Naughty By Nature, "It's On" (4 versions) / "Hip Hop Hooray (Pete Rock Remix)" (Tommy Boy 569)	1993		$3.50	$7.00
P.M. Dawn, "Set Adrift on Memory Bliss" (2 versions) / "Watchers Point of View" (2 versions) (Gee Street 866 095-1)	1991		$3.00	$6.00
Public Enemy, "You're Gonna Get Yours" (2 versions) / "Miuzi Weighs A Ton" / "Rebel Without A Pause" (Def Jam 06861)	1987	$3.00	$6.00	$12.00
Run-D.M.C., "Rock Box" (3 versions) (Profile 7045)	1984	$2.00	$4.00	$8.00
Run-D.M.C., "You Talk Too Much" (2 versions) / "Daryll & Joe (Krush Groove 3)" (Profile 7069)	1985	$3.00	$6.00	$12.00
Salt-n-Pepa, "Let's Talk About Sex" (3 versions) / "Swift" (Next Plateau 50157)	1991	$2.50	$5.00	$10.00
The Sugarhill Gang, "Rapper's Delight" (6:30) / "Rapper's Delight" (15:00) (Sugar Hill 542)	1979	$7.50	$15.00	$30.00
The Sugarhill Gang, "8th Wonder" / "Sugar Hill Groove" (Sugar Hill 542)	1980	$2.00	$4.00	$8.00

LPs	Year	VG	VG+	NM
The Beastie Boys, Paul's Boutique				
(if on Capitol C1-91743, single gatefold edition)	1989	$2.50	$5.00	$10.00
(if jacket says Capitol C1-92844, multi-gatefold edition, record still has catalog number C1-91743)	1989	$3.75	$7.50	$15.00
De La Soul, Three Feet High and Rising (Tommy Boy 1019)	1989	$2.50	$5.00	$10.00
Digital Underground, Sex Packets (Tommy Boy 1026)	1990	$3.00	$6.00	$12.00
Fatback, Fatback XII (Spring 6723)	1979	$2.50	$5.00	$10.00
Grandmaster Flash and the Furious Five, The Message (Sugar Hill 268)	1982	$3.75	$7.50	$15.00
Ice Cube, AmeriKKKa's Most Wanted (Priority 57120)	1990	$3.00	$6.00	$12.00
Ice-T, The Iceberg / Freedom of Speech ... Just Watch What You Say (Sire 26028)	1989	$3.00	$6.00	$12.00
Oran "Juice" Jones, Juice (Def Jam BFC 40367)	1986	$3.00	$6.00	$12.00
LL Cool J, 14 Shots To The Dome (Def Jam C 53325) (2 LPs)	1993	$3.75	$7.50	$15.00
Naughty By Nature, Naughty By Nature (Tommy Boy TBLP-1051)	1991	$3.75	$7.50	$15.00
Public Enemy, It Takes A Nation Of Millions To Hold Us Back (Def Jam BFW 44303)	1988	$3.00	$6.00	$12.00
Public Enemy, Apocalypse 91 ... The Enemy Strikes Back (Def Jam C2 47374) (2 LPs)	1991	$3.75	$7.50	$15.00
Run-D.M.C., King of Rock (Profile PRO-1205)	1985	$3.00	$6.00	$12.00
Run-D.M.C., Together Forever: Greatest Hits 1983-1991 (Profile PRO-1419) (2 LPs)	1991	$3.75	$7.50	$15.00
Salt-n-Pepa, A Salt With A Deadly Pepa (Next Plateau PL 1011)	1988	$3.00	$6.00	$12.00
Gil Scott-Heron, The Revolution Will Not Be Televised				
(if on Flying Dutchman BLD1-0613)	1974	$5.00	$10.00	$20.00
(if on Flying Dutchman BXL1-0613, reissue)	1978	$3.00	$6.00	$12.00
(if on Flying Dutchman AYL1-3818, reissue)	1980	$2.00	$4.00	$8.00
(if on Bluebird 6694-1-RB, reissue)	1988	$3.00	$6.00	$12.00
The Sugarhill Gang, Sugar Hill Gang (Sugar Hill 245)	1980	$3.00	$6.00	$12.00

RECORD CLUBS

History: What an inventive idea. Instead of going to a record store and purchasing the records you want, you could order twelve albums for a penny by filling out a postcard in a magazine. Of course, you might be required to purchase seven more albums at full price over the next three years, and if a little card came in the mail and you didn't send it back saying "no thanks," you received a record (and a bill for it) in the mail a few days later.

Record clubs were created in the early 1950s, as record companies were trying to find a way to counter record stores that offered deep discounts—some as high as 30 percent off the manufacturer's suggested retail price—without sacrificing a profit line. At first, the record companies tried to stop these stores from offering records at such a low price; some companies even threatened cutting off a record store's supply of prime product. But it wasn't long before record companies offered their own "discount programs" as well.

A Johnny Cash album from his days on Sun Records; this pressing was made available through the Capitol Record Club. Courtesy Last Vestige Music Store, Albany, N.Y.

In 1955, Columbia Records formed a mail-in record club. RCA followed suit with its own direct-to-the-consumer record club, and Capitol Records followed in 1958. Each club would offer its own label's records (as well as the recordings of licensed titles from some smaller independent labels), and the recordings could be bought by consumers as part of a subscription service. Throughout the 1960s and 1970s, each club advertised in magazines and comic books, hoping to acquire new subscribers. The club would send its members catalogs of albums available for purchase, mostly grouped into different musical genres for easier selectability.

In 1964, the Capitol Record Club issued a three-song flexi-disc to club members, featuring snippets of the Beatles' "Roll Over Beethoven," the Beach Boys' "Little Deuce Coupe," and the Kingston Trio's "When The Saints Go Marching In." All three songs are interspersed with plugs by a narrator, imploring listeners to join the Capitol Record Club and acquire more music for their collection.

A promotional 7" record on thin cardboard, featuring snippets of hits from Capitol's three biggest recording acts of the early 1960s, all available through the Capitol Record Club. From the Collection of Leonard and Judy Carney, provided courtesy of Steve and Laurie Arnold.

By 1968, however, the Capitol club was a distant third in sales behind the Columbia and RCA clubs. That year, Capitol Records sold the subscription service to the Longines-Wittnauer Company, and was merged with the watchmaker's Longines Symphonette prestige box set product. Capitol Record Club pressings through the Longines Symphonette Society will have three diagonal lines on the upper left corner of the album; the number "16" will be on the lower right corner of the back cover; and the serial number will have an "ST-8-" preceding it.

The Columbia and RCA Record Clubs still exist today (although the RCA club is now known as the BMG Direct Club, due to the Bertlesmann Group purchasing RCA's music division in the early 1990's). For many years, while some releases were available on compact disc and on cassette in record stores, these clubs still had a fair number of vinyl subscribers, and specially-created vinyl copies of many of these albums—in some cases, the only vinyl copies available anywhere—were released to club members who requested them.

As you can see from the digitally enhanced runout grooves in this copy of the Little River Band's *Greatest Hits* LP, these pressings were specifically made for Columbia Record and Tape Club subscribers. Notice the "CBS" engraved in the runout groove in the lower left of this photo. Across the top of the label perimeter, above the Capitol logo, is more information that the record was pressed for sale to Columbia House subscribers.

Thanks to the Internet, record club members can now purchase recordings through club online Web pages, as well as through the traditional magazine postcard inserts.

What To Look For: Of all the record clubs, the rarest and most collectible pressings come from the Capitol Record Club. Besides the Beatles and Beach Boys recordings, the Capitol Record Club also pressed Philles, Laurie, and Sun International ABC-Paramount releases for its subscribers. Although the labels will be similar to stock copies, Capitol Records pressings on the Capitol Record Club will begin with the prefix "8-." Non-Capitol records in the Capitol Record Club begin with a "T" and a five-digit serial number; stereo albums began with "ST" and the five digit serial number, with the first digit being a "9" in both cases.

In 1968, the Longines Symphonette Society purchased the Capitol Record Club operation, and operated it as part of its Longines Symphonette label until the subscription service finally folded in 1973. Longines pressings will have serial numbers that begin with the number 7. If a Capitol-based artist (the Beatles, the Beach Boys, Glen Campbell) had a record issued through the Longines-era club, the record covers will have three diagonal lines along the top, and the number "16" can be found on the back cover.

Trivia

The RCA Record Club mistakenly pressed copies of the Beach Boys' Reprise album Surf's Up with an Asylum label (Asylum R-113793), and those copies are worth $60-$150 in mint condition.

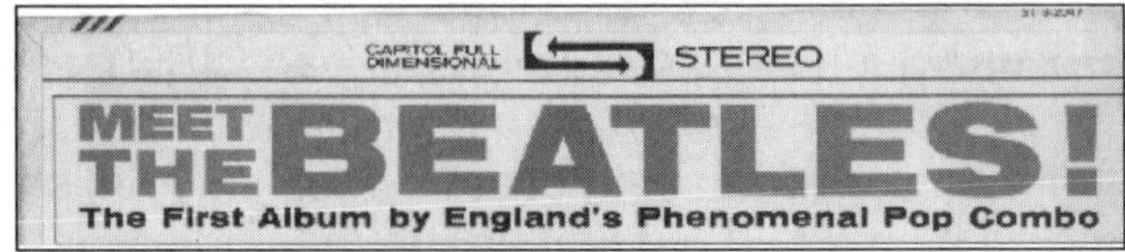

CAPITOL FULL DIMENSIONAL
STEREO
MEET THE BEATLES!
The First Album by England's Phenomenal Pop Combo

Notice the three diagonal lines along the top of this copy of *Meet the Beatles;* this is a Capitol Record Club pressing during the Longines Symphonette era. Photo Credit: From the Collection of Bruce Spizer.

The Columbia and RCA club pressings are almost indistinguishable from stock copy pressings; only the word "RCA Music Service" or "CRC" on the back cover denote these releases as being from a record club. A closer examination of RCA Record Club titles indicates that it, like the Capitol club, used a different serial number than on the copies available through stores (RCA Record Club serial numbers began with an "R" followed by a six-digit number).

Another way to tell if the record is a stock copy or from a record club is to look for a bar code. Most records made after 1982 will have a visible bar code on the back cover. Since there would be no need for a bar code on a record club pressing (the album would not have to pass through an electronic scanner at the checkout counter), many record club pressings will have a blank square where a bar code would normally exist.

Trivia

Don't bother trying to steam off the covers of The Beatles' *Yesterday and Today* album from the Capitol Record Club; all Capitol Record Club pressings contain the "trunk cover," with nothing underneath but cardboard. Longines pressings with green labels, however, have all eleven tracks in true stereo.

The back cover of Duran Duran's *Rio* album is missing its bar code; a clue that this record came from a record club, in this case, the RCA Direct Record Club.

Even though a smaller number of record club pressings were made than store pressings, many collectors will search out Record Club releases only if there is a unique mix unavailable in store pressings—i.e., copies of the Ronettes' *Presenting The Fabulous Ronettes Featuring Veronica* and the Beatles' *Yesterday and Today*, which feature true stereo in the grooves (the store copies used fake or rechanneled stereo).

Since 1987, the BMG Direct Club (the descendant of the RCA Club) presses its records in Canada, for export to the United States.

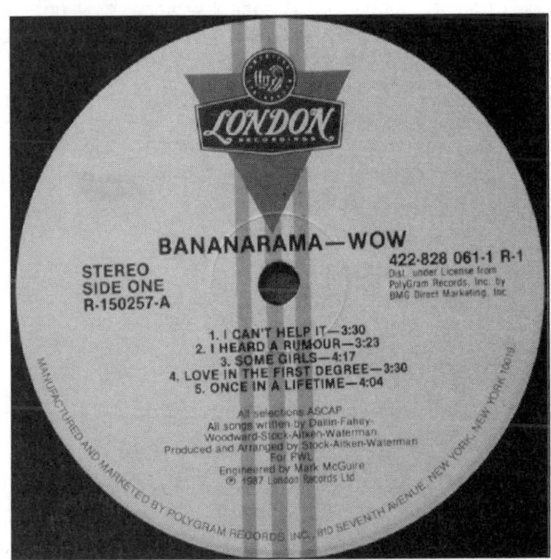

On this Bananarama LP, you can see the record's original serial number (on the right) and its BMG Direct serial number (on the left, begins with an "R").

Trivia

The Cars' Candy-O album is only identified as such by a sticker on the shrinkwrap—unless you joined the RCA Music Service; on those copies, the name of the band and the album are printed on the front cover for all to see.

The Cars' *Candy-O*, from the RCA Record Club.

References: Chapple, Steve; Garofalo, Reebee, *Rock 'n' Roll Is Here To Pay: The History And Politics of the Music Industry*, Nelson-Hall, Inc., Chicago, Ill, 1977; Neely, Tim, *The Goldmine Record Album Price Guide*, Krause Publications, Iola, Wisconsin, 1999; Spizer, Bruce, *The Beatles' Story on Capitol Records: Part One: Beatlemania and the Singles*, 498 Productions LLC, New Orleans, Louisiana, 2000—contains a history of the Capitol Record Club and its relation to the Beatles' releases.

Web pages: Columbia House, the company that evolved from the Columbia Record and Tape Club: *http://www.columbiahouse.com.*

Columbia Record Club	Year	VG	VG+	NM
The Beach Boys, Spirit of America (Capitol SVBB) (2 LPs)	1975	$5.00	$10.00	$20.00
A Surprise Gift from the Beatles, the Beach Boys and the Kingston Trio (Capitol/Evatone 8464, promotional soundsheet)	1964	$500.00	$1,000.00	$2,000.00
The Beatles, Beatle Talk (Great Northwest GNW-4007)	1978	$12.50	$25.00	$50.00
Garth Brooks, Ropin' The Wind (Capitol Nashville C1-596330)	1991	$12.50	$25.00	$50.00
Billy Ray Cyrus, Some Gave All (Mercury 1P-8218)	1992	$6.25	$12.50	$25.00
George Harrison, George Harrison (Dark Horse DHK 3255)	1979	$10.00	$20.00	$40.00
Alan Jackson, Don't Rock the Jukebox (Arista AS 8681)	1991	$10.00	$20.00	$40.00
George Jones, And Along Came Jones (MCA 10398)	1991	$5.00	$10.00	$20.00
Wynonna Judd, Wynonna (MCA 1P-8201) (label may have name misspelled "Wyonna")	1992	$6.25	$12.50	$25.00
John Lennon and Yoko Ono, Double Fantasy (Geffen GHS-2001) (if "CH" on label, cream label)	1981	$18.75	$37.50	$75.00

Columbia Record Club	Year	VG	VG+	NM
(if black Geffen label)	1986	$12.50	$25.00	$50.00
Lynyrd Skynyrd, Lynyrd Skynyrd 1991 (Atlantic A1-82258)	1991	$5.00	$10.00	$20.00
Madonna, The Immaculate Collection (Sire W1-26440) (2 LP's)	1990	$5.00	$10.00	$20.00
Paul McCartney, Tripping The Live Fantastic - Highlights (Capitol C1-595379)	1990	$6.25	$12.50	$25.00
Thelonious Monk, Monk's Miracles (Columbia Musical Treasury D5338)	1967	$6.25	$12.50	$25.00
Ricky Van Shelton, Backroads (Columbia C46855)	1990	$5.00	$10.00	$20.00
Skid Row, Slave To The Grind (Atlantic 1P-8136)	1991	$5.00	$10.00	$20.00
Sonny and Cher, Sonny and Cher's Greatest Hits, Atco A25 5178(2)	1967	$7.50	$15.00	$30.00
Travis Tritt, It's All About To Change (Warner Bros. W1-26589)	1991	$5.00	$10.00	$20.00
Tanya Tucker, What Do I Do With Me (Capitol Nashville 1P-8140)	1991	$5.00	$10.00	$20.00
Tina Turner, Simply The Best (Capitol 1P-8192) (2 LPs)	1991	$5.00	$10.00	$20.00
Van Halen, For Unlawful Carnal Knowledge (Warner Bros. W1-26594)	1991	$5.00	$10.00	$20.00

RCA Record Club / BMG Record Club	Year	VG	VG+	NM
Beach Boys, Endless Summer (Capitol R 223559) (2 LPs)	197??	$6.25	$12.50	$25.00
Beach Boys, Surf's Up (Asylum R 113793) (error on label, should have been Brother Records)	1972	$37.50	$75.00	$150.00
Garth Brooks, No Fences (Capitol Nashville R 173266)	1990	$12.50	$25.00	$50.00
The Cars, Candy-O (Elektra R 123334)	1979	$3.00	$6.00	$12.00
Vince Gill, Pocket Full of Gold, MCA R 173599)	1991	$5.00	$10.00	$20.00
Alan Jackson, Don't Rock the Jukebox, Arista R 143877)	1991	$6.25	$12.50	$25.00
Brenda Lee, Merry Christmas From Brenda Lee (Decca R 103619)	1971	$5.00	$10.00	$20.00
John Lennon and Yoko Ono, Double Fantasy (Geffen R 104689)	1981	$10.00	$20.00	$40.00
Madonna, The Immaculate Collection (Sire R 254164) (2 LPs)	1990	$5.00	$10.00	$20.00
Reba McEntire, Reba Live (MCA R 244602) (2 LPs)	1989	$6.25	$12.50	$25.00
Ronnie Milsap, Back to the Grindstone (RCA R 183710)	1991	$5.00	$10.00	$20.00
Elvis Presley, Worldwide Gold Award Hits, Vol. 1 and 2 (RCA R 213690) (2 LPs)				
(if one orange and one tan RCA label)	1974	$30.00	$60.00	$120.00
(if two tan RCA labels)	1974	$10.00	$20.00	$40.00
(if two black RCA labels with "His Master's Voice" trademark)	1977	$6.25	$12.50	$25.00
Elvis Presley, Aloha From Hawaii Via Satellite (RCA R 213736) (2 LP's) (stereo, not quadraphonic)				
(if two orange RCA labels)	1973	$17.50	$35.00	$70.00
(if two tan RCA labels)	1975	$15.00	$30.00	$60.00
(if two black RCA labels with "His Master's Voice" trademark)	1977	$7.50	$15.00	$30.00

RCA Record Club	Year	VG	VG+	NM
R.E.M., Out of Time (Warner Bros. R 124762)	1991	$4.00	$8.00	$16.00
Simple Minds, Live in the City of Light (A&M R 209526) (2 LPs)	1987	$5.00	$10.00	$20.00
Randy Travis, Heroes and Friends (Warner Bros. R 174597)	1990	$5.00	$10.00	$20.00
Roger Waters, The Wall - Live in Berlin (Mercury R 209833) (2 LPs)	1990	$5.00	$10.00	$20.00
Hank Williams, Jr., Pure Hank (Warner Bros. R-160351)	1991	$5.00	$10.00	$20.00

Capitol Record Club	Year	VG	VG+	NM
Roy Acuff, Great Train Songs (Hickory DT-90696) (rechanneled stereo)	1965	$6.25	$12.50	$25.00
Beach Boys, Smiley Smile (Capitol ST-8-2891) (rechanneled stereo)	1968	$75.00	$150.00	$300.00
The Beatles, Meet the Beatles (Capitol ST-8-2407) (some songs in stereo)				
(if label has rainbow perimeter)	1966	$125.00	$250.00	$500.00
(if label is lime green)	1969	$50.00	$100.00	$200.00
The Beatles, Revolver (Capitol ST-8-2576) (stereo)				
(if label has rainbow perimeter)	1966	$25.00	$50.00	$100.00
(if label is lime green)	1969	$10.00	$20.00	$40.00
(if label is orange, last year of pressing for Capitol Record Club)	1973	$50.00	$100.00	$200.00
The Beatles, Yesterday and Today (Capitol ST-8-2553)				
(if label has rainbow perimeter, some tracks in stereo)	1966	$75.00	$150.00	$300.00
(if label is lime green, all eleven tracks in true stereo)	1969	$37.50	$75.00	$150.00
Glen Campbell, Limited Collector's Edition (Capitol SWAK-93157)	1970	$5.00	$10.00	$20.00
Ray Charles, Live in Concert (ABC-Paramount ST-90144)	1965	$5.00	$10.00	$20.00
The Chiffons, Sweet Talkin' Guy (Laurie ST-90779)	1966	$50.00	$100.00	$200.00
The Crystals, Twist Uptown (Philles DT-90722)	1965	$300.00	$600.00	$1,200.00
The Everly Brothers, Roots (Warner Bros. ST-91601)	1968	$12.50	$25.00	$50.00
The Impressions, One By One (ABC-Paramount ST-90520) (stereo)	1965	$7.50	$15.00	$30.00
The Kinks, Arthur (Or the Decline And Fall of the British Empire) (Reprise SMAS-93034)	1970	$10.00	$20.00	$40.00
Led Zeppelin, Led Zeppelin IV (Atlantic SMAS-94019)	1972	$10.00	$20.00	$40.00
The Lovin' Spoonful, Do You Believe In Magic				
(if on Kama Sutra T-90597, mono)	1965	$7.50	$15.00	$30.00
(if on Kama Sutra ST-90597, stereo)	1965	$10.00	$20.00	$40.00
Paul Revere and the Raiders, In the Beginning (Jerden DT-90709) (rechanneled stereo)	1966	$12.50	$25.00	$50.00
The Ronettes, Presenting the Fabulous Ronettes Featuring Veronica				
(if on Philles T-90271, mono)	1965	$62.50	$125.00	$250.00
(if on Philles ST-90271, stereo)	1965	$100.00	$200.00	$400.00
Steely Dan, Can't Buy A Thrill (ABC-Dunhill SMAS-94976) (error on label, should have been on ABC)	1973	$6.25	$12.50	$25.00
Hank Williams, The Very Best of Hank Williams				
(if on MGM T-90511, mono)	1965	$10.00	$20.00	$40.00
(if on MGM ST-90511, stereo)	1965	$5.00	$10.00	$20.00

RHYTHM AND BLUES/SOUL

History: To cover the rich and vibrant history of soul and R&B music would go beyond the limits of this book. But for the many artists and musicians who recorded classic songs on tiny labels, artists who had signed recording contracts that bordered on perpetual servitude, artists who watched as the song they thought was rising up the pop charts was now being sung by a white artist—they can now see their original recordings selling for very high prices at Internet auctions and at record shows.

What we know today as rhythm and blues, or "R&B," evolved from the 1940s, as a mixture of gospel, jazz, and an uptempo big-band sound called "jump blues." R&B artists like Louis Jordan, Ruth Brown, and LaVern Baker took the blues, added horns and drums, and sang over the instruments as if they were shouting above the music.

One of Ruth Brown's biggest hits, and an R&B classic. From the Collection of Val Shively.

Of course, during the 1950s, one of the biggest obstacles R&B artists had to face was the "covering" of their songs by white artists. Whether designed to have two artists sell more records with one song, and thus enhance the songwriter's royalties, or whether it was an effort to create "instant hits" for various artists, many R&B artists would watch as their hit songs rose up the charts—only to discover a white singer or group recording that same song, often with the same arrangement, overtake the original in sales. On most occasions, the white "cover" record outsold the original R&B song—the Moonglows' "Sincerely" was covered by the McGuire Sisters; the Chords' "Sh-Boom" was appropriated by the Crew Cuts; LaVern Baker's "Tweedle Dee" was covered by Georgia Gibbs, and Pat Boone covered, of all things, Little Richard's "Tutti-Frutti."

Hank Ballard and the Midnighters' "The Twist" was later covered by Chubby Checker, who turned it into a monster hit and a national dance craze. But even though Ballard's version was not the hit, he received plenty of royalties as "The Twist"'s songwriter. From the Collection of Val Shively.

That being said, many R&B artists were able to "cross over" the unwritten-yet-enforced musical color barrier, as teenagers eventually eschewed the pale imitations and purchased instead the soulful originators. Some of these artists that were able to establish themselves to both black and white audiences eventually earned nicknames like "The Genius," "Mr. Excitement," "The Godfather of Soul," and "The Queen of Soul."

Ray Charles, "The Genius," recorded a series of R&B classics for Atlantic, including "Hallelujah I Love Her So" and "Rockhouse," as well as his soul-meets-gospel call-and-response classic "What'd I Say." Charles would later move to ABC Records and continue his soul classics with "Hit The Road Jack" and "Unchain My Heart." His album *Modern Sounds in Country and Western Music* became one of the biggest-selling albums of 1962, as Charles took, such classic country songs as "I Can't Stop Loving You" and "You Don't Know Me," and brought them to life with his own soulful arrangements.

Trivia

If you've always wondered about the lyrics in the Steve Miller Band song "The Joker," when he sings of "the pompatus of love," those words are from an old R&B song by the Medallions, "The Letter" (Dootone 347) and "pompatus" are the equivalent of private whispered conversations between lovers. By the way, the references to "space cowboy," "gangster of love," and "Maurice" are all from earlier Steve Miller songs.

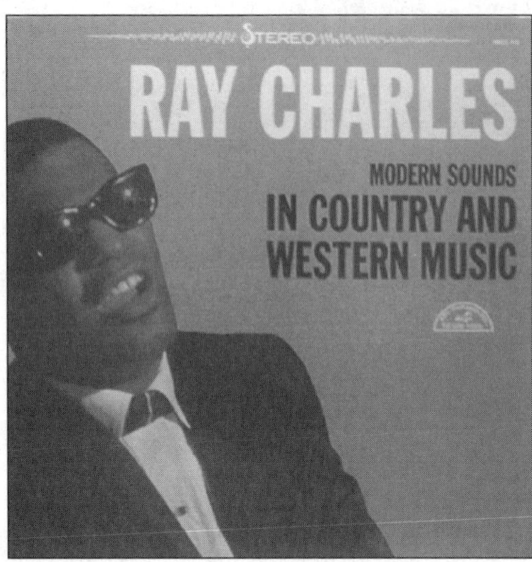

In the early 1960s, no album was able to combine the diverse musical genres as rhythm/blues and country/western as Ray Charles' *Modern Sounds in Country and Western Music.*

James Brown, "The Godfather of Soul," started his career as a gospel singer. The gospel group Brown joined, the Flames, was signed by Federal Records, and recorded the heartwrenching "Please, Please, Please" as "James Brown and the Famous Flames." A series of soul ballads and uptempo numbers followed, including "Try Me," "Think," and "Night Train." One of the crowning achievements in Brown's career was the release of a 1962 live album that captured all the energy and excitement of a James Brown concert. The album, *Live at the Apollo*, sold millions of copies and inspired a generation of performers who listened to that album every night and tried to emulate Brown's dance steps and moves.

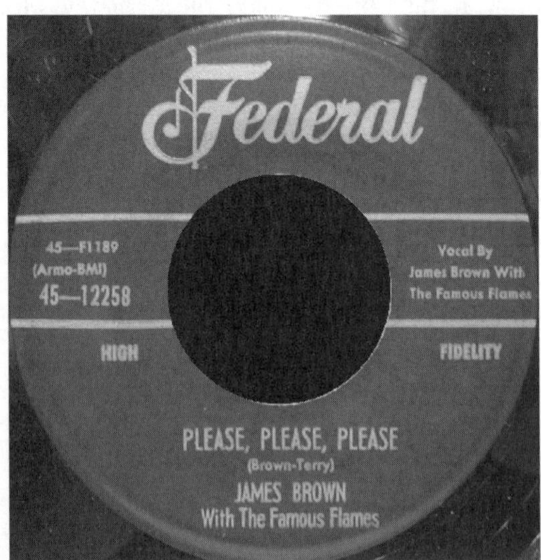

James Brown's signature soulful ballad "Please Please Please" was originally recorded for the Federal label; it would later re-chart for King Records. From the Collection of Val Shively.

The story of Jackie Wilson's career is both bitter and sweet. After initial hits with "Reet Petite" and "Lonely Teardrops," Wilson spent the next ten years recording in every musical style from pop to opera, at the request of his record company Brunswick. He earned the nickname "Mr. Excitement," as his talent and charisma would create pop hits like "Doggin' Around," "Baby Workout" and "(Your Love Keeps Lifting Me) Higher and Higher," despite all the overly lush orchestrations and banal background singers fostered upon him by Brunswick. Sadly, while on stage in a New Jersey club in 1975, Wilson was felled by a stroke, and died in a nursing home eight years later. His musical legacy, however, lives on in such singer-dancer-entertainers as Michael Jackson.

One of many albums Jackie Wilson recorded for Brunswick was this collection of standards. While Wilson made millions of dollars for the label, the singer died in a nursing home, penniless. Courtesy Last Vestige Music Store, Albany, N.Y.

The "Queen of Soul," Aretha Franklin, was also musically handcuffed by a record company—in this case, Columbia Records—which had her singing songs like "Rock-A-Bye Your Baby With A Dixie Melody." But when she signed with Atlantic Records, producer Jerry Wexler took Franklin to Muscle Shoals, Alabama, where she recorded with the legendary Muscle Shoals Sound Rhythm Section, a group of white musicians that played R&B with the same fervor as Motown's Van Dyke Six house band. The collaborations between Franklin and the Muscle Shoals band produced hits like "Respect," "I Never Loved A Man (The Way I Love You)," and "Chain of Fools."

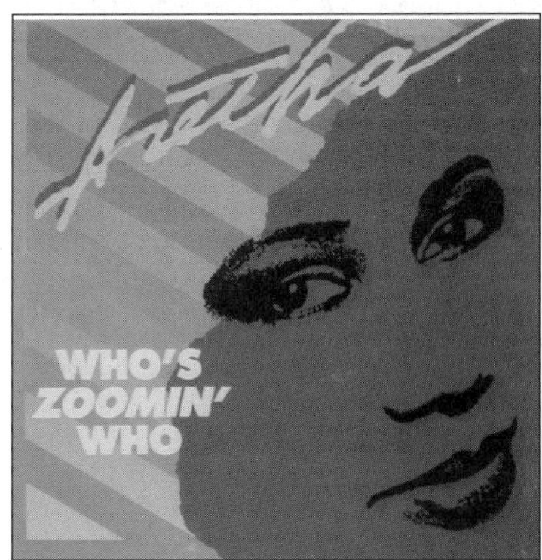

Twenty years after Aretha Franklin's biggest hits, her hit-making ability is still unmatched, as songs like "Who's Zoomin' Who," "Freeway of Love" and "Jumpin' Jack Flash" kept her on the charts well into the 1990s. Courtesy Last Vestige Music Store, Albany, N.Y.

The difference between "rhythm and blues" and "soul" music may be hard to define, but the best way to describe it is that as R&B music became more commercially acceptable, it eventually was renamed "soul" music (as in "music that reached into your soul").

Trivia

The Tymes' album *Somewhere* is hard enough to find, but try to find the 45 that was added as a bonus for people who purchased the album. Most copies of Somewhere either don't have the bonus 45, or the slot in the album jacket that held the 45 has split or torn over time.

A copy of the Tymes' *Somewhere* album, with the bonus 45 intact. Courtesy Last Vestige Music Store, Albany, N.Y.

While the Motown musical hit factory was working overtime in Detroit, another record company proved that soul music could still be made in the deep south. Originally formed in the 1950s as Satellite Records, Stax and its sister label Volt was the home of Otis Redding, the Staple Singers, Rufus Thomas, Sam & Dave, and the Dramatics, all of whom had hits for the label. Backing up the singers at Stax/Volt was its house band, Booker T. and the M.G.'s.

One of Stax/Volt's more successful combinations, Sam Moore and Dave Prater. Courtesy Last Vestige Music Store, Albany, N.Y.

The 1970s were filled with disco and funk music, as well as some sweet soul from the City of Brotherly Love. Kenny Gamble and Leon Huff, who had previously produced such artists as Jerry Butler, Wilson Pickett, and Dusty Springfield, set up their own recording studio and record label. Within twelve months, their label, Philadelphia International Records, had chart-topping hits from Billy Paul, Harold Melvin and the Blue Notes, the O'Jays, and the Three Degrees.

The O'Jays had recorded and toured for over 15 years before "Love Train," their first #1 single. The song was written and produced by Kenny Gamble and Leon Huff, and arranged by Thom Bell.

Trivia

When the Five Keys were photographed for their album The Five Keys On Stage!, the group posed with their hands spread out, as if they were sustaining a harmonic chord. But the right hand of the singer on the far left is in such a position that... well... Capitol eventually reissued the album with the offending "digit" airbrushed away, but that second pressing is actually rarer than the first!

Notice the difference in these two photos? On the top is the first pressing of *The Five Keys On Stage!*, which contains a prime example of why photographers should make sure nothing is in the background that could be misinterpreted as... well... The record on the top is the "airbrushed" copy, which had fewer copies printed and is rarer. Photo Credit: Courtesy Good Rockin' Tonight/ Collectors Universe.

Another producer working in Philadelphia, Thom Bell, produced a series of tender soul ballads for such harmony groups as the Stylistics, the Spinners, the Delfonics, and Blue Magic. Both Thom Bell and the Gamble-Huff team used the same house band, MFSB (Mother, Father, Sister, Brother), a 42-piece orchestra capable of playing anything from Beethoven's Fifth Symphony to the theme from *Soul Train* (which they did, and it topped the charts).

When the Jackson 5 first appeared on American Bandstand, Dick Clark asked them who their biggest influences were. Almost all the Jacksons mentioned the Delfonics as their biggest influence. Courtesy Last Vestige Music Store, Albany, N.Y.

Other cities produced groups with soulful sounds—the Tavares brothers from Boston, the Chi-Lites from Chicago, the Commodores from Alabama, and the Gap Band from Atlanta. In these cities, the sound of soul music represented the strengths and struggles of the urban communities. Tavares sang sweet ballads like "Check It Out," and dance tracks like "Heaven Must Be Missing An Angel." While the Chi-Lites sang sweet soul ballads like "Oh Girl" and "Have You Seen Her," they also sang "(For God's Sake) Give More Power to the People."

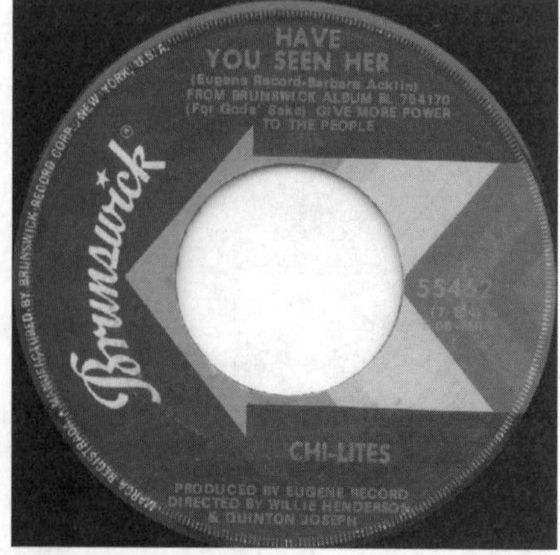

One of the most memorable soul ballads of the 1970s, the Chi-Lites' "Have You Seen Her" was covered in 1989 by M.C. Hammer as a rap ballad.

Soul music in the 1980s was now influenced by other musical styles, including funk, rap, and dance. Sexy male singers like Luther Vandross, Teddy Pendergrass, Babyface, and Kashif could melt hearts like ice in July. Meanwhile, singers like Anita Baker, Phyllis Hyman, Jennifer Holliday, and Whitney Houston showed they could also use every inch of their vocal cords to create such powerful recordings as "Sweet Love," "And I Am Telling You I'm Not Going," and "Don't Wanna Change the World."

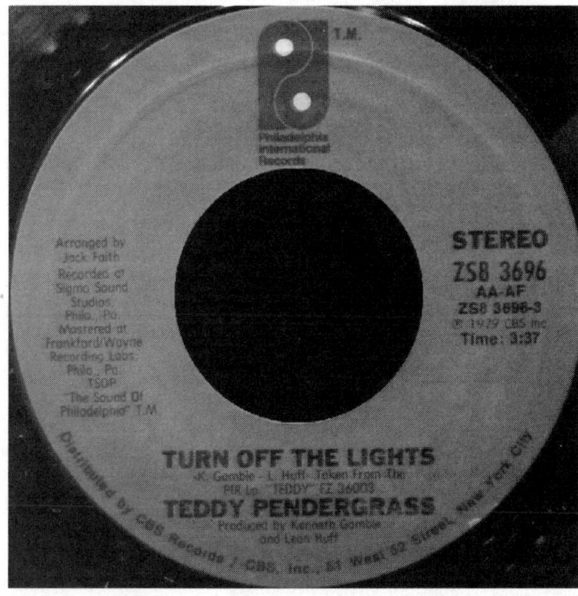

Teddy Pendergrass was the lead singer for Harold Melvin and the Blue Notes; his solo albums sold millions of copies, mostly to women who couldn't get enough of Pendergrass' sexy voice. From the Collection of Val Shively.

What To Look For: A good rule of thumb to follow when collecting R&B and soul records is, the older the record, the more it's worth. For example, early R&B and soul records from the Five Keys, the Orioles, and Ruth Brown are hard to find, and the few copies that have survived sell for very high prices. Conversely, most major label 45s and LPs from the 1970s are easily and readily available, and their collectible value has not risen. This is not to say that 1970s music is better or worse than 1950s music; but it is much easier to find a "million-selling" copy of Harold Melvin and the Blue Notes' "The Love I Lost" than it is to find any Aladdin recording of the Five Keys.

R&B albums from the 1950s are very rare, but 10-inch LPs can return thousands of dollars in near-mint condition. As for albums from the 1970s, the rarer and more collectible albums will be quadraphonic releases or half-speed mastered audiophile pressings, because of the low print run of these two formats.

Some R&B/soul artists continue to release 45s and LPs, but any 45s released today are usually only an artist's biggest hits.

Although the Boyz II Men song "Motownphilly" was released as a 45, the B-side features 45-second versions of five songs from the group's album *Cooleyhigh Harmony.*

Check the Motown chapter of this book for a selected price guide featuring artists from the Motown family of labels.

References: Graff, Gary, Freedom du Lac, Josh, McFarlon, Jim, Eds., *MusicHound R&B: The Essential Album Guide*, Visible Ink Press, Detroit, Mich., 1998; Gregory, Hugh, *Soul Music A-Z (Revised Edition)*, Da Capo Press, Inc., New York, N.Y. 1995; Whitburn, Joel, *Top R&B Singles 1942-1995*, Record Research, Inc., Menomonee Falls, Wisconsin, 1996.

Web pages: A page devoted to classic soul recordings: *http://www.soul-patrol.com/soul*; a fan-created Web site devoted to Aretha Franklin: *http://ntfp.globalserve.net/ebutler;* the Ray Charles homepage: *http://www.raycharles.com*; the Philadelphia International homepage, containing information on Gamble-Huff produced soul songs of the 1970s: *http://www.phillyinternational.com.*

Museums: Memphis Rock 'n' Soul Museum, 145 Lt. George W. Lee Avenue, Memphis, TN 38103; (901) 543-0800; *http://www.memphisrocknsoul.org.*

45s	Year	VG	VG+	NM
Ashford and Simpson, "Solid" / "Solid (Dub Version)" (Capitol B-5397)	1984			$3.00
The Bar-Kays, "Soul Finger" / "Knucklehead" (Volt 148)	1967	$2.00	$4.00	$8.00
Archie Bell and the Drells, "Tighten Up" / "Dog Eat Dog" (Ovide 228)	1967	$7.50	$15.00	$30.00
(if on Atlantic 2478)	1968	$3.00	$6.00	$12.00
(if on Atlantic 2478, B-side is "Tighten Up - Part 2")	1968	$2.00	$4.00	$8.00
Brook Benton, "It's Just A Matter of Time" / "Hurtin' Inside" (Mercury 71394)	1959	$3.75	$7.50	$15.00
The Midnighters, "Work With Me Annie" / "Until I Die" (Federal 12169) (if label top is silver, group listed as "The Midnighters (Formerly Known as the Royals)")	1954	$25.00	$50.00	$100.00

45s	Year	VG	VG+	NM
(if label is green, group listed as "The Midnighters (Formerly Known as the Royals)")	1954	$10.00	$20.00	$40.00
Hank Ballard and the Midnighters, "Teardrops on Your Letter" / "The Twist" (King 5171)	1959	$7.50	$15.00	$30.00
Bobby Bland, "Lovin' Blues" / "I.O.U. Blues" (Duke 105)	1952	$75.00	$150.00	$30.00
Bobby Bland, "Turn On Your Love Light" / "You're The One (That I Need)" (Duke 344)	1961	$5.00	$10.00	$20.00
Blue Magic, "Sideshow" / "Just Don't Want To Be Lonely" (Atco 6961)	1974		$3.00	$6.00
Booker T. and the M.G.'s, "Green Onions" / "Behave Yourself" (Stax 127)				
(if on gray label)	1962	$5.00	$10.00	$20.00
(if on blue label)	1962	$4.00	$8.00	$16.00
(if on Volt 102)	1962	$7.50	$15.00	$30.00
Boyz II Men, "Motownphilly" / "Under Pressure" (Motown 2090)	1991		$2.50	$5.00
James Brown, "Please Please Please" / "Why Do You Do Me?" (Federal 12258)	1956	$10.00	$20.00	$40.00
James Brown, "Try Me" / "Tell Me What I Did Wrong" (Federal 12337)	1958	$7.50	$15.00	$30.00
James Brown, "Please Please Please" / "In The Wee Wee Hours" (King 5853)	1964	$3.75	$7.50	$15.00
Jerry Butler, "He Will Break Your Heart" / "Thanks To You" (Vee Jay 354)	1960	$5.00	$10.00	$20.00
Jerry Butler, "Only the Strong Survive" / "Just Because I Really Love You" (Mercury 72898)	1969	$2.00	$4.00	$8.00
The Chairmen of the Board, "Give Me Just A Little More Time" / "Since the Days of Pigtails" (Invictus 9074)	1970		$3.00	$6.00
Gene Chandler, "Duke of Earl" / "Kissin' in the Kitchen" (Vee Jay 416)	1961	$6.25	$12.50	$25.00
(if second pressing, A-side credited to "The Duke of Earl")	1962	$5.00	$10.00	$20.00
Ray Charles, "Roll With Me Baby" / "The Midnight Hour" (Atlantic 976)	1952	$125.00	$250.00	$500.00
Ray Charles, "What'd I Say (Part I)" / "What'd I Say (Part II)" (Atlantic 2031)	1959	$5.00	$10.00	$20.00
Ray Charles, "Eleanor Rigby" / "Understanding" (ABC 11090)	1968	$2.00	$4.00	$8.00
The Clovers, "Don't You Know I Love You" / "Skylark" (Atlantic 934)	1951	$250.00	$500.00	$1,000.00
The Clovers, "Ting-A-Ling" / "Wonder Where My Baby's Gone" (Atlantic 969)	1952	$25.00	$50.00	$100.00
Arthur Conley, "Sweet Soul Music" / "Let's Go Steady" (Atco 6463)	1967	$2.50	$5.00	$10.00
Tyrone Davis, "Turn Back the Hands of Time" / "I Keep Coming Back" (Dakar 616)	1970	$2.00	$4.00	$8.00
The Delfonics, "La-La Means I Love You" / "Can't Get Over Losing You" (Philly Groove 150)	1968	$2.50	$5.00	$10.00
The Delfonics, "Didn't I (Blow Your Mind This Time)" / "Down Is Up, Up Is Down" (Philly Groove 161)	1970	$2.50	$5.00	$10.00
The Dells, "Tell the World" / "Blues at Three" (Vee Jay 134)	1955	$500	$1,000	$2,000
(if on red vinyl)	1955	$2,500	$3,750	$5,000
The Dells, "Oh What A Night" / "Believe Me" (Cadet 5649)	1969		$3.00	$6.00
The Dramatics, "Whatcha See is Whatcha Get" / "Thankful for Your Love" (Volt 4058)	1971	$2.00	$4.00	$8.00
The Esquires, "Get On Up" / "Listen To Me" (Bunky 7750)	1967	$2.50	$5.00	$10.00
The Five Keys, "The Glory of Love" / "Hucklebuck with Jimmy" (Aladdin 3099)	1951	$250.00	$500.00	$1,000.00
The Five Keys, "Red Sails in the Sunset" / "Be Anything, But Be Mine" (Aladdin 3127)	1952	$3,000	$4,500	$6,000
The Four Aims, "If Only I Had Known" / (B-side unknown) (Grady 012) (group later became the Four Tops)	1956	$150.00	$300.00	$600.00
Aretha Franklin, "Respect" / "Dr. Feelgood" (Atlantic 2403)	1967	$2.50	$5.00	$10.00
Aretha Franklin, "Who's Zoomin' Who" / "Bittersweet Love" (Arista 9410)	1985			$3.00
(with picture sleeve, add:)	1985			$3.00
Kenny Gamble, "Down by the Seashore" (Part 1) / "Down by the Seashore" (Part 2) (Arctic 107)	1965	$50.00	$100.00	$200.00
Major Harris, "Love Won't Let Me Wait" / "After Losing You" (Atlantic 3248)	1975		$2.00	$4.00
Jerry Butler and the Impressions, "For Your Precious Love" / "Sweet Was The Wine" (Vee Jay 280)	1958	$4,000	$6,000	$8,000
(if on Falcon 1013)	1958	$15.00	$30.00	$60.00
(if on Abner 1013)	1958	$10.00	$20.00	$40.00

45s	Year	VG	VG+	NM
The Impressions, "People Get Ready" / "I've Been Trying" (ABC Paramount 10622)	1965	$3.75	$7.50	$15.00
The Isley Brothers, "I Hear A Symphony" / "Who Could Ever Doubt My Love" (VIP 25020)	1965	$200.00	$400.00	$800.00
The Isley Brothers, "That Lady (Part 1)" / "That Lady (Part 2)" (T-Neck 2251)	1973		$2.50	$5.00
Ben E. King, "Stand By Me" / "On The Horizon" (Atco 6194)	1961	$5.00	$10.00	$20.00
(if on Atlantic 89361, B-side is the Coasters' "Yakety Yak")	1986			$3.00
(with picture sleeve promoting film "Stand By Me," add:)	1986			$3.00
King Floyd, "Groove Me" / "What Our Love Needs" (Chimneyville 435)	1970		$3.00	$6.00
Gladys Knight and the Pips, "Every Beat Of My Heart" / "Room In Your Heart"				
(if on Huntom 2510, group listed as "The Pips")	1961	$125.00	$250.00	$500.00
(if on Vee Jay 386, group listed as "The Pips")	1961	$5.00	$10.00	$20.00
(if on Vee Jay 386, B-side retitled "Ain'tcha Got Some Room (In Your Heart For Me)"	1961	$5.00	$10.00	$20.00
(if on Fury 1050, re-recordings)	1961	$6.25	$12.50	$25.00
Gladys Knight and the Pips, "Midnight Train to Georgia" / "Window Raising Granny" (Buddah 383)	1973		$2.50	$5.00
Love Unlimited, "Walking in the Rain with the One I Love" / "I Should Have Known" (Uni 55319)	1972		$3.00	$6.00
Love Unlimited Orchestra, "Love's Theme" / "Sweet Moments" (20th Century 2069)	1973		$2.50	$5.00
The Main Ingredient, "Just Don't Want To Be Lonely" / "Goodbye My Love" (RCA Victor APBO-0205)	1974		$2.50	$5.00
The Manhattans, "There Goes A Fool" / "Call Somebody Please" (Carnival 506)	1964	$10.00	$20.00	$40.00
The Manhattans, "Kiss and Say Goodbye" / "Wonderful World of Love" (Columbia 10310)	1976		$2.50	$5.00
Harold Melvin and the Blue Notes, "Yesterday I Had The Blues" / "Ebony Woman" (Philadelphia International 3525)	1973		$2.50	$5.00
(with picture sleeve, add:)	1973		$3.00	$6.00
The Moments, "Love On A Two-Way Street" / "I Won't Do Anything" (Stang 5012)	1970	$2.00	$4.00	$8.00
Aaron Neville, "Tell It Like It Is" / "Why Worry" (Par-Lo 101)				
(if on black-white label)	1966	$5.00	$10.00	$20.00
(if on turquoise label with silver print)	1966	$6.25	$12.50	$25.00
The O'Jays, "Deeper (In Love With You)" / "I've Got The Groove" (Neptune 22)	1970	$2.00	$4.00	$8.00
The O'Jays, "Back Stabbers" / "Sunshine" (Philadelphia International 3517)	1972		$2.50	$5.00
The Parliaments, "(I Wanna) Testify" / "I Can Feel The Ice Melting" (Revilot 207)	1967	$3.75	$7.50	$15.00
Wilson Pickett, "634-5789 (Soulsville, U.S.A.)" / "That's A Man's Way" (Atlantic 2320)	1966	$3.75	$7.50	$15.00
Lou Rawls, "In My Little Black Book" / "Just Thought You'd Like To Know" (Candix 305)	1960	$5.00	$10.00	$20.00
Lou Rawls, "You'll Never Find Another Love Like Mine" / "Let's Fall In Love All Over Again" (Philadelphia International 3592)	1976		$2.50	$5.00
Otis Redding, "Shake" / "You Don't Miss Your Water" (Volt 149)	1967	$3.00	$6.00	$12.00
Otis Redding, "(Sittin' On) The Dock of the Bay" / "Sweet Lorene" (Volt 157)				
(if black-red label)	1968	$3.00	$6.00	$12.00
(if multicolor label)	1968	$2.50	$5.00	$10.00
The Royals, "Work With Me Annie" / "Until I Die" (Federal 12169) (group later became the Midnighters)	1954	$62.50	$125.00	$250.00
Sam and Dave, "Soul Man" / "May I Baby" (Stax 231)	1967	$3.00	$6.00	$12.00
Sister Sledge, "We Are Family" / "Easier To Love" (Cotillion 44251)	1979		$2.00	$4.00
The Stylistics, "Betcha By Golly, Wow" / "Ebony Eyes" (Avco 4591)	1972		$2.50	$5.00
Tavares, "Heaven Must Be Missing An Angel (Part 1)" / (Part 2) (Capitol 4270)	1976		$2.50	$5.00
The Tymes, "So Much In Love" / "Roscoe James McClain" (Parkway 871)				
(if first pressing, A-side titled "So In Love")	1963	$6.25	$12.50	$25.00
(if second pressing, title corrected)	1963	$3.75	$7.50	$15.00
(with picture sleeve, add:)	1963	$7.50	$15.00	$30.00
The Tymes, "Isle of Love" / "I'm Always Chasing Rainbows" (Parkway 7039)				
(included as bonus single in "Somewhere" LP, value is for single alone)	1964	$3.75	$7.50	$15.00

45s	Year	VG	VG+	NM
The Whispers, "And The Beat Goes On" / "Can You Do The Boogie" (Solar YB-11894)	1980		$2.00	$4.00

LPs	Year	VG	VG+	NM
Ashford and Simpson, Is It Still Good To Ya (Warner Bros. BSK 3219)	1978	$2.50	$5.00	$10.00
Bobby Bland, Here's the Man! (Duke DLP-75) (mono)				
(if purple-yellow label)	1962	$50.00	$100.00	$200.00
(if orange label)	1962	$25.00	$50.00	$100.00
(if on Duke DLPS-75, stereo, with spoken intro to "36-22-36")	1962	$50.00	$100.00	$200.00
(if on Duke DLPS-75, stereo, no spoken intro to "36-22-36")	196??	$25.00	$50.00	$100.00
(if on ABC Duke DLP-75)	1974	$3.00	$6.00	$12.00
(if on MCA 27038, reissue)	198??	$2.00	$4.00	$8.00
Booker T. and the M.G.'s, And Now... Booker T. and the M.G.'s (Stax ST-711) (mono)	1966	$12.50	$25.00	$50.00
(if on Stax STS-711, stereo)	1966	$20.00	$40.00	$80.00
James Brown, Live at the Apollo (King 826)				
(if mono, custom back cover, "crownless King" label)	1963	$50.00	$100.00	$200.00
(if stereo, custom back cover, "crownless King" label)	1963	$75.00	$150.00	$300.00
(if mono, other King albums on back cover, "crownless King" label)	1963	$37.50	$75.00	$150.00
(if stereo, other King albums on back cover, "crownless King" label)	1963	$50.00	$100.00	$200.00
(if mono, "crowned King" label)	1966	$12.50	$25.00	$50.00
(if stereo, "crowned King" label)	1966	$17.50	$35.00	$70.00
James Brown, Raw Soul (King 1016) (mono)	1967	$12.50	$25.00	$50.00
(if on King KS-1016, stereo)	1967	$17.50	$35.00	$70.00
Jerry Butler, Jerry Butler, Esquire (Abner R-2001) (mono)	1959	$100.00	$200.00	$400.00
(if on Vee Jay LP-1027)	1960	$37.50	$75.00	$150.00
The Chairmen of the Board, Give Me Just A Little More Time (Invictus ST-7300)	1970	$10.00	$20.00	$40.00
Ray Charles, What'd I Say (Atlantic 8029) (mono)				
(if black label)	1959	$12.50	$25.00	$50.00
(if white "bullseye" label)	1960	$10.00	$20.00	$40.00
(if red-white label, white fan logo on right)	1960	$6.25	$12.50	$25.00
(if red-white label, black fan logo on right)	1962	$5.00	$10.00	$20.00
Ray Charles, Ingredients in a Recipe for Soul (ABC-Paramount 465) (mono)	1963	$5.00	$10.00	$20.00
(if on ABC-Paramount S-465, stereo)	1963	$6.25	$12.50	$25.00
The Clovers, The Clovers (Atlantic 1248) (mono)	1956	$150.00	$300.00	$600.00
(if on Atlantic 8009, reissue, black label)	1957	$100.00	$200.00	$400.00
(if on Atlantic 8009, white "bullseye" label)	1960	$75.00	$150.00	$300.00
(if on Atlantic 8009, mono, red-white label)	1961	$50.00	$100.00	$200.00
The Delfonics, The Sexy Sound of Soul (Philly Groove 1150)	1968	$20.00	$40.00	$80.00
The Dells, Oh What A Nite (Vee Jay LP 1010)				
(if maroon label)	1959	$200.00	$400.00	$800.00
(if black label with rainbow perimeter)	1961	$75.00	$150.00	$300.00
(if on VJLP 1010, late 1980's reissue, "Trade Mark Reg." on label)	198??	$2.50	$5.00	$10.00
The Dramatics, Whatcha See is Whatcha Get (Volt VOS-6018)	1972	$6.25	$12.50	$25.00
(if on Stax STX-4111, reissue)	1978	$2.50	$5.00	$10.00
The Esquires, Get On Up and Get Away (Bunky 300)	1968	$8.75	$17.50	$35.00
The Five Keys, The Best of the Five Keys (Aladdin LP-806) (mono) (pressings entitled "On the Town" are bootlegs)	1956	$1,000	$1,500	$2,000
The Five Keys, The Five Keys On Stage! (Capitol T 828)				
(if cover shows the lead singer's thumb sticking out in an angle that looks as if his zipper is open)	1957	$75.00	$150.00	$300.00
(if cover shows the lead singer's thumb airbrushed out, this copy is actually rarer than first pressing)	1957	$125.00	$250.00	$500.00
Aretha Franklin, I Never Loved A Man The Way I Love You (Atlantic 8139) (mono)	1967	$6.25	$12.50	$25.00

LPs	Year	VG	VG+	NM
(if on green-red label)	1969	$3.00	$6.00	$12.00
(if on Atlantic SD 8139, stereo, green-blue label)	1967	$5.00	$10.00	$20.00
Graham Central Station, Graham Central Station (Warner Bros. BS 2763)	1974	$2.50	$5.00	$10.00
(if on Warner Bros. BS4 2763, quadraphonic)	1974	$3.75	$7.50	$15.00
The Impressions, People Get Ready (ABC-Paramount 505) (mono)	1965	$7.50	$15.00	$30.00
(if on ABC-Paramount S-505, stereo)	1965	$10.00	$20.00	$40.00
The Intruders, Cowboys to Girls (Gamble G-5004)	1968	$12.50	$25.00	$50.00
The Isley Brothers, It's Our Thing (T-Neck TNS-3001)	1969	$5.00	$10.00	$20.00
Michael Jackson, Thriller (Epic QE 38112)	1982	$2.00	$4.00	$8.00
(if on Epic HE 48112, half-speed mastered edition)	1982	$10.00	$20.00	$40.00
(if on Epic 8E8 38867, picture disc)	1983	$3.75	$7.50	$15.00
Ben E. King, Spanish Harlem (Atco 33-133) (mono)				
(if yellow label with harp)	1961	$25.00	$50.00	$100.00
(if gold-gray label)	1962	$10.00	$20.00	$40.00
(if on Atco SD 33-133, stereo, yellow label with harp)	1961	$37.50	$75.00	$150.00
(if on Atco SD 33-133, stereo, purple-brown label)	1962	$12.50	$25.00	$50.00
Gladys Knight and the Pips, Claudine (Buddah BDS-5602)	1974	$7.50	$15.00	$30.00
Kool and the Gang, Ladies Night (De-Lite 9513)	1979	$2.50	$5.00	$10.00
Love Unlimited, Under the Influence Of... (20th Century T-414)	1973	$2.50	$5.00	$10.00
The Manhattans, Dedicated To You (Carnival CMLP-201) (mono)	1966	$62.50	$125.00	$250.00
(if on Carnival CSLP-201, stereo)	1966	$125.00	$250.00	$500.00
Harold Melvin and the Blue Notes, Wake Up Everybody (Philadelphia International PZ 33808)	1975	$3.00	$6.00	$12.00
(if on Philadelphia International PZQ 33808, quadraphonic)	1975	$5.00	$10.00	$20.00
The Midnighters, Their Greatest Hits (Federal 295-90) (10-inch LP)	1954	$4,000	$6,000	$8,000
(If on Federal 541, mono, red cover)	1955	$375.00	$750.00	$1,500.00
(if on Federal 541, mono, yellow cover)	1955	$250.00	$500.00	$1,000.00
Aaron Neville, Tell It Like It Is (Par-Lo 1) (mono)	1967	$20.00	$40.00	$80.00
(if on Par-Lo 1, stereo)	1967	$50.00	$100.00	$200.00
The O'Jays, Ship Ahoy (Philadelphia International KZ 32408)	1973	$2.50	$5.00	$10.00
(if on Philadelphia International PZQ 32408, quadraphonic)	1974	$3.75	$7.50	$15.00
(if on Philadelphia International PZ 32408, budget reissue)	198??	$2.00	$4.00	$8.00
Wilson Pickett, Wilson Pickett in Philadelphia (Atlantic SD 8270)	1970	$5.00	$10.00	$20.00
The Pointer Sisters, So Excited! (Planet BXL1-4355)	1982	$2.50	$5.00	$10.00
Lou Rawls, When You've Heard Lou, You've Heard It All (Philadelphia International JZ 35036)	1977	$2.50	$5.00	$10.00
Otis Redding, Pain in My Heart (Atco 33-161) (mono)	1964	$62.50	$125.00	$250.00
If on Atco SD-33-161, rechanneled stereo)	1968	$62.50	$125.00	$250.00
Sam and Dave, Hold On, I'm Comin' (Stax ST-708) (mono)	1966	$10.00	$20.00	$40.00
(if on Stax STS-708, stereo)	1966	$12.50	$25.00	$50.00
Sister Sledge, We Are Family (Cotillion SD 5209)	1979	$2.50	$5.00	$10.00
The Stylistics, Let's Put It All Together (Avco 69001)	1974	$3.75	$7.50	$15.00
Tavares, The Best of Tavares (Capitol ST-11701)	1977	$2.50	$5.00	$10.00
The Tymes, Somewhere (Parkway P 7039) (contains bonus single, deduct 20% if missing)	1964	$12.50	$25.00	$50.00

ROCK 'N' ROLL

History: There will always be arguments on what the first "rock 'n' roll" record was. Some people claim that the jump boogie song "Rocket 88," recorded by Ike Turner's Kings of Rhythm (and credited to "Jackie Brenston and his Delta Cats") at Sam Phillips' Sun Studios and released on Chess Records, is the first "rock 'n' roll" record. Others cite Bill Haley and His Comets' "(We're Gonna) Rock Around the Clock" for this honor, as it was the first "rock 'n' roll" record to hit #1 on the Billboard charts. There are also some arguments for the Chords' "Sh-Boom," Little Richard's "Tutti-Frutti," and Elvis Presley's "Heartbreak Hotel" as the first rock 'n' roll record. All of these songs could hold that claim, and so could many more.

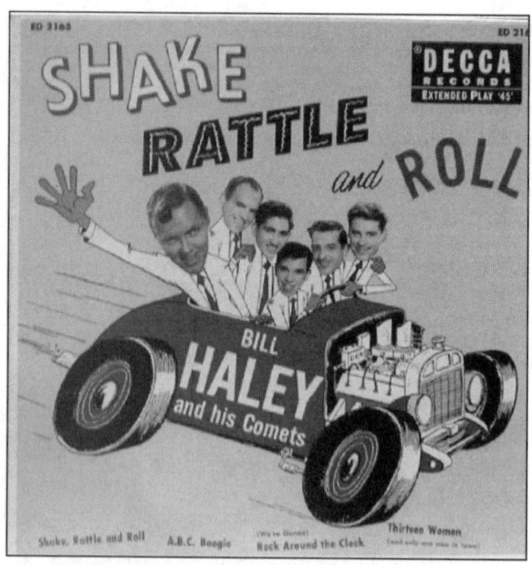

This EP contains Bill Haley and the Comets' biggest hit, "(We're Gonna) Rock Around The Clock." While the 45 itself has remained in print for over 30 years, Haley's albums and EPs containing this track are getting harder to find. From the Collection of Val Shively.

But no matter which song was first, the undeniable fact is that rock 'n' roll music, a genre blending rhythm and blues music with country-western twang and pop sensibility, took the 1950s by storm and continues, in a myriad of formats and styles, to this day.

Between 1955 and 1959, rock 'n' roll music was at its first great creative period. Artists used different musical styles—country and western music mixed with rhythm and blues, thick soul blended with musical sincerity—and created sounds and melodies and rhythms no one had ever heard before.

In Texas, Bill Haley and His Comets took their western bop music nationwide with their teen-dance classic "(We're Gonna) Rock Around the Clock." Buddy Holly and the Crickets followed the Comets out of Texas, and entered an international spotlight. Meanwhile, Elvis Presley had shaken up Memphis and was on his way to conquering the world, and following him from the south were Jerry Lee Lewis, Carl Perkins, and the Everly Brothers.

In Chicago, the Chess/Checker labels had two of the most successful influences in the early rock 'n' roll era—Chuck Berry on Chess, and Bo Diddley on Checker. Diddley, born Hubert Elias McDaniel, created the famous "Bo Diddley Beat," a clap-and-clap-and-clap-and-space-and-clap-clap rhythmic track featured in his hit "Bo Diddley," and later used by Buddy Holly, the Rolling Stones, George Michael, and others.

Meanwhile, Chuck Berry mixed the blues and intricate lyrics with his electric guitar, writing songs like "Johnny B. Goode" and "Sweet Little Sixteen," and influencing musicians on both sides of the Atlantic Ocean.

A rare picture sleeve featuring the legendary Chuck Berry. From the Collection of Val Shively.

Other cities began to add their sound to the rock 'n' roll fabric. In New Orleans, Fats Domino created a series of musical rock piano songs still being emulated by Louisiana musicians today. Other New Orleans artists added jazz and dixieland music to their own R&B and boogie-woogie music, creating music that was perfect for parties or for passion.

Also recording in New Orleans, but originally from Macon, Georgia, was "Little Richard" Penniman. Little Richard was one of the most charismatic performers in the early rock era, with his high-coiffed pompadour, mascara, and face powder, but there was no denying his musical talent and the influences it provided. He brought high-energy soul to the rock mix, and his songs "Tutti-Fruitti" and "Long Tall Sally" blasted from the nation's jukeboxes and radios.

Trivia

On this pressing of Jimmy Jones' "Handy Man," one can see how excited Cub Records was about this growing hit. The information, scribbled on the label by a Cub Records staffer, notes that "Handy Man" is big in Los Angeles and Pittsburgh, and that although Jones had a management contract with "Goldie Goldman," the singer had no long-term contract with Cub or MGM as of yet.

Jimmy Jones' first big hit—and, from the scribblings on the 45, a hot property that Cub Records desperately wanted to sign to a long-term deal. From the Collection of Val Shively.

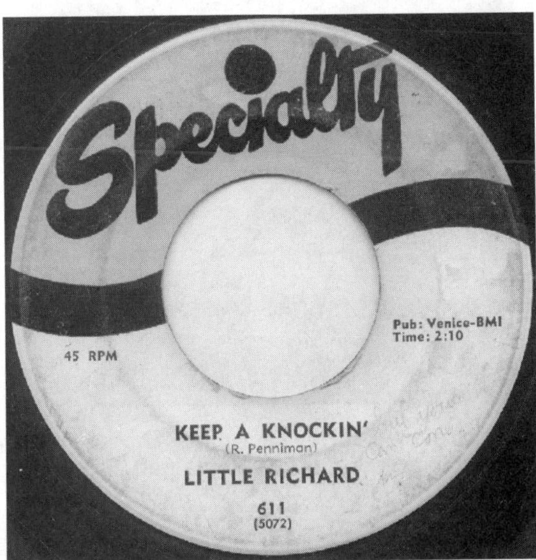

"Keep-a-Knockin" was one of many hits Little Richard recorded on the Specialty label.

The birth of rock 'n' roll also came at a time when the 7-inch, 45 rpm format achieved dominance over the 10-inch, 78 rpm disc. The 45 was created by RCA Records in 1948, and was designed as an alternative to the LP (long-playing) record, developed at that time by another label, Columbia Records. The 45 failed as a long-playing format, but survived instead as an alternative to fragile 10-inch 78s—the same amount of music could be placed on a lighter, more durable 45. By 1955, every major and minor record label produced both 45s and 78s. Just four years later, companies stopped making 78s and concentrated instead on 45s and LPs.

Along with rock 'n' roll and its purer derivatives, country/western and rhythm and blues, came doo-wop music. Part gospel, part harmony, part barbershop, doo-wop grew from the street corners of New York City, Boston, Philadelphia, and Pittsburgh, and teenagers whose intricate vocal harmonies produced some of the greatest sounds of the 1950s.

The first period of rock 'n' roll nearly ended in 1959, as a series of events derailed some careers and untimely ended others. Elvis Presley was drafted and served in the Army, away from his loyal fans. Jerry Lee Lewis married his 13-year-old cousin, and the negative publicity from the incestuous relationship destroyed his career. A plane crash took the lives of Buddy Holly, Ritchie Valens, and the Big Bopper. Chuck Berry spent time in jail; Little Richard ended his career and followed the path of the Lord.

The music that filled the void was ultimately provided by "teen idols," non-threatening singers whose good looks and adequate singing ability helped sell millions of singles and albums.

Although many of the early legends of rock 'n' roll had disappeared, others came to hold the torch high. One such group was the Kingsmen, who reached national fame with a half-mumbled, half-sung rocker called "Louie, Louie," which may or may not have had profane lyrics, depending on which elected official one speaks to.

Instrumentals were also extremely popular in the early rock 'n' roll era. Whether it involved Latin mambo, "twangy" guitar reverberations, or heavily orchestrated motion picture themes, it seemed that almost every third hit record on the radio in the 1950s did not have a lead singer on the track.

Some lucky rock artists turned their first hit into their biggest recording, and later built off that success to create a career. Del Shannon's "Runaway" was the first in a series of upbeat rockers with downbeat lyrics. Freddy Cannon's "Tallahassie Lassie" began a long line of rocking songs with booming bass drums. And Roy Orbison's impassioned, heartwrenching vocals on songs like "Only the Lonely" and "Crying" made him one of the top stars of the early 1960s.

Often cited as one of the earliest "garage rock" songs, "Louie Louie" has been covered by over 500 different singers and bands. The version by the Kingsmen is the most famous of them all.

Between 1959 and 1962, a new musical trend appeared—the "teen death" song. "Teen death" songs involved lovers caught in a desperate situation, usually a car crash or an accident of some sort, with either the boy dying (Ray Peterson's "Tell Laura I Love Her"), the girl dying (Mark Dinning's "Teen Angel"), or both of them dying (Johnny Preston's "Running Bear"). There were even songs about potential suicide (Joey Reynolds' "Endless Sleep") and commitment after death (J. Frank Wilson's "Last Kiss"). Although many of these songs were extremely ghoulish (in "Teen Angel," two teenagers escape from a car stalled on the railroad tracks, but the girl runs back to get the boy's high school ring and dies in the collision), it did create a new type of love song—where love is not stopped by earthly bonds.

Although the overall description of these genres is "fifties" music, music from as late as 1963 is grouped into this collection, as the arrival of the Beatles changed the musical landscape forever. Many artists who had hits on a constant basis in the 1950s and early 1960s were suddenly squeezed off the radio in favor of British singers and bands. But the Beatles were influenced by American rock 'n' roll as well; many of their earliest recordings were either covers of rock 'n' roll songs, or used riffs and melodies of previous rock songs.

The opening harmonica riff on Bruce Chanel's "Hey! Baby" was later re-interpreted by the Beatles for their song "Love Me Do." This pressing of the Bruce Chanel hit was the original release on LeCam; the song was later picked up for national distribution on Smash. From the Collection of Val Shively.

What To Look For: While well-played 45s can still be found in big cardboard boxes at the flea market or church sale, near-mint copies of 1950s records are becoming harder to find with every passing year.

Records were often removed from their picture sleeves, so that the sleeve could be tacked to a bedroom wall or trimmed for a scrapbook. This makes picture sleeves from the 1950s very difficult to find, and extremely collectible in near-mint condition.

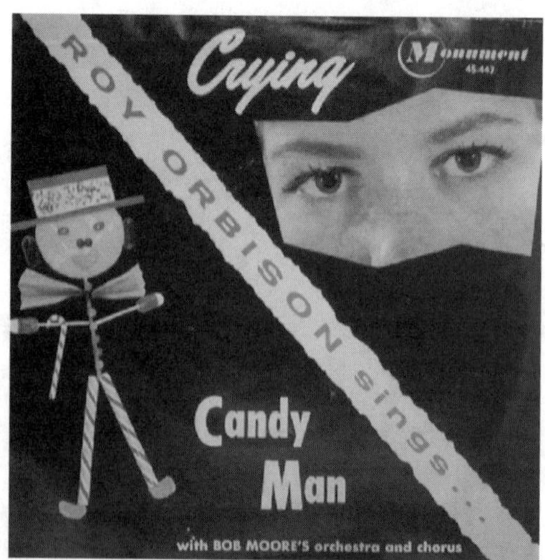

This picture sleeve of Roy Orbison's "Crying" is harder to find than the record it once contained. From the Collection of Val Shively.

In the 1950s, rock 'n' roll was driven by 45 RPM singles. Albums were recorded almost as an afterthought. Those "afterthoughts" are now worth hundreds of dollars in near-mint condition.

Trivia

Clarence Henry had a three-octave vocal range. Well, he actually had three voices. In his song "Ain't Got No Home," he sings in his normal voice—then in a falsetto to sing like a girl—then in a guttural grunt to sing like a frog. That's how he earned his nickname "Frog Man."

An early pressing of Clarence Henry's "Ain't Got No Home." Since the label artwork was printed on a blank background, along with the artist's name and title of the song, the label artwork can wear off over time.

While the existence of 45s eventually eliminated the need for 78 RPM records, both formats co-existed for a short time in the early rock 'n' roll era. By 1957, it was not economically feasible to press 78s for every record a label issued; only the biggest hits were issued on both formats. That being said, 78s pressed after 1957, because of their rarity in comparison to the mass-produced 45s, are worth much more than their 45 RPM counterparts.

A 78 pressing of one of the Everly Brothers' biggest hits. Courtesy Last Vestige Music Store, Albany, N.Y.

Trivia

Bobby Bare's first Top 40 hit was accidentally released under someone else's name. He and his friend Bill Parsons were in the studio working on one of Parsons' songs, "Rubber Dolly." As an afterthought, Bare recorded a novelty track, "The All-American Boy," a satire of Elvis Presley's career. Even though Bare's voice is on the record, the label erroneously credited Parsons with the hit.

Bobby Bare's biggest Top 40 hit, albeit credited to "Bill Parsons." Bare would have other pop and country hits, including "Shame on Me" and "DropKick Me Jesus."

As the 78 RPM record drifted into the history books, a new type of 45 emerged—the stereo pressing. Because these stereo 45s were pressed in fewer quantities, and because many of them actually contain true stereo recordings—not rechanneled or "fake" stereo, where the singer is in one speaker and the music is in the other—these records are collectible both for their rarity and their content.

References: Neely, Tim, *Goldmine Price Guide to 45 RPM Records*, Krause Publications, Iola, Wisconsin, 1999; Tobler, John, *The Buddy Holly Story*, Beaufort Books, N.Y., 1979; Whitburn, Joel, *Top Pop Singles 1955-1996*, Record Research, Inc., Menomonee Falls, Wisconsin, 1997.

Web pages: Chuck Berry's homepage: *http://www.chuckberry.com*; the official Jerry Lee Lewis homepage: *http://www.jerryleelewis.net*; a fanpage devoted to the career of Fats Domino: *http://www.fortunecity.com/tinpan/costello/472;* Roy Orbison's official Web site: *http://www.orbison.com*; Usenet newsgroups: *rec.music.rock-pop-r+b.1950s*.

Depending on the popularity of the artist, a "Stereo 45" can be worth two to three times the price of the same song on a monaural 45. From the Collection of Val Shively.

45s	Year	VG	VG+	NM
Jesse Belvin, "Goodnight My Love (Pleasant Dreams)" / "Let Me Love You Tonight" (Modern 1005	1956	$10.00	$20.00	$40.00
(if B-side is "I Want You With Me Xmas")	1956	$10.00	$20.00	$40.00
Chuck Berry, "Maybelline" / "Wee Wee Hours" (Chess 1604)	1955	$12.50	$25.00	$50.00
Chuck Berry, "Roll Over Beethoven" / "Drifting Heart" (Chess 1626)	1956	$12.50	$25.00	$50.00
Chuck Berry, "Sweet Little Sixteen" / "Reelin' and Rockin'" (Chess 1683)	1958	$7.50	$15.00	$30.00
The Big Bopper, "Chantilly Lace" / "The Purple People Eater Meets the Witch Doctor" (D 1008)	1958	$62.50	$125.00	$250.00
(if on Mercury 71343)	1958	$5.00	$10.00	$20.00
Gary "U.S." Bonds, "Quarter to Three" / "Time Ole Story" (Legrand 1008)				
(if record is credited to "U.S. Bonds", purple label)	1961	$10.00	$20.00	$40.00
(if record is credited to "Gary U.S. Bonds", gold-red label)	1961	$3.75	$7.50	$15.00
(with picture sleeve, add:)	1961	$10.00	$20.00	$40.00
Freddie "Boom Boom" Cannon, "Tallahassee Lassie" / "You Know" (Swan 4031)	1959	$5.00	$10.00	$20.00
Jimmy Clanton, "Go, Jimmy, Go" / "I Trusted You" (Ace 575)				
(if normal white label)	1959	$5.00	$10.00	$20.00
(if purple label)	1959	$6.25	$12.50	$25.00
(with picture sleeve, add:)	1959	$7.50	$15.00	$30.00
Dee Clark, "Raindrops" / "I Want To Love You" (Vee Jay 383)	1961	$5.00	$10.00	$20.00
The Coasters, "Yakety Yak" / "Zing Went the Strings of My Heart" (Atlantic 6116)	1958	$6.25	$12.50	$25.00
Eddie Cochran, "Summertime Blues" / "Live Again" (Liberty 55144)	1958	$7.50	$15.00	$30.00
Sam Cooke, "You Send Me" / "Summertime" (Keen 34013)	1957	$6.25	$12.50	$25.00
Sam Cooke, "Cupid" / "Farewell, My Darling" (RCA Victor 47-7883)	1961	$3.75	$7.50	$15.00
(with picture sleeve, add:)	1961	$6.25	$12.50	$25.00
The Crickets, "That'll Be The Day" / "I'm Looking For Someone To Love" (Brunswick 55009)	1957	$12.50	$25.00	$50.00
The Crickets, "Peggy Sue Got Married" / "Don't Cha Know" (Coral 62238)	1960	$10.00	$20.00	$40.00
Bobby Day, "Rock-N Robin" / "Over and Over" (Class 229)	1958	$7.50	$15.00	$30.00
Joey Dee and the Starliters, "Peppermint Twist - Part 1" / "Peppermint Twist - Part 2" (Roulette 4401)	1961	$4.00	$8.00	$16.00
Bo Diddley, "Bo Diddley" / "I'm A Man" (Checker 814)	1955	$12.50	$25.00	$50.00

45s	Year	VG	VG+	NM
Bo Diddley, "Say Man" / "Clock Strikes Twelve" (Checker 931)	1959	$7.50	$15.00	$30.00
(with picture sleeve, add:)	1959	$100.00	$200.00	$400.00
Fats Domino, "The Fat Man" / "Detroit City Blues" (Imperial 5058) (blue label, "script" logo)	1950	$500.00	$1,000.00	$2,000.00
Fats Domino, "Blueberry Hill" / "Honey Chile" (Imperial 5407)				
(if black vinyl, red label)	1956	$6.25	$12.50	$25.00
(if pressed on red vinyl)	1956	$37.50	$75.00	$150.00
(if black vinyl, black label)	1957	$3.75	$7.50	$15.00
Tommy Edwards, "It's All In The Game" / "Please Love Me Forever" (MGM 12688)	1958	$3.75	$7.50	$15.00
Everly Brothers, "Wake Up Little Susie" / "Maybe Tomorrow" (Cadence 1337)	1957	$7.50	$15.00	$30.00
(with picture sleeve, add:)	1957	$62.50	$125.00	$250.00
Everly Brothers, "Cathy's Clown" / "Always It's You" (Warner Bros. 5151)				
(if first pressing, pink labels)	1960	$5.00	$10.00	$20.00
(if second pressing, red labels with arrows)	1960	$3.75	$7.50	$15.00
(with picture sleeve, add:)	1960	$12.50	$25.00	$50.00
(if stereo pressing)	1960	$12.50	$25.00	$50.00
(if gold vinyl promo pressing)	1960	$25.00	$50.00	$100.00
The Fendermen, "Mule Skinner Blues" / "Torture"				
(if on Cuca 1003, first recording)	1960	$50.00	$100.00	$200.00
(if on Soma 1137, alternate recording)	1960	$6.25	$12.50	$25.00
Frankie Ford, "Sea Cruise" / "Roberta" (Ace 554)	1959	$7.50	$15.00	$30.00
Bill Haley and His Comets, "(We're Gonna) Rock Around the Clock" / "Thirteen Women (And Only One Man In Town)" (Decca 29124)				
(if lines on either side of "Decca")	1954	$15.00	$30.00	$60.00
(if star under "Decca")	1955	$5.00	$10.00	$20.00
Bill Haley and His Comets, "See You Later, Alligator" / "The Paper Boy (On Main Street, U.S.A.)" (Decca 29791)	1956	$6.25	$12.50	$25.00
Clarence "Frogman" Henry, "Ain't Got No Home" / "Troubles, Troubles" (Argo 5259)	1956	$5.00	$10.00	$20.00
Buddy Holly, "Peggy Sue" / "Everyday" (Coral 61885)				
(if orange label)	1957	$12.50	$25.00	$50.00
(if black label with color bars)	196??	$6.25	$12.50	$25.00
The Isley Brothers, "Shout (Part 1)" / "Shout (Part 2)" (RCA Victor 47-7588)	1959	$7.50	$15.00	$30.00
(if on RCA Victor 61-7588, stereo)	1959	$15.00	$30.00	$60.00
The Isley Brothers, "Twist and Shout" / "Spanish Twist" (Wand 124)	1962	$5.00	$10.00	$20.00
The Kingsmen, "Louie Louie" / "Haunted Castle" (Jerden 712)	1963	$15.00	$30.00	$60.00
(if on Wand 143)	1963	$5.00	$10.00	$20.00
(if on Wand 143, A-side is titled "Louie Louie 64-65-66...")	1966	$3.75	$7.50	$15.00
(if on Wand 143, B-side is "Little Green Thing")	196??	$3.75	$7.50	$15.00
Bobby Lewis, "Tossin' and Turnin'" / "Oh Yes I Love You" (Beltone 1002)	1961	$6.25	$12.50	$25.00
Little Richard, "Tutti-Frutti" / "I'm Just A Lonely Guy" (Specialty 561)	1955	$12.50	$25.00	$50.00
Little Richard, "Keep-a-Knockin'" / "Can't Believe You Wanna Leave" (Specialty 611)	1957	$7.50	$15.00	$30.00
(with picture sleeve, add:)	1957	$15.00	$30.00	$60.00
Gene McDaniels, "A Hundred Pounds of Clay" / "Take A Chance on Love" (Liberty 55308)	1961	$40.00	$8.00	$16.00
Chuck Miller, "The House of Blue Lights" / "Can't Help Wonderin'" (Mercury 70627)	1955	$5.00	$10.00	$20.00
The Mystics, "Hushabye" / "Adam and Eve" (Laurie 3028) (mono)	1959	$7.50	$15.00	$30.00
(if on Laurie S-3028, stereo)	1959	$30.00	$60.00	$120.00
Ricky Nelson, "I'm Walkin'" / "A Teenager's Romance" (Verve 10047)				
(if first pressing, orange-yellow label)	1957	$12.50	$25.00	$50.00
(if second pressing, black-white label)	1957	$10.00	$20.00	$40.00
Ricky Nelson, "Poor Little Fool" / "Don't Leave Me This Way" (Imperial 5528)	1958	$7.50	$15.00	$30.00
Ricky Nelson, "Travelin' Man" / "Hello Mary Lou" (Imperial 5741)	1961	$6.25	$12.50	$25.00
(if on red vinyl)	1961	$200.00	$400.00	$800.00
Roy Orbison, "Only the Lonely (Know the Way I Feel)" / "Here Comes That Song Again" (Monument 421)	1960	$6.25	$12.50	$25.00
Roy Orbison, "Crying" / "Candy Man" (Monument 447)	1961	$5.00	$10.00	$20.00
(with picture sleeve, add:)	1961	$10.00	$20.00	$40.00
Gene Pitney, "(The Man Who Shot) Liberty Valance" / "Take It Like A Man" (Musicor 1020)	1962	$3.75	$7.50	$15.00
The Platters, "I'll Cry When You're Gone" / "I Need You All The Time" (Federal 12164)	1954	$250.00	$500.00	$1,000.00

45s	Year	VG	VG+	NM
The Platters, "Only You (And You Alone)" / "You Made Me Cry" (Federal 12244)	1955	$75.00	$150.00	$300.00
The Platters, "Only You (And You Alone)" / "Bark, Battle and Ball" (Mercury 70633)				
(if first pressing, pink label)	1955	$12.50	$25.00	$50.00
(if second pressing, black label)	1955	$10.00	$20.00	$40.00
Elvis Presley, "Heartbreak Hotel" / "I Was The One" (RCA Victor 47-6420)	1956	$10.00	$20.00	$40.00
Elvis Presley, "Don't Be Cruel" / "Hound Dog" (RCA Victor 47-6604)	1956	$7.50	$15.00	$30.00
(with picture sleeve, if "Hound Dog!" is listed above "Don't Be Cruel", add:)	1956	$30.00	$60.00	$120.00
(with picture sleeve, if "Don't Be Cruel" is listed above "Hound Dog!", add:)	1956	$50.00	$100.00	$200.00
Elvis Presley, "Love Me Tender" / "Anyway You Want Me (That's How I Will Be)" (RCA Victor 47-6643)				
(if record refers to movie "Love Me Tender")	1956	$7.50	$15.00	$30.00
(if record has no reference to "Love Me Tender")	1956	$10.00	$20.00	$40.00
(with black/white picture sleeve, add:)	1956	$45.00	$90.00	$180.00
(with black/green picture sleeve, add:)	1956	$18.75	$37.50	$75.00
(with black/dark pink picture sleeve, add:)	1956	$10.00	$20.00	$40.00
(with black/light pink picture sleeve, add:)	1956	$7.50	$15.00	$30.00
Johnnie Ray, "Cry" / "The Little White Cloud That Cried" (Okeh 6840)	1951	$5.00	$10.00	$20.00
Johnnie Ray, "Just Walking In the Rain" / "In the Candlelight" (Columbia 40729)	1956	$2.50	$5.00	$10.00
The Royal Teens, "Short Shorts" / "Planet Rock" (ABC-Paramount 9882)	1958	$7.50	$15.00	$30.00
Santo and Johnny, "Sleep Walk" / "All Night Diner" (Canadian American 103)	1959	$6.25	$12.50	$25.00
Del Shannon, "Runaway" / "Jody" (Big Top 3067)	1961	$7.50	$15.00	$30.00
Del Shannon, "From Me To You" / "Two Silhouettes" (Big Top 3152)	1963	$15.00	$30.00	$60.00
Huey "Piano" Smith, "Don't You Just Know It" / "High Blood Pressure" (Ace 545)	1958	$6.25	$12.50	$25.00
Johnny Tillotson, "Poetry in Motion" / "Princess, Princess" (Cadence 1384)	1960	$5.00	$10.00	$20.00
Ike and Tina Turner, "A Fool In Love" / "The Way You Love Me" (Sue 730)	1960	$7.50	$15.00	$30.00
Ritchie Valens, "Donna" / "La Bamba" (Del-Fi 4110)				
(if first pressing, blue/green/black label with circles)	1958	$17.50	$35.00	$70.00
(if second pressing, green label)	1958	$10.00	$20.00	$40.00
(if third pressing, light blue label)	1958	$7.50	$15.00	$30.00
(if black label with blue sawtooth border)	196??	$3.75	$7.50	$15.00
(if light blue label, black sawtooth border)	196??	$6.25	$12.50	$25.00
Gene Vincent and his Blue Caps, "Be-Bop-A-Lula" / "Woman Love" (Capitol F3450)				
(with large Capitol logo)	1956	$17.50	$35.00	$70.00
(with smaller Capitol logo)	1956	$12.50	$25.00	$50.00
Billy Ward and the Dominoes, "Sixty Minute Man" / "I Can't Escape From You" (Federal 12022AA)	1951	$125.00	$25.00	$500.00
Jackie Wilson, "Lonely Teardrops" / "In The Blue of the Evening" (Brunswick 55105)	1958	$7.50	$15.00	$30.00

78s	Year	VG	VG+	NM
Chuck Berry, "Maybelline" / "Wee Wee Hours" (Chess 1604)	1955	$17.50	$35.00	$70.00
Chuck Berry, "Too Pooped to Pop" / "Let It Rock" (Chess 1747)	1960	$250.00	$500.00	$1,000.00
Eddie Cochran, "Summertime Blues" / "Live Again" (Liberty 55144)	1958	$125.00	$250.00	$500.00
The Crickets, "That'll Be The Day" / "I'm Looking For Someone To Love" (Brunswick 55009)	1957	$75.00	$150.00	$300.00
Sam Cooke, "You Send Me" / "Summertime" (Keen 34013)	1957	$15.00	$30.00	$60.00
Bo Diddley, "Bo Diddley" / "I'm A Man" (Checker 814)	1955	$15.00	$30.00	$60.00
Bo Diddley, "Say Man" / "Clock Strikes Twelve" (Checker 931)	1959	$30.00	$60.00	$120.00
Fats Domino, "Blueberry Hill" / "Honey Chile" (Imperial 5407)	1956	$7.50	$15.00	$30.00
Everly Brothers, "Wake Up Little Susie" / "Maybe Tomorrow" (Cadence 1337)	1957	$15.00	$30.00	$60.00
Bill Haley and His Comets, "(We're Gonna) Rock Around the Clock" / "Thirteen Women (And Only One Man In Town)" (Decca 29124)				
(if black label, gold print, "Decca Personality Series")	1955	$30.00	$60.00	$120.00
(if black label, silver print, star under "Decca")	1955	$10.00	$20.00	$40.00

78s	Year	VG	VG+	NM
Ricky Nelson, "It's Late" / "Never Be Anyone Else But You" (Imperial 5565)	1959	$100.00	$200.00	$400.00
Jackie Wilson, "Lonely Teardrops" / "In The Blue of the Evening" (Brunswick 55105)	1958	$75.00	$150.00	$300.00
Little Richard, "Tutti-Frutti" / "I'm Just A Lonely Guy" (Specialty 561)	1955	$12.50	$25.00	$50.00
Gene Vincent and his Blue Caps, "Be-Bop-A-Lula" / "Woman Love" (Capitol 3450)	1956	$30.00	$60.00	$120.00

LPs	Year	VG	VG+	NM
Chuck Berry, After School Session (Chess LP-1426) (mono)	1958	$50.00	$100.00	$200.00
(if on Chess LPS-1426, rechanneled stereo)	196??	$3.00	$6.00	$12.00
The Big Bopper, Chantilly Lace (Mercury MG-20402)				
(if black label)	1959	$125.00	$250.00	$500.00
(if on red label, with either black or black and white Mercury logo on top)	1964	$50.00	$100.00	$200.00
(if on red label, twelve Mercury logos around the perimeter)	196??	$6.25	$12.50	$25.00
(if Chicago skyline label)	1975	$3.75	$7.50	$15.00
(if on Mercury 832902-1, new number, black label)	1988	$3.75	$7.50	$15.00
(if on Pickwick SPC-3365, budget reissue)	1973	$3.75	$7.50	$15.00
Gary U.S. Bonds, Dance 'Til Quarter to Three (Legrand LLP-3001) (mono)	1961	$25.00	$50.00	$100.00
Freddie "Boom Boom" Cannon, The Explosive! Freddy Cannon (Swan LP-502) (mono)	1960	$30.00	$60.00	$120.00
(if on Swan LPS-502, stereo)	1960	$75.00	$150.00	$300.00
Sam Cooke, Twistin' the Night Away (RCA Victor LPM-2625) (mono)	1962	$7.50	$15.00	$30.00
(if on RCA Victor LSP-2555, stereo)	1962	$5.00	$10.00	$20.00
The Crickets, The "Chirping" Crickets (Brunswick BL 54038) (mono)				
(if textured cover)	1957	$200.00	$400.00	$800.00
(if regular cover)	1957	$150.00	$300.00	$600.00
The Crickets, In Style with the Crickets (Coral CRL 57230) (mono)	1960	$50.00	$100.00	$200.00
(if on Coral CRL 757230, stereo)	1960	$100.00	$200.00	$400.00
Bobby Day, Rockin' with Robin (Class LP-5002) (mono)	1959	$100.00	$200.00	$400.00
(if on Rendezvous M-1312, reissue)	196??	$20.00	$40.00	$80.00
Joey Dee and the Starliters, Doin' the Twist at the Peppermint Lounge (Roulette R-25166) (mono)	1961	$10.00	$20.00	$40.00
(if on Roulette SR-25166, stereo)	1961	$12.50	$25.00	$50.00
Bo Diddley, Bo Diddley (Checker LP 1431) (mono)	1958	$37.50	$75.00	$150.00
(if on Chess LP 1431)	1958	$50.00	$100.00	$200.00
(if on Checker LP-3007, titled "Boss Man")	1967	$20.00	$40.00	$80.00
(if on Checker LPS-3007, "Boss Man," rechanneled stereo)	1967	$12.50	$25.00	$50.00
(if on Chess CH-9194, reissue)	1986	$2.50	$5.00	$10.00
Fats Domino, Rock 'n' rollin' with Fats Domino (Imperial 9004)				
(if maroon label)	1956	$37.50	$75.00	$150.00
(if black label with stars on top)	1958	$20.00	$40.00	$80.00
(if black-pink label)	1964	$6.25	$12.50	$25.00
(if black-green label)	1967	$5.00	$10.00	$20.00
(if on Imperial LP-12388, retitled Rock 'n' rollin' with Fats Domino, rechanneled stereo)	1968	$3.00	$6.00	$12.00
The Everly Brothers, Songs Our Daddy Taught Us (Cadence CLP-3016) (mono)				
(if first pressing, metronome graphic)	1958	$25.00	$50.00	$100.00
(if second pressing, black border)	1962	$15.00	$30.00	$60.00
(if on Rhino RNLP-212, reissue)	1985	$2.50	$5.00	$10.00
The Everly Brothers, It's Everly Time! (Warner Bros. W 1381)	1960	$7.50	$15.00	$30.00
(if on Warner Bros. WS 1381, stereo)	1960	$10.00	$20.00	$40.00
(if on Warner Bros. PRO 134, 10-inch promo sampler)	1960	$150.00	$300.00	$600.00
The Fendermen, Mule Skinner Blues (Soma MG-1240)				
(if on blue vinyl)	1960	$2,000.00	$3,000.00	$4,000.00
(if on black vinyl)	1960	$300.00	$600.00	$1,200.00
Frankie Ford, Let's Take a Sea Cruise (Ace LP 1005) (mono)	1959	$75.00	$150.00	$300.00
Clarence "Frogman" Henry, You Always Hurt the One You Love (Argo LP-4009) (mono)	1961	$75.00	$150.00	$300.00
(if on Cadet LP-4009, mono, includes Cadet albums in Argo sleeves)	1966	$12.50	$25.00	$50.00
Buddy Holly, Buddy Holly (Coral CRL 57210) (mono)				
(if maroon label)	1958	$100.00	$200.00	$400.00
(if black label with color bars)	1964	$25.00	$50.00	$100.00
(if on MCA 25239, reissue)	1989	$3.00	$6.00	$12.00
(if on MCA 11161, audiophile reissue, gatefold cover)	1995	$10.00	$20.00	$40.00

LPs	Year	VG	VG+	NM
Buddy Holly, That'll Be The Day (Decca DL 8707)				
(if black label with silver print)	1958	$375.00	$750.00	$1,500.00
(if black label with color bars)	1961	$75.00	$150.00	$300.00
The Isley Brothers, Shout! (RCA Victor LPM-2156) (mono, "Long Play" on label)	1959	$30.00	$60.00	$120.00
(if on RCA Victor LSP-2156, stereo, "Living Stereo" on label)	1959	$50.00	$100.00	$200.00
Johnny and the Hurricanes, Johnny and the Hurricanes (Warwick W-2007) (mono)	1959	$37.50	$75.00	$150.00
(if on Warwick W-2007ST, stereo)	1959	$75.00	$150.00	$300.00
Bobby Lewis, Tossin' and Turnin' (Beltone 4000) (mono)	1961	$50.00	$100.00	$200.00
Little Richard, Here's Little Richard (Specialty 100) (mono)	1957	$175.00	$350.00	$700.00
(if on Specialty SP-2100, thick vinyl)	1957	$50.00	$100.00	$200.00
Gene McDaniels, In Times Like These (Liberty LRP-3146) (mono)	1960	$7.50	$15.00	$30.00
(if on Liberty LST-7146, stereo, blue vinyl)	1960	$50.00	$100.00	$200.00
(if on Liberty LST-7146, stereo, black vinyl)	1960	$10.00	$20.00	$40.00
Chuck Miller, After Hours (Mercury MG-20195) (mono)	1958	$20.00	$40.00	$80.00
Ricky Nelson, Ricky (Imperial LP 9048) (mono)				
(if black label with stars)	1957	$25.00	$50.00	$100.00
(if black label with pink and white at left)	1964	$6.25	$12.50	$25.00
(if black label with green and white at left)	1966	$5.00	$10.00	$20.00
(if on Imperial LP 12392, rechanneled stereo)	1968	$3.75	$7.50	$15.00
Roy Orbison, Crying (Monument M-4007) (mono)	1962	$30.00	$60.00	$120.00
(if on Monument SM-14007, stereo)	1962	$150.00	$30.00	$600.00
The Platters, The Platters (Federal 549) (mono)	1957	$400.00	$800.00	$1,600.00
The Platters, The Flying Platters Around the World (Mercury MG-20366)	1958	$7.50	$15.00	$30.00
(if on Mercury SR-60043, stereo)	1959	$12.50	$25.00	$50.00
Elvis Presley, Elvis Presley (RCA Victor LPM-1254) (mono)				
(if "Long Play" on label, "Elvis" in pale pink, "Presley" in pale green on cover, pale green logo box in upper right front cover)	1956	$125.00	$250.00	$500.00
(if "Long Play" on label, "Elvis" in pale pink, "Presley" in neon green on cover, neon green logo box in upper right front cover)	1956	$100.00	$200.00	$400.00
(if "Long Play" on label, "Elvis" in pale pink, "Presley" in neon green on cover, black logo box in upper right front cover)	1956	$62.50	$125.00	$250.00
(if "Long Play" on label, "Elvis" in neon pink, "Presley" in neon green on cover, black logo box in upper right front cover)	1958	$50.00	$100.00	$200.00
(if "Mono" on label, cover photo is off-center but resembles 1958 release)	1963	$30.00	$60.00	$120.00
(if "Monaural" on label)	1964	$15.00	$30.00	$60.00
(if on RCA Victor LSP-1254(e), "Stereo Electronically Reproduced" and silver "RCA Victor" on label)	1962	$50.00	$100.00	$200.00
(if on RCA Victor LSP-1254(e), same as above, except white "RCA Victor" on label)	1965	$10.00	$20.00	$40.00
(if on RCA Victor LSP-1254(e), orange label, stiff non-flexible vinyl)	1968	$7.50	$15.00	$30.00
(if on RCA Victor LSP-1254(e), tan label)	1975	$3.75	$7.50	$15.00
(if on RCA Victor LSP-1254(e), black label, dog near top)	1976	$3.00	$6.00	$12.00
(if on RCA Victor AFL1-1245(e), some copies have stickers over original catalog numbers)	1977	$3.00	$6.00	$12.00
Elvis Presley, Elvis (RCA Victor LPM-1382) (mono)				
(if matrix number is 15S, 17S or 19S, containing alternate take of "Old Shep" with lyrics "he grew old AND his eyes were growing dim")	1956	$200.00	$400.00	$800.00
(if songs are listed as "Band 1" through "Band 6" on label)	1956	$100.00	$200.00	$400.00
(if back cover has ads for other albums)	1956	$75.00	$150.00	$300.00
(if back cover has no ads for other albums, "Long Play" on label)	1956	$75.00	$150.00	$300.00

(if "Mono" on label)	1963	$20.00	$40.00	$80.00
LPs	**Year**	**VG**	**VG+**	**NM**
(if "Monaural" on label)	1965	$15.00	$30.00	$60.00
(if on RCA Victor LSP-1382(e), "Stereo Electronically Reprocessed" and silver "RCA Victor" on label)	1962	$50.00	$100.00	$200.00
(if on RCA Victor LSP-1382(e), same as above, except white "RCA Victor" on label)	1964	$12.50	$25.00	$50.00
(if on RCA Victor LSP-1382(e), orange label, non-flexible vinyl)	1968	$7.50	$15.00	$30.00
(if on RCA Victor LSP-1382(e), orange label, flexible vinyl)	1971	$5.00	$10.00	$20.00
(if on RCA Victor LSP-1382(e), tan label)	1975	$3.75	$7.50	$15.00
(if on RCA Victor LSP-1382(e), black label, dog near top)	1976	$3.00	$6.00	$12.00
(if on RCA Victor AFL1-1382(e), some copies have stickers over original catalog numbers)	1977	$3.00	$6.00	$12.00
Johnnie Ray, I Cry For You (Columbia CL 2510) (10-inch LP)	1955	$17.50	$35.00	$70.00
Santo and Johnny, Santo and Johnny (Canadian American CALP-1001) (mono)	1959	$15.00	$30.00	$60.00
(if on Canadian American SCALP-1001, stereo)	1959	$20.00	$40.00	$80.00
Del Shannon, Little Town Flirt (Big Top 12-1308)				
(if both sides are mono)	1963	$37.50	$75.00	$150.00
(if one side is mono, the other in stereo)	1963	$250.00	$500.00	$1,000.00
(if both sides are stereo; playing this title is the best way to identify if the record is stereo or mono)	1963	$375.00	$750.00	$1,500.00
Huey "Piano" Smith, Having a Good Time (Ace LP-1004) (mono)	1959	$100.00	$200.00	$400.00
Ike and Tina Turner, Ike and Tina Turner's Kings of Rhythm Dance (Sue LP 2003) (mono)	1962	$100.00	$200.00	$400.00
Ritchie Valens, In Concert at Pacoima Jr. High (Del-Fi DFLP 1214)	1960	$62.50	$125.00	$250.00
(if on Rhino RNLP 70233, reissue)	1987	$2.50	$5.00	$10.00
Billy Ward and the Dominos, Billy Ward and His Dominoes (Federal 295-94) (10-inch LP)	1955	$6,000	$9,500	$13,000

A mixture of doo-wop, soul and fantasy, the Cadets' "Stranded in the Jungle" is a popular staple on rock and roll oldies stations today.

ROCKABILLY

History: As its name suggests, "Rockabilly" is a hybrid of rock 'n' roll and hillbilly music. As musicians played blues and gospel music with an uptempo rocking beat, rockabilly music rose from the clubs and honky tonks throughout the South, and became one of the building blocks of modern rock 'n' roll.

The most famous haven for rockabilly music was the Sun Studios in Memphis, Tennessee. There, studio owner Sam Perkins cultivated rockabilly artists like Elvis Presley, Carl Perkins, Charlie Feathers, and Sleepy LaBeef on his Sun label. Rockabilly music also evolved in Texas, where Bill Haley and Buddy Holly's early hits, "Rock Around the Clock" and "That'll Be the Day" are rockabilly classics, even though the artists themselves called the music "western bop."

Charlie Feathers' "Tongue-Tied Jill" is one of the rarest rockabilly records ever pressed, either as a 78 or as a 45. Courtesy Good Rockin' Tonight/Collectors Universe.

At the same time, artists like Gene Vincent, Eddie Cochran, and Wanda Jackson garnered major label contracts with rockabilly smashes like "Summertime Blues," "Let's Have A Party," and "Be-Bop-A-Lula."

Although Elvis Presley's rockabilly output (his five singles on Sun and his early RCA recordings) are very collectible, one of the most collectible "pure rockabilly" artists is Charlie Feathers. Feathers, who mixed bluegrass music into his own version of rockabilly, recorded some singles on the Sun label, as well as for Sam Phillips' "Flip" subsidiary label. Even though his records did not have the same success as other rockabilly artists, Feathers finally received his due in the 1970s. While touring England, his live performances inspired a new generation of British rockabilly musicians, who today spend thousands of dollars for Feathers' 1950s recordings.

Trivia

Although he would later have a Top 10 hit with "You're Sixteen," Johnny Burnette's Coral releases are among the most collectible records of his career.

One of the highly collectible Johnny Burnette 45s on the Coral label. The song allegedly got its name when Burnette and his brother Dorsey watched their toddler sons, "Rocky" and "Billy," dance around the floor while the song was being rehearsed. Courtesy Good Rockin' Tonight/Collectors Universe.

The initial rockabilly wave lasted from 1954 to 1959. Over the years, some artists have revived the rockabilly sound and beat, most notably the Stray Cats, Billy Swan, and the Reverend Horton Heat.

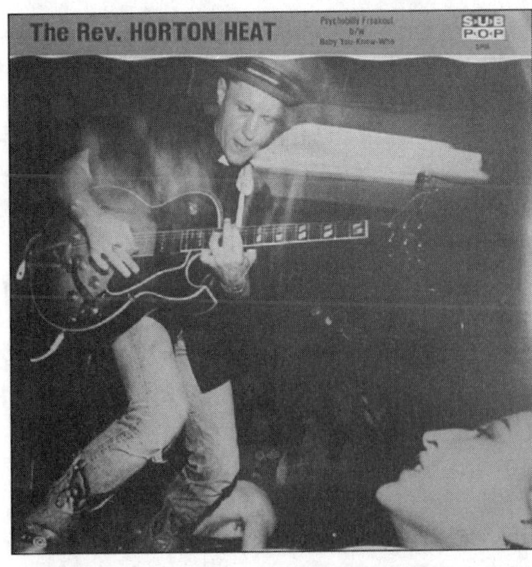

The Reverend Horton Heat's high-energy rockabilly-punk recordings prove that rockabilly music still stands the test of time today.

Trivia

Eddie Cochran's rockabilly classics include "Summertime Blues" and "C'mon Everybody." He also wrote "Twenty Flight Rock," which was used in the motion picture "The Girl Can't Help It."

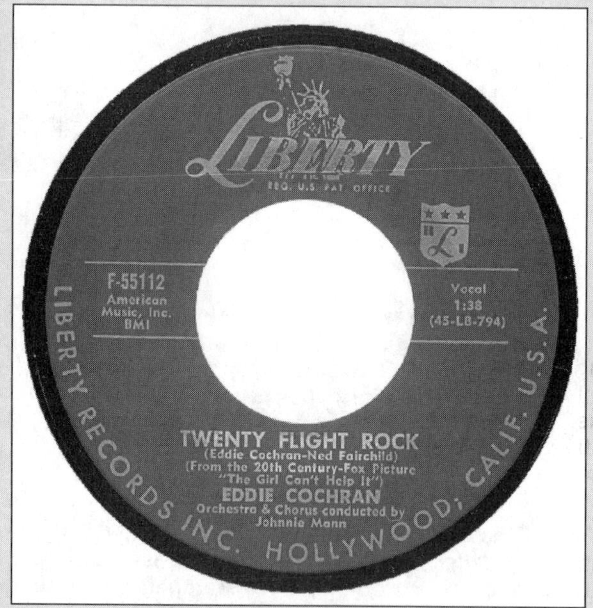

Eddy Cochran's 7-inch of "Twenty Flight Rock." Courtesy Good Rockin' Tonight / Collectors Universe.

What To Look For: Rockabilly records are highly collectible. In fact, almost anything rockabilly pioneer Charlie Feathers ever recorded is extremely desirous by rockabilly collectors.

Albums by rockabilly artists are also collectible, both for their rarity and their historical value. Gene Vincent's early albums can sell for as much as $2,000 in near-mint condition, and Wanda Jackson's Rockin' with Wanda can sell for three figures even in VG condition.

References: Floyd, John, *Sun Records: An Oral History*, Avon Books, New York, 1998; Morrison, Craig, *Go Cat Go: Rockabilly Music and Its Makers*, University of Illinois Press, Chicago, Ill., 1998.

Museums: The Rockabilly Hall of Fame, 211 College St., Burns, Tennessee 37029; (615) 740-ROCK.

Web pages: The Rockabilly Hall of Fame Web site: *http://www.rockabillyhall.com*; a site featuring published articles on rockabilly artists: *http://www.rockabilly.net*; Usenet newsgroup: alt.music.rockabilly.

45s	Year	VG	VG+	NM
Sonny Burgess, "Red Headed Woman" / "We Wanna Boogie" (Sun 247)	1956	$37.50	$75.00	$150.00
Johnny Burnette, "The Train Kept A-Rollin'" / "Honey Hush" (Coral 61719)	1956	$62.50	$125.00	$250.00
Johnny Burnette, "Rock Billy Boogie" / "If You Want It Enough" (Coral 61918)	1957	$75.00	$150.00	$300.00
Johnny and Dorsey Burnette, "Blues Stay Away From Me" / "Midnight Train" (Coral 62190)	1960	$50.00	$100.00	$200.00
Johnny Cash, "I Walk The Line" / "Get Rhythm" (Sun 241)	1956	$10.00	$20.00	$40.00
Gene Cochran, "Mean When I'm Mad" / "One Kiss" (Liberty 55070)	1957	$7.50	$15.00	$30.00
(with picture sleeve, add:)	1957	$500.00	$1,000.00	$2,000.00
Gene Cochran, "Summertime Blues" / "Live Again" (Liberty 55144)	1958	$7.50	$15.00	$30.00
The Crickets, "That'll Be The Day" / "I'm Looking For Someone To Love" (Brunswick 55009)	1957	$12.50	$25.00	$50.00
Charlie Feathers, "I've Been Deceived" / "Peeping Eyes"				
(if on Flip 503)	1955	$125.00	$250.00	$500.00
(if on Sun 503)	1956	$200.00	$400.00	$600.00
Charlie Feathers, "Tongue Tied Jill" / "Get With It" (Meteor 5032)				
(if on maroon label, first pressing)	1956	$500.00	$1,000.00	$1,500.00
(if on blue label)	1956	$100.00	$200.00	$400.00
Charlie Feathers, "Defrost Your Heart" / "Wedding Gown of White" (Sun 231)	1956	$200.00	$400.00	$600.00
Charlie Feathers, "When You Come Around" / "Too Much Alike" (King 5043)	1957	$100.00	$200.00	$400.00
Bill Haley and His Comets, "(We're Gonna) Rock Around the Clock" / "Thirteen Women (And Only One Man In Town)" (Decca 29124)				
(if lines on either side of "Decca")	1954	$15.00	$30.00	$60.00
(if star under "Decca")	1955	$5.00	$10.00	$20.00
Bill Haley and His Comets, "See You Later, Alligator" / "The Paper Boy (On Main Street, U.S.A.)" (Decca 29791)	1956	$6.25	$12.50	$25.00
Dale Hawkins, "Suzie-Q" / "Don't Treat Me This Way" (Checker 863)	1957	$12.50	$25.00	$50.00
Dale Hawkins, "Poor Little Rhode Island" / "Every Little Girl" (Checker 944)	1960	$5.00	$10.00	$20.00
(with picture sleeve, add:)	1960	$75.00	$150.00	$300.00
Buddy Holly and the Three Tunes, "That'll Be The Day" / "Rock Around with Ollie Vee" (Decca 30434)				
(if star under "Decca")	1957	$62.50	$125.00	$250.00
(if lines on either side of "Decca")	1957	$100.00	$200.00	$400.00
(if pink label promo)	1957	$62.50	$125.00	$250.00
Buddy Holly, "Peggy Sue" / "Everyday" (Coral 61885)				
(if orange label)	1957	$12.50	$25.00	$50.00
(if black color bars label)	196??	$6.25	$12.50	$25.00
Wanda Jackson, "Let's Have A Party" / "Cool Love" (Capitol 4397)	1960	$10.00	$20.00	$40.00
Sleepy LaBeef, "I'm Through" / "All Alone" (Starday 292)	1957	$37.50	$75.00	$150.00
(if on Mercury 71112)	1957	$25.00	$50.00	$100.00
Jerry Lee Lewis, "Whole Lotta Shakin' Goin' On" / "It'll Be Me" (Sun 267)	1957	$10.00	$20.00	$40.00
Ricky Nelson, "I'm Walkin'" / "A Teenager's Romance" (Verve 10047)				
(if first pressing, orange-yellow label)	1957	$12.50	$25.00	$50.00
(if second pressing, black-white label)	1957	$10.00	$20.00	$40.00
Ricky Nelson, "Be-Bop Baby" / "Have I Told You Lately That I Love You" (Imperial 5463)				
(if red label, first pressing)	1957	$12.50	$25.00	$50.00
(if black label)	1957	$10.00	$20.00	$40.00
(with picture sleeve, add:)	1957	$20.00	$40.00	$80.00
Roy Orbison, "Ooby Dooby" / "Go! Go! Go!" (Sun 242)	1956	$25.00	$50.00	$100.00
Carl Perkins, "Blue Suede Shoes" / "Honey Don't" (Sun 234)	1956	$15.00	$30.00	$60.00
Elvis Presley, "Good Rockin' Tonight" / "I Don't Care if The Sun Don't Shine" (Sun 210)	1954	$1,000.00	$2,000.00	$3,000.00
Billy Lee Riley, "Trouble Bound" / "Rock With Me, Baby" (Sun 245)	1956	$30.00	$60.00	$120.00
Billy Lee Riley, "Rockin' on the Moon" / "Is That All To The Ball" (Brunswick 55085)	1958	$50.00	$100.00	$200.00
Gene Vincent, "Be-Bop-A-Lula" / "Woman Love" (Capitol F3450)				
(with large Capitol logo)	1956	$17.50	$35.00	$70.00
(with smaller Capitol logo)	1956	$12.50	$25.00	$50.00
Gene Vincent, "The Night Is So Lonely" / "Right Now" (Capitol F4237)	1959	$12.50	$25.00	$50.00
(with picture sleeve, add:)	1959	$500.00	$1,000.00	$2,000.00

LPs	Year	VG	VG+	NM
Johnny Burnette, Johnny Burnette and the Rock 'n' Roll Trio (Coral CRL 57080) (mono) (originals have maroon labels, printing on jacket's spine, "Made in U.S.A." in lower right of back cover)	1956	$2,000	$4,000	$8,000
Johnny Cash, Johnny Cash With His Hot And Blue Guitar (Sun SLP-1220) (mono)	1956	$25.00	$50.00	$100.00
Eddie Cochran, Singin' To My Baby Liberty LRP-3061) (mono)				
(if green label)	1957	$200.00	$400.00	$800.00
(if black label, reissue)	1960	$75.00	$150.00	$300.00
(if on Liberty LN-10137, reissue)	198??	$3.00	$6.00	$12.00
The Crickets, The "Chirping" Crickets" (Brunswick BL 54038) (mono)				
(if textured cover)	1957	$200.00	$400.00	$800.00
(if regular cover)	1957	$150.00	$300.00	$600.00
Bill Haley and His Comets, Shake Rattle and Roll (Decca DL 5560) (10-inch LP)	1955	$200.00	$400.00	$800.00

LPs	Year	VG	VG+	NM
Dale Hawkins, Oh! Susie-Q (Chess LP-1429) (mono)	1958	$500.00	$1,000.00	$2,000.00
Wanda Jackson, Rockin' with Wanda (Capitol T 1384) (mono)				
(if black label with rainbow perimeter, Capitol logo at left)	1960	$100.00	$200.00	$400.00
(if gold "Star Line" label)	1962	$62.50	$125.00	$250.00
Roy Orbison, Roy Orbison at the Rockhouse (Sun SLP-1260) (mono)	1961	$150.00	$300.00	$600.00
Gene Vincent, Gene Vincent and the Blue Caps (Capitol T 970)				
(if yellow label promo)	1958	$250.00	$500.00	$1,000.00
(if black label promo)	1958	$250.00	$500.00	$1,000.00
(if turquoise label stock copy)	1958	$100.00	$200.00	$400.00
Gene Vincent, Crazy Times (Capitol T 1342) (mono) (black label with rainbow perimeter, Capitol logo at left)	1960	$75.00	$150.00	$300.00
(if on Capitol ST 1342, stereo, black label with rainbow perimeter, Capitol logo at left)	1960	$125.00	$250.00	$500.00

Buddy Holly's "That'll Be The Day," is a mixture of rockabilly and "western bop." This "sample copy" was pressed with a yellow label, and is much harder to find than a similar stock copy.

THE ROLLING STONES

History: Without a doubt, the Rolling Stones have earned their nickname, "The Greatest Rock 'n' Roll Band in the World." From their early years at the Ealing Club, performing with Alexis Korner's Blues Incorporated, to their years of cutting-edge live shows and envelope-opening lyrics, the Rolling Stones have done it all. They have lived the rock 'n' roll lifestyle—sometimes to excess, sometimes to distress. But other than the Beatles and Elvis Presley, the Rolling Stones are arguably the most collectible rock band worldwide.

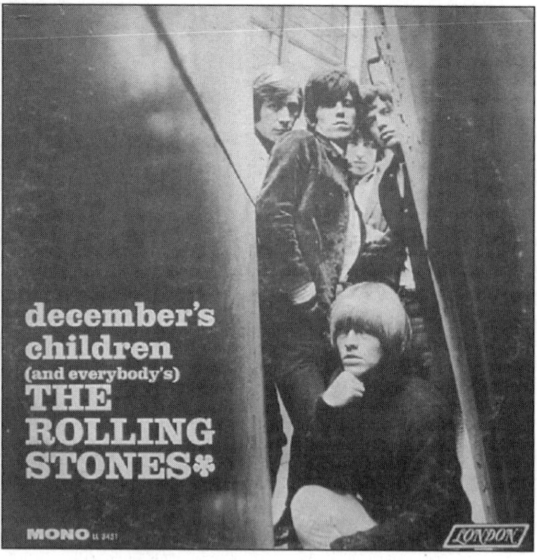

The World's Greatest Rock and Roll Band.

The nucleus of the Rolling Stones has always been lead singer Mick Jagger and guitarist Keith Richards. The songs they co-wrote have become rock anthems—"I Can't Get No Satisfaction," "Paint It, Black," "Honky Tonk Women," "19th Nervous Breakdown," "Brown Sugar," and "Start Me Up."

It was a love of early American blues music—Leadbelly, Muddy Waters, Willie Dixon, and Chuck Berry—that provided an early bond between schoolmates Jagger and Richards in 1961. As the story goes, while Jagger and Richards were waiting at a Dartford railway station, Richards noticed some blues records in Jagger's hands. Before long, both Jagger and Richards were singing and performing with mutual friend Dick Taylor in a band called "Little Boy Blue and the Blue Boys." They eventually added pianist Ian Stewart and guitarist Brian Jones to form an early combo.

Taking their name from the Muddy Waters classic "Rollin' Stone," the newly christened Rolling Stones made their live debut at England's Marquee Club. By 1963, the band added drummer Charlie Watts and bass player Bill Wyman (allegedly added because Wyman owned his own amplifier), and made a steady living performing at the Ealing Jazz Club and the Station Hotel Crawdaddy. A promoter named Andrew Loog Oldham signed the band to a management deal, and immediately began promoting the group as a musical alternative to the Beatles. He even created a successful newspaper campaign, taking out ads with the tagline, "Would you let your daughter marry a Rolling Stone?"

The campaign paid off, and the Stones signed a recording contract with the British label Decca (apparently by the person who passed on signing the Beatles to that label). The group's covers of "Not Fade Away" and "Come On" immediately brought them a new legion of fans—and some detractors, who couldn't understand why this band wasn't as sweet and polite as the Beatles.

Eventually the Stones' success translated into American hits—and some American controversy. Their first release on London Records, Decca's American subsidiary label, was the UK hit "I Wanna Be Your Man." The song's B-side, an instrumental called "Stoned," was quickly yanked from the shelves because of the "drug reference" of the song's title. Eventually "I Wanna Be Your Man" returned to the stores, as the B-side of the group's first hit, a remake of the Buddy Holly song "Not Fade Away." Their first Top 40 hit in America, "Tell Me (You're Coming Back)," was a Jagger-Richards original, and showed the band could write their own material, as well as perform killer versions of blues classics.

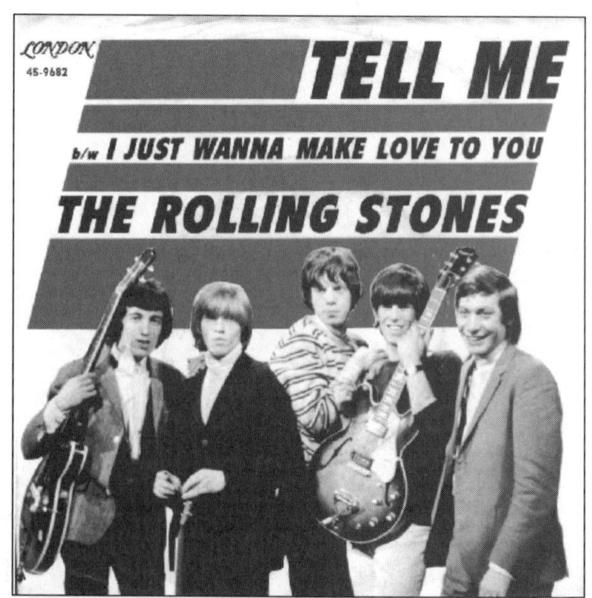

The Rolling Stones, "Tell Me (You're Coming Back)." From the Collection of Lothar Fohrn.

Other hits followed: "It's All Over Now," "Play With Fire," and "Time Is On My Side." In fact, by 1965, the Rolling Stones were chart-toppers in England, and their songs' airplay in America proved that there was more to British music than moptops, cheeky humor, and "Yeah, Yeah, Yeah."

While their fans enjoyed the Stones' music, the band was constantly harangued by reporters who were eager for a story on how "bad" the "bad boys of rock" really were. Everything from drug arrests to urinating on the wall of a gas station were fodder for journalists and reporters, but these news stories did not diminish the Stones' popularity; rather, it actually enhanced the group's reputation.

The Rolling Stones, "Not Fade Away." From the Collection of Lothar Fohrn.

And in 1965, the group recorded some of the most popular songs of its career—beginning with "I Can't Get No Satisfaction," and following with "Get Off of My Cloud," "As Tears Go By," "19th Nervous Breakdown," "Paint It, Black," "Mother's Little Helper," "Have You Seen Your Mother, Baby, Standing in the Shadow?" and "Ruby Tuesday." The group introduced new instruments into its repertoire, including Brian Jones' sitar on "Paint It, Black." The Stones' record sleeves also show a fiercer experimentation than in their previous efforts; while their early covers show the band standing at attention or relaxing on a grassy knoll, "Have You Seen Your Mother, Baby, Standing in the Shadow?" shows the band dressed as women. Another picture sleeve, this one for "Street Fighting Man," shows the violent aftermath of the police and protestors at the 1968 Democratic Convention.

By the late 1960s, the Rolling Stones continue to raise the bar, both musically and artistically. Songs like "Let's Spend the Night Together" and "Jumpin' Jack Flash" kept the Stones' music at the top of the charts, while their live performances and concert tours were greeted by frenzied fans worldwide.

The Rolling Stones' *"Jumpin' Jack Flash."*

The year 1969 should have been as successful for the Rolling Stones as any other. But that year will be remembered for two tragedies that nearly shook the band to its foundation. On June 8, 1969, Brian Jones left the Rolling Stones to form his own group, and was replaced by former Bluesbreaker Mick Taylor. Less than a month after Jones left the band, the founding Stones member was found dead in his swimming pool, the victim of an accidental drowning. The band continued on, performing a concert in Hyde Park in Jones' memory.

"Honky Tonk Women," one of the Stones' last hits on London.

The second tragedy happened in late December 1969. The Rolling Stones were part of a free concert at California's Altamont Speedway. During the concert, a fan was beaten to death by Hell's Angels, who were hired as concert security.

Trivia

Keith Richards woke up one night in his Florida hotel, with a catchy riff swirling in his head from his dreams. He instantly turned on a cassette player near his bed, grabbed his guitar, and played the riff into the cassette player before it faded into memory. Then he went back to sleep. The next morning, he found the tape which contained his midnight jamming session. That riff became the opening notes to "I Can't Get No Satisfaction."

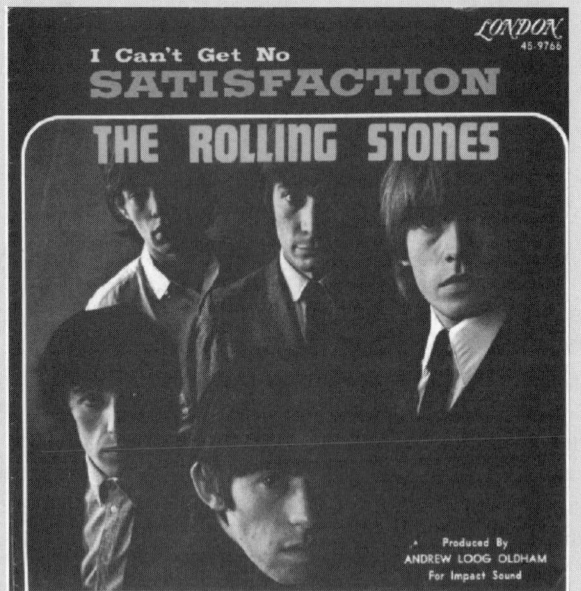

The Rolling Stones' "I Can't Get No Satisfaction." From the Collection of Lothar Fohrn.

In 1970, the Rolling Stones switched labels, from Decca/London to their own custom Rolling Stones Records (initially distributed by Atlantic Records). Their first single on their new label, "Brown Sugar," was a Top 5 hit, and the album *Sticky Fingers* (featuring an Andy Warhol-designed front cover of a pair of jeans, with a fully functional zipper) shot to #1 on the album charts.

By 1972, *Exile on Main Street* was released, hailed by critics as one of the greatest Stones albums ever released. By this time the band's tours outgrew concert halls and arenas, as its multimedia productions now required stadium tours. The next Stones personnel change occurred in 1974, when Mick Taylor left for a solo career. Ronnie Wood, formerly of Faces, joined the Stones as their new guitarist.

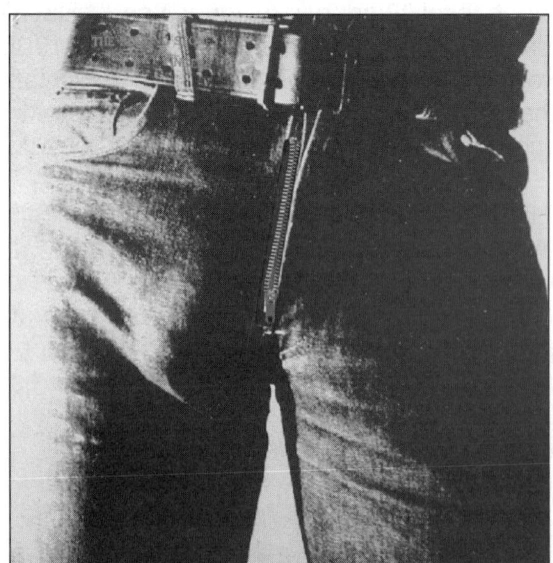

***Sticky Fingers* was the Rolling Stones' first LP on their own Rolling Stones label. Courtesy Last Vestige Music Store, Albany, N.Y.**

Even in the 1970s, the Stones never lost their love for blues and soul—or their reputation for controversy. Billboards promoting their album Black and Blue, featuring a rope-bound, bruised woman saying she loved the album, were quickly removed after protests from anti-abuse groups. Their 1978 album *Some Girls* featured images of Marilyn Monroe and Lucille Ball—until lawsuits forced changes to the artwork.

Later covers of *Some Girls* cover up the photos with an "Under Construction" banner. Courtesy Last Vestige Music Store, Albany, N.Y.

One of the tracks from *Some Girls*, "Miss You," not only became another #1 hit for the Rolling Stones, but also became a #1 hit in discos and clubs, forcing the release of a 12-inch "disco" version of the track.

Even in the 1980s, the Rolling Stones were still pushing the envelope as far as possible. Some of the lyrics to their 1981 song "Start Me Up," including "You make a dead man come," received a few edits on some conservative radio stations. While their 1985 single "Undercover of the Night" featured lyrics of militias and terrorism, their album *Undercover* featured a naked woman on the cover, her body parts covered by peelable stickers.

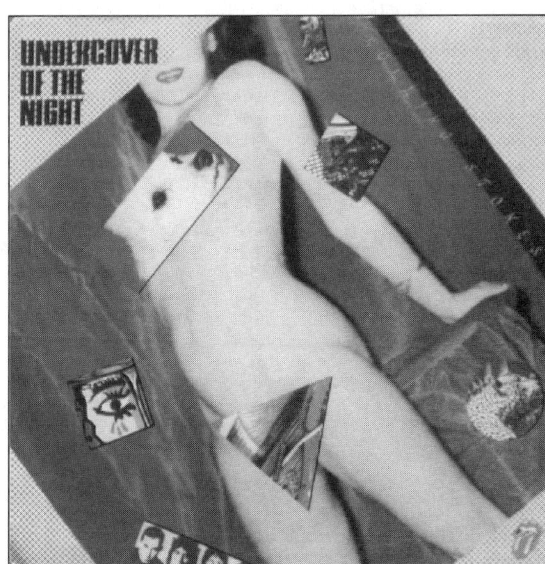

7-inch picture sleeve for "Undercover of the Night."

By 1985, Mick Jagger recorded his first solo album, *She's The Boss*, and collaborated with David Bowie for a remake of "Dancing In The Streets." The track, recorded for the world famine relief concert Live Aid, was a runaway smash. Keith Richards and Ronnie Wood also appeared at Live Aid, performing with Bob Dylan in the closing ceremonies.

Sadly, 1985 was also the year Ian Stewart, the Stones' piano player and road manager, died at the age of 47 of a massive heart attack. Stewart was an original member of the Stones, but eventually faded into the background, working behind the scenes and playing piano whenever the band needed him.

In 1986, the band changed distribution for its vanity label, from Atlantic to CBS. With their first song, "Harlem Shuffle," the Stones showed they still had a love for classic soul and blues ("Harlem Shuffle" was a midchart hit for Bob and Earl in the early 1960s).

But there was a growing friction in the band, most notably between Mick Jagger and Keith Richards. Both men recorded solo albums, and fans checked every lyric and liner note to find some clue to what each bandmember thought about each other. Eventually Jagger and Richards put their disagreements behind them and, with the Stones, recorded the album *Steel Wheels*, and the Top 40 hit "Mixed Emotions."

In 1993, after 30 years with the Rolling Stones, Bill Wyman retired from the band. The group still continues to record and tour, with Darryl Jones working as a "side musician" in place of Wyman. Like its bandname implies, the Rolling Stones continue to roll on.

What To Look For: Rolling Stones picture sleeves—especially those from the London years—are currently commanding high prices. Although most sleeves simply feature stock photos of the band itself, some sleeves contained controversial covers ("Street Fighting Man" and "Beast of Burden," for example) and were quickly deleted. Beware of counterfeits—most 1960s Rolling Stones picture sleeves have been counterfeited.

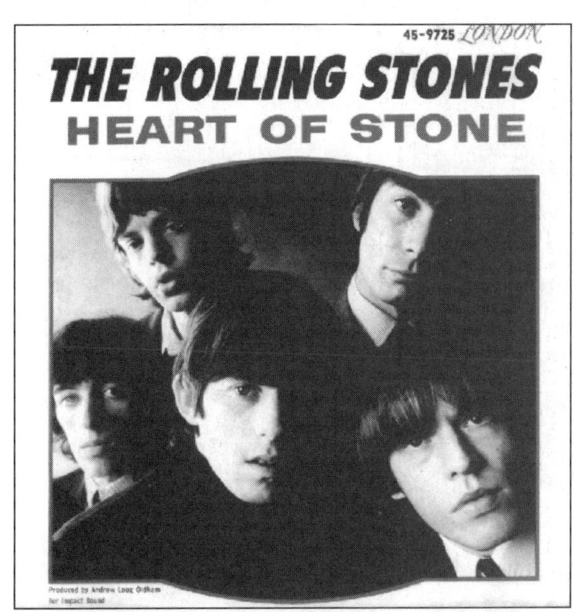

A hard-to-find Rolling Stones sleeve. From the Collection of Lothar Fohrn.

Conversely, the Stones' stock recordings from 1971 forward have not equally increased in value. Rare pieces from this period include stereo and mono radio pressings of *Sticky Fingers*, the aforementioned "Beast of Burden" picture sleeve, any stock copies of the single "Too Tough" with "Miss You" on the B-side, and a Mobile Fidelity multi-album audiophile boxed set. In 1986, ABKCO Records, which currently owns the Rolling Stones' London Records catalog, reissued those albums as part of an audiophile series. Although they did return some of the lost art and liner notes to public view—including the rare "toilet graffiti" from *Beggars Banquet*—these reissues have minimal collectible value when compared to the originals.

References: Booth, Stanley, *Dance With The Devil: The Rolling Stones And Their Times*, Random House, New York, 1984; Dowley, Tim, *The*

Rolling Stones, Hippocrene Books, Inc., New York, N.Y., 1983; Greenfield, Robert, *S.T.P.: A Journey Through America with the Rolling Stones*, Saturday Review Press / E.P. Dutton & Co., Inc., New York, 1974; Norman, Philip, *Symphony for the Devil: The Rolling Stones Story*, Linden Press/Simon and Schuster, New York, 1984; Wyman, Bill, with Coleman, Ray, *Stone Alone: The Story of a Rock and Roll Band*, Da Capo Press, New York, 1997.

Web pages: The Rolling Stones' official homepage: *http://www.therollingstones.com.* There are dozens of Rolling Stones record collecting sites, including Lothar Fohrn's Rolling Stones page (*http://members.aol.com/lfohrn*); The Rolling Stones Internet Index, *http://members.aol.com/hummer1954/links.html*; a page listing the Top 100 Rolling Stones Internet sites, *http://hometown.aol.com/lorand/index.html*; Usenet newsgroups: *alt.rock-n-roll.stones.*

Trivia

Rolling Stones LPs and picture sleeves are often more than just protective paper products. Many album covers have die-cut holes or edges, three-dimensional photos, and of course, working zippers.

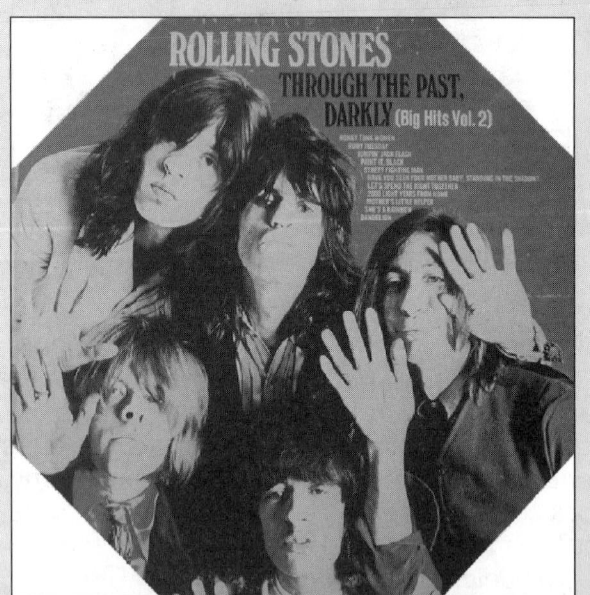

An octagonal cover for the album *Through The Past Darkly (Big Hits, Vol. 2)*. Courtesy Last Vestige Music Store, Albany, N.Y.

Rolling Stones 45s	Year	VG	VG+	NM
"I Wanna Be Your Man" / "Stoned" (London 9461)	1964	$4,000	$6,000	$8,000
(if on white label promo)	1964	$200.00	$400.00	$800.00
"Not Fade Away" / "I Wanna Be Your Man" (London 9657) (if on London purple-white label, first pressing)	1964	$10.00	$20.00	$40.00
(if on London blue-white swirl label)	1964	$2.00	$4.00	$8.00
(with picture sleeve, add:)	1964	$75.00	$150.00	$300.00

Rolling Stones 45s	Year	VG	VG+	NM
"Tell Me (You're Coming Back)" / "I Just Want To Make Love To You" (London 9682) (if on London purple-white label, first pressing)	1964	$10.00	$20.00	$40.00
(if on London blue-white swirl label)	1964	$2.50	$5.00	$10.00
(with picture sleeve, add:)	1964	$62.50	$125.00	$250.00
"(I Can't Get No) Satisfaction" / "The Under Assistant West Coast Production Man" (London 9766)	1965	$5.00	$10.00	$20.00
(with picture sleeve, add:)	1965	$50.00	$100.00	$200.00
"19th Nervous Breakdown" / "Sad Day" (London 9823)	1966	$3.75	$7.50	$15.00
(with picture sleeve, add:)	1966	$15.00	$30.00	$60.00
"Paint It, Black" / "Stupid Girl" (London 901)	1966	$3.75	$7.50	$15.00
(with picture sleeve, add:)	1966	$15.00	$30.00	$60.00
"Have You Seen Your Mother, Baby, Standing in the Shadow" / "Who's Driving My Plane" (London 903)	1966	$3.75	$7.50	$15.00
(with picture sleeve, add:)	1966	$15.00	$30.00	$60.00
"We Love You" / "Dandelion" (London 905)	1967	$5.00	$10.00	$20.00
(with picture sleeve, add:)	1967	$100.00	$200.00	$400.00
"Street Fighting Man" / "No Expectations"	1968	$5.00	$10.00	$20.00
(with picture sleeve, add:)	1968		$4,000.00	$7,000.00
$10,000.00				
"Honky Tonk Women" / "You Can't Always Get What You Want" (London 910)	1969	$3.75	$7.50	$15.00
(with picture sleeve, add:)	1969	$7.50	$15.00	$30.00
"Brown Sugar" / "Bitch" (Rolling Stones 19100)	1971		$2.50	$5.00
"Tumbling Dice" / "Sweet Black Angel" (Rolling Stones 19103)	1972		$2.50	$5.00
"Silver Train" / "Angie" (Rolling Stones 19105) ("Silver Train" listed as A-side)	1973	$3.00	$6.00	$12.00
"Angie" / "Silver Train" (Rolling Stones 19105) ("Angie" listed as A-side, or neither song listed as "A" side)	1973		$2.50	$5.00
"Fool To Cry" / "Hot Stuff" (Rolling Stones 19304)	1976		$2.00	$4.00
"Miss You" / "Far Away Eyes" (Rolling Stones 19307)	1978		$2.00	$4.00
(with picture sleeve, add:)	1978		$2.00	$4.00
"Beast of Burden" / "When The Whip Comes Down" (Rolling Stones 19309)	1978		$2.00	$4.00
(with picture sleeve, add:)	1978	$300.00	$600.00	$1,200.00
"Shattered" / "Everything Is Turning To Gold" (Rolling Stones 19310)	1978		$2.00	$4.00
(with picture sleeve, add:)	1978		$3.00	$6.00
"Start Me Up" / "No Use In Crying" (Rolling Stones 21003)	1981		$2.00	$4.00
(with picture sleeve, add:)	1981		$2.00	$4.00
"Going to a Go-Go" / "Beast of Burden" (Rolling Stones 21301)	1982		$2.00	$4.00
(with picture sleeve, add:)	1982		$2.00	$4.00
"Too Tough" / "Miss You" (Rolling Stones 99724)	1984	$10.00	$20.00	$40.00
(if on white label promo)	1984	$7.50	$15.00	$30.00
"Harlem Shuffle" / "Had It With You" (Rolling Stones 05802)	1986			$3.00
(with picture sleeve, add:)	1986			$3.00
"Love Is Strong" / "The Storm" / "Love Is Strong (Teddy Riley Remix)" (Virgin 38446)	1994		$2.50	$5.00
(with picture sleeve, add:)	1994		$2.50	$5.00
"Saint of Me" / "Anyway You Look At It" (Virgin NR-38626)	1998			$2.00
(with picture sleeve, add:)	1998			$2.00
Solo 45s	**Year**	**VG**	**VG+**	**NM**
Mick Jagger, "Just Another Night" / "Turn the Girl Loose" (Columbia 07473)	1985			$3.00
(with picture sleeve, add:)	1985		$2.00	$4.00
Mick Jagger and David Bowie, "Dancing In The Street" / (instrumental) (EMI America 8288)	1985			$3.00
(with picture sleeve, add:)	1985			$3.00
Rolling Stones 45s	**Year**	**VG**	**VG+**	**NM**
Mick Jagger, "Ruthless People" / "I'm Ringing"	1986		$3.00	
(with picture sleeve, add:)	1986		$2.00	$4.00
Mick Jagger, "Sweet Thing" / "Whispering Spirit" (Atlantic 87410)	1992		$2.00	$4.00
Keith Richards, "Run Rudolph Run" / "The Harder They Come" (Rolling				

Rolling Stones 45s	Year	VG	VG+	NM
Stones 19311)	1978	$5.00	$10.00	$20.00
Keith Richards, "Take It So Hard" / "I Could Have Stood You Up" (Virgin 99297)	1988			$3.00
(with picture sleeve, add:)	1988			$3.00
Keith Richards, "Eileen" / "Wicked As It Seems" (Virgin S7-56955)	1993		$2.00	$4.00
Mick Taylor, "Leather Jacket" / "Show Blues" (Columbia 11065)	1979		$2.50	$5.00
Ronnie Wood, "Breathe On Me" / "I Can Feel The Fire" (Warner Bros. 8036)	1974		$3.00	$6.00
Ronnie Wood, "Seven Days" / "Breakin' My Heart" (Columbia 11014)	1979		$3.00	$6.00
Bill Wyman, "White Lightning" / "I Wanna Get Me A Gun" (Rolling Stones 19111)	1974		$2.50	$5.00
Bill Wyman, "(Si Si) Je Suis Un Rock Star" / "Rio De Janeiro" (A&M 2367)	1981		$2.50	$5.00
(with picture sleeve, add:)	1981	$2.50	$5.00	$10.00

Rolling Stones LPs	Year	VG	VG+	NM
England's Newest Hit Makers -- The Rolling Stones (London LL 3375 mono, PS 375 stereo)				
(if on London LL 3375, white label promo)	1964	$750.00	$1,500.00	$3,000.00
(if on London LL 3375, maroon label, "Full Frequency Range Recording" inside horizontal lines that go through the center hole, lower left corner of cover advertises a bonus photo, mono)	1964	$75.00	$150.00	$300.00
(if on London PS 375, dark blue label, lower left-hand corner offers a bonus photo, rechaneled stereo)	1964	$75.00	$150.00	$300.00
(with bonus photo, add:)	1964	$50.00	$100.00	$200.00
(if on London LL 3375, maroon label, word "London" unboxed at top, mono)	1965	$15.00	$30.00	$60.00
(if on London PS 375, dark blue London label, word "London" unboxed at top, rechaneled stereo)	1965	$6.25	$12.50	$25.00
(if on London LL 3375, maroon or red label, "London" boxed at top, mono)	1966	$10.00	$20.00	$40.00
(if on London/ABKCO 73751, "Digitally Remastered from Original Master Recording," red label)	1986	$2.00	$4.00	$8.00
12 x 5 (London LL 3402 mono, London PS 402 rechaneled stereo)				
(If on London LL 3402, maroon label, "London/ffrr" boxed at top)	1964	$50.00	$100.00	$200.00
(if on London LL 3402, maroon label, "London" unboxed at top)	1964	$15.00	$30.00	$60.00
(if on London LL 3402, maroon label, "London" unboxed at top, blue vinyl pressing)	1964	$5,000	$7,500	$10,000
(if on London PS 402, dark blue label, "London" unboxed at top, rechaneled stereo)	1964	$6.25	$12.50	$25.00
(if on London LL 3402, red or maroon label, "London" boxed at top)	1965	$10.00	$20.00	$40.00
(if on London/ABKCO 74021, "Digitally Remastered from Original Master Recording," red label)	1986	$2.00	$4.00	$8.00
Big Hits (High Tide and Green Grass) (London NP 1 mono)				
(if on London NP 1, cover has two lines of type, in lower case letters)	1966	$2,000	$4,000	$8,000
(if on London NP 1, cover has five lines of type, in capital letters)	1966	$10.00	$20.00	$40.00
(if on London/ABKCO 80011, "Digitally Remastered from Original Master Recording," red label)	1986	$2.00	$4.00	$8.00
Their Satanic Majesties Request (London NP 2 mono, London NPS 2, stereo)				
(if on London NP 2, mono)	1967	$62.50	$125.00	$250.00
(if on London NPS 2, stereo, with 3-D cover)	1967	$10.00	$20.00	$40.00
(if on London/ABKCO 80021, "Digitally Remastered from Original Master Recording," red label)	1986	$2.00	$4.00	$8.00

Rolling Stones LPs	Year	VG	VG+	NM
Beggars Banquet (London PS 539)				
(if original "toilet graffiti" is on cover)	1968	$2,500	$5,000	$10,000
(if all songs are credited to "Jagger-Richard")	1968	$6.25	$12.50	$25.00
(if on London/ABKCO 73591, "Digitally Remastered from Original Master Recording," red label, restores previously censored toilet graffiti)	1986	$2.00	$4.00	$8.00

Rolling Stones LPs	Year	VG	VG+	NM
Hot Rocks 1964-1971 (London 2PS 606/7) (2 LP's)				
(if side 4 has "11-5-71" in the dead wax, this album contains alternate mixes of "Brown Sugar" and "Wild Horses")	1971	$250.00	$500.00	$1,000.00
(if stock pressing; all of side 1 and "Mother's Little Helper" and "19th Nervous Breakdown" on side 2 in mono, all other songs in stereo)	1971	$5.00	$10.00	$20.00
(if on London/ABKCO 66671, "Digitally Remastered from Original Master Recording," red label)	1986	$2.00	$4.00	$8.00
Sticky Fingers (Rolling Stones COC 59100)				
(if white label mono promo)	1971	$125.00	$250.00	$500.00
(if white label stereo promo)	1971	$75.00	$150.00	$300.00
(regular stock copy with working zipper)	1971	$2.50	$5.00	$10.00
(if on Mobile Fidelity 1-060, working zipper replaced by gold cardboard version)	1980	$12.50	$25.00	$50.00
(if on CBS FC 40488, photo of zipper)	1986	$2.00	$4.00	$8.00
(if on Virgin 47863, limited edition reissue, 180-gram virgin vinyl, working zipper)	1999	$6.25	$12.50	$25.00
Exile on Main St. (Rolling Stones COC 2-2900) (2 LP's)				
(if first pressing, Unipak design, cover has to be opened to remove the records)	1972	$3.75	$7.50	$15.00
(if postcards are still in the album jacket, add:)	1972	$1.25	$2.50	$5.00
(if later version with two pockets, one for each record)	1973	$3.00	$6.00	$12.00
(if on CBS CG2 40489, reissue)	1986	$2.50	$5.00	$10.00
(if on Virgin 47864, limited edition reissue, 180-gram virgin vinyl, with postcards)	1999	$12.50	$25.00	$50.00
Some Girls (Rolling Stones COC 39108)				
(if all women's' faces are visible - there are nine different color schemes, price is equal for each one)	1978	$3.75	$7.50	$15.00
(if "cover under reconstruction" on front, also with nine different color schemes)	1978	$2.50	$5.00	$10.00
(if on Mobile Fidelity 1-087, audiophile vinyl)	1982	$12.50	$25.00	$50.00
(if on CBS FC 40499, reissue)	1986	$2.00	$4.00	$8.00
(if on Virgin 47867, 180-gram vinyl, with inserts, still has "cover under construction" on sleeve)	1999	$6.25	$12.50	$25.00
Tattoo You (Rolling Stones COC 39108)	1981	$2.50	$5.00	$10.00
(if on CBS FC 40502, reissue)	1986	$2.00	$4.00	$8.00
Still Life (American Concert 1981) (Rolling Stones COC 39113)	1982	$2.50	$5.00	$10.00
(if on CBS FC 40503, reissue)	1986	$2.00	$4.00	$8.00
Undercover (Rolling Stones 90120) (with stickers intact)	1983	$3.00	$6.00	$12.00
(if stickers are missing)	1983	$2.00	$4.00	$8.00
(if on CBS FC 40504, no stickers)	1986	$2.00	$4.00	$8.00
Dirty Work (Rolling Stones OC 40250) (add 50% if red shrinkwrap is still on album)	1986	$2.00	$4.00	$8.00
Singles Collection: The London Years (ABKCO 1218-1) (4 LPs) (almost all tracks in mono)	1989	$12.50	$25.00	$50.00
Voodoo Lounge (Virgin V 2750 (39782) (2 LPs) (pressed in UK for export to USA)	1994	$5.00	$10.00	$20.00
Bridges to Babylon (Virgin 8 44712 1) (2 LPs) (pressed in UK for export to USA)	1997	$3.75	$7.50	$15.00

SEVENTIES ROCK

History: Rock and roll in the 1970s seemed to always compete against other musical formats, whether it was from punk, new wave, disco, or bubblegum music. Even with all these other influences, straight-ahead rock and roll found supportive audiences and millions of records (and 8-tracks and cassettes) sold. But despite the mirror-ball image of the 1970s, some of the greatest rock singers and bands began stellar careers. They may have come from hardscrabble industrial American cities, or from across the Atlantic Ocean.

Glam music became a British craze in the early 1970s. Artists in platform shoes, androgynous makeup and glittery outfits dominated the UK music scene for a time, and some of those artists, including Gary Glitter, T. Rex, and the Sweet did have some American chart success.

Two of the biggest acts to graduate from the world of glam music were David Bowie and Queen. Bowie, who changes his musical themes with almost every album released, began his career with the band David Jones and the Lower Third (his birth name was David Jones, but he changed it to David Bowie so as not to be confused with the Monkees' Davy Jones). While his early recordings featured him crooning over elaborate orchestrations, Bowie later adapted his style with albums like *Hunky Dory and The Rise and Fall of Ziggy Stardust and the Spiders From Mars.* In these recordings, Bowie created the character of Ziggy Stardust, an androgynous rock singer with cut-to-the-point sexual lyrics.

Although "Space Oddity" became David Bowie's first U.S. hit on RCA, it was released three years earlier on the Mercury label, and that version is much harder to find.

From this early glam period, Bowie seemed to change his singing style, his musical interpretations—as soon as audiences thought they knew his work, he would experiment with new sounds and images. His singles ran the gamut from trippy science fiction ("Space Oddity") to freeze-dried funk ("Fame") to interpolations from the rock pulpit ("Young Americans").

Although Queen was grouped with the rest of the glam bands of the early 1970s, their diverse influences included Led Zeppelin and Giuseppi Verdi. The combination of hard rock and full-blown opera culminated in their 1975 album *A Night At The Opera* and its six-minute aria "Bohemian Rhapsody." Like Bowie, Queen experimented with various musical styles, including rockabilly ("Crazy Little Thing Called Love"), funk ("Another One Bites The Dust") and anthems of conscience ("We Are The Champions").

Queen's rock-opera opus, "Bohemian Rhapsody," brought the group's theatrical performances to a whole new level.

The 1970s were also the most fertile musical period for singer-songwriter Elton John. His tender ballads and hard-rocking dance tracks helped propel his albums to the top of the charts; his over-the-top live performances made him a superstar. His piano style was influenced by both Fats Domino and Jerry Lee Lewis; he would pound the keys mercilessly in "Saturday Night's All Right For Fighting" and "Pinball Wizard"; he would gently caress the ivories with "Sorry Seems To Be The Hardest Word" and "Don't Let The Sun Go Down on Me." In fact, between 1972 and 1977, Elton John had 18 Top 40 hits, including six #1 songs.

Elton John's *Captain Fantastic and the Brown Dirt Cowboy,* one of many #1 albums he had in the 1970s. Courtesy Last Vestige Music Store, Albany, N.Y.

Bruce Springsteen didn't need flashy costumes in his performances; Springsteen's songs contained images of his South Jersey neighborhoods, the family and friends he knew, and the lyrics of American life. Some critics hailed him as a new Bob Dylan; others lionized him as the rock guitarist that could cut through all the phoniness with a single chord. His earliest 45s, including "Spirit in the Night" and "Blinded By The Light," are almost impossible to find today and can command high prices in near-mint condition.

By the late 1970s, a new form of rock music had appeared—arena rock. Arena rock bands were so named because their music was so popular, the bands could sell out stadiums and arenas on concert tours. Some of these groups reached fans on dual levels; they had hook-laden songs that dominated Top 40 radio, but their albums and concerts were all-out rock sessions. These groups included Kansas, Blue Öyster Cult, Styx, Kansas, and Boston.

Another type of rock music, "Southern Rock," grew to prominence in the 1970s. Groups such as Lynyrd Skynyrd and the Allman Brothers Band mixed the current hard rock music with blues and country influences, adding long guitar jams and butt-shaking boogie to their songs. Later 1970s groups that also were part of the "Southern Rock" genre were Black Oak Arkansas, .38 Special, Molly Hatchet, the Charlie Daniels Band, and the Marshall Tucker Band.

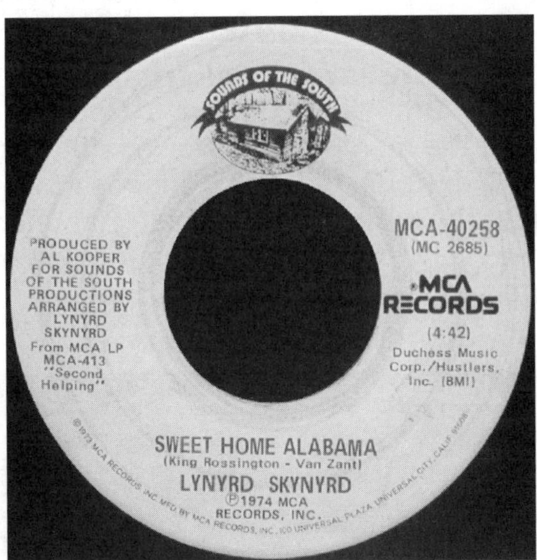

Lynyrd Skynyrd's first Top 10 hit, "Sweet Home Alabama," contains a response to Neil Young's songs "Alabama" and "Southern Man."

In fact, many of these rock bands could now be heard on "album-oriented rock" or AOR radio stations. Unfettered by a three-minute pop song time limit, many AOR radio stations would play album-length tracks like Led Zeppelin's "Stairway to Heaven," the Outlaws' "Green Grass and High Tides Forever," Lynyrd Skynyrd's "Free Bird," the Moody Blues' "Nights in White Satin," and both sides of Pink Floyd's "The Dark Side of the Moon," all on a regular rotation.

The 1970s were also the most fertile period for the solo Beatles. Each former member of the Fab Four had groundbreaking albums, and all of them have varying levels of collectibility. In fact, one of the Beatles' album tracks from the 1960s, "Got To Get You Into My Life," actually hit the Top 10 in 1976.

But it was a television compilation album of John Lennon singing classic hits from the 1950s and 1960s that became one of his most collectible albums to date.

Trivia

Billy Joel's first album, *Cold Spring Harbor,* was released on the Family Productions label. It was also mis-mastered at approximately 29 RPM, making Joel sound more like Alvin the Chipmunk on the record. A Columbia re-release returned the album to a proper speed, but the song "You Can Make Me Free" was shaved by three minutes on the reissue.

Trivia

In 1973, Brownsville Station had a Top 10 hit with "Smokin' in the Boys' Room." One of the members of Brownsville Station, Cub Koda, became a successful and influential rock and blues historian, and wrote many popular columns for *Goldmine* and *DISCoveries* magazines.

Brownsville Station's "Smokin' in the Boys' Room," featuring the legendary Cub Koda.

When the Beatles recorded the song "Come Together" for the *White Album*, music publisher Morris Levy claimed that "Come Together" had been plagiarized from a Chuck Berry song, "You Can't Catch Me." In 1973, as part of a settlement, John Lennon agreed to record an album of classic 1950s and 1960s songs, with three tracks from Levy's publishing catalog. But when Levy received an early master tape of the songs, he rush-released them on his Adam VIII label as a mail-order record, without Lennon's permission or consent. Lennon claimed the release of the album, *John Lennon Sings the Great Rock and Roll Hits: Roots* was an illegal use of the master tapes, and sued Levy. In 1975, Lennon received more than $100,000 in damages, and the *Roots* album was pulled off the market, in favor of Lennon's *Rock and Roll* album, which contained the "official" mixes from those tapes. (*Roots* contains two tracks that did not make it to *Rock and Roll*, "Be My Baby" and "Angel Baby," adding to the Adam VIII record's collectibility).

Original pressings of Roots will have the cover art printed directly on the cardboard, not colored onto slicks. The album's labels will be of ordinary size, with sharp print. The inner paper sleeve will have ads for other Adam VIII albums. Counterfeits of *Roots* have the album cover coated with slicks; the labels will be abnormally large, and will have the word "Greatest" on the cover spine.

With what has to be the ugliest photo of John Lennon ever taken, Morris Levy released John Lennon's remakes on Levy's on Adam VIII label. Ironically, this record is much more collectible than the "official" oldies album Lennon released, *Rock and Roll.* Courtesy Good Rockin' Tonight/Collectors Universe.

What To Look For: The rarest and most collectible recordings by '70s bands and artists are their first recordings. Look for their first single, especially if it came with a picture sleeve. Keep an eye out for promo copies, and remember that these discs would have a very short print run as compared to the stock copies sold in stores.

Just because you own an artist's first album, it does not mean you own a copy that was pressed in the artist's early career. Successful artists will have their albums remain in print for decades; and although the album cover may have the correct copyright date, the album inside may have label artwork from five to twenty years after that original pressing. And if the album contains a UPC bar code on the back cover, that indicates your disc was pressed in the late 1970s at the earliest—meaning you may be holding a 10-year-old reprint of Bruce Springsteen's first album.

Trivia

Boston's first Top 10 hit, "More Than A Feeling," has been influenced by more than a few songs. One can hear the song structure and melody of a song by the James Gang, "Tend My Garden," in the Boston hit. Also, the instrumental portions that lead to the refrain sound remarkably similar to "Louie, Louie."

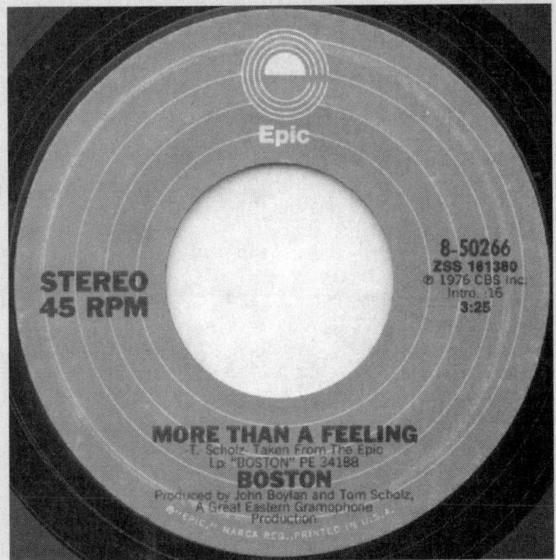

Many of Boston's album-length tracks were severely edited for radio and for 7" singles. When "More Than A Feeling" was edited for 45 pressings, the entire second verse was sliced out of the song.

As is discussed in another chapter of this book, the late 1970s was the era of picture discs. Designed for collectors and for fans who wanted to see their favorite artist rotate at 33 1/3 RPM speed on a turntable, picture discs have become a popular collectible today. Keep an eye out also for colored vinyl, promotional picture sleeves, and audiophile "heavy vinyl" album pressings.

As for 45s, many of the biggest hits have not risen above their original purchase price. Keep an eye out for original picture sleeves, or for rare 45s that either were not hits upon their original release, or were hits that had two different B-sides.

Reference: Alterman, Eric, *It Ain't No Sin To Be Glad You're Alive: The Promise Of Bruce Springsteen*, Little, Brown & Co., New York, N.Y., 1999; Graff, Garry, Durchholz, Daniel, Eds., *MusicHound Rock: The Essential Album Guide*, Visible Ink Press, Detroit, Mich., 1999; Naha, Ed., Compil., *Lillian Roxon's Rock Encyclopedia*, Grosset & Dunlap, N.Y., 1978; Neely, Tim, *Goldmine Standard Catalog of American Records* (2d Ed.), Krause Publications, Iola, Wisconsin, 2000; Osborne, Jerry, *The Official Price Guide to Records 2000*, House of Collectibles/Ballantine Publishing, New York 2000.

Web pages: Bowienet, David Bowie's Internet provider site: *http://www.davidbowie.com*; Queen's official homepage: *http://www.queenonline.com*; a site devoted for fans of Bruce Springsteen: *http://www.backstreeets.com*; a homepage for fans of the band Boston: *http://www.boston.org*; Elton John's homepage: *http://www.eltonjohn.com*; Usenet newsgroups: alt.music.bruce-springsteen, *alt.music.eagles, alt.music.queen.*

45s	Year	VG	VG+	NM
The Allman Brothers Band, "Ramblin Man" / "Pony Boy" (Capricorn 0007)	1973		$2.50	$5.00
America, "A Horse With No Name" / "Everyone I Meet Is From California" (Warner Bros. 7555)	1972		$3.00	$6.00
Bachman-Turner Overdrive, "You Ain't Seen Nothin' Yet" / "Free Wheelin'" (Mercury 73622)	1974		$2.00	$4.00
Black Oak Arkansas, "Jim Dandy" / "Red Hot Lovin" (Atco 6948)	1973		$2.50	$5.00
David Bowie, "Time" / "The Prettiest Star" (RCA Victor ABPO-0001)	1973		$3.00	$6.00
(with rare picture sleeve, add:)	1973	$200.00	$400.00	$800.00
David Bowie, "Young Americans" / "Knock on Wood" (RCA Victor PB-10152) (either tan or orange label)	1975		$3.00	$6.00
David Bowie, "Golden Years" / "Can You Hear Me" (RCA Victor PB-10441)	1975		$2.00	$4.00
Creedence Clearwater Revival, "Travelin' Band" / "Who'll Stop The Rain" (Fantasy 637)	1970		$3.00	$6.00
(with picture sleeve, add:)	1970	$3.00	$6.00	$12.00
The Doobie Brothers, "China Grove" / "Evil Woman" (Warner Bros. 7728)	1973		$2.00	$4.00
The Eagles, "Hotel California" / "Pretty Maids All In A Row" (Asylum 45386)	1977		$2.00	$4.00
The Electric Light Orchestra, "Evil Woman" / "10538 Overture (Live)" (United Artists XW 729	1975		$2.00	$4.00
Fleetwood Mac, "Rhiannon (Will You Ever Win)" / "Sugar Daddy" (Reprise 1345)	1976		$2.00	$4.00
Fleetwood Mac, "Go Your Own Way" / "Silver Springs" (Warner Bros. 8304) (non-LP B-side)	1976	$2.00	$4.00	$8.00
Foghat, "Slow Ride" / "Save Your Loving" (Bearsville 0306)	1975		$2.50	$5.00
Grand Funk Railroad, "Closer To Home" / "Aimless Lady" (Capitol 2877)	1970		$3.00	$6.00
George Harrison, "Blow Away" / "Soft-Hearted Hana" (Dark Horse 8763) (If first pressing, no reference to "Loka Productions S.A." or "RE-1" on label)	1979	$5.00	$10.00	$20.00
(if second pressing, label has "Loka Productions S.A." and "RE-1")	1979		$2.50	$5.00
(with picture sleeve, add:)	1979		$2.50	$5.00
Jefferson Starship, "Miracles" / "Al Garimaso (There Is Love)" (Grunt FB-10367)	1975		$2.50	$5.00
Billy Joel, "She's Got A Way" / "Everybody Loves You now" (Family Productions 0900)	1971	$6.25	$12.50	$25.00
Billy Joel, "Just The Way You Are" / "Get It Right The First Time" (Columbia 10646)	1977		$2.50	$5.00
Elton John, "Border Song" / "Bad Side of the Moon" (Congress 6022)	1970	$12.50	$25.00	$50.00
Elton John, "Lucy in the Sky With Diamonds" / "One Day At A Time" (MCA 40344)	1974		$2.50	$5.00
(with picture sleeve, add:)	1974	$2.50	$5.00	$10.00
Kansas, "Carry On Wayward Son" / "Questions of My Childhood" (Kirshner 4267)	1976		$2.50	$5.00
Lynard Skynard, "Need All My Friends" / "Michelle" (Shade Tree 101) (300 copies pressed, name spelled as seen)	1971	$375.00	$750.00	$1,500.00
Lynyrd Skynyrd, "Sweet Home Alabama" / "Take Your Time" (Sounds of the South 40258)	1974	$2.00	$4.00	$8.00

45s	Year	VG	VG+	NM
Lynyrd Skynyrd, "Free Bird" / "Down South Jukin'" (MCA 40328)	1974		$2.50	$5.00
The Marshall Tucker Band, "Heard It In A Love Song" / "Life in a Song" (Capricorn 0270)	1977		$2.50	$5.00
Paul McCartney and Wings, "Venus and Mars Rock Show" / "Magneto and Titanium Man" (Capitol 4175)	1975		$2.50	$5.00
Meat Loaf, "Two Out Of Three Ain't Bad" / "For Crying Out Loud" (Epic/Cleveland International 50613)				
(if "Two Out Of Three Ain't Bad" is only 3:50 long)	1978		$2.50	$5.00
(if "Two Out Of Three Ain't Bad" is 5:12 in length)	1978		$3.00	$6.00
The Steve Miller Band, "The Joker" / "Something To Believe In" (Capitol 3732)	1973		$2.50	$5.00
The New York Dolls, "Trash" / Personality Crisis" (Mercury 73414)	1973	$15.00	$30.00	$60.00
(with picture sleeve, add:)	1973	$3.75	$7.50	$15.00
Nilsson, "Me And My Arrow" / "Are You Sleeping" (RCA Victor 74-0443)	1971		$3.00	$6.00
Outlaws, "Green Grass and High Tides" / "Prisoner" (Arista 0213)	1976		$2.50	$5.00
Queen, "Bohemian Rhapsody" / "I'm In Love With My Car" (Elektra 45297)				
(if label has a butterfly)	1975	$2.00	$4.00	$8.00
(if label is red, a rare variation)	1976	$2.50	$5.00	$10.00
Queen, "We Are The Champions" / "We Will Rock You" (Elektra 45441)	1977		$3.00	$6.00
(with picture sleeve, add:)	1977	$2.50	$5.00	$10.00
Lou Reed, "Walk on the Wild Side" / "Perfect Day" (RCA Victor 74-0887)	1973		$3.00	$6.00
Lou Reed, "Sweet Jane" / "Lady Day" (RCA Victor APBO-0238)	1974	$7.50	$15.00	$30.00
Roxy Music, "Love Is The Drug" / "Both Ends Burning" (Atco 7042)	1975		$2.00	$4.00
Santana, "Oye Como Va" / "Samba Pa Ti" (Columbia 45330)	1971		$2.50	$5.00
(with picture sleeve, add:)	1971	$2.00	$4.00	$8.00
Bob Seger, "Night Moves" / "Ship of Fools" (Capitol 4369)	1976		$2.00	$4.00
Bob Seger, "Old Time Rock and Roll" / "Sunspot Baby" (Capitol 4702)	1979		$2.00	$4.00
(with picture sleeve, add:)	1979		$3.00	$6.00
Bruce Springsteen, "Blinded By The Light" / "The Angel" (Columbia 45805)	1972	$125.00	$250.00	$500.00
(with picture sleeve, add:)	1972	$100.00	$200.00	$400.00
Bruce Springsteen, "Born To Run" / "Meeting Across the River" (Columbia 10209)	1975	$5.00	$10.00	$20.00
Ringo Starr, "Drowning in the Sea of Love" / "Just A Dream" (Atlantic 3412)	1977	$30.00	$60.00	$120.00
Steely Dan, "Dallas" / "Sail the Waterway" (ABC 11323) (neither track ever appeared on a US Steely Dan album)	1972	$7.50	$15.00	$30.00
Steely Dan, "Reeling In The Years" / "Only A Fool Would Say That" (ABC 11352)	1973		$2.00	$4.00
Rod Stewart, "Maggie May" / "Reason To Believe" (Mercury 73224)	1971		$3.00	$6.00
Rod Stewart, "Da Ya Think I'm Sexy?" / "Scarred and Scared" (Warner Bros. 8724)	1978		$2.00	$4.00
(with picture sleeve, add:)	1978		$2.50	$5.00
Styx, "Lady" / "You Better Ask" (Wooden Nickel 65-0116)	1973	$2.50	$5.00	$10.00
Styx, "Lady" / "Children of the Land" (Wooden Nickel WB-10102)	1974		$2.50	$5.00
Supertramp, "Take The Long Way Home" / "Ruby" (A&M 2193)	1979		$2.00	$4.00
(with picture sleeve with yellow maze, add:)	1979		$2.00	$4.00
(with picture sleeve with green maze, red maze, or any other color, add:)	1979		$2.50	$5.00
The Sweet, "Little Willy" / "Man from Mecca" (Bell 45251)	1972		$3.00	$6.00
The Sweet, "Fox On The Run" / "Burn On the Flame" (Capitol 4157)	1975		$2.50	$5.00
T. Rex, "Bang A Gong (Get It On)" / "Raw Ramp" (Reprise 1032)	1971	$2.00	$4.00	$8.00
Thin Lizzy, "The Boys Are Back In Town" / "Jailbreak" (Mercury 73786)	1976		$2.50	$5.00
Joe Walsh, "Life's Been Good" / "Theme From Boat Weirdos" (Asylum 45493)	1978		$2.00	$4.00
Edgar Winter, "Frankenstein" / "Hangin' Around" (Epic 10945)	1973	$2.00	$4.00	$8.00
Edgar Winter, "Frankenstein" / "Undercover Man" (Epic 10967)				
(if yellow label)	1973		$3.00	$6.00
(if orange label)	1973		$2.00	$4.00
Neil Young, "Heart of Gold" / "Sugar Mountain" (Reprise 1065)				
(if no reference to "Harvest" album)	1971		$2.00	$4.00
(if "Harvest" album is mentioned on label)	1971		$2.50	$5.00
Neil Young, "Sugar Mountain" / "The Needle and the Damage Done" (Reprise 1393)	1978		$2.00	$4.00
ZZ Top, "Tush" / "Blue Jean Blues" (London 220)	1975		$2.50	$5.00
(with picture sleeve, add:)	1975	$2.00	$4.00	$8.00

LPs	Year	VG	VG+	NM
The Allman Brothers Band, Eat a Peach (Capricorn 2CP-0102) (2 LP's)	1972	$2.50	$5.00	$10.00
(if on Capricorn CX4-0102, quadraphonic)	1974	$7.50	$15.00	$30.00
Ambrosia, Somewhere Live Never Traveled (20th Century T-510)				
(if cover has a pyramid fold-over)	1976	$2.50	$5.00	$10.00
(if standard cover)	1976	$2.50	$5.00	
Bachman-Turner Overdrive, Not Fragile (Mercury SRM-1004)	1974		$2.50	$5.00
The Band, Rock of Ages (Capitol SABB-11045) (2 LPs)				
(if first pressing, Capitol label is red with purple "C" logo)	1972	$6.25	$12.50	$25.00
(if second pressing, with orange label)	1978	$2.00	$4.00	$8.00
Black Oak Arkansas, High on the Hog (Atco SD-7035)	1973		$2.50	$5.00
David Bowie, The Rise and Fall of Ziggy Stardust and the Spiders From Mars (RCA Victor LSP-4702)				
(if orange label)	1972	$3.75	$7.50	$15.00
(if tan label, reissue)	1975	$3.00	$6.00	$12.00
(if on RCA Victor AFL1-4702, reissue)	1977	$2.50	$5.00	$10.00
(if on Mobile Fidelity 1-064, audiophile pressing)	1983	$12.50	$25.00	$50.00
(if on Ryko Analogue RALP 1034, 2 LP's, clear vinyl, "limited edition" obi)	1990	$5.00	$10.00	$20.00
(if on Ryko Analogue LD-4702, promo with both LP and CD versions)	1990	$25.00	$50.00	$100.00
David Bowie, Diamond Dogs (RCA Victor CPL1-0576)				
(if first pressing, Bowie's dog genitals are clearly visible)	1974	$1,000	$2,000	$4,000
(if second pressing, Bowie's dog genitals are covered)	1974	$3.75	$7.50	$15.00
(if on RCA Victor AYL1-3889, reissue)	1980	$2.00	$4.00	$8.00
(if on Ryko Analogue RALP-0137, clear vinyl, dog genitals are restored)	1990	$5.00	$10.00	$20.00
Creedence Clearwater Revival, Cosmo's Factory (Fantasy F-8402)				
(if dark blue label)	1970	$3.75	$7.50	$15.00
(if brown label)	1973	$2.50	$5.00	$10.00
(if white label promo)	1970	$20.00	$40.00	$80.00
(if on Mobile Fidelity 1-037, audiophile pressing)	1979	$17.50	$35.00	$70.00
(if on Fantasy ORC-4516, reissue)	1981	$2.00	$4.00	$8.00
The Doobie Brothers, Takin' It To the Streets (Warner Bros. BS 2899)				
(if on "Burbank" label with palm trees)	1976	$2.50	$5.00	$10.00
(if on cream label)	1979	$2.00	$4.00	$8.00
(if on Mobile Fidelity 1-122, audiophile vinyl)	1983	$10.00	$20.00	$40.00
The Eagles, On the Border (Asylum 7E-1004)				
(clouds on label)	1974	$3.00	$6.00	$12.00
(if on Asylum EQ 1039, quadraphonic)	1975	$5.00	$10.00	$20.00
The Electric Light Orchestra, Eldorado (United Artists UA-LA339-G)				
(if tan label, first pressing)	1974	$3.00	$6.00	$12.00
(if sunrise label)	1977	$2.50	$5.00	$10.00
(if on Jet JZ 35526)	1978	$2.50	$5.00	$10.00
(if on Jet PZ 35526)	198??	$2.00	$4.00	$8.00
Fleetwood Mac, Rumours (Warner Bros. BSK 3010)				
(if record has 2:02 version of "Never Going Back Again")	1977	$2.50	$5.00	$10.00
(if record has 2:16 version of "Never Going Back Again")	1977	$2.00	$4.00	$8.00
(if on Nautilus NR-8, audiophile pressing)	1980	$10.00	$20.00	$40.00
Grand Funk Railroad, E Pluribus Funk (Capitol SW-853)	1971	$3.75	$7.50	$15.00
George Harrison, All Things Must Pass (Apple STCH-639) (3 LPs)	1970	$10.00	$20.00	$40.00
(1988 reissue, has Apple labels and Capitol cover, and large sticker on back cover)	1988	$20.00	$40.00	$80.00
George Harrison, Thirty Three and 1/3 (Dark Horse DH 3005) (deduct 30% for cutouts)	1976	$2.50	$5.00	$10.00
Jefferson Starship, Red Octopus (Grunt BFL1-0999)	1975	$2.50	$5.00	$10.00
(if on Grunt BFD1-0999, quadraphonic)	1975	$3.75	$7.50	$15.00

LPs	Year	VG	VG+	NM
(if on Grunt AYL1-3660)	1980	$2.00	$4.00	$8.00
(if on DCC Compact Classics LPZ-2036, audiophile vinyl)	1997	$6.25	$12.50	$25.00
Billy Joel, Cold Spring Harbor (Family Productions FPS-2700) (dark blue label, mastered at wrong speed)	1971	$10.00	$20.00	$40.00
(if on Columbia PC 38984, mastered at proper speed, "You Can Make Me Free" shortened by 3 minutes)	1983	$2.00	$4.00	$8.00
Billy Joel, The Stranger (Columbia JC 34987)	1977	$2.50	$5.00	$10.00
(if on Columbia PC 34987)	1979	$2.00	$4.00	$8.00
(if on Columbia HC 34987, half-speed mastered edition)	1981	$7.50	$15.00	$30.00
(if on Columbia HC 44987, half-speed mastered reissue)	1982	$6.25	$12.50	$25.00
Elton John, Goodbye Yellow Brick Road (MCA 10003) (2 LPs)	1973	$3.75	$7.50	$15.00
(if on MCA 6894, 2 LPs)	1980	$2.50	$5.00	$10.00
(if on Direct Disc SD-16614, audiophile pressing, 2 LPs)	1980	$12.50	$25.00	$50.00
(if on Mobile Fidelity 2-160, audiophile pressing, 2 LPs)	1984	$10.00	$20.00	$40.00
Kansas, Leftoverture (Kirshner JZ 34224)	1976	$2.50	$5.00	$10.00
(if on Kirshner PZ 34224, budget reissue)	198??	$2.00	$4.00	$8.00
(if on Kirshner HZ 44224, half-speed mastered edition)	1982	$10.00	$20.00	$40.00
John Lennon, John Lennon Sings the Great Rock and Roll Hits (Roots) (Adam VIII A-8018)	1975	$250.00	$500.00	$1,000.00
Lynyrd Skynyrd, Street Survivors (MCA 3029)				
(if first pressing, band in flames on cover)	1977	$6.25	$12.50	$25.00
(if second pressing, band on cover with black background)	1977	$2.50	$5.00	$10.00
(if on MCA 5223, reissue)	1980	$2.00	$4.00	$8.00
(if on MCA 37213, reissue)	1985	$2.00	$4.00	$8.00
The Marshall Tucker Band, Searchin' For A Rainbow (Capricorn CP 0161)	1975	$3.00	$6.00	$12.00
(if on Warner Bros. BSK 3609, reissue)	1982	$2.50	$5.00	$10.00
Paul McCartney and Wings, Band on the Run (Apple SO-3415) (with photo innersleeve and poster)	1973	$5.00	$10.00	$20.00
(if on Capitol SO-3415, custom label with MPL logo)	1975	$5.00	$10.00	$20.00
(if on Capitol SO-3415, black label, "Manufactured by Capitol Records...")	197??	$12.50	$25.00	$50.00
(if on Capitol SO-3415, black label, "Manufactured by MPL Communications Inc." at top)	197??	$5.00	$10.00	$20.00
(if on Columbia JC 36482, custom label)	1980	$3.75	$7.50	$15.00
(if on Columbia JC 36482, white "MPL" logo on lower left front cover)	198??	$25.00	$50.00	$100.00
(if on Columbia PC 36482, "PC" cover with "JC" label)	198??	$5.00	$10.00	$20.00
(if on Columbia PC 36482, "PC" cover with "PC" label)	198??	$7.50	$15.00	$30.00
(if on Columbia HC 46382, half-speed mastered audiophile edition)	1981	$12.50	$25.00	$50.00
(if on Capitol 99176, 2 LP's, 180-gram audiophile reissue, original LP on one disc, interviews on second)	1999	$10.00	$20.00	$40.00
Meat Loaf, Bat Out Of Hell (Epic/Cleveland International PE 34974)				
(if orange label with no bar code on back cover)	1977	$2.50	$5.00	$10.00
(if on Epic/Cleveland International E99 34974, picture disc)	1978	$5.00	$10.00	$20.00
(if on Epic/Cleveland International JE 34974, dark blue label)	1979	$2.00	$4.00	$8.00
(if on Epic/Cleveland International HE 44974, half-speed mastered edition)	1981	$10.00	$20.00	$40.00
(if on Epic/Cleveland International PE 34974, dark blue label, bar code on cover)	1985		$3.00	$6.00
The Steve Miller Band, Book of Dreams (Capitol SO-11630)	1977	$2.50	$5.00	$10.00
(if on Capitol SEAX-11903, picture disc)	1978	$3.75	$7.50	$15.00
(if on Capitol SN-16323, reissue)	1984	$2.00	$4.00	$8.00
The New York Dolls, In Too Much Too Soon (Mercury SRM-1-1001)	1974	$10.00	$20.00	$40.00
Nilsson, A Little Touch of Schmilsson in the Night (RCA Victor APL1-0097)	1973	$3.00	$6.00	$12.00
(if on RCA Victor AYL1-3761, reissue)	1980	$2.00	$4.00	$8.00
Queen, A Night at the Opera (Elektra 7E-1053)	1975	$2.50	$5.00	$10.00

LPs	Year	VG	VG+	NM
(if on Mobile Fidelity 1-067, audiophile pressing)	1980	$20.00	$40.00	$80.00
Lou Reed, Rock and Roll Animal (RCA Victor APL1-0472)	1974	$3.00	$6.00	$12.00
(if on RCA Victor AFL1-0472, reissue)	1977	$2.00	$4.00	$8.00
(if on RCA Victor AYL1-3664, reissue)	1980	$2.00	$4.00	$8.00
Linda Ronstadt, Heart Like A Wheel (Capitol ST-11358)	1974	$3.00	$6.00	$12.00
(if on Capitol SW-11358, reissue)	1975	$2.50	$5.00	$10.00
Roxy Music, Country Life (Atco SD 36-106)				
(if cover shows two semi-naked women on a grassy background)	1975	$6.25	$12.50	$25.00
(if cover deletes the women, leaving the grassy background)	1975	$2.50	$5.00	$10.00
Santana, Abraxas (Columbia KC 30130) (first pressings contain poster)	1970	$3.75	$7.50	$15.00
(without poster)	197??	$2.50	$5.00	$10.00
(if on Columbia HC 40130, half-speed mastered edition)	1981	$20.00	$40.00	$80.00
(if on Columbia PC 30130, reissue)	1985	$2.00	$4.00	$8.00
Bob Seger, Night Moves (Capitol ST-11557)	1976	$2.50	$5.00	$10.00
Bruce Springsteen, Born to Run (Columbia PC 33795)				
(if Jon Laudau's name is misspelled "John" on back cover)	1975	$6.25	$12.50	$25.00
(if a sticker on back cover has Jon Landau's name spelled correctly)	1975	$3.75	$7.50	$15.00
(if Jon Landau's name is spelled correctly, no sticker)	1975	$2.50	$5.00	$10.00
(if white label promo)	1975	$25.00	$50.00	$100.00
(if on Columbia HC 43795, half-speed mastered edition)	1982	$10.00	$20.00	$40.00
(if Classic Records reissue, no gatefold cover, "Classic Records" on back cover)	1999	$10.00	$20.00	$40.00
(if Classic Records reissue, gatefold cover, "Classic Records" on back cover)	1999	$6.25	$12.50	$25.00
Ringo Starr, Ringo's Rotogravure (Atlantic SD 18193) (if cover is notched or cut, deduct 2/3 from price)	1976	$3.75	$7.50	$15.00
(if "DJ Only" scrawled into trail-off area)	1977	$7.50	$15.00	$30.00
Steely Dan, Pretzel Logic (ABC 806)				
(if black label)	1974	$3.00	$6.00	$12.00
(if multicolor label)	1974	$2.50	$5.00	$10.00
(if on MCA 37042, reissue)	1980	$2.00	$4.00	$8.00
(if on MCA 1593, reissue)	1987	$3.00	$6.00	
Rod Stewart, Blondes Have More Fun (Warner Bros. BSK 3261)	1978	$2.50	$5.00	$10.00
(if on Warner Bros. BSP 3276, picture disc)	1978	$5.00	$10.00	$20.00
(if on Mobile Fidelity 1-054, audiophile pressing)	1980	$6.25	$12.50	$25.00
Styx, The Grand Illusion (A&M SP-4637)	1977	$2.50	$5.00	$10.00
(if on Mobile Fidelity 1-026, audiophile pressing)	1979	$7.50	$15.00	$30.00
(if on A&M SP-3223, reissue)	1984	$2.00	$4.00	$8.00
Supertramp, Even in the Quietest Moments, A&M SP-4634)	1977	$3.00	$6.00	$12.00
(if on A&M SP-3215, reissue)	1982	$2.00	$4.00	$8.00
(if on Sweet Thunder 5, audiophile vinyl)	198??	$10.00	$20.00	$40.00
The Sweet, Desolation Boulevard (Capitol ST-11395)	1975	$3.00	$6.00	$12.00
(if on Capitol SN-16287, reissue)	1981	$2.00	$4.00	$8.00
T. Rex, Tyrannosaurus Rex (A Beginning) (A&M SP-3514) (2 LP's)	1972	$3.75	$7.50	$15.00
T. Rex, Tanx (Reprise MS 2132)	1973	$3.00	$6.00	$12.00
Thin Lizzy, Thin Lizzy (London PS 594)	1971	$10.00	$20.00	$40.00
Thin Lizzy, Jailbreak (Mercury SRM-1-1081)	1976	$3.00	$6.00	$12.00
Joe Walsh, The Smoker You Drink, The Player You Get (ABC Dunhill DS-50140)	1973	$2.50	$5.00	$10.00
(if on ABC Command QD-40016, quadraphonic)	1974	$5.00	$10.00	$20.00
(if on MCA 37054, reissue)	1979	$2.00	$4.00	$8.00
The Edgar Winter Group, Edgar Winter's White Trash (Epic E 30512)				
(if yellow label)	1971	$3.75	$7.50	$15.00
(if orange label)	1973	$3.00	$6.00	$12.00
Neil Young, Harvest (Reprise MS 2032)				
(if first pressing, textured cover and lyric insert)	1972	$3.75	$7.50	$15.00
(if second pressing, flat cover)	1972	$2.50	$5.00	$10.00
(if on Reprise SMAS-92485, Capitol Record Club edition)	1972	$6.25	$12.50	$25.00
(if on Reprise R 113998, RCA Music Service edition)	1972	$3.00	$6.00	$12.00
(If on Reprise MSK 2277, reissue, brown "Reprise" label)	1978	$2.00	$4.00	$8.00
(if on Nautilus NR-44, audiophile vinyl)	1982	$37.50	$75.00	$150.00
ZZ Top, Fandango! (London PS 656)	1975	$3.00	$6.00	$12.00

FRANK SINATRA

History: The Voice. Pure and simple. No other words are necessary.

Frank Sinatra's career spanned more than 60 years, a career in which he found success as a singer, a performer, an actor and a cultural icon. From the days of the screaming bobbysoxers at the Brooklyn Paramount, to his Las Vegas encounters with the Rat Pack, to his award-winning Duets albums, Frank Sinatra saw highs and lows in his career, both triumphs and tragedies. Yet through it all, like the songs he sang, he always got through the troubles and tribulations - his way.

Frank Sinatra, with a wink and a song, on one of his many records for Capitol. Courtesy Last Vestige Music Store, Albany, N.Y.

Francis Albert Sinatra was born in Hoboken, New Jersey in 1915. By 1935, after attending a Bing Crosby concert, Sinatra decided he wanted to become a singer. Without any previous formal training, Sinatra sang well enough to win amateur talent contests, including a victory on the *Major Bowes Amateur Hour* radio program. In 1939, while working as a singing waiter in a restaurant in Englewood Cliffs, N.J., Sinatra was discovered by bandleader Harry James, and the two later toured and performed together.

Six months after signing with Harry James, Sinatra joined Tommy Dorsey's band. Sinatra told Dorsey he always wanted to sing the way Dorsey played his trombone. Dorsey eventually taught Sinatra special breathing techniques that allowed the singer to simultaneously draw breath and sing, allowing a performer to sustain notes for longer periods of time.

It was during his tenure with Dorsey's band that Sinatra became the target of adoration from teenage girls. These "bobby-soxers" would scream and swoon at the sound of Sinatra's voice. By the time Sinatra performed as a warmup act for Benny Goodman at the Brooklyn Paramount theater in New York City, the lines of screaming girls waiting to enter the theater stretched for three city blocks.

During World War II, Sinatra recorded songs for the V-Disc label, as did many of his fellow singers and musicians. These recordings were made for the enjoyment of soldiers and sailors in the theaters of war. Sinatra's V-Discs contain alternate recordings, airchecks and new interpretations of his classic Columbia-era songs, and although a two-CD set of his V-Disc recordings is currently available, clean copies of the original 78 RPM V-Discs are very hard to find today.

By 1942, Sinatra paid his way out of his contract with Dorsey, and signed with Columbia Records for a solo career. He also signed with MGM for a motion picture career, and Sinatra looked to be at the top of his game.

Sinatra's first albums were six-song 10-inch 33 1/3 RPM microgroove records for Columbia.

But by 1949, the exposure of his affair with actress Ava Gardner wrecked his marriage; both his MGM and Columbia contracts were not renewed. By 1951, the singer had hit rock bottom, reduced to borrowing money from Ava Gardner to sustain his rent.

In 1952, Sinatra returned to prominence, starring in the role of Maggio in the film *"From Here To Eternity."* His performance won him an Academy Award, and helped resurrect his performing career. Armed with a new contract from Capitol Records, Sinatra worked with arranger Nelson Riddle on new interpretations of classic 1940s compositions by George Gershwin and Cole Porter.

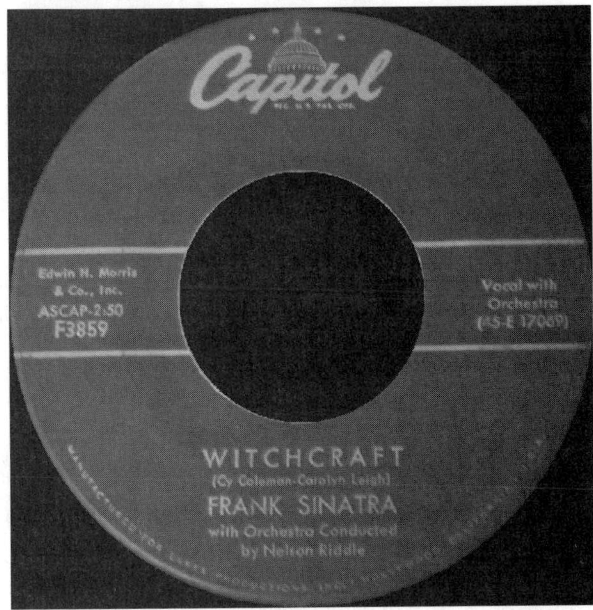

Among the many collaborations between Sinatra and Nelson Riddle was this song, "Witchcraft." Courtesy Last Vestige Music Store, Albany, N.Y.

What followed were a series of "concept" albums, a collection of songs built around a single theme. Sinatra's first successful concept album was *Songs For Young Lovers*, and was followed by the even more successful ballad collection *In The Wee Small Hours.* In fact, throughout the 1950s, Sinatra recorded two albums a year—one of uptempo songs, one of tender ballads.

Trivia

In 1955, Frank Sinatra sang "Love And Marriage" as part of a television production of Our Town. Thirty years later, that Sinatra recording appeared as the opening theme to another television series—the sitcom "Married ... With Children."

***In the Wee Small Hours* was released as a series of EPs, on two 10-inch LPs, and on a single 12-inch LP. But no matter what format, the songs themselves are compelling and stirring. Courtesy Last Vestige Music Store, Albany, N.Y.**

By 1961, Sinatra started his own record label, Reprise, and began recording albums for that label, as well as finishing up his recording contracts with Capitol. That year, six different Sinatra albums—two on Reprise, four on Capitol—all reached the Top 10 on the album charts.

Even though the Beatles dominated the album and singles charts in the mid-1960s, Sinatra was able to continually release successful albums on his Reprise label. He even garnered Top 40 hits like "Summer Wind," "That's Life," and a #1 hit, "Strangers in the Night."

Trivia

One of Sinatra's Capitol EP issues was the four-part, 45 RPM EP "Songs for Swingin' Lovers." If you have one of these EPs, look at the cover. If Sinatra is facing the romantic couple on the cover, the EP is worth $20, with an additional $20 for the cover. Now if Sinatra is facing away from the romantic couple, add an extra $5 to the price.

The collaboration between Sinatra and Nelson Riddle continued into the 1960s, with songs like "Summer Wind." From the Collection of Val Shively.

The picture sleeve for Sinatra's 1980 hit, "New York, New York." His rendition of this song eventually became the unofficial theme music for the New York Yankees. From the Collection of Val Shively.

During this time, while Frank Sinatra still had fans among the elder generation, the younger crowd was more interested in another Sinatra—Frank's daughter Nancy, who had hits with "These Boots Are Made For Walkin'" and "Sugartown." Father and daughter even sang together on a #1 hit in 1967, "Something Stupid."

In 1971, Frank Sinatra announced he was retiring from the professional stage, seeking instead to spend more time with his family. Three years later, he "un-retired" with a new series of albums. In 1980, Sinatra released a three-album set, *Trilogy*, and a song from that album, "New York, New York," put him back on the pop charts once again.

Trivia

How would you like to have the most popular singer of his era record a song for your presidential campaign? Frank Sinatra's "High Hopes" was pressed as a special commemorative 45, as "High Hopes with Jack Kennedy." A copy of this record in near-mint condition would sell for as much as $300 today.

Frank Sinatra's last recordings were a critically acclaimed series of *Duets* albums, in which the legendary singer sang his greatest hits, accompanied by other artists. His duet partners included Bono, Aretha Franklin, Barbra Streisand, Jimmy Buffett, Linda Ronstadt, Willie Nelson, and Frank Sinatra Jr.

After 50 years of performing, The Voice finally fell silent on May 14, 1998, when Frank Sinatra passed away in his sleep. His recordings, however, will continue to ensure that "Ol' Blue Eyes" will continue to enthrall listeners for generations to come.

What To Look For: Like Elvis Presley and the Beatles, Frank Sinatra sold millions of albums, 45s, and 78s. This means that millions of records exist, and the common releases can be acquired at a reasonable cost. What is harder to find, and by definition more collectible and expensive, are non-standard releases. Columbia Microgroove 7-inch small-holed 33 1/3 RPM records can sell for $150-$600 in near-mint condition, depending on the title. That same title on a standard 45 only commands $20-$25 in near-mint condition.

Sinatra often custom-pressed 45s and LPs for special occasions. The press runs on these titles ranged from 500 to 1,000 copies, and were given by Sinatra to charitable organizations, or to his family and friends. Some of his albums were also released with elaborate slipcases and autographed covers, and are very collectible today.

With almost sixty years of recorded material, there is no doubt that boxed sets of Sinatra's albums proliferate the market. Mobile Fidelity Sound Lab, the audiophile label, pressed sixteen of Sinatra's Capitol LPs in a boxed set. Other boxed sets are available from Time-Life Music, the Longines Symphonette Society, and from Sinatra's previously contracted record labels, Capitol, Columbia, RCA Victor, and Reprise.

Sinatra's recorded output appears on nearly every musical format, from 78 to CD. It also exists on 7-inch 33 RPM microgroove singles, as well as on 7-inch four-song 45 RPM extended play singles.

References: Mustazza, Leonard, *Ol' Blue Eyes: A Frank Sinatra Encyclopedia*, Greenwood Press, Westport, Conn. 1998.

Web pages: The official Frank Sinatra Store: *http://www.franksinatra.com*; "A Great Link," featuring dozens of Sinatra-based Web pages and fanpages. *http://www.agreatlink.com/agl/Sinatra/Sinatra.htm*; The Sinatra Music Society, a discussion group dedicated to the understanding of the music of Frank Sinatra: *http://www.sinatra-ms.com*; a Web page devoted to the history of Sinatra's music: *http://www.songsbysinatra.com.*

45s	Year	VG	VG+	NM
Frank Sinatra, "I'll Never Smile Again" / (B-side unknown) (RCA Victor 27-0077)	1949	$3.75	$7.50	$15.00
Frank Sinatra, "I'll Never Smile Again" / "I'll Be Seeing You" (RCA Victor 447-0116) (reissue of pre-World War II 78)	1950	$3.00	$6.00	$12.00
Frank Sinatra, "Love Means Love" / "Cherry Pies Ought To Be You" (Columbia 39141)	1951	$6.25	$12.50	$25.00
(if on Columbia 3-39141, microgroove 33 1/3 rpm 7" single, small hole)	1951	$200.00	$400.00	$600.00
Frank Sinatra and Dagmar, "Mama Will Bark" / "I'm A Fool To Want You" (Columbia 39425)	1951	$10.00	$20.00	$40.00
Frank Sinatra, "Night and Day" / "The Lamplighter's Serenade" (RCA Victor 447-0408)	1952	$3.00	$6.00	$12.00
Frank Sinatra, "My One And Only Love" / "I've Got The World On A String" (Capitol F2450)				
(with center spindle intact)	1953	$7.50	$15.00	$30.00
(with spindle popped out)	1953	$5.00	$10.00	$20.00
Frank Sinatra, "Young at Heart" / "Take a Chance" (Capitol F2703)	1953	$5.00	$10.00	$20.00
Frank Sinatra, "Melody of Love" / "I'm Gonna Live Till I Die" (Capitol F3018)	1954	$5.00	$10.00	$20.00
Frank Sinatra, "Love and Marriage" / "The Impatient Years" (Capitol F3260)	1955	$3.75	$7.50	$15.00
Frank Sinatra, "Jealous Lover" / "You Forgot All The Words" (Capitol F3552)	1956	$6.25	$12.50	$25.00
(if A-side is correctly titled "Hey! Jealous Lover")	1956	$3.75	$7.50	$15.00
Frank Sinatra, "Witchcraft" / "Tell Her You Love Her" (Capitol F3859)	1957	$3.00	$6.00	$12.00
Frank Sinatra, "High Hopes" / "All My Tomorrows" (Capitol F4214)	1959	$3.75	$7.50	$15.00
(with picture sleeve, add:)	1959	$50.00	$100.00	$200.00
Frank Sinatra, "High Hopes with Jack Kennedy" / "Jack Kennedy All The Way" (no label, KB 2077/8)	1960	$75.00	$150.00	$300.00
Frank Sinatra, "Nice 'n' Easy" / "This Was My Love" (Capitol 4408)	1960	$3.00	$6.00	$12.00
Frank Sinatra, "The Second Time Around" / "Tina" (Reprise 20001) (light blue label)	1961	$6.25	$12.50	$25.00
Frank Sinatra, "I'll Be Seeing You" / "The One I Love) (Reprise 20023) (peach label)	1961	$3.75	$7.50	$15.00

45s	Year	VG	VG+	NM
Frank Sinatra and Sammy Davis, Jr., "Me And My Shadow" / Sammy Davis, Jr. and Dean Martin, "Sam's Song" (Reprise 20128)	1962	$3.75	$7.50	$15.00
(with picture sleeve, add:)	1962	$12.50	$25.00	$50.00
Frank Sinatra, "California" / "America the Beautiful" (Reprise 20157) (promo only, no stock copies issued)	1963	$62.50	$125.00	$250.00
(with picture sleeve, add:)	1963	$187.50	$375.00	$750.00
(if same catalog number, 1978 reissue, private pressing for Sinatra's own use)	1978	$50.00	$10.00	$200.00
Frank Sinatra, “"My Kind of Town" / "I Like To Lead When I Dance" (Reprise 0279)	1964	$2.50	$5.00	$10.00
(with picture sleeve that was only issued for promo copies, add:)	1964	$37.50	$75.00	$125.00
Frank Sinatra, "It Was A Very Good Year" / "Moment to Moment" (Reprise 0429)	1965	$2.00	$4.00	$8.00
(with picture sleeve, add:)	1965	$6.25	$12.50	$25.00
Frank Sinatra, "Frank Sinatra Reads From Gunga Din" (Reprise 0493) (300 copies pressed for Sinatra's personal use)	1966	$125.00	$250.00	$500.00
Frank Sinatra, "Summer Wind" / "You Make Me Feel So Young" (Reprise 0509)	1966	$2.50	$5.00	$10.00
Frank Sinatra and Nancy Sinatra, "Something Stupid" / "I Will Wait For You" (Reprise 0561)	1967	$2.00	$4.00	$8.00
Frank Sinatra, "Love's Been Good To Me" / "A Man Alone" (Reprise 0852)	1969	$2.00	$4.00	$8.00
Frank Sinatra, "The Train" / "What's Now Is Now" (Reprise 0920) (label design contains "r:" in box)	1969	$2.00	$4.00	$8.00
Frank Sinatra, "I Sing The Songs (I Write The Songs)" / "Empty Tables" (Reprise 1347)	1976	$2.50	$5.00	$10.00
Frank Sinatra, "Theme from New York, New York" / "That's What God Looks Like To Me" (Reprise 29903)	1980	$2.50	$5.00	$10.00
(with picture sleeve, add:)	1980	$2.00	$4.00	$8.00
Frank Sinatra, "To Love A Child" (mono/stereo) (Reprise PRO-S-1007) (500 copies pressed, given to Nancy Reagan for a White House function)	1982	$75.00	$150.00	$300.00
Frank Sinatra, "L.A. Is My Lady" / "Until The Real Thing Comes Along" (Qwest 29223)	1984		$2.50	$5.00
(with picture sleeve, add:)	1984	$3.75	$7.50	$15.00
Frank Sinatra and Bono, "I've Got You Under My Skin" / U2, "Stay (Faraway, So Close)" (Island/Capitol 858076-7)	1994		$2.00	$4.00
(with picture sleeve, add:)	1994		$2.00	$4.00
Frank Sinatra and George Strait, "Fly Me To The Moon" / George Strait, "Check Yes Or No" (MCA 55127)	1995		$2.00	$4.00

LPs	Year	VG	VG+	NM
Frank Sinatra, Dedicated To You (Columbia CL 6096) (10-inch LP)	1952	$25.00	$50.00	$100.00
Frank Sinatra, Fabulous Frankie! (RCA Victor LPT-3063) (10-inch LP)	1953	$15.00	$30.00	$60.00
Frank Sinatra, In The Wee Small Hours, Part 1 (Capitol H1-581) (10-inch LP)	1955	$25.00	$50.00	$100.00
Frank Sinatra, In The Wee Small Hours, Part 2 (Capitol H2-581) (10-inch LP)	1955	$25.00	$50.00	$100.00
Frank Sinatra, In The Wee Small Hours (Capitol W 581) (mono)				
(if gray label original)	1955	$10.00	$20.00	$40.00
(if black label, rainbow perimeter)	1959	$6.25	$12.50	$25.00
(if on Capitol DW 581, rechanneled stereo)	196??	$3.00	$6.00	$12.00
(if on Capitol SM-581, reissue)	197??	$2.00	$4.00	$8.00
Frank Sinatra, Frank Sinatra Conducts Music of Alec Wilder (Columbia Masterworks ML 4271) (mono)	1955	$25.00	$50.00	$100.00
Frank Sinatra, Songs for Swingin' Lovers! (Capitol W 653) (gray label) (mono)				
(if Sinatra faces away from the embracing couple)	1956	$12.50	$25.00	$50.00
(if Sinatra faces toward the embracing couple)	1956	$10.00	$20.00	$40.00
(if black label, rainbow perimeter)	1959	$6.25	$12.50	$25.00
(if on Capitol DW 653, rechanneled stereo)	196??	$3.00	$6.00	$12.00
(if on Capitol SM-653, reissue)	197??	$2.00	$4.00	$8.00
Frank Sinatra, Frankie and Tommy (RCA Victor LPM-1569)	1957	$15.00	$30.00	$60.00
(if album is retitled Tommy Plays, Frankie Sings)	1957	$10.00	$20.00	$40.00
Frank Sinatra, Where Are You? (Capitol W 855) (mono)				
(if gray label)	1957	$7.50	$15.00	$30.00
(if black label, rainbow perimeter)	1959	$5.00	$10.00	$20.00
(if on Capitol SW 855, stereo, does not contain "I Cover the Waterfront")	1959	$10.00	$20.00	$40.00

LPs	Year	VG	VG+	NM
(if on Capitol SW 855, stereo, contains "I Cover the Waterfront")	196??	$7.50	$15.00	$30.00
(if on Capitol SN-16267, reissue)	198??	$2.00	$4.00	$8.00
Frank Sinatra, Come Fly With Me (Capitol W 920) (mono)				
(if gray label)	1958	$10.00	$20.00	$40.00
(if black label, rainbow perimeter)	1959	$5.00	$10.00	$20.00
(if on Capitol SW 920, stereo)	1959	$7.50	$15.00	$30.00
(if on Capitol SM-920, reissue)	197??	$2.00	$4.00	$8.00
Frank Sinatra, Nice 'N' Easy (Capitol W 1417) (mono)	1960	$5.00	$10.00	$20.00
(if on Capitol SW 1417, stereo)	1960	$6.25	$12.50	$25.00
(if on Mobile Fidelity 1-086, audiophile pressing)	1981	$10.00	$20.00	$40.00
(if on Capitol SN-16204, reissue)	198??	$2.00	$4.00	$8.00
Frank Sinatra, I Remember Tommy (Reprise F 1003) (mono)	1961	$5.00	$10.00	$20.00
(if on Reprise R9 1003, stereo)	1961	$6.25	$12.50	$25.00
Frank Sinatra, The Concert Sinatra (Reprise F 1009) (mono)	1963	$3.75	$7.50	$15.00
(if on Reprise R9 1009, stereo, first pressings declare the album was recorded in "35mm Stereo")	1963	$6.25	$12.50	$25.00
(if on Reprise R9 1009, stereo, no reference to "35mm Stereo")	196??	$5.00	$10.00	$20.00
Frank Sinatra, A Man And His Music (Reprise 2F 1016) (mono) (2 LPs)	1965	$5.00	$10.00	$20.00
(if on Reprise 2FS 1016, stereo)	1985	$6.25	$12.50	$25.00
(if records came with blue slipcase, embossed silver front, raised letters, booklet, signed card, add:)	1965	$50.00	$100.00	$200.00
Frank Sinatra, SinatraJobim (Reprise FS 1028) (only test pressings exist, value is for a single pressing)	1969	$2,000	$3,000	$4,000
Frank Sinatra, A Man Alone & Other Songs of Rod McKuen (Reprise FS 1030)	1969	$3.75	$7.50	$15.00
(if signed copy, gatefold cover, hardbound book included, only 400 pressed)	1969	$100.00	$200.00	$400.00
(if on Reprise SMAS-92081, Capitol Record Club edition)	1969	$5.00	$10.00	$20.00
Frank Sinatra, Sinatra: The Works (Longines Symphonette LS-308A)				
(if 10 LPs in set)	1972	$18.75	$37.50	$75.00
(if only 6 LPs, abridged set)	1973	$10.00	$20.00	$40.00
(with bonus LP, Sinatra Like Never Before, Longines Symphonette SYS-5637, add:)	1972	$6.25	$12.50	$25.00
Frank Sinatra, Ol' Blue Eyes Is Back (Reprise FS 2155)	1973	$3.00	$6.00	$12.00
(if on Reprise FS4 2155, quadraphonic)	1974	$6.25	$12.50	$25.00
Frank Sinatra, Trilogy: Past, Present, Future (Reprise 3FS 2300) (3 LPs; all crammed into cover designed to hold 1 LP)	1980	$5.00	$10.00	$20.00
Frank Sinatra, Sinatra (Mobile Fidelity SC-1) (16 LPs)	1983	$150.00	$300.00	$600.00
Frank Sinatra, L.A. Is My Lady (Qwest 25145)	1984	$3.00	$6.00	$12.00
Frank Sinatra, The Voice: The Columbia Years 1943-1952 (Columbia C6X 40343) (6 LPs)	1986	$20.00	$40.00	$80.00
Frank Sinatra, Sinatra Rarities (Columbia PC 44238)	1989	$10.00	$20.00	$40.00
Frank Sinatra, Duets (Capitol C1-89611)	1993	$5.00	$10.00	$20.00

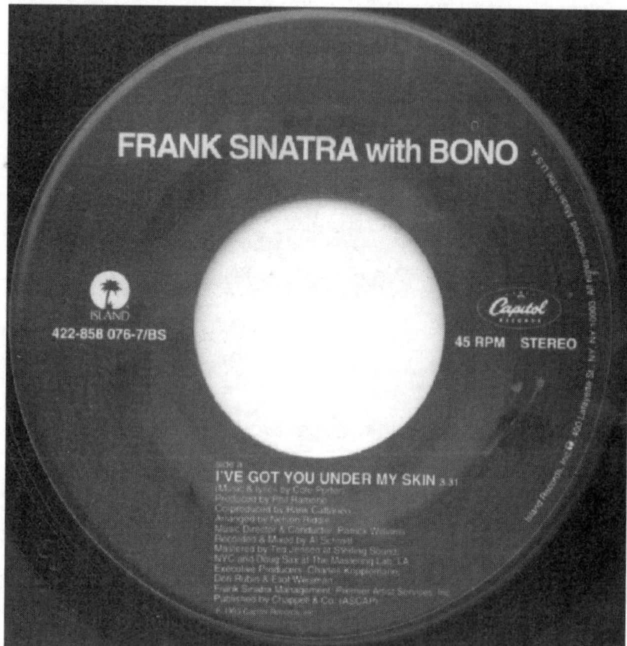

Some artists who recorded with Sinatra on his ***Duets*** albums released the collaborations on their own labels. That's why there are two label trademarks on this Island 45.

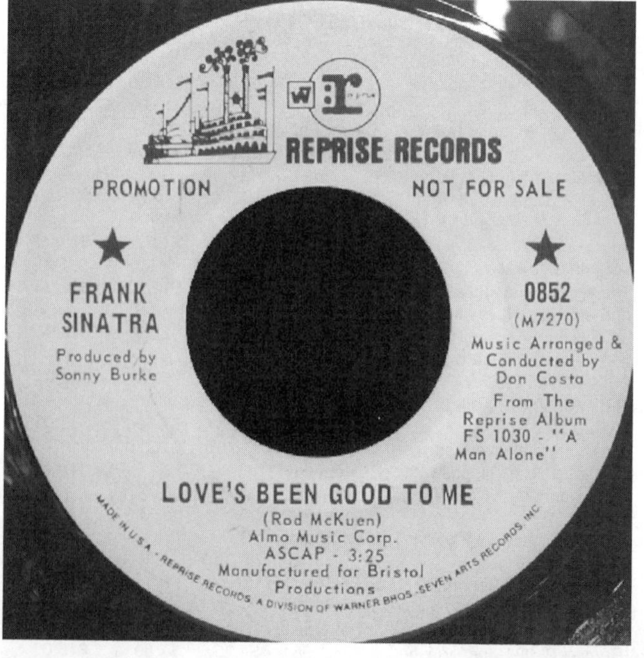

The album of Sinatra-interpreted Rod McKuen songs from which this single was taken, ***A Man Alone***, exists in a deluxe gatefold collection worth over $400 in near-mint condition. From the Collection of Val Shively.

SIXTIES ROCK

History: The British Invasion dominated the American music scene in the mid-1960s. But during that time, some American singers and bands were able to establish their own recording careers, and have their own hits and careers. Whether the songs were based in folk-rock, psychedelia, bayou rock, or straightforward pop songs, these artists reflected the changing values of the late 1960s—in many cases, their songs were testaments to the history of the late 1960s.

The biggest "folk-rock" group of the 1960s was the Byrds. Their first hit, "Mr. Tambourine Man," was given to them by Bob Dylan, and although the recording session featured only member Jim (later Roger) McGuinn and studio musicians, the song hailed a new musical era. Just as the British Invasion artists had recorded their own versions of American blues and soul hits, the Byrds recorded folk-rock songs as if they were re-interpreting the British Invasion's biggest hit-makers. Other folk-rock groups in the 1960s include the Association, Simon and Garfunkel, the Beau Brummels, and Buffalo Springfield.

A Byrds picture sleeve from one of their hits. From the Collection of Val Shively.

The summer of 1967 was also known as the Summer of Love. San Francisco and Los Angeles were the new epicenters of popular culture and music, and people could experience this new musical revolution whether they were traveling along the Sunset Strip, or standing at the corners of Haight and Ashbury. It was a perfect time for harmony groups like The Mamas and the Papas, or Spanky and Our Gang, to have hits.

Trivia

Chad Allen and the Expressions already had a Top 40 single, "Shakin' All Over," but they needed a new name. Someone at the record company suggested calling themselves "Guess Who?" until the band could think of a new name. Eventually the name "Guess Who" stuck, and is now the name Chad Allen and the Expressions are better known by.

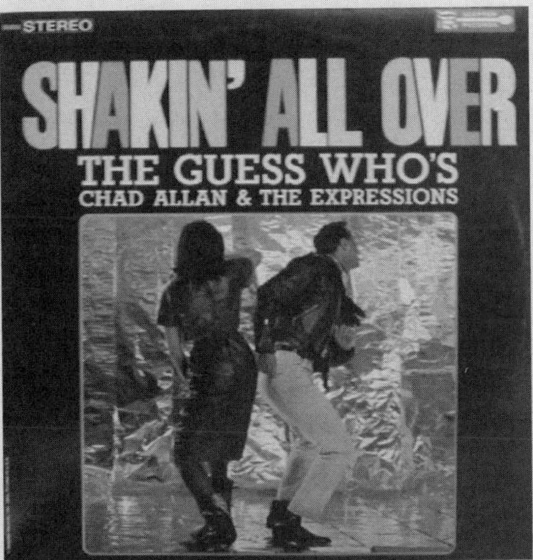

The Guess Who's lone album on Scepter contains the band's original name. From the Collection of Val Shively.

If you listen very closely as the Mamas and the Papas sing the first words to "California Dreamin'," you can hear a fifth voice. That's Barry McGuire of "Eve of Destruction" fame, it was his voice that was recorded with this song, but it was wiped off when the Mamas and the Papas were offered it.

Trivia

While listening to the radio, singer-songwriter John Fred thought he heard the Beatles singing about "Lucy in disguise with diamonds." Upon discovering he had misheard the lyric to the song "Lucy in the Sky With Diamonds," he turned that mistake into a hit song for himself, "Judy In Disguise (With Glasses)."

Depending on the color of this label, this record can sell for up to $12 in near-mint condition.

It was also the time for psychedelic music. Groups like the Jefferson Airplane, the Doors, Love, and the Grateful Dead mixed music and marijuana, breaking free from the three-minute, two-verse pop song into longer, free-flowing musical journeys. Many garage bands also drifted toward psychedelic recordings, including the Chocolate Watchband and the Thirteenth Floor Elevators.

One of the Doors' later releases, first pressings of *L.A. Woman* have a cellophane front cover. Courtesy Last Vestige Music Store, Albany, N.Y.

One group that dabbled for a while in psychedelic music was Tommy James and the Shondells, with songs like "Crimson and Clover" and "Crystal Blue Persuasion." The fact that James and his band even had the opportunity to record hits is amazing, considering that his first recording, "Hanky Panky," flopped. It wasn't until a disc jockey in Pittsburgh played it a few years later as an "exclusive" that the song finally became a hit, propelling James to a superstar recording career.

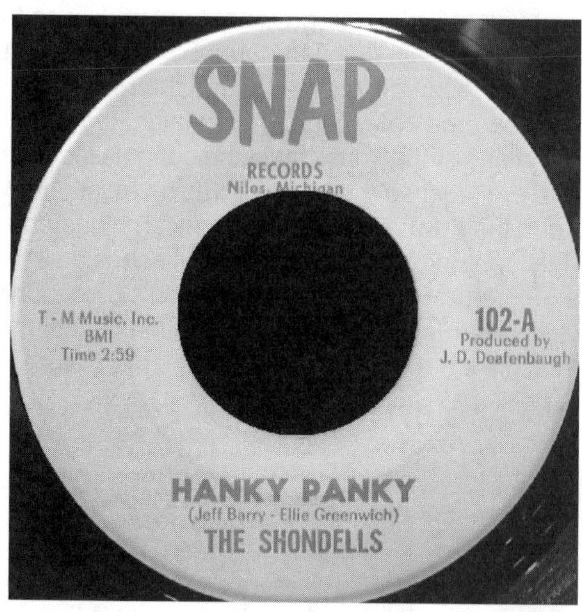

"Hanky Panky," as originally released in 1963 on the tiny Snap label. It would become a hit in 1966 on the Roulette label. From the Collection of Val Shively.

Over in New York, songwriters Lou Reed and John Cale formed the Velvet Underground, and over the course of three albums defined the punk and new wave movements that would appear a decade later. The Velvet Underground's songs contained stark realism about sex and drugs and life; tracks like "All Tomorrow's Parties," "Heroin," and "Sweet Jane" may have been too coarse for AM radio play, but were strong enough to achieve a dedicated following that still exists to this day.

Female rock singers were also finding success in the rock world. Janis Joplin fronted her rock band, Big Brother and the Holding Company, singing the blues with an energy previously unheard. Nancy Sinatra stepped out of her famous father Frank's shadow, recording a series of rough-and-tumble Top 40 singles like 'These Boots Are Made For Walkin'," "How Does That Grab You, Darlin?" and "Jackson."

One of the extremely rare Velvet Underground 45s. A picture sleeve for this item has been confirmed to exist. Courtesy Good Rockin' Tonight/Collectors Universe.

Trivia

When an artist becomes a superstar, everything he or she ever recorded in the past suddenly becomes collectible, even though those albums and 45s previously stiffed upon their initial release. Case in point: the Hassles may have been an average 1960s rock band with a couple of albums and a lifetime of obscurity. So why are their records collectible today? Well, it seems one of their members was a guy named Billy Joel.

The Hassles released two LPs in their short lifespan. Billy Joel performed on both of them. Courtesy Last Vestige Music Store, Albany, N.Y.

Rock 'n' roll musicians had appeared at multi-artist festivals for years, but the 1969 Woodstock Festival changed everything. What was originally planned as a small music festival grew into a 500,000 multi-artist three-day concert, featuring everyone from Jimi Hendrix to the Jefferson Airplane, from Melanie to Janis Joplin, from Joan Baez to Sly and the Family Stone. The "Woodstock Generation," as it would eventually be called, spent three days in mud and rain, absorbing not only the music and the performances, but also the positive message of peace and love—a message that would hopefully take them toward a new enlightenment.

What To Look For: For most of the 1960s, albums were available in both monaural and stereo formats. However, as more people purchased stereophonic equipment, record companies decided to eliminate monaural pressings altogether (although they continued to press monaural promo copies for AM radio stations). Therefore, monaural albums from the late 1960s are actually more collectible than the same title in stereo.

Also, with albums, check the back cover to make sure that there is no UPC bar code, which would immediately indicate you have purchased a reprint. No record company in the 1960s had the technology available to use bar codes, nor did any record store.

With 45s, try to avoid purchasing styrene pressings, especially if the record is also available as a normal vinyl pressing. The biggest offender is the Bell family of labels (which includes Mala, Amy, Philly Groove and Sphere Sound). These pressings were made to save money; in the end, the records wore out faster, and had more surface hiss after multiple plays.

References: Strong, Martin C., *The Great Psychedelic Discography*, Canongate Books Ltd., Edinburgh, U.K., 1997.

Web pages: A homepage devoted to fans of the Byrds: *http://www.lyon.edu/wedata/users/kadler/public_html/rmcguinn*; Nancy Sinatra's personal homepage: *http://www.nancysinatra.com*; a tribute site to the Velvet Underground: *http://www.velvetunderground.com;* if you want to relive the history of the Woodstock festival, click here: *http://www.woodstock.com.*

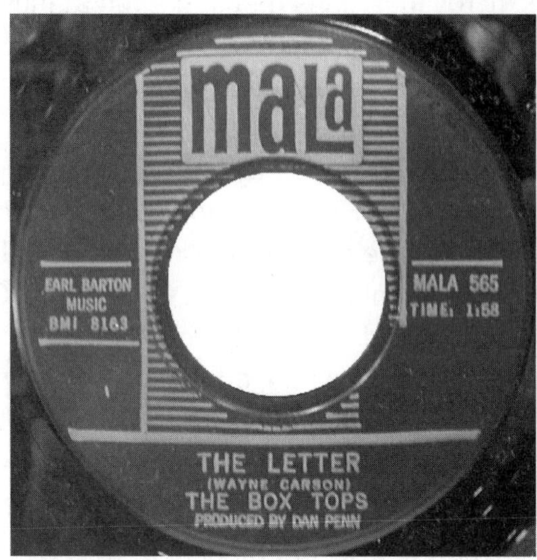

The Box Tops' "The Letter," on a styrene pressing. Almost every Box Tops single is available on a vinyl pressing with a paper label; styrene pressings should only be bought if you want a "playing" copy of a 45, as opposed to one that stays on the shelf. From the Collection of Val Shively.

45s	Year	VG	VG+	NM
The Association, "Cherish" / "Don't Blame It On Me" (Valiant 747)	1966	$3.00	$6.00	$12.00
The Association, "Windy" / "Sometime" (Warner Bros. 7041)	1967	$2.50	$5.00	$10.00
The Beau Brummels, "Laugh, Laugh" / "Still In Love With You Baby" (Autumn 8)				
(if white label)	1965	$3.75	$7.50	$15.00
(if tan label, second presssing)	1965	$3.00	$6.00	$12.00
Big Brother and the Holding Company, "Piece of My Heart" / "Turtle Blues" (Columbia 44626)	1968	$2.50	$5.00	$10.00
The Box Tops, "The Letter" / "Happy Times" (Mala 565)	1967	$3.00	$6.00	$12.00
The Byrds, "Mr. Tambourine Man" / "I Knew I'd Want You" (Columbia 43271)	1965	$3.75	$7.50	$15.00
(with picture sleeve that promotes the Byrds' appearance on the TV show Hullabaloo, add:)	1965	$75.00	$150.00	$30.00
(if "Mr. Tambourine Man" is on both sides, red vinyl promo)	1965	$37.50	$75.00	$150.00
The Byrds, "Eight Miles High" / "Why" (Columbia 43578)	1966	$3.00	$6.00	$12.00
(with picture sleeve, add:)	1966	$15.00	$30.00	$60.00
The Chambers Brothers, "Time Has Come Today" / "Dinah" (Columbia 43816)	1966	$3.00	$6.00	$12.00
(if on Columbia 44414, B-side is "People Get Ready")	1968	$2.00	$4.00	$8.00
The Cowsills, "The Rain, the Park and Other Things" / "River Blue" (MGM 13810)	1967	$2.50	$5.00	$10.00
(with picture sleeve, add:)	1967	$3.00	$6.00	$12.00
Creedence Clearwater Revival, "I Put A Spell On You" / "Walk on the Water" (Fantasy 617)	1968	$2.00	$4.00	$8.00
Creedence Clearwater Revival, "Proud Mary" / "Born on the Bayou" (Fantasy 619)	1969		$3.00	$6.00
The Doors, "Light My Fire" / "The Crystal Ship" (Elektra 45615)				
(if first pressing, yellow-black label)	1967	$7.50	$15.00	$30.00
(if second pressing, red-black-white label)	1967	$3.00	$6.00	$12.00
The Doors, "Hello, I Love You, Won't You Tell Me Your Name?" / "Love Street" (Elektra 45635)	1968	$5.00	$10.00	$20.00
(if second pressing, title shortened to "Hello I Love You")	1968	$3.00	$6.00	$12.00
The Electric Prunes, "I Had Too Much To Dream (Last Night)" / "Lovin" (Reprise 0532)	1966	$5.00	$10.00	$20.00
Every Mother's Son, "Come On Down To My Boat" / "I Believe In You" (MGM 13733)	1967	$2.50	$5.00	$10.00
John Fred and his Playboy Band, "Judy in Disguise (With Glasses)" / "When the Lights Go Out" (Paula 282)				
(if white label)	1967	$3.00	$6.00	$12.00
(if yellow label)	1967	$2.50	$5.00	$10.00

45s	Year	VG	VG+	NM
(if pink label)	1967	$2.00	$4.00	$8.00
Bobby Fuller Four, "I Fought The Law" / "She's My Girl" (Exeter 124)	1964	$87.50	$175.00	$350.00
(if on Mustang 3014, B-side is "Little Annie Lou")	1966	$3.75	$7.50	$15.00
The Guess Who, "Shakin' All Over" / "Till We Kissed" (Scepter 1295)	1965	$3.75	$7.50	$15.00
(if B-side is "Monkey in a Cage" by the Discotays)	1965	$7.50	$15.00	$30.00
The Guess Who, "These Eyes" / "Lightfoot" (RCA Victor 74-0102)	1969		$3.00	$6.00
Tommy James and the Shondells, "Hanky Panky" / "Thunderbolt"				
(if on Snap 102, group listed as the "Shondells," no mention of Red Fox Records on the label)	1963	$20.00	$40.00	$80.00
(if on Snap 102, group listed as the "Shondells," "Dist. by Red Fox Records, Pgh., Pa." on label)	1966	$7.50	$15.00	$30.00
(if on Red Fox 110, group is listed as "The Shondells")	1966	$10.00	$20.00	$40.00
(if on Roulette 4686)	1966	$2.50	$5.00	$10.00
The Jefferson Airplane, "White Rabbit" / "Plastic Fantastic Lover" (RCA Victor 47-9248)	1967	$3.75	$7.50	$15.00
Love, "My Little Red Book" / "Message to Pretty" (Elektra 45603)	1966	$2.50	$5.00	$10.00
Love, "Que Vida" / "Hey Joe" (Elektra 45613)	1967	$12.50	$25.00	$50.00
The Lovin' Spoonful, "Do You Believe In Magic" / "On The Road Again" (Kama Sutra 201)				
(if first pressing, orange-red label)	1965	$3.75	$7.50	$15.00
(if second pressing, yellow label, "Kama Sutra" in red)	1965	$2.50	$5.00	$10.00
(if third pressing, yellow label, "Kama Sutra" in black)	1965	$2.00	$4.00	$8.00
The Mamas and the Papas, "California Dreamin' "/ "Somebody Groovy" (Dunhill 4020)	1966	$2.50	$5.00	$10.00
(with promo picture sleeve, add:)	1966	$75.00	$150.00	$300.00
The McCoys, "Hang On Sloopy" / "I Can't Explain It" (Bang 506)	1965	$3.75	$7.50	$15.00
Moby Grape, "8:05" / "Mister Blues" (Columbia 44172)	1967	$2.00	$4.00	$8.00
(with picture sleeve, add:)	1967	$5.00	$10.00	$20.00
Gary Puckett and the Union Gap, "This Girl Is A Woman Now" / "His Other Woman" (Columbia 44967)	1969		$3.00	$6.00
The Young Rascals, "Groovin'" / "Sueno" (Atlantic 2401)	1967	$2.00	$4.00	$8.00
The Rascals, "People Got To Be Free" / "My World" (Atlantic 2537)	1968		$3.00	$6.00
(with picture sleeve, add:)	1968	$3.00	$6.00	$12.00
The Reflections, "(Just Like) Romeo and Juliet" / "Can't You Tell By The Look In His Eyes" (Golden World 9)	1964	$5.00	$10.00	$20.00
Paul Revere and the Raiders, "Kicks" / "Shake It Up" (Columbia 43556)	1966	$2.50	$5.00	$10.00
(if "Kicks" on both sides, red vinyl promo)	1966	$12.50	$25.00	$50.00
Mitch Ryder and the Detroit Wheels, "Sock It To Me - Baby!" / "I Never Had It Better" (New Voice 820)				
(if first version, lyric "feels like a punch" is mumbled and sounds obscene, most pressings with this lyric variation appear on multicolored labels)	1967	$6.25	$12.50	$25.00
(if second version, lyric "hits me like a PUNCH!!" clearly audible, most pressings with this lyric variation appear on blue-labeled copies, both with printed labels and "sprayed on" labels)	1967	$2.50	$5.00	$10.00
Sam the Sham and the Pharaohs, "Haunted House" / "How Does a Cheating Woman Feel" (Dingo 001)	1964	$50.00	$100.00	$200.00
Sam the Sham and the Pharaohs, "Wooly Bully" / "Ain't Gonna Move" (MGM 13322)	1965	$3.75	$7.50	$15.00
Simon and Garfunkel, "The Sounds of Silence" / "We've Got A Groovey Thing Goin'" (Columbia 43396)	1965	$2.50	$5.00	$10.00
(if "Sounds of Silence" is on both sides, red vinyl promo)	1965	$12.50	$25.00	$50.00
Nancy Sinatra, "These Boots Are Made For Walkin'" / "The City Never Sleeps At Night" (Reprise 0432)	1965	$3.00	$6.00	$12.00
Spanky and Our Gang, "Like To Get to Know You" / "Three Ways From Tomorrow" (Mercury 72795)				
(if orange-tan swirl label)	1968	$2.00	$4.00	$8.00
(if red label with white "Mercury" across top of label)	1968	$2.50	$5.00	$10.00
(with picture sleeve, add:)	1968	$2.50	$5.00	$10.00

45s	Year	VG	VG+	NM
Ike and Tina Turner, "Proud Mary" / "Funkier Than a Mosquito's Tweeter" (Liberty 56216)	1970		$3.00	$6.00
The Turtles, "Happy Together" / "Like the Seasons" (White Whale 244)	1967	$2.00	$4.00	$8.00
(with picture sleeve, add:)	1967	$5.00	$10.00	$20.00
The Ultimate Spinach, "(Just Like) Romeo and Juliet" / "Some Days You Just Can't Win" (MGM 14023)	1969	$3.00	$6.00	$12.00
The Velvet Underground, "All Tomorrow's Parties" / "I'll Be Your Mirror" (Verve 10427)	1966	$150.00	$300.00	$600.00
(if marked for promotional use only)	1966	$75.00	$150.00	$300.00
(with rare picture sleeve, add:)	1966	$2,000.00	$4,000.00	$8,000.00

LPs	Year	VG	VG+	NM
The Association, And Then... Along Comes the Association				
(if on Valiant VLM-5002, mono)	1966	$5.00	$10.00	$20.00
(if on Valiant VLS-25002, stereo)	1966	$6.25	$12.50	$25.00
(if on Warner Bros. W 1702, mono)	1967	$5.00	$10.00	$20.00
(if on Warner Bros. WS 1702, stereo, gold label)	1967	$5.00	$10.00	$20.00
(if on Warner Bros. WS 1702, stereo, "W7" logo on green label)	1967	$3.00	$6.00	$12.00
The Beau Brummels, Introducing the Beau Brummels (Autumn LP 103) (mono)	1965	$12.50	$25.00	$50.00
(if on Autumn SLP 103, stereo)	1965	$15.00	$30.00	$60.00
Big Brother and the Holding Company, Big Brother and the Holding Company (Mainstream 56099) (mono)	1967	$25.00	$50.00	$100.00
(if on Mainstream S-6099, stereo)	1967	$12.50	$25.00	$50.00
(if on Columbia C 30631, with two extra tracks)	1971	$5.00	$10.00	$20.00
The Box Tops, The Box Tops Super Hits (Bell S-6025)	1968	$5.00	$10.00	$20.00
The Byrds, Mr. Tambourine Man (Columbia CL 2372) (mono)				
(if label says "Guaranteed High Fidelity")	1965	$10.00	$20.00	$40.00
(if label says "360 Sound Mono")	1966	$7.50	$15.0	$30.00
(if on Columbia CS 9172, stereo, red label, "360 Sound" in black)	1965	$10.00	$20.00	$40.00
(if on Columbia CS 9172, stereo, red label, "360 Sound" in white)	1966	$6.25	$12.50	$25.00
(if on Columbia CG 33645, a double album with Turn! Turn! Turn!)	1976	$3.75	$7.50	$15.00
(if on Columbia PC 9172, reissue)	198??	$2.00	$4.00	$8.00
(if on Sundazed LP 5059, audiophile reissue)	1999	$3.75	$7.50	$15.00
The Cowsills, The Best of the Cowsills (SE-4619)	1969	$3.75	$7.50	$15.00
Creedence Clearwater Revival, Creedence Clearwater Revival (Fantasy F-8382)				
(if first pressing, no reference to "Susie Q" on front cover)	1968	$6.25	$12.50	$25.00
(if second pressing, "Susie Q" mentioned on front cover, dark blue label)	1968	$3.75	$7.50	$15.00
(if white label promo)	1968	$20.00	$40.00	$80.00
(if brown label)	1973	$2.50	$5.00	$10.00
The Doors, The Doors (Elektra EKL-4007) (mono)	1967	$50.00	$100.00	$200.00
(if on Elektra EKS-74007, stereo, brown label)	1967	$12.50	$25.00	$50.00
(if on Elektra EKS-74007, stereo, red label, large "E")	1969	$3.75	$7.50	$15.00
(if on Elektra EKS-74007, butterfly on label)	1971	$3.00	$6.00	$12.00
(if on Elektra EKS-74007, red label, Warner Communications logo in lower right)	1980	$2.50	$5.00	$10.00
(if on Elektra EKS-74007, red-black label)	1983	$2.00	$4.00	$8.00
(if on DCC Compact Classics LPZ-2046, audiophile vinyl)	1997	$6.25	$12.50	$25.00
The Electric Prunes, The Electric Prunes (Reprise R-6248) (mono)	1967	$12.50	$25.00	$50.00
(if on Reprise RS-6248, stereo)	1967	$10.00	$20.00	$40.00
The Bobby Fuller Four, The Bobby Fuller Four (I Fought The Law) (Mustang M-901) (mono)	1966	$20.00	$40.00	$80.00
(if on Mustang MS-901, stereo)	1966	$37.50	$75.00	$150.00
The Good Rats, The Good Rats (Kapp KS-3580)	1969	$10.00	$20.00	$40.00
The Guess Who's Chad Allen and the Expressions, Shakin' All Over (Scepter SP-533) (mono)	1966	$10.00	$20.00	$40.00
(if on Scepter SPS-533, some songs in stereo)	1966	$6.25	$12.50	$25.00
The Hassles, The Hassles (United Artists UAS-6631)	1968	$6.25	$12.50	$25.00

LPs	Year	VG	VG+	NM
Tommy James and the Shondells, I Think We're Alone Now (Roulette R 25353) (mono)	1967	$7.50	$15.00	$30.00
(if on Roulette SR 25353, footprints cover, "I Think We're Alone Now" is rechanneled stereo)	1967	$6.25	$12.50	$25.00
(if on Roulette SR 25353, photo cover)	1967	$3.75	$7.50	$15.00
Jefferson Airplane, Jefferson Airplane Takes Off! (RCA Victor LPM-3584) (mono)				
(if first version, "Runnin' Round This World" as last song on side 1, one has to count the number of tracks on the album to make sure the song is there, some jackets will list the song whether or not it's on the record)	1966	$1,500	$2,250	$3,000
(if second version, no "Runnin' Round This World," but "Let Me In" has lyrics "Don't tell me you want money", and "Run Around" has lyrics "that sway as you lay under me," must be heard to confirm)	1966	$250.00	$500.00	$1,000.00
(if third version, no "Runnin' Round This World," but "Let Me In" has lyrics "Don't tell me it's so funny," and Run Around" has lyrics "that sway as you stay here by me," must be heard to confirm)	1966	$6.25	$12.50	$25.00
(if on RCA Victor LSP-3584, stereo, format follows first version listed above)	1966	$2,000	$3,500	$5,000
(if on RCA Victor LSP-3584, stereo, format follows second version listed above)	1966	$450.00	$900.00	$1,800.00
(if on RCA Victor LSP-3584, stereo, format follows third version listed above)	1966	$6.25	$12.50	$25.00
(if on RCA Victor LSP-3584, orange label)	1969	$3.00	$6.00	$12.00
(if on RCA Victor LSP-3584, tan label)	1975	$2.50	$5.00	$10.00
(if on RCA Victor AYL1-3739)	1980	$2.00	$4.00	$8.00
Janis Joplin, I Got Dem Ol' Kozmik Blues Again Mama! (Columbia KCS 9913)				
(if "360 Sound Stereo" on label)	1969	$5.00	$10.00	$20.00
(if orange label)	1969	$5.00	$10.00	$20.00
(if on Columbia PC 9913, budget-line reissue)	198??	$2.00	$4.00	$8.00
Love, Love (Elektra EKL-4001) (mono)	1966	$25.00	$50.00	$100.00
(if white label promo)	1966	$75.00	$150.00	$300.00
(if on Elektra EKS-74001, stereo, brown label)	1966	$12.50	$25.00	$50.00
(if on Elektra EKS-74001, stereo, red label with large "E")	1969	$3.75	$7.50	$15.00
(if on Elektra EKS-74001, stereo, butterfly on label)	1971	$3.00	$6.00	$12.00
The Lovin' Spoonful, Daydream (Kama Sutra KLP-8051) (mono)	1966	$5.00	$10.00	$20.00
(if on Kama Sutra KLPS-8051) (stereo)	1966	$7.50	$15.00	$30.00
The Mamas and the Papas, If You Can Believe Your Eyes and Ears (Dunhill D-50006) (mono)				
(if first version, toilet clearly visible on front cover)	1966	$20.00	$40.00	$80.00
(if second version, scroll over toilet)	1966	$5.00	$10.00	$20.00
(if third version, black cover with photo cropped to render toilet invisible)	1966	$10.00	$20.00	$40.00
(If on Dunhill DS-50006, stereo, cover conforms to first version listed above)	1966	$25.00	$50.00	$100.00
(if on Dunhill DS-50006, stereo, scroll over toilet, says "Includes California Dreamin'")	1966	$6.25	$12.50	$25.00
(if on Dunhill DS-50006, stereo, scroll over toilet, says "Includes California Dreamin', "Monday Monday," "I Call Your Name"")	1966	$6.25	$12.50	$25.00
(if on Dunhill DS-50006, stereo, cover conforms to third version listed above)	1966	$12.50	$25.00	$50.00
(if on Dunhill ST-90797, stereo, Capitol Record Club, scroll proclaims "California Dremain'")	1966	$12.50	$25.00	$50.00
(if on ABC Dunhill DS-50006)	1968	$3.00	$6.00	$12.00
Moby Grape, Moby Grape (Columbia CL 2698) (mono)				
(if cover has Don Stephenson "giving the finger" on his washboard)	1967	$10.00	$20.00	$40.00
(if offending finger is airbrushed out)	1967	$5.00	$10.00	$20.00
(if on Columbia CS 9498, stereo, Don Stephenson "giving the finger" on his washboard)	1967	$10.00	$20.00	$40.00
(if offending finger is airbrushed out)	1967	$5.00	$10.00	$20.00
The Music Machine, (Turn On) The Music Machine (Original Sound 5015) (mono)	1966	$10.00	$20.00	$40.00
(if on Original Sound 8875, stereo)	1966	$12.50	$25.00	$50.00
Procol Harum, Shine On Brightly (A&M SP-4151)	1968	$6.25	$12.50	$25.00
Gary Puckett and the Union Gap, Young Girl (Columbia CS 9664)	1968	$5.00	$10.00	$20.00
The Young Rascals, The Young Rascals (Atlantic 8123) (mono)	1966	$7.50	$15.00	$30.00
(if on Atlantic SD 8123, stereo, green-blue label)	1966	$10.00	$20.00	$40.00

LPs	Year	VG	VG+	NM
(if on Atlantic SD 8123, stereo, purple-green label)	1966	$12.50	$25.00	$50.00
(if on Atlantic SD 8123, stereo, red-green label)	1969	$3.00	$6.00	$12.00
(if on Rhino RNLP 70237)	1988	$2.50	$5.00	$10.00
The Rascals, Time Peace / The Rascals' Greatest Hits (Atlantic 8190) (mono) (promo only)	1968	$12.50	$25.00	$50.00
(if on Atlantic SD 8190, stereo, green-blue label)	1968	$6.25	$12.50	$25.00
(if on Atlantic SD 8190, stereo, purple-gold label)	1968	$3.75	$7.50	$15.00
(if on Atlantic SD 8190, stereo, red-green label)	1969	$3.00	$6.00	$12.00
The Reflections, (Just Like) Romeo and Juliet (Golden World 300) (mono)	1964	$37.50	$75.00	$150.00
Paul Revere and the Raiders, Like, Long Hair (Gardena LP-G-1000) (mono)	1961	$150.00	$300.00	$600.00
Mitch Ryder and the Detroit Wheels, Take a Ride (New Voice 2000) (mono)	1966	$6.25	$12.50	$25.00
(if on New Voice S-2000, stereo)	1966	$7.50	$15.00	$30.00
The Shangri-Las, Leader of the Pack (Red Bird 20101) (mono)	1965	$37.50	$75.00	$150.00
Simon and Garfunkel, Bookends (Columbia KCL 2729) (red label, "mono" at bottom)	1968	$12.50	$25.00	$50.00
(if on Columbia KCS 9529, white label, "Special Mono Radio Station Copy")	1968	$7.50	$15.00	$30.00
(if on Columbia KCS 9529, stereo, "360 Sound Stereo" on label, add 25% for poster)	1968	$3.00	$6.00	$12.00

LPs	Year	VG	VG+	NM
(if on Columbia KCS 9529, stereo, orange label)	1970	$2.50	$5.00	$10.00
(if on Columbia PC 9529, budget reissue)	197??	$2.00	$4.00	$8.00
Ike and Tina Turner, Come Together (Liberty LST-7637)	1970	$3.75	$7.50	$15.00
The Turtles, Happy Together (White Whale WW 114) (mono)	1967	$5.00	$10.00	$20.00
(if on White Whale WWS 7114, stereo)	1967	$6.25	$12.50	$25.00
(if on Rhino RNLP 152)	1983	$2.50	$5.00	$10.00
The Velvet Underground, The Velvet Underground and Nico (Verve V-5008) (mono)				
(if first version, peel-off banana peel, photo of band framed by male torso)	1967	$75.00	$150.00	$300.00
(if second version, peel-off banana peel, torso obscured by sticker)	1967	$75.00	$150.00	$300.00
(if third version, peel-off banana peel, torso airbrushed off cover)	1967	$50.00	$100.00	$200.00
(if on Verve V6-5008, stereo, conforms to first version)	1967	$50.00	$100.00	$200.00
(if on Verve V6-5008, stereo, confirms to second version)	1967	$50.00	$100.00	$200.00
(if on Verve V6-5008, stereo, confirms to third version)	1967	$37.50	$75.00	$150.00
(if on Verve V6-5008, stereo, banana is part of cover and cannot be peeled off)	1968	$25.00	$50.00	$100.00
(if on Verve 825119-1, reissue)	1985	$3.00	$6.00	$12.00

Although most people consider this a sweet love song, the Turtles have said in interviews that there's an ironic twist in the lyrics—at the end, when the singer goes "And how is the weather," one realizes that the entire song up to that point was the singer's fantasy about what he would say if he could actually strike up a conversation with the girl in front of him. Courtesy Last Vestige Music Store, Albany, N.Y.

This single by the Premiers was originally released on the Faro label before Warner Bros. picked it up for national distribution. By the way, despite what the label says, the song is a studio recording; the audience are friends of the Premiers. From the Collection of Val Shively.

One of the many garage-turned-psychedelic bands of the 1960s, the Electric Prunes had Top 40 hits in "Get Me To The World On Time" and "I Had Too Much To Dream (Last Night)." Courtesy Last Vestige Music Store, Albany, N.Y.

SKA/REGGAE

History: Ska and reggae were the first successful musical styles to originate from the island of Jamaica, and both created an impact throughout the world. The original ska sound began in the early 1960s, as Jamaican musicians mixed popular music from American radio stations with Cuban percussive rhythms and a Jamaican musical style called *mente*. Ska was cultivated by Jamaican producers and musicians such as Clement "Sir Coxsone" Dodd, Arthur "Duke" Reed, Cecil "Prince Buster" Campbell, and Cluet "Clue J" Johnson. Johnson, in fact, is the person to whom the word "ska" is attributed; he often greeted people with the words "Love Skavoovie," which were later shortened into "ska."

Between 1962 and 1966, the Skatalites were ska's first musical superstars. The Skatalites were an amalgamation of the best musicians in Jamaica, with a thunderous horn section anchored by world-class trombonist Don Drummond.

This Skatalites reissue was part of a "Best of Reggae" series from United Artists Records. From the Collection of Mark Pisani.

With hits like "Man in the Street" and the theme to "The Guns of Navarone," the Skatalites established themselves as the premier ambassadors of ska. Unfortunately, the Skatalites' musical existence came to a crashing halt on January 1, 1965. Don Drummond, who had battled mental illness for much of his adult life, was arrested and charged with stabbing his girlfriend to death. Declared legally insane, Drummond was committed to a mental institution, dying in 1969 under mysterious circumstances (the official report was a suicide, but many believe Drummond was murdered and the evidence covered up). With the loss of Drummond, the Skatalites' popularity faded, although members of the band still perform under that name today.

As Jamaicans immigrated to England, they took the Skatalites' ska beat to a new musical home in the UK. One such Jamaican was Chris Blackwell, who later licensed many ska records to American and European labels. Blackwell eventually formed his own company, Island, which became a home to ska and reggae artists for decades.

Early ska music barely penetrated American radio in the 1960s, although Millie Small's classic "My Boy Lollipop" did crack the Top 10, as did Desmond Dekker and the Aces' "Israelites" and the Equals' "Baby Come Back." In fact, some Jamaican ska recordings were actually covered by Annette Funicello (Prince Buster's "Ska, Ska, Ska") and the Fleetwoods ("Ska Light, Ska Bright"). And when an extremely warm summer slowed the Jamaicans' desire for fast ska music, a slower musical style, rock steady, was born.

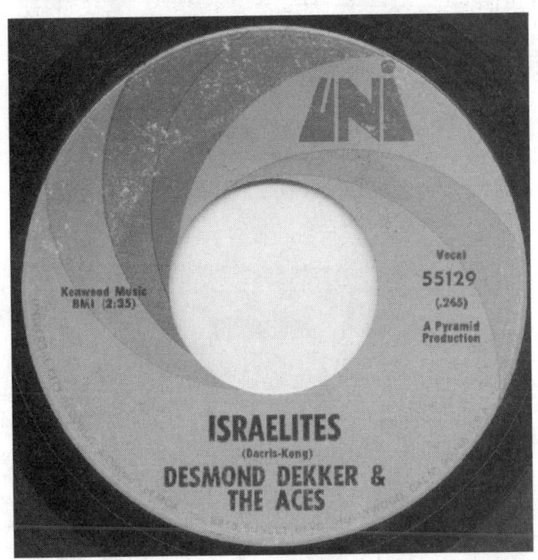

As ska slowly morphed into reggae, Desmond Dekker's "Israelites" hit the U.S. Top 10 in 1969.

That slower ska sound eventually morphed into reggae, which added elements of New Orleans jazz and Rastafarian beliefs and ideals. As much a musical style as it was a voice of protest, reggae songs were stories of struggle against the harsh Jamaican governmental system, mixed with a staccato down-beat rhythm. Artists such as Toots and the Maytals, Burning Spear, and Bob Marley and the Wailers began their careers during this period, with Bob Marley eventually reaching worldwide superstardom.

Trivia

"Walt Jabsco," the nattily-dressed logo for 2-Tone Records, was drawn by Jerry Dammers as a sketch of Peter McIntosh (later Peter Tosh) from the cover of The Wailing Wailers (Studio One S1001, Jamaica). Notice the resemblance? Tosh is the tall, skinny one on the right, next to Bob Marley (center), while Bunny Livingstone (later Bunny Wailer) is on the left.

Walt Jabsco appears on the Specials' "Gangsters" US 45 and company sleeve.

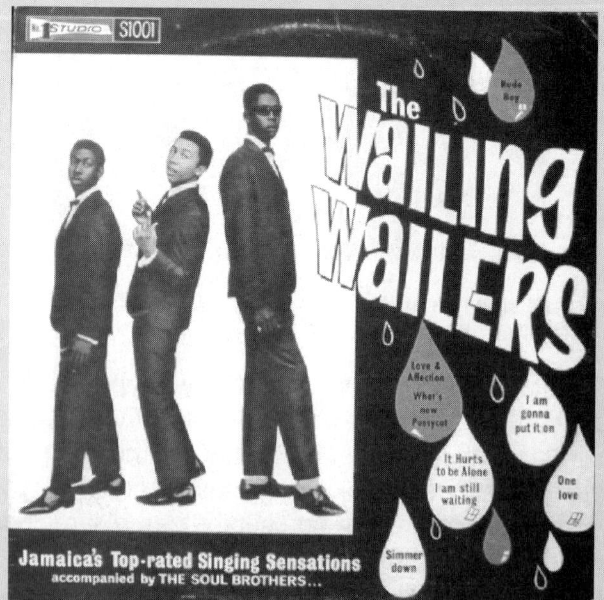

Peter Tosh, on the far right of the Wailing Wailers LP, was the inspiration for the 2-Tone logo.

Bob Marley was not just a reggae musician; he was the most prominent ambassador of this new rhythm, both musically and politically. Whether it was protest songs like "Get Up, Stand Up" and "I Shot The Sheriff," or love songs like "No Woman No Cry" and "Could You Be Loved," the music of Bob Marley and the Wailers reached the hearts and souls of millions. In some countries, a concert by Bob Marley was greeted with the same enthusiasm as an open-air mass by the Pope. When Marley succumbed to cancer in 1981, his death was mourned by reggae lovers and oppressed people worldwide.

Bob Marley originally wrote and performed "I Shot The Sheriff," and although Eric Clapton's version was the major hit, Marley's rendition was released as a U.S. single.

Ska songs often mention a person known as a "rude boy." This is not someone who calls an English teacher "Daddio." Rude boys in Jamaica were tough youths, many of whom were involved in some sort of underhanded activity. Many ska songs either decry "rude boys" or extol their virtues as Jamaican Robin Hoods. For more information on "rude boy" activity in 1960s Jamaica, consider renting the film *"The Harder They Come,"* starring singer Jimmy Cliff. Today's reference to "rude boy," however, simply means a ska music aficionado.

Any type of "rude boy" would appreciate the Equals' "Baby Come Back," featuring lead singer Eddy Grant.

Reggae music was also known for the "dub," remixed instrumental versions of popular A-sides. These "dubs" were used by Jamaican club DJs, who would rap or "toast" over the melodies. Among the remixing elite in rap circles are Sly Dunbar and Robbie Shakespeare, who have remixed nearly every ska and reggae record in existence.

Sly and Robbie have worked with hundreds of reggae artists, creating hit reggae songs and killer dub remixes. They produced this album by Jamaican rap sensation U-Roy. From the Collection of Mark Pisani.

In the late 1970s, British producer Jerry Dammers created a new record label, 2-Tone, to record many of the ska-influenced modern groups in England. This version of ska, a blending of reggae with funk, caught on with groups like the Coventry Automatics (who later became the Specials). Many of the ska bands on the 2-Tone label contained both black and white members, providing racial harmony with a killer beat. Such 2-Tone groups included the Selecter, Madness, the Beat (English Beat in the USA), and the Bodysnatchers. Other groups not signed to 2-Tone, but who had the ska beat down pat, were Bad Manners, The Friday Club, and Rico Rodriguez, who was musically trained by Don Drummond himself. Elvis Costello and the Clash also dabbled in ska rhythms on their early hits.

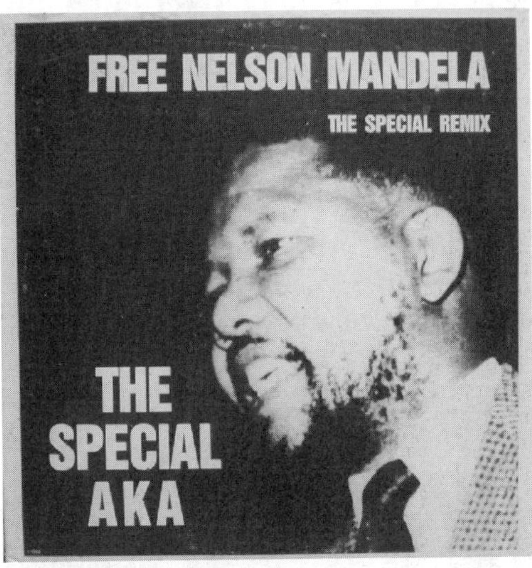

The Special A.K.A., along with other recording artists, created this dance classic about the wrongful imprisonment of African National Congress leader Nelson Mandela.

Although the 2-Tone label spawned many ska hits in the UK, those songs did not achieve the same popularity in America. Songs like Madness' "One Step Beyond," the English Beat's "Save It For Later," and the Specials' "Ghost Town" were hits on college radio stations, but not elsewhere.

Because an American power pop group also called itself the "Beat," the ska band with the same name was known as the "English Beat" in North America, and as the "Beat" everywhere else.

Trivia

UB40's cover of "Red Red Wine" may have been written by Neil Diamond, but they were actually covering the version sung by Jamaican singer Tony Tribe. The UB40 song was a #1 hit worldwide in 1983, but only creased the lower regions of the Top 40 in America. Five years later, a radio station in Phoenix played forgotten hits in heavy rotation, eventually giving UB40 a second chance on the radio. Other stations started playing "Red Red Wine" as an album track, and A&M Records reserviced stations with new copies of an old record. Five years after its original release, "Red Red Wine" hit #1 in America in 1988. And how did the band get its name? As out-of-work youths in Birmingham, England in the 1970s, they were very familiar with an Unemployment Benefits Form No. 40, or a "UB40."

The original American 7-inch pressing of "Red Red Wine" did not have Terence "Astro" Wilson's "toasting" rap at the end of the song.

The 1988 reissue of "Red Red Wine" features the entire album cut, including the rapping section at the end.

Reggae music did make its way to America, as artists like Paul Simon and Johnny Nash added reggae rhythms to songs like "I Can See Clearly Now" and "Mother and Child Reunion." Meanwhile, another successful reggae group, England's UB40, broke through with reggae-influenced versions of "I Got You Babe," "Can't Help Falling In Love," and "Red Red Wine," along with self-penned classics like "King," "One In Ten," and "If It Happens Again."

Because of the subject matter of some reggae songs, including the smoking of marijuana and ganja, some reggae classics had to have their lyrics changed in order to reach a larger audience. An example of this involves a song called "Pass the Coochie," by the Mighty Diamonds. When the British teen reggae group Musical Youth re-recorded the song, the name was changed to "Pass the Dutchie," as it would make more sense for kids to share a stewing pot (dutchie) than a spliff of ganja (coochie).

Eventually ska and reggae music reached America, and groups like the Untouchables, Fishbone, and the Toasters all modified the original sounds, mixing them with punk, new wave and other popular American musical styles. Other groups in the 1980s who took up the ska banner were Boston's Bim Skala Bim and the Mighty Mighty Bosstones, Fresno's Let's Go Bowling, Gainesville's Less Than Jake, and Anaheim's Din. Popular reggae artists in the 1980s and 1990s included Shabba Ranks, Maxi Priest, and Shaggy. Even Ziggy Marley, Bob Marley's son, had Top 40 hits with the reggae sound, including "Tomorrow People."

Less Than Jake's album *Hello Rockview* was released as a special edition 7-disc 45 rpm box set—complete with plastic insert adapters, as seen here.

Trivia

Terry Hall of the Fun Boy Three, a ska group formed after the Specials broke up, wrote "Our Lips Are Sealed" with the Go-Go's' Jane Wiedlin. Although the Go-Go's had the Top 40 hit in 1982 with "Our Lips Are Sealed," the Fun Boy Three released their ska-dub version in 1984.

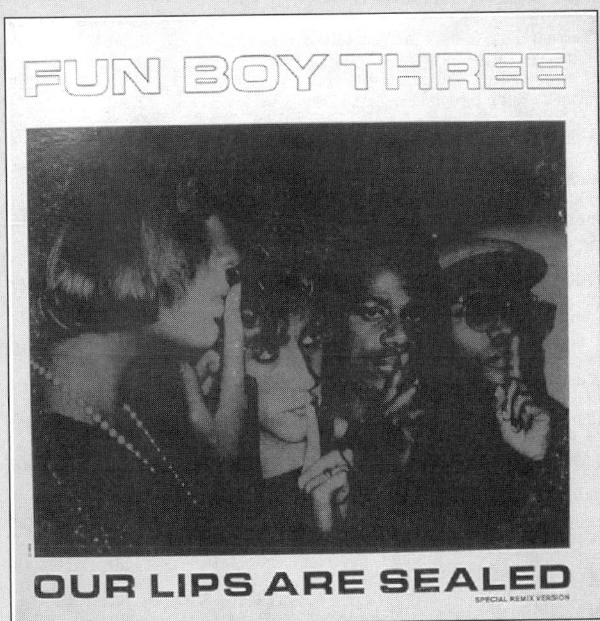

The Fun Boy Three's ska-dub hit, "Our Lips Are Sealed."

What To Look For: Some 1960s ska artists have had American releases, most notably Prince Buster, Desmond Dekker, and the Ska Kings. But the "second wave of ska" (the 2-Tone 1970s releases), which were heard through college radio stations nationwide, provided ska music with its first foothold onto American radio.

Collectors are more interested in British or Jamaican pressings of ska records, especially when looking for the Skatalites or the Specials. Current product from ska bands like No Doubt and the Mighty Mighty Bosstones are available on CD, although No Doubt's breakthrough album *Tragic Kingdom* does exist on vinyl.

The original Studio One and Tuff Gong pressings from Jamaica are certainly the most desirous for reggae collectors, but there are some American pressings—especially those that were pressed in limited numbers—that are prizes for anybody's reggae record collection.

One of these rare American pressings involves Bob Marley and the Wailers' *Catch A Fire*. The first copies were released with a cigarette-lighter-styled cover. Consumers opened the top of the jacket to remove the record. Later pressings returned the jacket opening to the side, making these first pressings extremely hard to find.

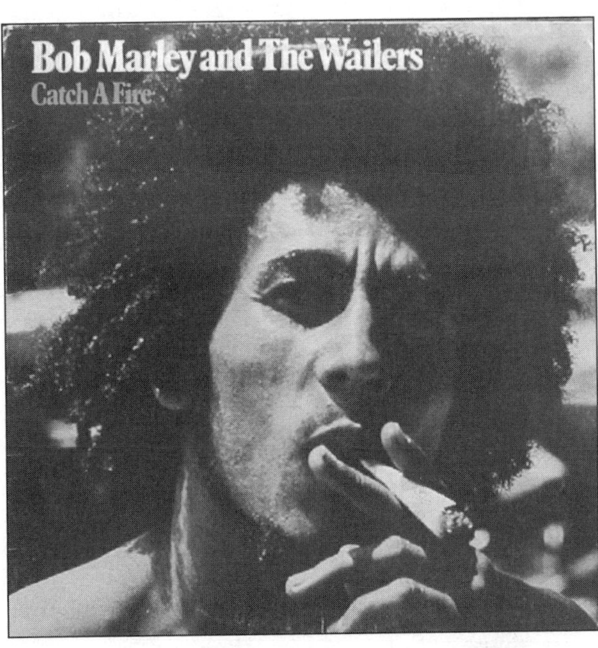

First pressings of *Catch A Fire* are in jackets that actually open like a cigarette lighter; the record shown here is the more common version.

Reference Books: Foster, Chuck, *Roots Rock Reggae: An Oral History of Reggae Music: From Ska to Dancehall,* Billboard Books, Watson-Guptill Publications, BPI Communications, New York, N.Y., 1999.

Web pages: The Skatalites, the Jamaican band who originated and popularized ska music in the 1960s, have their own Web site: *http://www.skatalites.com*; for another history of the Skatalites, this Web page is helpful: *http://www.profane.com/skatalites*; a page on the Specials: *http://www.eyeontomorrow.com/specials*; the Bob Marley official homepage: *http://www.bobmarley-foundation.com*; there are dozens of Web pages devoted to Bob Marley and the Wailers; this is a good starting point: *http://www.mac-net.or.jp/pa/akira/bob.html*; UB40's homepage: http://www.ub40-dep.com; a FAQ on the history of ska, the music and the culture: *ftp://rtfm.mit.edu/pub/usenet/news.answers/music/ska-faq/part1* (there are three parts); Usenet newsgroups: *alt.music.ska, alt.music.reggae.*

45s	Year	VG	VG+	NM
Bad Manners, "My Girl Lollipop (My Boy Lollipop)" / "Falling Out of Love" (Portrait 04602)	1984		$2.00	$4.00
Jimmy Cliff, "Wonderful World, Beautiful People" / "Waterfall" (A&M 1146)	1969	$2.00	$4.00	$8.00
(with picture sleeve, add:)	1969	$3.00	$6.00	$12.00
Jimmy Cliff, "The Harder They Come" / "Viet Nam" (Reprise 1383)	1977		$3.00	$6.00
Desmond Dekker and the Aces, "Israelites" / "My Precious World" (Uni 55129)	1969		$3.00	$6.00
Desmond Dekker and the Aces, "It Mek" / "Problems" (Uni 55150)	1969		$3.00	$6.00
The English Beat, "Tears Of A Clown" / "Twist and Crawl" (Sire 49265)	1980	$2.00	$4.00	$8.00
The Equals, "Baby Come Back" / "Hold Me Closer" (RCA Victor 47-9186)	1967	$3.75	$7.50	$15.00
(if on RCA 47-9583, second pressing)	1968	$2.50	$5.00	$10.00
Fun Boy Three, "Our Lips Are Sealed" / "We're All Having Fun" (Chrysalis 42710)	1983		$2.00	$4.00
General Public, "Tenderness" / "Limited Balance" (IRS 9934)	1984			$3.00
(with picture sleeve, add:)	1984			$3.00
Less Than Jake, Hello Rockview (Capitol 58723) box set, 7 45s , price is for entire box, records and two plastic custom adapters)	1998	$5.00	$10.00	$20.00
Madness, "One Step Beyond" / "Mistakes" (Sire 0204) (Canadian import)	1979	$2.50	$5.00	$10.00
Bob Marley and the Wailers, "Doppy Conquer" / The Upsetters, "Justice" (Shelter 7309)	1971	$3.00	$6.00	$12.00
Bob Marley and the Wailers, "Get Up Stand Up" / "Slave Driver" (Cotillion 1218)	1973	$2.00	$4.00	$8.00
Bob Marley and the Wailers, "I Shot The Sheriff" / "Put It On" (Island 004)	1974		$3.00	$6.00
Bob Marley and the Wailers, "No Woman No Cry" / "Kinky Reggae" (Island 037)	1975		$3.00	$6.00
Bob Marley and the Wailers, "Roots Rock Reggae" / "Cry To Me" (Island 060)	1976		$3.00	$6.00
Bob Marley and the Wailers, "Jamming" / "No Woman, No Cry" (Island 49755)	1981		$3.00	$6.00
Musical Youth, "Pass The Dutchie" / "Give Love A Chance" (MCA 52149)	1982			$3.00
(with picture sleeve, add:)	1982			$3.00
Prince Buster, "Everybody Ska" / "30 Pieces of Silver" (Amy 906)	1964	$3.75	$7.50	$15.00
Prince Buster, "Ten Commandments" / "Don't Make Me Cry" (Philips 40427)	1967	$3.00	$6.00	$12.00
Prince Buster, "Ten Commandments from Woman to Man" / "Ain't That Saying A Lot" (RCA Victor 47-9114)	1967	$3.00	$6.00	$12.00
Millie Small, "My Boy Lollipop" / "Something's Gotta Be Done" (Smash 1893)	1964	$3.75	$7.50	$15.00
Millie Small, "Tongue Tied" / "Blood Shot Eyes" (Atco 6384)	1965	$2.50	$5.00	$10.00
The Specials, "Gangsters" / "The Specials" (Chrysalis/ 2-Tone 2374) (B-side is by The Selecter)	1979	$2.00	$4.00	
(with "Specials" picture sleeve, add:)	1979	$2.00	$4.00	$8.00
The Special A.K.A., "Free Nelson Mandela" / "Break Down The Door" (Chrysalis 42794)	1984	$2.50	$5.00	$10.00
The Ska Kings, "Jamaica Sea" / "Oil In My Lamp" (Atlantic 2232)	1964	$2.50	$5.00	$10.00
UB40, "Red Red Wine" / "Sufferin'"				
(if on A&M 2600, red label, 3-minute version of A-side)	1983		$2.00	$4.00
(if on A&M 1244, black label, 5-minute version of A-side)	1988		$2.00	$4.00
UB40, "Can't Help Falling In Love" / "Jungle Love" (Virgin S7-17402)	1993		$2.00	$4.00

12-inch	Year	VG	VG+	NM
Bad Manners, "My Girl Lollipop" (4 versions) (Portrait 05009)	1984	$2.50	$5.00	$10.00
Jimmy Cliff, "Special" / "Peace Officer" (Columbia 03045)	1982	$2.50	$5.00	$10.00
The English Beat, "Tears Of A Clown" / "Hands Off .. She's Mine" / "Twist and Crawl" (Sire PRO-A-874) (DJ only)	1980	$3.75	$7.50	$15.00
General Public, "I'll Take You There" (8 versions) (Epic Soundtrax 77460)	1994	$6.25	$12.50	$25.00
Bob Marley and the Wailers, "Reggae on Broadway" (2 versions) (Cotillion PR 291)	1981	$3.00	$6.00	$12.00
Bob Marley and the Wailers, "Chances Are" (2 versions) (Cotillion PR 414)	1981	$3.75	$7.50	$15.00
Bob Marley and the Wailers, "Buffalo Soldier" / "Buffalo Dub" (Island DMD 628)	1983	$2.50	$5.00	$10.00
Bob Marley and the Wailers, "Iron Zion Lion" (4 versions) / "Could You Be Loved" (Tuff Gong 864693-1)	1992	$3.00	$6.00	$12.00
The Mighty Mighty Bosstones, "Kinder Words" / "Chocolate Pudding" / "Pirate Ship" (Mercury 1156)	1994	$2.50	$5.00	$10.00

12-inch	Year	VG	VG+	NM
Musical Youth, "She's Trouble" / "Incommunicado" (MCA L33-1147)	1983	$2.50	$5.00	$10.00
The Specials, "Ghost Town" / "Why" / "Friday Night, Saturday Morning" (Chrysalis/2-Tone CDS-2525)	1981	$2.50	$5.00	$10.00
UB40, "I've Got Mine" (2 versions) / "Dubmobile" / "One In Ten" (A&M 12703)	1983		$2.50	$5.00
UB40, "Red Red Wine" / "She Caught the Train" (A&M 12090)	1983		$3.00	$6.00

LPs	Year	VG	VG+	NM
Jimmy Cliff, Can't Get Enough of It (Veep VPS-16536)	1969	$10.00	$20.00	$40.00
Jimmy Cliff, Wonderful World, Beautiful People (A&M SP-4251)	1970	$6.25	$12.50	$25.00
(if on A&M 3189, reissue)	198??	$2.00	$4.00	$8.00
Desmond Dekker and the Aces, Israelites (Uni 73059)	1969	$7.50	$15.00	$30.00
The English Beat, I Just Can't Stop It				
(if on Sire SRK-6091)	1980	$3.75	$7.50	$15.00
(if on IRS SP-70606, reissue)	1983	$2.50	$5.00	$10.00
The English Beat, Special Beat Service (IRS SP-70032)	1982	$2.50	$5.00	$10.00
The Equals, Baby Come Back (RCA Victor LSP-4078)	1967	$5.00	$10.00	$20.00
Madness, One Step Beyond (Sire SRK 6085)	1979	$3.00	$6.00	$12.00
Madness, Madness (Geffen GHS 4003)	1983	$2.50	$5.00	$10.00
Bob Marley and the Wailers, Catch A Fire				
(if on Island SW-9241, flip-top cover, Capitol distribution)	1973	$12.50	$25.00	$50.00
(if on Island ILPS 9241, Island distribution, this and all other releases have cover with opening on right)	1975	$3.75	$7.50	$15.00
(if on Island ILPS 9241, Warner Bros. distribution)	1978	$3.00	$6.00	$12.00
(if on Island 90030, Atco distribution)	1983	$2.00	$4.00	$8.00
(if on Tuff Gong 846201-1)	1990	$3.00	$6.00	$12.00
(if on Mobile Fidelity 1-238, audiophile vinyl)	1995	$6.25	$12.50	$25.00
Bob Marley and the Wailers, Rastaman Vibration				
(if on Island ILPS 9383, promotional package with burlap box and press kit)	1976	$25.00	$50.00	$100.00
(if on Island ILPS 9383, Island distribution)	1976	$3.00	$6.00	$12.00
(if on Island ILPS 9383, Warner Bros. distribution)	1978	$2.50	$5.00	$10.00
(if on Island 90033, Atco distribution)	1983	$2.00	$4.00	$8.00
(if on Tuff Gong 846205-1)	1990	$3.00	$6.00	$12.00
Bob Marley and the Wailers, Exodus				
(if on Island ILPS 9498, Island distribution)	1977	$3.00	$6.00	$12.00
(if on Island ILPS 9498, Warner Bros. distribution)	1978	$2.50	$5.00	$10.00
(if on Island 90034, Atco distribution)	1983	$2.00	$4.00	$8.00
(if on Tuff Gong 846208-1)	1990	$3.00	$6.00	$12.00
(if on Mobile Fidelity 1-221, audiophile vinyl)	1995	$6.25	$12.50	$25.00
The Mighty Mighty Bosstones, Devils Night Out (Taang! 44)	1991	$3.75	$7.50	$15.00
Prince Buster, Ten Commandments (RCA Victor LPM-3792) (mono)	1967	$6.25	$12.50	$25.00
(if on RCA Victor LSP-3792, stereo)	1967	$7.50	$15.00	$30.00
The Selecter, Too Much Pressure				
(if on Chrysalis CHR 1274)	1980	$2.50	$5.00	$10.00
(if on Chrysalis PV 41274, reissue)	1983	$2.00	$4.00	$8.00
Millie Small, My Boy Lollipop (Smash MGS-27055) (mono)	1964	$12.50	$25.00	$50.00
(if on Smash SRS-67055, stereo)	1964	$10.00	$20.00	$40.00
The Specials, The Specials				
(if on Chrysalis CHR 1265)	1979	$3.75	$7.50	$15.00
(if on Chrysalis PV 41265, reissue)	1986	$2.50	$5.00	$10.00
Toots and the Maytals, Funky Kingston				
(if on Island ILPS 9330)	1975	$3.00	$6.00	$12.00
(if on Mango MLPS 9330, reissue)	197??	$2.50	$5.00	$10.00
Toots and the Maytals, Reggae Got Soul (Mango MLPS 9374)	1976	$3.00	$6.00	$12.00
Toots and the Maytals, Live Mango MLPS 9647)	1980	$3.00	$6.00	$12.00
UB40, Labour of Love (A&M SP6-4980)	1983	$3.00	$6.00	$12.00
(if on A&M R 100677, BMG Direct Marketing edition)	1988	$3.50	$7.00	$14.00
UB40, Little Baggariddim (A&M SP6-5090)				
(if first pressing, in clear plastic sleeve)	1985	$3.00	$6.00	$12.00
(if second pressing, in standard album cover)	1985	$2.00	$4.00	$8.00
Various Artists, Dance Craze (Chrysalis CHR 1299) (contains The Specials, the Selecter, Madness and others)	1981	$4.50	$9.00	$18.00
Various Artists, Reggae Christmas By the Joe Gibbs Family of Artists (Joe Gibbs Music 8077)	1982	$5.00	$10.00	$20.00

SOUNDTRACKS

History: In the days before DVDs and VCRs, in a time when motion pictures appeared only on the big theater screen, albums of motion picture soundtracks and film scores were the best way for film buffs and music collectors to "re-experience" the magic of their favorite films.

The soundtrack to *And God Created Woman*, with actress Brigitte Bardot as its main selling point. From the Collection of R. Michael Murray.

Some of the earliest motion picture soundtracks were actually that—the actual sound recording from a film (some studios in the 1910s and 1920s, most notably the Edison studios, experimented with flat discs and cylinders that could play sounds and voice to an audience as the film played on the screen). But when films such as *Lights of New York* and *The Jazz Singer* proved that motion pictures could be made with synchronous sound, a demand for purchasable soundtracks was born.

Up until the early 1950s, soundtrack collections consisted of selected music recorded onto a series of 78 RPM discs, each series of discs stored in a pocketed folio. While this format was perfect for musicals, as each side of a 78 could hold a popular song from the film, it was not until the development of the 12-inch 33 1/3 RPM long-playing record that more orchestral and incidental music could be stored on a purchasable disc.

Motion picture soundtracks can be broken down into three groups: atmospheric orchestral instrumental music or the "underscore"; songs from a musical or opera, as recorded by the original actors or their vocal substitutes; and songs that were "inspired by" the motion picture. Among soundtrack collectors, the underscore soundtracks are the most desired. As for the other soundtrack records, their collectible value is determined both by the record's rarity and by how much music from the film is actually on the record, and how much of the rest of the album is dominated by filler pop songs. Sometimes a soundtrack is mass-produced, depending on the popularity of the film; many of these titles can languish in cutout bins for years.

The soundtrack to *Dr. Dolittle*, featuring Anthony Newley and Samantha Eggar, was pressed in both a gatefold and a non-gatefold edition.

Soundtrack fans appreciate the underscores of motion pictures—classical music, jazz, new age, blues, rock, and ambient sound, all blended into sonic masterpieces. Composers whose names have become recognizable in the soundtrack field include James Horner, Jerry Goldsmith, Alfred Newman, Max Steiner, John Williams, Danny Elfman, John Barry, Miklos Hozsa, Henry Mancini, and Vangelis Papathanasiou.

Trivia

The soundtrack for the Warner Brothers film Jamboree contains a fantastic cross-section of early rock 'n' roll. This soundtrack has been counterfeited; originals have front cover slicks and back cover notes printed on the cardboard, and the dead wax will contain the machine-stamped words "Jam 1" and "Jam 2" (counterfeits will have them drawn or etched in the dead wax).

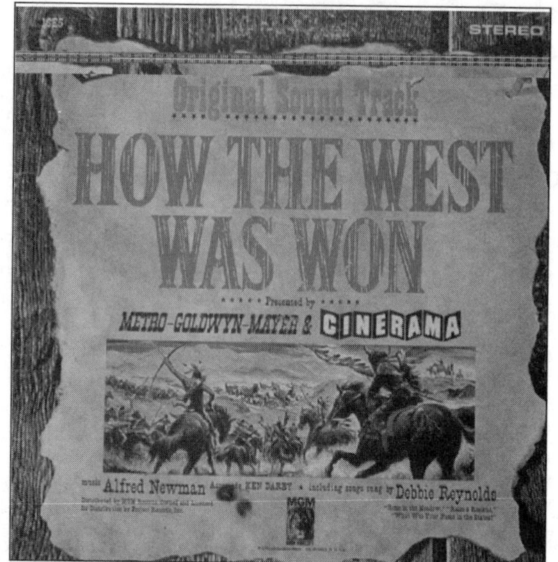

Alfred Newman's sweeping score for the Cinerama classic, *How The West Was Won.* Courtesy Good Rockin' Tonight/Collectors Universe.

Although these soundtrack composers have created the most recognizable and breathtaking motion picture scores, those artists' most collectible work are often the soundtracks to their earlier films. For example, while collectors of *Star Wars*-related material will quickly snap up John Williams' original scores for *Star Wars* and its sequels, collectors of John Williams' scores, those collectors who appreciate classical music, will avidly hunt for soundtracks to his earliest compositions, including *The Eiger Sanction, The Fury* and *The Missouri Breaks*.

In a perfect world, naturally every album would have an available soundtrack record. Unfortunately, this does not always happen. While a composer can use AFM union musicians for a film's orchestral music, a "re-use" fee must be paid for that music to appear in any other format—including a soundtrack album. If the "re-use" fee is not paid, the soundtrack album is not made.

Sometimes a soundtrack album can be recorded, the records pressed, the jackets printed—only to have the album yanked at the last minute. One such example of a last-minute album cancellation is the soundtrack for the film *The Caine Mutiny. The Caine Mutiny* soundtrack album featured Max Steiner's score, with film dialogue interspersed throughout the record. Herman Wouk, who received a Pulitzer Prize for the original *Caine Mutiny* book, disapproved of the dialogue-with-underscore concept of the album, and sent a blistering letter to Columbia Pictures president Harry Cohn, saying he would no longer offer his book projects to that studio. Cohn immediately contacted the record company and told it to stop pressing copies of *The Caine Mutiny.* Only a few records survived, and the surviving copies today can sell for as much as four figures in good condition. The record has been bootlegged twice: once in 1973 with a black-and-white cover; once in the late 1990s with the color cover, but no name on the jacket spine.

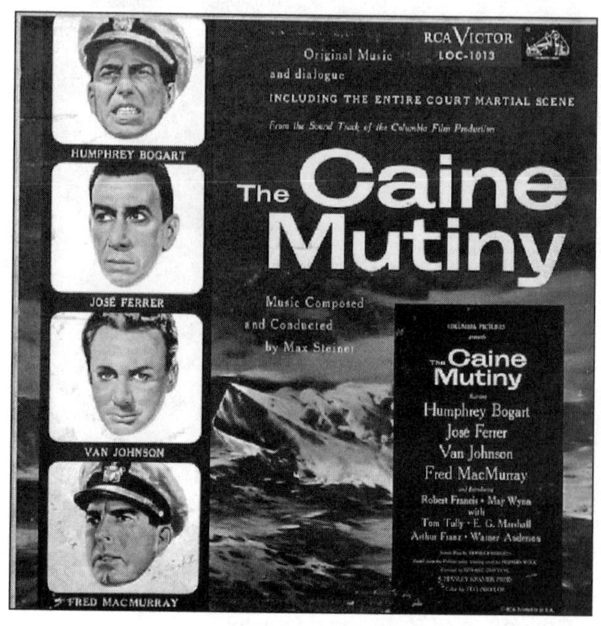

The soundtrack to *The Caine Mutiny* is one of the rarest albums, soundtrack or otherwise, of all time. Courtesy Good Rockin' Tonight/Collectors Universe.

Another factor that can affect a movie soundtrack's collectible price is whether the album has or will be re-released on compact disc. Because compact discs can hold more music per unit than can a vinyl album, more CD re-releases offer extra musical passages and film dialogue, in an effort to convince music lovers to pitch the old LP and switch to CD. Many soundtracks, however, have not been re-released on CD, which can cause fans to either cling to their old LPs or to seek out foreign pressings or bootleg CDs.

Soundtrack albums will nearly always contain a classic scene from its concomitant motion picture—whether the album jacket features the leading man in a loving embrace with an actress, or shows a doe-eyed ingenue staring wistfully into the horizon, the cover itself can be as collectible—if not more than the vinyl contained therein. And if the film contains a sexy starlet or pinup goddess, rest assured that the album soundtrack will also feature her on the front cover.

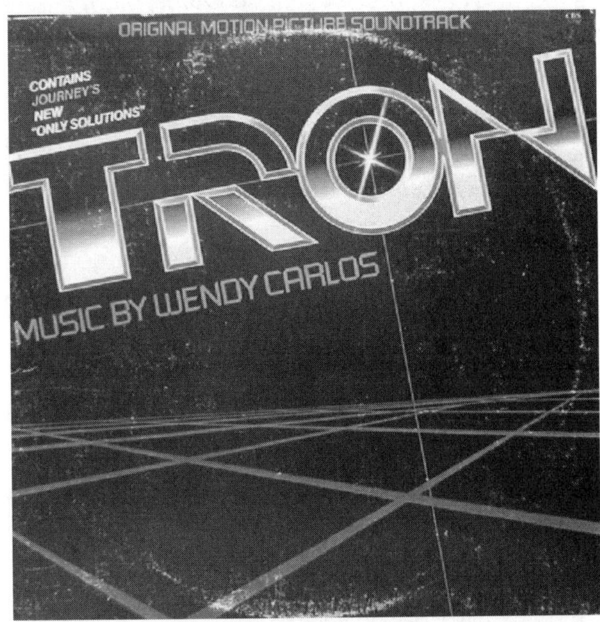

Wendy Carlos' soundtrack to the film *Tron* has not been released on CD; however, that hasn't stopped bootleggers from pressing their own CD's and trying to sell them as legitimate releases. Also notice that Journey, who contributed one song to the soundtrack, received higher billing than Carlos, who composed the entire score.

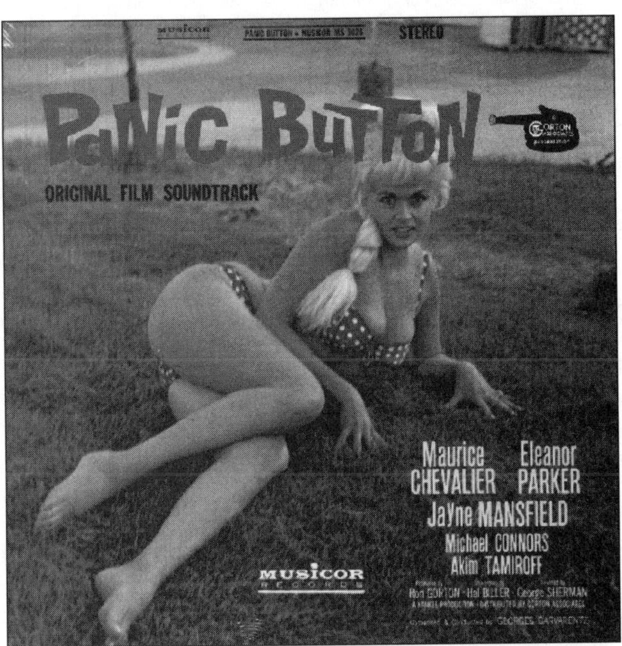

Jayne Mansfield received third billing in *Panic Button*, but she graces the front cover of the album soundtrack. By the way, Georges Garvarentz composed the underscore for this film. From the Collection of R. Michael Murray.

What To Look For: Purists will often want their soundtracks in the form they were originally released, while music lovers will want the soundtrack that contains the most music available. Compact disc releases of some vinyl soundtrack titles have caused the price of the original release to drop in value. In the mid-1970s, Johnny Green's soundtrack for the film *Raintree County* used to sell for almost $200 in near-mint condition. Because of CD reissues, however, the price for the vinyl album has dropped over the years.

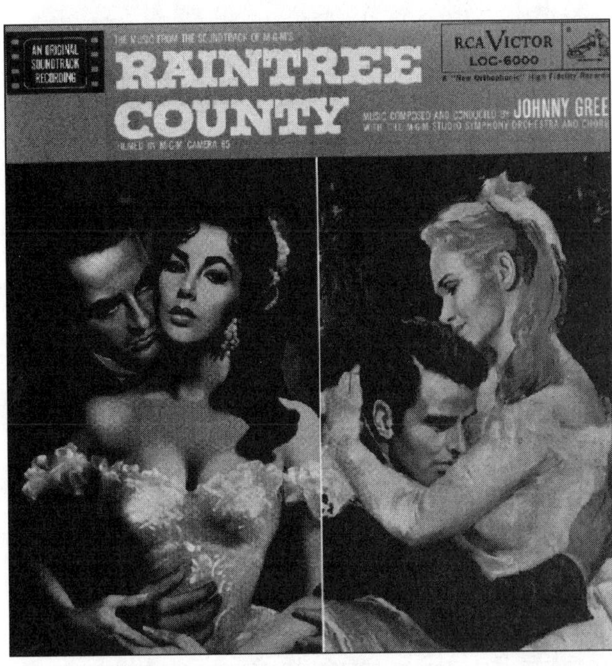

The soundtrack to *Raintree County*, one of many soundtrack LPs whose value has dropped due to the underscore's release on CD. From the Collection of R. Michael Murray.

Some soundtracks have increased in value not because of their musical content, but instead because the film itself has its own collector base (James Bond fans, Batman fans, pin-up girl collectors, horror movie buffs).

In 1973, MGM Records released some of its greatest soundtracks as "two-fers"—two or more 1950s soundtracks on a two-album set. The original releases were 10-inch LPs from the 1950s, and their collectible value is substantially higher than these reissues. These "two-fers" are worth only $20 in near-mint condition, with a coupling of "The Pirate," "Pagan Love Song," and "Hit The Deck" reaching $40 in near-mint condition.

An example of the MGM "two-fer" album series, listed as *"Those Glorious MGM Musicals."*

Trivia

Some MGM soundtrack albums in the 1950s and 1960s offered more than just an LP. "MGM Deluxe Editions" were soundtrack box sets for such motion pictures as Ben-Hur, King of Kings and Gone With The Wind. Inside each box was the soundtrack, as well as hardcover books, photos and other special additions.

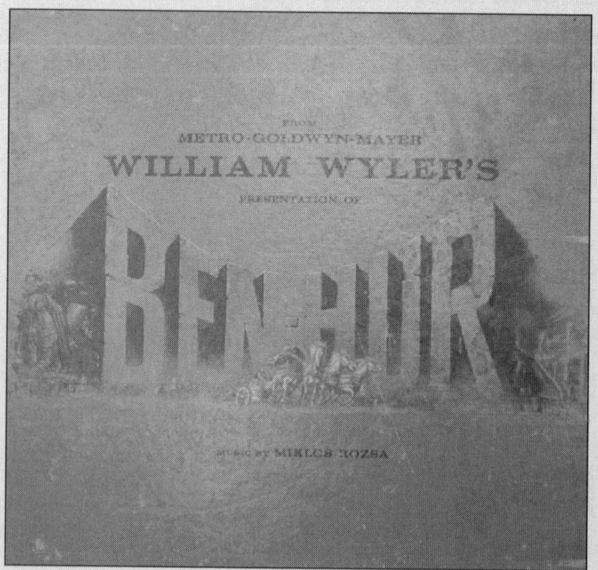

The soundtrack for *Ben-Hur* came with a behind-the-scenes booklet on the making of the motion picture, as well as the history of the original Ben-Hur 19th-century novel.

References: Karlin, Fred, *Listening to Movies*, Wadsworth Publishing Company, 1994; McNally, Keith; McNally, Dorie; *McNally's Price Guide for Collectible Soundtrack Records*, West Point Records, 1995; Osborne, Jerry; Maupin, Ruth; *The Official Price Guide to Movie/TV Soundtracks and Original Cast Albums*, House of Collectibles, New York, 1997.

Web pages: Soundtrack.net, a Web page for the art of film and television music. *http://www.filmmusic.com* or *http://www.soundtrack.net*; Filmscore Monthly Magazine, *http://www.filmscore-monthly.com.*

Motion Picture Soundtrack LPs	Year	VG	VG+	NM
Airport (Decca DL 79173) (stereo)	1970	$6.25	$12.50	$25.00
And God Created Woman (Decca DL 8685) (mono)	1957	$30.00	$60.00	$120.00
Batman (Warner Bros. 25977) (orchestral score by Danny Elfman)	1989	$5.00	$10.00	$20.00
Beach Banket Bingo (Capitol T 2323) (mono)	1965	$7.50	$15.00	$30.00
(if on Capitol ST 2323, stereo)	1965	$15.00	$30.00	$60.00
Ben-Hur (MGM 1E1) (mono) (with hardcover book)	1959	$10.00	$20.00	$40.00
(if on MGM S-1E1, stereo, with hardcover book)	1959	$12.50	$25.00	$50.00
Beyond the Valley of the Dolls (2oth Century Fox TFS-4211)	1970	$50.00	$100.00	$200.00
Blade Runner (Full Moon/Warner Bros. 23748)	1982	$5.00	$10.00	$20.00
Born Free (MGM SE-4368) (stereo)	1966	$5.00	$10.00	$20.00
A Boy Named Charlie Brown (Columbia Masterworks OS 3500)	1970	$5.00	$10.00	$20.00
The Caine Mutiny (RCA Victor LOC-1013) (mono)	1954	$4,000	$7,000	$10,000
(if with same catalog number, reissued in 1993, limited edition of 100 copies)	1993	$50.00	$100.00	$200.00
Casino Royale (Colgems COMO-5005) (mono)	1967	$7.50	$15.00	$30.00
(if on Colgems COSO-5005, stereo)	1967	$25.00	$50.00	$100.00
Cinderfella (Dot DLP-8001) (mono) (gatefold cover with game board, spinner, booklet, music stand, and other goodies)	1960	$15.00	$30.00	$60.00
(if on Dot SLP-38001, stereo, gatefold, with all the above parts)	1960	$25.00	$50.00	$100.00
The Color Purple (Qwest 25289) (2 LPs) (box set, "limited edition," purple vinyl, with booklet)	1985	$6.25	$12.50	$25.00
(if on Qwest 25336, 2 LPs, gatefold cover, purple vinyl)	1985	$5.00	$10.00	$20.00
Damn Yankees (RCA Victor LOC-1047) (mono) (with "Long Play" on label)	1958	$10.00	$20.00	$40.00
Desire Under The Elms (Dot DLP-3095) (mono)	1958	$25.00	$50.00	$100.00
Doctor Dolittle (20th Century Fox TCF-5101) (mono)	1967	$5.00	$10.00	$20.00
(if on 20th Century Fox TCS-5101) (stereo)	1967	$5.00	$10.00	$20.00
Doctor Zhivago (MGM S1E-6 ST) (stereo)	1965	$5.00	$10.00	$20.00
Dr. No (United Artists UAL-4108) (mono)	1963	$10.00	$20.00	$40.00
(if on United Artists UAS-5108, stereo)	1963	$12.50	$25.00	$50.00
Easy Rider (ABC Dunhill DSX-50063)	1969	$6.25	$12.50	$25.00
The Exorcist (Warner Bros. W 2774)	1974	$7.50	$15.00	$30.00
Fantasia (if on Disneyland WDX-101, 3 LPs, original issue, maroon-red labels, with 24-page booklet)	1957	$15.00	$30.00	$60.00
(if on Buena Vista WDX-101, 3 LPs, mono, blue labels, 24-page booklet)	1961	$7.50	$15.00	$30.00
(if on Buena Vista STER-101, 3 LPs, first stereo issue, black-yellow rainbow labels, 24-page booklet)	1961	$10.00	$20.00	$40.00
(if on Buena Vista 101, 2 LPs, stereo, no booklet)	1982	$5.00	$10.00	$20.00

Motion Picture Soundtrack LPs	Year	VG	VG+	NM
(if on Buena Vista V-104, digitally re-recorded music track, Mickey Mouse on front cover)	1982	$6.25	$12.50	$25.00
Fiddler on the Roof (United Artists UAS-10900) (2 LPs) (with booklet)	1971	$5.00	$10.00	$20.00
Fritz the Cat (Fantasy F-9406)	1972	$7.50	$15.00	$30.00
Gentlemen Prefer Blondes (MGM E-208) (mono)	1953	$30.00	$60.00	$120.00
The Girl In The Bikini (Poplar PLP 33-1002) (mono)	1952	$100.00	$200.00	$400.00
Gone With The Wind (MGM 1E-10) (mono) (with 32-page booklet)	1967	$5.00	$10.00	$20.00
(if on MGM S1E-10, stereo, with 32-page booklet)	1967	$5.00	$10.00	$20.00
The Greatest Show on Earth (RCA Victor LPM-3018) (10-inch LP)	1952	$50.00	$100.00	$200.00
Heavy Metal (Full Moon/Asylum 5E-547) (contains Elmer Bernstein's instrumental music)	1981	$12.50	$25.00	$50.00
(if on Full Moon/Asylum DP-90004, contains 2 LPs of pop-rock music)	1981	$5.00	$10.00	$20.00
Hoosiers (Polydor 831 475-1)	1987	$7.50	$15.00	$30.00
Howard the Duck (MCA 6173)	1986	$5.00	$10.00	$20.00
Ice Station Zebra (MGM S1E-14 ST)	1968	$10.00	$20.00	$40.00
It's A Mad, Mad, Mad World (United Artists UAL-4110) (mono)	1963	$5.00	$10.00	$20.00
(if on United Artists UAS-5110, stereo)	1963	$6.25	$12.50	$25.00
Jamboree! (Warner Bros., no number) (mono)	1957	$300.00	$600.00	$1,200.00
King of Kings (MGM 1E-2) (mono) (contains hardbound book and four 8 x 10 photos)	1961	$7.50	$15.00	$30.00
(if on MGM S1E-2, stereo, contains hardbound book and four 8 x 10 photos)	1961	$10.00	$20.00	$40.00
Little Shop of Horrors (Geffen GHS-24125)	1986	$5.00	$10.00	$20.00
Long John Silver (RCA Victor LPM-3279) (10-inch LP)	1954	$75.00	$150.00	$300.00
M*A*S*H (Columbia Masterworks OS-3520) (first pressings do not contain the Ahmad Jamal theme song)	1970	$5.00	$10.00	$20.00
A Man Called Flintstone (Hanna-Barbera HLP-2055) (mono)	1975	$25.00	$50.00	$100.00
Man of La Mancha (United Artists UAS-9906)	1972	$5.00	$10.00	$20.00
(if cover is cut or notched, making album a cutout budget release)	1972	$2.50	$5.00	$10.00
Midnight Cowboy (United Artists UAS-5198)	1969	$5.00	$10.00	$20.00
Mutiny on the Bounty (MGM 1E-4) (mono) (contains book and painting)	1962	$7.50	$15.00	$30.00
(if on MGM S1E-4, stereo, contains book and painting)	1962	$10.00	$20.00	$40.00
Never on Sunday (United Artists USA-5070) (stereo)	1960	$5.00	$10.00	$20.00
(if on United Artists SW-90834, stereo, Capitol Record Club edition)	196??	$5.00	$10.00	$20.00
The Odd Couple (Dot DLP-25862)	1968	$5.00	$10.00	$20.00
Once Upon A Time In The West (RCA Victor LSP-4736)	1969	$5.00	$10.00	$20.00
Our Man Flint (20th Century Fox TFM-3179) (mono)	1966	$10.00	$20.00	$40.00
(if on 20th Century Fox TFS-4179, stereo)	1966	$15.00	$30.00	$60.00
Panic Button (Musicor MM-2026) (mono)	1964	$20.00	$40.00	$80.00
(if on Musicor MS-3026, stereo)	1964	$30.00	$60.00	$120.00
Paper Moon (Paramount PAS-1012)	1973	$5.00	$10.00	$20.00
Peyton Place (RCA Victor LOC-1042) (mono) ("Long Play" at bottom of label)	1958	$7.50	$15.00	$30.00
(if on RCA Victor LSD-1042, stereo, "Living Stereo" at bottom of label)	1958	$25.00	$50.00	$100.00
(if on RCA Victor LOC-1042, mono, "Monaural" at bottom of label)	1965	$6.25	$12.50	$25.00
(if on RCA Victor LSD-1042, stereo, "Stereo" at bottom of label)	1965	$15.00	$30.00	$60.00
Planet of the Apes (Project 3 PR-5023 SD) (gatefold cover)	1968	$7.50	$15.00	$30.00
(if regular non-gatefold cover)	1968	$5.00	$10.00	$20.00
Raiders of the Lost Ark (DCC Compact Classics LPZ-2-2009) (2 LP's) (contains music not heard in other reissues)	1995	$7.50	$15.00	$30.00
Raintree County (RCA Victor LOC-6000) (mono) (2 LPs)	1957	$30.00	$60.00	$120.00
Motion Picture Soundtrack LPs	**Year**	**VG**	**VG+**	**NM**
(if on RCA Victor LOC-1038, one LP, mono)	1958	$7.50	$15.00	$30.00
(if on RCA Victor LSO-1038, one LP, stereo)	1958	$12.50	$25.00	$50.00
Riot on Sunset Strip (Tower T 5065) (mono)	1967	$5.00	$10.00	$20.00
(Tower DT 5065, rechanneled stereo)	1967	$6.25	$12.50	$25.00
Rock, Rock, Rock (Chess LP-1425) (mono)	1958	$50.00	$100.00	$200.00
(if demo version with no label or catalog number, 20 tracks)	1958	$375.00	$750.00	$1,500.00
Ryan's Daughter (MGM 1SE-27)	1970	$6.25	$12.50	$25.00
The Sand Pebbles (20th Century Fox 3189) (mono)	1966	$7.50	$15.00	$30.00
(if on 20th Century Fox S-4189, stereo)	1966	$12.50	$25.00	$50.00
The Seventh Voyage of Sinbad (Colpix CP-504) (mono)	1958	$50.00	$100.00	$200.00
(if on Varese Sarabande STV-81135, reissue)	1983	$5.00	$10.00	$20.00
Snow White and the Seven Dwarfs				
(if on Disneyland WDL-4005, mono, gatefold cover)	1956	$50.00	$100.00	$200.00
(if on Disneyland DQ-1201, mono, whirlpool-like design on cover)	1959	$12.50	$25.00	$50.00
(if on Disneyland DQ-1201, mono, reissue, cover is same as 1956 release, but no gatefold)	1968	$6.25	$12.50	$25.00
(if on Buena Vista 102, mail order, 3 LPs, contains entire movie soundtrack)	1975	$12.50	$25.00	$50.00
(if on Disneyland 3101, picture disc)	1981	$7.50	$15.00	$30.00
(if on Disneyland DQ-1201, reissue with high-gloss cover, cel photos on back)	1987	$7.50	$15.00	$30.00
Some Like It Hot (United Artists UAL-4030) (mono)	1959	$12.50	$25.00	$50.00
(if on United Artists UAS-5030, stereo)	1959	$18.75	$37.50	$75.00
The Sons of Katie Elder (Columbia Masterworks OL 6420) (mono)	1965	$12.50	$25.00	$50.00
(if on Columbia Masterworks OS 2820, stereo)	1965	$25.00	$50.00	$100.00
The Sterile Cuckoo (Paramount PAS-5009)	1970	$5.00	$10.00	$20.00
Thank God It's Friday (Casablanca NBLP-7099-3) (3 discs; 2 LPs plus one 12" of Donna Summer with blank B-side)	1978	$5.00	$10.00	$20.00
The Thin Blue Line (Nonesuch 79209-1)	1988	$5.00	$10.00	$20.00
The Threepenny Opera				
(if on RCA Victor LOC-1086, mono, pink and black drawing on cover, characters underneath)	1964	$37.50	$75.00	$150.00
(if on RCA Victor LSD-1086, stereo, pink and black drawing on cover, characters underneath)	1964	$50.00	$100.00	$200.00
(if on RCA Victor LSD-1086, stereo, orange drawing, Sammy Davis Jr. in foreground, "RE" at bottom)	1964	$5.00	$10.00	$20.00
True Grit (Capitol ST-263) (stereo)	1969	$7.50	$15.00	$30.00
(if on Capitol ST-8-0263, Capitol Record Club issue)	1969	$10.00	$20.00	$40.00
Up the Down Staircase (United Artists UAL-4169) (mono)	1967	$5.00	$10.00	$20.00
(if on United Artists UAS-5169, stereo)	1967	$10.00	$20.00	$40.00
Vertigo (Mercury MG-20384) (mono)	1958	$37.50	$75.00	$150.00
West Side Story (Columbia Masterworks OL-5670) (mono) (with gatefold cover, gray-black labels, six "eye" logos)	1961	$5.00	$10.00	$20.00
West Side Story (Columbia Masterworks OS-2070) (stereo) (with gatefold cover, gray-black labels, six "eye" logos)	1961	$6.25	$12.50	$25.00
Willy Wonka and the Chocolate Factory (Paramount PAS-6012)	1971	$10.00	$20.00	$40.00
Yojimbo (MGM E-4096) (mono)	1962	$25.00	$50.00	$100.00
(if on MGM SE-4096, stereo)	1962	$37.50	$75.00	$150.00
Zabriskie Point (MGM SE-4468)	1970	$5.00	$10.00	$20.00

SPACE-AGE POP

History: Space-age pop is a broadly-encompassing genre of instrumentals appearing through the 1950s and 1960s. Many of these records were a mixture of jazz, classical, Latin, and exotic music, and after years of being rejected and ignored as simple background music, space-age pop has recently come into its own. Collectors are now hunting for albums by Perez Prado, Martin Denny, Jackie Gleason, Ferrante and Teicher, Herb Alpert, and experimental stereo pressings by Esquivel and Enoch Light.

Space-age pop, also known as "bachelor-pad" music, was often used by single men who brought dates to a dimly-lit but fully stocked apartment on the pretense of viewing some "etchings." Among the leaders in this "mood music" were Percy Faith, Mantovani, and Jackie Gleason. Yes, *that* Jackie Gleason. Though "The Great One" could not read a musical scale, he knew that the most popular songs of the time, recorded with a smoky jazz cornet and lush strings, would sell lots of records. Gleason, along with arrangers Pete King and Billy May and cornetist Bobby Hackett, conducted more than twenty best-selling albums of mood music, and brought romance to millions of bachelors and bachelorettes everywhere.

Two of Jackie Gleason's biggest-selling albums, combined onto a budget LP for twice the romantic mood.

During this time period, instrumental artists experimented with new recording and performing techniques. The bandleader Esquivel composed classical pieces with unorthodox stereo separations—he once placed two orchestras in two separate studios blocks away from each other, then recorded them simultaneously to tape. The early recordings of Ferrante and Teicher featured "prepared piano" compositions, where the duo wedged items into the piano stringbed to create new vibration patterns—or plucked the piano strings with their fingers.

Juan Garcia Esquivel's early experiments with stereo separation were considered avant-garde in the 1960s—and are considered masterpieces by Space Age Pop collectors today.

Composer Les Baxter, who had hits with "The Poor People of Paris" and "Unchained Melody," was also part of the space-age pop genre. He added African, Asian, South American, and Polynesian sounds and melodies to his records, and introduced new and unique instruments, such as the theremin, to his orchestral albums. Baxter also produced albums for another space age pop legend, a Brooklyn housewife named Amy Camus, who became Peruvian princess and four-octave vocalist Yma Sumac.

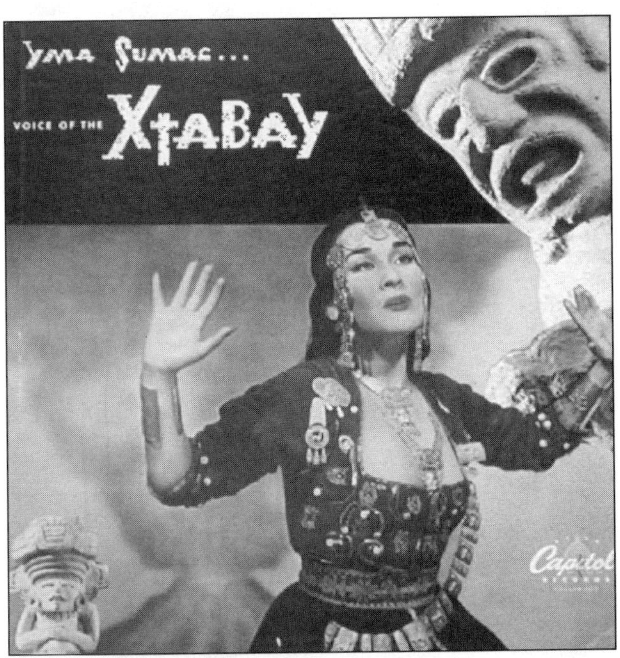

Yma Sumac's first 10-inch album, *Voice of the Xtabay,* became an underground hit and is today a hard-to-find collectible.

Space-age pop also encompasses the various Latin orchestras and conductors of the 1950s and 1960s. You could mambo to Perez Prado or Tito Puente, you could live la vida loca with Desi Arnaz or Xavier Cugat. In fact, Latin singers and orchestra leaders in the 1950s nearly held their own against the onslaught of rock and roll.

This stereo release contains re-recordings of Prez Prado's "Cherry Pink and Apple Blossom White" and "Patricia," but this album's "Mambo No. 5" was sampled for Lou Bega's 1999 hit.

Trivia

After guaranteeing Capitol Records he would sell 60,000 copies of his first album or pay for the pressings himself, Jackie Gleason's Music for Lovers Only sold more than 500,000 albums in its initial run.

Martin Denny's "exotic" aural rainforest instrumentals are also a major part of Space Age Pop. Denny, who had previously worked with Les Baxter, added even more rare and unique instruments to his own recordings, including gongs and temple bells. His recordings even had exotic bird calls, courtesy of his vibraphone player Arthur Lyman (who later recorded his own hit, "Yellow Bird," in 1961).

Martin Denny's version of the standard "Stranger in Paradise" featured bird calls, vibraphones, maracas and drums—truly a song for a stranger to visit paradise.

What To Look For: Ten years ago, many of these space-age pop records were gathering dust in thrift stores, or going unsold at yard sales. With the recent rise in 1950s kitsch/cool collectibles, this music is finding a new appreciation, and the prices for records in near-mint condition is starting to rise. This music has also returned to the forefront, thanks to the success of reissue packages on RCA, Rhino, and DCC Compact Classics.

However, most of the artists grouped in the space-age pop genre sold million of albums, so there are few "rare" recordings (albums by Herb Alpert and the Tijuana Brass are everywhere; although the music itself is spectacular, the records themselves have little "rarity" collectible value).

What are rare in space-age pop are any 10-inch LPs recorded by these artists, especially if the records were not subsequently released on a 12-inch LP a few short years later.

Stereo pressings are a must, if for no other reason than to hear how Enoch Light and Esquivel interpreted and used this new recording technique to their own advantage. Clean covers are also desired, especially if the front cover has a cheesecake model (Sandy Warner, for example, is a major visual selling point of most Martin Denny albums).

Current space-age pop revival bands include Combustible Edison, the Friends of Dave Martinez, and the Squirrel Nut Zippers.

Even though some space-age pop artists released 45s, this collecting genre is more driven by near-mint copies of 10-inch and 12-inch albums.

References: Kelly, Michael "Doc Rock," *Liberty Records: A History of the Recording Company and Its Stars, 1955-1971*, McFarland & Company, Inc., Jefferson, North Carolina, 1993; Martin Denny recorded for Liberty Records, and his story is part of this book; Wooley, John; Connor, Thomas; Brown, Mark; *Forever Lounge: A Laid-Back Price Guide to the Languid Sounds of Lounge Music*, Antique Trader Books, Dubuque, Iowa, 1999; *Incredibly Strange Music*, Vols. I and II, Re/Search Publications, San Francisco, 1993, 1994.

Web pages: The Space-Age Pop Music page, a great Web page for history and music, *http://home.earthlink.net/~spaceagepop*; cool and Strange Music, a magazine devoted to avant-garde songs: *http://members.aol.com/coolstrge/mainpage.html*; the Enoch Light Web page: *http://easyweb.easynet.co.uk/~rcb/light*; Record Collector's Heaven, which features links to many space age pop artists like Martin Denny and Les Baxter: *http://weirdomusic.freeservers.com.*

45s	Year	VG	VG+	NM
Ray Anthony, "Peter Gunn" / "Tango For Two" (Capitol F4041)	1958	$2.00	$5.00	$10.00
Chet Atkins, "In The Mood" / "Sweet Bunch of Daisies" (RCA Victor 47-4377)	1951	$6.25	$12.50	$25.00
Les Baxter, "The Poor People of Paris" / "Theme From 'Helen of Troy'" (Capitol F3336)	1956	$3.75	$7.50	$15.00
Al Caiola, "The Magnificent Seven" / "The Lonely Rebel" (United Artists 261)	1960	$3.00	$6.00	$12.00
Martin Denny, "Quiet Village" / "Llama Serenade" (Liberty 55162)	1958	$3.00	$6.00	$12.00
(if "Quiet Village" is on Liberty 56126, as B-side of "Midnight Cowboy")	1969		$2.50	$5.00
(if "Quiet Village" is on United Artists 0069, "Silver Spotlight Series" reissue)	1973		$2.00	$4.00
Esquivel, "Besame Mucho" / "Verda Tropical" (RCA Victor 47-5969)	1954	$5.00	$10.00	$20.00
Esquivel, "That Old Black Magic" / "Cielito Lindo" (RCA Victor 47-7316)	1958	$3.75	$7.50	$15.00
Percy Faith and his Orchestra, "I Love You" / "Long Ago (And Far Away)" (Decca 27542)	1951	$3.00	$6.00	$12.00
Percy Faith and his Orchestra, "Theme From 'A Summer Place'" / "Go-Go-Po-Go" (Columbia 41490)	1959	$2.00	$4.00	$8.00
(with picture sleeve, add:)	1959	$3.75	$7.50	$15.00
Ferrante and Teicher, "Exodus" / "Twilight" (United Artists 274)	1960	$3.00	$6.00	$12.00
(with picture sleeve, add:)	1960	$3.75	$7.50	$15.00
Jackie Gleason, "Terry's Theme From 'Limelight'" / "Peg o' My Heart" (Capitol F2507)	1953	$3.75	$7.50	$15.00
Al Hirt, "Janine" / "Elegie" (RCA Victor 47-7854)	1961	$2.50	$5.00	$10.00
(with picture sleeve, add:)	1961	$3.00	$6.00	$12.00
Al Hirt, "Java" / "I Can't Get Started" (RCA Victor 47-8280)	1963	$2.00	$4.00	$8.00
Bert Kaempfert, "Wonderland By Night" / "Dreaming The Blues" (Decca 31141)	1960	$2.00	$4.00	$8.00
Stan Kenton, "Sophisticated Lady" / "Begin the Beguine" (Capitol F2446)	1953	$3.00	$6.00	$12.00
Enoch Light, "Baby, It's Cold Outside Cha Cha" / "Chiquita Cha Cha" (Grand Award 1026)	1958	$3.00	$6.00	$12.00
Enoch Light, "Young At Heart Cha Cha" / "Travel Now, Pay Next Year, Pleasure Cruise" (Command 4009)	1960	$2.50	$5.00	$10.00
Arthur Lyman, "Jungle Fantasy" / "Koni Au I Ka Wai" (HIFI 599)	1960	$2.50	$5.00	$10.00
Henry Mancini, "Banzai Pipeline" / "Rhapsody in Blue" (RCA Victor 47-8184)	1963	$5.00	$10.00	$20.00
(with picture sleeve, add:)	1963	$6.25	$12.50	$25.00
Henry Mancini, "The Pink Panther Theme" / "It Had Better Be Tonight" (RCA Victor 47-8256)	1963	$2.00	$4.00	$8.00
(with picture sleeve, add:)	1963	$3.75	$7.50	$15.00
Mantovani, "Let Me Be Loved" / "Call of the West" (London 1761)	1957	$3.75	$7.50	$15.00
(with picture sleeve featuring James Dean, add:)	1957	$15.00	$30.00	$60.00
Sandy Nelson, "Let There Be Drums" / "Quite A Beat" (Imperial 5775)	1961	$3.75	$7.50	$15.00
Santo and Johnny, "Sleep Walk" / "All Night Diner" (Canadian-American 103)	1959	$5.00	$10.00	$20.00
Santo and Johnny, "Twistin' Bells" / "Bullseye!" (Canadian American 120)	1960	$4.00	$8.00	$16.00
(with picture sleeve, add:)	1960	$10.00	$20.00	$40.00
Yma Sumac, "Birds" / "Najalas Lament" (Capitol F1819)	1951	$5.00	$10.00	$20.00
(with picture sleeve, add:)	1951	$10.00	$20.00	$40.00

LPs	Year	VG	VG+	NM
Leo Addeo, Paradise Regained (RCA Victor LSA-2414) (stereo)	1961	$7.50	$15.00	$30.00
Ray Anthony, Jazz Session at the Tower, Capitol T-749) (mono)	1956	$10.00	$20.00	$40.00
Chet Atkins, Chet Atkins in Three Dimensions (RCA Victor LPM-1197)				
(if first pressing, with black-and-white guitar cover)	1956	$12.50	$25.00	$50.00
(if second pressing, with red guitar cover)	1961	$5.00	$10.00	$20.00
Les Baxter, Le Sacre Du Sauvage (Capitol 288)				
(if 10-inch record)	1952	$20.00	$40.00	$80.00
(if 12-inch record)	1954	$10.00	$20.00	$40.00
Vincent Bell, Pop Goes The Electric Sitar (Decca DL 4938) (mono)	1967	$5.00	$10.00	$20.00
Jerry Byrd, On The Shores of Waikiki				
(if on Mercury MG-20230, mono)	1960	$7.50	$15.00	$30.00
(if on Mercury SR-60230, stereo)	1960	$10.00	$20.00	$40.00
Al Caiola, The Magnificent Seven				
(if on United Artists UAL-3133, mono)	1960	$5.00	$10.00	$20.00
(if on United Artists UAS-6133, stereo)	1960	$6.25	$12.50	$25.00
Xavier Cugat, Mambo! (Columbia CL 2506) (10-inch LP)	1955	$12.50	$25.00	$50.00
Xavier Cugat, Relaxing with Cugat (Quiet Music, Volume VI) (Columbia CL 515)				
(if first pressing, black label, silver print, "GL" prefix)	1952	$12.50	$25.00	$50.00
(if second pressing, maroon label, gold print, "CL" prefix)	1953	$10.00	$20.00	$40.00
Martin Denny, Exotica				
(if Liberty LRP-3034, mono pressing, turquoise label)	1957	$10.00	$20.00	$40.00
(if Liberty LRP-3034, mono, black rainbow label)	1960	$6.25	$12.50	$25.00
(if Liberty LST-7034, rechanneled stereo, all-black label)	1958	$6.25	$12.50	$25.00
(if Liberty LST-7034, rechanneled stereo, black rainbow label)	1960	$5.00	$10.00	$20.00
Esquivel, Infinity In Sound				
(if RCA Victor LPM-2225, mono)	1960	$7.50	$15.00	$30.00
(if RCA Victor LSP-2225, stereo like you would not believe)	1960	$15.00	$30.00	$60.00

LPs	Year	VG	VG+	NM
Esquivel, Latin-Esque				
(if RCA Victor LPM-2418, mono)	1962	$5.00	$10.00	$20.00
(if RCA Victor LSP-2418, stereo, standard cover)	1962	$10.00	$20.00	$40.00
(if RCA Victor LSP-2418, stereo, die-cut cover that reveals the inner sleeve)	1962	$15.00	$30.00	$60.00
Percy Faith, Music From Hollywood (Columbia CL 577) (mono)	1955	$5.00	$10.00	$20.00
Percy Faith, A Night With Jerome Kern (Columbia CS 8181) (stereo)	1959	$5.00	$10.00	$20.00
Ferrante and Teicher, Heavenly Sounds in Hi-Fi (ABC-Paramount S-221) (stereo)	1958	$5.00	$10.00	$20.00
Ferrante and Teicher, Soundproof (Westminster SW 1045) (stereo)	195??	$6.25	$12.50	$25.00
Jackie Gleason, Music For Lovers Only				
(if Capitol H-352, 10-inch record)	1952	$7.50	$15.00	$30.00
(if Capitol W-352, 12-inch mono record)	1953	$6.25	$12.50	$25.00
Jackie Gleason, Music for Lovers Only / Music To Make You Misty (Capitol WAO 475) (2 LPs)	1954	$10.00	$20.00	$40.00
Morton Gould, Jungle Drums (RCA Victor LSC-1994) ("shaded dog" on label)	1958	$10.00	$20.00	$40.00
Skitch Henderson, Keyboard Sketches (Capitol H-110) (10-inch LP)	1950	$12.50	$25.00	$50.00
Al Hirt, Swingin' Dixie (At Dan's Pier 600 in New Orleans) (Audio Fidelity AFSD-57877) (stereo)	1959	$5.00	$10.00	$20.00
Al Hirt, "Pops" Goes The Trumpet (RCA Victor LSC-2729) (stereo) (with Arthur Fiedler and the Boston Pops Orchestra)	1964	$5.00	$10.00	$20.00
Bert Kaempfert, Wonderland By Night				
(if on Decca DL-4101, mono)	1960	$3.75	$7.50	$15.00
(if on Decca DL-74101, stereo)	1960	$5.00	$10.00	$20.00
Stan Kenton, A Presentation of Progressive Jazz				
(if on Capitol H 172, 10-inch record)	1950	$15.00	$30.00	$60.00

LPs	Year	VG	VG+	NM
(if on Capitol T 172, 12-inch record)	195??	$10.00	$20.00	$40.00
Stan Kenton, The Kenton Era (Capitol TBP 569) (4 LP set with 44-page book)	1955	$25.00	$50.00	$100.00
Enoch Light, Around The World In Eighty Days (Grand Award GA-214-SD)	1958	$6.25	$12.50	$25.00
Enoch Light, Stereo 35'MM (Command 826-SD)	1961	$3.75	$7.50	$15.00
Arthur Lyman, Hawaiian Sunset (HIFI R-807) (mono)	1959	$5.00	$10.00	$20.00
(if above is on HIFI SR-807, stereo)	1959	$7.50	$15.00	$30.00
Henry Mancini, The Music From Peter Gunn				
(if on RCA Victor LPM-1956, mono, words "Peter Gunn" on top of album jacket)	1959	$10.00	$20.00	$40.00
(if on RCA Victor LPM-1956, mono, words "Peter Gunn" in center of album jacket)	1959	$5.00	$10.00	$20.00
(if on RCA Victor LSP-1956, stereo, words "Peter Gunn" on top of album jacket)	1959	$12.50	$25.00	$50.00
(if on RCA Victor LSP-1956, stereo, words "Peter Gunn" in center of album jacket)	1959	$6.25	$12.50	$25.00
Mantovani, Mantovani Stereo Showcase (London SS 1)	1959	$5.00	$10.00	$20.00
Sandy Nelson, Sandy Nelson Plays Teen Beat				
(if on Imperial LP 9105, mono)	1960	$7.50	$15.00	$30.00
(if on Imperial LP 12044, stereo)	1960	$10.00	$20.00	$40.00
Santo and Johnny, Santo and Johnny				
(if on CALP-1001, mono)	1959	$15.00	$30.00	$60.00
(if on SCALP-1001, stereo)	1959	$20.00	$40.00	$80.00
Yma Sumac, Legend of the Sun Virgin				
(if on Capitol L 299, 10-inch record)	1952	$30.00	$60.00	$120.00
(if on Capitol T 299, 12-inch mono)	1955	$12.50	$25.00	$50.00
(if on Capitol SM-299, 1970's reissue)	197??	$3.00	$6.00	$12.00
Various Artists, Liberty Proudly Presents Stereo - The Visual Sound (Liberty LST-100) (stereo)	1959	$10.00	$20.00	$40.00

This stereo demonstration album contains excerpts from the Liberty Records stable, including Martin Denny, Julie London and a rare clip from the Chipmunks.

Bandleader Enoch Light formed his own labels, Command and Project 3, for his stereo experimentations. Although this copy of "In The Mood" is in mono, Light experimented with sound all the way into the quadraphonic era.

STAMPER NUMBERS AND VINYL GRAFFITI

History: The dead wax in the runout grooves of albums often contains an indecipherable series of numbers and letters, but in many cases, that alphanumeric code can tell you when and where a particular album was pressed, and whether it was one of the first pressings out of the factory. Knowledge of such information can help you in purchasing a record that is rarer than its print run would normally indicate.

For this book, we will decode for you the RCA Victor stamper number alphanumeric code. In the 1950s and 1960s, RCA's albums all contained a similar alphanumeric code, which will be deciphered here. Looking at the dead wax of a copy of SSgt Barry Sadler's album "Ballads of the Green Berets," we see the following numbers machine-stamped in the dead wax:

SPRM 6183 3S

In this enhanced photo, you can see little numbers and letters in the lower left corner of the runout groove of this record.

The stamper number for Side 1 of Ssgt Barry Sadler's *Ballads of the Green Berets* LP.

Trivia

Phil Spector collectors can tell when Phil and Annette Spector broke up by following the trail-off trail. Early Philles releases say "Phil and Annette" in the dead wax; by the time Veronica Bennett came into the picture, the graffiti stopped—only to resurface on some American Apple label 45s as "Phil and Ronnie."

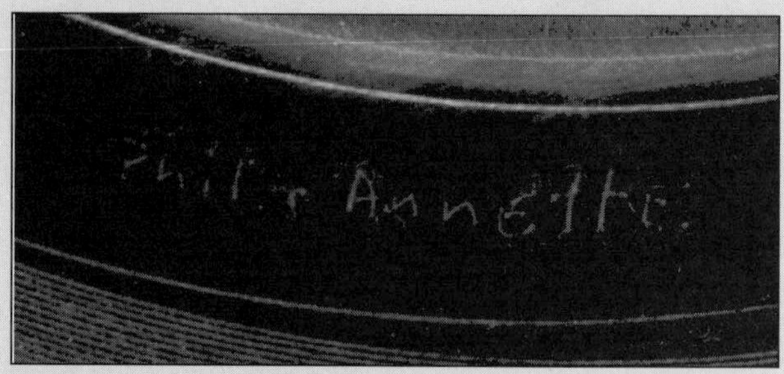

Phil and Annette Spector's names carved into the dead wax of the Crystals' "Then He Kissed Me."

A few years (and a new wife) later, "Phil and Ronnie" appeared in the dead wax of the Beatles' "The Long and Winding Road."

Flipping the record over, we see a different series of numbers on the B-side:

SPRM 6184 3S

First, some explanation of what happens after an artist records an album. The tapes are edited, remixed, and recorded onto a "master tape," which is carefully timed for the length of one side of an album. Metal stampers, which will be used to press the vinyl into records, are made from the master tape.

The first letter of the RCA code, "S," corresponds with the year the master tape was created. Before 1955, the first two alphanumeric characters in the code corresponded with the year of the original master tape. The first letter, "A" through "E," represents the decade of the master tape's creation, while the second character would be a number representing the year within that decade. "D9," for example, means the master was made in 1949, while "E3" means 1953.

Beginning in 1955, the two-character system was scrapped. Now the master tape's year of creation would be represented by a single letter—"F" for 1955, "G" for 1956, and so on. The letters "I," "O," "Q," and "V" are skipped in this sequence, so the pattern runs like this:

F = 1955
G = 1956
H = 1957
J = 1958
K = 1959
L = 1960
M = 1961
N = 1962
P = 1963
R = 1964
S = 1965
T = 1966
U = 1967
W = 1968
X = 1969
Y = 1970
Z = 1971

So an "S" recording means Sadler recorded his album in 1965.

The fourth letter of the RCA code corresponds with the recording format. "M" or "P" for mono, "Y" or "S" for stereo. So now we know this album is a mono release from 1965.

The four-digit number in the middle means that this album was made from the 6,183rd master tape produced by RCA in 1965 (and the B-side was created with the 6,184th master tape of the year). The alphanumeric code also appears on the label, usually underneath the catalog number (so if those numbers don't match up, you may have an Elvis Presley label that actually plays Neil Sedaka).

The last numbers, followed by an "S," indicate which metal stamper was used to create the album. An indication of "1S" means the record was pressed with the first stampers made for that album. This example has "3S"—meaning the pressing plants wore out two stampers before this record was even made. Since stampers wear out at different rates, it is not uncommon to find one side of a record with a higher or lower stamper number than the other.

After examining the code, if you want to find out where the record was made, look in another area of the dead wax, usually on the opposite side of the label from the code. There you will find a machine stamped or hand-drawn letter "I," "H," or "R." RCA records stamped with an "H" were made in its Hollywood, California factory. An "I" means the records were pressed in Indianapolis. And if the dead wax letter is "R," the record was manufactured in RCA's plant in Rockaway, New York.

By reading this code, one could tell that this record was recorded in 1957 ("H"), that it came from the 6,779th master tape recorded in that year, and that this record was one of the first pressings from the factory...

... and all that information came from the runout groove of Elvis Presley's "Jailhouse Rock."

This coding system works for RCA releases; other record companies used different numbering methods.

Another thing to look for in the runout grooves are mysterious messages. Some artists will add a whimsical or mystical phrase in the dead wax, perhaps something pertaining to the song or to the band's state of mind at the time.

For example, the first pressings of Led Zeppelin's 45 "Immigrant Song"/"Hey What Can I Do" (Atlantic 2777) has tiny words printed on the runout groove, just near the edge of the paper label, "Do What Thou Wilt Shall Be The Whole Of The Law." About the only time vinyl graffiti adds or detracts from the value of a record is if the record was also pressed "graffiti-less" in subsequent pressings. With regard to the Led Zeppelin quotation, The *Goldmine Price Guide to 45 RPM Records* says the statement was removed from the dead wax in the second and subsequent pressings. If you're a Led Zep completist, this news might help you discern the age of your copy of that 45.

Trivia

On Buchanan and Goodman's break-in record "Buchanan and Goodman on Trial," first pressings of the 45 contain the signatures of both Bill Buchanan and Dickie Goodman in the dead wax. Because the duo were in litigation over their use of sampled snippets for their comedy collages, a second pressing contain some replaced samples, but does not contain the duo's signatures in the dead wax.

Buchanan and Goodman's second single, "Buchanan and Goodman on Trial."

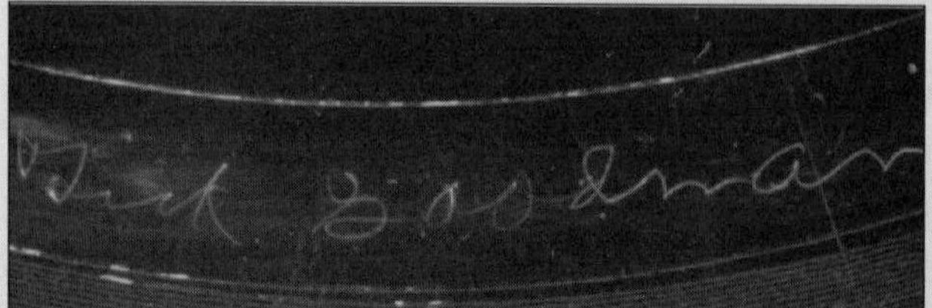

Bill Buchanan's and Dick Goodman's signature from the "On Trial" 45.

Look carefully at the label edge of Led Zeppelin's "Immigrant Song" 45...

... and you might see this vinyl graffiti that was removed from second and subsequent pressings.

And then there's the tale of Herbie.

In the late 1970s and early 1980s, hundreds of 12-inch dance singles that were pressed at the Frankford/Wayne mastering plant in New York City contained the signature of Herb Powers Jr. Go find an early 1980s 12-inch New York City dance club record. If you look into the dead wax and see "Herbie Jr.," along with an accompanying smiley face, you've found a record mastered by Herb Powers Jr.

Trivia

Among classical music collectors, a sonic performance can change from one stamper number to the next. Take for example LSC-2436, RCA's recording of the Chicago Symphony Orchestra's performance of Respighi's "Pines of Rome." Because of the thick bass in this recording, the tonearm sometimes mistracks and skips right off the disc, as if the needle itself reacts from the booming notes on the record. Later pressings corrected this defect, but a first pressing of this album in mint condition, with no ring wear on the jacket, can command nearly $1,000 to a classical collector.

Powers was a former club DJ who joined Frankford/Wayne in 1976, learning the art of mastering records. "Back then the job entailed converting the music from half-inch tape to vinyl," said Powers in a 1997 *Goldmine* interview. "I started putting my name on the dead wax on the first record, because I wanted to keep track of what I was doing. A lot of times, record companies did not give you credit on the records. It was a way for me to know that I actually mastered that record. It was also a way to tell that the record wasn't a reproduction made by a bootlegger."

The Jonzun Crew's funk-dance hit "Space Cowboy," with Herb Powers' signature in the dead wax.

By the late 1970s and early 1980s, Powers mastered some of the greatest New York City dance hits of the time—tracks like Run-D.M.C.'s "Rock Box" (Profile 7045), UTFO's "Roxanne, Roxanne" (Select 62254), the Beastie Boys' "Rock That" (Def Jam DJ002), and Keith Silverflash's "Funky Space Player" (Silver Flash Funk 21801), among others.

Sometimes the dead wax graffiti was little more than his nickname, the smiley face, and a stamp from Frankford/Wayne. But before long, Powers would put his wife's name on the record…then his kids' names…then messages about the record and its artist. "I started putting messages in around 1977, a year into my mastering career, when I got comfortable with what I was doing, comfortable with the client base that I had. For Tommy Boy Records, if you're doing their first record, and you're working together with the person and you say, 'You know something, I really like this song. Let's write something in the grooves about it.' That's something that happens as you get to know the people, the producers, the record company execs, the presidents, stuff like that. There were people that said they would not accept the record unless I inscribed something in there. Because they knew then that I did it. And on Cutting Records, I would put down Aldo, who was the owner of that label, he would always ask me to put his wife and kids' names on the record. It was a good luck thing for him," he told Goldmine.

A standard "Herbie Jr." signature, with smiley face, as well as the Frankford-Wayne pressing plant trademark.

If you own a copy of the Jonzun Crew's "Pack Jam" (Tommy Boy 826), you might see little Pac-Men in the runoff grooves. Once again, that was Herb Powers having fun. "We had a very sharp tool that looks like a dentist's drill. You have to have a very steady hand and a good eye, to sit there and draw it in. We're not using any magnifiers or anything, it's all free hand. One small slip into the groove, and you'd have to remaster the entire record. That happened at least twice in ten years at Frankford/Wayne. It's a very high pressure business—you don't want mistakes, because you don't have time to do it again."

Sometimes the stamper number can actually give a clue as to what type of mix a song was pressed with. The 45 of Naked Eyes' hit "Always Something There To Remind Me" exists in two formats: the introduction to the first pressing (with stamper number B-8155-5-45-501056-A-P-3) starts cold, as cathedral bells play in the drumless foreground; while the second pressing (with stamper number B-8155-5-45-501056-C-P-11) is a remix by John "Jellybean" Benitez that begins with a drum riff, and continues with a drum beat throughout the introduction.

What To Look For: For some collectors, stamper numbers are the DNA code of a record. With it, they can crack a record's history, audio content, even the home factory and date when it was pressed. It is not a be-all and end-all for collectors, but knowledge of the stamper-number codes never hurts.

An RCA record with a 24S stamper number does not necessarily mean the record was pressed years after its release. Millions of copies of Elvis Presley's "Are You Lonesome To-Night?" were pressed in the first few weeks, so a 24th master in that series may have been pressed only a month after the first master.

By the same token, a low master number does not necessarily mean you've purchased the best quality album or 45. Stampers were used until the records pressed failed quality inspections, or until the stampers cracked or melted under the intense pressure of pressing. Then a new stamper was made, and pressing resumed. So that 2S pressing may be the first with the new stamper, or the pressing just before the master was ruined.

When it comes to vinyl graffiti, the value of a record is not increased or decreased by the existence of cryptic phrases, autographs, or smiley faces in the dead wax. If the graffiti is removed or altered, however, then there is an increased value in the vinyl graffiti pressings. For example, the James Gang put humorous messages on many of their albums, but their records have very limited collectible value.

The mysterious runout groove graffiti can also inform you if the record you've purchased has a variation in the song; *i.e.*, alternate lyrics, a different mix, a disc mastered at an incorrect speed. It can also alert you as to the genuineness of the record—sometimes a variation in stamper number may mean the record you're purchasing is a bootleg or a reproduction. In the following price guide, you can use the information provided to determine—without dragging a phonograph with you to play the record—which version of a song is more collectible.

45s	Year	VG	VG+	NM
Big Star, "Watch the Sunrise" / "Don't Lie To Me" (Ardent 2902)				
(if label has the number "AS-01180" on it, B-side actually plays correct song)	1972	$6.25	$12.50	$25.00
(if label has the number "AS-01127" on it, B-side is listed as "Don't Lie To Me" but actually plays "Thirteen")	1972	$12.50	$25.00	$50.00
Lou Christie, "Rhapsody in the Rain" / "Trapeze" (MGM 13473)				
(if matrix number in the dead wax is "66-XY-308," the song contains the racy - by 1966 standards - lyrics, "We were makin' out in the rain / And in this car, our love went much too far," first pressing)	1966	$5.00	$10.00	$20.00
(if matrix number in the dead wax is "66-XY-308 D.J.," the song contains the tamer lyrics, "We fell in love in the rain / And in this car, love came like a falling star," second and subsequent pressings)	1966	$3.75	$7.50	$15.00
The Crystals, "(Let's Dance) The Screw" (Pt. 1) / (Pt. 2) (Philles 111)				
(if white label promo)	1963	$2,000.00	$3,000.00	$4,000.00
(if light blue label, machine-stamped numbers in dead wax. If numbers are hand-engraved, he record is a worthless reproduction)	1963	$3,000.00	$4,500.00	$6,000.00
Danny and the Juniors, "At The Hop" / "Sometimes" (Singular 711)				
(if blue label, machine-stamped numbers in dead wax, no mention of Artie Singer on label)	1957	$250.00	$500.00	$1,000.00
(if blue label, machine-stamped numbers in dead wax, "Orchestra Directed by Artie Singer" on label)	1957	$250.00	$500.00	$1,000.00
(if on black label, or without the machine-stamped numbers in the dead wax, record is a reproduction)				
The Fiestas, "So Fine" / "Last Night I Dreamed" (Old Town 1062)				
(if label has "ZTSP," Columbia pressing with piano intro)	1958	$12.50	$25.00	$50.00
(if label does not have "ZTSP," normal intro)	1958	$7.50	$15.00	$30.00
The Five Satins, "In The Still of The Nite" / "The Jones Girl" (Ember 1005) (red vinyl)				
(if record has "6016A" in the dead wax)	1956	$50.00	$100.00	$200.00
(if record has "E-2015-45" in the dead wax)	1956	$12.50	$25.00	$30.00
(if record has "E-1005" in the dead wax)	1956	$7.50	$15.00	$30.00
Ernie K-Doe, "Mother in Law" / "Wanted, $10,000 Reward" (Minit 623)				
(if numbers in the dead wax are "45-SO-738", "Mother-in-Law" accidentally mastered at 33 1/3 RPM)	1961	$50.00	$100.00	$200.00
(if numbers in the dead wax are "45-SO-738-2," "Mother-in-Law" mastered at proper speed)	1961	$6.25	$12.50	$25.00
Led Zeppelin, "Immigrant Song" / "Hey, Hey, What Can I Do" (Atlantic 2777)				
(if vinyl graffiti on A-side dead wax: "Do What Thou Wilt Shall Be The Whole Of The Law")	1970	$6.25	$12.50	$25.00
(if no vinyl graffiti, label has tall, thinner type)	1970	$3.75	$7.50	$15.00
(if no vinyl graffiti, text is smaller and fatter)	1970		$2.50	$5.00
Led Zeppelin, "D'yer Mak'er" / "The Crunge" (Atlantic 2986)				
(if defective pressing, left channel fades out halfway through the A-side, matrix number is followed by a "3" in the dead wax)	1973		$3.00	$6.00
(without the "3" in the dead wax, true stereo throughout)	1973	$2.50	$5.00	$10.00
The Miracles, "The Feeling Is So Fine" / "You Can Depend On Me" (Tamla 54028)				
(if matrix number is followed by "A" in trail-off wax, alternate take of B-side)	1960	$125.00	$250.00	$500.00
(without "A" on matrix number)	1960	$100.00	$200.00	$400.00
The Miracles, "Shop Around" / "Who's Lovin' You" (Tamla 54034)				
(if "H55518A" in trail-off wax, original first take of song, quickly withdrawn)	1960	$45.00	$90.00	$180.00
(if "L-1" in trail-off wax, hit version of song, horizontal lines on label)	1960	$7.50	$15.00	$30.00
(if "L-1" in trail-off wax, hit version of song, globe on label)	1960	$3.00	$6.00	$12.00
Mott the Hoople, "All The Young Dudes" / "One Of The Boys" (Columbia 45673)				
(if number in dead wax ends in "1" plus a letter, altered lyrics to avoid UK radio ban on brand names)	1972		$3.00	$6.00
(if number in dead wax ends in "2" or higher plus a letter, lyrics are "Marks and Sparks," as in LP)	1972	$2.00	$4.00	$8.00

45s	Year	VG	VG+	NM
Elvis Presley, "It's Now or Never" / "A Mess of Blues" (RCA Victor 47-7777)				
(if "It's Now or Never" is missing the piano part, stamper numbers L2WW-0100-3S or L2WW-0100-4S)	1960	$250.00	$500.00	$1,000.00
(if "It's Now or Never" has the overdubbed piano)	1960	$5.00	$10.00	$20.00
Elvis Presley, "He Touched Me" / "The Bosom of Abraham" (RCA Victor 74-0651)				
(if stamper number is AWKS-1277, "He Touched Me" incorrectly mastered at 35 rpm)	1972	$37.50	$75.00	$150.00
(if stamper number is APKS-1277, both songs play correctly)	1972	$2.00	$4.00	$8.00
Prince, "Crazay"				
(Label is blank white in an A&M sleeve. Three copies of this test pressing were made in Minneapolis by Prince as a cover to the newly released Jesse Johnson single, which is A&M 2878. The test pressing must have in the trail off vinyl: "AM-02904-AES2.")	1986	$125.00	$250.00	$500.00
Gerry Rafferty, "Baker Street" / "Big Change in the Weather" (United Artists XW1192)				
(if no "E" in the dead wax, mispress with full-length version of "Baker Street")	1978	$2.00	$4.00	$8.00
(with "E" in the dead wax, slightly sped-up version of "Baker Street," regular pressing)	1978		$2.00	$4.00
Silver Convention, "Fly Robin Fly" / "Chains of Love" (Midland International MB-10339)				
(if matrix number is 10339-A, "Fly Robin Fly" is over four minutes long)	1975		$3.00	$6.00
(if matrix number is 10339-Z, "Fly Robin Fly" is 3:05 long)	1975		$2.00	$4.00
Bruce Springsteen, "Cover Me" / "Jersey Girl" (Columbia 04561)				
(if dead wax contains a "-1" and a letter, spoken introduction to "Jersey Girl")	1984	$2.50	$5.00	$10.00
(if dead wax contains a "-2" or higher plus a letter, "Jersey Girl" has no introduction)	1984		$2.00	$4.00
The Surfaris, "Wipe Out" / "Surfer Joe" (Princess 50)				
(if "RE-1" in the dead wax, short versions of both songs)	1963	$37.50	$75.00	$150.00
(without "RE-1" in the dead wax, long versions of both songs)	1963	$100.00	$200.00	$400.00
Barry White, "Practice What You Preach" / "Come On" (A&M 31458 0924 7)				
(if label and dead wax numbers match)	1995		$3.00	
(if dead wax number is different, songs are actually "I Got A Thang 4 Ya" and "Sweet On U" by Lo-Key)	1995		$2.50	$5.00

Albums	Year	VG	VG+	NM
The Beatles, Yesterday and Today (Apple SST 2553)				
(if "Mfd. by Apple" on label, with triangle engraved in dead wax, all 11 tracks are true stereo)	1971	$6.25	$12.50	$25.00
(if "Mfd. by Apple" on label, no triangle in dead wax, some tracks in mono or rechanneled stereo)	1971	$5.00	$10.00	$20.00
David Bowie, The Man Who Sold The World (Mercury SR 61325)				
(if matrix numbers are stamped in the trail-off area) (no matrix numbers means it is a worthless bootleg)	1970	$10.00	$20.00	$40.00

Bob Dylan, The Freewheelin' Bob Dylan (Columbia CL 1986) (mono)

(if "Guaranteed High Fidelity" on label, plays "Let Me Die In My Footsteps," "Rocks and Gravel," "Uncle John Birch Blues," "Gamblin' Willie's Dead Man's Hand," Label does NOT list these songs.

Albums	Year	VG	VG+	NM
Stamper number in dead wax ends in "-1," followed by a letter)	1963	$5,000	$10,000	$15,000
Bob Dylan, Highway 61 Revisited (CS 9189) (stereo)				
(if matrix number on side 1 ends with "-1," followed by a letter, record contains alternate take of "From a Buick 6")	1965	$62.50	$125.00	$250.00
(if matrix number on side 1 ends with "-2" or higher, followed by a letter, record contains standard take of "From a Buick 6")	1965	$7.50	$15.00	$30.00
Bobby Hebb, Sunny (Philips PHM 200212)				
(if matrix number is "200-212" in dead wax, record is mono)	1966	$6.25	$12.50	$25.00
(if matrix number is "2/600-212" in dead wax, mono labeled but actually plays stereo)	1966	$6.25	$12.50	$25.00
(if label number is PHS 600212) (stereo)	1966	$7.50	$15.00	$30.00
The James Gang, James Gang Rides Again (ABC S-711)				
(if the dead wax does not contain "RE-1", the song "The Bomber" contains a snippet of Ravel's "Bolero")	1970	$6.25	$12.50	$25.00

45s	Year	VG	VG+	NM
(if the dead wax contains "RE-1," "Bolero" is not part of "The Bomber")	1970	$3.00	$6.00	$12.00
The James Gang, The Best of the James Gang Featuring Joe Walsh (ABCX-744)				
(if matrix number is ABCX-774-A, the song "The Bomber" contains a snippet of Ravel's "Bolero")	1973	$5.00	$10.00	$20.00
(if matrix number is ABCX-774-A-RE-1, "Bolero" is not part of "The Bomber")	1973	$3.00	$6.00	$12.00
Lost & Found, Everybody's Here (International Artists IA-3)				
(first pressing, no "Masterfonics" in dead wax)	1968	$25.00	$50.00	$100.00
(reissue, word "Masterfonics" in dead wax)	1979	$3.75	$7.50	$15.00
The Residents, George and James (Ralph RZ 8042)				
(first mix, eventually rejected and withdrawn, "Re-1" in the dead wax)	1984	$7.50	$15.00	$30.00
(second mix, "Re-5" in the dead wax)	1984	$2.50	$5.00	$10.00
Paul Revere and the Raiders, Paul Revere and the Raiders (Sande S-1001) (mono)				
(original version, with "Sande" and no mention of "Etiquette" in dead wax)	1963	$300.00	$600.00	$1,200.00
(reissue, with "Sande" and "Etiquette" in dead wax)	1979	$6.25	$12.50	$25.00
The Rolling Stones, Hot Rocks 1964-1971 (London 2PS 606/7) (2 LP's)				
(if side 4 has "11-5-71" in the dead wax, meaning this album contains alternate mixes of "Brown Sugar" and "Wild Horses")	1971	$250.00	$500.00	$1,000.00
(if stock pressing; all of side 1 and "Mother's Little Helper" and "19th Nervous Breakdown" on side 2 in mono, all other songs in stereo)	1971	$5.00	$10.00	$20.00
B.J. Thomas, Raindrops Keep Fallin' On My Head (Scepter SPS-580)				
(if dead wax number is "SPS-580-A-1B" on side A, and "SPS-580-B-1A" on side B, very muddy mix)	1970	$3.75	$7.50	$15.00
(if dead wax number is "SPS-580-A-1C" on side A, and "SPS-580-B-1C" on side B, remixed version)	1970	$3.00	$6.00	$12.00
Neil Young, Neil Young (Reprise RS 6317)				
(if brown and orange "Reprise W7" logo, no name on front cover, no "RE-1" in dead wax)	1968	$50.00	$100.00	$200.00
(if same as above, but four songs remixed - "RE-1" in dead wax)	1969	$15.00	$30.00	$60.00
(if brown "Reprise" label, Neil Young's name on front cover)	1970	$3.75	$7.50	$15.00

SUB POP SINGLES CLUB

History: The roster of Sub Pop Records, a Seattle-based label, has included many of the up-and-coming rock bands in the Rain City. It has also released 45s, albums, and CDs by the most popular alternative rock bands of the 1990s.

While the major record companies were phasing out their production of 7-inch 45s, Sub Pop used the format as part of a "Singles Club." By spending $40 for a yearly fee (or $25 for six months), you were guaranteed to receive at least one new Sub Pop 45 every month, a pressing by one of Seattle's new up-and-coming bands. And Sub Pop was guaranteed a steady cash flow in the form of music subscriptions.

4,000 copies of Love Battery's "Foot" were pressed; the B-side is a remake of Neil Young's "Mr. Soul." Courtesy Last Vestige Music Store, Albany, N.Y.

Just as Ken Griffey Jr.'s rookie trading card was #1 in the initial Upper Deck baseball card series, Sub Pop's first release in its singles club was "Love Buzz," a song by an up-and-coming grunge group called Nirvana. The first 1,000 copies of "Love Buzz" were hand-numbered on the picture sleeves, and contain the phrase, "Why don't you trade those guitars for shovels," written in the runout groove. These copies today, in near-mint condition and with the picture sleeve intact, can sell for as much as $150 apiece, although some collectors have paid as high as $1,000 for a copy. Not bad for a $40 yearly investment.

The first release in the Sub Pop Singles Club, Nirvana's "Love Buzz" was a remake of an old Shocking Blue song. From the Collection of Mike Bolton.

If Nirvana was the only release on Sub Pop worth collecting, the club would have cinched its place in history. But Sub Pop also released other legendary artists, both through its Singles Club and its commercially available retail outlets. Imagine a record company lineup featuring the Smashing Pumpkins, Hole, the Afghan Whigs, Fugazi, Mudhoney, Dinosaur Jr., the Velvet Monkeys, the Reverend Horton Heat, Sonic Youth, Urge Overkill, the Fastbacks, Shonen Knife, the John Spencer Blues Explosion, Ween, Combustible Edison, and Green River—with Cheap Trick and the Beach Boys, to top it all off.

Trivia

When a newly remastered version of the Beach Boys' *Pet Sounds* was released in 1996, Sub Pop licensed three tracks from the album, "I Just Wasn't Made For These Times," "Wouldn't It Be Nice," and "Here Today," and released them as a standard Sub Pop EP.

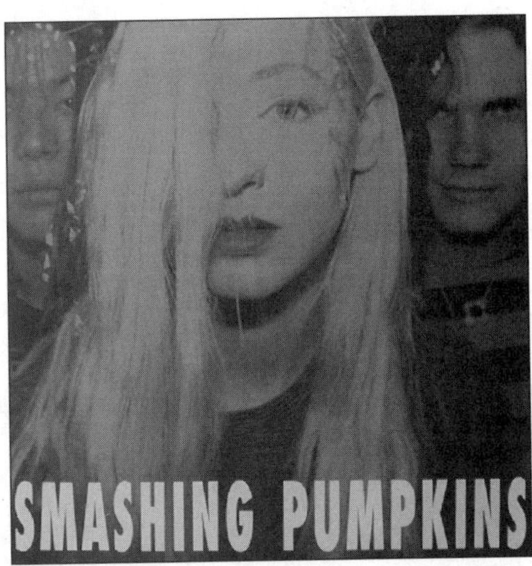

Before they achieved their own superstardom, the Smashing Pumpkins recorded this Sub Pop release, "Tristessa" backed with "La Dolly Vita." It is now the most collectible non-Nirvana release on the Sub Pop label. Courtesy Last Vestige Music Store, Albany, N.Y.

The first run of the Singles Club only lasted from 1988 to 1993. A second Sub Pop Singles Club began in 1997, and continues to this day.

What To Look For: Almost every release in the Sub Pop Singles Club has some variation from the standard stock copies of Sub Pop's releases. The first pressings were almost always on colored vinyl; the later pressings were pressed on black vinyl. Sub Pop limited its Singles Club run to anywhere from 10,000 pressings to as little as 1,500—and once they were gone, that was that. If you joined the club in 1992, you could not purchase 1991 club records from Sub Pop.

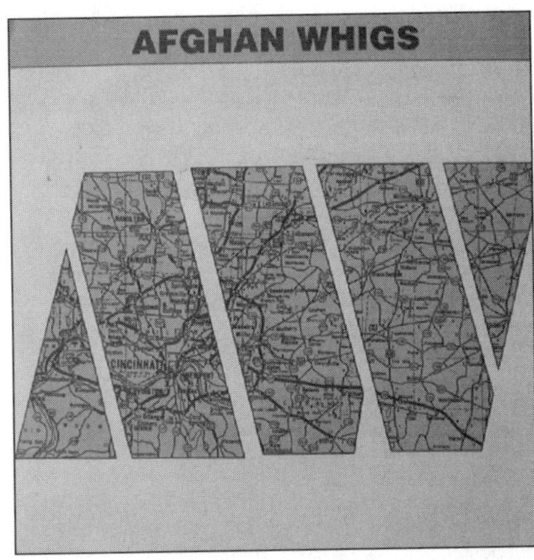

If you joined the club in April 1989, the first 45 you received may have been this pressing from the Afghan Whigs. Notice the map of Cincinnati inside the stylized *"AW"* on the front cover. Courtesy Last Vestige Music Store, Albany, N.Y.

Sub Pop's catalog numbers and "Singles Club" issue numbers may not match. Singles that were released as part of the Singles Club, and not as standard Sub Pop stock pressings, are listed separately in the discography below.

Known Counterfeits and Bootlegs: Because of their rarity, Sub Pop Singles Club releases have been heavily bootlegged and counterfeited. Some records were pressed on black vinyl when no legitimate black vinyl copy existed, or were pressed on a colored vinyl that was not part of the original print run. Some collectors believe that Nirvana's "Love Buzz" has been counterfeited so often, that bootleg copies outnumber original pressings.

One of the clues in identifying a Sub Pop Singles Club counterfeit is to look at the paper sleeve itself. Legitimate copies will have a perforated section where one can detach the application for the Sub Pop Singles Club. Counterfeits, because they are often printed with a laser printer, will not have this perforation feature.

Make sure to check the runout grooves of Sub Pop records for forgeries and counterfeit pressings. One collector found that although the counterfeit label may look identical to his legitimate Sub Pop pressing of Nirvana's "Molly's Lips"/"Candy" 45, authentic copies will have the following stamper number in the runout grooves: on the A-side, "L-37037 LATER SP-97-A Kdisc ch," and on the B-side, "L-37037X LATER SP-97-B Kdisc ch." The "disc ch" is handwritten, not printed. All the other alphanumeric listings are hand-printed, not machine stamped. Counterfeit copies have an "X" machine stamped. The SP-97A or SP-97B is also machine stamped. Thanks to Mike Bolton for that tip.

The first 1,000 copies of Nirvana's "Love Buzz" were hand-numbered in red magic marker. Counterfeits of the cover and the record do exist; check with an expert for authenticity. Photo Credit: From the Collection of Mike Bolton.

References: Neely, Tim, *Goldmine Price Guide to Alternative Records*, Krause Publications, Iola, Wisconsin, 1996.

Web pages: Sub Pop's current home page, along with information on how to join the new Singles Club: *http://www.subpop.com*; for more information on Nirvana's early Sub Pop recordings, visit this Web page: *http://www.nirvanadiscography.com*; the entire Sub Pop Singles Club discography, complete with release dates and colored vinyl issues, is available at this site: *http://members.tripod.com/cycletheory/singlesclub.html.*

45s	Year	VG	VG+	NM
Afghan Whigs, "I Am The Sticks" / "White Trash Party" (1,500 copies pressed, #6 in singles club)	1989	$5.00	$10.00	$20.00
(with picture sleeve, add:)	1989	$5.00	$10.00	$20.00
Babes in Toyland, "House" / "Arriba" (Sub Pop 66) (3,500 copies pressed, #19 in singles club)				
(if on gold vinyl, first 2,000 pressed)	1990	$10.00	$20.00	$40.00
(if on black vinyl, last 1,500 pressed)	1990	$2.50	$5.00	$10.00
(with picture sleeve, add:)	1990	$2.50	$5.00	$10.00
The Beach Boys, "I Just Want Made For These Times (Stereo Mix)" / "Wouldn't It Be Nice (vocals only)" / "Here Today" (stereo backing track) (Sub Pop 363)	1996		$2.50	$5.00
(with picture sleeve, add:)	1996		$2.50	$5.00
Beat Happening, "Red Head Walking" / "Secret Picnic Spot" (Sub Pop 74)				
(if on red vinyl, first 2,000 pressed)	1990	$2.00	$4.00	$8.00
(if on black vinyl)	1990		$2.00	$4.00
(with picture sleeve, add:)	1990		$2.00	$4.00
Beat Happening, "Nancy Sin" / "Left Behind" (Sub Pop 2000) (bonus release in singles club)				
(no picture sleeve)	1992	$3.00	$6.00	$12.00
Cheap Trick, "Baby Talk" / "Brontosaurus" (Sub Pop 393)	1997			$2.00
(with picture sleeve, add:)				$2.00
Combustible Edison, "Cry Me A River" / "Satan Says" (Sub Pop 236) (#59 in singles club)	1993	$2.50	$5.00	$10.00
(with picture sleeve, add:)	1993	$2.50	$5.00	$10.00
The Field, "Candy" / Nirvana, "Molly's Lips (Live)" (Sub Pop 97) (7,500 copies pressed, #27 in singles club)				
(if green vinyl, first 4,000 pressed)	1991	$8.75	$17.50	$35.00
(if black vinyl, last 3,500 pressed)	1991	$2.50	$5.00	$10.00
(with picture sleeve, add:)	1991	$2.50	$5.00	$10.00
Fugazi, "Joe #1" / "Break-in" / "Song #1" (Sub Pop 52) (2,000 copies pressed, #14 in singles club)				
(if on green vinyl, first 1,200 pressed)	1989	$18.75	$37.50	$75.00
(if on black vinyl, last 800 pressed)	1989	$6.25	$12.50	$25.00
(with picture sleeve, add:)	1989	$6.25	$12.50	$25.00
Hole, "Dicknail" / "Burn Black" (Sub Pop 93)				
(if on gray marble vinyl, first 3,500 pressed)	1991	$11.25	$22.50	$45.00
(if on black vinyl)	1991		$2.50	$5.00
(with picture sleeve, add:)	1991		$2.50	$5.00
L7, "Shove" / "Packin' A Rod" (Sub Pop 58) (3,000 copies pressed, #15 in singles club)				
(if on green vinyl, first 1,200 pressed)	1990	$5.00	$10.00	$20.00
(if on black vinyl, last 1,800 pressed)	1990	$2.50	$5.00	$10.00
(with picture sleeve, add:)	1990	$2.50	$5.00	$10.00
Mudhoney, "Touch Me I'm Sick" / "Sweet Young Thing" (Sub Pop 18)				
(if on brown vinyl, first 800 pressed)	1988	$22.50	$45.00	$90.00
(if on purple, red, yellow, blue vinyl, accidentally pressed but legit copies) 1988		$50.00	$100.00	$200.00
(if on black vinyl, toilet label)	1988	$25.00	$50.00	$100.00
(if on black vinyl, standard label)	1988		$3.75	$7.50
(with picture sleeve, add:)	1988		$3.75	$7.50
Nirvana, "Love Buzz" / "Big Cheese" (Sub Pop 23) (1,000 copies pressed, hand numbered, #1 in singles club)	1988	$18.75	$37.50	$75.00
(with picture sleeve, add:)	1988	$18.75	$37.50	$75.00
Nirvana, "Sliver" / "Dive" (Sub Pop 73)				
(if blue vinyl, first 3,000 copies)	1990	$10.00	$20.00	$40.00
(if clear pink-lavender vinyl)	1990	$12.50	$25.00	$50.00
(if black vinyl, with no California address on label)	1990	$2.50	$5.00	$10.00
(if yellow vinyl, California address on label)	1990		$3.50	$7.00
(if black vinyl, California address on label)	1990			$3.00
(with fold-over picture sleeve, add:)	1990	$2.50	$5.00	$10.00
(with standard picture sleeve, add:)	1990			$3.00
S.F. Seals, "Nowherica" / "Being Cheated" (2,000 copies pressed, all on clear pink vinyl, #55 in singles club)	1993		$2.50	$5.00
(with picture sleeve, add:)	1993		$2.50	$5.00
Smashing Pumpkins, "Tristessa" / "La Dolly Vita" (Sub Pop 90)				
(if on pink vinyl)	1991	$13.75	$27.50	$55.00
(if on black vinyl)	1991		$2.50	$5.00
(with picture sleeve, add:)	1991		$2.50	$5.00
Soundgarden, "Hunted Down" / "Nothing To Say" (Sub Pop 12a) (500 copies pressed) (blue vinyl)	1987	$16.25	$32.50	$65.00
(with blue company sleeve, add:)	1987	$16.25	$32.50	$65.00
Tsunami, "Left Behind" / Velocity Girl, "Warm" / "Crawl" (Sub Pop 137) (4,000 copies pressed, #39 in singles club)				
(all copies on strawberry red vinyl)	1992	$3.00	$6.25	$12.50
(with picture sleeve, add:)	1992	$3.00	$6.25	$12.50
Velocity Girl, "Crazy Town" / "Creepy" (Sub Pop 179)				
(if on green vinyl, 2,000 pressed)	1992	$5.00	$10.00	$20.00
(if on black vinyl)	1992		$2.50	$5.00
(with picture sleeve, add:)	1992		$2.50	$5.00
The Velvet Monkeys, "Rock the Nation" / "Why Don't We Do It In The Road?" (Sub Pop 102) (7,000 copies pressed, #28 in singles club)				
(if on clear vinyl, first 4,000 pressed)	1991	$5.00	$10.00	$20.00
(if on black vinyl, last 3,000 pressed)	1991		$2.50	$5.00
(with picture sleeve, add:)	1991		$2.50	$5.00
Ween, "Skycruiser" / "Cruise Control" (Sub Pop 214) (2,000 copies pressed, all on clear pink vinyl, #57 in singles club)	1993	$2.50	$5.00	$10.00
(with picture sleeve, add:)	1993	$2.50	$5.00	$10.00

EPs / LPs	Year	VG	VG+	NM
Afghan Whigs, Up In It (Sub Pop 60)				
(first pressings on orange vinyl)	1990	$6.25	$12.50	$25.00
(second pressings on black vinyl)	1990	$2.50	$5.00	$10.00
Afghan Whigs, Gentlemen (Sub Pop 238)	1993	$2.50	$5.00	$10.00
Beat Happening, Dreamy (Sub Pop 98)	1991	$2.50	$5.00	$10.00
Combustible Edison, I, Swinger (Sub Pop 244)	1994	$2.50	$5.00	$10.00
Green River, Dry As A Bone (Sub Pop 11) (EP)				
(with yellow inserts inside)	1987	$12.50	$25.00	$50.00
(with pink inserts inside)	1987	$8.75	$17.50	$35.00
Green River, Rehab Doll (Sub Pop 15) (EP)				
(if on green vinyl, 1,000 pressed)	1988	$8.75	$17.50	$35.00
(if on black vinyl)	1988	$6.25	$12.50	$25.00
L7, Smell The Magic (Sub Pop 79) (EP)				
(first pressings on purple vinyl)	1990	$10.00	$20.00	$40.00
(second pressings on black vinyl)	1990	$2.00	$5.00	$10.00
Mudhoney, Superfuzz Bigmuff (Sub Pop 21) (EP)				
(with poster included)	1988	$7.50	$15.00	$30.00
(without poster)	1988	$5.00	$10.00	$20.00
Mudhoney, Mudhoney (Sub Pop 44)				
(first 3,000 have gatefold sleeve and poster)	1989	$7.50	$15.00	$30.00
(later pressings, without gatefold sleeve or poster)	1989	$5.00	$10.00	$20.00
Nirvana, Bleach (Sub Pop 34)				
(if on white vinyl, first 1,000 copies pressed)	1989	$12.50	$25.00	$50.00
(if on red vinyl)	1989	$5.00	$10.00	$20.00
(with foldout poster)	1989	$7.50	$15.00	$30.00
Soundgarden, Screaming Life (Sub Pop 12) (EP)				
(if on orange vinyl, first 500 pressings)	1987	$37.50	$75.00	$150.00
(later pressings on black vinyl)	1987	$10.00	$20.00	$40.00
(subsequent pressings on other colors)	1987	$5.00	$10.00	$20.00

SUN RECORDS

History: Saying that the only thing Sun Records ever brought to rock 'n' roll was Elvis Presley, is equivalent to erroneously stating the New York Yankees are only known for Babe Ruth. During the 1950s, Sun Records and its creator, Sam Phillips, recorded seminal blues records, nurtured a new musical format called "rockabilly," and started the careers of rock 'n' roll legends.

Sam Phillips was born in 1923, the youngest of eight children born to an Alabama tenant farmer. After working in radio stations throughout Alabama and Tennessee, Phillips set up his own recording studio at 706 Union Avenue, Memphis, Tennessee, in 1950. His early recordings were sessions for local blues artists, such as B.B. King and Howlin' Wolf, whose recordings Phillips would then lease to national record labels like Chess, Modern and RPM.

During one of these sessions, Phillips produced "Rocket 88" by Ike Turner and his Kings of Rhythm. Chess Records licensed the track and credited it to "Jackie Brenston and his Delta Cats" (Brenston was a member of Turner's band, and sang lead on the track). The song, cited by many experts as the first true "rock and roll record," hit #1 on the R&B charts and gave Phillips his first national exposure.

Recordings by the Prisonaires, one of Sun Records' earliest groups, are extremely difficult to find today. Courtesy Good Rockin' Tonight/Collectors Universe.

Unfortunately, many of the blues artists that recorded for Sun eventually went north and recorded with Chess and the other Chicago labels, effectively eliminating the Memphis Recording Service middleman. Phillips eventually fought back by creating his own record label, Sun. Sun's first releases were by blues singers and disc jockeys around the Memphis area, including saxophonist Johnny London, disc jockey Rufus Thomas, and songwriter Little Junior Parker. Sun even had its own vocal group, the Prisonaires, a quintet of convicts from Tennessee State Penitentiary.

During this time, Phillips had an open-door policy at Sun; he would record anybody and everybody, all the while looking for someone who could be Sun's next big superstar—somebody who could sing the blues like he had lived it all his life, someone who could master country and western bop, somebody who could bring Sun Records the same national prominence it once had in the "Rocket 88" days.

In 1954, that person walked into the Memphis Recording Service, hoping to make an acetate recording for his mother. The legend of Elvis Presley was born that day.

Even though Phillips nurtured Presley's early talent and provided him with his top studio musicians Scotty Moore and Bill Black, Phillips continued to record other artists, experimenting with a new sound called "rockabilly"—a mixture of blues, bluegrass, and western bop, with a "slapback" echo and roadhouse energy. While Elvis Presley recorded his seminal Sun singles and performed with Scotty Moore and Bill Black on tour, other Sun recording artists, like Charlie Feathers, Billy Lee Riley, and Sonny Burgess, spread the gospel of rockabilly through every roadhouse and dance hall in the South.

Elvis Presley's "Milkcow Blues Boogie," with its false start—the band starts slow, but Elvis stops the session, and recreates the song as a rockabilly classic. Courtesy Good Rockin' Tonight/Collectors Universe.

Phillips eventually sold Presley's contract to RCA Victor for $35,000, which he invested into his Sun studio and into the new Holiday Inn motel organization. For an independent record label, losing its biggest singer might have meant a death knell for the label. But there was something new under the Sun, a stable of artists that would bring the label Top 10 hits of its own.

Jerry Lee Lewis recorded dozens of rock and country hits with Sun; "Whole Lot of Shakin' *Goin' On*" was his first. Courtesy Good Rockin' Tonight/Collectors Universe.

Carl Perkins' version of "Blue Suede Shoes" sold millions of copies for Sun—outselling a competing version of "Blue Suede Shoes" by Elvis Presley on his new RCA label.

Carl Perkins, who played in local clubs and bars around Memphis, brought Sun Records its first national Top 5 rock 'n' roll hit, "Blue Suede Shoes." Sun also had a string of hits from a flamboyant piano-pounder from Louisiana, Jerry Lee Lewis. Another Sun performer, Johnny Cash, brought a darker side to rockabilly, with songs like "Cry! Cry! Cry!," "Ballad of a Teenage Queen," and "I Walk The Line." A group from Texas called the Teen Kings had some minor hits on Sun, but it was the first musical exposure for the Teen Kings' singer and lead guitarist, Roy Orbison.

Trivia

In 1977, Sun International released an album of Elvis Presley material, including tapes of Presley talking to Sam Phillips during a recording session, as well as interviews Presley did with some radio stations. RCA sued and successfully removed this record from the market, creating yet another scarce Elvis Sun recording.

The glory era of Sun ended in the early 1960s. Although the label's hits at that time were few and far between (Cash and Perkins signed with Columbia, Orbison joined the Monument label, and Lewis' career never survived the negative publicity of his incestuous marriage), the label found success across the Atlantic, as the Beatles added two of Carl Perkins' hits, "Honey Don't" and "Matchbox," to their growing musical repertoire.

In 1969, Sam Phillips sold Sun Records to Shelby Singleton, and the company became a reissue label, selling re-releases of the classic 1950s hits. The legendary Sun Studio in Memphis is now a museum, and equipment from the Elvis Presley recording sessions is now on permanent display at the Rock and Roll Hall of Fame in Cleveland, Ohio.

What To Look For: Where to start? Sun has a little bit of everything for collectors—early blues legends, the evolution of rockabilly, the Million Dollar Quartet (the solo recordings of Presley, Cash, Perkins. and Lewis).

Sun 45s with a catalog number lower than 222 will have "push marks" on the label, three circular indentations around the spindle hole, caused when the record label was pressed onto the vinyl. Counterfeits will not have push marks. Because Sun was an independent record label and had its records pressed at other factories, there are variations in how the labels were attached to the vinyl. And although "push marks" make the record a legitimate copy, the absence of "push marks" does not necessarily mean the record is not an original. If you're unsure about the legitimacy of your Sun 45, don't be afraid to consult an expert, especially one versed in Elvis Presley recordings.

In this enhanced photo, the "push marks"—three circular indentations in the label—were made by the pressing plant Sun Records used. Four of Elvis Presley's 45s contain these "push marks," the last one ("Mystery Train") does not.

All five of Elvis Presley's Sun 45s have been replicated in one form or another. Many will say "Reproduction" in the dead wax. Others will be pressed in colored vinyl; legitimate Presley 78s were pressed only on black vinyl. Presley never had a picture sleeve or a four-song EP during his Sun career; any that exist are counterfeits.

There is a Sun 45, catalog number 1129, with the songs "That's All Right" and "Blue Moon of Kentucky," with no artist listed. This record also appears under Sun catalog number 1136 in 1978, as part of a four-song EP with "Misty" and "D.O.A." These are **not** rare Elvis recordings; the tracks are actually by singer Jimmy Ellis. Ellis, who also recorded under the name Orion, was capable of sounding almost like the King—enough to fool some people into thinking Presley was recording under a pseudonym. In the late 1970s, Ellis sang some duets with Jerry Lee Lewis, which some people mistook as Presley-Lewis duets from the 1950. How confusing did it get? In 1978, Ellis recorded a song on the Boblo label, called "I'm Not Trying To Be Like Elvis."

Elvis records may be tough to find, but regional hits by the Prisonaires and blues harmonica player Hot Shot Love are even tougher to uncover. Rockabilly legend Charlie Feathers also recorded for Sun, and his sides are among the most difficult titles to find for Feathers and rockabilly collectors.

One of Charlie Feathers' Sun releases. Courtesy Good Rockin' Tonight/Collectors Universe.

During Sun's hitmaking days, the label released only 12 albums, concentrating instead on its singles hits. The Sun albums included tracks from Johnny Cash, Carl Perkins, Roy Orbison, and Jerry Lee Lewis, as well as one "Best of Sun" album. After 1969, when Phillips sold the label to Shelby Singleton, much of the Sun catalog was reissued, especially on the Sun International label. There is a distinct redesign of the Sun label artwork, and the following was added to the label's bottom perimeter: "Sun International Corp.—A Division of the Shelby Singleton Corp.—Nashville, U.S.A." Many of the albums in the Sun International 1000 series are available both in gold vinyl and in black vinyl.

For a couple of years, Sun also had a sister label, Phillips International. Artists on that label included Charlie Rich and Bill Justis.

References: Kennedy, Rick; McNutt, Randy, *Little Labels - Big Sound*, Indiana University Press, Bloomington, Indiana, 1999; Morrison, Craig, *Go Cat Go: Rockabilly Music and Its Makers*, University of Illinois Press, Chicago, Ill., 1998.

Web pages: Mike Callahan's Both Sides Now: Sun Label Discography, *http://www.bsnpubs.com/suna.html*; the official Sun Records homepage, *http://www.sunrecords.com*; take a tour of the original Sun Studios, *http://www.sunstudio.com*.

Trivia

There is a design change for Sun International 45s that can help you in determining whether the 45 you purchased is an original or a repressing. Although both 45 labels have the music scale perimeter and the letters "SUN" against a sunbeam background, Sun International pressings have two-tone "bullseyes" on the lower half of the label, and the numbering system begins with "S1."

An example of a Shelby Singleton-owned Sun International label, with the Gentrys covering a Neil Young hit.

45s	Year	VG	VG+	NM
Johnny Cash, "Folsom Prison Blues" / "So Doggone Lonesome" (Sun 232)	1956	$7.50	$15.00	$30.00
Johnny Cash, "I Walk The Line" / "Get Rhythm" (Sun 241)	1956	$10.00	$20.00	$40.00
Johnny Cash, "Ballad of a Teenage Queen" / "Big River" (Sun 283)	1958	$6.25	$12.50	$25.00
Johnny Cash, "Guess Things Happen That Way" / "Come In Stranger" (Sun 295)	1958	$6.25	$12.50	$25.00
(with picture sleeve, add:)	1958	$10.00	$20.00	$40.00
Johnny Cash, "Mean Eyed Cat" / "Port of Lonely Hearts" (Sun 347)	1960	$5.00	$10.00	$20.00
Jimmy Ellis, "That's All Right" / "Blue Moon of Kentucky" (Sun 1129)				
(with no singer credit, pressed so that people would mistake the record as Elvis Presley's recording)	1973		$2.50	$5.00
(with Jimmy Ellis credited)	1973		$2.00	$4.00
Jimmy Ellis, "D.O.A." / "Misty" / "That's All Right" / "Blue Moon of Kentucky" (Sun 1136)	1977		$2.00	$4.00
Charlie Feathers, "Defrost Your Heart" / "Wedding Gown of White" (Sun 231)	1956	$200.00	$400.00	$600.00
Charlie Feathers, "Peeping Eyes" / "I've Been Deceived" (Sun 503)	1956	$200.00	$400.00	$600.00
Jerry Lee Lewis, "Crazy Arms" / "End of the Road" (Sun 259)				
(as "Jerry Lee Lewis")	1957	$25.00	$50.00	$100.00
(as "Jerry Lee Lewis and his Pumping Piano")	1957	$12.50	$25.00	$50.00
Jerry Lee Lewis, "Whole Lot of Shakin' Goin' On" / "It'll Be Me" (Sun 267)	1957	$10.00	$20.00	$40.00
Jerry Lee Lewis, "Great Balls of Fire" / "You Win Again" (Sun 281)	1957	$10.00	$20.00	$40.00
(with picture sleeve, add:)	1957	$20.00	$40.00	$80.00
Jerry Lee Lewis, "What'd I Say" / "Livin' Lovin' Wreck" (Sun 356)	1961	$5.00	$10.00	$20.00
Jerry Lee Lewis, "Save The Last Dance For Me" / "Am I To Be The One" (Sun 1139)	1978		$2.00	$4.00

45s	Year	VG	VG+	NM
(uncredited "duet" partner is Jimmy "Orion" Ellis, an attempt to fool purchasers into thinking Lewis was duetting with Elvis Presley on a "lost" track)				
Hot Shot Love, "Wolf Call Boogie" / "Harmonica Jam" (Sun 196)	1954	$1,000	$2,000	$4,000
Roy Orbison, "Ooby Dooby" / "Go! Go! Go!" (Sun 242)	1956	$25.00	$50.00	$100.00
Roy Orbison, "Rockhouse" / "You're My Baby" (Sun 251)	1956	$15.00	$30.00	$60.00
Roy Orbison, "Devil Doll" / "Sweet And Easy To Love" (Sun 265)	1957	$20.00	$40.00	$80.00
Roy Orbison, "Chicken Hearted" / "Like Love" (Sun 284)	1958	$12.50	$25.00	$50.00
Roy Orbison, "Devil Doll" / "Sweet And Easy To Love" (Sun 353)	1960	$62.50	$125.00	$250.00
Carl Perkins, "Gone, Gone, Gone" / "Let The Jukebox Keep On Playing" (Sun 224)	1955	$25.00	$50.00	$100.00
Carl Perkins, "Blue Suede Shoes" / "Honey Don't" (Sun 234)	1956	$15.00	$30.00	$60.00
Carl Perkins, "Boppin' The Blues" / "All Mama's Children" (Sun 243)	1956	$10.00	$20.00	$40.00
Carl Perkins, "Matchbox" / "Your True Love" (Sun 261)	1957	$7.50	$15.00	$30.00
Carl Perkins, "Glad All Over" / "Lend Me Your Comb" (Sun 287)	1958	$7.50	$15.00	$30.00
Elvis Presley, "That's All Right" / "Blue Moon of Kentucky" (Sun 209)	1954	$2.000	$3,000	$4,000
Elvis Presley, "Good Rockin' Tonight" / "I Don't Care if The Sun Don't Shine" (Sun 210)	1954	$1,000	$2,000	$3,000
Elvis Presley, "Milkcow Blues Boogie" / "You're A Heartbreaker" (Sun 215)	1955	$2,000	$3,000	$4,000
Elvis Presley, "Baby Let's Play House" / "I 'm Left, You're Right, She's Gone" (Sun 217)	1955	$1,000	$2,000	$3,000
Elvis Presley, "I Forgot To Remember To Forget" / "Mystery Train" (Sun 223)	1955	$500.00	$1,000.00	$2,000.00
The Prisonaires, "Just Walking In The Rain" / "Baby Please" (Sun 186)				
(on red vinyl)	1953	$2,500	$3,750	$5,000
(on black vinyl)	1953	$75.00	$150.00	$300.00
The Prisonaires, "Softly and Tenderly" / "My God Is Real" (Sun 189)	1953	$175.00	$350.00	$700.00
The Prisonaires, "A Prisoner's Prayer" / "I Know" (Sun 191)	1953	$125.00	$250.00	$500.00
The Prisonaires, "There Is Love In You" / "What'll You Do Next" (Sun 207)	1954	$5,000	$8,500	$12,000
Rufus Thomas, "Bear Cat" / "Walking In The Rain" (Sun 181)				
(if A-side is subtitled "The Answer to Hound Dog")	1953	$87.50	$175.00	$350.00
(without subtitle)	1953	$50.00	$100.00	$200.00
Rufus Thomas, "Tiger Man (King of the Jungle)" / "Save Your Money" (Sun 188)	1953	$125.00	$250.00	$500.00

78s	Year	VG	VG+	NM
Johnny Cash, "I Walk The Line" / "Get Rhythm" (Sun 241)	1956	$6.25	$12.50	$25.00
Jerry Lee Lewis, "Whole Lot of Shakin' Goin' On" / "It'll Be Me" (Sun 267)	1957	$50.00	$100.00	$200.00
Jerry Lee Lewis, "Great Balls of Fire" / "You Win Again" (Sun 281)	1957	$50.00	$100.00	$200.00
Hot Shot Love, "Wolf Call Boogie" / "Harmonica Jam" (Sun 196)	1954	$150.00	$300.00	$600.00
Roy Orbison, "Ooby Dooby" / "Go! Go! Go!" (Sun 242)	1956	$50.00	$100.00	$200.00
Elvis Presley, "That's All Right" / "Blue Moon of Kentucky" (Sun 209)	1954	$750.00	$1,500.00	$3,000.00
Elvis Presley, "Good Rockin' Tonight" / "I Don't Care if The Sun Don't Shine" (Sun 210)	1954	$450.00	$900.00	$1,800.00
Elvis Presley, "Milkcow Blues Boogie" / "You're A Heartbreaker" (Sun 215)	1955	$625.00	$1,250.00	$2,500.00
Elvis Presley, "Baby Let's Play House" / "I 'm Left, You're Right, She's Gone" (Sun 217)	1955	$375.00	$750.00	$1,500.00
Elvis Presley, "I Forgot To Remember To Forget" / "Mystery Train" (Sun 223)	1955	$250.00	$500.00	$1,000.00
The Prisonaires, "Just Walking In The Rain" / "Baby Please" (Sun 186)	1953	$25.00	$50.00	$100.00
The Prisonaires, "Softly and Tenderly" / "My God Is Real" (Sun 189)	1953	$125.00	$250.00	$500.00
Rufus Thomas, "Bear Cat" / "Walking In The Rain" (Sun 181)	1953	$12.50	$25.00	$50.00

LPs	Year	VG	VG+	NM
Johnny Cash, Johnny Cash With His Hot And Blue Guitar (Sun SLP-1220) (mono)	1956	$25.00	$50.00	$100.00
Johnny Cash, The Songs That Made Him (Sun SLP-1235) (mono)	1958	$25.00	$50.00	$100.00

LPs	Year	VG	VG+	NM
Johnny Cash, Johnny Cash Sings Hank Williams (Sun SLP-1245) (mono)	1960	$12.50	$25.00	$50.00
Johnny Cash, Johnny Cash - The Legend (Sun LP-118) (2 LPs) (electronically rechanneled stereo)	1970	$5.00	$10.00	$20.00
Jerry Lee Lewis, Jerry Lee Lewis (Sun SLP-1230) (mono)	1958	$50.00	$100.00	$200.00
Jerry Lee Lewis, Jerry Lee's Greatest (Sun SLP-1265) (mono)	1961	$62.50	$125.00	$250.00
(if white label promo)	1961	$200.00	$400.00	$800.00
Roy Orbison, Roy Orbison at the Rockhouse (Sun SLP-1260) (mono)	1961	$150.00	$300.00	$600.00
Roy Orbison, The Original Sun Sound of Roy Orbison (Sun 113)	1969	$3.00	$6.00	$12.00
Carl Perkins, The Dance Album Of Carl Perkins (Sun SLP-1225) (mono)	1957	$300.00	$600.00	$1,200.00
Carl Perkins, Teen Beat - The Best of Carl Perkins (Sun LP-1225) (mono) (same as above, with new title and cover)	1961	$125.00	$250.00	$500.00
Carl Perkins, Original Golden Hits (Sun LP-111)	1969	$3.00	$6.00	$12.00
Elvis Presley, The Sun Years – Interviews and Memories (Sun International 1001)	1977	$6.25	$12.50	$25.00

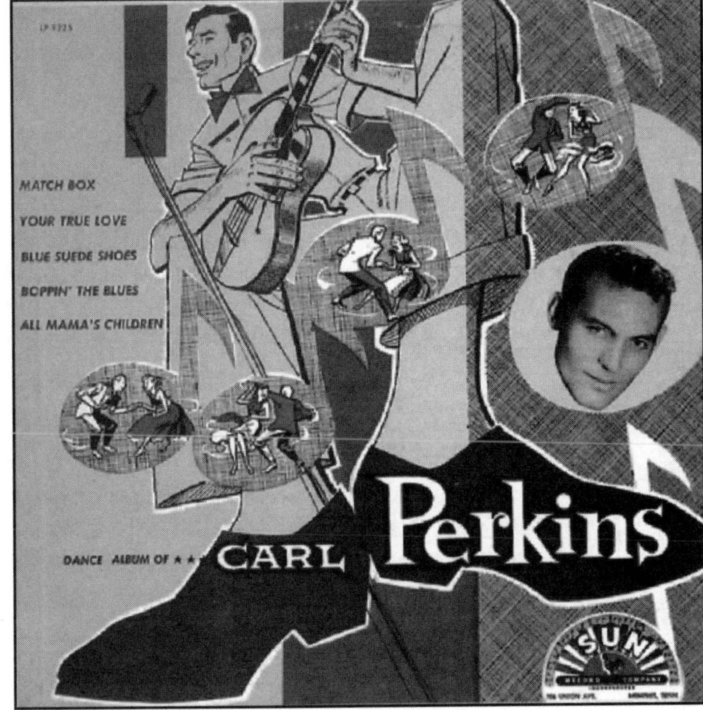

The rarest LP Sun produced was The Dance Album of Carl Perkins. Four years later, it was reissued under the title Teen Beat—The Dance Album of Carl Perkins. Both records have the same catalog number, but the one not mentioning "Teen Beat" is the rarer record. Courtesy Good Rockin' Tonight/Collectors Universe.

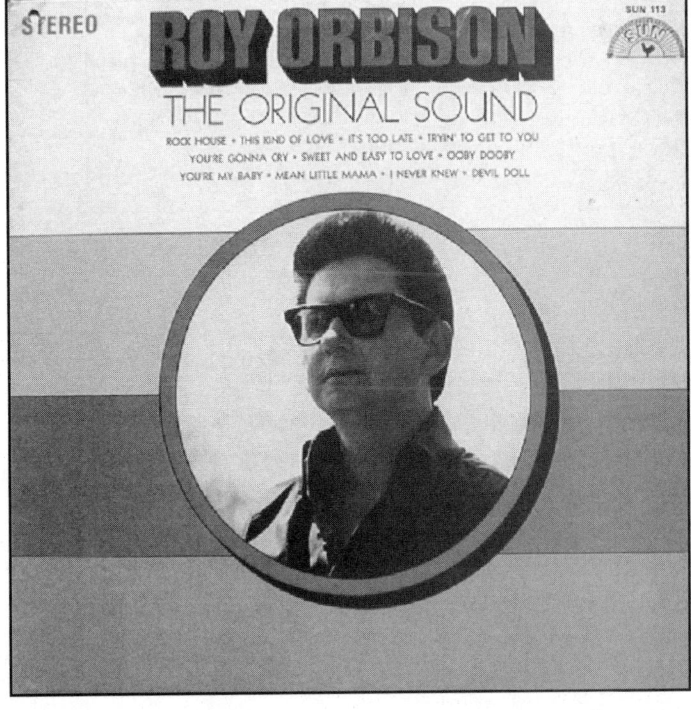

"The Original Sun Sound" was a series of reissue LPs in the early 1970s. Their value is approximately the same, barely more than $10 in near-mint condition.

SURF MUSIC

Trivia

The Surfaris' "Wipe Out" was actually planned as the B-side for the song "Surfer Joe." In fact, "Wipe Out" was virtually the instrumental track for "Surfer Joe." Eventually, the song went from a hot local track on an independent label, to a Top 10 national track for Dot Records.

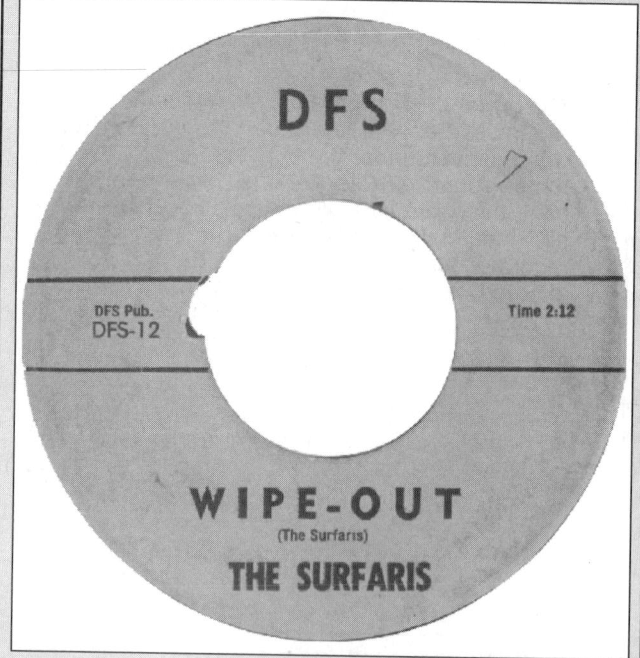

This is the original "DFS" label for the Surfaris' hit "Wipe Out." Thousands of amateur drummers have replicated this song's famous drum solo. Courtesy Good Rockin' Tonight/Collectors Universe.

History: Surf music, both vocal and instrumental, began in the late 1950s. Instrumental surf music has a twangy guitar or bass guitar lead, and is best represented by artists such as Duane Eddy, Dick Dale and the Del-Tones, and the Ventures. Song titles may have a reference to surfing or beach sports, such as "Pipeline" by the Chantay's and "Wipe Out" by the Surfaris. But the main component of instrumental surf music is that it provides the listener with the sensation and energy of hanging ten on their boards, shooting the curl, and trying not to wipe out. Surfing was the original "extreme sport," and the surf instrumental music reflected the energy of that sport.

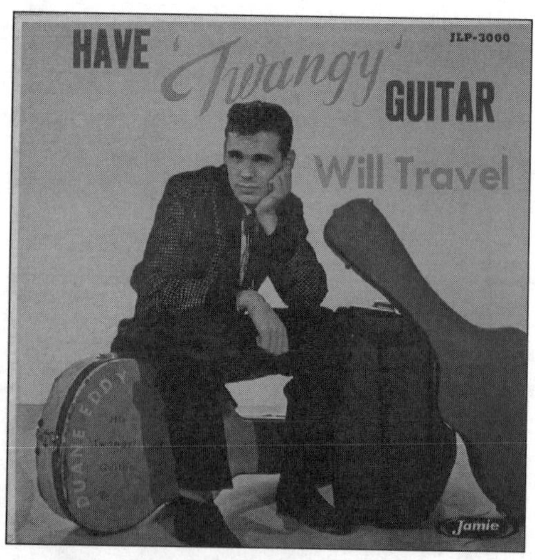

By playing his bass the way most people would play an acoustic guitar, Duane Eddy revolutionized rock instrumental music—and provided early inspirations for surf bands everywhere. Courtesy Last Vestige Music Store, Albany, N.Y.

Vocal surf music added doo-wop lyrics about cars, girls, the beach, surfing, swimming—in short, having a good time at the Southern California shorelines. The Beach Boys and Jan & Dean crafted car-song masterpieces ("Little Deuce Coupe," "409," "Little Old Lady from Pasadena"), as well as beach songs ("Surfin' U.S.A." and "Surf City"), and introspective pop songs about teen life ("In My Room," "A Surfer's Dream"). Other vocal surf groups include the Hondells ("Little Honda"), Ronny and the Daytonas ("GTO"), the Rip Chords ("Hey Little Cobra"), and the Sunrays ("Andrea").

The original pressing of the Beach Boys' first hit, "Surfin'," on the tiny "X" label. Since there was another "X" record company in existence, this title was also released on "Candix" Records. Courtesy Good Rockin' Tonight / Collectors Universe.

Surf music has made a small comeback in recent years, especially in movies and on television. Biopics of Jan and Dean and of the Beach Boys were ratings-winners when they aired on TV, the Ventures' theme from "Hawaii Five-O" became their most recognized hit since "Walk—Don't Run," and Dick Dale's instrumental "Miserlou" was prominently featured in the film "Pulp Fiction."

One of Dick Dale's earliest pressings, on his own custom "Del-Tone" label, before he joined Capitol Records. From the Collection of Val Shively.

Surf music should not be confused with "Beach" music, the predominant dance music of the Carolinas. Beach music, like Northern Soul in England, involves danceable songs by both popular and unknown artists of the 1960s. Some pop/soul/rock groups whose music also can be classified as "beach music" include Spanky and Our Gang, Jay and the Techniques, and General Johnson.

What To Look For: Surf music has been reissued on countless CDs and greatest hits packages. Finding 45s is not hard, but finding the accompanying picture sleeves in near-mint condition is extremely tough.

The Ventures have released more albums than any instrumental group in the rock era, and have new titles available even today. Their earliest albums, which were recorded for Dolton Records, are very collectible. Make sure if you do purchase a Ventures album that contains "Walk—Don't Run," that it contains the original version, as the group re-recorded the track in 1964 for use in a motion picture of the same name.

Trivia

Jan & Dean and the Beach Boys were two separate groups, but their members did work together on certain projects. Jan Berry and Brian Wilson co-wrote Jan & Dean's biggest hit, "Surf City." And Jan & Dean can be heard in the background on the Beach Boys' hit "Barbara Ann."

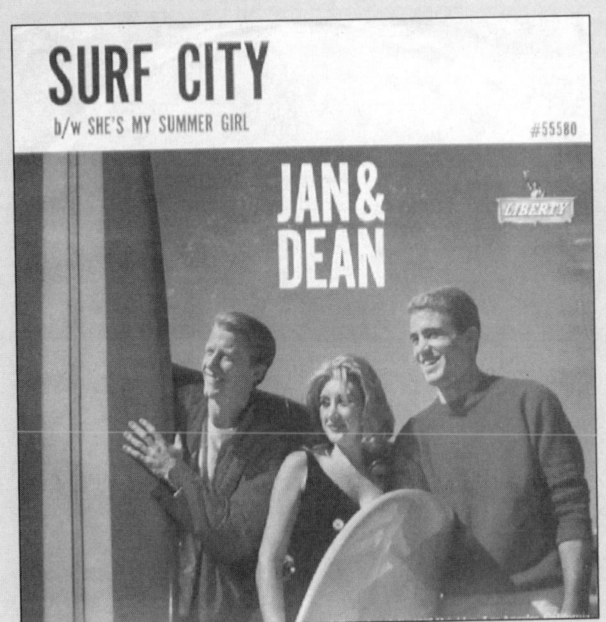

The picture sleeve for the Jan Berry/Brian Wilson collaboration of "Surf City." From the Collection of Val Shively.

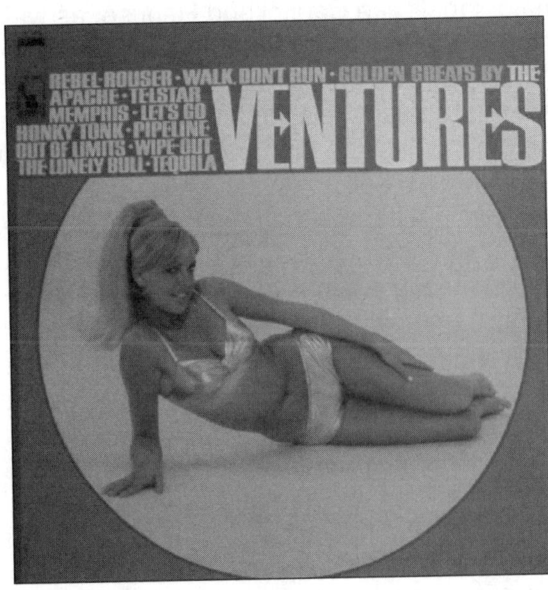

The Ventures covered many different surf classics, including some of their own hits, for this *Golden Greats* LP.

Trivia

Duane Eddy's "twangy" sound came from his work with producer Lee Hazlewood. It was Hazlewood who suggested that Eddy play notes on the lower strings of the electric guitar, then added reverb to the final mix, giving America the "twangy" sound.

Duane Eddy's first recording, "Moovin' 'n' Groovin'," for the Jamie label. Lee Hazlewood's partner in this production, Lester Sill, would later become the "Les" of Philles Records. From the Collection of Val Shively.

The lion's share of the Beach Boys' catalog exists on major labels like Capitol and Reprise, as well as their own custom label Brother. A series of recordings they made before signing with Capitol exist and have been regularly reissued by low-budget labels (these albums include the Beach Boys' first recording, "Surfin'," as well as an a capella version of "Surfer Girl"). Although the original 45 pressings of these tracks on the "X" and Candix labels are rare and collectible, pressings on other labels do not have this same collectible value.

References: Blair, John, T*he Illustrated Discography of Surf Music 1961-1965* (3d Ed.), Popular Culture, Ann Arbor, Mich., 1995; Dalley, Robert J., *Surfin' Guitars: Instrumental Surf Bands of the Sixties* (2d Ed.), Popular Culture, Ann Arbor, Mich., 1996.

Web pages: The Tsunami Soul Surf Music Page, with many links to other surf music homepages: *http://www.oberlin.edu/~serials/Surf.html*; the official homepage for Dick Dale and the Del-Tones: *http://www.dickdale.com*; an unofficial site for Beach Boys fans, with links to other pages: *http://www.beachboys.com*; Usenet newsgroups: *rec.music.artists.beach-boys, alt.music.beach-boys.*

45s	Year	VG	VG+	NM
The Beach Boys, "Surfin'" / "Luau"				
(if on X 301, first pressing)	1961	$250.00	$500.00	$1,000.00
(if on Candix 301, no mention of Era Records on the label)	1961	$75.00	$150.00	$300.00
(if on Candix 301, "Distributed by Era Records Sales, Inc." on label)	1961	$50.00	$100.00	$200.00
(if on Candix 331)	1962	$50.00	$100.00	$200.00
The Beach Boys, "Surfin' Safari" / "409"				
(Capitol 4777)	1962	$6.25	$12.50	$25.00
(with picture sleeve, add:)	1962	$50.00	$100.00	$200.00
The Beach Boys, "Surfin' U.S.A." / "Shut Down" (Capitol 4932)				
(first version lists Brian Wilson as writer, second version lists Chuck Berry as writer, value is equal)	1963	$6.25	$12.50	$25.00
The Beach Boys, "Barbara Ann" / "Girl Don't Tell Me")				
(Capitol 5561)	1965	$5.00	$10.00	$20.00
(with picture sleeve, glossy finish, add:)	1965	$37.50	$75.00	$150.00
(if picture sleeve does not have glossy finish, add:)	1965	$50.00	$100.00	$200.00
The Beach Boys, "Sloop John B"/ "You're So Good To Me" (Capitol 5602)				
(if original pressing, with orange-yellow swirl on label)	1966	$5.00	$10.00	$20.00
(with picture sleeve, add:)	1966	$7.50	$15.00	$30.00
(if reissue pressing, red and orange "target" label)	1969	$2.50	$5.00	$10.00
(if reissue pressing, orange label, "Capitol" at bottom of label)	1973	$2.00	$4.00	$8.00
(if reissue pressing, purple label)	1978	$2.00	$5.00	
The Challengers, "Hot Rod Show" / "K-39"				
(Vault 913)	1964	$7.50	$15.00	$30.00
The Chantays, "Pipeline" / "Move It"				
(If on Downey 104)	1963	$15.00	$30.00	$60.00
(if on Dot 16440)	1963	$6.25	$12.50	$25.00
(if on Dot 145, reissue on black label)	1966	$2.00	$4.00	$8.00
(if on Dot 145, reissue on orange-red label)	1969		$3.00	$6.00
Dick Dale and the Del-Tones, "Jesse's Pearl" / "St. Louis Blues" (Deltone 5014)	1960	$25.00	$50.00	$100.00
Dick Dale and the Del-Tones, "Miserlou" / "Eight Till Midnight"				
(If on Deltone 5019)	1962	$6.25	$12.50	$25.00
(if on Deltone 4939, a release distributed by Capitol)	1963	$5.00	$10.00	$20.00
Dick Dale and the Del-Tones, "King of the Surf Guitar" / "Havah Nagilah"	1963	$5.00	$10.00	$20.00
(with picture sleeve, add:)	1963	$20.00	$40.00	$80.00
Duane Eddy, "Moovin' 'n' Groovin'" / "Up and Down" (Jamie 1101)				
(if first pressing with pink label)	1958	$12.50	$25.00	$50.00
(if second pressing with yellow label)	1958	$6.25	$12.50	$25.00
Duane Eddy, "Rebel-'Rouser" / "Stalkin'"				
(Jamie 1104)	1958	$6.25	$12.50	$25.00
Duane Eddy, "Forty Miles of Bad Road" / "The Quiet Three"				
(if on Jamie 1126, mono)	1959	$5.00	$10.00	$20.00
(if on Jamie 1126, stereo)	1959	$12.50	$25.00	$50.00
(with picture sleeve for mono pressing only, add:)	1959	$12.50	$25.00	$50.00
The Honeys, "Surfin' Down the Swanee River" / "Shoot the Curl" (Capitol 4952)	1963	$37.50	$75.00	$150.00
(with rare picture sleeve, add:)	1963	$200.00	$400.00	$800.00
Jan and Dean, "Surf City" / "She's My Summer Girl" (Liberty 55580)	1963	$3.75	$7.50	$15.00
(with picture sleeve, add:)	1963	$10.00	$20.00	$40.00
Jan and Dean, "Ride the Wild Surf" / "The Anaheim, Azuza and Cucamonga Sewing Circle, Book Review and Timing Association"				
(Liberty 55724)	1964	$3.75	$7.50	$15.00
(with picture sleeve, add:)	1964	$10.00	$20.00	$40.00
The Sunrays, "Andrea" / "You Don't Phase Me"				
(Tower 191)	1966	$3.00	$6.00	$12.00
The Surfaris, "Wipe Out" / "Surfer Joe"				
(if on DFS 11/12)	1963	$1,500	$2,250	$3,000
(if on Princess 50, with short versions of the songs - short versions have "RE-1" in the dead wax)	1963	$37.50	$75.00	$150.00
(If on Princess 50, with long versions of the songs - long versions do not have the "RE-1" in the dead wax)	1963	$100.00	$200.00	$400.00
(if on Dot 16479)	1963	$3.75	$7.50	$15.00
(if on Dot 144)	1966	$2.50	$5.00	$10.00
(if on Dot 144 DJ, red vinyl, "Wipe Out" on both sides)	1966	$25.00	$50.00	$100.00

45s	Year	VG	VG+	NM
(if on Dot 144 DJ, red vinyl, "Surfer Joe" erroneously listed on both sides)	1966	$37.50	$75.00	$150.00
The Trashmen, "Surfin' Bird" / "King of the Surf" (Garrett 4002)	1963	$7.50	$15.00	$30.00
The Ventures, "Walk - Don't Run" / "Home" (Blue Horizon 101)	1960	$625.00	$1,250.00	$2,500.00
The Ventures, "Walk - Don't Run" / "Home" (Dolton 25)	1960	$6.25	$12.50	$25.00
(if B-side is "The McCoy," catalog number is 25X)	1960	$5.00	$10.00	$20.00
The Ventures, "Hawaii Five-O" / "Soul Breeze" (Liberty 55068)	1968	$2.00	$4.00	$8.00

LPs	Year	VG	VG+	NM
The Beach Boys, Surfin' Safari (Capitol T 1808) (mono)	1962	$10.00	$20.00	$40.00
(if on Capitol DT-1808, rechanneled stereo, "Duophonic" on top of jacket)	1962	$6.25	$12.50	$25.00
(if on Capitol DT-1808, "Capitol Full Dimensional Stereo" under "Duophonic" banner on jacket)	1962	$20.00	$40.00	$80.00
The Beach Boys, Surfer Girl (Capitol T 1981) (mono) (two versions exist, one referencing the Four Freshmen, one referencing their new single, "Little Deuce Coupe," value is equal)	1963	$10.00	$20.00	$40.00
(if on Capitol ST-1981, stereo, same two variations exist, value is equal)	1963	$12.50	$25.00	$50.00
The Beach Boys, Summer Days (And Summer Nights) (Capitol T-2354) (mono)	1965	$7.50	$15.00	$30.00
(if on Capitol DT-2354, rechanneled stereo, "Duophonic" on top of jacket)	1965	$6.25	$12.50	$25.00
(if on Capitol DT-2354, "Capitol Full Dimensional Stereo" under "Duophonic" banner on jacket)	1965	$12.50	$25.00	$50.00
The Beach Boys, Pet Sounds (Capitol T-2458) (mono)	1966	$10.00	$20.00	$40.00
(if on Capitol DT 2458, rechanneled stereo)	1966	$7.50	$15.00	$30.00
(if on Brother/Reprise 2MS 2083, as a 2-LP set with "Carl and the Passions - So Tough")	1972	$7.50	$15.00	$30.00
(if above Brother/Reprise issue is a white label promo)	1972	$12.50	$25.00	$50.00
(if on Brother/Reprise MS 2197, mono)	1974	$5.00	$10.00	$20.00
(if on Capitol SN-16156, mono)	1981	$2.00	$4.00	$8.00
(if on Capitol C1-48421, mono)	1994	$3.75	$7.50	$15.00
(if on DCC Compact Classics LPZ-2006, mono, audiophile vinyl)	1995	$6.25	$12.50	$25.00
The Challengers, Surfbeat (Vault LP-100) (mono)	1963	$12.50	$25.00	$50.00
(if on Vault VS-100, stereo, black vinyl)	1963	$20.00	$40.00	$80.00
(if on Vault VS-100, stereo, pressings exist in yellow, red or orange vinyl, value is equal)	1963	$62.50	$125.00	$250.00
The Chantays, Pipeline				
(If on Downey DLP-1002, mono)	1963	$50.00	$100.00	$200.00
(if on Downey DLPS-1002, stereo)	1963	$75.00	$150.00	$300.00
(if on Dot DLP 3516, mono)	1963	$12.50	$25.00	$50.00
(if on Dot DLP 25516, stereo)	1963	$20.00	$40.00	$80.00
Dick Dale and the Del-Tones, Surfer's Choice				
(If on Deltone LPM-1001, mono)	1962	$25.00	$50.00	$100.00
(If on Deltone DT 1886, rechanneled stereo)	1962	$10.00	$20.00	$40.00
(If on Deltone T-1886, mono)	1962	$12.50	$25.00	$50.00
Dick Dale and the Del-Tones, King of the Surf Guitar				
(If on Capitol ST-1930, stereo)	1963	$12.50	$25.00	$50.00
(If on Capitol T-1930, mono)	1963	$10.00	$20.00	$40.00
Dick Dale and the Del-Tones, King of The Surf Guitar: The Best of Dick Dale and the Del-Tones, 1961-1964 (Rhino RNLP-70074)	1986	$3.00	$6.00	$12.00
Duane Eddy, Have "Twangy" Guitar - Will Travel (Jamie JLP-3000) (mono)				
(if first pressing, Eddy sitting with guitar case, title on cover in white)	1958	$30.00	$60.00	$120.00
(if second pressing, Eddy sitting with guitar case, title on cover in green and red)	1959	$25.00	$50.00	$100.00
(if third pressing, Eddy standing with guitar)	1959	$12.50	$25.00	$50.00

LPs	Year	VG	VG+	NM
Duane Eddy, Have "Twangy" Guitar - Will Travel (Jamie JLPS-3000) (stereo)				
(if first pressing, Eddy sitting with guitar case, title on cover in white)	1958	$100.00	$200.00	$400.00
(if second pressing, Eddy sitting with guitar case, title on cover in green and red)	1959	$75.00	$150.00	$300.00
(if third pressing, Eddy standing with guitar)	1959	$25.00	$50.00	$100.00
(if Eddy standing with guitar, album is in rechanneled stereo)	196??	$12.50	$25.00	$50.00
Jan and Dean, Jan and Dean Take Linda Surfin' (Liberty LRP-3294) (mono)	1963	$12.50	$25.00	$50.00
(if on Liberty LST-7294, stereo)	1963	$20.00	$40.00	$80.00
Jan and Dean, Surf City and Other Swingin' Cities (Liberty LRP-3314) (mono)	1963	$10.00	$20.00	$40.00
(if on Liberty LST-7314, stereo)	1963	$12.50	$25.00	$50.00
The Sunrays, Andrea (Tower T 5017) (mono)	1966	$12.50	$25.00	$50.00
(if on Tower ST 5017, stereo)	1966	$15.00	$30.00	$60.00
The Surfaris, Wipe Out (Dot DLP-3535) (mono)				
(if back cover photo shows five Surfaris)	1963	$12.50	$25.00	$50.00
(if back cover photo shows four Surfaris)	1963	$10.00	$20.00	$40.00
(if back cover photo shows NO Surfaris)	1963	$7.50	$15.00	$30.00
The Surfaris, Wipe Out (Dot DLP-25535) (stereo)				
(if back cover photo shows five Surfaris)	1963	$20.00	$40.00	$80.00
(if back cover photo shows four Surfaris)	1963	$12.50	$25.00	$50.00
(if back cover photo shows NO Surfaris)	1963	$10.00	$20.00	$40.00
The Trashmen, Surfin' Bird (Garrett GA-200) (mono)	1964	$55.00	$110.00	$220.00
(if on Garrett GAS-200, rechanneled stereo)	1964	$87.50	$175.00	$350.00
(if on Beat Rocket BR-107, audiophile reissue)	1999	$3.00	$6.00	$12.00
The Ventures, Walk Don't Run (Dolton BLP-2003) (mono)				
(if pale blue label, dolphins on top)	1960	$12.50	$25.00	$50.00
(if dark label, logo on left)	1963	$5.00	$10.00	$20.00
The Ventures, Walk Don't Run (Dolton BST-8003) (stereo)				
(if pale blue label, dolphins on top)	1960	$15.00	$30.00	$60.00
(if dark label, logo on left)	1963	$6.25	$12.50	$25.00

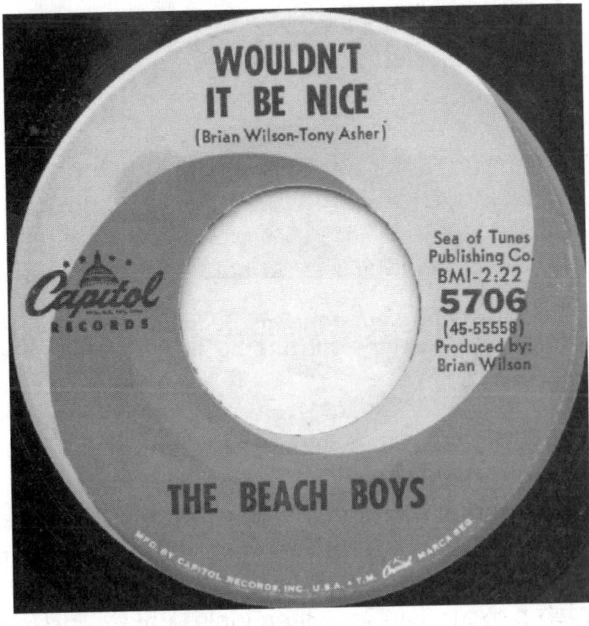

"Wouldn't It Be Nice," besides achieving Top 10 status, was also the opening track on the Beach Boys' opus album *Pet Sounds*.

TEEN IDOLS

History: Teen idols, young pop singers whose clean-cut looks and demeanor made them the magnets of popular music culture, have been around popular music for decades. Frank Sinatra, in fact, was a teen idol to every bobbysoxer who braved the cold temperatures in line at the Brooklyn Paramount for one of his concerts. Elvis Presley and the Beatles were teen idols upon their debuts, both driving their audiences into frenzies.

But over the years, the term "teen idol" has been linked to artists whose looks were more important than their music. Whether they were popular actors who released a one-off single, or vocalists whose voices were just the final touch in a record company's factory-produced project, teen idols have often been reviled as "all looks and no talent." Today, however, these albums and 45s are very collectible, especially among fans who once got rid of their record collection when they reached adulthood, but today hunt for the songs they still love.

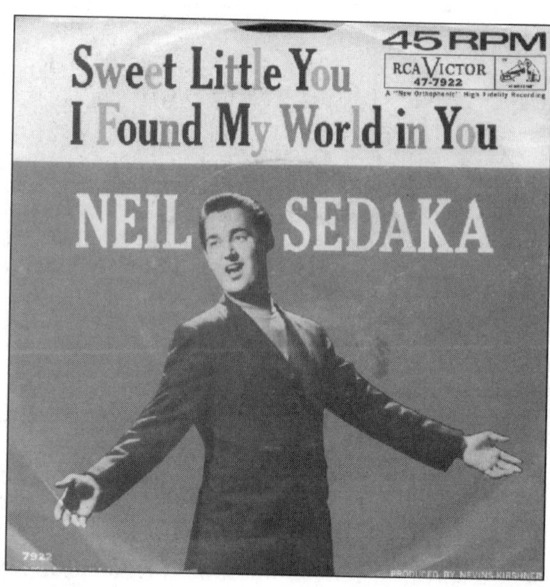

Neil Sedaka, who went from Brill Building songwriter to worldwide superstar—with a stop in the 1960s as a teen idol.

With the rise of television and its ability to bring new performers into millions of homes, teen idols became part of the popular music culture. Artists such as Pat Boone, Gail Storm, and Kay Starr were an alternative to the "rock 'n' roll" permeating the airwaves. Many of these teen idols, Pat Boone in particular, were involved in a practice in the 1950s called "cover records." As a song by a black artist or group was rising up the charts, a teen idol like Pat Boone or Georgia Gibbs would record the song themselves, eventually stalling the black artist's chart movement and record sales to the benefit of the white artist (the songwriter and publisher continued to receive all their royalties, however). With covers of "Ain't That A Shame," "I Almost Lost My Mind," and "Tutti-Fruitti," Pat Boone was able to sell millions of records to white audiences whose parents wouldn't allow them to purchase black music—in effect, according to apologists for "cover" artists, increasing the profits for the songwriters and copyright holders.

Some of the first teen idols of the rock era, however, were capable of writing their own songs; Paul Anka, for example, hit #1 with "Diana," his self-penned song about the love for his baby-sitter. A capable songwriter as well as an accomplished vocalist, Anka later wrote "She's a Lady" for Tom Jones, provide English lyrics for the Frank Sinatra standard "My Way," and composed the theme music for *"The Tonight Show."*

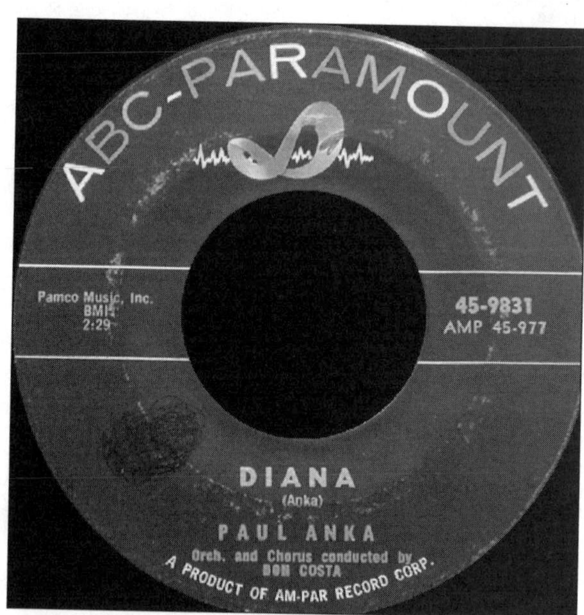

Paul Anka's song "Diana," the first hit in his four-decade performing career.

Another teen idol who had a long and fruitful career was Bobby Darin. Although Darin was marketed as a teen idol with songs like "Splish Splash" and "Queen of the Hop," he showed the ability to sing more mature songs like "Mack the Knife," "Lazy River," and "If I Were A Carpenter."

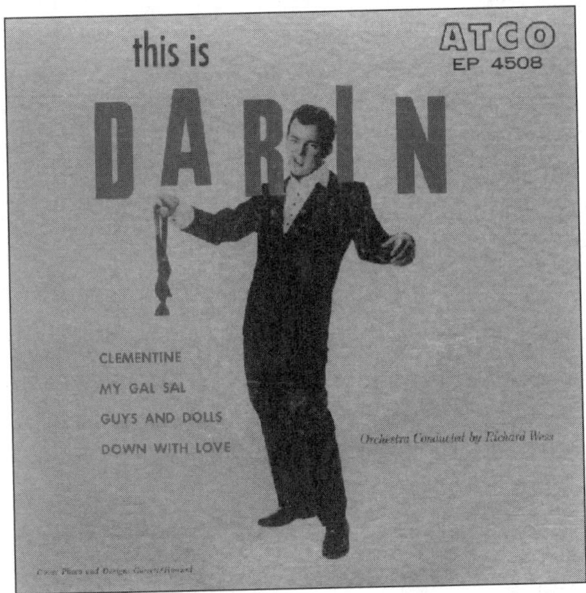

A rare four-song EP from Bobby Darin.

As many of rock 'n' roll's first stars faded away from the scene in 1959, manufactured teen idols took their place. Artists such as Frankie Avalon, Fabian, Bobby Rydell, Bobby Vinton, and Annette Funicello were promoted on TV shows like *"American Bandstand"* and *"The Mickey Mouse Club,"* and their record companies promoted these singers as wholesome, clean-cut, non-threatening pop singers. Although Frankie Avalon sang about Venus, the goddess of love, he never appeared in anything more salacious than some beach party motion pictures with Annette Funicello, who always wore a two-piece bathing suit in those films.

Almost every one of Frankie Avalon's hits on the Chancellor label came with picture sleeves, here's one of them.

The *"American Bandstand"* connection was extremely crucial for many teen idols, for an appearance on Dick Clark's weekly show could translate into millions of records sold. And since many of the labels that had teen idols on their roster, like Chancellor and Cameo, were in Philadelphia (where *"American Bandstand"* was first broadcast), the teen idols provided a steady stream of music and good looks to TV viewers across the country.

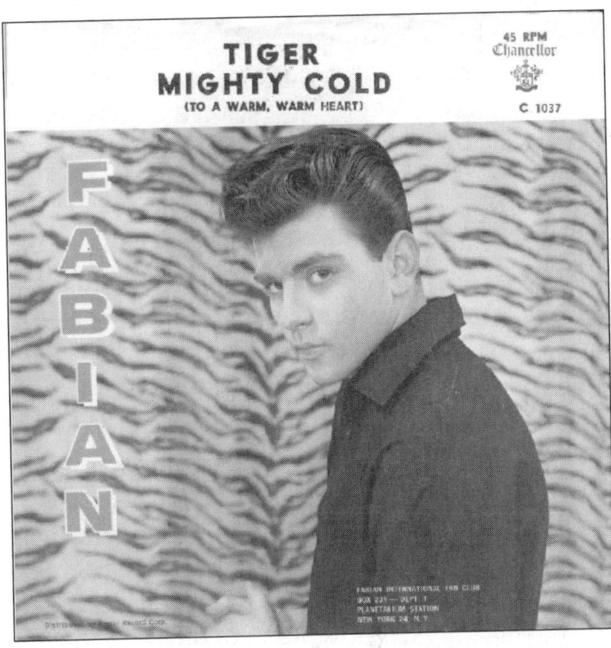

Fabian Forte provided a rough swagger—but not too rough—for his millions of fans, as shown on this picture sleeve for "Tiger."

These 1950s and 1960s "teen idols" actually returned control of pop music to hired songwriters. Teen idols were not expected to write their own material (Paul Anka notwithstanding); they would sing whatever was put in front of them, songs written by established tunesmiths. The Brill Building in New York City and the Cameo studios in Philadelphia were havens for teen-idol songwriting teams like Gerry Goffin and Carole King; Neil Sedaka and Howard Greenfield; or Kal Mann, Bernie Lowe, and Dave Appel.

Trivia

Bobby Rydell once recorded a giveaway record for the Steel Pier performing center at Atlantic City. This record is one of the hardest to find for Rydell completists.

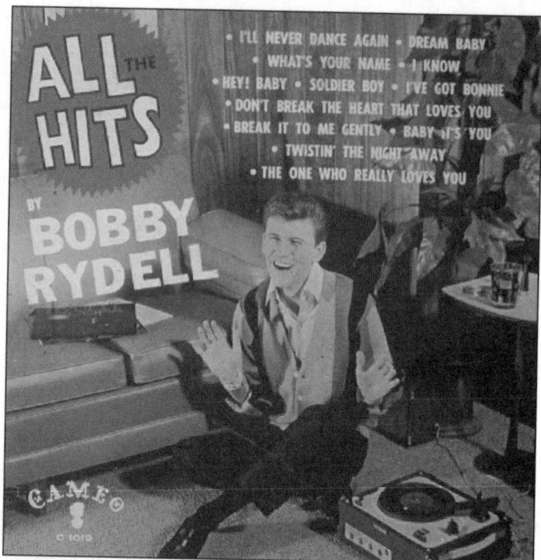

Bobby Rydell enjoyed teen idol success in the early 1960s; you can see his album *Rydell at the Copa* on the couch in the background of this album cover. Courtesy Last Vestige Music Store, Albany, N.Y.

By the early 1960s, singing teen idols came from popular television shows such as *"The Donna Reed Show" or "The Adventures of Ozzie and Harriet."* Colpix Records took actors like Shelley Fabares, James Darren, and Paul Petersen, placed them in the studio, and recorded some lightweight pop songs like "Goodbye Cruel World" and "She Can't Find Her Keys." While Petersen and Darren had some minor hits, Shelley Fabares took her song "Johnny Angel" to #1 on the pop charts.

Colpix 45s, with their dark golden label, will often wear down around the edge, causing ringwear, as can be seen on this copy of Shelley Fabares' "Johnny Angel."

One exception to the television-manufactured teen idols was Ricky Nelson. Although he had built-in exposure through *"The Adventures of Ozzie and Harriet,"* Nelson could play his own instruments, he surrounded himself with a top-notch band, he mixed rockabilly and country-pop with his teen idol output; and continued to have hits on the pop charts long after his TV show left the airwaves.

Ricky Nelson's first hit, "I'm Walkin'," was recorded to impress a girl who was more interested in what was on the jukebox than on their date.

The music careers of many of these 1960s teen idols came to a screeching halt in 1964, when the Beatles, the Rolling Stones, and the rest of the British Invasion forced them off the pop charts. Some teen idols turned to the stage or screen, appearing in beach pictures or light comedy movies. Bobby Darin, for example, earned an Oscar nomination for his work in the film *"Captain Newmann, M.D."* James Darren co-starred in *"The Time Tunnel,"* while Shelley Fabares had a long-standing role in the TV show, *"Coach."*

Television shows in 1970 helped create the next series of teen idols. Whether it was drama shows like *"Here Come the Brides,"* situation comedies like *"The Partridge Family,"* or variety shows starring the Osmonds, new teen idols began to re-dominate the pop charts. Artists like Bobby Sherman and David Cassidy dominated pop music in the early 1970s, while Donny Osmond, Leif Garrett, and Shaun Cassidy started their careers with remakes of 1960s pop songs.

Leif Garrett was a teen idol sensation in the late 1970s. While his early hits were remakes of "Runaround Sue" and "Put Your Head on My Shoulder," this song, his biggest, was an original.

Although these 1970s teen idols all sold millions of albums and 45s, their recordings are so plentiful that even the near-mint value of their recorded product has not risen above a few dollars per album. Only David Cassidy's records command reasonably normal aftermarket prices, as Cassidy's affiliation with the *"Partridge Family"* TV show has kept his recordings hot among both record collectors and TV-program collectors.

One of David Cassidy's solo hits, a remake of the Association's "Cherish."

In fact, many teen idols from the 1950s and 1960s found new life on the pop charts, thanks to TV shows like *"Happy Days"* and movies like *"Grease,"* which featured a school called "Rydell High," and appearances by both Fabian and Frankie Avalon. Paul Anka had a series of Top 40 hits in the mid-1970s, including the songs "(You're) Having My Baby," "Times of Your Life," and "I Don't Like To Sleep Alone." Another teen idol, Neil Sedaka, had hits with "Bad Blood," "Laughter in the Rain," and a piano-ballad remake of his 1962 hit "Breaking Up Is Hard To Do."

Television teen idols seemed to come and go, as everyone from *"Welcome Back, Kotter"* teen heart-throb John Travolta, to *"Starsky and Hutch's"* David Soul, to commercial pitchman Rodney Allen Rippy recorded albums and singles, many with mixed success.

Long before *Saturday Night Fever* and *Urban Cowboy* and *Pulp Fiction* and *Battlefield Earth,* John Travolta had a minor singing career during his off-days with *Welcome Back, Kotter*.

Today's teen idols are a throwback to the manufactured teen singing sensations of the 1960s, as groups such as the Backstreet Boys, N'Sync, Destiny's Child, and the Spice Girls have all commenced their singing careers with casting calls. With these groups, everything is important—the songs, the image, the wardrobe, the outward press releases. Television shows can still make teen idols popular, as artists like Britney Spears, Christina Aguilera, and N'Sync's Justin Timberlake were all graduates of the *"Mickey Mouse Club."*

Trivia

Paul Anka's song "Diana" was written about his unrequited love for his baby-sitter. He apparently didn't get over it—in the 1960s, he recorded a follow-up song, "Remember Diana."

A sequel of sorts to his classic hit, "Remember Diana" barely squeaked into the Top 40.

What To Look For: The vinyl 45s on many of the teen idols of the 1950s and 1960s are very plentiful. Finding albums for these artists is very difficult, and stereo pressings of 1960s original albums will command much more than the same title in mono (unless the recordings are "rechanneled stereo," at which point a knowledgeable collector will settle for the mono pressings).

Teen idol collectors also hunt for picture sleeves, as most record companies made sure that person's face was attached to that record in one way or another. If these picture sleeves have pin holes or tape marks (as these sleeves were notoriously separated from their vinyl and tacked or taped to a bedroom wall or to a scrapbook), then the grade on the sleeves is VG+ at best.

Some picture sleeves may also contain information on how to join a fan club or to receive a special mail-in album. Because so few "mail-in" albums were pressed in relation to songs available at the record store, the "mail-in" pressings can command high prices. And if two or more teen idols are on the same mail-in pressing, the record's value rises exponentially.

Annette Funicello is one of the most collectible teen idols of them all. Her picture sleeves usually contained fan club and mail-order information; finding an intact one is not easy.

Even today's crop of teen idols have pressed their Top 40 songs on vinyl. These pressings can be found through Internet record stores, but because their music is also available on CD and cassette, many buyers will either ignore the 45 release or be oblivious to its existence. Because the print runs on these 45s are so low, grabbing a few copies of a Britney Spears or Christina Aguilera 45 might provide you with a collectible record that someone may want in the future.

Christina Aguilera's first hit was pressed on a 7" 45, proof that today's artists still have 45s in their catalogue.

References: Darin, Dodd; Paetro, Maxine, *Dream Lovers: The Magnificent Shattered Lives of Bobby Darin and Sandra Dee by Their Son*, Warner Books, Inc., New York, 1994; DiOrio, Al, *Borrowed Time: The Thirty-Seven Years of Bobby Darin,* Running Press Book Publishers, Philadelphia, Pa., 1986; Funicello, Annette; Romanowski, Patricia, *A Dream Is A Wish Your Heart Makes: My Story,* Hyperion, New York 1995; Selvin, Joel, *Ricky Nelson: Idol for a Generation*, Contemporary Books, Chicago, 1990.

Web pages: The late Rick Nelson's Web page: *http://www.rickynelson.com*; Bobby Rydell's homepage: *http://www.bobbyrydell.com*; Fabian's homepage: *http://www.fabianforte.com*; a page for Annette Funicello, maintained by fan Jim Banks: *http://www.cowtown.net/users/annette/.*

45s	Year	VG	VG+	NM
Paul Anka, "Diana" / "Don't Gamble With Love" (ABC-Paramount 9831)	1957	$5.00	$10.00	$20.00
Paul Anka, "Put Your Head On My Shoulder" / "Don't Ever Leave Me" (ABC-Paramount 10040) (mono)	1959	$3.75	$7.50	$15.00
(with picture sleeve, add:)	1959	$6.25	$12.50	$25.00
(if on ABC-Paramount S-10040, stereo)	1959	$12.50	$25.00	$50.00
Paul Anka, "Puppy Love" / "Adam and Eve" (ABC-Paramount 10082) (mono)	1960	$3.75	$7.50	$15.00
(with picture sleeve, add:)	1960	$6.25	$12.50	$25.00
(if on ABC-Paramount S-10082, stereo)	1960	$12.50	$25.00	$50.00
Annette, "First Name Initial" / "My Heart Became of Age" (Buena Vista 349)	1959	$3.75	$7.50	$15.00
(with picture sleeve, add:)	1959	$7.50	$15.00	$30.00
Annette, "Pineapple Princess" / "Luau Cha Cha Cha" (Buena Vista 362)	1960	$3.75	$7.50	$15.00
(with picture sleeve, add:)	1960	$7.50	$15.00	$30.00
Annette, "Teenage Wedding" / "Walkin' and Talkin'" (Buena Vista 414)	1962	$5.00	$10.00	$20.00
(with extremely rare picture sleeve, add:)	1962	$150.00	$300.00	$600.00
Frankie Avalon, "Venus" / "I'm Broke" (Chancellor 1031) (mono)	1959	$5.00	$10.00	$20.00
(with picture sleeve, add:)	1959	$10.00	$20.00	$40.00
(if on Chancellor S-1031, stereo)	1959	$10.00	$20.00	$40.00
Frankie Avalon, "Why" / "Swingin' on a Rainbow" (Chancellor 1045) (mono)	1959	$3.75	$7.50	$15.00
(with picture sleeve, add:)	1959	$7.50	$15.00	$30.00
(if on Chancellor S-1045, stereo)	1959	$10.00	$20.00	$40.00
Frankie Avalon, "Voyage to the Bottom of the Sea" / "Summer of '61" (Chancellor 1081)	1961	$3.00	$6.00	$12.00
(with picture sleeve, add:)	1961	$6.25	$12.50	$25.00
The Bay City Rollers, "Saturday Night" / "Marlina" (Arista 0149)	1975		$2.00	$4.00
(with picture sleeve, add:)	1975		$3.00	$6.00
The Backstreet Boys, "Quit Playing Games (With My Heart)" / "Lay Down Beside Me" (Jive 42453)	1997			$3.00
The Backstreet Boys, "Everybody (Backstreet's Back)" / "As Long As You Love Me" (Jive 42510)	1998			$3.00
David Cassidy, "Cherish" / "All I Want To Do Is Touch You" (Bell 45150)	1971		$2.50	$5.00
(with picture sleeve, add:)	1971		$3.00	$6.00
Bobby Darin, "Mack the Knife" / "Was There A Call For Me" (Atco 6147)	1959	$5.00	$10.00	$20.00
(with picture sleeve, add:)	1959	$10.00	$20.00	$40.00
James Darren, "Goodbye Cruel World" / "Valerie" (Colpix 609)	1961	$3.75	$7.50	$15.00
(with picture sleeve, add:)	1961	$6.25	$12.50	$25.00
DeFranco Family featuring Tony DeFranco, "Heartbeat" - It's A Lovebeat" / "Sweet, Sweet Loretta" (20th Century 2030)	1973		$2.00	$4.00
(with picture sleeve, add:)	1973		$2.00	$4.00
Shelley Fabares, "Johnny Angel" / "Where's It Gonna Get Me" (Colpix 621)	1962	$5.00	$10.00	$20.00
(with rare picture sleeve, add:)	1962	$125.00	$250.00	$500.00
Shelley Fabares, "Football Season's Over" / "He Don't Love Me" (Colpix 721) (produced by Jan and Dean's Jan Berry)	1963	$25.00	$50.00	$100.00
Fabian, "Turn Me Loose" / "Stop Thief!" (Chancellor 1033) (mono)	1959	$5.00	$10.00	$20.00
(with picture sleeve, add:)	1959	$10.00	$20.00	$40.00
(if on Chancellor S-1033, stereo)	1959	$12.50	$25.00	$50.00
Fabian, "Kissin' and Twistin'" / "Long Before" (Chancellor 1061)	1960	$3.00	$6.00	$12.00
(with picture sleeve, add:)	1960	$7.50	$15.00	$30.00
Connie Francis, "Who's Sorry Now?" / "You Were Only Fooling" (MGM 12588)	1958	$5.00	$10.00	$20.00
Connie Francis, "Everybody's Somebody's Fool" / "Jealous of You" (MGM 12899)	1960	$3.75	$7.50	$15.00
(with picture sleeve, add:)	1960	$5.00	$10.00	$20.00
Lesley Gore, "It's My Party" / "Danny" (Mercury 72119)	1963	$3.75	$7.50	$15.00
(with picture sleeve, add:)	1963	$7.50	$15.00	$30.00
Lesley Gore, "You Don't Own Me" / "Run, Bobby, Run" (Mercury 72206)	1963	$3.75	$7.50	$15.00
(with picture sleeve and insert, add:) (deduct 25% from picture sleeve price if insert is missing)	1963	$10.00	$20.00	$40.00
Lesley Gore, "Sunshine, Lollipops and Rainbows" / "You've Come Back" (Mercury 72433)	1965	$5.00	$10.00	$20.00
(with picture sleeve, add:)	1965	$2.50	$5.00	$10.00
Hayley Mills, "Let's Get Together" / "Cobbler, Cobbler" (Buena Vista 385)	1961	$3.00	$6.00	$12.00
(with picture sleeve, add:)	1961	$6.25	$12.50	$25.00
Ricky Nelson, "I'm Walkin'" / "A Teenager's Romance" (Verve 10047) (if first pressing, orange-yellow label)	1957	$12.50	$25.00	$50.00
(if second pressing, black-white label)	1957	$10.00	$20.00	$40.00
Ricky Nelson, "Travelin' Man" / "Hello Mary Lou" (Imperial 5741)	1961	$6.25	$12.50	$25.00
(if on red vinyl)	1961	$200.00	$400.00	$800.00
Rick Nelson, "Young World" / "Summertime" (Imperial 5805)	1962	$5.00	$10.00	$20.00
(with picture sleeve, add:)	1962	$10.00	$20.00	$40.00
Rick Nelson, "Fools Rush In" / "Down Home" (Decca 31533)	1963	$3.75	$7.50	$15.00
(with picture sleeve, add:)	1963	$7.50	$15.00	$30.00
Wayne Newton, "Danke Schoen" / "Better Now Than Later" (Capitol 4989)	1963	$3.00	$6.00	$12.00
Donny Osmond, "Go Away Little Girl" / "Time To Ride" (MGM 14285)	1971		$3.00	$6.00
(if B-side is "The Wild Rover (Time to Ride)":)	1971		$2.50	$5.00
Donny and Marie Osmond, "Deep Purple" / "Take Me Back Again" (MGM 14840)	1975		$2.00	$4.00
Paul Petersen, "She Can't Find Her Keys" / "Very Likely" (Colpix 620)	1962	$3.75	$7.50	$15.00
(with picture sleeve, last name misspelled "Peterson", add:)	1962	$7.50	$15.00	$30.00
Paul Petersen, "She Rides With Me" / "Poorest Boy In Town" (Colpix 720) (A-side produced by Brian Wilson)	1964	$20.00	$40.00	$80.00
Rodney Allen Rippy, "Take Life A Little Easier" / "World of Love" (Bell 45403)	1973	$2.00	$4.00	$8.00
Bobby Rydell, "Kissin' Time" / "You'll Never Tame Me" (Cameo 167)	1959	$3.75	$7.50	$15.00
(with picture sleeve, add:)	1959	$6.25	$12.50	$25.00
Bobby Rydell, "Volare" / "I'd Do It Again" (Cameo 179)	1960	$3.75	$7.50	$15.00
(with picture sleeve, add:)	1960	$6.25	$12.50	$25.00
Bobby Rydell, "Wildwood Days" / "Will You Be My Baby" (Cameo 252)	1963	$3.00	$6.00	$12.00
(with picture sleeve, add:)	1963	$5.00	$10.00	$20.00
Neil Sedaka, "Ring-a-Rockin'" / "Don't Fly On Me" (if on Legion 133)	1958	$25.00	$50.00	$100.00
(if on Guyden 2004)	1958	$12.50	$25.00	$50.00
Neil Sedaka, "Calendar Girl" / "The Same Old Fool" (RCA Victor 47-7829)	1960	$3.75	$7.50	$15.00
(with picture sleeve, add:)	1960	$6.25	$12.50	$25.00
Neil Sedaka, "Breaking Up Is Hard To Do" / "As Long As I Live" (RCA Victor 47-8064)	1962	$3.75	$7.50	$15.00
(with picture sleeve, add:)	1962	$6.25	$12.50	$25.00
Helen Shapiro, "Walkin' Back To Happiness" / "Kiss and Run" (Capitol 4662)	1961	$3.00	$6.00	$12.00
Bobby Sherman, "It Hurts Me" / "Give Me Your Word" (Decca 31741)	1965	$3.75	$7.50	$15.00
(with picture sleeve, add:)	1965	$12.50	$25.00	$50.00
Bobby Sherman, "Little Woman" / "One Too Many Mornings" (Metromedial 121)	1969		$2.50	$5.00
(with picture sleeve, add:)	1969		$2.50	$5.00

45s	Year	VG	VG+	NM
Joanie Sommers, "Johnny Get Angry" / "Theme From 'A Summer Place'" (Warner Bros. 5275)	1962	$5.00	$10.00	$20.00
Rick Springfield, "Speak To The Sky" / "Why" (Capitol 3340)	1972	$2.00	$4.00	$8.00
(with picture sleeve, add:)	1972	$3.75	$7.50	$15.00
Johnny Tillotson, "It Keeps Right On A-Hurtin" / "She Gave Sweet Love To Me" (Cadence 1418)	1962	$3.75	$7.50	$15.00
Johnny Tillotson, "Talk Back Trembling Lips" / "Another You" (MGM 13181)	1963	$3.00	$6.00	$12.00
(with picture sleeve, add:)	1963	$5.00	$10.00	$20.00
Bobby Vee, "Devil or Angel" / "Since I Met You Baby" (Liberty 55270)	1960	$5.00	$10.00	$20.00
(with picture sleeve, add:)	1960	$7.50	$15.00	$30.00
Bobby Vee with the Crickets, "Punish Her" / "Someday (When I'm Gone From You") (Liberty 55479)	1962	$5.00	$10.00	$20.00
(with picture sleeve, add:)	1962	$7.50	$15.00	$30.00

LPs	Year	VG	VG+	NM
Paul Anka, Paul Anka Sings His Big 15 (ABC-Paramount 323) (mono)	1960	$12.50	$25.00	$50.00
(if on ABC-Paramount S-323, rechaneled stereo)	196??	$7.50	$15.00	$30.00
Paul Anka, Anka at the Copa (ABC-Paramount 353) (mono)	1960	$7.50	$15.00	$30.00
(if on ABC-Paramount S-353, stereo)	1960	$10.00	$20.00	$40.00
Annette, Annette Sings Anka (Buena Vista BV-3302) (mono)	1960	$25.00	$50.00	$100.00
Annette, Annette's Pajama Party (Buena Vista BV-3325) (mono)	1964	$10.00	$20.00	$40.00
(if on Buena Vista STER-3324, stereo)	1964	$25.00	$50.00	$100.00
Annette and Hayley Mills, Annette and Hayley Mills (Singing 10 Of Their Greatest All-Time Hits) (Disneyland DL-3508) (only available through TV mail-in offer, issued in paper jacket, mono)	1964	$250.00	$500.00	$1,000.00
Frankie Avalon, Swingin' on a Rainbow (Chancellor CHLX-5004) (mono)	1959	$10.00	$20.00	$40.00
(if on Chancellor CHLXS 5004, stereo)	1959	$12.50	$25.00	$50.00
Frankie Avalon, Young and in Love (Chancellor 69801) (if LP is in felt cover and 3-D portrait, all in box)	1960	$20.00	$40.00	$80.00
(if LP does not contain the box)	1960	$10.00	$20.00	$40.00
The Bay City Rollers, Bay City Rollers (Arista 4049)	1975	$2.50	$5.00	$10.00
Pat Boone, Pat Boone Sings Guess Who?" (Dot DLP-3501) (mono)	1963	$12.50	$25.00	$50.00
(if on Dot DLP-25501, stereo)	1963	$20.00	$40.00	$80.00
Pat Boone, My 10th Anniversary With Dot Records (Dot DLP-3650) (mono)	1965	$3.00	$6.00	$12.00
(if on Dot DLP-25650, stereo)	1965	$3.75	$7.50	$15.00
David Cassidy, David Cassidy's Greatest Hits (Bell 1321)	1974	$3.75	$7.50	$15.00
David Cassidy, The Higher They Come... (RCA Victor APL1-1066)	1975	$3.75	$7.50	$15.00
(if pressed on blue vinyl)	1975	$25.00	$50.00	$100.00
Bobby Darin, This Is Darin (Atco 33-115) (mono) (if mono, with harp on label)	1960	$10.00	$20.00	$40.00
(if mono, with gold-dark blue label)	1962	$5.00	$10.00	$20.00
(if stereo, with harp on label)	1960	$20.00	$40.00	$80.00
(if stereo, with purple-brown label)	1962	$6.25	$12.50	$25.00
James Darren, James Darren (Album No. 1) (Colpix CLP-406)	1960	$10.00	$20.00	$40.00
(if pressed on green vinyl)	1960	$37.50	$75.00	$150.00
James Darren, Shelley Fabares, Paul Petersen, Teenage Triangle (Colpix CP-444) (mono)	1963	$10.00	$20.00	$40.00
(if on SCP-444, rechaneled stereo)	1963	$10.00	$20.00	$40.00
The DeFranco Family featuring Tony DeFranco, Heartbeat, It's A Lovebeat (20th Century T-422)	1973	$2.50	$5.00	$10.00
Shelley Fabares, Shelley! (Colpix CLP-426) (mono)	1962	$37.50	$75.00	$150.00
(if on Colpix CST-426, stereo)	1962	$150.00	$300.00	$600.00
Fabian, The Fabian Facade: Young and Wonderful (Chancellor CHL-69802) (felt gatefold cover with cutout window)	1960	$20.00	$40.00	$80.00
Fabian, Fabian's 16 Fabulous Hits (Chancellor CHL-5024) (mono)	1962	$18.75	$37.50	$75.00

LPs	Year	VG	VG+	NM
Fabian and Frankie Avalon, The Hit Makers (Chancellor CHL-5009) (mono)	1960	$25.00	$50.00	$100.00
Connie Francis, Rock 'n Roll Million Sellers (MGM E-3794) (mono)	1960	$7.50	$15.00	$30.00
(if on MGM SE-3794, stereo)	1960	$10.00	$20.00	$40.00
Connie Francis, Never On Sunday and Other Title Songs from Motion Pictures (MGM E-3965) (mono)	1961	$7.50	$15.00	$30.00
(if on MGM SE-3965, stereo)	1961	$10.00	$20.00	$40.00
Lesley Gore, I'll Cry If I Want To (if on Mercury MG 20805, mono, no blurb for "It's My Party")	1963	$7.50	$15.00	$30.00
(if on Mercury MG 20805, mono, with blurb for "It's My Party")	1964	$5.00	$10.00	$20.00
(if on Mercury SR 60805, stereo, no blurb for "It's My Party")	1963	$10.00	$20.00	$40.00
(if on Mercury SR 60805, stereo, with blurb for "It's My Party")	1964	$7.50	$15.00	$30.00
(if on Mercury ML-8016, reissue of stereo version)	1980	$2.50	$5.00	$10.00
Hayley Mills, Let's Get Together (Buena Vista BV-3311) (mono)	1962	$6.25	$12.50	$25.00
(if on Buena Vista STER-3311, stereo)	1962	$10.00	$20.00	$40.00
Ricky Nelson, Teen Time (Verve V 2083) (mono) (only has three Ricky Nelson songs)	1957	$125.00	$250.00	$500.00
Ricky Nelson, Ricky (Imperial LP 9048) (mono) (if black label with stars)	1957	$25.00	$50.00	$100.00
(if black label with pink and white at left)	1964	$6.25	$12.50	$25.00
(if black label with green and white at left)	1966	$5.00	$10.00	$20.00
(if on Imperial LP 12392, rechanneled stereo)	1968	$3.75	$7.50	$15.00
Donny and Marie Osmond, I'm Leaving It All Up To You (MGM M3G-4968)	1974	$2.50	$5.00	$10.00
Paul Petersen, My Dad (Colpix CP-442) (mono)	1963	$12.50	$25.00	$50.00
(if on Colpix SCP-442, stereo)	1963	$15.00	$30.00	$60.00
Rodney Allen Rippy, Take Life A Little Easier (Bell 1311)	1974	$5.00	$10.00	$20.00
Bobby Rydell, Bobby Sings (Cameo 1007) (mono)	1960	$12.50	$25.00	$50.00
Bobby Rydell, Wild (Wood) Days (Cameo C-1055) (mono)	1963	$5.00	$10.00	$20.00
(if on Cameo SC-1055, stereo)	1963	$10.00	$20.00	$40.00
Neil Sedaka, "Little Devil" and His Other Hits (RCA Victor LPM-2421) (mono)	1961	$12.50	$25.00	$50.00
(if on RCA Victor LSP-2421, stereo)	1961	$15.00	$30.00	$60.00
Bobby Sherman, Here Comes Bobby (Metromedia MD 1028)	1970	$3.75	$7.50	$15.00
Joanie Sommers, Johnny Get Angry (Warner Bros. W 1470) (mono)	1962	$10.00	$20.00	$40.00
(if on Warner Bros. WS 1470, stereo)	1962	$12.50	$25.00	$50.00
Rick Springfield, Comic Book Heroes (if on Capitol SMAS-11206, briefly issued and then withdrawn)	1973	$10.00	$20.00	$40.00
(if on Columbia KC 32704)	1973	$3.75	$7.50	$15.00
(if on Columbia PC 32704, budget reissue)	1981	$2.00	$4.00	$8.00
Rick Springfield, Working Class Dog (RCA Victor ARL1-3697)	1981	$2.50	$5.00	$10.00
(if on RCA Victor AYL1-4766, "Best Buy Series" reissue)	1983	$2.00	$4.00	$8.00
Johnny Tillotson, It Keeps Right On A-Hurtin' (Cadence CLP-3058) (mono)	1962	$7.50	$15.00	$30.00
(if on Cadence CLP-25058, stereo)	1962	$10.00	$20.00	$40.00
Bobby Vee, Bobby Vee Sings Your Favorites (Liberty LRP-3165) (mono)	1960	$12.50	$25.00	$50.00
(if on Liberty LST-7165, stereo)	1960	$20.00	$40.00	$80.00
Bobby Vee, The Night Has A Thousand Eyes (Liberty LRP-3285) (mono)	1962	$7.50	$15.00	$30.00
(if on Liberty LST-7285, stereo)	1963	$10.00	$20.00	$40.00

TELEVISION RECORDS

History: If you have a popular television show, the next thing to do is to exploit its popularity. And in many cases, this meant a television-soundtrack album. Whether it involved the show's dialogue or music, or if the actors attempted (in the literal sense of the word) to sing, television soundtracks have their own special collectible value, as both record collectors and fans of that particular TV show will hunt down rare albums and 45s pertaining to that show or actor.

Many of the early television soundtracks featured variety-show performances, or recorded sketches. By the late 1950s, actors such as Ricky Nelson found that performing their songs on television—in Nelson's case, as part of the show *"Ozzie and Harriet"*—guaranteed fans would mob record stores to acquire that new single. Even "The Ballad of Davy Crockett," as heard in a three-part Walt Disney miniseries, had dozens of artists singing about the coonskin-capped frontier legend.

Bill Hayes, who later appeared on the soap opera Days of Our Lives, sung the most popular of more than 20 versions of "The Ballad of Davey Crockett" that were released in the 1950s.

Many of the "swinging detective" shows of the 1950s, like *"77 Sunset Strip"* and "Hawaiian Eye," had their soundtracks pressed by Warner Bros. Records, including a Top 40 hit by *"77 Sunset Strip's"* Edd "Kookie" Byrnes ("Kookie, Kookie, Lend Me Your Comb"). Of course, it didn't hurt that the show was also produced by Warner Bros. Studios, with its own built-in record company.

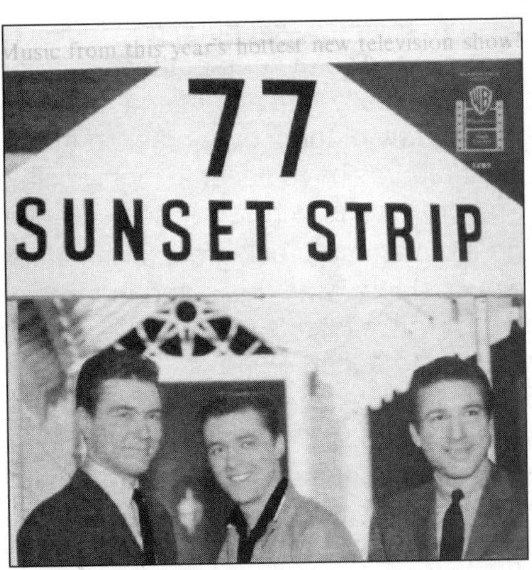

Featuring Efrem Zimbalist, Jr. and Edd "Kookie" Byrnes, the soundtrack for the popular 1950s detective series 77 Sunset Strip. Courtesy Last Vestige Music Store, Albany, N.Y.

Many soundtrack collectors avidly hunt for albums from Saturday morning TV shows. From the early 1960s until 1975, such Hanna-Barbera programs as *"Huckleberry Hound," "Yogi Bear"* and *"Top Cat"* often had simultaneous albums in the record stores, many of which featured the voices of Mel Blanc, Don Messick, and Jean Vander Pyl in audio-only adventures of the Saturday morning shows. Of course, in the 1960s, Hanna-Barbera was a division of Columbia/Screen Gems Pictures and benefited from its affiliation with Columbia's Colpix label.

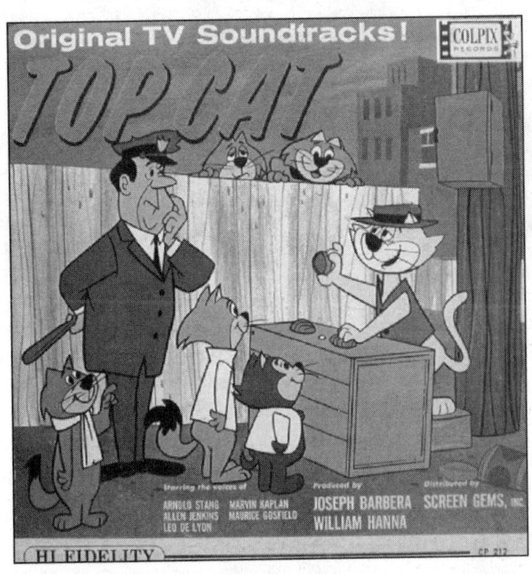

Top Cat, featuring the entire vocal cast of the TV show. This was one of many Hanna-Barbera Colpix releases in the 1960s.

By 1968, with the success of the Archies as both a TV series and a top-selling recording act, instantly every Saturday morning cartoon featured its characters in a band, ready to belt out a pop tune at a moment's notice. And of course, these cartoon characters eventually had album and 45 releases. Although very few of them ever cracked the Top 40 charts, their albums have become highly collectible, both for record fans and 1970s kitsch collectors.

Among the animated rock groups with at least one album or single were Josie and the Pussycats (featuring the voice talents of both Cheryl Ladd, ten years before she became one of Charlie's Angels; and Patrice Holloway, who found success in the "Northern Soul" British clubs), the Hardy Boys (Frank and Joe, along with at least three other friends, who solved crimes and played to sold-out rock concerts long before Parker Stevenson and Shaun Cassidy ever met each other), the Bugaloos (a psychedelic live-action series featuring four singing insects with thick-as-London-fog British accents), and the Groovie Goolies (an animated monster cartoon series from which one song, "Chick-a-Boom," became a hit for Daddy Dewdrop).

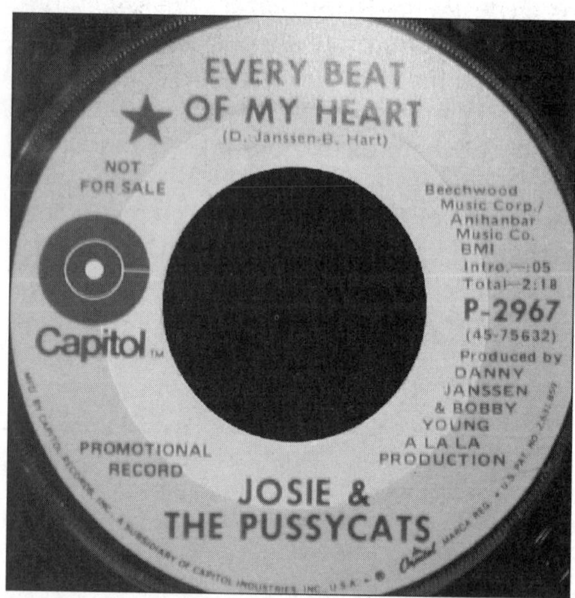

With the release of a live-action motion picture based on the classic Saturday morning cartoon, original recordings by Josie and the Pussycats will increase in value. From the Collection of Val Shively.]

By the early 1970s, the Harlem Globetrotters had an animated Saturday morning show, and yes, it included a tie-in 45. There was even an all-simian band, Lancelot Link and the Evolution Revolution, whose songs on the *"Lancelot Link, Secret Chimp"* show were released on an LP.

At least these shows were designed so that the concept of singing cartoon characters was within the moderate suspension of disbelief involved with watching Saturday morning programs. And if "The Senses Of Our World," "Sha La Love You," and "Inside, Outside, Upside Down" didn't set your toes to tapping, be thankful you did not have to hear William Shatner sing. Or Jack Klugman. Or Telly Savalas. Or Jack Webb.

Yet that's exactly what happened—not only were there album tie-ins for Saturday morning shows, but also for prime time programs as well. Oftentimes the albums only contained snippets from the TV show (as did the popular "All in the Family" albums). Other albums allowed their actors and actresses to sing—either in character or as themselves—with mixed results.

The next wave of TV shows with concomitant soundtracks occurred in the late 1970s. The opening themes of shows like *"Welcome Back, Kotter," "Happy Days," "The Greatest American Hero," and "Laverne and Shirley"* eventually migrated (and, with extra lyrics, were filled out from their 30-second TV theme length to a 3-minute pop version) to Top 40 radio. Even actors from these 1970s TV shows—John Travolta, David Soul, Shaun Cassidy—were able to crack the pop charts with songs of their own. In fact, the opening themes from shows that received poor ratings, such as *"Angie"* and *"Makin' It,"* still found a home on Top 40 radio.

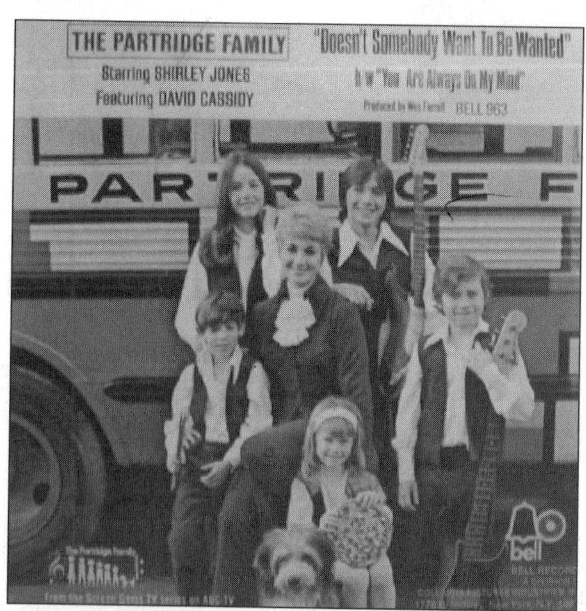

A successful marriage of TV and music, long before the existence of MTV, the Partridge Family had a string of Top 40 hits. Near-mint picture sleeves from this band are getting harder to find. From the Collection of Val Shively.

Trivia

In an ironic twist in 1992, "The Heights," a show about a struggling rock band, premiered. The opening theme, "How Do You Talk To An Angel?" became a #1 hit—in the same week the show was canceled for low ratings.

TV soundtracks in the 1980s, for shows like *"Moonlighting"* and *"Miami Vice,"* actually were a mixture of the show's catchy opening theme song, and various songs by other artists in the same musical theme or vein. Some songs that were featured on episodes of *"Miami Vice"* actually spurred radio to play these songs once again—songs such as Phil Collins' "In The Air Tonight" and Glenn Frey's "Smuggler's Blues."

Today, many TV shows insert pop songs into their shows, and announce where fans can purchase the songs heard on the program. Shows such as *"Buffy the Vampire Slayer," "7th Heaven," "Charmed" and "Dawson's Creek"* have given previously no-hit wonders vital exposure—and their first pop hits.

And among collectors of classic soundtracks, names like Henry Mancini, Mike Post, Bill Conti, and Alexander Courage often appear. Mancini added jazz to *"Peter Gunn"*; Mike Post created the opening themes for *"The Rockford Files"* and *"Hill Street Blues"*; Bill Conti scored such shows as *"Dynasty"*; and the opening theme to *"Star Trek"* was written by Alexander Courage.

Both TV soundtrack collectors and jazz buffs appreciate the soundtrack work of Henry Mancini.

Trivia

Even TV commercials have produced charted pop hits. These include the Hillside Singers and the New Seekers, each of whom had a hit with a Coca-Cola jingle "I'd Like To Teach The World To Sing"; The California Raisins, studio singers who parlayed a series of raisin commercials into a remake of "I Heard It Through The Grapevine"; and the T-Bones, whose song "No Matter What Shape (Your Stomach's In)" was previously heard in an antacid commercial.

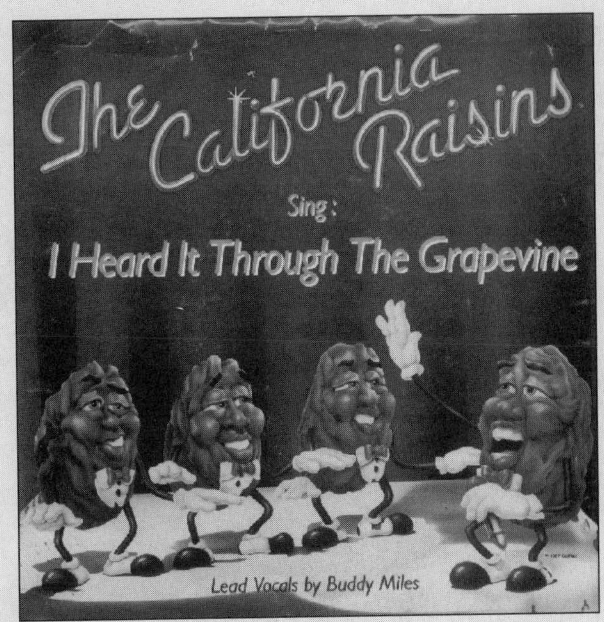

Buddy Miles, who had previously worked with Jimi Hendrix, is the lead "raisin" in this studio group, based on the popular commercial.

What To Look For: The most desirable TV soundtracks today are the Saturday morning cartoon albums, of which some titles can range into the high hundreds. Very few of these records had any chart or radio success, so copies are rare. Condition is also key—many TV soundtrack collectors appreciate the kitschy cover art as much as the album contained therein.

Another desirable TV theme package involves the music and actors from the *"Star Trek"* television series. Not only are the themes and underscores available on LP and CD, but many of the series' stars—including William Shatner, Leonard Nimoy, Grace Lee Whitney, and Nichelle Nichols—have recorded albums at one time or another.

Trivia

While the theme song for the late-1980s show "Beauty and the Beast" was released as a single, love-struck fans of the show bought the soundtrack album to hear actor Ron Perlman, who played the beast-like character "Vincent" on the show, read love poems and sonnets, as atmospheric music played in the background.

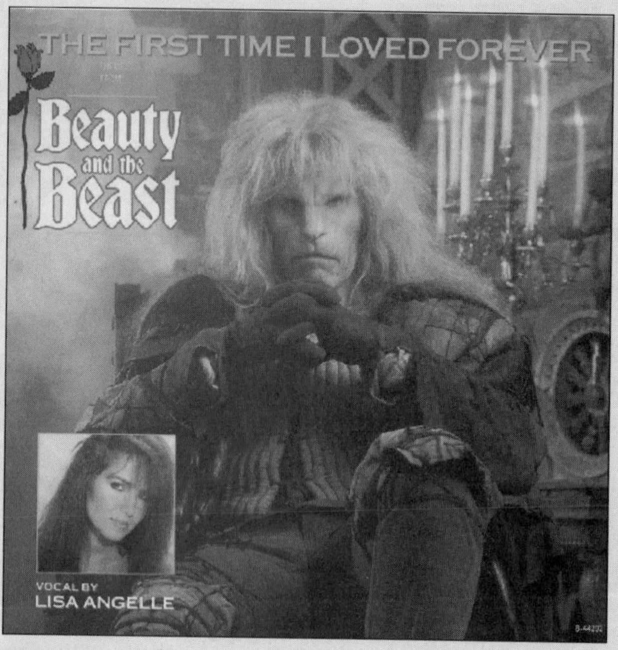

The opening theme to the TV version of "Beauty and the Beast," with lyrics written by Melanie, was sung by Lisa Angelle.

TV soundtrack collecting is a cross-hobby field—not only are record collectors looking for these albums and 45s, but also fans of the TV show and of the actors and actresses on that show. For example, the various soundtracks released during the 18-month popularity of the 1960s TV show *"Batman"* are searched out by record collectors, comic book collectors, TV program collectors, Batman fans, and camp/kitsch collectors.

References: Lofman, Ron, *Goldmine's Celebrity Vocals*, Krause Publications, Iola, Wisconsin, 1994.

Neal Hefti composed the theme for the TV series Batman, but his 7" single of the opening theme was eclipsed on the Top 40 by a surf-rock version performed by the Marketts. From the Collection of Val Shively.

45s	Year	VG	VG+	NM
The Bugaloos, "Senses Of Our World" / "For A Friend" (Capitol 2946)	1970	$3.00	$6.00	$12.00
Edd "Kookie" Byrnes with Connie Stevens, "Kookie, Kookie, Lend Me Your Comb" / Edd Byrnes, "You're the Top" (if on Warner Bros. 5047, mono)	1959	$5.00	$10.00	$20.00
(if on Warner Bros. S-5047, stereo)	1959	$12.50	$25.00	$50.00
(with picture sleeve, add:)	1959	$10.00	$20.00	$40.00
Richard Chamberlain, "Theme from Dr. Kildare (Three Stars Will Shine Tonight)" / "A Kiss To Build A Dream On" (MGM 13075)	1962	$2.50	$5.00	$10.00
(with picture sleeve, add:)	1962	$5.00	$10.00	$20.00
Lorne Greene, "Ringo" / "Bonanza" (RCA Victor 47-8444)	1964	$2.00	$4.00	$8.00
The Groovie Goolies, "The First Annual Semi-Formal Combination Celebration Meet-The-Monster Population Party" / "Save Your Good Lovin' For Me" (RCA Victor 74-0383)	1970	$2.50	$5.00	$10.00
The Hardy Boys, "Wheels" / "Sha-La-La" (RCA Victor 47-9795)	1969	$2.00	$4.00	$8.00
Josie and the Pussycats, "Letter to Mama" / "Inside, Outside, Upside Down" (Capitol CP 58-1)	1970	$5.00	$10.00	$20.00
(with picture sleeve, add:)	1970	$7.50	$15.00	$30.00
Josie and the Pussycats, "Every Beat of My Heart" / "It's All Right With Me" (Capitol 2967)	1970	$5.00	$10.00	$20.00
Lancelot Link and the Evolution Revolution, "Sha La Love You" / "Blind Date" (ABC 11278)	1970	$2.50	$5.00	$10.00
Lancelot Link and the Evolution Revolution, "Daydreams" / "Magic Feelings" (ABC 11285)	1970	$2.50	$5.00	$10.00
Laverne and Shirley (Penny Marshall and Cindy Williams), "Sixteen Reasons" / "Chapel of Love" (Atlantic 3367)	1976		$3.00	$6.00
The New Seekers, "Buy the World a Coke" / "Bring a Little Sunshine" "It's The Real Thing" (Coca-Cola, no cat no.)	1971	$3.00	$6.00	$12.00
The New Seekers, "I'd Like To Teach The World To Sing" / "Boom Town" (Elektra 45762)	1971		$3.00	$6.00
Nichelle Nichols, "Beyond Antares" / "Uhura's Theme" (R-Way RW 1001)	1979	$2.50	$5.00	$10.00
(with picture sleeve, add:)	1979	$3.75	$7.50	$15.00
Leonard Nimoy, "Theme from 'Star Trek'" / "Visit to a Sad Planet" (Dot 17038)	1967	$5.00	$10.00	$20.00
(with picture sleeve, add:)	1967	$12.50	$25.00	$50.00
Holly Robinson, "21 Jump Street" / the dB's, "Change with the Changing Times" (IRS 53468)	1988		$3.00	$6.00
John Sebastian, "Welcome Back, Kotter" / "Warm Baby" (Reprise 1349)	1976	$2.00	$4.00	$8.00

45s	Year	VG	VG+	NM
(if A-side simply says "Welcome Back")	1976		$2.00	$4.00
William Shatner, "How Insensitive" / "Transformed Man" (Decca 32399)	1969	$5.00	$10.00	$20.00
David Soul, "Don't Give Up On Us" / "Black Bean Soup" (Private Stock 45,129)	1977		$2.00	$4.00
Burt Ward, "Boy Wonder I Love You" / "Orange Colored Sky" (MGM K13632) (produced by Frank Zappa)	1967	$17.50	$35.00	$70.00
Jack Webb, "Try A Little Tenderness" / "You'd Never Know The Old Place Now" (Warner Bros. 5003)	1967	$2.50	$5.00	$10.00
Grace Lee Whitney, "Disco Trekkin'" / "Star Child" (Star Enterprises, no catalog number)	1976	$2.50	$5.00	$10.00

LPs	Year	VG	VG+	NM
The Banana Splits, We're The Banana Splits (Decca DL 75075)	1969	$50.00	$100.00	$200.00
Batman (20th Century Fox TFM-3180) (mono)	1966	$15.00	$30.00	$60.00
(if on 20th Century Fox TFS-4180, stereo)	1966	$25.00	$50.00	$100.00
The Beverly Hillbillies (Columbia CL 2402) (mono)	1965	$10.00	$20.00	$40.00
(if on Columbia CS 9202, stereo)	1965	$15.00	$30.00	$60.00
The Bugaloos, The Bugaloos (Capitol SW-621)	1970	$7.50	$15.00	$30.00
The Catanooga Cats, The Catanooga Cats (Forward ST-F-1018)	1969	$10.00	$20.00	$40.00
Dark Shadows (Philips PHS 600314) (with poster)	1969	$7.50	$15.00	$30.00
The Flintstones (Colpix CP-302) (mono)	1961	$50.00	$100.00	$200.00
Get Smart (United Artists UAL-3533) (mono)	1965	$10.00	$20.00	$40.00
(if on United Artists USA-6566, stereo)	1965	$15.00	$30.00	$60.00
The Globetrotters, The Globetrotters (Kirshner KES-108)	1971	$5.00	$10.00	$20.00
Lorne Greene, Michael Landon and Dan Blocker, Bonanza - Ponderosa Party Time! (RCA Victor LPM-2583) (mono)	1962	$7.50	$15.00	$30.00
(if on RCA Victor LSP-2583, stereo)	1962	$10.00	$20.00	$40.00
How the Grinch Stole Christmas! (Leo LE-901) (mono)	1966	$12.50	$25.00	$50.00
(if on Leo LES-901, stereo)	1966	$17.50	$35.00	$70.00
The Groovie Goolies, The Groovie Goolies (RCA Victor LSP-4420)	1970	$6.25	$12.50	$25.00

LPs	Year	VG	VG+	NM
The Hardy Boys, Here Come The Hardy Boys (RCA Victor LSP-4217)	1969	$5.00	$10.00	$20.00
Josie and the Pussycats, Josie and the Pussycats (Capitol ST-665)	1970	$50.00	$100.00	$200.00
Lancelot Link and the Evolution Revolution, Lancelot Link and the Evolution Revolution (ABC S-715)	1970	$10.00	$20.00	$40.00
Love, American Style (Capitol ST-11250)	1973	$10.00	$20.00	$40.00
The Man From U.N.C.L.E. (RCA Victor LPM-3475) (mono)	1965	$15.00	$30.00	$60.00
The Music From Marlboro Country (United Artists SP-107)	1967	$12.50	$25.00	$50.00
Donny and Marie Osmond, Donny & Marie - Featuring Songs From Their Television Show (Polydor PD-1-6068)	1976	$2.00	$4.00	$8.00
Ozzie and Harriet (Imperial LP-9049) (mono)	1957	$50.00	$100.00	$200.00
Peyton Place (Epic LN 24147) (mono)	1965	$7.50	$15.00	$30.00
(if on Epic BN 26147, stereo)	1965	$10.00	$20.00	$40.00
Mike Post, Theme From L.A. Law and Otherwise (Polydor 833985-1)	1987	$2.00	$4.00	$8.00
Rocky and His Friends (Golden LP-64) (gold label)	1961	$50.00	$100.00	$200.00
Rudolph The Red-Nosed Reindeer (Decca DL 4815) (mono)	1964	$15.00	$30.00	$60.00
(if on Decca DL 34327, mono, custom reissue)	1965	$10.00	$20.00	$40.00
(if on Decca DL 74815, stereo)	1964	$20.00	$40.00	$80.00
(if on MCA 15003, reissue with dark rainbow label)	1973	$5.00	$10.00	$20.00
William Shatner, The Transformed Man (Decca DL 75043)	1969	$15.00	$30.00	$60.00
Space: 1999 (RCA Victor ABL1-1422)	1975	$5.00	$10.00	$20.00
Victory at Sea				
(if on RCA Victor LM-1779, original recording)	1954	$6.25	$12.50	$25.00
(if on RCA Victor LM-2335, mono, re-recording)	1959	$5.00	$10.00	$20.00
(if on RCA Victor LSC-2335, stereo recording)	1959	$5.00	$10.00	$20.00
(if on Mobile Fidelity 3-150, 3 LPs, audiophile vinyl)	1984	$25.00	$50.00	$100.00

Not only has there been a soundtrack album for The Flintstones, but Alan Reed and Mel Blanc have recorded various children's albums as "Fred Flintstone" and "Barney Rubble" since this album's initial release. Courtesy Good Rockin' Tonight / Collectors Universe.

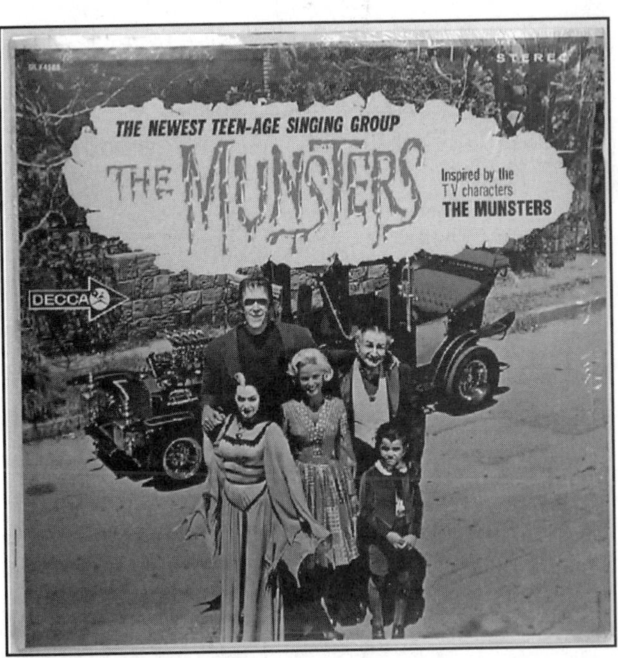

The Munsters TV series spawned this TV soundtrack, in which the characters form a singing group. The collectibility of this album is not for its vocal value, as one can imagine. Courtesy Good Rockin' Tonight / Collectors Universe.

FRANK ZAPPA AND THE MOTHERS OF INVENTION

History: Satirist, iconoclast, innovator, auteur. Those adjectives—and many more—describe Frank Zappa. In Zappa's music, you can hear the influences of such varied artists as Edgard Varese, Howlin' Wolf, and Karlheinz Stockhausen; you can also hear the scathing humor of Lenny Bruce and Richard Pryor. Through Zappa's compositions, everything from the rock 'n' roll lifestyle to ambient social lifestyles, from hippies to groupies, from mall rats to ethnocentric social climbers, were put on display—and eventually skewered.

Frank Zappa was born in Baltimore in 1940, the son of a government research scientist (Zappa was not, as urban legends have claimed for years, the son of Lumpy Brannum, *"Captain Kangaroo's"* Mr. Green Jeans). His family eventually moved to California, where Zappa cultivated a love for classic R&B and doo-wop music, along with the works of Edgard Varese ("Ionisation") and Igor Stravinsky ("Rites of Spring").

Zappa's first band, the Mothers of Invention, recorded for Verve between 1967 and 1969. Their albums, a mixture of satire, social commentary, and shock, made them darlings of the Los Angeles and New York counter-culture generation.

Zappa later recorded albums with roots in doo-wop (*Cruising with Ruben & The Jets*) classical music (*Lumpy Gravy*, featuring the Abnuceals Emuukha Electric Symphony Orchestra and Chorus), and burlesque comedy (*Live at the Fillmore East*), but his most popular recordings are satirical views of the freak-out counterculture, the life of a rock star, politics, religion, and the world in general.

Trivia

Besides his own performing career, Frank Zappa produced and performed on albums for such diverse artists as Grand Funk Railroad (he produced the Good Singin', Good Playin' album), George Duke (Zappa played guitar on Duke's album Feel) and John Lennon (who joined Zappa and the Mothers of Invention at a live jam at the Fillmore East, which later appeared on Lennon's Some Time In New York City album).

This parody of the Beatles' *Sgt. Pepper's Lonely Hearts Club Band* cover can be found inside gatefold copies of the Mothers of Invention's We're Only In It For The Money. Courtesy Last Vestige Music Store, Albany, N.Y.

By 1970, Zappa had disbanded the Mothers of Invention, concentrating on solo work, but often inviting the top musicians and songwriters to join him in the studio. His jazz-rock album *Hot Rats* featured such guest stars as Captain Beefheart and Jean-Luc Ponty, while his 1971 album *Live at the Fillmore East* featured a new Mothers of Invention, including the Turtles' Howard Kaylan and Mark Volman. In fact, during the early 1970s, Zappa's musical output was delineated as two polar opposites—the no-holds-barred satirist who was also a gifted and talented jazz and classical composer.

This dichotomy continued throughout the 1970s and 1980s; Zappa recorded avant-garde classical and jazz compositions (including the *Shut Up 'n Play Yer Guitar* series), while continuing with his satire and parodies (*Sheik Yerbouti, Ship Arriving Too Late To Save A Drowning Witch*).

During the 1980s, Zappa changed from recording star to political activist, testifying and lobbying in Congress against music-industry censorship and against the Parents Music Resource Center. He also gathered his entire music catalog, including all the original master tapes, and began a series of reissues on the Rykodisc label. In fact, at the time of his death in 1993, more than 50 different Zappa albums were available through this small independent label.

Frank Zappa's orchestral album *Lumpy Gravy*, complete with background conversations and studio experiments using recording tape.

What To Look For: The early Zappa albums, especially those with the Mothers of Invention, can be found without too much hunting. Finding them in near-mint condition, however, is difficult. The stereo version of the album *We're Only In It For The Money* may contain minimal censorship edits on two songs, "Who Needs the Peace Corps?" and "Let's Make the Water Turn Black"; but because so few of those records were actually pressed and sold, those edited records are actually worth more than the original pressings.

Trivia

In the winter of 1971, Zappa and his Mothers of Invention performed a concert at the Montreux Casino in Switzerland. During the concert, a misguided fan discharged a flare gun and the flaming projectile hit the ceiling of the casino. With the building burning to the ground, Zappa and his band escaped with their lives. Meanwhile, the band Deep Purple had brought a portable recording studio to Montreux, planning to record their next album in the acoustically superior Casino. As the Casino turned into smoldering rubble, Deep Purple turned that tragedy into their biggest hit, "Smoke on the Water."

Trivia

Although Frank Zappa released many critically-acclaimed albums, his 7-inch songs rarely dented the Billboard Hot 100 charts. In fact, of the four songs that actually did hit the charts, only one of those cracked the Top 40—"Valley Girl," his duet with his daughter Moon Zappa.

Using his daughter Moon Zappa's off-the-cuff impersonation of Southern California teenage airheads, "Valley Girl" became Frank Zappa's first Top 40 single, totally, fer sher, fer sher.

Because Zappa concentrated on albums rather than singles, his 7-inch recordings are extremely rare. During his *Cruising with Ruben and the Jets* phase, MGM's Verve subsidiary released "Jelly Roll Gum Drop," a song from that album, as a single—but credited it not to Zappa, but to *"Ruben and the Jets."* And in the case of life imitating art, some of the Mothers who were part of the Ruben and the Jets project recorded an LP, *For Real*, with Zappa producing.

References: Kostelanetz, Richard, *The Frank Zappa Companion: Four Decades of Commentary,* Schirmer Books, New York, 1997; Walley, David, *No Commercial Potential: The Saga of Frank Zappa,* De Capo Press, New York 1996; Zappa, Frank, with Peter Occhiogrosso, *The Real Frank Zappa Book*, Poseidon Press, New York 1989.

Long a devotee of doo-wop music, one of Frank Zappa's side affiliations was with his doo-wop group, Ruben and the Jets.

Web pages: The Frank Zappa home page: *http://www.zappa.com*; St. Alphonso's Pancake Homepage, Robbert Heederik's Zappa tribute page: *http://www.science.uva.nl/~robbert/zappa/;* Brian L. Knight compares Frank Zappa's music to that of jazz legend Sun Ra: *http://members.tripod.com/vermontreview/essays/razappa.htm*; Usenet newsgroups: *alt.fan.frank-zappa, alt.music.frank-zappa.*

45s	Year	VG	VG+	NM
Ned and Nelda (Frank Zappa with Ray Collins), "Hey Nelda" / "Surf Along" (Vigah 002)	1963	$37.50	$75.00	$150.00
The Mothers of Invention, "How Could I Be Such A Fool" / "Help I'm A Rock (3rd Movement: It Can't Happen Here)" (Verve 10418)	1966	$50.00	$100.00	$200.00
(with picture sleeve, add:)	1966	$25.00	$50.00	$100.00
The Mothers of Invention, "Who Are The Brain Police" / "Trouble Comin' Every Day" (Verve 10458)	1966	$50.00	$100.00	$200.00
(with picture sleeve, add:)	1966	$25.00	$50.00	$100.00
The Mothers of Invention, "Why Don't You Do Me Right" / "Big Leg Emma" (Verve 10513)	1967	$50.00	$100.00	$200.00
(if promo copy)	1967	$25.00	$50.00	$100.00
Ruben and the Jets, "Jelly Roll Gum Drop" / "Any Way The Wind Blows" (Verve 10632)	1968	$37.50	$75.00	$150.00
(with picture sleeve, add:)	1968	$18.75	$37.50	$75.00
The Mothers of Invention, "My Guitar" / "Dog Breath" (Bizarre 0840)	1969	$12.50	$25.00	$50.00
Frank Zappa, "Peaches En Regalia" / "Little Umbrellas" (Bizarre 0889)	1970	$12.50	$25.00	$50.00
The Mothers of Invention, "WPLJ" / "My Guitar" (Bizarre 0892)	1970	$12.50	$25.00	$50.00
Junior Mintz, "Tears Begin To Fall" / "Junior Mintz Boogie" (Bizarre 1027)	1971	$12.50	$25.00	$50.00
Frank Zappa and the Mothers of Invention, "Tears Begin to Fall" / "Junior Mintz Boogie" (Bizarre 1052)	1971	$12.50	$25.00	$50.00
Frank Zappa, "Magic Fingers" / "Daddy, Daddy, Daddy" (United Artistts 50857)	1971	$12.50	$25.00	$50.00
The Mothers, "Cletus Awreetus-Awrightus" / "Eat That Question" (Bizarre 1127)	1972	$8.75	$17.50	$35.00
Frank Zappa, "Don't Eat The Yellow Snow" / "Cosmic Debris" (Discreet 1312)	1974	$3.75	$7.50	$15.00
Frank Zappa, "Dancin' Fool" / "Baby Snakes" (Zappa Z-10)	1979	$2.50	$5.00	$10.00
Frank Zappa, "I Don't Wanna Get Drafted" / "Ancient Armaments (Live)" (Zappa ZR-1001)	1980		$2.00	$4.00
(with picture sleeve, add:)	1980	$2.50	$5.00	$10.00
Frank and Moon Zappa, "Valley Girl" / Frank Zappa, "You Are What You Is" (Barking Pumpkin 02972)	1982			$3.00
(with picture sleeve, add:)	1982		$3.50	$7.00

LPs	Year	VG	VG+	NM
The Mothers of Invention, Freak Out! (Verve V-5005-2) (2 LPs)				
(if mono, white label promo)	1966	$100.00	$200.00	$400.00
(if mono, cover has a blurb on inside gatefold on how to get a map of "freak-out-hot-spots" in Los Angeles)	1966	$50.00	$100.00	$200.00
(if mono, cover has no "freak-out-hot-spots" blurb)	1966	$37.50	$75.00	$150.00
(if stereo, Verve V6-5005-2, yellow label promo)	1966	$75.00	$150.00	$300.00
(if stereo, Verve V6-5005-2, with "freak-out-hot-spots" blurb)	1966	$20.00	$40.00	$80.00
(if stereo, Verve V6-5005-2, no "freak-out-hot-spots" blurb)	1966	$15.00	$30.00	$60.00
The Mothers of Invention, We're Only In It For The Money (Verve V-5045)				
(if mono, white label promo)	1968	$75.00	$150.00	$300.00
(if mono, contains insert with "Sergeant Pepper's Lonely Hearts Club Band"-like cutouts)	1968	$37.50	$75.00	$150.00
(if stereo, Verve V6-5045, uncensored version, contains cutout sheet)	1968	$15.00	$30.00	$60.00
(if stereo, Verve V6-5045, "Who Needs the Peace Corps?" and "Let's Make The Water Turn Black" edited)	1968	$37.50	$75.00	$150.00
Frank Zappa and the Mothers of Invention, Cruising With Ruben and the Jets (Verve 5055)	1968	$15.00	$30.00	$60.00
(if yellow label promo)	1968	$37.50	$75.00	$150.00
Frank Zappa, Uncle Meat (Bizarre MS 2024) (2 LPs)				
(if original blue label pressing, with booklet)	1969	$8.75	$17.50	$35.00
(if reissue on brown Reprise label)	1973	$5.00	$10.00	$20.00
Frank Zappa, Hot Rats (Bizarre RS 6356)				
(if original blue label pressing)	1969	$12.50	$25.00	$50.00
(if reissue on brown Reprise label)	1973	$3.75	$7.50	$15.00
Frank Zappa, Weasels Ripped My Flesh (Bizarre MS 2028)				
(if original blue label pressing)	1970	$6.25	$12.50	$25.00
(if reissue on brown Reprise label)	1970	$3.75	$7.50	$15.00
Frank Zappa, Apostrophe (') (Discreet Ds 2175)				
(if record is white label promo)	1974	$12.50	$25.00	$50.00
(if record is on DSR 2175, quadraphonic)	1974	$8.75	$17.50	$35.00
Frank Zappa, Shut Up 'n Play Yer Guitar (Barking Pumpkin BPR-1111) (mail order only)	1981	$5.00	$10.00	$20.00
Frank Zappa, Shut Up 'n Play Yer Guitar Some More (Barking Pumpkin BPR-1112) (mail order only)	1981	$5.00	$10.00	$20.00
Frank Zappa, Return of the Son of Shut Up 'n Play Yer Guitar (Barking Pumpkin BPR-1113) (mail order only)	1981	$5.00	$10.00	$20.00
Frank Zappa, Shut Up 'n Play Yer Guitar (Barking Pumpkin W3X-38290) (3 LP's) (box set of three prior titles)	1981	$6.25	$12.50	$25.00
Frank Zappa, Ship Arriving Too Late To Save A Drowning Witch (Barking Pumpkin FW 38066)	1982	$3.00	$6.00	$12.00
Frank Zappa, Rare Meat" The Early Productions of Frank Zappa (Rhino/Del-Fi RNEP-604)	1984	$10.00	$20.00	$40.00
Frank Zappa, The Old Masters, Box 1 (Barking Pumpkin 7777) (8 LPs)	1984	$15.00	$30.00	$60.00
(two more 8-LP sets were released with catalog numbers 8888 and 9999, value is same for each set)				
Frank Zappa, Frank Zappa Meets the Mothers of Prevention (Barking Pumpkin ST-74203)	1985	$2.50	$5.00	$10.00
Frank Zappa, Beat the Boots (Foo-EEE RI-70907) (10 LP's) (Rhino box set of eight previously bootlegged concerts)	1991	$25.00	$50.00	$100.00
Frank Zappa, Beat the Boots #2 (Foo-EEE RI-70372) 11 LP's) (same as above, but eleven more concerts)	1992	$25.00	$50.00	$100.00
Frank Zappa, Strictly Commercial: The Best of Frank Zappa (Ryko Analogue RALP 40500) (2 LP's with obi strip)	1995	$5.00	$10.00	$20.00

A

B

C

H

I

J

K

L

M

N

O

P

Q

R

S

T

U

V

W

X

Y

Z